# HGTV
## HOME & GARDEN TELEVISION

# BEFORE & AFTER DECORATING

**HGTV Before & After Decorating**
Editor: Amy Tincher-Durik
Art Director: Chad Owen, Owen Design
Contributing Editor: Paula Marshall
Copy Chief: Terri Fredrickson
Copy and Production Editor: Victoria Forlini
Editorial Operations Manager: Karen Schirm
Managers, Book Production: Pam Kvitne, Marjorie J. Schenkelberg, Rick von Holdt
Contributing Copy Editor: Jane Woychick
Contributing Proofreaders: Sara Henderson, Nancy Ruhling, Margaret Smith
Illustrator: Tom Buchs
Indexer: Elizabeth Parson
Electronic Production Coordinator: Paula Forest
Editorial and Design Assistants: Kaye Chabot, Karen McFadden, Mary Lee Gavin

**Meredith® Books**
Editor in Chief: Linda Raglan Cunningham
Design Director: Matt Strelecki
Executive Editor, Home Decorating and Design: Denise L. Caringer

Publisher: James D. Blume
Executive Director, Marketing: Jeffrey Myers
Executive Director, New Business Development: Todd M. Davis
Executive Director, Sales: Ken Zagor
Director, Operations: George A. Susral
Director, Production: Douglas M. Johnston
Business Director: Jim Leonard

Vice President and General Manager: Douglas J. Guendel

**Meredith Publishing Group**
President, Publishing Group: Stephen M. Lacy
Vice President-Publishing Director: Bob Mate

**Meredith Corporation**
Chairman and Chief Executive Officer: William T. Kerr

In Memoriam E. T. Meredith III (1933-2003)

All of us at Meredith® Books are dedicated to providing you with information and
ideas to enhance your home. We welcome your comments and suggestions. Write
to us at: Meredith Books, Home Decorating and Design Editorial Department, 1716
Locust St., Des Moines, IA 50309-3023.

If you would like to purchase any of our home decorating and design, cooking,
crafts, gardening, or home improvement books, check wherever quality books are
sold. Or visit us at: meredithbooks.com

For more information on the topics included in this book as well as additional
projects, visit HGTV.com/beforeandafterbook

Cover photograph: Lark Smothermon/Woolly Bugger Studios

# Table of Contents

# Introduction

Like the programs on HGTV, this book takes the guesswork out of restyling your home. The makeovers are achievable—and this book will give you the confidence and inspiration to realize your dreams.

Time marches on, and so do personal tastes. If you have purchased a new home, are preparing your home for life changes, need a room to function in a new way, or merely feel the urge to infuse your home with a new style, this book contains the inspiration and expert advice you need to make the change a reality. The focus of this book is redecorating, not time-consuming, costly remodeling that alters the structure of a room. You may be surprised how simple changes in surfaces—paint, fabrics, flooring, countertops—can take a room from woeful to wonderful.

To help you find the specific decorating ideas you want, this book of dramatic before-and-after transformations is organized by room. Within each section you will find a variety of home types, from old to new constructions, featuring different forms of architecture and decorated in all styles, including cottage, country, traditional, and contemporary. Even if you don't find a home or room that matches your own, the decorating principles at work will help you apply what you learn to your individual needs or project.

## USE WHAT YOU HAVE

Sometimes the easiest way to make over a room is to use what you have in a new, innovative way. Many of the rooms pictured incorporate the existing furnishings and accessories, but fresh fabrics and paint bring new life to the space. Even simple changes in room arrangement that you can achieve in an afternoon can make your space more functional and appealing.

## ONE ROOM TWO OR THREE WAYS

Options—that's what this book is about, so some rooms are shown redecorated in more than one way. This proves that good basic elements lend themselves to multiple decorating styles.

## PROJECTS

You can certainly opt for store-bought decorating accessories, but why not make them yourself? This allows you to personalize ready-made items, often at a fraction of the price, and gives you a sense of pride for doing it yourself. Throughout this book, you will find dozens of projects, which range from pillow construction to beaded-board paneling installation. Many projects are presented with materials lists and step-by-step instructions that make completion quick and easy.

## MORE IDEAS

Following each makeover you'll find additional information about one feature in that room—for example, lighting options for kitchens and bathrooms, or molding installations that add architectural interest in a living room. Look at the options and choose the one that best suits your home and lifestyle.

## TRIED-AND-TRUE DECORATING TIPS AND TECHNIQUES

Want to know how to make a bedroom grow with your child or how to select the best paint color for a room? You will find the answers to your decorating questions in special sidebars throughout this book. These foolproof techniques and everlasting decorating principles will help you transform your home into the comfortable, stylish haven you've always dreamed of.

## RESOURCES

Do you want the fabric or the paint color featured in one of the rooms? This section includes everything you need to know to find the materials you want quickly and easily.

Whether you want to turn your bedroom into a restful retreat or restyle your kitchen to make it a place where your family will want to linger long after a meal is over, this collection of inspiring makeovers will encourage you to get started today. The rooms are real, and the problems and solutions are believable. This is a book you will turn to again and again for practical advice and information to make your home a reflection of your personal style.

# LIVING ROOMS

# Arranged for the SEASONS

Updating a room for seasonal changes goes beyond decorative touches: Give your room a new attitude by moving the furniture to take advantage of all nature has to offer, bringing in colors and textures that reflect the time of year, and rethinking accessories. The best part? By using what you already have in innovative ways, you can capture the mood of the season.

In this long, narrow living room, a new furniture arrangement and a few seasonally appropriate touches create different looks for summer and winter. The furnishings and neutral-color slipcovers remain the same, resulting in an inexpensive afternoon makeover.

## VERSION ONE: SIMPLY SUMMER

If you have a large picture window in your living room, make the most of the natural light and views it provides. In this room, two large sofas are positioned face-to-face in front of the window. This arrangement creates a conversation space for family and friends—and a comfortable place to catch a nap in the warm sun or read by natural daylight. A coffee table between the sofas provides a place to rest feet and set beverages.

**Summery accessories set the tone.** An additional conversation area camps in front of the fireplace. This intimate setting with two dark-color rattan chairs and a petite round table is ideal for casual

dining. The shutters on the mantel evoke a feeling of breezy summer days. Other summery accessories include bright table linens, a vase of colorful flowers on the coffee table, and natural woven baskets that could easily be used for trips to the farmer's market.

**Mix warm and cool colors.** Colorwise, the white walls, warm wood floor (sans rug so that you can feel the cool, smooth floor under your bare feet), and neutral gray and eggplant-color slipcovers are a pleasing backdrop for crisp cotton pillows and vintage-look polka-dot-pattern throws in ocean blues, cream, and purple. This color scheme keeps the look cool and serene. Green, another "low-temperature" color, appears as an accent throughout the room. Orange and yellow, the complements of blue and purple, respectively, add a touch of warmth.

*Continued on page 10*

## SUMMER STYLE

Refer to these strategies when planning a summery space:

- **Color.** Consider a cool and relaxing scheme of blues, greens, and purples, with calm neutrals, such as white and beige, as the backdrop. Punch up the scheme with warm accents in red, yellow, and orange.
- **Fabrics.** Crisp cottons and linens are great fabrics to use for summer decorating, and gauzy fabrics are perfect for breezy window treatments. For the bedroom, use 100 percent cotton bedding for comfortable sleeping.
- **Textures.** Bring in natural textural finishes, including woven wicker and rattan, sisal, bamboo, and grasses.
- **Accents.** Seashells. Fresh flowers. Fruits and vegetables. Bringing the outdoors in is an ideal way to enjoy all that Mother Nature has to offer.

## VERSION TWO: WINTER

*VERSION ONE: SUMMER*

## VERSION TWO: WINTER WARMTH

When winter winds begin to howl and the temperature starts to drop, it's time to think about cuddling into comfort. Focusing on the fireplace, stashing summer fabrics and accents, and bringing in warm color accents and soft textures transform this room into an inviting haven from the cold.

**Arrange the furnishings for function.** The sofas stand back-to-back, creating distinct areas for different functions. The purple-covered sofa joins the two rattan chairs—now dressed with plump pillows—and coffee table for a cozy place to relax or converse around the warming glow of the fire. Graphic prints adorn the mantel: The bell pepper print sticks with the new color scheme and evokes memories of the season that recently passed. When the fireplace isn't in use, filling it with candles gives a pleasing glow. On the other side of the room, the gray-covered sofa faces a piano (not shown) in an intimate concert space.

**Heat up the space with color.** Warm color floods the space, from the red pillows to the orange-patterned rug beneath the gray sofa. Purple accents make an appearance in a pillow and throw, linking the two areas of the room and providing a splash of cool contrast. The tables are now uncovered, revealing warm wood tones.

**Invite cozy comfort.** Texture also defines this winter space. The summer arrangement featured crisp cottons and woven baskets; soft chenille pillows and throws pamper the space for winter.

## NICE AND NEUTRAL

A neutral palette—dominated by white, cream, or brown—is very versatile, as this room demonstrates. These colors blend into the background, allowing the warm and cool colors to take center stage, and are able to temper dominant hues. To give a neutral scheme visual interest, introduce texture, such as wood furniture and woven baskets.

## VERSION TWO: WINTER

*VERSION ONE: SUMMER*

## WINTER WONDERLAND

Consider these strategies when planning a space for the winter months:

- **Color.** Neutrals work well as an overall palette. These colors can easily be accented with warm hues—red, orange, and yellow—to take the chill out of the room on cold winter days and nights.
- **Fabrics and Textures.** Bring out the flannel, wool, fleece, velvet, and chenille for snuggling.
- **Accents.** Light up a room with candles and sparkling ornaments in a bowl. Give a nod to Mother Nature with sprigs of holly and pine displayed on the mantel or in vases.

# Seasonal Decorating

Spring. Summer. Autumn. Winter. When the seasons change, you have the opportunity to create an environment that reflects all of Mother Nature's splendor. At the onset of each season, look around and notice the colors, textures, and motifs that best reflect it. Think beyond traditional holiday decorating strategies. Assemble more universal collections that can be changed slightly for holidays, if desired. For example, the fall display *opposite above right* incorporates Halloween-motif items, such as a luminary, at the end of October and a cornucopia around Thanksgiving. The four examples shown here demonstrate how you can dress a mantel for each season. Follow these cues for tabletop and other displays throughout your home.

**Spring**. It's the time for new beginnings, so start on the right foot by filling a mantel with objects that invite light indoors. Eliminate dark, wintry decorations and bring in mirrors, empty glass containers that provide translucent sparkle, and fresh botanical prints.

**Summer.** Seaside symbols bring home the feeling of warm waves and ocean breezes—regardless of where you live. On this mantel, blond-wood frames resemble sun-bleached driftwood, and small buckets filled with sand and long grasses add breezy informality. Seashells complete the mood.

**Autumn.** When the leaves begin to change from green to brilliant oranges, reds, and yellows, look to Mother Nature for decorating inspiration. The focal point of this arrangement is a wreath placed off-center for an informal look. Copper vessels anchor the scene; melons, squashes, and pumpkins of varying sizes, colors, and textures fill in the spaces between. The slow-ripening produce can be used for seasonal recipes.

**Winter.** As the days grow short, find ways to take advantage of light. Glowing tea light candles line this mantel, and a taller candle hangs in front of the mirror. A winter landscape is further created by an oval-shape mirror, which looks like an icy pond. Topiary forms covered with miniature evergreen garlands and topped with red ribbons resemble tiny Christmas trees.

# Stylish CHOICES

S ometimes one feature of a room is so overpowering it becomes difficult to see other possibilities. In this room the dominating feature was the dark green walls. The traditional-style accessories were compatible with the color, but they were too small—and there were too few to make an impact. Everything in the room seemed featherlight, too insubstantial to balance the weighty walls.

**Identify key framework elements.** Once the walls were "neutralized" with two coats of soft ecru-beige paint, style possibilities could be more easily determined. Three steps helped build the style foundation for the space. First, two parsons chairs and a large club chair (shown on page 18), which fit the scale for the room, are dressed in fresh, simple off-white slipcovers. The chairs are comfortably positioned to form two sides of a conversation grouping, creating a good layout for finishing the room. Second, the room's windows lacked coverings; sailcloth Roman shades installed inside the frames provide the background for tab-topped panels. Finally, the addition of a plain sisal rug completes the framework on the floor.

The two styles shown, contemporary and French, illustrate how to take those critical next steps to creating style in a neutral space.

*Continued on page 16*

BEFORE

CHANEL Jean Leymarie

VERSION ONE: FRENCH

VERSION TWO: CONTEMPORARY

## VERSION ONE: FINELY FRENCH

This option gives the room a fresh approach to traditional. Pieces with curving lines and classic contours provide the French flavor. The warm cherry red from the toile curtains repeats in several pieces around the room to unify the space.

**Accessorize with color, texture, and shape.** One problem area is a long, blank wall. A white antique secretary and large oval mirror nicely fill the space while keeping the look light. Accent pieces in rattan add warm tones and gentle texture; iron pieces add curves and punctuating black touches. Cream-color curvy pitchers and urns are the perfect accessories to give this room a relaxed but stately feeling. For a little glimmer, silver vases and frames dot the room.

The sisal rug gets a celadon green banding to define the edges of the conversation grouping without adding too strong a color.

Inside the antique secretary, contoured pottery, silver-tone frames, and old books complement the overall French feel of the room.

Cherry red and deep pink accents bring warm color into the mostly neutral space.

## CREATING YOUR STYLE

Making big changes in a room that's firmly planted in one style can be a daunting task. Here are some ideas to help you formulate a new style for any room.

- **Go beyond neutral.** In this room, it would have been easy to stop with neutral everything—and after such an overwhelming wall color (dark green) such a decision would have been understandable. However, the room would have looked bland. If you start with a clear idea of the desired end result and work toward it, you'll have the motivation to complete the project.
- **Think of style as a layer.** If committing to upholstery, wall color, and window treatments in a particular style is more than you feel comfortable doing, create a neutral base, as was done here, and start choosing accessories and inexpensive, yet quality, furniture of a particular style for one area of the room. If you don't like it, your investment is minimal; if you do like it, you're halfway to completion.
- **Pick a point to start from—and follow it for every decision.** In this room, two approaches to defining a starting point are shown. In the contemporary version, a large painting is the key feature, setting the style and color selection. In the French version, the style itself guided the choices. Whatever your starting point, compare all your choices to it. You needn't follow a style or a color slavishly, but keeping your starting point as the focus helps unify the space.
- **Appreciate the good points.** Rarely is a room redecorated from scratch, and unless you do major remodeling, windows and doors will stay in place. So start on a positive note. This room had big windows and very nice seating pieces. Built from those elements, the makeover was easier to accomplish—and less expensive.
- **Pinpoint the trouble spots.** Note what makes a room uncomfortable and have a plan to deal with troublesome areas. Too much glare from the windows? Put filtering window treatments on the list. In this room, the wall color wasn't working, the windows needed subtle coverings, and a dark corner and long blank wall needed special attention. In the contemporary redo, the dark corner became a focal point; in the French-style redo, the long blank wall received two good-size pieces (the secretary and the mirror).

## VERSION TWO: CONTEMPORARY CREATION

This style choice started with a dramatic abstract painting; the style of the room radiates from this focal point, formerly a dark corner. Peachy pink and light blue from the painting are repeated in fabrics and accessories throughout the room. The sleek torchiére indirectly lights the painting and illuminates the corner.

**Bring purpose—and focus—to a corner.** Four framed contemporary prints form a single visual unit on the long wall opposite the painting, and a trio of upholstered cubes take up residence underneath the drawings. These are multipurpose pieces: The cushioned tops pop off to reveal storage space, and the cubes can be pulled into seating service when needed. A large urn filled with curly willow branches adds height and texture to this corner— and balances the painting in the opposite corner.

**Ground the design.** Between the parsons chairs sits a glass-top table, an airy piece perfect in front of a window. It could, however, look too lightweight, so a light-color contemporary drawing is casually propped in the window to visually anchor the space.

**Punctuate with black.** In the center of the room, an ottoman draped with an animal-print throw sits on the sisal rug. The sharp angles of the decor are reflected in the black banding on the rug, and black accents spot the room to carry the contemporary theme.

**Bring balance with simple window treatments.** With strong style statements throughout the room, the curtains are subdued; simple sailcloth panels frame the windows.

*AFTER*

If luxurious fabrics such as silk are out of your price range, use them sparingly—as accents only—on pillows and other small items. This pillow has a quilted envelope fold and is embellished with a beaded tassel for a hint of romance.

## FABRIC STRATEGIES

- The quality of upholstered furniture can vary. Pieces from the 1940s and 1950s often are constructed better than newer pieces; therefore, it might be worth spending the money to reupholster or slipcover them.
- Love an old sofa but not its droopy fabric and sagging seat cushions? If it has good lines and is well-constructed, a good workroom can add or replace batting and foam to make it comfortable again.
- Inexpensive fabrics can be enlivened with details. Chambray, twill, and cotton duck are sturdy, inexpensive materials that can be dressed up or dressed down. Trims, buttons, bows, and other dressmaker details can make plain fabric on a chair more interesting. Adding pillows covered in sumptuous fabrics is another way to dress up plain fabrics.
- If your windows are an odd size or have an odd configuration, don't assume that you'll have to have custom curtains made. Carry the measurements with you as you shop; you may be surprised by the variety of sizes of ready-made window treatments.

# MORE IDEAS FOR

# Freshening with Fabric

Fabrics, with all their pattern and color, have the power to transform a room. If your living room needs a punch of style, but you love your furnishings and the wall color, consider adding doses of fabric by way of slipcovers, pillows, window treatments, and small accessories such as lampshades and fabric-covered storage containers. When choosing fabric, consider the style of your room and how the room is used. For example, select tough, hard-wearing denim and corduroy if children frequently use the room. Antique fabrics with a faded, timeworn patina are perfect for window treatments and pillow covers in casual cottage-style settings.

If your living room suffers from textured drywall, cracked plaster, or dated paneling, hide the flaws with fabric. This stylish, drapey muslin panel swags between playful hooks screwed into a 1x4. This treatment provides the perfect camouflage for walls in need of repair. Coordinating checked fabric brings bold pattern to the window and chair cushion.

Loose, skirted chair slipcovers are an ideal choice for this relaxed cottage-style living room. The mix of patterned fabrics in similar colors—from florals of different sizes to the bold checks—adds interest to the room without overpowering it. The living room and adjoining kitchen are unified by the use of the same large floral-motif fabric on pillows and valances. See page 112 for more information on mixing fabric motifs and colors.

Fabrics can be more than slipcovers, window treatments, and other typical soft furnishings. If you have a prized collection of textiles, such as Native American blankets like those shown, antique quilts, or hand-dyed African fabrics, show them off! Hang them on rods or ladders propped against a wall. Frame those that are delicate or that require special care. Two caveats: To prevent fading, display textiles away from direct sunlight, and to avoid permanent creasing where textiles have been folded and hung, unfold them every so often and refold in a different way.

Fabrics in bright, sunny yellows and fresh pinks offset the dark woodwork and tiny windows in this living room. The slipcovers unite an assortment of traditional and contemporary furnishings. Patterned accent fabrics, such as covered lampshades and the banding on the sisal rug, add a feminine touch.

# Boxy to BEAUTIFUL

You can revitalize any humdrum space—just take cues from this makeover. In this modular home, the living room is a boxy space with almost no architectural character. Adding visual interest is the key to making this a successful transformation; creating visual softness and defining a focal point are essential to the task.

**Frame the space with wood.** The thin walls in this home required attention first. They were originally covered with pale green painted paneling. Instead of ripping it down and starting from scratch, the paneling now wears a disguise of evenly spaced 1x4 boards, which make the old paneling seams less noticeable. The 60-inch-tall boards are capped with a plate rail, which runs around the perimeter of the room, providing visual interest and display space. The wall is topped with a hefty crown molding that visually flows right into the ceiling and is finished with an extra-tall baseboard. All the woodwork is painted a creamy white—a traditional cottage-style accent.

**Create a sense of spaciousness.** Although the ceiling is only 8 feet high in this room, the ornate moldings give it a grand appearance, and smart color choices make the space seem larger. Between the plate rail and crown molding, the walls are painted a deep purple; the ceiling is painted in a softer purple. This use of color visually heightens the walls and draws attention to the moldings.

**Windows can take center stage.** The wall with large windows had the potential of becoming a focal point, but there were no details to catch the eye. To start, new white energy-efficient windows are installed. For impact, boards are mounted between the windows, and a header is mounted above the windows to make them appear to be one unit. Simple wood blinds rather than window-blocking fabric treatments keep the focus on the architecture.

*Continued on page 24*

**BEFORE**

*AFTER*

**Rethink furniture arrangement for increased function.** After the "frame" of the room was complete, the furnishings and function of the space needed evaluation. Originally, the loves seat was floating in the room; it wasn't anchored to the chairs for a conversation grouping, and it was at an awkward angle for viewing the television. The newly slipcovered furniture pieces face the pine armoire, which moved from the corner to the wall adjacent to the windows. For additional

seating, a white bench (shown on page 23) joins the grouping. A large area rug, which is placed atop new neutral carpeting, anchors the arrangement.

**Cottage-style colors and accents complete the look.** The rug brings together the room's soft palette of cream, green, and purple. These three colors convene in a coordinated set of fabrics, which cover the love seat, chairs, and plump ottoman. The fabrics provide visual softness against the crisp, defined lines of the molding. The striped and floral fabrics are in scale with one another and set the stage for casual cottage-style accessories, including numerous shapes and sizes of candles, tin tiles that flank the armoire, and smooth-lined lamps and tables. Touches of silver join the mix in photo frames, lamp bases, and candle accessories.

**Consider multifunction pieces.** The finishing touch in this living room is the combination flip-top bench and coatrack, which provides practical storage. The bench serves as a convenient place to change footwear.

BEFORE

AFTER

## Storage Box

This versatile storage box can work in any room of your home. It's a great place to stash stuff, and the top can serve as a place to sit to take off and put on shoes. This box has been mounted to the wall to appear as part of a single unit with the coat hooks above, but keeping it freestanding gives you the flexibility to move it where it's needed.

### You Will Need

Poplar board cut to the following: 18x24" front and back (2); 15x18" sides (2); 15x24" top and bottom (2)
Hammer, nails
Trim, cut in sizes to cover corner seams
Wood glue

Sandpaper, primer, latex paint in the desired color and finish, paintbrush
2 piano hinges
Screwdriver, screws
2 glass beads, tacky glue

**1** Construct the box by nailing together the front, back, sides, and bottom, following the illustration.

**2** Apply trim to the box edges with wood glue, covering the seams.

**3** Lightly sand the box and the top piece (lid). Prime; let dry. Paint; let dry.

**4** Attach the lid to the box with the piano hinges. Mount the hinges on the inside of the box and underside of the lid.

**5** To form the lip on the box lid, use tacky glue to attach a glass bead to each front corner on the underside of the lid.

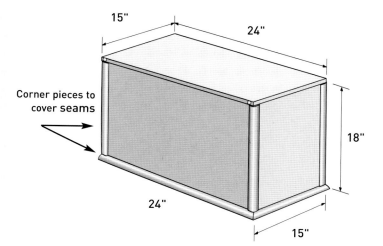

15"
24"
Corner pieces to cover **seams**
18"
24"
15"

Adding Architecture with Moldings

Fresh from the lumberyard shelf, a combination of stock moldings in different shapes packs lots of personality for relatively little cost.

Built-in hutches are an asset to any home. Windowsill, Colonial, and standard molding pieces replicate a built-in hutch in this dining room; using the same wallpaper within the plate racks and below the chair rail enhances the illusion. For a similar look, draw the dimensions of the hutch on the wall; wallpaper within this area. Build the outer frame from poplar strips and cut windowsill stock for the shelves; paint the pieces and nail the shelves to the frame. Glue a piece of screen molding to the top of each windowsill piece, 2½ inches from the back, to form a lip. Mount the box to the wall. Cut the Colonial molding to fit the windowsill stock and paint each piece. Glue to the underside of each windowsill strip, aligning back edges. Attach quarter round to the front of the Colonial molding with glue and nails.

Vertical and horizontal molding strips can break up a tall wall, making it appear shorter. If you have high ceilings and want to visually shorten the walls, divide the wall horizontally; paint one color above the line and another below. For a look similar to this, paint dots in a contrasting color below the line. Cut screen molding strips to fit between the baseboard and where the under-cap molding will sit (at or near the line). Paint the screen molding, then glue and nail it to the wall, evenly spacing it. Cut the under-cap molding to fit the wall; paint, then glue and nail to the wall. Top the under-cap molding with painted doorstop molding cut to size.

Shaker pegs, topped with a shelf that's ideal for display space, act as hangers for photographs. To create this shelf, cut 1x8 pine boards the length of the wall; rip the boards to 4 inches wide for the shelf and 3⅜ inches for the peg rails. Paint the boards. Glue and nail the shelf to the rail, with the back edges flush at right angles. Cut decorative molding to fit the joint between the shelf and rail; paint, then glue and nail in place. Drill holes for the pegs, evenly spacing them along the rail. Mount the rail to the wall, drilling through some of the peg holes. Paint the pegs and glue in place.

# Crisp and
# CONTEMPORARY

Once a barren study space used as a pass-through, this room lacked real purpose. The challenge was transforming the under-utilized room into a functional space where people would want to linger. Help came in the form of paint, comfortable furnishings, and a mix of clean-lined contemporary accessories.

**Mask damaged walls with paint.** Romantic harlequin diamonds in a two-tone colorwash create a dramatic focal point in this room. Because the overall pattern is busy—and time-consuming to create—the treatment is reserved for one wall behind the sofa. The adjoining walls are painted in the darker of the diamond colors, keeping the focus on the pattern. The colorwashing technique is ideal for walls in ill condition, like the walls in this room: The paint will settle into any cracks and crevices, producing a highly textural appearance that enhances blemishes, making them a part of the design. The ceiling and crown molding have a fresh coat of white paint that visually lifts the ceiling.

**Clean lines accentuate the focal point wall.** The rich, warm color scheme on the walls defines the space and serves as a subtle backdrop for the brown upholstered sofa and chair and for natural wood furnishings in finishes from light to dark. The coffee table and metal-base lamps have a contemporary edge that blends well with the simple lines of the overstuffed sofa and chair. The clean lines throughout the room keep the attention on the diamond-painted wall. The area rug warms the wood floor and unifies the conversation grouping.

*Continued on page 30*

## HOW COLOR AFFECTS A ROOM

When selecting paint colors for a room, first consider the size of your room, then decide whether you want to enhance its features or trick the eye into seeing the space in a different way. Follow these cues to help you select the colors that are right for your particular needs.

- **Closer** Warm colors advance, making walls seem closer.
- **Farther Away** Cool colors recede, making walls appear farther away.
- **Narrower** White or light-color ceilings make a room look narrower—and taller—when paired with dark walls.
- **Larger** Light-color walls make a room look larger because they reflect a lot of light rather than absorb it.
- **Lower** Dark painted ceilings visually make a room shorter.
- **Smaller** Walls in dark colors make a room appear smaller because they absorb light rather than reflect it.
- **Higher** White ceilings appear higher.
- **Wider** If you desire a wider-looking room, combine a dark ceiling with light walls.

BEFORE

*AFTER*

*AFTER*

**Use shapes and lines as contrast.** To keep the strong lines from making the room seem too hard-edged, plump pillows with stylized flowers grace the sofa. An oversize round clock, a graphic print on the desk (shown on page 29), and a tall floral arrangement with naturally flowing lines help balance the formal harlequin pattern.

The room still serves its original function (as an office), but now the space also is a place to relax or entertain.

The defined lines of the painted harlequin diamond wall are balanced by accessories with soft curves, including the floral motif on the pillows.

 For more information on sensational paint treatments, visit **HGTV**.com/beforeandafterbook

# Harlequin Diamond Walls

This classic design, with diamonds that are taller than they are wide, is versatile: Large or small, diamond patterns lend a sophisticated feel to rooms decorated in any manner. When choosing the size of your diamond pattern, keep the scale of the room and its furnishings in mind. Remember that the smaller the pattern, the more time-consuming the process will be (because you will need to measure, mark, and paint more diamonds). For ease in creating a diamond pattern, work with a partner and use a chalk line, as described below.

The diamonds in this living room/office are colorwashed in light and medium yellow for subtle contrast. For basic colorwashing, start with a light (white or cream) base coat and mix the top coat paint with glaze, a transparent medium that allows the paint to stay workable longer than plain paint. The glaze/paint mixture will create depth when applied to the walls with a sponge in circular strokes or with a paintbrush in a crosshatching motion. This design features two colors, but you can use a palette of colors for the technique.

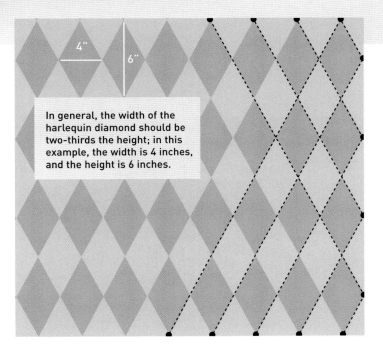

In general, the width of the harlequin diamond should be two-thirds the height; in this example, the width is 4 inches, and the height is 6 inches.

## You Will Need

Satin or semi-gloss latex paint for base coat, white or cream
Satin or semi-gloss latex paint for top coat, two colors
Tape measure
Colored pencil that matches top coat paint
Chalk line
Optional: Painter's tape
Glaze
Bucket and mixing tool
Roller and paint tray
Paintbrushes or sea sponges

1. Apply the base coat paint to the wall; let dry.

2. Measure the height and width of the wall. Using these measurements, determine the size (height and width) of the individual diamonds in the design.

3. Using the illustration as a guide, measure and mark the width of the diamonds along the top and bottom of the wall using the tape measure and colored pencil. Measure and mark the height along each side in the same manner.

4. Working with a partner, snap a chalk line to join the marks. This creates the diagonal lines of the design.

5. If you desire crisp diamonds, use painter's tape to mask off (tape around as an outline to be filled in with paint) diamonds in the first color you would like to paint. If you prefer a more freehand look, use the chalk lines as a guide. For either method, put a small piece of tape in the diamonds reserved for the second top coat color to prevent a pattern mishap.

6. Mix 4 parts glaze to 1 part top coat paint (first color).

7. Using either a paintbrush in a crosshatching X motion or a damp sea sponge in a circular motion, apply the glaze/paint mixture to the diamonds. Work quickly to ensure the mixture stays wet and workable. Remove painter's tape, if used, and let dry.

8. Remove the small pieces of tape in the remaining diamonds; mask off these diamonds if desired. Mix 4 parts glaze to 1 part of the second top coat paint. Paint the diamonds as in Step 7. Remove painter's tape, if used, and let dry.

Adding Drama with Paint

Any room will benefit from a fresh coat of paint, whether you're using a solid color or a decorative technique. Areas where people tend to gather, such as living and family rooms, are natural places to showcase color. Match colors and decorative techniques to the style of your room, taking cues from the furnishings, carpeting, window treatments, and accessories.

Embossed wallcoverings, available at specialty paint stores and home improvement centers, can be found in multiple motifs to suit nearly every decorating style. While the wallcoverings may be left white—or painted with a solid color of paint—using a squeegee to reveal the raised portions creates visual depth (the raised details stand out against the darker recessed areas). For this technique, first paint the wallcovering with a base coat of semi-gloss paint; let dry. Mix 1 part top coat paint (semi-gloss) with 4 parts glaze, paint over the base coat, and immediately remove some of the top coat glaze/paint mixture with a squeegee. In this contemporary living room, a light blue paint is used as the base coat; a darker blue top coat is used on portions of the wall, creating wide vertical stripes. A solid dark blue horizontal stripe breaks up the busy wall and serves as a stately backdrop for four framed photographs.

Polka dots make a lighthearted addition to a casual setting. In this room, inexpensive and easy-to-use dauber sponges, commonly used for stenciling and stamping, create layered dots. Paint the wall with the desired background color; let dry. Randomly paint dots onto the wall with one dauber; let dry. Using a marker, draw a row of scallops around the outer edge of another dauber and use scissors to cut along the line; draw and cut a row of scallops around the center, forming a ring. Use the cut dauber and another color of paint to stamp over the existing dots.

Fresco is a classic paint technique that can produce a contemporary feel, as in this spirited living area. Apply a layer of drywall joint compound to the wall, using a spackling knife and sweeping motions; let dry. Sand down protruding ridges and prime the wall with a high-nap roller. Paint the wall in a light base coat color like white or off-white; the top coat glaze/paint mixture will have more depth when applied over a light base coat. Mix a darker top coat color (1 part) with glaze (4 parts) and apply to the wall in a random fashion, allowing some of the base coat to show.

# Easy-Going yet Elegant
## FAMILY STYLE

Vaulted ceilings, big windows, and wood floors give the family room of this suburban home a lot of interest and plenty of light. The intent of this redo is to add that missing layer of comfort and ease that say "home." The challenge is creating the evolved look of casual style in a single pass.

**Flowing window treatments balance distinct lines.** A pretty, lightweight floral fabric serves as the window covering, which features several stylish design elements: The elegant draping swags capped with white decorative iron pieces celebrate the vaulted ceiling and the Palladian window's glorious height. The neatly pleated valances on all but the tallest window add a little structure. The combination of blinds and swags softens the sharp edges of the window frames and permits control of the bright sunlight that pours into the room. A warm taupe wall color accentuates the windows.

**Consider all the elements in a room when hanging fixtures.** A delicate Italian chandelier that's painted white brings the eye to the height of the Palladian window, but no higher. As one enters the room, the chandelier is perfectly framed by the window.

**Classic cottage style: warm wood tones and pastels.** Rich wood floors are easy to care for, a necessary asset for this busy room. They provide the perfect anchor for the white-slip-covered sofas and chair that make up the conversation area. The pink and white color scheme travels from the window treatments to throw pillows—plain and ruffled—in solids, prints, and checks. A whitewashed coffee table with a wood top centers the conversation group and firmly establishes the casual yet chic look.

*Continued on page 36*

**BEFORE**

*AFTER*

**Curvy lines accentuate the space.** Two corners of the room are softened considerably with a pair of round tables from the 1940s (shown on page 35). Painted creamy white, the tables feature curving legs and edges that perfectly complement this room and provide a stylish surface for delicate lamps embellished with crystal drops.

**Give an armoire focal-point status.** An antique armoire, also painted creamy white, stands against the one solid wall as a commanding but not overpowering focal point. The light color keeps the piece from looking top-heavy or bulky in this airy room. The recessed areas of the doors are covered in a delicately patterned wallpaper, adding elegant detail to the large armoire. Inside this older piece are the accoutrements necessary for the modern family room: video and stereo equipment. Storing these pieces behind doors keeps them readily accessible without allowing them to be the center of attention; that compromise maintains the beauty of the room without impeding the function.

**Slipcovers can give importance.** Although this room serves casual family needs, attention to detail fosters elegance. Consider, for example, the slipcover for the wing chair: Because this tall chair sits at the entrance to the room, the pleated skirt that wraps the bottom of the chair sits 4 inches off the floor. This gives the significant piece a lighter, airier look than if the slipcover draped to the floor, as those on the sofas do.

## CREATING INFORMAL ELEGANCE

At first glance this room looks as though it has evolved easily into its casual, refined state. Even if the homeowners had had the leisure of developing the look over time, they would have employed many of the same principles (explained below) used in doing it all at once.

- **Choose core colors.** Choosing a white and pink theme accented with warm tones keeps the look clean, but choosing a basic color scheme in a room needn't tie you down. Rather, choose something that allows you creative flexibility while helping you focus on a final goal.
- **Fear not white!** Even though a rambunctious young family tramples through this room, white slipcovers work well. They are removable, so they can be washed easily when too many spills have occurred. The inviting drape of white slipcovers is casual, not sloppy, and the light color is an inviting backdrop for many styles.
- **Include dressmaker details.** Casually drooping slipcovers and loose swags of curtains are offset by the universal neatness accent: pleats. Pleated valances, slipcover skirts, and lampshades add visual order throughout the room.
- **Choose shapes that provide a framework for the space.** Keeping the sofas saved a lot of money, but on their own, the pieces are a bit nondescript. Accenting them with a wing chair, curvy end tables, and an armoire with graceful lines gives them—and the entire room—a more complete personality. The lamps and swagged curtains add complementary curving lines.

The crisply pleated valances in this living room display two romantic touches: White iron pieces grace the top of each valance, and beaded fringe dances playfully on the bottom.

Floral-motif embossed wallpaper, installed in the recessed panels of the armoire, adds elegance to the painted piece.

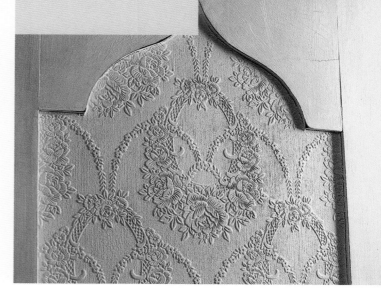

# Painted and Papered Armoire

Wood armoires—vintage and new—make impressive focal points in any room. But when left unfinished, they can sometimes be more of an eyesore. Painting an armoire and adding a subtly patterned wallpaper to the recessed areas can make it a more pleasing focal point in your room.

## You Will Need

Soap, water, bucket, rags
Wood putty, scraper
Fine-grit sandpaper, tack cloth
Paper, pencil, scissors

Embossed wallpaper, wallpaper paste, wallpaper smoother, sponge
Primer, latex paint in cream or white and any finish, paintbrushes
Brown glaze, rag

1. Remove the doors and drawers from the armoire. Thoroughly clean the armoire; dry.

2. Fill in any gouges, cracks, and holes with wood putty. When dry, sand to a smooth finish.

3. Sand the entire armoire to prepare it for painting. Using the tack cloth, remove any dust particles.

4. If your armoire has recessed panels similar to the ones pictured here, use paper and pencil to create a pattern for the wallpaper. Cut out the pattern and transfer it to the wallpaper; cut out.

5. Using wallpaper paste, adhere the wallpaper to the recessed panel. Carefully smooth out any wrinkles with a wallpaper smoother and use a damp sponge to wipe up any paste that has seeped from behind the paper. Repeat for all recessed areas.

6. Prime the armoire, including the recessed wallpapered portions; let dry.

7. Paint the armoire cream or white; let dry.

8. Sand the raised edges (i.e., corners) for a worn, distressed look.

9. Lightly rub brown glaze onto the armoire, including the wallpapered portions, to further age it.

# Cottage-Style Decorating

FURNISHED
ROOMS

Cottage style is all about calm, relaxation, and creating a retreat you can enjoy as an everyday getaway. Imagine your dream vacation home or ideal home-away-from-home: Is it a cottage on a lake you visited as a child? Or do you long for a rustic haven in the middle of the woods? Which elements do these places have? Comfortable furnishings that invite you to curl up in front of the fireplace with a good book? Vintage textiles, worn wood tables, and a soft color palette? Go to flea markets, thrift and antiques stores, and salvage yards to find charming timeworn furnishings and accessories that will transform your living spaces into the getaway you've always longed for.

Embellished pillows, furnishings painted a creamy white, and flea market finds fill this cozy, cottage-style living room. A mix of textures and architectural elements, from the gauzy fabric draped over the old three-panel floor screen to the large tin tile, gives the room a luxurious feel.

If your home lacks a porch, bring the outdoors in with wicker furnishings, vintage textiles, and garden-inspired accessories. Placing the chairs in front of the windows heightens the effect.

Cottage touches bloom on fabrics, hatboxes, and framed embroidery in this comfortable home. Distressed furnishings and found objects such as seashells complete the look. If you are unable to find authentic distressed pieces, see page 63 for instructions on giving wood furnishings and doors an aged, antique look.

It's all in the details: When decorating in a casual style, look for old discarded items such as this metal screen-door protector, which now serves as a place to display cherished photographs.

# Designed for LIVING

Living rooms are used for many activities, including reading, relaxing, watching television, and a playspace for children. It's little wonder, then, that these rooms often become cluttered with books and magazines, audiovisual equipment, and toys. Finding stylish storage solutions can be a problem, but this living room handles it with grace. A bookcase is converted into an entertainment center that conceals the television when it's not in use; footlockers covered in imitation suede become deep storage chests that also serve as extra seating; new benches that flank the fireplace corral CDs and magazines.

**Punch up the scheme with a mix of color and pattern.** Storage wasn't the only challenge, however. The nearly mono-chromatic scheme lacked excitement—green covered the walls, furnishings, and accessories, accented only by cream. The fresh, light green is still the foundation for the scheme in the newly transformed space, but lavender accents and a mix of striped, floral, and solid fabrics enliven the room. A custom floorcloth replaces the chenille rug and anchors the room by bringing together all the colors in the furnishings, fabrics, and accessories.

**Ample seating for all.** Because this room hosts many visitors, sufficient seating space is a must. The green chair is still in place, but the old taupe sofa has been replaced with a larger, more comfortable cream-color sofa. The benches placed on each side of the fireplace and the ottomans set on casters provide seating and practical storage; both can be moved around the room to suit various needs and configurations. Piles of pillows beckon guests to the seating pieces; they also can be tossed on the floor for casual seating.

**Draw attention to the fireplace.** Originally, the fireplace, the focal point of the room, stood out against the unadorned green walls, but it lacked emphasis because of mismatched, cluttered accessories set atop the mantel. The mantel display is now simplified with three clean-line vintage vases; on the wall four photographs transferred onto canvas flank the mantel. A stack of hatboxes covered in art papers provides additional storage and can even serve as an impromptu end table.

## PAINTED FLOORCLOTHS

Floorcloths are an inexpensive, easy way to add style, color, and pattern to any room. Preprimed canvas—canvas treated with artist's gesso—is available by the yard, by the ounce, per square foot, or by a number and name at crafts and art supply stores (the higher the number, the stronger the canvas). Cut canvas to the desired size and shape with scissors or a rotary cutter, or purchase precut canvas, such as rectangles and circles. Most canvas is nonfraying, but some types may require "hemming" with an adhesive, such as hot glue. This floorcloth is divided into 11½-inch squares and painted with acrylic paint in dark and light lavender, green, teal, and cream (note that latex paint also may be used); the crisp lines are created with the aid of painter's tape. To protect a floorcloth against wear, two coats of clear acrylic polyurethane are applied to the top.

❋ For additional floorcloth ideas and projects,
visit **HGTV.com/beforeandafterbook**

**BEFORE**

*AFTER*

# Storage Bench

Stylish storage is easy to create: With bullnose wood panels and a couple of hours you can build a simple bench that can be used for storage and seating.

## You Will Need

3/4" bullnose wood panels, cut to the following: 33x11¼" seat and bottom shelf (2); 21x11¼" sides (2)
Pencil
Drill or screwdriver
2" wood screws
Optional: L brackets

Wood putty, scraper
Sandpaper, tack cloth
Primer, latex paint in the desired color and finish, paintbrush
11¼x33x3" piece of foam
1 yard decorator fabric, 45" wide
Scissors, needle, matching thread

**1** Following the illustration, make pencil lines on the side panels where the seat and bottom shelf will be.

**2** Drill pilot holes on each side panel, where they will be attached to the shelves.

**3** Screw the shelves to the side panels. If additional support is needed, attach L brackets.

**4** Using wood putty, fill in the gaps where the shelf meets each side panel at the front bullnose; let dry.

**5** Lightly sand the bench; remove dust with the tack cloth. Prime; let dry. Paint; let dry.

**6** Wrap the fabric around the foam as if wrapping a present; trim excess fabric. Secure the fabric to the underside of the foam with a few stitches. Place the covered cushion on the bench seat.

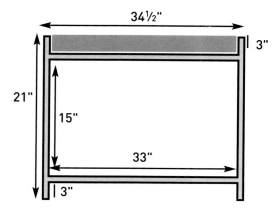

34½"
3"
21"
15"
33"
3"

# Trunk Ottoman

Ottomans can be more than a place to rest your feet; they can provide hidden storage. For an affordable storage ottoman, take a footlocker or trunk and cover it in soft, strong, nonfraying imitation suede.

## You Will Need

Trunk or footlocker (the top of this example is 16x30")
Pencil or marker
Latex paint to match faux suede, paintbrush
2" thick foam, cut to fit top of footlocker or trunk
Quilt batting to cover sides and top of trunk
Staple gun, staples
Screwdriver or drill
4 screw-in casters with screws/nuts
2 yards faux suede in the desired color
Scissors
Long needle, matching thread
Thin-gauge wire
Straight pins
1 drawer pull
Braided trim to match faux suede
10 buttons with shanks to match faux suede

**1** Mark the location of the hinges on the inside of the trunk. Remove all hardware (handles, hinges and latches) from the trunk or footlocker.

**2** Paint the inside of the trunk; let dry.

**3** Place the foam on top of the lid. Center six layers of quilt batting on top of the foam. Cut a small square from each corner of batting so that it easily folds around the foam and lid; staple batting to the sides of the lid, keeping in mind that too many staples can create a rippled effect when the faux suede is pulled taut inside the lid.

**4** Staple four layers of batting to the outside of the trunk.

**5** Turn over the trunk. Predrill holes for the casters; screw the casters into place.

**6** Cut the faux suede to cover the top and sides of the trunk. Place the fabric right side down on top of the trunk. Pin the corners to sew a seam and create a fitted top; turn right side out and slip over the top of the trunk. Staple the fabric to the inside of the trunk lid, pulling the fabric taut.

**7** Cut slits for the hinges on the back of the trunk; fold any excess fabric up and under.

**8** On the inside of the trunk lid, drill 10 holes for tufting (every 5 inches in two rows). Using a long needle and long double thread, place the needle into the hole and bring through the lid. Place thin-gauge wire into the needle hole and pull the needle back through hole with thread. Take out the wire, thread the button, and poke the shank through to the top. Place the button on the thread, pull the thread tight to tuft, and tie off, clipping the threads close to the button. Repeat for each button.

**9** For the sides, sew the front and one side piece of the faux suede together with right sides facing. Repeat with the back and remaining side piece. Place the fabric on the trunk; pin the pieces together to create a fitted slipcover; remove. Sew the two sections together, place on the trunk, and staple to the inside. Check that the fabric is even around the bottom as you staple to the inside of the trunk.

**10** Attach the drawer pull to the center front of the trunk lid.

**11** Cut the braided trim into pieces to cover the inside of the trunk and lid. Glue the pieces in place over the staples.

**12** Reattach the trunk hinges in the marked locations (Step 1).

TV Storage

Convenience and easy viewing are priorities for rooms that house televisions and audiovisual equipment, but when these items are located in the main living area, they tend to take center stage. If you love watching movies and catching up on the latest news, and you aren't willing to find another location for the TV, at least make its presence more discreet. If you have an entertainment center, consider adding doors or a fabric curtain to hide the equipment when it's not in use. Scout out underused space—for instance, beneath a staircase—to keep the room's attention on furnishings, artwork, and collections.

A niche for a television and stereo equipment makes the most of space beneath the stairs in this home. Doors hide the equipment when it's not in use. When planning spaces for electronic gear, allow for the manufacturer's suggested ventilation space and for electrical outlets and appropriate wiring.

Although this fireplace is no longer used for its original purpose, it still has an important function: The doors above the circa-1850 mantel conceal a television.

Armoires are wonderful places to store televisions and related equipment: Doors hide what's stashed within, and myriad techniques can be used to make even the most ordinary armoire a striking focal point in any room. The nature-inspired color scheme and motif painted on this armoire blend in with the knotty pine paneling and lodge-look accessories. See page 37 for an armoire that has been whitewashed and wallpapered to suit a cottage-style setting.

# KITCHENS &
# DINING ROOMS

# Light but not WHITE

Design axioms are best interpreted rather than blindly applied. For example, "use white to make a space look larger" can sometimes create a stark and boring room if you follow only the letter of the law. Instead, select an eye-pleasing blend of light tones. In this tiny condo kitchen, a $1,000 makeover created a space that's bright, inviting, and functional.

**Warm the space with color and wood tones; add visual punch with hardware.** A "butter and cream" combination of mellow white and soft yellow paint softens the harsh contrast of heavily grained oak cabinets and muddy-blue walls. The repositioned refrigerator and ominously black dishwasher receive coverings to reduce their visual prominence. Large, shiny drawer and cabinet pulls make way for small, brushed-silver-tone knobs that do the job inconspicuously. New wood laminate flooring topped with an apple green rug completes the surface warming.

**Good lighting is a kitchen essential.** With two doors but no windows, the room required a good lighting plan. The soft yellow walls and one-shade-from-white cabinets stretch and soften the light from existing sources: a ceiling fixture, a fluorescent strip over the sink, and a single-bulb fixture in the stove hood. To improve the countertop lighting, two brushed-nickel lamps stand at the ready, an unexpected but elegant addition to the lighting pool.

**Keep an eye on the details.** Because everything is exposed in a small kitchen, think aesthetics as well as function. The new faucet upgrades the plain stainless-steel sink. New towels and a rug complement the new look. The lamps and a gathering of simple white pitchers pretty up the countertop landscape. A wood stool provides a handy place to sit but easily can be moved out of the way when the cooking action heats up.

BEFORE

*AFTER*

Lamps with brushed-nickel bases and understated white shades add elegant task lighting. The lamp base complements other brushed-nickel elements in the room, including the new faucet (shown below).

The top of this refrigerator is used as storage space; keeping the items in baskets reduces clutter.

## SIZEWISE

- In a small kitchen, appliances can visually dominate and make the room feel crowded. Here, turning the refrigerator 90 degrees increases the usable floorspace and downplays the visual impact of the appliance. Covering the black facade of the dishwasher with a custom panel makes it blend neatly with the freshly painted cabinetry.
- Baskets maximize the storage potential of the refrigerator. A large wicker basket tucked in the back corner stores paper towels, a second basket holds other kitchen essentials, and a small basket-tray at the fore holds bottled water. When the design or packaging of a product looks good, use it as part of your display (especially in a grouping like the water bottles on top of this refrigerator) to free up precious closed-cabinet storage space.
- If your space is small, you may be able to splurge on one item, such as flooring or countertops, because you don't need much of it. About half the budget in this makeover went for flooring labor and materials.

# PROJECTS

## Refrigerator Bulletin Board

If one side or both sides of your refrigerator is exposed, this is a great project to put that unused space to good decorative use.

### You Will Need

36x48" bulletin board
Newspapers or other protective floor covering
Matte spray paint, black or other desired color
Tape measure
Scissors

1½ yards fabric, in the desired color and motif
Spray adhesive
Tacky glue
Decorative buttons
Brass thumbtacks
Double-sided carpet tape

**1** Place the bulletin board on the newspapers or other protective floor covering.

**2** Carefully paint the frame of the bulletin board; let dry and spray a second coat. **Note:** *It doesn't matter if paint gets on the bulletin board portion, because it will be covered with fabric.*

**3** Measure the bulletin board portion (inside the frame). Get the exact measurement so the fabric will completely cover the area. Cut the fabric to this size.

**4** Thoroughly spray the bulletin board portion with spray adhesive, following the manufacturer's instructions. Starting at the top left corner, carefully press on the fabric, smoothing it so there are no bubbles.

**5** Using tacky glue, adhere the decorative buttons to the brass thumbtacks. Press the buttons along the outer edge of the bulletin board to resemble upholstery tacks.

**6** Turn the bulletin board over. Attach double-sided carpet tape around the outside edges. Adhere the bulletin board to the side of the refrigerator.

## Dishwasher Panel

Creating a panel to disguise an off-color dishwasher is an inexpensive alternative to having a panel custom-made or purchasing a new dishwasher. This example has been painted to resemble the cabinets, but you could top the panel with magnetic or chalkboard paint to make a child's drawing space. If you do not own a saw to cut the plywood and lathing strips, note that many home improvement centers will make cuts free of charge or for a minimal fee; mitered cuts may cost extra.

### You Will Need

Tape measure
½" plywood
Optional: Saw, miter saw
1" lathing strips
Wood glue
Finishing nails

Hammer
1½" molding that matches cabinetry
Sandpaper, tack cloth
Primer, latex paint in the desired color and finish, paintbrush
Hook-and-loop tape
Scissors

**1** Measure the exact length and width of the dishwasher front. Cut the plywood to these measurements.

**2** Measure the length and depth of the dishwasher sides, top, and bottom. **Note:** *This measurement is usually about 1 inch deep by the same length (sides) or width (top and bottom) as the dishwasher front.* Cut lathing strips to match each measurement.

**3** Glue the lathing strips to each side of plywood front piece. Secure in place with several finishing nails on each side.

**4** Using the measurements from Step 1, miter four pieces of molding to fit the plywood panel. Glue the mitered pieces to the panel; let dry.

**5** Sand the panel; remove dust particles with the tack cloth. Prime; let dry. Paint; let dry.

**6** Attach hook-and-loop tape to the back of the panel and to the front of the dishwasher so that the tape aligns. Press the panel to the dishwasher front.

# Lighting

Lighting is a major consideration for any kitchen. Kitchens require a blend of general, task, and accent lighting, with each type serving a different need. General or ambient lights provide a uniform, overall glow. Task lights are positioned to give light where you need it for specific jobs, for instance, doing dishes or chopping vegetables. Accent lights focus light on an object or surface to highlight it.

Unobtrusive recessed can lights are a popular choice for all three types of lighting. Can lights are available in downlight, accent, and wall-washing models. Track lights are another versatile option: Because the lights swivel on the track, they can be used for general, task, and accent needs. Pendent lights are another popular choice. Hung from a ceiling, pendants can be used for general and task lighting; when grouped, they are a great choice above islands and tables. Finally, undercabinet fixtures provide wonderful task lighting. These fixtures include slim energy-efficient fluorescents, miniature track lights, and strips of low-voltage mini halogens.

An average-size kitchen, measuring about 120 square feet, requires approximately 150 to 200 watts of incandescent general lighting, or 60 to 80 watts of fluorescent lighting. For larger kitchens, allow 2 to 3 watts of incandescent light or ¾ to 1 watt of fluorescent light per square foot.

Three pendent fixtures over the island provide light where it's needed most. Recessed can lights provide general lighting, while undercabinet fixtures create additional task lighting.

Accent lighting is a great way to bring focus to prized collections. Items on display in a niche get special attention, thanks to a single accent light.

Lights tucked inside glass-fronted cabinets offer a warm glow; glass shelves allow the light to flow through the cabinet. Note the recessed task lighting above the countertop run.

Sunshine can provide lovely ambient light in kitchens with large windows.

## LIGHTBULBS

Choosing the correct bulbs will make your general, task, and accent lighting as efficient and effective as possible. Keep the following in mind the next time you shop for lightbulbs.

**Incandescent** These bulbs traditionally are used throughout the home. While they are inexpensive, they produce more heat than light, so they are inefficient unless used only sparingly.

**EnergyMiser or Supersaver** This type of incandescent bulb uses 5 to 13 percent less energy than a traditional incandescent. These bulbs cost a little more than the traditional type, but their longer life makes them more cost-effective.

**Halogen** These bulbs are more efficient than incandescents: They last three to four times longer, and a lower-wattage halogen bulb will give the same illumination as a larger-watt incandescent.

**Compact fluorescent** These bulbs screw into the same sockets as incandescents but use about 75 percent less energy than incandescent bulbs—and last 10 times longer. They can be expensive, but over time they save many times their initial cost.

**Linear fluorescents** These thin tubes produce even, glare-free, shadow-free illumination, which is ideal for general lighting. Linear fluorescents also can be used for undercabinet lighting.

A large pendant light provides general lighting in this contemporary kitchen. A light-color ceiling and pale flooring prevent the black cabinets and countertops from absorbing too much of the light.

# Sleek Design on a

## BUDGET

Even the most budget-conscious kitchen remodeling projects require thoughtfulness and care. In this kitchen, the main objective was refreshing the surfaces (walls, floors, and countertops), but three smaller details—covering an unsightly electrical box, consolidating cooking appliances, and creating a clever window treatment—completed the transformation.

Initially, the soffit and cabinets were painted white, a blue and white border circled the room, and a gray laminate covered the entire backsplash. The white laminate counters were showing their age, as was the vinyl flooring that had a sad coat of paint over it.

**Pull the look together with paint and wallcoverings.**
To give the room a unified appearance, the cabinets and soffit were painted a soft, neutral beige. A commercial-grade vinyl wallpaper embellished with silvery squares covers the backsplash. The overall environment of the kitchen is addressed in applying these elements: A wallpaper paste designed for humid conditions was used to attach the wallpaper. The counter edge of the wallpaper is protected with a strip of quarter round that's held firmly in place with waterproof caulk.

*Continued on page 56*

## PAINTING CABINETS

A fresh coat or two of paint is a cost-effective way to dress up a dreary kitchen. A little prep work will make the job last.

- Determine which type of paint is on the cabinets: Put rubbing alcohol on a clean rag and wipe an inside surface. If the paint comes up, it's latex (water-base); if the paint is unaffected, it's alkyd (oil-base). You can paint oil over latex, but only certain latex paints will adhere to oils, so check the label before you buy.
- Some paints are designed to stand up to the moisture and temperature changes in kitchens and baths. These usually cost a little more but are worth the expense. A smooth paint finish will make kitchen cleanup easier; eggshell and semi-gloss paints fit the bill, without giving the excess shine of gloss paint.
- Thoroughly clean cabinets to remove dirt and cooking grease residue. Trisodium phosphate (TSP) is a popular cleaning agent.
- If you're replacing cabinet hardware, patch the old holes.
- Lightly sand the surface and prime to help the new paint adhere.

BEFORE

AFTER

▲

The new flooring is actually vinyl tiles that have the look of authentic terra-cotta tiles—and cost just a fraction of the real thing.

▲ ▶

Easy-care commercial-grade wallpaper that is decorated with a silvery square motif covers the backsplash. The wallpaper echoes the kitchen's new brushed-metal accents.

**Versatile vinyl.** The old flooring was scraped down to the concrete subfloor. New high-quality vinyl tiles with the look of terra-cotta now cover the floor and give the room a warm glow. In an older house, vinyl tile is a good choice: After you've made the subfloor as clean and level as possible, remaining imperfections will be hidden by the flexible vinyl (ceramic tiles may break). Vinyl tile also is easy to install.

**Cost-effective countertop.** Because the existing countertops were structurally sound, new granite-look laminate has been glued directly over the surface. To ensure a smooth, seamless look, a professional tackled the job; the gleaming results reflect the skill of the artisan.

**Copper fusion.** The warm tone of the flooring repeats throughout the kitchen. The counter laminate has flecks of coppery terra-cotta. New copper-tone cabinet pulls decorate drawers and doors. The window treatment deserves kudos for cleverness: A sheet of copper screen wire was folded and crinkled to look like a sheet curtain. This shimmery curtain welcomes the breeze and lightly filters sunlight.

**Conceal an eyesore.** A custom cover disguises the unsightly electrical box. Because the box was in so obvious a location (next to the sink), wallpaper with a swirl pattern in copper tones was applied on the front panel; a strip of hooks was added below to make the space useful.

**Consolidation equals efficiency.** New surfaces can give a kitchen a unified look, but they don't change the functionality of the space. This kitchen already worked quite well. Cabinets provided sufficient storage and the major appliances were positioned effectively. However, one simple change perfected the setup: The varying cabinet heights create a few odd voids along the walls, and one of those open spots was right next to the wall oven. That's where a shelf was added for the microwave; the bread machine found a new home in the same corner; thus, a neatly consolidated cooking area was created.

# Crinkly
# Copper Wire Curtain

If you are looking for a nonstandard, nonfabric window treatment, consider this clever option.

## You Will Need

Tape measure
Optional: work gloves
Aluminum or copper screen wire
Utility scissors or knife

Optional: Spray paint, copper or
   other desired color
Cafe curtain brackets
Screwdriver
Dowel rod cut to the desired width

1 ◼ Measure the window length and width. Unroll the screen wire and cut to match the height of the window plus ½ inch; then cut across so the screen is double the width of the window plus 1 inch. Fold the cut edges ½ inch. **Note:** *The factory edge can be used as a finished edge.*

2 ◼ If desired, spray-paint both sides of the screen; let dry.

3 ◼ Crumple the screen to give it a wrinkled look. Gently flatten and accordion-fold the screen. **Note:** *If you've painted the screen, a little paint may flake off.*

4 ◼ Attach the brackets to the wall or window frame.

5 ◼ Cut an X at the top of each fold in the screen. Run the dowel rod through the holes and hang the rod in the brackets.

3

❋ For additional window treatment projects, including shades, curtains, and valances, visit **HGTV.com/beforeandafterbook**

# Backsplashes

Backsplashes play an important role in the kitchen: They stop messy spills, splashes, and splatters from seeping behind the cabinets. It's a messy job, but that doesn't mean backsplashes can't be beautiful. Backsplashes come in many styles and materials, from popular ceramic tile and treated beaded board to more exotic glass and granite, so they can be as attractive as they are functional.

Ceramic tiles of all shapes, sizes, and motifs can be used effectively as a backsplash. The large tiles shown here were inspired by 1920s seed packets. Search tile stores and home improvement centers for the right tiles for your decorating scheme.

Wood usually isn't associated with areas that receive frequent washings, but if you treat it with a coat of polyurethane, it will perform beautifully. Beaded-board back-splashes look particularly at home in country decorating styles.

Granite often is used for countertops because of its durability. However, it rarely is seen as a backsplash. Here, a type of granite known as emerald pearl covers both surfaces (see page 71 for a larger look at this kitchen). Pieces of mica create the sparkle in the dark material.

This painted masterpiece was created on artist's canvas and adhered to the wall with wallpaper paste. Three coats of polyurethane protect the acrylic paint from the elements, and a narrow row of glazed tiles with a leaf motif anchors the canvas to the counter.

Copper in any form brings warmth to a kitchen. The patina on this golden copper backsplash provides a rich backdrop for cherry cabinets.

Mosaics are an artistic take on the backsplash. This example is made from broken tiles and found objects such as seashells. The dark grout helps to hide food splatters, and the shelf above displays dishware.

# Mix-It-Up MAKEOVER

Sometimes a room is so dark, dull, and outdated it's hard to know where to begin, especially when the budget is tight. If you are faced with a similar situation, take heart: By evaluating what works—and what doesn't—and thinking about ways to freshen items that still function but aren't aesthetically pleasing, you can transform a space for a lot less money than you might think.

**Update with paint.** In this kitchen the cabinets had to be addressed first. Purchasing new cabinets is costly: They can consume up to 40 percent of a kitchen remodeling budget. Why not dedicate that money to other uses—such as new appliances—or even keep the money in your pocket by painting your existing cabinets and replacing the hardware? That's what was done here: Two colors—sunny yellow and barn red—now cover the cabinets in a distressed finish. The red paint could have been overpowering, but it is covered with a dark stain, which softens the look. New, clean-lined hardware in brushed nickel adds a sleek, contemporary edge, which contrasts nicely with the paint treatment.

**Smooth transitions.** The fresh-looking vinyl floor was retained, but the dark backsplash tiles and worn laminate countertops needed to be replaced. The tiles were removed, and the backsplash area now wears a traditional red and white toile-print wallpaper. The print adds visual interest to the space and complements the red and yellow painted cabinets. A single row of white ceramic tile functions as a short, easy-clean backsplash. To reduce project costs, the existing counter stays put, but it's now covered with a light wood-tone laminate. The edge is painted red and distressed for a seamless transition between the counter and the cabinets below.

**Continued on page 62**

## CABINET HARDWARE

One of the easiest ways to add a spark to cabinets is with hardware. The selection available at home improvement centers and through Internet or mail-order sources is impressive. Styles include metal shapes with interesting curves and ceramic knobs and pulls with painted-on motifs. Wood knobs can be personalized with paint that complements the cabinets and overall decorating style.

BEFORE

*AFTER*

**Dress the window for success.** The once bare window over the sink now is dressed with a matchstick wood shade. The textured treatment is a fun, natural touch that adds contemporary flair to the overall traditional scheme. The white-painted window frame blends with the newly decorated space.

**Appliances blend in for a seamless look.** Because the homeowners saved money by salvaging the cabinets (the doors had been removed and were retained for reuse) and flooring and covering the countertop, they purchased new white appliances— a dishwasher, range, and microwave oven—that give the room a more uniform look; the dark dishwasher and range would have drawn too much attention in the now lighter, brighter space.

**Pay attention to details.** As in many rooms, it's the finishing touches that pull a look together, and this kitchen is no exception. A brushed-nickel gooseneck faucet, red and white collectibles and ceramic pieces, and a white chair that's handy for sorting mail or looking for a recipe unify the space.

BEFORE

AFTER

## Distressed Cabinets

Refreshing tired cabinets or giving brand-new cabinets an aged appearance is easy. When selecting colors, remember that the base coat color will only peek through the top coat where the top coat is sanded away. For an authentic aged appearance, do most of the sanding where natural wear would occur—for instance around handles and on raised portions of the project surface.

### You Will Need

Screwdriver
Latex primer
Medium-grit sandpaper, tack cloth
Paintbrushes, paint tray
Latex paint for base coat in the
    desired color and finish
Latex paint for top coat in the
    desired color and finish
Water-base stain in desired finish
Lint-free cloths
Wax or water-base polyurethane

1. Remove the doors and drawers from the cabinets. Remove any hardware.

2. Prime the cabinets, doors, and drawer fronts; let dry.

3. Lightly sand the surfaces. Wipe away dust with a tack cloth.

4. Apply the base coat to all surfaces; let dry.

5. If desired, apply wax to the surfaces.

6. Apply the top coat paint to all surfaces; let dry.

7. Sand the raised portions of the door and drawer surfaces as well as the cabinet edges, rubbing away paint in the natural wear areas. Wipe away dust with a tack cloth.

8. Randomly brush stain onto one area of one surface. Quickly wipe away some of the stain with a lint-free cloth, allowing the stain to sink into the recessed areas. Continue applying and removing stain until the entire surface has been covered. Repeat for the doors, drawers, and cabinet surfaces.

9. Rub the painted surface with wax or apply polyurethane for protection.

7

8

# Cabinet Doors

Cabinets can consume a large part of any kitchen makeover budget, so if your existing cabinets still function well, consider some easy updates: Paint them. Remove the doors and add fabric curtains. Incorporate inserts of nearly any material on the doors. Add new pulls and knobs.

Decades ago, glass inserted into a cabinet door was most prized for its practicality: You could see what was inside the cabinet without opening the door. Glass is now also valued for the many looks it can create. In this kitchen, complete with stainless-steel appliances and soapstone countertops, frosted glass enhances the contemporary feel. Other options include various glass colors and patterns and art paper laminated between glass layers.

Old, dingy cabinets get a fresh coat of paint and well-placed fabric details in this 1917 kitchen. The blue and white color scheme was inspired by a border of delft accent tiles. Coordinating delft fabric dresses the windows and lines the glass-fronted upper cabinets. Strategically placed fabric covers unsightly areas: A pretty pleated skirt hides lower cabinets made of metal.

Placing inserts in cabinet doors is a great way to add charm—and to replace worn surfaces. Most commonly, inserts are made of beaded board, glass, or even wallpaper that covers a portion of the door. Punched and painted tin is a less common material that adds flair to any kitchen. The tin inserts here feature Mexican motifs, a perfect complement for the backsplash tiles.

# Style on the

# SURFACE

Kitchens—along with bathrooms—are the most often remodeled rooms of the home, but updating them doesn't have to entail costly demolition. As this kitchen demonstrates, rethinking surface treatments, including wallcoverings, cabinet doors, hardware, and countertops, can refresh a tired space within the existing floor plan. This saves time, money, and the inconveniences that accompany more extensive remodeling.

**Fresh color and interesting motifs set the stage.** First, a light-color striped wallpaper replaces fruit motif paper. The light walls keep the small room from seeming even smaller, and the vertical stripes visually lift the ceiling, which is now covered in a dramatic chocolate brown wallpaper with an intricate swirling design. This design repeats in decorative elements throughout the room, including the rustic-looking chandelier that provides much-needed light above the island.

*Continued on page 68*

## KITCHEN COMFORT

Living rooms are the obvious conversational center of a home, but kitchens are a natural gathering place. In fact, a recent study shows that during waking hours, people tend to spend more time in the kitchen than any other room of the home. What can you do to encourage family and friends to linger while you cook and after a meal is served?

- **Pull up a chair.** If you have an island or a peninsula, arrange stools or high-back chairs around it to allow people to socialize while you cook. Guests can be close to the cook without interfering with meal preparation or traffic flow.
- **Personalize it.** Kitchens often open or flow into other living spaces, so decorate accordingly. Paint. Add pattern. Incorporate fabric. Showcase a collection. When your kitchen is filled with what you love, it becomes a welcoming place—a home within a home for you and your family and friends.
- **Set the mood.** Put on some music that suits the occasion. Get your family or guests involved in making the meal. They can set the table or chop vegetables while you prepare the main dishes. Keep snacks and beverages close at hand. Provide adequate lighting for special activities, for instance, overhead lighting above a table if you want to play after-dinner board or card games.

**BEFORE**

*AFTER*

**Casual country style.** Newly installed beaded board dramatically changes the overall look of this now fresh country kitchen. Cut to fit between the cabinets and countertops, ¼-inch beaded-board panel is glued on top of the existing laminate backsplash; the rest is cut to size and glued into the recessed areas of the cabinet doors. The birch cabinets were previously left with a natural finish; now they sport an aged glazed finish. Two coats of polyurethane protect both the backsplash and cabinets from splatters.

**Creative countertop.** The once plain laminate countertop now has a custom look, thanks to 15-inch glazed tiles in a rustic blue that complements the aged cabinets. The tiles were first set on the countertop to determine a pleasing arrangement; then the corner tiles were cut to size and the tiles were attached to the countertop with thin set. A light sand-color grout fills in the spaces between the tiles. To complete the look, flexible trim painted to match the aged cabinets covers the laminate edge.

**Pull the look together.** For added style, the porcelain cabinetry knobs have been replaced with stylish wrought iron, which complements the new iron light fixture over the island. The island chairs are spiffed up with distressed blue paint finish similar to the color of the glazed countertop tiles.

The vertical-stripe motif of the wallpaper resembles beaded board, the material that serves as the backsplash and covers the recessed portions of the cabinet doors.

## GETTING THE LOOK: AGED CABINETS

The cabinets in this kitchen were once plain-panel birch in a natural finish. Beaded-board panels and an aged paint finish give the cabinets a fresh decorative look. To achieve a similar aged look for your cabinets, first remove the cabinet doors. Lightly sand the cabinets and doors; then prime and let dry. Paint with white or off-white paint; let dry. Mix 4 parts glaze to 1 part walnut stain and generously wipe onto the doors and cabinets, allowing the glaze/stain mixture to accumulate in the recessed areas of the panels. Oil-base (alkyd) products were used for this project, but water-base (latex) paints, stains, and glazes will produce equally impressive results. Water-base products are easier and safer to use than oil-base products, and they will not yellow over time as oil-base products tend to do. If you choose to use oil-base products for this or any project, carefully follow the manufacturer's instructions. For more information on distressing cabinets, see page 63.

# MORE IDEAS FOR
# Countertops

Countertops, usually noted for their functionality, have taken on new status as a kitchen focal point in recent years. Standard laminate, butcher-block, and ceramic tile countertops are readily available, but marble, granite, and stainless steel examples offer broader design possibilities. This exciting range of options allows you to choose the surface that best fits your decorating scheme and your normal cooking routine: Butcher block is great for cutting food; marble and granite make wonderful baking prep surfaces. Regardless of which you choose, keep in mind the cost of the material and its installation, the durability of the material, and ease of maintenance and cleanup.

This kitchen features three counter-top materials: butcher block, stainless steel, and granite.

Solid butcher-block countertops provide an ideal place for chopping vegetables, eliminating the need to soil a cutting board each time you prepare a salad. Made of hardwood strips, butcher block brings a sense of warmth to a kitchen, but it must be sealed for protection from moisture.

Most commonly associated with commercial kitchens, stainless steel has become a popular option in private residences. Besides being easy to clean, this material withstands the heat of pots and pans. Stainless steel is available in various finishes and treatments, from bright and mirrorlike to brushed or embossed.

Though expensive, granite is a beautiful and nearly indestructible counter surface. Ultracool and virtually stain-proof, it is perfect for rolling and kneading dough. To protect the surface, periodic application of a nontoxic penetrating sealant is required.

Concrete offers a tough, durable surface that withstands heat, but it stains easily. Because concrete can be tinted, it is at home in nearly any decorating scheme.

Marble countertops are a popular choice for baking and candy making because of their cool surface. This natural material is softer and more porous than granite and needs to be sealed like granite. Still, even when sealed, marble is less durable. The two materials are similar in price.

# Streamlined for LIVING

Open floor plans are wonderful for creating a sense of spaciousness, but blurring the line between a kitchen and a living area gives the kitchen decor added importance. Achieving the perfect blend of function and aesthetics is no small task. Here, a glaring fluorescent light fixture, black appliances, and visually heavy upper cabinets that have seen brighter days spoil the view from the adjacent family room. A well-considered remodeling added layers of charm while keeping all the function.

**Work within the layout.** In this transformation what stayed in place is as surprising as what moved: The stove, sink, dishwasher, and refrigerator all occupy the same spaces, leaving the basic layout and size of the room unchanged. However, with the upper cabinets and soffit removed and storage consolidated along one wall, the room looks and feels completely different. Two other elements are simply enhanced: A single metal window is replaced with two wood-frame windows, and the peninsula is lengthened and deepened to provide a larger work area that doubles as a casual eating area.

**Re-evaluate the space.** Next to the refrigerator a door leading to the dining room prohibited good use of the entire wall. Eliminating the door caused no inconvenience; an opening to the living and dining rooms is only a few feet down the wall, and it was enlarged to open up the floor plan even more. The result is a wall dedicated to storage needs—a desirable feature in any kitchen.

**Visually expand the room.** Along the same wall, a visual trick makes the room look larger: The cabinets closest to the living area are not as deep as the pantry cabinets, which are in turn less deep than the wraparound cabinet for the refrigerator. The staggered cabinets exaggerate the distance to the rear door, making the kitchen look grandly large.

*Continued on page 74*

## BLENDING KITCHENS WITH LIVING AREAS

- Choose quiet appliances (especially dishwashers) and exhaust fans so that cooking and cleaning noises don't overwhelm the living area. Further, keep appliance colors muted; if possible, choose colors and finishes that blend with the cabinets or walls. Hidden dials and displays also make appliances less noticeable.
- Flow colors and styles between rooms. In this kitchen the flooring and white walls flow from one room to the other, making the transition to the living area seamless. Also consider the flow of window styles and coverings, light fixtures, and furniture styles.
- Add comfortable features to the kitchen, such as unfitted cabinets with the look of furniture and glass insets on upper cabinets for display areas. In this kitchen counter stools that look like chairs function perfectly and also seem at home from the living area.
- Nothing says "kitchen" more than a counter full of jars and other cooking accoutrements. For an open kitchen plan, be sure to include plenty of storage so utensils, cookware, and serving pieces are at hand but out of sight. Plan a spot for dirty dishes too; some homeowners add a second dishwasher so dirty dishware is never in view.

BEFORE

AFTER

To keep clutter off the countertops, tall drawers hold canisters and other bulky items.

**Warm the room with wood.** With plenty of natural light and an overall white color scheme, both rooms are bright, but the warm wood floor and butcher-block countertops prevent the space from feeling cold. Beaded board covers the cabinets and walls for visual interest and adds a strong vertical element to the space.

**Take the focus off the appliances.** Every effort is made to reduce the visual prominence of appliances: The black-fronted stove and dishwasher are replaced with new white models, and the new stove has a downdraft feature, eliminating the need for a hood. The microwave oven resides behind the pantry doors. To save money, the existing almond-color refrigerator is still in place, but new white cabinets that surround it minimize its visibility.

**Consider flexible lighting options.** Lighting an open kitchen can be a challenge: How do you get enough light without creating glare? Using a bank of recessed ceiling fixtures and adding dimmers will give you great flexibility; the lighting can be easily adjusted according to need.

# Beaded-Board Paneling

You can buy tongue-and-groove beaded-board kits from a lumber supply or home improvement center. The wood comes in a variety of lengths and qualities: A higher-quality wood contains fewer knots, thus being easier to paint. Before purchasing beaded board, measure your walls carefully and consider which extras (for example, molding for baseboards) you may need to complete your project. Keep in mind that manufacturers recommend buying the paneling and bringing it indoors at least two weeks before attaching it to your wall. This gives it time to acclimate to the temperature of the room, so it won't shrink after installation.

The beaded-board paneling in this kitchen hangs directly from vertical studs and horizontal bracing. Find the position of the framing and mark it as a guide for nailing in the panels. Note that some kits contain clips for affixing the panels to the wall.

When applying beaded board, be sure the paneling is straight, or plumb. If the wall has any slope, you will need to trim the panel for a good fit so the piece will stand straight. Scribe the panel by holding it in its proper place and running a pencil down the wall so that the pencil marks a line that matches the slope of the wall. Cut the board along the marked line and nail in place.

## You Will Need

Screwdriver or drill
Tape measure
Pencil
Beaded board
Saw
Carpenter's level
Hammer
6-penny finishing nails
Miter box (power or manual)

Molding, as desired
Surface compound, spackling knife
Optional: primer, semi-gloss enamel
   paint in the desired color,
   paintbrush
Optional: Water-base polyurethane

1. Remove all outlet covers, switchplates, and molding (including baseboards).

2. Cut the first piece of beaded board to the correct height for your particular project needs. Beginning in one corner, set the beaded board against the wall. Use a carpenter's level to check that it is perfectly straight and fits tightly against the corner. Nail the panel into place.

3. Continue around the room, keeping the top edge level at the height line until you have completed the entire wall surface. Cut the boards to special widths and lengths as needed to fit under windows and around doors. At corners, you can either overlap the boards or make miter cuts to join the boards at 45-degree angles (depending on the thickness of the paneling).

4. When the wall surface is complete, add molding for base boards and window trim, as desired.

5. Spackle over any knots in the wood and fill any nail holes; let dry.

**Optional:** If you don't want to leave the panel in its natural finish, prime and paint, allowing it to dry between applications. If the beaded board is in a kitchen or other room where it may need to be cleaned, apply a coat of polyurethane for protection.

# MORE IDEAS FOR

## Storage

Whether you spruce up your kitchen or completely remodel it, take some time to evaluate your current storage situation. Consider how and where food, cooking utensils, and small appliances are housed. Are related items grouped together? Are small appliances positioned close to the countertop where you use them? Do you keep the items you use most frequently near the front of a cabinet or drawer? Do you have space that isn't used as efficiently as it could be, for instance, a broom closet that could be converted into a pantry? Even if you believe you have ample storage, could you benefit from pullout shelves that make finding items easier? With a little planning, you can maximize your space to make cooking and other kitchen-related tasks more enjoyable.

For hundreds of tips to help organize your kitchen, visit **HGTV.com/beforeandafterbook**

▷ Pullout shelves are a handy way to reach pots and pans and any items that may be stored near the back of the cabinet.

▲ A narrow slice of space on each side of a cooktop can be used to store slim items, such as spices and seasonings.

◁ Islands can accommodate full-size storage on one side and shallow shelves for spices, seasonings, and oils on the other. Some islands are open on one or both ends to allow storage and display space.

▲ A space-saving pullout pantry keeps supplies handy for cooking and blends in with the rest of the cabinetry when it is closed.

◁ This cabinet features a pullout shelf on the bottom and a pop-up shelf specially designed for a stand mixer. The mixer shelf eliminates the need to bring the heavy item up to the countertop for use.

# Inviting

## DINING

Sometimes starting with nothing is scary, because it's hard to know where to begin. It would have been easy to simply move into this dining room without addressing the worn carpeting or dull white walls, but by evaluating the space and uncovering an unseen gem, the homeowner brought the dining space beyond its humble beginnings to create a room with style and grace.

**Work with the floor plan.** Like many ranch-style homes with open floor plans, this home featured a long, narrow living and dining area with a low ceiling. The dark, uninspired space needed a boost. Warm taupe paint on the walls now makes the room inviting; a fresh coat of white paint overhead gives the ceiling a visual lift. Before, dingy carpeting concealed beautiful hardwood flooring. Now refinished, the floor provides visual warmth. A sisal rug, which brings in natural texture, protects the area beneath the table.

**Define the spaces.** Although the light colors helped visually widen and heighten the open space, the two areas still lacked definition. The solution is a movable wall that defines the living and dining areas and introduces a playful splash of orange in the mostly neutral space. This wall is shorter than the ceiling to make the room appear taller—and because the wall is only half the width of the room, the room seems wider.

*Continued on page 80*

BEFORE

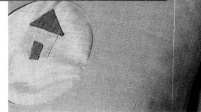

AFTER

## PHOTO FUN

Family photos become original artwork in this dining room. To create similar artwork, enlarge your chosen photos at a copy center and have them transferred to white canvas. **Note:** *In most cases, copy stores can make these types of canvases up to 3 feet wide and any length.* Sandwich the top and bottom edges of each canvas panel between pairs of 1x4s cut slightly longer than the canvas width and brushed with polyurethane. Screw the boards together. To hang, mount the bottom edge of the top board on nails driven into the wall.

**Mix it up.** The most essential feature in the room is the refinished round dining table. The table is covered with a tailored white tablecloth and surrounded by contemporary metal office chairs for a successful rendition of old-meets-new. A simple upholstered bench provides additional seating; its pipe legs complement the metal chairs and the legs of the divider wall.

**A neutral backdrop is versatile.** What makes this room so much fun are the splashes of color against the neutral background. The bright graphic pillows on the patterned bench and a green and blue Roman shade bring in cool tones that contrast nicely with the orange wall. A trio of family photos serves as bold, oversize artwork.

# Freestanding Divider Wall

With basic woodworking skills, you can make a movable divider wall similar to this. This project will likely take a weekend to complete, but the result is worth the effort.

## You Will Need

2x4s, cut two each of the following lengths: 69" (A); 48" (B); 16" (C); 45" (D)

¼-inch birch plywood, cut to the following dimensions: 3½x48" (E); 3½x72¼" (F); 3½x36" (G); 3½x15½" (H); 48½x71¼" (I)

No. 8x2½" deck screws

1" pipe flanges (2)

1"-diameter galvanized pipes (2), 40" long, threaded on both ends

Wood glue

6-penny finishing nails

1" galvanized pipe tees (2)

9" lengths of 1" galvanized pipe (4)

1" galvanized 90-degree pipe elbows (4)

Wood putty, putty knife

Primer, latex paint in the desired color and finish, paintbrush

Tape measure, pencil

Circular saw

Drill

Pipe wrench

Hammer

Jigsaw

Router with flush-trim bit

Handsaw

Sandpaper

Screwdriver

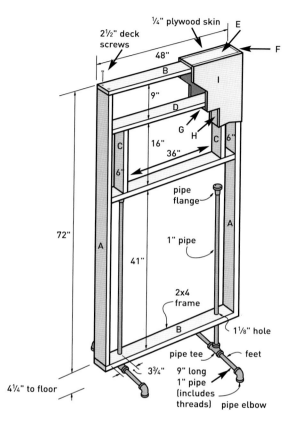

1 ▦ Assemble the frame stiles (A) and rails (B) with 2½-inch screws. Position the window stiles (C) between the window rails (D) as shown in the illustration; attach with screws. Position the assembled window frame within the wall frame; screw into place.

2 ▦ Attach two 1-inch pipe flanges to the underside of the lower window rail, centering one under each window stile. Drill two 1⅛-inch-diameter holes in the lower frame rail where shown. Insert the pipes through the holes, using a pipe wrench to tighten them into the flanges. (These pipes give the wall rigidity.)

3 ▦ Attach the top and side frame skins (E and F) to the frame with glue and 6-penny finishing nails. Install the window rail skins (G) next, then the window stile skins (H).

4 ▦ With a tape measure and pencil, mark the window opening on the panel skins (I); then use a jigsaw to cut about ¼ inch inside the lines. Apply a thin bead of wood glue to one side of the frame assembly, position one panel skin squarely on the frame, and nail the skin to the frame. Flip the frame over and attach the other skin in the same manner.

5 ▦ Using a router with a flush-trim bit, trim the skin panels flush with the surface of the window frame skins. Carefully square the corners with a handsaw.

6 ▦ Use a pipe wrench to assemble the pipe feet from tees, 1-inch pipe, and elbows, as in the illustration. Thread them onto the pipe extending from the lower frame rail.

7 ▦ Fill any nail holes with putty, sand the surfaces smooth, and paint the wall with one coat of primer and two coats of paint, allowing the primer and paint to dry between coats.

# MORE IDEAS FOR
# Window Treatments

Window treatments can be more than a practical way to provide privacy, block glare on the television screen, and shelter you from the sun. They bring color, pattern, and texture into a room, carrying through the decorating scheme you have chosen. When preparing to purchase or create window treatments, consider the following: What is your style? Choose treatments and hardware that complement the mood you want to achieve (for instance, heavy velvet panels may have a place in a formal dining room but not in a cottage-style room). How is the room used? Do you need the treatments to block out the sun to protect artwork on the walls? If so, look for room-darkening treatments. Finally, consider the architecture of the space. Do the treatments need to hide flaws in the walls or windows or can the treatments show off these features? For extra style, use interesting curtain rods and finials to punctuate your overall scheme.

Valances—those little pieces of fabric that grace the top of a window—add softness, color, and pattern to a hard architectural element. These treatments are purely decorative, framing both the window and views. In rooms where privacy isn't a concern, valances may hang alone, but pairing them with shades, blinds, or panels offers privacy and more light control. The valances shown in this country-inspired kitchen are tab-top, with loops or "tabs" of fabric sewn into or onto the top seam.

Roller shades are an inexpensive window treatment option, but they often lack personality and style. This patchwork shade brings pattern and color into the room. The squares are arranged randomly for punches of color that aren't too predictable, but a precise checkerboard could also be created. A similar shade can be made with squares of paper-back silk ironed onto a standard shade.

Rod-pocket panels are a popular option because of their simplicity: The curtain rod simply slips through a channel (the pocket) sewn into the top edge of the panel. Often these panels are made of lightweight fabric and left unlined for a casual appearance. In this room ordinary panels gain interest and style with the addition of a contrasting fabric liner and trim.

Hinged to either side of a window frame interior, louvered shutters lend a fitted look to any setting. The slats can be opened and shut accordingly to your lighting, privacy, and ventilation needs. White is an ever-popular choice for shutters, but they are available in a multitude of colors and wood tones. These shutters provide a classic look; the crisp and clean appearance complements the summery blue and white scheme.

# Fine DINING

The typical dining room plays a chameleonlike role in the house. The basic surroundings need to be interesting, and oftentimes elegant, but not express too much style. Rather, the mood and style of the dining event plays the lead. Creating that style can be quick and easy if you use items you already have on hand.

**Start with the basics.** Setting a fresh mood for any meal is an achievable goal; all it takes is a little planning. Start by creating a universal backdrop. In this dining area the pretty table and chairs, antique cupboard, and French doors are all a soft white. That makes the good lines of each element stand out when the room is not in use. A simple but elegant Italian art glass chandelier and an extensive selection of red and white transferware pieces keep the room pleasantly and adequately decorated even when the table isn't set. The red and white sets the tone for three different events: breakfast, brunch, and a formal dinner.

## VERSION ONE: BREAKFAST

**Keep it simple.** For a casual breakfast, no tablecovering is necessary. The red and white plates help determine the choice of flowers: A pot of bright gerbera daisies set in a miniature gazebo creates a cheerful look with minimal effort. The vintage wood farm chairs have simple tied-on seat cushions with a skirt of old valance lace around three sides. Everyday meals provide added enjoyment when served in such pleasant surroundings.

*Continued on page 86*

VERSION ONE: BREAKFAST

*VERSION TWO: BRUNCH*

## VERSION TWO: BRUNCH

**Dressed up but not stuffy.** For a slightly more formal Sunday brunch (shown on page 85), three square tablecloths create a colorful geometric pattern that's much more interesting than a single tablecloth. If company is coming for the meal, set aside the everyday (in this case, transferware from the cabinet) and bring out something special (in this case, white ironware). Slipcovered parsons chairs sit at either end of the table to add to the dressed-up look of the room. The centerpiece is a classic cement bust ringed with ivy and topped with a garden cloche, bringing a touch of the outdoors to the room.

## VERSION THREE: DINNER

**Pull out all the stops.** The most formal occasions call for the most refined dinnerware and decor. In this dining area the good silver is put on display in the cabinet, adding gleam and shine to the space. The curl-top parsons chairs show their elegant green Jacquard upholstery. And the table is topped with layers of lace tablecloths and filmy fabrics. The best china with gold rims is mixed with antique teacups to create a unique place setting for each guest. The centerpiece only looks expensive: It's a candy dish topped with a glass vase; together they display flowers (set in florist's foam) and a candle.

## CUSTOM SLIPCOVERS

Slipcovers are becoming more readily available in various styles, but you may prefer a custom slipcover for that special chair or sofa. One of the most cost-effective ways to have slipcovers made, or to have any custom sewing work done, is to find a good workroom. Firms are often listed under Upholstery or Drapery in the Yellow Pages, but the best source is word of mouth. Ask friends for the names of firms they've used. You're looking for someone who knows the ins and outs of working with textiles and furniture. Expensive fabric may make you swoon, but if it isn't expertly sewn, it will be a disappointment. These skills are so much in demand that some of the best workrooms do work only for interior designers. If you find a workroom through the Yellow Pages or a similar source, have the shop make a pillow first so you can check the quality of the work. Get the specifics written down and agreed upon before the work starts, as you would for any professional service, and stay in touch with the workroom throughout the project to ensure the work is progressing on schedule and on budget.

Slipcovers allow the same chair to be dressed for completely different occasions. This dining chair has a lace-trim cushion for casual affairs and a more elaborate cover with dressmaker details for special events.

*VERSION THREE: DINNE*

## SERVING UP STYLE

To create beautiful settings quickly and convenientchy, you'll need key elements on hand. Start by picturing the kinds of meals you plan to serve.

- **Begin with breakfast.** If your dining room is in use daily, start by gathering the items you'll need for family meals. A good, sturdy table that can handle constant use is a must. Here, the painted table and chairs have good lines, but they're basic pieces that won't suffer from a few dings and nicks. Tableware, too, needs to be sturdy. In this house a collection of red and white transferware is at the ready in the cabinet. The pieces are complementary, not matching, and most are vintage. A few chips or the loss of a piece won't upset the balance.

- **Plan for regular events.** Casual entertaining calls for a second layer of decorating. Here, the better china, the slipcovers for chairs, and the tablecloths are all of the same caliber and well-suited to each other. Have more than you need for any one occasion if you entertain regularly to give you the flexibility to create a variety of settings. If you have these special second-level items on hand, it will take no time at all to make Sunday dinner, birthday gatherings, and relaxed entertaining even more special.

- **Be ready for formal only if you'll really do formal.** There's no point in having formal dinner service for 12 if you'll use it only once a year. If, however, you don't have good china and a big event is coming, consider renting the good stuff. It may be expensive, but the cost is a fraction of what you'd pay to buy and store good china and silver for the rare use. If you entertain frequently, keep the good china and linens easily accessible so you'll use them often.

- **Use a little creative thinking.** Repurposed candy dishes, layered linens, and mix-and-match dishware all contribute to a dining area with interest and charm. As you collect favorite items, consider how they can be used; gather and group enough of them to adequately cover the table.

- **Plan the table when you plan the meal.** If you're planning to entertain, imagine how you want the table to look. That way, if there's something you've been longing to add to your collection or something that needs replacing, you can address the need ahead of time, not at the last minute. Once table planning becomes habit, you'll do it without stress. A little think time also allows you to experiment with ideas just for fun.

# Slipcovers

If you have dated, dingy furniture in need of rescue—or if your living spaces could benefit from some fresh color and fabrics—slipcovers may be the solution. Slipcovers let you introduce new style into any space, and slipcovering is much more affordable than reupholstering. Outdated or tattered upholstery disappears when topped with a pretty slipcover. Heavily patterned winter fabrics can give way to refreshing whites and light prints for summer. Perhaps best of all, if you have mismatched furnishings, slipcovers can unify the pieces.

Even the simplest of chairs can take on a whole new look with a slipcover. This tailored example in a summery fabric is dressy enough for a formal gathering yet still looks comfortable and inviting.

Delicate rose embellishments and dressy piping detail this slipcover. The full skirt, reminiscent of a flowing ball gown, is a classy touch.

If the thought of making a slipcover is daunting and you can't find the right ready-made for your particular chair, think of other ways to dress it up. This once-tired chair sports a fresh coat of paint; a flanged pillow and tufted seat cushion add comfort.

## SLIPCOVER BASICS

- When making or purchasing slipcovers, choose low-maintenance fabrics that can be machine-washed with ease.
- Look beyond current furnishings for slipcovering potential: Old chairs with simple lines are an easy fit and an inexpensive option.
- Before purchasing, check the sturdiness of any old furnishings you select for slipcovering. Also check that the old upholstery is clean, so that old stains won't show through the new fabric.
- If your chosen chair isn't comfortable, cut new foam for the cushion and wrap it with batting for extra loft.
- Add details, such as piping, fringe, rope, or braiding to customize a ready-made slipcover.

# Simply CHARMING

Sometimes it's the quick, inexpensive changes that transform a space. In this dining area adding fabrics and expanding the colorful plate collection make the space more inviting. This is a great example of using what you have—in this case, the dining set, a grouping of plates, and pleasing paint colors on the wall and wainscoting—as the basis for a fresh take on a room.

**Give a collection purpose.** To create a focal point with lots of impact, two plates are added, and the grouping is rearranged in an arched fashion. The walls of this room are tall, and the pale yellow visually expands the space even more, so additional plates make the collection more effective. The new bright green and blue plates provide a punch of color against the cheerful walls.

**Use fabric to unify the space.** The dark-stained dining set looked out of place against the crisp white wainscoting and yellow walls. To tie the table and chairs to the other elements in the space, coordinating blue and white plaid fabrics are introduced in a tablecloth and new drop-in seat covers. The seat covers replace a predominantly dark green plaid that made the chairs look outdated.

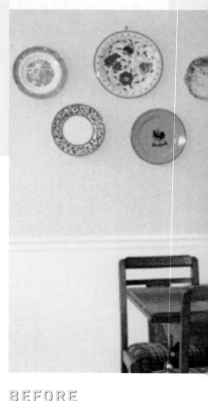

## QUICK AND EASY TABLECLOTH

Even if you don't own a sewing machine you can easily create a tablecloth for a square or rectangular table. Choose a fabric in a color and motif that coordinates with other elements in the room. Wash and dry the fabric to remove any sizing; iron. Cut the fabric into the desired shape and size for your table, adding a $\frac{1}{4}$- or $\frac{1}{2}$-inch seam allowance to each side. A drop of 8 inches is recommended (it won't drape onto diners seated at the table). Following the manufacturer's directions, use $\frac{1}{4}$- or $\frac{1}{2}$-inch-wide fusible hem tape to finish the edges of the cloth.

✳ For more simple tablecloth ideas,
visit **HGTV.com/beforeandafterbook**

BEFORE

*AFTER*

## ARTFUL ARRANGEMENTS

Having difficulties imaging how your collection of plates, artwork, or family photographs will look on a wall? By following this easy technique, you'll create stunning displays.

- Trace the outline of each item onto paper; cut out.

- Using low-tack tape, adhere the paper shapes to the wall, grouping them in several combinations until you find a visually pleasing one.

- Once you are satisfied with the design, use the paper as a map for nail holes: Nail through the paper outlines, remove the paper, and hang each item in the appropriate place.

## Drop-In Seats

Consider the power of fabric in dining areas: The addition of a tablecloth and new drop-in dining chair seats in a coordinating fabric can introduce much needed doses of color and pattern. Re-covering old, worn drop-in seats is a quick way to freshen dining chairs. For this project, select a fabric with a tight weave that can stand up to stretching; choose one that is lightweight so it won't add bulk to the seat and make it difficult to fit into the frame.

### You Will Need

Screwdrivers, flat and phillips
Fabric in the desired color and motif
Pins
Scissors

Optional: high-density upholstery foam and polyester batting in desired loft, sized to fit seat
Optional: spray adhesive
Staple gun, staples

Remove the seat from the chair, using a screwdriver if necessary.

Using the flat screwdriver, carefully remove the staples that hold the fabric to the seat. Use caution; you will use the old fabric as a pattern.

Lay the new fabric flat, right side down. Place the old fabric on the new fabric; pin in place and cut around the edge of the old fabric.

If the old foam and batting are flat and stained, replace them with new high-density foam and polyester batting. Adhere the foam to the wood seat with spray adhesive; top with the batting.

With the fabric right side down, center the foam- and batting-covered seat on the fabric, foam side down. Starting on one side, pull the fabric to the underside of the wood seat and staple in the center. Repeat on the remaining sides, pulling the fabric taut. Continue stapling around the fabric until it is secured. At the corners, neatly fold and staple. After stapling is complete, trim any excess fabric.

Replace the seat in the chair.

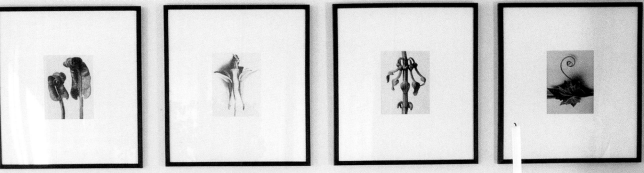

# Arranging Wall Art

Arranging artwork on your walls can be one of the more daunting decorating tasks you face—but it doesn't have to be. Here are some basic rules to follow the next time you want to do an arrangement. Generally, place artwork at eye level, giving consideration to the piece you're hanging and who will be viewing it. In a child's room, for example, place the piece at his or her eye level for easy viewing. Choosing the right hardware to hang your pieces is important. Use picture hooks that can withstand the weight of your pieces, and consider decorative hangers, such as drawer pulls, that go beyond their intended function. Choose frames and mats that enhance the artwork: If you have simple art, treat it to a decorative frame; let elaborate art stand out by giving it a modest mat and frame.

Grouping like objects creates drama; these four pansy watercolors lend an airy, arty mood to this space. Consistency in framing ties the paintings together, and the symmetry of the arrangement creates a more formal look.

Artwork can be a strong focal point when matted and framed in the same manner and arranged symmetrically. This series of photos hangs above a sofa; a similar arrangement would work above a long table or buffet in a dining room.

Pictures don't always have to be hung in a row; frames don't have to match. This interesting arrangement pairs illustrations in different sizes and frames with a few ornate mirrors. The stimulating grouping keeps the eye moving.

# A Matter of
COLOR

Introducing fresh, strong color. Rethinking furniture placement. Balancing furnishings and accessories. Creating a focal point. Blending a television with its surroundings. These are the keys to making this combination dining/sitting room more functional, cozy, and comfortable. If you have a space with similar needs, use this room as a guide for your makeover.

**Behold the power of paint.** What was once a sterile, uninspired place is now enveloped in warm color. The striking red complements the dark wood table and the plaid furnishings and window treatments. It also brings out the best in the accessories, including prints of guinea fowl. The new color defines all these elements and makes them stand out even more.

**Find a focal point.** Because the furnishings were small and out of scale with each other, the dining portion of the room lacked a clear focal point. A corner armoire replaces the small dresser that held the TV—and becomes an instant focal point. Treated to a distressed paint finish in black and dark brown, the armoire holds a smaller television, as well as a collection of porcelain dishware, vases, and bowls. To accommodate the electrical cords from the TV, a hole is drilled in the back of the armoire. To best display the collections and television, the doors on the armoire are always open. Because the door fronts are more attractive than the backs, the doors are reversed so that the fronts face outward into the room.

**Balance and proportion are key.** Four prints hung in a grid pattern balance the armoire and add rich gold color against the red walls. The large platter that hung above the table finds a new home on the opposite wall, beneath a wall-mounted display cabinet, where its size is more appropriate. The dresser that served as the TV stand now sits between the two chairs in the sitting area, providing additional space for displays and beverages.

**Make room for diners.** At the table, taller Windsor chairs look better—and are much more comfortable for diners—than the old short barrel chairs. The table has grown by a leaf and stands parallel to the wall, allowing diners to sit all around it instead of three sides only.

*Continued on page 98*

BEFORE

AFTER

BEFORE

AFTER

**Comfort for two.** Initially, only one ottoman served the sitting area, and it typically held a tray for snacks and coffee. Now, two ottomans allow a pair to put up their feet while watching TV. The ottomans can also serve as extra seating if necessary.

**Look beyond the intended use.** The new floor covering is actually a fringed tapestry tablecloth, which was given a pad backing to prevent it from slipping.

## CHOOSING PAINT COLORS

Paint is undoubtedly one of the easiest, least expensive ways to make a dramatic impact in any room. If you are ready to bring color into your home but are unsure of how to evaluate colors before making a commitment, use painted sample boards to audition your selections. Prime a piece of foam-core board. Use a board that has the same texture as your wall, because textured surfaces will appear darker than smooth surfaces painted the same color. Paint the board, allowing it to dry completely (paint usually looks darker dry than when it's wet). Move the sample board around the room, observing how it appears in different light, from morning to night and near different light sources. Notice how the color interacts with furnishings, artwork, and accessories in the room. When selecting paint for this exercise, keep in mind that the sheen, or finish, will also affect appearance. Flat paint will look darker than semi-gloss, and semi-gloss will look darker than gloss (the shinier the paint, the lighter it will appear).

# MORE IDEAS FOR

## Focal Points

Living rooms are where most people consciously set out to create a focal point. However, any room that is used for sitting and conversation needs a focus, an item or area that draws the eye and unifies the furnishings. In living rooms, fireplaces, large picture windows, and pieces of art are obvious candidates for focal points; in dining areas, the same items can be the focus. In addition, impressive pieces of furniture, such as armoires, china cabinets, and buffets, can command attention and anchor the space.

Artwork can be a dramatic focal point, as this contemporary piece demonstrates. The spindle-back chairs, which originally had cane seats, are upholstered in red to complement the painting.

Fireplaces are a typical focal point in living rooms, but how about in a dining room? To create ambience around this table, a salvaged antique fireplace mantel is mounted on the wall. A crackle finish gives the mantel an old-time feel, and an upholstered bench tucked into the firebox transforms the mantel into a banquette.

The focal point of this Swedish-style dining room is made up of two pieces that appear as one unit: a painted sideboard and a plate rack.

Customized screens are an inexpensive way to bring interest to a room. This focal point screen is painted with blocks and swirls of color and has cutouts that display a sponged wall treatment behind it.

# BEDROOMS

# Tiny to TERRIFIC

At first glance, design oddities detract from this small bedroom in a 1950s ranch, but smart design strategies turn them into unique opportunities. Paint and tailored Roman shades unify the windows; a headboard becomes a fitting focal point and adds storage space; light-color berber replaces old commercial-grade carpet; and—voilá—this room is now as comfortable as it is classy.

**Unify with paint.** The horizontal row of louvered windows set high in the wall is spaced unevenly, and one window had been replaced with an air-conditioning unit that created an eyesore. Rather than camouflage the home's midcentury roots, the home-owner emphasized the horizontal nature of the windows by painting a stripe on the walls between the windows (thus turning the windows and wall sections between them into one sleek unit). Now the eye notices the windows without noticing they are off-center. The soft layered design of the Roman shades adds subtle horizontal lines, which accent the painted stripe. The space with the air-conditioner is treated like the other windows; the shade is left down when the unit is not in use.

**Emphasize the focal point.** The feature attraction is the new headboard, which fits neatly under the high windows. The headboard design incorporates two built-in side tables, offering a place to stash reading materials, an alarm clock, and matching lamps. The outer edge is trimmed with black, and the interior is padded with a dark gray flannel. The black and gray, blue walls, white trim, and multicolor bed linens make for a crisp, masculine look.

*Continued on page 106*

BEFORE

AFTER

**Ordinary doors can have design flair.** French doors leading to a small office create an offbeat look. The stiles separating the 15 glass panes are boxy, without a routed edge, and the bottom edge of the doors is no wider than the top. Now painted in the same black as the headboard, the doors are drawn into the overall design of the room. Translucent film (available at home improvement centers) covers the glass panes, so these once odd doors now resemble a shoji screen. This adds a contemporary edge that complements the look of the room.

# Padded Storage Headboard

This headboard—intended for use with a queen-size bed—is constructed of plywood and medium-density fiberboard (MDF), with padded squares of foam-core board as the interior. The back of the unit is made from a full sheet of sturdy plywood. MDF, which has a clean, paintable edge, makes up the two end tables. MDF is quite heavy; consider having it cut at a home improvement center so the pieces are easier to handle.

## You Will Need

4x8' sheet of ¾" MDF cut to the following: 4'x14" (2); 12x16" (4); 6x12" (4)
4x8' sheet of plywood
15' 1x2
6 penny nails
1¼" wood screws
4x8' sheets of foam core (2)
Polyester batting

3 yards decorator fabric in the desired color and motif, 45" wide
Spray adhesive
Packing tape
Construction adhesive
Utility knife, scissors
Drill
Primer, latex paint, black and color that coordinates with wall color, paintbrush

1 ▲ Attach the 4-foot-by-14-inch pieces of MDF to the sides of the plywood. This creates the headboard unit.

2 ▲ Following the illustration, make two side tables with the four 12x16-inch pieces and four 6x12-inch pieces of MDF, gluing and then nailing the pieces together. (Illustration 1) Note that the front and back of the tables will be open.

3 ▲ Attach the two side tables to the headboard unit with screws. Position the top edge of the tables 21 inches above the bottom of the unit. (Illustration 2)

4 ▲ Cut and adhere 1x2 to the side and top edges of the headboard.

5 ▲ Prime the entire unit; let dry. Paint the interior and inward-facing 1x2 edges black. Paint the top and sides of the unit in a coordinating color; let dry.

6 ▲ Determine where you will need to run electrical cords through the back of the unit (near the side tables). Drill holes where desired.

7 ▲ Cut 16 of the following for the back of the unit: 15-inch squares of foam-core board, 16-inch squares of batting, and 17-inch squares of fabric. Cut 4 of the following for the sides of the unit: 12½x13-inch pieces of foam-core board, 13½x14-inch pieces of batting, and 13½x15-inch pieces of fabric. Spray each piece of foam-core board with spray adhesive; wrap batting around the board. Spray the batting with spray adhesive; wrap the fabric around the batting-covered board. Trim any excess batting and fabric; use packing tape to secure the edges, if needed.

8 ▲ Starting at the top of the unit, glue the 15-inch-square batting- and fabric-covered pieces of foam core to the back wall of the unit. Glue six squares across to form the top two rows; glue four squares in the bottom row, between the two side tables. Glue two 13x15-inch batting- and fabric-covered pieces to each of the sidewalls, above the side tables.

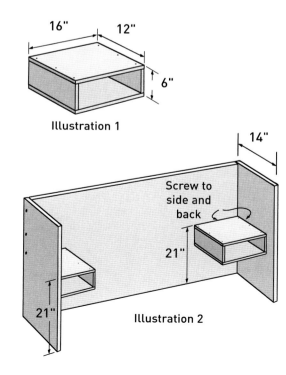

16" 12"

6"

**Illustration 1**

14"

Screw to side and back

21"

21"

**Illustration 2**

❄ For more do-it-yourself headboard projects, visit **HGTV.com/beforeandafterbook**

# Headboards

Beds are often the focal point of a bedroom, but they can't reach this status with bedding and pillows alone. To truly make your bed take center stage, consider adding a headboard. Any of these ideas can be implemented in an afternoon, but keep other options in mind too, such as a folding screen with fabric panels that complements your bedding or an artist's canvas the width of your bed covered with fabric or paint accents. If your bed already has a headboard, find ways to emphasize it, for example, with a fabric slipcover.

Ordinary fence pickets can add cottage charm to any bedroom. To construct a similar headboard, use pickets of different lengths; this example uses 11 pickets cut into graduated lengths, from 50 inches (the tallest middle piece) to 34 inches (the shortest end pieces). Two cross boards are bolted to the pickets, one 1 inch from the bottom and the other 27 inches from the bottom. For a similar weathered look, prime the headboard unit and paint two coats, sanding between coats. Attach the unit to the wall or bed frame using drywall screws or anchor bolts.

Bring the outdoors into your bedroom with a bright floral headboard. These fun flowers are painted freehand on a piece of plywood with various colors of acrylic paints and artists' paintbrushes; then, the outline of each flower is carefully cut out with a saw. To complete the headboard, the cut edges of the motifs are painted, and then the unit is attach to the bed frame (the bed shown has a low headboard with posts).

Decorating doesn't get any easier than this: Old tin tiles lined up behind a bed provide instant vintage charm. If you have difficulty finding antique tiles at flea markets or antiques shops, look for reproduction tiles at home improvement centers or crafts stores.

Vintage textiles are sometimes too fragile to use as bedcoverings, such as this 1837 quilt, but they make beautiful faux headboards. Displayed vertically, the pieced quilt makes the walls appear taller than they are.

This stylish headboard treatment puts soft gusseted pillows to work as decorative accents. For a similar look, choose three coordinating seat cushions with ties already attached and add them to a window treatment rod mounted above your bed.

# Traditional RETREAT

A bedroom should be a retreat, a private oasis from the rest of the world. This bedroom had all the basics in place—a comfortable, high-quality bed, a makeup table, and an easy chair—but the dominant blues of the large Oriental rug and painted walls created a chilly feeling.

**Temper strong color with pattern.** The bright blue rug, with peach and terra-cotta accents, needed to stay in place to warm the hardwood floors, but finding appropriate wallcoverings and fabrics to complement the rug required careful planning: The rug needed strong elements and strong colors to balance it. A pretty blue and white trellis-pattern wallpaper and predominantly red floral fabrics—used for the romantic bed draperies, bed skirt, and window treatments—introduce a jolt of color and add vertical lines to offset the horizontal "weight" of the rug.

**Window treatments can emphasize—or disguise.** Fabrics play an important role throughout the room. The old window treatment was a simple valance and louvered shutters. The new treatment has full-length panels with blue-check trim and a valance for a fuller, more finished look. The unusual round window over the bed posed an interesting challenge. Instead of following the arc of the window, the treatment covers the entire section of wall behind the bed; stationary lace sheers stretch between the two bed drapery panels.

**Unify the elements with fabric and color.** The chairs in front of the window, once covered in a striped fabric, are now upholstered in neutral beige that blends with the other furnishings in the room. Another chair sits at the makeup table; its drop-in seat features the same blue-check fabric that appears in accents throughout the room, visually connecting the elements.

**Choose one item to bring it all together.** To tie together all the elements in the room—the Oriental rug, trellis-print wallpaper, neutral bed coverlet and upholstered chairs, and floral and checked fabrics—a bright patchwork quilt is placed at the end of the bed. This simple accessory unifies the room, acting like a visual bridge for all the colors to come together.

BEFORE

*AFTER*

# PROJECT

## Wallpaper Like a Pro

Wallpaper choices are almost limitless: Hundreds of patterns in a myriad of colors to suit nearly every decorating style are available. Wallpapering an entire room may seem daunting, but with planning, forethought, and patience, you can dramatically change the look of the room.

Before choosing a wallcovering, consider your experience level, the features of the room, and the look you want to create. Some papers, such as stripes, are easier for beginners to hang because there is no pattern to match. However, stripes can be hard to hang straight on crooked walls and will accentuate flaws in the wall surface. Papers with floral designs require matching, but the busyness of the design often disguises flaws in the hanging or in the walls.

△ This window treatment features floral and checked fabrics.

## MIXING PATTERNS SUCCESSFULLY

Keep the following points in mind when incorporating different patterns in a room.

- **Limit the color palette.** In this bedroom, red is the dominant force, but touches of blue and white link the soft furnishings, the wallpaper, and the rug.
- **Consider scale.** Varying the size of the patterns adds interest, but keep the size of the room in mind too. Large patterns will overpower a small space but look at home in bigger rooms; small patterns won't have impact in large areas but are perfect for little spaces.
- **Keep it simple.** Introduce a limited number of patterns: Sticking to three—for instance, a floral, stripe, and plaid—adds interest to a room without overwhelming the eye.
- **Balance the patterns.** Distributing patterns throughout a room will make for a smooth transition; positioning them together in groups, or clumps, creates too many focal points.

## You Will Need

Wallpaper primer
Chalk line
Scissors
Wallpaper
Water tray
Optional: wallpaper paste

Wallpaper brush
Damp cloth or sponge
Straightedge
Razor knife with several extra blades
Seam roller

1. Clean the wall and cover it with a primer designed for wallcovering applications. To help conceal any small gaps in seams, tint the primer to match the wallcovering background. The primer seals the wall, helps the wallpaper bond better, and creates a surface with good "slide," making the wallpaper easier to manipulate for pattern matching.

2. Choose an inconspicuous corner—for instance, behind a door, where pattern mismatching will be least obvious—for a starting point. Snap a chalk line to mark a straight vertical line on the wall. This line indicates a true vertical. Establish another true vertical line when you turn a corner or start a new wall.

3. Cut the first strip of wallpaper 6 inches longer than the section of the wall you're covering to allow for trimming. For prepasted wallpaper, roll the strip, print side up, and immerse it in a tray filled with water. Let the paper soak for the time specified in the manufacturer's directions. Unroll the paper and lay the strip on a clean, washable surface, paste side up. If you are using wallpaper that isn't prepasted, don't soak it in water; instead apply paste to the dry wallpaper. "Book" the strip by loosely folding—but not creasing—both ends to the middle; this keeps the paste from touching the front of the paper. Let the strip sit for the time indicated by the manufacturer; this allows the paste to activate and the paper to expand and contract.

4. Hang the first strip by unfolding the top end (leave the bottom end folded for the time being), holding it up by the corners, and lining it up with the chalk line. Allow 3 inches of wallpaper to overlap the top edge, for trimming. Unfold the bottom half of the strip and continue to align it with the vertical chalk line. Allow the bottom 3 inches of the strip to overhang for trimming.

5. Smooth out wrinkles and bubbles using a soft brush and sweeping movements. Use this technique for each strip as you hang it: Start at the top middle of each strip and work the brush diagonally to the right. Go back to the top middle and brush to the left so your motions form a triangle. Sponge off any wet paste that seeps from the edges to the front of the paper.

6. Continue applying successive strips, aligning the pattern and smoothing the covering.

7. Trim any excess wallpaper from the top and bottom edges, using a straightedge and sharp razor knife. Change the blade frequently to avoid tearing the paper. Trim each strip while the paste is still damp; then flatten the seams gently but firmly with a seam roller. Sponge off any wet paste that seeps from the edges to the front of the paper.

8. To paper around doors and windows, cut a rough opening with 3 extra inches on all sides from the dry strip that extends over the door or window opening. Moisten the strip and hang it. Make diagonal cuts near the corners of the opening. Smooth the paper around the frame; trim, then clean with a damp sponge.

9. To wallpaper around outlets and light switches, turn off the electricity to the outlets and remove the covers. Position the wallcovering over the outlet or switch opening, cut an X with a razor knife over the opening, and smooth the paper into place. Trim the four flaps made by the X. When you are finished, reattach the covers and turn on the electricity.

## WALLPAPERING TIPS, TRICKS, AND TECHNIQUES

- Fix wall damage, such as cracks, flaking paint, and holes, before priming and hanging wallpaper.
- To avoid mildew growth, prime walls with a mildew-proof wallpaper primer before papering.
- When trying to match a pattern, peel back the paper and reposition it. Overworking the paper can stretch it.
- Press gently on the seam roller. Otherwise, you may force out too much paste and cause curling at the seams.
- Use only high-quality washable paints near wallpapered surfaces, because paste smears can be difficult, if not impossible, to remove from unwashable paint.
- Apply wallcoverings in normal room temperature and humidity conditions. Extreme heat and humidity can cause drying problems.
- Use good lighting to ensure a quality application.

# Canopies

If your bedroom lacks charm, consider surrounding your bed with a canopy, which will create an instant focal point. Even if you don't have a canopy bed, luxury and romance can be yours if you install some hardware and a fabric that complements your decorating scheme.

Lightweight scrim provides a gauzy cover when strung through two chrome-finish brass towel rings attached to the ceiling.

Four-poster beds can look charming with canopies, but draping fabric all around may be cumbersome and look too childlike. For a stylish solution, hang one panel at the head of the bed; this treatment softens the space and gives the appearance of a headboard.

In this charming bedroom, four wrought-iron rods, forming the main rectangle of the canopy, hang from the ceiling. A blue and white check cotton fabric is tied between the rods, and floor-length panels are tied in the same manner. Brass finials provide a finishing touch in the corners.

This bedroom looks like a romantic bed-and-breakfast retreat, thanks to vintage linens and cottage decor. Fabric hung from a J hook in the ceiling drapes over unused swing-arm lamps flanking the bed, creating a lovely canopy.

# Hand-Me-Downs
## Get DRESSED UP

Is your bedroom filled with dissimilar furnishings or lack cohesion? Many homeowners are often faced with a mismatched group of furnishings and hand-me-downs from family members and friends. Such was the case in this bedroom. The young home-owners had a nice queen-size bed and functional storage pieces, but the window treatments were different, and there were no nightstands on which to set an alarm clock or reading lamp. Rearranging the room, restyling the mismatched pieces for unity, and adding Mediterranean-inspired colors made the room into a welcoming oasis from everyday stress.

**Let the bed take center stage.** First, the bed is moved closer to the window. To make the bed a more suitable focal point, it is set at a slight angle for a commanding presence, and a shutter screen serves as a makeshift headboard (the actual headboard is low). The screen also helps channel the heat from a heating vent near the bed. Slipcovers in muted beige, green, and red cover the headboard and footboard. These colors set the stage for an inviting room that is bathed in soft colors and textures and natural finishes.

**Dual window treatments are versatile.** The old, mismatched window treatments give way to bamboo window shutters and rice paper shades that are versatile enough to let in ample light during the day and block out streetlights at night. The horizontal lines of the shutters and folding screen are a nice visual contrast to the strong vertical pattern on the head- and footboard slipcovers.

**Mix and match storage pieces and furnishings for visual interest.** A dark-stained dresser and white cubes provided ample storage space opposite the bed, but they weren't unified. The storage cubes are moved to the closet, where they stack on the existing closet shelf and organize sweaters and little-used

clothing. The dresser wears a fresh coat of white paint to help lighten the main space. Additional storage enters the room in the form of a blanket chest at the foot of the bed. The mix of white-painted furnishings and molding and natural woven elements—the bamboo shutters, the nightstands, the wicker blanket chest and chair—is inviting rather than distracting.

*Continued on page 118*

BEFORE

*AFTER*

AFTER

BEFORE

**Carve out comfort.** With the storage cubes moved to the closet, a vacant corner becomes an intimate reading nook where a chandelier hangs above a comfortable chair. The room lacks overhead lights, so this fixture brings in much-needed general lighting. Additional lighting also comes from petite lamps with beaded-fringe shades, which occupy the new nightstands.

**Anchor the space with color and texture.** To complete the makeover, the dingy carpeting is replaced with hardwood flooring, which has been painted white. The white flooring combined with the beige walls and white ceiling creates an airy space. An area rug beside the bed ushers in additional textures and color.

# Bamboo Shutters

In this bedroom, a dual window treatment effectively lets in light and provides privacy. A white rice paper shade plays a supporting role, but the homemade bamboo shutters are the real attraction. With basic woodworking skills and easy-to-find materials you can create these shutters. The instructions are for making one shutter; repeat the process for a pair.

## You Will Need

Tape measure
Wood trim
Sander or sandpaper and tack cloth
Radial arm saw
Bamboo sheets
Latex paint in the desired color and
    finish, paintbrush
Small nails

Hammer
Optional: wood glue
6 L-brackets, screws
Nail set
Wood filler
Router
Cabinet hinges
Shade to fit window dimensions

1 ▲ Measure the window around the frame interior where you will attach the hinges. Cut two pieces of wood trim to fit the height measurement (lateral pieces) and three pieces of wood cross members to fit between the two longer pieces. Sand the wood pieces; remove dust with the tack cloth.

2 ▲ On one edge of the lateral pieces create a slot by ripping to a ½-inch depth, ¼ inch wide (two blade kerfs) or slightly wider than the bamboo.

3 ▲ Cut the cross members (horizontal pieces) in half thickwise so you have six narrow pieces that will be placed back-to-back over the bamboo.

4 ▲ Cut the bamboo to size, allowing for the width of the cross member as well as the depth of the slots. The slots will be used to hold the material in place.

5 ▲ Paint the wood pieces; let dry.

6 ▲ Nail the cross members together, sandwiching the bamboo between. For more stability, glue these pieces together. Slide the bamboo into the slot of one lateral piece until the lateral piece meets the cross member at the top corner. Place an

L-bracket at this corner and screw on to stabilize the corner. Nail the cross members onto the shade as you did the top. Place an L-bracket at the bottom corner and screw on.

7 ▲ Place the two center cross members on the middle of the shutter, one on the back and one on the front; nail together. Place an L-bracket on the corner where the lateral piece and the cross member meet; screw on.

8 ▲ Slide the second lateral piece onto the remaining edge of the bamboo until the top of the piece meets the top cross member. Place an L-bracket at the top, middle, and bottom corners where the cross members meet the second lateral piece; screw on.

9 ▲ Use a nail set to countersink small nails into the cross members. Fill in the holes with wood filler.

10 ▲ Rout pockets in the finished shade on the side that will be hung on the window frame. The hinges will sit in these pockets.

11 ▲ Touch up over the wood filler and L-brackets with paint; let dry. **Note:** *To completely cover the L-brackets. use several coats.*

12 ▲ Affix the hinges to the window frame to hang the shutters.

Screens

Folding screens—constructed of everything from wood to metal and embellished with papers, ribbons, photographs, and hand painting—add something special to almost any room. These versatile design elements can set off a cozy corner for reading, hide clutter, or create architectural dimension in a blank square space. Ready-made screens are plentiful and easily personalized. If you can't find a premade screen you like, make one from bifold closet doors, louvered panels, or even a garden trellis.

The colors, patterns, and textures of Asian design take center stage in this bedroom. Behind a stream-lined, diagonally set Art Deco bed stands a dark wood screen with a hand-painted ginkgo leaf design.

Colorful paper cutouts resembling origami shapes are combined with rice paper and a clean-lined frame to create a screen with Asian flair. Rather than block light, this tall screen diffuses it through panels fitted with rice paper and chicken wire.

Bifold closet doors, available at home improvement centers, can easily be made into a screen with two-way hinges. This screen is covered with wallpaper and topped with a coordinating border. Ribbons tacked to the top of the doors hold framed artwork.

A playfully hand-painted screen set in the corner of this formal bedroom provides a much needed break from the expanse of blue walls.

# Colorize, TEXTURIZE

A great bedroom starts with a great bed. The bed is where you sleep, relax, and read; it's also most often the focal point of the room. Give your bed the status it deserves with stacks of pillows and cozy bedding, and surround it with furnishings and accessories that complement rather than detract from it.

This bedroom had a lot going for it, including a beautiful wrought-iron bed and coordinating full-length oval mirror. However, the pale lavender walls—while restful—were lifeless, and the cotton bedding, gauzy bed skirt, wood nightstand, and unadorned paper chandelier shades were void of much-needed pattern, color, and texture.

**Punch up the scheme with fresh color and textures.** To take this room up a notch on the style chart, a warmer shade of lavender paint now covers the walls, and bright, cheery colors make their entrance via pillows made of woven satin ribbons and a coordinating suite of projects: a chandelier, nightstand topper, and flowing bed skirt. These accessories not only bring in color, but they also set the stage for new textures, which can both be seen and felt. Textures also make their way into this cheerful space via a soft chenille throw and a green Jacquard duvet cover.

**Use artwork to unify.** Matted and framed artwork is added to one wall to break up the expanse of lavender. This piece of art brings together all the colors now present in the room.

## RIBBON BED SKIRT

Creating a custom bed skirt is quick and easy with a flat sheet, ribbons, and fusible hem tape. Cut a flat sheet to fit the box spring, allowing an extra ¾ inch at the foot end and sides. Hem the edges. Measure from the top of the box spring to the floor and cut ribbons of the same length in various colors to attach to the sides and foot end of the sheet. (In this example, 1½-inch-wide ribbons in six colors are used.) Using a wood-burning tool as described on page 124 to cut the ribbons will prevent the ends from fraying. Cut fusible hem tape to the length of each side and the foot end; remove the paper and temporarily adhere to the sheet edges. Press the ribbons to the tape and iron, following the manufacturer's instructions.

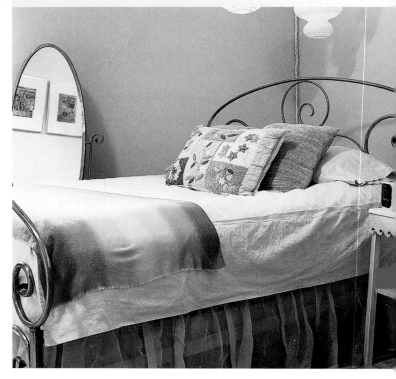

BEFORE

## Woven Ribbon Pillow

Satiny soft pillows made of interwoven ribbons are a luxurious place to rest your head. These instructions are for two colors of ribbon, but choose as many colors as you desire to complement your decor.

### You Will Need

Scissors, crafts knife
Foam-core board
Tape measure
1½" wide single-face satin ribbon, two colors
Straight pins

Fusible interfacing, iron
Fabric for pillow back (i.e., cotton or satin)
Sewing machine, needle, matching thread
20" pillow insert

1. Cut the foam core to a 22-inch square with the crafts knife.

2. Cut 28 ribbons, 14 of each color, each 21 inches long.

3. Line the ribbons of one color in a row on the foam-core board, with the shiny side down. Allow no gaps between the ribbons. Secure each end of the ribbon strips with straight pins.

4. Beginning with one piece of the remaining color of ribbon, secure one end to the foam core with a straight pin, shiny side down. Weave the ribbon through the ribbons placed in Step 3, going over and under the ribbons. When complete, secure with a straight pin. Repeat this process with the remaining ribbons, alternating the ribbon weave to create a checkerboard pattern.

5. After the entire panel is woven, adjust any ribbons that are not tightly secured in the weave.

6. Cut a 21-inch-square piece of fusible interfacing. Iron the fusible interfacing to the woven ribbons, following the manufacturer's instructions and removing pins as you iron. Discard the foam core.

7. From the backing fabric cut a 21-inch square. With the right side of the fabric and shiny side of the ribbon unit together and a ½-inch seam allowance, stitch three of the sides together. Turn right side out, insert the pillow form, and whipstitch the opening closed.

### USING A WOOD-BURNING TOOL

To prevent ribbon ends from fraying, use a wood-burning tool to cut the ribbons. Use caution when working with a wood-burning tool, because it will be very hot. Also note that you will need a nonmelting cutting surface and a metal ruler for cutting straight edges.

# Woven Nightstand Top

This fun table topper is a great way to spruce up a nightstand. An ornate iron plant stand was used for this example, but this versatile design will work equally well on any standard wood nightstand or other tabletop.

## You Will Need
Tape measure
Foam-core board
Scissors, crafts knife
Nightstand
1½"-wide single-face satin ribbon,
 two or more colors
Fusible interfacing, iron
Straight pins
2 pieces of ⅛"-thick framing glass,
 cut to size of nightstand top with
 the edges sanded

1 ■ Measure the edges of the nightstand top and add 2 inches to each measurement. Using a crafts knife, cut the foam core to match these measurements.

2 ■ Cut as many 1½-inch-wide ribbons as needed to cover the length and width of the foam-core board. If using two colors, cut equal amounts of each color; if using more than two colors, cut as many of each color as desired.

3 ■ Follow Steps 3 to 6 for the Woven Ribbon Pillow, cutting the fusible interfacing to size (1 inch smaller than the foam-core board).

4 ■ Sandwich the woven ribbon panel between the two pieces of glass. Place the completed topper on the nightstand.

# Woven Chandelier

Lampshades are available in every shape, size, and color imaginable, but few are as pretty as this. This chandelier has an ordinary paper shade, metal rings at top and bottom for structure, and a hanging cord. Similar inexpensive fixtures can be found at home decorating and discount stores.

## You Will Need
Hanging lamp kit
Tape measure
Scissors
1½"-wide single-face satin ribbon,
 two or more colors
Low-temperature hot-glue gun and
 nonflammable glue sticks

1 ■ Assemble the lamp, following the manufacturer's instructions.

2 ■ Measure the circumference of the shade and the length from top to bottom (from metal ring to metal ring).

3 ■ Cut as many ribbons as required to cover the circumference of the shade in the desired colors. If using two colors, cut equal amounts of each color; if using more than two colors, cut as many of each color as desired. Set aside.

4 ■ Cut as many ribbons as required to cover the length of the shade in the desired colors. If using two colors, cut equal amounts of each color; if using more than two colors, cut as many of each color as desired. Set aside.

5 ■ Adhere the circumference ribbon ends to the shade in a row, shiny side up, aligning the seams at the back of the shade. Allow no gaps between the ribbons.

6 ■ Beginning with one piece of the length ribbon, adhere one end to the shade at the top (near the metal ring). Weave the ribbon through the ribbons placed in Step 5, going over and under the ribbons. When complete, secure the end at the bottom metal ring with hot glue. Repeat this process with the remaining ribbons, alternating the ribbon weave to create a checkerboard pattern.

# Pillows

Pillows are one of the most versatile decorating accessories around. They can be purchased or made in nearly every shape, size, color, and fabric motif imaginable, to complement the decor of every room of the home. Better yet, they are easy to personalize with any number of details, from trims and fringe to appliqués and buttons. Take pillows beyond the bedroom: In large sizes they can serve as seating in family rooms; smaller cushion-type pillows add comfort to dining room chairs.

For more pillow projects you can make, visit **HGTV**.com/beforeandafterbook

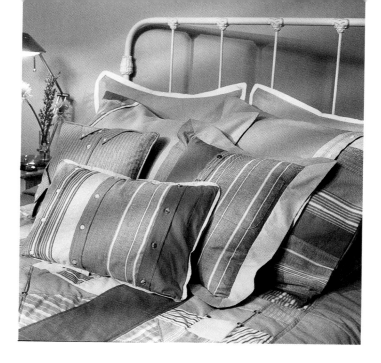

Outgrown shirts make a fun, tailored addition to this bedroom; customized pillows and a pieced and quilted bedspread dress the bed for success. Pillows similar to these can be easily constructed from one shirt or many shirts when they are cut and pieced together. When cutting old shirts to make pillows, quilts, and other projects, use the tailored features, such as plackets, cuffs, and pockets, as interesting details instead of only using the larger areas of shirt fabric.

Ribbons, rickrack, fabric scraps, and ready-made appliqué flowers combine in a sweet, country-inspired pillow. Embellish a purchased pillow cover in a similar fashion by first stitching "stems" of ribbon or rickrack onto the pillow front. Cut floral shapes from scrap fabrics and appliqué them over the stems. To complete the look, attach an appliqué shape, such as a flower or circle, to the center of each flower, using fabric glue or by hand-stitching.

Fleece is one of the easiest, most forgiving fabrics for sewing and crafts projects. It doesn't fray, which means you don't have to be concerned with raw edges. This cozy square pillow features four equal-size squares on its front. To create a similar pillow, cut two 13½-inch squares (for the pillow front and back) from one color of fleece; cut four squares or other shapes from a contrasting color. Glue the small shapes to the pillow front; use perle cotton and a large-eye needle to create a running stitch around the shapes. Put the pillow front and back right sides together and stitch three sides, using a ½-inch seam allowance. Turn right side out, insert a pillow form, and hand-stitch the opening closed.

# Good As GOLD

If you entertain overnight guests and you are lucky enough to have a designated space to accommodate them, consider the room a guest getaway. When planning a guest room space, imagine yourself in the guest's position. When you are a guest in someone's home, what amenities do you prefer? A television? Places to sit and relax? This guest room had a comfortable queen-size bed, plenty of natural light for daytime activities, a beautiful refinished hardwood floor, and a place to stash clothing and personal items. The overall neutral palette, while restful, was uninspired. It took some paint and French-style accents to make this room a warm, inviting space.

**Wake it up with paint.** The most obvious difference in this makeover is the paint color. When selecting a paint color, it is often easiest to use what's in the room—furnishings, flooring, accessories—as inspiration. In this room, however, the opposite occurred: The homeowner chose paint colors to audition, then decorated around the chosen color (see page 98). A vivid yellow-orange won the lead part and now enlivens the room. Fortunately, the homeowner remembered a piece of French crewel in cream, gold, and brown, dating from the mid-1800s, at a local antiques store. Although the piece is only large enough to cover a twin-size bed, it provides the mix of color and texture the space needed.

**Layer in softness.** To make the bed an interesting focal point, textiles are layered on top of it. The crewel is the top layer. Below, a piece of cream-color antique linen visually lengthens the crewel, and the original taupe bed skirt adds a tailored finish. Two large pillows are covered in old linens and a grain sack, providing additional texture and old-world charm.

Layers also appear on the windows: The long drapery is tied back with hemp twine, and another piece of antique linen serves as a long valance. Combined, the two neutral-color pieces of fabric let in light while providing the privacy that guests require.

*Continued on page 131*

BEFORE

*AFTER*

*AFTER*

BEFORE

**Use neutral hues and wood tones to tone down bold color.** Although the new, energizing color dominates the space, it is neutralized by the crisp white moldings, freshly painted dresser, and touches of silver throughout. Silver—seen in the bedside lamp and accessories, curtain rod, and dresser hardware—acts almost like an ice cube, cooling down the space. The wood floor now glows in the presence of the bold walls, but the warm tone of the wood also neutralizes the space.

**Refresh tired furnishings.** The dark-stained dresser, a hand-me-down that served as an entertainment center, was too dominating. To soften its harsh appearance it got a coat of white paint, which complements the molding; the original pulls are painted silver. Now the dresser does more than serve as storage space: The TV is gone, and a much needed mirror and stylish topiaries grace the dresser top.

**Complete the look with elegant accessories.** To round out the room, the once bare walls display a white platter and two elegant French-inspired wall sconces, featuring curved lines and drop crystals for a spark of romance. The new bedside table—which took the place of a chair—has ample space for a reading lamp, a clock, and other bedroom necessities.

## GUEST ROOM CHECKLIST

The next time you are expecting overnight guests, have these items on hand—or similar items that cater to the preferences of your guest (for instance, a CD player and CDs your teenage niece enjoys).

- Bedside light and clock
- Extra pillows, blankets, and fresh linens
- Bottle or carafe of water and glasses, electric kettle and tea bags or other beverage service, and a fruit basket
- Reading materials, writing paper, and a pen
- Mirror
- Comfortable chair
- Clean towels and washcloths and travel-size toiletries
- Clothes hangers and a place to stash luggage
- Flowers

## THE GREAT PAINT EXPERIMENT

Painting colors directly on a wall will give you the most accurate indication of how a color will appear. You can also use primed sample boards, as described on page 98, and move them around the room to see how the colors change throughout the day in different lighting conditions.

# Guest Rooms

When planning a room for your overnight guests, keep your own wish list in mind. When you are away from home, do you like a place to lounge while reading the morning paper or a fresh robe you can slip into after a shower? To see if your guests will be comfortable, sleep in the space yourself. If you don't have a special room to dedicate to guests, consider underused areas, like lofts or basements; or temporarily convert a den or office into a guest haven with a movable screen.

Complete with romantic netting, this "napping couch" invites guests to drift off to sleep in the summer breeze. If it's too chilly at night, the door at far right leads to the main house, where other sleeping quarters can be found.

What used to be a workshop is now a guesthouse that opens to a patio. Painted finishes on an open-beam ceiling, plywood walls, and a concrete floor dress up the space, which is filled with flea market finds.

A little-used loft space can be the perfect hideaway for guests—and a place you can use as a get-away-from-it-all retreat when you don't have overnight visitors.

This room is filled with everything a guest could desire in a home-away-from-home, including a table for primping or writing notes, a comfortable place to enjoy a cup of tea, and an inviting bed with mounds of pillows.

# Room for TWO

It is not uncommon for children to share rooms when they are young and receive separate spaces as they grow older. In this case, however, two boys who once had their own rooms—but usually ended up sleeping in each other's rooms—now share a space that inspires fun and creativity.

**A loft saves space—and offers more than a place to sleep.** Sleeping quarters were addressed first. The existing full-size bed stays in place, but to conserve space a custom loft is constructed above it to hold another mattress. The ends of the loft structure are open storage and display space—an important feature for a room that contains possessions of two instead of one.

**Storage for two.** To further tackle storage needs, each child has his own red-painted dresser, and the closet is divided into two separate areas. Bins and hanging storage (shown on page 136) allow plenty of space for clothing, footwear, and sports gear. The dressers face each other, creating a designated changing area.
*Continued on page 136*

## GROWTH CHART

This growth chart resembles a football field—a nod to the favorite sport of the two boys. The chart is painted on a wall that was first coated with magnetic paint; the footballs are homemade magnets that can be moved as the children grow. Nearly any motif can be used—including animals, musical notes, and racecars—to suit your child's interests.

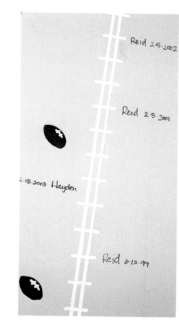

BEFORE

*AFTER*

Stacked bins and hanging storage create plenty of space for two boys' possessions.

**BEFORE**   **AFTER**

## ROOMS THAT GROW

When planning a room for your child or children, keep an eye on the future. When you purchase versatile furnishings, select a lasting color scheme and choose enduring design motifs so the room will grow with your child. Use these cues as a starting point for creating a safe, comfortable haven your child will enjoy for years to come.

- When planning a nursery, select a crib that converts into a toddler's daybed. Often, the bedding can be used for both, saving you money. This also makes the child's transition from crib to bed easier.
- Look beyond traditional kid colors, such as blue for boys and pink for girls. Gender-neutral colors, such as reds, greens, and yellows, can create a timeless look.
- Avoid trendy motifs, such as the latest cartoon character, that your child will quickly outgrow. To appease your child, incorporate these motifs through inexpensive, easy-to-change accessories, including throw pillows, lampshades, and photo frames.
- Theme decorating often makes selecting fabrics and accessories easy, but choose themes that have stood the test of time, such as floral, nautical, and Americana motifs.
- When selecting fabrics, opt for easy-care cottons in geometrics, stripes, florals, and solids that can be easily mixed and matched.
- If planning a room two children will share, consider current and future needs (for instance, play spaces when they are young and study spaces as they grow older). Create a room where each child has space for his or her possessions and provide common areas where lessons on compromise and sharing can be learned.

**Bold color and graphic motifs bring excitement.** The room was originally painted a soft yellow, with bright furnishings, bedding, and accessories. This color scheme was invigorating, but there was no real style theme. The room required a more sophisticated scheme that could grow with the boys. The new color and design scheme is inspired by contemporary striped fabrics in white, brown, and red, found on the new chair and ottomans, and fun red circle mobiles hung by the windows. Stripes and dots—both reminiscent of sports symbols—are now present throughout the space, on the custom duvet covers and pillows, wall art painted by the residents, and storage containers. A crisp stripe treatment is even painted below the window. A neutral light brown paint on the walls allows the shapes and bold red to take center stage.

**Personalize with paint.** To encourage creative play and display, sections of the wall and dressers are covered with magnetic paint, providing a surface on which to showcase favorite photographs and artwork. Homemade magnets in letters and sports motifs can be moved from surface to surface with ease.

**Time for rest.** Finally, to give the children a spot to sit, relax, and read a book with Mom or Dad, a comfy chair now sits beneath a large window, which features a scallop-shape valance and brown Roman shades. Ottomans provide a place for the boys to put up their feet and can be used for extra seating.

# Dressed-Up Dresser

Dressers serve an important purpose in a bedroom—storage on the inside and display space on top—but why not make a dresser a place for fun too? This dresser has both cork and magnetic surfaces for kids to tack up pictures and mementos. Magnetic paint is readily available at crafts stores and home improvement centers; most often, it can be covered with paint in any color for a truly personalized look. To dress up the magnetic surface, create custom magnets.

## You Will Need

Dresser
Sandpaper, tack cloth
Primer
Paintbrushes
Magnetic paint
Latex enamel paint in the desired
    color and finish

Tacky glue
Cork squares
Crafts knife
Scissors
Jumbo rickrack

1 Remove the drawers and any doors from the dresser. Lightly sand the dresser, drawers, and doors; remove dust with the tack cloth. Prime; let dry.

2 Select areas to be painted with magnetic paint; on this dresser, the sides and back are painted. Paint the desired areas, following the manufacturer's instructions; let dry.

3 Paint the entire dresser the desired color of latex enamel paint; let dry.

4 Using tacky glue, adhere cork squares to the top portion of the dresser back. If necessary, cut the squares with a crafts knife to fit the width of the dresser.

5 Cut jumbo rickrack to serve as a border for the cork section. Adhere to the cork with tacky glue.

# MORE IDEAS FOR

# Kids' Rooms

Children's rooms are some of the most fun to decorate: They are a great place to experiment with color, pattern, interesting paint treatments, and even furniture arrangement. When decorating a child's room keep safety foremost in your mind; among other items, always choose child-safe paints as well as beds that meet current safety standards. After safety, aim for enduring style. Selecting versatile furnishings—for instance, a crib that converts into a toddler bed—and a lasting color scheme not dependent on a new, popular superhero will help you create a room that will grow with your child. The rooms shown here are decorated in a primary color scheme, but pastels, jewel tones, or even neutrals may also convey a child's interests and personality.

Select colors, motifs, and furnishings that can grow with your child. The look of this room can easily mature through the conversion of bunk beds into side-by-side twins, a change of bedding, and the removal of the throw rugs. Ample storage that is easily within reach of a child is a key to a well-functioning room. This room features built-in shelving as well as a tall cupboard that resembles an athletic locker.

Clean and uncluttered, this young child's room features headboard shelves that store and display toys and tic-tac-toe pieces; platform beds offer extra storage. The clean white framework will coordinate with any decor as the child grows older and develops different tastes. Bright fabrics and accessories in primary colors, accompanied by geometric patterns, look crisp against the white walls and furniture.

For lasting style, choose a theme that isn't too childlike. The nautical look of this room makes it appealing for a child of any age. Washable 100-percent-cotton fabrics in a bold check motif, chambray blue walls, and white-painted furnishings contribute to the timeless feel of the room.

# From Country Cousin to CITY SOPHISTICATE

A common decorating mistake is to fill a room with too much of a favorite thing. In this case, the bed and bath were too cute and too pink: pink walls, pink floors, and pink textiles. Every accent was dated, over-the-top country. With no contrast and no established focal points, the rooms felt visually adrift.

**Use color as the starting point.** An about-face gave the bedroom the balance it needed. The color scheme—a neutral camel beige with black accents—is the foundation for the new look. The walls and floors are similar shades of honey-beige; the carpet is a textured berber with a hearty look and feel. Furniture in dark tones adds needed contrast.

**Window treatments can do more than block sunlight.** New window treatments also add texture and color. The old drawn-back panels make way for honey-tone bamboo Roman shades that are mounted outside the window molding to visually maximize the size of the window and control light and privacy. Layered on top are sailcloth panels attached by silver ring clips to brushed-silver rods. The rods are hung almost at the ceiling, and the panels hang to the floor, another design trick to accent the height and size of a window.

**Continued on page 142**

## ACCENTING IS EVERYTHING

When a room gets a complete overhaul, be prepared to change everything. In this room it's difficult to imagine anything coming forward unchanged; only the dresser's classic lines saved it from going to the resale shop.

- **Lamps.** The rounded pink lamps are replaced with a slender, brushed-nickel lamp with a translucent shade next to the bed and a classic urn-shape lamp on the dresser. Mixing, rather than matching, makes the room more visually interesting

- **Side chair.** Next to the bedside table, a light and airy wicker chair replaces a pink rocker. The wicker's texture adds depth and contrast while continuing the warm, natural tones in the room.

- **Wall art.** A pink and blue heart-motif quilt hung above the bed; aside from the color scheme, it is much too childlike for an adult's bedroom. The matted architectural bridge drawing is not only more appropriate, but it adds a nice horizontal element to balance the bed's strong vertical lines.

- **Bedding.** In this room the new bedding is not only appropriate for the redo, but the layering makes the bed much more inviting and pleasing to look at: beige sheets, an off-white cotton blanket, a wool camel-hair blanket, and a stack of pillows.

- **Tabletop accessories.** Every picture frame, basket, and vase is new to the space. The new room simply couldn't accommodate any of the style of the old room.

BEFORE

*AFTER*

BEFORE

**Splurge on style.** The old bed was the only item with no redeeming style qualities. Now a slatted mahogany bed that stands taller resides in the room, along with a nightstand of the same style. Two black leather bedside footstools complement the deep, rich wood.

**If it still functions—and has good lines—salvage it.** An old dresser had nice lines but a bad finish and an unappealing three-panel mirror. Clunky hardware and stain that exaggerated the wood grain gave way to a smooth black satin paint finish and simple silver hardware. Now the curving lines of the piece rightly dominate in cool dramatic fashion. A simple black-frame mirror rests casually on the dresser top. Polishing the look of the old dresser helped it fit in with the new furniture.

**If you don't need it, pitch it.** The second tall dresser shared the same good lines, but crowded the small room, which has two large closets. In its place a tall tropical plant fans out to fill the space, adding a natural touch.

## ARTFUL ADDITIONS

Improved printing processes and readily available standard-size picture frames have made adding wall art to any room easier and less expensive than ever before. In a streamlined setting like this suite, using one simple frame style in similar sizes throughout creates cohesiveness. For personalized artwork similar to that shown here, purchase standard-size frames with precut mats. Even if the mat doesn't have exactly the right size of opening, it may be close enough to fit or you may be able to re-create the photo. By scanning the image—either at home or at a drugstore or copy center—and printing it on photographic paper, you can resize it to fit whatever frame you choose. You can also adjust the color (heightening or muting the tones) to better suit a room. In this master suite black and white photos provide a fitting graphic look.

AFTER

The long window treatments are hung close to the ceiling to emphasize the height and size of the window. ▶

The master bath shared the same unfortunate look as the bedroom, with the additional dismay of a visually vibrating pink sponge treatment on all the walls. The floor was not spared; it sported pink heart-motif linoleum. The wood tones offered no visual relief; there was a plethora of poorly grained wood.

**Unify two spaces with compatible colors.** To revive this space, the same style modus operandi is employed: Wash the room with warm tones and accent with black. The walls were sanded down to remove the residual texture from the sponge painting; then they were painted a neutral honey-beige two tones darker than the bedroom. Painting adjoining rooms the same basic color but a touch lighter or darker adds enough contrast to link and separate the spaces. The same goes for the window treatments: In the bedroom bamboo shades and full-length curtain panels in cream are used; a complementary cream-color Roman shade with a custom ribbon edge covers the bathroom window.

## CUSTOMIZING PURCHASED SHADES

A band of black grosgrain ribbon adds punch to plain shades. For a similar look, iron the shade flat to make it easier to attach the ribbon. Cut the ribbon to fit about 1 inch inside the edge of each side. Carefully attach the ribbon with fabric glue or fusible hem tape, following the manufacturer's instructions.

BEFORE

AFTER

A brushed-nickel faucet complements the new cabinetry hardware.

Ceramic floor tiles are an easy-clean option in a bath.

**Brushed nickel lends a sophisticated feel.** A brushed-nickel, two-handle faucet gives the plain white oval sink a fresh new look. The vanity and storage cabinet have the same black paint covering and brushed-nickel hardware as the bedroom dresser. New towel bars also sport a brushed-nickel finish. Over the vanity, a new four-light fixture with ribbed, frosted-glass shades provides plenty of light. Replacing the wood toilet seat with plain white, a minimal expense, makes it less noticeable.

**Tiles are a smart flooring choice.** In this bath redo, the biggest expense is new flooring: Creamy white tiles in 4x4 squares now cover the floor. Designers often disagree on whether a small bath should have small or large tiles, so choose which you prefer. The key is in the grout color; match the grout to the tile to blend rather than contrast, and the space is bound to look bigger. Of course, the light color choice helps too. A small sisal rug is the perfect accent for this floor.

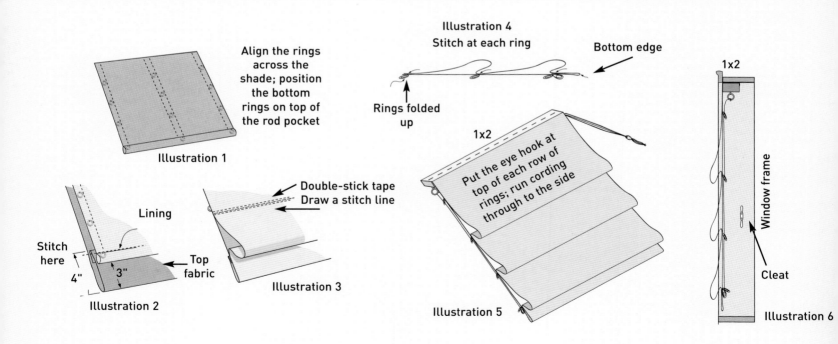

Align the rings across the shade; position the bottom rings on top of the rod pocket

Illustration 1

Stitch here
4"
3"
Lining
Stitch here
Top fabric

Illustration 2

Double-stick tape
Draw a stitch line

Illustration 3

Illustration 4
Stitch at each ring
Bottom edge
Rings folded up

1x2
Put the eye hook at top of each row of rings; run cording through to the side

Illustration 5

1x2
Window frame
Cleat

Illustration 6

# PROJECT

## Roman Shades

Roman shades, a classic window treatment, are actually quite easy to make. Despite the simple construction, ready- or custom-made Roman shades will cost you—far more than the materials for this project. The shades are made so that the top fabric hangs in folds; the lining hangs straight, and the top is stitched to the lining across the width of the shade at each ring. The overhanging fabric hides the stitching.

### You Will Need

Tape measure
1x2*
Table saw
Scissors
Lining fabric*
Decorator fabric, in the desired color and motif*
Rings
Sewing machine

Double-stick tape
Disappearing-ink marker
Staple gun, staples
Eye hooks
Cording*
Cleats
1½" wood screws, screwdriver
¼" metal rod
*Measure window prior to purchasing and cutting materials

1. Cut the 1x2 one-half inch shorter than the window width.

2. Cut the lining fabric ¼ inch shorter than the window width and the same as the window height. This allows 1 inch at the bottom for a rod pocket and 2 inches at the top to attach the shade. Finish the raw edges and fold over the bottom 1 inch to form a rod pocket; stitch.

3. Cut the decorator fabric ½ inch wider than the window width and 48 inches longer than the window height. Finish the raw edges. Fold over the bottom 4 inches to form a rod pocket; stitch.

4. Starting at the bottom edge of the lining, right side up, evenly space three rings across the lining width. Continue spacing rings across the lining, placing them 5 inches apart along the length of the lining. (Illustration 1)

5. Place the lining right side up on top of the decorator fabric, also right side up, aligning the rod pockets. Stitch the lining to the decorator fabric where the rod pockets meet. There will be 3 inches of decorator fabric exposed at the bottom. (Illustration 2) Fold the joined lining and fabric so that the front of the lining faces the back of the decorator fabric.

6. With the lining on the bottom, fold 10 inches of the decorator fabric to align with the row of rings above the lining rod pocket. Fold the rings up so that you will not stitch over them. Using double-stick tape, temporarily adhere the lining to the decorator fabric right above the line of rings. If desired, draw a stitch line with the disappearing-ink marker, right below the line of rings. (Illustration 3) Stitch.

7. Repeat Step 6, folding 10 inches of decorator fabric to align with the additional rows of rings. (Illustration 4)

8. Staple the remaining top 2 inches of decorator fabric to the 1x2. Attach three eye hooks to the 1x2, aligning them with the three rings spaced across the width of the fabric. For the left-hand and middle cords, cut lengths 2 times the window length plus the width. For the right-hand cord, cut a cord half that length. Tie one end of each cord to the ring at the bottom (near the rod pockets). Thread the cords through each loop in the corresponding column and run them all through the right-hand eye hook. (Illustration 5)

9. Secure the cleat to the right-hand side of the window frame with screws.

10. Attach the 1x2 to the window frame with the 1½-inch wood screws. (Illustration 6)

11. Put the metal rod through the rod pocket.

# Unifying a Bedroom and Bath

If your bedroom/bathroom suite doesn't feel like a unified space, use the following tips to create flow between them. First, consider color of paint, wallcoverings, fabrics, and even flooring and decorative accessories. Choose dominant and accent colors that work well in both spaces, regardless of their architectural features. Besides being perfect places to display color, fabrics used as window treatments, slipcovers, and bedding are a great way to bring complementary patterns and motifs into the bedroom and bath. Next, notice the surfaces and finishes that appear in each room: If you have a marble-top vanity, consider adding marble-top or marble-accented bedside tables. Finally, use accessories, including artwork and collections, to forge a link between the spaces.

A taupe and white color scheme—and graceful decorating—unifies this bedroom and bath. In the bath the white fixtures, tile, and cabinetry create a sense of spaciousness. The taupe and white wallpaper adds warmth to the light that streams in from the windows. Additional color in the bedroom—green plants, pink flowers—blend well with the taupe and white theme. The architectural piece above the bed recalls the bathroom wallpaper pattern.

The colors, textures, and imagery of the sea combine to create a bedroom and bath filled with a sun, sea, and surf atmosphere. In the bathroom light pours in through a large tub window; the breezy blue and white palette found throughout, including the glazed ceramic tiles, captures the colors of ocean waves. The bedroom, complete with a round window that resembles a porthole, shares the maritime atmosphere of the bath and boasts an impressive view.

# BATHROOMS

# Cottage-Style RETRE

A bathroom needs to be functional, but that doesn't mean it can't be a beautiful, soothing space where you can escape from daily stress. Before this bathroom was treated to fresh fabrics, an inviting color scheme, charming beaded-board panel, and friendlier lighting and storage, it was a sterile, unwelcoming space. Devoid of charm, the room featured dry-walled walls, bare-bulb lighting centered over small medicine cabinets, and pedestal sinks with narrow rims that barely accommodated soap and toothbrushes. Further, storage was an issue: Wire shelving near the sinks held toiletries and other bath essentials but looked cluttered.

**Emphasize the assets.** The focal point of this bathroom, the beautiful claw-foot tub, set the stage for the makeover: The vintage look and feel served as the inspiration for the new cottage style. The tub is too large to remove—and too expensive to replace—

## BLANK-SLATE DECORATING

If you have an all-white room with little personality—and it doesn't function the way you want it to—here are some ways to jump-start the makeover process:

- **Evaluate what works and what doesn't.** Do you have enough space for the activities you do in the room? Is there ample storage and lighting? Does your room have great architectural features you want to play up? Thinking about the good (and how you can play it up) and the bad (and how to remove or restyle it) is the right place to start.

- **Consider your budget.** It's important to prioritize and decide what changes you can make to get the most bang for the buck. The tub in this bath would have been difficult to remove and expensive to replace. With new reproduction hardware and a few coats of special epoxy paint to spiff up the porcelain, the tub looks good as new. Keeping the tub left money for fresh fabrics, wallcoverings, and even new wall-mounted sinks.

- **Get inspired.** Do you love a particular color or decorating style but haven't had the opportunity to try it yet? Is there an element in the room, for instance, an outside view or architectural detail, that can drive the decorating? In this room, the paneled door and vintage claw-foot tub lent themselves to a cottage style. If you aren't sure where to begin, review collections of coordinated wallcoverings and fabrics, which take the guesswork out of choosing.

- **Address the details.** The little things, such as new hardware and light fixtures, can provide major style. Often, these details are inexpensive but their decorative impact is significant.

but it required a makeover of its own. With a few coats of specially formulated epoxy paint to refresh the tired porcelain, and a coat of soft green paint on the outside, the tub regains its charm and status. Reproduction brass hardware and a pretty shower curtain accent the new look. A spindle-back chair provides seating—and serves as a makeshift table for towels and reading materials during long, relaxing baths.

**Coordinated fabrics and wallcoverings unify.** Fabric and color play a big role in this bath: Floral and striped fabrics in cream, green, and pastel pink provide visual and real softness in the shower curtain, valances, sink skirts, and chair cushion. A coordinating wallpaper and rickrack border continue the cottage-style scheme above the newly installed beaded-board panel and on the storage chest.

*Continued on page 152*

BEFORE

*AFTER*

**Store in style.** Storage was a problem in this bath, but the newly decorated space handles it with grace. The once dark, grungy chest is now a pretty place to store toiletries and display personal items. The chest is painted the same soft green as the tub and treated to decoupaged cutouts from a coordinated wallcovering. Pleated sink skirts hide bathroom necessities; exposed storage above the toilet (not shown) holds towels, toiletries, and collectibles. Even the ledge above the beaded-board panel gets in on the act, serving as a display shelf for accessories.

**Consider function and aesthetics.** The original pedestal sinks, while functional, are replaced with wall-hung sinks, which have wider rims for holding everyday items. Above, the old-fashioned medicine cabinets carry the vintage feel one step further, and vintage-style light fixtures provide a polished alternative to the harsh bare bulbs.

## SINK SKIRTS

Sink skirts are a charming—and functional—addition to any pedestal or wall-hung sink. Besides providing color and pattern to coordinate with other fabrics in the room, they can hide essentials such as tissues, toiletries, and cleaning paraphernalia. The pleated skirts featured in this bathroom are attached to the sinks with hook-and-loop tape, making them easy to remove for washing.

To make a simple gathered version, measure around the sink or vanity from wall to wall; multiply the measurement by 3 to allow enough fabric for pleating. Measure the height of the sink or vanity from where you plan to hang the skirt down to the floor; add 3 inches to allow for top and bottom hems (a wide hem adds body and weight to the bottom of the skirt). Sew a 2-inch bottom hem and a 1-inch top hem. To pleat the skirt, use a toothpick to push equal amounts of fabric beneath the sewing machine foot and stitch across 1/4- to 1/2-inch-wide pleats. Stitch one pleat at a time and then use the toothpick to push through more fabric. Cover the pleating stitches with jumbo rickrack, braiding, cord, or ribbon. Attach the skirt to the sink or vanity with hook-and-loop tape.

## Decoupaged Chest

Dressing up a tired piece of furniture—or a new unfinished piece—is easier than you might think with paint and decoupage papers. Decoupage is a simple technique—you cut out the desired images and adhere them to a surface—but skill is required for even, accurate cutting. Use a small pair of sharp scissors to cut out decoupage motifs; hold the scissors at an angle close to the edge of the motif as you cut; turn the paper as you cut so that you get a clean edge. If desired, use a crafts knife and a self-healing cutting mat.

Look for decoupage papers in crafts and art supply stores as well as on the Internet. If you can't find special decoupage papers in motifs you like, use wrapping paper or wallpaper, but don't use magazines: The images on the reverse side of the paper will bleed through when you apply the decoupage medium.

### You Will Need

Chest or other piece of furniture
Screwdriver
Sandpaper, tack cloth
Paintbrush
Primer
Latex enamel paint in the desired
  color and finish

Small, sharp scissors
Decoupage papers, wrapping papers,
  or other desired paper
Decoupage medium, paintbrush or
  foam brush, sponge, wallpaper
  smoother

1. Remove any drawers, doors, and hardware from the piece of furniture. Lightly sand each portion; remove any dust with the tack cloth.

2. Prime the piece of furniture; let dry. Paint; let dry.

3. Cut the desired motifs from the paper. Using a paintbrush or foam brush, apply decoupage medium to the back of each motif and adhere to the piece of furniture. If excess decoupage medium seeps from beneath the motifs, quickly wipe it away with a damp sponge.

4. After all motifs are placed, cover the entire surface with a thin, even layer of decoupage medium, using a foam brush to seal. Use the wallpaper smoother to flatten the edges of the papers; this ensures they will adhere to the surface.

5. Reattach the hardware or doors and reinsert the drawers.

❋ For more fresh furniture ideas, visit
HGTV.com/beforeandafterbook

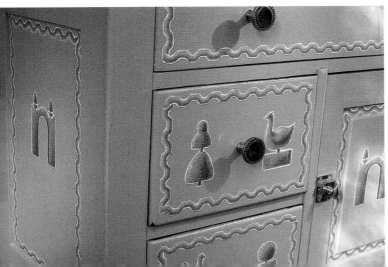

# MORE IDEAS FOR

## Softening a
# Sterile Space

White bathrooms offer a clean, crisp, fresh look, but a lack of color can make a monochromatic room feel devoid of personality. The good news is nearly any color, from primaries to pastels, can work well with white. If your walls are white and you don't want to paint them, bring in color by way of fabrics, for instance, shower curtains, rugs, towels, and accessories.

Wainscoting and board-and-batten molding in crisp white are paired with a white honeycomb tile floor, a vintage bathtub, a terry cloth-covered bench, and sheer curtains in this sunny, style-savvy bath. Walls painted in pale blue set off the white moldings and fixtures.

White fixtures and a black and white tile floor are classics—as are the etched frameless mirror and delicate glass shelf. Hints of pale lilac—paint on the walls, an upholstered stool, and items placed on the sink and glass shelf—breath life into this small powder room.

This attic bath, with its sloping ceilings and limited standing room, is filled with casual charm, from the white beaded board to the lively mix of black and white checked, floral, and dotted patterns. Because moving or replacing a bathtub is messy and costly, painting it is a great option. To paint the outside of a tub similar to this, clean the sides with a trisodium phosphate cleaner, apply a coat of high-quality latex primer, and paint the desired motif with latex or acrylic paints. To clean a painted tub, use a damp sponge and avoid abrasive cleaners.

# Respecting the ROOTS

This bathroom in a 1950s ranch hadn't been altered much since its creation. It still functioned well enough, but the dated tiles, dark wood vanity, and worn bathtub were in need of attention. Help came in the form of a fresh color scheme, a dresser-turned-vanity, and sleek accessories that respect—and even enhance—the midcentury roots of this home. If your bathroom still functions well enough but has a dated look, take cues from this stylish transformation.

**Start with a clean slate.** The first step in this makeover was reevaluating the walls. The paneled walls had been painted white in an earlier redecorating, but rather than try to salvage or recover them, fresh drywall is installed. This provides a clean, even starting point. The fresh turquoise blue paint that now covers the walls is a nod to the '50s; olive green accents throughout the room are the perfect period partner.

**Update a tub with paint and graphic elements.** To keep the project under budget, the tub is retained, but it required a deep cleaning and repainting with do-it-yourself epoxy paint formulated for the job. To further freshen the tub area, 12x12-inch tile replaces the small yellow tiles, and stainless-steel fixtures are now in place. Finally, ½-inch glass shower screen is mounted to the tub and wall, extending to the ceiling beam for support. The glass is sandblasted in a graphic circular pattern within 12-inch squares.

**Restyle furniture for new function.** The dark, dual-sink vanity was in good condition, but its boxy shape lacked pizzazz. The rest of the home is filled with midcentury furnishings and accessories, so a vintage dresser found at a secondhand shop seemed a perfect remedy: Fitted with a stainless-steel sink and faucet, the dresser now serves as a hip vanity—and fitting focal point. Above, a green-frame mirror replaces the old plain one, and retro lamps replace uninspired lighting choices. Track lighting is installed on the ceiling beam for good measure.

*Continued on page 158*

BEFORE

*AFTER*

**Look for storage in unlikely places.** The new vanity provides some storage, but not enough. Ready-made cabinet boxes with doors offer a solution. Typically, such boxes are stacked, but here they are staggered on the wall opposite the vanity, where framed photographs once hung. Inside, toiletries and hand towels are stored; black and white photographs grace the exterior doors. The staggered placement allows the tops to be used for displaying period collectibles.

**Continue the sleek style throughout the space.** To complete the makeover, the vinyl flooring gave way to large ceramic tiles, which link the space with the connecting hallway tiles. The old inefficient toilet is replaced with a contemporary one-piece unit that complements the sleek styling throughout the room.

BEFORE

AFTER

# Dresser Vanity

Transforming a dresser into a vanity is a fun way to make your bathroom one of a kind. First, choose a dresser that's in good condition and in dimensions that suit your space; check that it will accommodate the size and style of sink you desire. If you are skilled at plumbing, you can hook up the plumbing yourself; otherwise, hire a professional plumber to do the work for you.

## You Will Need
Dresser
Sink, faucet
Optional: pencil, scissors, paper
Marker, masking tape
Jigsaw
Screwdriver

1. Decide where you want the sink to be placed on the dresser top. Remove the drawers and any drawer supports that will interfere with the plumbing.

2. Most sinks come with a positioning template; if yours does not, trace the sink outline and create one with paper. Tape the template in the desired place on the dresser top; trace. If you will be mounting the faucet outside the sink, as in this example, mark its placement too.

3. Determine the location of the water supply and drain lines. Mark this location on the back of the dresser.

4. Using a jigsaw, cut the sink, faucet, and water supply/drain line openings.

5. Set the sink and faucet, following the manufacturer's instructions. Hook up the plumbing.

6. Cut the backs of the drawers that surround the sink and/or plumbing so that they fit perfectly into place. Use the jigsaw to remove the necessary portions.

7. Reinsert the drawers.

Storage

Any bathroom—large or small, new or old—can benefit from increased storage capacity. Whether you need a place to keep grooming and cleaning supplies, or a place for towels and linens, or both, finding attractive, space-savvy options can be problematic. Many of the ideas shown can be incorporated into a new or remodeled bath. Also, put to use overlooked spaces such as your walls and the back of a door; hooks, racks, and pegs can hold towels and robes.

These may look like swing-out doors, but they actually glide like drawers so that nothing becomes hidden in the back. Even the space around the plumbing is put to good use, thanks to a ring that holds a hand towel.

Decorative panels on the front of a vanity can also serve a purpose: Use them for handy tilt-out storage. Kits available at home improvement centers often include hinges and a shelf that attaches to the back of the panel. The panel shown here hides an electrical outlet.

If your medicine chest is an eyesore, replace the door with a cut-to-fit wooden panel inside a wooden frame and apply a print for instant appeal. Nonglare glass protects the paper from moisture.

The space between bathroom wall studs is an ideal place for a tall, narrow storage niche. This in-shower space has plenty of room for towels; a small glass shelf keeps bath oils and other accessories within reach.

A sliding drawer pulls out easily, and everything stored within is in plain view. Dividers keep the items organized. Tall bottles are placed on the side; small items stay in the shallow middle section beneath the plumbing.

# Warming Up a
# MASTER BATH

Left with typical builder finishes after construction, a master bath like this one has all the warmth and charm of a high school locker room. All it takes, however, is a little vision and a pinch of cash to turn lackluster into luxurious.

**Play up what you have.** If your bath looks similar to this, create a plan that allows you to keep the existing fixtures and cabinetry, for cost-effectiveness. The cabinets in this bath were plain white, but rich brown paint really warms up the room; the gold-tone faucets already on the tub and sink added a nice glamorous touch, so they are kept; the cabinet hardware is replaced with brass-tone traditional pieces that match the new style of the room. The green marble-look flooring was not worn, so the smart choice was to keep the flooring and develop a color scheme that would complement—rather than match—the dark green.

**Color and pattern add interest.** A chocolate-brown on cream toile wallpaper is the perfect backdrop for the relaxed, high-country look. The scenic toile pattern flows in an easy manner across the large expanse of wall. Two plush rugs in a cream color break up the field of marble and brighten the floor.

*Continued on page 164*

## STYLISH FURNISHINGS

Once you've made the color and style choices for a room, start planning complementary touches, items that give a room—even a bath—its style. These details make the difference between a functional and uninviting bathroom and a relaxing, spa-like space. Go beyond the obvious towels, rugs, and soap holders and add the elements you'd find in any comfortable room:

- **Upholstered chair.** Include a small, comfortable chair to sit on after a bath or when getting dressed. An armless parsons chair, like the one in this room, is small and light enough to be easily moved around the bath as needed.
- **Cushioned bench.** A bench provides a nice focal point on a long, blank wall. The open legs on the bench shown here keep the look light. The cushioned seat is the perfect place to lay a robe or slippers. Cover the cushion with fabric that matches or complements other fabric used in the room.
- **Wall art.** High-quality artwork in interesting frames makes any bathroom seem more luxurious. When choosing artwork, choose pieces that will resist temperature and humidity. Mirrors with interesting frames, unusual shapes, or decorative etching are both functional and artistic additions to a bathroom.
- **Accessories.** In any room little things make the difference, so include an artful mix of small ceramic, glass, or porcelain pieces in your bath. For a garden touch, use these pieces to hold fresh flowers or small plants.
- **Plant stand.** In a bathroom with a large soaking tub like this one, include a tubside table to keep a cup of tea, a book, or a loofah at hand. It's perfect for keeping items away from the edge of the tub but at your fingertips.

**BEFORE**

AFTER

BEFORE

**Layered window treatments offer versatility.** A pair of windows placed side by side create the effect of one large window over the tub. This arrangement lets in lots of light, but it needed the right window treatment to provide privacy. A brown-check custom-made valance hung well over the top of the window frame—only 2 inches from the ceiling—makes the window unit look even larger. Behind the valance is a custom Roman shade in an off-white diamond matelassé with a brown-check banding to provide the required privacy.

**Bathrooms need display space too.** A narrow shelf runs the width of both windows. Painted a glossy white and held in place with decorative brackets, the shelf extends the lower frame of the window and is the perfect place for a few plants to accent the green tile.

## SMART MONEY

Window treatments can be budget-busters, but in a room where the window is a key feature, custom window treatments can be worth the investment. This Roman shade, made of a good fabric with custom trim and a perfectly pleated valance, would be a hard project for anyone who hasn't done it before. Because this window is a relatively modest size, the cost of the custom work wasn't overwhelming.

# Display Shelf

Simple shelves below or above a window make a stylish statement, whether they display keepsakes or everyday items. Your local home improvement center has everything you need, including MDF (medium-density fiberboard) to make a shelf such as this. Choose a bracket style and size that complements the look of the room and has the right depth for the shelf.

## You Will Need

Tape measure
Saw
MDF (see Step 1 for size)
Primer, latex paint in the desired
    color and finish, paintbrush

2 decorative brackets with hardware
Stud finder
Screwdriver

1. Measure the window width. Cut the MDF to this length and 6 to 8 inches wide.

2. Prime the shelf and brackets; let dry. Paint; let dry.

3. Install the brackets on the wall studs so they align with the edges of the frame; this makes the shelf look as though it is part of the window.

4. Top the brackets with the shelf.

## FAUX-CHERRY CABINETS

The cabinets in this bath received a rich cherry-look paint treatment. For a similar effect, after priming, apply a light brown paint; let dry. Apply a dark brown glaze to the surface, working in 1-foot-square sections. Immediately wipe off excess glaze using a dry cotton rag to achieve a mottled effect. Continue the process until all surfaces are covered and ragged; let dry. Apply a brown-red glaze with a 2-inch-wide paintbrush, working in a 1-foot-square area. While the glaze is still wet, drag a wood-graining tool over the area, revealing some of the base coat paint and mottled glaze. Continue the process until the entire piece is covered. Seal with a coat of polyurethane.

For more do-it-yourself shelf projects,
visit **HGTV.com/beforeandafterbook**

# MOR OR

# Fabric Touches

Like any other room of the house, bathrooms can benefit from doses of fabric color and pattern. Whether your bath is large or small or has charming vintage fixtures or brand-new features, it can be softened or given a high-energy spark with shower curtains, sink and toilet skirts, window treatments, and even upholstered chairs and footstools. If you have fabric scraps left from a project, use them to cover a photo frame, embellish a ready-made towel, or line a basket that holds toiletries.

Hand-painted stripes on the walls, along with cottage-style fabrics in various prints and patterned picture frames, give this basic bath a colorful spark. The sink skirt conceals unsightly pipes, while the minimal window treatments let in maximum sunlight.

A mix of fabrics, including terry cloth, a sheer stripe, and a black and beige check, bring pattern into this bath. The floor-length curtain is tucked behind the ceiling soffit; fringed trim edges the soffit and is attached to the shower side of the overhang with hook-and-loop tape. A fabric valance hides a 1x1 that has a sheer striped fabric stapled to it. To embellish ordinary hand towels, use snaps or hook-and-loop tape to attach pompom trim and rickrack, which can be removed for washing.

## CHOOSING BATHROOM FABRICS

When selecting fabrics for your bathroom, keep these tips in mind:

- **Who will use it—and how often.** If the bathroom is used infrequently—and by adults only—luxurious fabrics that will receive little handling work fine. If the bathroom is strictly for children, purchase practical laminated shower curtains that can stand up to wear and tear.
- **Choose washable, natural fabrics that are easy to care for, including cotton, cotton blend, or linen.** Wash them in cold water, dry on low heat, and smooth out wrinkles with a cool iron.
- **Avoid using stain-prone fabrics or ones that have to be dry-cleaned.** Silk will show water stains, and heavy upholstery fabric often requires dry cleaning.

Vintage floral fabrics impart a cottage-style look to this bath. Bedsheets are fashioned into a shower curtain; the window treatment is a restyled curtain panel. The corners of the panel are nailed into the beaded board, and the nailheads are hidden by large glued-on buttons. Strips of fabric accent the treatment and give it shape. Another piece of fabric is attached to the underside of the vanity with hook-and-loop tape to conceal the sink pipes.

A remnant of white and green plaid fabric acts as a simple window shade that lets in sunlight. A tighter green plaid serves as a shower curtain. The bright green fabrics, along with a hand-painted green and blue wave border, enliven the space.

# Country Checks to
# CLEAN AND SERENE

Boxy rooms with no architectural detail are easy spaces to wallpaper, but they may lack character. This bathroom suffered from exactly that, with a dated checked wallcovering, a generic vanity, plain plate glass mirror, and exposed-bulb lighting. Help came in the form of beaded-board wainscoting, a light-color patterned wallcovering, and molding details that transform the space from dowdy to dramatic.

**Beaded board adds charm.** Sixty-inch-tall beaded-board paneling covers the lower portion of the walls. The white-painted paneling is only ¼ inch thick, which works especially well for small rooms that can't afford to lose square footage to the walls. To install, the tiled baseboard was removed, and the paneling was glued and nailed to the drywall. The decorative molding cap adds much-needed detailing. Beaded board also makes an appearance on the vanity doors.

**Use color to provide a sense of spaciousness.** To visually expand the small space, a light-color wallpaper with a swirling scroll motif covers the upper portion of the walls and flows onto the ceiling for a seamless transition. The white-painted vanity and mirror frame keep the room light and airy. The new white countertop—actually 12-inch marble tiles adhered to the existing countertop—freshens the surface for little cost. The tiles are attached with thin set, and latex grout fills in the gaps between tiles. A 1½-inch wood trim covers the tile and old laminate edge.

*Continued on page 170*

BEFORE

**Give the mirror focal-point status.** The most dramatic change in this space is the made-over mirror. The homemade frame fills the space between the vanity and ceiling and gives the once plain mirror a grand appearance. A new light fixture is attached directly to the mirror for effective general lighting.

**Pay attention to details.** Completing the look, new towel bars have the same finish and style as the light fixture and brushed-nickel cabinetry hardware. The vanity basket contains soaps and other small items previously jumbled on the vanity corner. Framed artwork fills the space between the door frame and mirror, taking the place of two small wreaths that were out of proportion in the room.

## PAINTING CABINETS AND OTHER WOOD FURNISHINGS

The misconception that all wood is good wood needs to be let go. Good wood tones do warm a room, but many wood surfaces are not meant to be exposed and are best painted over. The cabinets in this bathroom are a case in point.

Painting over lesser-grade woods isn't difficult, but it does require some care to get a good finish. First, wash the surface with a good-quality wood cleaner. Anything that's been in the air could be on the furniture surface.

Remove all hardware; if you're changing it, use wood putty to close the holes. Completely fill the holes and sand the surface completely smooth. Give the entire surface a good sanding to add some tooth for the best paint adhesion. Wipe down the entire piece with a tack cloth to remove all dust particles. A smooth surface is crucial for a good painted finish. Wood grain can be rather forgiving; some minor nicks and dings aren't noticeable. Furniture painted a solid color will show every nuance in the surface.

A satin-finish paint will give a final surface that's luxurious but not slick or glossy-looking. It will also be easy to take care of. Most pieces require two coats or more, and to ensure the best finish, allow adequate drying time between coats and sand between coats.

On heavily used surfaces, such as the top of a dresser or cabinet doors that may require scrubbing, adding a couple of coats of water-base polyurethane will help seal the surface and protect it from everyday scratches, nicks, and water rings.

# Framed Mirror

One of the easiest ways to give a mirror importance is with molding. This framing project will dress up any bath. In the example shown, a light fixture is mounted directly onto the mirror. If you choose to do this, you will need to cut a hole in the mirror over the light box.

## You Will Need

Tape measure
Saw
1x6 boards (4)
Hammer, nails
1x4 boards (2)
Sandpaper, tack cloth

Primer, paint in the desired color
  and finish, paintbrush
1x2 trim
Mirror
5" crown molding
Glue
Mirror mounting hardware
Stud finder

1 Measure the mirror. Cut the 1x6 board into four pieces to frame the mirror; nail together.

2 Rip the 1x4 boards to 3 inches wide; cut to fit around the frame. Nail in place.

3 Sand the frame; remove any dust with the tack cloth. Prime; let dry. Paint; let dry. Also sand, prime, and paint the 1x2 trim and crown molding.

4 Glue the mirror into the frame; let dry. Cut the 1x2 trim to serve as the innermost frame that will keep the mirror secure. Nail in place.

5 Top the frame with the crown molding; nail in place.

6 Mount the framed mirror to the wall, attaching it to the wall studs.

**5" crown molding**

**1x6**

**1x4 ripped to 3" wide**

**1x2 inner edge**

# Mirrors and Lights

Because bathrooms are the designated place for grooming, mirrors and lights are essential to their function. To ensure your bathroom mirror is evenly illuminated and free of shadows, light sources need to be evenly distributed around it. If movie star lights—exposed bulbs that surround the entire mirror—don't appeal to you, plan to install one or two fixtures above the mirror that cast light over the front edge of the sink and countertop; two additional lights—one centered on each side of the mirror—will ensure even lighting. If there isn't enough room for lights on the sides of your mirror, consider a light above the mirror that is longer than the mirror itself. When paired with a light-color countertop, more light will reflect on your face. When purchasing bulbs for your bathroom, select those designed for vanity illumination, which create light in the daylight spectrum range; bulbs that are too yellow or white will not create an accurate reflection of how you look outside the bathroom. For more information on lightbulb selection and the three types of lighting—general, task, and accent—see pages 52 and 53.

Matching the width of each vanity, the framed mirrors feature tubes of incandescent lighting that emphasize the other strong vertical lines in the room.

Wall sconces and light fixtures recessed in an overhang illuminate tall mirrors set into the maple-clad wall in this bathroom.

Rectangular mirrors above both vanities play up the rectangular sinks and rows of small windows (reflected in the mirror), unifying the space. Thanks to the multiple windows, natural light fills this room so the sconces beside the mirrors provide adequate light.

A thrift store mirror makes a bold statement in this dramatic bath. It hangs from the ceiling on a piece of black and gold rope. Recessed lights above the vanity supplement natural light from a large window behind the vanity.

The mirrors in this bathroom have curved tops, which repeat the curves of the vanity below. Light fixtures installed on the sides of each mirror pair with recessed fixtures above for even illumination. The white walls help reflect light.

## MIRROR HEIGHT

To ensure that people of different heights can comfortably use a mirror, it is generally recommended that the bottom edge of a mirror be hung no more than 40 inches from the floor. If the top of the mirror is tilted away from the wall, its bottom edge can be as much as 48 inches above the floor.

# Options, Options, OPTIONS

Sometimes a bathroom has everything going for it—great flooring, plenty of natural light, a roomy tub—but without creative accessorizing, even the most stylish elements don't live up to their potential. Two different looks, bold contemporary and French country, are created in this bath, using three basic elements: functional bathroom items, such as towels, candles, and soaps; simple window treatments; and wall art, rugs, and natural elements for warmth and texture.

## OPTION ONE: CONTEMPORARY

The black and white floor tiles lend themselves to this punchy color scheme of chartreuse and salmon and interesting graphic elements.

**Make a bold, graphic statement.** Squares appear throughout the space, from the houndstooth check of the window valance to the square artwork that flanks the tub. The bright fruit paintings, typically reserved for kitchens and dining areas, bring a playful element into the bath. Another piece of art, an abstract painting, is propped against the wall on the tub ledge.

**Don't forget the fun.** The flowers and greenery, including a flat of grass on the tub ledge and gerbera daisies on the vanity, keep the look fresh and springlike. The vase with green and bronze-color dots adds a contemporary note; so do the black accents, including a mesh storage basket that holds towels at the base of the tub.

**Repeat the colors for emphasis.** Chartreuse and salmon accents abound in towels, candles, and other inexpensive vanity accessories. The bright green also makes an appearance on the bench cushion and funky floral-motif rug.

*Continued on page 176*

BEFORE

*OPTION ONE: CONTEMPORARY*

Although black and white looks perfect in a contemporary scheme, it can easily suit a more refined look when paired with muted colors—in this case, soft peach-pink and celadon green—and thoughtfully placed accessories.

**Fabric changes the look.** The window treatments are of the same design as the ones in the contemporary bath, but the black and white toile fabric gives them a completely different, more tailored, look. This same toile now graces the bench cushion.

**Refine with texture.** Wicker and copper are the dominant textural elements in this refined bath. From the French wall basket filled with greenery and the basket urn on the tub ledge to the various copper pots throughout the room, a high-country look prevails. A toile-lined basket provides stylish storage for towels and slippers, and a basket tray artfully contains vanity clutter.

## ARTFULLY CONTAINED

To reduce clutter in the bath—and bring in interesting shapes, colors, and textures—group lotions, soaps, and other necessities on pretty trays and platters or in baskets and bowls. In the French take on this bath a white-painted urn stores cotton swabs on the sink vanity tray, and a glass jar filled with soaps echoes the smooth lines of the tub. In the bold, contemporary version a bright green plate holds colorful bathroom accessories on the vanity.

*OPTION TWO: FRENCH COUNTRY*

# Accessorizing the Bath

Envision a relaxing sanctuary; then picture it in your own bathroom. Start with a mental image or a real image, such as a picture, postcard, or another source of inspiration. After you envision the perfect scene, select a color palette. Determine which colors evoke the setting you want to capture; pick one or two dominant colors as well as a complementary accent or neutral tone. Next, what textures work in your theme? Can they be incorporated in flooring or window treatments? Finally, to pull your theme into focus, add decorative accents, including pictures, keepsakes, artwork, or plants.

Seemingly diverse elements—antique Dutch tiles, chartreuse paint, and beaded-board wainscoting—come together and dress up a once dingy, dark bath. The colorful wall art is the perfect accompaniment to the deep molding display shelf, which holds a collection of pottery from the '40s and '50s. The sink features chrome pipe fittings and a marble top.

This tiny bath gets a boost in style from wallpaper that features large architectural elements such as columns and busts. Books on built-in shelves, an antique dresser, and framed prints in black and white create a library look.

Vintage photographs and antique accessories—along with a claw-foot tub, oak plank floors, and tongue-and-groove siding used as wainscoting—transport this bath to the country. All the wood surfaces have been antiqued to impart the feeling of an old rural dwelling.

Can there be too much of a good theme? The answer is no in this delightful dog-theme bath. Dogs march across the walls, and paw prints embellish the sink and medicine cabinet. Neutral striped fabrics appear as a sink skirt and a clever window valance that includes dog biscuits attached with twine.

# SPECIAL SPACES

# Refining a
# FOCAL POINT

With only minor changes, yesterday's dark and dated fireplace can become a bright and fresh focal point. The fireplace here had ample display and storage space in the form of bookcases, but the dark wood and brick and cluttered shelves created an eyesore rather than a pleasing visual bonus. In addition, dark beams, which served only a decorative purpose, made the room feel small and cavernlike. A new color palette and enhanced architectural details—with some contemporary elements thrown in for interest—give the room sophisticated flair.

**Remove the old.** First, the ceiling beams were removed. Fortunately, only minor patching was required where the beams were attached. The heavy brown crown molding also was removed; white crown molding now frames the entire room. A fresh coat of white paint covers the ceiling and a light marble-pattern wallpaper (applied in pieces to look like a painted faux finish) makes the room look larger and more open.

**Update and unify with paint and moldings.** The elements in the wall unit lacked unity: A mantel shelf was hung with little consideration for the style of the hearth or fireplace surround. A new mantel, made of crown molding and fluted pilasters, now surrounds the fireplace to make it the center of the focal point. The brickwork and the bookcase are painted white. To further emphasize the center, the bricks are treated to a subtle beige colorwashing, and a crackle-finish screen rests on the hearth.

**Continued on page 184**

BEFORE

*AFTER*

**Create visual impact.** Before painting, the bookcases received their own special treatment: Extra moldings add heft to balance the heavy visual weight of the brick. Doors are added to the lower portions of the cases for closed storage; the vertical lines of the doors break up the strong horizontal lines created by the stacked shelves. Built-in benches provide extra seating and ground the focal point wall. Gentle arches make an appearance in the curved top of the bookcases, doors, and bench fronts. The curves soften distinct lines present throughout the space and create a cohesive look; if one curve motif alone were introduced, it would look out of place, but repeating the motif enhances its impact.

**Visually soften the hearth.** To complete the focal-point makeover, tile replaces the brick on the hearth. Framed in wood, the tile has a softer visual appearance than the brick, and it is much easier to clean.

**Complete the look with color—and comfort.** New wood laminate flooring, which replaced worn gray carpeting, warms up the floor and updates the overall look. The black-trim rug defines the space. To add further character, wood-tone accessories, both old and new, soften the dominant white and make it appear less formal. The chair is re-covered in soft, supple imitation suede, which takes it from dowdy to dramatic; with a side table and reading lamp, it's now a great place to relax and read a book. For a contemporary kick, curved track lighting and door hardware in brushed nickel add a touch of modern simplicity.

 Cabinet doors and a pair of benches provide hidden storage. A gentle curve motif on the door and bench fronts mimics the arch on the top of the bookcases.

▶ Updating a tired but stylish chair is as easy as reupholstering it. In this case, faux suede in a soft brown covers the chair cushions, complementing the warm tones in the room. Details include black circles, cut from more faux suede, and nailhead tacks, both of which repeat the cutwork detailing on the original chair.

◀ Crown molding frames the room and poses as the new mantel shelf. Repetition and reuse of key elements strengthens any design scheme.

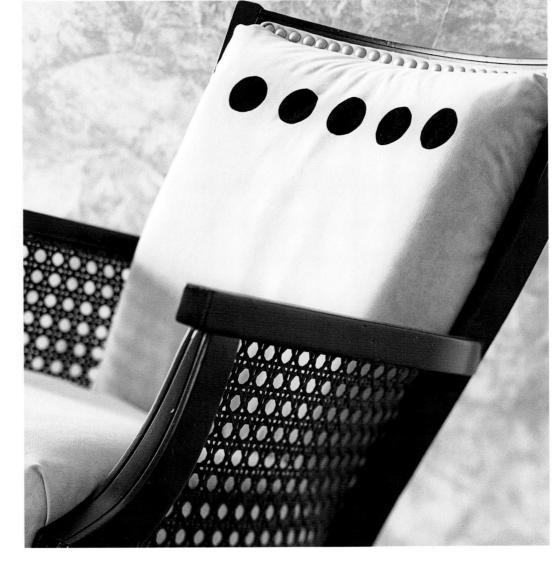

# MORE IDEAS FOR

# Fireplace Mantels

Fireplaces usually take center stage in a room—but is your focal point lacking pizzazz? Whether your mantel is new or old, brick or wood, it can benefit from a makeover. Use these examples as a springboard to create a space that commands attention.

Paint is one of the easiest ways to freshen a mantel. Once a generic builder mantel, this example now sports a neutral beige paint with red details that complement the surrounding wall. The recessed areas are painted with a contemporary-look marble finish.

Layered tiles in woodsy colors and motifs form a fresh facade over a dingy, outdated brick fireplace. Because ripping out the brick would have been labor-intensive, a layer of cement mortar was troweled on and allowed to cure for a week to provide a smooth, solid surface. The tiles are applied with thin-set tile adhesive; terra-cotta-color sanded grout fills in the seams.

Columns and a mercury-glass mirror frame an old wood fireplace surround that has a well-worn painted finish. These details bring a sense of history and architectural significance to the living room. The surround replaced faux stones.

A flat brick-face fireplace is given the royal treatment with a wood cover-up. The basic structure is covered with a combination of stock moldings—including fluted pilasters, dentil trim, and a deep crown—and painted with a fresh coat of semi-gloss white to brighten the room and lend simple elegance.

# Underutilized to STYLIZED

A clean, uncluttered entryway may appear open and bright, but it isn't necessarily functional. Rather than leave this space unused, make it say "Wow!" In this new home, the entryway was bare, with little more than a table in place. A clean, modern look steps in, courtesy of thoughtfully placed storage and seating pieces and a new paint treatment. If you are faced with a similar situation, take advantage of the underused area. How would you like it to function? Do you need a place to change footwear or primp before heading to work or an evening on the town? Can you take advantage of storage possibilities? Here, all these issues are addressed.

**Readymade seating and storage increase functionality.** First, a set of ready-made cubes—some open and others with drawers and doors—is arranged in a step system that draws the eye to the window, the only existing architectural element in the space. The cubes are used for display, and the low, comfy seating area is a great place to sort mail. This unit effectively fills the space between the coat closet to the left and the pillar that divides the entry from the main living space.

**Define the space with color.** The ceiling in this space is high. To bring the walls down to scale—and to keep the eye interested in what's happening down low—the wall behind the unit is painted in two colors. Using the top of the pillar as a natural breaking point, soft blue-green is painted below, and white is painted above, framing the space for an intimate setting. Where the two colors meet, dentil molding is painted metallic silver. Squares stenciled in silver leaf, spaced randomly on the walls, complement the metallic look. The square motif imitates the cube design and provides a shiny accent on the walls.

*Continued on page 190*

BEFORE

**AFTER**

**Mirror magic.** A mirror is always a welcome addition to an entryway. Here, a custom-cut oval mirror fills the space between the window and the higher cubes. Mounted on pivot brackets, it can accommodate users of any height. The nearby lamp provides functional and task lighting for mirror use and accent lighting for the display.

**Accessorize with contrasting color and shapes.** Modern clean-line accessories in a variety of shapes introduce color and contrast against the predominantly green and black space. Silver makes an appearance in photo frames and the lamp base, complementing the cube hardware and legs. A piece of pottery, painted in two colors, and the striped rug continue the strong graphic lines that define the space.

### STENCILED IN SILVER

Metallic silver leaf in a random square design brings subtle color into this space. For a similar look, purchase a square stencil, or create one yourself with a piece of clear acetate and a crafts knife. Using stencil adhesive, adhere the stencil to the wall in the desired location. Following the manufacturer's instructions, carefully apply the leaf to the wall (the material is delicate and tears easily). Move the stencil to the next desired location and apply the leaf in the stencil opening.

# PROJECT

## Hinged Mirror

Mirrors play a necessary role in entryways, but ensuring that a guest or resident of any height can use the mirror is an important consideration. This mirror is set on pivoting hinges so it can be angled upward or downward to accommodate all who use it. Evaluate the space you need to fill. Mirrors are available in many shapes and sizes, but you may need to have one cut to best fit your needs. Be aware that brackets will not hold a beveled-edge mirror.

### You Will Need
Tape measure               Mirror
Scissors                   Screwdriver
Adhesive-back foam         Stud finder
2 pivoting brackets and hardware

1. Measure the mirror and determine the best placement of the side brackets; center the brackets on the sides to ensure the mirror will hang straight.

2. Cut four pieces of adhesive-back foam the same size as the portion of the bracket that will hold the mirror in place. Peel off the backing and press the foam onto the mirror in the location determined in Step 1.

3. Using the screwdriver, tighten the brackets to secure the mirror.

4. Mount the mirror to the wall, directly to the wall studs.

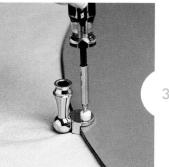

3

✳ For hundreds of ideas on using mirrors effectively in your home, visit **HGTV.com/beforeandafterbook**

# Functional Entryways

Entryways offer guests the first glimpse into your home and its style. Encourage guests to linger—and make a strong first impression—by filling the space with personal touches, such as collections, or by placing comfortable furnishings nearby for removing footwear. Include a rack or pegs for hanging jackets and hats and a mirror that will both visually enlarge the space and provide a practical place to groom before leaving the house.

White wainscoting beneath soft blue walls sheathes this entryway, a former bedroom. Hooks provide spots to hang jackets and hats, and an antique table is the perfect spot to drop mail and keys.

Greeting guests with things you love gives them a taste for what's beyond the entryway. In this space a 300-year-old table, black tole tray, and flow-blue pieces introduce guests to a home filled with history.

This entryway, with its vivid painted walls, moon-motif clock, and playful bench, prepares visitors for more visual excitement inside. The tile floor is easy to clean, and the mirror permits last-minute primping before departure.

This entry/mudroom features nautical references: Color copies of French nautical charts are pasted above the tall wainscoting; the round mirrors are reminiscent of portholes. Hooks accept jackets and beach bags, and a large basket on the floor can hold umbrellas and other outdoor necessities.

# Carving Out a Corner for COMFORT

Small homes often have less than abundant storage space. This 900-square foot home is a case in point. Although the homeowners haven't amassed a huge number of possessions, they still require a place to store blankets, pillows, books, and keepsakes in their bedroom. Rather than purchase or create freestanding storage units that might take up too much precious space, they found an ingenious solution: a window seat with storage beneath (the lid lifts for easy access to items). The cozy space is perfect for catching a nap or reading beneath the window.

**The look of a bump-out—without remodeling.** This window seat, which is nearly the dimensions of a twin-size bed, was constructed against a flat interior bedroom wall. Typically, window seats are added via a bump-out, but the architecture of the home and an old tree right outside the window ruled out that option. A vertical box forms a closet to the left of the window seat, and the window seat itself is a horizontal box, which fills in the space between the closet and the wall to create the feel of a bump-out.

**Luxurious fabrics add color and comfort.** Upholstered medium-density foam tops the bench, making it a haven for the homeowners—or young overnight visitors who can use it as a bed. Pillows of varying sizes invite people to come and stay for a while. The pillows are made of silks in a mix of warm and cool colors that spice up the overall neutral color palette. Light affects how the silks appear: During the day they are a bold counterpoint to the beige walls, but in the evening the colors deepen for a more romantic appearance.

The lid of this window seat lifts to reveal storage space. The seat holds seasonal bedding, books, and magazines. The contents are kept organized thanks to dividers.

BEFORE

*AFTER*

## Obi Pillow

Pillows can serve as jewelry for your room—and this dynamic design with an obi (which resembles the sash traditionally worn with a kimono) is no exception. Splurging on luxurious fabrics gives this pillow a special feel and look. Anyone with basic sewing skills can stitch pillows. If you choose to use silk brocade and douppioni silk, as shown here, you will need to use special care: These fabrics unravel quickly, so carefully cut on the straight of grain with clean, sharp scissors or a rotary cutter. Serge the edges or use a specially formulated ravel preventer. Otherwise, use an easier-to-handle fabric such as cotton.

### You Will Need

Scissors or rotary cutter
13x12" pieces of silk brocade for
    pillow back (2)
13x17" piece of silk brocade for
    pillow front
Sewing machine, matching thread,
    70/10H needle, presser foot

Pins
Iron, ironing board
Chopstick
Satin cording
Ravel preventer
4x26" pieces of douppioni silk (2)
12x16" pillow form
Tailor's chalk

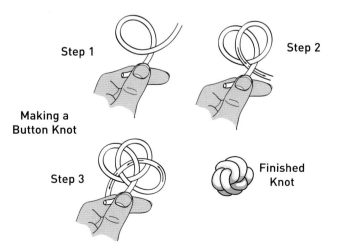

**Step 1**

**Step 2**

**Making a Button Knot**

**Step 3**

**Finished Knot**

1 Create a double-fold machine hem on the inside edge of each pillow back piece. Place the back flaps on the pillow front with right sides facing, overlapping the hemmed edges of the back pieces. Carefully pin the pieces together and stitch around the perimeter, using a ½-inch seam allowance. To avoid pointy dog-ear corners, taper the seam at each corner.

2 Turn the pillow cover right side out, using the chopstick to gently push out the corners; press.

3 To create the button knots for the obi sash, you will need 8 to 10 inches of satin cording. Loop the cord as shown in the illustrations, then ease the knot together into a ball shape and finish with a simple knot. Squeeze and pinch to define the ball shape. Repeat the process to make a second knot. Trim the ends of each knot and treat with ravel preventer.

4 To make the button loops, use 3 inches of satin cording and shape into a teardrop large enough to accommodate the button, leaving ½-inch-long tails; baste. Repeat the process to make a second loop.

5 To make the obi, use the 4x26-inch pieces of douppioni silk. Pin the two pieces together with right sides facing and stitch around the perimeter, using a ½-inch seam allowance and leaving one end open. Turn the obi right side out and gently push out the corners with the chopstick. Fold in the open end of one piece of silk approximately ½ inch. Baste the loops made in Step 4 to the folded-in piece of silk, 1⅛ inches from each side. Fold in the other piece of silk approximately ½ inch and slip-stitch closed. Fit the sash around the pillow, overlapping the ends with the loops on the top. Using the loops as a guide, carefully mark the spot for each button on the obi with tailor's chalk. Blindstitch each button in place.

# Storage Window Seat

This window seat, which is essentially a horizontal box, measures 76 inches long by 28 inches high by 27 inches deep. Your project size will be determined by the space available, any architectural restrictions (for instance, window trim), and the cushion thickness, so measure carefully, taking these items into consideration when planning. Note that kickspace is not figured into these instructions; kickspace will be determined by your baseboard molding.

## You Will Need

¾" thick medium-density fiberboard (MDF) (3 sheets)
4 pressed-brass surface-mounted hinges or a piano hinge
2 childproof lid supports
6¾" thick x 3" wide x 8' long stock pine
Yellow construction glue
Screws, nails, brads
Primer, latex paint in the desired color and finish, paintbrush
Drill
Hammer
Screwdriver

### CONSTRUCTION NOTES

- Follow the illustration to construct the box with a series of dado joints (joints made with rectangular grooves cut into the wood).
- For added strength—and more-organized storage—divide the box into three sections using dado joints.
- The top of the bench box is trimmed with 3-inch-wide pine to support the lid and finished cabinet. The lid is one large, heavy piece of MDF, but you could divide the lid into smaller, more manageable, sections.
- Use childproof lid supports so the lid won't accidentally slam shut on fingers. Use the appropriate size supports for the weight of the lid.
- For added safety, consider drilling ventilation holes into the box cabinet face, using a decorative pattern, so that a child trapped inside could still breathe.
- The applied panel-style face frame is a series of ½-inch-thick by 3-inch-wide MDF strips spaced to suit, then glued and nailed with brads. This gives the window seat a classic finish detail.
- The window seat pictured here is permanently installed in an older home. To compensate for the uneven floor, a basic kick space base was fabricated on-site; the box was made level front to back and side to side with shims and a 4-foot level. The bench box was then placed on the preinstalled kickspace base (it was screwed down and trimmed out, and the lid was added).
- Although the interior of this seat is left unfinished, you could paint it or line it with cedar veneer.

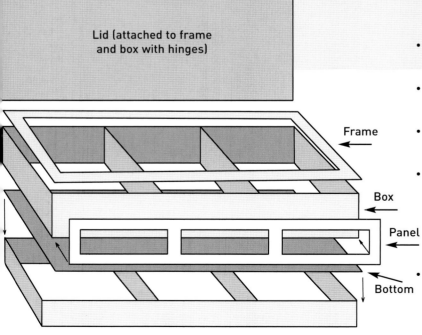

Lid (attached to frame and box with hinges)

Frame

Box

Panel

Bottom

Kick space

MORE IDEAS FOR
Cozy Nooks

Everyone needs a peaceful place to call his or her own—that place where you can hide away for a few moments and read a book, catch a nap, or merely watch the outside world go by. If you don't currently have such a refuge, or the opportunity to create a built-in window seat, take heart: A carefully placed sofa can fulfill your getaway needs.

This entryway niche near the staircase is a convenient place to change footwear. The wood sofa isn't a built-in, but it nestles quite naturally into the spot. A cushion and decorative pillows add comfort.

In this bedroom, a graceful contoured sofa sits between two tall bookcases. It is large enough to accommodate an afternoon napper.

The window seat in this kitchen boasts garden views. It is a wonderful place to chat with the cook while meals are prepared. The drawers beneath hold files.

Nestled between built-in armoires that store clothing and a TV, a gracious window seat is right at home in this bedroom. The seat is a great place to curl up with a book, and the drawers beneath the seat provide additional storage.

# Collect It,

# DISPLAY IT

If you are a collector—or merely have lots of stuff to stash—you undoubtedly have many items to contain and display in one space. If you have a bookcase or open shelving, you may be wondering where to begin. How do you group items? What about incorporating objects of different colors or types? Can you hang art on the walls around the display? In this example, a bookcase is filled with three types of collections; use it as a road map to plot your display strategy.

The bookcase features closed storage below and open shelving above. The shelves can be completely exposed or viewed through glass-fronted doors. The interior of the case has a green distressed paint treatment that provides a subtly aged backdrop against which the items stand out.

## VERSION ONE: THE GARDEN THEME

Garden books—vintage and new. Wooden gardening supplies. Brightly colored sap buckets. A small antique landscape painting. Seed packets. An old watering can. If you love gardening and all things natural, you probably have a similar collection gathering dust in your potting shed. Bringing these items together in an artful way transforms them into a unified collection.

**Continue a theme throughout a space for added impact.** On the wall surrounding the bookcase, tin sap buckets serve as art. These are left empty, but they could easily be filled with flowers, grasses, or even twigs to bring in more of the outside. More

buckets—tall, short, cylindrical—stand on top of the cabinet, creating a colorful focal point against the soft beige walls.

To round out the garden theme, floral-motif pillows occupy the chair, and the coffee table houses stacks of garden and landscaping books.

*Continued on page 202*

Version One: The Garden Theme

Version Two: The White Theme

▶ When arranging a collection in a bookcase or cabinet that has glass-fronted doors, consider how the contents will appear when the doors are closed. Will some items disappear completely behind the door frame? Will some be only partially visible? Plan your design with this in mind, rearranging the items if necessary for viewing.

### VERSION TWO: THE WHITE THEME

Mixing old and new items is a breeze when you concentrate on color as a visual link. A mix of objects will make the collection look as if it grew over time; having too many similar items can make your display look like a gift shop shelf. In a group the white ironstone and stoneware platters, pitchers, cake plates, and bowls placed in and on this bookcase (shown on page 201) take on importance—much more than if the pieces were spread throughout the house. Against the green-painted cabinet interior, the white visually "pops."

**Complement the collection with neutral-color accents.** Four egg engravings in matching frames and mats add elegance to the wall surrounding the cabinet. An additional print is placed atop the cabinet, along with large and tall items that wouldn't fit within the cabinet.

The overall neutral palette in this room is well-suited to the collection. The taupe leather chair now holds comfy white pillows, one in cotton duck stamped with a green leaf motif.

### VERSION THREE: THE DOG THEME

Dog collectibles of every shape, size, and vintage fill the bookcase and find a home atop or next to it. Statues, books, baskets, and dog-motif photo frames fill the case; larger statues and a print in an ornate frame are placed on top.

**Unify the look with artwork and textiles.** To balance the display, more vintage dog etchings and drawings in antique frames are hung on the wall, and a dark-stained shelf holds an additional dog figure. Dog-theme literature and needlepoint pillows with dog motifs pull the look together.

Ironstone and stoneware of various shapes and sizes create a unified collection because they share a common color: white.

## DISPLAY DOS AND DON'TS

When you are ready to create your own artful arrangement, keep the following in mind:

- **Do** use a tried-and-true formula: Starting at the top left corner of the bookcase or shelving unit, trace the letter Z. Place the largest items first at the "points" of the letter (upper left, upper right, vertically down and across the shelves, and then lower left and right). Fill in the remaining spaces with shorter, smaller vertical- and horizontal-oriented accessories. Reverse the zigzag pattern on an adjoining or flanking set of shelves if you are working with a large bookcase wall.
- **Do** stack items for additional height and visual interest; for instance, top a stack of books with a basket or framed piece of artwork.
- **Do** take a step back after you have arranged your collection. Is it too full? Are there areas that still need filling in? Taking a snapshot of the display can help you get a better sense of how it works together. Check the balance of your design; your eyes tend to go toward the voids, or empty spaces, on the shelves.
- **Don't** let overflow find its way onto tables. Keep tabletops clean for contrast.
- **Don't** feel that you have to purchase new items to fill a too empty bookcase. Rethink the objects that you already have and love. Consider arranging and grouping them in new ways to give them unity.
- **Don't** place too small items in a bookcase. They may look great when grouped on a tabletop, but they can become lost when tucked on shelves with larger, more visually dominating elements. For example, a large tole tray on a stand has more visual impact on a shelf than a dozen tiny boxes would.

# Displaying Collections

Even if you don't consider yourself a collector, you no doubt have items that you cherish and want to display. Whether you have vintage photographs of ancestors, found items from walks along the beach or in the woods, or toys from your childhood, personalize your home by showcasing what you love.

A beautiful collection of Native American bowls lines the perimeter in this kitchen. This is a great way to display any type of collectible bowl or other dishware.

If you have a collection you love, why not take it one step further? This collection of miniature teapots is thoughtfully arranged in custom teapot-shape shadow boxes. Translate the idea for other collections, perhaps using a spool of thread to hold a thimble collection.

Grouping a collection is a great way to showcase it: These clocks have found a home in an old divided crate.

The corner of this kitchen is filled with a treasure trove of antiques and collectibles. A collection of Red Wing pottery and spongeware resides in the vintage pie safe. Inexpensive whisk brooms create a makeshift valance.

Greenhouse windows in a breakfast room host a collection of birdhouses, bringing a fresh, springlike feel to the space. The birdhouses are grouped with other outdoor collectibles, including watering cans and garden tools.

## ARRANGING COLLECTIONS

Follow these guidelines when displaying a collection or group of items on a shelf or a tabletop or in a cabinet.

- **Vary the height.** Incorporate items of different heights, from short to tall. If all your items are of similar height, boost some of them up on pedestals or stacks of books for interest.
- **Ponder proportion.** Besides the height of an item, it is also important to consider its proportion—and how it interacts with other items. An enormous chair in a small room looks awkward and out of place. The same is true of a display space, such as a tabletop.
- **Consider weight.** Due to their size, color, and shape, some items appear heavy to the eye, while others are light. When you arrange your items, pretend you're balancing them on a scale. The visual weight of the pieces should be equal.
- **Be aware of balance.** When items are paired, they lack interest. In an overall symmetrical arrangement, incorporate a small asymmetrical vignette to add some drama.
- **Appeal to your senses.** Items often have implied texture you can see, and actual texture you can touch. Freely mix items with varying textures.
- **Be true to the palette.** Display items that work in the larger scope of the entire room. Are the colors complementary to the wall, the furnishings, and the flooring?

For more tips on decorating with collectibles, visit **HGTV.com/beforeandafterbook**

# More Than a
## PORCH

This long, narrow enclosed porch is too small to be used as a stand-alone room, but it's a perfect buffer zone between indoors and out. To make this dreary space an appealing entry, outdoor elements are brought inside.

**Bring the feeling of the outdoors in.** Boldly striped wallpaper hangs like an awning along the sloped ceiling and onto a scalloped-edge plywood window valance. The walls are papered in a faux-stone pattern, and the bench cushions are covered in a black background ivy-trellis pattern. Clunky metal windows hide behind white, wood-slatted blinds that control light levels and provide privacy.

Completing the outdoor theme are botanical prints on the wall, a high-quality outdoor light fixture near the door, a bound sea grass rug, and silk topiaries.

### QUICK BENCHES

If you'd like to have a bench under a bank of windows, but don't want to make it from scratch, use prefab kitchen cabinets available in home improvement stores. The cabinet designed to go over a refrigerator is about the right height once it sits on a base. Buy as many as you need to fill the space and create filler strips from board stock the same width as the cabinet frames. You'll need to build a 1- or 2-inch-high base and create a top from plywood. Check that all pieces are held together tightly and firmly attached to the wall, the same as you would if the cabinets were being hung in the kitchen. Choose door hardware that's fairly flat so it doesn't bump people in the back of the legs when they sit on the bench.

BEFORE

*AFTER*

## CREATE AN INDOOR AWNING

Measure the length of the wall or windows to be covered. Use that measurement to make a valance from ¼-inch birch plywood cut 11½ inches wide, with rounded notches cut on the bottom edge to look like scalloped-edge fabric.

Sand and prime the valance sections before putting them in place above the windows. Hold the valance in place with screws on the window frames, so it can be removed at a later date. Then caulk the spaces between boards and the joint between ceiling and valance to give a smooth edge that hides all the joints.

To hang the wallpaper, size the walls and wood valance. That makes it easier to remove wallpaper at a later date. Even if the paper is prepasted, use wallpaper paste to ensure good adhesion to the ceiling.

Hang the wallpaper with the stripes forming one continuous line from the high point of the ceiling down to the edge of the valance. Using a sharp razor blade, cut the wallpaper at the edge of the valance; don't try to wrap it around the bottom. With matching paint and some patience, paint stripes the same width as the wallpaper motif on the valance to complete the look.

# Bench Cushion Cover

Creating a custom cushion is easier than you might have imagined. If you cover a long bench, such as this one (which is 14 feet long), making two or three smaller cushions is more manageable than making one. Look for 3-inch-thick foam with good density; squeeze the foam and choose one that's fairly firm rather than one that squishes easily. Cutting the foam to the length and width of the final cushion plus ½ inch all around ensures a tight fit with a firm surface.

## You Will Need

Tape measure
3"-thick foam, cut to size of bench
   plus ½" all around
Polyester batting
45"-wide decorator fabric

Scissors
Sewing machine, matching thread
Zipper, the length of the cushion
Premade piping

1   Measure the bench. Purchase 3-inch-thick foam cut to this size plus ½ inch all around. Wrap the foam in polyester batting.

2   Cut the top and bottom fabric to the same length and width as the foam plus 1 inch all around for seam allowances.

3   Cut two 3-inch-wide fabric strips the length of the cushion back. Using a basting stitch, stitch the pieces together lengthwise.

4   Place an upholstery zipper that's slightly shorter than the length of the back facedown over the basted seam. Stitch the two sides of the zipper to the fabric. Pull out the basting stitches.

5   With the zipper in the center of the fabric, trim the piece to 4 inches wide (3-inch cushion depth plus two ½-inch seam allowances).

6   Cut the fabric 4 inches wide along the length of the pattern to wrap around the remaining three sides of the cushion and wrap around the back to the ends of the zipper section. You may need to sew several pieces together.

7   Overlap the strips on the zipper.

8   Stitch the piping to the top and bottom pieces of the cushion, ½ inch from the edge. (Illustration 1) Stitch the zipper section to the back edge of the top and bottom sections, ½ inch from the edge. (Illustration 2)

9   Starting at one end of the zipper section, sew the strip to the top of the cushion; work your way around the cushion. You'll finish at the other end of the zipper section, and you'll be able to remove any extra fabric. Repeat by sewing along the bottom of the cushion.

10   Trim the corners and turn the piece inside out. Insert the batting-wrapped foam into the cushion cover.

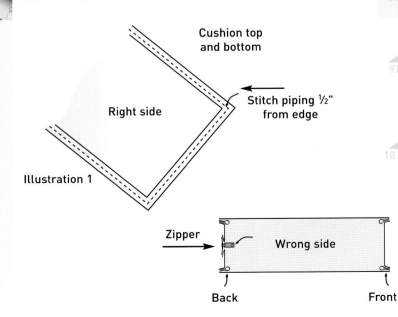

Cushion top
and bottom

Right side

Stitch piping ½"
from edge

Illustration 1

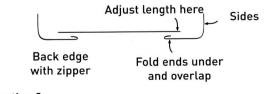

Zipper

Wrong side

Back      Front

Adjust length here   Sides

Back edge
with zipper

Fold ends under
and overlap

Illustration 2

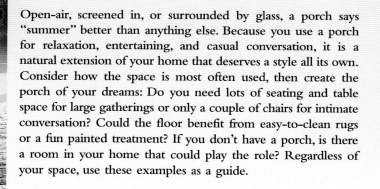

# MORE IDEAS FOR

# Porches

Open-air, screened in, or surrounded by glass, a porch says "summer" better than anything else. Because you use a porch for relaxation, entertaining, and casual conversation, it is a natural extension of your home that deserves a style all its own. Consider how the space is most often used, then create the porch of your dreams: Do you need lots of seating and table space for large gatherings or only a couple of chairs for intimate conversation? Could the floor benefit from easy-to-clean rugs or a fun painted treatment? If you don't have a porch, is there a room in your home that could play the role? Regardless of your space, use these examples as a guide.

This back porch is actually an addition. The wide open space allows guests to linger and admire the garden and immaculate yard, including an antique birdhouse.

Screen porches let in fresh air and sunlight and keep out unwanted bugs. Awning-stripe fabrics in springlike colors complement the painted wicker, wood, and metal furnishings.

This rambling sunporch is an ideal place to chat or have a midafternoon snack. The floor is painted in a diamond pattern of white and periwinkle blue; no-sew window treatments carry through the blue and white theme.

If you don't have a porch and long for one, bring in the outdoors with plants, summery fabrics, and a place to lounge. Positioned next to large windows, this daybed is a get-away-from-it-all retreat.

# Credits & Resources

**PAGES 8–11.**
**Designer/Stylist:** Becky Jerdee. **Photographer:** Bill Hopkins.

**PAGES 14–19.**
**Designer/Stylist:** Donna Talley, Ivy Vine Design. **Photographer:** Michael Partenio. **Slipcovers:** Jean Fleming. **Both Versions:** Paint: SW6135 Ecru, Sherwin-Williams (www.sherwinwilliams.com); Window treatments: Country Curtains, (www.countrycurtainscatalog.com); Curtain rods: Home Depot (www.homedepot.com); Parsons chairs: Herb 'n' Country, Great Barrington, MA. **Version One, French:** Sisal rug: Pier 1 Imports, (www.pier1.com); White pitcher: Target (www.target.com). **Version Two, Contemporary:** Faux fur throw, torchiéré light, round glass table: Target (www.target.com); Oil painting: Steven Spann (www.stevenspann.com); Sisal rug: Calico Corners (www.calicocorneronline.com).

**PAGES 22–25.**
**Designer/Stylist:** Cathy Kramer, Cathy Kramer Design. **Photographer:** Bill Hopkins. **Slipcovers:** Sonja Carmon. **Storage Box Project:** Cathy Kramer, Cathy Kramer Design. Chair fabric: 667042 Melrose Stripe-Amethyst, Waverly (www.waverly.com); Love seat fabric: Silas-10 (floral), 22656-10 (stripe), 11759-10 (piping), Kravet (www.kravet.com). Ottoman fabric: 990104-110 Marguerite Weave, thistle, Kravet (www.kravet.com). Accent pillows: 2001117-10 Pansy Matelasse, amethyst, Kravet (www.kravet.com). Lamps: Luna candlestick lamp with medium square bell shade in silk celadon, Small Genie table lamp in silver with small hourglass shade in silk celadon, Jamie Young (call 888-671-5883 for a retailer near you); Glass jars, acrylic frames: tag (773.697.6300/www.tagltd.com); Beaded photo frames, tall glass candle holder: Pier 1 (www.pier1.com); Banded rug, Colonial Mills (www.colonialmills.com); Carpet: Opening night 7F768 (S), Oyster #00102, 12-foot width, Shaw www.shawfloors.com; Windows: Simonton Windows (www.simontonwindows.com).

**PAGES 28–31.**
**Designer/Stylist:** Susan Andrews. **Photographer:** Bob Greenspan. **Decorative Painter:** Tina Blanck. Paint: HC-7, HC-13, HC-16, 2158-20, Benjamin Moore (www.benjaminmoore.com); Lamps: Target (www.target.com); Rug: Pottery Barn (www.potterybarn.com).

**PAGES 34–37.**
**Field Editor:** Linda Krinn. **Interior Designer:** Nancy Hilliard. **Photographer:** Ross Chapple. **Armoire Project:** Nancy Hilliard. Window treatments: Sewn by J&L Interiors, designed by Beekeeper's Cottage. Furnishings, fabrics, slipcovers, lighting, and accessories: Beekeeper's Cottage, 43738 Hay Rd., Ashburn, VA 20147 (703-726-9411/www.beekeeperscottage.com).

**PAGES 40–43.**
**Designer/Stylist:** Gayle Schadendorf. **Photographer:** Ed Gohlich. **Bench and Ottoman Projects:** Gayle Schadendorf. Fabric (stripe): Sidewalk Stripe, Mint, #666212, Waverly, (www.waverly.com); Fabric (floral): U-Dorable/spring #0006728, Calico Corner Fabrics (www.calicocorneronline.com; Sheer ribbon: Midori Ribbon (www.midoriribbon.com); Vases, window treatments, curtain rods: Cost Plus World Market (www.costplus.com); Sleeper sofa: Kelly's Furniture, San Diego, CA (858-874-6880); Artwork: David Hebble Photography, Coronado, CA (619-203-6919); Trunk: Target (www.target.com); Faux suede, Field's Fabrics (www.fieldsfabrics.com); Magazine boxes and storage boxes: IKEA (www.ikea.com).

**PAGES 48–51.**
**Designer/Stylist:** Donna Talley, Ivy Vine Design. **Photographer:** Michael Partenio. **Refrigerator Bulletin Board and Dishwasher Panel Projects:** Donna Talley, Ivy Vine Design. Knobs: Bruce Hall Corporation (607-547-9961); Paint (cabinets): SW7105, Sherwin-Williams (www.sherwinwilliams); Paint (walls): 8186, Martha Stewart (www.marthastewart.com); Flooring: SwiftLock laminate, Armstrong (www.armstrong.com); Lamps, bowl, pitcher, dishtowel: Target (www.target.com); Wood stool: A.C. Moore (www.acmoore.com).

**PAGES 54–57.**
**Designer/Stylist:** Deborah Hastings. **Photographer:** Sylvia Martin. **Curtain Project:** Deborah Hastings. Paint (cabinets and walls): Beachcomber 20 YY 58/082, Glidden (www.glidden.com); Paint (trim): Swiss Coffee 2012, ICI Paints (www.glidden.com); Countertop: Bronze Legacy 4656-60, Wilson Art (www.wilsonart.com).

**PAGES 60–63.**
**Designer/Stylist:** Cathy Kramer, Cathy Kramer Design. **Photographer:** Kent Clawson. **Cabinet Painting:** Patty Mohr Kramer. Base Coat (walls): #2012 Swiss Coffee, Glidden (www.glidden.com); Base Coat (yellow cabinets): Yellowhammer, Ralph Lauren (www.ralphlauren.com); Base Coat (red cabinets): Barn Red Ralph Lauren; Toile wallpaper: Classics Lifestyles, #564300, Wavelly (www.waverly.com); Toile fabric: Classic Lifestyles book, Country Life fabric, #659430, Waverly; Countertop: Manitoba Maple, #7911-60, Wilsonart (www.wilsonart.com); Faucet: #K-690, Vinnata Kitchen Sink Faucet with Pull-Down Spray, Brushed Nickel, Kohler (www.kohler.com); Hardware: #BP9365-G10 Bin Pulls, #BP1586-G10 Knobs, Amerock (www.amerock.com); Woven shade: Tahiti, Straw Hut #WWTA245A96F, Hunter Douglas (www.hunterdouglas.com); Appliances: G.E. (www.ge.com).

**PAGES 66–69.**
**Designer/Stylist:** Deborah Hastings. **Photographer:** Sylvia Martin. Wallpaper: Terra Verde (walls) and Sunny Tuscany (ceiling), Seabrook (www.seabrookwallcoverings.com).

**PAGES 72–75.**
**Designer/Stylist:** Diane Carroll. **Photographer:** Colleen Duffley. **Beaded-Board Project:** Diane Carroll. Oven/range: JennAir (www.jennair.com); Dishwasher: Asko (www.askousa.com); Toaster, coffee maker: Michael Graves, Target (www.target.com); Stand mixer: KitchenAid (www.kitchenaid.com); Artwork: Scott Carroll, through Kristy Stubbs French Gallery (214-871-9311/mail@stubbsgallery.com); Butcher-block countertops: John Boos and Co. (www.homedepot.com). Beaded-board panel kit: Home Depot (www.homedepot.com).

**PAGES 78–81.**
**Designer/Stylist:** Jeni Hilpipre. **Photographer:** Tim Murphy/Foto Imagery. Cake stand on table: Bimboveloce, Chiasso (www.chiasso.com); Dining chairs: Design Within Reach (www.dwr.com); Wineglass area rug: Pottery Barn (www.potterybarn.com); Glass container for fish: Crate and Barrel (www.crateandbarrel.com); Fabric: Duralee Fabrics, Ltd. (www.duralee.com).

**PAGES 84–87.**
**Designers/Stylists:** Linda Krinn. **Interior Designer:** Nancy Hilliard. **Photographer:** Ross Chapple. **Slipcover information:** Donna Talley, Ivy Vine Design, and Jean Fleming. Furnishings, fabrics, slipcovers, lighting, and accessories: Beekeeper's Cottage, 43738 Hay Rd., Ashburn, VA 20147 (703-726-9411/www.beekeeperscottage.com).

**PAGES 90–93.**
**Designer/Stylist:** Joetta Moulden (www.shelterstyle.com; info@shelterstyle.com).
**Photographer:** Janet Lenzen.

**PAGES 96–99.**
**Designer/Stylist:** Joetta Moulden (www.shelterstyle.com; info@shelterstyle.com).
**Photographer:** Janet Lenzen. Paint: #1301, Benjamin Moore (www.benjaminmoore.com).

**PAGES 104–107.**
**Designer/Stylist:** Deborah Hastings. **Photographer:** Sylvia Martin. **Headboard Project:** Deborah Hastings. Paint: Mexican Springs 1441 (walls), Swiss Coffee 2012 (trim), ICI Paints (www.glidden.com); Chair: Pier 1 Imports (www.pier1.com); Bedding: Garnet Hill (www.garnethill.com).

**PAGES 110–113.**
**Designer/Stylist:** Deborah Hastings. **Photographer:** Sylvia Martin. Wallpaper: Tropical Breezes (walls) and Cyprus Garden (ceiling), Seabrook (www.seabrookwallcoverings.com); Quilt: Pottery Barn (www.potterybarn.com).

**PAGES 116–119.**
**Designer/Stylist:** Becky Jerdee. **Photographer:** Bill Hopkins. **Shutter Project:** David Underwood. Closet storage: Qbits Modular Furniture System by Sauder and Lynette Jennings (www.sauder.com).

**PAGES 122–125.**
**Designer/Stylist:** Gayle Schadendorf. **Photographer:** Ed Gohlich. **Pillow, Nightstand Top, and Chandelier Projects:** Gayle Schadendorf. Ribbon: Offray. Paint: SW6521, Sherwin-Williams (www.sherwinwilliams.com); Bed coverlet, blue chenille throw, night stand: Ross Stores (www.rossstores.com); Hanging lamp: IKEA (www.ikeausa.com).

**PAGES 128–131.**
**Designer/Stylist:** Stacy Kunstel. **Photographer:** Paul Whicheloe/Anyway Productions. Crewel fabric, antique linens, tassels, alarm clock, mirror, lamp: Red Chair Antiques & Collectibles, Peterborough, NH (603-924-5953); Nightstand, wall platter, candle sconces, curtain rod: Yankee Candle Company (www.yankeecandle.com); Iron planters: Friend of a Gardner, Peterborough, NH (603-924-9278); Paint (wall): 4C4-3, Behr (www.behr.com); Paint (wall trim and chest): Magnolia White, Martha Stewart (www.marthastewart.com).

**PAGES 134–137.**
**Designer/Stylist:** Cathy Kramer, Cathy Kramer Design. **Photographer:** Andy Lyons. **Dresser Project:** Cathy Kramer, Cathy Kramer Design. **Decorative Painter:** Patty Mohr Kramer. **Duvet Cover:** Sonja Carmon. **Loft Bed:** Designed by Phillip Crum (978-475-4991). Chest: Maple Shaker Mule Chest, CCM511, Woodcraft Industries (www.woodcraftindustries.com); Blinds: Zig-Zag blind in Walnut, Kirsch (www.kirsch.com); Paint (magnetic): Magic Wall magnetic paint, Kling Magnetics (www.kling.com); Paint: 6607 (walls), 6635 (dressers), Sherwin Williams (www.sherwinwilliams.com); Chair: Conrad in #100271 Jade/Raisin, Mitchell Gold (www.mitchellgold.com); Ottomans: Link in #11245 Jamboree/Raisin, Mitchell Gold (www.mitchellgold.com); Faux Suede: Kanto Italiano in #3714 Red Ultra Suede, #3705 Brown, #3701 Tan, Synergized Fabrics, Inc. (617-889-4150); Closet storage: Closits Modular Storage System by Sauder and Lynette Jennings and Qbits Modular Furniture System by Sauder and Lynette Jennings (www.sauder.com); Rickrack: Wrights (www.wrights.com)

**PAGES 140–145.**
**Designer/Stylist:** Donna Talley, Ivy Vine Design. **Photographer:** Michael Partenio. **Roman Shade Project Instructions:** Deborah Hastings. **Both Rooms:** Photographs: Target (www.target.com). **Bedroom:** Paint: SW6127, Sherwin Williams (www.sherwinwilliams.com); Bed, nightstand: Retro Ve Collection, Thomasville Furniture (www.thomasville.com); Carpet: LA747 Castlebury in 5757 Honey, Laura Ashley at Lowe's (www.lowes.com); Lamp (dresser): Eddie Bauer Home (www.eddiebaurehome.com); Lamp (nightstand), suede pillows (bed): Linens 'n Things (www.lnt.com); Window treatments: Sailcloth panels in Natural #5053, Tortoise Shell Roman Shades #48515, Country Curtains (www.countrycurtainscatalog.com); Picture Target (www.target.com); Leather pillow (chair): Pottery Barn (www.potterybarn.com); Wicker chair: Pier 1 (www.pier1.com). **Bathroom:** Paint: SW6129, Sherwin Williams (www.sherwinwilliams.com); Light fixture: Hampton Bay at Home Depot (www.homedepot.com); Flooring: Rialto 4x4 ceramic tile, Lowe's (www.lowes.com); Window treatments: Sailcloth Roman Shade in Natural #485e, Country Curtains (www.countrycurtainscatalog.com); Towel bars: Linens 'n Things (www.lnt.com).

**PAGES 150–153.**
**Designer/Stylist:** Joetta Moulden (www.shelterstyle.com; info@shelterstyle.com). **Interior Design:** John Kidd & Associates. **Photographer:** Hal Lott. **Chest Project:** Joetta Moulden. All brass hardware, plumbing, and lighting fixtures: The Renovator's Supply (www.rensup.com). Fabrics: Classic Ticking in Khaki, Polka, Glosheen Lining in White, Waverly (www.waverly.com); Wallpaper: Boxer in Antique Linen, Waverly (www.waverly.com).

**PAGES 156–159.**
**Designer/Stylist:** Susan Andrews. **Photographer:** Bob Greenspan. **Dresser Project:** Susan Andrews. **Contractor:** Greg Heiman, Heiman Development, Kansas City, MO (816-942-0000). Paint: 90GG49/159 (wall), 90YY48/255 (accent on mirror), Glidden (www.glidden.com); Faucet: HansGrohe, Axor Phillipe Starck design (www.hansgrohe.com); Sink, toilet: Kohler (www.kohler.com); Lamps: Home Depot (www.homedepot.com); Tile (floor): Metro Ceramincs Grey, Home Depot (www.homedepot.com); Tile (wall): 12x12 Cream, Lowe's (www.lowes.com).

**PAGES 162–165.**
**Designer/Stylist:** Donna Talley, Ivy Vine Design. **Photographer:** Michael Partenio. **Display Shelf Project:** Donna Talley, Ivy Vine Design. Roman shade: Created by Val Papero, The Shade Place. Valance: Created by Susan Cuda, Designer's Choice. Fabric: Calico Corners (www.calicocorneronline.com); Wallpaper: Thibault (purchased at Signature Interiors, Saratoga Springs, NY, saratogasignature.com).

**PAGES 168–171.**
**Designer/Stylist:** Deborah Hastings. **Photographer:** Sylvia Martin. **Mirror Project:** Deborah Hastings. Wallpaper: Remembered Places, Seabrook (www.seabrookwallcoverings.com).

**PAGES 174–177.**
**Designer/Stylist:** Donna Talley, Ivy Vine Design. **Photographer:** Tria Giovan. **Both Versions:** Window treatments: Country Curtains (www.countrycurtains.com).

# Credits & Resources

**PAGES 182–185.**
**Designer/Stylist:** Cathy Kramer, Cathy Kramer Design. **Photographer:** Bill Hopkins. **Chair Upholstery:** Sonja Carmon. Wallpaper: Village PaperIllusion Color Multi #5805265, FSC Wallcoverings (www.villagehome.com); Lights: Bendable rail system, Tiella (www.tiella.com); Hearth: Thermo-Rite, ultraview, satin-nickel finish, clear glass, HearthCraft (www.hearthcraft.com); Hardware: Handles #19205 WN, Amerock Corporation (www.amerock.com); Pillows: Pier 1 (www.pier1.com); Faux suede fabric: Kanto Italiano #3733 Black Ultra Suede (chair), #3702 Camel (chair), #3730 Gray (built-in seating), Synergized Fabrics (617-889-4150); Upholstery tacks: #1585 Brass 54, Pewter Zinc finish, Turner and Seymour (www.turnerseymour.com); Architectural trims: Georgia-Pacific Corp. (www.gp.com); Rug: Sausalito #2280 in Ebony #300, Capel, Inc. (www.capelrugs.com); Firewood holder: Umbra (www.umbra.com); Floor: Bruce Hardwood Floors, 4¼" Bruce Birchall Plank in Adobe, Armstrong (www.bruce.com/www.armstrong.com).

**PAGES 188–191.**
**Designer/Stylist:** Cathy Kramer, Cathy Kramer Design. **Photographer:** Kent Clawson. **Mirror Project:** Cathy Kramer, Cathy Kramer Design. Storage Units and Furniture: Closits Modular Storage System by Sauder and Lynette Jennings and Qbits Modular Furniture System by Sauder and Lynette Jennings (www.sauder.com); Blinds: Ty Reed in Umber, Kirsch (www.kirsch.com); Rugs: 2x6 runner in wide stripe black and taupe, Colonial Mills (www.colonialmills.com); Mirror brackets: #MP6408 in Chrome Victorian, Advance Glass (www.advanceglasscreations.com); Pillows and accessories: Pier 1 (www.pier1.com).

**PAGES 194–197.**
**Designer/Stylist:** Stacy Kunstel. **Photographer:** Paul Whicheloe, Anyway Productions. **Pillow Project:** Wendy Hiraoka, Hiraoka Home, Honolulu, HI (www.hiraokahome.com). **Window Seat Project:** Steve Copplestone, Copplestone Woodcrafts, 79 Winter Harbor, Wolfeboro, NH 03894 (603-569-9290). Candlestick table, chair, crystal lamp: American Home Gallery, Wolfeboro, NH (603-569-8989); Merino wool throw: Out of the Blue, Wolfeboro, NH (603-569-8644); Paint (walls): Jackson Antique, California Paints (www.californiapaints.com); Paint (floor): Thundercloud, Glidden (www.glidden.com); Mirror: Ethan Allen (www.ethanallen.com).

**PAGES 200–203.**
**Designer/Stylist:** Joetta Moulden (www.shelterstyle.com; info@shelterstyle.com). **Photographer:** Fran Brennan. **Cabinet:** Interior painting by Sammie Cockrell, Faux FX, 11418 Lakeside Place Dr., Houston, TX 77077 (sjcockrell@houston.rr.com). Framing: Arden's Picture Framing, 1631 West Alabama, Houston, TX 77006 (713-522-5281). Custom dog portraits, tramp art frame, sap buckets, pails, cake pedestals, pitchers: Shelter Style (www.shelterstyle.com).

**PAGES 206–209.**
**Designer/Stylist:** Deborah Hastings. **Photographer:** Sylvia Martin. **Cushion Project:** Deborah Hastings. Wallpaper: The Art of Cheri Blum (walls), Tropical Breezes (ceiling), Seabrook (www.seabrookwallcoverings.com).

# Index

# Index

# Disorders
# of
# Thrombosis

# Disorders
# of
# Thrombosis

**Russell Hull, M.B.B.S., M.Sc.**
Director, Clinical Trials Unit
Department of Medicine
Foothills Hospital
Calgary, Alberta
Canada

**Graham F. Pineo, M.D.**
Director, Clinical Trials Unit
Department of Medicine
Calgary General Hospital
Calgary, Alberta
Canada

**W.B. SAUNDERS COMPANY**
*A Division of Harcourt Brace & Company*
Philadelphia    London    Toronto    Montreal    Sydney    Tokyo

**W.B. SAUNDERS COMPANY**
*A Division of Harcourt Brace & Company*

The Curtis Center
Independence Square West
Philadelphia, Pennsylvania 19106

**Library of Congress Cataloging-in-Publication Data**

Disorders of thrombosis / [edited by] Russell Hull, Graham F.
Pineo. — 1st ed.

p.   cm.

ISBN 0–7216–5278–6

1. Thrombosis.     2. Thromboembolism.     3. Coronary heart
disease.     4. Cerebrovascular disease.     I. Hull, Russell.
II. Pineo, Graham F.     [DNLM: 1. Thrombosis.
QZ 170 D612 1996]

RC647.C55D58 1996     616.1′57—dc20

DNLM/DLC                                              95–4086

Disorders of Thrombosis                                              ISBN 0–7216–5278–6

Printed in the United States of America

Last digit is the print number:     9     8     7     6     5     4     3     2     1

*To our wives*
*Patricia and Elizabeth*
*to whom we owe an enormous debt.*

10/17/96

# Contributors

Gregory W. Albers, M.D.
Assistant Professor, Neurology and Neurological Sciences, Stanford University School of Medicine; Director, Stanford Stroke Center, Stanford University Medical Center, Stanford, California, United States
*Atrial Fibrillation*

Melvin A. Andersen, M.D., F.R.C.P.(C)
Clinical Associate Professor, Pathology, University of Calgary Faculty of Medicine; Head, Division of Anatomic Pathology, Calgary General Hospital, Calgary, Alberta, Canada
*Anticoagulants and Bone Demineralization*

Jack Ansell, M.D.
Professor of Medicine, Boston University School of Medicine; Vice Chair of Clinical Affairs, Boston University Medical Center, Boston, Massachusetts, United States
*Oral Anticoagulants (Antithrombotic Agents) for Cardiovascular Disorders; Oral Anticoagulants for the Treatment of Venous Thromboembolism*

W. R. Auger, M.D.
Associate Director, Pulmonary Vascular Program, University of California San Diego Medical Center, San Diego, California, United States
*Chronic Pulmonary Thromboembolism*

B. R. Bagg, R.T.
Registered Respiratory Therapist, Respiratory Care, Calgary General Hospital, Calgary, Alberta, Canada
*Chronic Pulmonary Thromboembolism*

Linda Barbour, M.D., M.S.P.H.
Assistant Professor in Internal Medicine and Obstetrics and Gynecology, University of Colorado School of Medicine, University of Colorado Health Sciences Center, Denver, Colorado, United States
*Management of Common Thrombotic Disorders During Pregnancy*

Henry J. M. Barnett, O.C., M.D., F.R.C.P.(C)
Professor Emeritus, Department of Clinical Neurological Sciences, The University of Western Ontario Faculty of Medicine; Scientist, The John P. Robarts Research Institute, London, Ontario, Canada
*Stroke Prevention*

Kenneth A. Bauer, M.D.
Associate Professor of Medicine, Harvard Medical School, Boston; Chief, Hematology-Oncology Section, Brockton-West Roxbury Veterans Affairs Medical Center, West Roxbury; Associate in Medicine, Beth Israel Hospital, Boston, Massachusetts, United States
*Pathogenesis of Venous Thromboembolism*

Richard C. Becker, M.D.
Associate Professor of Medicine, University of Massachusetts Medical School; Director, Thrombosis Research Center; Director, Anticoagulation Services; Director, Coronary Care Unit, University of Massachusetts Medical Center, Worcester, Massachusetts, United States
*Oral Anticoagulants (Antithrombotic Agents) for Cardiovascular Disorders*

David Bergqvist, M.D., Ph.D.
Professor of Vascular Surgery, Department of Surgery, University Hospital, Uppsala, Sweden
*Cost-Effectiveness of Preventing Postoperative Deep Vein Thrombosis*

Mark A. Bisesi, M.D.
Diagnostic Radiology Resident, Michigan State University College of Human Medicine, Grand Rapids Program; Diagnostic Radiology Resident, Grand Rapids Area Medical Education Center, Grand Rapids, Michigan, United States
*Ventilation-perfusion Lung Scans for the Diagnosis of Acute Pulmonary Embolism*

**Lars C. Borris, M.D.**

Specialist of Orthopedic Surgery, The Venous Thrombosis Group, Department of Orthopedics, Aalborg Hospital, Aalborg, Denmark
*Prevention in Orthopedic Surgery and Trauma*

**Harry R. Büller, M.D., Ph.D.**

Department of Hemostasis, Thrombosis, Atherosclerosis, and Inflammation Research, Academic Medical Center, Amsterdam, The Netherlands
*Objective Tests for the Diagnosis of Venous Thrombosis*

**John A. Cairns, M.D., F.R.C.P.(C)**

Professor and Chair, Department of Medicine, McMaster University School of Medicine; Active Staff Cardiologist, Hamilton General Hospital and Chedoke-McMaster Hospital, Hamilton, Ontario, Canada
*Coronary Thrombolysis*

**Demetra Callas, B.S.**

Graduate Fellow, Loyola University of Chicago Stritch School of Medicine, Maywood, Illinois, United States
*New Antithrombotic Drugs*

**Cedric J. Carter, M.B., F.R.C.P., F.R.C.P.(C)**

Associate Professor, Pathology, University of British Columbia Faculty of Medicine; Head, Haematology/Immunohaematology, Vancouver Hospital and Health Sciences Centre, Vancouver, British Columbia, Canada
*Pathogenesis of Arterial Thrombosis; Epidemiology of Venous Thromboembolism*

**G. Patrick Clagett, M.D.**

Professor of Surgery, University of Texas Southwestern Medical Center at Dallas Southwestern Medical School, Dallas, Texas, United States
*Overview of Prevention*

**Alexander T. Cohen, M.B.B.S., M.Sc., F.R.A.C.P.**

Lecturer, King's College School of Medicine and Dentistry, London; Director of Clinical Studies, Thrombosis Research Institute, Chelsea, England, United Kingdom
*Prevention of Venous Thromboembolism in General Surgery*

**Philip C. Comp, M.D., Ph.D.**

Professor of Medicine, University of Oklahoma Health Sciences Center, University of Oklahoma College of Medicine; Associate Chief of Staff for Research, Veterans Administration Medical Center, Oklahoma City, Oklahoma, United States
*Congenital and Acquired Hypercoagulable States*

**J. Conard, Ph.D.**

Maître de Conférence des Universités, Faculté de Médecine, Université Pierre et Marie Curie; Praticien Hospitalier, Service d'Hématologie Biologique, Hôtel-Dieu, Paris, France
*Laboratory Tests for the Diagnosis of Venous Thromboembolism*

**Richard L. Edwards, M.D.**

Associate Professor of Medicine, University of Connecticut School of Medicine; Associate Medical Director, American Red Cross Blood Services, Farmington, Connecticut, United States
*Thrombosis and Cancer*

**Bo Eklof, M.D., Ph.D.**

Clinical Professor of Surgery, University of Hawaii John A. Burns School of Medicine; Vascular Surgeon, Straub Clinic and Hospital, Honolulu, Hawaii, United States
*Vena Caval Filters*

**Greg Elliott, M.D.**

Professor of Medicine, University of Utah School of Medicine; Chief, Pulmonary Division, LDS Hospital, Salt Lake City, Utah, United States
*Venal Caval Filters*

**Jawed Fareed, Ph.D., F.A.C.A.**

Professor, Loyola University of Chicago Stritch School of Medicine, Maywood, Illinois, United States
*New Antithrombotic Drugs*

**William Feldstein, B.Sc., M.B.A.**

Research Coordinator, Clinical Trials Unit, University of Calgary Faculty of Medicine, Calgary, Alberta, Canada
*Cost-Effectiveness of Diagnosis: Deep Vein Thrombosis in Symptomatic Patients* and *Pulmonary Embolism*

**G.T. Ford, M.D., F.R.C.P.C., F.A.C.P., F.C.C.P.**

Professor, Department of Medicine, Division of Respiratory Medicine, University of Calgary Faculty of Medicine; Director, Division of Respiratory Medicine, Calgary General Hospital, Calgary, Alberta, Canada
*Chronic Pulmonary Thromboembolism*

**A.S. Gallus, M.B., F.R.A.C.P., F.R.C.P.A., F.R.C.P.(C)**

Associate Professor, School of Medicine, Flinders University of South Australia; Chairman, Division of Laboratory Medicine, Flinders Medical Centre, Bedford Park, South Australia, Australia
*Prevention in Medical Patients*

**David Garcia-Dorado, M.D., F.A.C.C.**

Clinical Chief, Service of Cardiology, Hospital General Universitari Vall d'Hebron, Barcelona, Spain
*Antithrombotic Therapy in Chronic Ischemic Heart Disease*

**James N. George, M.D.**

Professor of Medicine, Chief, Hematology-Oncology Section, Department of Medicine, University of Oklahoma Health Sciences Center, University of Oklahoma College of Medicine, Oklahoma City, Oklahoma, United States
*Heparin-associated Thrombocytopenia*

**Samuel Z. Goldhaber, M.D.**

Associate Professor of Medicine, Harvard Medical School; Staff Cardiologist, Brigham and Women's Hospital, Boston, Massachusetts, United States
*Thrombolytic Therapy for Venous Thrombo-embolism*

**Scott H. Goodnight, M.D.**

Professor of Medicine and Pathology, Oregon Health Sciences University School of Medicine, Portland, Oregon, United States
*Antiplatelet Therapy in Cardiovascular Disease*

**Alexander Gottschalk, M.D.**

Professor of Radiology, Michigan State University College of Human Medicine, East Lansing; Residency Program Director, University Affiliated Hospitals of Flint, Flint; Grand Rapids Area Medical Education Center, Grand Rapids, Michigan, United States
*Ventilation-perfusion Lung Scans for the Diagnosis of Acute Pulmonary Embolism*

**David Green, M.D., Ph.D.**

Professor of Medicine, Northwestern University Medical School; Chief of Medicine, Rehabilitation Institute of Chicago, Chicago, Illinois, United States
*Prevention in Neurosurgery and Spinal Cord Injury*

**David A. Hanley, M.D., F.R.C.P.C.**

Professor of Medicine, Head, Division of Endocrinology and Metabolism, Department of Medicine, Foothills Hospital and University of Calgary Faculty of Medicine; Head, Division of Endocrinology and Metabolism, Foothills Hospital; Endocrine Tumour Group Leader, Tom Baker Cancer Centre, Calgary, Alberta, Canada
*Anticoagulants and Bone Demineralization*

**Debra Hoppensteadt, M.S., M.T. (A.S.C.P.)**

Loyola University of Chicago Stritch School of Medicine, Maywood, Illinois
*New Antithrombotic Drugs*

**M.H. Horellou, M.D.**

Maître de Conférence des Universités, Université Pierre et Marie Curie; Praticien Hospitalier, Service d'Hématologie Biologique, Hôtel-Dieu, Paris, France
*Laboratory Tests for the Diagnosis of Venous Thromboembolism*

**Walter Jeske, B.S.**

Graduate Fellow, Loyola University of Chicago Stritch School of Medicine, Maywood, Illinois, United States
*New Antithrombotic Drugs*

**Vijay V. Kakkar, F.R.C.S., F.R.C.S.E.**

Professor of Surgical Science, National Heart and Lung Institute, University of London and King's College School of Medicine and Dentistry; Director, Thrombosis Research Institute, Chelsea, England, United Kingdom
*Prevention of Venous Thromboembolism in General Surgery*

**Michael R. Lassen, M.D.**

Orthopedic Surgeon, The Venous Thrombosis Group, Department of Orthopedics, Aalborg Hospital, Aalborg, Denmark
*Prevention in Orthopedic Surgery and Trauma*

**Andreas Laupacis, M.D., M.Sc., F.R.C.P.(C)**

Associate Professor, Departments of Medicine and Community Medicine and Epidemiology, University of Ottawa Faculty of Medicine; Director, Clinical Epidemiology Unit, Loeb Medical Research Institute, Ottawa Civic Hospital, Ottawa, Ontario, Canada
*Atrial Fibrillation*

**Anthonie W.A. Lensing, M.D., Ph.D.**

Academic Medical Center, Department of Hemostasis, Thrombosis, Atherosclerosis, and Inflammation Research, Amsterdam, The Netherlands
*Objective Tests for the Diagnosis of Venous Thrombosis*

**Henri R. Lijnen, Ph.D.**

Associate Professor, University of Leuven, Leuven, Belgium
*Novel Thrombolytic Agents*

**Björn Lindgren, Ph.D.**

Professor of Health Economy, University of Lund, Malmö General Hospital, Malmö, Sweden
*Cost-Effectiveness of Preventing Postoperative Deep Vein Thrombosis*

**Gordon D.O. Lowe, M.D., F.R.C.P.**

Professor of Medicine, University of Glasgow; Honorary Consultant and Co-Director, Haemophilia Centre, Royal Infirmary, Glasgow, Scotland, United Kingdom
*Acute Stroke*

**Victor J. Marder, M.D.**

Professor of Medicine, Chief of the Hematology Unit, and Associate Chair for Academic Affairs, Department of Medicine, University of Rochester School of Medicine and Dentistry; Attending Physician, Strong Memorial Hospital, Rochester, New York, United States
*Acute Arterial Obstruction*

**Thomas Mätzsch, M.D., Ph.D.**

Associate Professor of Surgery, University of Lund, Malmö General Hospital, Malmö, Sweden
*Cost-Effectiveness of Preventing Postoperative Deep Vein Thrombosis*

**H.E. Meldrum, B.A.**

Director, North American Symptomatic Carotid Endarterectomy Trial, The John P. Robarts Research Institute, London, Ontario, Canada
*Stroke Prevention*

**Michael M. Millenson, M.D.**

Assistant Professor of Medicine, Temple University School of Medicine; Director of Hematology, Fox Chase Cancer Center, Philadelphia, Pennsylvania, United States
*Pathogenesis of Venous Thromboembolism*

**Kenneth Ouriel, M.D.**

Clinical Associate Professor of Surgery, University of Rochester School of Medicine and Dentistry; Attending Surgeon, Rochester General Hospital and The Strong Memorial Hospital, Rochester, New York, United States
*Acute Arterial Obstruction*

**J. Pickard, M.D.**

Clinical Assistant Professor in Internal Medicine, University of Colorado School of Medicine, University of Colorado Health Sciences Center, Denver; Family Medical Clinic, Estes Park Colorado, Estes Park Medical Clinic, Estes Park, Colorado, United States
*Management of Common Thrombotic Disorders During Pregnancy*

**Simon W. Rabkin, M.D., F.R.C.P.(C), F.A.C.C.**

Professor of Medicine, University of British Columbia, Faculty of Medicine, Vancouver, British Columbia, Canada
*Epidemiology of Arterial Thromboembolism*

**Gary E. Raskob, M.Sc.**

Assistant Professor, Department of Biostatistics and Epidemiology, and Department of Medicine, University of Oklahoma Health Sciences Center, University of Oklahoma College of Medicine; Director, Clinical Epidemiology Unit, Veterans Administration Medical Center, Oklahoma City, Oklahoma, United States
*Evidence-Based Recommendations for the Diagnosis and Treatment of Thromboembolic Disease: Rules of Evidence for Assessing the Literature; Heparin Therapy for Acute Cardiac Disorders; Deep Vein Thrombosis in Symptomatic Patients; Heparin Treatment of Venous Thromboembolism; Calf-Vein Thrombosis*

**Frederick R. Rickles, M.D.**

Professor of Medicine and Pediatrics, Emory University School of Medicine; Deputy Chief, Hematologic Disease Branch, Division of HIV/AIDS, National Center for Infectious Diseases, Centers for Disease Control and Prevention, Atlanta, Georgia, United States
*Thrombosis and Cancer*

**M.M. Samama, M.D., Ph.D.**

Professor des Universités, Faculté de Médicine; Praticien Hospitalier, Service d'Hématologie Biologique, Hôtel-Dieu, Paris, France
*Laboratory Tests for the Diagnosis of Venous Thromboembolism*

**Paul D. Stein, M.D.**

Professor of Medicine (Henry Ford), Case Western Reserve University School of Medicine, Cleveland, Ohio; Medical Director, Levine Health Enhancement Center, Henry Ford Heart and Vascular Institute, Detroit, Michigan, United States
*Clinical Features of Deep Vein Thrombosis and Pulmonary Embolism; Ventilation-perfusion Lung Scans for the Diagnosis of Acute Pulmonary Embolism; Cost-Effectiveness of Diagnosis: Pulmonary Embolism*

**William D. Suggs, M.D.**

Assistant Professor of Surgery, Albert Einstein College of Medicine of Yeshiva University; Chief, Vascular Surgical Services, North Central Bronx Hospital; Assistant Attending Surgeon, Montefiore Medical Center, Bronx, New York, United States
*Chronic Arterial Obstruction*

**Pierre Théroux, M.D., F.R.C.P.(C), F.A.C.C.**

Professor of Medicine, Université de Montréal Faculty of Medicine; Chief, Coronary Care Unit, Institute de

Cardiologie de Montréal, Montréal, Quebec, Canada
*Antithrombotic Therapy in Chronic Ischemic Heart Disease*

**A.G.G. Turpie, M.D.**

Professor, Department of Medicine, McMaster University, Hamilton, Ontario, Canada
*Prevention in Neurosurgery and Spinal Cord Injury*

**K. Valentine, M.D., Ph.D.**

Hematology Fellow, Division of Hematology, Department of Internal Medicine, University of Calgary, Faculty of Medicine, Calgary, Alberta, Canada
*Management of Common Thrombotic Disorders During Pregnancy*

**Frank J. Veith, M.D.**

Professor of Surgery, Albert Einstein College of Medicine of Yeshiva University, New York; Director of Vascular Surgical Services, Montefiore Medical Center, Bronx, New York, United States
*Chronic Arterial Obstruction*

**Marc Verstraete, M.D., Ph.D., F.R.C.P. (Edin), F.A.C.P. (Hon)**

Professor of Medicine, University of Leuven, Leuven, Belgium
*Novel Thrombolytic Agents*

**S. Viner, M.D.**

Assistant Director, Department of Intensive Care, Calgary General Hospital, Calgary, Alberta, Canada
*Chronic Pulmonary Thromboembolism*

**Jeanine M. Walenga, Ph.D., F.A.C.A.**

Associate Professor, Loyola University of Chicago Stritch School of Medicine, Maywood, Illinois, United States
*New Antithrombotic Drugs*

# Foreword

Disorders of thrombosis have long been recognized as the cause of venous thromboembolism. We now recognize that systemic thromboembolism has an even greater impact on population health. In the 1980s, coronary thrombosis was "rediscovered" as the cause of acute myocardial infarction in patients with coronary atherosclerosis. In the 1990s, the very significant impact of left ventricular mural thrombosis in patients with coronary artery disease and cardiomyopathy, and of left atrial thrombosis in patients with atrial fibrillation, on the etiology of stroke has been clarified. We now recognize that approximately 20% of all ischemic strokes are caused by emboli arising from the heart.

Modern diagnostic techniques facilitate the identification of coronary artery thrombi as well as left ventricular thrombi and left atrial thrombi. Our improved understanding of the importance of disorders of thrombosis in the etiology of two of our most prevalent and lethal diseases—myocardial infarction and stroke—has led to a search for more effective and safer antithrombotic treatment.

Each of the most frequently used antithrombotic agents—heparin, warfarin, and aspirin—was introduced more than 40 years ago, before the era of randomized clinical trials. As a result, the indications, dosages, and monitoring techniques of these commonly used agents have undergone re-evaluation in multiple clinical trials in the past few years. The indications for each of these agents have undergone further clarification but require more study. The appropriate dosages and monitoring techniques of these agents have also undergone significant positive changes that have enhanced their safety.

Trials currently in progress are evaluating the combination of these agents, especially the combination of aspirin and warfarin, at much lower dosages than have been given in the past.

As our understanding of the pathophysiology of thrombotic disorders increases, we can anticipate the evolution of multiple, new antiplatelet and other antithrombotic agents.

The morbidity and mortality of thrombotic diseases are truly staggering. New insights into the pathophysiology, prevention, and treatment of these disorders will have an enormous impact on population health.

This text correlates current laboratory and clinical knowledge of disorders of thrombosis to assist in the prevention and treatment of systemic and venous thromboembolism.

JAMES E. DALEN, M.D.
VICE PROVOST FOR HEALTH SCIENCES
DEAN, COLLEGE OF MEDICINE
THE UNIVERSITY OF ARIZONA
TUCSON, ARIZONA

# Preface

Disorders of thrombosis continue to be major causes of morbidity and mortality. Tremendous advances have been made over the past two decades with respect to pathogenesis, diagnosis, prevention, and treatment of these problems. Clinical trials in the treatment of arterial and venous thromboembolism have set the pace for the development of other high-quality (Level I), multicenter clinical trials involving a number of disorders. In this book, we have compiled the latest information on all aspects of both arterial and venous thrombotic disorders by an international panel of experts. Progress in the field has been made because of the rigorous dedication by many to the improvement of health care.

A unique feature of this book is the application of the rules of evidence to all references related to diagnostic tests and to prevention and treatment of thrombotic disorders. In so doing, we have identified the large number of high-quality clinical trials that have been performed while, at the same time, demonstrating the numerous areas where further trials are required. We have applied the rules of evidence as defined by Dr. David Sackett and his colleagues at McMaster University School of Medicine. Studies graded as Level I provide the clinical anchor. This feature, however, is not intended to distract from the efforts and achievements of investigators performing non-Level I trials. In pioneering a field, it may be necessary to precede Level I trials with pilot studies. In certain other situations, Level I trials may not be possible. It is evident on review of the literature in this domain that findings of Level I trials, if consistent, rapidly become the standard of clinical practice. In reviewing this book, firm recommendations regarding diagnostic tests or approaches to prevention and treatment of thrombotic disease are best made where Level I evidence is available.

In establishing these levels of evidence, we have tried to avoid harshness, particularly in distinguishing between Levels I and II trials. In the further application of rules of evidence to the references, we must acknowledge the assistance provided by Gary Raskob, Assistant Professor, Department of Biostatistics and Epidemiology and Department of Medicine at the University of Oklahoma Health Sciences Center.

*Disorders of Thrombosis* is designed to be a companion to *Disorders of Hemostasis,* third edition, edited by Drs. Oscar D. Ratnoff and Charles D. Forbes. It is our goal from the outset to provide periodic revisions in the form of future editions of *Disorders of Thrombosis.*

*Disorders of Thrombosis* should be of interest to subspecialists as well as to general internists and primary care physicians. It is our hope that the application of the rules of evidence will be of assistance to the experienced clinician, to medical students and residents, as well as to others wishing to approach this subject in an evidence-based fashion.

The authors would like to thank the following individuals for their assistance in the preparation of this book: Toni McGee, Laurie Nairn, Marisa Reibin, Marian Rooney, Darlene McKeage, Karen Fettes, and Laurie Genert.

RUSSELL HULL
GRAHAM F. PINEO

# Contents

**SECTION III**

# SPECIAL PROBLEMS  337

# Chapter 1

# Evidence-Based Recommendations for the Diagnosis and Treatment of Thromboembolic Disease: Rules of Evidence for Assessing the Literature

Gary E. Raskob

In recent years, there has been increasing emphasis for clinicians to practice "evidence-based" medicine. Evidence-based medicine stresses the evaluation of evidence from clinical trials as the basis for clinical decisions and patient care.[1] For many clinicians, this requires a change from the traditional approach, which emphasizes pathophysiologic understanding and clinical experience as the basis for clinical decisions. To practice evidence-based medicine, the clinician must understand and apply formal rules of evidence for evaluating the clinical literature.[1] Over the past 15 years, scientific criteria for clinical studies evaluating new diagnostic tests[2–4] and treatments[5–8] have been defined, and rules of evidence for assessing the literature and making clinical recommendations have been developed.[9, 10]

Thromboembolic disease is well suited to the practice of evidence-based medicine because of the wealth of data from rigorously designed clinical trials evaluating new approaches for treatment and diagnosis. This chapter reviews the study design requirements for studies evaluating new therapies and diagnostic approaches in the context of thromboembolic disease. Rules of evidence for assessing the clinical literature are outlined. These rules are used throughout the remainder of the book to qualify the strength of evidence supporting specific recommendations. Firm recommendations are made only when supported by "level I" evidence. In

the absence of level I evidence, firm recommendations are not made. In these instances, the alternative clinical approaches are described.

## STUDY DESIGN REQUIREMENTS FOR ANTITHROMBOTIC THERAPY

There has been increasing recognition in recent years that study designs commonly used in the past to evaluate antithrombotic therapy, such as uncontrolled case series or studies utilizing historic controls, are subject to many potential biases that may lead to spurious estimates of effectiveness and safety. General agreement now exists that properly designed and executed clinical trials are required to adequately evaluate the effectiveness and safety of new antithrombotic treatments. The essential design features required to avoid bias have been defined[5–8] and applied in many clinical trials evaluating antithrombotic therapy. These essential design features are:

1. The study should be performed prospectively and should include a concurrent control group
2. The patients should be randomly allocated to the alternative treatment groups
3. Comparability of the alternative treatment groups for patient characteristics and important prognostic variables should be demonstrated

4. Well defined objective measures should be used to evaluate effectiveness and safety, and bias in the assessment of outcomes should be avoided

5. All clinically relevant outcomes should be assessed and reported

6. A sufficient number of patients must be studied to allow valid conclusions, and appropriate statistical methods should be used to analyze data.

Retrospective studies are susceptible to numerous potential biases, particularly in the selection of patients and the allocation of treatment, and are not adequate for evaluating new therapies. In an uncontrolled study, it is impossible to determine whether an observed outcome is a true effect of treatment or whether the outcome would have occurred even in the absence of the treatment being evaluated. Studies utilizing historic (non-concurrent) controls are subject to the potential for bias resulting from changes in the demographic and clinical characteristics of a particular population of patients with time, changes in patient management, and improvements in health care. Thus, a concurrent control group is required to make valid inferences about the relative effectiveness and safety of a new therapy.

The use of random allocation is the only technique that will ensure the treatment groups are comparable with respect to the *unknown* as well as the known characteristics influencing patient outcome. Several alternate procedures for allocating patients to the treatment groups have been proposed to replace random allocation.[11] However, none of these alternative approaches can ensure that the treatment groups will be comparable with respect to variables that may influence the patient's outcome, but that are *unknown* at the time the study is conducted. For this reason, random allocation of patients to the treatment groups remains a mandatory requirement for the definitive evaluation of the effectiveness and safety of new therapy.[11]

The knowledge of a patient's treatment may influence both the intensity and the result of the search for a particular outcome (known as diagnostic-suspicion bias). Therefore, the assessment of outcome should be performed without knowledge of the patient's treatment group, and should be based on well defined objective outcome measures. Ideally, a double-blind design should be used in which neither the patient nor members of the health care team know which treatment the patient is receiving. In the context of antithrombotic therapy, procedures have been developed to enable double-blind designs for clinical trials evaluating treatments that require laboratory monitoring and dose titration, such as heparin[12-14] or oral anticoagulant therapy.[14-17] In these studies, adjustments in the drug regimen were made by a physician who was not involved in the assessment of patient outcome. The results of laboratory monitoring of coagulation tests, which could reveal the nature of the patient's treatment, were released only to this designated physician. The remaining members of the health care team, including the patient's attending physician and those involved in assessing the outcome, did not know which treatment the patient was receiving. This approach has been used successfully to enable double-blind designs in randomized trials evaluating alternative approaches for the initial treatment of venous thrombosis,[12-14] the prevention of venous thrombosis,[15] and long-term anticoagulant therapy for myocardial infarction[16] or atrial fibrillation.[17]

If a double-blind design is not possible, the potential for diagnostic-suspicion bias can be avoided by using objective tests to assess the outcome and by performing these tests routinely at fixed intervals in all patients. The test results should be interpreted without knowledge of the patient's treatment group and without knowledge of other test results or the patient's clinical findings. This approach was used successfully to evaluate the effectiveness of alternative regimens for the long-term treatment of venous thrombosis when the nature of the interventions did not allow the use of a double-blind design.[18, 19]

A sufficient number of patients should be evaluated to minimize the possibility of two important statistical errors. These are the alpha error (a false positive conclusion) and the beta error (a false negative conclusion). If the number of patients evaluated in a clinical trial is small, even differences in outcome between treatments that are considered clinically important may not be statistically significant.[8] This may lead to the erroneous conclusion that no difference in outcome between treatment exists, when in fact it does (the beta error). A sufficient number of patients should be studied to ensure that the probability of a beta error is low (less than 10%).

In assessing the results of a clinical trial of therapy, the clinician should routinely address two questions:

1. If a statistically significant ($p < .05$) difference in outcome between treatments is found, is this difference clinically important?

2. If a statistically significant difference is not

found, was the study large enough to exclude the existence of a true, clinically important difference?

The 95% confidence interval for the observed difference in the outcomes of effectiveness or safety between treatments should always be provided.[20] If the minimum clinically important difference, as defined by the reader, lies outside the 95% confidence interval for the observed difference, the reader can conclude that the existence of a true clinically important difference is unlikely.[7] An advantage of using the 95% confidence interval to determine if a clinically important difference has been excluded is that it enables individual readers to apply their own values for the "minimum clinically important difference."

Appropriate procedures should be used to analyze the data. If interim analyses are performed during the course of the study, appropriate statistical procedures to account for these multiple analyses should be used. Subgroup analyses should be based on a well defined, scientific rationale established before the study begins, and should be kept to a minimum.[21] Ideally, these subgroups will have been defined by stratifying patients before random allocation to the experimental or control treatment.

## LEVELS OF EVIDENCE FOR THERAPY STUDIES

Levels of evidence for clinical studies evaluating antithrombotic therapy have been defined and used to qualify the strength of evidence supporting a specific clinical recommendation.[9, 10] The levels of evidence are defined based on the study design as shown in Table 1–1. The strongest level of evidence is level I and the weakest is level V. The levels I and II are distinguished from levels III, IV, and V based on two key design features: (1) the nature of the control group, either concurrent, historic, or absent; and (2) the use of random allocation to the alternative treatment groups. Both levels I and II evidence use a concurrent control group with random allocation of patients to the alternative treatments. The distinction between level I and level II evidence is statistical. Both level I and level II evidence come from randomized control designs, but level II evidence has a higher likelihood of either false positive results (alpha error) or false negative results (beta error).

Two factors determine whether a given randomized trial will be classified as level I or level

Table 1–1. **Levels of Clinical Evidence for Therapy***

| Level | | Study Design Features |
|-------|------|------------------------|
| I | Strongest | Large randomized trials with definite results (low chance of alpha or beta error) |
| II | | Small randomized trials with uncertain results (moderate to high alpha or beta error) |
| III | | Nonrandomized studies with concurrent controls |
| IV | | Nonrandomized studies with historic controls |
| V | Weakest | Case series with no controls |

*From Sackett DL: Rules of evidence and clinical recommendations on the use of antithrombotic agents. Chest 95(Feb Suppl): 2s–4s, 1989.

II. These are (1) the sample size, and (2) the size of the observed treatment effect. There is no arbitrary sample size that distinguishes a level I or level II study. Studies with relatively small sample sizes but that identify profound treatment effects may provide level I evidence. For example, a randomized trial evaluating alternative approaches to the longterm treatment of proximal deep vein thrombosis documented a clinically striking and statistically significant difference in the rates of recurrent venous thromboembolism in patients treated with warfarin (none of 17) compared with patients who received low-dose subcutaneous heparin (9 of 19) ($p<.001$).[18] This study provides level I evidence for the effectiveness of warfarin in this setting. Conversely, studies with larger sample sizes may be classified as level II if they do not enroll sufficient patients to exclude a clinically important difference in outcomes between treatments. For example, two randomized trials evaluating longterm oral anticoagulant therapy after myocardial infarction,[22, 23] which enrolled 200 to 300 patients per group, are classified as level II[24] because these studies could not exclude a risk reduction in mortality of 20% in favor of oral anticoagulant treatment (a clinically important difference). Subsequently, larger trials with 400 to 600 patients per group established the effectiveness of longterm oral anticoagulant therapy for improving survival in patients with myocardial infarction.[16, 25]

The levels of evidence approach was used by the American College of Chest Physicians (ACCP) working group on antithrombotic therapy to evaluate the literature and make clinical recommendations.[9, 10] This approach has several advantages over past approaches to the development of clinical recommendations and practice guidelines.[26] First, it avoids recommendations based on "expert" opinion, which may be incorrect and potentially harmful. Second, the rules of evidence are explicit, and the practitioner can judge for himself or herself the validity of a specific recommendation based on the evidence cited. Third, those clinical scenarios that lack firm evidence for a particular approach can be identified, and research can be targeted to these areas. This latter point is illustrated by the case of oral anticoagulant treatment for patients with nonvalvular atrial fibrillation.[27] At the time of the second ACCP consensus conference, the value of longterm anticoagulant treatment in patients with nonvalvular atrial fibrillation remained uncertain because of a lack of level I evidence. By the time the third ACCP consensus conference was held in 1992, four level I trials had been completed, providing firm evidence for the benefit of oral anticoagulants.[27] This enabled the third conference to make a firm recommendation based on level I evidence.[27]

The levels of evidence approach is used throughout the remainder of this book to qualify the strength of evidence for specific clinical recommendations about therapy.

## STUDY DESIGN REQUIREMENTS FOR DIAGNOSIS

Many diagnostic tests are introduced into clinical practice and accepted enthusiastically, but with further evaluation are shown to be limited in clinical application or even useless. The uncritical acceptance of a diagnostic test for thromboembolic disease has serious implications. Patients with false positive results may receive unnecessary, potentially harmful treatment, and patients with false negative findings may have necessary and highly effective treatment withheld. In the past, the evaluation of diagnostic tests has often been based on studies that have failed to include the essential design features required to avoid bias. In more recent years, essential design features for studies evaluating diagnostic tests have been defined[2-4] and applied in the setting of diagnostic tests for thromboembolism.

The essential study design features for studies evaluating diagnostic tests are:

1. The study should include a consecutive series of patients
2. All patients should undergo both the test under evaluation and the diagnostic reference

test ("gold standard") to determine the four indices of diagnostic efficacy: sensitivity, specificity, positive predictive value, and negative predictive value
3. The test should be evaluated in a broad spectrum of patients, both with and without the disease of interest, with varying severity of the disease, and with a variety of comorbid conditions that are commonly confused with the disease of interest
4. The results of the test under evaluation and the reference test should be interpreted independently and without knowledge of the results of the other or the patient's clinical or ancillary test findings
5. A sufficient number of patients should be studied to make valid conclusions, based on 95% confidence intervals, for the indices of sensitivity, specificity, and positive and negative predictive values
6. There should be studies including longterm followup to determine the safety of withholding treatment in patients with negative results by the test under evaluation.

It is important that consecutive patients be evaluated to avoid selection bias. A broad spectrum of patients should be included to provide valid estimates of sensitivity, specificity, and predictive values. This should include patients with comorbid conditions that may produce false positive or false negative results to determine the usefulness of the test in various patient subgroups. Failure to evaluate the test in a broad spectrum of patients may result in falsely high indices of efficacy.[4]

"Work-up" bias should be avoided. This bias occurs when the results of the test under evaluation influence the decision to perform the reference ("gold standard") test. Work-up bias is avoided by performing both the test under evaluation and the reference test in all patients. Interpretation bias occurs when knowledge of the result of one test influences the interpretation of another test. Interpretation bias should be avoided by interpreting the new test and the reference test independently, without knowledge of the other, and without knowledge of the patient's clinical findings or ancillary test results.

The final step in the process of evaluating a new diagnostic test is to confirm the clinical validity of a negative result. Clinical validity should be determined by longterm followup of consecutive patients in whom treatment has been withheld based on negative test results. This approach has been used to validate negative findings by objective testing for deep vein thrombosis[28–32] or pulmonary embolism[33, 34], and for thallium scanning in patients with chest pain.[35]

The validity of a new test can also be assessed by a randomized comparison with a gold standard and assessing clinical outcome in patients managed on the basis of either the gold standard or the new test. This approach can be used if the disease being studied is responsive to treatment, and if inadequate management leads to clinical complications (e.g., recurrent thromboembolism) that can be objectively measured. These complications can be used as outcome measures for comparing the diagnostic efficacy of the two approaches. This randomized trial approach has been used to evaluate diagnostic tests in patients with clinically suspected venous thrombosis.[30, 32]

## LEVELS OF EVIDENCE FOR DIAGNOSTIC STUDIES

The diagnostic studies are classified as level I evidence if the essential design features outlined above are met. Thus, to qualify as level I evidence, there must be either an independent, blind comparison with a reference test and longterm followup to assess clinical validity of negative results or a randomized comparison with a reference test measuring clinical outcome of patients on longterm followup. In either case, a sufficient number of patients should be included to provide valid conclusions based on the 95% confidence intervals for sensitivity, specificity, and predictive values and for the clinical outcomes. Firm recommendations for diagnosis of thromboembolism are made only when supported by level I evidence. If the study design fails to meet the essential design criteria outlined above, the study is designated as non-level I, and recommendations are not made based on this data.

## References

1. Evidence-based Medicine Working Group: Evidence-based medicine. A new approach to teaching the practice of medicine. JAMA 268:2420–2425, 1992.
2. Department of Clinical Epidemiology and Biostatistics, McMaster University: How to read clinical journals: II. To learn about a diagnostic test. Can Med Assoc J 124:703–710, 1981.
3. Jaeschke R, Guyatt G, Sackett DL, for the Evidence-based Medicine Working Group: Users' guides to the medical literature, III. How to use an article about a diagnostic test. A. Are the results of the study valid? JAMA 271:389–391, 1994.
4. Ransohoff D, Feinstein AR: Problems of spectrum and bias in evaluating the efficacy of diagnostic tests. N Engl J Med 299:926–930, 1978.
5. Department of Clinical Epidemiology and Biostatistics, McMaster University: How to read clinical journals: V. To distinguish useful from useless or even harmful therapy. Can Med Assoc J 124:1156–1162, 1981.
6. Guyatt GH, Sackett DL, Cook DJ, for the Evidence-based Medicine Working Group: Users' guides to the medical literature, II. How to use an article about therapy or prevention. A. Are the results of the study valid? JAMA 270:2598–2601, 1993.
7. Guyatt GH, Sackett DL, Cook DJ, for the Evidence-based Medicine Working Group: Users' guides to the medical literature, II. How to use an article about therapy or prevention. B. What were the results and will they help me in caring for my patients? JAMA 271:59–63, 1994.
8. Frieman JA, Chalmers TC, Smith H, Kuebler RR: The importance of beta, the type II error, and sample size in the design and interpretation of the randomized controlled trial: Survey of 71 "negative" trials. N Engl J Med 299:690–694, 1978.
9. Sackett DL: Rules of evidence and clinical recommendations on the use of antithrombotic agents. Chest 95[Feb Suppl]:2s–4s, 1989.
10. Cook DJ, Guyatt GH, Laupacis A, Sackett DL: Rules of evidence and clinical recommendations on the use of antithrombotic agents. Chest 102[Oct Suppl]:305s–311s, 1992.
11. Sackett DL: Readers' guides for therapy: Was the assignment of patients to treatment randomized? ACP Journal Club May/June:A–12, 1991.
12. Hull R, Raskob G, Rosenbloom D, et al: Heparin for 5 days compared with 10 days in the initial treatment of proximal venous thrombosis. N Engl J Med 322:1260–1264, 1990.
13. Hull R, Raskob G, Pineo G, et al: Subcutaneous low molecular weight heparin compared with continuous intravenous heparin in the treatment of proximal vein thrombosis. N Engl J Med 326:975–982, 1992.
14. Brandjes DPM, Heijboer H, Buller HR, et al: Acenocoumarol and heparin compared with acenocoumarol alone in the initial treatment of proximal-vein thrombosis. N Engl J Med 327:1485–1489, 1992.
15. Hull R, Raskob G, Pineo G, et al: A comparison of subcutaneous low-molecular weight heparin with warfarin sodium for prophylaxis against deep-vein thrombosis after hip or knee implantation. N Engl J Med 329:1370–1376, 1993.
16. Report of the Sixty Plus Reinfarction Study Research Group: A double-blind trial to assess long-term anticoagulant therapy in elderly patients after myocardial infarction. Lancet 2:989–994, 1980.
17. Connolly S, Laupacis A, Gent M, et al: Canadian Atrial Fibrillation Anticoagulation (CAFA) study. J Am Coll Cardiol 18:349–355, 1991.
18. Hull R, Delmore T, Genton E, et al: Warfarin sodium vs. low-dose heparin in the long-term treatment of venous thrombosis. N Engl J Med 301:855–858, 1979.
19. Hull R, Delmore T, Carter C, et al: Adjusted subcutaneous heparin versus warfarin sodium in the long-term treatment of venous thrombosis. N Engl J Med 306:189–194, 1982.
20. Braitman LE: Confidence intervals assess both clinical significance and statistical significance. Ann Intern Med 114:515–517, 1991.
21. Oxman AD, Guyatt GH: A consumer's guide to subgroup analysis. Ann Intern Med 116:78–84, 1992.
22. Second Report of the Working Party on Anticoagulant Therapy in Coronary Thrombosis to the Medical Research Council: An assessment of long-term anticoagulant administration after cardiac infarction. Br Med J 2:837–843, 1964.

23. Breddin D, Loew D, Lechner K, et al: The German-Austrian Aspirin Trial: A comparison of acetylsalicylic acid, placebo, and phenproucoumon in secondary prevention of myocardial infarction. Circulation 62[Suppl 5]:63–72, 1980.

24. Cairns JA, Hirsh J, Lewis HD, et al: Antithrombotic agents in coronary artery disease. Chest 102[Oct Suppl]:456s–481s, 1992.

25. Smith P, Arnesen H, Holme I: The effect of warfarin on mortality and reinfarction after myocardial infarction. N Engl J Med 323:147–152, 1990.

26. Hirsh J, Haynes B: Transforming evidence into practice: Evidence-based consensus. ACP Journal Club January/February:A–16, 1993.

27. Laupacis A, Albers G, Dunn MI, Feinberg WM: Antithrombotic therapy in atrial fibrillation. Chest 102[Oct Suppl]:426S–433S, 1992.

28. Hull R, Hirsh J, Sackett DL, et al: Clinical validity of a negative venogram in patients with clinically suspected venous thrombosis. Circulation 64:622–625, 1981.

29. Hull R, Carter CJ, Jay R, et al: The diagnosis of acute recurrent deep-vein thrombosis: A diagnostic challenge. Circulation 67:901–906, 1983.

30. Hull R, Hirsh J, Carter CJ, et al: Diagnostic efficacy of impedance plethysmography for clinically suspected deep-vein thrombosis: A randomized trial. Ann Intern Med 102:21–28, 1985.

31. Huisman MV, Buller HR, ten Cate JW, Vreelsen J: Serial impedance plethysmography for suspected deep-vein thrombosis in outpatients. The Amsterdam General Practitioner Study. N Engl J Med 314:823–828, 1986.

32. Heijboer H, Buller HR, Lensing AW, et al: A comparison of real-time compression ultrasonography with impedance plethysmography for the diagnosis of deep-vein thrombosis in symptomatic outpatients. N Engl J Med 329:1365–1369, 1993.

33. Kipper MS, Moser KM, Kortman KE, Ashburn WL: Long-term follow-up of patients with suspected pulmonary embolism and a normal lung scan. Chest 82:411–415, 1982.

34. Hull R, Raskob G, Coates G, Panju A: Clinical validity of a normal perfusion lung scan in patients with suspected pulmonary embolism. Chest 97:23–26, 1990.

35. Pamelia FX, Gibson RS, Watson DD, et al: Prognosis with chest pain and normal thallium-201 exercise scintigrams. Am J Cardiol 55:920–926, 1985.

# Cardiac and Arterial Disease

# Chapter 2

# Epidemiology of Arterial Thromboembolism

Simon W. Rabkin

Epidemiology can be conveniently defined as the study of the distribution (who? when? where? how much?) and determinants (why? and why not?) of human disease. In Western industrialized countries, there is an excessive amount (excess prevalence), or an epidemic, of atherosclerotic and thromboembolic diseases in the coronary arteries, cerebral arteries, and peripheral arteries as the clinical manifestations relating to these abnormalities, such as myocardial infarction and stroke, are found in excess in these countries. Indeed, in many industrialized countries these conditions are the leading causes of death.

For ischemic or coronary heart disease there was a dramatic increase in the age-adjusted cause of death from the early 1920s to the early 1970s in the United States.[2] The epidemic of coronary atherosclerosis is not limited to the male gender. Of the 550,000 people who die each year in the United States from heart-related disease, about 250,000 women die from coronary heart disease. About 100,000 of the deaths are considered premature, that is, prior to the average life expectancy.[15] Although the incidence of ischemic or coronary artery disease is declining in some countries, in other countries, such as some in Eastern Europe, incidence rates are increasing.

## DETERMINATION OF RISK FACTORS FOR ARTERIAL THROMBOEMBOLIC DISEASE

Many factors have been identified in individuals free of vascular disease that predict the subsequent development of atherosclerotic and thromboembolic vascular disease. These have been called *risk factors* for the disease. A large number of factors have been identified as risk factors or determinants or predictors of arterial thromboembolism (Table 2–1). The proof of whether a factor is a cause of thromboembolic disease is rigorous, and not all risk factors have proven with any degree of certainty whether or

Table 2–1. **Some Factors Related to Arterial Thromboembolism**

Age
Sex
Race
Genetic (family history)
Diet—fat, glucose, consumption
Socioeconomic status
Occupation
Personality
Psychologic stress
Cigarette smoking
Obesity, overweight
Abdominal obesity
Diabetes mellitus
Physical activity—excessive activity/physical inactivity
Elevated blood pressure
Hormones, estrogen

**Laboratory Factors**

Alpha$_2$ globulin
Blood group other than O
Carboxyhemoglobin
Coagulation disorders
Total cholesterol
Reduced high-density-lipoprotein cholesterol
Elevated low-density-lipoprotein cholesterol
Elevated Lp (a)
Low apoproteins AI and AII
Elevated apo B concentration
Elevated plasma homocysteine levels
Electrocardiographic abnormalities
Glucose intolerance
Reduced lung (vital) capacity
Hyperestrogenemia in men
Low iron binding capacity
Rheumatoid factor
Elevated serum selenium concentration
Elevated uric acid

9

not they are involved in the process leading to thromboembolic disease. An association does not prove causality; a factor can be associated with a disease because of its association to another factor. The first factor is thereby unrelated in a causal way to disease. A frequently used example is the increase in number of television sets that paralleled the increase in coronary artery disease in the 1950s; there was an association but not a causal relationship. For many factors, the data strongly suggest a causal relationship between them and the clinical manifestations of thromboembolic disease. This is a complex issue, and several concepts must be discussed.

The clinical event is our primary concern, but we do not always know the underlying pathophysiologic events in each case. Using the example of acute myocardial infarction, the pathophysiologic concept is coronary thromboembolism. The process involves (1) factors that trigger the thromboembolic event (i.e., coronary thrombosis), and (2) the factors responsible for the setting in which thromboembolism occurs, namely on an atherosclerotic plaque. Of course, the pathophysiology of a disease may involve less common conditions that are unrelated to the usual pathophysiology. Examples are severe spasm of a coronary artery without atherosclerosis or excessive metabolic demands of the myocardium such as in extreme overexertion without coronary thrombosis. Thus, there are risk factors for thromboembolism and there are risk factors for atherosclerosis.

Furthermore we must always bear in mind that clinicians play the "substitution game" of substituting the pathophysiologic event *thromboembolism* for the more complex *clinical event*. Other chapters in this book deal in more detail with the triggering events leading to arterial thrombosis; this chapter will deal with factors that predict the clinical event. Readers must be aware of the substitution process in this chapter; factors cannot always be clearly distinguished as risk factors for atherosclerosis and risk factors for thrombosis because some of the risk factors such as cigarette smoking may play a role in the process of thrombosis as well as the development of atherosclerosis.

Establishing a high probability of a causal relationship between a factor and arterial thromboembolism requires different kinds of data (Table 2–2). An example is if a study revealed low selenium concentration in the blood of patients with thromboembolic stroke. To establish a causal relationship, various kinds of data would be necessary. The most convincing data would be a randomized, double-blind, pla-

**Table 2–2. Kinds of Data or Evidence or Kinds of Questions That Must be Answered to Establish a High Probability of a Causal Relationship Between a Factor and a Disease**

### Evidence of a True Experiment in Humans

Are these randomized, double-blind, placebo-controlled trials, with the appropriate number of people, in which the factor under study is increased and the incidence of the disease is increased?

### Experimental Data in Humans

Are these randomized, double-blind, placebo-controlled trials, with the appropriate number of people, in which the factor under study is reduced and the incidence of the disease is reduced?

### Evidence of a Strong Association

Is the association of the factor with the disease highly statistically significant or is there a high relative risk of the disease in individuals with the factor under study?

### Consistency of the Association From Study to Study

A Dose-response Relationship

Is the association of the factor with the disease in a manner such that the greater its amount the greater the likelihood of disease?

### Epidemiologic Sense

Is the factor in a high prevalence in populations or countries with high prevalence of disease and vice versa?

### Biologic Evidence

Does the association make biologic sense? Are there biologic data in animal models to support the relationship, ie., is there replication of disease in animal models with the factor under study producing a credible biologic basis for the relationship?

cebo-controlled trial with the appropriate number of people, with individuals representative of the population, that are randomized to high or low selenium diets, preferably with a range of diets that would ensure different blood selenium levels. Subjects would be followed for a designated time period and the number of strokes in the different groups examined. Verification that selenium supplementation actually increased serum selenium concentration would be an important part of that study. Such a study is extremely expensive. In addition, preferably several similar studies should be conducted by different investigators to ensure that the first study's results were valid. Thus, other kinds of studies are required compatible with the hypothesis that there is a causal relationship between a given factor and thromboembolic disease. Studies include (1) *case-control studies,* indicating a higher prevalence of reduced serum selenium in stroke patients. Cases with the disease of interest are compared with controls, individuals free of the disease, and the relative odds or risk of disease are calculated. These kinds of studies are often called "retrospective" as they "look backward" and suggest that the factor had been present before the event. They are susceptible to a number of biases producing erroneous results but are inexpensive and relatively easy to perform. (2) *Repeatability or consistency* studies are those consistently showing the same findings. (3) **Epidemiologic data** of higher stroke rates in populations with low selenium concentrations and low stroke rates in populations with high selenium concentrations. (4) **Gradients of risk** studies are demonstrations that the lower serum selenium levels are associated with greater stroke rates and vice versa. (5) **Experimental data in animal models** provide plausible biologic explanations for the association of stroke and serum selenium. Proof would be established if introduction of the factor produced the condition. This is not an ethical possibility for most factors, in humans, because trials of factors that produce disease are unacceptable.

How can sense be made of these different kinds of data or studies? The best approach is to rate or grade the kinds of data. Thus, a randomized, placebo-controlled, double-blind trial in a sufficiently large patient or population group would be rated as a Level I, whereas an observational study would be rated as Levels III to IV.[61] It must be recognized that for some factors a rigorous proof of causality involving all of the kinds of studies is not possible. It is not acceptable to do a randomized clinical trial of cigarette smoking by randomizing individuals to a smoking group and encouraging them to do so for years to establish the incidence in a group that does not select itself as a smoking group. Similarly, the difficulties of conducting a randomized trial of physical exercise, ensuring that the other factors such as body adiposity and serum lipids levels remain constant, may be too difficult to accomplish.

The last few years have provided a greater understanding of existing risk factors, identification of new ones, and an appreciation of their interrelationship.

## RISK FACTORS FOR THROMBOEMBOLIC DISEASE

Some of the more important risk factors for arterial thromboembolic disease are discussed.

## Age

Death from coronary atherosclerotic or ischemic heart disease (myocardial infarction and/or sudden death) and cerebrovascular disease (strokes) increases with increasing age. Thus, the older an individual the greater the likelihood that death will occur from thromboembolic disease.

## Cigarette Smoking

Cigarette smoking has been accepted as a risk factor for arterial thromboembolism for a long time. The data are based on (1) observational studies of a higher prevalence of atherosclerosis in autopsy of cigarette smokers compared with nonsmokers.[62] The association between atherosclerosis and cigarette smoking has been established for women as well as men.[73] Other evidence of smoking risk includes (2) the higher prevalence of cigarette smokers among individuals presenting with the clinical manifestations of thromboembolic disease such as myocardial infarction[56]; (3) the higher incidence of thromboembolic disease in cigarette smokers in prospective cohort studies[45]; and (4) the lower incidence of atherosclerotic vascular disease in former smokers compared with current smokers.[21]

Compared with observational studies, the strength of the association between cigarette smoking and thromboembolic arterial disease is not as strong as earlier studies in intervention trials that randomized high-risk individuals to groups that were given and complied with advice on cigarette smoking cessation.[59] In those trials not everyone randomized to smoking cessation quit smoking, and thus a selection bias may have been operative. Considering the strength of the evidence between cigarette smoking and thromboembolic disease and the consistency of the observation in large-scale investigations within and between countries, a causal link between cigarette smoking and arterial thromboembolic disease is generally accepted.

## Hypertension

Elevated blood pressure is an accepted risk factor for thromboembolic disease and an even greater risk factor for heart failure and hemorrhagic stroke. Either systolic or diastolic blood pressure is a risk factor, but most studies show a stronger correlation with systolic than diastolic blood pressure. The relationship between hypertension and atherosclerotic vascular disease is based on (1) the association in patients with atherosclerotic vascular disease of elevated blood pressure compared with patients without vascular disease, and (2) epidemiologic data showing the increased incidence of atherosclerotic vascular disease in individuals initially free of disease with elevated blood pressure.[3, 16, 28, 45, 52] Evidence of a gradient of risk with higher blood pressures is associated with greater incidence of cardiovascular disease. Other evidence of the relationship between hypertension and atherosclerotic disease includes (1) the accelerated production of atherosclerosis in experimental animal models with hypercholesterolemia that are made hypertensive; (2) increases in atherosclerotic vascular disease prevalence and incidence in countries with higher blood pressure compared with those with lower blood pressure; (3) the prognostic value of blood pressure before a myocardial infarction or stroke as a determinant of survival after the event (i.e., the greater the blood pressure, the greater the likelihood of an adverse survival even up to 10 years after myocardial infarction and up to 3 years after stroke[51, 53]; and (4) reduction in the incidence of cardiovascular disease events in individuals treated for elevated blood pressure parallels their blood pressure reduction.[10, 64]

Although current antihypertensive medications do not reduce coronary heart disease incidence to the level expected from the degree of blood pressure reduction, there is no doubt that incidence of this disease is reduced with antihypertensive drug treatment. The value of systolic blood pressure elevation as a predictor of cardiovascular disease incidence extends to the condition of "isolated systolic hypertension," in which systolic blood pressure but not diastolic blood pressure is elevated. Treatment of isolated systolic hypertension in the elderly significantly reduced the incidence of coronary artery disease and stroke.[63]

## Obesity

The relationship between obesity and atherosclerotic vascular disease has been controversial, but controversy was resolved when better standardization methods for measurement of obesity were developed and cohorts with longer followup were examined. Retrospective or case control studies noted the association of arterial thromboembolic disease in overweight individuals. Prospective or cohort studies had shown varying results, which may be explained by the age of the cohort and length of followup.[50] For men, the younger the age at being overweight the greater the likelihood of development of

manifestations of thromboembolic disease, but a long exposure to obesity is required.[50] Obesity has been difficult to define. Standard body weight for height tables provide a range but are not precise enough. Standardization of weight for height squared or the body mass index ($BMI = wt/ht^2$) has shown a gradient of risk with increasing incidence of thromboembolic disease with BMI over 25 $kg/m^2$. Obesity type has emerged as an even more important factor.[33, 34] Increased abdominal adiposity, the male pattern obesity with an increased girth compared with the female pattern of obesity with increased hip circumference, is a more dangerous kind of obesity.[74] An increase in the waist-to-hip ratio in men and women is significantly associated with a higher incidence of myocardial infarction, stroke, and death in prospective epidemiologic study.

## Dyslipidemia

Consideration of the relationship of coronary atherosclerosis to abnormalities of serum lipids must take into account the different kinds of lipids, namely, total serum cholesterol, low-density lipoprotein cholesterol (LDL-C), high-density lipoprotein cholesterol (HDL-C), Lp(a), and the various apolipoproteins—apo AI, apo AII, apo B, and apo E phenotypes.

## Total Serum Cholesterol

Total serum cholesterol has been established as a risk factor for atherosclerosis based on the association between increased cholesterol and atherosclerotic disease in patients, and the increased risk of development of atherosclerotic vascular disease in individuals free of disease with elevated cholesterol.[8, 26, 29, 31, 58] Interestingly, elevated cholesterol is associated with an increased incidence of nonhemorrhagic stroke, but inversely associated with intracranial hemorrhage.[45] Further evidence includes the production of atherosclerosis in experimental animal models of hypercholesterolemia; linkage of genetic hypercholesterolemia and development of premature atherosclerosis; increases in atherosclerotic vascular disease prevalence and incidence in countries with higher cholesterol; reduction in the incidence of cardiovascular disease events in individuals treated for elevated cholesterol in parallel with their reduction in cholesterol; and regression of atherosclerotic lesions in patients who have been treated for their hypercholesterolemia.

## High-density Lipoprotein Cholesterol

High density lipoprotein cholesterol (HDL-C) has been established as a risk factor for atherosclerosis based on results of many studies. These include the association between low HDL-C and increased incidence of atherosclerotic events,[20, 41] and the association of low HDL-C and angiographically defined atherosclerosis in coronary arteries and other vessels. Indeed, Miller and coworkers[76] focused only on patients who had total cholesterol less than 5.2 mmol/L in a retrospective case-control study of 1,000 persons who had coronary angiography at Johns Hopkins Hospital. Of the 244 men and 107 women with total cholesterol less than 5.2 mmol/L, 76% of men and 44% of women had significant coronary artery stenosis. Luria and coworkers[77] found that total cholesterol-to-HDL-C ratio was highly correlated to the presence and extent of coronary stenosis in a series of 380 patients who had coronary angiograms. These investigators also found that this ratio was a marker for the clustering of other risk factors, namely, high hemoglobin and fibrinogen levels and a history of cigarette smoking. The link between HDL-C and coronary stenosis is strengthened by two other kinds of observations.

It has been observed that genetic abnormalities may be associated with extremely low concentrations of HDL-C and apo AI. However, normal total cholesterol and triglycerides can be associated with angiographically documented premature coronary artery disease in persons in their late twenties and early thirties.[78] Observers have seen reduction in the incidence of cardiovascular disease events in individuals treated for low HDL-C in parallel with an elevation in HDL-C.[79]

## Triglycerides

Whether serum triglyceride levels are related to the development of atherosclerotic vascular disease has been a controversial subject. Data in univariate analysis show an association between serum triglycerides and (1) the presence of atherosclerotic vascular disease, (2) the increased risk of development of atherosclerotic vascular disease in individuals free of disease, and (3) reduction in clinical manifestations of coronary disease events in individuals with elevated triglycerides. However, although there is a relationship in univariate analysis in 14 of 18 studies with a total of over 10,000 men and women, multivariate analysis does not always show that triglycerides remain a significant factor.[4] High serum triglycerides may be more strongly associated with atherosclerosis in women than men.[6]

HDL-C and triglycerides are inversely correlated, and HDL-C is closely linked to atherosclerotic vascular disease. Therefore, in many studies, after HDL-C is considered, triglycerides are no longer significant risk factors predicting thromboembolic disease.[40] However, the nature of the metabolic abnormality producing the hypertriglyceridemia may be more important, and this may be defined by concomitant abnormalities of LDL-C.[11]

## Apolipoprotein B

Apo B levels were first shown by Sniderman and coworkers[65] to identify individuals with greater probability of coronary atherosclerosis. In an observational study of 64 men with a first myocardial infarction before the age of 45 years in Sweden, the degree of coronary atherosclerosis on coronary angiography was most strongly related to plasma apo B concentration.[67] The ability of apo B to predict the development of coronary events has been consistently found, but the question remains whether it is more useful than total serum cholesterol as a routine test in the general population.[54]

## Lipoprotein (a)

Lp(a) consists of a low-density lipoprotein (LDL) particle linked by a disulfide bridge from apolipoprotein B-100 to apoprotein (a) (apo [a]). Observational studies have demonstrated that elevated Lp(a) levels are more frequently associated with angiographic evidence of more extensive coronary atherosclerosis[12] and greater likelihood of progression of coronary atherosclerosis[38] or occluded coronary arteries after myocardial infarction.[43] Some prospective epidemiologic data have supported the relationship between increased Lp(a) and increased incidence of atherosclerotic coronary artery disease.[57] Biologic data have linked Lp(a) with coagulation and atherosclerotic lipid particles. Problems with methodology of Lp(a) measurement and standardization as well as optimal treatment of elevated Lp(a) include the limited research on establishing whether or not Lp(a) is an important risk factor. Furthermore, recent data in large prospective studies of the ability of high Lp(a) to predict the development of the clinical manifestations of coronary disease have been disappointing,[54] and thus routine use of this lipid in assessment of cardiovascular risk is not warranted.[54]

## Apolipoprotein E

Three apo E alleles determine six apo E genotypes. The relationship of the corresponding apo E phenotype to coronary atherosclerosis on coronary angiography has been reviewed by Davignon and coworkers.[14] The frequency of apo E phenotypes in patients with angiographically documented coronary artery disease was similar to that without coronary atherosclerosis. Apo E phenotypes are similar in patients with hypertension compared with those in the general population and do not influence the lipid changes associated with antihypertensive treatment with alpha or beta blockers.[49]

## Diabetes Mellitus

Diabetes mellitus is a recognized predictor of thromboembolic disease. The relationship between diabetes and atherosclerotic vascular disease is based on (1) the association in patients with atherosclerotic vascular disease with diabetes mellitus, and (2) epidemiologic data showing the increased incidence of atherosclerotic vascular disease in individuals free of disease but with diabetes mellitus or impaired glucose tolerance.[18, 19, 45] Men with diabetes mellitus have a markedly increased incidence of stroke compared with nondiabetic men.[45] Evidence of a gradient of risk is present as the higher the blood sugar, the greater the incidence of cardiovascular disease. Furthermore, accelerated production of atherosclerosis occurs in experimental animal models with diabetes mellitus with hypercholesterolemia. The necessary data from randomized control trials of noninsulin-dependent diabetics randomized to rigorous control of their hyperglycemia have yet to show that this therapy diminishes the occurrence of atherosclerotic vascular disease.

## Coagulation Factors

Other chapters in this book describe in greater detail the coagulation factors and their link to arterial thromboembolism. However, a recent prospective cohort study is of interest. Patients in Northern Italy with documented cardiovascular disease had baseline coagulation studies and were followed for the development of disease. Coagulation factors were important predictors of subsequent recurrent cardiovascular disease (Table 2–3). Interestingly, the predictive value of the factors was different, depending on whether the patients had myocardial infarction, angina pectoris, transient ischemic attacks, or peripheral vascular disease.

## Physical Exertion

Physical exertion is a factor that has been implicated as a risk factor for triggering of myocardial infarction and for protecting against myocardial infarction. In retrospective, in case-control studies of several thousand patients with acute myocardial infarction, the relative risk of myocardial infarction has been reported to be from 5.9 (i.e., an individual is 5.9 times more likely to have a myocardial infarction after heavy physical exertion[42]) to 2.1.[72] The increased risk is for the few-hour period after the heavy physical exertion. The risk of myocardial infarction is reduced for individuals who engage in regular physical exertion.[42, 72]

Lower levels of physical exercise may be associated with an increased risk of peripheral vascular as well as coronary artery disease.[6]

## COMBINATION OF RISK FACTORS

The combination of risk factors produces a more than additive increase in incidence of ath-

Table 2–3. **Coagulation Factors and the Risk of Recurrent Cardiovascular Disease***

|  | Myocardial Infarction | Angina | TIA | PVD† |
|---|---|---|---|---|
| Number | 297 | 120 | 146 | 304 |
| High | fibrinogen<br>Factor VIII:C<br>vWF:Ag | vWF:Ag†<br>Leukocyte† | Factor VIII:C<br>Leukocyte† | Factor VIII:C |
| Low | Factor VII<br>Protein C |  |  | Protein C<br>Factor VII<br>Antithrombin III |

*Recurrent cardiovascular events include fatal and nonfatal myocardial infarctions or strokes and sudden death in patients with different kinds of cardiovascular disease.
†vWF = von Willebrand factor; leukocyte refers to elevated leukocyte count.
TIA = transient ischemic attack(s); PVD = peripheral vascular disease.

erosclerotic vascular disease. The combination of hypertension (systolic blood pressure greater than 141 mm Hg) and cigarette smoking is associated with an age-adjusted death rate from stroke that is almost 10 times greater than the risk in nonsmoking men with blood pressures of less than 125 mm Hg.[45]

## INTERRELATIONSHIP OF RISK FACTORS

A major trend over the past several years is the tendency to evaluate constellations of risk factors and to suggest that they may have a common origin. High blood pressure and hypercholesterolemia are more likely to occur together than by chance alone. Families have been described with this combination segregating in a pattern to suggest a potential common inheritance.[71] This may be linked to a gene that will eventually be defined. It may also be related to the postulated "atherosclerosis gene."

Another concept that has received a great deal of attention has been the interrelationship of obesity, hypertriglyceridemia, hypertension, and glucose intolerance. Reaven has advanced the concept that the four factors are interrelated, with a common pathophysiologic mechanism being insulin resistance of tissues.[55] Epidemiologic data have revealed that hyperinsulinemia increases an individual's risk of subsequent occurrence of coronary disease. Hyperinsulinemia is more likely to be present in individuals who are overweight, and who have hypertriglyceridemia and hypertension.[30, 75] Hyperinsulinemia may accelerate the process of atherosclerosis by being a stimulus for the changes in vascular smooth muscle that lead to atherosclerosis.

Alteration of coagulation factors is associated with the insulin resistance syndrome.[27] In addition, hypercoagulability and reduced fibrinolysis are linked to hyperlipidemia.[1]

Multiple intervention strategies for the prevention of atherosclerotic events have become the usual approach to patients, because most have more than one risk factor. The benefit of this approach has been demonstrated in a study of 300 men and women with angiographically documented coronary atherosclerosis who were randomly assigned to a multiple risk factor reduction individualized program or the usual care.[23] The intensive risk factor reduction program favorably altered the rate of narrowing of the coronary arteries and decreased hospitalizations for clinical cardiac events.

In summary, this chapter has outlined some of the concepts that are necessary to establish a causal relationship between any factor and the development of thromboembolic disease. Establishing a causal relationship benefits our understanding of the pathophysiology of the disease. Even when the factor is not treated, such as alterations in estrogens or testosterone as a risk factor for coronary disease in men.[47] The cholesterol reduction strategy or multiple intervention strategies to reduce the progression of coronary atherosclerosis and decrease coronary and cerebral vascular events is important for disease prevention. It also provides the spark to search for as yet undiscovered risk factors for thromboembolic disease.

## REFERENCES

1. Andersen P: Hypercoagulability and reduced fibrinolysis in hyperlipidemia: Relationship to the metabolic cardiovascular syndrome. J Cardiovasc Pharm 20[Suppl 8]:S29–31, 1992.
2. Anderson TW: The male epidemic. In Proceedings of the Conference on the Decline in Coronary Heart Disease Mortality. US HEW NIH publication 79–1610, 1979.
3. Armstrong VW, Cremer P, Eberle E, et al: The association between serum Lp(a) concentrations and angiographically assessed coronary atherosclerosis—dependence on serum LDL levels. Atherosclerosis 62:249, 1986.
4. Austin M: Plasma trigycerides and coronary heart disease. Arteriosclerosis 11:2–14, 1991.
5. Beaglehole R, Bonita R, Stewart A: Cardiovascular disease mortality trends in the western Pacific 1968–84. NZ Med J 101:441–413, 1988.
6. Bergstrand L: Femoral and coronary atherosclerosis in patients with hyperlipidemia. Arteriographic findings correlated to clinical and biochemical parameters. Acta Radiol 392[Suppl]: 1–27, 1994.
7. Berkson DM, Stamler J: Epidemiological factors on cerebrovascular disease. J Arterioscler Res 5:189–202, 1965.
8. Chapman JM, Coulson AH, Clark VA, et al: The differential effect of serum cholesterol, blood pressure and weight on the incidence of myocardial infarction and angina pectoris. J Chronic Dis 23:631–645, 1971.
9. Chapman JM, Reeden LC, Rowen ER, et al: Epidemiology of vascular lesions affecting the central nervous system. Am J Public Health 56:191–201, 1966.
10. Collins R, Peto R, MacMahon S, et al: Blood pressure, stroke and coronary heart disease. Part 2. Short-term reductions in blood pressure: Overview of randomized drug trials in their epidemiological context. Lancet 335:827–838, 1990.
11. Coresh J, Kwiterovich PO, Smith HH, Bachorik PS: Association of plasma triglyceride concentration and LDL particle diameter, density, and chemical composition with premature coronary artery disease in men and women. J Lipid Res 34:1687–1697, 1993.
12. Dahlen G, Guyton JR, Attar M, et al: Association of levels of lipoprotein Lp(a), plasma lipids and other lipoproteins with coronary artery disease documented by angiography. Circulation 74:758, 1986.
13. Davies JW, Semenciw RM, Mao Y: Cardiovascular disease mortality trends and related risk factors in Canada. Can J Cardiol 4[suppl A]:16A–20A, 1988.

14. Davignon J, Gregg RE, Sing CF: Apolipoprotein E polymorphism and atherosclerosis. Arteriosclerosis 8:1–21, 1988.

15. Eaker ED: Coronary heart disease in women. Reviewing the evidence. Identifying the needs. NHLBI, NIH, Bethesda, Maryland, 1987.

16. Epstein FH: The epidemiology of coronary heart disease: A review. J Chronic Dis 18:735–774, 1965.

17. Fienleib M: The magnitude and nature of the decrease in coronary heart disease mortality rate. Am J Cardiol 54:2c–7c, 1984.

18. Fuller JN, Shipley MJ, Rose G, et al: Coronary heart disease risk and impaired glucose tolerance. The Whitehall Study. Lancet 1:1373, 1980.

19. Garcia MJ, McNamara PM, Gordon T, Kannel WB: Morbidity and mortality of diabetes in the Framingham population. Sixteen year followup study. Diabetes 23:105, 1976.

20. Gordon T, Castelli WP, Hyortland MC, et al: High-density lipoprotein as a protective factor against coronary heart disease: The Framingham study. Am J Med 62:707–714, 1977.

21. Gordon T, Castelli WP, McGee D, Dawber TR: Death and coronary attacks in men after giving up cigarette smoking. A report from the Framingham Study. Lancet 2:1345, 1974.

22. Hammond EC, Horn D: Smoking and death rates: Report on forty-four months of follow-up of 187,783 men. II. Death rates by cause. JAMA 166:1294–1308, 1958.

23. Haskell WL, Alderman EL, Fair JM, et al: Effects of intensive multiple risk factor reduction on coronary atherosclerosis and clinical cardiac events in men and women with coronary artery disease. The Stanford Coronary Risk Intervention Project (SCRIP). Circulation 89:975–990, 1994.

24. Havlick RJ, Feinleib M: Proceedings of the Conference on the Decline in Coronary Heart Disease Mortality. US Dept HEW NIH 79–1610, 1979.

25. Inter-Society Commission for Heart Disease Resources: Primary prevention of atherosclerotic disease. Circulation 42:A55–95, 1970.

26. Iso HJR, Wentworth D, Neaton JD, Cohen JD: Serum cholesterol levels in six year mortality from stroke in 350,977 men screened from the Multiple Risk Factor Intervention Trial. N Engl J Med 320:904–910, 1989.

27. Juhan-Vague I, Thompson SG, Jespersen J: Involvement of the hemostatic system in the insulin resistance syndrome. A study of 1500 patients with angina pectoris. The ECAT Angina Pectoris Study Group. Arterioscler Thromb 13:1865–1873, 1993.

28. Kannel WB: Role of blood pressure in cardiovascular morbidity and mortality. Prog Cardiovasc Dis 17:5–24, 1974.

29. Kannel WB, Castelli WP, Gordon T, McNamara PF: Serum cholesterol, lipoproteins and the risk of coronary heart disease: The Framingham study. Ann Intern Med 74:1–12, 1974.

30. Kaplan NM: The Deadly Quartet. Upper-body obesity, glucose intolerance, hypertriglyceridemia, and hypertension. Arch Intern Med 149:1514–1520, 1989.

31. Keys A, Taylor HL, Blackburn H, et al: Coronary heart disease among Minnesota business and professional men followed fifteen years. Circulation 28:381–395, 1963.

32. Kleenbaum DG, Kupper LL, Casel JC, et al: Multivariate analysis of risk of coronary heart disease in Evans County, Georgia. Arch Intern Med 123:943–948, 1971.

33. Lapidus L, Bengtsson C, Larsson B, et al: Distribution of adipose tissue and risk of cardiovascular disease and death: A 12 year follow-up of participants in the population study of women in Gothenburg, Sweden. Br Med J 289:1257–1261, 1984.

34. Larsson B, Svardsudd K, Welin L, et al: Abdominal adipose tissue distribution, obesity and risk of cardiovascular disease and death; 13 year follow-up of participants in the study of men born in 1913. Br Med J 288:1401–1404, 1984.

35. Luepka RV, Jacobs DR, Folsom AR, et al: Cardiovascular risk factor change 1973–74 to 1980–82. The Minnesota Heart Survey. J Clin Epidemiol 41:825–833, 1988.

36. McFarland KF, Boniface ME, Hornung CA, et al: Risk factors and noncontraceptive estrogen use in women with and without coronary disease. Am Heart J 117:1209–1214, 1989.

37. Maciejko JJ, Holmes DR, Kottke BA, et al: Apolipoprotein A-I as a marker of angiographically assessed coronary artery disease. N Engl J Med 309:385–389, 1983.

38. Marburger C, Hambrecht R, Niebauer J, et al: Association between lipoprotein (a) and progression of coronary artery disease in middle aged men. Am J Cardiol 73:742–746, 1994.

39. Marmot MG: Interpretation of trends in coronary heart disease mortality. Acta Med Scand 701[Suppl]:58–65, 1985.

40. Menotti A, Scanga M, Morisi G: Serum triglycerides in the prediction of coronary artery disease. Am J Cardiol 73:29–32, 1994.

41. Miller NE, Forde OH, Thalle DS, et al: The Tromso study. Lancet 1:965–967, 1977.

42. Mittleman MA, Maclure M, Tofler GH, et al: Triggering of acute myocardial infarction by heavy physical exertion. Protection against triggering by regular exertion. N Engl J Med 329:1677–1683, 1993.

43. Moliterno DJ, Lange RA, Meidell RS, et al: Relation of plasma lipoprotein(a) to infarct artery patency in survivors of myocardial infarction. Circulation 88:935–940, 1993.

44. Morris JN, Kagan A, Pattison DC, et al: Incidence and prediction of ischemic heart disease in London businessmen. Lancet 2:553–559, 1966.

45. Neaton JD, Wentworth DN, Cutler J, et al: Risk factors for death from different types of stroke. Am J Epidemiol 3:493–499, 1993.

46. Paul O, Lepper MH, Phelan WH, et al: A longitudinal study of coronary heart disease. Circulation 23:20–31, 1963.

47. Phillips GB, Pinkernell BH, Jing TY: The association of hypotestosteronemia with coronary artery disease in men. Arterioscler Thromb 14:701–706, 1994.

48. Pisa Z, Uemura K: International differences in developing improvements in cardiovascular health. Ann Med 21:193–197, 1989.

49. Rabkin SW, Huff M, Newman C, et al: Lipids and lipoproteins during antihypertensive drug therapy: Comparison of doxazosin and atenolol in a randomized double-blind trial: The Alpha Beta Canada study. Hypertension 24:241–248, 1994.

50. Rabkin SW, Mathewson FAL, Hsu PH: Relationship of body weight to incidence of ischemic heart disease in a cohort of North American men followed for twenty-six years. Manitoba study. Am J Cardiol 39:452–458, 1977.

51. Rabkin SW, Mathewson FAL, Tate RB: Prognosis after acute myocardial infarction in a prospective cardiovascular study. Am J Cardiol 40:604–610, 1977.

52. Rabkin SW, Mathewson FAL, Tate RB: Predicting the risk of ischemic heart disease and cerebrovascular disease from systolic and diastolic blood pressure. Ann Intern Med 88:342–345, 1978.

53. Rabkin SW, Mathewson FAL, Tate RB: The relation of blood pressure to stroke prognosis. Ann Intern Med 89:15–20, 1978.

54. Rader DJ, Hoeg JM, Brewer HB: Quantitation of plasma apolipoproteins in the primary and secondary prevention of coronary artery disease. Ann Intern Med 120:1012–1025, 1994.

55. Reaven GM, Hoffman BB: A role for insulin in the aetiology and course of hypertension. Lancet 2:435–436, 1987.

56. Report of the Surgeon General: Smoking and Health. US Dept HEW Public Health Service publication 79–50066, 1979.

57. Rhoades GG, Dahlen G, Berg K, et al: Lp(a) lipoprotein as a risk factor for myocardial infarction. JAMA 256:2540, 1986.

58. Rhoades GG, Gulbrandsen CL, Kagan A: Serum lipoproteins and coronary heart disease in a population study of Hawaiian Japanese men. N Engl J Med 294:293–298, 1976.

59. Rose G, Hamilton PJS: A randomized controlled trial of the effects on middle aged men of advise to stop smoking. J Epidemiol Community Health 32:275, 1978.

60. Rosenmen RH, Brand RJ, Scholtz RI, Friedman M: Multivariate prediction of coronary heart disease during 8.5 year follow-up in the Western Collaborative Group study. Am J Cardiol 37:903–910, 1976.

61. Sackett DL: Rules of evidence and clinical recommendations on the use of antithrombotic agents. Chest 95:2S–5S, 1989.

62. Sackett DL, Gibson RW, Bross IDJ, Pickern JW: Relation between aortic atherosclerosis and the use of cigarettes and alcohol. N Engl J Med 279:1413–1420, 1968.

63. SHEP Cooperative Research Group. Prevention of stroke by antihypertensive drug treatment in older persons with isolated systolic hypertension: Final results of the Systolic Hypertension in the Elderly Program (SHEP). JAMA 265:3255–3264, 1991.

64. Simons-Morton DG, Cutler JA, Allender PS: Hypertension treatment trials and stroke occurrence revisited a quantitative overview. Ann Epidemiol 3:555–562, 1993.

65. Sniderman A, Shapiro S, Marpole D, et al: Association of coronary atherosclerosis with hyperapobetalipoproteinemia (increased protein but normal cholesterol levels in human low density (beta) lipoproteins). Proc Natl Acad Sci USA 77:604–608, 1980.

66. Tejada C, Strong JP, Montenegro MR, et al: Distribution of coronary and aortic atherosclerosis by geographic location, race and sex. In McGill HC (ed): The Geographic Pathology of Atherosclerosis. Baltimore, Williams & Wilkins, 1968.

67. Tornvall P, Bavenholm P, Landou C, et al: Relation of plasma levels and composition of apolipoprotein B-containing lipoproteins to angiographically defined coronary artery disease in young patients with myocardial infarction. Circulation 88:2180–2189, 1993.

68. Tuomilehto J, Giboers J, Salonen JT, et al: Decline in cardiovascular mortality in North Karelia and other parts of Finland. Br Med J 293:1068–1071, 1986.

69. Uemura K, Pisa Z: Trends of cardiovascular disease: mortality in industrialized countries since 1950. World Health Stat Q 41:155–178, 1988.

70. United States Department of Health and Human Services: The Health Consequences of Smoking: Cardiovascular Disease. Washington, DC: US Dept HHS Public Health Services, Office on Smoking and Health, DHHS publication (PHS) 84:50204, 1983.

71. Williams RR, Hunt SC, Hopkins PN, et al: Familial dyslipidemic hypertension. Evidence from 58 Utah families for a syndrome present in approximately 12% of patients with essential hypertension. JAMA 259:3579–3586, 1988.

72. Willich SN, Lewis M, Lowel H, et al: Physical exertion as a trigger of acute myocardial infarction. N Engl J Med 329:1684–1690, 1993.

73. Witteman JCM, Grobbee DE, Valkenburg HA, et al: Cigarette smoking and the development and progression of aortic atherosclerosis. A 9-year population-based follow-up study in women. Circulation 88:2156–2162, 1993.

74. Zamboni M, Armellini F, Sheiban I, et al: Relation of body fat distribution in men and degree of coronary narrowing in coronary artery disease. Am J Cardiol 70:1135–1138, 1992.

75. Zavaroni I, Bonora E, Pagliara M, et al: Risk factors for coronary artery disease in healthy persons with hyperinsulinemia and normal glucose tolerance. N Engl J Med 320:702–706, 1989.

76. Miller M, Mead LA, Kwiterovich PO, Pearson TA: Dyslipidemia with desirable plasma total cholesterol levels and angiographically demonstrated coronary artery disease. Am J Cardiol 65:1–5, 1990.

77. Luria MH, Erel J, Sapoznikov D, Gotsman MS: Cardiovascular risk factor clustering and the ratio of total cholesterol to high-density lipoprotein cholesterol in angiographically documented coronary artery disease. Am J Cardiol 67:31–36, 1991.

78. Norum RA, Lakier JB, Goldstein S, et al: Familial deficiency of apolipoproteins A-I and C-III and precocious coronary-artery disease. N Engl J Med 306:1513–1519, 1982.

79. Frick MH, Elio O, Haapa K, et al: Helsinki heart study: Primary prevention trial with gemfibrozil in middle-aged men with dyslipidemia. N Engl J Med 317:1237–1245, 1987.

80. Cortellaro M, Boschetti C, Cofrancesco E, et al: The Plat Study: hemostatic function in relation to atherothrombotic ischemic events in vascular disease patients. Principal results. Arterioscler Thromb 12:1063–1070, 1992.

# Chapter 3

# Pathogenesis of Arterial Thrombosis

Cedric J. Carter

Acute organ death such as that occurring in an acute myocardial infarction or an acute stroke is usually the result of intra-arterial thrombus. A consistent observation is that arterial thrombi usually occur in abnormal vessels. There is almost invariably evidence of some atherosclerotic change, and in some instances these changes are of a degree that may cause major hemodynamic disturbance. These findings are very different from venous thrombosis, in which the degree of vessel abnormality is often modest or not discernible using simple light microscopy. It is therefore apparent that atherosclerosis and acute arterial thrombosis are closely linked. What is not clear is whether, in terms of etiology, they are the result of parallel but largely independent processes or whether they are closely linked by a unifying primary pathologic process. One of the unexplained aspects of arterial thrombosis is why, when there may be a very high general degree of atheroma in a population, certain individuals experience early and catastrophic arterial thrombosis, and other individuals do not. This suggests that there is some degree of independence of process between acute arterial thrombosis and atherosclerosis.

Acute arterial thrombosis has three important clinical foci—ischemic thrombotic heart disease, thrombotic stroke, and acute peripheral arterial disease. The degree of vigor with which the etiology of arterial thrombosis at each site has been pursued has varied with both clinical significance and the availability of diagnostic methods. In general, acute coronary thrombosis has been most carefully studied, followed by peripheral arterial disease, in which repeat imaging studies and biopsies are relatively easy tasks. The least studied area has been acute stroke.

Careful biopsy or autopsy studies over many decades have delineated the anatomic pathology of arterial thrombosis. The demonstration of abnormalities of varying degree in the vessel wall has been a consistent finding. In coronary artery thrombosis two general patterns have been observed.[1] In approximately 75% of the cases, the thrombi are associated with a clear break in the endothelial layer that extends beyond the intima. In its minimal form this is now referred to as plaque fissuring. The remaining 25% of the lesions are often associated with severe stenosis and show much more superficial damage to the endothelium. These descriptions of the anatomy of thrombotic lesions have largely relied on light microsopy using conventional polychromatic stains. They represent the end result of what in most cases has been a chronic process. Recent advances in the understanding of arterial thrombosis have built on these observations and have moved into various, more biologically oriented fields. These include the application of hemodynamic models, investigations into fundamental endothelial cell biology, and extension and refinement of knowledge concerning the regulation of the coagulation system.

Virchow's prescient observations concerning the etiology of intravascular thrombosis are still pertinent today.[2] The aspect that has changed is the ability to directly address the issues of changes in the vessel wall, in the flow of blood, and in the nature of blood.

Arterial thrombosis is believed to be the result of variable contributions of the constituents of Virchow's triad. According to the location and anatomy of particular vessels, the relative contribution of the pathologic components varies. In terms of being able to provide a biologic background to the pathophysiology of arterial thrombosis, some understanding of vascular physiology is required.

18

## VESSEL WALL FUNCTION

The function of a normal blood vessel is to deliver and remove substances from organs and tissues. This involves the provision of a suitable conduit for fluid transmission and the ability to allow interchange of molecules and cells between the vascular, cellular, and extracellular spaces, while at the same time protecting the body from the adverse effects of hemorrhage. To fulfill these biologic commitments, blood vessels have to be able to show rapid and dramatic responses to physiologic and pathologic stimuli.

## VESSEL CONTRACTILITY

All blood vessels are able to alter their diameters. There appear to be multiple mediators of vasoconstriction including endothelin,[3] thromboxane $A_2$,[4] and the alpha adrenergic system.[5] Vasoconstriction helps to maintain perfusion pressure to organs and to limit hemorrhage from damaged vessels. Conversely, vasoconstriction can adversely alter hemodynamics and in extreme situations can induce relative or complete stasis and thus predispose to thrombosis. Vasoconstrictive forces are opposed by vasodilatory substances such as prostaglandin $I_2$ ($PGI_2$)[6] and EDRF[7] (nitric oxide). A more current term for EDRF is endothelium-derived nitric oxide, or ENDO.[8] Both $PGI_2$ and ENDO generation are influenced by sheer forces and pulsatile pressure and may explain the historic observation that blood vessels seem to be able to sense high velocity blood flow and dilate.[9, 10]

## VESSEL PERMEABILITY

The endothelium has to permit the passage of gases, molecules of various sizes, and in some circumstances whole cells. Electron microscopy of normal endothelium shows the presence of various pores that may permit molecules as large as lipoproteins to enter and exit endothelial cells.[11] The presence of vesicles suggests a vesicular transit system. Gases (e.g., nitric oxide) can cross the endothelial barrier by simple diffusion. What is not clear is how cells can traverse intact normal endothelium in the general circulation. In specific sites, such as the splenic sinusoids, lymph nodes, the kidney, the liver, and the bone marrow, the endothelial lining is discontinuous, and this is probably a major means of physiologic cellular transit.

## ANTITHROMBOTIC AND PROTHROMBOTIC ENDOTHELIAL COMPONENTS

Normal endothelium, both in an anatomic and functional sense, is the least thrombogenic surface known to man. The formation of a thrombus involves platelet adhesion, platelet release and aggregation, activation of the coagulation cascade, and modulation of fibrinolysis. To prevent thrombosis, normal endothelium must be able to prevent or neutralize these prothrombotic forces.

## ANTITHROMBOTIC PLATELET INTERACTIONS

Platelets are thought to circulate in a resting state and become activated by a variety of biologic stimuli. The development of a platelet plug, in the absence of a hemorrhagic breach in a vessel, is clearly undesirable. There are several means by which endothelium can limit vessel wall platelet accumulation.

ENDO and $PGI_2$, both vasodilators, maintain blood flow and help prevent stasis.[6, 7] They synergize to inhibit platelet endothelial cell and platelet-platelet interaction.[6, 12] Both of these substances are produced in the endothelial cell. $PGI_2$ levels can be increased in endothelial cells by shear stress[13] (see Rheology). $PGI_2$ synthesis can be increased by thrombin.[14] Acetylcholine causes ENDO release; however, the importance of this mechanism in vivo is not clear.[15] It is of interest, however, that ENDO release is decreased in hypertension, diabetes, and atherosclerosis.[16]

Adenosine nucleotides are important modulators of platelet function. Adenosine diphosphate (ADP) and adenosine triphosphate (ATP) are released upon platelet activation. ADP is proaggretory.[17, 18] The endothelium contains enzymes that can convert ADP and ATP to adenosine and adenosine monophosphate (AMP), which are both antiaggregatory.[19]

## PROTHROMBOTIC PLATELET INTERACTIONS

Loss of normal endothelium or alteration of its function diminishes the protective effects of $PGI_2$, ENDO, and the enzymes that break down ADP and ATP. In experimental models, if just the endothelial cells are carefully removed with minimal subendothelial damage, vessels retain much of their resistance to platelet adhesion and aggregation.[20] More substantive subendothelial disruption results in extensive platelet release and aggregation.[21] It is thought that the disruption exposes platelets to collagen fibrils that activate platelets by interaction with the platelet membrane. In addition, various adhesins, including von Willebrand factor (VWF) and fibronectin, are localized in this area.[22] VWF is synthesized in endothelial cells and stored in Weibel-Palade bodies and can be rapidly released by a variety of stimuli.[23–25] At the biochemical level, thrombin causes the release of VWF, but there are clearly other mediators of release, because in humans severe exercise greatly increases plasma VWF levels in the absence of significant thrombin generation.[26]

If a platelet plug forms, it contains a variable amount of fibrin. The endothelium also contains or exhibits substances that will inhibit the formation or the removal of vessel wall fibrin (see later).

## ANTICOAGULANT PROPERTIES

The coagulation cascade that eventually converts soluble fibrinogen into fibrin consists of a series of zymogens that upon activation become serine proteases, which themselves can generate further serine proteases. This process, whether initiated via factor XI in the intrinsic pathway or via factor VII in the extrinsic pathway, eventually generates thrombin.[27, 28] Thrombin, in addition to converting fibrinogen to fibrin, has multiple other effects on the coagulation system of both a pro- and an anticoagulant nature. With respect to serine protease activation of the clotting proteins, there are two important cofactors—thrombin-activated factors V and VIII. These cofactors are part of the so-called prothrombinase and tenase complexes that localize procoagulant activity onto surfaces such as the platelet and the endothelium. Modulation of thrombin activity at the endothelial surface is of potential importance in preventing thrombosis.

Regulation of the serine protease generation of fibrin clot is mediated by several well characterized inhibitory proteins. With respect to direct inhibition of serine proteases is a family of inhibitors called serpins. On the basis of in vitro experiments and clinical observations on the effects of specific deficiencies, antithrombin III (ATIII) appears to be the most important serpin for thrombin regulation. In vitro, the rate of inhibition of thrombin is slow; however, glycosaminoglycans greatly improve the rate of thrombin inhibition by ATIII.[29] Endothelial cells are a rich source of glycosaminoglycans

and, in particular, it is likely that heparan sulphate is an important component of the anticoagulant properties of the vessel wall.

Procoagulant serine protease generation activity is facilitated by the two cofactors Va and VIIIa. In the presence of protein S, activated protein C (APC) will destroy Va and VIIIa.[31] In vitro experiments showed that APC was derived from its zymogen precursor, protein C, by the action of thrombin. On the basis of the requisite kinetics, it seemed very unlikely that sufficient quantities of free thrombin would be available in the body to directly activate protein C. The enigma was solved by the demonstration of large amounts of thrombomodulin on the surface of normal endothelial cells.[32] Thrombin, when it docks onto endothelial cell thrombomodulin, becomes a much more efficient activator of protein C but at the same time loses its other procoagulant activities.[33]

Clinical and laboratory observation plus kinetic considerations suggest that the traditional model for the coagulation cascade is wrong. The historic view included the concept that contact activation of factor XII was an important procoagulant principle, in vivo. The observation of lack of bleeding in congenital factor XII deficiency cases demonstrated that other means of thrombin generation must exist. In terms of kinetics, the extrinsic pathway was an obvious candidate, and current views of the coagulation cascade are that the initial thrombin generation is via the extrinsic pathway. This thrombin, as part of its activities, feeds back to factor XI, bypassing factor XII, and priming the intrinsic pathway.[27] This hypothesis, although attractive, has some shortcomings. If thrombin is kept generating via the extrinsic pathway, intrinsic factor deficiencies such as hemophilia should not cause bleeding. The discovery of a natural inhibitor of the extrinsic pathway, now called Tissue Factor Pathway Inhibitor (TFPI), but previously known as EPI or LACI, appears to provide an explanation for hemostatic dependency on the intrinsic pathway.[34] TFPI is generated during the initiation of the extrinsic pathway, and after a period of time it down-regulates its activities and hence enhances the relative prohemostatic role for the intrinsic pathway.[35] Endothelial cells can synthesize TFPI and are thought to be a major source of this antithrombotic protein.[36]

## PROCOAGULANT PROPERTIES OF ENDOTHELIUM

Endothelial cells can act as a template for the assembly of clotting complexes. The very low concentrations of many of the coagulation factors mean that liquid phase interactions cannot explain the rapid reaction of the coagulation cascade, and some form of reactive surface is needed to support the protein-protein interactions. This concept has been clearly demonstrated; and at least three defined examples of activation complexes appear to be active. In the activation of factor VII, a factor bound to various tissues is involved. Tissue factor is expressed following trauma in a variety of situations. In keeping with the nonthrombogenic properties of normal endothelium, intact endothelial cells do not appear to express tissue factor activity; however, the exposure of endothelial cells to numerous stimuli initiates expression. These stimuli include cellular elements such as polymorphs, lymphocytes, macrophages, and soluble substances including thrombin, kinins, immune complexes, and interleukins.[37] The two other situations in the coagulation cascade wherein procoagulant complexes have been demonstrated are the "tenase" and "prothrombinase" complexes. In the tenase complex, the vitamin K–dependent factors IXa and X together with the cofactor VIIIa are assembled via calcium bridging onto areas of the platelet membrane that are thought to express negatively charged phospholipids. In this conformation, there is rapid activation of zymogen X to Xa. This Xa, in conjunction with cofactor Va, and prothrombin in a similar fashion generate thrombin, hence the term "prothrombinase" complex. Given that the endothelium, although nonthrombogenic in normal circumstances, also has to be prohemostatic in the event of injury, a biologic advantage may be obtained in having a means of localizing efficient coagulation complexes on the endothelium. Some evidence is available to support this concept.[37]

## PROFIBRINOLYTIC PROPERTIES

It is clear from the earlier description that intact, normal endothelium can exhibit antithrombotic properties in a variety of ways. However, despite these defenses, fibrin generation can occur. In addition to the regulatory proteins described earlier, one factor that prevents occlusive thrombosis is the presence of a fibrinolytic system. Cellular fibrinolysis by leukocytes can occur but has never been reliably quantified. What has become apparent in recent years is the importance of plasminogen activators. In a manner similar to that of the coagulation cascade, attempts have been made to define both an intrinsic and an extrinsic

plasminogen activation system. The intrinsic fibrinolytic activation system appears to be factor XII–dependent and involves the kallikrein system.[38] Although this system can be demonstrated in vitro, its importance in vivo is not clear, although it has been suggested that the clinical effect of factor XII deficiency may, in fact, be thrombosis.[39] On the basis of both experimental work and the clinical correlation with ex vivo measurements, the primary plasminogen activator appears to be tissue plasminogen activator (TPA).[40] The endothelial cell is a major source of TPA synthesis and release.[41] In humans, TPA levels rapidly increase following exercise and the injection of active substances such as nicotine, epinephrine, and DDAVP. The rapidity of this response suggests that this is release of preformed TPA.[42] In systems using cultured endothelial cells, it has been proved possible to demonstrate that various agents can increase TPA synthesis as measured by TPA messenger ribonucleic acid (mRNA).[41] In terms of potential physiologic significance, it is of interest that thrombin and shear stress both appear to increase TPA synthesis.[43]

TPA converts plasminogen to plasmin. This enzymatic conversion is greatly enhanced by the binding of TPA to fibrin.[40] With respect to profibrinolytic properties of the endothelial cells, receptors for TPA and plasminogen have been demonstrated on intact endothelial cells, suggesting that fibrin in the ternary complex of fibrin, TPA, and plasmin has the potential to be rapidly lysed.

## ANTIFIBRINOLYTIC PROPERTIES

The main inhibitor of TPA is plasminogen activator inhibitor, type 1 (PAI-1).[44] This substance is also produced and secreted by endothelial cells. It is particularly effective at inhibiting free (versus receptor-bound) TPA (see Profibrinolytic Properties). In addition, TPA that is bound to fibrin is relatively resistant to PAI-1 neutralization. The current theory is that the fibrinolytic potential in any particular situation is a balance between the effects of TPA and those of PAI-1. If the latter predominate, fibrinolysis is decreased.[44] Thrombin, in addition to increasing TPA synthesis, will also increase mRNA of PAI-1. It is unclear as to which effect predominates in vivo.

Several physiologic mediators of increased PAI-1 synthesis do not concomitantly affect TPA production. These include transforming growth factor-beta (TGF-beta), tumor necrosis factor

(TNF), endotoxin, and interleukin-1 (IL-1). The action of any one of these agents represents a prothrombotic situation.[44]

In the event of TPA being able to generate plasmin, further antifibrinolytic and presumably prothrombotic mechanisms are in effect. If plasmin is generated and bound to fibrin or endothelial cell plasmin receptors, it is relatively resistant to its primary inhibitor $\alpha_2$-antiplasmin. In contrast, free plasmin is rapidly inhibited by $\alpha_2$-antiplasmin.[45] The importance of low $\alpha_2$-antiplasmin levels, unlike that of increased PAI-1 levels, in the genesis of arterial thrombosis is not clear.

## RHEOLOGY

In normal circumstances, blood moves freely from organ to organ. Normal endothelium presents a smooth and relatively low-resistance surface. The amount of blood flow determines the rate of delivery and the rate of removal of both cellular and protein elements to the endothelial and vessel surface. In view of the variable size of blood vessels and the huge pressure differences, it is obvious that there are major differences in the local rheologic milieu in normal vessels. On the basis of adaptive evolution, it can be assumed that the normal conditions have been optimized for prolonged efficient function and therefore altered vessel anatomy should have deleterious consequences.[46]

On the basis of a variety of observations, it appears that the initial process in the genesis of a thrombus is platelet adhesion to the vessel wall. This involves several phases, starting with an initial contact. The presumption is that if the endothelial surface is normal, flow is normal, and the platelet is in a resting state; as a consequence, this will be a transient event without sequelae. The next phase of interaction would occur if the above conditions were not satisfied and there was physical attachment of the platelet to the vessel. Subsequently, if the process progressed, shape change, spreading, and eventually platelet release would occur. Once this has occurred, platelets can activate and attract further platelets.[47]

A basic concept in the understanding of the contribution of rheology to the coagulation system is that of the shear force. The term *shear* refers to the sliding motion between two planes. Blood is a viscous substance; if a vessel wall and flowing blood are envisioned, a view of the blood divided into a series of concentric laminae can be made. In cross-section it would look like a horizontal cross-section of an onion. At the most peripheral lamina, which is in direct contact with the vessel wall, the velocity of the blood should approximate to zero. With movement away from the vessel wall, the velocity increases to a maximum in the center of the vessel, assuming that the vessel is of uniform circular shape. In these circumstances, the shear rate is maximal at the vessel wall and zero at the centerline. The difference in relative velocities gives rise to the concept of the shear rate. The interaction between the layers of flowing viscous blood and the vessel wall at varying velocities of the lamina consumes energy, and the force required per unit area necessary to maintain the relative velocities of the laminar flows is termed the *shear stress*. Viscosity is defined as the ratio of the shear stress to the shear rate.[46]

These concepts can be applied to platelet vessel wall interactions. The arrival of platelets at a surface relates to the flow rate, which in turn relates to the wall shear rate. In general, increased platelet adhesion relates to the flow rate and hence the shear rate.[47]

Conditions of extreme high shear stress do not occur in normal arteries, but they can do so in relation to an atherosclerotic plaque or severe stenosis. Under these conditions, there is a marked tendency for platelets to be deposited onto de-endothelialized areas of the vessel.[48] Conversely, in situations of lower shear, predominantly fibrin deposition occurs in de-endothelialized areas. These observations are congruent with the classic pathologic description of venous and arterial thrombi in which, in high flow and hence high shear regions, as in arterial thrombosis, platelet-rich thrombi form.[49] In lower flow regions, whether venous or arterial, the thrombi are mixed and contain an abundance of fibrin together with entrapped red cells.

The issue has become even more interesting with respect to the issue of the role of tissue factor. As described in the section on anticoagulant properties of the endothelium, it has become apparent that the initiation of thrombosis is largely performed via the extrinsic pathway. The kinetics of the extrinsic pathway interactions have traditionally been worked out under highly nonphysiologic conditions. These conditions are usually called *thermodynamically closed static systems*. Recently, several investigators have devised systems to examine the effects of various shear rates on the coagulation enzyme kinetic interactions and have shown them to be shear-dependent.[50] Thus, shear seems to have a role in activation of both platelets and the coagulation cascade. These interactions would appear to be particularly important in relation to the vessel wall and may explain both the location and magnitude of thrombotic changes that occur in relation to atherosclerosis.

## Development of the Atherosclerotic Plaque

As described, the cardinal feature of normal endothelium is its ability to actively prevent the development of thrombosis. Obviously numerous mechanisms damage endothelium, including simple direct trauma, or other mechanisms such as infections, and metabolic toxins such as raised homocysteine levels. The most important damage is the development of what is probably the end result of the endothelial cell insults—atherosclerotic change and plaque formation.

The contribution of atherosclerosis to thrombosis has two components. One part is the direct alteration in endothelial function; the other is the hemodynamic disturbance that will interact with remaining endothelial cell function and the other components of the coagulation system.

Atherosclerosis and thrombosis are clearly related during the process of plaque fissuring and acute thrombosis. What is less clear is the nature and extent of coagulation-atherosclerosis interactions in the earlier phases of the generation of atherosclerosis. In animal models using repeat mechanical injuries, particularly in the presence of high lipid concentrations, atherosclerotic lesions can be generated.[51] In these models there is repeated endothelial cell damage and loss, and the classic platelet adhesion-aggregation-secretion model can be implicated. This is clearly a somewhat artificial system. Repetitive mechanical insults to the vessel wall are not part of normal human physiology, but in the general population, time-dependent generation of atherosclerotic changes is ubiquitous. This implies that there must be more subtle mechanisms operating in the population.

Atherosclerotic lesions can be conveniently divided into three phases of a continuum.[52] The first phase is termed the fatty streak. This consists of the demonstration of collections of lipid-laden macrophages immediately under the intact endothelium. These lesions can be duplicated in animals and nonhuman primates by the prolonged ingestion of high cholesterol diets.[53–55] Platelet deposition is not an initial feature of this lesion, but adherence and invasion by macrophages and lymphocytes are observed.[56] Some of these findings are thought to be related to the effects of oxidized lipoproteins. These lesions progress to intermediate or fibrofatty lesions.[57] They consist of multiple lay-

ers of lipid-containing foam cells together with smooth muscle cells and lymphocytes. The third phase of this process is the development of the fibrous plaque–type lesion. The components of fibrous tissue and necrotic tissue are observed in addition to the foam cells and smooth muscle cell proliferation seen in less mature lesions. At this stage, there may be frank encroachment into the vessel lumen. Unlike the less mature lesions, there may be some loss of endothelial covering, which will expose macrophages. Platelets may adhere to these macrophages, thus providing an early link with the coagulation system.[58] Accumulation of platelets occurs in hemodynamically favorable sites for cell adhesion.[59] This may explain the areas of atherosclerosis observed in the vicinity of vessel branches and bifurcations. Platelets adhering to macrophages can release TGF-alpha and TGF-beta as well as platelet derived endothelial cell growth factor (PD-ECGF).[57] These platelet products complement similar products derived from both macrophages and damaged endothelium and influence the appearance of smooth muscle cells. These smooth muscle cells exhibit a synthetic phenotype and are thought to synthesize much of the extracellular matrix that characterizes the advanced fibrous lesion.[52] From meticulous pathologic studies, it appears that acute occlusive thrombosis largely occurs as a consequence of the interaction of the coagulation system with complications of the advanced fibrous lesion.

## Acute Arterial Thrombosis

Atherosclerotic changes in the form of fatty streaks are present from puberty onward.[60] At this stage of the atherosclerotic lesion, acute arterial thrombosis is exceedingly rare. It is the progression of some of these early lesions over the next few decades that is one of the determinants of acute arterial thrombosis.

Necropsy material of thrombosed coronary arteries shows two principal types of lesions associated with arterial thrombosis. The minority are so-called type I lesions.[1] These lesions are characterized by the presence of a severe but smooth stenosis. There is substantial loss of endothelium, to a degree that is greater than the very patchy loss described in the genesis of the atherosclerotic lesion. This sort of lesion supports the theoretic role of abnormal rheology in the development of acute arterial thrombosis. There is a region of extremely high shear at the entrance to the stenosis, which, in addition to contributing to endothelial loss, may also be of a magnitude to directly activate platelets.[61] Distal to the stenosis is disturbed flow with eddies and an area that facilitates platelet–vessel wall and coagulation interactions.[59]

The other main lesion is termed the type II lesion.[1] This is three times more common in coronary arteries than the type I lesion. The type II change is characterized by the presence of a deep intimal tear or plaque fissure. This results in a ragged stenosis. The common feature between type I and type II lesions is loss of the protective endothelial layers, which has a variety of consequences. The most obvious is the loss of the physical barrier between vessel contents and the subendothelium, permitting both protein and cellular interactions. Local concentrations of the vasodilatory and antiplatelet ENDO and PGI-2 are reduced.[6, 7, 12] The various adhesins, as described in the section on prothrombotic features of the endothelium, are able to interact with their tissue or cellular receptors.[22] Anticoagulant material on the endothelial surface, such as heparan sulfate, is lost.[30] With respect to type II lesions, several aspects are related to the deeper intimal changes. The deep tear exposes considerable amounts of types I and III collagen, which causes platelet adhesion and release.[22] In addition, various monocytes and macrophages are exposed. These cells can express tissue factor.[62] A third aspect is that the thrombus initially forms within the interior of the fissured plaque. This is an area that is relatively protected from shear forces, which tend to remove thrombotic material. A further consequence of the development of the intraplaque thrombosis is further narrowing of the arterial lumen. Narrowing, in turn, introduces new rheologic components into the region. When complete occlusion occurs, it is of interest that the distal thrombus is more of the classic "venous" type organization that reflects the effects of low shear forces.[63]

The importance of the effects of plaque fissuring raises several issues. One obvious question is what determines plaque rupture. Is it the structure of the plaque, the location of the plaque, the physical stresses, or a combination of all these factors? Structure does seem to be important. Plaques that fissure tend to do so at the junction of the plaque cap and the normal intima. Another feature is that a fairly consistent finding in relation to the fissure zone is an area of marked cholesterol deposition that is associated with very scanty collagen development.

Another major issue is that which determines if a plaque rupture proceeds to thrombosis while others do not. This issue is raised because careful examination of coronary blood vessels in people both with and without acute arterial thrombosis shows a surprisingly high frequency (circa 9%) of plaque fissuring in the group that is thrombosis free.[64] If the size of the fissure is factored out, there remain many "benign" fissured plaques. The explanation probably lies in the interaction of many of the other factors, including platelet function, the level of activity of the coagulation system, fibrinolytic activity, and the rheologic milieu.

## Correlations and Interactions of the Components of Acute Thrombosis

From the demonstration of specific risk factors and some understanding of the underlying physiologic components of thrombosis, various themes for investigation have developed. As the focus in a particular area increases, there is a tendency to diverge from the global approach to acute thrombosis espoused by the classical descriptive and experimental pathologists. A series of research disciplines with relatively special interests has developed. A current problem in the advancement of an understanding of the development of acute arterial thrombosis is identification and development of cross-disciplinary interactions.

To try to complelely relate all advances in all areas into a concise unified hypothesis, and do every scientific stakeholder justice, is a formidable, probabably insurmountable task. Using the information discussed in this chapter, including normal and some abnormal physiology, there may be an advantage in re-examining each area and highlighting interactive areas. To simplify the task, this discussion is sequential. However, this is not an ideal format because in reality the interrelationships are a three-dimensional matrix or more properly a three-dimensional Venn diagram. This means, rather like regression analysis, that the factor which is discussed first will cannibalize the discussion of later factors. Without any acknowledgment of scientific or clinical precedent, the components are discussed in the order (1) rheology, (2) platelets, (3) lipids, (4) coagulation, and (5) fibrinolysis.

### Rheology

The effects of rheology on acute thrombosis seem to be largely mediated through platelets, coagulation factors, and possibly some effects on lipid deposition. Experimental stenoses of 80% in flow chambers lead to extensive platelet deposition at the apex of the stenosis.[65] This effect is dependent on the degree of stenosis, and this effect is no longer observed with stenoses of less than 35%. This information correlates with the information from the NASCET study, in which surgical benefit of carotid surgery was most marked in patients with severe stenoses.[66] The executive mechanisms governing platelet deposition in these circumstances are still under investigation, but severe shear conditions can directly activate platelets and modify platelet glycoproteins, and hence, adhesive function is shear-dependent.[61] A further observation of interest is that at higher shear rates, von Willebrand factor rather than fibrinogen seems to be an important determinant of platelet-platelet interaction. This observation is not in keeping with putative explanations of the current epidemiologic observation concerning high fibrinogen levels and myocardial infarction.

There has been much recent interest in reevaluating coagulation enzyme interactions under various shear conditions and correlating these findings with the structure of thrombi. In addition to the work on tissue factor activity and shear, there is some evidence for shear affecting the rate of fibrin polymerization.[67] The observations are in keeping with the distribution of fibrin thrombi in the recirculation region of branching flow.

The effects of rheologic factors on lipids have been little studied. In the development of fatty streaks and eventually plaque lesions, an important component seems to be low-density lipoprotein (LDL) accumulation in the subendothelium. Radio-labeled LDL can show increased endothelial internalization in response to increased shear stress. This stress may also modify the number of LDL receptors.[68]

Information on the effects of shear on fibrinolysis is limited, and this should be an area for future research.

## Platelets

Some aspects of rheology and platelet function have been discussed. This relationship can be approached from a reverse direction, in that platelet deposition alters vessel anatomy and hence its own rheologic environment. This has not been directly studied using platelets but can be simulated in vitro using various models and devices.

Very little information of direct involvement on lipid metabolism by platelets is available. There is an indirect relationship via the various cytokines and growth factors (e.g., PD-EGF, TGF-alpha and TGTF-beta) that are released by secreting platelets.[52] These substances have effects on endothelial cells and macrophages and hence lipid metabolism.

Platelets, when activated by a variety of means, actively enhance the forward rate of the coagulation cascade. The primary facilitator is the presentation of a solid-phase template for the assembly of the essential "tenase" and "prothrombinase" coagulation complexes.[69]

Most noncellular fibrinolysis seems to be mediated by the relationship between TPA and PAI-1. Both of these substances are produced by endothelium and are released at thrombotic sites. Conditions that permit a relatively high level of PAI-1 favor thrombosis.[40] Platelets can facilitate high PAI-1 levels by two mechanisms. Platelets contain high concentrations of PAI-1 that can be released to give high local concentrations. In addition, platelet TGF-beta may enhance PAI-1 production from other cells such as endothelial cells.[70]

Another area in which platelets may influence thrombus generation is by the release of platelet factor 4 (PF4). Endothelial cells are a major source of glycoaminoglycans (GAGs). Some of these substances have a heparin-like activity. In fact, heparin is also a GAG but is present in very small amounts compared with other GAGs such as heparan sulfate.[30] There is direct evidence from animals that PF4 released from animals can neutralize the antithrombotic effects of GAGs.[71] Systemic levels of PF4 are often transient and modest, but as in the case of PAI-1, the key issue may be the generation of high local concentrations at the thrombus site.

## Coagulation System

As described, there is clearly an intimate relationship between the cellular platelets and the coagulation system.[69] The latter in its simplest form can be regarded as simply a system for converting fibrinogen, a sol, into fibrin, a gel.

The earlier section on endothelial cell biology made a case for the importance of the endothelium for both pro- and antithrombotic processes. Until the recent development of human tissue cultures, it has been very difficult to address some of these issues. On the other hand, there has been a long tradition of measurement of liquid coagulation proteins to try to explain the origin of arterial thrombosis. The original concept was that a simple increase in component members of the coagulation cascade would be prothrombotic. Much work has been done in this area, particularly by the Northwick Park group in England.[72] Initially, it appeared as if a variety of clotting proteins showed a correlation with thrombosis. As the epidemiologic techniques were refined, it became apparent that only two factors had much statistical explanatory effect—factor VII and fibrinogen. Platelet effects of a raised fibrinogen are unlikely to be a major contributor to a thrombotic tendency. Similarly, fibrinogen levels are not usually rate-limiting in fibrin generation. With respect to rheologic interactions, the major effect of a high fibrinogen level might be expected to be felt at the microcirculation level, but atherosclerosis is a disease of the larger vessels. We are, therefore, left with a firm epidemiologic observation on fibrinogen levels that is difficult to reconcile with our understanding of acute arterial thrombosis.

Increased levels of factor VII, particularly when measured as total coagulant VII or as circulating active factor VII (VIIa), do provide some biologic rationale for the epidemiologic observations.[73] Two aspects are probably related. First, factor VII appears to be the only clotting factor that can circulate in appreciable amounts in an active form.[74] As discussed, much of the interest in the coagulation cascade in terms of thrombotic response has shifted to the extrinsic pathway. For a long time there has been a concept that an intrinsic level of low-grade activity of the coagulation system was required to permit a rapid thrombotic response. Attempts were made to implicate the factor XII–prekallikrein system, but kinetically the factor VII–tissue factor complex seems a better candidate. If this is indeed the case, high levels of factor VII, in particular factor VIIa, in conjunction with the tissue factor expressing monocytes and macrophages described in the type II plaque fissure, would be an ideal combination to rapidly generate fibrin and, hence, a stable thrombus. The other area of potential interaction is the interaction of factor VII with raised lipids and in particular triglycerides (see Lipids).

Although, strictly speaking, this is negative information, a discussion of the role of the coagulation system would not be complete without specific reference to the role of the natural inhibitors of the coagulation cascade. It is clear from clinical studies that deficiencies of ATIII, protein C and protein S are all associated with an increase in the rate of venous thrombosis. It was naturally anticipated that there would be an increase in arterial thrombosis, either in the coronary arteries or elsewhere. This has proved not to be the case, and the odd case report of an individual association probably reflects the relatively high frequency of these deficiencies in the general population rather than a causal relationship.[75] One highly topical new development is the demonstration of a mutant factor V

that confers a resistance to activated protein C and appears to show a very strong association with venous thrombosis.[76] This new entity has not been evaluated in arterial thrombosis to date, but the negative results associated with primary protein C deficiency suggests that it will probably not be a major risk factor.

## Lipids

Two main areas of activity in arterial thrombosis research have been in lipid biology and the study of the coagulation system, the latter encompassing both the coagulation cascade and associated platelet activities. The rationale for lipid research was initiated by several observations. Classic pathology studies showed the presence of lipid infiltration on atheroma, and clinical studies confirmed a positive relationship between a series of lipid fractions and atherosclerosis.[76] Much of the interest has focussed on cholesterol and its associated lipoproteins such as LDL. Although lipid abnormalities can explain some aspects of atheroma, other studies show platelet participation in the evolution of atheromatous lesions.[78] In addition, there is the observation that acute thrombosis, the final mediator of the adverse effects of atheroma, occurs in an abnormal lipid environment. This biologically intimate relationship has always suggested that it should be possible to establish direct biochemical links between lipid abnormalities and abnormal coagulation. In practice, showing the links has proved to be a difficult task.

An obvious point to start looking for interactions between abnormal lipids and the coagulation system is in the effects of lipids on platelets. In support of this relationship have been a variety of in vitro studies showing that increases in various forms of LDL increase platelet aggregation as well as more sensitive measures of platelet activation, such as increases of intracellular free calcium ion concentrations.[79, 80] Conversely high-density lipoprotein (HDL) has inhibitory effects on platelet function.[81] Attempts to show increased platelet reactivity in vivo in humans by the use of activation markers such as PF4 have given conflicting results. Feeding lipids to African green monkeys, however, did cause a rise in circulating beta thromboglobulin (BTG).[82] As indicated, BTG and PF4 may not be sufficiently sensitive to detect minor degrees of platelet activation, and studies using flow cytometry and antibodies that detect activated subpopulations would be of interest.

Studies both in Europe and North America have implicated raised factor VII levels as a risk factor for acute myocardial infarction.[72, 73] These studies were either cross-section surveys or prospective studies, and they incorporated various measures of lipid levels. A consistent finding has been a positive correlation between plasma triglyceride levels and factor VII levels. This seems to be true whether coagulant factor VII or just the factor VII antigen is measured.[83] It has been shown that the raised factor VII levels in some cases represent an interaction between a particular factor VII genotype and plasma triglycerides.[84] What has not been demonstrated is whether the factor VII levels in hypertriglyceridemics are an additional predictive risk factor.

One of the lipoproteins, Lp(a), shows a strong correlation with both atherogenesis and thrombosis.[85] A component of this lipoprotein, apo(a), shows a strong homology with plasminogen. There is some evidence to show it can compete with plasminogen for its binding sites to both cells and fibrin, again providing a link between lipid abnormalities and the coagulation system.[85]

Raised triglyceride levels appear to decrease fibrinolysis. The nature of this relationship is discussed in more detail.

## Fibrinolysis

Fibrin is found incorporated into developing atherosclerotic plaques. It provides support for the "encrustation" hypothesis of the genesis of atherosclerosis.[1, 52, 86] Fibrin in the form of thrombus is also found in the ubiquitous plaque fissures that are present in the healthy as well as the thrombotic population.[64] This suggests that fibrin deposition is an ongoing process that is related to both the evolution of atherosclerotic plaque and acute thrombotic events. This concept receives indirect support from the demonstration that D-dimer levels increase after TPA infusion in healthy individuals.[87] It therefore seems reasonable that factors that diminish fibrinolysis should show an association with arterial thrombotic events such as coronary thrombosis or thrombotic stroke. The problem with the evaluation of the fibrinolytic system has been inadequate technology. This is particularly true for the assessment of the in vivo activity. Despite these limitations, there is an extensive literature on global fibrinolysis tests such as the euglobulin lysis time and dilute whole blood clot lysis time, but these tests tend to show poor reproducibility and poor standardization. Recent advances in the understanding of the relationship between TPA and PAI-1 have simplified the field somewhat. Several groups have identified raised levels of PAI-1 as a risk factor for coronary artery disease.[88-91] An interaction with

lipids appears possible, in that PAI-1 levels have been shown to have a positive correlation with both triglyceride levels and cholesterol levels.[92-94] The origin of the increased PAI-1 observed in these circumstances has been the subject of considerable investigation. Experiments with human umbilical vein endothelial cell cultures in the presence of various lipid fractions suggest that endothelial release is a more likely source.[95, 96] This work has been extended in a similar fashion to that for factor VII, and it is suggested that the PAI-1 regulation by triglycerides is genotype specific for a PAI-1 gene polymorphism.[97]

## The Future

In summary, the multifactorial nature of arterial thrombosis gives rise to a huge number of potential interactions. The only constant feature seems to be the prerequisite for a damaged endothelium. The ability to grow endothelial cells and advances in molecular biology have opened up a new area of endothelial biology that is still in its infancy but could lead to therapeutic options.

An area that remains underdeveloped is the study of the role of rheology in both thrombosis and fibrinolysis. This may explain some of the apparent anomalies that have been derived from experiments in static or nonphysiologic conditions.

Animal models have given some useful information but usually permit the study of only one variable. The anticipated development of larger transgenic mammals such as rabbits or pigs offers the opportunity to introduce several of the interactive factors that have been described.

A further area of interest is the interpretation of some of the ongoing interventional trials addressing several of the putative underlying pathologies. It will be interesting to see if the successful induction of atheroma regression is accompanied by the anticipated decrease in acute thrombotic events. It is already clear that antiplatelet agents decrease acute thrombosis, but longterm trials in younger patients may answer the vexing question as to the actual contribution of platelets to the evolution of the primary atheromatous lesion.

An area in which an interventional study would be of interest is in the modification of the rheologic properties of blood.

The role of increased factor VII in the acute thrombotic event remains tantalizing, and the results of current trials of longterm anticoagulants are awaited with interest.

The prevalence of preatheromatous lesions

in juveniles suggests that acute arterial thrombosis will never be eradicated. However, by increasing our understanding of its genesis, and hence opportunities for intervention, it may be possible to ensure that thrombotic events occur at a suitably advanced age.

## REFERENCES

1. Davies MJ: A macro and micro view of coronary vascular insult in ischaemic heart disease. Circulation 82[Suppl II]:38, 1990.
2. Virchow R: Phlogose und thrombose in Gefässsystem. I Virchow R (ed): Gesammelte Abhandlungen zur Wissenschaftlichen Medicin. Frankfurt, Germany, Von Meidinger Sohn, 1856, pp 458–636.
3. Walder CE, Thomas R, Thiemermann C, et al: The hemodynamic effects of endothelin-1 in the pithed rat. J Cardiovasc Pharmacol 13[Suppl 5]:S93, 1989.
4. Hirsh PD, Hillis LD, Campbell WB, et al: Release of prostaglandins and thromboxane into the coronary circulation in patients with ischemic heart disease. N Engl J Med 304:685, 1981.
5. Dhital KK, Burnstock G: Adrenergic and non-adrenergic neural control of the arterial wall. In Camilleri J-P, Berry CL, Fiessinger J-N, Bariety J (eds): Diseases of the Arterial Wall. New York, Springer-Verlag, 1989, pp 97–126.
6. Bunting S, Gryglewski R, Moncada S, et al: Arterial walls generate from prostaglandin endoperoxides, a substance which relaxes strips of mesenteric and coeliac arteries and inhibits platelet aggregation. Prostaglandins 12:897, 1976.
7. De Mey JG, Claeys M, Vanhoutte PM: Endothelium-dependent inhibitory effects of acetylcholine, adenosine triphosphate, thrombin, and arachidonic acid in the canine femoral artery. J Pharmacol Exp Ther 222:166, 1982.
8. Palmer RM, Ferrige AG, Moncada S: Nitric oxide release accounts for the biological activity of endothelium-derived relaxing factor. Nature 327:524, 1987.
9. Vane JR, Anggard EE, Botting RM: Regulatory functions of the vascular endothelium. N Engl J Med 323:27, 1990.
10. Zarins CK, Zatina MA, Giddens DP, et al: Shear stress regulation of artery lumen diameter in experimental atherogenesis. J Vasc Surg 5:413, 1987.
11. Grega GJ, Adamski SW, Dobbins DE: Physiological and pharmacological evidence for the regulation of permeability. Fed Proc 45:96, 1986.
12. Radomski MW, Palmer RM, Moncada S: The anti-aggregating properties of vascular endothelium: Interactions between prostacyclin and nitric oxide. Br J Pharmacol 92:639, 1987.
13. Bhagyalakshmi A, Frangos JA: Mechanism of shear-induced prostacyclin production in endothelial cells. Biochem Biophys Res Commun 158:31, 1989.
14. Weksler BB, Ley CW, Jaffe EA: Stimulation of endothelial prostacyclin production by thrombin, trypsin, and the ionophore A23187. J Clin Invest 62:923, 1978.
15. Ludmer PL, Selwyn AP, Shook TL, et al: Paradoxical vasoconstriction induced by acetylcholine in atherosclerotic coronary arteries. N Engl J Med 315:1046, 1986.
16. Gryglewski RJ, Botting RM, Vane JR: Mediators produced by the endothelial cell. Hypertension 12:530, 1988.
17. Born GV: Aggregation of platelets by adenosine diphosphate and its reversal. Nature 194:927, 1962.
18. Fisher GJ, Bakshian S, Baldessare JJ: Activation of human platelets by ADP causes a rapid rise in cytosolic free calcium without hydrolysis of phosphatidylinositol-4,5-biphosphate. Biochem Biophys Res Commun 129:958, 1985.
19. Pearson JD, Gordon JL: Metabolism of adenosine nucleotides by ectoenzymes of vascular endothelial cell and smooth muscle cells in culture. Biochem J 190:421, 1980.
20. Groves HM, Kinlough-Rathbone RL, Richardson M, et al: Platelet interaction with damaged rabbit aorta. Lab Invest 40:194, 1979.
21. Badimon L, Badimon JJ, Galvez A, et al: Influence of arterial damage and wall shear rate on platelet deposition. Ex vivo study in a swine model. Arteriosclerosis 6:312, 1986.
22. Houdijk WPM, Sakariassen KS, Nievelstein PFEM, et al: Role of factor VIII-von Willebrand factor and fibronectin in the interaction of platelets in flowing blood with monomeric and fibrillar human collagen types I and III. J Clin Invest 75:531, 1985.
23. Levine JD, Harlan JM, Harker LA, et al: Thrombin-mediated release of factor VIII antigen from human umbilical vein endothelial cells in culture. Blood 60:531, 1982.
24. Hamilton K, Sims PJ: Changes in cytosolic $Ca^{2+}$ associated with von Willebrand factor release in human endothelial cells exposed to histamines. J Clin Invest 79:600, 1987.
25. Ribes JA, Francis CW, Wagner DD: Fibrin induces release of von Willebrand factor from endothelial cells. J Clin Invest 79:117, 1987.
26. Andrew M, Carter C, O'Brodovich H, et al: Increase in factor VIII complex and fibrinolytic activity are dependent on exercise intensity. J Appl Physiol 60:1917, 1986.
27. Gailani D, Broze GJ: Factor XI activation in a revised model of blood coagulation. Science 253:909, 1991.
28. Nemerson Y, Repke D: Tissue factor accelerates the activation of coagulation factor VII: The role of the bifunctional cofactor. Thromb Res 49:351, 1985.
29. Rosenberg RD, Damus PS: The purification and mechanism of action of human antithrombin-heparin cofactor. J Biol Chem 248:6490, 1973.
30. Marcum JA, Rosenberg RD: Heparinlike molecules with anticoagulant activity are synthesized by cultured endothelial cell. Biochem Biophys Res Commun 126:365, 1985.
31. Marlar RA, Kleiss AJ, Griffin JH: Mechanism of action of human activated protein C, a thrombin-dependent anticoagulant enzyme. Blood 59:1067, 1982.
32. Maruyama I, Bell CE, Majerus PW: Thrombomodulin is found on endothelium of arteries, veins, capillaries, lymphatics, and on syncytiotrophoblast of human placenta. J Cell Biol 101:363, 1985.
33. Jakubowski HV, Kline MD, Owen WG: The effect of bovine thrombomodulin on the specificity of bovine thrombin. J Biol Chem 261:3876, 1986.
34. Broze GJ Jr, Miletich JP: Characterization of the inhibition of tissue factor in serum. Blood 69:150, 1987.
35. Broze GJ Jr, Warren LA, Novotny WF, et al: The lipoprotein-associated coagulation inhibitor that inhibits the factor VII-tissue factor complex also inhibits factor $X_a$: Insight into its possible mechanism of action. Blood 71:335, 1988.
36. Bajaj MS, Rana SV, Wysolmerski RB, et al: Inhibitor of the factor $VII_a$-tissue factor complex is reduced in patients with disseminated intravascular coagulation but not in patients with severe hepatocellular disease. J Clin Invest 79:1874, 1987.
37. Jaffe EA: Biochemistry, immunology, and cell biology of endothelium. In Colman RW, Hirsh J, Marder VJ,

Salzman EW (eds): Hemostasis and Thrombosis, ed 3. Philadelphia, JB Lippincott, 1994, pp 724–725.

38. Kaplan AP, Silverberg M: The coagulation-kinin pathway of human plasma. Blood 70:1, 1987.

39. McPherson RA: Thromboembolism in the Hageman trait. Am J Clin Pathol 68:420, 1977.

40. Bachmann F, Kruithof EKO: Tissue plasminogen activator: Chemical and physiological aspects. Semin Thromb Hemost 10:6, 1984.

41. Levin EG, Loskutoff DJ: Cultured bovine endothelial cells produce both urokinase and tissue-type plasminogen activators. J Cell Biol 94:631, 1982.

42. Prowse CV, Cash D: Physiologic and pharmacologic enhancement of fibrinolysis. Semin Thromb Hemost 10:51, 1984.

43. Diamond SL, Sharefkin JB, Dieffenbach C, et al: Tissue plasminogen activator messenger RNA levels increase in cultured human endothelial cells exposed to laminar shear stress. J Cell Physiol 143:364, 1990.

44. Loskutoff DJ, Sawdey M, Mimuro J: Type 1 plasminogen activator inhibitor. In Coller B (ed): Progress in Hemostasis and Thrombosis, vol 9. Philadelphia, WB Saunders, 1989, pp 87–116.

45. Aoki N, Harpel PC: Inhibitors of the fibrinolytic system. Semin Thromb Hemost 10:24, 1984.

46. Goldsmith HL, Turitto VT: Rheological aspects of thrombosis and haemostasis: Basic principles and applications. Thromb Haemost 55:415, 1986.

47. Turitto VT, Baumgartner HR: Initial deposition of platelets and fibrin on vascular surfaces in flowing blood. In Colman RW, Hirsh J, Marder VJ, Salzman EW (eds): Hemostasis and Thrombosis, ed 3. Philadelphia, JB Lippincott, 1994, 805–822.

48. Baumgartner HR, Turitto VT, Weiss HJ: Effect of shear rate on platelet interaction with subendothelium in citrated and native blood. II. Relationships among platelet adhesion, thrombus dimensions, and fibrin formation. J Lab Clin Med 95:208, 1978.

49. Weiss HJ, Turitto VT, Vivic WJ, et al: Fibrin formation, fibrinopeptide A release, and platelet thrombus dimensions on subendothelium exposed to flowing native blood: Greater in factor XII and XI than in factor VIII and IX deficiency. Blood 63:1004, 1994.

50. Contino P, Repke D, Nemerson Y: A continuous flow reactor system for the study of blood coagulation. Thromb Haemost 66:138, 1991.

51. Moore S: Injury mechanisms in atherogenesis. In Moore S (ed): Vascular Injury and Atherosclerosis. New York, Marcel Dekker, 1981, pp 131–148.

52. Ross R: The pathogenesis of atherosclerosis: A perspective for the 1990s. Nature 362:801, 1993.

53. Gerrity Rg, Naito HK, Richardson M, et al: Dietary induced atherogenesis in swine: Morphology of the intima in prelesion stages. Am J Pathol 95:775, 1979.

54. Rosenfeld ME, Tsukada T, Chait A, et al: Fatty streak initiation in Watanabe hereditable hyperlipemic and comparably hypercholesterolemic fat-fed rabbits. Arteriosclerosis 7:9, 1987.

55. Faggiotto A, Ross R, Harker L: Studies of hypercholesterolemia in the non-human primate. I. Changes that lead to fatty streak formation. Arteriosclerosis 4:323, 1984.

56. Tsukada T, Rosenfeld M, Ross R, et al: Immunocytochemical analysis of cellular components in atherosclerotic lesions. Use of monoclonal antibodies with the Watanabe and fat-fed rabbit. Arteriosclerosis 6:601, 1986.

57. Ross R: The pathogenesis of atherosclerosis—An update. N Engl J Med 314:488, 1986.

58. Faggiotto A, Ross R: Studies of hypercholesterolemia in the non-human primate. II. Fatty streak conversion to fibrous plaque. Arteriosclerosis 4:341, 1984.

59. Zarins Ck, Giddens DP, Bharadvaj BK, et al: Carotid bifurcation atherosclerosis: Quantitation of plaque localization with flow velocity profiles and wall shear stress. Circ Res 53:502, 1983.

60. Stary HC: Evolution and progression of atherosclerotic lesions in coronary arteries of children and young adults. Arteriosclerosis 9[Suppl]:I–19, 1989.

61. Ruggeri ZM: Mechanisms of shear-induced platelet adhesion and aggregation. Thromb Haemost 70:119, 1993.

62. Wilcox JN, Smith KM, Schwartz SM, et al: Localization of tissue factor in the normal vessel wall and in the atherosclerotic plaque. Proc Natl Acad Sci USA 86:2839, 1989.

63. Freiman DG: The structure of thrombi. In Colman RW, Hirsh J, Marder VJ, Salzman EW (eds): Hemostasis and Thrombosis, ed 2. Philadelphia, JB Lippincott, 1987, pp 1123–1135.

64. Davies MJ, Bland JM, Hangartner JRW, et al: Factors influencing the presence or absence of acute coronary thrombi in sudden ischaemic death. Eur Heart J 10:203, 1989.

65. Turitto VT, Badimon L, Gemmell C: Basic mechanisms of thrombosis on stenotic lesions: Mediation of platelet and coagulation events by blood flow. In Grepaldi G, Gotto AM, Manzato E, Baggio G (eds): Atherosclerosis VIII. Amsterdam, Excerpta Medica, 1989, pp 437–442.

66. North American Symptomatic Carotid Endarterectomy Trial Collaborators: Beneficial effects of carotid endarterectomy in symptomatic patients with high-grade stenosis. N Engl J Med 325:445, 1991.

67. Tippe A, Muller-Mohnssen H: Shear dependence of the fibrin coagulation kinetics in vitro. Thromb Res 72:379, 1993.

68. Nerem RM, Levesque MJ, Logan SA, et al: Biologic responses of vascular endothelial cells to shear stress. In Grepaldi G, Gotto AM, Manzato E, Baggio G (eds): Atherosclerosis VIII. Amsterdam, Excerpta Medica, 1989, pp 421–424.

69. Mann KG: Membrane-bound enzyme complexes in blood coagulation. In Spaet TH (ed): Progress in Hemostasis and Thrombosis 7. Orlando, Grune & Stratton, 1984, pp 1–38.

70. Laiho M, Saksela O, Keski-Oha J: Transforming growth factor-beta induction of type-I plasminogen activator inhibitor. J Biol Chem 262:17467, 1987.

71. Marcum JA, McKenney JBM, Rosenberg RD: The acceleration of thrombin-antithrombin complex formation in rat hind quarters via naturally occurring heparin-like molecules bound to the endothelium. J Clin Invest 74:2003, 1984.

72. Meade TW, Mellows S, Brozivic M, et al: Haemostatic function and ischaemic heart disease: Principal results of the Northwick Park Heart Study. Lancet 2:533, 1986.

73. Hoffman C, Shah A, Sodums M, et al: Factor VII activity state in coronary artery disease. J Lab Clin Med 111:475, 1988.

74. Morrissey JH, Macik BG, Neuenschwander PF, et al: Quantification of activated factor VII levels in plasma using a tissue factor mutant selectively deficient in promoting factor VII activation. Blood 81:734, 1993.

75. Nachman RL, Silverstein R: Hypercoagulable states. Ann Intern Med 119:819, 1993.

76. Bertina RM, Koeleman BPC, Koster T, et al: Mutation in blood coagulation factor V associated with resistance to activated protein C. Nature 369:64, 1994.

77. Castelli WP: Epidemiology of coronary heart disease. The Framingham Study. Am J Med 76:4, 1984.

78. Davies MJ, Woolf N, Rowles PM, et al: Morphology of

the endothelium over the atherosclerotic plaques in human coronary arteries. Br Heart J 60:459, 1988.

79. Knorr M, Locher R, Vogt E, et al: Rapid activation of human platelets by low concentrations of low density lipoproteins via phosphatidylinositol cycle. Eur J Biochem 172:753, 1988.

80. Katzman PL, Bose R, Henry S, et al: Serum lipid profile determines platelet reactivity to native and modified LDL-cholesterol in humans. Thromb Haemost 71:627, 1994.

81. Colli S, Maderna P, Tremoli E, et al: Prostacyclin-lipoprotein interactions: Studies on human platelet aggregation and adenylate kinase. Biochem Pharmacol 34:2451, 1985.

82. Lewis JC, Taylor RG: Effects of varying dietary fatty acid ratios on the plasma lipids and platelet function in the African green monkey. Atherosclerosis 77:167, 1989.

83. Hoffman CJ, Miller RH, Hultin MB: Correlation of factor VII activity and antigen with cholesterol and triglycerides in healthy young adults. Arterioscler Thromb 12:267, 1992.

84. Humphries DE, Lane A, Green F, et al: Factor VII coagulant activity and antigen in healthy men are determined by interaction between factor VII genotype and plasma triglyceride concentration. Arterioscler Thromb 14:193, 1994.

85. Loscalzo J: Lipoprotein(a). A unique risk factor for atherothrombotic disease. Arterioscler Thromb 10:672, 1990.

86. Smith EB, Keen GA, Grant A, et al: Fate of fibrinogen in human arterial intima. Arteriosclerosis 10:263, 1990.

87. Siefried E, Rijken DC, Hoegee E, et al: Fibrin degradation products—FbDPs—appear in blood of healthy volunteers upon infusion of recombinant tissue type plasminogen activator (rt-PA). In Lowe GDO, Douglas JT, Forbes CD, Henschen A (eds): Fibrinogen 2: Biochemistry, Physiology, and Clinical Relevance. Amsterdam, Excerpta Medica, 1987, pp 289–292.

88. Anzar J, Estelles A, Tormo G, et al: Plasminogen activator activity and other fibrinolytic variables in patients with coronary artery disease. Br Heart J 59:535, 1988.

89. Paramo JA, Colucci M, Collen D, et al: Plasminogen activator inhibitor in the blood of patients with coronary artery disease. Br Med J 291:573, 1985.

90. Hamsten A, Blomback M, Wiman B, et al: Haemostatic function in myocardial infarction. Br Heart J 55:58, 1986.

91. Hamsten A, Wiman B, De Faire U, et al: Increased plasma levels of a rapid inhibitor of tissue plasminogen activator in young survivors of myocardial infarction. N Engl J Med 313:1557, 1985.

92. Lowe GDO, McArdle BM, Stromberg P, et al: Increased blood viscosity and fibrinolytic inhibitor in type II hyperlipoproteinaemia. Lancet 1:472, 1982.

93. Mehta J, Mehta P, Dawson D, et al: Plasma tissue plasminogen activator levels in coronary artery disease: Correlation with age and serum triglyceride concentrations. J Am Coll Cardiol 9:263, 1987.

94. Raccah D, Alessi MV, Scelles C, et al: Plasminogen activator inhibitor in various types of endogenous hypertriglyceridemia. Fibrinolysis 7:171, 1993.

95. Mussoni L, Mannucci L, Sirtori M, et al: Hypertriglyceridemia and regulation of fibrinolytic activity. Arterioscler Thromb 12:19, 1992.

96. Stiko-Rahm A, Wiman B, Hamstem A, et al: Secretion of plasminogen activator inhibitor-1 from cultured human umbilical vein endothelial cells is induced by very low density lipoprotein. Arteriosclerosis 10:1067, 1990.

97. Dawson S, Hamsten A, Wiman B, et al: Genetic variation at the plasminogen activator inhibitor-1 locus is associated with altered levels of plasminogen activator inhibitor-1 activity. Arterioscler Thromb 11:183, 1991.

# PART ONE

# CORONARY ARTERY DISEASE AND CARDIOVASCULAR DISEASE

## Chapter 4

# Antiplatelet Therapy in Cardiovascular Disease

Scott H. Goodnight

Clinical trials have clearly shown that antiplatelet agents substantially lower rates of arterial occlusion in patients with cardiovascular disease.[1, 2, 3II, 4I, 5I, 6I] Other sections of this volume analyze these trials in detail and make specific recommendations for treatment of specific vascular disorders. This chapter examines antiplatelet therapy from a broader perspective and covers the medically relevant pharmacology of the currently available antiplatelet drugs (particularly aspirin and ticlopidine), the benefits and risks of antiplatelet therapy combined with anticoagulants, and the rationale for the use of antiplatelet agents in the treatment of arterial disease. Thereafter, an assessment of the overall efficacy of these agents is presented. The concluding section reviews some promising new antiplatelet agents, several of which are now being tested in humans.

## ASPIRIN

### Antithrombotic Effects of Aspirin

Salicylic acid (from plant sources) has been used for thousands of years for symptomatic treatment of fever and rheumatic pain.[7] In the late 1890s, acetylsalicylic acid for therapeutic use was synthesized and, because of its effectiveness, quickly replaced salicylic acid in medical practice. Vane discovered in 1971 that aspirin inhibited prostaglandin synthesis in guinea pig lung, and that same year Smith and Willis showed that aspirin blocked prostaglandin production in human platelets.[8, 9] Subsequently it has been amply demonstrated that aspirin irreversibly inhibits platelet cyclooxygenase with reduced thromboxane synthesis. Because of this effect, platelet aggregation (but not platelet adhesion) is impaired, and the skin bleeding time is prolonged. The effects of aspirin on platelet function are widely regarded as the primary mechanism by which aspirin inhibits platelet-mediated thrombosis.[2] Aspirin also inhibits cyclooxygenase in endothelial cells, which limits prostacyclin synthesis, a potentially detrimental effect that could reduce the antithrombotic efficacy of the drug.[10]

### Low-dose or High-dose Aspirin for Treatment of Thrombosis?

The optimal dose of aspirin to prevent thromboembolism with the least risk of bleeding remains controversial. Conceptually, a dosage regimen that substantially impairs platelet thromboxane synthesis but spares endothelial cell prostacyclin production would seem ideal. Therapeutic strategies to maximize benefit have included the use of ultra low doses of aspirin (e.g., 30–60 mg daily) and prolongation of the interval between doses to 48 hours (e.g., 325 mg every other day). To monitor these effects, plasma or serum thromboxane, $PGI_2$, or the urinary metabolites of these eicosanoids have been measured as surrogate indices of antithrombotic efficacy.[11] However, these data do not necessarily predict success when controlled clinical studies are performed. For example, large trials have now shown evidence of efficacy with doses of aspirin as low as 30 mg and as high as 3,000 mg daily, which suggests that diminution of prostacyclin synthesis may not be clinically relevant.[12] Low-dose therapy is associated with less bleeding and is now generally preferred by clinicians. However, not all investigators would accept this contention. Some neurologists suggest (based on clinical trial data) that higher doses of aspirin (e.g., 650 mg twice daily) are more effective than lower doses in the prevention of transient ischemic attacks (TIA) or stroke.[13, 14] One trial suggested that 900 mg daily of aspirin was better than 50 mg daily in preventing enlargement of carotid atherosclerotic plaques as measured by ultrasound.[15] Perhaps higher doses of aspirin are required to prevent atherosclerotic plaque growth than are needed to inhibit platelet-mediated thrombosis. In addition, very-low-dose aspirin regimens may not effectively inhibit platelet aggregation in all patients, so that individualization of therapy may be required.[16V]

## New Formulations of Aspirin

Two new formulations of aspirin have been developed and tested in humans. The first of these is a low-dose controlled-release preparation in which 75 mg of aspirin has been imbedded in a wax matrix that allows 10 mg of aspirin to be released every hour.[17] The low concentrations of aspirin cause acetylation of platelet cyclooxygenase in the presystemic (portal) circulation, but the aspirin is then rapidly inactivated in the liver so that systemic prostacyclin production is not affected. Urinary thromboxane metabolites are substantially reduced (equivalent to 162.5 mg/day of rapid-release aspirin), but the excretion of $PGI_2$ metabolites is preserved. Because it takes 2 to 4 days to maximally suppress thromboxane synthesis with this product, a loading dose of 162.5 mg of regular aspirin is required if immediate antiplatelet effects are desired. Additional studies will be needed to determine if controlled-release aspirin does indeed have therapeutic advantages over traditional low-dose aspirin, that is, less gastrointestinal toxicity and enhanced antithrombotic effect.

A dermal preparation of aspirin has been developed that also selectively inhibits platelet cyclooxygenase but spares prostacyclin biosynthesis.[18] A dermal solution that contains 750 mg of aspirin is applied to the skin. It requires approximately 10 days for maximal (greater than 95%) inhibition of platelet thromboxane as measured in serum and urine, whereas urinary prostacyclin metabolites decrease by only 20% in that time. $PGI_2$ synthesis stimulated by bradykinin infusions was unaltered in this trial. Benefits from this aspirin preparation could include an enhanced efficacy and a reduced rate of gastrointestinal hemorrhage. A side effect was mild skin irritation in half of the patients.

## Risks of Bleeding With Aspirin

Some assessment of the risks of bleeding due to aspirin is necessary for comparison with the antithrombotic benefits of the drug. Minor bleeding such as bruising or mild epistaxis is consistently increased in patients taking aspirin, but serious hemorrhage that leads to disability or death is of more clinical importance. Overall rates of central nervous system (CNS) hemorrhage with aspirin are slightly, but not significantly, increased over bleeding with placebo in most of the major clinical trials. For example, in a group of otherwise well physicians (Physicians Health Study—PHS) who took either 325 mg of aspirin every other day or placebo, the relative risk of CNS hemorrhage in the aspirin group was 2.14% ($p=.06$).[19I] In the British Doctors Trial, disabling (but not total) stroke was significantly increased ($p=.05$), although it is unclear which of these events were hemorrhagic rather than thrombotic in origin.[20II] In contrast, rates of CNS bleeding were not increased with aspirin therapy in the large Nurses Prospective Trial[21III] or in ISIS-2.[22I] In a more elderly and possibly higher risk population of patients enrolled in the Swedish Aspirin Low-dose Trial (SALT), there was a slight but statistically significant increase in CNS bleeding (1.5% with 75 mg of aspirin per day versus 0.45% with placebo; $p=.03$).[23I]

Major gastrointestinal (GI) bleeding is also increased in patients taking aspirin in many of the large clinical trials. For example, in the PHS study, 3.3% of patients on aspirin reported melena compared with 2.2% receiving the placebo ($p<.00001$).[191] One patient died of GI hemorrhage in the trial, and he was enrolled in the aspirin arm. In the SALT (low-dose aspirin), severe GI bleeding was reported in 1.6% of patients receiving aspirin compared with 0.6% of patients receiving placebo.[231]

In a 1993 study, a group of 406 healthy elderly subjects (over 70 years) were followed for 1 year.[241] Half of them received 100 mg of enteric-coated aspirin daily; the other half were given placebo. Overt GI bleeding occurred in 3% of the subjects receiving aspirin compared with none in the placebo group. Moreover, a small but significant decrease in mean hemoglobin levels was observed in those taking aspirin (i.e., a fall of 0.33 versus 0.11 g/dl; $p<.05$). Although there are few data available for a direct comparison of bleeding risks with increasing doses of aspirin, there appears to be a clearcut dose-response relationship between the amount of aspirin consumed and rates of bleeding. For example, in the Dutch TIA trial, major bleeding complications were found to be 2.6% in the 30 mg/day group, which was increased to 3.2% in the 283 mg/day cohort.[251] In the UK-TIA aspirin trial (2,435 patients), GI hemorrhage occurred in 5% of the patients receiving 1,200 mg/day, 3% in those receiving 300 mg/day, and 1% in those receiving placebo.[261]

Overall, most large trials report statistically significant increases in total and major bleeding, with small increases in CNS or GI bleeding. The magnitude of the increased risk of major bleeding is small (e.g., 1–2% of patients). These figures must be compared with the sometimes substantial benefits of therapy (e.g., reductions in cardiovascular morbidity or mortality that can range from 15% to more than 75%).

## TICLOPIDINE

Ticlopidine is a thienopyridine derivative that effectively inhibits platelet function and is approved for clinical use in the United States.[27] In contrast to aspirin, ticlopidine blocks adenosine diphosphate (ADP)–induced platelet aggregation, perhaps by impairing the binding of fibrinogen to the glycoprotein IIb/IIIa receptor.[28V, 29V] The bleeding time is prolonged to a greater degree than with aspirin.[30] The major effect of ticlopidine is most likely on the megakaryocyte because it takes 3 to 5 days to induce platelet inhibition, and the effect persists for about 1 week after the drug has been stopped.[30] The recommended dose is 250 mg twice daily. The drug is normally taken with meals to enhance absorption and decrease GI side effects.[31II]

This antiplatelet agent has been shown to be effective for treatment of patients with vascular disease. Large clinical trials have shown benefit in patients with recent thromboembolic stroke (The Canadian American Aspirin Study—CATS),[321] TIA (Ticlopidine Aspirin Stroke Study—TASS),[331] and unstable angina.[341, 35] Other studies have suggested efficacy of ticlopidine in patients with intermittent claudication, coronary artery bypass grafts,[361] and diabetic retinopathy.[371]

An important question is whether ticlopidine is superior to aspirin. In the TASS trial, more than 3,000 patients received either ticlopidine (250 mg bid) or aspirin (650 mg bid) if they had suffered a recent TIA, retinal ischemic episode, or minor stroke. Nonfatal stroke and death from all causes were the primary outcome events. At 3 years, death or nonfatal stroke was 17% in the ticlopidine group and 19% in the aspirin group (12% relative risk reduction, $p=.048$).[331]

In CATS, ticlopidine was compared with placebo in 1,053 patients who developed a recent atherothrombotic or lacunar stroke. Of the patients taking ticlopidine, 10.8% per year developed a primary outcome event (ischemic stroke, myocardial infarction, or vascular death) compared with 15.3% in the placebo group (risk reduction 30%, $p=.006$).[321] Because previous trials in stroke patients have not shown a benefit of aspirin, it is possible that ticlopidine may prove superior to aspirin for patients who have suffered a completed stroke. To clarify the issue, a direct comparison of the two agents in a randomized clinical trial will be necessary.

Data from these trials showed that there is no difference in efficacy in men and women. A 1993 published analysis of a subgroup of patients from TASS showed that ticlopidine was effective in nonwhites, and the benefit was similar in magnitude to that of the total series.[381]

Several side effects have occurred in patients taking ticlopidine.[39] About 20% develop diarrhea (compared with 10% in aspirin-treated patients), and 12% develop skin rash (5% with aspirin). There is an increase in serum cholesterol of about 10%. Of greater concern, approximately 1% of patients develop severe neutropenia (absolute neutrophil count of less than 500/mm$^3$), which almost always occurs in the first 3 months of therapy and is rapidly reversible with discontinuation of the drug. Of interest, neutropenia did not occur in the subgroup of nonwhite patients enrolled in TASS. Because of the neutropenia, complete blood counts at

2-week intervals after therapy have been initiated and are considered mandatory.

Rare complications of treatment include a thrombotic thrombocytopenic purpura–(TTP)-like syndrome, which is often fatal,[40] and aplastic anemia.[41] One study described a drug interaction with cyclosporin A (CsA) in heart transplant patients. CsA levels fell substantially (136 ng/ml to 72 ng/ml; $p<.001$) despite constant dosing with the CsA.[42]

At the present time, the use of ticlopidine should be considered in patients who cannot tolerate aspirin or who are refractory to it. Examples include patients who are allergic to aspirin (e.g., asthmatics), those who have peptic ulcer or other gastric disease, and patients who develop recurrent thromboembolism while on aspirin.

## DIPYRIDAMOLE

Dipyridamole is a phosphodiesterase inhibitor that has been given alone or in combination with aspirin to prevent thrombosis in patients with mechanical cardiac valves or other cardiovascular abnormalities.[43, 44] However, a review of prior clinical trials suggests that dipyridamole is not a very effective antithrombotic agent when used alone, and it does not add significantly to the benefits of aspirin.[12] One possible indication for dipyridamole is as an adjunct to warfarin in patients with mechanical cardiac valves who develop thromboembolism while on oral anticoagulants and who cannot tolerate low doses of aspirin.[45]

## COMBINED ANTITHROMBOTIC THERAPY—ASPIRIN PLUS WARFARIN

Combination therapy with an anticoagulant such as warfarin plus an antiplatelet agent such as aspirin appears attractive, at least on the surface. If enhanced antithrombotic efficacy can be obtained without a major increase in risk, combined therapy would clearly be worthwhile. Oral anticoagulants are classically used for venous thromboembolism, and antiplatelet agents are used for arterial occlusion, but sometimes the opposite strategy can also be effective. For example, in two studies coumarin anticoagulants have been shown to be very effective in reducing recurrent myocardial infarction (MI), stroke, and death in patients with a history of MI.[46I, 47I] Conversely, antiplatelet therapy may sometimes be of benefit in situations in which anticoagulants are often used, such as in prevention of cerebral emboli in patients with nonvalvular atrial fibrillation (NVAF).[48I]

Potential beneficial effects of combined therapy can be examined in three clinical trials in which oral anticoagulants were studied with or without the addition of aspirin. All three studies involved patients with mechanical cardiac valves. In a trial reported by Chesebro and coworkers in 1983, warfarin (International Normalization Ratio [INR] approximately 3–6) plus aspirin (500 mg/day) was no better than warfarin alone in the prevention of thromboembolism (1.8/100 patient-years versus 1.2/100 patient-years).[52] In another randomized trial, warfarin plus 1 g of aspirin per day was shown to be associated with fewer thromboembolic complications than warfarin alone.[50]

A 1993 published trial from Canada showed a striking risk reduction of 77% in major systemic emboli or death from vascular causes ($p<.001$) when delayed release enteric-coated low-dose aspirin (100 mg/day) was added to warfarin (INR 3–4.5).[51I] Therefore, the composite data suggest that the addition of low-dose aspirin to warfarin produces sharply decreased mortality, particularly from vascular causes, as well as major systemic embolization in patients with cardiac valve replacement.

Four controlled studies have addressed the risks of bleeding in patients receiving combined therapy as compared with warfarin alone.[51I, 53I] As seen in Figure 4–1, total bleeding in each of the trials was significantly increased when aspirin was used. However, major hemorrhage (requiring transfusion or hospitalization or producing death) was increased to the greatest extent in patients on higher doses (500–1,000 mg/day) of aspirin. Patients on low-dose aspirin (75–100 mg/day) had only modest increases in serious bleeding. Importantly, therefore, the increase in major bleeding seemed to be more closely associated with aspirin dose than with the intensity of the warfarin therapy. Even high-intensity warfarin when given with low-dose aspirin appeared to be relatively safe.[51I]

Turpie and coworkers performed a risk-benefit analysis in their patients treated with high-intensity warfarin and low-dose aspirin.[51I] If rates of nonfatal intracranial hemorrhage and death from hemorrhage are combined with those of major systemic emboli and death from vascular causes, a risk reduction of 65% was observed (11.6%/year versus 4.2%/year; $p<.001$), suggesting that the increase in major bleeding was more than compensated by a reduction in thromboembolism (Fig. 4–2).

Although the indications for combined treatment continue to evolve, it would seem prudent

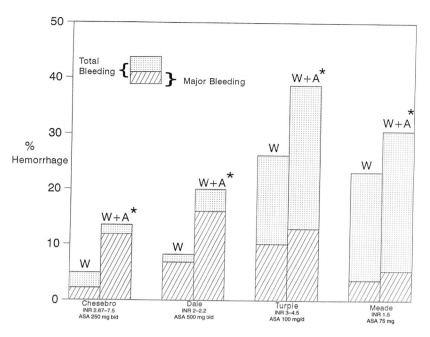

**Figure 4–1.** A comparison of total and major bleeding in four trials of warfarin with aspirin (W + A) or warfarin alone (W). An asterisk (*) indicates a statistically significant difference between (W) and (W + A) groups. (Data from Guwitz, et al;[49] Dale, et al;[50] Turpie, et al;[51] and Meade, et al.[53])

to employ the lowest effective dose of oral anticoagulants, such as INR 3 (in the case of artificial heart valves) or INR 2 to 3 for other indications, and a low dose of aspirin (e.g., 65 mg/day). Patients in whom combined therapy should be considered include (1) those with artificial cardiac valves, (2) those who develop recurrent thromboembolism on optimal oral anticoagulant therapy, and (3) those who have a clear indication for oral anticoagulant therapy, but who also may benefit from antiplatelet agents (e.g., patients with both venous and arterial thromboembolic disease).

Combination anticoagulant-antiplatelet therapy should be considered only in patients in whom the risk of major thromboembolism is quite high (such as those with mechanical cardiac valves) to justify the increased risk of major

bleeding. Other indications may become clearer in the future. For example, the results of a large primary prevention trial in which patients with myocardial infarction are being treated with very-low-dose oral anticoagulants (INR 1.5) along with very-low-dose aspirin (75 mg/day) should soon be complete.[54]

## RATIONALE FOR ANTIPLATELET AGENTS IN CARDIOVASCULAR DISEASE

Although the treatment is often the same (e.g., low-dose aspirin), the rationale for antiplatelet agents often varies depending on the nature of the underlying disorder. As new therapies are developed, treatment is likely to be-

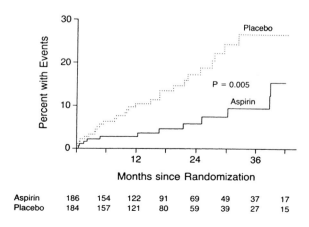

**Figure 4–2.** Cumulative risk of major systemic embolism, nonfatal intracranial hemorrhage, death from hemorrhage, or death from vascular causes in patients with heart valve replacement receiving warfarin plus placebo or warfarin plus aspirin (100 mg/day). (Used with permission from Turpie AGG, et al: A comparison of aspirin with placebo in patients treated with warfarin after heart-valve replacement. N Engl J Med 329:524–529, 1993.)

| | | | | | | | | |
|---|---|---|---|---|---|---|---|---|
| Aspirin | 186 | 154 | 122 | 91 | 69 | 49 | 37 | 17 |
| Placebo | 184 | 157 | 121 | 80 | 59 | 39 | 27 | 15 |

come more specific and better tailored to a specific pathologic process. Indications for antiplatelet therapy are listed in the following sections.

## Reduction of Platelet Hyperreactivity

Mounting evidence suggests that platelets may be persistently or sometimes transiently "hyperactive" in patients with cardiovascular disease.[55, 56V] For example, platelet counts are often elevated,[56V] the mean platelet volume (MPV) is high,[57] and platelets show increased reactivity in the early morning hours.[58] The latter observation is of interest because two studies have shown that a preponderance of acute myocardial infarctions occur early in the morning.[59, 60I] The frequency of stroke peaks in the late morning.[61]

Intense platelet activation occurs following thrombolytic therapy for acute coronary artery occlusion.[62, 63V, 64] Increased platelet reactivity has also been identified by the measurement of platelet membrane activation antigens (e.g., CD62, CD63, thrombospondin) utilizing flow cytometry in patients scheduled for percutaneous coronary angioplasty (PTCA).[65V] In this study, rates of postoperative ischemic events were found to be higher in the patients who had evidence of activated platelets.

There is evidence that aspirin can suppress the heightened platelet reactivity in some of these patients. For example, low-dose enteric-coated aspirin eliminated the early morning increase in platelet reactivity in a group of normal individuals.[66] Of interest, in the PHS the higher incidence of MI in the early morning was suppressed in subjects who were enrolled in the low-dose aspirin arm of the trial.[60I]

## Prevention of Vascular Occlusion at Sites of Atherosclerotic Plaque

Most acute MI cases result from the rupture of an atherosclerotic plaque with the formation of an occlusive platelet-rich thrombus in the coronary artery.[67, 68] Because antiplatelet therapy reduces rates of primary and recurrent MI, it seems likely that treatment blocks platelet aggregation and subsequent thrombus formation. Experimental studies conducted in animals clearly show that antiplatelet therapy can reduce platelet accumulation at sites of vascular injury.[67] Data from the PHS indicate that low-dose aspirin reduces acute vascular occlusion in the coronary and lower extremity circulations but does not delay the onset of chronic stable

angina or intermittent claudication, suggesting that aspirin's primary action is to inhibit acute thrombosis rather than atherogenesis.[69I, 70I]

## Prevention of Platelet Emboli Originating From Sites of Vascular Injury

Many instances of TIA, amaurosis fugax, and reversible ischemic neurologic deficits (RIND) are caused by the embolization of platelet clumps from ulcerated nonocclusive carotid artery or proximal aortic atherosclerotic plaques.[71] Arrhythmias in patients with unstable angina could also be triggered by platelet emboli. Antiplatelet therapy is often dramatically effective in the treatment of these disorders, most likely by decreasing the number and size of platelet clumps produced at the site of the vascular lesions.[72I]

## Prevention of Acute Vascular Occlusion Following Mechanical Injury to Endothelial Surfaces

Aspirin reduces rates of early vascular occlusion following PTCA in humans.[73I, 74II] As evidenced by experimental studies in animals, balloon angioplasty[75] and surgical endarterectomy[76] are potent stimuli to platelet deposition at sites of vascular injury.

## Prevention of Platelet-mediated Thromboembolism in Patients With Nonvalvular Atrial Fibrillation

Direct experimental data to support this possibility are rather limited. One small study suggested that platelets are hyperreactive in the majority of atrial fibrillation patients receiving warfarin, and that aspirin failed to suppress platelet aggregation in seven of 17 patients treated with aspirin alone.[77V] These data suggest that platelet-dependent mechanisms may be operative in some patients with stroke secondary to atrial fibrillation. The Stroke Prevention in Atrial Fibrillation (SPAF) trials clearly demonstrate that aspirin reduces the risk of systemic embolization in many patients with nonvalvular atrial fibrillation.[48I]

## Prevention of Vascular Intimal Proliferation or Atherogenesis in Patients with Vascular Disease

As indicated previously, the evidence is very strong that antiplatelet therapy inhibits acute platelet-mediated thrombosis. However, it is far less clear that blocking platelet reactivity reduces the progression of atherosclerosis or the development of reactive intimal proliferation following vascular injury (e.g., following carotid endarterectomy or coronary angioplasty). Some evidence indicates that platelets are, in fact, involved in atherogenesis, either as the source of growth factors (e.g., platelet-derived growth factor [PDGF]) or as part of a repetitive process of vascular injury and platelet adhesion leading to incorporation of platelets into the enlarging atherosclerotic plaque.[67, 68, 78, 79]

Several studies suggest that low-dose aspirin treatment does not inhibit atherogenesis. In the PHS, aspirin promptly reduced the incidence of first MI in otherwise healthy men but failed to delay the onset of angina pectoris.[69I] In another subgroup analysis, the need for vascular surgery in patients with peripheral vascular disease was significantly reduced (relative risk 0.54; $p = .03$), but there appeared to be no major effect of aspirin on the time to new onset claudication.[70I]

Aspirin also failed to lower the rate of carotid artery restenosis in patients following carotid endarterectomy[80II] and had only modest ability to lower restenosis following PTCA, which remains a major unsolved limitation of that procedure.[73I] In contrast, one study that employed high-resolution duplex ultrasound found that 900 mg, but not 50 mg, of aspirin daily for 1 year slowed the progression of carotid plaques,

suggesting that high doses of aspirin might be required to limit atherogenesis.[15]

On balance, the available evidence seems to suggest that low-dose aspirin does not have a major antiatherosclerotic effect or the ability to retard intimal proliferation following vascular injury. Additional studies are warranted to learn if higher doses of aspirin are more effective or whether alternative antiplatelet agents might even be superior.

## MAGNITUDE OF THE EFFECT OF ANTIPLATELET THERAPY IN CARDIOVASCULAR DISEASE

Tables 4–1 and 4–2 list the results of some of the large trials of antiplatelet therapy in patients with cardiovascular and cerebrovascular disease in simplified form to provide an estimate of the benefits of antiplatelet therapy. In some studies, the effects are quite striking; for example, a 50 to 70% reduction in mortality is seen in patients treated with aspirin for unstable angina. For other indications, the benefits of antiplatelet therapy are more modest. The ability of aspirin or ticlopidine to reduce stroke or death in patients following TIA is limited to a 10 to 20% reduction in risk. However, as previously indicated, the risks of therapy are rather low. Overall risks of major CNS or GI hemorrhage range

Table 4–1. **Risk Reductions (Compared With Placebo) With the Use of Antiplatelet Agents in Patients With Cerebrovascular Disease**

| Indication | Trial | Treatment | Outcome Measure | Risk Reduction (%) |
|---|---|---|---|---|
| Primary prevention of stroke | PHS[19] | Aspirin 325 mg every other day | Stroke | None |
| | British Doctors Trial[20] | Aspirin 500 mg daily | Stroke | None |
| | Nurses Prospective Cohort Study[21] | Aspirin 325 mg 1–6 times weekly | Stroke | None |
| Secondary prevention of stroke after TIA | Canadian Cooperative Study Group[93] | Aspirin 650 mg twice daily | Stroke and death | 52 (in men) |
| | UK-TIA Study Group[26] | Aspirin 300 mg or 1,200 mg daily | Stroke, MI, or death | 15 |
| | European Stroke Prevention Study[94] | Aspirin 330 mg plus dipyridamole 75 mg three times daily | Stroke or death | 44 |
| | Swedish Aspirin Low-Dose Trial[23] | Aspirin 75 mg daily | Stroke or death | 18 |
| Secondary prevention of stroke after completed stroke | Canadian-American Ticlopidine Study[32] | Ticlopidine 250 mg twice daily | Stroke, MI, or vascular death | 30 |
| | European Stroke Prevention Study[94] | Aspirin 330 mg or dipyridamole 75 mg three times daily | Stroke or death | 32 |

Table 4–2. **Risk Reductions (Compared With Placebo) With the Use of Antiplatelet Agents in Patients With Cardiovascular Disease**

| Indication | Trial | Treatment | Outcome Measure | Risk Reduction (%) |
|---|---|---|---|---|
| Primary prevention of MI | PHS[19] | Aspirin 325 mg every other day | MI | 44 |
| | British Doctors Trial[20] | Aspirin 500 mg daily | MI | 10 |
| | Nurses Prospective Cohort Study[21] | Aspirin 325 mg 1–6 times weekly | MI | 32 |
| Secondary prevention of MI | Antiplatelet Trialists[95] | Aspirin (variable doses) | Vascular mortality | 15 |
| | ISIS-2[22] | Aspirin 160 mg daily | Reinfarction | 50 |
| Coronary thrombolysis | ISIS-2[22] | Aspirin 160 mg daily | Vascular mortality | 42 |
| Unstable angina | VA Cooperative Study[96] | Aspirin 325 mg daily | Mortality | 51 |
| | Canadian Multi-center Trial[97] | Aspirin 325 mg four times daily | Cardiac or all-cause mortality | 71 |
| | Montreal Heart Institute Trial[74] | Aspirin 325 mg twice daily | MI | 72 |
| | RISC[98] | Aspirin 75 mg daily | MI and death | 64 |
| Chronic stable angina | PHS[99] | Aspirin 325 mg every other day | MI | 70 |
| | | | Angina pectoris | None |
| | Swedish Angina Pectoris Aspirin Trial[100] | Aspirin 75 mg daily | MI or sudden death | 34 |
| Coronary artery bypass grafts | Mayo Clinic study[101] | Aspirin 325 mg plus dipyridamole 75 mg three times daily | Vein graft occlusion | 36 |
| | VA Cooperative Study[102] | Aspirin 325 mg 1 or 3 times daily | Vein graft occlusion | 31 |
| Percutaneous transluminal coronary angioplasty | Montreal Heart Institute Trial[73] | Aspirin 330 mg plus dipyridamole 75 mg three times daily | Acute MI (periprocedural) | 77 |
| | | | Restenosis | None |
| Nonvalvular atrial fibrillation | SPAF[48] | Aspirin 325 mg daily | Systemic emboli | 42 |

from 1 to 4%, and the death rate as a result of antiplatelet therapy is less than 1%.

In some instances, for example in lower extremity peripheral vascular disease, antiplatelet therapy does not seem to be very effective in maintaining the patency of vascular grafts or preventing reoperation for vascular occlusion.[1] However, almost all patients with peripheral vascular disease have coronary or carotid atherosclerosis, so that antiplatelet therapy can be recommended to reduce MI and/or stroke.[81]

## NEW ANTIPLATELET AGENTS

After decades of reliance on aspirin for inhibition of platelet function, several new antiplatelet agents either have become available (ticlopidine) or are undergoing clinical testing in human cardiovascular disease. This latter group of agents is discussed briefly.

## Platelet Membrane Receptor Inhibitors

Monoclonal antibodies (e.g., 7E3) directed against the platelet integrin glycoprotein IIb/IIIa were developed and tested in 1987 by Coller and coworkers.[82] Because the first unmodified monoclonal antibodies stimulated the formation of antimurine antibodies, more purified preparations (e.g., Fab fragments) and novel "humanized" chimeric antibodies (e.g., c7E3) that have a human constant region and a murine variable region have been developed.[83] The chimeric antibodies have remarkably low antigenicity when infused into humans. These antibodies effectively block platelet receptors for fibrinogen and perhaps other adhesive proteins.

Doses of antibody that prolong the bleeding time to greater than 30 minutes also produce blockade of 80 to 95% of the fibrinogen receptors. ADP-induced platelet aggregation is dramatically inhibited (Fig. 4–3). Thrombocytopenia following infusion of the antibodies has not been a clinical problem.

Pilot trials with several monoclonal antireceptor antibodies have been carried out in three disorders: unstable angina; following thrombolytic therapy for acute MI; and during PTCA to prevent acute coronary artery occlusion.[83] So far, the results have been promising. For example, in a pilot study by the European Cooperative Group in refractory unstable angina, c7E3 reduced total event rates of death, MI, or urgent coronary artery revascularization from 20% to 3% ($p=.03$).[84]

A second strategy to block glycoprotein IIb/

IIIa receptors is through the specific peptides that bind directly to the glycoprotein heterodimer.[83] When such peptides are infused into experimental animals or humans, marked reduction (e.g., 85%) in platelet aggregation can be achieved. Several products are now undergoing testing in patients with unstable angina and elective PTCA. The use of these peptides is theoretically attractive because platelet inhibition is rapidly reversible and the agents have extremely short half lives in vivo, suggesting that rapid modulation of the antiplatelet effects can be achieved, along with reduced bleeding in high-risk situations.

## Direct Antithrombins

Thrombin is an extraordinarily potent platelet agonist that undoubtedly plays a pivotal role

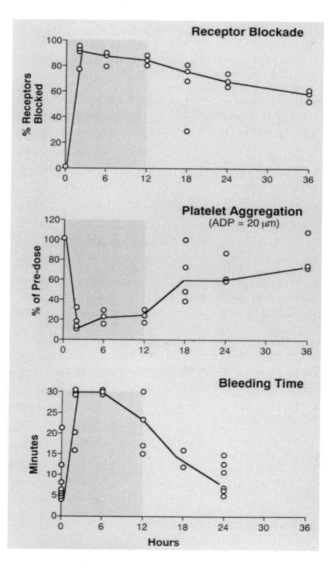

**Figure 4–3.** Receptor blockade, platelet aggregation, and bleeding time in high-risk angioplasty patients receiving a c7E3 infusion for 12 hours. The dose was 0.25 mg/kg bolus and 10 µg/minute for 12 hours. (Used with permission from Topol EJ and Plow EF: Clinical trials of platelet receptor inhibitors. Thromb Haemost 70:94–98, 1993.)

in arterial thrombogenesis.[85] Consequently, pharmacologic inhibition of this enzyme should effectively interrupt arterial thrombus formation in vivo. A family of specific thrombin inhibitors has been derived from hirudin, a protein found in the saliva of the leech *Hirudo medicinalis* that blocks the active site of thrombin. These hirudin analogs are likely to prove superior to heparin for inhibition of thrombin action in vivo. Thrombin bound to fibrin or subendothelial matrix retains its enzymatic activity but is protected from inactivation by the complex of heparin-antithrombin III. In contrast, the direct thrombin inhibitors effectively block thrombin action in these sites. In contrast to heparin, specific thrombin inhibitors have a more predictable effect on coagulation tests, an excellent bioavailability, and a reproducible dose-response curve in vivo.[86V] Currently, several of these preparations are undergoing clinical testing in patients with unstable angina and PTCA,[87] and following thrombolytic therapy in patients with acute MI. For example, some studies have suggested that Hirulog (Biogen, Inc., Cambridge, MA) is safe and apparently effective when given to patients following cardiac catheterization[88II] or during coronary angioplasty.[87II]

Another thrombin inhibitor is the antithrombin peptide D-Phe-Pro-Arg CH$_2$Cl (PPACK). In a study in a baboon thrombosis model, intravenous infusion of the synthetic antithrombin peptide for only 1 hour abolished coronary artery thrombosis in an injured vessel for at least 24 hours thereafter.[76] Platelet deposition was dramatically reduced at the injury site when compared with controls receiving heparin. The bleeding time was markedly increased (greater than 30 minutes), as were the partial thromboplastin time and the prothrombin time. However, because of the very short half life of the peptide, all of these parameters returned to normal within 30 minutes after stopping the infusion. Thus, the inhibitor appeared to permanently inactivate thrombin at sites of vascular injury following a relatively brief 1-hour infusion. Clinical trials of this agent in humans have yet to be reported.

### n-3 Fatty Acids

The n-3 fatty acids are highly unsaturated long-chain fatty acids found in marine oils and a few terrestrial plants.[89] Various formulations are now commercially available, ranging from relatively unmodified fish oil, to triglycerides enriched in n-3 fatty acids, to highly purified ethyl esters of eicosapentaenoic acid (EPA-C20:5 n-3) and docosahexaenoic acid (DHA-C

22:6 n-3). The n-3 fatty acids have been shown to reduce platelet adhesion and aggregation, prolong the bleeding time, and impair platelet deposition at sites of vascular injury.[90] One study suggested that intimal proliferation following carotid endarterectomy was markedly inhibited 30 days after vascular injury in baboons.[91]

Several clinical trials of fish oil or more purified n-3 fatty acids have been performed in patients undergoing PTCA to determine if restenosis rates might be reduced with this therapy.[92] The results of these trials have been mixed, but a meta-analysis suggested that the relative risk of restenosis was decreased by 27% ($p = .05$).[92] However, the results of a larger trial of n-3 fatty acids in coronary angioplasty patients showed no benefit of purified n-3 fatty acids in angioplasty patients.[103]

## REFERENCES

1. Goodnight SH, Coull BM, McAnulty JH, et al: Antiplatelet therapy—Part 1 and 2. West J Med 158:385–392, 506–514, 1993.
2. Fuster V, Dyken ML, Vokonas PS, Hennekens C: Aspirin as a therapeutic agent in cardiovascular disease. Circulation 87:659, 1993.
II 3. Miller KP, Frishman WH: Platelets and antiplatelet therapy in ischemic heart disease. Med Clin North Am 72:117, 1988.
I 4. The E.P.S.I.M. Research Group: A controlled comparison of aspirin and oral anticoagulants in prevention of death after myocardial infarction. N Engl J Med 307:701, 1982.
I 5. Willard JE, Lange RA, Hillis LD: Current concepts: The use of aspirin in ischemic heart disease. N Engl J Med 327:175, 1992.
I 6. Dalen JE, Hirsh J: Third ACCP consensus conference on antithrombotic therapy. Chest 102:303S, 1992.
7. Vane JR, Flower RJ, Botting RM: History of aspirin and its mechanism of action. Stroke 21[Suppl IV]:IV–12, 1990.
8. Vane JR: Inhibition of prostaglandin synthesis as a mechanism of action for aspirin-like drugs. Nature 231:232, 1971.
9. Smith JB, Willis AL: Aspirin selectively inhibits prostaglandin production in human platelets. Nature 231:235, 1971.
10. Jaffe EA, Weksler BB: Recovery of endothelial cell prostacyclin production after inhibition by low doses of aspirin. J Clin Invest 63:532, 1979.
11. FitzGerald F, Oates J, Hawiger J, et al: Endogenous biosynthesis of prostacyclin and thromboxane and platelet function during chronic administration of aspirin in man. J Clin Invest 71:676, 1983.
12. Hirsh J, Dalen JE, Fuster V, et al: Aspirin and other platelet-active drugs; The relationship between dose, effectiveness, and side effects. Chest 102[Suppl]:327S, 1992.
13. Samuelsson K, Svensson J: Aspirin: Optimal dose in stroke prevention. Stroke 24:1259, 1993.
14. Dyken ML: Controversies in stroke: Past and present: The Willis lecture. Stroke 24:1251, 1993.
15. Ranke C, Hecker H, Creutzig A, Alexander K: Dose-

dependent effect of aspirin on carotid atherosclerosis. Circulation 87:1873, 1993.

V 16. Voss R, Geissler BS, Tillmanns H, Matthias FR: In vitro and ex vivo effects of aspirin in patients on a low-dose aspirin therapy. Thromb Res 72:49, 1993.

17. Clarke RJ, Mayo G, Price P, et al: Suppression of thromboxane $A_2$ but not of systemic prostacyclin by controlled-release aspirin. N Engl J Med 325:1137, 1991.

18. Keimowitz RM, Pulvermacher G, Mayo G, Fitzgerald DJ: Transdermal modification of platelet function: A dermal aspirin preparation selectively inhibits platelet cyclooxygenase and preserves prostacyclin biosynthesis. Circulation 88:556, 1993.

I 19. Steering Committee of the Physicians' Health Study Research Group: Final report on the aspirin component of the ongoing physicians' health study. N Engl J Med 321:129, 1989.

II 20. Peto R, Gray R, Collins R, et al: Randomized trial of prophylactic daily aspirin in British male doctors. Br Med J 296:313, 1988.

III 21. Manson JE, Stampfer MJ, Colditz GA, et al: A prospective study of aspirin use and primary prevention of cardiovascular disease in women. JAMA 266:521, 1991.

I 22. ISIS Collaborative Group: Randomised trial of intravenous streptokinase, oral aspirin, both, or neither among 17,187 cases of suspected acute myocardial infarction: ISIS-2. Lancet 13:349, 1988.

I 23. The SALT Collaborative Group: Swedish aspirin low-dose trial (SALT) of 75 mg aspirin as secondary prophylaxis after cerebrovascular ischemic events. Lancet 338:1345, 1991.

I 24. Silagy CA, McNeil JJ, Donnan GA, et al: Adverse effects of low-dose aspirin in a healthy elderly population. Clin Pharmacol Ther 54:84, 1993.

I 25. The Dutch TIA Trial Study Group: A comparison of two doses of aspirin (30 mg vs. 283 mg a day) in patients after a transient ischemic attack or minor ischemic stroke. N Engl J Med 325:1261, 1991.

I 26. Farrell B, Godwin J, Richards S, Warlow C: The United Kingdom transient ischaemic attack (UK-TIA) aspirin trial: Final results. J Neurol Neurosurg Psychiatry 54:1044, 1991.

27. Editorial: Ticlopidine. Lancet 337:459, 1991.

V 28. DiMinno G, Cerbone AM, Mattioli PL, et al: Functionally thrombasthenic state in normal platelets following the administration of ticlopidine. J Clin Invest 75:328, 1985.

V 29. Cattaneo M, Akkawat B, Lecchi A, et al: Ticlopidine selectively inhibits human platelet responses to adenosine diphosphate. Thromb Haemost 66:694, 1991.

30. Saltiel E, Ward A: Ticlopidine. A review of its pharmacodynamic and pharmacokinetic properties, and therapeutic efficacy in platelet-dependent disease states. Drugs 34:222, 1987.

II 31. Shah J, Fratis A, Ellis D, et al: Effect of food and antacid on absorption of orally administered ticlopidine hydrochloride. J Clin Pharmacol 30:733, 1990.

I 32. Gent M, Easton JD, Hachinski VC, et al: The Canadian-American ticlopidine study (CATS) in thromboembolic stroke. Lancet 1:1215, 1989.

I 33. Hass WK, Easton JD, Adams HP Jr, et al: A randomized trial comparing ticlopidine hydrochloride with aspirin for the prevention of stroke in high-risk patients. N Engl J Med 321:501, 1989.

I 34. Balsano F, Rizzon P, Violi F, et al: Studio Ticlopidina Angina Instabile: Antiplatelet treatment with ticlopidine in unstable angina: A controlled multicenter clinical trial. Circulation 82:17, 1990.

35. FitzGerald GA: Ticlopidine in unstable angina: A more expensive aspirin? Circulation 82:296, 1990.

I 36. Limet R, David JL, Mogotteaux P, et al: Prevention of aorta-coronary bypass graft occlusion. J Thorac Cardiovasc Surg 94:773, 1987.

I 37. TIMAD Study Group: Ticlopidine treatment reduces the progression of nonproliferative diabetic retinopathy. Arch Ophthalmol 108:1577, 1990.

I 38. Weisberg LA: The efficacy and safety of ticlopidine and aspirin in non-whites: Analysis of a patient subgroup from the Ticlopidine Aspirin Stroke Study. Neurology 43:27, 1993.

39. Albers GW: Role of ticlopidine for prevention of stroke. Stroke 23:912, 1992.

40. Page Y, Tardy B, Zeni F, et al: Thrombotic thrombocytopenic purpura related to ticlopidine. Lancet 337:774, 1991.

41. Khelif A, Assouline D, Ffrench M, et al: Ticlopidine and aplastic anaemia. Br J Haematol 83:678, 1993.

42. De Lorgeril M, Boissonnat P, Dureau G, et al: Evaluation of ticlopidine, a novel inhibitor of platelet aggregation, in heart transplant recipients. Transplantation 55:1195, 1993.

43. Harker LA, Fuster V: Pharmacology of platelet inhibitors. J Am Coll Cardiol 8:21, 1986.

44. FitzGerald GA: Dipyridamole. N Engl J Med 316:1247, 1987.

45. Stein PD, Alpert JS, Copeland J, et al: Antithrombotic therapy in patients with mechanical and biological prosthetic heart valves. Chest 102[Suppl]:445S, 1992.

I 46. Report of the Sixty Plus Reinfarction Study Group: A double-blind trial to assess long-term oral anticoagulant therapy in elderly patients after myocardial infarction. Lancet 2:989, 1980.

I 47. Smith P, Arnesen H, Holme I: The effect of warfarin on mortality and reinfarction after myocardial infarction. N Engl J Med 323:147, 1990.

I 48. Stroke Prevention in Atrial Fibrillation Investigators: Stroke Prevention in Atrial Fibrillation Study: Final results. Circulation 84:527, 1991.

49. Gurwitz JH, Goldberg RJ, Holden A, et al: Age-related risks of long-term oral anticoagulant therapy. Arch Intern Med 148:1733, 1988.

50. Dale J, Myhre E, Storstein O, et al: Prevention of arterial thromboembolism with acetylsalicylic acid: A controlled clinical study in patients with aortic ball valves. Am Heart J 94:101, 1977.

I 51. Turpie AGG, Gent M, Laupacis A, et al: A comparison of aspirin with placebo in patients treated with warfarin after heart-valve replacement. N Engl J Med 329:524, 1993.

52. Chesebro JH, Fuster V, Elveback LR, et al: Trial of combined warfarin plus dipyridamole or aspirin therapy in prosthetic heart valve replacement: Danger of aspirin compared with dipyridamole. Am J Cardiol 51:1537, 1983.

I 53. Meade TW, Roderick PJ, Brennan PJ, et al: Extracranial bleeding and other symptoms due to low dose aspirin and low intensity oral anticoagulation. Thromb Haemost 68:1, 1992.

54. Meade TW: Low-dose warfarin and low-dose aspirin in the primary prevention of ischemic heart disease. Am J Cardiol 65:7C, 1990.

55. Trip MD, Cats VM, van Capelle FJL, Vreeken J: Platelet hyperreactivity and prognosis in survivors of myocardial infarction. N Engl J Med 322:1549, 1990.

V 56. Thaulow E, Erikssen J, Sandvik L, et al: Blood platelet count and function are related to total and cardiovascular death in apparently healthy men. Circulation 84:613, 1991.

57. Martin JF, Bath PMW, Burr ML: Influence of platelet size on outcome after myocardial infarction. Lancet 338:1409, 1991.

58. Tofler GH, Brezinski D, Schafer AI, et al: Concurrent morning increase in platelet aggregability and the risk of myocardial infarction and sudden cardiac death. N Engl J Med 316:1514, 1987.

59. Goldsmith JC: Contributions of the subendothelium to prostacyclin release after vascular injury. J Lab Clin Med 100:574, 1982.

I 60. Ridker PM, Manson JE, Buring JE, et al: Circadian variation of acute myocardial infarction and the effect of low-dose aspirin in a randomized trial of physicians. Circulation 82:897, 1990.

61. Marler JR, Price TR, Clark GL, et al: Morning increase in onset of ischemic stroke. Stroke 20:473, 1989.

62. Fitzgerald DJ, FitzGerald GA: Role of thrombin and thromboxane A$_2$ in reocclusion following coronary thrombolysis with tissue-type plasminogen activator. Proc Natl Acad Sci USA 86:7585, 1989.

V 63. Fitzgerald DJ, Catella F, Roy L, FitzGerald GA: Marked platelet activation in vivo after intravenous streptokinase in patients with acute myocardial infarction. Circulation 77:142, 1988.

64. Kerins DM, Roy L, FitzGerald GA, Fitzgerald DJ: Platelet and vascular function during coronary thrombolysis with tissue-type plasminogen activator. Circulation 80:1718, 1989.

V 65. Tschoepe D, Schultheiss HP, Kolarov P, et al: Platelet membrane activation markers are predictive for increased risk of acute ischemic events after PTCA. Circulation 88:37, 1993.

66. McCall NT, Tofler GH, Schafer AI, et al: The effect of enteric-coated aspirin on the morning increase in platelet activity. Am Heart J 121:1382, 1991.

67. Badimon L, Chesebro JH, Badimon JJ: Thrombus formation on ruptured atherosclerotic plaques and rethrombosis on evolving thrombi. Circulation 86[Suppl]:74, 1992.

68. Badimon JJ, Fuster V, Chesebro JH, Badimon L: Coronary atherosclerosis: A multifactorial disease. Circulation 87[Suppl]:113, 1993.

I 69. Ridker PM, Manson JE, Buring JE, et al: The effect of chronic platelet inhibition with low-dose aspirin on atherosclerotic progression and acute thrombosis: Clinical evidence from the Physicians' Health Study. Am Heart J 122:1588, 1991.

I 70. Goldhaber SZ, Manson JE, Stampfer MJ, et al: Low-dose aspirin and subsequent peripheral arterial surgery in the Physicians' Health Study. Lancet 340:143, 1992.

71. Byer JA, Easton JD: Therapy of ischemic cerebrovascular disease. Ann Intern Med 93:742, 1980.

I 72. Theroux P, Ouimet H, McCans J, et al: Aspirin, heparin, or both to treat acute unstable angina. N Engl J Med 319:1105, 1988.

I 73. Schwartz L, Bourassa MG, Lesperance J, et al: Aspirin and dipyridamole in the prevention of restenosis after percutaneous transluminal coronary angioplasty. N Engl J Med 318:1714, 1988.

II 74. Lindblad B, Persson NH, Takolander R, Bergqvist D: Does low-dose acetylsalicylic acid prevent stroke after carotid surgery? A double-blind, placebo-controlled randomized trial. Stroke 24:1125, 1993.

75. Lam JYT, Chesebro JH, Steele PM, et al: Antithrombotic therapy for deep arterial injury by angioplasty: Efficacy of common platelet inhibition compared with thrombin inhibition in pigs. Circulation 84:814, 1991.

76. Lumsden AB, Kelly AB, Schneider PA, et al: Lasting safe interruption of endarterectomy thrombosis by transiently infused antithrombin peptide D–Phe-Pro-Arg Ch$_2$Cl in baboons. Blood 81:1762, 1993.

V 77. Helgason CM, Hoff JA, Kondos GT, Brace LD: Platelet aggregation in patients with atrial fibrillation taking aspirin or warfarin. Stroke 24:1458, 1993.

78. Loscalzo J: The relation between atherosclerosis and thrombosis. Circulation 86[Suppl]:95, 1992.

79. Ross R: The pathogenesis of atherosclerosis: A perspective for the 1990s. Nature 362:801, 1993.

II 80. Harker LA, Bernstein EF, Dilley RB, et al: Failure of aspirin plus dipyridamole to prevent restenosis after carotid endarterectomy. Ann Intern Med 116:731, 1992.

81. Hertzer NR, Bevan ZG, Young JR, et al: Coronary artery disease in peripheral vascular patients. A classification of 1000 coronary angiograms and results of surgical management. Ann Surg 199:223, 1984.

82. Coller BS, Scudder LE, Berger HJ, Iuliucci JD: Inhibition of human platelet function in vivo with a monoclonal antibody. With observations on the newly dead as experimental subjects. Ann Intern Med 109:635, 1988.

83. Topol EJ, Plow EF: Clinical trials of platelet receptor inhibitors. Thromb Haemost 70:94, 1993.

84. Simoons ML: Randomized trial of monoclonal platelet antibody for refractory unstable angina pectoris. Presented at the European Congress of Cardiology, Barcelona, Spain, 1992.

85. Maraganore JM: Thrombin, thrombin inhibitors, and the arterial thrombotic process. Thromb Haemost 70:208, 1993.

V 86. Fox I, Dawson A, Loynds P, et al: Anticoagulant activity of hirulog, a direct thrombin inhibitor, in humans. Thromb Haemost 69:157, 1993.

II 87. Topol EJ, Bonan R, Jewitt D, et al: Use of a direct antithrombin, hirulog, in place of heparin during coronary angioplasty. Circulation 87:1622, 1993.

II 88. Cannon CP, Maraganore JM, Loscalzo J, et al: Anticoagulant effects of *hirulog*, a novel thrombin inhibitor, in patients with coronary artery disease. Am J Cardiol 71:778, 1993.

89. Goodnight SH: Fish oil and vascular disease. Trends Cardiovasc Med 1:112, 1991.

90. Goodnight SH: The effects of n-3 fatty acids on atherosclerosis and the vascular response to injury. Arch Pathol Lab Med 117:102, 1993.

91. Harker LA, Kelly AB, Hanson SR, et al: Interruption of vascular thrombus formation and vascular lesion formation by dietary n-3 fatty acids in fish oil in nonhuman primates. Circulation 87:1017, 1993.

92. Goodnight SH, Cairns JA, Fisher M, FitzGerald GA: Assessment of the therapeutic use of n-3 fatty acids in vascular disease and thrombosis. Chest 102:374, 1992.

I 93. Canadian Cooperative Study Group: A randomized trial of aspirin and sulfinpyrazone in threatened stroke. N Engl J Med 299:53, 1978.

I 94. ESPS Group: European Stroke Prevention Study. Stroke 21:1122, 1990.

95. Antiplatelet Trialists' Collaboration: Secondary prevention of vascular disease by prolonged antiplatelet treatment. Br Med J 296:320, 1988.

I 96. Lewis HD, Davis JW, Archibald DG, et al: Protective effects of aspirin against acute myocardial infarction and death in men with unstable angina. Results of a

Veterans Administration Cooperative Study. N Engl J Med 309:396, 1983.

I 97. Cairns JA, Gent M, Singer J, et al: Aspirin, sulfinpyrazone, or both in unstable angina. N Engl J Med 313:1369, 1985.

98. RISC Group: Risk of myocardial infarction and death during treatment with low dose aspirin and intravenous heparin in men with unstable coronary artery disease. Lancet 336:827, 1990.

I 99. Ridker PM, Manson JE, Gaziano M, et al: Low-dose aspirin therapy for chronic stable angina. A randomized, placebo-controlled clinical trial. Ann Intern Med 114:835, 1991.

I 100. Juul-Möller S, Edvardsson N, Jahnmatz B, et al: Double-blind trial of aspirin in primary prevention of myocardial infarction in patients with stable chronic angina pectoris. Lancet 340:1421, 1992.

I 101. Chesebro JH, Clements IP, Fuster V: A platelet-inhibitor-drug trial in coronary-artery bypass operations: Benefits of perioperative dipyridamole and aspirin therapy on early postoperative vein-graft patency. N Engl J Med 307:73, 1982.

I 102. Goldman S, Copeland J, Moritz T, et al: Improvement in early saphenous vein graft patency after coronary artery bypass surgery with antiplatelet therapy: Results of a Veterans Administration Cooperative Study. Circulation 77:1324, 1988.

103. Leaf A, Jorgensen MB, Jacobs AK, et al.: Do fish oils prevent restenosis after coronary angioplasty? Circulation 90:2248, 1944.

# Chapter 5

# Coronary Thrombolysis

J. A. Cairns

## HISTORY AND RATIONALE

The evolution of coronary thrombolytic therapy began with the work of Tillett and Garner,[1] demonstrating that human isolates of Lancefield group A beta hemolytic streptococci excreted a potent fibrinolytic substance into their culture medium. Studies of this "streptococcal fibrinolysin" led to an understanding of the role of plasminogen activation in fibrinolysis and fibrinogenolysis.[2] A sequence of laboratory and clinical studies culminated in the availability of a preparation of streptokinase (SK) for intravenous (IV) use, which was relatively safe and efficacious for thrombolysis.[3]

The clinical description of acute myocardial infarction (AMI) by Herrick[4] in 1912 embodied the concept that acute coronary thrombosis was responsible, and this view was widely accepted. The possibility of lysing primary or secondary occlusive thrombi was the principal rationale for the first published trial of thrombolytic therapy for AMI in 1959.[5] Additional benefit was anticipated by the mechanisms of protection and preservation of flow in the microcirculation of the peri-infarction zone, diminished blood viscosity, and reduced platelet aggregation. By 1960, a small study of intracoronary SK in patients with suspected AMI had been reported.[6] Over the next 25 years, 24 randomized studies of intravenous thrombolytic therapy were conducted, primarily in Europe.[7] Treatment protocols varied widely and, in many instances, there were long delays from onset of AMI to start of treatment. Nevertheless, five trials showed statistically significant mortality reductions, and several more showed trends favoring therapy. Despite the encouraging results, in particular those from the European Cooperative Study,[8] thrombolytic therapy was not commonly used to treat AMI in Europe and virtually never used in North America. In addition to having a natural conservatism toward new and potentially dangerous therapies, physicians were presented with a number of autopsy studies reporting a low incidence of coronary thrombosis in fatal MI,[9] and the pathogenetic role of the coronary artery thrombus was seriously questioned.[10] There was also a general decrease in the enthusiasm for anticoagulant therapy in AMI.

In the late 1970s, there was a reawakening of interest in the potential for thrombolytic therapy for AMI for three principal reasons: (1) demonstration that coronary thrombosis is a very early event in most AMI;[11] (2) recognition that infarct size is of prognostic importance;[12] and (3) evidence that infarct size might be limited by interventions early in the course of AMI,[13] with the expectation that reperfusion might lead to marked limitation of infarct size.

The renewed interest in thrombolytic therapy was directed initially at intracoronary administration, first reported by Chazov in 1976.[14] The expectation that local delivery of the thrombolytic agent would result in less systemic thrombolysis, and the initial studies reporting reperfusion rates of 70 to 80% with intracoronary SK,[15V] encouraged the conduct of randomized trials. These confirmed the presence of occlusion in the infarct-related artery in about 85% of AMIs and demonstrated reperfusion in 70%.[16] The reality that most hospitals do not have cardiac catheterization laboratories, and the recognition of the economic and logistic impediments to emergency cardiac catheterization even in referral hospitals, stimulated a re-evaluation of intravenous (IV) thrombolytic therapy.[17, 18] Several studies showed that, in many instances, reperfusion could be achieved with IV thrombolysis more quickly than with intracoronary administration by avoiding the delay arising from the requirement for coronary angiography with the intracoronary strategy.

The initial agent in clinical use was SK. Urokinase (UK), a direct endogenous plasminogen activator secreted by human kidney cells, was extracted and purified in 1957,[19] and was compared with SK in trials in patients with pulmonary embolism[20I] and was studied in early trials in patients with AMI.[7] The agent rt-PA was first used in humans in 1983.[21V] Subsequently, randomized controlled studies were undertaken to assess the efficacy of IV rt-PA in achieving coronary artery reperfusion and patency[22I, 24I] and in preserving left ventricular (LV) myocardium by the measurement of LV function.[25I–27I] Anisoylated plasminogen streptokinase activator complex (APSAC) offers theoretic advantages over SK[28] and has been evaluated in a number of clinical trials. Single chain UK plasminogen activator (scu-PA), a precursor of UK, also offers theoretic advantages, and clinical evaluation has been undertaken.[29I]

## CLINICAL TRIALS OF MORTALITY REDUCTION

### Thrombolytic Agents Versus Control

A definitive overview[7] of 24 trials of IV thrombolytic therapy conducted between 1959 and 1979 found that the pooled odds reduction in mortality was $22 \pm 5\%$ ($p<.001$) (Table 5–1). However, generalizations to clinical practice were of uncertain relevance. Subsequent trials were designed to be of sufficient size to individually allow the evaluation of mortality.

The Gruppo Italiano per lo Studio della Streptochinasi nell Infarto Miocardico (GISSI) Study[30I] was conducted in 176 cardiac care units throughout Italy, with the enrollment of 11,806 patients randomized to SK (1.5 MU over 1 hour) or conventional therapy (i.e., no placebo control). At the discretion of the treating physician, 21% of patients in each group received IV heparin and/or oral anticoagulants, whereas 14% received antiplatelet therapy. Hospital mortality was reduced from 13.0% to 10.7%, representing an 18% risk reduction ($p=.0002$). The Second International Study of Infarct Survival (ISIS-2) study[31I] was conducted in 417 hospitals throughout Europe, Australia, New Zealand, the United States, and Canada. There were 17,187 patients randomized with placebo control to SK (1.5 MU over 1 hour), acetylsalicylic acid (ASA) (160 mg enteric-coated preparation daily for a month, the first tablet chewed at the time of study entry), both, or neither, according to a factorial design. The 5-week vascular mortality was reduced from 12.0% to 9.2%, representing a 23% risk reduction (25% odds reduction) ($p<.00001$) by SK when compared with no SK, and from 13.2% to 8.0%,

representing a 39% risk reduction (42% odds reduction, $p<.00001$) by the combination of SK and ASA when compared with no SK or ASA. In a third study[32I] of 219 patients, 30-day mortality was reduced by SK from 12.5% to 3.7%, representing a 72% risk reduction ($p=.016$). Three other clinical trials showed trends favoring SK.[33I–35I]

The APSAC Intervention Mortality Study (AIMS) trial[36I, 37I] evaluated APSAC, which is usually given intravenously over 5 minutes and is slowly activated in the circulation. There were 1,258 patients randomized to 30 U of APSAC or placebo, and 30-day mortality was reduced from 12.1% to 6.4%, a 50.5% odds reduction of mortality (Cl = 26–67%, $p=.0006$). However, the trial was stopped early by the data-monitoring committee, and thus the magnitude of the true benefit may have been overestimated. APSAC has also been compared with heparin in the first few hours following onset of AMI, with reduction of hospital mortality from 9.6% to 6.6% ($p$ = not significant [NS]) in a trial involving 149 patients,[38II] and from 12.6% to 5.6% ($p$ = .032) in another trial involving 313 patients.[39I] A comparison of APSAC with intracoronary SK in a study of 240 patients[40I] indicated a trend in favor of APSAC for reduction of in-hospital mortality (7.7% vs 4.1%, $p$ = NS).

The Anglo-Scandinavian Study of Early Thrombolysis (ASSET) trial[41II] was designed to test the effect of IV rt-PA on 1-month mortality. There were 5,011 patients randomized to IV rt-PA (10-mg bolus, 50 mg additional in first hour, 20 mg in hour 2, 20 mg in hour 3, total 100 mg) or placebo. All patients received IV heparin for 24 hours; no ASA was given. The 1-month all-cause mortality was reduced by rt-PA from 9.8% to 7.2%, representing a 28% odds reduction ([Cl] = 19–37%, $p=.0011$). The European Cooperative Trial comparing rt-PA with placebo was designed to assess the effects of rt-PA on ventricular function, infarct size, and morbidity.[42I] There were 722 patients randomized to rt-PA (100-mg single chain) or placebo infusion over 3 hours, all patients receiving heparin and low-dose ASA. At 21 days, there was a nonsignificant difference in mortality (3.7% with rt-PA and 6.8% with placebo). The pooled odds reduction in mortality for rt-PA versus placebo is 29% (Cl = 15–41%, $p<.0003$), based upon the results of six trials.[43]

### Comparison Among Various Thrombolytic Agents

The availability of rt-PA offered the promise of greater efficacy and fewer complications from

TABLE 5–1. **Mortality Outcomes in Large Trials of Thrombolytic Therapy**

| Study (Reference) | Patients | Agent, Dose | Time | Followup | Mortality Therapy (%) | Mortality Control (%) | Risk Reduction | p |
|---|---|---|---|---|---|---|---|---|
| **Intravenous SK vs Placebo** | | | | | | | | |
| GISSI[30] | 11,806 | SK 1.5 MU, 1 h | <12 h | Hospital | 10.7 | 13.0 | 18 | .0002 |
| ISIS-2[31] | 17,187 | SK 1.5 MU, 1 h | <24 h | 5 wk | 9.3 | 12.0 | 23 | <.0001 |
| White[32] | 219 | SK 1.5 MU, 1 h | <4 h | 30 da | 3.7 | 12.5 | 70 | .016 |
| EMERAS[58] | 3,568 | SK 1.5 MU, 1 h | 6–24 h | 5 wk | 11.2 | 11.8 | 6 | NS |
| **Intravenous APSAC vs placebo** | | | | | | | | |
| AIMS[36, 37] | 1,258 | APSAC 30 U | <6 h | 30 da | 6.4 | 12.1 | 47 | .0006 |
| **Intravenous rt-PA vs placebo** | | | | | | | | |
| ASSET[41] | 5,011 | rt-PA 100 mg, single, 3 h | <5 h | 1 mo | 7.2 | 9.8 | 26 | .0011 |
| European Coop[42] | 721 | rt-PA 100 mg, single, 3 h, ASA 250 mg heparin 5000 U → angio (oral agent after 3 da) | <5 h | 14 da | 2.8 | 5.7 | 51 | NS |
| LATE[53] | 5,711 | rt-PA, 100 mg, single, 3 h, ASA, heparin IV 48 h | 6–24 h | 35 da | 8.9 | 10.3 | 14 | .07 |
| **Intravenous SK vs intravenous APSAC** | | | | | | | | |
| Anderson (TEAM 2)[125] | 370 | APSAC 30 U 5 min SK 1.5 MU 1 h + heparin bolus → infusion 24 h | <4 h | Hospital | SK 7.1 | APSAC 5.9 | | .61 |
| **Intravenous SK vs intravenous rt-PA** | | | | | | | | |
| GISSI-2[44] | 12,490 | rt-PA 100 mg, single, 3 h vs SK 1.5 MU, 0.5–1 h | <6 h | Hospital | SK 8.6 | rt-PA 9.0 | | NS |
| International Study Group[45] | 20,891 | rt-PA 100 mg, single, 3 h vs SK 1.5 MU, 0.5–1 h | <6 h | Hospital | SK 8.5 | rt-PA 8.9 | | NS |

Intravenous SK vs Intravenous scu-PA

| Trial | N | Regimen | Entry | Endpoint | | | | | | p |
|---|---|---|---|---|---|---|---|---|---|---|
| PRIMI[74] | 401 | SK 1.5 MU, 1 h, vs scu-PA 80 mg, 1 h + heparin bolus at 3 h, infusion → oral | <4 h | Hospital | **SK** 4.9 | | **scu-PA** 3.5 | | | NS |

**Intravenous APSAC vs Intravenous rt-PA**

| TAPS[48] | 435 | APSAC 30 U, rt-PA 100 mg single, 1.5 h + heparin | <6 h | Hospital | **APSAC** 8.1 | | **rt-PA** 2.4 | 70 | | .0095 |

**Intravenous rt-PA vs Intravenous UK**

| GAUS[84] | 245 | rt-PA 70 mg, single, 1.5 h vs UK 3 MU, 1.5 h + heparin → oral | <6 h | Hospital | **rt-PA** 4.8 | | **UK** 4.1 | | | NS |

**IV SK, vs IV APSAC vs IV rt-PA**

| ISIS-3[46] | 46,091 | SK 1.5 MU 1 h, APSAC 30 U, 3–5 min, rt-PA 0.6 mU/kg duteplase, 4 h | <24 h | 35 da | **SK** 10.5 | **APSAC** 10.6 | **rt-PA** 10.3 | | | NS |

**IV SK vs IV SK/rt-PA vs IV rt-PA**

| GUSTO[50] | 41,021 | SK 1.5 MU 1 h + heparin sc or IV, SK 1.0 MU 1 h + rt-PA (alteplase) 1.0 mg/kg, 1 h + heparin, or rt-PA up to 100 mg 1.5 h + heparin | <6 h | 30 da | **SK-sc HEPARIN** 7.2 | **sk-iv HEPARIN** 7.4 | **SK/ rt-PA** 7.0 | **rt-PA** 6.3 | **ACCEL rt-PA vs SK** 14 | .001 |

47

bleeding, hypotension, and allergic reactions, and the initial studies of coronary reperfusion rates supported this expectation (Table 5–1). It was also anticipated that APSAC would result in less bleeding than SK and possibly greater efficacy because of somewhat greater fibrin specificity. The only major trial of APSAC versus placebo[361, 371] did indeed show a benefit considerably greater than that observed with SK compared with placebo. Surprisingly, the first major placebo-controlled mortality trial of rt-PA (ASSET)[411] reported a mortality reduction similar to that observed with SK. No distinct advantage of any available thrombolytic agent had emerged from the individual placebo-controlled trials, and it became clear that direct comparison in large trials was necessary to determine relative efficacies and side effect profiles.

The GISSI-2[441] was a multicenter, randomized, open-label trial designed to compare SK (1.5 MU IV over 30–60 min) with alteplase (single chain rt-PA, 10-mg bolus, 50 mg over next 1 hour, 40 mg over next 2 hours; total 100 mg). In this 2 × 2 factorial design, patients were also randomly allocated to heparin (12,500 units subcutaneously commencing at 12 hours, and repeated every 12 hours to hospital discharge) or usual therapy. Oral ASA (300–325 mg/day) and atenolol (IV followed by oral, using the ISIS-1 regimen) were recommended for all patients and were administered in 87% and 45.3% of patients, respectively. Hospital mortality was 8.6% with SK and 9% with rt-PA (p=NS). The International tPA/SK Mortality Trial[451] was a collaboration of the Italian GISSI-2 centers and those in several additional countries following the GISSI-2 protocol. Whereas the primary outcome of the GISSI-2 trial was to be a composite of mortality and extent of LV damage, the International Trial was to include sufficient patients to detect an important difference in the effects of rt-PA and SK on in-hospital and 6-month mortality, as well as the effect of heparin on mortality and safety. An additional 8,401 patients were recruited for a total of 20,891. ASA was given to 91% of patients, atenolol to 36%. There was no difference in hospital mortality between patients treated with SK (8.5%) and those who received rt-PA (8.9%).

The ISIS-3,[461] a multicenter, randomized trial, was designed to address the following questions. (1) Which of the three commonly used thrombolytic agents (SK, APSAC, and rt-PA) if any, is the most effective? (2) Which patients should receive thrombolytic therapy? (3) What are the effects of adding heparin to thrombolytic-aspirin regimens? Eligible patients were those with a clinically suspected diagnosis of AMI, within 24 hours of onset. Physicians were asked to decide whether there was a clear indication for thrombolytic therapy, and, if so, such a patient was randomly allocated to one of the three thrombolytic agents. If the physician believed there was an uncertain indication for thrombolytic therapy (i.e., no ST segment elevation, many hours since onset of AMI, very elderly patient, relative contraindication to thrombolytic therapy), the patient was randomly allocated to one of the three agents or to no thrombolytic therapy. Patients were further randomized in a factorial design to calcium heparin (12,500 U subcutaneously, the first dose about 4 hours post randomization, and then every 12 hours for 7 days), or no heparin. All patients were expected to receive ASA (162 mg/day orally, commencing on diagnosis of AMI) and 97% did so. A total of 46,091 patients were recruited (75% certain indication, 25% uncertain indication).

The vascular mortality rates at 35 days post randomization were as follows—rt-PA 10.3%, SK 10.6%, APSAC 10.5% (p=NS). In the subset of patients randomized within 6 hours of onset of AMI, and with ST segment elevation at the time of randomization, there was no difference in mortality among the three agents. Mortality among the heparin-treated patients was 10.3% and among the no heparin patients was 10.6% (p=NS). However, during the 7-day period of heparin administration, the comparative mortalities were 7.4% and 7.9% (2p=.06). For each thrombolytic agent, 35-day mortality rates for heparin versus no heparin were not significantly different: rt-PA (heparin 10.0%, no heparin 10.7%), SK (heparin 10.5%, no heparin 10.6%), and APSAC (heparin 10.5%, no heparin 10.6%).

An overview[461] of the GISSI-2 and ISIS-3 data, based upon analysis of 48,293 patients, found that 35-day mortality was 10.0% with both rt-PA and SK. An overview of the heparin effect for the two trials, based upon 40,754 patients, indicated a mortality of 10.0% with heparin and 10.2% with no heparin (p=NS). During the 7-day heparin treatment period, mortality rates were 6.8% with heparin and 7.3% without (2p=.01).

The GISSI-2 and ISIS-3 trials detected no important differences in the 35-day vascular mortality among rt-PA, SK, and APSAC. However, these results are specific to the dose regimens of the thrombolytic agents and of the heparin used in the two trials. The case was made that in the GISSI-2 and ISIS-3 studies, the heparin regimens were insufficiently vigorous to obtain the maximal benefit from rt-PA or, indeed, from SK. New evidence acquired since these studies had been designed indicated the beneficial effect of full-dose intravenous heparin (APTT 1.5–2 times normal) in sustaining infarct vessel patency among patients treated with rt-PA.[47] Other studies suggested that new dose regimens of rt-PA and combinations of fibrin-specific and nonspecific agents might be more effective than the standard regimens previously employed in the large randomized trials.[48I, 49I] The rt-PA-APSAC Patency Study (TAPS) group[48I] randomized 435 patients within 6 hours of onset of MI to "front-loaded" rt-PA (15-mg bolus, 50 mg over 30 min, 35 mg over 60 min) or to APSAC (30 U IV over 5 min). All patients received a bolus of 5,000 U of heparin IV, with the infusion begun after 90 minutes in the rt-PA group and after 6 hours in the APSAC group with anticoagulation maintained throughout the hospital stay. Among the 421 patients who received the allocated therapy, in-hospital death was 2.4% with rt-PA and 8.1% with APSAC ($p=.0095$).

Concerns that the heparin regimens in GISSI-2 and ISIS-3 might have been suboptimal, and encouraging results from the studies of new thrombolytic dose regimens, prompted the initiation of the multinational Global Utilization of Streptokinase and Tissue Plasminogen Activator for Occluded Coronary Arteries (GUSTO) trial.[50I, 51I] The primary objective of the trial was to determine whether a regimen designed to produce rapid and sustained infarct vessel recanalization was associated with improved survival. Patients with suspected AMI (characteristic pain and ST segment elevation) within 6 hours of onset were eligible for study entry. All patients received chewable aspirin, two 80-mg tablets, as soon as possible. They were randomized to one of four regimens:

1. rt-PA (alteplase) IV 15-mg bolus, then 0.75 mg/kg over 30 minutes not to exceed 50 mg, then 0.50 mg/kg over 60 minutes not to exceed 35 mg, the total dose not to exceed 100 mg. Simultaneously, heparin was commenced with a 5,000 U IV bolus, followed by a 1,000 to 1,200 U per hour continuous infusion for at least 48 hours, maintaining APTT at 60 to 85 seconds.
2. Streptokinase 1.5 mU IV over 1 hour *plus* heparin IV in an identical regimen to that for the rt-PA group.
3. SK 1.5 MU IV over 1 hour *plus* heparin 12,500 U subcutaneously commencing at 4 hours after initiation of SK and repeated every 12 hours for 7 days (or until prior discharge).
4. rt-PA IV 1.0 mg/kg over 60 minutes, maximum total dose 90 mg, including an initial bolus of 10% of the total amount, *plus* simultaneous SK 1.0 MU IV over 60 minutes, *plus* heparin in an identical regimen to that for the rt-PA group.

IV beta blockade (atenolol 5 mg, repeated once) followed by oral maintenance was recommended for patients without contraindications. Nitrates, calcium channel blockers, antiarrhythmics, and ACE inhibitors were prescribed at the discretion of the attending physician and were recorded.

There were 41,021 patients randomized after a mean of 2 hours who began thrombolytic therapy a mean of 2.75 hours after infarct onset. Mortalities at 24 hours and 30 days were, respectively, for rt-PA 2.3, 6.3%; for rt-PA/SK 2.8, 7.0%; for SK (subcutaneous heparin) 2.8, 7.2%; and for SK (IV heparin) 2.9, 7.4%. The relative mortality reduction with accelerated rt-PA versus the SK alone groups was 14% ($p=.001$), and the absolute mortality reduction was 1%. Hemorrhagic and total stroke were more common with the accelerated rt-PA than the SK alone groups (0.72% versus 0.52%, $p=.03$, and 1.55% versus 1.31%, $p=.09$).

Major bleeding was not different among the four regimens. The composite outcome of death and nonfatal disabling stroke was less with accelerated rt-PA than SK (6.9% versus 7.8%, $p=.006$). These findings would suggest that for 1,000 patients with evidence of acute myocardial infarction, treated within 6 hours of onset using accelerated rt-PA rather than SK, there would be ten fewer deaths, or nine fewer occurrences of a composite of death plus nonfatal disabling stroke. Currently the cost of rt-PA is substantially more than that of SK, and the investigators calculated an excess cost of $29,000 per year of life saved with accelerated rt-PA rather than SK. The benefit of accelerated rt-PA over SK varies with patient age, time from infarct onset, and location of AMI. Hence, in arriving at decisions about appropriate use of limited health care resources, physicians and health care planners will have to develop cost-effectiveness analyses in these different patient groups.

## Relative and Absolute Mortality Reduction Among Various Patient Subgroups

There is evidence for the reduction of early (up to about 35 days) and late (up to 5 years) mortality by SK, APSAC, and rt-PA, each compared with placebo, for patients treated intravenously within the first few hours of onset of AMI. However, the benefit may vary considerably depending upon a variety of characteristics of the individual patient and the timing of the thrombolytic therapy. Relative reduction in mortality is simply the difference between the mortality of the thrombolytic-treated group and the mortality of the group not treated with thrombolytic therapy, expressed as a percentage of the mortality in the untreated group. Hence, if mortality is 10% in the untreated group and 9% in the thrombolysis-treated group, the relative mortality (or risk) reduction is 10%. The absolute mortality reduction is simply the difference between the two mortalities—in this case 1%. The absolute mortality reduction may be calculated from knowledge of the mortality in the untreated group and the relative mortality reduction.

(Absolute mortality reduction) = (mortality in untreated group) × (relative mortality reduction) = (mortality in untreated group) − (mortality in treated group)

This absolute mortality reduction is often expressed in terms of the number of lives saved per 100 or per 1,000 patients treated. An absolute mortality reduction of 1% is equivalent to the saving of 1 life per 100 patients treated with the thrombolytic agent compared with not using it (or 10 lives per 1,000 patients treated).

The relative mortality reduction with thrombolysis has been evaluated in a number of large clinical trials. The greatest interest has attended variations in relative mortality reductions in relation to age, infarct location, previous infarction, blood pressure, heart rate, and time from onset of AMI to therapy. The large trials have demonstrated some variability in relative risk reduction in relation to age. In the GISSI[301] and ISIS-2[311] trials, the relative benefit among patients over 75 or 70 years was much less than that among the younger patients. Conversely, the ASSET trial[411] and the AIMS trial[361, 371] showed greater relative risk reduction among the older patients. However, all of these trials have shown a higher baseline risk in the elderly, and accordingly, all show greater absolute benefits in the elderly even though relative risk reductions have varied. Among patients over age 65, there is consistent evidence of many more lives saved per 1,000 patients treated than the number among the younger patients. Hence, age over 70 itself, rather than being a contraindication to thrombolytic therapy, is actually a strong indication for the treatment.

In most of the large trials, the relative mortality reduction appears to be greater with anterior than with inferior MI. Whereas a statistically significant reduction in mortality has generally been noted with anterior MI, there has generally been only a favorable trend with inferior MI. Even in the Fibrinolytic Treatment Trialists' Collaboration (FTT) with over 60,000 patients randomized to fibrinolytic or placebo, the benefit with inferior MI does not quite reach statistical significance.[52] The mortality of anterior MI is generally twice that of inferior MI; hence, the absolute benefit among patients with anterior MI is much greater than that among those with inferior MI, for whom there is not absolute proof of benefit. Patients who present with bundle branch block have a large and statistically significant reduction of mortality with thrombolytic therapy in the FTT. Perhaps surprisingly, patients who present with a history suggestive of AMI, but with only ST segment depression, show a trend toward harm from thrombolytic therapy. It is highly likely that among patients presenting with ST segment depression, there are many who might benefit from thrombolytic therapy,[531] but currently there are no clinical trial data to help in the selection of potentially responsive patients from this group. Patients with a history suggestive of AMI but with a normal electrocardiogram (ECG) have a very low mortality and do not benefit from thrombolytic therapy. It is likely that AMI is an incorrect diagnosis in many such patients (in whom thrombolytic therapy could only cause harm).

Although relative benefits may vary somewhat, thrombolytic therapy is efficacious in patients with first and subsequent MI and a full range of presenting heart rates. It is efficacious, too, across the range of presenting blood pressures with the probable exception of those with very high systolic or diastolic levels.[311, 52]

Studies in animals show a clear relationship between the duration of coronary artery occlusion and the extent of myocardial necrosis.[54] When coronary occlusion has developed in patients in the cardiac care unit (CCU), the rapid institution of thrombolytic therapy or immediate PTCA has, at times, resulted in the prevention of MI. There is considerable clinical evidence to indicate that thrombolytic therapy begun within the first few hours after the onset of AMI results in greater benefit than when it is begun many hours after the onset.[55]

In the GISSI study,[301] the most striking mortality reduction (47%) occurred in those patients randomized within 1 hour of infarct onset. Patients entering within 6 hours of infarct onset had a 22.6% reduction in mortality ($p<.00006$), whereas the reduction was only 10.6% among those entered between 6 and 9 hours of onset, and there was a trend against SK among those entered between 9 and 12 hours. In the ISIS-2 study,[311] wherein the overall odds reduction for mortality with SK was 25%, the reduction was 29.6% ($2p<.00001$) for those entered in 0 to 6 hours of onset, but only 18% ($2p=.02$) for those entered between 6 and 24 hours after infarct onset.

An overview[311] of the results for mortality reduction in relation to time, based upon six randomized trials of SK, found that the odds reduction was 31% ($p<.00001$) for the 0- to 3-hour group, 22% ($2p<.00001$) for the 3- to 6-hour group, and 14% ($2p<.02$) for the 6- to 24-hour group. The AIMS trial[36I, 37I] of APSAC versus placebo showed no statistically significant difference in relative mortality reduction between patients treated within 4 hours and those treated at 4 hours or more. Similarly, the ASSET trial[41I] of rt-PA versus placebo showed no statistically significant difference in relative mortality reduction between patients treated at less than 3 hours of onset and those treated at 3 hours or more. The FTT collaboration found an odds reduction of mortality of 24% ($p<.0001$) for the 0- to 6-hour group, 15% ($p=.004$) for the 7- to 12-hour group, and 4% ($p=NS$) for the 13- to 24-hour group.[52]

The most recent data from the GUSTO trial[50aI] showed that by comparison with the SK alone regimens, the accelerated rt-PA regimen reduced mortality by 20% among patients treated at 0 to 2 hours after infarct onset, and 17% among patients treated at 2 to 4 hours. There was a statistically insignificant reduction of 9% at 4–6 hours, and none beyond 6 hours.

From all these observations, there appear to be good reasons to develop methods to administer thrombolytic therapy very early to patients with symptoms indicative of AMI. Several studies have documented the delays that occur in the management of patients before and following the diagnosis of AMI.[56, 57II] Because substantial delays occur in the hospital emergency department and an even greater delay is present in patients who are transferred to the CCU before starting lytic therapy, a number of investigators have evaluated the feasibility of starting thrombolytic therapy prior to hospitalization. In phase 1 of the Myocardial Infarction Triage and Intervention (MITI) Study, in which the diagnosis of MI was made by paramedics using a portable electrocardiogram (ECG) machine and remote physician consultation, a saving of 73 ± 44 minutes was estimated if thrombolytic therapy had been initiated prior to hospitalization.[56] The European Myocardial Infarction Project[57] randomized 5,469 patients within 6 hours of onset of AMI to prehospital or inhospital ad-

ministration of APSAC 30 U IV. Thrombolytic therapy was begun a mean of 55 minutes earlier in the prehospital group. Overall mortality at 30 days was 9.7% in the prehospital group and was 11.1% in the hospital group (risk reduction 13%, $p=.08$). Cardiac mortality was reduced to 8.3% from 9.8% (risk reduction 16%, $p=.049$). An overview of five such trials found a reduction in short-term mortality of 17% ($p=.03$) among the patients who received thrombolytic therapy before admission.[57II]

The possibility of benefit among patients treated many hours after infarct onset was apparent even in the early trials. An overview of randomized trials of SK[311] has demonstrated a statistically significant reduction in the odds of mortality among patients entered 6 to 24 hours after infarct onset. The Estudio Multicentrico Estreptoquinasa Republica de America de Sur (EMERAS) trial[58II] randomized 3,586 patients to SK (1.5 MU over 1 hour) or placebo within the period 6 to 24 hours following onset of AMI. Overall mortality was 11.9% with SK and 12.4% with placebo (4% odds reduction, $p=NS$). Among the patients presenting 7 to 12 hours from onset of symptoms, hospital mortality was 11.7% with SK and 13.2% with placebo (odds reduction 14%, $p=NS$), whereas in the 13- to 24-hour group hospital mortality was 11.4% with SK and 10.7% with control (odds increase 8%, $p=NS$). The entry windows in the large placebo-controlled trials of APSAC and rt-PA had not extended beyond 6 hours until the Late Assessment of Thrombolytic Efficacy (LATE) Study[53I] was done. This trial randomized 5,711 patients with AMI between 6 and 24 hours of pain onset to IV rt-PA or matching placebo. Overall, 35-day mortality was 8.9% with rt-PA and 10.3% with placebo, a nonsignificant 14.1% relative risk reduction. However, among patients entered under 12 hours, the 35-day mortality was 8.9% versus 12% (relative risk reduction 25.6%, $p=.02$). Among patients entered at 12 to 24 hours, the mortality was 8.7% versus 9.2% (relative risk reduction 5.4%, $p=NS$). The FTT Collaboration overview of over 60,000 patients randomized to a fibrinolytic therapy or control found a mortality reduction from 12.7% to 11.1% in the 7- to 12-hour group (odds reduction 14%, $2p=.005$), and from 10.5% to 10.0% in the 13- to 24-hour group (odds reduction 5%, $2p=NS$).

## Longterm Results of Thrombolytic Therapy

The relatively high rate of late mortality previously observed in patients with non-Q wave infarction led to concerns that any benefit of reduced inhospital mortality from thrombolytic therapy might be lost subsequently as patients with incomplete infarctions were exposed to a risk of recurrent MI over subsequent months. However, the initial gains were not lost during 1-year followup in the large trials of SK,[31I, 59I] APSAC[37I] and rt-PA,[60I] and similar observations were made in the smaller trials.[34II, 61II–63II]

Mortality between hospital discharge and 1-year followup was about 7% in treated and untreated groups in the GISSI trial,[59I] and between 5 weeks and 1 year was 5.6% with SK and 6.5% with placebo in the ISIS-2 trial.[31I] In these large trials, the reduction in total 1-year mortality by SK remains statistically significant. These observations now extend out to 4 years with maintenance of the initially observed benefit.[64] Mortalities between hospital discharge and 1 year were 4.7% and 5.7% in the APSAC and placebo groups of the AIMS trial,[37I] and the overall mortalities were APSAC 11.1% and placebo 17.8% ($p = .0007$). In the ASSET trial,[60I] mortalities by 1 year were rt-PA 13.2% and placebo 15.1% ($p < .05$). During the 1-year followup, rates of percutaneous transluminal coronary angioplasty (PTCA) and aortocoronary bypass surgery were low in the GISSI trial (SK 3.3%, placebo 3%), the AIMS trial (APSAC 4.3%, placebo 3.9%), and the ASSET trial (rt-PA 4.9%, placebo 4.8%), suggesting that routine invasive investigation and therapy may not be necessary to preserve the initial mortality reductions in thrombolytic therapy. Of course, the longterm benefits of thrombolytic therapy might well be greater if the fatal and nonfatal hazards of severe residual coronary artery stenosis and ischemia could be reduced, but the potential contribution of more aggressive investigation and revascularization is unknown.

During the 21-day to 12-month followup of TIMI-1,[65I] patients' rates of coronary artery bypass grafting or PTCA (35% rt-PA, 38.7% SK) were high by comparison with the ISIS-2, AIMS, and ASSET trials, whereas the interval mortalities were not different (6.3% rt-PA and 6.2% SK).

## STUDIES DELINEATING CORONARY ARTERY PATENCY AND LEFT VENTRICULAR FUNCTION

The early trials of thrombolytic therapy had focused on the clinically important outcomes of death and reinfarction. The reawakened interest in thrombolytic therapy in the early 1980s was associated with extensive angiographic evaluations of infarct-related artery patency rates.[43] From these studies, the following observations emerged.

1. Coronary angiography done in the first 6 hours of a transmural MI in evolution revealed completely occlusive thrombosis in 85% of cases.[11]

2. Spontaneous reperfusion rate was about 10% during acute coronary angiographic observation.[66, 67, 68I] The spontaneous patency rate was about 35% among patients undergoing angiography at 12 to 24 hours (DeWood) and up to 83% by 3 weeks.[69I]

3. Reocclusion occurred in 5 to 30% of vessels, which initially reperfused, most of it by 24 hours, but with additional reocclusions over subsequent days.[70II]

The terminology used in reports of angiographic outcomes requires some discussion. Reperfusion and reocclusion rates can be determined only when a pretreatment angiogram has been done. Reperfusion (recanalization) rate is the proportion of initially occluded infarct-related vessels that are subsequently opened; reocclusion rate is the proportion of vessels observed to reperfuse and then reocclude. The patency rate is assessed by performing an angiogram at a given point in time and is an aggregate of the rates of initial patency, reperfusion occurring spontaneously and as the result of thrombolytic therapy, and reocclusion. Because pretreatment angiography has usually been omitted to avoid delay in IV thrombolytic therapy, true reperfusion and reocclusion rates have been determined in relatively few studies and were routinely available only when intracoronary thrombolytic therapy was common. Even with serial studies, the rates of reperfusion and reocclusion calculated vary with the timing of the second and subsequent angiograms. Careful specification of the timing of angiography is essential to the meaningful interpretation of results.

Seven randomized trials of intracoronary SK versus control treatment and three comparing intracoronary SK with IV SK have been published. Recanalization rates at 60 to 90 minutes were very high, ranging from 60 to 79% with intracoronary SK. Recanalization rates were consistently higher with intracoronary than with IV SK.[43]

Angiographic studies have generally demonstrated the highest 90-minute reperfusion and patency rates with rt-PA, the next highest with APSAC, and the lowest with SK. The most useful data are from studies in which direct comparisons of these agents were made.

The European Cooperative Trial[23] randomized 129 patients to IV rt-PA (0.75 mg/kg) or IV SK (1.5 MU over 1 hour) within 6 hours of infarction. Angiography was undertaken within 75 to 90 minutes, and at 90 minutes the patency was 70% in the rt-PA group and 55% in the SK group ($p=.054$). In the TIMI-1 study,[221] coronary angiography was performed on 316 patients within 7 hours of onset of AMI. They were then randomized to receive either rt-PA (80 mg over 3 hours) or IV SK (1.5 MU over 1 hour); 290 patients actually received treatment. Within 90 minutes of starting therapy, reperfusion was observed in 62% of the rt-PA patients and 31% of the SK patients ($p<.001$). When all patients treated were considered, whether or not there was initial patency, final patency rates at 90 minutes were 70% among those given rt-PA and 43% among those given SK, similar to the rates observed in the European Cooperative Trial.

In the largest study comparing IV SK with IV APSAC,[711] 370 patients were randomly allocated double-blind to APSAC (30 U IV over 2 to 5 minutes) or SK (1.5 MU IV over 1 hour) within 4 hours of the infarction. Angiography at a mean of 140 minutes revealed patencies of 72% with APSAC and 73% with SK. In the other studies comparing APSAC with SK, the 90-minute patencies were, respectively, 72% versus 56%[72II] and 55% versus 53%.[73II] Ninety-minute patency with APSAC is probably less than with rt-PA but is probably not much different from that with SK, with no difference observed by 140 minutes.

The German Activator Urokinase Study (GAUS)[84I] compared rt-PA with UK and found no significant difference in patencies at 90 minutes; the Pro-Urokinase in Myocardial Infarction (PRIMI) trial[29I] compared SK with scuPA and found no significant difference in 90-minute patency.

The most recent data come from trials utilizing combinations of SK and rt-PA and accelerated dose regimens of rt-PA. The comparison of rt-PA with a combination of rt-PA/SK found a higher 90-minute patency with the combination regimen (79% versus 64%, $p<.05$).[49I] The TAPS study[48I] found that compared with APSAC, accelerated-dose rt-PA produced greater 90-minute patency (84.4% versus 70.3%, $p=.0007$).

The GUSTO study had an angiographic component that constituted a trial of much greater size than any previously done.[51I] A group of 2,034 patients were selected; 1,200 had angiography at 90 minutes and 7 days, and groups of 400 each had angiography at 3 hours, or 24 hours, or 7 days. Infarct-related artery (IRA) patency was designated in the presence of TIMI-

2 flow (patency with opacification of the entire distal vessel but with delayed filling or washout of contrast agent) or TIMI-3 flow (normal flow). The 90-minute patencies were for accelerated rt-PA 81%, rt-PA/SK 73%; for SK (IV heparin) 61%, and for SK (subcutaneous heparin) 54%. TIMI-3 flow at 90 minutes was strikingly higher with accelerated-dose rt-PA than with the SK regimens (54% versus 32%). As in previous trials, the investigators noted a marked catchup phenomenon in coronary artery patency with SK by 180 minutes, when patencies were for accelerated rt-PA 76%, rt-PA/SK 85%; SK (IV heparin) 74%, and SK (subcutaneous heparin) 73%. Of vessels demonstrated to be patent at 90 minutes, reocclusion rates at 5 to 7 days were for accelerated rt-PA 5.9%, rt-PA/SK 4.9%, SK (IV heparin) 5.5%, and SK (subcutaneous heparin) 6.4%.

The measurement of left ventricular function reflects the extent of infarct size and is a strong independent determinant of late prognosis following AMI.[75] This observation has been confirmed in the thrombolytic era in a report from the GISSI-2 trial, in which LV function was the strongest predictor of 6-month mortality.[76] Several randomized studies have evaluated the effects of thrombolytic therapy on left ventricular function.

Three studies have measured LV function in patients randomized to IV SK versus placebo.[77I, 78II, 79I] Treatment was begun in under 6 hours, and in each of the studies, the left ventricular ejection fraction (LVEF) as measured by contrast angiography or radionuclide angiography (RNA) at least 3 weeks after MI was significantly higher in the treated group.

There have been five randomized, placebo-controlled trials of IV rt-PA that have measured LV function. Each showed statistically significantly better LVEF in the rt-PA-treated patients, whether by contrast angiography[27I, 42I, 80I] or by RNA.[28I, 81II]

The comparative effects of IV SK and rt-PA on LV function have been assessed in four studies. In TIMI-I[25I] and the White study,[82I] LVEF by contrast angiography at hospital discharge was identical for IV SK and IV rt-PA. In the Plasminogen Activator Italian Multicenter Study (PAIMS),[83II] there was a slight advantage to rt-PA over SK. The GAUS trial[84I] measured LVEF by radiographic contrast at 10 days or more after therapy and found no difference between IV rt-PA and IV UK.

The GUSTO trial[51II] carried out by far the largest evaluation of comparative LV function employing various regimens of thrombolytic therapy. The ejection fractions of the various regimens ranged from 57 to 59% and were not significantly different either at 90 minutes or at 5 to 7 days. The trial also related LVEF to TIMI-3 patency (without regard to thrombolytic therapy) at 90 minutes and 5 to 7 days and found a close relationship.

It is therefore apparent that infarct-related artery (IRA) patency at 60 to 90 minutes is greatest with rt-PA, next with APSAC, and least with SK (1.5 MU over 1 hour). The regimen of accelerated rt-PA in TAPS and GUSTO appears to give the highest rates of perfusion at 90 minutes, and is better than the t-PA/SK regimen, which in turn is more effective than standard regimens of SK. Although there is a marked gradient of IRA patency at 90 minutes among the various thrombolytic agents and regimens, the difference disappears by 180 minutes. By 3 weeks, there is very little difference in IRA patency between thrombolytic agents and placebo. Nevertheless, the 90-minute patency is a strong predictor of inhospital survival. Patients with TIMI-3 patency at 90 minutes have a better prognosis than patients with TIMI-2 patency. Differences in LV function as a result of thrombolytic therapy have generally been detected only when patients are treated early, and even then the difference between thrombolytic therapy and placebo has been rather small. The majority of comparisons of thrombolytic regimens have found no difference in LV function.

## COMPLICATIONS AND SIDE EFFECTS

### Bleeding

The thrombolytic agents (Tables 5–2 and 5–3) are thought to produce their benefit by lysing coronary thrombi, but, of course, this is nonselective, and morbidity may result from the lysis of thrombi at other sites where hemostasis is required. In addition, the plasminemia produced by thrombolytic agents leads to a reduction of circulating fibrinogen and factors V and VIII, to the generation of fibrin and fibrinogen degradation products (FDPs) with anticoagulant properties, and to a platelet function defect,[85, 86] resulting in hemostatic incompetence. The risk of bleeding with SK might be expected to be greater than with rt-PA because of the relatively long half life of SK and the much greater systemic rather than local generation of plasmin. However, considerable bleeding may also arise with rt-PA because of its greater thrombolytic efficacy, the significant systemic plasmin generation that occurs with the current dosage regimens, and the use of hepa-

rin subsequently. The true incidence of bleeding may be determined only in large trials of thrombolytic therapy.

In most reports, bleeding is divided into major and minor episodes, but the definition varies somewhat. Generally the term ''major hemorrhage'' includes fatal hemorrhage and those requiring transfusion. The definition may also include hemorrhage leading to hospitalization or operative intervention, in certain critical areas (retroperitoneal, spinal, retinal), and overt blood loss with an arbitrary fall in hemoglobin. The greatest concern attends cerebral bleeding, which is often classified separately from other major bleeding.

In the trials of IV SK without angiography, bleeding, apart from that at local venipuncture sites, was reported in about 4% of patients, with an absolute excess over control patients of about 3%. Major bleeding, defined in terms of a transfusion requirement, occurred in only about 0.5% of patients, and cerebral hemorrhage occurred in 0.1% of patients. The total incidence of stroke was about equal in SK and placebo groups in the ISIS-2 trial.[311] It is possible that bleeding and stroke were under-reported in the larger trials of SK, which were of simple design and focused on mortality as a major outcome event. In the AIMS trial,[361, 371] total bleeding in hospital was 13.8% with APSAC and 4.1% with placebo, and transfusion was required in 0.8% of each group. Stroke and cerebral hemorrhage rates were 1.3% and 0.5%, respectively, with APSAC, and 0.6% and 0.2% with placebo (absolute excess of cerebral hemorrhage 0.3%). In the ASSET trial,[411] among the rt-PA patients, minor bleeding occurred in 6.3% and major bleeding in 1.4% (absolute excess 6% and 0.9%, respectively). Cerebral hemorrhage rates were 0.3% with rt-PA and 0.01% with placebo.

The expectation that bleeding and, in particular, cerebral hemorrhage may be reduced with APSAC and rt-PA by comparison with SK has been evaluated in larger studies allowing direct comparisons. In the International Study Group t-PA/SK mortality trial,[45] major bleeding and intracerebral bleeding occurred with the following respective frequencies—SK 0.9% and 0.3%, rt-PA 0.6% and 0.4%.

In the ISIS-3 trial,[461] bleeding was slightly more common in APSAC- and rt-PA-treated patients than in SK-treated patients, but the rates of major bleeding were not different (SK 0.9%; APSAC 1%; rt-PA 0.8%). The rates of definite or possible cerebral hemorrhage were SK 0.2%; APSAC 0.7%; rt-PA 0.5% ($p<.0001$). In both of these trials, the heparin-treated patients had

Table 5–2. **Hemorrhage in Large Noninvasive Trials of Thrombolytic Therapy**

| Study | Patients | Agents | Major Noncerebral Hemorrhage (%) | Cerebral Hemorrhage (%) |
|---|---|---|---|---|
| *Thrombolytic Agents vs Control* | | | | |
| GISSI[30] | 11,806 | SK, 21% IV heparin ± oral anticoagulant | SK 0.3 · CONTROL | SK 0.1 · CONTROL 0 |
| ISIS-2[31] | 17,187 | SK, 30% IV heparin ± oral anticoagulant | SK 0.6 · PLACEBO 0.2 | SK 0.1 · PLACEBO 0 |
| AIMS[36, 37] | 1,004 | APSAC, IV heparin—warfarin 3 mo | APSAC 0.8 · PLACEBO 0.8 | APSAC 1 · PLACEBO 0.3 |
| ASSET[41] | 5,011 | rt-PA, IV heparin 24 h | rt-PA 1.4 · PLACEBO 0.5 | rt-PA 0.3 · PLACEBO 0.01 |
| *Comparisons of Thrombolytic Agents* | | | | |
| International Study Group[45] | 20,891 | SK vs rt-PA factorial with sc heparin | SK 0.9 · rt-PA 0.6 | SK 0.3 · rt-PA 0.4 |
| ISIS-3[46] | 46,091 | SK vs APSAC vs rt-PA factorial with sc heparin | SK 0.9 · APSAC 1.0 · rt-PA 0.9 | SK 0.2 · APSAC 0.7 · rt-PA 0.5 |
| GUSTO[50] | 41,021 | SK 1.5 MU 1 h + heparin sc or IV, or SK 1.0 MU 1 h + rt-Pa (alteplase) 1.0 mg/kg, 1 h + heparin, or rt-PA up to 100 mg, 1.5 h + heparin | SK-SC HEPARIN 0.3 · SK-IV HEPARIN 0.5 · SK/rt-PA 0.6 · rt-PA 0.4 | SK-SC HEPARIN 0.49 · SK-IV HEPARIN 0.54 · SK/rt-PA 0.94 · rt-PA 0.72 |

55

Table 5–3. **Hemorrhage in Small Invasive Trials of Thrombolytic Therapy**

| Study | Patients | Agents | Major Noncerebral Hemorrhage (%) | | | Cerebral Hemorrhage (%) | | |
|---|---|---|---|---|---|---|---|---|
| TIMI-I[22] | 290 | rt-PA vs SK | rt-PA 29 | | SK 27 | rt-PA 0 | | SK 0 |
| European Cooperative[23] | 129 | rt-PA vs SK | rt-PA 7.7 | | SK 6.3 | rt-PA 0 | | SK 0 |
| TAMI-5[126] | 575 | rt-PA vs SK vs combination | rt-PA 8.7 | SK 10 | COMBINATION 12 | rt-PA 2.1 | SK 1.5 | COMBINATION 0 |
| Bassand[127] | 169 | rt-PA vs APSAC | rt-PA 2 | | APSAC 1 | rt-PA 0 | | APSAC 0 |
| TAPS[48] | 433 | accelerated rt-PA vs APSAC | rt-PA 2.8 | | APSAC 8.1 | rt-PA 1 | | APSAC 1 |
| PRIMI[74] | 401 | rscu-PA vs SK | rscu-PA 4.0 | | SK 11.3 | rscu-PA 1.0 | | SK 0.5 |

significantly more major bleeding, whereas cerebral hemorrhage was significantly increased with heparin only in the ISIS-3 trial.

In the GUSTO trial[501] the rates of all stroke and hemorrhagic stroke with the various regimens were, respectively, for accelerated rt-PA 1.55 (0.72%); rt-PA/SK: 1.64 (0.94%); SK (IV heparin) 1.40 (0.54%); and SK (subcutaneous heparin) 1.22 (0.49%). The differences in overall stroke rate were attributable to differences in the incidence of hemorrhagic stroke. All-cause mortality was reduced by about 10 per 1000 patients treated by accelerated rt-PA compared with the SK-alone groups, whereas the composite rate of death plus nonfatal disabling stroke was reduced to about nine per 1,000 patients treated. The incidence of severe or life-threatening bleeding was not significantly different among the groups. There were no statistically significant differences in cerebral or major extracranial bleeding between the IV and subcutaneous heparin arms of the SK group.

Female sex, low body weight, and increasing age, as well as a history of cerebral vascular disease, are risk factors for cerebral hemorrhage in thrombolytic trials.[85] Uncontrolled hypertension and a history of chronic hypertension may be risk factors, although evidence is sparse. It is likely that higher doses of rt-PA increase the risk of cerebral hemorrhage.

Major noncerebral bleeding was increased among the heparin-treated patients in GISSI-2 and ISIS-3. However, in the GUSTO trial, there was no difference in rates of severe, life-threatening bleeding between IV and subcutaneous (sc) heparin in the SK-treated patients. Although ASA increased the rate of minor bleed-

ing in ISIS-2, the rate of major bleeding was not increased.

The most important determinant of the rate of noncerebral bleeding is the degree of vascular invasion. Even with optimal operator skills, small-bore catheters, and groin sheath maintenance for 24 hours after angiography, large hematomas are common, often requiring transfusion. The risk of major bleeding is increased several-fold. In two studies involving invasive vascular procedures, and comparing SK with rt-PA, the proportion of patients requiring transfusion was not different for the two agents. When IV APSAC was compared with intracoronary SK in a trial in which all patients first underwent coronary angiography,[401] bleeding was more frequent with APSAC, and the transfusion requirement in 17% of APSAC cases was similar to that in angiographic studies of IV SK and IV rt-PA.

## Allergy and Anaphylaxis

Streptokinase is produced by type B streptococci and is a foreign protein to which most humans have antibodies.[87] These antibodies inactivate exogenously administered SK, although the current high-dose regimens usually overwhelm the levels of naturally occurring antibodies. Within 3 to 4 days of SK administration, the level of neutralizing antibodies becomes sufficiently high to inactivate the usual therapeutic dose of 1.5 MU SK. Persistence of neutralizing antibodies sufficient to inactivate the usual dose of SK is observed in up to 80% of patients at 1 year following SK therapy, and in about 50% of patients at 2 to 4 years.[88, 89] Once a patient has received SK, absolute assurance of efficacy of repeat thrombolytic therapy at any subsequent time beyond the first 3 or 4 days would require rt-PA. Routine measurement of SK neutralizing antibody titre at 6 to 12 months following administration of SK or APSAC might provide further guidance as to the likely efficacy of repeat therapy with SK or APSAC. Further evaluation of such approaches is required.[90]

Allergic reactions may occur with even low levels of SK antibodies, and although they are probably less common with the purified preparations of SK now available, they are not rare. Anaphylaxis is indeed rare. The problem of under-reporting is likely for minor allergic manifestations, although in blinded trials, there should be no expectation bias, and the relative frequency with SK versus placebo should be evident. The incidence of possible allergic manifestations (fever, rash, rigor, bronchospasm) appears to be about 5%, with about a five-fold excess over placebo. Anaphylactic shock is likely to be over-reported in a setting in which hypotension and minor allergic manifestations due to treatment are fairly common. The reported incidence in GISSI[30I] was 0.1%, whereas in ISIS-2, possible anaphylactic shock was reported in 0.2%, although review of these cases failed to reveal characteristic features of anaphylactic shock in most.[311]

APSAC may be expected to have a risk of allergic manifestations similar to that of SK. In the AMIS trial,[36I] reversible anaphylactic reactions occurred in 0.6% of APSAC patients and in no placebo patients. The rates of more minor allergic reactions were 1.8% with APSAC and 2.7% with placebo ($p = .3$). The ISIS-3 trial[46I] provides the best comparative data for possible allergic and anaphylactic reactions. A possible allergic reaction with persistent shock occurred with the following frequencies in ISIS-3—SK 0.3%, APSAC 0.5%, and rt-PA 0.1%. The relatively high rate with APSAC may have arisen from the bolus infusion of this drug in contrast to the slower infusion of SK. It is doubtful that rt-PA causes true allergic reactions.

The GUSTO trial[50I] provides data on the comparative frequencies of allergy and anaphylaxis between tPA and SK. However, the open label design would permit ascertainment bias.

## Hypotension

Hypotension is often observed during the administration of SK and has been attributed to the systemic plasminemia, which leads to bradykinin release from kallikrein, from activation of complement, and possibly from endothelial prostacyclin secretion.[91] Hypotension may occur

as a result of vagal reflexes precipitated by posterior wall reperfusion.[92] Hypotension may of course be precipitated by LV dysfunction produced by the infarct process, and it is the absolute difference between SK and placebo-treated patients that must be considered. The absolute excess of hypotension and/or bradycardia with SK reported in ISIS-2[311] was 7.9%, generally during the 60-minute infusion or shortly thereafter. In the AIMS trial[36I, 371] treatment produced a more marked fall in blood pressure than did placebo, although cardiogenic shock was more common among placebo-treated patients.

The ISIS-3 trial[46I] again provides the best comparative data. Profound hypotension requiring drug therapy occurred with the following frequencies—SK 6.8%; APSAC 7.2%; and rt-PA 4.3%. It is also possible in this trial to compare rates of profound hypotension among the thrombolytic agents and open control, in which the rates were as follows—SK 5.8%; APSAC 5.9%; rt-PA 2.8; and open control 0.96%, although there could be some bias in this unblinded comparison.

## Arrhythmias

Although there was an impression in early trials of thrombolytic therapy that ventricular arrhythmias were more frequent at the time of reperfusion, and that ventricular fibrillation (VF) appeared to be precipitated by reperfusion on some occasions, randomized controlled trials have shown no increase in the incidence of serious ventricular arrhythmias[33II, 93] and a reduction in the incidence of ventricular fibrillation,[30I, 31I, 94, 95] particularly late VF occurring after the first day of hospitalization.[94] Followup data from the GISSI-2 study have demonstrated that the prevalence of ventricular premature depolarizations (VPDs) with a frequency of greater than 10 per hour is similar to that in the prethrombolytic era, although the percentage of patients with VPDs is somewhat lower.[76]

## Recurrent Ischemia and Reinfarction

Following recanalization, the vessel usually remains severely stenotic from a combination of atherosclerosis and residual thrombus and is subject to a risk of reocclusion and reinfarction.[96] The definitions of reinfarction vary, although simple clinical criteria of the recurrence of prolonged ischemic pain, accompanied by a second rise in cardiac enzymes, are likely to be employed in a large mortality trial. More sensitive criteria involving closer attention to enzyme monitoring are likely to reveal higher rates of reinfarction.

The incidence of reinfarction in the trials of IV SK is remarkably consistent, at about 4% among patients allocated to SK, with an absolute excess over control patients of 1 to 2%. In the AIMS trial,[36I, 37I] the rate of reinfarction during the hospital stay was not significantly increased in the APSAC group (6.1%) versus placebo (4.7%) ($p$=.3). In the ASSET study,[41I] there was no excess of reinfarction with rt-PA compared with placebo. In the GISSI-2 study,[44I] the rates of reinfarction during hospital stay were 2.6% with rt-PA and 3% with SK ($p$=NS). A similar tendency to slightly less reinfarction with rt-PA was observed in the ISIS-3 trial[46I] (SK 3.5%, APSAC 3.6%, rt-PA 2.9%, $2p$<.05 rt-PA versus SK). In the GUSTO trial, reinfarction rate was 3.4 to 4% in all treatment groups with no significant differences.

An excessive rate of reinfarction following thrombolysis could mitigate the potential benefit of early recanalization. This concern led to a substantial research effort to determine whether reocclusion could be avoided by more vigorous antithrombotic therapy or coronary angioplasty.

### Angina

Successful thrombolysis would be expected to preserve myocardium prone to residual ischemia, leading to an increased incidence of angina. Post-infarct angina has been reported with greatly varying frequency among the various trials, most likely reflecting differences in criteria and completeness of reporting, but randomized blinded comparisons reveal no differences in frequency between SK and conventional therapy,[59I, 63II] between APSAC and placebo,[37I] or between rt-PA and placebo.[60I] Rates of revascularization following thrombolytic therapy were not significantly increased,[37I, 60I, 63II] except in one trial.[61II] The rates of reinfarction during followup were higher with all three thrombolytic agents, however.[36I, 60I, 61II, 63II] In the trials directly comparing thrombolytic agents, there has been no difference in rates of recurrent ischemia among the various thrombolytic agents.

### ADJUVANT THERAPY

### Aspirin

The rationale for the use of aspirin along with thrombolytic therapy lies in the relatively high risk of reocclusion of 5 to 30% and a rate of reinfarction of about 4% without aspirin. The ISIS-2[31I] trial directly assessed the benefit of aspirin. Employing a factorial design, the trial demonstrated a 5-week reduction in the odds of death of 23% with aspirin ($p$<.00001), 25% with streptokinase, and 42% with the combination. Among patients receiving streptokinase, the reinfarction rate was reduced from 4 to 2%. The addition of aspirin to SK caused less than a 1% increase in minor bleeding and no increase in major bleeding, and stroke incidence fell significantly. Although there has been no evaluation of the contribution of aspirin to treatment with APSAC or rt-PA, the conjoint administration has become standard. The Antiplatelet Trialists' overview[97] indicated that aspirin may be expected to reduce vascular mortality by about 13% and fatal and nonfatal vascular events by about 23% over an approximate 2-year period following the inhospital phase of AMI. These observations indicate that additional benefits of aspirin may be anticipated if it is continued beyond the 1-month protocol of the ISIS-2 study.

### Anticoagulation

The value of heparin in conjunction with thrombolytic therapy was evaluated in two large trials. The GISSI-2 trial[44I] and its international extension[45] randomized a total of 20,891 patients using a 2 × 2 factorial design to either IV rt-PA or SK, followed at 12 hours after randomization by calcium heparin 12,500 U sc or no heparin, and continued every 12 hours until hospital discharge. Most patients received aspirin. There was no difference in mortality between heparin (8.5%) and no heparin (8.9%). Heparin significantly increased the absolute risk of major bleeding by 0.5%, and there was no difference in the risk of cerebral hemorrhage or reinfarction.

In ISIS-3,[46I] most patients received aspirin, and in addition to the random allocation to fibrinolytic therapy, they were randomized to heparin or no heparin in a factorial design. At 35 days, the vascular mortality was 10.3% in the heparin group and 10.0% in the no heparin group. During the 7-day treatment period, mortalities were 7.4% (heparin) and 7.9% (no heparin) ($2p$=.06). There was a trend to reduced inhospital reinfarction with heparin (3.2%) compared with no heparin (3.5%) ($2p$=.09). Probable cerebral hemorrhage was slightly increased (0.6 versus 0.4%, $2p$<.05), whereas rates of all stroke did not differ (1.2% in each group). Major bleeding requiring transfusion was increased by heparin (1.0 versus 0.8%,

$2p<.01$). An overview[46I] of the results of both trials calculated 35-day mortality to be 10.0% with heparin and 10.2% without ($p=$NS), and 7-day heparin treatment period mortality of 6.8% with heparin and 7.3% with no heparin ($2p<.01$).

Several trials among patients who had received rt-PA evaluated angiographic patency of the infarct-related artery in relation to the administration of heparin. In the Bleich trial,[98I] no aspirin was given, and IRA patency at a mean of 57 hours was improved by heparin. In the Heparin-Aspirin Reperfusion Trial (HART),[99I] heparin was compared with aspirin, 80 mg per day, and achieved a higher rate of 18-hour patency. In the European Cooperative Study Group-6 study,[100II] all patients received aspirin and were randomized to heparin or not. IRA patency at 81 hours was slightly better with heparin. Other studies indicated that immediate heparin did not improve 90-minute patency,[101II] and that probably after 24 hours,[102II] and certainly after 48 hours,[103I] heparin had no advantage over aspirin alone.

Concerns that the heparin regimens employed in GISSI-2 and ISIS-3 may have been suboptimal prompted the use of aggressive IV regimens in three of the four thrombolytic regimens evaluated in the GUSTO trial.[50I] Heparin as a bolus of 5,000 U IV was given immediately and followed by an infusion of 1,000 to 1,200 U per hour to maintain APTT at 60 to 85 seconds in the accelerated rt-PA, the rt-PA/SK combination, and in one SK group. The other SK group received heparin according to the ISIS-3 protocol. Among the SK-treated patients, there were no differences in mortality, reinfarction, major hemorrhage, cerebral hemorrhage, IRA patency, or reocclusion in relation to the heparin regimen. Hence, there was no evidence to support that IV heparin is superior to subcutaneous heparin among patients receiving SK. There was minimal evidence for a benefit of subcutaneous heparin in the overview of the GISSI-2 and ISIS-3 trials. Accordingly, there is no reason to routinely administer heparin along with SK, and it appears rational to reserve it for those patients at high risk of systemic embolization because of congestive heart failure, large infarction, or atrial fibrillation. There has been no study among patients receiving rt-PA that has assessed the value of adjunctive heparin in relation to important patient outcomes. However, the results from the angiographic trials, together with the short half life and lesser systemic fibrinolytic effect of rt-PA, provide a rationale for adjunctive heparin for about 48 hours following the administration of rt-PA.

## Beta Blockers

The evidence for reduction of early mortality from AMI by about 13% by the administration of IV beta blocker[104I] and the improvement of some secondary outcomes by IV metoprolol in the TIMI-IIB study[105I] prompted the recommendation for their use in GISSI-2 and GUSTO. Although definitive evidence is lacking for an incremental benefit of IV beta blocker among patients receiving thrombolytic therapy, it is unlikely that further trials will be done.

## Nitrates, Angiotensin Converting Enzyme (ACE) Inhibitors, Magnesium

Although an overview of trials of IV nitroglycerin in patients with AMI showed a 49% reduction in the odds of death ($p<.001$)[106] in the prethrombolytic era, trials have not demonstrated significant benefit. The ISIS-4 trial,[107, 108] using a $2 \times 2 \times 2$ factorial design, randomly allocated 58,000 patients to oral isosorbide 5'-mononitrate or placebo, captopril or placebo, and magnesium sulfate or control, and thus patients could receive any of these agents alone, any two agents, all three agents, or placebo only.

Among those patients who received the mononitrate, there was only a slight and nonsignificant favorable trend (absolute reduction 0.23%, $p=$NS). The benefit was no different among the 70% of patients who received thrombolytic therapy. An overview of the ISIS-4 and GISSI-3 results showed no significant benefit of nitrate.

ACE inhibitors have been shown to reduce mortality when given to patients with large infarction[109I] or congestive heart failure,[110I] beginning about 3 days after MI. The ISIS-4 and GISSI-3 trials evaluated captopril and lisinopril, respectively, begun within 24 hours of MI onset. In ISIS-4[111IIII] the mortality was reduced from 7.63% to 7.10% among the patients receiving captopril (absolute reduction 0.53%, $2p=0.02$). An overview of ISIS-4, GISSI-3, and a Chinese trial of captopril was consistent with the ISIS-4 results. The results were similar whether or not patients were given thrombolytic therapy.

An overview[112] of several small trials of magnesium sulfate ($MgSO_4$) among patients with AMI demonstrated a marked reduction in mortality (odds reduction 55%, $p=.001$). The Leicester Intravenous Magnesium Intervention Trial (LIMIT-2)[113I] demonstrated a 24% reduction in the odds of mortality with $MgSO_4$. Thrombolytic therapy had been given to 36% of the patients, and the benefit of $MgSO_4$ did not differ from that of thrombolytic therapy. In the ISIS-4 study,[113a] there was a trend toward an increase in mortality with $MgSO_4$ (absolute increase 0.39%, $2p = NS$). An overview of all trials shows an absolute excess mortality of 0.19% ($p = NS$) with $MgSO_4$.

## Coronary Angioplasty (Percutaneous Coronary Angioplasty and Coronary Artery Bypass Grafting)

Percutaneous coronary angioplasty (PTCA) has been evaluated as a potential adjunct to thrombolytic therapy, based upon the rationale that IRA flow might be optimized by decreasing the degree of occlusion resulting from residual coronary thrombus and underlying atherosclerosis. The TIMI-II trial, in part A,[114II] randomized patients who had received rt-PA into three groups, including those having (1) immediate coronary angiography and PTCA, (2) coronary angiography and PTCA if still indicated at 18 to 48 hours, and (3) no PTCA unless required by evidence of spontaneous or provoked ischemia. At hospital discharge there was no difference in LV function or IRA patency between the immediate and the 18- to 48-hour PTCA groups.

In the European Cooperative Study,[115II] 367 patients who had received rt-PA were randomized to immediate coronary angiography and PTCA if possible, or to ongoing medical therapy with coronary angiography and PTCA only if indicated by clinical events. Mortality at 14 days were 7% in the early invasive therapy group and 3% in the elective intervention group, and recurrent ischemia within 24 hours occurred, respectively, in 17% and 3%. Hypotension, ventricular fibrillation, and bleeding were more frequent with immediate PTCA, and the study was stopped early because of trends toward harm in the invasive group. In the TAMI Study,[116I] 197 patients who had patent IRAs 90 minutes following IV rt-PA were randomized to immediate PTCA or to deferred (elective) PTCA if still indicated 7 to 10 days after MI. No benefit of early over delayed PTCA was observed.

In part B of the TIMI-II trial,[105I] 3,262 patients who had received rt-PA were randomly allocated to an invasive strategy (coronary angiography 18 to 48 hours after rt-PA followed by PTCA if appropriate) or to a conservative strategy (coronary angiography and PTCA to be performed only for the occurrence of spontaneous or exercise-induced ischemia). Reinfarction or death occurred in 10.9% of the invasive group and 9.7% of the conservative group ($p = NS$). Ejection fraction at rest and exercise at hospital discharge and at 6 weeks did not differ significantly for the invasive and conservative groups.

The Should We Intervene following Thrombolysis? (SWIFT) trial[117I] recruited 800 patients who had received APSAC within 3.5 hours of AMI onset. They were randomly allocated to early angiography (2–7 days) plus appropriate intervention (PTCA in 43%, CABG in 15%) or conservative care (PTCA in 3% and CABG in 2% during initial admission). By 12 months there were no differences in mortality (5.8% intervention group, 5% conservative group), reinfarction (15.1% intervention group, 12.9% conservative group), occurrence of angina, or LV ejection fraction. Hospital stay was longer in the intervention group (11 days versus 10 days, $p < .0001$).

These trials may be summarized as follows. There is no advantage of immediate PTCA over a policy of delayed PTCA done at 18 to 48 hours,[114II] or at 7 to 10 days,[116I] or only if indicated by clinical and ECG events.[114II, 115II] PTCA delayed to 18 to 48 hours[105I] or until 2 to 7 days[117I] has no advantage over a policy of no PTCA during the hospital stay unless clinically indicated. Although there were much higher rates of post-hospital coronary angiography and revascularization in the conservative management groups in the TIMI-IIB and SWIFT trials, the 1-year mortality rates were no different from those in the early intervention groups. Hence, for most patients who have received thrombolytic therapy, early coronary angiography and prophylactic PTCA are not indicated. The development of ischemia spontaneously or on stress testing may be safely employed to indicate a need for angiography and possible revascularization. PTCA is generally preferable to revascularization surgery when the clinical course of AMI becomes complicated by recurrent ischemia or hemodynamic instability. However, surgery is preferred when there are contraindications to PTCA; when there is significant stenosis of two major vessels, all three vessels, or the left main coronary artery; or when PTCA has failed.

The need for angiography and the role of revascularization among patients in whom reperfusion has failed or in whom major hemodynamic deterioration has occurred in the early hours of AMI are not clearly delineated at present. In the RESCUE study,[118I] 151 patients with first anterior MI who had received IV thrombolytic therapy but had only TIMI grade 0 or 1 flow at 1.5 to 8 hours after MI onset were randomized to PTCA or medical therapy. Although there was no difference in the primary outcome of resting ejection fraction, the PTCA group had a significantly higher exercise ejection fraction and a reduction in mortality and congestive heart failure.

Among patients with cardiogenic shock, the mortality rate is exceedingly high. A number of case series of PTCA for cardiogenic shock have been reported, with observed mortality rate considerably lower than those for previously reported patients with cardiogenic shock.[119] In the absence of clear data from randomized trials, coronary angiography followed by PTCA or CABG as appropriate is a rational approach among patients with cardiogenic shock in the early hours of AMI.[120]

Immediate PTCA without prior administration of thrombolytic therapy (primary PTCA) has been compared with conventional thrombolytic regimens in three 1993 trials.[121I, 122I, 123II] Composite clinical outcomes of death and recurrent MI were favorably influenced by primary PTCA in comparison to both rt-PA and SK. However, the relatively high rate of outcomes in the non-PTCA groups in comparison to observations in large clinical trials suggests that the true benefit may be less than was observed.

## CLINICAL USE OF THROMBOLYTIC THERAPY

The initial aims in the management of AMI are to prevent death from ventricular fibrillation, to limit infarct size, and to relieve ischemic pain. These have not changed since the 1960s and, in the era of thrombolytic therapy, remain central to patient management. Hence, vigorous programs of education of the public and physicians about the signs and signals of heart attack, the provision of rapid response mobile emergency care systems, and the maintenance of expertly staffed and well-equipped emergency rooms continue to be prerequisites to optimal care of patients with AMI.

Within a few minutes of arrival in the emergency room (ER), the patient with suspected MI should be in a bed, under surveillance with continuous ECG monitoring, and provided with a large-bore IV. An ECG and more detailed history should be obtained shortly thereafter. The earlier thrombolytic therapy is started, the greater the reduction in mortality. Accordingly, hospital personnel must establish a new level of urgency that does not resolve with immediate stabilization and monitoring of the patient, but must persist until thrombolytic therapy is started or is determined to be contraindicated. The current reality is that a CCU bed is generally not immediately available, and hospitals should ensure that patients with suspected AMI may have thrombolytic therapy commenced in the ER. This will be most expeditious if emergency room physicians have the necessary skills to initiate the therapy. In most settings, waiting for an on-site consultation by an internist or cardiologist will cause undesirable delay in beginning thrombolytic therapy. Telephone consultation and facsimile (fax) transmission of an ECG may be helpful and yet not delay the initiation of therapy unduly.

If the patient had a half hour of ischemic pain in the chest or characteristic referral areas, and has at least 1 mm of ST segment elevation in two standard leads or two contiguous chest leads, the likelihood of an infarct in evolution is very high. A rapid additional history should be taken to discern any contraindications to aspirin or thrombolytic therapy. Aspirin should be administered as soon as the diagnosis of significant myocardial ischemia is formulated. The dose is 160 to 325 mg and is most conveniently given and optimally tolerated as two children's aspirins (80 mg each) to be chewed and swallowed.

The contraindications to thrombolytic therapy may be considered to be absolute when the patient has a condition that mimics AMI and would be aggravated by thrombolytic therapy, or when the patient has uncontrolled bleeding. A patient with an elevated titer of SK neutralizing antibody could not benefit from streptokinase, but rt-PA would be effacious. The relative contraindications generally are related to a predisposition to the risk of hemorrhage because of the presence of a preformed hemostatic plug that may be lysed, to disorders of coagulation, or to vascular pathology (Table 5–4).[124]

Aortic dissection and pericarditis may be confused with AMI, and these alternative diagnoses should always be borne in mind during the history and physical examination. Most relative contraindications arise from preceding events and patient characteristics that increase the chance of hemorrhage from thrombolytic therapy and are readily discerned by appropriate questioning. When a relative contraindication is present, the physician must give consideration to the relative potential benefits of therapy and the potential risks of life-threatening hemorrhage. A patient with a high risk of death from the AMI should receive thrombolytic therapy even if there is a substantial risk of hemorrhage. A patient with a low risk from AMI should not receive thrombolytic therapy if there is a substantial risk of hemorrhage.

If the patient has received SK or APSAC more than 4 days previously, there will be a sufficient titer of SK antibodies present to neutralize con-

Table 5–4. **Contraindications to Thrombolytic Therapy**

**Contraindications**

| Absolute Contraindications | Relative Contraindications |
|---|---|
| Aortic dissection<br>Acute pericarditis<br>Active bleeding<br>Problematic SK antibodies (substitute rt-PA)<br>Previous well-documented allergic reaction to SK or APSAC—rtPA should be used<br>Repeat SK or APSAC therapy is unlikely to be effective when SK neutralizing antibody (NA) levels are markedly elevated. It is recommended that following an initial dose of SK or APSAC, once 4 days has passed, neither therapy be repeated, unless measurement of SK NA titer has shown resolution of resistance; rt-PA should be substituted. Routine measurement of SK NA titer at 6 to 12 months following administration of SK or APSAC may provide further guidance as to the likely efficacy of repeat therapy with SK or ASPAC | Potential hemorrhagic focus. Thrombolytic agents are capable of lysing hemostatic plugs in many locations, and it appears that most hemorrhage occurs as a result of lysis of a hemostatic plug. The risk of bleeding diminishes as the time from formation of a hemostatic plug increases. The following suggestions for time limits following various clinical events are arbitrary and conservative:<br>At any time—cerebral hemorrhage, known intracerebral vascular disease (malignancy, AV malformation)<br>Within past 6 months—GI or GU hemorrhage or stroke<br>Within past 2 to 4 weeks—major surgery, organ biopsy, puncture of noncompressible vessel, prolonged chest compression (CPR) in a patient who has evidence of resulting chest trauma or who remains unconscious, major trauma, even minor head trauma<br>Diabetic proliferative retinopathy<br>Severe, uncontrolled hypertension (systolic BP >200 mm Hg and/or diastolic BP >120 mm Hg)<br>Pregnancy<br>History of bleeding diathesis; hepatic dysfunction, cancer |

ventional doses of SK or APSAC, and accordingly, rt-PA must be given. There is some uncertainty about the duration of the elevated antibody levels, but some studies have indicated resistance persists up to 4 years after SK treatment in up to 50% of patients. If SK neutralizing antibodies have been measured at some point after infarction (i.e., 6–12 months) and found to have returned to low levels, SK or APSAC will again be efficacious. If no such measurement has been made, rt-PA should be given for repeat therapy in every patient who has received SK or APSAC more than 4 days prior to the present event.

The choice of thrombolytic agent is controversial. It is clear that SK, APSAC, and rt-PA all result in marked reductions in mortality. The GUSTO trial has demonstrated that an accelerated dose regimen of rt-PA is superior to the conventional regimen of SK. The incremental benefit is modest, and yet the incremental cost of rt-PA over SK is substantial. Physicians in hospitals are obligated to discuss the difficult issue of cost effectiveness and to develop guidelines for the administration of these two agents. The unequivocal and largest saving of lives in the GUSTO trial occurred among patients under age 75 years, patients with anterior MI, and patients whose therapy was started within 4 hours of onset of MI. These may represent reasonable guidelines for the use of rt-PA in preference to SK.

The dose regimens for the thrombolytic agents have been widely utilized in clinical trials and are known to be effective and safe. They are as follows: SK, 1.5 MU given IV over about 1 hour; APSAC (anistreplase), 30 U given IV over 5 minutes; rt-PA (alteplase), the most widely used and currently approved regimen is 100 mg over 3 hours, with 60 mg in hour 1 (6 mg in the first 1–2 minutes), and 20 mg in each of hours 2 and 3. However, the accelerated dose regimen employed in GUSTO appears to be preferable and is as follows: 15-mg bolus, then 0.75 mg/kg over 30 minutes not to exceed 50 mg, then 0.5 mg/kg over 60 minutes not to exceed 35 mg, the total dose not to exceed 100 mg.

Hypotension during the infusion of SK should be managed by stopping the infusion and, if necessary, placing the patient in the head-down position (Trendelenburg), infusing volume, and, if bradycardia has occurred, atropine. Intravenous dopamine or dobutamine is only occasionally required. The episode will usually resolve, and the aim should be to complete the infusion, which can usually be accomplished without recurrence of hypotension. Similar measures are undertaken when hypotension follows the administration of APSAC, although generally the infusion has been completed before the hypotension occurs. In general, there is no reason to modify an infusion of rt-PA if hypotension occurs.

Hypotension is not rare in MI and may, of course, occur in the absence of thrombolytic therapy. Consideration must always be given to the possibilities of acute LV dysfunction, papillary muscle dysfunction or rupture, ventricular septal defect (VSD), external myocardial rupture, excessive vagal tone, and hemorrhage.

Physicians and nurses must familiarize themselves with measures to predict, prevent, detect, and treat hemorrhage. Relative contraindications to thrombolysis arise mainly from the presence of markers of increased hemorrhagic risk. Some patients at particularly high risk for their AMI may be given thrombolytic therapy even if they are at risk of hemorrhage, and special precautions may then be warranted. Precautions include a previous history of peptic ulcer or gastrointestinal (GI) bleeding (prophylactic $H_2$ blocker infusion), current use of oral anticoagulants (reduced dose of thrombolytic agent and avoidance of heparin), and severe hypertension (treat before administering thrombolytic agent). Even with careful attention to contraindications, major bleeding occurs in 0.5 to 1% of patients and cerebral bleeding in 0.2 to 1% of patients.

Every effort must be made to minimize invasive procedures and trauma (careful turning in bed, extra attention to bed rails, careful mobilization). Medical and nursing staff must be alert to early warnings of hemorrhage, watching for hematemesis, epistaxis, hematuria, hemorrhoidal bleeding, and melena. Abdominal discomfort or femoral nerve palsies may suggest GI or retroperitoneal hemorrhage. Daily hemoglobin and urinalysis samples should be obtained for the first 48 hours. The onset of sinus tachycardia and/or hypotension should precipitate an evaluation for possible hemorrhage.

Minor bleeding (epistaxis, bruising, blood-stained emesis) generally requires no special measures apart from increased vigilance and evaluation of PT and APTT, hemoglobin, and anticoagulant regimens, which may require modification. Major bleeding requires a staged response, depending upon severity.

Bleeding may occur at sites of preformed hemostatic plugs as a result of lysis, or at sites of new vascular injury as a result of the joint influences of lysis and the coagulopathy resulting from the thrombolytic action and the administration of antithrombotic agents (aspirin, heparin, warfarin). The lytic effect of rt-PA is fairly short-lived—the half life of rt-PA is only about 5 minutes. That of SK is about 90 minutes, and therefore significant lysis may persist for several hours.

Minor bleeding requires only heightened observation, including measurement of hemoglobin, platelets, and APTT. If bleeding is from an accessible site, direct compression is appropriate and usually effective. If severe bleeding is

occurring, the thrombolytic agent should be stopped and coagulation factor replacement undertaken with fresh frozen plasma and cryoprecipitate. Fresh frozen plasma contains about 500 mg of fibrinogen per unit plus factors V and VIII, whereas cryoprecipitate contains 250 mg of fibrinogen per 5 ml, and is thus a much more concentrated form of factor replacement. Life-threatening bleeding will require still more vigorous measures, including whole blood replacement for volume and coagulation factors.

If severe bleeding occurs within a few hours of the administration of SK, there may be significant persisting plasminemia, which can be corrected by the infusion of epsilon aminocaproic acid (Amicar). This is usually given as 5 g diluted in 250 ml of 5% dextrose and water infused over 1 hour and followed by 1 g/hour as necessary.

Patients who are to receive rt-PA should also receive heparin, as a 75 U/kg IV bolus at the time of initiating the rt-PA infusion, with an initial maintenance infusion of 1,000 to 1,200 U/hour to maintain APTT at 1.5 to 2 times control. A 48-hour infusion is likely to be sufficient, if aspirin is being given, and high-dose heparin should be sustained only if there appears to be a high risk of systemic embolism (large anterior MI, congestive heart failure, previous systemic embolus, atrial fibrillation). Otherwise, only low-dose heparin (7,500 U sc every 12 hours) is indicated for prophylaxis against venous thrombosis for at least 7 days and until the patient is fully ambulatory. If the patient has received SK or APSAC, high-dose heparin should be administered only if there appears to be a high risk of systemic embolism.

There is no good evidence for routine prophylactic administration of antiarrhythmic therapy among patients with MI. The incidence of ventricular fibrillation has decreased in trials of thrombolytic therapy,[14, 15V, 93, 94] and accordingly, antiarrhythmic therapy should be reserved for patients with ventricular arrhythmias who are symptomatic or have a high risk of progression to VF.

Intravenous beta blockade confers a modest additional benefit among patients receiving thrombolytic therapy and was given safely to 45% of patients in GISSI-2 and 46% of patients in GUSTO. It is likely to be most beneficial when given to patients without significant heart failure who have sinus tachycardia or marked hypertension. It is often prudent to delay administration until the thrombolytic infusion has been completed.

Prophylactic sublingual and IV nitroglycerin have been widely used in acute MI. Large trials have provided no strong evidence for an overall benefit, and it seems wise to reserve nitroglycerin for patients who have a systolic BP greater than 100 mm Hg and who have persistent or recurrent ischemic pain and/or congestive heart failure. ACE inhibitor therapy, beginning about day 3, has been demonstrated to improve outcome when given to patients with large myocardial infarction or congestive heart failure. The benefit of beginning on day 1 is likely to be minimal, based upon the results of large trials; therefore, it seems reasonable to reserve the therapy for patients with large infarcts and to avoid commencing therapy until day 2 or 3, when any initial tendency to hypotension has usually resolved. There appears to be no role for routine $MgSO_4$ therapy.

The recurrence of possibly ischemic pain should prompt a careful assessment to rule out pericarditis, pulmonary embolus, chest wall pain, or other problems that may mimic myocardial ischemia. A vigorous attempt to reduce factors that increase myocardial oxygen demand and the optimal administration of nitrates, beta blockers, and calcium antagonists are indicated. A failure to respond to optimal medical therapy is an indication for coronary angiography and consideration for PTCA or coronary artery bypass grafting in appropriately equipped centers, or for transfer of the patient to such a center from one not so equipped. If the pain is unresponsive, and particularly if further ST segment elevation is occurring, repeat thrombolytic therapy may be indicated for recurrent infarction. SK will be effective and may be repeated within 4 days of previous use, but beyond this point, rt-PA should be substituted. In a center with individuals appropriately skilled in emergency PTCA with a delivery system allowing rapid response (less than 1 hour) and with surgical backup, PTCA represents a reasonable alternative to repeat thrombolysis.

In general, the management of patients following thrombolysis is similar to that of other post-MI patients. General prophylactic interventions include attention to all coronary risk factors and the institution of longterm aspirin and beta blockade for every possible patient. Most patients should have an assessment of residual ischemia and some measure of LV function. Patients with recurrent or induced ischemia, congestive heart failure, or symptomatic arrhythmias require further investigation in addition to vigorous medical therapy.

In summary, randomized controlled trials of various thrombolytic agents have been conducted in over 60,000 patients, and trials comparing thrombolytic agents have been done in a further 100,000 patients. This unprecedented body of excellent data has provided unequivocal evidence for the benefit of SK, APSAC, and rt-PA and quite good evidence for the benefit of UK and scu-PA for the reduction of inhospital and longterm mortality among patients with AMI. The overall absolute reduction of mortality over approximately the 35 days following AMI is about 1.9%, or a saving of 19 lives per 1,000 patients treated. Among patients with ST segment elevation or bundle branch block treated within 12 hours of onset of AMI, about 30 lives were saved per 1,000 patients treated, at a cost of about two nonfatal strokes and four major bleeding episodes. The risk-benefit ratio is clearly in favor of thrombolytic therapy.

There are few absolute contraindications to thrombolytic therapy; most are relative and arise from an increased potential for hemorrhage in certain patients. The physician must weigh the absolute potential benefits and risks of therapy. In general, thrombolytic therapy is beneficial for patients with anterior or inferior infarction, with first or subsequent infarction, and of any age. The most marked absolute benefits are achievable among patients treated very early; the earlier therapy is started, the greater the benefit. However, many patients presenting within 7 to 12 hours from symptom onset may benefit, and some presenting even 13 to 24 hours from infarct onset may benefit.

Direct comparisons of thrombolytic agents have generally not shown clear benefits of one agent over another. However, one large trial has shown a statistically significant reduction in frequency of the composite outcome of death and disabling stroke with a regimen of accelerated-dose rt-PA plus heparin over conventional-dose SK plus heparin.

To use thrombolytic therapy safely and to achieve maximal benefit, physicians and nurses must take measures to predict, prevent, detect, and treat bleeding. Allergic reactions to SK and APSAC are not uncommon and are generally readily managed, as is hypotension. Anaphylaxis is rare. Dangerous arrhythmias are less frequent than in the absence of thrombolytic therapy, but in any case are managed no differently. Recurrent ischemia is common, and reinfarction occurs in about 4% of patients. Vigorous anti-ischemic drug therapy is indicated, with judicious progression to coronary angiography and PTCA or coronary artery bypass grafting as appropriate.

Aspirin alone reduces 35-day mortality almost as much as does thrombolytic therapy, and the combination produces an almost additive reduction in mortality. Aspirin should be given to every patient once the diagnosis of acute myocardial ischemia is formulated, unless there is a specific contraindication. There is good evidence that early patency of the infarct-related artery is enhanced by heparin in conjunction with rt-PA, although there are no data to indicate a reduction in mortality. Heparin is routinely given with rt-PA. Heparin does not appear to be necessary in conjunction with SK, unless there is a high risk of systemic embolism. Intravenous beta blocker therapy is probably beneficial in appropriate patients. Routine use in the first 24 hours of $MgSO_4$, IV and oral nitrates, and ACE inhibitors appears to confer no clear advantages. Prophylactic PTCA is not indicated at any time during the hospital course and may be reserved for patients who have spontaneous or exercise-induced ischemia and appropriate coronary anatomy.

The maximal potential benefit of thrombolytic therapy will be achieved only by widespread efforts to educate physicians and other health professionals as to the benefits of thrombolytic therapy and its optimal and safe use. A new urgency in bringing patients with suspected AMI to the hospital emergency room must be communicated to the health care system and to the lay public. The early administration of a thrombolytic agent to appropriately selected patients can markedly reduce mortality.

# REFERENCES

1. Tillett WS, Garner RL: The fibrinolytic activity of hemolytic streptococci. J Exp Med 58:485–502, 1933.
2. Sherry S: The origin of thrombolytic therapy. J Am Coll Cardiol 14:1085–1092, 1989.
3. Sherry S, Fletcher AP, Alkjaersig N, Smyrniotis FE: An approach to intravascular thrombolysis in man. Trans Assoc Am Physicians 70:288–296, 1957.
4. Herrick JB: Clinical features of sudden obstruction of the coronary arteries. JAMA 59:2015–2020, 1912.
5. Fletcher AP, Sherry S, Alkjaersig N, et al: The maintenance of a sustained thrombolytic state in man. II. Clinical observations on patients with myocardial infarction and other thromboembolic disorders. J Clin Invest 38:1111–1119, 1959.
6. Boucek HJ, Murphy WP: Segmental perfusion of the coronary arteries with fibrinolysis in man following a myocardial infarction. Am J Cardiol 5:525–533, 1960.
7. Yusuf S, Collins R, Peto R, et al: Intravenous and intracoronary fibrinolytic therapy in acute myocardial infarction: Overview of results on mortality, reinfarction and side effects from 33 randomized controlled trials. Eur Heart J 6:556–585, 1985.
8. European Cooperative Study Group for Streptokinase Treatment in Acute Myocardial Infarction: Streptokinase in acute myocardial infarction. N Engl J Med 301:797–802, 1979.
9. Ehrlich JC, Shinohara Y: Low incidence of coronary thrombosis in myocardial infarction: A restudy by serial block technique. Arch Pathol 78:432–445, 1964.
10. Chandler AB, Chapman I, Erhardt LE, et al: Coronary thrombosis in myocardial infarction. Am J Cardiol 34:823–832, 1974.
11. DeWood MA, Spores J, Notske R, et al: Prevalence of total coronary occlusion during the early hours of transmural myocardial infarction. N Engl J Med 303:897–902, 1980.
12. Sobel BE, Bresnahan GF, Shell WE, et al: Estimation of infarct size in man and its relation to prognosis. Circulation 46:640–648, 1972.
13. Rude RE, Muller JE, Braunwald E: Efforts to limit the size of myocardial infarcts. Ann Intern Med 95:736–761, 1981.
14. Chazov EL, Mateeva LS, Mazaer AV, et al: Intracoronary administration of fibrinolysis in acute myocardial infarction. Ter Arkh 48:8–19, 1976.
V 15. Rentrop KP, Blanke H, Karsch KR, et al: Selective intracoronary thrombolysis in acute myocardial infarction and unstable angina pectoris. Circulation 63:307–317, 1981.
16. O'Neill WW, Topol EJ, Pitt B: Reperfusion therapy of acute myocardial infarction. Prog Cardiovasc Dis 30:235–266, 1988.
17. Schroeder R, Biamino G, Leitner E-R, et al: Intravenous short-term infusion of streptokinase in acute myocardial infarction. Circulation 67:536–548, 1983.
18. Lo YSA: Intravenous versus intracoronary streptokinase in acute myocardial infarction. Clin Cardiol 8:609–619, 1985.
19. Ploug J, Kjeldgaard NO: Urokinase as an activator of plasminogen from human urine. I. Isolation and properties. Biochem Biophys Acta 24:282–289, 1957.
I 20. Urokinase-streptokinase Pulmonary Embolism Trial. Phase II results: A national cooperative trial. JAMA 229:1606–1613, 1974.
V 21. Van de Werf F, Ludbrook PA, Bergmann SR, et al: Clot-selective coronary thrombolysis with tissue-type plasminogen activator in patients with evolving myocardial infarction. N Engl J Med 310:609–613, 1984.
I 22. Cheseboro JH, Knatterud G, Roberts R, et al: Thrombolysis in myocardial infarction (TIMI) trial, phase 1: A comparison between intravenous plasminogen activator and intravenous streptokinase. Circulation 76:142–154, 1987.
I 23. Verstraete M, Bernard R, Bory M, et al: Randomized trial of intravenous recombinant tissue-type plasminogen activator versus intravenous streptokinase in acute myocardial infarction. Lancet 1:842–847, 1985.
I 24. Verstraete M, Bleifeld W, Brower RW, et al: Double blind randomized trial of intravenous tissue-type plasminogen activator versus placebo in acute myocardial infarction. Lancet 2:965–969, 1985.
I 25. Sheehan FH, Braunwald E, Canner P, et al: The effect of intravenous thrombolytic therapy on left ventricular function: A report on tissue-type plasminogen activator and streptokinase from the thrombolysis in myocardial infarction (TIMI Phase 1) trial. Circulation 75:817–829, 1987.
I 26. Guerci AD, Gerstenblith G, Brinker JA, et al: A randomized trial of intravenous tissue plasminogen activator for acute myocardial infarction with subsequent randomization to elective coronary angioplasty. N Engl J Med 317:1613–1618, 1987.
I 27. National Heart Foundation of Australia Coronary

Thrombolysis Group: Coronary thrombolysis and myocardial salvage by tissue plasminogen activator given up to 4 hours after onset of myocardial infarction. Lancet 1:203–208, 1988.

28. Monk JP, Heel RC: Anisoylated plasminogen streptokinase activator complex (APSAC): A review of its mechanism of action, clinical pharmacology and therapeutic use in acute myocardial infarction. Drugs 34:25–49, 1987.

I 29. PRIMI Trial Study Group: Randomised double-blind trial of recombinant prourokinase against streptokinase in acute myocardial infarction. Lancet 1:863–868, 1989.

I 30. Gruppo Italiano per lo Studio della Streptochinasi nell Infarto Miocardico (GISSI): Effectiveness of intravenous thrombolytic treatment in acute myocardial infarction. Lancet 1:397–402, 1986.

I 31. ISIS-2 (Second International Study of Infarct Survival) Collaborative Group: Randomised trial of intravenous streptokinase, oral aspirin, both or neither among 17,187 cases of suspected acute myocardial infarction. Lancet 2:349–360, 1988.

32. White HD, Norris RM, Brown MA, et al: Effect of intravenous streptokinase on left ventricular function and early survival after acute myocardial infarction. N Engl J Med 317:850–855, 1987.

II 33. The ISAM Study Group: A prospective trial of intravenous streptokinase in acute myocardial infarction (ISAM): Mortality, morbidity, and infarct size at 21 days. N Engl J Med 314:1465–1471, 1986.

II 34. ISIS Pilot Study Investigation: Randomized factorial trial of high-dose intravenous streptokinase, of oral aspirin, and of intravenous heparin in acute myocardial infarction. Eur Heart J 8:634–642, 1987.

II 35. Kennedy JW, Martin GV, Davis KB, et al: The Western Washington intravenous streptokinase in acute myocardial infarction randomized trial. Circulation 77:345–352, 1988.

I 36. AIMS Trial Study Group: Effect of intravenous APSAC on mortality after acute myocardial infarction: Preliminary report of a placebo-controlled clinical trial. Lancet 1:545–549, 1988.

I 37. AIMS Trial Study Group: Long-term effects of intravenous anistreplase in acute myocardial infarction: Final report of the AIMS study. Lancet 335:427–431, 1990.

II 38. Ikram S, Lewis S, Bucknall C, et al: Treatment of acute myocardial infarction with anisoylated plasminogen streptokinase activator complex. Br Med J 293:786–789, 1986.

I 39. The APSAC Multicenter Trial Group: The German multicenter trial of anisoylated plasminogen streptokinase activator complex versus heparin for acute myocardial infarction. Am J Cardiol 62:437–451, 1988.

I 40. Anderson JF, Rothburd RI, Hackworthy RA, et al: Multicenter reperfusion trial of intravenous anisoylated plasminogen activator complex (APSAC) in acute myocardial infarction: Controlled comparison with intracoronary streptokinase. J Am Coll Cardiol 11:1153–63, 1988.

I 41. Wilcox RG, Van der Lippe G, Olsson CG, et al: Trial of tissue plasminogen activator for mortality reduction in acute myocardial infarction. Anglo-Scandinavian Study of early thrombolysis (ASSET). Lancet 2:525–530, 1988.

I 42. Van de Werf F, Arnold AER: Intravenous tissue plasminogen activator and size of infarct, left ventricular function, and survival in acute myocardial infarction. Br Med J 287:1374–1379, 1988.

43. Cairns JA, Fuster V, Kennedy JW: Coronary thrombolysis. Chest 102:482S–507S, 1992.

I 44. Gruppo Italiano per lo Studio della Sopravvivenza nell'Infarto Miocardico. GISSI-2: A factorial randomized trial of alteplase and heparin versus no heparin among 12,490 patients with acute myocardial infarction. Lancet 336:65–71, 1990.

I 45. The International Study Group: In-hospital mortality and clinical course of 20,891 patients with suspected acute myocardial infarction randomized between alteplase and streptokinase with or without heparin. Lancet 336:71–75, 1990.

I 46. ISIS-3 Collaborative Group: ISIS-3: A randomized comparison of streptokinase vs tissue plasminogen activator vs anistreplase and of aspirin plus heparin vs aspirin alone among 41,299 cases of suspected acute myocardial infarction. Lancet 339:753–770, 1992.

47. Rapold HJ, de Bono D, Arnold AER, et al: Plasma fibrinopeptide A levels in patients with acute myocardial infarction treated with alteplase. Correlation with concomitant heparin, coronary artery patency, and recurrent ischemia. Circulation 85:928–934, 1992.

I 48. Neuhaus K-L, Von Essen R, Tebbe U, et al: Improved thrombolysis in acute myocardial infarction with front-loaded administration of alteplase: Results of the rt-PA-APSAC Patency Study (TAPS). J Am Coll Cardiol 19:885–891, 1992.

I 49. Grines CL, Nissen SE, Booth DC, et al: A prospective randomized trial comparing combination half-dose tissue-type plasminogen activator and streptokinase with full-dose tissue-type plasminogen activator. Circulation 84:540–549, 1991.

I 50. The GUSTO Investigators: An international randomized trial comparing four thrombolytic strategies for acute myocardial infarction. N Engl J Med 329:673–682, 1993.

I 50a. Topol E, Califf R, Lee K: Letter. N Engl J Med 331:277–278, 1994.

I51. The GUSTO Angiographic Investigators: The effects of tissue plasminogen activator, streptokinase, or both on coronary patency, ventricular function, and survival after acute myocardial infarction. N Engl J Med 329:1615–1622, 1993.

52. Fibrinolytic Therapy Trialists' (FTT) Collaborative Group: Indications for fibrinolytic therapy in suspected acute myocardial infarction: Collaborative overview of early mortality and major morbidity results from all randomised trials of more than 1000 patients. Lancet 343:311–322, 1994.

I 53. LATE Study Group. Late assessment of thrombolytic efficacy (LATE) study with alteplase 6–24 hours after onset of acute myocardial infarction. Lancet 342:759–766, 1993.

54. Reimer KA, Lowe JE, Rasmussen MM, et al: The wave front phenomenon of ischemic cell death: 1. Myocardial infarct size vs duration of coronary occlusion in dogs. Circulation 56:786–794, 1977.

55. Koren G, Weiss AT, Hasin Y, et al: Prevention of myocardial damage in acute myocardial ischemia by early treatment with intravenous streptokinase. N Engl J Med 313:1384–1389, 1985.

56. Weaver WD, Eisenberg M, Martin J, et al: Myocardial Infarction Triage and Intervention Project-Phase I: Patient characteristics and feasibility of prehospital initiation of thrombolytic therapy. J Am Coll Cardiol 15:925–931, 1990.

II 57. The European Myocardial Infarction Project Group: Prehospital thrombolytic therapy in patients with suspected acute myocardial infarction. N Engl J Med 329:383–389, 1993.

II 58. EMERAS (Estudio Multicentrico Estreptoquinasa Republica de America de Sur) Collaborative Group: Randomised trial of late thrombolysis in patients with suspected acute myocardial infarction. Lancet 342:767–772, 1993.

I 59. GISSI: Long-term effects of intravenous thrombolysis in acute myocardial infarction: Final report of the GISSI study. Lancet 2:871–874, 1987.

I 60. Wilcox RG, von der Lippe G, Olsson CG, et al: Effects of alteplase in acute myocardial infarction: 6-months results from the ASSET Study. Lancet 335:1175–1178, 1990.

II 61. Simoons ML, Vos J, Tijssen JGP, et al: Long-term benefit of early thrombolytic therapy in patients with acute myocardial infarction: 5 year follow-up of a trial conducted by the Interuniversity Cardiology Institute of the Netherlands. J Am Coll Cardiol 14:1609–1615, 1989.

I 62. Kennedy JW, Ritchie JL, Davis KB, et al: Western Washington randomized trial of intra-coronary streptokinase in acute myocardial infarction: A 12-month follow-up report. N Engl J Med 312:1073–1078, 1985.

II 63. Schroder F, Neuhaus KI, Leizorovicz A, et al: Trial of intravenous streptokinase in acute myocardial infarction (ISAM): long-term mortality and morbidity. J Am Coll Cardiol 9:197–203, 1987.

64. Baigent C, Collins R, for the ISIS Collaborative Group: ISIS-2: 4-year mortality follow-up of 17,187 patients after fibrinolytic and antiplatelet therapy in suspected myocardial infarction. Circulation 88[Suppl I]:1–291, 1993.

I 65. Dalen JE, Gore JM, Braunwald E, et al: Six- and twelve-month follow-up of phase 1 Thrombolysis in Myocardial Infarction (TIMI) trial. Am J Cardiol 62:179–185, 1988.

66. Khaja F, Walton JA, Brymer JF, et al: Intracoronary fibrinolytic therapy in acute myocardial infarction: Report of a prospective randomized trial. N Engl J Med 308:1305–1311, 1983.

67. Leiboff RH, Katz RJ, Wasserman AG, et al: A randomized, angiographically controlled trial of intracoronary streptokinase in acute myocardial infarction. Am J Cardiol 53:404–407, 1984.

I 68. Rentrop KP, Feit F, Blanke H, et al: Effects of intracoronary streptokinase and intracoronary nitroglycerin infusion on coronary angiographic patterns and mortality in patients with acute myocardial infarction. N Engl J Med 311:1457–1463, 1984.

I 69. Van de Werf F, Arnold AER: Intravenous tissue plasminogen activator and size of infarct, left ventricular function, and survival in acute myocardial infarction. Br Med J 287:1374–1379, 1988.

II 70. Verstraete M, Arnold AER, Brower RW, et al: Acute coronary thrombolysis with recombinant human tissue-type plasminogen activator: Initial patency and influence of maintained infusion on reocclusion rate. Am J Cardiol 60:231–237, 1987.

I 71. Anderson JL, Sorensen SG, Moreno FL, et al: Multicenter patency trial of intravenous anistreplase compared with streptokinase in acute myocardial infarction. Circulation 83:126–140, 1991.

II 72. Brochier ML, Quilliet L, Kulbertus H, et al: Intravenous anisoylated plasminogen streptokinase activator complex versus intravenous streptokinase in evolving myocardial infarction: Preliminary data from a randomised multicentre study. Drugs 33 [Suppl 3]:140–145, 1987.

II 73. Hogg KJ, Gemmill JD, Burns JMA, et al: Angiographic patency study of anistreplase versus streptokinase in acute myocardial infarction. Lancet 335:254–258, 1990.

I 74. PRIMI Trial Study Group: Randomised double-blind trial of recombinant prourokinase against streptokinase in acute myocardial infarction. Lancet 1:863–869, 1989.

75. The Multicenter Postinfarction Research Group: Risk stratification and survival after myocardial infarction. N Engl J Med 309:331–336, 1983.

76. Volpi A, DeVita C, Franzosi MG, et al: Determinants of 6-month mortality in survivors of myocardial infarction after thrombolysis. Results of the GISSI-2 data base. Circulation 88:416–429, 1993.

I 77. White HD, Norris RM, Brown MA, et al: Effect of intravenous streptokinase on left ventricular function and early survival after acute myocardial infarction. N Engl J Med 317:850–855, 1987.

II 78. Kennedy JW, Martin GV, Davis KB, et al: The Western Washington intravenous streptokinase in acute myocardial infarction randomized trial. Circulation 77:345–352, 1988.

I 79. Simoons ML, Serruys PW, Brand M, et al: Improved survival after early thrombolysis in acute myocardial infarction: A randomized trial by the Interuniversity Cardiology Institute in the Netherlands. Lancet 2:578–581, 1985.

I 80. O'Rourke M, Baron D, Keogh A, et al: Limitation of myocardial infarction by early infusion of recombinant tissue-type plasminogen activator. Circulation 77:1311–1315, 1988.

I 81. Armstrong PW, Baigrie RS, Daly PA, et al: Tissue plasminogen activator: Toronto (TPAT): Placebo-controlled randomized trial in acute myocardial infarction. J Am Coll Cardiol 13:1469–1476, 1989.

I 82. White HD, Rivers JT, Maslowski AH, et al: Effect of intravenous streptokinase as compared with that of tissue plasminogen activator on left ventricular function after first myocardial infarction. N Engl J Med 320:817–821, 1989.

II 83. Magnani B for the PAIMS Investigators: Plasminogen Activator Italian Multicenter Study (PAIMS): Comparison of intravenous recombinant single-chain human tissue-type plasminogen activator (rt-PA) with intravenous streptokinase in acute myocardial infarction. J Am Coll Cardiol 13:19–26, 1989.

I 84. Neuhaus K-L, Tebbe U, Gottwik M, et al: Intravenous recombinant tissue plasminogen activator (rt-PA) and urokinase in acute myocardial infarction: Results of the German Activator Urokinase Study (GAUS). J Am Coll Cardiol 12:581–587, 1988.

85. Hirsh J: Coronary thrombolysis: Hemorrhagic complications. Can J Cardiol 9:505–511, 1993.

86. Coller BS: Platelets and thrombolytic therapy. N Engl J Med 322:32–42, 1990.

87. Massel D: Clinical use of coronary thrombolytic therapy. Previous streptokinase therapy. Can J Cardiol 9:518–520, 1993.

88. Massel D, Turpie AGG, Cairns JA, et al: Persistence of neutralizing antibodies at one year following IV streptokinase for acute myocardial infarction. Circulation 82[Suppl III]:III-254, 1990.

89. Elliot JM, Cross DB, Cederholm-Williams S, et al: Streptokinase titers 1 to 4 years after intravenous streptokinase. Circulation 84[Suppl II]:II-116, 1991.

90. Massel D, Turpie AGG, Oberhardt BJ, et al: Estimation of resistance to streptokinase: A preliminary

report of a rapid bedside test. Can J Cardiol 9:134E, 1993.

91. Lew AS, Laramee P, Cercek B, et al: The hypotensive effect of intravenous streptokinase in patients with acute myocardial infarction. Circulation 72:1321–1326, 1985.

92. Wei JY, Markis JE, Malagold M, et al: Cardiovascular reflexes stimulated by reperfusion of ischemic myocardium in acute myocardial infarction. Circulation 67:796–801, 1983.

93. Burney RE, Walsh D, Kaplan LR, et al: Reperfusion arrhythmia: Myth or reality. Ann Emerg Med 18:240–243, 1989.

94. Vermeer F, Simoons ML, Lubsen J: Reduced frequency of ventricular fibrillation after early thrombolysis in myocardial infarction. Lancet 1:1147–1148, 1986.

95. Volpi A, Cavalli A, Santoro E, et al: Incidence and prognosis of secondary ventricular fibrillation in acute myocardial infarction: Evidence for a protective effect of thrombolytic therapy. Circulation 82:1279–1288, 1990.

96. Harrison DG, Ferguson DW, Collins SM, et al: Rethrombosis after reperfusion with streptokinase: Importance of geometry of residual lesions. Circulation 69:991–999, 1984.

97. Antiplatelet Trialists' Collaboration: Collaborative overview of randomised trials of antiplatelet therapy—I: Prevention of death, myocardial infarction, and stroke by prolonged antiplatelet therapy in various categories of patients. Br Med J 308:81–106, 1994.

I 98. Bleich SD, Nichols TC, Schumacher RR, et al: Effect of heparin on coronary arterial patency after thrombolysis with tissue plasminogen activator in acute myocardial infarction. Am J Cardiol 66:1412–1417, 1990.

I 99. The Heparin-Aspirin Reperfusion Trial (HART) Investigators: A comparison between heparin and low-dose aspirin as adjunctive therapy with tissue-type plasminogen activator for acute myocardial infarction. N Engl J Med 323:1433–1437, 1990.

II 100. The European Cooperative Study Group (ECSG): The effect of early intravenous heparin on coronary patency, infarct size and bleeding complications after alteplase thrombolysis: Results of a randomized double blind European Cooperative Study Group trial. Br Heart J 67:122–128, 1992.

II 101. TAMI Study Group: A randomized controlled trial of intravenous tissue plasminogen activator and early intravenous heparin in acute myocardial infarction. Circulation 79:281–286, 1989.

II 102. Thompson PL, Aylward PE, Federma J, et al: A randomized comparison of intravenous heparin with oral aspirin and dipyridamole 24 hours after recombinant tissue-type plasminogen activator for acute myocardial infarction. Circulation 83:1534–1542, 1991.

I 103. Meijer A, Verheugt FWA, Werter CJPJ, et al: Aspirin versus coumadin in the prevention of reocclusion and recurrent ischemia after successful thrombolysis: A prospective placebo-controlled angiographic study. Results of the APRICOT study. Circulation 87:1524–1530, 1993.

I 104. ISIS-1 Collaborative Group: A randomized trial of intravenous atenolol among 16,027 cases of suspected acute myocardial infarction. Lancet 2:57–66, 1986.

I 105. The TIMI Study Group: Comparison of invasive and conservative strategies after treatment with intravenous tissue plasminogen activator in acute

myocardial infarction: Results of the Thrombolysis in Myocardial Infarction (TIMI) phase II trial. N Engl J Med 320:618–627, 1989.

106. Yusuf S, Collins R, MacMahon S, et al: Effect of intravenous nitrates on mortality in acute myocardial infarction: An overview of the randomised trials. Lancet 1:1088–1092, 1988.

107. ISIS-4 Collaborative Group: Fourth International Study of Infarct Survival: Protocol for a large simple study of the effects of oral mononitrate, of oral captopril, and of intravenous magnesium. Am J Cardiol 68:87–100, 1991.

III 108. ISIS-4 Collaborative Group: ISIS-4: Randomised study of oral isosorbide mononitrate in over 50,000 patients with suspected acute myocardial infarction. Circulation 88[Suppl 1]:1–394, 1993.

I 109. Pfeffer MA, Braunwald E, Moye LA, et al: Effect of captopril on mortality and morbidity in patients with left ventricular dysfunction after myocardial infarction. N Engl J Med 327:669–677, 1992.

I 110. The Acute Infarction Ramipril Efficacy (AIRE) Study Investigators: Effect of ramipril on mortality and morbidity of survivors of acute myocardial infarction with clinical evidence of heart failure. Lancet 342:821–828, 1993.

111. ISIS Collaborative Group: ISIS-4: Randomised study of oral captopril in over 50,000 patients with suspected acute myocardial infarction. Circulation 88[Suppl 1]:1–394, 1993.

112. Teo KT, Yusuf S, Collins R, et al: Effects of intravenous magnesium in suspected acute myocardial infarction. Br Med J 303:1499–1503, 1991.

I 113. Woods KL, Fletcher S, Roffe C, Haider Y: Intravenous magnesium sulphate in suspected myocardial infarction: Results of the second Leicester Intravenous Magnesium Intervention Trial (LIMIT-2). Lancet 339:1553–1558, 1992.

113a. ISIS Collaborative Group: ISIS-4: Randomised study of intravenous magnesium in over 50,000 patients with suspected acute myocardial infarction. Circulation 88[Suppl 1]:1–292, 1993.

II 114. The TIMI Research Group: Immediate vs delayed catheterization and angioplasty following thrombolytic therapy for acute myocardial infarction: TIMI IIA results. JAMA 260:2849–2858, 1988.

II 115. Simoons ML, Arnold AER, Betriu A, et al: Thrombolysis with tissue plasminogen activator in acute myocardial infarction: No additional benefit from immediate percutaneous coronary angioplasty. Lancet 1:197–203, 1988.

I 116. Topol EJ, Califf RM, George BS, et al: A randomized trial of immediate versus delayed elective angioplasty after intravenous tissue plasminogen activator in acute myocardial infarction. N Engl J Med 317:581–588, 1987.

I 117. SWIFT (Should We Intervene Following Thrombolysis?) Trial Study Group: SWIFT trial of delayed elective intervention vs conservative treatment after thrombolysis with anistreplase in acute myocardial infarction. BMJ 302:555–560, 1991.

I 118. Ellis SG, daSilva ER, Heyndrickx GR, et al: Randomized comparison of rescue angioplasty with conservative management of patients with early failure of thrombolysis for acute anterior myocardial infarction. Circulation 90:2280–2284, 1994.

119. Knudtson M: Coronary thrombolysis: adjuvant coronary angioplasty. Can J Cardiol 9:528–536, 1993.

120. O'Neill WW: Angioplasty therapy of cardiogenic shock: Are randomized trials necessary? J Am Coll Cardiol 19:915–917, 1992.

I 121. Grines CL, Browne KF, Marco J, et al: A comparison of immediate angioplasty with thrombolytic therapy for acute myocardial infarction. N Engl J Med 328:673–679, 1993.

I 122. Zijlstra F, deBoer MJ, Hvorntje JCA, et al: A comparison of immediate angioplasty with intravenous streptokinase in acute myocardial infarction. N Engl J Med 328:680–684, 1993.

II 123. Gibbons RJ, Holmes DR, Reeder GS, et al: Immediate angioplasty compared with the administration of a thrombolytic agent followed by conservative treatment for myocardial infarction. N Engl J Med 328:685–691, 1993.

124. Cairns JA, Hirsh J, Sackett DL: Clinical use of coronary thrombolytic therapy. Contraindications. Can J Cardiol 9:516–522, 1993.

125. Anderson JL, Sorensen SG, Moreno FL, et al: Multicenter patency trial of intravenous anistreplase compared with streptokinase in acute myocardial infarction. Circulation 83:126–140, 1991.

126. Califf RM, Topol EJ, Stack RS, et al: Evaluation of combination thrombolytic therapy and timing of cardiac catheterization in acute myocardial infarction. Circulation 83:1543–1556, 1991.

II 127. Bassand J-P, Cassagnes J, Machecourt J, et al: Comparative effects of APSAC and rt-PA on infarct size and left ventricular function in acute myocardial infarction. A multicentre randomized study. Circulation 84:1107–1117, 1991.

# Chapter 6

# Heparin Therapy for Acute Cardiac Disorders

Graham F. Pineo, Gary E. Raskob, and Russell D. Hull

Heparin has been used in clinical practice for 50 years, but the major advances in the clinical use of heparin are relatively recent. Over the past 10 years or more, rigorously designed and conducted clinical trials have resulted in important advances in heparin therapy.[1I–8I, 9II, 10I–12I, 13, 14II, 15, 16, 17II] In patients with venous thromboembolism, virtually all of the uncertainties that a clinician commonly encountered in selecting an appropriate course of heparin therapy have now been resolved.[1I–6I] There have also been major clinical advances in the use of heparin in patients with unstable angina[7I, 8I, 9II] or myocardial infarction (MI),[10I–12I] and as adjunctive therapy in patients undergoing percutaneous transluminal coronary angioplasty (PTCA).[13, 14II, 15] In contrast to venous thromboembolism, however, several important issues concerning the use of heparin for these latter clinical indications remain unresolved.

This chapter reviews the recent advances in heparin therapy for patients with acute coronary syndromes (unstable angina or myocardial infarction), and as adjunctive therapy in patients undergoing PTCA. An emerging common theme in all of these conditions is the relation between the intensity of heparin anticoagulant effect and the clinical effectiveness of therapy.

The practical clinical use of heparin and the evidence supporting this practice are emphasized in this chapter; the biochemistry, pharmacology, and adverse effects of heparin have been reviewed.[16] (See also Chapter 27.)

## ACUTE CORONARY SYNDROMES

Several indications dictate heparin treatment in patients with acute coronary syndromes (unstable angina or myocardial infarction). These indications are (1) initial treatment of patients with unstable angina to prevent myocardial infarction; (2) treatment in patients with myocardial infarction, to improve short-term survival and reduce morbidity by preventing the complications of left ventricular mural thrombosis and systemic embolism, and venous thromboembolism; (3) adjunctive treatment in patients undergoing PTCA to prevent thrombosis and abrupt closure of the treated coronary artery; and (4) adjunctive treatment with thrombolytic therapy in patients with myocardial infarction to prevent rethrombosis of infarct-related artery. The clinical use of heparin in patients with unstable angina or following acute myocardial infarction or PTCA is reviewed in this section. The use of heparin as an adjunct to thrombolytic therapy for acute myocardial infarction is reviewed by Dr. J. Cairns in Chapter 5.

## PRIMARY TREATMENT

### Unstable Angina

In a landmark trial, Théroux and colleagues randomly allocated 479 patients with acute unstable angina to receive aspirin, continuous intravenous heparin, both, or neither (placebo).[7I] The results of this trial demonstrated that both aspirin and intravenous heparin are effective in reducing the incidence of MI in patients with unstable angina (Table 6–1). In addition, heparin, but not aspirin, was associated with a statistically significant and clinically important reduction in the frequency of refractory angina (Table 6–1).[7I] Major bleeding, defined as the need for transfusion or as a fall in hemoglobin of 2 g/dl or more, occurred with low frequency (1.6–3.2%) in each of the treatment groups. The heparin and aspirin arms of this study were continued until a total of 484 patients were

Table 6–1. **Practical Approaches for Heparin Treatment in Unstable Angina and Myocardial Infarction Without Thrombolysis***

| Clinical Indication | Route | Dose and Monitoring | Evidence Level |
|---|---|---|---|
| Unstable angina | Intravenous | 5,000 Units IV bolus<br>Continuous infusion of 1,000 Unit/hour<br>Adjust to maintain APTT ratio between 1.5 to 2.0 | I |
| Myocardial infarction without thrombolysis | Intravenous | 5,000 Units IV bolus<br>Continuous infusion of 1,250 Units/hour<br>Adjust to maintain APTT ratio between 1.5 to 2.0 | I |
| | Subcutaneous | 12,500 Units q 12 hours† | I |

*Firm recommendations are not possible at the present time for heparin treatment in patients with myocardial infarction who receive thrombolysis, or for patients who undergo PTCA (see text for discusson).

†The level I clinical trials evaluated the subcutaneous regimen of 12,500 U given every 12 hours. Other suggested regimens (e.g., 17,500 U every 12 hours) have not been evaluated by randomized clinical trials.

enrolled (240 on heparin and 244 on aspirin). The study was started $8.3 \pm 7.8$ hours after the last episode of pain and endpoints were assessed at $5.7 \pm 3.3$ days. Myocardial infarction occurred in two of 240 patients (0.8%) on heparin and nine of 244 patients on aspirin (3.7%, $p = 0.035$). The Cox regression logistic analysis showed that the improvement in survival without myocardial infarction with heparin ($p = 0.035$) was independent of other baseline characteristics.

In another randomized trial performed in patients with refractory unstable angina, heparin was effective in reducing the frequency of anginal attacks and the duration of ischemic episodes.[81] Heparin was shown to be as effective as intravenous urokinase with or without aspirin in preventing intractable angina or myocardial infarction in patients with unstable angina who were placed on treatment at a mean of 8.7 hours after their last ischemic symptoms.[17II]

Patients with acute myocardial ischemia (either unstable angina at rest or non-Q wave myocardial infarction), were randomized to receive either aspirin alone or aspirin plus intravenous heparin with warfarin starting on day 2 or 3 and continued throughout the 12-week treatment period.[18I] The primary endpoints were recurrent angina with electrocardiographic changes, myocardial infarction, and/or death. The treatment started $9.5 \pm 8.8$ hours after the initial qualifying pain and was continued in both arms of the study for 12 weeks. There was a significant reduction in all ischemic events in the aspirin, heparin, warfarin group (10.5%) compared with the group on aspirin alone (27%, $p = 0.004$).[18I] Bleeding was seen more commonly in the patients on combination therapy.

In another trial by Théroux and associates, the clinical outcomes after discontinuing heparin or aspirin therapy were evaluated.[9II] Early

reactivation of unstable angina was more common in patients who received heparin than in those who were given aspirin. However, concomitant aspirin administration lowered the incidence of early reactivation following discontinuation of heparin (Table 6–1). The recurrent ischemic events were clinically important (that is, they resulted in infarction or the need for urgent intervention with thrombolysis, angioplasty, or coronary bypass surgery). Most of the ischemic events occurred early after heparin was discontinued (mean 9.5 hours). This phenomenon could explain why intermittent intravenous heparin, which may result in periods of inadequate anticoagulation, was ineffective in one randomized trial of patients with acute unstable coronary artery disease.

A synthetic competitive thrombin inhibitor, argatroban, was studied in 43 patients with unstable angina in a phase I clinical trial.[19V] The drug was given by intravenous infusion 0.5 to 5.0 µg/kg/minute over a 4-hour period. Symptoms of myocardial ischemia did not occur during the infusion, but nine of 43 patients (20.9%) developed an episode of unstable angina at a mean of $5.8 \pm 2.6$ hours after the infusion was completed. Symptoms of angina were seen more frequently in patients on higher doses of argatroban and with a greater prolongation of activated partial thromboplastin time (APTT). This rebound phenomenon, which was similar to that seen after intravenous heparin treatment, remains unexplained. A better understanding of this rebound phenomenon may allow optimized treatment of thromboembolic disease with either heparin or specific thrombin inhibitors.

The findings of these clinical trials confirm that both aspirin and continuous intravenous heparin are effective in patients with unstable angina. Level I evidence indicates that heparin by continuous intravenous infusion is more effective than aspirin for reducing the incidence of refractory angina. It remains uncertain, however, whether combined heparin and aspirin treatment is more effective than aspirin alone for reducing the incidence of MI. This issue should be addressed by further clinical trials.

The American College of Chest Physicians (ACCP) Consensus Conference on Antithrombotic Therapy recommended that all patients with unstable angina be treated with aspirin (160–325 mg/day).[13] Treatment should start as soon as the clinical impression of unstable angina is formed, and it should be continued indefinitely.

Patients who have more severe angina should receive heparin in addition to aspirin. However, if warfarin is commenced, aspirin therapy should be discontinued until the planned course of warfarin is completed.[20]

## Myocardial Infarction

Heparin is effective for preventing the development of left ventricular mural thrombosis and systemic embolism, and for preventing the complication of venous thromboembolism in patients with MI.[10I, 11I, 20] Based on the available clinical trial data, the Consensus Conference on Antithrombotic Therapy recommended that patients at increased risk of systemic embolism or pulmonary embolism receive therapeutic heparin either intravenously or subcutaneously, followed by oral anticoagulant therapy with warfarin (level I).[20] These patients include those with severe left ventricular dysfunction, congestive heart failure, echocardiographic evidence of mural thrombosis, a past history of systemic or pulmonary embolism, and those with atrial fibrillation. At the least, all patients with MI should receive treatment with low-dose subcutaneous heparin (5,000 U every 8 hours) to prevent venous thromboembolism.[20]

A clinical trial in patients with acute anterior MI has provided important information about the relation between heparin dose, anticoagulant response, and the effectiveness of heparin therapy for preventing left ventricular mural thrombosis. Turpie and colleagues[10I] randomly allocated 221 patients with acute anterior transmural myocardial infarction to receive treatment with either low-dose subcutaneous heparin (5,000 U every 12 hours) or higher doses of subcutaneous heparin (12,500 U every 12 hours). Left ventricular mural thrombosis occurred in 28 of 88 patients (32%) in the low-dose group, compared with 10 of 95 patients (11%) in the high-dose group ($p=0.0004$).[10I]

The frequency of bleeding complications was low and similar in the two treatment groups (4–5%), and major bleeding was rare (<1%). The mean APTT response was 47.8 seconds in patients who received the higher doses, compared with 34.8 seconds in patients who received the low-dose regimen ($p<0.001$). The mean APTT responses over the course of therapy were higher among patients who did not develop mural thrombosis than in those patients in whom mural thrombosis was detected. Thus, the findings indicate that treatment with a subcutaneous heparin regimen of 12,500 U every 12 hours resulted in a more intense anticoagulant response and was more effective for preventing mural thrombosis than the low-dose regimen of 5,000 U every 12 hours.

A subsequent randomized trial confirmed the effectiveness of subcutaneous heparin (12,500 U every 12 hours) for reducing the frequency of left ventricular mural thrombosis.[11I] This latter trial also reported that heparin treatment resulted in a 41% risk reduction in hospital mortality (from 9.9% to 5.8%, $p=0.03$).[11I]

Evidence exists from one clinical trial[12I] that longterm subcutaneous heparin may be of benefit in patients with MI. Neri Serneri and colleagues[12I] randomly assigned 728 patients who had Q wave myocardial infarction 6 to 18 months earlier to receive subcutaneous heparin (12,500 U once daily) in addition to the usual care, or a control group who received the usual care without heparin. Treatment was continued for an average of 2 years. Myocardial re-infarction occurred in 13 of 365 patients (3.6%) in the control group, compared with five of 363 patients (1.4%) in the heparin group ($p=0.05$), a 61% risk reduction.[12I] The mortality rate from all causes was 6.3% in the control group (23 patients) compared with 4.1% in the heparin group (15 patients); this difference did not achieve statistical significance, but represents a potentially clinically important 34% risk reduction. Mortality attributable to thromboembolism (fatal re-infarction, stroke, or pulmonary embolism) was strikingly reduced by heparin treatment (from 1.9% to 0.3%, risk reduction 86%, $p<0.05$). Bleeding complications were rare (1%). Clinically important osteoporosis, a potential complication of longterm heparin use, occurred in only two of the 363 patients (0.6%). However, 90% of the patients enrolled were male; because only a small number of female patients were entered, the risk of osteoporosis associated with longterm heparin use in postmenopausal female patients remains uncertain.

The impressive risk reductions observed with subcutaneous heparin treatment in this study warrant investigation by further clinical trials. The subcutaneous heparin regimen was well tolerated and safe and has the practical advantage that it does not require laboratory monitoring. The practical recommendations for heparin treatment in patients with MI are shown in Table 6–1.

## Adjunctive Treatment to Coronary Angioplasty (PTCA)

Heparin is commonly used as adjunctive treatment in patients undergoing PTCA.[13] It is common practice to administer heparin as an intravenous bolus immediately prior to the procedure, followed by a continuous intravenous infusion of heparin. However, the need for continued heparin treatment, the duration of treatment, and the optimal heparin regimen and intensity of therapy remain uncertain. These issues remain incompletely resolved because of a lack of adequately designed clinical trials (level I) addressing these issues. In patients who have an uncomplicated PTCA procedure, the findings of one level II randomized trial[14II] suggest that heparin for 18 to 24 hours may not confer additional benefit over heparin given only during the procedure. Definitive conclusions about the benefit of continued heparin infusion after PTCA are not possible based on this one trial. This study entered only patients who had an uncomplicated procedure[14II]; the benefit of heparin in patients with complex lesions or a complicated angioplasty, for example with dissection, remains unevaluated.

Based on the available data, the ACCP Consensus Conference recommended that heparin be given to patients undergoing PTCA.[13] The suggested regimen is a 10,000-U bolus intravenously, followed by a continuous intravenous infusion adjusted to maintain the APTT at 1.5 to 2.0 times control. This group recommended that heparin be continued for 2 to 4 hours in patients with an uncomplicated procedure, and for 16 to 24 hours in patients with unstable angina, complex lesions, multivessel angioplasty, and a suboptimal PTCA result.[13] It should be emphasized, however, that firm clinical trial data (level I evidence) to support these recommendations is lacking.

A retrospective study[15] provides interesting data on the relation between the intensity of heparin treatment and the clinical outcome of PTCA. McGarry and coworkers[15] reported a review of 336 patients who had elective PTCA and were treated with intravenous heparin. All patients received an intravenous bolus of 10,000 U at the beginning of the procedure followed

by a continuous infusion of 2,000 U/hour. At the conclusion of the procedure, the infusion dose was reduced to 1,000 U/hour and continued for 18 to 24 hours. The outcome in patients with an APTT ratio of 3.0 or more (271 patients) was compared with the outcome in 65 patients who had a less intense anticoagulant response (APTT ratio less than 3.0). There was a statistically significant and clinically important lower frequency of abrupt coronary artery closure in the group with the more intense heparin response. Abrupt closure occurred in seven of 65 patients (10.7%) with an APTT response less than 3.0, compared with only seven of 271 patients (2.5%) in patients with a more intense APTT response (ratio 3.0 or more).[15] In the group with a less intense APTT response, two of the 65 patients (3.0%) died, compared with only one of 271 patients (0.4%) with a more intense APTT response (not statistically significant). Major bleeding complications requiring transfusion occurred with a similar low frequency in the more intense and less intense groups (2.9% and 4.6%, respectively).

Because of the retrospective study design, the findings cannot be used to make definitive recommendations on the use of adjuvant heparin in patients undergoing PTCA. The results provide an interesting hypothesis, however, that intense heparin therapy (APTT ratio 3.0 or more) may be of benefit for reducing the incidence of abrupt coronary closure after PTCA. This possibility should be investigated by randomized clinical trials.

## REFERENCES

I 1. Salzman EW, Deykin D, Shapiro RM, Rosenberg R: Management of heparin therapy: Controlled prospective trial. N Engl J Med 292:1046–1050, 1975.
I 2. Hull RD, Raskob GE, Hirsh J, et al: Continuous intravenous heparin compared with intermittent subcutaneous heparin in the initial treatment of proximal-vein thrombosis. N Engl J Med 315:1109–1114, 1986.
I 3. Gallus AS, Jackaman J, Tillett J, et al: Safety and efficacy of warfarin started early after submassive venous thrombosis or pulmonary embolism. Lancet 2:1293–1296, 1986.
I 4. Hull RD, Raskob GE, Rosenbloom D, et al: Heparin for 5 days as compared with 10 days in the initial treatment of proximal venous thrombosis. N Engl J Med 322:1260–1264, 1990.
I 5. Brandjes DPM, Heijboer H, Buller HR, et al: Acenocoumarol and heparin compared with acenocoumarol alone in the initial treatment of proximal-vein thrombosis. N Engl J Med 327:1485–1489, 1992.
I 6. Hull RD, Raskob GE, Rosenbloom DR, et al: Optimal therapeutic level of heparin therapy in patients with venous thrombosis. Arch Intern Med 152:1589–1595, 1992.
I 7. Theroux P, Ouimet H, McCans J, et al: Aspirin, heparin or both to treat acute unstable angina. N Engl J Med 319:1105–1111, 1988.

I 8. Neri Serneri GG, Gensini GF, Poggesi L, et al: Effect of heparin, aspirin or alteplase in reduction of myocardial ischaemia in refractory unstable angina. Lancet 335:615–618, 1990.

II 9. Theroux P, Waters D, Lam J, et al: Reactivation of unstable angina after the discontinuation of heparin. N Engl J Med 327:141–145, 1992.

I 10. Turpie AG, Robinson JG, Doyle DJ, et al: Comparison of high-dose with low-dose subcutaneous heparin to prevent left ventricular mural thrombosis in patients with acute transmural anterior myocardial infarction. N Engl J Med 320:352–357, 1989.

I 11. Scati Group: Randomized controlled trial of subcutaneous calcium heparin in acute myocardial infarction. Lancet 2:182–186, 1989.

I 12. Neri Serneri GG, Rovelli F, Gensini GF, et al: Effectiveness of low-dose heparin in prevention of myocardial reinfarction. Lancet 1:937–942, 1987.

13. Stein PD, Dalen JE, Goldman S, et al: Antithrombotic therapy in patients with saphenous vein and internal mammary artery bypass grafts and following percutaneous transluminal coronary angioplasty. Chest 102[Suppl]:508S–515S, 1992.

II 14. Ellis SG, Roubin GS, Wilentz J, et al: Effect of 18- to 24-hour heparin administration for prevention of restenosis after uncomplicated coronary angioplasty. Am Heart J 117:777–782, 1989.

15. McGarry TF, Gottlieb RS, Morganroth J, et al: The relationship of anticoagulation levels and complications after successful percutaneous transluminal coronary angioplasty. Am Heart J 123:1445–1451, 1992.

16. Hirsh J, Dalen JE, Deykin D, Poller L: Heparin: Mechanism of action, pharmacokinetics, dosing considerations, monitoring, efficacy and safety. Chest 102[Suppl]:337S–351S, 1992.

II 17. Schreiber TL, Rizik D, White C, et al: Randomized trial of thrombolysis versus heparin in unstable angina. Circulation 86:1407–1414, 1992.

I 18. Cohen M, Adams PC, Parry G, et al: Combination antithrombotic therapy in unstable rest angina and non-Q-wave infarction in nonprior aspirin users: Primary end points analysis from the ATACS trial. Circulation 89:81–88, 1994.

V 19. Gold HK, Torres FW, Garabedian HD, et al: Evidence for a rebound coagulation phenomenon after cessation of a 4-hour infusion of a specific thrombin inhibitor in patients with unstable angina pectoris. Am Coll Cardiol 21(5):1039–1047, 1993.

20. Cairns JA, Hirsh J, Lewis HD, et al: Antithrombotic agents in coronary artery disease. Chest 102[Suppl]: 456S–481S, 1992.

# Chapter 7

# Oral Anticoagulants (Antithrombotic Agents) for Cardiovascular Disorders

Richard C. Becker and Jack Ansell

The coumarin-type oral anticoagulants have been in use for over 50 years and are well established weapons in the armamentarium against thrombotic disease.[1, 2] Their discovery evolved from investigations into the hemorrhagic disease of cattle occurring early in the twentieth century, which was attributed to the consumption of spoiled sweet clover. Link[3] eventually isolated the responsible agent in spoiled sweet clover, dicumarol (3-3' methyl-bis-4-hydroxy coumarin), which quickly entered the clinical arena through work at the Mayo Clinic in 1941.[4] Link subsequently synthesized a related compound (warfarin), initially popularized as a rodenticide in the late 1940s. Warfarin entered clinical practice in the 1950s and quickly became the major oral anticoagulant in clinical use.

## WARFARIN

## Mechanism of Action

Warfarin produces its anticoagulant effect by interfering with the cyclic interconversion of vitamin K and its 2,3 epoxide (vitamin K epoxide).[5] Vitamin K is an essential cofactor in the post-translational γ-carboxylation of several glutamic acid residues in the vitamin K–dependent coagulation Factors II, VII, IX, and X (Fig 7–1). In the absence of γ-carboxylation, these proteins are unable to bind calcium and phospholipid, and depending on the level of carboxylation, they manifest a reduced coagulant (i.e., enzymatic) potential.[2] Warfarin exerts this effect by inhibiting vitamin K epoxide reductase (see Fig. 7–1).

## Pharmacokinetics

Because of its excellent bioavailability and favorable pharmacokinetics, warfarin is the most commonly used oral anticoagulant in North America. It is highly water soluble and rapidly

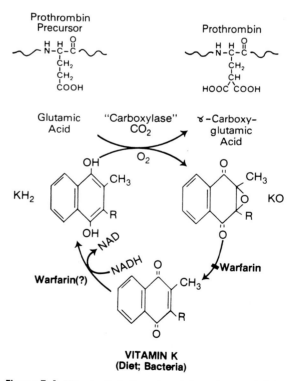

**Figure 7–1.** Vitamin K, in its reduced form, is essential for the γ-carboxylation reaction of glutamic acid residues within vitamin K–dependent coagulation factors. Reduced vitamin K is subsequently oxidized in the carboxylation reaction. Warfarin sodium interferes with the recycling (reduction) of oxidized vitamin K.

absorbed from the gastrointestinal tract after oral ingestion.[6] Peak absorption occurs in 60 to 90 minutes. Food may delay the rate of absorption but is said not to reduce the extent of absorption.

Warfarin is a racemic mixture of stereoisomers, each with distinctive metabolic pathways, half lives, and potency.[2] Racemic warfarin, however, has an average half life of 36 to 42 hours with a range from 15 to 60 hours. Variability in warfarin half life, as a result of either natural differences in metabolism or disease and drug-induced alterations in metabolic rate, accounts for the marked variations in an individual's initial response to, or maintenance requirement for, warfarin. Warfarin's effect also varies inversely with the amount of vitamin K absorbed (from the diet and from metabolic byproducts of gastrointestinal bacteria) and varies directly with the amount of warfarin absorbed or available to exert its anticoagulant effect (Table 7–1).[1]

## Therapeutic Range of Monitoring of Oral Anticoagulants

The concept of a safe and effective therapeutic range developed largely as a consequence of trial and error and clinical empiricism in the 1940s and 1950s.[1] A prothrombin time (PT) ratio of 2.0 to 2.5 or 3.0, using a human brain thromboplastin reagent sensitive to a reduction in the vitamin K-dependent coagulation factors, was felt to represent this therapeutic range. In

North America in the 1950s and 1960s, manufacturers switched to a less sensitive rabbit brain thromboplastin reagent, resulting in the need for a higher average warfarin dose to achieve the same prolongation of the PT.[7] Despite this change, physicians did not adjust their treatment by altering the therapeutic range and, consequently, patients were more intensely anticoagulated. Hull and coworkers[8] demonstrated the consequences of this situation in a study of patients with deep venous thrombosis treated with warfarin by documenting a higher incidence of bleeding in those monitored with the less sensitive rabbit brain thromboplastin. They found no increase in recurrent thromboembolism in those monitored by the more sensitive reagent when both groups were maintained in a similar therapeutic range.

To correct for differences in thromboplastin sensitivity, the World Health Organization recommended the use of an international standard PT.[9] This is achieved by equilibrating all thromboplastins against a sensitive international reference thromboplastin and then using that equilibration factor (the International Sensitivity Index or ISI) to convert PT ratios (PT divided by the mean of the normal range) to an international ratio (the International Normalized Ratio or INR). The INR is essentially the PT ratio obtained if the international reference thromboplastin had been used to measure the PT. Table 7–2 illustrates how a local PT ratio is converted to an INR, which is performed automatically by laboratory instrumentation. By con-

## Table 7–1. **Causes of Nontherapeutic Prothrombin Time**

| Considerations | PT |
|---|---|
| Major | |
| Too much or too little vitamin K | |
|     Decrease in dietary vitamin K | Increase |
|     Malabsorption of vitamin K | Increase |
|     Suppression of gut bacteria | Increase |
|     Increase in dietary vitamin K | Decrease |
| Too much or too little warfarin sodium | |
|     Decrease in absorption | Decrease |
|     Changes in metabolism | Increase/decrease |
|     Drug effects | Increase/decrease |
| Minor | |
| Changes in factor production/metabolism | |
|     Liver disease | Increase |
|     Hypermetabolic states (fever) | Increase |
|     Other illnesses | Increase |
| Technical/laboratory factors: Problems with | |
|     Phlebotomy | Increase/decrease |
|     Evacuated collection tube | Increase/decrease |
|     Handling | Increase/decrease |
|     Instrumentation | Increase/decrease |
|     Different thromboplastin reagents | Increase/decrease |

## Table 7–2. **Use of ISI to Calculate an INR**

ISI = International Sensitivity Index
    A comparative rating of different
    thromboplastins
INR = International Normalized Ratio
    A comparative rating of prothrombin time
    ratios for individuals with stable therapeutic
    anticoagulation

To convert a prothrombin time (PT) ratio to an INR
  equivalent:
    $INR = PT\ Ratio^X\ (X = ISI)$

Example:
    17.9 s = PT
    12.2 s = Mean of normal range
    2.3 = ISI of thromboplastin
Then:
    $\dfrac{17.9}{123}$ = 1.47 PT ratio

    $1.47^{2.3}$ = 2.4 INR

verting all PT ratios to INRs, a patient's PT result can be interpreted regardless of where it is performed, and then the guidelines of international consensus groups can be followed for therapeutic effectiveness, as outlined in Table 7–3.

## Complications of Therapy and Their Management

Hemorrhage is the most common complication of oral anticoagulation therapy.[10] The frequency of bleeding correlates with the elevation of the PT, as well as other factors, such as a history of stroke or gastrointestinal bleeding, a serious comorbid condition, or instability of control.[11] The cumulative risk of hemorrhage is also directly related to the duration of anticoagulant treatment, although most events occur early in the course of therapy.[12] The overall risk of hemorrhage (major and minor) is 2 to 3% during the first month of treatment, 0.8% per month during the first year, and 0.2% per month thereafter. The total average annual risks for major bleeding (retroperitoneal, gastrointestinal, or those requiring transfusion, hospitalization, or surgical intervention) and fatal bleeding with longterm oral anticoagulant therapy are 6%, 2%, and 0.8%, respectively.

Management of serious bleeding requires immediate correction of the PT by replacement of the vitamin K-dependent coagulation factors. This can be achieved by the administration of fresh frozen plasma, but sufficient plasma must be given to be effective (approximately 15 ml/ kg is an appropriate estimated dose). Vitamin K

can be given for less serious degrees of excessive anticoagulation, but small doses are recommended (1 mg parenterally) because larger doses may predispose to relative degrees of warfarin resistance for patients who need to remain anticoagulated after excessive anticoagulation is corrected.[13] Vitamin K will take 12 to 24 hours to improve the PT in individuals with normal hepatic function. Excessive prolongations of the PT without bleeding can be corrected simply by withholding warfarin for a few days. Table 7–4 summarizes recommendations adapted from the American College of Chest Physicians[14] for management of an elevated INR with or without bleeding.

Gastrointestinal and genitourinary bleeding in the presence of a therapeutic degree of anticoagulation may result from an unsuspected lesion of clinical significance and should be evaluated, especially to exclude an underlying malignancy.[1]

Warfarin-induced skin necrosis is another serious, but rare, complication of oral anticoagulant therapy.[15] It typically produces necrosis of subcutaneous fatty tissue within the first few days of initiating therapy, and in some cases appears to be related to an excessive reduction in protein C, a naturally occurring, vitamin K-dependent coagulation inhibitor.[16] Reduction in protein C may occur in subjects who are heterozygous for protein C deficiency. However, the condition is sufficiently rare that it is not cost-effective to screen patients for protein C deficiency, nor must all patients be covered with heparin when warfarin is started unless a deficiency is suspected.

## Invasive Procedures During Warfarin Therapy

For patients on longterm anticoagulation requiring invasive procedures, physicians must as-

## Table 7–3. **Indications and Recommended Therapeutic Range for Oral Anticoagulation**

| Indication | INR |
|---|---|
| Prophylaxis of venous thrombosis (high-risk surgery) | 2.0–3.0 |
| Treatment of venous thrombosis | |
| Treatment of pulmonary embolism | |
| Prevention of systemic embolism | |
|   Tissue heart valves | 2.0–3.0 |
|   Acute myocardial infarction (to prevent systemic embolism) | |
|   Valvular heart disease | |
|   Atrial fibrillation | |
| Recurrent systemic embolism | 2.5–3.5 |
| Mechanical prosthetic valves | |

**Table 7-4. American College of Chest Physicians Recommendations for Elevated INR**

1. If the INR is above the therapeutic range but below 6.0, the patient is not bleeding, and rapid reversal is not indicated for reasons of surgical intervention, then the next few doses can be omitted and warfarin commenced at a lower dose when the patient is in the therapeutic range.
2. If the INR is above 6.0 but below 10.0 and the patient is not bleeding, or more rapid reversal is required because the patient requires elective surgery, then vitamin $K_1$ intravenously in a dose of 0.5 to 1 mg can be given with the expectation that a demonstrable reduction of the INR will occur at 8 h, and many patients will be in the therapeutic range of 2.0 to 3.0 in 24 h. If the INR is still too high at 24 h, the dose of 0.5 mg can be repeated. Warfarin treatment can then be resumed at a lower dose.
3. If the INR is above 10.0 but below 20.0 and the patient is not bleeding, a higher dose of vitamin K of 3 to 5 mg intravenously should be given with the expectation that INR will be reduced substantially at 6 h. The INR should be checked every 6 to 12 h, and vitamin K can then be repeated if necessary (the risk of anaphylaxis, albeit small, is increased with intravenous vitamin K administration).
4. If a rapid reversal of an anticoagulant effect is required because of serious bleeding or major warfarin overdose (e.g., INR>20.0), vitamin K in a dose of 10 mg should be given by intravenous injection and the INR checked every 6 h. Vitamin K may have to be repeated every 12 h and supplemented with plasma transfusion of factor concentrate depending on the urgency of the situation (the risk of anaphylaxis, albeit small, is increased with intravenous vitamin K administration).
5. In case of life-threatening bleeding or serious warfarin overdose, replacement with factor concentrates is indicated supplemented with intravenously given vitamin K, 10 mg, to be repeated as necessary depending on the INR.
6. If continued warfarin therapy is indicated after high doses of vitamin K administration, then heparin can be given until the effects of vitamin K have been reversed, and the patient becomes responsive to warfarin.

Used with permission from Dalen JE, Hirsh J (eds): Third ACCP Conference on Antithrombotic Therapy. Chest 102:3035–5495, 1992.

sess the risk of thromboembolism if anticoagulation is stopped versus the risk of bleeding if anticoagulation is continued at the same or lower intensity.[1] Based on that assessment there are three general choices, including: (1) discontinuing warfarin several days before the procedure to allow the PT to return to normal and restarting therapy shortly after surgery; (2) lowering the warfarin dose so as to maintain a lower or subtherapeutic range during the procedure; (3) discontinuing warfarin, admitting the patient to the hospital before surgery, and reinstituting heparin that will be discontinued 2 to 4 hours before surgery and reinstituted after surgery when it is considered safe, followed by oral anticoagulation. The last of these options provides the shortest interval free of anticoagulation if surgery cannot be done on an anticoagulated patient. The cost-effectiveness of the latter approach must be assessed carefully, and many individuals can be entirely off anticoagulation for short periods of time without undue risk.

## Coronary Artery Disease

Coronary artery disease is the leading cause of death in the United States, Canada, and other industrialized nations. Moreover, the treatment of patients with coronary artery disease is responsible for a substantial portion of the United States health care budget, approaching 55 billion dollars annually. Therefore, treatment strategies designed to reduce morbidity and

mortality among patients with proven, as well as those at risk for, atherosclerotic coronary artery disease would be expected to have a significant impact on the current health care system.

The association between atherosclerosis, coagulation, and thrombosis is recognized widely and currently is the target of intensive investigation. Fueled by recent observations revealing an incontrovertible link between acute coronary thrombosis and cardiac events, including acute myocardial infarction and post-reperfusion arterial reocclusion, the field of thrombocardiology is developing at an extraordinary pace.

## CORONARY ARTERY DISEASE

### Pathobiology of Atherosclerosis

A comprehensive description of coronary atherosclerosis in its various stages of development has been provided recently by Stary.[17] The classification includes five distinct phases and details the contributory role of nonocclusive thrombosis in the natural history of this common process.

TYPE I LESION. The earliest coronary arterial abnormality consists of macrophages with lipid-droplet inclusions.

TYPE II LESION. This stage is characterized by layers of cells extended with lipid-droplet inclusions. Macrophage foam cells begin to accumulate in the deeper portions of the subendothelial proteoglycan intima.

TYPE III LESION. The preatheroma stage is characterized by a transition from fatty streak to the more advanced atheroma. Pool-like aggregates of extracellular lipid particles begin to form in the musculoelastic layer.

TYPE IV LESION. Also known as the atheromatous stage, this lesion contains a large extracellular lipid pool referred to as the "lipid" or "necrotic" core.

TYPE V LESION. The fibroatheromatous stage contains an atheroma as well as a proteoglycan layer with smooth muscle cells embedded in a matrix of collagen and capillaries (fibrous cap). The formation of the fibrous cap is accelerated when platelets and fibrin, deposited on the vessel's endothelial surface, are incorporated within the intimal layer. During this sequence of events, intraluminal thrombosis is intimately involved in the plaque's growth and development. A majority of patients experiencing unstable angina and acute myocardial infarction are known to have type V lesions within one or more epicardial coronary arteries (Fig. 7–2).

It is important to realize that the atherosclerotic process begins early in the second decade of life and progresses at a variable pace. Indeed,

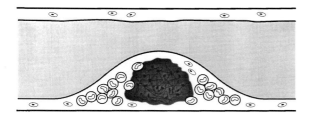

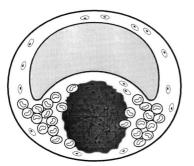

**Figure 7–2.** Longitudinal and cross-sectional schematic representations of an advanced atherosclerotic plaque (type V lesion). A large, centrally located lipid "necrotic" core is separated from the vessel's lumen by a fibrous cap. Macrophages are shown (see text).

a recent autopsy series of 111 victims of noncardiac trauma (mean age 26 ± 6 years) identified signs of coronary atherosclerosis in 78.3% of the total group, with more than 50% narrowing in 20.7% and more than 75% narrowing in 9%. Proximal vessel involvement was a common observation. Furthermore, left main or significant two- and three-vessel involvement was found in 20% of the group studied.[18]

## Coronary Arterial Thrombogenesis

A classification of vascular injury preceding coronary arterial thrombosis has been proposed by Ferrel, Fuster, and coworkers.[19]

TYPE 1 INJURY. Type I injury is localized to the vascular endothelium and most often is caused by alterations in coronary arterial blood flow at either branch points or areas of eccentric intimal thickening. It represents a stage of mild, chronic injury, predisposing to platelet adherence but not, under normal circumstances, to occlusive thrombosis.

TYPE II INJURY. In contrast to type I vascular injury, type II injury is not localized to the endothelial surface. Instead, it involves deeper layers of the atherosclerotic plaque, inciting platelet activation, aggregation, and thrombosis.

TYPE III INJURY. Type III injury is characterized by extensive plaque disruption with exposure of the vascular subendothelial connective tissue matrix. Given the strong stimulus for thrombosis, type III injury represents the most common pathobiologic precipitant for occlusive coronary arterial thrombosis. Of interest, recent evidence suggests that the atheromatous core (containing cholesterol crystals and other substrate) is the most thrombogenic component of human atherosclerotic plaques (Fig. 7–3).

## The Link Between Atherosclerosis and Coagulation

Fibrin is a common component of coronary arterial atherosclerotic plaques, suggesting that the coagulation mechanism is a participant in the atherosclerotic process. Even in the earliest stage of development (type I lesion), a uniform pattern of antifibrin antibody binding is observed, suggesting that fibrinogen derived from the infiltration of plasma is converted to fibrin within the vessel's intima. Advanced atherosclerotic plaques (type V lesion) contain a localized

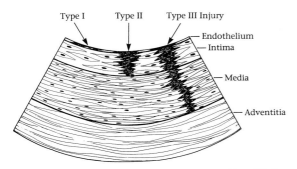

**Figure 7–3.** A classification of vascular injury. Type I injury is superficial and rarely leads to thrombosis; however, it may contribute to plaque growth and endothelial cell dysfunction. Type II and type III injury patterns involve deeper portions of the vessel wall. They are thrombosis-prone (see text).

banded pattern of antifibrin antibody binding, consistent with direct incorporation of polymerized fibrin within the fibrous cap.[20, 21]

Platelets are also felt to be important participants in atherosclerosis. They can support macrophage foam cell formation in cultured aortic smooth muscle cells.[22] Mendelsohn and Loscalzo demonstrated that, in the absence of other sources of free cholesterol, platelets aggregated with collagen can produce lipid-rich particles that are avidly taken up by monocytes (macrophages) in tissue culture.[23] It has also been observed that platelet depletion dramatically reduces the mitogenic response to vessel wall injury.[24] Thrombin, a serine protease of broad specificity and many potential effects on atherosclerosis, can induce macrophage interleukin-1 synthesis, a cytokine capable of provoking smooth muscle cell proliferation and expression of leukocyte adhesion molecules on the endothelial surface. Smith and coworkers[25] have shown a direct correlation between the level of fibrin-related antigen and low-density lipoprotein (LDL) cholesterol in advanced atherosclerotic lesions. Fibrinogen itself has received considerable attention and is believed to contribute to the atherosclerotic process through (1) induction of endothelial cell disorganization and migration[26, 27]; (2) the provision of a surface for LDL cholesterol binding[28]; and (3) stimulation of smooth muscle cell proliferation.[29] Fibrin(ogen) degradation products may also play an active role by (1) increasing vascular permeability; (2) inducing disorganization of endothelial cells; and (3) stimulating smooth muscle cell proliferation.

A novel lipoprotein composed of LDL cholesterol and apo A, Lp(a) has been shown by several investigative groups to compete with plasminogen for cell surface binding sites on monocytes, endothelial cells, and platelets.[30–32] Lp(a) can also adhere to fibrin monolayers, reducing fibrin's ability to augment the conversion of plasminogen to plasmin.[33] Lastly, Lp(a) induces the expression and secretion of plasminogen activator inhibitor,[34] reducing vascular fibrinolytic capacity and thromboresistance.

## Thrombin Activity in Coronary Artery Disease

Thrombin generation is common to all thrombotic processes. Thrombin, a 308 amino acid serine protease, in turn (1) potentiates the tenase and prothrombinase complexes; (2) converts fibrinogen to fibrin; (3) exposes fibrin monomer polymerization sites; (4) accelerates factor XIII-mediated fibrin monomer crosslinking; (5) activates platelets; (6) induces platelet and endothelial cell plasminogen activator inhibitor-1 (PAI-1) release; and (7) provokes tissue factor release.

Accumulating evidence suggests that coronary atherosclerosis, from a pathologic and biochemical perspective, is a chronic active process with intermittent acute events. Rosenberg and coworkers have shown that thrombin activity and generation remain heightened in patients with coronary artery disease, supporting a chronic state of prothrombotic potential.[35] In a study of 225 patients with angina pectoris undergoing coronary angiography, plasma levels of prothrombin activation fragment 1.2 (F1.2) and of thrombin-antithrombin III complexes (TAT) were increased among individuals with angiographically verified coronary atherosclerosis, as well as those with a previous history of myocardial infarction.[36]

Plasma samples obtained from patients experiencing acute myocardial infarction typically reveal increased levels of fibrinopeptide A, F1.2, and TAT, suggesting thrombin activation and generation.[37] These abnormalities persist for 3 to 5 days after the acute event,[38] and have been shown to correlate with recurrent thrombotic events.[39–41]

## Epidemiologic Experience With Coagulation Factors and Cardiac Events

Epidemiologic studies have examined factor VII and fibrinogen, two components of the natural hemostatic mechanism. In the Northwick Park Study,[42, 43] factor VII coagulant activity was shown to correlate with cardiovascular mortality.[44] Fibrinogen also correlated strongly, as did factor VIII, although less strongly than the other hemostatic markers. The potential importance of factor VIII, however, is strengthened by the low incidence of atherosclerotic coronary artery disease in patients with hemophilia.[45] In the Atherosclerosis Risk in Communities (ARIC) Study consisting of 15,800 individuals from four diverse areas in the United States, baseline measurements of factor VIII and von Willebrand factor were performed to determine their relationship to the development of coronary atherosclerosis. In univariate analysis, both factors were positively associated with plasma triglycerides and negatively associated with high-density lipoprotein (HDL) cholesterol.[46]

As with the Northwick Park Study, several large-scale epidemiologic studies have identified an association between both factor VIII activity and fibrinogen and the incidence of atherosclerotic coronary artery disease. In the Leigh Study,[47] fibrinogen and coronary disease correlated in men between 40 and 69 years of age. Interestingly, this association was stronger than the association between cholesterol (and other standard risk factors) and coronary disease. The Framingham[48] and Caerphilly[49] studies both identified an association between fibrinogen levels and the incidence of coronary disease among men and women in their fifth to eighth decades of life.

Involvement of the fibrinolytic system in the development of acute coronary syndromes has recently led investigative groups to explore several markers as predictors of thrombotic cardiovascular events. In a study of 213 consecutive patients with angina pectoris and angiographically confirmed coronary artery disease, t-PA mass concentration was the only laboratory marker significantly associated with mortality at a mean followup of 7 years.[50] High circulating (PAI-1) levels have also been shown to correlate with an increased risk of ischemic thrombotic events.[51]

With a strong framework provided by observational epidemiologic studies, the primary objective of the ongoing Thrombosis Prevention Trial[52I, 53I] is to demonstrate a 30% reduction in the incidence of ischemic heart disease in approximately 6,000 high-risk men between the ages of 45 and 69 attributable to low-dose warfarin, low-dose aspirin (75 mg controlled release), or the combination. An aim of the trial's warfarin component is to reduce factor VII activity from a high-risk level of 120% (as determined in the Northwick Park Study) to approxi-mately 70% (a level seen in patients with little or no atherosclerotic coronary artery disease).

## ORAL ANTICOAGULANTS IN CLINICAL PRACTICE

### Myocardial Infarction

#### Secondary Prevention

An association between atherosclerotic coronary artery disease, coagulation, and thrombotic events, including unstable angina, myocardial infarction, and systemic thromboembolism, has led to the investigation of oral anticoagulant use in clinical practice.

#### Early Outcome

In 1977, Chalmers and coworkers[54] pooled the results from 37 published reports examining the role for anticoagulant therapy among patients with acute myocardial infarction and concluded that treatment reduced mortality by approximately 20%. Reanalysis of the data using more rigorous statistical methods later confirmed Chalmers' conclusions.[55]

It is important to recognize, however, that many of the anticoagulant trials performed over the years have been nonrandomized, poorly controlled, and either historic or observational in design. As a result, and in the final analysis, they have provided limited information for practicing clinicians. Overall, only three trials included in Chalmers and Peto's analyses were randomized, controlled, and of sufficient sample size—the British Medical Research Council Trial,[56II] The Bronx Municipal Hospital Study,[57I] and the Veterans Administration Cooperative Study (Table 7–5).[58II]

The Medical Research Council (MRC) Trial was a single-blind, controlled trial of 1,427 patients with acute myocardial infarction.[56II] Patients were randomized to heparin (15,000 U intravenous bolus, followed by 10,000 U every 6 hours for five doses) or no heparin. Heparin-treated patients received an oral anticoagulant (phenindione) simultaneously, adjusted to maintain the thrombosis test level between 10 and 20% (INR 1.6–2.1), whereas the no-heparin group received low-dose phenindione (maintenance dose 0.5 mg twice daily). In the high-dose anticoagulation group, mortality (all-cause) decreased from 18.2 to 16.2%, reinfarction from 13 to 9.7%, and the composite endpoint of death or reinfarction decreased from 31 to 29.5% (risk reduction 16%). In addition, a significant reduction in overall thrombo-

Table 7–5. **Anticoagulation in the Early Postinfarction Phase**

| Trial | | Patients (N) | Mortality (%) | p Value | Reinfarction | p Value | Thromboembolism (%) | p Value |
|---|---|---|---|---|---|---|---|---|
| Medical Research Council Trial | High-dose OA | 712 | 16.2 | NS | 9.7 | NS | 2.2 | <0.01 |
| | Low-dose OA | 715 | 18.0 | | 13.0 | | 5.6 | |
| Bronx Municipal Hospital Study | OA | 745 | 14.8 | <0.01 | 12.5 | <0.05 | 0.1 | NS |
| | Placebo | 391 | 21.2 | | 18.7 | | 0.2 | |
| VA Cooperative Study | OA | 500 | 9.6 | NS | 4.0 | NS | 3.6 | 0.005 |
| | Placebo | 499 | 11.2 | | 6.0 | | 10.8 | |

OA—Oral Anticoagulants, NS—Not specified

embolic events, including deep venous thrombosis, pulmonary embolism, and stroke, was observed. Although hemorrhagic events were more common in the high-dose anticoagulation group, no deaths resulted.

The Bronx Municipal Hospital Center Trial[57] randomized 1,136 men and women with acute myocardial infarction to either anticoagulation (heparin 5,000 U bolus, followed by 10,000 U subcutaneously every 8 hours for five doses and phenindione [INR 2.0–2.5]) or placebo. Treatment was continued throughout the hospital stay. Mortality (all-cause) decreased from 21.2 to 14.9% in the anticoagulation group, and reinfarction decreased from 13 to 11.8%. A reduction in mortality was particularly evident in women over 55 years of age in whom a reduction from 31 to 14.9% was observed. As in the MRC trial, thromboembolic events were lower and hemorrhagic events were higher in the anticoagulation group. There were, however, no fatal hemorrhagic events.

The Veterans Administration Cooperative Study[58] included 999 men with acute myocardial infarction. Patients randomized to anticoagulation received heparin (10,000 U subcutaneously every 8 to 12 hours, adjusted to a clotting time of twice normal) and warfarin (PT 25–30 seconds), whereas control patients received matching placebos. The observation period on treatment was 28 days. Among anticoagulated patients, inhospital mortality (all cause) decreased from 11.2 to 9.6%, and reinfarction from 4 to 2%. The rate of pulmonary embolism and stroke was substantially decreased—2.6 to 0.2% and 3.8 to 0.8%, respectively. Although anticoagulant therapy was discontinued because of bleeding in five patients, major hemorrhage was uncommon and there were no deaths. Thus, the early use of anticoagulant therapy following acute myocardial infarction is associated with a modest reduction in thromboembolism-related morbidity and mortality. It must be recognized, however, that the care of patients has changed substantially over the past two to three decades, raising questions over the direct applicability of previous observations to current practice.

## Mural Thrombosis and Embolic Events

Left ventricular mural thrombus is observed either echocardiographically or at the time of autopsy among patients with acute myocardial infarction,[59III, 60IV] especially in those with anterior infarction involving the apex.[69II, 70II, 72I] In large clinical trials of anticoagulant therapy, researchers reported an incidence of cerebral embolism of 2 to 4% among the control patients, frequently causing either severe neurologic deficits or death.[56II, 57I, 58II] Of these trials, two showed a statistically significant reduction in stroke with early anticoagulation, whereas the third trial demonstrated a positive trend.

A recent meta-analysis performed by Vaitkus and coworkers[75] supports the findings of three previous studies published in the early 1980s.[76–78] The odds ratio for increased risk of systemic embolism in the presence of echocardiographically demonstrated mural thrombus was 5.45 (95% confidence interval [CI] 3.02–9.83) and the event rate difference was 0.09 (95% CI 0.003–0.14). The odds ratio of anticoagulation versus no anticoagulation in preventing embolization was 0.14 (95% CI 0.04–0.52) with an event rate difference of −0.33 (95% CI −0.50 to −0.16). The odds ratio of anticoagulation versus control in preventing mural thrombus formation was 0.32 (95% CI 0.20–0.52) and the event rate difference was −0.19 (95% CI −0.09 to −0.28). The available data support the following conclusions, that (1) mural thrombosis following acute myocardial infarction increases the risk of systemic embolism; (2) anticoagulation can reduce mural thrombus formation; and (3) the risk of systemic embolism can be substantially reduced by anticoagulation (Fig. 7–4).

It is recommended that patients at increased risk of systemic or pulmonary embolism because of severe left ventricular dysfunction (ejection fraction <40%), congestive heart failure, a his-

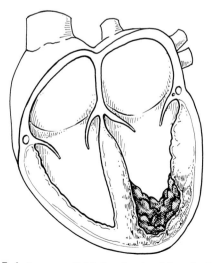

**Figure 7–4.** A myocardial infarction involving the left ventricular apex is not uncommonly associated with mural thrombosis. Systemic embolism, primarily stroke, can be reduced with anticoagulant therapy.

tory of venous or arterial embolism, echocardiographic evidence of mural thrombosis, or atrial fibrillation without contraindications receive heparin (intravenous or subcutaneous) in a dose sufficient to increase the activated partial thromboplastin time 1.5 to 2.5 times control, followed by warfarin (INR 2.0–3.0) for 1 to 3 months. Continued treatment should be considered strongly in patients with recurrent embolic events, persistent left ventricular dysfunction, and chronic atrial fibrillation.

## Long-term Outcome of Myocardial Infarction

At least 26 clinical trials examining the safety and efficacy of oral anticoagulants in the secondary prevention of cardiac events have been conducted over the past three decades.[80III, 82III, 83III, 85III, 86I] As with studies investigating the benefits of anticoagulation in the early postinfarction phase, many were designed poorly, precluding firm conclusions from being drawn. Pooled data from several studies with an acceptable design, however, suggest that oral anticoagulants (given from 1–6 years) reduce the combined endpoint of death and reinfarction by approximately 20% (Table 7–6).

In the 60-plus Reinfarction study,[88I] 878 patients older than 60 years of age (mean 67.6 years) who had experienced a prior Q wave myocardial infarction (at least 6 months earlier; mean 6 years) and were receiving oral anticoagulant therapy (acencoumarin or phenoprocoumon) were randomly allocated to either continued treatment (INR 2.7–4.5) or placebo. Mortality among patients randomized to oral anticoagulant therapy decreased from 13.4 to 7.6% (risk reduction 43%). Recurrent myocardial infarction decreased from 15.7 to 11.6% (risk reduction 26%). Stroke rates were also decreased with active treatment. There were no fatal hemorrhagic events.

In the Warfarin Reinfarction Study (WARIS),[89I] researchers recruited 1,214 patients who had sustained an acute myocardial infarction (mean 27 days previously). They were randomized in a double-blind fashion to receive either warfarin (INR 2.8–4.8) or placebo. During an average followup of 37 months, mortality (allcause) decreased from 20 to 15% (risk reduction 24%), reinfarction decreased from 20.4 to 13.5% (risk reduction 34%), and stroke decreased from 7.2 to 3.3% (risk reduction 55%). Serious bleeding was observed in 0.6% of warfarin-treated patients per year.

As with experience investigating early outcome, the longterm beneficial effects of anticoagulation following myocardial infarction appear modest. It would seem likely that patients at moderate to high risk for experiencing a thromboembolic event derive the greatest overall benefit. The comparative benefits of warfarin over aspirin for longterm use cannot be determined from the available information.

## Oral Anticoagulants After Thrombolytic Therapy

A major assumption, albeit with rapidly growing support, in the treatment of patients with acute myocardial infarction is that the speed of coronary arterial reperfusion correlates directly with the overall extent of myocardial salvage, which in turn determines the absolute reduction in patient mortality. Thus, improvements in the efficacy and stability of reperfusion would likely have a significant impact on patient outcome.

While novel strategies designed to achieve earlier and more complete coronary arterial reperfusion are being investigated, it is important not to overlook the problem of reocclusion. Indeed, coronary reocclusion remains a major obstacle to achieving optimal patient outcome. In the Antithrombotics in the Prevention of Reocclusion in Coronary Thrombolysis (APRICOT) 300 patients with angiographically validated infarct-related artery patency after thrombolytic therapy were randomly assigned to treatment with either warfarin (INR 2.8–4.0), aspirin (300 mg/day), or placebo. Patency on a second angiographic study after 3 months was the primary endpoint of the study.[90I] The rate of reocclusion was 25% with aspirin, 39% with warfarin, and 32% with placebo ($p$ = NS). Coronary arterial lesions with <90% stenosis reoccluded more frequently than did those with >90% stenosis (42 and 23%, respectively; $p<.01$). In lesions with >90% stenosis, no differences occurred among the three groups in preventing reocclusion. In lesions of less than 90% occlusion, however, the reocclusion rate was lower with aspirin (17%) than with warfarin (25%) or placebo (30%) ($p<.01$). In complex angiographic lesions (sharp angles or intraluminal filling defects), the reocclusion rate was lower with aspirin (14%) than with warfarin (32%) or placebo (25%) ($p<.02$).[91II]

The potential benefit of combining warfarin and aspirin is unknown. The angiographic substudy of the Coumadin Aspirin Reinfarction Study (CARS) will likely provide important insights.

Table 7–6. **Oral Anticoagulants in the Late Postinfarction Phase**

| Trial | | Patients | Follow-up | Target INR | Mortality (%) | p Value | Reinfarction (%) | p Value | Hemorrhage (%) | p Value |
|---|---|---|---|---|---|---|---|---|---|---|
| Sixty Plus Reinfarction Study | OA | 439 | 2 years | 2.7–4.5 | 51 (1.6) | | 29 (6.6) | | 84 (19.1) | |
| | Placebo | 439 | | | 69 (15.7) | 0.07 | 64 (14.5) | 0.0005 | 10 (2.2) | <0.05 |
| Warfarin Aspirin Reinfarction Study | OA | 607 | 37 months (mean) | 2.8–4.8 | 94 (15.5)* | | 82 (13.5)* | | 52 (8.5)* | |
| | Placebo | 607 | | | 123 (20.3) | 0.02 | 124 (20.4) | 0.0007 | 25 (4.1) | <0.005 |

*Intention to treat
OA—Oral Anticoagulants, INR—International Normalized Ratio

## Ongoing Clinical Trials

The benefits of oral anticoagulants, coupled with the benefits of antiplatelet therapy (primarily with aspirin) in patients with atherosclerotic coronary artery disease provide a solid rationale for investigating their combined use after myocardial infarction. The Coumadin Aspirin Reinfarction Study (CARS) is a randomized, double-blind clinical trial comparing the safety and efficacy of fixed low-dose warfarin plus aspirin versus aspirin alone in the prevention of nonfatal reinfarction, cardiovascular death, and nonfatal stroke. It is anticipated that 6,000 patients will be enrolled in the trial and followed for up to 3 years (Fig. 7–5).

Oral anticoagulation is also being investigated in patients with unstable angina and non–Q wave myocardial infarction. Indeed, a recent study of 214 patients with unstable rest angina and non–Q wave myocardial infarction suggested that combination therapy (aspirin plus anticoagulation) significantly reduces recurrent ischemic events.[92I] The group Organization to Assess Strategies for Ischemic Syndromes (OASIS) is conducting a randomized controlled trial of antithrombotic therapy designed to compare hirudin and heparin in preventing death, reinfarction, refractory angina, and recurrent angina. After completion of the hirudin/heparin infusions (72 hours), patients will be randomized to treatment with either warfarin (INR about 1.5) or placebo. Treatment will be continued for 6 months, at which time the incidence of cardiovascular death and myocardial infarction will be evaluated. Overall, this study is expected to enroll between 10,000 and 12,000 patients worldwide.

A brief overview of several major clinical trials either in progress or in the advanced planning phase follows.

**WARFARIN/ASPIRIN FOLLOWING CORONARY ARTERY BY-PASS GRAFTING.** In this Canadian-based study of 300 patients, an ability to prevent unstable angina and revascularization following bypass surgery will be investigated. The three arms of the study include aspirin 100 mg daily, warfarin (INR 2.0–3.0), and the combination aspirin 100 mg daily plus warfarin (INR 2.0–3.0).

**SECONDARY PREVENTION FOLLOWING CORONARY ARTERY BYPASS GRAFTING.** This United States–based study of nearly 1,500 patients will examine the adjunctive role of cholesterol-lowering agents and antithrombotic strategies in preventing recurrent thrombotic events after bypass surgery. The four arms of the trial include (1) Lovastatin (low-intensity) plus aspirin 80 mg daily; (2) Lovastatin (low-intensity) plus aspirin 80 mg daily plus warfarin (INR 2.0–3.0); (3) Lovastatin (high-intensity) plus aspirin 80 mg daily; and (4) Lovastatin (high-intensity) plus aspirin 80 mg daily plus warfarin (INR 2.0–3.0).

**ARTERIAL DISEASE MULTI-INTERVENTION (ADMIT) PILOT.** The primary prevention of fatal and nonfatal myocardial infarction and stroke will be assessed in a trial of 600 individuals. The major objectives of this United States–based study are to assess feasibility, recruitment, efficacy, and safety of HDL-raising strategies, antioxidant therapy, low-dose anticoagulation (warfarin 1–4 mg daily) and their combination (all patients receive aspirin 325 mg daily).

**COMBINATION THERAPY IN ISCHEMIC HEART DISEASE.** This trial of 450 patients, scheduled to be completed in 1996, will assess the ability of either aspirin 75 mg daily or aspirin 75 mg daily plus warfarin (INR 1.5) to prevent myocardial infarction and unstable angina. The study is being carried out in the United Kingdom.

**VETERANS ADMINISTRATION COOPERATIVE TRIAL.** Scheduled for completion in 1998, this trial of 8,000 patients will examine the secondary prevention of myocardial infarction using either aspirin 160 mg daily or aspirin 80 mg daily plus warfarin (INR 1.5–2.5).

In summary, the coumadin-type oral anticoagulants have been used for greater than one-

### Coumadin Aspirin Reinfarction Study (CARS)

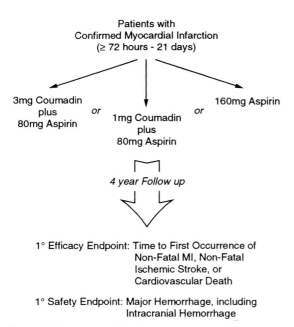

Patients with
Confirmed Myocardial Infarction
(≥ 72 hours - 21 days)

3mg Coumadin plus 80mg Aspirin    or    1mg Coumadin plus 80mg Aspirin    or    160mg Aspirin

4 year Follow up

1° Efficacy Endpoint: Time to First Occurrence of Non-Fatal MI, Non-Fatal Ischemic Stroke, or Cardiovascular Death

1° Safety Endpoint: Major Hemorrhage, including Intracranial Hemorrhage

**Figure 7–5.** Design of the Coumadin Aspirin Reinfarction Study (CARS).

half century in the prevention and treatment of thromboembolic diseases. Beyond their widely recognized role in venous thromboembolism, oral anticoagulants also offer benefit in arterial thromboembolism, reducing early and long-term recurrent thrombotic events after myocardial infarction in patients at moderate to high risk. They may also have a place in the management of unstable angina. Ongoing clinical trials will address several important questions, including which patients are most likely to derive benefit, the associated risks, the value of combination (antiplatelet and anticoagulant) therapy, and the impact of very low intensity anticoagulation. It appears likely that anticoagulant therapy will remain a major area of interest in the years to come.

# REFERENCES

1. Ansell J: Oral anticoagulant therapy—50 years later. Arch Intern Med 153:586–596, 1993.
2. Hirsh J: Oral anticoagulant drugs. N Engl J Med 324:1865–1875, 1991.
3. Link KP: The discovery of dicumarol and its sequels. Circulation 19:97–107, 1959.
4. Butt HR, Allen EV, Bollman JL: A preparation from spoiled sweet clover which prolongs coagulation and prothrombin time of the blood: Preliminary report of experimental and clinical studies. Mayo Clin Proc 16:388–395, 1941.
5. Whitlon DS, Sadowski JA, Suttie JW: Mechanism of coumarin action: Significance of vitamin K epoxide reductase inhibition. Biochemistry 17:1371–1377, 1978.
6. Porter RS, Sawyer WT, Lowenthal DT: Warfarin. In Evans WE, Scentag JJ, Jusko WJ (eds): Applied Pharmacokinetics, 2nd ed. Spokane, WA, Applied Therapeutics, 1986, pp 1057–1104.
7. Hirsh J: Is the dose of warfarin prescribed by American physicians unnecessarily high? Arch Intern Med 147:769–771, 1987.
8. Hull R, Hirsh J, Jay R, et al: Different intensities of anticoagulation in the long term treatment of proximal venous thrombosis. N Engl J Med 307:1676–1681, 1982.
9. Kirkwood TBL: Calibration of reference thromboplastins and standardization of the prothrombin time ratio. Thromb Haemost 49:238–244, 1983.
10. Levine MN, Hirsh J, Landerfeld S, Raskob G: Hemorrhagic complications of anticoagulant treatment. Chest 102[Suppl]:352S–363S, 1992.
11. Fihn SD, McDonell M, Martin D, et al: Risk factors for complications of chronic anticoagulation: A multicenter study. Ann Intern Med 118:511–520, 1993.
12. Landefeld CS, Beyth RJ: Anticoagulant-related bleeding: Clinical epidemiology, prediction, and prevention. Am J Med 95:315–328, 1993.
13. Shetty HG, Backhouse G, Bentley OP, et al: Effective reversal of warfarin-induced excessive anticoagulation with low dose vitamin K₁. Thromb Haemost 67:13–15, 1992.
14. Dalen JE, Hirsh J (eds): Third ACCP Conference on Antithrombotic Therapy. Chest 102:303S–549S, 1992.
15. Cole MS, Minifee PK, Wolma FJ: Coumarin necrosis: A review of the literature. Surgery 103:271–276, 1988.
16. McGehee WG, Klatz TA, Epstein DJ, Rapaport SI: Coumarin necrosis associated with hereditary protein C deficiency. Ann Intern Med 100:59–60, 1984.
17. Stary HC: Evolution and progression of atherosclerotic lesions in coronary arteries of children and young adults. Arteriosclerosis 9[Suppl I]:I–19:I–32, 1989.
18. Joseph A, Achkerman D, Talley D, et al: Manifestations of coronary atherosclerosis in young trauma victims—an autopsy study. J Am Coll Cardiol 22:459–467, 1993.
19. Ferrell M, Fuster V: Mechanisms of acute myocardial infarction. In Becker RC (ed): The Modern Era of Coronary Thrombolysis. Boston, Kluwer Academic Publishers, 1994, pp 1–13.
20. Woolf N, Carstairs K: Infiltration and thrombosis in atherogenesis—a study using immunofluorescent techniques. Am J Pathol 51:373–386, 1967.
21. Hudson J, McCaughey W: Mural thrombosis and atherogenesis in coronary arteries and aorta. Atherosclerosis 19:543–553, 1974.
22. Kurth HS: Platelet mediated cholesterol accumulation in cultured smooth muscle cells. Science 227:1243–1245, 1985.
23. Mendelsohn ME, Loscalzo J: Role of platelets in cholesteryl ester formation by U-937 cells. J Clin Invest 81:62–68, 1988.
24. Friedman RJ, Stemerman MB, Wenz B, et al: The effect of thrombocytopenia on experimental atherosclerotic lesion formation in rabbits. J Clin Invest 60:1191–1201, 1977.
25. Smith EB, Keene GA, Grant A, Stirk G: Fate of fibrinogen in human arterial intima. Arteriosclerosis 10:263–275, 1990.
26. Kadish JL, Butterfield CE, Folkman J: The effects of fibrin on cultured vascular endothelial cells. Tissue Cell 11:99–108, 1979.
27. Lough J, Moore S: Endothelial injury induced by thrombin or thrombi. Lab Invest 33:130–135, 1975.
28. Thompson WD, Smith EB: Atherosclerosis and the coagulation system. J Pathol 159:97–106, 1989.
29. Ishida T, Tanaka K: Effects of fibrin and fibrinogen degradation products on the growth of rabbit aortic smooth muscle cells in culture. Atherosclerosis 44:161–174, 1982.
30. Loscalzo J, Weinfeld M, Fless GM, Scanu A: Lipoprotein(a), fibrin binding, and plasminogen activation. Arteriosclerosis 10:240–245, 1990.
31. Hajjar KA, Gavish D, Breslow JL, Nachman RL: Lipoprotein(a) modulation of endothelial surface fibrinolysis and its potential role in atherosclerosis. Nature 339:303–305, 1989.
32. Miles LA, Fless GM, Levin EG, et al: A potential basis for the thrombotic risks associated with lipoprotein(a). Nature 339:305–307, 1989.
33. Simon DI, Fless G, Scanu AS, Loscalzo J: Tissue type plasminogen activator binds to and is inhibited by lipoprotein(a) and low density lipoprotein. Biochemistry 30:6671–6677, 1991.
34. Etingen OR, Hajjar DP, Hajjar KA, et al: Lipoprotein(a) regulates plasminogen activator inhibitor-1 expression in endothelial cells. A potential mechanism for thrombogenesis. J Biol Chem 226:2459–2465, 1991.
35. Merlini PA, Bauer KA, Oltrona L, et al: Persistent activation of the coagulation mechanism in unstable angina and myocardial infarction. Circulation 90:61–68, 1994.

36. Kienast J, Thompson SG, Raskino C, et al: Prothrombin activation fragment 1 + 2 and thrombin antithrombin III complexes in patients with angina pectoris: Relation to the presence and severity of coronary atherosclerosis. Thromb Haemost 4:550–553, 1993.

37. Eisenberg P, Sherman LA, Schechtman K, et al: Fibrinopeptide A: A marker of acute thrombosis. Circulation 71:912–918, 1985.

38. Becker RC, Bovill EG, Corrao JM, et al: Thrombin and platelet activity do not correlate in unstable angina and non-Q wave myocardial infarction. Circulation 8[Suppl]:I–609, 1993.

39. Gulba DC, Barthels M, Westhoff-Bleck M, et al: Increased thrombin levels during thrombolytic therapy in acute myocardial infarction. Relevance for the success of therapy. Circulation 83:937–944, 1991.

40. Eisenberg PR, Abednschein DR, Becker RC, et al: Lack of suppression of thrombin activity in vivo: A determinant of failure of recanalization (abstract). J Am Coll Cardiol 21[Suppl A]:464A, 1993.

41. Scharfstein JS, George D, Burchenal JEB, et al: Hemostatic markers predict clinical events in patients treated with rt-PA and adjunctive antithrombin therapy. J Am Coll Cardiol Suppl:56A, 1994.

42. Brozovic M, Stirling Y, Harricks C, et al: Factor VII in an industrial population. Br J Haematol 28:381–391, 1974.

43. Meade TW, North WRS, Chakrabarti R, et al: Haemostatic function and cardiovascular death: Early results of a prospective study. Lancet 1:1050–1054, 1980.

44. Meade TW, Mellows S, Brozovic M, et al: Haemostatic function and ischaemic heart disease: Principal results of Northwick Park Heart Study. Lancet 2:533–537, 1986.

45. Rosendaal FR, Varekamp I, Smit C, et al: Mortality and causes of death in Dutch haemophiliacs. 1973–86. Br J Haematol 71:71–76, 1989.

46. Conlan MG, Folsom AR, Finch A, et al: Associations of Factor VII and vonWillebrand Factor with age, race, sex and risk factors for atherosclerosis. Thromb Haemost 3:380–385, 1993.

47. Kannel WB, Wolf PA, Castelli WP, D'Agostino RB: Fibrinogen and risk of cardiovascular disease. JAMA 258:1183–1186, 1987.

48. Kannel WB, Castelli WP, Meeks SL: Fibrinogen and cardiovascular disease. Abstract of paper for 34th annual Scientific Session of the American College of Cardiology, March 1985, Anaheim, California.

49. Yarnell JWG, Baker IA, Sweetnam PM, et al: Fibrinogen, viscosity and white blood cell count are major risk factors for ischemic heart disease. The Caerphilly and Speedwell Collaborative Heart Disease Studies. Circulation 83:836–844, 1991.

50. Jansson JH, Olofsson BO, Nilsson TK. Predictive value of tissue plasminogen activator mass concentration on long term mortality in patients with coronary artery disease. A 7 year follow up. Circulation 88[Part I]:2030–2034, 1993.

51. Cortellaro M, Confrancesco E, Boschetti C, et al: Increased fibrin turnover and high PAI-1 activity as predictors of ischemic events in atherosclerotic patients. A case control study. Arterioscler Thromb 13:1412–1417, 1993.

I 52. Meade TW, Wilkes HC, Stirling Y, et al: Randomized controlled trial of low dose warfarin in the primary prevention of ischaemic heart disease in men at high risk: Design and pilot study. Eur Heart J 9:836–843, 1988.

I 53. Meade TW, Roderick PJ, Brennan PJ, et al: Extracranial bleeding and other symptoms due to low dose aspirin and low intensity oral anticoagulation. Thromb Haemost 1:1–6, 1992.

54. Chalmers TC, Matta RJ, Smith H, Kunzler A-M: Evidence favoring the use of anticoagulants in the hospital phase of acute myocardial infarction. N Engl J Med 297:1091–1096, 1977.

55. Peto R: Clinical trial methodology. Biomed Pharmacol Ther 28:24–36, 1978.

II 56. Medical Research Council Group: Assessment of short term anticoagulant administration after cardiac infarction: Report of the working party on anticoagulant therapy in coronary thrombosis. Br Med J 1:335–342, 1969.

I 57. Drapkin A, Merskey C: Anticoagulant therapy after acute myocardial infarction. JAMA 222:541–548, 1972.

II 58. Veterans Administration Cooperative Study: Anticoagulants in acute myocardial infarction: Results of cooperative clinical trial. JAMA 225:724–729, 1973.

III 59. Tulloch JA, Gilchrist AR: Anticoagulants in treatment of coronary thrombosis. Br Med J 2:965–971, 1950.

IV 60. Burton CR: Anticoagulant therapy of recent cardiac infarction. Can Med Assoc J 70:404–408, 1954.

61. Drapkin A, Merskey C: Anticoagulant therapy after acute myocardial infarction. JAMA 222:541–548, 1972.

62. Anticoagulants in acute myocardial infarction. JAMA 225:724–729, 1973.

63. Davies MJ, Woolf N, Robertson WB: Pathology of acute myocardial infarction with particular reference to occlusive coronary thrombi. Br Heart J 38:659–664, 1976.

64. Asinger RW, Mikell FL, Elsperger J, Hodges M: Incidence of left ventricular thrombosis after acute transmural myocardial infarction. N Engl J Med 305:297–302, 1981.

65. Friedman MJ, Carlson K, Marcus FI, Woolfenden JM: Clinical correlations in patients with acute myocardial infarction and left ventricular thrombus detected by two dimensional echocardiography. Am J Med 72:894–898, 1982.

66. Keating EC, Gross SA, Schlamowitz RA, et al: Mural thrombi in myocardial infarctions. Am J Med 74:989–995, 1983.

67. Visser CA, Kan G, Lie KI, Durrer D: Left ventricular thrombus following acute myocardial infarction: A prospective serial echocardiographic study of 96 patients. Eur Heart J 4:333–337, 1983.

68. Spiriot P, Bellotti P, Chiarella F, et al: Prognostic significance and natural history of left ventricular thrombi in patients with acute anterior myocardial infarction: A two dimensional echocardiographic study. Circulation 72:774–780, 1985.

II 69. Davis MJ, Ireland MA: Effect of early anticoagulation on the frequency of left ventricular thrombi after anterior wall acute myocardial infarction. Am J Cardiol 57:1244–1247, 1986.

II 70. Arvan S, Boscha K: Prophylactic anticoagulation for left ventricular thrombi after acute myocardial infarction: A prospective randomized trial. Am Heart J 113:688–693, 1987.

71. Johannessen KA, Nordrehaug JE, von der Lippe G, Vollset SE: Risk factors for embolization in patients with left ventricular thrombi and acute myocardial infarction. Br Heart J 60:104–110, 1988.

I 72. Turpie AG, Robinson JG, Doyle DJ, et al: Comparison of high dose with low dose subcutaneous heparin to prevent left ventricular mural thrombosis in patients with acute transmural anterior myocardial infarction. N Engl J Med 320:352–357, 1989.

73. Nihoyannopoulos P, Smith CG, Maseri A, Foale RA: The natural history of left ventricular thrombus in myocardial infarction: A rationale in support of masterly inactivity. J Am Coll Cardiol 14: 903–911, 1989.

74. Keren A, Goldberg S, Gottlieb S, et al: Natural history of left ventricular thrombi: Their appearance and resolution in the posthospitalization period of acute myocardial infarction. J Am Coll Cardiol 15:790–800, 1990.

75. Vaitkus PT, Barnathan ES: Embolic potential, prevention and management of mural thrombus complicating anterior myocardial infarction: A meta-analysis. J Am Coll Cardiol 22:1004–1009, 1993.

76. Weinreich DJ, Burke JF, Pauletto FJ: Left ventricular mural thrombi complicating acute myocardial infarction: Long term follow up with serial echocardiography. Ann Intern Med 100:789–794, 1984.

77. Keating EC, Gross SA, Schlamowitz RA, et al: Mural thrombi in myocardial infarctions: Prospective evaluation of two dimensional echocardiography. Am J Med 74:989–995, 1983.

78. Friedman MF, Carlson K, Marcus FI, et al: Clinical correlation in patients with acute myocardial infarction and left ventricular thrombus detected by two dimensional echocardiography. Am J Med 72:894–898, 1982.

79. Mitchell JRA: Anticoagulants in coronary heart disease—retrospect and prospect. Lancet I:257–262, 1981.

III 80. Wright IS, Marple CD, Beck DF: Anticoagulant therapy of coronary thrombosis with myocardial infarction. JAMA 138:1074–1079, 1948.

81. Gifford RH, Feinstein AR: A critique of methodology in studies of anticoagulation for acute myocardial infarction. N Engl J Med 280:351–357, 1969.

III 82. Carleton RA, Sanders CA, Burack WR: Heparin administration after acute myocardial infarction. N Engl J Med 263:1002–1005, 1960.

III 83. Wasserman AJ, Gutterman LA, Yoe KB, et al: Anticoagulants in acute myocardial infarction: The failure of anticoagulants to alter mortality in randomized series. Am Heart J 71:43–49, 1966.

84. International Anticoagulant Review Group: Collaborative analysis of long term anticoagulant administration after acute myocardial infarction. Lancet 1:203–209, 1970.

III 85. Loeliger EA, Hensen A, Kroes F, et al: A double blind trial of long term anticoagulant treatment after myocardial infarction. Acta Med Scand 182:549–566, 1967.

I 86. Meuwissen OJAT, Vervoorn AC, Cohen O, et al: Double blind trial of long term anticoagulant treatment after myocardial infarction. Acta Med Scand 186:361–368, 1969.

87. Loeliger EA: The optimal therapeutic range in oral anticoagulation. History and proposal. Thromb Haemost 42:1141–1152, 1979.

I 88. The Sixty Plus Reinfarction Study Research Group: A double blind trial to assess long term oral anticoagulant therapy in elderly patients after myocardial infarction. Lancet 2:989–993, 1980.

I 89. Smith P, Aresen H, Holme I: The effect of warfarin on mortality and reinfarction after myocardial infarction. N Engl J Med 323:147–152, 1990.

I 90. Meijer A, Verheugt FWA, Werter CJPJ, et al: Aspirin versus coumadin in the prevention of reocclusion and recurrent ischemia after successful thrombolysis: A prospective placebo-controlled angiographic study. Circulation 87:1524–1530, 1993.

II 91. Veen G, Meyer A, Verheugt FWA, et al: Culprit lesion morphology and stenosis severity in the prediction of reocclusion after coronary thrombolysis: Angiographic results of the APRICOT study. J Am Coll Cardiol 22:1755–1762, 1993.

I 92. Cohen M, Adams PC, Parry G, et al: Combination antithrombotic therapy in unstable rest angina and non–Q wave infarction in non prior aspirin users. Primary end points analysis from the ATACS Trial. Circulation 89:81–88, 1994.

# Chapter 8

# Antithrombotic Therapy in Chronic Ischemic Heart Disease

Pierre Théroux and David Garcia-Dorado

The rationale for the use of anticoagulants and antiplatelet therapy in coronary artery disease has been reviewed in previous chapters. Acute coronary syndromes are caused by formation of intracoronary thrombi impeding coronary artery blood flow at rest or minimal exercise to produce myocardial ischemia.[1] In patients with chronic disease, the manifestations of myocardial ischemia are the consequence of an increased myocardial oxygen consumption in the presence of a fixed stenosis with possibly some degree of focal vasoconstriction. This distinction between acute and chronic disease is valuable for patient management but is a simplification of the continuous remodelling process that occurs in diseased coronary arteries. Thus, acute syndromes[2, 3] and subclinical activation of lesions[1] may lead to rapid progression of coronary artery disease and accelerated atherosclerosis. Clinical trials not only help define the role of various therapeutic interventions, but, when powerful enough, they can provide insights into the mechanisms of disease.

Antiplatelet therapy has been tested in a variety of clinical conditions from asymptomatic populations to patients with acute life-threatening conditions.[4] Aspirin is easy to use and is inexpensive; low doses are both efficacious and free of important side effects.[5] Anticoagulants are more difficult to titrate and are associated with a higher risk of serious bleeding complications. Adequate monitoring methods have only recently been defined[6]; still we do not know whether lower doses could provide adequate prophylaxis in secondary prevention.

This chapter will review the most important trials that have been performed in the chronic phase of ischemic heart disease with antiplatelet and anticoagulant drugs to try to define the

modalities for their clinical usefulness. Many of these trials have been performed after an acute coronary event. As risk improves in the months following myocardial infarction, the findings probably also apply to patients with chronic coronary artery disease.

## ANTIPLATELET THERAPY

### Evidence for Platelet Activation

One study prospectively assessed spontaneous platelet aggregation 3 months after a myocardial infarction in 149 patients. The results were classified as positive when aggregation occurred within 10 minutes, intermediate when it occurred between 10 and 20 minutes, and negative when no aggregation was observed within 20 minutes. During a followup of 5 years, cardiac death or recurrent myocardial infarction supervened in 14.9% of the negative patients, 24.1% of the intermediate patients, and in 46.2% of the positive patients.[7] The results of this study are shown in Figure 8–1.

The Caerphilly Collaborative Heart Disease Study examined platelet aggregation induced by collagen, thrombin, and adenosine diphosphate (ADP) in a case-control study of 1,811 men aged 49 to 66 years.[8] Patients taking aspirin were excluded from the study. Significant correlations were found between past myocardial infarction, electrocardiographic evidence of ischemic heart disease, and platelet aggregation response to ADP. Subjects in the highest fifth of platelet aggregability had a twofold increase in odds of a past myocardial infarction as compared with patients in the lowest fifth.

In a prospective cohort study of 487 healthy

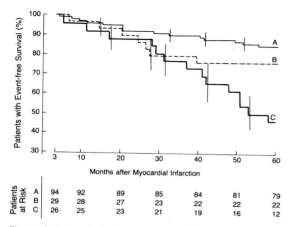

**Figure 8–1.** Survival without myocardial infarction during 5 years of followup in patients with no spontaneous platelet aggregation at baseline (A), in patients with intermediate aggregation (B), and in patients with positive aggregation. Spontaneous platelet aggregation was determined as an increase of 20% or more in light transmission of platelet-rich plasma. (Trip MD, Cats VM, van Capelle FJJ, et al: Platelet hyperreactivity and prognosis in survivors of myocardial infarction. N Engl J Med 322:1549–1554, 1990. Reprinted by permission of The New England Journal of Medicine © 1990. Massachusetts Medical Society.)

men, higher fasting platelet counts and hyper-aggregability to ADP predicted a higher mortality during a 13.5 year followup period.[9] Total mortality was 0.73 per year in the lower quartile of platelet counts and 1.52 in the upper quartile (relative risk 2.6, 95% confidence limits 1.4–4.9). When platelet aggregation to ADP was above the median, cardiac mortality reached 0.98 per year compared with 0.2 when it was below. In a prospective angiographic study of progression of coronary artery disease with angiograms repeated after 2 years, patients with progression had a higher platelet responsiveness to thrombin as compared with patients with no progression with odds ratios for progression of 2.49 (95% confidence limits 1.10–5.66).[10] Clinical events, in that study, were also more frequent in hyperresponders.

Higher plasma levels of von Willebrand factor could predict subsequent prognosis in two studies performed in outpatients after myocardial infarction.[11, 12] The von Willebrand factor is present in the subendothelium and is secreted by platelets. It binds platelet membrane receptors glycoprotein Ib and IIb/IIIa to mediate platelet adhesion and, in high-shear stress conditions, platelet aggregation. In the first study of 123 patients followed for a period of 4.9 years, the Cox regression analysis retained the level of von Willebrand factor as the most powerful predictor of fatal and nonfatal myocardial infarction.[11] The Progetto Lombardo Athero-

Thrombosis study followed 335 patients for 2 years[12]; the levels of von Willebrand antigen could predict death, myocardial infarction, and stroke with a standardized regression effect of 1.68 ($p<.001$).

These observations of a prognostic value of platelet hyperreactivity support previous observations of shortened platelet survival time and increased platelet secretion products in stable angina,[13] and a subclinical state of platelet activation associated with various risk factors, such as diabetes mellitus,[14] hypercholesterolemia,[15] and smoking.[16] Although they do not document a causal relationship, they suggest that platelets have a major pathophysiologic role in acute ischemic syndromes. Therapeutic intervention trials with antiplatelet drugs, however, help better define the cause-effect relationship.

## Angina Pectoris, Progression of Disease, and Aspirin Use

Whether antiplatelet therapy could be useful in angina pectoris has been evaluated in many small trials. These trials have not suggested a benefit. In one early study, aspirin did not influence short-term severity of angina or exercise tolerance.[17III] Dipyridamole was evaluated in more studies because of its known coronary vasodilatory effects; it did not improve angina[18V, 19II] and a coronary steal was documented.[20]

Small pilot studies have nevertheless suggested that antiplatelet therapy could be useful in some circumstances. In one study, pyridimolcarbanate, a synthetic agent with an effect on vascular wall, reduced the incidence of exercise-induced chest pain.[21] Ticlopidine was also reported to reduce the frequency of episodes of ST segment depression detected by Holter monitoring, especially episodes occurring at night.[22] Another study did not confirm a benefit of ticlopidine on exercise-induced ischemia.[23II] Controversial results were also obtained with prostacyclin, dazoxiben (a thromboxane synthetase inhibitor), and iloprost (a synthetic prostacyclin analogue).[24II, 25I]

Clinical trials, often quoted for the benefits they reported with aspirin, failed to document a favorable impact on the incidence of angina. In the Research Group from Southeast Sweden, aspirin initiated in hospital for unstable angina reduced the incidence of severe angina requiring referral to coronary angiography during the following year[26I]; this effect was however limited to the first few months of followup with no additional benefit thereafter. Other randomized trials with a longterm followup after an episode of unstable angina have not shown a reduction in recurrent angina.[27, 28I] The Physicians' Health Study enrolled men without a previous history of myocardial infarction, stroke, or transient ischemic attack and was stopped prematurely because of a reduction in the rate of myocardial infarction with aspirin compared with placebo; aspirin, however, did not prevent the appearance of angina during a 60.2-month followup. New angina appeared in 331 of the 22,071 men enrolled, 173 in the aspirin group, and 158 in the placebo group.[29]

The question of whether aspirin could influence the rate of angiographic progression of coronary artery disease was examined in only one trial, from the Mayo Clinic.[30] Patients randomized to aspirin-dipyridamole or to placebo showed similar progression or regression rates of established coronary lesions in the angiograms repeated after $4.6 \pm 0.1$ years. Definite lesion progression occurred in 41% of treated patients and in 39% of placebo patients, probable progression in 11 and 13% of patients, respectively, and regression in 4 and 2% (NS). Fewer new coronary lesions, however, developed in patients receiving the antiplatelet therapy.

Thus, both the aspirin-dipyridamole trial of the Mayo Clinic, in patients with stable angina, and the Physicians' Health Study, in a healthy population, showed reductions in the incidence of myocardial infarction with antiplatelet therapy, suggesting effective prevention of thrombus formation. That aspirin blunts the morning peak incidence in myocardial infarction is also supportive of this protective effect against acute thrombosis.[31] This benefit, however, is not translated in a favorable effect on angina; a direct clinical evidence of a role of aspirin to prevent disease progression is also missing. Alternative but unlikely explanations for the benefit of aspirin could be an antithrombotic effect mediated by mechanisms other than inhibition of the cyclooxygenase pathway at higher doses,[32] anti-inflammatory effects,[33] and possibly modification of plaque composition. These effects, at the present time, remain speculative. Recent noninvasive studies have nevertheless suggested that aspirin could delay progression of peripheral occlusive vascular disease,[34I] and aspirin slows plaque growth in the carotid artery in a dose-dependent fashion.[35]

## Aspirin and Primary Prevention

The first observation on the potential benefit of aspirin in primary prevention was made by Craven, a general practitioner from California, with no instances of coronary artery disease reported in his practice of 1,465 patients treated with aspirin 650 mg daily over a 10-year period.[36] A subsequent, placebo-controlled study of 430 aged patients suggested no benefit,[37] whereas case-control observations from Boston showed a negative association between regular aspirin intake and hospitalization for nonfatal myocardial infarction.[38, 39] A cohort study involving 1 million people who had answered an oriented questionnaire[40III] and a case-control study of 568 married men who died suddenly[41IV] reported no differences in death rate between aspirin users and nonusers.

More recent prospective trials have better delineated the role of aspirin in primary prevention. A cohort study of 87,678 nurses in the United States, age 34 to 65 years, free of coronary artery disease at baseline, was conducted for 6 years.[42III] The adjusted relative risk for a first myocardial infarction was 0.68 ($p = .005$) for women taking one to three, or four to six, aspirins per week; the benefit was confined to women age 50 years or more and was not present with use of more than six aspirins per week.

Two randomized trials studied male physicians. The British trial had an open-labeled design and included 5,139 cases; two-thirds of the population were allocated to aspirin 500 mg per day and one-third to avoidance.[43II] Total mortality was 1.44% per year with aspirin and 1.6% without (NS); vascular mortality was, respectively, 0.84% and 0.79% per year (NS) and myocardial infarction 0.9% and 0.93% per year for a nonsignificant risk reduction of 3%. Disabling strokes occurred more frequently with aspirin (risk ratio 2.58, $p < .05$). The Physicians' Health Study performed in the United States was double-blind, placebo-controlled, and involved 22,071 men free of coronary artery disease and age between 40 and 80 years at entry.[44I] The aspirin dose used was 325 mg every other day. Total mortality was the same with aspirin, 0.4% per year, and without, 0.42%, as was cardiovascular mortality, 0.23% and 0.24%, respectively.

A striking reduction was observed in the incidence of myocardial infarction with aspirin, 0.255% per year versus 0.437% with placebo for a risk reduction of 44% ($p < .00001$). Overall stroke rate was higher with aspirin, 0.22% versus 0.18 ($p = .15$) and particularly hemorrhagic stroke, which was twice as frequent, 0.04% versus 0.02% ($p = .06$). Benefits were absent in the age group below 50 years and increased in age groups between 50 to 59, 60 to 69, and 70 to 84 years.

Combining the results of the two randomized

trials showed no difference in mortality with aspirin, a risk reduction of myocardial infarction of 32% ($p<.0001$), and a trend to increased nonfatal stroke (risk increase 18%).[45]

## Aspirin in Secondary Prevention

### Stable Angina

The Mayo Clinic trial on coronary progression followed patients randomized to the combination of aspirin plus dipyridamole or to placebo for a period of 54 months.[30] Each of the two study groups involved 185 patients. A nonfatal myocardial infarction developed in 10 patients in the treated group and in 22 in the control group ($p=.007$); there exists no differences in total mortality (6% in each group) or cardiac death (4% in each group). The largest aspirin study in stable angina was the Swedish Angina Pectoris Aspirin trial (SAPAT).[46l] In this trial, 2,035 patients were randomized double-blind to low-dose aspirin, 75 mg daily, or to placebo and were followed for 50 months. Sotalol was routinely administered to control symptoms. Figure 8–2 shows the results of this study on the primary endpoint of first occurrence of nonfatal or fatal myocardial infarction or sudden death. Aspirin plus the beta blocker reduced the risk by 34% (95% confidence limits 24–49%) compared to placebo plus the beta blocker. Vascular events, vascular death, stroke, and total mortality were all also significantly reduced by 22 to 32%. As in other trials, the number of coronary artery bypass surgeries was not influenced by aspirin use. Major bleeding occurred in 1.98% of aspirin patients and in 1.26% of placebo patients. Bleeding events consisted of hemorrhagic stroke in, respectively, 0.5% and 0.2% of patients. These figures are in accordance with the reports of the benefits of aspirin in patients with acute or prior unstable angina and myocardial infarction, with the benefits reported in patients with other atherosclerotic conditions such as post bypass surgery, post coronary angioplasty, peripheral vascular disease, prior stroke or transient ischemic attacks, and with the benefits observed in nonatherosclerotic conditions such as atrial fibrillation, rheumatic valve disease and valve surgery, as reviewed by the Antiplatelet Trialists' Collaboration.[4]

### Unstable Angina

The most striking benefits of aspirin in secondary prevention have been observed in the followup of patients with unstable angina. Three double-blind, randomized placebo-controlled trials have been performed with aspirin and one with ticlopidine. The dosage of aspirin in the Veterans Administration Cooperative Study,[27] which included 1,338 males, was 324 mg per day; in the Canadian Multicenter trial of 555 patients of either sex, 325 mg four times a day;[28l] and in the RISC study group of 796 men analyzed among the 945 enrolled, 75 mg per day.[47] Durations of followup were, respectively, 12 months, 2 years, and 30 days. The relative risk reductions for the major endpoint of cardiac death or nonfatal myocardial infarction were 51% in the two former studies and 68% in the latter. The Canadian study had a factorial design with sulfinpyrazone used in two treatment arms; this drug resulted in no significant benefit or interaction with aspirin. The ticlopidine trial included 652 male or female patients randomized to ticlopidine 250 mg bid or to placebo and followed for 24 months. The reduction in the risk of vascular death and nonfatal myocardial infarction in that study was 46.3% ($p=.009$), similar to that observed with

**Figure 8–2.** Cumulative patients with a primary endpoint event (sudden death, fatal and nonfatal myocardial infarction) among 2,035 patients with stable angina pectoris randomized to aspirin, 75 mg daily, or placebo and followed for a median of 50 months. All patients received a beta blocker to control symptoms. The risk reduction with aspirin compared with placebo was 34% (95% confidence limits 24 to 49). (Used with permission from Juul-Möller S, Edvardsson N, Jahnmatz B, et al, for the Swedish Angina Pectoris Trial (SAPAT): Double-blind trial of aspirin in primary prevention of myocardial infarction in patients with stable chronic angina pectoris. Lancet 2:1421–1424, 1992. © by The Lancet Ltd. 1992.)

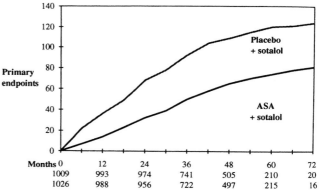

Number of patients at risk in each of the two treatment arms.

aspirin.[481] No direct comparison has been made between ticlopidine and aspirin in unstable angina.

## Myocardial Infarction

Trials in the secondary prevention after myocardial infarction with antiplatelet drugs have studied aspirin versus placebo (six trials),[49II, 50II, 51II, 52II, 53, 54II] the combination of aspirin plus dipyridamole versus placebo (two trials),[54II, 55I] sulfinpyrazone versus placebo (two trials),[56I, 57] and aspirin versus oral anticoagulants (two trials).[51II, 58II] Ticlopidine has not yet been evaluated in that setting.

The Antiplatelet Trialists' Collaboration meta-analysis of these trials showed a $25 \pm 4\%$ (SD) reduction in the odds of myocardial infarction, stroke or vascular death, a $29 \pm 5\%$ reduction in the odds of nonfatal myocardial infarction, and a $12 \pm 5\%$ reduction in the odds of death from any cause.[4] None of the trials considered separately, however, had sufficient statistical power to document a significant effect on mortality. All showed a trend to reduced mortality except for the largest, the Aspirin Myocardial Infarction Study (AMIS),[53] which suggests a detrimental effect. The incidence of myocardial infarction was, however, favorably influenced in all trials, including the AMIS trial, and the reduction achieved was statistically significant in one trial, the second Persantine-Aspirin study (PARIS II).[55I] Dipyridamole added to aspirin did not provide additional benefit compared to aspirin alone.[54II] The first sulfinpyrazone study, the Anturane Reinfarction Trial, had suggested a reduction in sudden death over the first 6 months of followup[56I]; these results were, however, subsequently much discussed and questioned.[59] The second Anturane trial, performed in Italy, involved 727 patients and did not show a reduction in sudden death and in overall death rate; it nevertheless showed a 56% (NS) reduction in the rate of recurrent myocardial infarction during a followup of 19 months.[57]

## Aortocoronary Bypass Surgery

Early graft occlusion is most often of thrombotic origin and late occlusion is caused by atherosclerosis.[60] Based on the important role of platelets and thrombosis in both phenomena, many trials examined the utility of antiplatelet therapy and a few, of anticoagulants.[61] In general, the trials that have initiated aspirin before surgery or within 24 hours after have shown benefits to prevent graft occlusion; these were less apparent when aspirin was started 2 or more days after surgery. Dipyridamole was used concomitantly with aspirin in the majority of these trials.

In the Mayo Clinic study, 407 patients were randomized to aspirin plus dipyridamole or to placebo.[62I] Dipyridamole was started 2 days before surgery at a dose of 100 mg four times a day and maintained after surgery at doses of 75 mg three times a day. Aspirin was started 7 hours after surgery at the dose of 325 mg three times a day. Early angiography obtained in 88% of patients at a median of 8 days after surgery showed all grafts patent in 92% of treated patients and in 79% of placebo patients ($p<.05$).

The Veterans Administration Cooperative Study tested four drug regimens, (1) aspirin 325 mg daily; (2) aspirin 975 mg daily; (3) aspirin 975 mg daily plus dipyridamole 225 mg daily; and (4) sulfinpyrazone 800 mg per day.[63I] Dipyridamole and sulfinpyrazone treatments were initiated 2 days before and aspirin 12 hours before surgery. Greater graft patency was observed with aspirin use (92–94%) than without (85%, $p<.05$). A nonstatistically significant trend also existed for better graft patency with sulfinpyrazone (90%). The benefits of aspirin were attenuated by a greater rate of reoperation required with its use (6.5% versus 1.7%, $p<.01$).

One study compared the risks and benefits of beginning aspirin 325 mg the night before, in comparison with 6 hours after, surgery.[64] Similar occlusion rates were observed at 8 days, 7% of 457 grafts with aspirin before and 8% of 451 grafts with aspirin after surgery. Postoperative use was associated with a lesser need for reoperation, 2% versus 6% ($p=.04$) and with significantly less chest tube drainage.

Another sulfinpyrazone trial confirmed the favorable trend that has been observed in the Veterans Administration Collaborative Study: graft patency was 96% with the drug compared to 91% with placebo ($p<.025$).[65I] Ticlopidine, started after surgery in a small size study, was also shown to be useful.[66I]

The longterm followup of these studies is of particular interest for this chapter on chronic coronary artery disease. The Mayo Clinic trial showed that the benefits were maintained at the time of angiogram obtained after 1 year with grafts patent in 88% of treated patients and in 53% of placebo patients.[67I] A new occlusion developed in 16% of treated patients and in 27% of control patients. The intimal proliferation, however, was not blunted by treatment, as was also shown in other studies.[68I]

Studies in coronary angioplasty have shown similar results to those of bypass surgery with clear reduction in acute thrombotic complication with antiplatelet use[69I, 70II] and sustained longterm benefit,[71III] but no significant effect on intimal proliferation leading to restenosis.[72I]

## Can Aspirin Attenuate the Severity of the Manifestations of Acute Coronary Syndromes?

Considering that aspirin benefits are mainly explained by its antiplatelet properties, it can be assumed that the drug would have the potential of modifying the natural course of manifestations of acute coronary syndromes by possibly attenuating its severity. Although three small retrospective studies have suggested that this was not the case,[29, 73, 74] a more recent prospective observation on a large population has suggested that previous aspirin use could produce a shift in the clinical manifestation from more severe to less severe.[75] In a first report, which included only 31 patients, Schreiber and coworkers described more frequent three-vessel disease in patients developing unstable angina while on aspirin therapy.[73] Cohen and coworkers, on the other hand, described no differences in the clinical characteristics and quantitative angiographic analysis of coronary artery disease in 93 patients with either unstable angina or myocardial infarction.[74] In the Physicians' Health Study of primary prevention among 22,071 male physicians, the use of aspirin reduced the incidence of myocardial infarction but had no influence on the site, size, electrocardiographic features, and resulting ejection fraction when an infarction occurred.[29] The case-control study by Garcia-Dorado and coworkers was the first to examine prospectively this question in a large population of consecutive patients admitted to a coronary care unit of a large community hospital.[75] The diagnosis of Q wave and non-Q wave myocardial infarction and of unstable angina was retained for the analysis. The index event in this study was unstable angina in 312 patients and myocardial infarction in 227 patients. It was unstable angina in 76% of aspirin users compared with 46% of nonusers ($p = .0000$). The relative risk for developing unstable angina rather than myocardial infarction with aspirin use was 1.64 (95% confidence limits 1.43–1.89). The proportion of non-Q versus Q wave myocardial infarction was also modified with more non-Q wave events in aspirin users, 38% versus 24% in nonusers, for a relative risk of non-Q versus Q wave myocardial infarction with aspirin use of 1.6 (95% confidence limits of 1.04–2.4) (Fig. 8–3). The results were similar in patients without or with pre-

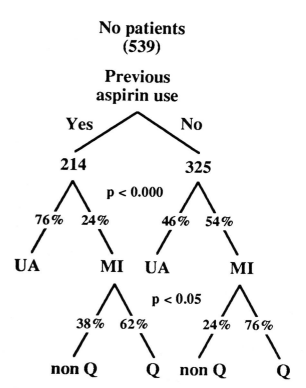

**Figure 8–3.** Distribution of acute coronary events by previous use of aspirin (or not) in a consecutive series of patients admitted to a coronary care unit. Previous aspirin use produced a shift to more patients with unstable angina (UA) and fewer patients with myocardial infarction (MI) and a shift to more patients with non-Q-wave infarction (non-Q) and fewer with Q-wave infarction, compared with patients not previously taking aspirin. The relative risk for developing unstable angina versus myocardial infarction with previous aspirin use was 1.64 (95% confidence limits 1.43 to 1.89) and for developing non-Q versus Q-wave infarction, 1.6 (95% confidence limits 1.04 to 2.47). The $p$ values indicate the relative proportion of unstable angina versus myocardial infarction and of non-Q versus Q-wave myocardial infarction in patients taking aspirin compared with patients not taking it.

viously documented coronary artery disease, suggesting a similar benefit in primary prevention.

## Clinical Usefulness of Antiplatelet Therapy

At the present time, aspirin is recommended for all patients with chronic coronary artery disease to prevent myocardial infarction and death. Lower doses appear as useful as higher doses and are associated with fewer side effects. The second best therapy for patients not tolerating aspirin is ticlopidine. This treatment should be reserved for higher risk patients because it can be associated with more serious side effects.

Observations derived from the various clinical trials have helped define the role of antiplatelet therapy in the continuous process of acute-chronic-acute coronary artery disease. The benefits are most apparent in the acute phase, when the role of thrombus is predominant, such as in unstable angina, myocardial infarction, and angioplasty. The benefits extend to secondary prevention; they are more marked after an episode of unstable angina or myocardial infarction, when the risk of recurrent thrombosis is higher, but they apply also to lower risk situations such as chronic coronary artery disease and asymptomatic individuals. Aspirin, further, can attenuate the natural history of acute coronary artery syndromes when they occur. No benefits are to be expected in situations not directly explained by thrombus formation such as stable angina pectoris, progression of coronary artery disease, graft disease, and restenosis after balloon angioplasty.

## ANTICOAGULANT THERAPY

### The Hypercoagulable State

The association between thrombosis and acute coronary syndromes has been clearly demonstrated by autopsy studies and by various invasive and noninvasive diagnostic procedures.[1] The etiologic role of thrombosis is further documented by the high efficacy of thrombolytic and antithrombotic therapy in these conditions. Thrombosis in acute settings is precipitated by the local response to exposition of subendothelial procoagulant material from a ruptured plaque to circulating blood. Evidence further exists of a more chronic state of activation of the coagulation system in chronic coronary disease and in various high-risk situations; this hypercoagulable state may contribute to an increased risk of acute thrombosis. The extreme situation is illustrated by deficiencies of natural anticoagulants such as low levels or functional defects in antithrombin III, heparin cofactor II, protein C or protein S, plasminogen, or tissue plasminogen activator.[76] Congenital defects are associated with venous and arterial thrombosis occurring at a relatively young age, before the appearance of atherosclerosis. Acquired hypercoagulable states are more frequent; examples are the antiphospholipid syndromes,[77] malignancies, myeloproliferative diseases, and others. Much more general situations associated with a hypercoagulable state are aging, smoking, dyslipidemia, atherosclerosis, and cardiovascular disease. The exact role of the hypercoagulable state in these situations is less clear; it can be causative, contributive, epiphenomenal, or the consequence of the disease state. The hypercoagulable state can be recognized in vivo by an elevation of various zymogens of the coagulation cascade, of their serine proteases, or of the activation peptides released in the circulation following activation of the zymogens (Table 8–1).[78]

Case-control and cohort studies have established a close correlation between the plasma levels of some of the coagulation factors and the risk of future cardiac events in an apparently healthy population, in individuals at risk of the disease, and in patients with known disease.

### Fibrinogen

This association is particularly strong for fibrinogen. An early prospective study of 120 survivors of myocardial infarction showed that reinfarction occurred exclusively in patients with initial fibrinogen levels exceeding 7.5 g/l during the acute phase.[79] A meta-analysis of six prospective epidemiologic studies performed between 1980 and 1992 including 92,147 person-years showed odds ratios of 2.3 (95% confidence limits 1.9–2.8) for the occurrence of myocardial infarction, stroke and peripheral disease, for individuals in the high tertile group versus those in the low tertile of fibrinogen levels.[80] Figure 8–4 shows a summary of the results of this meta-analysis. Higher fibrinogen levels correlated with the presence of most risk factors including aging, smoking, male sex, menopause, higher body mass index, low socioeconomic class, physical inactivity, hypertension, and lipid parameters.[81] Multivariate analy-

Table 8–1. **Abnormalities of the Coagulation State Detected in Blood and Possibly Associated with a Thrombogenic State**

| **Platelets** | **Endothelial Factors** |
|---|---|
| Platelet count | Protein C |
| Platelet aggregability to ADP | von Willebrand factor |
| Platelet aggregability to thrombin | Thrombomodulin |
| **Coagulation Factors** | **Fibrinolytic System** |
| Plasma viscosity | t-PA mass |
| Fibrinogen | PAI-1 |
| Factor VII | |
| Factor VIII | |

ADP = adenosine diphosphate, t-PA = tissue plasminogen activator, PAI-1 = inhibitor of tissue plasminogen activator.

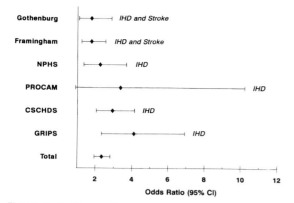

**Figure 8-4.** Meta-analysis of six prospective studies performed between 1980 and 1992 of fibrinogen levels as a risk factor for cardiovascular events. NPHS = Northwick Park Heart Study, PROCAM = Prospective Cardiovascular Münster Study, CSCHDS = Caerphilly and Speedwell Collaborative Heart Disease Studies, GRIPS = Göttinger Risk, Incidence and Prevalence Study, IHD = Ischemic heart disease. Data are odds ratios and 95% confidence limits for cardiovascular events in people with fibrinogen levels in the upper tertile compared with the lower tertile. (Used with permission from Ernst E and Reech KL: Fibrinogen as a cardiovascular risk factor: A metaanalysis and review of the literature. Ann Intern Med 118:956–963, 1993.)

sis of all data, however, retained fibrinogen plasma levels as an independent predictor of prognosis.[82] This association was particularly pronounced in younger men, whether or not they had coronary artery disease. A strong interaction of fibrinogen levels with higher blood pressure existed for risk of stroke[83-85] and with LDL cholesterol for risk of cardiovascular events.[86] The risk for people with low fibrinogen did not increase with increasing levels of LDL cholesterol. It did, however, increase by a factor of 2.5 in people with low LDL cholesterol values, with fibrinogen levels in the upper tertile compared to the lower tertile. People with LDL cholesterol and fibrinogen concentrations both in the upper tertile had a 6.1-fold increase in risk.

Numerous mechanisms can explain the correlation observed between higher fibrinogen plasma levels and acute coronary disease. Some are greater fibrin formation with a given stimulus, direct involvement of fibrinogen and fibrin in the evolution of the atherosclerotic plaque generating mitogenic and chemotactic fragments, increased plasma viscosity, and enhanced platelet aggregability.[80]

## Factor VII

Factor VII, in contrast to fibrinogen, is not an acute phase reactant; any elevation may thus indicate a more fundamental disease process. The Northwick Park Heart Study demonstrated that plasma factor VII coagulant activity was a strong predictor of coronary thrombosis as manifested by fatal or nonfatal myocardial infarction among 1,511 middle-aged men followed for 5 years (Fig. 8–5).[87] The independent predictors of prognosis in this study were older age and higher plasma levels of factor VIIa and of fibrinogen. An increase of one standard deviation in factor VII activity or in fibrinogen levels increased risk of ischemic heart disease death within 5 years of recruitment by, respectively, 62% and 84%. The prognostic value of factor VII and fibrinogen persisted after 10 years of followup with an increase of 30% or more in the risk of ischemic heart disease. The prognostic value of cholesterol plasma levels was less in that study than that of factor VII and of fibrinogen.

Several other cross-sectional studies have reported increase in factor VII mass and activity in patients with, or at risk of, coronary artery disease.[87-90] Plasma factor VII activity is determined largely by the concentration of factor VII antigen, and both are positively associated with plasma lipid levels.[91] A strong correlation can be found between the concentration of factor VII coagulant activity and total fat consumption in the previous 24 hours, with a lag of approximately 3 hours. Increased levels are also encountered with increasing age, menopause, obesity, and diabetes mellitus.[92]

## von Willebrand Factor and Factor VIII

The von Willebrand factor circulates in the plasma complexed with factor VIII procoagulant. The Northwick Park Heart Study described an association between factor VIII level and the risk of future cardiac events.[87] The Progetto Lombardo Athero Thrombosis (PLAT) Study also reported significant associations between von Willebrand antigen level, factor VIII plasma activity and future death, myocardial infarction and stroke in 335 patients studied 3 months after a myocardial infarction and followed for 2 years.[12] The multivariate analysis in that study retained elevated levels of factor VIII, of fibrinogen, and of protein C as predictive of an unfavorable clinical course. The plasma von Willebrand factor levels correlated closely with levels of factor VIII and predicted cardiac events by univariate analysis. The Atherosclerotic Risks in Communities (ARIC) Study demonstrated in nearly 15,000 men and women age 45 to 64 years higher fibrinogen, factor VIII and von

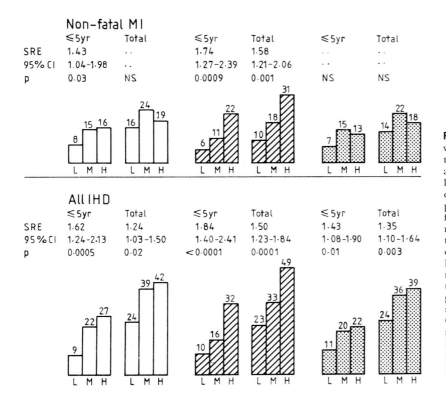

**Non-fatal MI**

|  | ≤5yr | Total | ≤5yr | Total | ≤5yr | Total |
|---|---|---|---|---|---|---|
| SRE | 1.43 | .. | 1.74 | 1.58 | .. | .. |
| 95% CI | 1.04-1.98 | .. | 1.27-2.39 | 1.21-2.06 | .. | .. |
| p | 0.03 | NS | 0.0009 | 0.001 | NS | NS |

**All IHD**

|  | ≤5yr | Total | ≤5yr | Total | ≤5yr | Total |
|---|---|---|---|---|---|---|
| SRE | 1.62 | 1.24 | 1.84 | 1.50 | 1.43 | 1.35 |
| 95% CI | 1.24-2.13 | 1.03-1.50 | 1.40-2.41 | 1.23-1.84 | 1.08-1.90 | 1.10-1.64 |
| p | 0.0005 | 0.02 | <0.0001 | 0.0001 | 0.01 | 0.003 |

**Figure 8–5.** Data from the Northwick Park Heart Study showing the value of factor VII coagulant activity (open bars), of fibrinogen levels (cross-hatched bars), and of cholesterol levels (dotted bars) for predicting nonfatal myocardial infarction (top), fatal and nonfatal myocardial infarction (IHD, bottom). Events at 5 and at 10 years of followup are shown. L, M, and H represent respectively the low, middle, and high third of distributions. SRE is the standardized regression effect. (Used with permission from Meade TW, Brozovic M, Chakrabarti RR, et al: Haemostatic function and ischaemic heart disease: Principal results of the Northwick Park Heart Study. Lancet 2:533–537, 1986. © by The Lancet Ltd. 1992.)

Willebrand factor levels in both sexes in patients with cardiovascular disease compared with patients free of disease.[93]

## Fibrinolytic Activity

### Tissue Plasminogen Activator and Plasminogen Activator Inhibitor

Beyond its role in blood clot formation, fibrin contributes to plaque growth by stimulating smooth muscle proliferation. Reduced plasma fibrinolytic activity is a common finding in patients with coronary artery disease. The fibrinolytic activity is essentially attributed to the inhibitor of plasminogen activator (PAI-1), which is the physiologic inhibitor of tissue-type and urokinase-type plasminogen activators.[94] PAI-1 is secreted by a number of cells, including liver, endothelial, and smooth muscle cells. Measurement of plasma PAI-1 mass concentration assesses PAI-1 plasma activity but also the inactive PAI-1 complexed with t-PA. Similarly, measurement of t-PA mass accounts for t-PA activity and for the t-PA–PAI-1 complex. An inverse correlation exists between t-PA activity and mass, because t-PA mass is mainly determined by higher plasma PAI-1 levels complexing t-PA.[95] Increased expression of PAI-1 is also found in the

atherosclerotic vessel wall. The LDL receptor in hepatocytes is involved in the clearance of the complex formed between t-PA, urokinase, and PAI-1.

An early study described that higher levels of PAI-1 activity in young survivors of myocardial infarction were associated with a higher risk of recurrence within 3 years.[96] In the European Concerted Action on Thrombosis and Disabilities Angina Pectoris Study (ECAT) of 3,033 patients undergoing coronary angiography because of angina pectoris, higher levels of t-PA antigen, PAI-1 antigen, fibrinogen, and C-reactive protein correlated with subsequent coronary events after 2 years of observation.[97] A smaller study of 213 consecutive patients with stable angina documented by multivariate analysis that t-PA mass concentration predicted all cause mortality and the need for bypass surgery during a 7-year followup.[95] Two large cohort studies of healthy populations have shown a strong relationship between the markers of fibrinolytic activity and the development of coronary artery disease.[98, 99] The Northwick Park Heart Study has followed 1,382 men for 17 years; fibrinolytic activity assessed indirectly in that study by the dilute blood clot lysis time correlated with the development of coronary artery disease as strongly as fibrinogen.[98] The

Physicians' Health Study followed 5,000 men for 5 years with a measure of t-PA antigen levels at entry in 231 patients[99]; higher levels could predict a future myocardial infarction, but not independently of lower HDL cholesterol values.

PAI-1 plasma levels are not influenced by smoking, cholesterol, or lipoprotein (a) plasma levels; however, they increase with age and are closely correlated with body mass, body fat distribution, triglyceride levels, systolic blood pressure, and with fasting insulin levels; high levels of PAI-1 can now indeed be considered as part of the metabolic syndrome of insulin resistance.[94]

## ANTICOAGULANTS IN CHRONIC ISCHEMIC HEART DISEASE

### Stable Angina and Anticoagulants

No large-scale studies have been undertaken to examine the influence of anticoagulants on angina pectoris. This is so because anticoagulants are not expected at first sight to be beneficial in situations primarily caused by an increase in myocardial oxygen demand. However, anticoagulants and, specifically, heparin possess physiologic effects that can be potentially useful. Thus, the dysfunctional endothelium may express procoagulant moiety facilitating local adhesion of blood cells and vasoconstriction. Fibrinogen is the major determinant of plasma viscosity and red cell aggregation; high levels may impair blood rheology and limit blood fluidity in the microcirculation to favor ischemia. Heparin is also a potent angiogenic factor[100] to promote development of collateral circulation in the heart.[101] Indeed, small pilot studies in men with stable angina have suggested that heparin plus exercise to the ischemic threshold can rapidly improve, within a few weeks, the functional class of the patients, the duration of exercise before the appearance of ischemia, and they may reduce the number of episodes of ST segment depression detected by ambulatory monitoring (Fig. 8–6).[101, 102I, 103I, 104I] The benefits of heparin in these studies were of similar magnitude as observed with the use of classic antianginal drugs. In one study, this effect was associated with decreased fibrinogen levels from $387 \pm 90$ to $333 \pm 65$ mg/dl ($p = .035$) and decreased platelet aggregability in response to thrombin from $17.9 \pm 10.8$ to $2.2 \pm 4.6$ ohms ($p < .001$)[103I] Platelet aggregation to ADP and to collagen was unchanged. Another study has shown that exercise was required for this effect of heparin, suggesting that the drug could in-

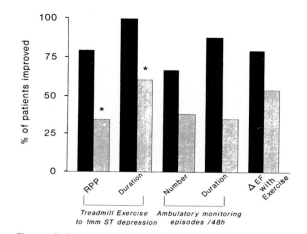

**Figure 8–6.** Results of one of the pilot studies that have shown a benefit of heparin combined with exercise to improve the angina threshold. Delteparin sodium 5,000 IU subcutaneously per day in this study was compared with placebo. The dark bars show the percentage of patients in the treatment group and the gray bars in the control group show those who demonstrated improvement after 1 month of therapy in pressure-rate product (RPP) at the onset of 1 mm of ST segment depression during treadmill exercise, duration of exercise to the onset of 1 mm of ST segment depression, number and duration of episodes of ST segment depression during ambulatory monitoring and change in left ventricular ejection fraction ($\Delta$EF) with exercise. (Quyyumi AA, Diodati JG, Lakatos E, et al: Angiogenic effects of low molecular weight heparin in patients with stable angina pectoris: A pilot study. J Am Coll Cardiol 22:635–641, 1993. Reprinted with permission from the American College of Cardiology.)

crease collaterals by potentiating the action of an ischemia-derived angiogenic factor.[104I]

Of interest is the study by Neri Serneri and coworkers who evaluated subcutaneous heparin in the longterm management of 30 patients with angina at rest and evidence of ischemia on the Holter monitoring.[105I] Patients were randomized, double-blind to calcium heparin 2,500 units subcutaneously daily or placebo for 6 months and were then crossed over to the alternate therapy for another 6 months. The frequency of angina and the levels of fibrinopeptide A were significantly decreased with heparin therapy as compared with placebo.

### Unstable Angina

Anticoagulants have not been tested in a large-scale trial for secondary prevention after an episode of unstable angina, although early pilot studies have suggested striking benefits. Wood and coworkers in 1961 prematurely stopped an unblinded trial of sequential allocation to anticoagulants or no anticoagulants after enrollment of the first 40 patients because of the benefits of treatment.[106] The trial was subsequently continued as a cohort study, the control group being formed by patients with a contraindication to anticoagulants; the incidence of myocardial infarction after 2-month followup was 3% in the 100 anticoagulated patients and of death 2%, as compared with 22% and 16%, respectively, in patients without anticoagulants. Vakil and coworkers reported a myocardial infarction rate of 36% in 190 treated patients and 50% in 156 nontreated, well-matched patients in an uncontrolled study with a followup of 3 months.[107] Telford and Wilson showed that the benefits observed with heparin during the acute phase were maintained after 3 months of treatment with an oral anticoagulant.[108I] Williams and coworkers also provided some data supporting benefits in a small randomized open-labeled trial of 102 patients[109]; patients received heparin for 48 hours and warfarin for 6 months. After 6 months, a 65% reduction in the risk of coronary event was observed in anticoagulated patients; most events were recurrent unstable angina.

## Myocardial Infarction

Trials performed with oral anticoagulants after myocardial infarction have included fewer patients than trials that have used aspirin, but they have, in general, showed as good if not better benefits. The mechanism for benefit could be, among other possible reasons, inhibition of vitamin K-dependent blood coagulation factor VII, which is elevated in these patients. The Medical Research Council Trial, published in 1964, reported risk reductions of 30% for death (NS) and of 60% for myocardial infarction ($p < .0001$) in 383 patients followed for 3 years.[110II] The Veterans Administration Study followed 747 patients for 7 years to document no differences in mortality but a reduction of 25% in the risk of myocardial infarction.[111II] In the German-Austrian trial of 629 patients, the mortality rate after 2 years was reduced by 20% and the reinfarction rate by 38% with the use of anticoagulants (NS).[112II]

Four important trials have been reported since 1980. The 60-Plus Study randomized 878 patients older than 60 years who had been treated with anticoagulants for a median of 6 years after a myocardial infarction to either continued anticoagulants or a matching placebo.[113I] Two years later, treated patients showed a 45% reduction in mortality ($p = .07$) and a 62% reduction in the rate of myocardial infarction ($p = .0001$).

In an Italian study, 728 patients were randomized, 6 to 18 months after a myocardial infarction, to heparin calcium (calciparine) 12,500 U subcutaneously daily or no treatment.[114I] During the following 23 months, the mortality rate was 48% lower with treatment (NS) and the reinfarction rate 63% lower ($p < .05$). The Warfarin Reinfarction Study (WARIS) enrolled 1,214 patients at the time of hospital discharge in a double-blind, randomized placebo-controlled trial of warfarin to an International Normalized Ratio (INR) of 2.8 to 4.8.[115I] The duration of the followup was 37 months. Total mortality was reduced with the anticoagulants from 20.2 to 15.4% (risk reduction 24%, $p = .02$), the reinfarction rate from 20.4 to 13.5% (risk reduction 34%, $p = .0007$), and the stroke rate from 7.2 to 3.2% (risk reduction 55%, $p = .001$). The results of the most recent study, from Holland, the ASPECT trial, were presented at the Fifteenth Congress of the European Society of Cardiology[116]; 3,404 patients were randomized to oral anticoagulation to an INR of 2.8 to 4.8 or to placebo within 6 weeks after hospital discharge. The active therapy resulted in no significant effect on total mortality and vascular death. It was, however, associated with a significant decrease in first reinfarction (2.3% versus 5.1%, hazard ratio 0.47, 95% confidence limits 0.38–0.59), first cerebrovascular event (0.7% versus 1.2%, hazard ratio 0.60, 95% confidence limits 0.40–0.90), and combined vascular event (4.8% versus 7.9%). The risk of bleeding was 1.4% with the anticoagulant compared with 0.4% with placebo.

The cumulative results of these studies showed that benefits of anticoagulation can be very substantial in secondary prevention after myocardial infarction, particularly for the prevention of recurrent infarction. As a consequence, these benefits may also apply to patients with stable angina and to other higher risk populations. Anticoagulants are not used in these circumstances considering the absence of documented benefits, the need for close monitoring, the higher risk of bleeding, and the benefit and lack of side effects of low-dose aspirin. The effectiveness and safety of low doses of warfarin are now being investigated in clinical trials examining secondary prevention after myocardial infarction, in unstable angina, and after coronary bypass surgery.

## Bypass Surgery and Balloon Angioplasty

Two early small studies have shown controversial results with warfarin used to maintain patency of bypass graft.[117, 118II] A larger trial of 489 patients showed significantly more patent grafts at 2 months with coumadin than with placebo, 90% versus 84% (*p*<.02), and a higher proportion of patients with all grafts opened, 81% versus 66%.[119] Heparin and dipyridamole were administered three times daily in that trial for 7 days after surgery to be followed by oral anticoagulants or no further therapy; patency was assessed 8 weeks after surgery.

Heparin is routinely administered during coronary angioplasty. Anticoagulants do not affect the restenosis rate.[120II, 121]

## ANTICOAGULANTS VERSUS ASPIRIN OR THE COMBINATION

The interpretation of the various trials performed with antiplatelet and anticoagulant drugs in coronary artery disease is confounded by the lack of adequate treatment in the control groups according to actual standards with known efficacy of the antithrombotic therapy. Only a few trials have directly compared antiplatelet and anticoagulant therapy.

Two randomized, double-blind trials have tested aspirin, heparin, and the combination or two placebos in unstable angina using a factorial design.[47, 122I] In one of the trials, involving 479 patients, aspirin and heparin both afforded protection during the acute phase with no additional benefit gained with the combination.[122I] In the second trial of 796 men, only the combination was associated with a significant protection after 5 days of treatment. Reactivation of the disease, however, was observed in the former trial[123II] and probably in the latter, shortly after the discontinuation of heparin in the group that received this drug alone without concomitant aspirin (Fig. 8–7). The patients who did best during followup in the two studies were those who received the combination therapy as initial therapy and uninterrupted aspirin thereafter. A smaller trial of 93 patients compared open-labeled aspirin 325 mg daily, aspirin 80 mg daily plus heparin plus warfarin, and heparin plus warfarin for a period of 12 weeks.[124I] The rate of infarction and death appeared lowest in the group that received a combination therapy, but the study was stopped prematurely because of a recruitment problem and frequent bypass surgery in these patients; consequently, the study has little power.

Two studies have compared anticoagulants and aspirin in the secondary prevention of acute myocardial infarction. The German-Austrian study used double-blind aspirin or placebo and open-labeled anticoagulants in 946 pa-

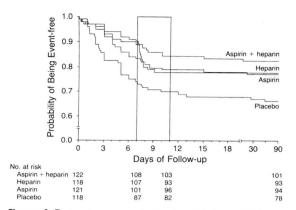

**Figure 8–7.** Cardiac events in the first 30 days of followup in a study that has compared aspirin, heparin, both, and neither during the acute phase of unstable angina. Treatment was administered for a mean of 6 days; the rectangle includes events that occurred early after the discontinuation of the study drugs. During the treatment period, the two groups that received heparin did better; a high attrition rate is clustered, a median of 9.5 hours following the discontinuation of the drug in the heparin-alone group. This rebound was less pronounced in patients who received the combination of heparin and aspirin, resulting longterm, at 90 days, in a better benefit of the combination therapy. (Théroux P, Waters D, Lam J, et al: Reactivation of unstable angina following discontinuation of heparin. N Engl J Med 327:141–145, 1992. Reprinted by permission of The New England Journal of Medicine. © 1992. Massachusetts Medical Society.)

tients.[112II] A trend to better benefit was observed with aspirin over placebo but not with the anticoagulant. The Enquête de Prévention Secondaire de l'Infarctus du Myocarde (E.P.S.I.M.) study randomized 1,303 patients 11 days after myocardial infarction to aspirin 500 mg three times a day or oral anticoagulant for a period of 29 months.[58II] Death rate was similar with the two treatments, 11% with anticoagulants and 10% with aspirin; the relative risk of myocardial infarction was reduced by 39% with the anticoagulants from 5 to 3%, but the reduction was not statistically significant (*p*=.07). Severe bleeding was also more frequent with the anticoagulant, 3% versus 1% (*p*<.002).

A few trials have compared graft patency with antiplatelets and anticoagulants. One study showed an occlusion rate of 16% with ticlopidine and of 18% with acenocoumarol.[125I] Another study of 235 patients also found the same occlusion rate at 3 months with aspirin started 24 hours before surgery, or heparin started 6 hours after followed by phenprocoumon, 22% and 20%, respectively.[126] A study compared graft patency at 2 weeks and at 1 year in 249 patients randomized to aspirin 50 mg and dipyridamole 400 mg daily started preoperatively or to oral anticoagulants started on the first operative day.[1271] Early graft occlusion occurred in 7% of patients in both groups. Treatment was replaced by placebo in half of the patients in each group after 3 months. Late graft occlusion was less frequent—16% with therapy maintained for 1 year—than when patients were switched to placebo after 3 months, which was 23%. These studies with antiplatelets and anticoagulants suggest that the modalities for the clinical benefit with each class of medication may be different and that the combination might be useful in many clinical circumstances.

## REFERENCES

1. Fuster V, Badimon L, Badimon JJ, et al: The pathogenesis of coronary artery disease and the acute coronary syndromes. N Engl J Med 326:242–250, 1992.
2. Moise A, Théroux P, Taeymans Y, et al: Unstable angina and progression of coronary atherosclerosis. N Engl J Med 309:685–689, 1983.
3. Ambrose JA, Winters SL, Arora RR, et al: Angiographic evolution of coronary artery morphology in unstable angina. J Am Coll Cardiol 7:472–478, 1986.
4. Antiplatelet Trialists' Collaboration: Collaborative overview of randomized trials of antiplatelet treatment. Part 1: Prevention of death, myocardial infarction by prolonged antiplatelet therapy in various categories of patients. Br Med J 308:81–106, 1994.
5. Willard JE, Lange RA, Hillis DL: The use of aspirin in ischemic heart disease. N Engl J Med 327:175–181, 1992.
6. Hirsh J, Dalen JE, Deykin D, et al: Oral anticoagulants. Mechanisms of action, clinical effectiveness, and optimal therapeutic range. Chest 102[Suppl]:312S–326S, 1992.
7. Trip MD, Cats VM, van Capelle FJJ, et al: Platelet hyperreactivity and prognosis in survivors of myocardial infarction. N Engl J Med 322:1549–1554, 1990.
8. Elwood PC, Renaud S, Sharp DS, et al: Ischemic heart disease and platelet aggregation. The Caerphilly Collaborative Heart Disease Study. Circulation 83:38–44, 1991.
9. Thaulow E, Erikssen J, Sandvik L, et al: Blood platelet count and function are related to total and cardiovascular death in apparently healthy men. Circulation 84:613–617, 1991.
10. Lam JYT, Latour JG, Lespérance J, et al: Platelet aggregation, coronary artery disease progression, and future coronary events. Am J Cardiol, in press.
11. Jannson JH, Nilsson TK, Johnson O: von Willebrand factor in plasma: A novel risk factor for recurrent myocardial infarction and death. Br Heart J 66:351–355, 1991.
12. Cortellaro M, Boschetti C, Cofrancesco E, et al: The PLAT study: Hemostatic function in relation to atherothrombotic ischemic events in vascular disease patients. Principal results. Arterioscler Thromb 12:1063–1070, 1992.
13. Conti CR, Feldman RL, Nichols WW, et al: Myocardial ischemia, platelets and prostaglandins. In Mehta J, Mehta P (eds): Platelets and Prostaglandins in Cardiovascular Disease. New York, Futura Publishing, 1981, pp 301–315.
14. Sagel J, Colwell JA, Crook L, et al: Increased platelet aggregation in early diabetes mellitus. Ann Intern Med 82:733–738, 1975.
15. Avirum M, Brook JG: Platelet activation by plasma lipoproteins. Prog Cardiovasc Dis 30:61–72, 1987.
16. Davis JW, Davis RF: Prevention of cigarette smoking-induced platelet aggregate formation by aspirin. Arch Intern Med 141:206–207, 1981.
III 17. Frishman WH, Christodoulou J, Weksler B, et al: Aspirin therapy in angina pectoris: Effects on platelet aggregation, exercise tolerance, and electrocardiographic manifestations of ischemia. Am Heart J 92:3–10, 1976.
V 18. Newhouse MT, McGregor M: Long-term dipyridamole therapy for angina pectoris. Am J Cardiol 16:234–237, 1965.
II 19. Sbar S, Schlant RC: Dipyridamole in the treatment of angina pectoris. A double-blind evaluation. JAMA 201:865–867, 1967.
20. Editorial: Dipyridamole in myocardial scintigraphy. Lancet 2:1346, 1980.
21. Yamazaki H, Sano T, Odakura T, et al: Electrocardiographic and hematologic changes by exercise test in coronary patients and pyridimolcarbanate pretreatment. Am Heart J 79:640–647, 1970.
22. Fox KM, Jonathan A, Selwyn AP: Effects of platelet inhibition on myocardial ischemia. Lancet 2:727–730, 1982.
II 23. Berglund U, Wallentin L: Effects of ticlopidine on platelet function and on coronary insufficiency in patients with angina pectoris. Adv Prost Thromb Leuk Res 13:277–280, 1985.
II 24. Reuben SR, Kuan P, Cairns T, et al: Effect of dazoxiben on exercise performance in chronic stable angina. Br J Clin Pharmacol 15[Suppl]:83S–86S, 1983.
I 25. Bugiardini R, Galvani M, Fenini D, et al: Effects of iloprost, a stable prostacyclin analog, on exercise capacity and platelet aggregation in stable angina pectoris. Am J Cardiol 58:453–459, 1986.
I 26. Wallentin LC, the Research Group on Instability in Coronary Artery Disease in Southeast Sweden: Aspirin (75 mg/day) after an episode of unstable coronary artery disease: Long-term effects on the risk of myocardial infarction, occurrence of severe angina and the need for revascularization. J Am Coll Cardiol 18:1587–1593, 1991.
27. Lewis HD, Davis JW, Archibald DG, et al: Protective effects of aspirin against acute myocardial infarction and death in men with unstable angina. N Engl J Med 309:396–403, 1983.
I 28. Cairns JA, Gent M, Singer J, et al: Aspirin, sulfinpyrazone or both in unstable angina. N Engl J Med 313:1369–1375, 1985.
29. Ridker PM, Manson JAE, Buring JE, et al: Clinical characteristics of nonfatal myocardial infarction among individuals on prophylactic low-dose aspirin therapy. Circulation 84:708–711, 1991.
30. Jonker JJC, Chesebro JH: Chronic coronary disease. In Fuster V, Verstraete M (eds): Thrombosis in Cardiovascular Disorders. Philadelphia, WB Saunders, 1992, pp 363–373.
31. Ridker PM, Manson JAE, Buring JE, et al: Circadian variation of acute myocardial infarction and the effect of low-dose aspirin in a randomized trial of physicians. Circulation 82:897–902, 1990.
32. Hanson SE, Harker LA: Effects of platelet modifying drugs on arterial thromboembolism in baboons: Aspirin potentiates the antithrombotic actions of dipyridamole and sulfinpyrazone by mechanism(s) independent of cyclooxygenase inhibition. J Clin Invest 75:1591–1599, 1985.
33. Hansen GK: Immune antiinflammatory mechanism in the development of atherosclerosis. Br Heart J 69[suppl]:S38–S41, 1993.

I 34. Hess H, Mietaschk A, Deichfel G: Drug induced inhibition of platelet function delay progression of peripheral occlusive vascular disease. A prospective double-blind arteriographical control trial. Lancet 1:415–419, 1985.

35. Ranke C, Hecker H, Greutzig A, Alexander K: Dose dependent of aspirin on carotid atherosclerosis. Circulation 87:1873–1879, 1993.

36. Craven LL: Experiences with aspirin (acetylsalicylic acid) in the nonspecific prophylaxis of coronary thrombosis. Mississippi Valley Med J 75:38, 1953.

37. Heikinheimo R, Jarvinen K: Acetylsalicylic acid and arteriosclerotic-thromboembolic diseases in the aged. J Am Geriatr Soc 19:403–405, 1971.

38. Boston Collaborative Drug Surveillance Group: Regular aspirin intake and acute myocardial infarction. Br Med J 1:440–443, 1974.

39. Boston Collaborative Drug Surveillance Program: Regular aspirin use and myocardial infarction. Br Med J 1:1057, 1976.

III 40. Hammond EC, Garfinkel L: Aspirin and coronary artery disease: Findings of a prospective study. Br Med J 2:269–271, 1975.

IV 41. Hennekens CH, Karlson LK, Rosner B: A case control study of regular aspirin use and coronary deaths. Circulation 58:35–38, 1978.

III 42. Manson JE, Stampfer J, Colditz GA, et al: A prospective study of aspirin use and primary prevention in cardiovascular disease in women. JAMA 266:521–527, 1991.

II 43. Peto R, Gray R, Collins R, et al: Randomized trial of prophylactic daily aspirin in British male doctors. Br Med J 296:313–316, 1988.

I 44. The Steering Committee of the Physicians' Health Study. Final report of the aspirin component of the ongoing Physicians' Health Study. N Engl J Med 321:129–135, 1989.

45. Hennekens CH, Buring JE, Sandercock P, et al: Aspirin and other antiplatelet agents in the secondary and primary prevention of cardiovascular disease. Circulation 80:749–756, 1989.

I 46. Juul-Möller S, Edvardsson N, Jahnmatz B, et al, for the Swedish Angina Pectoris Trial (SAPAT): Double-blind trial of aspirin in primary prevention of myocardial infarction in patients with stable chronic angina pectoris. Lancet 2:1421–1424, 1992.

47. The RISC Group: Risk of myocardial infarction and death during treatment with low-dose aspirin and intravenous heparin in men with unstable coronary disease. Lancet 336:827–830, 1990.

I 48. Balsano F, Rizzon P, Violi F, et al: Antiplatelet treatment with ticlopidine in unstable angina: A controlled multicenter trial. Circulation 82:17–26, 1990.

II 49. Elwood PC, Cochrane AL, Burr ML, et al: A randomized controlled trial of acetylsalicylic acid in the secondary prevention of mortality from myocardial infarction. Br Med J 1:436–440, 1974.

II 50. The Coronary Drug Project Research Group: Aspirin in coronary heart disease. J Chronic Dis 29:625–642, 1976.

II 51. Breddin K, Loew D, Lechner K, et al: Secondary prevention of myocardial infarction: A comparison of acetylsalicylic acid, placebo and phenprocoumon. Hemostasis 9:325–344, 1980.

I 52. Elwood PC, Sweetnam PM: Aspirin and secondary mortality after myocardial infarction. Lancet 2:1313–1315, 1979.

53. Aspirin Myocardial Infarction Study Research Group: A randomized, controlled trial of aspirin in persons recovered from myocardial infarction. JAMA 243:661–669, 1980.

II 54. The Persantine-Aspirin Reinfarction Study Research Group: Persantine and aspirin in coronary heart disease. Circulation 62:449–461, 1980.

I 55. Klimt CR, Knatterud GL, Stamler J, et al: Persantine-Aspirin Reinfarction Study: Part II: Secondary coronary prevention with persantine and aspirin. J Am Coll Cardiol 7:251–269, 1986.

I 56. The Anturane Reinfarction Trial Research Group: Sulfinpyrazone in the prevention of cardiac death after myocardial infarction: The Anturane Reinfarction Trial. N Engl J Med 298:289–300, 1978.

57. Report from the Anturane Reinfarction Italian Study: Sulfinpyrazone in postmyocardial infarction. Lancet 1:237–248, 1982.

II 58. The E.P.S.I.M. Research Group: A controlled comparison of aspirin and oral anticoagulants in prevention of death after myocardial infarction. N Engl J Med 307:701–708, 1982.

59. Temple R, Pladger GW: The FDA's critique of the Anturane Reinfarction Trial. N Engl J Med 303:1488–1492, 1980.

60. Fuster V, Chesebro JH: Coronary artery bypass grafting. A model for the understanding of the progression of atherosclerotic disease and the role of pharmacologic intervention. Adv Prost Thromb Leuk Res 13:285–299, 1985.

61. Stein PD, Dalen JE, Goldman S, et al: Antithrombotic therapy in patients with saphenous vein and internal mammary artery bypass grafts following percutaneous transluminal coronary angioplasty. Chest 102[Suppl]:502S–515S, 1992.

I 62. Chesebro JH, Clements IP, Fuster V, et al: A platelet-inhibitor-drug trial in coronary artery bypass operations: Benefit of perioperative dipyridamole and aspirin therapy on early post-operative vein-graft patency. N Engl J Med 307:73–78, 1982.

I 63. Goldman S, Copeland J, Moritz T, et al: Improvement in early saphenous vein graft patency after coronary artery bypass surgery with antiplatelet therapy: Results of a Veterans Administration Collaborative Study. Circulation 77:1324–1332, 1988.

64. Goldman S, Copeland J, Moritz T, et al: Starting aspirin therapy after operation. Effects on early graft patency. Circulation 84:520–526, 1991.

I 65. Baur HR, VanTassel RA, Pierach CA, et al: Effects of sulfinpyrazone on early graft closure after myocardial revascularization. Am J Cardiol 49:420–424, 1982.

I 66. Limet R, David JL, Magotteaux P, et al: Prevention of aorto-coronary bypass graft occlusion. J Thorac Cardiovasc Surg 94:773–783, 1987.

I 67. Chesebro JH, Fuster V, Elveback LR, et al: Effect of dipyridamole and aspirin on late vein-graft patency after coronary bypass operations. N Engl J Med 310:209–214, 1984.

I 68. Sanz G, Pajaron A, Alegria E, et al: Prevention of early aortocoronary bypass occlusion by low-dose aspirin and dipyridamole. Circulation 82:765–773, 1990.

I 69. Schwartz L, Bourassa MG, Lespérance J, et al: Aspirin and dipyridamole in the prevention of restenosis after percutaneous transluminal coronary angioplasty. N Engl J Med 318:1714–1719, 1988.

II 70. Lembo NJ, Black AJR, Roubin GS, et al: Effect of pretreatment with aspirin versus aspirin plus dipyridamole on frequency and type of acute complications of percutaneous transluminal coronary angioplasty. Am J Cardiol 65:422–426, 1990.

II 71. Heiss HW, Just H, Middleton D, et al: Reocclusion prophylaxis with dipyridamole combined with acetylsalicylic acid following PTCA. Angiology 41:263–269, 1990.

72I. Schwartz L, Bourassa MG, Lespérance J, et al: Aspirin and dipyridamole in the prevention of restenosis after percutaneous transluminal coronary angioplasty. N Engl J Med 318:1714–1719, 1988.

73. Schreiber TL, Macina G, Bunnell P, et al: Unstable angina or non Q wave myocardial infarction despite long term aspirin: Response to thrombolytic therapy with implications on mechanisms. Am Heart J 120:248–255, 1990.

74. Cohen M, Merino A, Hawkins L, et al: Clinical and angiographic characteristics and outcome of patients with rest-unstable angina occurring during regular aspirin use. J Am Coll Cardiol 18:1458–1462, 1991.

75. Garcia-Dorado D, Théroux P, Tornos P, et al: Previous aspirin use attenuates the severity of the manifestations of acute ischemic syndromes. Lancet (submitted)

76. Hirsh J, Prins MH, Samana M: Approach to the thrombophilic patient for hemostasis and thrombosis: Basic principles and clinical practice. In Colman RW, Hirsh J, Marder VJ, Salzman EW (eds): Hemostasis and Thrombosis. Basic Principles and Clinical Practice. Philadelphia, JB Lippincott, 1993, pp 1543–1561.

77. Hughes GRV: The antiphospholipid syndrome—Ten years on. Lancet 342:341–344, 1993.

78. Bauer KA, Rosenberg RD: The pathophysiology of the prethrombotic state in humans: Insight gained from studies using markers of the hemostatic system activation. Blood 70:343–350, 1987.

79. Fulton RM, Duckett K: Plasma fibrinogen and thromboemboli after myocardial infarction. Lancet 2:1161–1164, 1976.

80. Ernst E, Reech KL: Fibrinogen as a cardiovascular risk factor: A metaanalysis and review of the literature. Ann Intern Med 118:956–963, 1993.

81. Folsom AR, Wu KK, Conlun MG: Fibrinogen and cardiovascular risk in the Atherosclerotic Risk in Communities (ARIC) study. In Ernst E, Koenig W, Lowe GDO, Meade TW (eds): Fibrinogen: A "New" Cardiovascular Risk Factor. Vienna, Blackwell-MZV, 1992, pp 124–129.

82. Yarnell JWG, Baker IA, Sweetman PM, et al: Fibrinogen, viscosity, and white blood count are major risk factors for ischemic heart disease: The Caerphilly and Speedwell Collaborative Heart Disease Studies. Circulation 83:836–844, 1991.

83. Wilhelmsen L, Svardsudd K, Korsan-Bengtsen K, et al: Fibrinogen as a risk factor for stroke and myocardial infarction. N Engl J Med 311:501–505, 1984.

84. Stone MC, Thorp JM: Plasma fibrinogen—A major coronary risk factor. J Royal Coll Gen Pract 35:565–569, 1985.

85. Kannel WB, Wolf PA, Castelli WP, et al: Fibrinogen and risk of cardiovascular disease. JAMA 258:1183–1186, 1987.

86. Martin JF, Bath PM, Burr ML: Influence of platelet size on outcome after a myocardial infarction. Lancet 338:1409–1411, 1992.

87. Meade TW, Brozovic M, Chakrabarti RR, et al: Haemostatic function and ischaemic heart disease: Principal results of the Northwick Park Heart Study. Lancet 2:533–537, 1986.

88. Broadhurst P, Kelleher C, Hugues L, et al: Fibrinogen, factor VII clotting activity and coronary artery disease severity. Atherosclerosis 85:169–173, 1990.

89. Hoffman CJ, Miller RH, Lawson WE, et al: Elevation of factor VII activity and mass in young adults at risk of ischemic heart disease. J Am Coll Cardiol 14:941–946, 1989.

90. Suzuki T, Yamauchi K, Matsushita T, et al: Elevation of factor VII activity and mass in coronary artery disease of varying severity. Clin Cardiol 14:731–736, 1991.

91. Skartlien AH, Lyberg-Beckmann S, Holme I, et al: Effects of alteration in triglyceride levels on factor VII-phospholipid complexes in plasma. Arteriosclerosis 9:798–801, 1989.

92. Miller GJ, Martin JC, Webster J, et al: Association between dietary fat intake and plasma factor VII coagulant activity—a predictor of cardiovascular mortality. Atherosclerosis 60:269–277, 1986.

93. Folsom AR, Wu KK, Shahar E, et al for the Atherosclerotic Risk in Communities (ARIC) Study Investigators: Association of hemostatic variables with prevalent cardiovascular disease and asymptomatic carotid artery atherosclerosis. Arterioscler Thromb 13:1829–1836, 1993.

94. Juhan-Vague I, Alessi MC: Plasminogen activator inhibitor I and atherothrombosis. Thromb Haemost 70:138–143, 1993.

95. Jansson JH, Olofsson BO, Nilsson TK: Predictive value of tissue plasminogen activator mass concentration on long-term mortality in patients with coronary artery disease. A 7 year follow-up. Circulation 88:2030–2034, 1993.

96. Hamsten A, De Faire U, Walldins G, et al: Plasminogen activator inhibitor in plasma: Risk factor for recurrent myocardial infarction. Lancet 2:3–9, 1987.

97. Van De Loo JCW: Predictive value of hemostatic variables in cardiovascular disease. In Neri Serneri GG, Gensini GF, Abbate R, Prisco D (eds): Thrombosis. An Update. Florence, Scientific Press, 1992, pp 731–737.

98. Ogden V, Meade TW: Fibrinolytic activity and the incidence of ischemic heart disease in the Northwick Park Heart Study (abstract). Blood Coagul Fibrinol 4:381, 1993.

99. Ridker PM, Vaughan DE, Stampfer MJ, et al: Endogenous tissue-type plasminogen activator and risk of myocardial infarction. Lancet 341:1165–1168, 1993.

100. Carroll SM, White FC, Roth DM, et al: Heparin accelerates coronary collateral development in a porcine model of coronary artery occlusion. Circulation 88:198–207, 1993.

101. Fujita M, Sasayam S, Asanoi H, et al: Improvement of treadmill capacity and collateral circulation as a result of exercise with heparin pretreatment in patients with effort angina. Circulation 77:1022–1029, 1988.

I 102. Quyyumi AA, Diodati JG, Lakatos E, et al: Angiogenic effects of low molecular weight heparin in patients with stable angina pectoris: A pilot study. J Am Coll Cardiol 22:635–641, 1993.

I 103. Melandri G, Semprini F, Cervi V, et al: Benefit of adding low molecular weight heparin to the conventional treatment of stable angina pectoris. Circulation 88:2517–2523, 1993.

I 104. Fujita M, Yamanishi K, Hirai T, et al: Comparative effects of heparin treatment with and without strenuous exercise on treadmill capacity in patients with stable angina. Am Heart J 122:453–457, 1991.

I 105. Neri Serneri GG, Abbate R, Prisco D, et al: Decrease in the frequency of anginal episodes by control of thrombin generation with low-dose heparin: A controlled cross-over randomized study. Am Heart J 115:60–66, 1988.

106. Wood P: Acute and subacute coronary insufficiency. Br Med J 1:1779–1782, 1961.

107. Vakil RJ: Preinfarction syndrome—management and follow-up. Am J Cardiol 14:55–63, 1964.

I 108. Telford AM, Wilson C: Trial of heparin versus atenolol in prevention of myocardial infarction in intermediate coronary syndrome. Lancet 1:1225–1228, 1981.

109. Williams DO, Kirby MG, McPherson K, et al: Anticoagulant treatment in unstable angina. Br J Clin Pract 40:114–116, 1986.

II 110. Second Report of the Working Party on Anticoagulant Therapy in Coronary Thrombosis to the Medical Research Council: An assessment of long-term anticoagulant administration after cardiac infarction. Br Med J 2:837–843, 1964.

II 111. Ebert RV, Borden CV, Hipp HR, et al: Long-term anticoagulant therapy after myocardial infarction: Final report of the Veterans Administration Cooperative Study. JAMA 207:2263–2267, 1969.

II 112. Breddin D, Loew D, Lechner K, et al: The German-Austrian Aspirin trial: A comparison of acetylsalicylic acid, placebo and phenprocoumon in secondary prevention of myocardial infarction. Circulation 62[Suppl V]:63–72, 1980.

I 113. Sixty Plus Reinfarction Study Research Group: Risks of long-term and anticoagulant therapy in elderly patients after myocardial infarction. Lancet 1:64–68, 1982.

I 114. Neri Serneri GG, Rovelli F, Gensini GF, et al: Effectiveness of low-dose heparin in prevention of myocardial reinfarction. Lancet 1:937–942, 1987.

I 115. Smith P, Arnesen H, Holme I: The effect of warfarin on mortality and reinfarction after myocardial infarction. N Engl J Med 323:147–152, 1990.

116. van Bergen PFMM, Azar AJ, Jonker JJC, et al: The effect of long-term treatment with anticoagulants on mortality and cardiovascular morbidity after myocardial infarction. Results of the ASPECT trial (abstract). Eur Heart J 14[Suppl]:118, 1993.

117. Pantely GA, Goodnight SH Jr, Rahimtoola SH, et al: Failure of antiplatelet and anticoagulant therapy to improve patency of grafts after coronary artery bypass: A controlled, randomized study. N Engl J Med 301:967–969, 1979.

II 118. McEnamy MT, Salzman EW, Mundth ED, et al: The effect of antithrombotic therapy on patency rates of saphenous vein coronary artery bypass grafts. J Thorac Cardiovasc Surg 83:81–89, 1982.

119. Gohlke H, Gohlke-Bärwolf C, Stürzenhofecker P, et al: Improved graft patency with anticoagulant therapy after aortocoronary bypass surgery: A prospective randomized study. Circulation 64[Suppl II]:22–27, 1981.

II 120. Urban P, Buller N, Fox K, et al: Lack of effect of warfarin on the restenosis rate or on clinical outcome after balloon coronary angioplasty. Br Heart J 60:485–488, 1988.

121. Thornton MA, Gruentzig AR, Hollman J, et al: Coumadin and aspirin in prevention of recurrence after transluminal coronary angioplasty: A randomized study. Circulation 69:721–727, 1984.

I 122. Théroux P, Ouimet H, McCans J, et al: Aspirin, heparin, or both to treat acute unstable angina. N Engl J Med 319:1105–1111, 1988.

II 123. Théroux P, Waters D, Lam J, et al: Reactivation of unstable angina following discontinuation of heparin. N Engl J Med 327:141–145, 1992.

I 124. Cohen M, Adams PC, Hawkins L, et al: Usefulness of antithrombotic therapy in resting angina pectoris or non-Q-wave myocardial infarction in preventing death and myocardial infarction. A pilot study from the Antithrombotic Therapy in Acute Coronary Syndrome Study Group. Am J Cardiol 66:1287–1292, 1990.

I 125. Rothlin ME, Pfluger N, Speiser K, et al: Platelet inhibitors versus anticoagulants for prevention of aorto-coronary bypass graft occlusion. Eur Heart J 6:168–175, 1985.

126. Weber MAJ, Hasford J, Taillens L, et al: Low-dose aspirin versus anticoagulants for prevention of coronary graft occlusion. Am J Cardiol 66:1464–1468, 1990.

I 127. Pfisterer M, Jockers G, Regenass S, et al: Trial of low-dose aspirin plus dipyridamole versus anticoagulants for prevention of aortocoronary vein graft occlusion. Lancet 2:1–6, 1989.

# Chapter 9

# Atrial Fibrillation

Andreas Laupacis and Gregory W. Albers

Atrial fibrillation is one of the most common arrhythmias. It is rare in young people but occurs in approximately 5% of individuals over 65 years of age. In the Framingham study, atrial fibrillation was present in 0.5% of individuals in their fifth decade, 1.8% in their sixth decade, 4.8% in their seventh decade, and 8.8% in their eighth decade.[1] In addition to increasing age, the most important risk factors for the development of atrial fibrillation are hypertension and heart failure.[2] Rheumatic heart disease was the most common cause of atrial fibrillation in the past, but it has decreased in importance. Other causes of atrial fibrillation include ischemic heart disease (although it is not a strong independent risk factor), hyperthyroidism, pulmonary embolism, and congenital heart disease. Atrial fibrillation can be present constantly (hence, it is known as constant atrial fibrillation) or intermittently (known as intermittent or paroxysmal atrial fibrillation).

The risk of stroke is increased approximately five-fold in individuals with atrial fibrillation, after controlling for other risk factors for stroke.[3] Thus, atrial fibrillation is an important cause of stroke and is present in approximately 15% of individuals with a stroke.[4III] In the Framingham study, the percentage of strokes attributable to atrial fibrillation increased from 2% in patients 50 to 59 years of age, to 24% in those in their eighth decade.[1] The most common mechanism for stroke in patients with atrial fibrillation is believed to be embolism from a thrombus in the left atrium. However, patients with atrial fibrillation often have other risk factors for stroke, such as left ventricular dysfunction and atherosclerosis of the aortic arch and the carotid, vertebral, or intracranial vessels.

## STROKE PREVENTION WITH WARFARIN

Because the primary cause of stroke in patients with atrial fibrillation is cardiac emboliza-tion, warfarin has been extensively evaluated for stroke prevention. Five randomized studies comparing the efficacy of warfarin with either placebo (two studies)[5I, 6II] or control (three studies)[7I, 8I, 9I] have been completed. In one of the studies, 46% of the patient years in the control group was contributed by patients who were taking aspirin.[9I] The target level of anticoagulation varied among the studies, ranging from as high as an International Normalized Ratio (INR) of 2.8 to 4.2[7I] to as low as a prothrombin time (PT) ratio of 1.2 to 1.5.[5I, 9I] Stroke was a primary outcome in all studies, but some studies also included noncerebral embolism, intracranial hemorrhage, and fatal hemorrhage (Table 9–1). The vast majority of outcome events were strokes. The mean followup ranged from 1.2 years to 2.2 years. Characteristics of the study designs and patient populations are shown in Tables 9–1 and 9–2.

All five studies stopped earlier than planned, four because interim analyses indicated that warfarin was highly efficacious, and one because the investigators were convinced of warfarin's efficacy by the results of two of the other studies.[10] The results are summarized in Table 9–3. All studies found a benefit of warfarin, which was statistically significant in four. A subsequent

Table 9–1. **Design of the Five Primary Prevention Trials**

| Study | Mean Followup (Years) | Primary* Outcome Event | Target INR | Total Sample Size |
|---|---|---|---|---|
| AFASAK[7I] | 1.2 | S, SE TIA | 2.8–4.2 | 1,007 |
| SPAF I[8I] | 1.3 | S, SE | 2.0–4.5 | 1,330 |
| BAATAF[9I] | 2.2 | S | 1.5–2.7 | 420 |
| CAFA[6II] | 1.3 | S, SE, TIA, ICB, FB | 2.0–3.0 | 383 |
| SPINAF[5I] | 1.8 | S | 1.5–2.5 | 525 |

*S = stroke; SE = systemic embolism; TIA = transient ischemic attack; ICB = intracranial bleed; FB = fatal bleed.

Table 9–2. **Patient Characteristics in the Five Primary Prevention Trials**

|  | AFASAK | SPAF | BAATAF | CAFA | SPINAF |
|---|---|---|---|---|---|
| Mean age | 74 | 67 | 68 | 68 | 67 |
| Male (%) | 54 | 71 | 73 | 75 | 100 |
| Intermittent atrial fibrillation (%) | 0 | 34 | 17 | 7 | 0 |
| Hypertension (%) | 32 | 52 | 51 | 39 | 59 |
| Heart failure (%) | 52 | 19 | 26 | 22 | 31 |
| Diabetes (%) | 8 | N/A | 15 | 12 | 19 |
| Previous stroke/TIA (%) | 6 | 7 | 3 | 4 | 0 |

collaborative analysis by the Atrial Fibrillation Investigators (see later) using individual patient data from the five studies found a relative risk reduction of 68% (95% confidence limits [CI] 50–79%, $p<.001$).[11] The absolute annual risk of stroke was decreased from 4.5 to 1.4%. In the collaborative analysis, all-cause mortality was decreased by 33% (95% CI 9–51%, $p=.01$).

In the collaborative analysis, the annual rate of major hemorrhage (defined as an intracranial hemorrhage, a hemorrhage requiring two units of blood, or hemorrhage requiring hospital admission) was 1.3% in warfarin-treated patients and 1.0% in the placebo-treated patients.[11] The annual rates of intracranial hemorrhages were 0.3% and 0.1%, respectively. Thus, these five studies provide convincing evidence that warfarin decreases the risk of stroke in patients with atrial fibrillation, and that the risk of intracranial hemorrhage is low in carefully selected patients whose anticoagulation is expertly controlled.

Although warfarin is efficacious in patients with atrial fibrillation, its bleeding side-effects and the inconvenience of monitoring have led to an attempt to identify subgroups of patients whose risk of stroke without anticoagulation is

so low that warfarin therapy is not required. The Atrial Fibrillation Investigators formed a common database that contained patient-specific data from all five trials. Although three of the trials evaluated risk factors in their individual studies,[91, 121, 13] the sample size achieved with the collaborative analysis makes this the most reliable study to identify risk factors. Four factors were found to independently increase the risk of stroke in placebo-treated or control patients—increasing age (relative risk [RR] 1.4 for each decade), diabetes (RR 2.0), a history of hypertension (RR 1.6), and a previous stroke or transient ischemic attack (RR 2.5). In patients less than 65 years of age with none of the other risk factors, the annual risk of stroke in patients on no antithrombotic treatment was 1.0% per year (Table 9–4). These patients represented 15% of all patients in the five trials. Patients over 65 years of age or any patient with one or more of the other three risk factors had an annual risk of stroke of 4% or greater. Warfarin dramatically decreased the risk of stroke in all subgroups of patients except those with no risk factors, whose risk of stroke was already low (Table 9–4).

The risk of stroke was virtually identical in

Table 9–3. **Efficacy of Warfarin for the Prevention of Stroke\***

| Variable | AFASAK | SPAF | BAATAF | CAFA | SPINAF |
|---|---|---|---|---|---|
|  | Control group | | | | |
| Person-years of followup | 413 | 244 | 435 | 250 | 440 |
| Strokes (n) | 19 | 17 | 13 | 9 | 19 |
| Stroke events/100 person-years | 4.6 | 7.0 | 3.0 | 3.6 | 4.3 |
|  | Warfarin | | | | |
| Person-years of followup | 412 | 260 | 487 | 240 | 456 |
| Strokes (n) | 8 | 6 | 2 | 5 | 4 |
| Stroke events/100 person-years | 1.9 | 2.3 | 0.4 | 2.1 | 0.9 |
| Risk reduction (95% CI), % | 58 | 67 | 86 | 41 | 79 |
|  | (7–81) | (21–86) | (51–96) | (−68–80) | (52–90) |
| p values† | .03 | .01 | .002 | >.2 | .001 |

\*Intention-to-treat analysis. Strokes represent all strokes, regardless of suspected cause. Transient ischemic attacks, systemic emboli, and intracranial hemorrhages are not included.
†By chi-square analysis.

Table 9–4. **Annual Event Rates (and 95% Confidence Limits) Per Age Groups and Risk Factors**

| Risk Categories* | Placebo/Control | | | Warfarin | | |
|---|---|---|---|---|---|---|
| | %† | Number of Events | Event Rate (95% CI) | %† | Number of Events | Event Rate (95% CI) |
| **Age <65** | | | | | | |
| No risk factors | 15 | 3 | 1.0% (0.3–3.1) | 17 | 3 | 1.0% (0.3–3.0) |
| One or more risk factors | 17 | 16 | 4.9% (3.0–8.1) | 17 | 6 | 1.7% (0.8–3.9) |
| **Age 65–75** | | | | | | |
| No risk factors | 20 | 16 | 4.3% (2.7–7.1) | 20 | 4 | 1.1% (0.4–2.8) |
| One or more risk factors | 27 | 27 | 5.7% (3.9–8.3) | 27 | 7 | 1.7% (0.9–3.4) |
| **Age >75** | | | | | | |
| No risk factors | 11 | 6 | 3.5% (1.6–7.7) | 11 | 3 | 1.7% (0.5–5.2) |
| One or more risk factors | 9 | 13 | 8.1% (4.7–13.9) | 9 | 2 | 1.2% (0.3–5.0) |

*Risk factors are history of hypertension, history of diabetes and history of prior stroke or TIA.
†% refers to the percent of people in each risk category.

patients with constant or intermittent atrial fibrillation. Similarly, the length of time since atrial fibrillation was diagnosed did not affect the risk of stroke, indicating that even patients who have been in atrial fibrillation for many years should be considered for antithrombotic therapy.

## STROKE PREVENTION WITH ASPIRIN

Two studies have compared aspirin with placebo for the prevention of stroke in patients with atrial fibrillation. The doses of aspirin used were 75 mg daily[71] and 325 mg daily.[81] The results were qualitatively similar, but quantitatively different. The Atrial Fibrillation, Aspirin, Anticoagulation study, using an intention-to-treat analysis, found a 16% relative risk reduction associated with aspirin ($p<.05$),[14] compared with a 42% risk reduction in the first Stroke Prevention in Atrial Fibrillation Study (SPAF I) ($p=.02$).[81] The collaborative group's analysis of these two studies found an overall relative risk reduction for stroke of 36% (95% CI 4–57%, $p=.03$). All-cause mortality was decreased by 17% (95% CI −20–40%), but this was not statistically significant. Thus, in these two studies the magnitude of the benefit associated with aspirin was approximately half that of warfarin. The two studies differed in their estimate of benefit for reasons that are not clear, but the result may simply be because of

chance. There were no unexpected side-effects of aspirin. The annual rate of major hemorrhage was 1%, both in aspirin and placebo-treated patients.

## SECONDARY PREVENTION OF STROKE

The European Atrial Fibrillation Trial was a secondary prevention study.[151] One thousand and seven patients who had a transient ischemic attack (TIA) or a minor stroke within the previous 3 months were entered into the trial. Patients who were felt to be eligible for oral anticoagulation therapy were randomized to receive anticoagulants, aspirin, or placebo (group 1). Patients who were felt to be ineligible for anticoagulants were randomized to aspirin or placebo (group 2). The baseline characteristics of the patients are shown in Table 9–5. Approximately 43% of patients were randomized less than 15 days after the neurologic event. The target INR was 2.5 to 4.0. Mean followup was 2.3 years. There was a 66% (95% CI 43–80%) relative risk reduction for stroke in patients treated with anticoagulants, corresponding to an annual risk of stroke of 12% in control patients and 4% in anticoagulant-treated patients. The primary constellation of outcome events in this trial was stroke, systemic embolism, myocardial infarction, or vascular death. This was decreased from 17% in control patients to 8% in anticoag-

Table 9–5. **Characteristics of Patients in the EAFT**

|  | Group 1 | Group 2 |
|---|---|---|
| Mean age | 71 | 77 |
| Male (%) | 59 | 49 |
| Intermittent atrial fibrillation (%) | 25 | 22 |
| Hypertension (%) | 44 | 52 |
| Heart failure (%) | 9 | 13 |
| Diabetes (%) | 13 | 13 |

ulant-treated patients, for a risk reduction of 47% (95% CI 21–64%). Total mortality was 9% in control patients and 8% in anticoagulant-treated patients. For aspirin, the results were a reduction in stroke from 12% to 10% per year; in stroke, systemic embolism, myocardial infarction, or death from 19% to 15%; and in total mortality from 12% to 11%. None of these differences reached conventional statistical significance. No intracranial hemorrhages occurred in any of the three groups.

Thus, in this study the relative risk reduction associated with anticoagulants was almost identical to that seen in the primary prevention trials. However, the risk of stroke in placebo-treated patients was approximately three times higher than in patients who have never had a neurologic event. Thus, the absolute decrease in stroke rate associated with anticoagulants is much higher in these patients than in patients with no previous neurologic event. Aspirin was considerably less effective than anticoagulants. The relative risk reduction of 14% was less than the overall estimate from the collaborative analysis of the primary prevention trials. However, when the European Atrial Fibrillation Trial (EAFT), AFASAK, and SPAF I results are combined, the benefit of aspirin is similar to the 25% risk reduction found in the meta-analysis of studies of aspirin for cardiac and cerebral vascular disease by the Antiplatelet Trialists.[16] It is reassuring that the risk of intracranial bleeding in anticoagulant-treated patients with a previous neurologic event was no greater than in the other studies, although patients with large strokes were not entered into the trial. This study does not help with the difficult clinical question about the optimal time after stroke to initiate anticoagulation.[17]

## WARFARIN COMPARED WITH ASPIRIN FOR THE PRIMARY PREVENTION OF STROKE

Data from the five previously described primary prevention trials, as well as the one sec-ondary prevention trial, suggest that warfarin is substantially more effective than aspirin. The SPAF investigators performed a second study (SPAF II) to directly compare warfarin and aspirin. Patients were prospectively stratified into those over or under 75 years of age, and randomized within these strata to receive either warfarin or aspirin.[181] The reason for this stratification was that a subgroup analysis of SPAF I suggested that aspirin was highly effective in patients less than 75 years of age, but ineffective in those older than 75.[19] The target INR in the warfarin group was 2.0 to 4.5 and the dose of aspirin used was 325 mg daily. Patients were followed for a mean of 2.3 years.

In patients less than or equal to 75 years of age (mean age 65), the annual risk of stroke or systemic embolus was 1.3% in warfarin-treated patients and 1.9% in aspirin-treated patients (RR 33%, 95% CI −30%–66%, $p=.24$). In those over 75 years of age (mean age 80) the annual risk of stroke or systemic embolus was 3.6% in warfarin-treated patients and 4.8% in aspirin-treated patients (RR 27%, 95% CI −50%–63%, $p=.39$). However, the risk of intracranial hemorrhage was 1.8% per year in those on warfarin, compared with 0.8% in those on aspirin. Thus, patients over 75 years of age who were on warfarin had slightly more disabling intracranial events than those on aspirin (4.6% versus 4.3%, $p=.82$).

The investigators found that patients assigned to aspirin who had none of the clinical risk factors for stroke identified in SPAF I (history of hypertension, previous thromboembolism, or recent heart failure) had a low annual rate of stroke on aspirin: 0.5% in patients younger than 75 and 1.8% in those older than 75.

The results of SPAF II appear different from the results of the other studies; in SPAF II aspirin appears to be as effective as warfarin. This is the result of the high rate of intracranial hemorrhage in the patients over 75 years of age on warfarin, as well as the relatively high rate of ischemic stroke in these patients. The Atrial Fibrillation Investigators evaluated the rate of intracranial hemorrhage and ischemic stroke in all patients over 75, except those in the SPAF I Study (who were included in SPAF II). There was only one intracranial hemorrhage in the 223 warfarin-treated patients (0.3% per year), and the rate of ischemic stroke was 1.2% annually.[20] It is not clear whether the differences between SPAF II results and those of the other trials are because of patient characteristics, intensity of anticoagulation, or chance.

The relatively low rate of stroke in patients on aspirin who did not have any of the four risk factors identified in SPAF II should be confirmed in a second study. If this is confirmed in SPAF III, which is ongoing, it will be possible to avoid warfarin in a considerable number of patients with atrial fibrillation (46% of patients in SPAF II were in the low-risk group). However, at present it is reasonable to use warfarin in most patients with atrial fibrillation except those identified to be at low risk in the collaborative analysis of the five primary prevention trials.[11]

## PATIENTS EXCLUDED FROM THE RANDOMIZED TRIALS

All of the randomized trials described to date had a number of exclusion criteria. Patients with atrial fibrillation who have mitral stenosis or mechanical or bioprosthetic heart valves are at high risk of stroke and clearly require anticoagulation. Although patients with congenital heart disease, hyperthyroidism, or severe cardiomyopathy were excluded from the trials, these patients also have a significant stroke rate, and it seems reasonable to think that warfarin is also effective in them. Finally, patients either at high risk of bleeding or likely to be noncompliant (e.g., patients on nonsteroidal anti-inflammatory drugs, or patients who are alcoholics) were usually excluded from these trials. As always, clinicians must consider whether the risks and benefits of antithrombotic therapy determined in the trials are likely to be applicable to their patients.

## MECHANISM OF STROKE IN PATIENTS WITH ATRIAL FIBRILLATION

In patients with atrial fibrillation, differentiating a cardioembolic stroke from strokes due to other mechanisms is particularly difficult. For this reason, the studies of stroke prevention in atrial fibrillation have used all strokes as the primary outcome measure (a minor exception was the Canadian Atrial Fibrillation Anticoagulation Study [CAFA], which excluded lacunar strokes).[6II] The SPAF investigators attempted to estimate the proportion of strokes that were cardioembolic by reviewing all strokes without knowledge of the treatment allocation, using predetermined criteria.[2II] Sixty-five percent of the strokes were presumed to be cardioembolic. Interestingly, aspirin was significantly more effective in reducing the occurrence of noncardioembolic strokes than it was in reducing cardioembolic strokes. Whatever the exact proportion of cardioembolic and noncardioembolic strokes, it is clear that many risk factors for stroke such as hypertension, cerebrovascular disease and left ventricular dysfunction coexist in patients with atrial fibrillation, and both aspirin and warfarin may influence more than one of the mechanisms.

## ECHOCARDIOGRAPHY

It is widely believed that echocardiographic findings can help identify patients with atrial fibrillation who are at increased risk for systemic embolization. However, despite a large number of studies, uncertainty remains regarding the predictive value of specific echocardiographic findings in patients with atrial fibrillation.

### Transthoracic Echocardiography

The majority of studies that have examined echocardiographic risk factors in atrial fibrillation have relied on transthoracic echocardiography. Echocardiographic risk factors for stroke identified in these trials include left atrial size, left ventricular dysfunction, and mitral annular calcification. However, these factors have been inconsistently identified, and none has clearly emerged as a definite independent predictor of stroke risk in atrial fibrillation patients.

No consistent relationship between left atrial size and stroke risk has been demonstrated in nonvalvular atrial fibrillation patients.[22–25V] The importance of left atrial size as a risk factor for stroke was evaluated in three of the five randomized, primary prevention trials.[5I, 9I, 26I] Only the SPAF I study found that left atrial size was a significant independent predictor of thromboembolism.[26I] This relationship was even stronger when left atrial size was corrected for body surface area. Patients in the placebo group of SPAF I who had a left atrial size less than 2.0 cm/m² had a thromboembolic rate of 3.1% per year. Patients with left atria between 2.0 and 2.5 cm/m² had an event rate of 5.0% per year, whereas patients whose left atria was greater than 2.5 cm/m² had an 8.7% per year rate of thromboembolism ($p = .01$).

In addition to left atrial size, the SPAF I study also found left ventricular dysfunction to be a significant risk factor for thromboembolism. Global left ventricular dysfunction was an independent predictor of thromboembolic events (RR 2.9, $p < .001$). Moderate to severe regional left ventricular dysfunction was also a potent predictor of stroke risk.

Mitral annular calcification was shown to be

an independent predictor of stroke risk in the Framingham study (RR 2.1).[27] However, whether mitral annular calcification itself actually increases stroke risk or is merely associated with high-risk cardiac disorders remains controversial. Mitral annular calcification was associated with an increased embolic rate in the Boston Area Anticoagulation Trial for Atrial Fibrillation (BAATAF) Study.[91] However, only 15 strokes occurred in this trial. Therefore, the strength of the association between mitral annular calcification and stroke in atrial fibrillation patients remains unclear.

In summary, left atrial size, left ventricular dysfunction, and mitral annular calcification have all been identified in some, but not all, studies evaluating echocardiographic risk factors for stroke in patients with atrial fibrillation. Further study is needed to conclusively determine the true importance of these risk factors, especially how much they add to simpler clinical assessments of risk.

## Transesophageal Echocardiography

Transesophageal echocardiography has a much higher sensitivity than transthoracic echocardiography for identifying a variety of potential cardioembolic sources including left atrial thrombus, spontaneous echo contrast, atrial septal aneurysm, and interatrial shunts.[28] Currently, however, only limited data are available from prospective studies regarding the association between transesophageal-detected echocardiographic abnormalities and stroke risk in patients with atrial fibrillation.

Autopsy studies have clearly demonstrated a high association between left atrial thrombi and systemic embolism.[29] Patients with atrial fibrillation associated with left atrial thrombi have been found to have a six-fold increased risk of embolism compared with atrial fibrillation patients without intracardiac thrombi.[30] Transthoracic echocardiography, however, has a low sensitivity for detecting left atrial thrombi and is rarely able to visualize the left atrial appendage, which is the most common site of thrombus formation in atrial fibrillation patients.[29, 31]III Studies comparing transesophageal echocardiography with the transthoracic approach have documented at least a five-fold increase in sensitivity for detection of intra-atrial thrombi using transesophageal echocardiography.[32, 33] Therefore, transesophageal echocardiography is clearly the procedure of choice for identification of intra-atrial or atrial appendage thrombi.

Spontaneous echo contrast (also known as "swirling echoes" or "smoke") is thought to be the result of red cell aggregation related to slow blood flow velocities. Spontaneous echo contrast has been associated with intracardiac thrombus formation and is generally regarded as a risk factor for systemic embolism.[28] This finding was initially described in patients with mitral stenosis but has subsequently been associated with several other cardiac disorders, including atrial fibrillation. In preliminary studies, spontaneous echo contrast within atria has been found in approximately 50% of patients with atrial fibrillation with atrial thrombi or recent systemic embolization.[34] Whether spontaneous echo contrast represents an independent risk factor for stroke in atrial fibrillation is unclear.[35] The efficacy of anticoagulation or antiplatelet therapy for prevention of thromboembolism in patients with spontaneous echo contrast has not been studied. Prospective trials designed to address these issues are currently in progress.

Patients with atrial fibrillation of unclear cause should be evaluated with transthoracic echocardiography to help clarify the etiology and identify potential risk factors for thromboembolism. Patients found to have significantly enlarged left atria, substantial left ventricular dysfunction, and possibly, mitral annular calcification may be at increased risk for thromboembolic events. Transesophageal echocardiography appears to be particularly useful for patients with atrial fibrillation who are considered to be at low risk for thromboembolism and in whom anticoagulant therapy is not anticipated. The finding of a left atrial or appendage thrombus, or spontaneous echo contrast, may significantly alter the management of these patients. However, the effectiveness and costs of doing transesophageal echocardiograms in all low-risk patients with atrial fibrillation are not known, and the procedure needs further study before it can be routinely recommended.

## CARDIOVERSION AND ANTICOAGULATION

Cardioversion from atrial fibrillation may be achieved with either direct-current electrocardioversion or pharmacologic agents. The most significant complication of cardioversion is systemic embolization. The pathophysiologic mechanisms responsible for embolization following cardioversion are unclear. Either the electric shock itself or the resumption of normal atrial contraction may dislodge intracardiac thrombi. A variety of clinical factors (age, duration of atrial fibrillation, underlying cardiac disease, atrial size, etc.) are likely to influence the risk of embolization associated with cardioversion. However, these factors have not been evaluated in appropriate studies.

No randomized trials have evaluated the efficacy of antithrombotic agents for prevention of cardioversion-related systemic embolization. A prospective cohort study in the 1960s[36III] found that patients who underwent electrocardioversion from atrial fibrillation without anticoagulation had an embolism rate of 5.3% compared with a 0.8% incidence in anticoagulated patients. More recent retrospective studies[37, 38] also support a high rate of systemic embolism in nonanticoagulated patients undergoing cardioversion and a substantial protective effect of anticoagulants. Finally, warfarin therapy is now known to be effective in patients with atrial fibrillation who are not being cardioverted.[11] Therefore, most authorities have strongly recommended that anticoagulation therapy be initiated prior to direct-current cardioversion.

No clinical studies have addressed the duration of anticoagulation required prior to or following cardioversion. The American College of Chest Physicians recommends 3 weeks of anticoagulation prior to elective cardioversion and continuation of anticoagulation until normal sinus rhythm has been maintained for 4 weeks.[39] These guidelines are based on the assumption that it takes approximately 2 weeks for a thrombus to organize and adhere to the atrial wall and the observation that normal atrial contractions may not resume for days to weeks following electrocardiographic resumption of sinus rhythm.[40V]

It is generally accepted that new-onset atrial fibrillation of very brief duration (less than 48 hours) does not require anticoagulation prior to cardioversion. This recommendation is based on the assumption that thrombus formation requires several days. However, no clinical studies have specifically addressed this issue.

For patients who undergo emergency cardioversion without anticoagulation because of rapid ventricular rates resulting in hemodynamic compromise or angina, anticoagulation is recommended following cardioversion. Anticoagulation is particularly important for patients with other risk factors for systemic embolism or for those in whom recurrent atrial fibrillation is considered likely to occur.

No studies have evaluated the role of anticoagulant therapy for prevention of thromboembolic complications related to pharmacologic cardioversion. A review of all the studies that have reported the frequency of stroke at the time of pharmacologic cardioversion suggests that stroke frequency is similar to that of electric cardioversion.[36III] It is likely that anticoagulation therapy is also efficacious for preventing complications of pharmacologic cardioversion, and the American College of Chest Physicians recommends that anticoagulants also be administered to individuals undergoing chemical cardioversion.[39]

Transesophageal echocardiography may be used to identify a subgroup of patients with atrial fibrillation who can be safely cardioverted without prolonged anticoagulation. In one prospective trial, patients with atrial fibrillation in whom transesophageal echocardiography did not detect an intracardiac thrombus were cardioverted without prolonged anticoagulation.[31III] Seventy-eight patients were successfully cardioverted in this study. In 11 patients, anticoagulation was considered contraindicated because of associated medical conditions. These patients underwent successful direct-current cardioversion without any anticoagulant therapy. Twenty patients were treated with short-term heparin (mean duration 2.1 days) and underwent successful electrocardioversion after failing a brief trial of pharmacologic cardioversion. Successful pharmacologic cardioversion was achieved in an additional 47 patients who received short-term heparin. In general, patients in all subgroups were treated with oral anticoagulant therapy for 1 month following successful cardioversion. No patient suffered a cardioversion-related systemic embolus.

This study raises the possibility that cardioversion may be performed safely in selected patients with atrial fibrillation without prolonged anticoagulation. However, the utility of this approach is controversial. Only a small number of patients were treated using this protocol, and only 11 patients were cardioverted without any anticoagulant treatment. In addition, transesophageal echocardiography may be unable to detect small thrombi, particularly in the left atrial appendage, which is the most common site for thrombus formation. Fresh thrombi also may have acoustic characteristics similar to those of surrounding blood.[41] A case report of a patient who suffered a stroke following cardioversion without anticoagulation after a negative transesophageal echocardiogram has been reported.[42] Furthermore, if this protocol is used, it is critical that an experienced echocardiographer using a biplane or multiplane transesophageal probe perform the examination. More data are required before this practice can be recommended.

## UNANSWERED QUESTIONS

During the last few years, much new information has become available to guide the therapy of patients with atrial fibrillation. However, a number of important clinical questions still remain to be answered.

### Which Patients Can Confidently Be Treated With Aspirin?

The collaborative analysis identified a relatively small group of patients who have an annual risk of stroke of approximately 1% when not treated with either aspirin or warfarin (those younger than 65 years old who do not have diabetes, a history of hypertension, or a previous TIA or stroke). Because of the large number of patients in this analysis, the results are reasonably robust, and warfarin does not seem justified in them. It is an individual clinical decision whether to treat these patients with aspirin or no antithrombotic therapy.

SPAF II identified a group of patients with an annual risk of stroke of 1.8% on aspirin. They were male patients who did not have a systolic blood pressure greater than 160 mm Hg, were not diabetic, and had no previous TIA or stroke; and females younger than 75 years of age with none of the above risk factors. Because these patients were identified as part of a subgroup analysis, this result should be confirmed in a second group of patients before routinely being incorporated into practice. The SPAF investigators have embarked on a third study (SPAF III) that includes following a large cohort of "low-risk" patients on aspirin in an attempt to confirm these results.

### What Is the Optimal Intensity of Anticoagulation When Using Warfarin?

In disorders other than atrial fibrillation, studies have clearly shown that the risk of hemorrhage is directly correlated with the intensity of anticoagulation (most accurately measured by the INR). This is almost certainly the case in patients with atrial fibrillation as well. However, there is also a level of anticoagulation below which the risk of stroke is increased. The lowest target level of anticoagulation occurred in the Stroke Prevention in Nonrheumatic Atrial Fibrillation (SPINAF) and BAATAF trials. They aimed for a prothrombin time ratio (PTR) of 1.2 to 1.5, corresponding to an INR of 1.4 to 2.8. The most recent American College of Chest Physicians (ACCP) Consensus Conference on Antithrombotic Therapy recommended an INR of 2.0 to 3.0, which was near the middle range of the five studies.[39] Two ongoing studies will provide more information about this issue. PATAF is a study in the Netherlands in which patients are randomized to aspirin 150 mg a day or two different levels of oral anticoagulant therapy (an INR of 2.5–3.5 or an INR of 1.1–1.6). The AFASAK investigators are conducting a second study in which patients are randomized to one of four treatments—warfarin 1 mg a day, aspirin 300 mg a day, warfarin 1 mg a day and aspirin 300 mg a day, or warfarin INR 2.0 to 3.0.

### When Should Warfarin Be Started in a Patient With Atrial Fibrillation Who Has Recently Had a Stroke?

Unfortunately, no reliable data are available to answer this question. The clinical decision should be based upon the fact that a previous stroke is a risk factor for a subsequent one, that recent studies have indicated that the risk of stroke during the week after an atrial fibrillation-related stroke is less than 5%,[43V, 44III] and that the risk of hemorrhagic transformation is higher in patients with large strokes. The recommendation of the recent ACCP Consensus Conference seems reasonable.[39] Anticoagulation should not be started until a computed tomography (CT) scan done 48 hours or more after the stroke shows no spontaneous hemorrhagic transformation, and it should be delayed for at least 5 to 14 days in patients with large strokes or with uncontrolled hypertension.

### What is the Role of Echocardiography for Risk Stratification in Atrial Fibrillation?

The SPAF investigators found that left ventricular function and left atrial size on transesophageal echocardiography added slightly to the risk stratification possible from clinical risk factors alone.[26I] They were able to lower the risk of stroke in the lowest subgroup of patients from 2.5 to 1.0% per year. However, the true additive role of transthoracic or transesophageal echocardiography to clinical risk factor stratification is not known. Similarly, the role of transesophageal echocardiography in identifying patients with atrial fibrillation who do not need to be anticoagulated at the time of cardioversion is not known. Ongoing studies should provide information to determine the true value of these technologies in patient management.

# REFERENCES

1. Wolf PA, Abbott RD, Kannel WB: Atrial fibrillation as an independent risk factor for stroke: The Framingham study. Stroke 22:983, 1991.
2. Cairns JA, Connolly SJ: Nonrheumatic atrial fibrillation. Risk of stroke and role of antithrombotic therapy. Circulation 84:469, 1991.
3. Wolf PA, Dawber TR, Thomas HE, et al: Epidemiologic assessment of chronic atrial fibrillation and risk of stroke: The Framingham Study. Neurology 28:973, 1978.
III 4. Sandercock P, Bamford J, Dennis M, et al: Atrial fibrillation and stroke: Prevalence in different types of stroke and influence on early and long term prognosis (Oxfordshire community stroke project). Br Med J 305:1460, 1992.
I 5. Ezekowitz MD, Bridgers SL, James KE, et al, for the Veterans Affairs Stroke Prevention in Nonrheumatic Atrial Fibrillation Investigators: Warfarin in the prevention of stroke associated with nonrheumatic atrial fibrillation. N Engl J Med 327:1406, 1992.
II 6. Connolly SJ, Laupacis A, Gent M, et al, for the CAFA Study Coinvestigators. Canadian Atrial Fibrillation Anticoagulation (CAFA) Study. J Am Coll Cardiol 18:349, 1991.
I 7. Petersen P, Boysen G, Godtfredsen J, et al: Placebo-controlled, randomised trial of warfarin and aspirin for prevention of thromboembolic complications in chronic atrial fibrillation: The Copenhagen AFASAK study. Lancet 1:175, 1989.
I 8. Stroke Prevention in Atrial Fibrillation Investigators: Stroke Prevention in Atrial Fibrillation Study. Final Results. Circulation 84:527, 1991.
I 9. The Boston Area Anticoagulation Trial for Atrial Fibrillation Investigators: The effect of low-dose warfarin on the risk of stroke in patients with nonrheumatic atrial fibrillation. N Engl J Med 323:1505, 1990.
10. Laupacis A, Connolly SJ, Gent M, et al: How should the results from completed studies influence ongoing clinical trials? The CAFA study experience. Ann Intern Med 115:818, 1991.
11. Atrial Fibrillation Investigators: Risk factors for stroke and efficacy of anti-thrombotic therapy in atrial fibrillation: Analysis of pooled data from five randomized controlled trials. Arch Intern Med 154:1449, 1994.
III 12. The Stroke Prevention in Atrial Fibrillation Investigators: Predictors of thromboembolism in atrial fibrillation: I. Clinical features of patients at risk. Ann Intern Med 116:1, 1992.
13. Petersen P, Kastrup J, Helweg-Larsen S, et al: Risk factors for thromboembolic complications in chronic atrial fibrillation: The Copenhagen AFASAK study. Arch Intern Med 150:819, 1990.
14. Petersen P, Boysen G: Stroke in atrial fibrillation. N Engl J Med 482, 1990.
I 15. EAFT (European Atrial Fibrillation Trial) Study Group: Secondary prevention in nonrheumatic atrial fibrillation after transient ischaemic attack or minor stroke. Lancet 342:1255, 1993.
16. Antiplatelet Trialists' Collaboration: Collaborative overview of randomized trials of antiplatelet therapy—I: Prevention of death, myocardial infarction, and stroke by prolonged antiplatelet therapy in various categories. Br Med J 308:81, 1994.
17. Sherman DG, Dyken ML, Fisher M, et al: Antithrombotic therapy for cerebrovascular disorders. Chest 102:529S, 1992.
I 18. Stroke Prevention in Atrial Fibrillation Investigators: Warfarin versus aspirin for prevention of thromboembolism in atrial fibrillation. Stroke Prevention in Atrial Fibrillation II Study. Lancet 343:687, 1994.
19. The Stroke Prevention in Atrial Fibrillation Investigators: A differential effect of aspirin on prevention of stroke in atrial fibrillation. J Stroke Cerebrovasc Dis 3:181, 1993.
20. Connolly S, for the Atrial Fibrillation Investigators: Stroke Prevention in Atrial Fibrillation II Study. Lancet 343:1509, 1994.
I 21. Miller VT, Rothrock JF, Pearce LA, et al, on behalf of the Stroke Prevention in Atrial Fibrillation Investigators: Ischemic stroke in patients with atrial fibrillation: Effect of aspirin according to stroke mechanism. Neurology 43:32, 1993.
22. Cerebral Embolism Task Force: Cardiogenic brain embolism. Arch Neurol 46:727, 1989.
23. Wiener I: Clinical and echocardiographic correlates of systemic embolization in nonrheumatic atrial fibrillation. Am J Cardiol 59:177, 1987.
24. Tegler CH, Hart RG: Atrial size, atrial fibrillation and stroke. Ann Neurol 21:315, 1987.
V 25. D'Olhaberriague L, Hernandez-Vidal A, Molina L, et al: A prospective study of atrial fibrillation and stroke. Stroke 20:1648, 1989.
I 26. The Stroke Prevention in Atrial Fibrillation Investigators: Predictors of thromboembolism in atrial fibrillation: II. Echocardiographic features of patients at risk. Ann Intern Med 116:6, 1992.
27. Benjamin E, Plehn J, D'Agostino R: Mitral annular calcification and the risk of stroke in an elderly cohort. N Engl J Med 327:374, 1992.
28. DeRook FA, Comess KA, Albers G, et al: Transesophageal echocardiography in the evaluation of stroke. Arch Intern Med 117:922, 1992.
29. Aberg H: Atrial fibrillation. I. A study of atrial thrombosis and systemic embolism in a necropsy material. Acta Med Scand 185:373, 1969.
30. Hinton R, Kistler P, Fallon J, et al: Influence of etiology of atrial fibrillation on incidence of systemic embolism. Am J Cardiol 40:509, 1977.
III 31. Manning WJ, Silverman DI, Gordon SPF, et al: Cardioversion from atrial fibrillation without prolonged anticoagulation with use of transesophageal echocardiography to exclude the presence of atrial thrombi. N Engl J Med 328:750, 1993.
32. Slany J, Stollberger D, Kronik G: Value of echocardiography in atrial fibrillation. Wien Klin Wochenschr 104:10, 1992.
33. Mugge A, Kuhn H, Daniel W: The role of transesophageal echocardiography in the detection of left atrial thrombi. Echocardiography 10:405, 1993.
34. Castello R, Pearson AC, Labovitz AJ: Prevalence and clinical implications of atrial spontaneous contrast in patients undergoing transesophageal echocardiography. Am J Cardiol 65:1149, 1990.
35. Chimowitz M, DeGeorgia M, Poole M, et al: Left atrial spontaneous echo contrast is highly associated with previous stroke in patients with atrial fibrillation or mitral stenosis. Stroke 24:1015, 1993.
III 36. Bjerkelund C, Orning O: The efficacy of anticoagulant therapy in preventing embolism related to DC electrical conversion of atrial fibrillation. Am J Cardiol 23:208, 1969.
37. Arnold A, Mick M, Mazurek R, et al: Role of prophylactic anticoagulation for direct current cardioversion in patients with atrial fibrillation or atrial flutter. J Am Coll Cardiol 19:851, 1992.
38. Weinberg D, Mancini J: Anticoagulation for cardioversion of atrial fibrillation. Am J Cardiol 745, 1989.

39. Laupacis A, Albers G, Dunn M, et al: Antithrombotic therapy in atrial fibrillation. Chest 102:426S, 1992.

V 40. Manning W, Leeman D, Gotch P, et al: Pulsed Doppler evaluation of atrial mechanical function after electrical cardioversion of atrial fibrillation. J Am Coll Cardiol 13:617, 1989.

41. Daniel W: Should transesophageal echocardiography be used to guide cardioversion? N Engl J Med 328:803, 1993.

42. Ewy G: Optimal technique for electrical cardioversion of atrial fibrillation. Circulation 86:1645, 1992.

V 43. Sacco RL, Foulkes MA, Morh JP, et al: Determinants of early recurrence of cerebral infarction. The Stroke Data Bank. Stroke 20:983, 1989.

III 44 Rothrock JF, Dittrich HC, McAllen S, et al: Acute anticoagulation following cardioembolic stroke. Stroke 20:730, 1989.

# PART TWO

# CEREBRAL VASCULAR DISEASE

## Chapter 10

# Acute Stroke

Gordon D.O. Lowe

Acute completed stroke is a common cause of death and disability, especially in the elderly. It has been estimated that 1.5 million people suffer a new stroke each year in the United States and in the European Community. One year after a stroke, two-thirds of patients are either dead or dependent on others in activities of daily living. Both hospital management of stroke and community care are expensive and account for a significant percentage of health care costs.

Preventive measures against stroke include:

1. The identification and management of hypertension, which is of proven benefit[1]
2. Potentially, reduction in cigarette smoking[2] and in hyperlipidemia,[3] which have recently been confirmed as risk factors for stroke in meta-analyses
3. Potentially, hormone replacement therapy in menopausal women[4III]
4. Antithrombotic drug prophylaxis and therapy.

Antithrombotic prophylaxis against stroke (reviewed in detail in Chapter 11) includes primary prevention with aspirin in healthy persons. This is not recommended routinely, because an overview of the two randomized controlled trials suggested an increase in risk of probably or definitely hemorrhagic strokes from 0.2 to 0.3% during aspirin treatment ($2p < .05$), and an increase in the risk of all strokes from 1.2 to 1.4% ($2p > .05$).[5] Further studies of primary

prevention by antithrombotic drugs in high risk persons (e.g., those with high levels of cigarette smoking, blood pressure, serum cholesterol, or plasma fibrinogen) are required.

Antithrombotic prophylaxis also includes primary prevention in persons with potential cardiac sources of thromboembolism, for example, atrial fibrillation. This is now well established for warfarin[6] and to a lesser extent for aspirin.[7, 8II]

In addition, prophylaxis includes secondary prevention in persons with transient cerebral ischemic attacks (TIA) or previous ischemic stroke. This is now well established for antiplatelet agents such as aspirin or ticlopidine[7]; and in the case of persons with atrial fibrillation or other cardiac sources of embolism, for warfarin.[6, 8II, 9]

Finally, antithrombotic prophylaxis includes prevention with antiplatelet agents such as aspirin in persons with documented symptomatic ischemic heart disease or peripheral arterial disease.[7]

Although much can therefore be done to *prevent* stroke (or recurrent stroke) by risk factor control, and in selected persons by antithrombotic prophylaxis, the role of antithrombotic therapies in *acute stroke* remains controversial.[10–12] Two main reasons exist for this controversy.

First is the fact that reported trials have not been large enough to yield confident estimates of the risks and benefits of such therapies regarding important clinical endpoints (death and disability). It is possible that prevention of further thromboembolism or thrombus extension by antithrombotic drugs may be balanced or outweighed by increased risk or extent of intracranial bleeding, especially hemorrhagic transformation of softened cerebral infarcts. This uncertainty is compounded by variations in physician practice concerning the timing of introduction of such antithrombotic treatment. Second is the pathologic heterogeneity of acute stroke and hence the probable inclusion of patients with intracranial hemorrhage (or hemorrhagic infarction) in studies performed before the introduction of computed tomography (CT) or magnetic resonance imaging (MRI), which allow more accurate diagnosis of stroke pathology.

Ongoing large, randomized, controlled trials in acute stroke patients, of whom a high percentage have accurate subtype diagnosis, should yield more confident assessments of the role of antithrombotic therapies, including thrombolytic drugs,[11] aspirin,[12] and heparins.[12] Meanwhile, published evidence to early 1994 will be reviewed.

## GENERAL MANAGEMENT OF ACUTE STROKE

Management has been reviewed[13] and is not considered in detail. However, two main themes in stroke care have emerged in the 1990s.

First is the advantage of organized stroke services, especially early institution of assessment and rehabilitation by a multidisciplinary stroke team or stroke unit. In a meta-analysis of randomized trials, such care appeared to significantly reduce both morbidity and mortality.[14, 15]

Second is the importance of early, accurate diagnosis of stroke subtype—subarachnoid hemorrhage; intracerebral hemorrhage; lacunar infarction; and atherothrombotic or cardioembolic infarction, which may involve the cerebral hemispheres or brainstem and cerebellum (Fig. 10–1). Diagnosis is usually confirmed by CT scanning, which is increasingly available in district general hospitals.[16] Although such diagnosis is less important for stroke rehabilitation, it is essential for appropriate use of antithrombotic therapy, both as treatment of acute stroke and as secondary prophylaxis. One possible approach in stroke diagnosis and specific therapy is shown in Figure 10–1.

## MANAGEMENT OF PRIMARY INTRACRANIAL HEMORRHAGE

Approximately 15% of all strokes in Western countries are the result of primary intracerebral hemorrhage or subarachnoid hemorrhage. Urgent CT scanning is appropriate in patients with clinically suspected primary intracranial bleeding, to confirm or refute the diagnosis; to establish the site and extent of bleeding; and to assess the need for surgery (see Fig. 10–1). In all patients with suspected stroke in whom longterm secondary prophylaxis with antithrombotic drugs will be considered (the great majority), CT scanning should be performed within 14 days of onset if possible, because the signs of intracerebral bleeding may have resolved thereafter and the diagnosis will be missed. Demonstration of intracranial bleeding often contraindicates secondary prophylaxis with antithrombotic drugs.

The main principles of treatment of primary intracranial bleeding are as follows.[17, 18]

1. Neurosurgical consultation and assessment of need for surgery (e.g., evacuation of intracranial hematomas; treatment of aneurysms or angiomas).

2. Measures to prevent vasospasm and secondary thrombosis in patients with subarachnoid hemorrhage, such as intravenous infusion of the calcium antagonist, nimodipine.[18] Fibrinolytic inhibitors such as tranexamic acid reduce the risk of rebleeding in patients with subarachnoid hemorrhage but increase the risk of cerebral infarction, resulting in no net benefit regarding overall outcome.[18]

3. Identification and reversal of hemostatic defects (e.g., thrombocytopenia, hemophilias, and the hemostatic defects induced by antithrombotic drugs such as anticoagulants or thrombolytic agents). Difficult decisions may have to be made for patients who have mechanical prosthetic heart valves and intracranial hemorrhage, because complete reversal of anticoagulation may result in fatal valve thrombosis. Early CT scanning is advisable in all such patients who have suspected strokes, to identify the stroke subtype.[10] The balance of risks and benefits with continued anticoagulation often requires discussion between cardiac surgeons and neurosurgeons.[10]

4. Control of hypertension if this is marked, but avoiding hypoperfusion in the acute stage.

5. Prophylaxis of venous thromboembolism.

Although small studies of low-dose subcutaneous heparin (5,000 U 8-hourly) have suggested efficacy,[19] they have not been of sufficient size

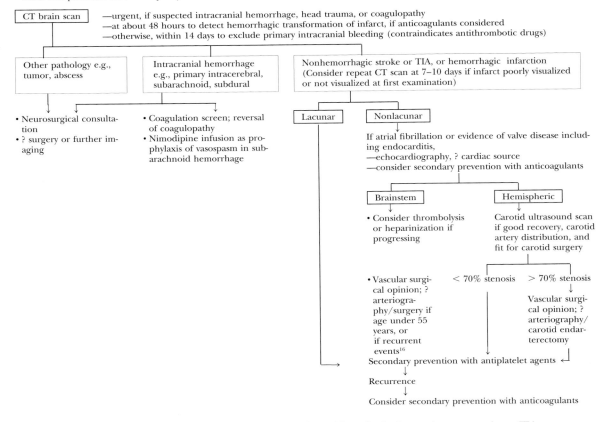

**Figure 10–1.** Guidelines for diagnosis and specific antithrombotic therapy in acute stroke or TIA.

to assess the possibly increased risk of further intracranial bleeding. At present, therefore, use of mechanical methods of prophylaxis (graduated elastic compression stockings and/or intermittent pneumatic compression), which are unlikely to increase the risk of bleeding, may be preferred. These prophylactic methods have not yet been evaluated in patients with hemorrhagic stroke, but it seems reasonable to extrapolate from studies demonstrating their efficacy in potential neurosurgical patients[201] and in other groups of surgical patients at moderate risk of venous thromboembolism.[21]

## RATIONALE FOR ANTITHROMBOTIC TREATMENTS IN ACUTE ISCHEMIC STROKE

About 85% of all strokes are the result of cerebral infarction. Of these, about 20% are

lacunar infarctions, usually ascribed to degenerative changes and occlusive thrombus in a small, subcortical perforating artery.[22] Most of the remaining 80%, non-lacunar, infarctions are the result either of thromboembolism from the heart (or occasionally from "paradoxical" venous thromboembolism through a patent foramen ovale); to thromboembolism arising in the atherosclerotic aortic arch, carotid arteries (often at the carotid bifurcation) or vertebrobasilar system; or to thrombosis in situ arising in the latter two systems. A small percentage are "watershed" or "boundary-zone" infarctions occurring in parts of the brain supplied by the terminal distributions of cerebral arteries when perfusion pressure falls (e.g., owing to hypotension or to internal carotid artery occlusion).[23] It is therefore important to establish by an appropriate scheme of investigations the site and probable cause of infarction, because of the implications for further investigations and for appropriate use of antithrombotic treatment (see Fig. 10–1).

Arterial thromboembolism causing cerebral infarction or TIA most commonly arises at the carotid bifurcation, where atheromatous plaques ulcerate, resulting in episodic thrombus formation. Thrombi may embolize to occlude distal arteries (transiently, causing TIA, or for several hours, causing cerebral infarction). Alternatively, thrombi may grow to occlude the artery at the site of plaque rupture or may be incorporated into the arterial plaque, causing an increase in stenosis (and hence in the risk of subsequent plaque ulceration, thrombus formation, and ischemic episodes).[24–29] This dynamic spectrum of carotid atherogenesis and thrombogenesis appears similar to that in the coronary arteries, which results in a spectrum of ischemic myocardial syndromes.[30]

Carotid artery thrombi, like thromboemboli arising from the heart, are composed mainly of platelets and fibrin. Studies of plasma levels of activation markers of platelets (e.g., beta thromboglobulin), coagulation (e.g., fibrinopeptide A) or fibrinolysis (e.g., B $\beta_{15–42}$ fibrin fragment and other fibrin degradation products) have shown elevated levels in patients with TIA or acute stroke, which were predictive of adverse clinical outcome (continued TIA, or 1-year mortality after stroke onset).[31, 32] These results suggest that activation of platelets, coagulation, and fibrinolysis occur in acute cerebral infarction and may also play a role in progression of infarction (for example, by promoting recurrent arterial or cardiac thromboembolism; extension of cerebral arterial thrombotic occlusion; microthrombosis in ischemic brain; or venous thromboembolism in the lower limbs of immobilized stroke patients).[12] If this is true, early treatment with platelet inhibitors (e.g., aspirin), anticoagulants (e.g., heparins), or thrombolytic drugs (e.g., streptokinase, urokinase, or tissue plasminogen activator) may reduce the volume of cerebral infarction, the risk of venous thromboembolism, and through these mechanisms both early mortality and late disability in patients with ischemic stroke.

The demonstrated efficacy of thrombolytic agents and aspirin in acute Q wave myocardial infarction,[33] and of heparin and aspirin in acute non-Q wave myocardial infarction or unstable angina,[34] support the case for large randomized controlled trials of aspirin, heparins, and thrombolytic agents in acute cerebral infarction,[10–12] especially because the thrombotic pathogenesis of acute coronary syndromes and acute carotid syndromes appears similar. Meanwhile, the wide variation in use of antithrombotic therapy in the treatment of acute ischemic stroke, revealed by a survey of neurologists in the United States,[35] probably reflects the lack of firm conclusions that can be drawn from analyses of published trials (and supports the case for further, larger trials).

## ANTIPLATELET AGENTS IN ACUTE ISCHEMIC STROKE

Meta-analyses of randomized, controlled trials of aspirin or other antiplatelet drugs show their efficacy in secondary prevention of cardiovascular events following recovery from ischemic stroke or from myocardial infarction, as well as in patients with TIA, angina (especially if unstable), peripheral arterial disease, or acute myocardial infarction.[7] However, despite biochemical evidence of platelet activation in acute ischemic stroke,[32, 36, 37] no large reported trials of the effect of aspirin (or other antiplatelet agents, including intravenous prostacyclin) exist on clinical outcome in *acute* ischemic stroke.[12] This lack of trials may reflect concern that use of platelet inhibitors in acute infarction may increase the risk of intracerebral bleeding, even if prior CT scanning is performed to exclude intracranial bleeding. Such a concern is supported by studies showing that patients with hemorrhagic stroke have impaired platelet function compared with patients with ischemic stroke[38]; that primary prevention[5] and secondary prevention[7] with aspirin increased the risk of hemorrhagic stroke (although this was outweighed by a decrease in risk of ischemic stroke and of total stroke in the case of secondary prevention[7]); and that immediate administration of aspirin in a rabbit model of embolic ischemic stroke was associated with a high risk of intracerebral bleeding.[39]

At present, therefore, the balance between antithrombotic benefit and hemorrhagic risk when antiplatelet agents are given to patients with acute ischemic stroke is unclear. On the principle of "primum non nocere," it may be prudent to defer routine institution of secondary prophylaxis with antiplatelet agents for about 14 days after the onset of acute ischemic stroke, by which time the risk of bleeding is small.[40] The ongoing International Stroke Trial (IST), a randomized trial of aspirin, heparin, both drugs, or neither in 20,000 patients with acute ischemic stroke within 48 hours after onset of symptoms,[12] should clarify the balance of risks and benefits for earlier administration of aspirin. This trial should also yield reliable estimates of benefits in subgroups (e.g., early versus later start of treatment; age under 75 years versus over 75; strokes due to large vessel occlusion versus small vessel lacunar strokes).[12] A trial of similar size of aspirin is being performed in China, and a smaller trial of 1,500 patients given aspirin or streptokinase (MAST) is proceeding in Europe.[12]

## ANTICOAGULANTS IN ACUTE STROKE

Sandercock and coworkers[12] performed a formal statistical overview of all truly randomized trials of anticoagulants in patients with acute stroke. Ten trials (including 1,047 patients) tested heparins (standard, unfractionated heparin in six trials; or a low molecular weight heparin or heparinoid in four trials) in acute ischemic stroke. One trial[41II] that included only 51 patients tested an oral anticoagulant in patients with acute presumed or confirmed ischemic stroke. Another small trial[19] tested low-dose heparin in acute *hemorrhagic* stroke. The results of the 10 trials of heparins in acute ischemic stroke are summarized in Figure 10–2.

The incidence of deep vein thrombosis (detected by routine screening with [125]I-fibrinogen leg scanning or with venography) was significantly lower in heparin-treated patients than in control patients (17.2% versus 54.1%); a proportional reduction of 81% (standard deviation [SD] 8%; $2p < .00001$). Only three of these

trials systematically identified pulmonary emboli. These were observed in 2.3% of heparin-treated patients and in 5.7% of controls ($2p > .05$). Likewise, mortality was rather low in the trials of ischemic stroke. Death occurred in 15.9% of heparin-treated patients and in 19.4% of controls ($2p > .05$). In those trials that scanned patients at the end of treatment to detect hemorrhagic transformation of cerebral infarction, this endpoint was also rather low—7.5% of heparin-treated patients and 6.9% of controls ($2p > .05$).

In the light of these results, what current recommendations can be made for routine use of heparin in acute stroke? Heparin is clearly effective in preventing about two-thirds of cases of deep vein thrombosis detected by routine screening; subcutaneous low-dose heparin (5,000 U 8-hourly) appears as effective as higher doses.[42I] This prophylactic effect of low-dose heparin appears comparable to its effects in acute myocardial infarction, in other conditions of general medical patients, and in surgical patients.[43, 44] The 58% proportional reduction in pulmonary embolism, and the 18% reduction in mortality, observed in patients with acute ischemic stroke randomized to heparins are likewise comparable to the effects of subcutaneous low-dose heparin[43, 44] or of low molecular weight heparins[45, 46] in surgical patients. However, because of the relatively small numbers of patients with acute stroke randomized in controlled trials of heparins, the 95% confidence

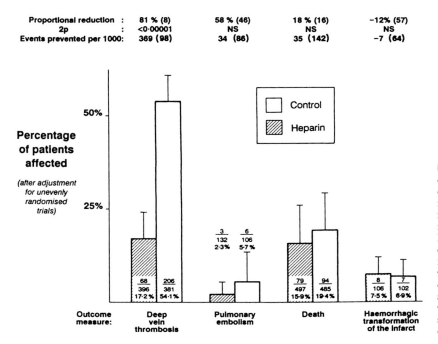

**Figure 10–2.** Overview analysis of deep vein thrombosis, pulmonary embolism, death, and hemorrhagic transformation of the infarct in randomized trials of heparins in acute ischemic stroke. Figures in parentheses are standard deviations. (Used with permission from Sandercock PAG, van den Belt AGM, Lindley RI, et al: Antithrombotic therapy in acute ischaemic stroke: An overview of the completed, randomised trials. J Neurol Neurosurg Psychiatry 56:17, 1993).

intervals for estimates of reductions in pulmonary embolism or mortality, and for estimates of any increase in hemorrhagic transformation of cerebral infarction, are wide.[12] Furthermore, no data on disability in survivors is available from trial reports,[12] and it is possible that death or disability from increased cerebral hemorrhage in patients treated with anticoagulants (even in low doses) may balance, or outweigh, reductions in venous thromboembolism, recurrent arterial or cardiogenic thromboembolism, or local extension of cranial or cerebral arterial thrombosis.

Despite the possibility of cerebral hemorrhage, therapeutic enthusiasts may wish to prescribe low-dose heparin, or low molecular weight heparin or heparinoid, for prevention of venous thromboembolism in patients with confirmed acute ischemic stroke, on the basis that such prophylaxis is highly effective in level-1 studies.[12] They can also point out that failure to give effective prophylaxis not only increases the risk of fatal pulmonary embolism,[421] but probably also increases the risk of nonfatal, symptomatic deep vein thrombosis or pulmonary embolism, which may require invasive investigations (venography, pulmonary angiography) and invasive and potentially hazardous therapy (full-dose anticoagulation, which may carry a much higher risk of intracranial bleeding, or insertion of an inferior vena caval filter). Heparin or low molecular weight heparin or heparinoid prophylaxis in patients with acute ischemic stroke with lower limb paralysis has recently been recommended by three consensus groups in the United Kingdom, Europe, and North America[44, 47, 48]; hence, physicians giving such prophylaxis can quote widespread peer support. The North American Consensus Group[44] stated that such a recommendation was grade A, based upon level-1 data.

It may, however, be prudent to exclude intracranial hemorrhage (usually by early CT scanning) prior to institution of heparin prophylaxis, until ongoing trials (such as the IST) establish whether low-dose heparin has an overall beneficial (or adverse) effect on morbidity and mortality in patients in whom CT scanning is not performed, or in whom CT scanning shows primary or secondary intracerebral bleeding. If CT scanning is delayed, mechanical methods of prophylaxis against venous thromboembolism can be instituted meantime (see Fig. 10–1; see later), and heparins added or substituted when CT scanning has excluded hemorrhage. Further studies are required to establish whether low molecular weight heparins (or heparinoids) are more efficacious than

standard, unfractionated heparin, as has been shown for surgical patients.[45, 46]

Therapeutic skeptics may wish to avoid even low-dose heparins or heparinoids in patients with acute stroke, pending the results of further, larger trials.[12] They should, however, consider that the consequences of such a policy may include an increased incidence of symptomatic venous thromboembolism, which may require invasive and hazardous therapy (see earlier). Although mechanical means of prophylaxis (graduated elastic compression stockings and/or intermittent pneumatic compression) may be substituted for heparin prophylaxis, these are grade C recommendations based on extrapolation of data from other patient groups,[44] such as general surgical patients[21] and potential neurosurgical patients.[201] The choice of prophylaxis against venous thromboembolism in stroke patients is discussed also in Chapter 19.

If low-dose heparin (or low-molecular-weight heparins or heparinoids) is effective in prophylaxis of venous thromboembolism following acute ischemic stroke, what is the role of full-dose anticoagulation (with heparin and warfarin) in prevention of recurrent arterial thromboembolism or extension of arterial thrombosis in situ? A North American Consensus Statement[10] provided a review of the literature and a statement that full-dose anticoagulants are either of no value or are harmful, in patients with completed strokes. However, heparin anticoagulation for 3 to 5 days was stated to be reasonable in patients with a progressing ischemic stroke, especially those involving the vertebrobasilar circulation. This grade B recommendation was based on two level-2 studies, each showing a favorable trend. However, the statement acknowledged that some experts do not give anticoagulants to such patients because of the paucity of clinical data, and they recommend aspirin instead.[10]

A subgroup of patients with acute ischemic stroke in whom early, full-dose anticoagulation may be indicated are those with a potential cardiac source of embolism. The management dilemma in such patients is the timing of full-dose anticoagulation, based upon estimation of the relative risks of early recurrent thromboembolism and of anticoagulant-induced bleeding,[10] especially bleeding into large cerebral infarcts, which are commonly observed in patients with a cardiac source of large, fibrin-rich thrombi. The risk of recurrent embolism in the 14 days after cardioembolic stroke is about 10%, but the rate varies with the cardiac abnormality: patients with nonvalvular atrial fibrillation appear to have a low risk of stroke recurrence,[10] possibly no greater than that in stroke patients without atrial fibrillation.[49]

Recommendations by a North American Consensus Group[10] are as follows.

1. Heparin, followed by warfarin (at a dose that prolongs the International Normalized Ratio [INR] of the prothrombin time between 2.0 and 3.0) should be instituted in nonhypertensive patients with small- to moderate-sized cardioembolic strokes in whom a CT scan, performed 48 hours or more after stroke onset, documents the absence of spontaneous hemorrhagic transformation.

2. Anticoagulant prophylaxis should be postponed 5 to 14 days in patients with large cardioembolic strokes or uncontrolled hypertension, because of the predisposition of these patients to hemorrhagic transformation.

3. In patients with nonvalvular atrial fibrillation as the presumed embolic source, initiation of warfarin (following CT at 48 hours or over) without initial heparin seems reasonable, in view of the low risk of early recurrent embolism.

## THROMBOLYTIC THERAPY IN ACUTE ISCHEMIC STROKE

As in acute myocardial infarction, judicious use of thrombolytic agents in patients with early acute ischemic stroke may in theory restore blood flow in the ischemic penumbra of an evolving infarct, and hence reduce infarct size and consequently reduce both death and disability. On the other hand, several practical problems have been suggested for thrombolysis in acute stroke, as compared with thrombolysis in acute myocardial infarction.[11, 50]

One of the problems is the relatively slow admission rate of patients with acute stroke to the hospital, compared with that for patients with acute myocardial infarction. However, thrombolytic therapy in acute myocardial infarction may be beneficial for up to 24 hours after onset of symptoms, albeit with diminishing benefit.[33] This efficacy of later therapy may be because arterial thrombosis and resulting infarction is not an "all-or-none" event as was traditionally supposed, but a dynamic, multistage process involving plaque rupture at an arterial stenosis; fluctuating blood flow and vasospasm; growth and distal embolization of thrombi; development of collateral blood flow; and microcirculatory blood flow, which is strongly affected by the flow properties of blood (rheology). Thrombolytic therapy greatly reduces plasma fibrinogen levels, and hence reduces plasma viscosity, red cell aggregation and the viscosity of blood, which may improve blood flow in the ischemic heart or brain.

A second problem is the greater delay in obtaining CT scanning to exclude hemorrhagic stroke, compared with the time to obtain an electrocardiogram to establish an indication for thrombolytic therapy in acute myocardial infarction (ST segment elevation or bundle branch block).[33] However, organization of urgent CT scanning for all patients with acute stroke who may benefit from thrombolytic therapy (in the event that ongoing randomized controlled trials show beneficial effects) should not be an insuperable problem for hospitals admitting emergencies. Urgent CT scanning is already indicated in such hospitals for assessment of patients with traumatic head injury and (as argued earlier) for clinically suspected spontaneous intracranial bleeding.

A third problem is the possibility that post thrombolytic reperfusion injury, edema, and hemorrhage in the ischemic brain are more injurious than in the ischemic heart. However, overall there is little evidence to support a significant excessive incidence of such events.[11] It should also be noted that although thrombolytic therapy in acute myocardial infarction *increases* acute mortality (probably owing to hemorrhage including intracranial hemorrhage, and to myocardial reperfusion injury), this short-term disadvantage is greatly outweighed by the *longer term decrease* in mortality.[33] The same may be true of thrombolytic therapy in acute ischemic stroke.

Finally, a problem is the possibility that thrombolytic therapy may dislodge intracardiac thrombus, resulting in a further cardioembolic stroke.

Wardlaw and Warlow[11] have reviewed the six randomized trials of thrombolytic therapy in acute ischemic stroke. The results are summarized in Figure 10–3. After removing the two trials conducted without a prior CT scan to exclude intracranial bleeding, this overview showed a 37% (SD 35%) reduction in the odds of death (95% confidence intervals, 74% reduction to 40% excess); and a significant 56% reduction (SD 21%) in the odds of death or deterioration (95% confidence intervals, 20 to 76% reduction; $2p = .007$). The reviewers concluded that the available evidence was sufficiently encouraging to warrant proper evaluation of thrombolysis in large, well-designed randomized trials.[11] Several such trials, including the European MAST Study, are currently in progress. Meanwhile, some clinicians use thrombolytic therapy on an individual, named-patient basis

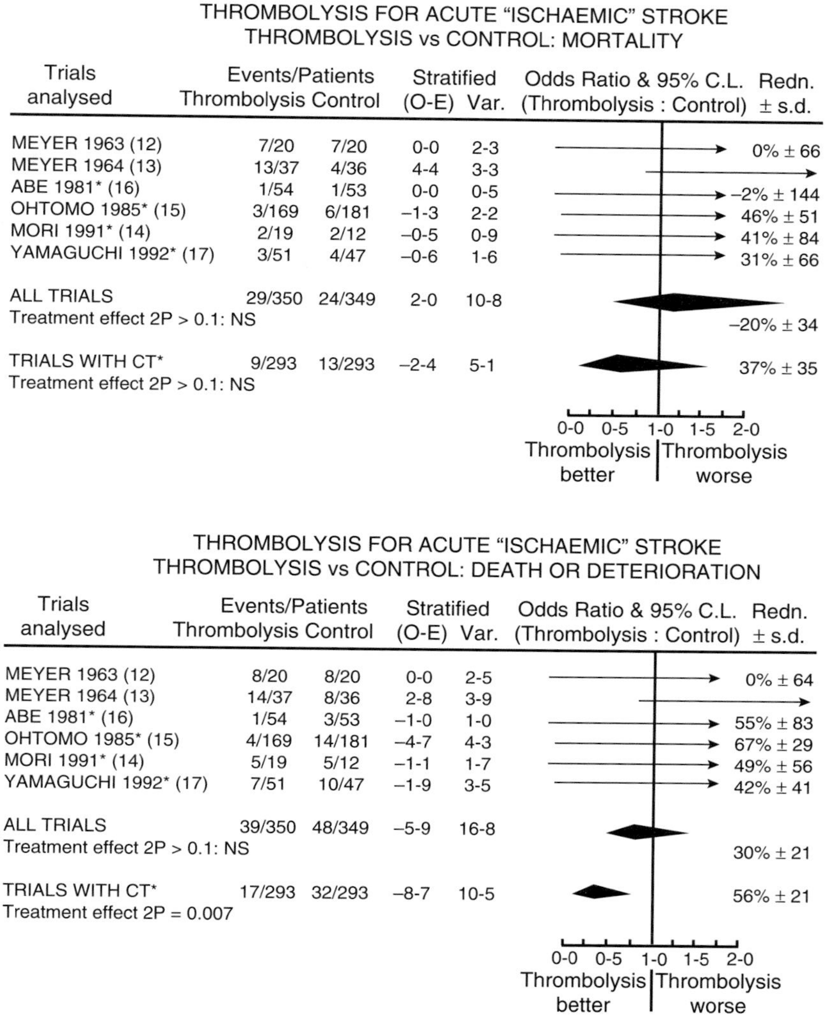

## THROMBOLYSIS FOR ACUTE "ISCHAEMIC" STROKE
## THROMBOLYSIS vs CONTROL: MORTALITY

| Trials analysed | Events/Patients Thrombolysis Control | | Stratified (O-E) Var. | | Odds Ratio & 95% C.L. (Thrombolysis : Control) | Redn. ± s.d. |
|---|---|---|---|---|---|---|
| MEYER 1963 (12) | 7/20 | 7/20 | 0-0 | 2-3 | | 0% ± 66 |
| MEYER 1964 (13) | 13/37 | 4/36 | 4-4 | 3-3 | | |
| ABE 1981* (16) | 1/54 | 1/53 | 0-0 | 0-5 | | −2% ± 144 |
| OHTOMO 1985* (15) | 3/169 | 6/181 | −1-3 | 2-2 | | 46% ± 51 |
| MORI 1991* (14) | 2/19 | 2/12 | −0-5 | 0-9 | | 41% ± 84 |
| YAMAGUCHI 1992* (17) | 3/51 | 4/47 | −0-6 | 1-6 | | 31% ± 66 |
| ALL TRIALS Treatment effect 2P > 0.1: NS | 29/350 | 24/349 | 2-0 | 10-8 | | −20% ± 34 |
| TRIALS WITH CT* Treatment effect 2P > 0.1: NS | 9/293 | 13/293 | −2-4 | 5-1 | | 37% ± 35 |

```
        0-0  0-5  1-0  1-5  2-0
       Thrombolysis | Thrombolysis
         better     |    worse
```

## THROMBOLYSIS FOR ACUTE "ISCHAEMIC" STROKE
## THROMBOLYSIS vs CONTROL: DEATH OR DETERIORATION

**Figure 10–3.** Overview analysis of the randomized trials of thrombolysis for acute ischemic stroke. (Panel A) Odds of death. (Panel B) Odds of death or deterioration for thrombolytic therapy versus placebo. The two trials by Meyer were excluded from the analysis of trials with CT brain scanning. (Used with permission from Wardlaw JM and Warlow CP: Thrombolysis in acute ischemic stroke: Does it work? Stroke 23:1826, 1992. Copyright 1992 American Heart Association.) [Updated versions can be obtained through *Cochrane Data Base of Systematic Reviews*, BMJ, PO Box 295, London WC1H9TE.]

| Trials analysed | Events/Patients Thrombolysis Control | | Stratified (O-E) Var. | | Odds Ratio & 95% C.L. (Thrombolysis : Control) | Redn. ± s.d. |
|---|---|---|---|---|---|---|
| MEYER 1963 (12) | 8/20 | 8/20 | 0-0 | 2-5 | | 0% ± 64 |
| MEYER 1964 (13) | 14/37 | 8/36 | 2-8 | 3-9 | | |
| ABE 1981* (16) | 1/54 | 3/53 | −1-0 | 1-0 | | 55% ± 83 |
| OHTOMO 1985* (15) | 4/169 | 14/181 | −4-7 | 4-3 | | 67% ± 29 |
| MORI 1991* (14) | 5/19 | 5/12 | −1-1 | 1-7 | | 49% ± 56 |
| YAMAGUCHI 1992* (17) | 7/51 | 10/47 | −1-9 | 3-5 | | 42% ± 41 |
| ALL TRIALS Treatment effect 2P > 0.1: NS | 39/350 | 48/349 | −5-9 | 16-8 | | 30% ± 21 |
| TRIALS WITH CT* Treatment effect 2P = 0.007 | 17/293 | 32/293 | −8-7 | 10-5 | | 56% ± 21 |

```
        0-0  0-5  1-0  1-5  2-0
       Thrombolysis | Thrombolysis
         better     |    worse
```

(because thrombolytic agents are not currently licenced for use in stroke) in patients with vertebrobasilar system infarcts who have a poor prognosis in the absence of specific treatment.[50, 51]

The European MAST Study has reported that they terminated recruitment to their multicenter trial of streptokinase (1,500,000 units by intravenous infusion over 1 hour) versus placebo, after reviewing 10-day safety data in 270 patients.[52] The hazard ratio for 10-day mortality was twice as high in the streptokinase arm (2.16; 95% CI 1.32–3.53; $p$ .001); long-term mortality (median follow-up 108 days) was also higher (hazard ratio 1.44; 95% CI 0.99–211; $p$ .05). The relative risk of symptomatic intracranial hemorrhage was 5.82 (95% CI 2.40–14.11; $p$ .001) and of any intracranial hemorrhage was 2.80 (95% CI 1.77–4.43; $p$ .001). Although long-term follow-up and analysis of this and other ongoing trials of thrombolytic therapy are awaited, the investigators have suggested that the use of thrombolytics in acute stroke should be reserved for patients taking part in clinical trials, with careful monitoring for safety.[52]

## RHEOLOGIC THERAPY IN ACUTE ISCHEMIC STROKE

The aim of rheologic therapies in acute ischemic stroke is to restore or improve blood flow in the ischemic brain, particularly in the microcirculation where changes in the flow properties of blood may have most effect.[53] The two rheologic approaches that have been evaluated in clinical trials are hemodilution with plasma expanders such as dextrans, hydroxyethyl-starch and albumin; and defibrination with the snake venom enzyme, ancrod.[53] Both of these approaches have antithrombotic, as well as flow-enhancing, effects. Although several randomized controlled trials of hemodilution with dextrans (including two large Italian and Scandinavian studies) showed no benefit in terms of outcome in acute ischemic stroke,[54] results may reflect adverse effects on blood volume and plasma viscosity (which is increased by dextran).[53] Furthermore, patients with high hematocrit, who have increased mortality[55] and who might be expected to benefit most from hematocrit reduction, were usually excluded from hemodilution trials. A more recent study of hemodilution with albumin, adjusted to individual patients' hemodynamic state and hematocrit, has shown more promising results.[56] Further trials are required of such customized hemodilution, which requires treatment in intensive care units.

Defibrination with ancrod has to date been studied in only a few small trials.[57]

## REFERENCES

1. Collins R, Peto R, McMahon S, et al: Blood pressure, stroke, and coronary heart disease. Part 2. Short-term reductions in blood pressure: Overview of randomised drug trials in their epidemiological context. Lancet 335:827, 1990.
2. Shinton R, Beevers G: Meta-analysis of relation between cigarette smoking and stroke. Br Med J 298:789, 1989.
3. Qizilbash N, Duffy SW, Warlow C, et al: Lipids are risk factors for ischaemic stroke: Overview and review. Cerebrovasc Dis 2:127, 1992.
III 4. Paganini-Hill A, Ross RK, Henderson BE: Postmenopausal oestrogen treatment and stroke: A prospective study. Br Med J 297:519, 1988.
5. Hennekens C, Buring JE, Sandercock P, et al: Aspirin and other antiplatelet agents in the secondary and primary prevention of cardiovascular disease. Circulation 80:749, 1989.
6. Hart RG: Cardiogenic embolism to the brain. Lancet 339:589, 1992.
7. Antiplatelet Trialists' Collaboration: Collaborative overview of randomised trials of antiplatelet therapy—I. Prevention of death, myocardial infarction, and stroke by prolonged antiplatelet therapy in various categories of patients. Br Med J 308:81, 1994.
8. Atrial Fibrillation Investigators: Risk factors for stroke and efficacy of antithrombotic therapy in atrial fibrillation. Arch Intern Med 154:1449, 1994.
9. Albers GW: Atrial fibrillation and stroke. Arch Intern Med 154:1443, 1994.
10. Sherman DG, Dyken ML Jr, Fisher M, et al: Antithrombotic therapy for cerebrovascular disorders. Chest 102[Suppl]:529S, 1992.
11. Wardlaw JM, Warlow CP: Thrombolysis in acute ischemic stroke: Does it work? Stroke 23:1826, 1992.
12. Sandercock PAG, van den Belt AGM, Lindley RI, et al: Antithrombotic therapy in acute ischaemic stroke: An overview of the completed randomised trials. J Neurol Neurosurg Psychiatry 56:17, 1993.
13. Warlow CP (ed): Stroke Octet. London, The Lancet, 1992.
14. Langhorne P, Williams BO, Gilchrist W, et al: Do stroke units save lives? Lancet 342:395, 1993.
15. Dennis M: Stroke services. Lancet 339:793, 1992.
16. Donnan GA: Investigation of patients with stroke and transient ischaemic attacks. Lancet 339:473, 1992.
17. Caplan LR: Intracerebral haemorrhage. Lancet 339:656, 1992.
18. van Gijn J: Subarachnoid haemorrhage. Lancet 339:653, 1992.
19. Dickmann U, Voth E, Schicha H, et al: Heparin therapy, deep vein thrombosis and pulmonary embolism after intracerebral haemorrhage. Klin Wochenschr 66:1182, 1988.
I 20. Turpie AGG, Hirsh J, Gent M, et al: Prevention of deep vein thrombosis in potential neurosurgical patients: A randomized trial comparing graduated compression stockings alone or graduated compression stockings plus intermittent pneumatic compression with control. Arch Intern Med 149:679, 1989.
21. Wells PS, Lensing AWA, Hirsh J: Graduated compression stockings in the prevention of postoperative venous thromboembolism. A meta-analysis. Arch Intern Med 154:67, 1994.
22. Bamford JM, Warlow CP: Evolution and testing of the lacunar hypothesis. Stroke 19:1074, 1988.
23. Mohr JP, Caplan LR, Melski JW, et al: The Harvard Cooperative Stroke Registry: A prospective registry. Neurology 28:754, 1978.
24. Fisher CM: Concerning recurrent transient cerebral ischemic attacks. Can Med Assoc J 86:1091, 1962.
25. Gunning AJ, Pickering GW, Robb-Smith AH, et al: Mural thrombus of the internal carotid artery and subsequent embolism. Q J Med 33:155, 1964.
26. Battacharji SK, Hurchinson EC, McCall AJ: Stenosis and occlusion of vessels in cerebral infarction. Br Med J 3:270, 1967.
27. Persson AV, Robichaux WT, Silverman M: The natural history of carotid plaque development. Arch Surg 118:1048, 1983.
28. Norris JW, Bornstein NM: Progression and regression of carotid stenosis. Stroke 17:755, 1986.
29. van Damme H, Vivario M: Pathologic aspects of carotid plaques: Surgical and clinical significance. Int Angiol 12:299, 1993.
30. Davies M, Thomas AC: Plaque fissuring: The cause of acute myocardial infarction, sudden ischaemic death, and crescendo angina. Br Heart J 53:363, 1985.
31. Stewart ME, Douglas JT, Lowe GDO, et al: Prognostic value of beta-thromboglobulin in patients with transient cerebral ischaemia. Lancet 2:479, 1983.
32. Douglas JT, Lowe GDO, Balendra R, et al: Prognostic significance of fibrinogen derivatives in acute stroke. In Lowe GDO, Douglas JT, Forbes CD, et al (eds): Fibrinogen 2: Biochemistry, Physiology and Clinical Relevance. Amsterdam, Elsevier, 1987, pp 241–244.
33. Fibrinolytic Therapy Trialists' (FTT) Collaborative Group: Indications for fibrinolytic therapy in suspected acute myocardial infarction: Collaborative overview of early mortality and major morbidity results from all randomised trials of more than 1000 patients. Lancet 343:311, 1994.
I 34. Cohen M, Adams PC, Parry G, et al: Combination antithrombotic therapy in unstable rest angina and non-Q-wave infarction in nonprior aspirin users. Primary end points analysis from the ATACS Trial. Circulation 89:81, 1994.
35. Marsh EE, Adams HP, Biller J, et al: Use of antithrombotic drugs in the treatment of acute ischemic stroke: A survey of neurologists in practice in the United States. Neurology 39:1631, 1989.
36. Koudstaal PJ, Ciabattoni G, van Gijn J, et al: Increased

thromboxane biosynthesis in patients with acute cerebral ischemia. Stroke 24:219, 1993.

37. van Kooten F, Ciabattoni G, Patrono C, et al: Evidence for episodic platelet activation in acute ischemic stroke. Stroke 25:278, 1994.

38. Mulley GP, Heptinstall S, Taylor PM, Mitchell JRA: ADP-induced platelet release reaction in acute stroke. Thromb Haemostas 50:524, 1983.

39. Clark WM, Madden KP, Lyden PD, et al: Cerebral hemorrhagic risk of aspirin or heparin treatment with thrombolytic treatment in rabbits. Stroke 22:872, 1991.

40. Sandercock P, Lindley R, Wardlaw J: Antiplatelet, anticoagulant and fibrinolytic agents in acute ischaemic stroke and TIA. Br J Hosp Med 47:731, 1992.

II 41. Marshall J, Shaw DA: Anticoagulant therapy in acute cerebrovascular accidents: A controlled trial. Lancet 1:995, 1960.

I 42. McCarthy ST, Turner J: Low-dose subcutaneous heparin in the prevention of deep-vein thrombosis and pulmonary emboli following acute stroke. Age Ageing 15:84, 1986.

43. Collins R, Scrimgeour A, Yusuf S, et al: Reduction in fatal pulmonary embolism and venous thrombosis by perioperative administration of subcutaneous heparin. N Engl J Med 318:1162, 1988.

44. Clagett GP, Salzman EW, Wheeler HB, et al: Prevention of venous thromboembolism. Chest 102[Suppl]:391S, 1992.

45. Nurmohamed MT, Rosendaal FT, Buller HR, et al: Low molecular weight heparin versus standard heparin in general and orthopaedic surgery: A meta-analysis. Lancet 340:152, 1992.

46. Leizorovicz A, Haugh MC, Chapius FR, et al: Low-molecular weight heparin in the prevention of perioperative thrombosis. Br Med J 305:913, 1992.

47. Thromboembolic Risk Factors (THRIFT) Consensus Group: Risk of and prophylaxis for venous thromboembolism in hospital patients. Br Med J 305:567, 1992.

48. European Consensus Statement: Prevention of venous thromboembolism. Int Angiol 11:151, 1992.

49. Sandercock P, Bamford J, Dennis M, et al: Atrial fibrillation and stroke: Prevalence in different types of stroke and influence on early and long term prognosis (Oxfordshire community stroke project). Br Med J 305:1460, 1992.

50. Sloan MA, del Zoppo GJ, Brott TG: Thrombolysis and stroke. In Julian D, Kübler W, Norris RM, et al (eds): Thrombolysis in Cardiovascular Disease. Basel, Marcel Dekker, 1989, pp 361–380.

51. Hacke W, Zeumer H, Ferbert A, et al: Intraarterial fibrinolytic therapy improves outcome in patients with acute vertebrobasilar occlusive disease. Stroke 19:1216, 1988.

52. Hommel M, Boissel JP, Cornu C, et al: Termination of trial of streptokinase in severe acute ischaemic stroke. Lancet 345:57, 1995.

53. Hartmann A, Kuschinsky W (eds): Cerebral Ischemia and Hemorheology, Berlin, Springer-Verlag, 1987.

54. Asplund K: Hemodilution in acute stroke. Cerebrovasc Dis 1[Suppl]:129, 1991.

55. Lowe GDO, Japp AJ, Forbes CD: Relation of atrial fibrillation and high haematocrit to mortality in acute stroke. Lancet 1:784, 1983.

56. Goslinga H, Eijzenbach V, Heuvelmans JHA, et al: Custom-tailored hemodilution with albumin and crystalloids in acute ischemic stroke. Stroke 23:181, 1992.

57. Hossman V, Heiss WD, Bewermeyer H, et al: Controlled trial of ancrod in ischemic stroke. Arch Neurol 40:803, 1983.

# Chapter 11

# Stroke Prevention

Henry J. M. Barnett and H. E. Meldrum

## PRIMARY STROKE PREVENTION

Various advances in stroke prevention and possibly the major reason for the reduction in stroke mortality is related to the identification of primary vascular risk factors that predispose to stroke. The most important ones to emerge have been age, gender, hypertension (both systolic and diastolic), cigarette smoking, and diabetes.[1] Less common or of less certain relationship have been excessive use of alcohol, hyperlipidemia, hyperfibrinogenemia, thrombocytosis, hemocystinuria, and the occurrence of antiphospholipid antibodies. Incontrovertible data have emerged that determine the benefit of controlling blood pressure and eliminating smoking.[2, 3III] There is no doubt that control of systolic and diastolic blood pressure in any age group will reduce the occurrence of stroke, and the elimination of cigarette smoking will reduce the risk within 5 years to the equivalent of those who have not used cigarettes.[3III, 4, 5] Whether either or both of these strategies has been the main cause in reducing stroke mortality is unknown, but it is reasonable to conjecture that they have played an important role.

Two studies in primary prevention, one involving 22,000 male United States physicians, and a second involving 5,000 male British physicians with an average followup of 5 years, attempted to determine whether 325 mg every other day in the United States study and 500 mg in the British study of acetylsalicylic acid (ASA) would reduce heart attack and stroke.[6I, 7II] Researchers in the United States study reported a 46% reduction in myocardial infarction but no reduction in stroke. Researchers in the British study reported no reduction in either and, if anything, a slight trend toward increase in stroke. Thus, to date, no trial has identified a primary stroke prevention by antithrombotic strategy. It was suggested that the failure of the British trial to reduce stroke was the result of too much aspirin being used. This suggestion seems improbable because the United States trial was equally negative in stroke prevention, using less than half of the dose employed in the British trial.

## SECONDARY STROKE PREVENTION

### Anticoagulants

There is significant risk on an annual basis of stroke for individuals with nonvalvular atrial fibrillation.[8] Five trials have examined the benefit of antithrombotic therapy in patients afflicted with nonvalvular atrial fibrillation.[9I, 10, 11I, 12I, 13I, 14I] The evidence is clear that anticoagulants in the form of warfarin have been shown to be of benefit in these trials. The level of anticoagulation varied between the trials with an International Normalization Ratio (INR) in the low to middle range (1.4–4.2) and concluded without convincing evidence that one level was better than the other. Bleeding complications occur with higher levels, and the evidence is suggestive that the lower level is adequate and therefore to be preferred. The results of the North American trial (SPAF) have determined that younger patients without any of the identified risk factors (evidence of congestive heart failure, left atrial enlargement, or hypertension) are at a vanishingly small risk and may not need to be treated.[15III, 16, 17] This matter requires further exploration. At the same time the concern that anticoagulants carry an increased risk of hemorrhagic complications for patients at or above 75 years of age leaves some doubt as to whether anticoagulants should be used in this age group.[18V, 19]

Anticoagulants for patients threatened with thromboembolic cerebral events consequent upon left ventricular ischemic infarction have been studied in one small randomized trial.[20II] Unfortunately, the trial was stopped after a mere 43 patients had been entered but the number of events in the group of patients receiving anticoagulants was substantially fewer than that in patients receiving placebo. This result bore out what had been observed in several case-control trials when random assignment had not been utilized.[21, 22III, 23V] The hazard of converting a bland ischemic infarction into a hemorrhagic infarction exists with stroke due to infarction from a cardiac embolic source. More of them become spontaneously hemorrhagic than do those that arise as atherothrombotic ischemic lesions. Nevertheless, if anticoagulants are withheld in patients with very large infarctions and if individuals are given the benefit of preliminary computed tomography (CT) examination, this complication can be reduced, although not entirely eliminated.

No recent trials have been conducted to determine the benefit of anticoagulant medication among patients who have atrial fibrillation in association with valvular disease. Early trials of imperfect design presented evidence that benefit was obtained.[24] The decline in rheumatic heart disease makes it improbable that there will be new trials in the foreseeable future for this phenomenon.

Ischemic cerebral infarction secondary to cerebral venous and sinus thrombosis is comparatively rare, but there is evidence that stroke may be prevented or reduced with anticoagulant treatment. Venous infarction is known to produce hemorrhagic infarction, and the use of anticoagulants would appear to be contraindicated. Nevertheless, a series of careful observations made by Ameri and Bousser cast doubt on this hypothesis.[25] The extension of the infarction and the severity of the neurologic deficit was decreased rather than increased by the judicious use of anticoagulant medication in this nonrandomized study. A subsequent small randomized trial has confirmed this report, and warfarin must now be considered when this condition is diagnosed.[26I]

## Platelet Inhibiting Drugs

Five platelet inhibiting drugs have been submitted to large-scale multicenter randomized clinical trials. Three may be dismissed from further discussion because they have not been shown to be of any value in stroke prevention; they are sulfinpyrazone, dipyridamole, and suloctidil.

Aspirin was the first platelet inhibitor shown to be effective in stroke reduction. The Canadian Aspirin Trial was launched in 1971. In 585 patients with transient ischemic attack (TIA) and minor stroke there was a reduction in combined stroke and death of 30%. No benefit was found in the 200 females taking 1,300 mg of aspirin used in the aspirin arms of this factorial-design study.[27I] A subgroup analysis of the male patients revealed a 50% reduction in stroke and stroke-death. Since that time, 16 trials of patients with TIA and minor stroke have been submitted to platelet inhibiting drug trials and, although the benefit has varied, it can be stated that 23 to 25% risk reduction is to be anticipated in such patients with the use of aspirin therapy.[28]

The female unresponsiveness in the Canadian trial has not been seen in other trials. It now appears that this failure to find a female responsiveness is related to the fact that women who suffer TIA and minor stroke have a relatively more benign outlook than do men. There were insufficient numbers of women in the Canadian trial to overcome the fact that this subgroup was at low risk. It would have required more female patients to have sufficient power in the trial to prove benefit.

The optimal dose of aspirin in stroke prevention remains uncertain.[29] Low dose (as little as 81 mg per day) has been administered successfully to patients with unstable angina and after myocardial infarction. An equal benefit has been found with the low dose as with higher dosage. The low dose has gone into popular use for the prevention of both heart attack and stroke. The popularity is understandable. Studies identified that the production of prostacyclin by the endothelial cells caused inhibition of platelet aggregation. This suggested that a large dose given to interfere with platelet aggregation through the thromboxane pathway might, in fact, not be as effective in preventing thrombosis and conceivably could lead to increased thrombosis. Close analysis, however, discloses that there has never been an increase in outcome events experienced in any group of vascular patients who are on a higher rather than a lower dose. The laboratory-generated hypothesis that less aspirin was better than more aspirin did not stand up to clinical observation. It was recognized that the gastrointestinal complications of higher dose are greater than with lower dose. However, when the reported complications are reviewed, those that can be described as major complications (requiring hospitalization or transfusion or causing death) are not dose-related.* A second hypothesis favoring low-dose aspirin has not been substantiated.

The question remains unanswered as to what is truly the optimal dose for stroke prevention

---

*Matchar D, personal communication, 1993.

in the stroke-threatened patient. Table 11–1 indicates that when low dose has been used, there has been a benefit, but never at the same level as the higher dose. The best answer will be found with a large multicenter trial when low dose (e.g., 81–325 mg) is compared directly with high dose (e.g., 625–1,300 mg). Until this is done, the authors' recommendation is that 650 to 950 mg be considered a reasonable daily dose schedule and that the enteric variety be used to assure tolerance.

Ticlopidine, a new platelet inhibitor that acts on the platelet by a route other than through the cyclooxygenase pathway, has emerged as an effective drug in preventing stroke and in reducing stroke recurrence. Claims for its moderate superiority to aspirin in stroke prevention rest upon one study. Although well designed and optimally conducted, the study suffers from being a single trial without corroboration.[30] The effectiveness of ticlopidine against placebo was established in a population of patients with completed stroke.[31] A significantly fewer number had recurrent stroke in the active treatment arm than in those taking placebo.

The claim has been made that for women and for those who have had a completed stroke, this could be the treatment of choice. The single trial of moderate size that detected no benefit for women, the Canadian Cooperative Study, appears now to have dealt with too few women

(200 in all). Women are at lower risk compared with men after TIA and minor stroke. There was not sufficient power in this trial to find benefit. Meta-analyses find no gender differences in platelet inhibition by platelet inhibiting drugs, including aspirin. It is notable too, that the Parisian, the Canadian, and the European aspirin trials involved patients with TIA and minor and even moderate stroke. It is unreasonable to claim that ticlopidine has a unique ability to reduce thrombosis-induced stroke further in patients whose presenting symptoms include stroke.

Ticlopidine, like aspirin, is not without some serious side effects. In this regard, it probably presents more of a concern than the universally used aspirin. Reversible bone marrow suppression (in 1%) and chronic diarrhea (in a range from 6–12% of users) add to the burden of its administration.

Many subgroup analyses have been published regarding the value of ticlopidine. To these writers, it is an excellent second choice to be used (250 mg bid) when patients cannot tolerate aspirin or continue to have disturbing ischemic events despite aspirin.

## Surgery for Asymptomatic Carotid Disease

Asymptomatic carotid disease due to arteriosclerosis principally centered in the region of

**Table 11–1. Major Prospective Studies of TIA and Minor Stroke With an ASA Effect**

| Study and Combined Outcome Events | Specific Outcome Events | mg/day | ASA Events | n | % | NO ASA Events | n | % | Risk Reduction* (%) |
|---|---|---|---|---|---|---|---|---|---|
| **Stroke and death** | | | | | | | | | |
| UK-TIA[50,51] | (DsS, VD) | 300 & 1,200 | 215 | 1,621 | 13 | 111 | 814 | 14 | 3 |
| UK-TIA[50,51] | (MS, SD) | 300 & 1,200 | 167 | 1,621 | 10 | 95 | 814 | 12 | 12 |
| SALT[52] | (S, D) | 75 | | 676 | 20 | 171 | 684 | 25 | 18 |
| Parisian[53] | (S, SD) | 1,000 | 35 | 400 | 9 | 31 | 204 | 15 | 42 |
| European[54] | (S, D) | 975** | 190 | 1,250 | 15 | 283 | 1,250 | 23 | 33 |
| Canadian[27] | (S, D) | 1,300 | 46 | 290 | 16 | 68 | 295 | 23 | 31 |
| US Medical[55] | (S, D) | 1,300 | 13 | 88 | 15 | 19 | 90 | 21 | 30 |
| **Stroke, myocardial infarction, and vascular death** | | | | | | | | | |
| SALT[52] | (S, MI, VD) | 75 | 151 | 676 | 22 | 184 | 684 | 27 | 17 |
| UK-TIA[50,51] | (S, MI, VD) | 300 & 1,200 | 354 | 1,621 | 22 | 204 | 814 | 25 | 13 |
| Parisian[53] | (S, MI, VD) | 1,000 | 55 | 400 | 14 | 47 | 204 | 23 | 40 |

TIA = transient ischemic attack; ASA = acetylsalicylic acid; Ds = disabling; S = stroke; V = vascular; D = death; M = major; MI = myocardial infarction.

*1 (observed/expected events on ASA)/(observed/expected events on NO ASA).

**Plus 225 mg dipyridamole.

The major trials that tested various doses of aspirin against placebo are listed according to the outcome events that were sought. The percentage risk reduction for each combination of outcome events is indicated in the right-hand column. The dotted line differentiates between the trials that utilized lower dose (above the dotted line) or were of low risk patients plus a low-dose cadre of patients (the UK-TIA trial). In all instances the low-dose and low-risk patients did less well than those on higher doses. (Modified and reproduced with permission from Dyken ML, Barnett HJM, Easton JD, et al: Low-dose aspirin and stroke: ``It ain't necessarily so.'' Stroke 23:1395–1399, 1992.)

the carotid sinus is a common phenomenon and increases with age. Longterm studies of hundreds of individuals with this condition have been carried out, particularly by Norris and Hennerici.[32III, 33] These prospective observational studies have determined that until the degree of stenosis reaches 75 to 80%, the annual risk of stroke is approximately 1%. When the stenosis increases beyond these levels, the annual stroke rate for ipsilateral ischemic events is in the neighborhood of 2.5%. Of equal importance is the observation that individuals with severe stenosis have a serious predilection to fatal myocardial infarction with three times the likelihood of experiencing this event than of having an ischemic stroke.

Scores of the thousands of individuals with asymptomatic carotid disease have been subjected to endarterectomy. These have included individuals who have had symptomatic disease on one side and have an asymptomatic lesion on the opposite side or patients who have never had symptoms on either side. Often the procedure has been carried out in patients who are to receive another surgical procedure such as coronary artery bypass grafting. There is no published evidence as yet that these procedures have conferred benefit upon the patients.

Three randomized clinical trials have been published. The first of these, the Carotid Artery Stenosis with Asymptomatic Narrowing; Operation Versus Aspirin (CASANOVA) Trial involved 410 patients.[34II] The protocol excluded from the study all patients who had 90% stenosis or greater. This was unfortunate because this group is the one most likely to benefit. It allowed surgery to be carried out in patients randomized to medical therapy if they had bilateral disease or if the disease progressed during the period of the study to reach 90% or greater. Thus, more than half of the patients assigned to the medical group were also subjected to surgery. In addition to this flaw in design, the study had a sufficiently high perioperative rate (6.9%) that the medical patients fared somewhat better than did those who had endarterectomy.

The second trial, at the Mayo Clinic, was designed so that aspirin was not given to the surgical patients.[35I] After randomizing only 71 patients, eight instances of myocardial infarction and three instances of ischemic cerebral infarction occurred in the surgical group and none occurred in the medical group during the same period. The study was stopped by the Safety and Monitoring Committee.

The most recent trial, the Veterans Affairs Trial, randomly assigned 444 patients with asymptomatic disease to receive either best medical care or best medical care plus endarterectomy.[36I] They reported that, including transient ischemic attack as an outcome event, there was a benefit from the surgical procedure. When the more important outcome events of stroke and death were counted, there was no difference between the medical and surgical groups. In the 30 days postoperatively, there were five strokes and four deaths in 203 patients. In four years, the stroke and death rate in the medical group was 44% and the surgical group was 41%. Again, there was no difference in the longterm outlook for these patients.

Two large trials continue to randomize and study this question. The Asymptomatic Carotid Atherosclerosis Study and a trial recently launched in Europe under the direction of Dafydd Thomas* will together examine the benefit among approximately 5,000 patients randomized to receive best medical care or best medical care plus endarterectomy.[37] Until these trials are complete, there is no compelling evidence that carotid endarterectomy benefits any group of patients with asymptomatic carotid artery disease.

## Surgery for Symptomatic Carotid Disease

### Extracranial Carotid Endarterectomy

Surgery on the accessible internal carotid artery for patients with transient ischemic attacks and minor strokes appropriate to this arteriosclerotic lesion was introduced in 1954. Between then and 1985, it has been estimated that approximately 1 million patients had extracranial carotid endarterectomy, and the evidence suggests that about two-thirds were symptomatic.[38] Two randomized trials were attempted in the 1960s.[39I, 40II] A forbidding perioperative complication rate prevented either of them from detecting benefit in approximately 400 patients randomized between the two trials.

The North American Symptomatic Carotid Endarterectomy Trial (NASCET) and the European Carotid Surgical Trial (ECST) both concluded in February 1991 that patients with severe stenosis significantly benefitted by carotid endarterectomy.[41I, 42I] The benefit as reported by the NASCET investigators may be indicated most readily by the following quotation from the paper reporting the results.[41]

Life-table estimates of the cumulative risk of any ipsilateral stroke at two years were 26% in the 331

*Personal communication, 1993.

medical patients and 9 percent in the 328 surgical patients—an absolute risk reduction ($\pm$SD) of 17 $\pm$ 3.5 percent ($p<0.001$). For a major or fatal ipsilateral stroke, the corresponding estimates were 13.1 percent and 2.5 percent—an absolute risk reduction of 10.6 $\pm$ 2.6 percent ($p<.001$). Carotid endarterectomy was still found to be beneficial when all strokes and deaths were included in the analysis ($p<.001$).

The investigators in ECST declared a reduced level of benefit. Instead of a 17% difference between the medical and surgical results for any ipsilateral stroke at 2 years, as shown by NASCET, the benefit was only 14% in 3 years. They reported a reduced risk in the medical patients and a slightly higher perioperative risk. The essential difference between the two studies proved to be the method of measurement of the degree of stenosis. The NASCET method employs the narrowest linear diameter of the stenosis in the minimum of two planes from the arteriogram as the numerator and the diameter of the internal carotid artery beyond the bulb and beyond the disease as the denominator (Fig. 11–1). The European trial utilized a larger denominator when it employed the probable original diameter of the carotid sinus in the equation for identifying the percentage of stenosis. When the arteriograms were remeasured with the NASCET method, it was apparent that 46% of the "severe" patients would have been in the moderate group in the NASCET study. Thus, what investigators in NASCET described and reported as 70% was the equivalent of what the investigators in ECST reported, by NASCET method of measurement, at 82%. Reanalyzing the survival curves from the ECST, including only those who fell within the NASCET description of "severe," identifies the fact that there was very little difference between the benefits of the two studies (Fig. 11–2). Both were convincingly significant and have established that the patients with this severity of stenosis should be submitted to carotid endarterectomy, provided they have appropriate symptoms.

The other provision that is essential to the generalization of the results of these two trials is that the carotid surgery must be carried out with less than a 10% perioperative complication rate of stroke and death. The complication rate for any events lasting more than 24 hours in the NASCET study was 5.8%. When this was calculated to include only those who had persisting disabling stroke or who had died, the perioperative morbidity and mortality rate was 2.1%.

There is no evidence available yet to indicate that patients with less than 70% stenosis by the

**Measurement of % Stenosis of Internal Carotid Artery**

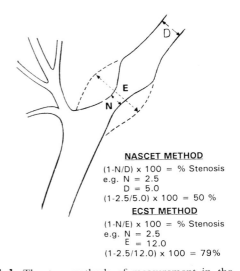

**NASCET METHOD**
(1-N/D) x 100 = % Stenosis
e.g. N = 2.5
D = 5.0
(1-2.5/5.0) x 100 = 50 %

**ECST METHOD**
(1-N/E) x 100 = % Stenosis
e.g. N = 2.5
E = 12.0
(1-2.5/12.0) x 100 = 79%

**Figure 11–1.** The two methods of measurement in the NASCET and ECST studies are portrayed. The ECST method allows more patients to be described as afflicted with "severe" stenosis than does the NASCET method. This variability accounts for the better outlook for medical patients in the severe category in ECST compared with NASCET and for the lesser benefit for patients with severe stenosis in ECST than in NASCET. (Used with permission from Barnett HJM: Stroke prevention by surgery for symptomatic disease in carotid territory. In Barnett HJM, Hachinski VC (eds): Neurologic Clinics. Philadelphia: W. B. Saunders, 1992, pp 281–292.)

NASCET method of measurement benefit from carotid endarterectomy. The benefit obtained from carotid endarterectomy was proportional to the degree of stenosis. Patients with 90 to 99% stenosis had an impressive 26% absolute difference between the medical outlook for ipsilateral stroke at 2 years compared with the surgical outlook. This absolute risk reduction declined in the patients between 80 to 89% to 17% and to 12% for the patients in the 70 to 79% range of stenosis. Because no figures are available for benefit below 70%, both the NASCET and the ECST trials continue to randomize patients to determine at what level of stenosis the benefit will continue to be identifiable.

The study of patients in NASCET and ECST with symptoms due to moderate stenosis may not identify an absolute cutoff point based only on the degree of stenosis. It might prove that patients with a high risk profile will be identified. This profile may have to be coupled with the degree of stenosis in making a decision as to who will benefit. During the period of NASCET when severely ill patients were being evaluated, a 16-risk profile was compiled and the patients in the medical group were separated into those who had five or fewer of the individual risks, those who had six of them, and those who had more than six. The risk criteria that were used in this profile were age (over 70 years), sex (male), systolic blood pressure (higher than 160 mm Hg), diastolic blood pressure (higher than 90 mm Hg), recency (less than 31 days) and type of prior cerebrovascular events (stroke, not transient ischemic attack). In addition, degree of stenosis (more than 80%); presence of ulceration on the angiogram; and a history of smoking, current smoking, hypertension, myocardial infarction, congestive heart failure, diabetes, intermittent claudication, or high blood lipid lev-

els were criteria. The likelihood of stroke or death at 2 years was 17% in those with the fewest number of risks, 23% in those with the median number (six), and 39% in those who had seven or more of these risk factors present.

Other prognostic variables have been studied since NASCET was completed for the severely ill patients. It has been found that when ulceration can be detected in the arteriogram, there is an increased likelihood in the medical patients of ipsilateral stroke occurring compared with those who do not have an identifiable ulcer in the arteriogram.[43] Furthermore, this risk rises sharply as the degree of stenosis increases from the eighth to the tenth decile (Fig. 11–3). Patients with retinal ischemic events only as a consequence of severe carotid stenosis had diminished risk (17% stroke and stroke death at 2 years) compared with those who had experienced hemisphere events (42% risk at 2 years).

Patients with transient ischemic attacks, and even asymptomatic patients with carotid artery lesions, have been found to have an increased number of lesions suggestive of brain infarction visualized in the CT examinations when compared with patients who do not have arterial disease or transient ischemic attacks. At first glance, it appeared that there was an increased risk imposed by the occurrence of these silent brain infarcts among the patients with severe disease in NASCET compared with those in whom the infarcts were not present. When regression analyses were carried out, looking at potential confounding variables, it was determined that, by itself, silent brain infarction in this group of patients did not confer an increased risk. The increased risk that was initially observed related predominantly to the fact that they were patients who had hemisphere rather than retinal events and who had ulcerative rather than nonulcerative carotid artery lesions.*

The presence of thrombus within the lumen of the artery beyond the stenosis was found to be a serious prognostic phenomenon. Twenty-five such patients were identified in the group of severely ill NASCET patients. The 30-day outlook for ipsilateral stroke in this small group was 25% in the medical group and still stood at 22% in the surgical group. This importance of intraluminal thrombus has been recognized in other publications.[44, 45] It appears probable, based on empirical and anecdotal evidence only, that such patients should be treated in a preliminary way for 30 days with anticoagulant

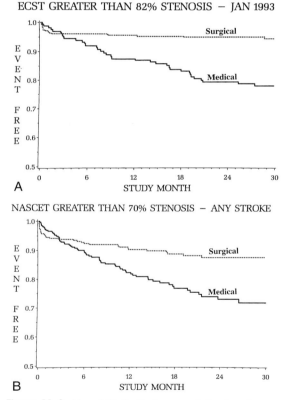

**Figure 11-2.** (A and B) Preliminary analysis of angiograms of patients randomized to no-surgery in ECST suggests that 82% stenosis measured using the ECST method is approximately equivalent to 70% stenosis measured using the NASCET method. ECST results have been reanalyzed for ECST patients with greater than 82% stenosis by the ECST method. The survival curves for ECST (A) and those previously published by NASCET (B) look remarkably similar. Stroke risk at 2 years in the medical groups ranges from 20 to 25%, and a ''crossover'' point in both studies occurs at about 3 months. (Used with permission from Barnett HJM and Warlow CP: Editorial: Carotid endarterectomy and the measurement of stenosis. Stroke 24:1281–1284, 1993.)

*NASCET unpublished data.

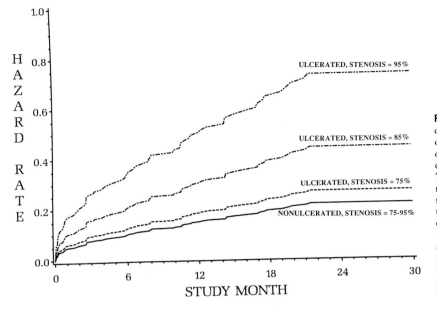

**Figure 11–3.** Cumulative hazard curves showing risk (hazard rate) of any ipsilateral stroke for medically treated patients with nonulcerated and ulcerated lesions with 75 to 95% stenosis. Patients with nonulcerated lesions are represented by only one curve, because the cumulative hazards are identical at all degrees of stenosis. (Used with permission from Eliasziw M, Streifler JY, Fox AJ, et al: Significance of plaque ulceration in symptomatic patients with high grade carotid stenosis. Stroke 25: 304–308, 1994.)

therapy prior to proceeding to surgical intervention.

## Extracranial-intracranial Bypass Surgery

The perfection of microvascular surgical anastomoses attracted neurosurgeons. Yasargil and Donaghy were able to obtain a good filling of the cortical branches of the middle cerebral artery from the superficial temporal artery.[46] Anecdotal case reports in small series began to appear in the literature with some claims of clinical improvement and reduction of the numbers of transient ischemic attacks, and some with purported improvement in neurologic deficit. These reports referred to patients whose carotid arteries were occluded or those in whom there was stenosis or occlusion of the intracranial carotid artery and its major branches. These reports were accompanied at times by improvement in regional cerebral blood flow. They lacked controls. A multicenter trial was launched in which the patients were randomized to receive best medical care or best medical care plus superficial temporal to middle cerebral artery anastomosis.[471] From 1979 to 1984, a total of 1,377 patients with carotid artery occlusion with or without continuing symptoms since the occlusion was detected, with intracranial carotid occlusion or stenosis or with stenosis or occlusion of the middle cerebral artery, were randomized to best medical care alone or best medical care plus bypass surgery. They were followed for an average of 5 years. At the end of the trial it was detected that patients on medical therapy survived stroke-free slightly more often than did the patients treated with the superficial temporal to middle cerebral artery anastomoses. This occurred despite the fact that the perioperative complication rate was very low at 2.5% and the patency rate was 97%.

The reason for the failure of this operation to demonstrate benefit for the total population randomized or for any of the subgroups is uncertain. However, it is very instructive to note that the patients whose anastomoses in the postoperative arteriograms were seen to produce the most luxuriant intracranial inflow, as judged by the number of well-filled middle cerebral artery branches, did less well than those whose anastomoses were poor. The best anastomoses would seem to have developed when the pressure in the intracranial middle cerebral branches was below that in the contributing superficial temporal artery. Conversely, the poorest anastomoses developed when the pressure differential was less marked, the middle cerebral branches were well filled to start with, and the stimulus to the passage of blood through the newly created channel was weaker. It appears reasonable to conclude that when nature has provided good anastomotic channels and the pressure in the intracranial arteries is good, the patients do well and the anastomosis does not flourish. When the development of poor collateral channels has occurred naturally, that which is provided by the bypass is inadequate even though the connections from the anastomosis itself look quite reasonable.

Perfusion and hemodynamic studies of a sophisticated nature were not performed either as a prelude or as a sequel to these operations. Many have suggested that there may be a subgroup of patients with hemodynamic compromise in whom the operation will be beneficial. A number of attempts to establish this benefit using positron emission tomography and single photon emission computed tomography have been conducted. In these anecdotal series, the hemodynamic disturbances have been reported to be correctable by the procedure. They are known to be correctable also with the passage of time. No series, small or large, has been reported using these technologies to establish evidence of efficacy for any subgroup. The bypass procedure has been virtually abandoned in North America. The United States Federal Government decreed in the Federal Register that federal money cannot be used for reimbursement related to this procedure in arteriosclerotic obliterative disease.[48]

Those who did not wish to accept the finality of the results continue to be concerned that in obliterative disease we may yet find an indication for the procedure. Certainly the condition of Moya Moya disease is worth studying in a strictly disciplined, randomized trial. It is also reasonable to consider the procedure as a prelude to the deliberate ligation of a major cerebral artery to allow the excision of an otherwise inoperable vascular tumor at the base of the brain or obliteration of a large and formidable aneurysm. A disorder dubbed "disabling transient ischemic attacks" has been described recently with the unacceptable claim that a group of patients appears to have been identified who will benefit from bypass surgery.[49V] The definition for "disabling" appears to be that the transient events continue despite medical therapy and interfere with the normal life of the patients. Nineteen such patients were described, of whom 17 received either anterior circulation or posterior circulation anastomoses. The total failure rate was 39% in this small series, including perioperative stroke in 22%, perioperative death in 5.5%, and continuation of attacks in some of the others. These chilling figures in an uncontrolled study confirm the negative conclusions of the Extracranial/Intracranial (EC/IC) Bypass Study and do not support any alteration in the conclusion that this procedure has failed to live up to claimed expectations.

Despite the spate of criticism from those disappointed with the loss of this elegant procedure to clinical practice, the Bypass Study confirmed that multicenter trials of surgical procedures can be conducted on a global scale.

The study was important also because it established negative benefit for a procedure that would have become commonplace and would have had a significant impact on the economics of stroke prevention. Because of its resounding negativity it has forced us to turn to other strategies and spend neither research nor health care money on an ineffective procedure.

## REFERENCES

1. Wolf PA, Belanger AJ, D'Agostino RB: Management of risk factors. In Barnett HJM, Hachinski VC (eds): Neurologic Clinics. Cerebral Ischemia: Treatment and Prevention, Vol 10. Philadelphia, W. B. Saunders, 1992, pp 177–191.
2. Gifford RW Jr.: Review of the long-term controlled trials of usefulness of therapy for systemic hypertension. Am J Cardiol 63:8B–16B, 1989.
III 3. Wolf PA, D'Agostino RB, Kannel WB, et al: Cigarette smoking as a risk factor for stroke. JAMA 259:1025–1029, 1988.
4. MacMahon S, Peto R, Cutler J, et al: Blood pressure, stroke, and coronary heart disease. Part 1, prolonged differences in blood pressure: Prospective observational studies corrected for the regression diluted bias. Lancet 335:765–774, 1990.
5. Collins R, Peto R, MacMahon S, et al: Blood pressure, stroke, and coronary heart disease. Part 2, short-term reductions in blood pressure: Overview of randomised drug trials in their epidemiological context. Lancet 335:827–838, 1990.
I 6. Steering Committee of the Physicians' Health Study Research Group: Final report on the aspirin component of the ongoing physicians' health study. N Engl J Med 321:129–135, 1989.
II 7. Peto R, Gray R, Collins R, et al: Randomised trial of prophylactic daily aspirin in British male doctors. Br Med J 296:313–316, 1988.
III 8. Wolf PA, Dawber TR, Thomas HE, et al: Epidemiologic assessment of chronic atrial fibrillation and risk of stroke: The Framingham Study. Neurology (Minneapolis) 28:973–977, 1978.
I 9. Petersen P, Boysen G, Godtfredsen J, et al: Placebo-controlled, randomised trial of warfarin and aspirin for prevention of thromboembolic complications in chronic atrial fibrillation: The Copenhagen AFASAK Study. Lancet 1:175–179, 1989.
10. Special Report: Preliminary report of the stroke prevention in atrial fibrillation study. N Engl J Med 322:863–868, 1990.
I 11. Stroke Prevention in Atrial Fibrillation Investigators: Stroke Prevention in Atrial Fibrillation Study: Final Results. Circulation 84:527–539, 1991.
I 12. The Boston Area Anticoagulation Trial for Atrial Fibrillation Investigators: The effect of low-dose warfarin on the risk of stroke in patients with nonrheumatic atrial fibrillation. N Engl J Med 323:1505–1511, 1990.
I 13. The Veterans Affairs Stroke Prevention in Nonrheumatic Atrial Fibrillation Investigators: Warfarin in the prevention of stroke associated with nonrheumatic atrial fibrillation. N Engl J Med 327:1406–1412, 1992.
II 14. Connolly SJ, Laupacis A, Gent M, et al: Canadian Atrial Fibrillation Anticoagulation (CAFA) Study. J Am Coll Cardiol 18:349–355, 1991.

III 15. Stroke Prevention in Atrial Fibrillation Investigators: Predictors of thromboembolism in atrial fibrillation: I. Clinical features of patients at risk. Ann Intern Med 116:1–5, 1992.

16. Moulton AW, Singer DE, Haas JS: Risk factors for stroke in patients with nonrheumatic atrial fibrillation: A case-control study. Am J Med 91:156–161, 1991.

17. Halperin JL, Hart RG: Atrial fibrillation and stroke: New ideas, persisting dilemmas. Stroke 19:937–941, 1988.

18. Warfarin Optimized Outpatient Follow-up Study Group: Risk factors for complications of chronic anticoagulation: A Multicenter Study. Ann Intern Med 118:511–520, 1993.

V 19. Gurwitz JH, Avorn J, Ross-Degnan D, et al: Aging and the anticoagulant response to warfarin therapy. Ann Intern Med 116:901–904, 1992.

II 20. Cerebral Embolism Study Group: Immediate anticoagulation of embolic stroke: A randomized trial. Stroke 14:668–676, 1983.

21. Cerebral Embolism Task Force: Cardiogenic Brain Embolism. Arch Neurol 43:71–84, 1986.

III 22. Weinreich DJ, Burke JF, Jo Pauletto F: Left ventricular mural thrombi complicating acute myocardial infarction: Long-term follow-up with serial echocardiography. Ann Intern Med 100:789–794, 1984.

V 23. Friedman MJ, Carlson K, Marcus FI, et al: Clinical correlations in patients with acute myocardial infarction and left ventricular thrombus detected by two-dimensional echocardiography. Am J Med 72:894–898, 1982.

24. Szekely P: Systemic embolism and anticoagulant prophylaxis in rheumatic heart disease. Br Med J 1:1209–1212, 1964.

25. Ameri A, Bousser MG: Cerebral venous thrombosis. Neurol Clin 10:87–111, 1992.

I 26. Einhaupl KM, Villringer A, Meister W, et al: Heparin treatment in sinus venous thrombosis. Lancet 338:597–600, 1991.

I 27. Canadian Cooperative Study Group: A randomized trial of aspirin and sulfinpyrazone in threatened stroke. N Engl J Med 299:53–59, 1978.

28. Barnett HJM: Aspirin in stroke prevention: An overview. Stroke 21 [Suppl IV]:40–43, 1990.

29. Dyken ML, Barnett HJM, Easton JD, et al: Low-dose aspirin and stroke: "It ain't necessarily so." Stroke 23:1395–1399, 1992.

I 30. Hass WK, Easton JD, Adams HP, et al: A randomized trial comparing ticlopidine hydrochloride with aspirin for the prevention of stroke in high-risk patients. N Engl J Med 321:501–507, 1989.

I 31. Gent M, Blakely JA, Easton JD, et al: The Canadian American Ticlopidine Study (CATS) in thromboembolic stroke. Lancet 1:1215–1220, 1989.

III 32. Norris JW, Zhu CZ, Bornstein NM, et al: Vascular risks of asymptomatic carotid stenosis. Stroke 22:1485–1490, 1991.

33. Hennerici M, Hulsbomer HB, Hefter H, et al: Natural history of asymptomatic extracranial arterial disease. Results of a long-term prospective study. Brain 110:777–791, 1987.

II 34. The CASANOVA Study Group: Carotid surgery versus medical therapy in asymptomatic carotid stenosis. Stroke 22:1229–1235, 1991.

I 35. Mayo Asymptomatic Carotid Endarterectomy Study Group: Results of a randomized controlled trial of carotid endarterectomy for asymptomatic carotid stenosis. Mayo Clin Proc 67:513–518, 1992.

I 36. Hobson RW II, Weiss DG, Fields WS, et al: Efficacy of carotid endarterectomy for asymptomatic carotid stenosis. N Engl J Med 328:221–227, 1993.

37. The Asymptomatic Carotid Atherosclerosis Study Group: Study design for randomized prospective trial of carotid endarterectomy for asymptomatic atherosclerosis. Stroke 20:844–849, 1989.

38. Dyken ML: Carotid endarterectomy studies: A glimmering of science. Stroke 17:355–358, 1986.

I 39. Fields WS, Maslenikov V, Meyer JS, et al: Joint study of extracranial arterial occlusion. V. Progress report of prognosis following surgery or nonsurgical treatment for transient cerebral ischemic attacks and cervical carotid artery lesions. JAMA 211:1993–2003, 1970.

II 40. Shaw DA, Venables GS, Cartlidge NEF, et al: Carotid endarterectomy in patients with transient cerebral ischemia. J Neurol Sci 64:45–53, 1984.

I 41. North American Symptomatic Carotid Endarterectomy Trial Collaborators: Beneficial effect of carotid endarterectomy in symptomatic patients with high-grade carotid stenosis. N Engl J Med 325:445–453, 1991.

I 42. European Carotid Surgery Trialists' Collaborative Group. MRC European Carotid Surgery Trial: Interim results for symptomatic patients with severe (70–99%) or with mild (0–29%) carotid stenosis. Lancet 337:1235–1243, 1991.

43. Eliasziw M, Streifler JY, Fox AJ, et al: Significance of plaque ulceration in symptomatic patients with high grade carotid stenosis. 25:304–308, 1994.

44. Buchan A, Gates P, Pelz D, et al: Intraluminal thrombus in the cerebral circulation. Stroke 19:681–687, 1988.

45. McCrory DC, Goldstein LB, Samsa GP, et al: Predicting complications of carotid endarterectomy. Stroke 24:1285–1291, 1993.

46. Donaghy RMP, Yasargil MG (eds): Microvascular Surgery. Report of First Conference, October 6–7, 1966. St. Louis, CV Mosby, 1967.

I 47. The EC/IC Bypass Study Group: Failure of extracranial-intracranial arterial bypass to reduce the risk of ischemic stroke: Results of an international randomized trial. N Engl J Med 313:1191–1200, 1985.

48. Health Care Financing Administration: Medicare program: Withdrawal of coverage of extracranial-intracranial arterial bypass surgery for the treatment of prevention of stroke. Federal Register 55:13321–13324, 1990.

V 49. McCormick PW, Tomecek FJ, McKinney J, et al: Disabling cerebral transient ischemic attacks. J Neurosurg 75:891–901, 1991.

I 50. UK-TIA Study Group: United Kingdom Transient Ischaemic Attack (UK-TIA) Aspirin Trial: Interim results. Br Med J 296:316–320, 1988.

I 51. UK-TIA Study Group: United Kingdom Transient Ischaemic Attack (UK-TIA) Aspirin Trial: Final results. J Neurosurg Psychiatry 54:1044–1054, 1991.

I 52. The SALT Collaborative Group: Swedish aspirin low-dose trial (SALT) of 75 mg aspirin as secondary prophylaxis after cerebrovascular ischaemic events. Lancet 338:1345–1349, 1991.

I 53. Bousser MG, Eschwege E, Haguenau M, et al: "A.I.C.L.A." controlled trial of aspirin and dipyridamole in the secondary prevention of atherothrombotic cerebral ischemia. Stroke 14:4–14, 1983.

I 54. European Stroke Prevention Study Group: ESPS: Principal end points. Lancet 2:1351–1354, 1987.

I 55. Fields WS, Lemak NA, Frankowski RF: Controlled trial of aspirin in cerebral ischemia: Part II. Surgical group. Stroke 9:309–318, 1978.

# PART THREE

# PERIPHERAL VASCULAR DISEASE

## Chapter 12

# Acute Arterial Obstruction

Kenneth Ouriel and Victor J. Marder

Acute arterial obstruction accounts for a significant loss of life and limb. The disease is traditionally subcategorized into acute and chronic varieties, differentiated from one another on the basis of the time course of the associated signs and symptoms. Acute arterial occlusion is said to occur when the patient experiences sudden onset of a change in the clinical status of an extremity so that the precise onset of clinical deterioration can be identified; chronic occlusions are associated with a more insidious mode of onset. The clinical deterioration in patients with acute peripheral arterial occlusion may represent a change from a baseline asymptomatic state to claudication, baseline claudication to pain at rest, or any other change in the status of limb viability. The exact nature of the change may provide the clinician with a clue as to the etiology of the occlusion, either embolic or thrombotic. Embolic events are most often associated with rapid progression from an asymptomatic state to nonviability as a result of the absence of well-developed collateral channels at the time of the occlusion. In contrast, thrombotic processes usually occur in the setting of a pre-existing stenotic lesion and therefore tend to be associated with antecedent symptoms. The presence of plentiful collateral arterial channels may provide a margin of safety when an arterial segment undergoes sudden thrombosis, preventing the development of severe ischemia.

The management of acute limb ischemia is complex, principally as a result of the multisystem nature of the disorder. In cases of chronic arterial occlusion, outcome is principally dependent on the restoration of arterial supply.[1, 2I] In contrast, in cases of acute arterial occlusion effective arterial revascularization is not the only parameter with which to gauge success[3V]; the duration of ischemia may have rendered the limb useless on the basis of extensive nerve and muscle damage. Coexistent medical illnesses such as myocardial dysfunction and malignancy are common in these patients and must be addressed from both a physiologic and psychosocial perspective. Furthermore, release of the by-products of tissue ischemia into the systemic circulation, the so-called reperfusion syndrome, may be associated with myoglobinuric renal failure and a wide variety of other life-threatening metabolic and electrolyte derangements.[4III] Thus, limb salvage and patient demise are all too frequently encountered in the treatment of the acutely ischemic extremity. This scenario illustrates the importance of a multisystem approach to the treatment of patients with acute limb ischemia, rather than isolating care solely to the target extremity. In addition, studies of patients with acute limb ischemia are meaningless unless the endpoints include patient outcome measures such as survival and not merely the status of the involved limb.

## ETIOLOGY

Obstruction of a major arterial channel is the final common pathway in acute limb ischemia; all etiologic mechanisms terminate in this one physiologic event. The most meaningful classification of the causes of acute arterial occlusion divides the entity into three subgroups—thrombosis, embolization, and traumatic injury. These subgroups are not mutually exclusive; embolization and traumatic injury are associated with thrombosis in the form of prograde and retrograde propagation of clot, and primary thrombosis may be accompanied by distal embolization of thrombotic debris both before and during therapeutic intervention. Nevertheless, assigning the patient to one of these three categories is useful in the design of therapeutic strategies and in determining the prognosis of the problem. For the purposes of this chapter, traumatic arterial injury will not be considered further.

Thrombosis is the most frequent etiology of acute limb ischemia in an institution with an active vascular surgical team (Table 12–1). In reported series of patients presenting with an acutely ischemic extremity, thromboses of native arteries or bypass conduits were present in 80 to 90% of instances,[5, 61] with embolism accounting for fewer than one in five cases. Thrombosis of a bypass graft is slightly more frequently encountered than native arterial thrombosis by a ratio of three to two. In general, a stenotic lesion is almost always present when a native artery or autogenous conduit occludes, whereas thrombosis of prosthetic conduits is frequently observed in the absence of such a lesion.[7] It is important to note that hypercoagulability is a frequent accompaniment of acute thrombosis, whether the process involves a prosthetic bypass conduit, an autogenous graft, or

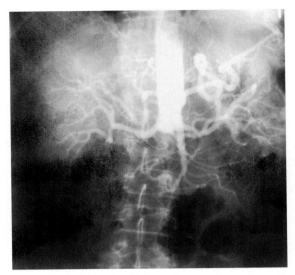

**Figure 12–1.** A transbrachial arteriogram of a patient with known aortoiliac occlusive disease who acutely progressed to juxtarenal aortic occlusion when a distal aortic stenosis advanced to occlusion.

the patient's own arterial vessel.[8, 9] It is likely that the prevalence of an underlying hypercoagulable state is much higher in the subset of patients who experience occlusion without an underlying anatomic lesion.

Native arterial thrombosis uncommonly results in acute ischemic symptoms. Most affected patients present with more chronic complaints because the slow progression of the underlying atherosclerotic stenosis provides time for the development of collateral channels around the process. Nevertheless, precipitous occlusion of a previously hemodynamically insignificant arterial stenosis may occasionally produce an abrupt worsening in symptomatology and an acutely threatened extremity (Fig. 12–1).

The expanded use of peripheral arterial bypass procedures has been associated with a corresponding increase in the number of patients presenting with acute limb ischemia on the basis of a thrombosed graft. The durability of bypass conduits is dependent on two important parameters—the conduit material and the site of the outflow anastomosis.[2] Infrainguinal prosthetic conduits such as those composed of expanded polytetrafluoroethylene or Dacron are associated with a lower patency rate than saphenous vein conduits, especially when the distal anastomosis is at the infragenicular popliteal or tibial level. Thus, it is not surprising that the number of patients presenting with occlusion of a prosthetic graft far exceeds the number presenting with occluded vein grafts, even in institutions where venous conduits are

Table 12–1. **Etiology of Acute Limb Ischemia**

| Diagnosis | Frequency (%) |
|---|---|
| Embolic occlusion | 21 |
| Thrombotic occlusion | 79 |
|   Native artery | 24 |
|     Atherosclerotic lesion | 16 |
|     Popliteal aneurysm thrombosis | 6 |
|     Antiphospholipid syndrome | 2 |
|   Bypass graft | 55 |
|     Aortofemoral | 9 |
|     Infrainguinal | 43 |
|     Axillofemoral | 4 |

placed in the majority of primary bypass procedures.[7] Differences exist in the etiology of graft occlusion in autogenous and nonautogenous conduits. Prosthetic grafts tend to fail without a demonstrable anatomic lesion significantly more often than do autogenous grafts (Table 12–2). This observation suggests that a large proportion of prosthetic grafts occlude as a result of transient perturbations in the dynamic interactions between the blood elements and the prosthetic surface. By contrast, autogenous grafts rarely occlude without an underlying lesion. The nonthrombogenic blood flow surface resists the deposition of platelet-fibrin thrombus, often despite markedly reduced graft flow as encountered with compromised inflow or outflow beds. Thus, thrombosis of venous bypass grafts is typically associated with critical stenoses, most often in the body of the graft or at one of the anastomoses.

Several unusual hypercoagulable states have been implicated in acute arterial occlusion.[9] The antiphospholipid syndrome is perhaps the most common of these entities, wherein the patient develops anticardiolipin antibodies and manifests a classic triad of venous and arterial thrombosis, habitual abortion, and a false positive serum test for syphilis.[10III] Disorders of plasminogen and fibrinogen and deficiencies of protein C and S are associated with vascular thromboses, as are the hypercoagulable states of malignancy or following operation.[11] The arterial defect underlying thrombosis may be so trivial in these instances that identification is never made, with microscopic changes limited to the endothelial layer.

Arterial emboli most often originate in the heart.[5] It has been estimated that 90% of peripheral emboli are of cardiac origin, although surface echocardiography is usually unable to detect mural thrombi.[12] A history of atrial fibrillation, recent myocardial infarction, or cardiac valvular disease is usually present in these patients. The proximal arterial tree represents a second source of arterial emboli. These "arterio-arterial" emboli are being recognized with increasing frequency, especially in the case of

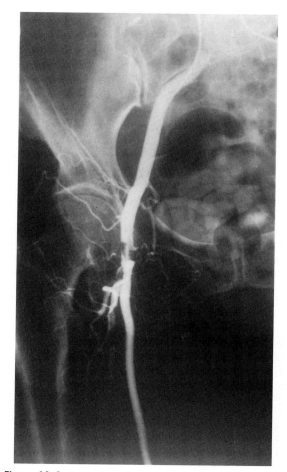

**Figure 12–2.** An arteriogram performed through a left femoral approach in a patient with an embolus to the common femoral artery. Note the additional thromboembolus in the profunda femoris vessel.

small embolic phenomena to the digital arteries as observed in the "blue-toe syndrome." Large emboli uniformly lodge at arterial bifurcations. The common femoral bifurcation is the most frequent site in the lower extremity, with embolic material obstructing the superficial and profunda femoral outflow (Fig. 12–2).[5, 13IV] Patients manifest easily palpable femoral pulses, which are occasionally "waterhammer" in na-

Table 12–2. **Etiologic Lesions in Occlusion of Autogenous and Nonautogenous Bypass Grafts**

| Conduit | Inflow Disease (%) | Outflow Disease (%) | Proximal Anastomosis (%) | Distal Anastomosis (%) | Body of Graft (%) | No Lesion (%) |
|---|---|---|---|---|---|---|
| Autogenous (N = 30) | 7 | 17 | 23 | 7 | 37 | 10 |
| Nonautogenous (N = 79) | 4 | 9 | 9 | 18 | 1 | 59 |

ture as a result of the obstructed, high resistance outflow. The femoral pulse disappears later, with retrograde thrombosis of the external iliac artery. Whereas a pulseless, rubbery femoral artery may be palpable in patients with an embolus, the patient with thrombosis of a chronically diseased vessel may manifest a rigidly calcific common femoral artery at the groin level. This finding may serve as a differentiating feature of an embolic versus thrombotic process.

The popliteal trifurcation represents the next most common location of lower extremity emboli, but their frequency is an order of magnitude behind that of femoral emboli.[12] Patients with popliteal emboli usually have palpable femoral and popliteal pulses, with absent pulses at the ankle. Upper extremity emboli usually lodge at the terminus of the brachial artery, at its bifurcation into the radial and ulnar vessels. The proximal brachial artery narrows at the origin of the profunda brachial artery, and this site represents the second most frequent location of upper extremity emboli. The brachial pulse is palpable at the antecubital fossa when the embolus lodges at the brachial bifurcation; radial and ulnar pulses are absent. In contrast, only a high axillary pulse is palpable when the embolus lodges at the origin of the profunda brachial artery.

## DIAGNOSIS

The diagnosis of acute limb ischemia is readily made with a thorough patient history and an examination of the affected extremity. Patients classically present with a variety of signs and symptoms that all begin with the letter p; pulselessness, pallor, pain, paresthesia, poikilothermia (coolness of the extremity), and paralysis. All patients present with pulselessness and most complain of pain; however, only a minority progress to total paralysis (Table 12–3).[61] Salvage of the extremity is dependent on the severity of the ischemia. As expected, a successful result is less likely in patients with complete motor and sensory loss, and salvage is so improbable in patients with true muscle rigor that aggressive attempts at revascularization are unwarranted.

The diagnosis of thrombosis or embolus is not always possible and sometimes is irrelevant, but several caveats may be stated. Thrombosis is most likely in the presence of known peripheral vascular disease and especially when a bypass graft has been placed. A history of claudication may precede acute thrombosis in patients with

Table 12–3. **Frequency of Presenting Signs and Symptoms in Acute Peripheral Arterial Occlusion**[22]

| Signs/Symptoms | Frequency (%) |
|---|---|
| Pulselessness | 100 |
| Pain | 92 |
| Pallor | 80 |
| Poikilothermic | 80 |
| Paresthesia | 52 |
| Paralysis | 30 |

Data from Ouriel K, Shortell CK, DeWeese JA, et al; J Vasc Surg 19:1021–1030, 1994.

native arterial occlusion. In contrast, normal contralateral pulses predict an embolic process, especially when patients have a history of cardiac arrhythmias or recent myocardial infarction.

Doppler segmental pressure measurements may pinpoint the involved arterial segments, and a gradient of 30 mm Hg between adjacent segments is indicative of occlusion.[14] Doppler signals are frequently inaudible at the ankle level, and examination at the popliteal level is occasionally necessary to obtain above-knee pressure measurements. Duplex ultrasound examination of the peripheral vessels is not usually necessary in the diagnosis of acute arterial occlusion, but when performed it may document the presence of thrombus within a bypass graft or native artery.

Arteriography remains the mainstay of diagnosis, accurately localizing the process and often characterizing its etiology. The site of puncture attains great importance in the arteriographic evaluation of an acutely ischemic extremity, principally because of a possible need for subsequent thrombolytic therapy. Generally, a contralateral approach is most appropriate for catheter insertion, keeping the arterial puncture far from the site of lytic infusion. Attempts at antegrade catheter insertion should be reserved for patients with occlusive processes well beyond the site of cannulation, because failure to gain arterial access may result in hemorrhage through the puncture sites when lytic infusion is begun in proximity to the defects.

## THERAPY

Amputation remained the sole treatment modality for ischemia of the extremity until the 1940s. Dos Santos is credited with pioneering lower extremity revascularization, employing femoral endarterectomy to restore arterial perfusion in chronic superficial femoral artery occlusion.[15] Saphenous vein bypass attained popularity in the 1950s and 1960s,[16] and operative technique improved over the following two decades to the point where bypass to the tibial and pedal arteries became feasible.[17V] Intra-arterial infusion of thrombolytic agents in cases of acute arterial occlusion was first reported by Cliffton in 1957, using a mixture of plasminogen, streptokinase, and streptodornase.[4]

Great controversy exists over the issue of whether operation or thrombolysis is most appropriate as the initial therapeutic intervention in patients with acute limb ischemia.[19] The champions of operative therapy have been stimulated by the excellent limb salvage results achieved with immediate surgical revascularization, with the vast majority of extremities salvaged by this approach. However, costs are associated with immediate operative intervention, the most striking of which is patient survival. Patients with acute limb ischemia are often in a most fragile medical state. Concurrent morbidities, including myocardial compromise, advanced malignancy, and metabolic derangements, are added to the problems originating in the ischemic extremity itself, producing a patient group least likely to tolerate aggressive interventions.

Blaisdell was the first to proclaim the high morbidity associated with early operation in peripheral arterial embolization, documenting a mortality rate exceeding 25% in an analysis of 35 surgical series published between 1964 and 1977.[4III] This finding led Blaisdell and coworkers to advocate a protocol of immediate high-dose heparinization, reserving operation for a time when the patient had been further stabilized and evaluated. Jivegard corroborated Blaisdell's observations in a later review of 201 patients with acute native arterial occlusions, documenting an early mortality rate of over 20%.[20V] Yeager more recently reported an experience with surgical management in 74 patients presenting with severe acute lower extremity ischemia.[3V] Although limb salvage was initially achieved in 70% of the cases, 15% of patients expired within 30 days of operation and over one-third of the patients were dead at 12 months. Only one conclusion can be drawn from these studies of operation in acute limb ischemia; immediate surgical revascularization is associated with a most satisfactory rate of limb salvage, but this result is achieved at the cost of patient mortality.

Nevertheless, operation is the treatment modality that provides the most rapid restoration of arterial flow in patients with acute peripheral arterial occlusion. Operative intervention may or may not be preceded by arteriography, but in many cases preoperative arteriography will provide information as to the exact etiology and location of the occlusive process. Two major subcategories of operative procedures exist—simple thromboembolectomy and arterial reconstruction. Thromboembolectomy is defined as the removal of an embolus and its propagated thrombus from the arterial tree. Prior to the early 1960s, this was accomplished through the performance of a multiplicity of arteriotomies, irrigating and directly excising the thrombotic material.[13V]

The introduction of the Fogarty balloon catheter in 1963 offered a mechanism to efficiently remove thrombi through a single strategically placed arteriotomy.[21] The catheter is inserted through the arteriotomy and threaded proximally or distally beyond all thrombus. The balloon is then inflated and the catheter is withdrawn, removing the thrombus and extruding it through the arteriotomy. The procedure is repeated until no residual thrombus is returned. Care must be taken not to overinflate the balloon, or damage to the arterial wall will result. Some degree of de-endothelialization is inherent in this procedure, possibly leading to an appreciable incidence of postoperative rethrombosis. Balloon catheter thromboembolectomy is appropriate as the sole therapy in cases of arterial emboli or in situ thrombosis without an underlying anatomic defect. Early rethrombosis may follow the procedure, however, when the diagnosis of an arterial stenosis has been missed.

## Arterial Reconstruction

Arterial reconstructive procedures play an important role in the restoration of limb viability when an arterial defect is present. The procedures include operative bypass, endarterectomy, and balloon or patch angioplasty. Each of these procedures may be combined with balloon catheter thrombectomy to remove proximal or distal thrombus. Bypass procedures are most frequently employed in cases of acute native arterial occlusion; endarterectomy and angioplasties are seldom appropriate in these cases. The goals of the bypass procedure are identical to those of chronic arterial occlusion—bypass from an inflow site free of disease to an outflow vessel distal to the occlusive process.

Acute occlusion of a previously placed bypass conduit may be treated with thrombectomy and lesser, directed methods designed to correct the responsible anatomic defect. Thrombosed aortofemoral graft limbs are usually treated with thrombectomy and a distal anastomotic procedure (patch angioplasty) designed to improve inflow to the profunda femoris artery, by the reasoning that a stenotic lesion at the profunda orifice is the most common lesion responsible for failure of these grafts. A frequently employed method of treating a failed prosthetic femoropopliteal bypass has been thrombectomy and patch angioplasty of a distal anastomotic stenosis. Many practitioners, however, believe that placement of a new bypass conduit is a more appropriate means of addressing an occluded infrainguinal graft.[22V] We are advocates of this approach, inserting a new autogenous vein graft in reoperative infrainguinal surgery whenever possible.

## Thrombolysis

Thrombolysis is a second method of restoring arterial circulation in acute peripheral arterial occlusion. The goal of thrombolysis is not to replace operation in this regard; rather, the strategy is to unmask the defect responsible for the occlusive event and directly address this lesion with a variety of operative or endovascular techniques.[23] Thrombolytic therapy offered a potential solution to the high mortality associated with immediate operative intervention. In addition, thrombolytic therapy provided a significant benefit over heparin therapy in its potential to achieve recanalization of the occluded arterial segment.

Urokinase is presently the most frequently utilized lytic agent in peripheral arterial occlusion, but streptokinase is still employed in a large number of European centers. Systemic heparinization or aspirin therapy has been utilized to prevent pericatheter thrombus formation during intra-arterial thrombolysis. A variety of thrombolytic techniques are in routine use, but all require placement of the catheter infusion holes into the substance of the thrombus. Unlike coronary thrombolysis, systemic infusion and infusion near but not within peripheral arterial thrombi are destined to fail in all but the most exceptional cases.[61] Bolusing of lytic agent into the thrombus and "pulse-spray" techniques are in widespread use to increase the rate of thrombolysis.[24, 25] Although this contention may prove valid, sound comparative data are presently unavailable, and the potential for increasing the risk of distal embolization is an issue that must be considered with these more aggressive techniques. We do not continue with thrombolytic infusion when the catheter tip cannot be positioned within the substance of the

thrombus or when no lytic progress is observed after a 12- to 18-hour duration of infusion. We do not continue therapy beyond 48 hours, regardless of clinical outcome, based on a perceived increase in thrombolytic complications beyond this point.

Early retrospective studies reported mortality rates of less than 5%, with limb salvage in over 90% of cases.[25, 26V] These initial results were probably overly optimistic, and prospective studies have documented somewhat higher rates of death and amputation. A rational basis for decisions regarding the most appropriate initial management in acute limb ischemia awaited the results of well designed, randomized trials comparing operation and thrombolytic intervention.

To date, two randomized, prospective trials of thrombolysis versus operation have been completed. A small series comparing 11 patients randomized to intra-arterial rt-PA and nine patients randomized to surgical treatment appeared in the European literature in 1992.[27II] This study was deficient in its statistical power, precluding meaningful conclusions regarding comparative outcome. The study did, however, serve to reinforce the concept of the adjuvant nature of thrombolytic infusion, with thrombolysis serving to unmask the arterial lesion responsible for the occlusion and early correction of the defect with operation or percutaneous balloon angioplasty.

A second study was performed at the University of Rochester, randomizing 114 patients with acute limb ischemia to initial operation or intra-arterial urokinase therapy.[61] Statistically meaningful conclusions were generated from this larger study; thrombolysis was associated with improved patient survival without an increase in the requirement for amputation, and intervention with operation or balloon angioplasty was avoided in one-third of the patients undergoing thrombolysis.

The completed randomized trials of thrombolytic therapy suffered from the inability to acquire large enough numbers of patients to stratify outcome by patient category. It is reasonable to assume that subsequent large multicenter trials will define specific categories of patients that are most appropriately treated with one treatment modality or the other. Until data become available, the rational treatment of limb ischemia must be individualized, based on the surgeon's and the angiographer's experience and beliefs. Currently, we take patients directly to operation when the ischemia is so severe that the delays associated with thrombolysis are predicted to result in an unacceptable risk of limb loss and when a localized common femoral or brachial embolus occurs without extensive distal thrombotic propagation. Otherwise, an attempt at catheter-directed thrombolysis is undertaken.

## Fasciotomy

Fasciotomy of the calf compartments may be necessary when operative or thrombolytic reperfusion results in excessive muscle edema, elevated compartment pressure, and nerve and muscle compromise. The need for fasciotomy can be gauged on the basis of the compartment pressure; tissue damage is unlikely until the pressures exceed 30 cm $H_2O$.[28] Subcutaneous fasciotomy may be appropriate when extensive edema is not present, using a small skin incision and running a long scissors down the fascia beneath the skin. This is usually performed over the lateral aspect of the calf to decompress the anterior compartment alone. A more extensive fasciotomy is necessary when the edema is severe, opening all four calf compartments through long skin incisions and leaving the wounds open until resolution of the edema allows the performance of a delayed primary closure or skin graft.

In summary, acute peripheral arterial occlusion is a disorder characterized by a substantial risk of limb loss and mortality. Prompt diagnosis and treatment are mandatory, and early arteriography can provide useful insights into the location and mechanism of occlusion. To date, the most effective method of restoring perfusion remains unclear. It is likely that therapy will need to be tailored to the individual patient, with thrombolysis most appropriate in some patient categories and operation in others. The results of future large controlled studies with the potential for subgroup analysis should provide data on which to base these decisions.

## REFERENCES

1. Bergamini TM, Towne JB, Bandyk DF, et al: Experience with in situ saphenous vein bypasses during 1981 to 1989: Determinant factors of long-term patency. J Vasc Surg 13:137–147, 1991.
I 2. Veith FJ, Gupta SK, Ascer E, et al: Six-year prospective multicenter randomized comparison of autologous saphenous vein and expanded polytetrafluoroethylene grafts in infrainguinal arterial reconstructions. J Vasc Surg 3:104–114, 1992.
V 3. Yeager RA, Moneta GL, Taylor LM, Jr., et al: Surgical management of severe acute lower extremity ischemia. J Vasc Surg 15:385–393, 1992.
III 4. Blaisdell FW, Steele M, Allen RE: Management of acute lower extremity arterial ischemia due to embolism and thrombosis. Surgery 84:822–834, 1978.
5. Elliott JP, Hageman JH, Szilagyi DE, et al: Arterial embolization: Problems of source, multiplicity, recurrence and delayed treatment. Surgery 88:833, 1980.
I 6. Ouriel K, Shortell CK, DeWeese JA, et al: A comparison of thrombolytic therapy with operative revascularization in the initial treatment of acute peripheral arterial ischemia. J Vasc Surg 19:1021–1030, 1994.
7. Ouriel K, Shortell CK, Green RM, et al: Differential mechanisms of late failure of autogenous and prosthetic bypass conduits. Paper presented at the ISCVS Meeting: Lisbon, Portugal, 1993.
8. Donaldson MC, Mannick JA, Whittemore AD: Causes of primary graft failure after in situ saphenous vein bypass grafting [published erratum appears in J Vasc Surg 15(4):611, 1992]. J Vasc Surg 15:113–118, 1992.
9. Whittemore AD: Failure of peripheral arterial reconstruction. Acta Chir Scand 550[Suppl]:74–80, 1989.
III 10. Shortell CK, Ouriel K, Green RM, et al: Vascular disease in the antiphospholipid syndrome: A comparison with the patient population with atherosclerosis. J Vasc Surg 15:158–165, 1992.
11. Comp PC, Esmon CT: Recurrent venous thromboembolism in patients with a partial deficiency of protein S. N Engl J Med 311:1525–1528, 1984.
12. Abbott WM, Maloney RD, McCabe CC, et al: Arterial embolism: A 44 year prospective. Am J Surg 143:460–464, 1982.
IV 13. Green RM, DeWeese JA, Rob CG: Arterial embolectomy before and after the Fogarty catheter. Surgery 77:24, 1975.
14. Fronek A, Coel M, Bernstein EF: The importance of combined multisegmental pressure and Doppler flow velocity studies in the diagnosis of peripheral arterial occlusive disease. Surgery 84:840, 1978.
15. Dos Santos JC. Sur la des obstruction des thrombus arterielles anciennes. Mem Acad Chir 73:409, 1947.
16. Kunlin J: Le traitement de l'arterite obliterante par la greffe veineuse. Arch Malad Coeur et Vaiss 42:371, 1949.
V 17. Wengerter KR, Yang PM, Veith FJ, et al: A twelve-year experience with the popliteal-to-distal artery bypass: The significance and management of proximal disease. J Vasc Surg 15:143–149, 1992.
18. Cliffton EE: The use of plasmin in humans. Ann NY Acad Sci 68:209–229, 1957.
19. Earnshaw JJ: Thrombolytic therapy in the management of acute limb ischaemia. Br J Surg 78:261–269, 1991.
V 20. Jivegard L, Holm J, Schersten T: Acute limb ischemia due to arterial embolism or thrombosis: Influence of limb ischemia versus pre-existing cardiac disease on postoperative mortality rate. J Cardiovasc Surg 29:32–36, 1988.
21. Fogarty TJ, Cranley JJ, Drause RJ, et al: A method for extraction of arterial emboli and thrombi. Surg Gynecol Obstet 116:241, 1963.
V 22. Edwards JE, Taylor LM, Jr., Porter JM: Treatment of failed lower extremity bypass grafts with new autogenous vein bypass grafting. J Vasc Surg 11:136–145, 1990.
23. Ouriel K, Shortell CK: Thrombolysis in acute peripheral arterial occlusion: Predictors of immediate success. Ann Vasc Surg 8:59–65, 1994.
24. Durham JD, Gellar SC, Abbott WM, et al: Regional infusion of urokinase into occluded lower-extremity bypass grafts: Long-term clinical results. Radiology 172:83–90, 1989.
25. Graor RA, Olin J, Bartholomew JR, et al: Efficacy and safety of intraarterial local infusion of streptokinase,

urokinase, or tissue plasminogen activator for peripheral arterial occlusion: A retrospective review. J Vasc Med Biol 2:310–315, 1990.

V 26. McNamara TO, Fischer JR: Thrombolysis of peripheral arterial and graft occlusions: Improved results using high-dose urokinase. Am J Roentgenol 144:769–775, 1985.

II 27. Nilsson L, Albrechtsson U, Jonung T, et al: Surgical treatment versus thrombolysis in acute arterial occlusion: A randomised controlled study. Eur J Vasc Surg 6:189–193, 1992.

28. Whitesides TE, Haney TC, Morimoto K, et al: Tissue pressure measurements as a determinant for the need for fasciotomy. Clin Orthop 113:43, 1975.

# Chapter 13

# Chronic Arterial Obstruction

William D. Suggs and Frank J. Veith

In the last two decades, enormous advances have been made in the treatment of lower limb ischemia from infrainguinal and aortoiliac arteriosclerosis. In the late 1960s, most patients with a threatened ischemic limb were subjected to a major amputation because they had arterial occlusive disease that was deemed too difficult or risky to treat, particularly distal occlusive disease. This was especially true in diabetic patients who were often regarded as having such advanced distal or small artery occlusive disease that they were considered inoperable. Although some patients were undergoing successful aorto-femoral or femoropopliteal bypasses for segmental occlusive disease of the iliac or superficial femoral arteries, many of them had only intermittent claudication. Most patients with rest pain or necrosis had complex, multilevel occlusive disease in patterns that were deemed unfavorable to treat surgically, and they were often subjected to primary amputation. This situation has changed dramatically in the last 20 to 25 years as interventional management strategies have been developed to treat virtually all patterns of arteriosclerotic disease underlying severe limb ischemia.[1] Moreover, the resulting aggressive, therapeutic approach to lower limb-threatening ischemia has proved to be effective and worthwhile.[1, 2] This form of treatment has gained increasing acceptance throughout the world, even though some still question its value and cost-effectiveness.[3] Despite this residual skepticism, most vascular surgeons, physicians, and virtually all patients acknowledge the value of the aggressive surgical and radiologic approach to limb-threatening ischemia.

Arteriosclerosis involves the entire arterial system in varying degrees. This involvement generally begins early in adult life and progresses slowly to the point where a flow-reducing stenosis or occlusion occurs in the aorta, in the iliac arteries, or in one or more of the arteries below the inguinal ligament. As the average age of our population increases, the number of individuals with hemodynamically significant arteriosclerosis, particularly in the infrainguinal area, also increases.

Obviously, the disease is associated in varying degrees with arteriosclerotic involvement elsewhere in the body, and this fact must always be considered when making therapeutic decisions in afflicted patients. It is this consideration that guides those caring for the patient to correctly seek palliation rather than cure and to attempt a lesser intervention or operation that maintains function rather than one that will restore a normal circulation. The generalized and slowly progressive nature of the disease process and the imperfect results of all interventional treatments should also deter any who might be unwisely tempted to treat asymptomatic or minimally disabling arteriosclerotic occlusive lesions. In the management of the increasingly common entity of infrainguinal arteriosclerosis, diagnostic and therapeutic restraint and the desire to minimize risks and avoid doing harm must be paramount considerations if the disease is not producing major functional impairment or tissue necrosis. On the other hand, despite the advanced age and poor generalized condition of many afflicted patients, aggressive intervention for both diagnosis and treatment is justified if limb loss is truly threatened by the disease process.

## CLINICAL PRESENTATION

The reserve of the human arterial system is enormous. Hemodynamically significant stenoses or major artery occlusions can exist in the arterial tree with few or no symptoms. This is particularly true if collateral pathways are normal or the patient's activity level is limited by

Supported by grants from the U.S. Public Health Service (HL 02990-01), the James Hilton Manning and Emma Austin Manning Foundation, the Anna S. Brown Trust, and the New York Institute for Vascular Studies.

coronary arteriosclerosis or other disease processes. Arteriosclerotic disease may produce a complete occlusion of the distal aorta or one or both of the common iliac arteries with extension into the external iliac arteries (Fig. 13–1). Patients with aortoiliac disease are generally male cigarette smokers who present with intermittent buttock, thigh, or calf claudication and often have some degree of sexual impotence. The most common manifestation of a short, segmental occlusion of the superficial femoral artery (the usual site of major arteriosclerotic involvement below the inguinal ligament) is mild, intermittent claudication. Similarly, this lesion will often be totally asymptomatic, and this is usually the case if only one or two tibial arteries are occluded without other significant lesions. Thus, the patient who usually presents with severe, disabling intermittent claudication or tissue necrosis has multiple, sequential occlusions or so-called combined segment disease with hemodynamically significant lesions at the aortoiliac level and the superficial femoral/popliteal level, or either of these combined with severe infrapopliteal disease.[1]

## Staging

Patients with hemodynamically significant infrainguinal arteriosclerosis may be classified into one of five stages, depending on their pre-

**Table 13–1. Staging of Infrainguinal Arteriosclerosis With Hemodynamically Significant Stenoses or Occlusions**

| Stage | Presentation | Invasive Diagnostic and Therapeutic Intervention |
|---|---|---|
| 0 | No signs or symptoms | Never justified |
| I | Intermittent claudication (>1 block) No physical changes | Sometimes justified for work-related function |
| II | Severe claudication (<1/2 block) Dependent rubor Decreased temperature | Sometimes justified; may remain stable |
| III | Rest pain Atrophy, cyanosis Dependent rubor | Usually indicated |
| IV | Nonhealing ischemic ulcer or gangrene | Usually indicated |

sentation (Table 13–1). Patients in stages III and IV are those whose limbs may be considered imminently threatened, although some with mild ischemic rest pain may remain stable for many years and occasionally one with a small patch of gangrene or an ischemic ulcer will have the lesion heal with conservative treatment.[4] With the exception of these few patients, invasive diagnostic procedures, such as angiography, are justified for those with stages III and IV disease, because these stages are usually associated with disease at several levels.

Rest pain as an isolated symptom can be difficult to evaluate unless it is accompanied by other findings. Many patients with significant arterial lesions have pain at rest from causes other than their arteriosclerosis, such as arthritis or neuritis. Such pain will not be relieved even by a successful revascularization. Significant ischemic rest pain is almost always associated with decreased pulses and other objective manifestations of ischemia, such as atrophy, decreased skin temperature when compared with the other extremity, marked rubor, and relief of pain with dependency. In some patients with a complex etiology of their rest pain, it may be necessary to perform noninvasive laboratory and angiographic evaluations before the predominant cause of the symptom can be determined and appropriate treatment instituted. Every patient with pain at rest and decreased pulses is not a candidate for angiography and an arterial intervention or operation. Some of these patients will be relieved of pain by appro-

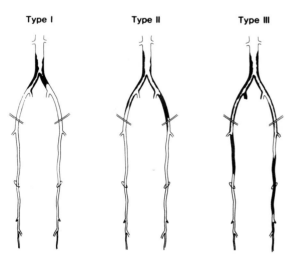

**Type I          Type II          Type III**

**Figure 13–1.** Patterns of aortoiliac occlusive disease. In type I, localized disease is confined to the distal abdominal aorta and common iliac arteries. In type II, more widespread abdominal disease is present, whereas a type III pattern denotes multilevel disease with associated infrainguinal occlusive lesions. (Used with permission from Brewster DC: Direct reconstruction for aortoiliac occlusive disease. In Rutherford RB (ed): Vascular Surgery, ed 3. Philadelphia, WB Saunders, 1989, pp 667–691.)

priate treatment for gout or osteoarthritis. Others can have their disease appropriately managed with simple analgesics and reassurance that their limb is not in jeopardy. Reassurance generally suffices for patients with stage I disease and those with stage II disease who are elderly (over 80 years) or at high risk because of intercurrent disease or atherosclerotic involvement of other organs such as the heart, the kidneys, or the brain.

A conservative approach consisting of exercise and smoking cessation is employed to treat patients with stage I involvement.[5] This approach appears to be justified based on the numerous reports of the slow progression of stage I disease to more advanced stages.[6-8] Only 1% per year of patients with claudication develop a threatened limb. Moreover, without treatment, 10 to 15% of patients in stage I will have their symptoms improve over 5 years, and 60 to 70% will not have symptoms progress over the same period. The 10 to 15% who do worsen are best treated with a primary operation or other therapeutic intervention after their disease progresses.

Some patients with stage II and a few with stage III or IV disease may have their disease remain stable and easily managed without operation for protracted periods of 1 or more years. Thus, a conservative, nonoperative approach is justified for selected patients in these stages.[4] Moreover, this conservative, nonoperative approach is particularly indicated if the patient is elderly and a poor surgical risk. An example of this would be an octogenarian with intractable congestive heart failure in whom a difficult distal small vessel bypass would be required to alleviate stage III signs and symptoms. Close observation of such a patient can often suffice for several months or even years; however, we would not hesitate to revascularize the limb when the patient's rest pain became intolerable or a small progressive patch of gangrene developed.[1, 2]

## Differential Diagnosis

*Intermittent claudication* is a crampy pain brought on by exertion and relieved by rest, and it is a distinct symptom that is usually a manifestation of arteriosclerotic occlusive disease. Mild calf claudication can be produced by a significant stenotic lesion in the iliac, superficial femoral, or popliteal artery. Occasionally, a patient will describe the claudication as a sense of heaviness, weakness, or fatigue in the limb without pain, and such patients may be mistakenly diagnosed as having neuromuscular disorders. Sometimes claudication-like symptoms can be produced by lesions compressing the lower spinal cord or cauda equina.[9, 10] Such *pseudoclaudication* is most often produced by spinal stenosis and can easily be suspected when peripheral pulses are normal. Occasionally, neurologic problems coexist with arterial occlusive disease, making an exact determination of the cause of the patient's symptoms a difficult challenge for the neurologist and the vascular surgeon. In these circumstances, angiography, computed tomography (CT) scan, or magnetic resonance imaging (MRI) of the lumbar spine and even myelography may be necessary.

Some of the problems that can be encountered in differentiating pain at rest from *true ischemic rest pain* have already been discussed. Again, difficulties are greatest when arterial occlusive disease coexists with another pathology. Similar problems can be encountered when determining the primary cause of ulcerating lesions in the ankle region and on the foot. The typical *venous ulcer* poses no problem in differential diagnosis. It occurs in a setting of chronic venous disease, is associated with stasis changes and normal arterial pulses, is usually relatively painless, and heals with elevation and compressive measures. The typical *arterial or ischemic ulcer* is far more painful and is associated with other manifestations of ischemia. It usually has a more necrotic base and is located at an area of chronic pressure or trauma, such as over the malleoli or the bunion area. Arterial or ischemic ulcer can also occur between the toes. Both ulcer conditions may be improved by hospitalization, bed rest, and local care. The differential diagnosis is usually difficult only when chronic venous and arterial disease coexist and venography and arteriography may be required. In some patients the primary cause of the ulcer can be determined only when arterial reconstruction produces healing after a period of intense, conservative management has failed to do so.

When a patient presents with a *gangrenous (black) or pregangrenous (blue) toe*, etiologies other than progression of chronic arteriosclerotic occlusive disease must be considered. *Local infection* can be the sole or a contributing cause of the toe lesion. This is particularly common in diabetics. If foot pulses or noninvasive tests of arterial function are normal, the gangrenous condition can be presumed to result from local arterial or arteriolar thrombosis secondary to infection. Radical local excision and drainage of all involved tissue usually result in a healed foot. Diagnosis is more difficult when infection coexists with arterial occlusive disease. Noninvasive studies and arteriography are usually required before it can be determined whether treatment should consist of excision and drainage alone or in combination with an arterial reconstruction. Decision-making under these conditions can be among the most difficult in vascular surgery.

Black or blue toes may also be the result of an embolic process. *Emboli* may originate from the heart, a proximal aneurysm, or any proximal atherosclerotic lesion. In the latter circumstance, small cholesterol, platelet, or fibrin emboli may lodge in interosseous or digital arteries. Peripheral pedal pulses may be normal, and spontaneous improvement of the resulting blue toe often occurs. This sequence of events has been termed the blue-toe syndrome, and its pathogenesis is thought to be analogous to that of transient ischemic attacks from atherosclerotic disease at the carotid bifurcation.[11] If a single, dominant, large artery lesion can be identified by angiography, it should be treated by endarterectomy or, more commonly, by an appropriate bypass. However, in our experience it has been difficult to identify a single lesion in the arterial tree of these patients, and we usually operate on them only after they have had several embolic episodes.

In a patient with the sudden onset of ischemia, the possibility of a major embolus from the heart or a proximal aneurysm must be considered. In these circumstances, angiography is indicated even if limb viability is not in question, because major emboli should be removed or lysed as soon as they are identified.

In the last several decades, with progress in cardiac surgery for rheumatic heart disease, almost all patients that we have seen with major arterial emboli and acute arterial occlusions have had them superimposed on extensive arteriosclerosis. Even with *arteriography,* which we employ routinely in such cases, the diagnosis and treatment of embolic disease are difficult and the results imperfect.[12] The only certain diagnostic feature of embolus is multiplicity. Furthermore, the location of the embolus may be atypical, and the vascular surgeon treating a presumed embolus in the presence of extensive arteriosclerosis must be prepared to perform an extensive arterial reconstruction or bypass even if the operation is undertaken soon after the acute event.[12] Because acute thrombosis cannot always be differentiated from embolus, complete preoperative arteriography should be mandatory in any suspected embolic occlusion of the lower extremity in a patient who could have arteriosclerosis.

Exploration of the distal popliteal artery is usually the best surgical approach in patients with severe ischemia due to an acute occlusion of the popliteal or the distal superficial femoral arteries.[13] Use of intra-arterially administered lytic agents, particularly urokinase, may have significant therapeutic advantages in the management of acute thromboembolic occlusions. Moreover, the care and surgical treatment of these cases should be undertaken only by an experienced vascular surgeon.

## PATIENT EVALUATION

### Local Factors and Physical Examination

As already indicated, the findings on physical examination of the involved extremity contribute to the staging of the atherosclerotic process and provide a rough guide for whether diagnostic or therapeutic intervention is justified and needed. Discoloration and swelling on physical examination should provide evidence of the presence and extent of infection in the involved foot. As a general rule, the extent of infection and necrosis deep to the skin is greater than one might expect from an examination of the skin. Exploration of suspicious areas can sometimes be carried out without anesthesia if the patient has diminished sensation from diabetic neuropathy. If neuropathy is not present, exploration and necessary débridement should be performed in the operating room under anesthesia.

In the initial examination of a patient with suspected arterial disease, careful inspection for previous operative scars is essential, because patients may be unaware of a prior sympathectomy or the nature and extent of previous arterial surgery. The site of scars can provide clues as to whether the arteries below the knee were violated, whether ipsilateral saphenous vein was utilized, and, if so, how much is left. Physical examination can also reveal evidence of associated chronic disease. In evaluating an ischemic limb, particular attention must be given to careful inspection of the heel and between the toes where unsuspected ischemic ulcers or infection may be present. A flashlight is extremely helpful in this regard. The uninvolved extremity must also be examined carefully. Because of the symmetry of atherosclerosis, the opposite extremity may harbor unsuspected ischemic lesions. Moreover, findings such as coolness and bluish discoloration are far more meaningful if they are asymmetrical, because cool or dusky extremities may sometimes be present without major arterial disease.

## Pulse Examination

Pulse examination in the lower extremities of a patient with suspected ischemia is extremely important. It requires considerable experience and must be performed with proper technique and with care.[14] The strength of a pulse as assessed by an experienced examiner is a valuable, semiquantitative assessment of the arterial circulation at that level.

In examining a patient with diminished pulses it is extremely helpful to count the pulse to an assistant who is palpating the patient's radial pulse to ensure that the examiner's own pulse or spurious muscular activity are not being felt. Before the examiner describes a pulse as being absent, considerable time and effort must be expended and ectopic localization of pulses, such as the lateral tarsal artery pulse, must be accomplished. In this era of too frequently performed noninvasive arterial tests, the value of a carefully performed and recorded pulse examination cannot be overemphasized. It provides a basis for comparison if subsequent disease progression occurs, and it is a simple way of accurately assessing the arterial circulation in the lower extremities at a given point in time. Careful pulse examination also provides an indicator of the type of approach that will be required to save a threatened foot.

If a patient with a gangrenous toe lesion has a pedal pulse, local treatment without reconstructive arterial surgery is usually the correct approach to achieve a healed foot, although there are rare exceptions.[15] If a patient with an ischemic foot lesion has a normal popliteal pulse but no pedal pulses, some form of infrapopliteal or small vessel bypass almost always is the correct approach to obtain a healed foot. If a patient with an ischemic foot lesion has a normal ipsilateral femoral pulse without distal pulses, some form of infrainguinal arterial reconstruction, preferably a femoropopliteal bypass, is the correct approach to achieve a healed foot. If a patient has a diminished femoral pulse, often with an associated bruit, some form of proximal arterial reconstruction or angioplasty above the inguinal ligament almost certainly is required.

## SYSTEMIC FACTORS

Systemic factors that are important in the patient who is a candidate for interventional treatment for arteriosclerosis include all factors in the history, physical examination, and routine laboratory tests that might indicate major organ failure. Most important is evidence of heart disease, diabetes, kidney disease, hypertension, chronic pulmonary disease, and atherosclerotic involvement of the arteries to the brain. All of these intercurrent diseases, if present, require appropriate medical management before, during, and after diagnostic and therapeutic interventions so that the risks are minimized. A detailed discussion of this management is beyond the scope of this chapter. Evidence of myocardial ischemia and congestive heart failure should be sought. If severe angina pectoris is present, some patients should be subjected to coronary arteriography and aortocoronary bypass prior to treating their limb ischemia. Patients with recent myocardial infarctions and those in congestive heart failure should have a Swan-Ganz catheter inserted and their fluid and volume replacement optimized before, during, and after operation on the basis of appropriate cardiac output and pressure measurements.[16, 17] It is also especially important to monitor renal function repetitively after an angiographic procedure because transient renal failure is common. If detected and appropriately treated, renal failure is generally reversible.

## NONINVASIVE VASCULAR LABORATORY TESTS

In the early stages during which interventional measures are not required, segmental arterial pressures and pulse volume recordings provide an objective and semiquantitative assessment of the circulation and help to confirm the diagnosis made by the history and physical examination, including the careful pulse examination. These tests also provide a baseline against which future changes can be measured. In addition, they give a rough index of the localization of occlusive lesions and the degree of ischemia in the foot. However, the correlation is not absolute, and flat ankle and forefoot wave tracings with ankle pressures less than 35 mm Hg can be dissociated from foot lesions or serious symptomatology. Furthermore, decreased thigh waveforms and pressures may be associated entirely with disease below the inguinal ligament as well as aortoiliac disease. The differentiation between these two types of lesions can be made only by femoral pulse examination and arteriography.

Noninvasive testing can be extremely helpful in predicting when a toe amputation or local procedure on the foot has virtually no chance of healing. A flatline forefoot tracing with an ankle pressure below 50 mm Hg indicates that a toe amputation or other foot operation for an ischemic lesion will not heal without prior revascularization. Because these tests do not evaluate the severity or extent of infection, the opposite is not always true. Good forefoot pulse waves and ankle pressures do not guarantee healing of foot operations, although they suggest that it will occur if infection can be eliminated. Furthermore, there is a gray zone of intermediate values in which the noninvasive tests are of little value and a therapeutic trial of a local foot procedure is justified and appropriate.

## ANGIOGRAPHIC EVALUATION

As in other areas of vascular surgery, proper high-quality arteriography is essential to make an assessment of the extent of arteriosclerosis and determine whether therapeutic intervention is possible. Arteriography also allows planning of the optimal form that this intervention should take.[1, 2] Adequate arteriography also defines the localization and extent of arteriosclerotic involvement in the infrarenal aorta and iliac arteries, which can be supplemented by direct pressure measurements taken at the time of arteriography to assess the hemodynamic significance of isolated stenoses.

To provide adequate information about the infrainguinal arterial system, the arterial tree from the groin to the forefoot should be well visualized in continuity, preferably by the transfemoral route. This is generally possible only if a long film changer, multiple exposures, large boluses of contrast, and other technical modifications described elsewhere[18] are employed. Oblique views may be required to completely visualize the origin and proximal portion of the deep femoral artery. Good preoperative distal artery visualization is, in our opinion, the key to performing optimal bypass surgery to arteries in the foot and lower leg. Reactive hyperemia, digitally augmented views, and delayed films may be necessary to achieve the needed visualization, although in our recent experience these measures were rarely required. Although others have advocated intraoperative arteriography to achieve this end,[19] we have found it less effective and very rarely necessary. Magnetic resonance imaging of flowing blood (MR angiography) has provided preoperative evaluation of patent distal leg and foot arteries without the need for dye injection. However, these techniques are not yet widely available.

## TREATMENT PRINCIPLES, PROCEDURES, AND JUDGMENT ISSUES

### General Considerations

For patients whose limbs are threatened because of arterial occlusive disease, limb salvage should be considered and attempted, except when gangrene extends into the deeper tissues of the tarsal region of the foot or when the patient has severe organic mental syndrome with an inability to ambulate, communicate, or provide self-care.[1, 2] Patients in the latter categories should undergo primary below- or above-knee amputation. Primary above-knee amputation should also be employed if a patient with foot gangrene is unable to stand or walk because of longstanding, severe flexion contractures.

### Medical Considerations

It can be expected that in affected patients a high incidence of other arteriosclerotic manifestations exists, and more than 60% may have diabetes mellitus.[2] The mean age is over 70 years, and many patients are in their eighties. Many have suffered documented myocardial infarction, some are in uncompensated congestive heart or renal failure, some have had myocardial infarctions within 3 weeks of presentation, and some have concurrent carcinomas.[2, 17]

The general plan of medical management is to achieve maximal improvement of cardiac, renal, and diabetic status before proceeding with arteriographic examination and operation. In some instances, the urgency of the ischemic situation, coupled with progressive infection in the foot, makes it necessary to perform angiographic examination and operation before ideal medical control can be achieved. Almost without exception, age, medical status, incurable malignancy and/or a contralateral amputation are not considered reasons to withhold arterial reconstruction.[1, 2]

## SURGICAL CONSIDERATIONS AND CRITERIA FOR RECONSTRUCTIBILITY

### Aortofemoral Bypass

Patients with disabling claudication or rest pain should have an aortofemoral bypass when the distal aorta or the bilateral iliac arteries are stenotic or occluded on aortogram. An example of such a patient is seen in Figure 13–2. Reconstructive procedures are performed from the

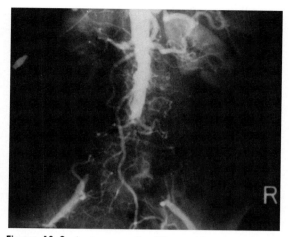

**Figure 13–2.** Aortogram of a 58-year-old woman demonstrating complete bilateral occlusion of the distal aorta and common iliac arteries. This patient underwent an aortofemoral bypass graft.

infrarenal aorta to the bilateral common femoral arteries using a bifurcated synthetic graft of either polytetrafluoroethylene (PTFE) or Dacron. If the superficial femoral arteries are occluded, the femoral anastomosis is constructed across the orifice of the profunda artery acting as a patch to widen the origin of the vessel. This technique has provided improved patency of aortofemoral grafts.

Patients with unilateral iliac artery occlusion are candidates for a femorofemoral or an aortounifemoral bypass to improve flow to the affected limb.

### Femoropopliteal Bypass

Patients whose limbs are clearly threatened and who have undergone arteriographic examination should undergo femoropopliteal bypass when the superficial femoral or popliteal artery is occluded and the patent popliteal artery segment distal to the occlusion has luminal continuity, on arteriographic examination, with any of its three terminal branches. This is true even if one or more of these branches ends in an occlusion anywhere in the leg. Even if the popliteal artery segment into which the graft is to be inserted is occluded distally, femoropopliteal bypass to this isolated segment can be considered.[20V, 21V, 22III] If the isolated popliteal segment is less than 7 cm in length or there is extensive gangrene or infection in the foot, a femoral to distal artery bypass or sequential bypass is sometimes performed in one or two stages.[21, 23] All femoropopliteal bypasses can be classified on the basis of their relationship to the knee

joint and runoff from the popliteal artery, as determined radiographically by previously described criteria.[21V, 24] However, it should be noted that all angiographic evaluations of popliteal runoff are imperfect and correlate in only a limited way with outflow resistance and bypass patency.[25]

### Infrapopliteal Bypass

Bypasses to arteries beyond the popliteal (small vessel bypasses) are performed only when femoropopliteal bypass is not deemed possible, according to the foregoing criteria. These small vessel bypasses are performed to the posterior tibial, the anterior tibial, or the peroneal arteries, in that order of preference. A tibial artery is generally used only if its lumen runs without obstruction into the foot, although vein bypasses to isolated tibial artery segments and other disadvantaged outflow tracts have been performed and have remained patent over 4 years.[26V, 27V] A peroneal artery is usually used only if it is continuous with one or two of its terminal branches that communicate with foot arteries. Absence of a plantar arch and vascular calcification are not considered contraindications to a reconstruction.[2, 26V] Some patients require a bypass to an artery or arterial branch in the foot.[1, 2, 26V, 27V] Very few patients fail to have an artery that meets these requirements in their leg or foot, and thus less than 1% of our patients are now considered inappropriate candidates for reconstruction on the basis of angiographic findings.[1]

In the case of both femoropopliteal and small vessel bypasses, stenosis of less than 50% of the diameter of the vessel is acceptable at or distal to the site chosen for the distal anastomosis. Although an effort is made to find the most disease-free segment of artery to use for the distal anastomosis, this may be tempered by the advisability of using the most proximal patent segment possible to shorten the length of the bypass.

The common femoral artery has generally been used as the site of origin for all bypasses to the popliteal and more distal arteries. However, over the last 18 years, we have also used as inflow sites the superficial femoral, popliteal, or tibial arteries when these vessels were relatively undiseased or vein length was limited.[26V, 28III] The superficial femoral and popliteal arteries are now used preferentially whenever there is no proximal luminal stenosis in excess of 40% of the cross-sectional diameter.[29V]

## Bypasses to Ankle or Foot Arteries

Some patients have no patent or usable artery above the level of the ankle, and they require a bypass to the very distal perimalleolar and inframalleolar arteries (Fig. 13–3). Visualization of these very distal arteries requires excellent preoperative angiography. Bypasses to dorsalis pedis arteries have yielded results comparable to those performed to more proximal tibial vessels, with 3-year primary patency rates of 58 to 60% and limb salvage rates of 75 to 95%. With careful followup, the assisted primary patency rates for these grafts have been substantially improved.[30–32] In addition, bypasses to the plantar and tarsal arteries have provided limb salvage when the dorsalis pedis and posterior tibial arteries were unsuitable for bypass (Fig. 13–4). Visualization of the dorsalis pedis and posterior tibial arteries and their branches and our use of them for bypass insertion have been major factors in reducing the proportion of patients whose arterial disease was so distal that they were "unsuitable for an attempt at limb salvage" or inoperable.[26V, 27V] The effectiveness of these bypasses to pedal arteries and their main branches has been documented, and these procedures are now being more widely performed and advocated.[1, 2, 26V, 27V]

## MANAGEMENT OF FOOT LESIONS

Approximately 75% of our patients have gangrenous or necrotic foot or toe lesions.[1, 2] Small (less than 2 cm²), uninfected, gangrenous le-

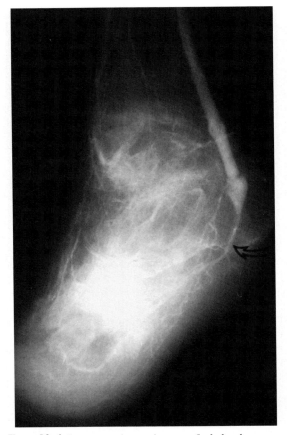

**Figure 13–4.** Intraoperative angiogram of a below-knee popliteal artery to lateral plantar artery bypass with reversed saphenous vein. Note the partially intact plantar arch (arrow).

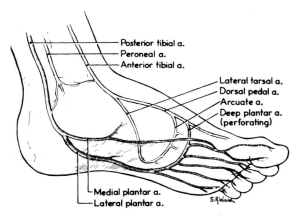

**Figure 13–3.** Diagram of named arteries in the ankle region and foot. Any of the main arteries or their branches, if patent, may be approached surgically and used as the distal outflow for a limb salvage bypass. (Used with permission from Ascer E, Veith FJ, Gupta SK: Bypasses to plantar arteries and other tibial branches: An extended approach to limb salvage. J Vasc Surg 8:434, 1988.)

sions on the toe or foot are not treated. Larger gangrenous lesions and areas of infection associated with necrosis are usually extensively débrided at the end of an arterial reconstruction. These débridements often require excision of one or more toes, and they frequently consist of a partial (medial or lateral) transmetatarsal amputation. An attempt is made to excise enough bone so there is overhanging skin and soft tissue. These wounds are usually left open, and drying of the soft tissues is prevented by placing the involved portion of the foot in a normal saline wet dressing within a plastic bag or plastic seal. Subsequent débridement of foot lesions is often required on the ward or in the operating room. Débridement is performed to remove all infected or necrotic tissue and exposed cartilage without regard for anatomic landmarks.

It is sometimes necessary, particularly in diabetic patients, to perform multiple, secondary operative procedures to achieve a healed foot.

Skin grafts are used to cover large cutaneous defects but are placed only when the wound is covered by clean granulation tissue. In some patients with extensive gangrene at the metatarsal or tarsal level, below-knee amputation is required despite functioning femoropopliteal bypass. This clinical presentation is particularly common in patients with end stage renal disease and diabetes.[33] In some instances, it has been possible to obtain foot healing in these patients by performing a secondary bypass to an artery distal to the popliteal segment.[21V, 22III, 33] Occasionally, however, a patient has extensive infection and necrosis, and a healed foot cannot be obtained even with straight-line arterial flow in pedal arteries.[33] This is particularly common in patients with end stage kidney disease and diabetes.[33, 34]

## FAILING GRAFT CONCEPT

Intimal hyperplasia, progression of proximal or distal disease, or lesions within the graft itself can produce signs and symptoms of hemodynamic deterioration in patients with a prior arterial reconstruction without producing concomitant thrombosis of the bypass graft.[35V, 36V, 37V, 38V, 39] We have referred to this condition as a "failing graft" because, if the lesion is not corrected, graft thrombosis will almost certainly occur.[37] The importance of this failing graft concept lies in the fact that many difficult lower extremity revascularizations can be salvaged for protracted periods by relatively simple interventions if the lesion responsible for the circulatory deterioration and diminished graft blood flow can be detected before graft thrombosis occurs.

Over the last 10 years we have been able to detect approximately 190 failing grafts and have corrected the lesions before graft thrombosis has occurred.[37V, 40V, 41V, 42] Invariably, the corrective procedure is simpler than the secondary operation that would be required if the bypass went on to thrombose. Vein grafts tend to fail as the result of hyperplastic lesions associated with the body or anastomotic areas of the graft. In contrast, PTFE grafts tend to fail as the result of proximal or distal progression of atherosclerotic disease. Solitary vein graft lesions of 15 mm or less in length can be treated by percutaneous transluminal angioplasty (PTA). Longer or multiple vein graft lesions should be treated by an interposition graft or a proximal or distal graft extension, depending on the lesion location.

Some of the transluminal angioplasties of these lesions have failed and required a second reintervention; others have remained effective in correcting the responsible lesion, as documented by arteriography more than 2 to 5 years later. If the failing graft is a vein bypass, detection of the failing state permits accurate localization and definition of the responsible lesion by arteriography as well as salvage of any undiseased vein. In contrast, if the graft is allowed to thrombose, the responsible lesion may be difficult to identify and the vein may be difficult or impossible to thrombectomize. Most importantly, the results of reinterventions for failing grafts, in terms of both continued cumulative patency and limb salvage rates, have been far superior to the results of reinterventions for grafts that have thrombosed and failed.[37V, 38V, 39, 40V, 41V, 42–44, 45III] The inflow and outflow arterial lesions responsible for the failing state of PTFE grafts can be treated with PTA when they are short occlusions (3–5 cm) or stenoses. Longer or more complex lesions require a graft extension to either above or below the responsible lesion.

The improved results associated with reintervention for failing grafts mandate that surgeons performing bypass operations follow their patients closely in the postoperative period and indefinitely thereafter. Ideally, noninvasive laboratory tests, including duplex studies, should be performed with similar frequency.[40V, 41V, 42, 44, 45III] If the patient has recurrence of symptoms or if the surgeon detects change in peripheral pulse examination or other manifestations of ischemia, the circulatory deterioration must be confirmed by noninvasive parameters and urgent arteriography.

## REOPERATION

All patients whose bypasses thrombose in the first month after operation undergo reoperation.[1, 2] The techniques employed have been described elsewhere.[46V, 47] Intraoperative angiographic examination is used routinely after graft thrombectomy. Vein grafts that fail immediately after operation usually require interposition of a segment of PTFE or total replacement with this material, although in our experience an occasional thrombectomized vein graft will remain patent if no etiologic lesion is present.

Patients whose bypasses thrombose after the first postoperative month are considered for aggressive reoperation, and femoral angiography is usually performed; however, they are subjected to reoperation only if the bypass failure is associated with a renewed threat to limb viability. If the patient has originally undergone operation elsewhere and details of the first operation are not known or the distal anastomosis is at or below the knee joint, a totally new bypass is performed. This is best accomplished using a variety of unusual approaches that permit access to infrainguinal arteries via unscarred, uninfected tissue planes.[47, 48] These unusual approaches include a direct approach to the distal two zones of the deep femoral artery,[49] lateral approaches to the popliteal artery above and below the knee,[50] and medial or lateral approaches to all three of the infrapopliteal arteries.[51] In addition to permitting dissection in virginal tissue planes, these unusual access routes facilitate use of shorter grafts, which enable the surgeon to use the patient's remaining segments of good vein when the ipsilateral greater saphenous vein has been used or injured by the primary operation.[47]

Failed below-knee PTFE femoropopliteal and small vessel bypasses can be similarly managed but are probably best treated by performance of an entirely new bypass, preferably with vein and using previously undissected arteries, if possible.[47, 52]

## LYTIC AGENTS

Although we believe that a totally new bypass is the best treatment for a thrombosed graft that is associated with limb-threatening ischemia, investigators have published reports advocating the use of intra-arterially administered urokinase to restore patency to thrombosed infrainguinal grafts.[53V] Treatment with thrombolytic agents allows for restoration of graft flow and permits detection of the cause of graft failure. PTA or surgical graft revision is then almost always required to correct the lesion causing the thrombosis. Late results with these lysed grafts have been mixed, although better methods for using these lytic agents are constantly being developed. Moreover, these agents have real value in the treatment of patients with native artery occlusions, such as those occurring with a popliteal aneurysm.[54]

## OPERATIVE MORTALITY

The perioperative mortality rates for patients undergoing aortic reconstructions range from 1 to 5%.[55, 56] The mortality rates for all patients undergoing infrainguinal arterial reconstructions for threatened limbs range from 2 to 6%.[1, 2, 57III] Operative mortality is slightly greater for infrapopliteal than for femoropopliteal bypasses, probably because the former operations are required in patients with more advanced, generalized disease, particularly in the lower extremity. Myocardial infarction is the principal cause of death from these operations.

These low operative mortality rates contrast with the high late death rates in that only 48% of all patients who had arterial reconstructions were alive 5 years later.[2] Almost all late deaths were unrelated to the original operation—most were the result of intercurrent arteriosclerotic events, chiefly myocardial infarction. Once again, these findings reflect the advanced stage of generalized arteriosclerosis present in these patients.

## TREATMENT RESULTS

The longterm patency rates of aortofemoral reconstruction have been excellent. Reports have documented patency rates of 85% at 5 years and 70% at 10 years. Initially about 95% of patients become asymptomatic or markedly improved, and 80% remain improved at 5 years.[58, 59]

Femoropopliteal bypasses performed with greater saphenous vein have 4-year primary patency rates that range from 68 to 80% with limb salvage rates from 75 to 80%.[60V, 61V, 62I] Femoropopliteal bypasses done with PTFE have patency rates that are similar to those of vein if the bypass is to the above-knee popliteal artery, but bypasses constructed with PTFE to the below-knee popliteal artery do not perform as well.[63]

Bypasses to tibial arteries should be performed with autogenous vein either by the reversed or the in situ technique. These bypasses should have 5-year primary patency rates that range from 60 to 67% with limb salvage rates of 70 to 75%.[60V, 61V, 62I, 64II] The secondary patency rates for all these grafts are improved with close patient followup and graft surveillance.

## ROLE OF ANGIOPLASTY

Angioplasty is a useful modality in the treatment of occlusive arterial disease, particularly in the iliac arteries. Our own[1, 2, 65] and others' experience[66, 67] suggest that with appropriate patient selection and in skilled hands, the complication rate is low. Moreover, when complications or failure of PTA do occur, they can generally be well treated by relatively simple surgical procedures with little if any increased patient morbidity or mortality.[65]

On this basis we presently attempt a PTA on

any patient with sufficiently severe disease to warrant intervention and in whom the procedure is deemed suitable.[1, 2] Patients with stage III or IV ischemia who have a hemodynamically significant segmental iliac stenosis and infrainguinal arteriosclerosis generally have a PTA (without or with a stent) of the iliac lesion as their first therapeutic intervention. If the PTA is unsuccessful, a bypass to the femoral level is performed. If the PTA is successful, further arterial intervention (usually some form of femorodistal bypass) is performed only if the ischemia is unrelieved and a healed foot cannot be achieved. We do not hesitate to perform a bypass to an iliac artery treated by PTA, and subsequent experience has borne out the effectiveness of this approach.[1, 2, 68, 69, 70V, 71V]

PTA is also used as the primary therapeutic intervention in patients without hemodynamically significant iliac artery disease who have a short (≤5 cm), segmental stenosis of the superficial femoral or popliteal artery, if this lesion is judged hemodynamically significant on the basis of pulse examination or noninvasive testing. In slightly less than half of our cases treated with angioplasty, some form of direct arterial surgery has also been required, usually a bypass of a second lesion distal to the one that was successfully treated by angioplasty.[1, 2]

Eleven percent of our iliac angioplasties and 8% of our femoropopliteal angioplasties were initially unsuccessful. If one considers the durability of those angioplasties that were initially successful, cumulative life table patency at 4 years was 78% for the iliac angioplasties and 50% for the femoropopliteal angioplasties. In a large, cooperative study, iliac angioplasty was performed for 2,264 cases with a 5-year patency rate of 84.6%. The use of stents may further improve the results of angioplasties of the iliac arteries. In addition, when an angioplasty fails and a limb is rethreatened, appropriate surgery results in protracted limb salvage in more than 70% of cases.[1, 2, 65] Generally, the operative procedure required is the same one that would have been performed had the angioplasty not been selected as the initial interventional treatment.[65] These facts, coupled with our angioplasty mortality rate of less than 1% in this elderly, sick group of patients, indicate that the risk of angioplasty failure is not excessive. We therefore continue to regard PTA, when performed by a committed radiology and surgery team, as an important part of an aggressive approach to salvaging limbs.[1, 68] However, 81% of patients with threatened limbs will require operative treatment at some point in their course; only 19% can be treated by PTA alone.[1]

PTA has also been effective in the treatment of stenotic lesions in tibial arteries and stenoses developing in or proximal or distal to a still-functioning vein or PTFE graft.[1, 2, 40V, 67, 72III, 73V]

## RECENT EVALUATIONS OF AGGRESSIVE APPROACHES TO LIMB SALVAGE

Two decades ago, most patients with limb-threatening ischemia were treated by a primary major amputation above or below the knee. With improved arteriography and the interventional and operative techniques already outlined, efforts to save more and more threatened lower limbs have become increasingly widespread around the world. Although the aggressive approach to saving limbs threatened because of ischemia seemed to be worthwhile, a recent analysis of a single decade's experience from the State of Maryland casts doubt on the value of balloon angioplasty and bypass techniques as methods for preventing major amputations.[3] This article purported to show that amputation rates in Maryland remained stable while the use of angioplasty and reconstructive arterial surgery increased markedly over the period of the study. The value of the procedures and their cost-effectiveness were questioned. Unfortunately, these conclusions were based on flawed analyses of flawed data. For example, transmetatarsal amputations, a most successful component of many limb salvage efforts, were considered major amputations in this study. Moreover, many of the reported angioplasties and bypasses in the study were performed for claudication and not for limb salvage. Amputation was obviously not an appropriate index of success in these cases. Finally, the Maryland study did not consider the possibility that as the population aged and became more infirm, amputation rates would have increased without the benefits of the increasing numbers of angioplasties and bypasses performed.

Further conclusive evidence that interventional techniques are effective in preventing amputation was presented in a recent analysis of major amputation rates from our own institution over a 16-year period.[1] In this study of all patients with limbs threatened because of arteriosclerotic ischemia, primary amputation rates fell from 41 to 7% over the 16 years (Fig. 13–5). This was an index of increasing operability as our ability to perform bypasses to more distal and disadvantaged outflow tracts increased. Less than 1% of patients were inoperable because of the pattern of their arterial

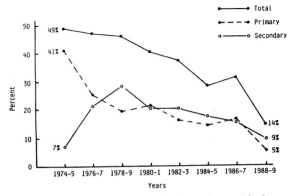

**Figure 13–5.** Amputation rates in all patients with threatened limbs. Primary amputations were those at the above-knee or below-knee levels without previous vascular interventions. Secondary amputations were major amputations performed any time after an arterial intervention. Total amputations were all major amputations. (Used with permission from Veith FJ, Gupta SK, Wengerter KR, et al: Changing arteriosclerotic disease patterns and management strategies in lower-limb-threatening ischemia. Ann Surg 212:402, 1990.)

disease. Over the same period, secondary amputations were also decreasing (see Fig. 13–5) so that we were not, by our aggressive use of bypass operations, merely converting primary amputations to secondary procedures. More importantly, total major amputation rates fell from 49 to 14%, showing conclusively that our limb salvage efforts were effective in preventing amputations, usually until the patient died from a cause other than the threatened limb or the procedure employed to save it.[1, 2]

## ECONOMIC IMPACT OF LIMB SALVAGE

The dollar cost of an aggressive approach to salvage limbs is high, with a mean cost of $19,000 for femoropopliteal bypasses and $29,000 for small vessel bypasses. These figures include all physician, hospital, and rehabilitation costs, including those of reoperations. On the other hand, the mean total cost of below-knee amputation, which in 26% of our patients resulted in failed rehabilitation with a need for chronic institutional care or professional assistance at home, was $27,000. Thus, limb salvage surgery is expensive but no more so than the less attractive alternative of amputation.[74, 75]

## REFERENCES

1. Veith FJ, Gupta SK, Wengerter KR, et al: Changing arteriosclerotic disease patterns and management strategies in lower-limb-threatening ischemia. Ann Surg 212:402, 1990.
2. Veith FJ, Gupta SK, Samson RH, et al: Progress in limb salvage by reconstructive arterial surgery combined with new or improved adjunctive procedures. Ann Surg 194:386, 1981.
3. Tunis SR, Bass EB, Steinberg EP: The use of angioplasty, bypass surgery, and amputation in the management of peripheral vascular disease. N Engl J Med 325:556, 1991.
4. Rivers SP, Veith FJ, Ascer E, Gupta SK: Successful conservative therapy of severe limb threatening ischemia: The value of nonsympathectomy. Surgery 99:759, 1986
5. Donaldson MC, Mannick JA: Femoropopliteal bypass grafting for intermittent claudication. Is pessimism warranted? Arch Surg 115:724, 1980.
6. Boyd AM: The natural course of arteriosclerosis of the lower extremities. Proc R Soc Med 55:591, 1962.
7. Coran AG, Warren R: Arteriographic changes in femoropopliteal arteriosclerosis obliterans: A five year follow-up study. N Engl J Med 274:643, 1966.
8. Imparato AM, Kim GE, Davidson T, Crowley JG: Intermittent claudication: Its natural course. Surgery 78:795, 1975.
9. Goodreau JJ, Greasy JK, Flanigan DP, et al: Rational approach to the differentiation of vascular and neurogenic claudication. Surgery 84:749, 1978.
10. Kavanaugh GJ, Svien HJ, Holman CB, Johnson RM: "Pseudoclaudication" syndrome produced by compression of the cauda equina. JAMA 206:2477, 1968.
11. Karmody AM, Powers SR, Monaco VJ, Leather RP: Blue toe syndrome: An indication for limb salvage surgery. Arch Surg 111:1263, 1976.
12. Haimovici HC, Moss CM, Veith FJ: Arterial embolectomy revisited. Surgery 78:409, 1975.
13. Gupta SK, Samson RH, Veith FJ: Embolectomy of the distal part of the popliteal artery. Surg Gynecol Obstet 153:254, 1981.
14. Calligaro KD, Veith FJ: Proper technique of lower extremity pulse examination. Contemp Surg 40:49, 1992.
15. Rivers SP, Scher LA, Veith FJ: Indications for distal arterial reconstruction in the presence of palpable pedal pulses. J Vasc Surg 12:552, 1990.
16. Whittemore AD, Clowes AW, Hechtman HB, Mannick JA: Aortic aneurysm repair: Reduced operative mortality associated with maintenance of optimal cardiac performance. Ann Surg 192:414, 1980.
17. Rivers SP, Scher LA, Gupta SK, Veith FJ: Safety of peripheral vascular surgery after recent acute myocardial infarction. J Vasc Surg 11:70, 1990.
18. Sprayregen S: Principles of angiography. In Haimovici H (ed): Vascular Surgery: Principles and Techniques. New York, McGraw-Hill, 1976, pp 39–66.
19. Flanigan DP, Williams LR, Keifer T, et al: Prebypass operative arteriography. Surgery 92:627, 1982.
V 20. Mannick JA, Jackson BT, Coffman JD: Success of bypass vein grafts in patients with isolated popliteal artery segments. Surgery 61:17, 1967.
V 21. Veith FJ, Gupta SK, Daly V: Femoropopliteal bypass to the isolated popliteal segment: Is polytetrafluoroethylene graft acceptable? Surgery 89:296, 1981.
III 22. Kram HB, Gupta SK, Veith FJ, et al: Late results of 217 femoropopliteal bypasses to isolated popliteal segments. J Vasc Surg 14:386, 1991.
V 23. Flinn WR, Flanigan DP, Verta MJ, et al: Sequential femoral-tibial bypass for severe limb ischemia. Surgery 88:357, 1980.
24. Rutherford RB, Flanigan DP, Gupta SK, et al: Sug-

gested standards for reports dealing with lower extremity ischemia. J Vasc Surg 4:90, 1986.

25. Ascer E, Veith FJ, Morin L, et al: Components of outflow resistance and their correlation with graft patency in lower extremity arterial reconstructions. J Vasc Surg 1:817, 1984.

V 26. Veith FJ, Ascer E, Gupta SK, et al: Tibiotibial vein bypass grafts: A new operation for limb salvage. J Vasc Surg 2:552, 1985.

V 27. Ascer E, Veith FJ, Gupta SK: Bypasses to plantar arteries and other tibial branches: An extended approach to limb salvage. J Vasc Surg 8:434, 1988.

III 28. Veith FJ, Gupta SK, Samson RH, et al: Superficial femoral and popliteal arteries as inflow sites for distal bypasses. Surgery 90:980, 1981.

V 29. Wengerter KR, Yang PM, Veith FJ, et al: A twelve-year experience with the popliteal-to-distal artery bypass: The significance and management of proximal disease. J Vasc Surg 15:143, 1992.

30. Harrington EB, Harrington ME, Schanzer H, et al: The dorsalis pedis bypass—moderate success in difficult situations. J Vasc Surg 15:409, 1992.

31. Andros G, Harris RW, Salles-Cunha SX, et al: Bypass grafts to the ankle and foot. J Vasc Surg 7:785, 1988.

32. Schneider JR, Walsh DB, McDaniel MD, et al: Pedal bypass versus tibial bypass with autogenous vein: A comparison of outcome and hemodynamic results. J Vasc Surg 17:1029, 1993.

33. Dietzek AM, Gupta SK, Kram HB, et al: Limb loss with patent infrainguinal bypasses. Eur J Vasc Surg 4:413, 1990.

34. Sanchez LA, Goldsmith J, Rivers SP, et al: Limb salvage surgery in end stage renal disease: Is it worthwhile? J Cardiovasc Surg 33:344, 1992.

V 35. Szilagyi DE, Smith RF, Elliot JP, et al: The biologic fate of autogenous vein implants as arterial substitutes: Clinical, angiographic and histopathologic observations in femoropopliteal operations for atherosclerosis. Ann Surg 178:232, 1973.

V 36. O'Mara CS, Flinn WR, Johnson ND, et al: Recognition and surgical management of patent but hemodynamically failed arterial grafts. Ann Surg 193:467, 1981.

V 37. Veith FJ, Weiser RK, Gupta SK, et al: Diagnosis and management of failing lower extremity arterial reconstructions. J Cardiovasc Surg 25:381, 1984.

V 38. Whittemore AD, Clowes AW, Couch NP, et al: Secondary femoropopliteal reconstruction. Ann Surg 193:35, 1981.

39. Berkowitz HD, Hobbs CL, Roberts B, et al: Value of routine vascular laboratory studies to identify vein graft stenosis. Surgery 90:971, 1981.

V 40. Sanchez L, Gupta SK, Veith FJ, et al: A ten-year experience with one hundred fifty failing or threatened vein and polytetrafluoroethylene arterial bypass grafts. J Vasc Surg 14:729, 1991.

V 41. Sanchez LA, Suggs WD, Veith FJ, et al: Is surveillance to detect failing polytetrafluoroethylene bypasses worthwhile? Twelve-year experience with ninety-one grafts. J Vasc Surg 18:981, 1993.

42. Sanchez LA, Suggs WD, Marin ML, et al: Is percutaneous balloon angioplasty appropriate in the treatment of graft and anastomotic lesions responsible for failing vein bypasses? Am J Surg 168:97, 1994.

43. Smith CR, Green RM, DeWeese JA: Pseudoocclusion of femoropopliteal bypass grafts. Circulation 68 [Suppl II]:88, 1983.

44. Bandyk DF, Cata RF, Towne JB: A low flow velocity predicts failure of femoropopliteal and femoro-tibial bypass grafts. Surgery 98:799, 1985.

III 45. Bandyk DF, Bergamini TM, Towne JB, et al: Durabil-

ity of vein graft revision: The outcome of secondary procedures. J Vasc Surg 13:200, 1991.

V 46. Veith FJ, Gupta SK, Daly V: Management of early and late thrombosis of expanded polytetrafluoroethylene (PTFE) femoropopliteal bypass grafts: Favorable prognosis with appropriate reoperation. Surgery 87:581, 1980.

47. Veith FJ, Gupta SK, Ascer E, et al: Improved strategies for secondary operations on infrainguinal arteries. Ann Vasc Surg 4:85, 1990.

48. Veith FJ, Ascer E, Nunez A, et al: Unusual approaches to infrainguinal arteries. J Cardiovasc Surg 28:58, 1987.

49. Nunez A, Veith FJ, Collier P, et al: Direct approach to the distal portions of the deep femoral artery for limb salvage bypasses. J Vasc Surg 8:576, 1988.

50. Veith FJ, Ascer E, Gupta SK, et al: Lateral approach to the popliteal artery. J Vasc Surg 6:119, 1987.

51. Dardik H. Dardik I, Veith FJ: Exposure of the tibial-peroneal arteries by a single lateral approach. Surgery 75:372, 1974.

52. Ascer E, Collier P, Gupta SK, et al: Reoperation for PTFE bypass failure: The importance of distal outflow site and operative technique in determining outcome. J Vasc Surg 5:298, 1987.

III 53. McNamara TO, Fischer JR: Thrombolysis of peripheral arterial and graft occlusions: Improved results using high dose urokinase. Am J Roentgenol 144: 769, 1985.

54. Schwarz W, Berkowitz HD, Taormina V, et al: The preoperative use of intraarterial thrombolysis for a thrombosed popliteal artery aneurysm. J Cardiovasc Surg 25:465, 1984.

55. Bunt TJ: The role of a defined protocol for cardiac risk assessment in decreasing perioperative myocardial infarction in vascular surgery. J Vasc Surg 15:626, 1992.

56. Lette J, Waters D, Lassonde J, et al: Multivariate clinical models and quantitative dipyridamole thallium imaging to predict cardiac morbidity and death after vascular reconstruction. J Vasc Surg 14:160, 1991.

III 57. Reichle FA, Tyson R: Comparison of long-term results of 364 femoropopliteal or femorotibial bypasses for revascularization of severely ischemic lower extremities. Ann Surg 182:449, 1975.

58. Crawford ES, Bomberger RA, Glaeser DH, et al: Aortoiliac occlusive disease: Factors influencing survival and function following reconstructive operation over a twenty-five year period. Surgery 90:1055, 1981.

V 59. Brewster DC, Perier BA, Robison JG, et al: Aortofemoral grafts for multilevel occlusive disease: Predictors of success and need for distal bypass. Arch Surg 117:1593, 1982.

V 60. Bergamini TM, Towne JB, Bandyk DF, et al: Experience with in situ saphenous vein bypasses during 1981 to 1989: Determinant factors of long-term patency. J Vasc Surg 13:137, 1991.

V 61. Taylor LM, Edwards JM, Porter JM: Present status of reversed vein bypass grafting: Five-year results of a modern series. J Vasc Surg 11:193, 1990.

I 62. Veith FJ, Gupta SK, Ascer E, et al: Six-year prospective multicenter randomized comparison of autologous saphenous vein and expanded polytetrafluoroethylene grafts in infrainguinal arterial reconstructions. J Vasc Surg 3:104, 1986.

63. Quinones-Baldrich WJ, Busuttil RW, Baker JD, et al: Is the preferential use of polytetrafluoroethylene grafts for femoropopliteal bypass justified? J Vasc Surg 8:219, 1988.

II 64. Wengerter KR, Veith FJ, Gupta SK, et al: Prospective

randomized multicenter comparison of in situ and reversed vein infrapopliteal bypasses. J Vasc Surg 13:189, 1991.

65. Samson RH, Sprayregen S, Veith FJ, et al: Management of angioplasty complication, unsuccessful procedures and early and late failures. Ann Surg 199:234, 1984.

66. Gruntzig A, Kumpe DA: Technique of percutaneous transluminal angioplasty with the Gruntzig balloon catheter. Am J Roentgenol 132:547, 1979.

67. Ring EJ, Alpert JR, Freiman DB, et al: Early experience with percutaneous transluminal angioplasty using a vinyl balloon catheter. Ann Surg 191:438, 1980.

68. Veith FJ, Gupta SK, Wengerter KR, et al: Impact of nonoperative therapy of the clinical management of peripheral arterial disease. Circulation 83:137, 1991.

69. Alpert JR, Ring EJ, Freiman DB, et al: Balloon dilatation of iliac stenosis with distal arterial surgery. Arch Surg 115:715, 1980.

V 70. Kadir S, Smith GW, White RI Jr, et al: Percutaneous transluminal angioplasty as an adjunct to the surgical management of peripheral vascular disease. Ann Surg 195:786, 1982.

V 71. Brewster DC, Cambria RP, Darling RC, et al: Long-term results of combined iliac balloon angioplasty and distal surgical revascularization. Ann Surg 210:324, 1989.

III 72. Kent KC, Whittemore AD, Mannick JA: Short-term and midterm results of an all autologous tissue policy for infrainguinal reconstruction. J Vasc Surg 9:107, 1989.

V 73. Bakal CW, Sprayregen S, Scheinbaum K, et al: Percutaneous transluminal angioplasty of the infrapopliteal arteries: Results in 53 patients. Am J Roentgenol 154:171, 1990.

74. Gupta SK, Veith FJ, Ascer E, et al: Cost factors in limb-threatening ischaemia due to infrainguinal arteriosclerosis. Eur J Vasc Surg 2:151, 1988.

75. Gupta SK, Veith FJ: Inadequacy of diagnosis related group (DRG) reimbursements for limb salvage lower extremity arterial reconstructions. J Vasc Surg 11:348, 1990.

# Venous Thromboembolism

# Chapter 14

# Epidemiology of Venous Thromboembolism

Cedric J. Carter

Epidemiology can be defined as the study of the distribution and determinants of disease in the population. In modern usage this involves the study of any type of illness or injury. In the past there was a concept that epidemiologic principles were to be applied only to classic epidemics such as plague or typhoid. Although this is still a suitable application of the discipline, most epidemiologic studies are now targeted at less acute and more subtle diseases.

Epidemiology differs from practical clinical medicine. It is not directly a study of the specifics of an individual's illness. It is an examination of how information from that individual can be recorded and analyzed in conjunction with information from other patients in a defined population. This community perspective should not impair immediate patient management because epidemiologic studies are usually observational. In fact, in many cases over time studies can be used to enhance patient management. Judicious investigational and statistical techniques in a whole population can ascertain linkages and causes that are not apparent in bedside clinical medicine. This new knowledge can then be applied to the population in the form of preventive or therapeutic measures. An obvious example of this application is in the field of venous thrombosis in which the epidemiologic studies provided the scientific basis for the various antithrombotic regimens that are now extremely important parts of medical and surgical care.

To study disease frequencies and distributions, measurements have to be made in the population of interest. Sometimes this is the whole population, but more often it is a specific population. In the case of venous thrombosis, much of the epidemiologic emphasis has been on the hospitalized population, and relatively few studies have addressed the total population. There are several reasons for this imbalance.

Specific subpopulations (e.g., orthopedic surgery patients) have a very high thrombotic risk. In these circumstances, close epidemiologic investigation is clearly justified and has helped to develop preventive regimens. From a logistic point of view such hospital groups are attractive groups to study. They are a discrete group with relativity homogenous demographics. They have a high occurrence rate of thrombosis and are in a setting where definitive diagnosis is possible. This situation contrasts sharply with that of the general population which is obviously much more heterogeneous. In addition, the frequency of thrombosis in the general population is relatively low, and the type of diagnostic testing used for high-risk hospital cases is often neither appropriate nor, in many cases, available to the general population.

Epidemiology requires measurements and the use of various rates and indices that permit the generation of data for the purposes of comparison and the calculation of risks. For population- or community-based studies, rates are usually expressed by a convenient denominator of the relevant population (e.g., cases per 100,000). For small populations, such as a specific surgical group, percentages or fractions are often used. If it is known how the specific group is related to the whole population, extrapolations can be made, but unless a linked database exists this is usually not possible. In the general medical literature the term "rate" may be employed rather than the terms "incidence," "prevalence," or "case frequency." These are different but not independent measures. Prevalence is the number of cases in a population at a given time. Because this is a point estimate there is no temporal component. The incidence refers to the number of new cases occurring in a population in a specified time (e.g., per month or per year). According to the chronicity of a disease, these rates can give a very different perspective. Usually incidences are more informative. For small or very specific groups the case frequency is often given. This is often the equivalent of an incidence. It involves an observation period, but because the time period is usually not specified, a simple rate is reported.

Epidemiologic studies are based on certain principles and requirements. For a study to be useful it cannot simply be a numeric description of events from an ill-defined population. The starting point of a study must be a clear idea of what is to be studied and why. Once this is decided, the specific methodologic and logistic issues have to be addressed.

## DEFINITION OF THE POPULATION OF INTEREST

The key starting point of any study is the definition and identification of the population of interest. Except for a few exceptions such as death, wherein the diagnostic endpoint is obvious and reporting is often mandatory, study populations are a subset of the general population. It is usually neither possible nor necessary to study a whole population. If a sample is carefully assembled, extrapolations to the parent population are often reasonable. The important issue is to ensure, when a population is subsampled, that the relationship of this sample to the parent population is clearly understood. Although this may appear to be self-evident, it is also one of the primary faults of many epidemiologic studies. Various statistics are generated or risks calculated but the recipients of this information are often unable to identify if the sample is representative of their group of interest.

For practical reasons, true population studies are rare. Some of the more developed counties have centralized statistics. The value of these data is influenced by both the accuracy and completeness of reporting. On the few occasions when the veracity of this type of record has been tested, it has often proved to be inaccurate.[1]

A more common approach is to address a specific population which, on the basis of previous observations, is thought to be at high risk for the variable under study. In the case of venous thrombosis, this type of study is often hospital based. This is partly because certain procedures or diseases that are associated with hospitals have a high incidence of venous thrombosis, and partly because many of the diagnostic tests are not readily available in the community. These studies can provide reliable but somewhat limited information because their relationship to the whole population may be difficult to ascertain. Obviously, all statistics are dependent on the quality of the diagnosis.

## INFLUENCE OF DIAGNOSTIC METHODS

Methods of diagnosis in venous thromboembolic disease are discussed in detail in Chapters 22 to 25. Certain general principles that apply to diagnostic tests are relevant to epidemiologic studies. The primary performance of a diagnostic test is defined by the relationship of the sensitivity and specificity. In terms of clinical utility, these parameters are influenced by the prevalence of venous thrombosis in the population under study. In certain circumstances the requirements of a diagnostic test for epidemiologic purposes differ from those for patient management. When a test is being done to determine immediate patient management, very stringent requirements are necessary for sensitivity and specificity of diagnostic accuracy. Although this is also an ideal for epidemiologic study, this level of rigor is often not possible, and suboptimal testing technology or incompleteness of application may occur. The issue then becomes whether this suboptimal testing introduces major bias into estimates.

The impact of imperfections in diagnosis varies according to circumstance. One extreme is the simple clinical diagnosis of deep-vein thrombosis (DVT). Clearly, the poor sensitivity and specificity of clinical diagnosis make this less than an ideal situation but it could be argued that for comparing relative rather than absolute rates in different subgroups or populations simple clinical diagnosis may not be of major importance. In many cases, even relative measurements are too unreliable. Pain and swelling in elderly adults have a series of causes not present in young adults. Sometimes the bias may be more insidious. An elegant example occurred when a group of investigators compared the objective diagnosis of DVT with clinical diagnosis in young women. It became apparent that knowledge of oral contraceptive use by the women led to a much higher rate of clinical diagnosis of DVT.[2]

There are situations in which suboptimal diagnosis may be less critical. One example is a situation in which a noninvasive test for DVT is applied in lieu of bilateral ascending venography. This test may not be sufficiently accurate for clinical management decisions but may permit intergroup comparisons of relative rates.

Indeed, if the relationship of the sensitivity of the noninvasive test relative to venography is known, a substitute estimate of incidence or prevalence can be made.

## STUDY DESIGN

The simplest and traditionally most common type of study is the descriptive study. The investigator defines the population of interest, applies the most readily available diagnostic test, and then demonstrates the incidence, prevalence, or case rate for the particular population. This may indicate the magnitude of the problem, but in many cases the information is retrieved with a view to some form of intervention, and additional information is required. Obtaining additional information normally takes the form of subgroup analyses following either prospective or retrospective stratification. Investigation starts with primary demographic variables such as age and sex and progresses to more specific categories such as recent surgery, presence of malignancy, or other clinically pertinent variables. Descriptive studies lack formal controls; however, different patterns of incidence or prevalence among the variables provide the hypotheses for more rigorous studies.

An alternative and often complementary type of study to the descriptive study is the case-control study. Case control studies permit a rapid, albeit retrospective, estimate of the apparent strength of association between the putative risk factors and clinical events. The primary attraction of the case-control design is that the investigator can "capture" the cases from previously recorded data rather than wait for new events to occur, as in a prospective study. This makes case-control studies particularly attractive for investigation of relatively rare conditions. The low frequency of some conditions makes primary prospective studies daunting from both a practical and financial point of view.

There is often confusion about the derivation of the strength of the association from case-control studies. What are being measured are the relative rates of exposure to a risk factor for cases and controls and not the effects of exposure. The investigator identifies cases and determines the rate of exposure to a putative risk factor (e.g., DVT cases versus the rate of oral contraception usage). Concomitantly, the investigator identifies one or more control groups and ascertains its exposure to the same putative risk factor. Subsequently, the investigator compares the exposure rate between cases and controls. The validity of the subsequent calculations depends on several assumptions. These include a low frequency of events in the population, an assurance that the controls are representative, and a certainty that all cases in a given population have been identified. If these assumptions appear reasonable, it is possible to calculate a "risk." To avoid confusion with the directly calculated risk, as determined by prospective cohort analytic studies (see later), this risk is termed an "odds ratio."

The mirror image of the case-control study previously described is the prospective cohort analytic study. In this type of study, subjects who are free of the condition of interest are identified. A proportion of them are exposed to the putative risk factor, whereas the remainder are not, and the case frequency of events that develop in each group is then directly compared. This result is a direct estimate and is termed the "relative risk." For the results to have any meaning, the inception cohorts should be similar. The usual practice is to match from the nonexposed population for individuals with similar overall characteristics. A practical example is the study conducted in England by family practitioners to assess the prothrombotic effects of oral contraception.[3] In this study, each time a physician placed a young female patient on the oral contraceptive, a female patient not on the oral contraceptive, but of similar age, was identified from the family practitioner's file to act as a control. Both cohorts were then followed to observe the incidence of clinically apparent DVT. Putting aside the logistic problems of sample size, the preferred study design is a cohort analytic study rather than a case-control study because the former avoids artifacts such as recall bias and can yield incidence rates as well as relative risks. A major drawback of the cohort analytic study is that it is impossible to control for hidden imbalance of characteristics between the treated or exposed cohort and the untreated or nonexposed cohort. To minimize this imbalance, the investigator needs a randomized controlled trial.

The randomized controlled clinical trial, with blinding whenever possible, is the most powerful study design. This type of study is only possible when the investigator can control the exposure to the potentially positive or negative risk factor. An example is the evaluation of a new medication. The advantages of the randomization process are that investigators can minimize the effects of occult or previously unconsidered sources of bias. The drawback for many epidemiologic studies is that the investigator is seldom in a position to control the exposure to the putative positive or negative risk factor.

The classic study of the epidemiology of a disease is closely linked to the natural history of the condition. In the field of venous thrombosis, these observational aspects are often preempted by interventions.

Interventions can have both informative and uninformative effects. On the positive side, interventions have often been devised on the scientific understanding of putative risk factors. If an untreated cohort is available for comparison, the intervention can be used to validate the importance of the risk factor. A practical example is the role of active increase in venous flow in patients in whom stasis is a possible risk factor for thrombosis.

## CAUSATION AND BIOSTATISTICAL CONSIDERATIONS

Epidemiologic techniques vary according to the target information. The field of venous thrombosis has a variety of objectives. A primary requirement, as indicated earlier, is the basic demography and the demonstration of the groups in whom thrombosis occurs, and how often. Surprisingly, there are still major deficiencies in this area when it comes to community studies. In the areas in which substantive information is available, the next task becomes one of determining the probability of a causal relationship, rather than a mere association. This is a complex area that combines basic epidemiology; biologic and pathologic knowledge or hypotheses; and the results of general or, preferably, specific interventions. In general these disciplines are complementary, and it is often difficult to define the investigative boundaries.

For the simpler investigative boundaries, such as the recording of measures of rate, the issues are the definition of the population of interest, accuracy of the diagnostic test or tests, and careful compilation of the data in a manner that facilitates retrieval and linkage. In simple descriptive studies the biostatistical contribution is usually minimal. The confidence intervals can be calculated on a single proportion, but in a large descriptive series confidence intervals add little further information beyond the simple rate of events.

Descriptive surveys can be used for the purposes of hypothesis forming. Provided the investigator records the population characteristics in a uniform and often stratified fashion, the data can be examined for correlations. There are various statistical approaches. The more sophisticated methods employ multivariate analytic techniques. With a sufficiently large sample, covariance techniques can be applied to correct for confounding variables. The use of multivariate rather than univariate methods is important, because in the etiology of venous thrombosis there is often linkage between risk factors, which can cause spurious associations. Multivariate techniques are somewhat cumbersome, and one approach that has been successful is a two-stage procedure. An initial univariate analysis is performed to identify possible individual risk factors, and these results form the basis of a secondary multivariate analysis.

In comparative trials (such as in case control and cohort studies), analytic trials can be utilized to generate estimates of risk. In case control studies, as explained earlier, these are indirect estimates and are termed odds ratios. In the case of cohort analytic trials, the direct estimates are termed the relative risks. If no association exists between the putative risk factor and the outcome, the odds ratios or relative risk ratios will approximate to unity. Values that are substantially greater or lesser than unity suggest an association. The simplest form of analysis of these data involves the use of the chi square statistic. This can be modified to weigh for the effects of relative risks for individual subcategories, as described by Mantel and Haenszel.[4]

If the investigator is able to randomize patients or populations to putative risk factors, analysis is clearly more straightforward because post hoc corrections are usually not required.

If a randomized trial is performed that challenges the importance of one discrete variable, a positive outcome supports a causal relationship for this variable. The problem is that most epidemiologic studies cannot employ this rigorous experimentation. Inferences have to be made on less direct information. In these circumstances, several ploys are used to examine possible causality. For the most part, inferences are intuitively obvious. Consistency of an association across several often varied studies supports the possibility of a causal association. The magnitude of the relative risk or odds ratio is important. When it is possible to examine for dosage, a dose effect (e.g., years of cigarette exposure versus lung cancer rates) is supportive of causation. In fact, all these maneuvers are an attempt to compensate for suboptimal experimental design.

## COMMUNITY-BASED SURVEYS OF INCIDENCE AND PREVALENCE OF VENOUS THROMBOEMBOLIC DISEASE

Systematic application of objective tests for the presence of venous thromboembolic disease to a sizeable community obviously presents major logistic problems. Early studies relied on suboptimal technology or indirect measures. Clinical diagnosis of venous thrombosis was used in earlier studies, but it is now clear that this approach is unreliable. Other studies, seeking a slightly more objective endpoint, attempted to assess the incidence of fatal pulmonary embolus. This substitute endpoint was used because it was realized that pulmonary embolism was a reflection of the presence of major venous thrombosis. It was also assumed that sudden death from pulmonary embolism would result in an accurate death certificate. In practice this approach was too crude. The use of death certificate information to ascertain the definitive cause of death has been shown to be inaccurate.[1] The quality of this information is also undermined by the fact that the relationship between the incidence of venous thrombosis and embolism in the general population was not and is still not known. In view of these limitations, a more direct approach to determining the incidence and importance of venous thromboembolic disease in the community was required.

Early attempts to directly study deep venous thrombosis in the general population were greatly hampered by suboptimal diagnostic methods. Reliance was based on simple clinical examination plus physician records or hospital record information. In addition, it was assumed in some studies that varicose ulceration was synonymous with previous deep venous thrombosis. Employing this methodology, an early study from Sweden indicated a prevalence of deep venous thrombosis of 5%.[5]

A later study from the United States involved a longitudinal survey, over an 11-year period, in and around the small industrial town of Tecumseh, Michigan.[6] The diagnostic methods were primarily periodic physical examinations and accompanying health status questionnaires. In general, objective tests for deep venous thrombosis were not used. In retrospect, some reservations also concerned the primary sampling process. Voluntary participation was involved, and certain groups that are now known to be at high risk for venous thromboembolic disease, such as the elderly, were underrepresented. Accepting these methodologic flaws, there was a general population incidence of 23 per 100,000 per year for pulmonary embolism and 122 per 100,000 for deep venous thrombosis. If the figures were extrapolated to the 1970 United States census, this study indicated that there were 250,000 new cases of clinically recognized deep venous thrombosis in the United States.

Because of the relatively undeveloped diagnostic methods used in this study, these figures may not be entirely accurate, but they do permit some more general observations. In this study females were at slightly higher risk of developing deep venous thrombosis, but it was of interest that under the age of 46 years deep venous thrombosis was three to four times more common in women. Approximately half of these cases could be attributed to complications of pregnancy. The other obvious feature of this study was the age dependency of deep venous thrombosis in both sexes. The sixth and seventh decades showed a dramatic increase in events. The breakdown of hospital-associated events and those in the ambulant population was not available; however, it is likely that some of the age-dependent increase is related to a greater frequency of prothrombotic surgical procedures, such as orthopedic surgery, and an age-dependent increase in cancer.

The Tecumseh Community Health Study remained the yardstick for community-based estimates of thromboembolic disease for many years. For three decades little additional work was done in this area. This is in contrast to the intense research into hospital-associated venous thromboembolic disease. A second community-based study was reported in 1991 from the United States.[7] This study took place in Worcester, Massachusetts, and took advantage of a linked system whereby 16 acute care hospitals reported to a discrete statistical census area. The rationale was that significant cases of deep venous thrombosis would not be treated and diagnosed at home and that, provided deep vein thrombosis was a primary diagnosis or a significant complication, cases could be retrospectively retrieved from the hospital records. In essence this was a straightforward retrospective attempt to determine incidence. The success of this type of descriptive study is dependent on the quality of the diagnostic testing, the completeness of the sample, and the accurate recording of events. Because the study was based on medical records, patient recollection was not a primary issue. In addition, it was possible to challenge the quality and completeness of the data because of the permanent records. A potential weakness was the employment of the International Classification of Disease Codes (ICD-9-CM) but, again, internal validation was possible.

The authors of this study acknowledged some potential shortcomings, such as events occurring in long-term care units and other less acute care institutions. However, the main probable effect of these cases would be that their reported figures may be a slight underestimate. The basic findings were an incidence for deep venous thrombosis of 48 per 100,000 per year with an incidence of 23 per 100,000 for all pulmonary emboli. The latter figure may be less reliable because of limited postmortem data. Various subanalyses were performed. As in the Tecumseh study, deep venous thrombosis acquired in the community showed a striking correlation with advancing age. Nearly all patients had at least one major risk factor for venous thromboembolic disease, and the majority had three or more. These risk factors are discussed in more detail later, but they included cancer, congestive heart failure, limb fracture, stroke, and surgery. An important positive feature in this study was that 82% of the deep venous thrombosis cases had an objective diagnosis. If these figures are extrapolated to the whole of the United States, an annual incidence for deep venous thrombosis of 170,000 cases is obtained. This estimate is similar to the estimate of 250,000 from the Tecumseh study, allowing for the fact that the Worcester study used objective diagnostic criteria and was performed approximately 30 years later. The Worcester study was also conducted after the introduction of antithrombotic prophylaxis.

From Sweden, a report in 1992 described the incidence in the Malmo area.[8] This study had many of the features of the Worcester study in that it relied on the fact that the medical area within a district was reasonably circumscribed and could be used to generate a community estimate. Some additional advantages were available to the Swedish investigators. One obvious positive feature was the fact that ascending venography was the means of diagnosis. This technique remains the absolute standard for the diagnosis of venous thrombosis, but for a variety of reasons it is less commonly performed in many Western countries. Another positive feature was a prospectively applied entry format that specifically required identification of risk factors and other potentially pertinent data. In keeping with the Worcester study, the overall male-to-female ratio was approximately equal, and age dependency was noted. The distribution of risk factors was similar, and concomitant cancer was noted in one fifth of all cases. This study differed from the Worcester study in that there appeared to be more events, with an annual incidence of approximately 150 per 100,000 compared with the Worcester estimate of approximately 50 per 100,000 of the population. The reason for the magnitude of difference is not clear. From the Swedish report it appears that recurrent deep venous thrombosis

was included in the event total. It is unclear whether patients who presented with pulmonary embolism were also included in the total if the patients were subsequently found to have deep venous thrombosis. In contrast, it appeared that the Malmo study was more likely to have encompassed the whole population, and ascending venography is the most sensitive diagnostic technique.

Ascending venography identifies calf vein thrombi more accurately than most noninvasive techniques. Using these two studies as the current best guides, it is reasonable to deduce that a likely estimate of incidence for first-event deep venous thrombosis would probably be somewhere between the two study estimates and could be in the region of 100 per 100,000, which, in a country the size of the United States, means 250,000 to 300,000 new cases of deep venous thrombosis per year. Unfortunately, in the case of pulmonary embolism, fatal or otherwise, very little reliable data exist. Probably the best estimate is that derived from the Worcester study, in which the conservative estimate was 23 per 100,000 per year. This figure included cases with and without detectable associated venous thrombosis, but because of practical constraints, such as a low postmortem rate, this figure is almost certainly an underestimate.

## HOSPITAL-BASED STUDIES AND THE DEVELOPMENT OF RISK FACTOR PROFILES

The incidence of venous thromboembolic disease derived from community-based studies is largely a reflection of symptomatic venous thrombosis. The three community-based studies cited earlier included cases from hospitalized patients, but cases were not detected by uniformly applied screening tests for venous thrombosis. Some clinically silent cases were detected by the presence of symptoms of pulmonary embolus, but the majority of asymptomatic cases are undetected. In contrast to this situation, various hospital-based studies included all patients in a particular clinical circumstance that had undergone objective, and often accurate, testing to detect the presence of venous thrombosis. Perhaps the most obvious example is the existence of multiple studies on the occurrence of deep venous thrombosis in orthopedic surgery. This more substantive database also facilitates the delineation of risk factors. The other new variable that is introduced into the hospital-based studies is a component of intervention. In many instances, intervention permits the testing of a hypothesis for either a risk factor or a mediating disease mechanism.

Initial studies concerning venous thromboembolic disease were based on simple clinical observation. Orthopedic surgeons rapidly became aware that acute sudden death was a complication of 2 to 3% fractured hips and hips undergoing elective surgery.[9] Subsequent venographic procedures confirmed the presence of proximal venous thrombosis in approximately half of the surviving patients. It also became apparent that symptomatic cases, whether with limb symptoms alone or with associated pulmonary emboli, represented a small fraction of the overall problem of venous thromboembolic disease. This information was the stimulus to the numerous descriptive studies that followed and the impetus for the development of various antithrombotic regimens. The use of the antithrombotic regimens has gained such widespread acceptance that it is no longer possible to justify the use of an untreated control group to study the incidence of deep venous thrombosis in major orthopedic surgery to the lower limbs. Thrombosis rates vary greatly according to clinical circumstances. Because particular groups have identified risk factors that are related to our understanding of the pathophysiology of venous thrombosis, the hospital-based epidemiology is discussed by major disease group.

## Orthopedic Surgery and Trauma

Orthopedic surgery and trauma provide an ideal opportunity to challenge the concept of Virchow's triad—damage to the vessel wall, changes in the nature of blood, and changes in the flow of blood.[10] Trauma, whether by accident or as a consequence of orthopedic procedures, causes direct damage to vessels, acute phase-reactant changes in the blood, and altered blood flow, both from direct effects on vessels and from stasis. On a theoretical basis, it would be expected that major orthopedic surgery cases would have the highest incidence of thromboembolic disease, and indeed this is the case.

From a diagnostic point of view, orthopedic cases present some practical problems. Local trauma with concomitant fibrin deposition makes radiofibrinogen leg scanning less useful. A similarly noninvasive test such as impedance plethysmography and the various forms of Doppler ultrasound are not thought to be sufficiently accurate, and thus formal contrast venography remains the standard diagnostic test for these cases.

Patients having major trauma or major surgery, such as knee replacement, appear to be at particularly high risk of developing deep venous thrombosis. Venographically confirmed rates in the region of 50% were commonly reported in the absence of aggressive antithrombotic prophylaxis.[11-13] It is also of interest that venography in patients who have received such prophylaxis shows the presence of a substantial number of thrombi.[14] This resistance to prophylactic measures supports the concepts that major knee surgery or trauma is a special situation. The biologic explanations for this extremely high incidence are not clear, in that hip surgery shares the same obvious risk factors as the knee group but in general shows a slightly lower incidence of thrombi.

Patients having fractured hips and hip replacements have a thrombosis rate varying from 30 to 50%.[15, 16] Although calf-vein thrombi, as seen in a whole variety of surgical and medical conditions, are common, a particular feature of hip cases is the proximal thrombosis rate. Often venography demonstrates thrombosis in the immediate traumatized or operative area.[17, 18] The other observation of interest is that in fractured hips the site, and by association the extent of trauma, seems to be an important variable. Peritrochanteric fractures are associated with more thrombi than subcapital fractures. Thrombi are most commonly seen in the operated limb, but the local induction of thrombosis is only part of the story. A consistent finding in all series has been an appreciable incidence of thrombosis in the nonoperated limb. Bilateral venous thrombosis occurs in at least 25% of cases, suggesting that both limbs should always be investigated.[17, 18] This has particular relevance in the case of new symptomatology in the nonoperated limb at a remote date. These symptoms may be post-phlebitic in nature.

The majority of cases of hip and knee replacement are performed for the effects of osteoarthritis. Replacements for rheumatoid arthritis cases tend to be done in a younger age group who have received additional longterm medications including corticosteroids and analgesics with antiplatelet effects. Although the data are limited, it appears that in the case of hip replacement the thrombosis rate is lower than that in the more frequent osteoarthritis-related cases.[20] This decrease in thrombosis rate was less evident in patients with knee replacements.

The overall features of both knee- and hip-associated thrombosis relative to thrombosis of patients with general abdominal surgery are a higher incidence, more proximal thrombi, and relative resistance to antithrombotic prophylaxis.

## Abdominal and Pelvic Surgery

Although orthopedic surgery has a particularly high case rate of thrombosis, nonorthopedic procedures are more prevalent in the hospital population and in the absence of prophylaxis are still an important source of fatal pulmonary emboli. The study of the incidence of venous thrombosis associated with abdominal surgery was greatly facilitated by the development of radiofibrinogen leg scanning. Patients are injected with radiofibrinogen and the lower limbs are scanned for the development of abnormal accumulations of radioactivity. This system worked well because the scanning was in an area remote from the surgical trauma and because isolated proximal thrombi were unusual in this patient group. In general, the thrombosis rates for patients with general abdominal surgery, whether diagnosed by venography or leg scan positivity, have been in the region of 10 to 20%.[21] An unexplained observation is that the incidence of leg scan positivity in European studies has tended to be higher than that in similar studies in North America.

Pelvic surgeries are associated with a considerable risk of thrombosis. The two best-studied areas are urologic surgery and gynecologic surgery. Most studies were performed in the 1960s and 1970s and relied heavily on radiofibrinogen as a detection test.

Prostatic surgery provides an interesting model for the demonstration of risk factors for venous thrombosis. The two main surgical procedures differ in their degree of invasiveness. An additional variable is that some surgery is for cancer rather than for benign prostatic enlargement.

When the major studies on prostatectomy are reviewed, the overall incidence of venous thrombosis for transvesical surgery is approximately 40% and for transurethral surgery, 10%.[22, 23] It is unclear why this difference is so great. Certainly the transvesical procedure is more invasive and is associated with more prolonged immobility. The issue of an additional risk of cancer has been addressed in one study; however, cancer cases were overrepresented in the transurethral group, and thus cannot account for the difference in thrombosis rate. Prostatic surgery is one of the few conditions in which there is frequent use of antifibrinolytics. One of the putative pathophysiologic factors in surgical thrombosis is the result in a series of studies showing that the postoperatively fibrinolytic potential is reduced. This, combined with results of studies of fibrinolytic activity that demonstrate a decrease in idiopathic venous thrombosis, led to a series of studies to examine whether antifibrinolytic treatment increased the postprostatectomy thrombosis rate. Controlled studies showed no increase in thrombosis in the group receiving antifibrinolytics.[24] Results of this study and three similar studies suggest that the importance of decreased fibrinolysis, although attractive as a scientific hypothesis, has a relatively minor role in the etiology of surgically associated thrombosis.

Gynecologic surgery, despite the fact that it involves surgery in the region of the iliofemoral veins, shows a relatively modest rate of thrombosis. In the case of hysterectomy, as in prostatectomy, the magnitude of surgery seems to correlate with the thrombosis rate. In the largest published series, vaginal hysterectomy had a thrombosis rate of 7% compared with 12% with vaginal hysterectomy.[25] These results achieved statistical significance, but it should be noted, as in the prostatic surgery results, that these are cohort analytic studies and selection to the procedure was not random. In the same gynecologic study, patients with malignancy appeared to have a major prothrombotic incidence. This may account for the wide variation in thrombosis rates observed among patients in various gynecologic series.

## Other Surgeries

Studies on other surgeries are limited. In general it has been assumed that the thrombotic risk can be estimated from the pre-existing abdominal, pelvic, and orthopedic studies.

Because studies of other surgeries are limited, it is difficult to put isolated rates into an overall perspective, but in some studies rates of thrombosis have been quite high. For example, in one thoracotomy study a thrombosis incidence of 50% was noted.[26] One area that has not received enough attention is reconstructive arterial vascular surgery. Because there is often associated trauma to the venous system with this type of surgery, venous thrombosis might be expected. In practice, the rates vary greatly, from as low as 10% up to 40%.[27, 28] Although not formally studied, the variable practice of using considerable amounts of heparin during and after these procedures may be an important determinant. As might be anticipated, radiofibrinogen is not a useful diagnostic test in these cases, and there is a reluctance to perform routine ascending venography in relatively ischemic limbs.

## Pregnancy and the Puerperium

Pregnancy is associated with considerable changes in the coagulation system that at face value might be expected to predispose to thrombosis. Similarly, the immediate postpartum period also involves these changes plus the additional risks of pelvic trauma and associated changes in hematocrit and blood viscosity. In theory, pregnancy-related thrombosis should be an interesting area for research. In practice, studies are limited and show an overdependence on clinical diagnosis. The reasons are multiple, but the main problem seems to be a lack of suitable diagnostic techniques. Radiofibrinogen leg scanning in the antepartum period is contraindicated. Ascending venography with appropriate fetal shielding is probably safe but has been underutilized. The role of conventional auditory ultrasound is not clear. The compression B-mode ultrasound approach is too recent for complete evaluation. Impedance plethysmography has had limited application in pregnancy. This is, in part, the result of theoretical concerns about false-positive findings. Whatever the various reasons, the net result is that most information on the epidemiology of pregnancy-related thrombosis is based on descriptive studies that utilized suboptimal diagnostic technology. Therefore, this information must be interpreted with some caution. This is particularly unfortunate given the North American practice of aggressive heparin prophylaxis for the duration of subsequent pregnancies after a previous pregnancy-related event has been ''diagnosed.''

A summary of a series of studies reporting clinically diagnosed cases of venous thrombosis indicated that pregnancy represented a high-risk period for thrombosis in young women.[29] Reanalysis of these data to give a monthly incidence, which included the puerperium, indicated that additional antepartum risk was minimal or none. Postpartum, the risk appeared to be considerable.[30] This information conforms to the anticipated pathophysiology. The interpretation of the variability of risk over the duration of the pregnancy is supported by a retrospective venography-based series from Sweden that documented only 11 cases of DVT over a 5-year study of 15,000 women. Nine of these cases were diagnosed postpartum, thus confirming the impressions derived from clinically diagnosed series.[31] A notable feature was the low rate of positive venograms in the suspected antepartum cases (2 of 17 suspected cases). This gave an absolute antepartum risk of at least one order of magnitude lower than the results of studies based on clinical diagnosis. Although it is diffi-cult to interpret across studies from different populations and time periods, this information strongly suggests that the earlier clinical reports describe an incidence of thrombosis that is no longer accurate for the present day.

Despite the obvious low incidence of venous thrombosis in the antepartum period, the undesirability of prolonged anticoagulation has led to studies that address the question of whether each antepartum trimester carries an equal risk. At the clinical level, it had been suggested that the later trimesters carried a higher risk and that prophylaxis, if indicated at all, could be reserved for the second half of pregnancy. This issue has been the subject of a multicenter study.[32] Two interesting findings emerged. Of the 60 events reported, the distribution was 13 events in the first trimester, 28 in the second, and 19 in the third. The distribution is compatible with random chance and does not support the concept of a high-risk third trimester. An unexpected finding in this study was that 58 of the 60 episodes occurred in the left leg and no cases of isolated right leg thrombosis occurred. The diagnosis was made predominantly by either impedance plethysmography or B-mode Doppler examination in the first two trimesters and included the addition of venography in the third trimester. Even if there was a possibility of a few false-positive findings by either of the two noninvasive techniques in the first two trimesters, the laterality is striking and may be related to the anatomic stenosis of the left iliac vein by the branching of the right femoral artery.

No comprehensive studies exist using objective techniques to examine for any additional thrombotic tendency that may be associated with cesarean section rather than normal delivery. Indirect support for such an increase can be derived from maternal mortality figures from fatal pulmonary embolism.[33–35]

## Surgically-related Thrombosis to Define Risk Factors

Orthopedic surgery, such as hip replacement, is largely restricted to a fairly homogeneous elderly group of patients with osteoarthritis. In contrast, abdominopelvic surgery involves all ages and has a wide range of primary and secondary illnesses. This means that with the relative facility of diagnosis, coupled with large numbers, the cases could be examined for particular risk factors. Defining risk factors started with simple description but rapidly evolved into the use of sophisticated models, such as linear logistic models and discriminate function.

There are several attractions to this sort of

analysis. One is using the various permutations of apparently independent risk factors, such as age, extent of surgery, presence of malignancy, and history of previous venous thrombosis, and developing a risk profile that would have a predictive capacity. Several attempts have been made at developing a profile, with varying success, but analysis has enabled broad recommendations to be developed. In general, the need for prophylaxis is less for a young, previously healthy individual who is to undergo relatively minor elective surgery.

Another attraction of analysis is the use of this information to gain insight into pathophysiologic mechanisms. Because these observations are not specific to disease or procedure, they are discussed in a more general fashion in a later section of this chapter.

## Venous Thrombosis in Medical Conditions

Factors are common to both surgical and medical patients, such as prolonged immobilization. Early postmortem series described pulmonary embolism and associated deep venous thrombosis in both medical and surgical patients.[36, 37] It seemed logical to apply the diagnostic technology that had largely been developed for surgical cases to certain medical conditions. Although it is likely that any medical condition that is associated with prolonged immobilization places patients at a high risk for venous thrombosis, some conditions seem to be particularly indicated.

## Cardiac Disease

Patients with myocardial infarction when studied in the 1960s showed an appreciable incidence of venous thrombosis. The reported figures of the case rates varied from 20 to 40%.[38–41] Most of these studies involved radiofibrinogen leg scanning, and the majority of the thrombi were calf thrombi. The rates of venous thrombosis reported in these studies are, if anything, somewhat higher than those reported in general surgery patients in the 1960s. Myocardial infarction in this era was treated somewhat differently than it is today. Prolonged bedrest was still the custom in some institutions, and aggressive anticoagulation was unusual in most units. There may be a partial explanation of this high thrombosis rate from information showing that there is considerable thrombin generation in acute myocardial ischemic attacks.[42] One study compared the venous thrombosis rate of patients who were subsequently confirmed to have

myocardial infarction with the rate in those whose diagnosis was not subsequently confirmed.[40] Patients with true infarction had a higher incidence, suggesting that the conditions that precipitated the coronary thrombosis may also have caused the deep venous thrombosis, but no attempt was made in this study to control for other variables such as duration of bedrest. The current incidence of venous thrombosis in myocardial infarction cases is unknown. It is likely to be much lower than the historical figures cited earlier. A variety of reasons account for the reduction. Patients are much more rapidly mobilized. Cardiac failure is more efficiently treated, and most patients now receive some form of fibrinolytic or anticoagulant treatment.

The other area of cardiac disease that was studied during this period was congestive heart failure. Autopsy studies have shown a high prevalence of pulmonary emboli. Autopsy-based studies, although they satisfy the criterion of an objective diagnosis, also pose other methodologic problems. In general, they represent an extreme of a disease spectrum, and in many cases the thrombi or emboli are agonal events. Despite the limitations of interpretation of autopsy data, congestive heart failure cases showed a similar frequency of venous thrombosis to that of myocardial infarction.[43] In congestive heart failure it is difficult to implicate tissue damage or thrombin generation and thus presumably stasis and altered rheology are the primary factors. No further studies have readdressed the venous thrombosis aspects of congestive failure; the current incidence is unknown but, as in the case of myocardial infarction, it is likely to be lower than the figures reported from the early studies.

## Neurologic Disease

Leg swelling in the paralyzed limb in hemiplegia is a common finding. Prior to the development of relatively convenient tests to detect the presence of venous thrombosis, many of these cases were thought to be the result of loss of vasomotor tone secondary to denervation. The advent of radiofibrinogen leg scanning and associated venography showed that the majority of post-stroke swollen legs were the result of deep vein thrombosis. Stroke results in a general immobility, but also an additional degree of immobility is related to the paralyzed limb. The effects of the degree of immobility are demonstrated by the fact that the thrombosis rate is up to 10 times higher in the paralyzed side. The overall rate of thrombosis is extremely high and has been reported to be as high as 60% in the paralyzed limb if radiofibrinogen is the sole diagnostic method.[44] Ascending venography results have shown rates varying from 28% to 50%.[45] These rates are similar to those in major orthopedic surgery or trauma. Regarding potential mechanisms, it is difficult to implicate tissue necrosis as a primary etiologic factor. Hemiplegia often results from small thrombi in the middle cerebral artery distribution. Compared with the damage from cerebral gunshot wounds, the tissue destruction is minimal. On the stasis side, denervation may cause loss of venous tone and thus may introduce an additional rheologic component.

## GENERAL RISK FACTORS FOR VENOUS THROMBOSIS

One of the most important aims of the epidemiologic study of venous thrombosis is to develop information that can be used to predict the likelihood of the development of thrombosis. The key issue is to maximize this information so that it can be applied to an individual. For example, does a 45-year-old patient with rheumatoid arthritis who is to have a noncemented hip replacement have the same risk of thrombosis as an 80-year-old patient with osteoarthritis who is to receive a cemented prosthesis? Most thrombosis expert would say not, but they would have difficulty in quantifying this difference. A further question is whether this information is likely to be useful. Obviously, if there is an antithrombotic regimen that is both highly effective and without side effects, relative risk is less of an issue. In many cases, ideal medications are not available and additional information is of potential value.

In general risk factor identification has proved to be only partially successful. Some of the broad disease categories and their risk of thrombosis have been described earlier. One issue not discussed so far is the development of a laboratory-derived risk profile that may summate or interact with the clinical risk profile. In the discussion about the pathogenesis of venous thrombosis (see Chapter 15), it can be seen that many hemostatic variables can be used to develop a laboratory component to the risk profile. In general, laboratory-derived risk has added little to the clinical risk factors for individual patients. The reason is not clear. It may partly be related to the relative lack of sophistication of the tests compared with the complexity of the coagulation system. It almost certainly is related to the fact that the laboratory-derived

risks are not independent of some of the clinical risk factors, and therefore the additional risk ascertained in the laboratory will only make a partial contribution to the outcome.

Descriptive studies have demonstrated some clinical risk factors that appear to have some prognostic importance.[46] This information has been modified in some instances by the application of multivariate analytic techniques.[47] Some of the areas of interest are summarized in the following section.

### Age

The Tecumseh, Malmo, and Worcester studies all showed a strong correlation between increasing age and venous thrombosis development.[6–8] The effect appeared to be most marked after the fifth decade. These studies were descriptive, and the published data do not permit correction for confounders such as malignancy, which is an age-dependent but probably also an independent risk factor.

With nonmultivariate techniques, increasing age has shown a consistently positive association with postoperative venous thrombosis that is independent of the type of surgery. Multivariate analysis confirmed the association.[47]

### Malignancy

In most clinical series describing postoperative thrombosis, malignancy is overrepresented in the deep venous thrombosis cases.[46, 47] The association appears to be strongest in patients with adenocarcinoma. There is biochemical evidence of cancer procoagulants that may explain this association.[48] In view of these descriptions it is of interest that upon multivariate analysis, involving 624 patients, malignancy was not a significant independent risk factor. However, when using stepwise regression techniques, closely associated risk factors may not be as detectable as two independent risk factors. In the same series of 624 patients, previous venous thrombosis was a statistically significant risk factor, whereas previous pulmonary embolism was not, thus exemplifying this problem.

In the series of 624 patients, malignancy was identified prior to surgery and in many instances was the reason for the surgery. Because malignancy is often an occult finding, yet still capable of manifesting biologic prothrombotic activity, an alternative approach to the study of malignancy is to follow postoperative deep venous thrombosis positive and negative cohorts and to ascertain the rates of development of malignancy over a time period. A 30-month followup of approximately 1,400 patients showed that in the younger patients (less than age 50) cancer developed 19 times more commonly ($p<.001$). Above the age of 50 the relative risk was still greater than 2.0, but the value did not achieve statistical significance.[49]

A multicenter European study employed a slightly different approach in which 250 documented venous thrombosis cases were followed for 2 years after the initial diagnosis.[50] The cohorts were 105 patients with secondary thrombosis (causes other than cancer) and 145 cases of thrombosis that were judged to be idiopathic in patients who were free of any evidence of cancer at the time of diagnosis. This case-control–type study showed a subsequent 7.6% incidence of cancer development in the idiopathic cohort as compared with a 1.9% incidence in the secondary thrombosis group. This odds ratio achieved statistical significance ($p = .043$). An additional finding was that among the 35 patients of the 145 idiopathic cases who developed recurrent thrombosis during followup, there were six cases of cancer detected. This result differed statistically with an odds ratio of 9.8 compared with the secondary venous thrombosis cohort and an odds ratio of 4.3 when compared with the primary cohort that did not recur.

The numerous descriptive studies and the two case-control studies described support a probable causal association between cancer and venous thrombosis.

### Obesity

Obesity clearly has an association with the development of postoperative venous thrombosis. The association has been shown by univariate analysis and by the contribution of obesity as a prospective predictive variable for the development of postoperative thrombosis.[51] The problem of interpretation of closely linked risk factors is evidenced by the fact that with multivariate analysis obesity was not an independent risk factor.[47] From a practical point of view, this need not invalidate obesity as a positive predictor of thrombosis but suggests that the association may be mediated through, or in conjunction with, other factors such as prolonged surgery times, increased postoperative immobility, or wound infection.

### Previous Venous Thrombosis

The etiology of venous thrombosis is presumed to be multifactorial. Although much of this chapter has concentrated on extraneous risk factors of some magnitude (e.g., major orthopedic surgery), it is also of interest that many patients in these "prothrombotic" circumstances do not develop venous thrombosis. This suggests an interaction between genetic and nongenetic factors. From a scientific point of view, the clearest genetic examples are the various thrombophilias described in Chapter 32.

Both univariate and multivariate analyses have confirmed previous venous thrombosis to be a risk factor for recurrence of venous thrombosis as detected by radiofibrinogen scanning.[46, 47] These studies were conducted before there was an adequate understanding of congenital thrombophilia. Since then it has become apparent that the gene frequency of these conditions is considerably higher than was previously realized. The other issue that continues to cause some controversy is whether residual anatomic changes, from previous thrombosis, on their own make a significant contribution to recurrent thrombosis. In the older textbooks this is stated to be the case, but it may well be a false conclusion. At least three potential confounding issues are present. First, many cases of apparent recurrent thrombosis are post-phlebitic episodes. Second, the genetic predisposition that precipitated the initial episode will continue to be present, independent of venous anatomic changes. Third, if altered venous anatomy was of primary importance, recurrent "idiopathic" thrombosis would be a common sequela to previous thrombosis secondary to major orthopedic surgery. Further study of hospital-related recurrent thrombosis is largely being preempted by the appropriate antithrombotic prophylaxis.

With respect to community-based studies, various reports have suggested previous thrombosis as a risk factor. However, there are problems with the quality of documentation. Because the acquisition of new defects detected on ascending venography is a relatively certain endpoint, the Malmo study, in which 14% of the cases had a previous documentation of an earlier venous thrombosis episode, is probably the strongest community-based evidence for previous thrombosis as a risk factor.[8]

### Immobilization

Comparison of thrombosis rates detected postmortem in cases with varying periods of immobilization prior to death suggests that immobility was a positive risk factor for deep venous thrombosis.[52] Similarly, the laterality of venous thrombosis in hemiplegia as compared with paraplegia provides an experimental support for this concept.[44] Clearly, as with other general risk factors, it is difficult to exclude a role for confounding variables, but from the clinical perspective the concept of utilizing the nonhemiplegic leg as the control is probably the strongest available evidence in humans.

In the experimental field, most models of venous thrombosis involve a component of stasis, although it is clear that stasis alone will not cause thrombosis in these models, and an additional prothrombotic stimulus is required.[53]

Interventional evidence in humans supports stasis as a risk factor. In general, anesthesia radioisotopic markers or cinevenography showed marked pooling of blood in the soleal venous plexi.[54, 55] This is often the site of calf-vein thrombosis. This information was the basis for instituting mechanical devices that prevent venous stasis and prevent postoperative venous thrombosis.

## Anesthesia

The suggestion that various forms of local or spinal anesthesia may result in a lower frequency of postoperative venous thrombosis than general anesthesia has been the subject of investigation since the early 1970s. The rationale for these investigations was a series of indirect observations. With epidural anesthesia, venous drainage was more rapid than with general anesthesia. Similarly, with epidural rather than general anesthesia there was less postoperative elevation of factor VIII and less depression of fibrinolytic potential.[56] Despite these promising biologic observations, the clinical evidence to support local rather than general anesthesia to prevent thrombosis is not convincing. Study results have varied, and multivariate analysis did not support the merits of epidural or spinal anesthesia.[47] Unfortunately, most of the clinical studies lacked adequate controls and none randomly assigned patients to different types of anesthesia.

## Blood Groups

Epidemiologic surveys of patients with DVT show that blood group O is overrepresented relative to the group frequency in the general population.[56, 58] So far, no explanation of this disequilibrium has been forthcoming. In the general population, linkage of blood groups to prothrombotic coagulation factors (e.g., von Willebrand factor) have been noted. However, paradoxically, individuals with blood group O have the lowest levels of von Willebrand factor.

## Oral Contraception and Estrogen Preparations

Oral contraceptives are prescribed to millions of women annually. Most preparations consist of a mixture of estrogen and a progestogen. Early preparations often had five times the estrogen dose relative to the currently prescribed preparations. In most countries, medications containing more than 50 μg of ethinyl estradiol or its equivalent are no longer available except as a short-term postcoital medication. The evolution of modern low estrogen–dose medications was the result of a series of studies starting in the 1960s. The impetus for these studies was case reports of venous thrombosis in young women, often in unusual sites (i.e., sites other than the lower limbs). Over the next decade, a series of comparative studies was undertaken. Early studies were of case-control design. As explained in the introduction to this chapter, this study architecture is ideal for studying relatively low-frequency events, which, despite the large amount of adverse publicity, is the frequency of oral contraceptive–associated thrombosis. From the case-control studies of idiopathic thrombosis, odds ratios varying from 4.1 to 8.3 were obtained.[59, 60–62] Odds ratios for secondary thrombosis gave statistically significant but slightly lower odds ratios.[63, 64] These studies as a whole showed a consistently positive effect on venous thrombosis for oral contraceptives, and in most cases the apparent association was substantial. Notwithstanding this information, the limitations of case-control studies are well recognized, and there are many opportunities for positive bias. For this reason, although the nonexperimental evidence looked compelling, two cohort analytic studies and one attempted randomized trial ensued.

Because the case frequency of venous thrombosis with the contraceptive medication is low, it was important that any prospective trial be of sufficient size to reliably detect differences between thrombotic rates in users and nonusers. A United States study compared the thrombosis rates of 16,000 users and nonusers and demonstrated a relative risk of approximately 7 for DVT, but in retrospect this study was insufficiently large to permit subgroup analyses.[65] The other cohort analytic study was from the United Kingdom and involved roughly one-third more subjects.[3] This study gave a relative risk of 4.2 for DVT and did permit some additional analyses. The social climate in Europe and North America precluded the performance of a proper randomized controlled trial of the oral contraceptive versus alternate contraception. Unfortunately, the attempt at such a trial in a less medically developed community resulted in inconclusive findings because of the low event rate and difficulties in endpoint validation.[66]

All the relevant information gathered during this period supported the hypothesis that the oral contraceptives increased the risk of venous thrombosis. This information, combined with that of some earlier noncontraceptive estrogen trials that used very high dosage, supported the concept that for venous thrombosis the estrogen component was the most important.[67, 68] One of the components of nonexperimental research that supports the possibility of a causal relationship is the demonstration of a dosage effect. Such an effect with contraceptive estrogen has never been satisfactorily established.[69–71] In general, the data have supported the concept but have had insufficient statistical power to achieve a conclusive result. Active study of the thrombogenic effects of oral contraception has effectively ceased, and current information has been reduced to interpretations of descriptive statistical data based on national reporting to disease registries. Therefore, this information is of less scientific substance than many of the earlier studies. In terms of patient management, the general points, on the basis of the epidemiologic studies, are patient selection to exclude high-risk cases and the use of an estrogen dose that is as low as possible.

An area of interest is the potential thrombogenicity of postmenopausal hormone replacement therapy. Various epidemiologic studies have shown that the postmenopausal state, whether occurring naturally or after oophorectomy, is associated with osteoporosis and an increase in atherosclerosis. Assuming that other side effects are minimal, a case can be made for routine replacement therapy. Considering the venous thrombogenicity associated with the oral contraceptive pill, many physicians assumed that hormonal replacement therapy would also cause venous thrombosis. So far this has not proven to be the case. A positive bias in clinicians' minds should have resulted in numerous case reports of thrombosis akin to those in the early days of oral contraception. This has not occurred. In addition, case-control studies have shown no evidence of a significant venous thrombotic effect.[72, 73]

Postmenopausal estrogen replacement has been prescribed usually with a natural conjugated estrogen that, despite its apparent dose, actually represents a very small dose of estrogen when expressed as an equivalent of ethinyl estradiol. The development that needs further study is the effect of dermal patches that deliver estrogen directly into the bloodstream. Both oral conjugated estrogens and dermal patches cause similar minor changes in the coagulation system, and this information is being substituted for direct studies.[74] As shown in both hospital- and community-based studies, because venous thrombosis is age-dependent, the lack of thrombogenicity of the new estrogen patch preparations should not be assumed.

## Other Miscellaneous Risk Factors

A variety of relatively rare conditions show a positive association with venous thrombosis. These include myeloproliferative conditions, metabolic disorders such as homocystinuria, Behçet's disease, and various collagen vascular disorders.[75, 76] These conditions contribute a small number of cases of DVT to the general population, although the case frequency in conditions such as lupus erythematosus can be quite high.[77–79]

In summary, epidemiology for most physicians is seen as an integral part of the study of a disease. The hope is that epidemiologic techniques will generate information that will be of use in a variety of areas. One aspect of study is how the disease is related to the population as a whole. A further issue is whether this information can be utilized to develop treatment or preventive strategies on a community basis. Another consideration is the utilization of this population-derived information to develop an understanding of the pathophysiology of a disease. A benefit that may be obtained by combining the study results is the development of treatment that can be directly applied to an individual patient.

To a certain extent, many of these objectives have been achieved. The impact of venous thrombosis on hospital-related thrombosis has been amply quantified for many high-risk conditions and naturally has led to the development of general preventive measures, when possible. Obviously and closely related is the increased understanding of pathophysiology. This is perhaps best exemplified by the demonstration of the effects of immobility in hemiplegia and the frequency of cancer-related thrombosis. Information has led to confirmatory direct experimental validation. With respect to the development of treatment for an individual patient, epidemiologic studies have provided somewhat less guidance. The various predictive formulas for thrombotic risk are still not sufficiently refined to give each patient an accurate and reliable individual risk of thrombosis. Appropriate antithrombotic prophylaxis is largely given on a group basis rather than a definitive individual risk basis.

A final issue that must be addressed is the future role of epidemiologic studies in venous thrombosis. Despite the progress in the last few decades, there are still areas of important study. The effects of an aging population and its impact on venous thrombotic disease is important. New technologies and increasing intensity of invasive procedures are generating new cases of thrombosis. A further but by no means final area of interest is the necessity for careful studies to ascertain the reasons for the relatively poor compliance in some countries and in some clinical specialties with respect to antithrombotic prophylaxis.

## REFERENCES

1. Rossman I: True incidence of pulmonary embolization and vital statistics. JAMA 230:1677, 1974.
2. Barnes RW, Kraph T, Hoak JC: Erroneous diagnosis of leg vein thrombosis in women on oral contraceptives. Obstet Gynecol 51:556, 1978.
3. Royal College of General Practitioners' Oral Contraception Study: Oral contraceptives, venous thrombosis, and varicose veins. J R Coll Gen Pract 28:393, 1978.
4. Mantel N, Haenszel W: Statistical aspects of analysis of data from retrospective studies of disease. J Natl Cancer Inst 22:719, 1959.
5. Gjores JE: The incidence of venous thrombosis and its sequelae in certain districts in Sweden. Acta Chir Scand 111[Suppl 206]:16, 1956.
6. Coon WW, Willis PW, Keller JB: Venous thrombosis and other venous disease in the Tecumseh Community Health Study. Circulation 48:839, 1973.
7. Anderson FA, Wheeler HB, Goldberg RJ, et al: A population-based perspective of the hospital incidence and case-fatality rates of deep vein thrombosis and pulmonary embolism. The Worcester DVT Study. Arch Intern Med 151:933, 1991.
8. Nordstrom M, Lindblad B, Berqvist D, Kjellstrom T: A prospective study of the incidence of deep-vein thrombosis within a defined urban population. J Intern Med 232:155, 1992.
9. Bergqvist D: Postoperative Thromboembolism. Berlin, Springer-Verlag, 1983, p 27.
10. Virchow R: Phlogose und thrombose. In Virchow R (ed): Gesammelte Abhandlungen zur Wissenschaftlichen Medicin. Frankfurt, Germany, Von Meidinger Sohn, 1856, p 458.
11. Hjelmstedt A, Bergvall U: Incidence of thrombosis in patients with tibial fractures. Acta Chir Scand 134:209, 1968.
12. Cohen SH, Ehrlich GE, Kaufman MS, et al: Thrombophlebitis following knee surgery. J Bone Joint Surg 55(1):106, 1973.
13. Hull R, Delmore TJ, Hirsh J, et al: Effectiveness of an intermittent pulsatile elastic stocking for the prevention of calf and thigh vein thrombosis in patients undergoing elective knee surgery. Thromb Res 16:37, 1979.
14. Leclerc J, Desjardins L, Geerts W, et al: A randomized trial of enoxaparin for the prevention of deep vein thrombosis after knee surgery. Thromb Haemost 65[Suppl]:753, 1991.
15. Hirsh J, Levine MN: Low molecular weight heparin. Blood 79:1, 1992.
16. Hull RD, Raskob GE: Prophylaxis of venous thromboembolic disease following hip and knee surgery. J Bone Joint Surg 68:146, 1986.
17. Nillius A, Nylander G: Deep vein thrombosis after total hip replacement: A clinical and phlebographic study. Br J Surg 66:324, 1979.
18. Culver D, Crawford JS, Gardiner JH, et al: Venous thrombosis after fractures of the upper end of the femur. A study of incidence and site. J Bone Joint Surg 52B:61, 1970.
19. Field ES, Nicolaides AN, Kakkar VV, et al: Deep-vein thrombosis in patients with fractures of the femoral neck. Br J Surg 59:377, 1972.
20. Buchanan RRC, Kraag G: Is there a lower incidence of deep venous thrombosis after joint replacement in rheumatoid arthritis? J Rheumatol 7:4, 1980.
21. Bergqvist D: Frequency of thromboembolic complications. In Bergqvist D (ed): Postoperative Thromboembolism. Berlin, Springer-Verlag, 1983, pp 12–13.
22. Nicolaides AN, Field ES, Kakkar VV, et al: Prostatectomy and deep-vein thrombosis. Br J Surg 59:487, 1972.
23. Mayo M, Halil T, Browse NL: The incidence of deep vein thrombosis after prostatectomy. Br J Urol 43:738, 1971.
24. Gordon-Smith IC, Hickman JA, El Masri SH: The effect of the fibrinolytic inhibitor epsilon-amino caproic acid on the incidence of deep-vein thrombosis after prostatectomy. Br J Surg 59:522, 1972.
25. Walsh JJ, Bonnar J, Wright FW: A study of pulmonary embolism and deep vein thrombosis after major gynaecological surgery using labelled fibrinogen-phlebography and lung scanning. J Obstet Gynaecol Br Commonw 81:311, 1974.
26. Jackman FR, Perry BJ, Siddons H: Deep vein thrombosis after thoracotomy. Thorax 33:761, 1978.
27. Porter J, Lindell T, Lakin P: Leg edema following femoropopliteal autogenous vein bypass. Arch Surg 105:883, 1972.
28. Hamer JD: Investigation of oedema of the lower limb following successful femoropopliteal bypass surgery: The role of phlebography in demonstrating venous thrombosis. Br J Surg 59:979, 1972.
29. Drill VA, Calhoun DW: Oral contraceptives and thromboembolic disease. JAMA 206:77, 1968.
30. Carter CJ, Gent M, Leclerc JR: The epidemiology of venous thrombosis. In Colman RW, Hirsh J, Marder VJ, Salzman EW (eds): Hemostasis and Thrombosis, 2nd ed. Philadelphia, JB Lippincott, 1987, pp 1185–1198.
31. Kierkegaard A: Incidence and diagnosis of deep vein thrombosis associated with pregnancy. Acta Obstet Gynecol Scand 62:239, 1983.
32. Ginsberg JS, Brill-Edwards P, Burrows RF, et al: Venous thrombosis during pregnancy: Leg and trimester of presentation. Thromb Haemost 67:519, 1992.
33. Department of Health and Social Security: Report on Confidential Enquiries into Maternal Deaths in England and Wales, 1979–1981. London, HMSO, 1986.
34. Department of Health: Report on Confidential Enquiries into Maternal Deaths in England and Wales, 1982–1984. London, HMSO, 1989.
35. Department of Health, Welsh Office, Scottish Home and Health Department and Department of Health and Social Services, Northern Ireland: Report on Confidential Enquiries into Maternal Deaths in the United Kingdom 1985–87. London, HMSO, 1991.
36. Morell MT, Dunill MS: The post mortem incidence of pulmonary embolism in a hospital population. Br J Surg 55:347, 1968.

37. MacIntyre IMG, Ruckley CV: Pulmonary embolism—a clinical and autopsy study. Scot Med J 19:20, 1974.

38. Maurer BJ, Wray R, Shillingford JP: Frequency of venous thrombosis after myocardial infarction. Lancet 2:1385, 1971.

39. Kotilainen M, Ristola P, Ikkala E, et al: Leg vein thrombosis diagnosed by $^{125}$I-fibrinogen test after acute myocardial infarction. Ann Clin Res 5:365, 1973.

40. Murray TS, Lorimer AR, Cox FC, et al: Leg-vein thrombosis following myocardial infarction. Lancet 2:792, 1970.

41. Nicolaides AN, Kakkar VV, Renney JTG, et al: Myocardial infarction and deep-vein thrombosis. Br Med J 1:432, 1971.

42. Theroux P, Latour J-G, Leger-Gauthier C, et al: Fibrinopeptide A and platelet factor 4 levels in unstable angina. Circulation 75:156, 1987.

43. Anderson GM, Hull E: The effect of dicoumerol upon the mortality and incidence of thromboembolic complications of congestive heart failure. Am Heart J 39:697, 1950.

44. Warlow C, Ogston D, Douglas AS: Deep venous thrombosis of the legs after strokes. Br Med J 1:1178, 1976.

45. Cope C, Reyes TM, Skversky NJ: Phlebographic analysis of the incidence of thrombosis in hemiplegia. Radiology 109:581, 1973.

46. Kakkar VV, Howe CT, Nicolaides AN, et al: Deep vein thrombosis of the leg. Is there a "high risk" group? Am J Surg 120:527, 1970.

47. Nicolaides AN, Irving D: Clinical factors and the risk of deep venous thrombosis. In Nicolaides AN (ed): Thromboembolism: Aetiology, Advances in Prevention and Management. Lancaster, England, MTP Press, 1975, pp 193–204.

48. Gordon SG, Cross BA: A factor X-activating cysteine protease from malignant tissue. J Clin Invest 67:1665, 1981.

49. Goldberg RJ, Seneff M, Gore JM, et al: Occult malignant neoplasms in patients with deep venous thrombosis. Arch Intern Med 147:251, 1987.

50. Prandoni P, Lensing AWA, Buller HR, et al: Deep-vein thrombosis and the incidence of subsequent symptomatic cancer. N Engl J Med 327:1128, 1992.

51. Clayton JK, Anderson JA, McNocol GP: Preoperative prediction of postoperative deep vein thrombosis. Br Med J 2:911, 1976.

52. Gibbs NM: Venous thrombosis in the lower limbs with particular reference to bed rest. Br J Surg 45:15, 1957.

53. Wessler S, Yin ET: Experimental hypercoagulable state induced by factor X: Comparison of non-activated and activated forms. J Lab Clin Med 72:256, 1960.

54. Doran FSA, Drury M, Sivyer A: A simple way to combat the venous stasis which occurs in the limbs during surgical operations. Br J Surg 51:486, 1964.

55. Clark C, Cotton LT: Blood flow in deep veins of leg: Recording technique and evaluation of methods to increase flow during operation. Br J Surg 55:211, 1968.

56. Rem J, Feddersen C, Brandz MR, et al: Post operative changes of coagulation and fibrinolysis independent of neurogenic stimuli and adrenal hormones. Br J Surg 68:229, 1981.

57. Jick H, Stone D, Westerholm B, et al: Venous thromboembolic disease and ABO blood type. Lancet 1:539, 1969.

58. Westerholm B, Wiechel B, Eklund G: Oral contraceptives, venous thromboembolic disease, and ABO blood type. Lancet 2:664, 1971.

59. Inman WHW, Vessey MP: Investigation of death from pulmonary, coronary, and cerebral thrombosis and embolism in women of child-bearing age. Br Med J 1:193, 1968.

60. Vessey MP, Doll R: Investigation of relation between use of oral contraceptives and thromboembolic disease. Br Med J 1:199, 1968.

61. Sartwell PE, Masi AT, Arthes FG, et al: Thromboembolism and oral contraceptives: An epidemiologic case-control study. Am J Epidemiol 90:365, 1969.

62. Vessey MP, Doll R, Fairburn AS, et al: Postoperative thromboembolism and the use of oral contraceptives. Br Med J 2:123, 1970.

63. Greene GR, Sartwell PE: Oral contraceptive use in patients with thromboembolism following surgery, trauma, or infection. Am J Public Health 62:680, 1972.

64. Boston Collaborative Drug Surveillance Program: Oral contraceptives and venous thromboembolic disease, surgically confirmed gall bladder disease and breast tumours. Lancet 1:1399, 1973.

65. Porter JB: Oral contraceptives and nonfatal vascular disease—recent experience. Obstet Gynecol 59:299, 1982.

66. Fuertes-De La Haba A, Curet JO, Pelegrina I, et al: Thrombophlebitis among oral and nonoral contraceptive users. Obstet Gynecol 38:259, 1971.

67. Jeffcoate TNA, Miller J, Roos RF, et al: Puerperal thromboembolism in relation to the inhibition of lactation by oestrogen therapy. Br Med J 4:19, 1968.

68. Coronary Drug Project Research Group: The coronary drug project; initial findings leading to modifications of its research protocol. JAMA 214:1303, 1970.

69. Stolley PD, Tonascia JA, Tockman MS, et al: Thrombosis with low-estrogen oral contraceptives. Am J Epidemiol 102:197, 1975.

70. Bottinger LE, Boman G, Eklund G, et al: Oral contraceptives and thromboembolic disease; effects of lowering oestrogen content. Lancet 1:1097, 1980.

71. Kierkegaard A: Deep vein thrombosis and the oestrogen content in oral contraceptives—an epidemiological analysis. Contraception 31:29, 1985.

72. Boston Collaborative Drug Surveillance Program: Surgically confirmed gall bladder disease, venous thromboembolism, and breast tumours in relation to post-menopausal estrogen therapy. N Engl J Med 290:15, 1974.

73. Devor M, Barrett-Connor E, Renvall M, et al: Estrogen replacement therapy and the risk of venous thrombosis. Am J Med 92:275, 1992.

74. Chetkowski RJ, Meldrum DR, Steingold KA, et al: Biologic effects of transdermal estrogen. N Engl J Med 314:1615, 1986.

75. Chievitz E, Thiede D: Complications and causes of death in polycythaemia vera. Acta Med Scand 172:513, 1962.

76. Schimke RN, McKusick VA, Huang T, et al: Homocystinuria: Studies of 20 families with 38 affected members. JAMA 193:711, 1965.

77. Gladman DD, Urowitz MB: Venous syndromes and pulmonary embolism in systemic lupus erythematosus. Ann Rheum Dis 39:340, 1980.

78. Roscove MNH, Petronella MC, Brewer RN: Antiphospholipid thrombosis: Clinical course after first thrombotic event in 70 patients. Ann Intern Med 117:303, 1992.

79. Long AA, Ginsberg JS, Brill-Edwards P, et al: The relationship of antiphospholipid antibodies to thromboembolic disease in systemic lupus erythematosus: A cross sectional study. Thromb Haemost 66:520, 1991.

# Chapter 15

# Pathogenesis of Venous Thromboembolism

Michael M. Millenson and Kenneth A. Bauer

The pathogenesis of venous thromboembolism was conceptualized in the modern era by Virchow, who in 1856 described three common alterations in vascular homeostasis that either individually or together may culminate in thrombus formation.[1] These three factors, now referred to as *Virchow's triad,* consist of (1) alterations in blood flow (stasis or turbulence); (2) alterations in the coagulability of blood (hypercoagulability); and (3) alterations in the vessel wall. Although considerable progress has been made in our understanding of the thrombotic process as a result of advances in cell biology, biochemistry, and molecular biology, the factors comprising Virchow's triad remain a useful starting point in discussing the pathogenesis of venous thromboembolism.

Thrombosis results from a disturbance in the balance between prothrombotic and antithrombotic forces that normally exist within the bloodstream.[2] Under normal circumstances, the endothelium is maintained as a nonthrombogenic surface as a result of several protective mechanisms that are in place to ensure the maintenance of blood fluidity.[3] In the event of vascular injury, these natural anticoagulant mechanisms limit and localize thrombus formation to this site. Thrombosis results when this process becomes unregulated, and endovascular clot forms at an inappropriate place and time. This chapter will review our current understanding of the factors that promote thrombogenesis, the mechanisms that normally protect the endothelium from inappropriate thrombus formation, and the ways in which these protective mechanisms may be disrupted, resulting in venous thromboembolism.

## OVERVIEW OF THE THROMBOTIC PROCESS

Thrombi are composed predominantly of fibrin strands and enmeshed aggregates of blood cells, with the relative composition differing between arterial and venous thrombi. Arterial thrombi arise in the setting of high flow and high shear forces in regions of disturbed blood flow related to atherosclerotic plaques. Vessel wall injury in this locale leads to platelet activation, which plays a major role in the pathogenesis of thrombosis on the arterial side of the circulation. This is manifest pathologically in the observation that *arterial* thrombi are composed primarily of platelet aggregates with relatively minor amounts of interspersed fibrin. In contrast, *venous* thrombi are formed in regions of static blood flow, and are composed predominantly of red cells entrapped within an extensive fibrin meshwork, with relatively few platelets intermixed. These pathologic differences may provide insight into the differing pathogenesis between arterial and venous thrombosis. Platelet-vessel wall interactions appear to be preeminent in causing arterial thrombosis, whereas vessel wall injury and platelet activation are generally regarded as being less important factors in the pathogenesis of venous thrombosis.

Instead, activation of the coagulation mechanism, often in the setting of static blood flow, has traditionally been implicated as the major factor leading to venous thrombosis, resulting in a "hypercoagulable state" as manifested by clinical situations in which patients display an unusual predisposition to thrombosis. Although thrombosis has been described in a variety of

Supported in part by National Institutes of Health Grant POI HL 33014 and the Medical Research Service Department of Veterans Affairs. Dr. Bauer is a recipient of an Established Investigatorship from the American Heart Association anatomic sites, the most common and clinically significant sites are the deep veins of the lower extremities. Venous thrombi arise in regions of slow blood flow, where local activation of blood coagulation by a variety of thrombogenic stimuli results in the formation of small deposits of fibrin. These deposits often originate within the venous sinuses and deep veins of the calf or thigh and may serve as a nidus for thrombus growth, with subsequent entrapment of blood cells and formation of additional fibrin gel.[4] If the evolving thrombus extends proximally and grows large enough to cause obstruction to venous outflow, the patient may experience pain and swelling in the affected limb as a result of venous engorgement and inflammation of the vein wall.

Alternatively, portions of the thrombus may dislodge and travel proximally (i.e., upwards), resulting in pulmonary embolism. Many pulmonary emboli are clinically "silent" and detectable only by perfusion lung scans. Recent evidence suggests that 40 to 50% of patients with documented deep venous thrombosis have objective evidence of pulmonary emboli at the time of presentation.[5, 6] Conversely, a substantial proportion of patients presenting with symptomatic pulmonary embolism confirmed by objective testing are found to have asymptomatic deep venous thrombosis on venography.[7] Pulmonary embolism and deep venous thrombosis are therefore best regarded as clinical manifestations of a common underlying pathophysiologic process. In general, pulmonary emboli occur more frequently and are more likely to cause symptoms in patients with large thrombi in proximal leg veins than in patients with calf vein thrombosis.[4]

Thromboembolic events may occur either "spontaneously" as isolated incidents, or in association with various predisposing risk factors that have been defined on clinical and epidemiologic grounds. In practice, patients suspected of having a thrombotic tendency are grouped into two general pathophysiologic categories— the primary and the secondary hypercoagulable states.[8, 9] These are listed in Table 15-1. The primary hypercoagulable states are those in which a specific inherited defect in one of the major natural anticoagulant mechanisms is identified. From the standpoint of biologic evidence and plausibility, these defects are accepted as having a causal role in the pathogenesis of venous thromboembolism in affected individuals.

The secondary hypercoagulable states consist of a heterogeneous array of clinical conditions that are widely recognized as being associated

**Table 15-1. The Primary and Secondary Hypercoagulable States**

| Primary | Secondary |
|---|---|
| Antithrombin III deficiency | Immobilization |
| Protein C deficiency | Postoperative state (orthopedic, gynecologic) |
| Protein S deficiency | Trauma |
| APC-resistance | Advanced age |
| Dysfibrinogenemia | Malignancy (occult or overt) |
| | Advanced congestive heart failure |
| | Chronic venous stasis, varicose veins |
| | Pregnancy, postpartum state |
| | Oral contraceptive use |
| | Obesity |
| | Nephrotic syndrome |
| | Lupus anticoagulant/ antiphospholipid antibody syndrome |

with an increased risk of venous thromboembolism, and these conditions account for the majority of patients with thrombotic disease encountered by the clinician. The primary and secondary hypercoagulable states should not be regarded as mutually exclusive categories; in fact, patients with any of the primary hypercoagulable states are particularly prone to developing thromboembolism when exposed to the high-risk situations that comprise the secondary hypercoagulable states (e.g., postoperative state, postpartum, etc.). For the most part, a precise understanding of the pathophysiologic mechanisms underlying the thrombotic tendency in these disorders is lacking. Table 15-2 summarizes some of the possible mechanisms contributing to the pathogenesis of thrombosis in these disorders, using the conceptual framework originally put forth by Virchow. It must be emphasized that many of these mechanisms are speculative and have proved difficult to substantiate scientifically. In the sections that follow, the evidence supporting many of these proposed mechanisms of thrombogenesis will be presented in detail.

## ROLE OF VENOUS STASIS

The importance of venous stasis in the pathogenesis of venous thromboembolism cannot be overstated, and many of the disorders listed in Table 15-2 have in common the tendency to cause impairment of venous blood flow in the lower extremities. From an epidemiologic point of view, one of the most important mechanisms protecting against thrombus formation in vivo appears to be the normal luminal flow of blood. Such flow serves to dilute and clear the local buildup of activated clotting factors, to minimize the interactions of activated clotting factors and platelets with the endothelial surface, and to mix activated clotting factors with the various physiologic anticoagulants, thereby neutralizing local procoagulant activity. The loss of these features in the setting of slow or absent flow (venous stasis) creates a permissive environment for local thrombus formation.

The role of venous stasis in promoting throm-

Table 15–2. **Potential Thrombogenic Mechanisms in the Secondary Hypercoagulable States**

| Risk Factor | Venous Stasis | Vascular Injury | Hemostatic Activation | Comments |
|---|---|---|---|---|
| Immobilization | + + + | – | + | Venous pooling from loss of muscular pumping action[10–12]; decreased fibrinolytic activity due to loss of flow[18, 19] |
| Surgery, postoperative state | + + | + + + | + | Forced immobilization; direct vascular injury, (particularly in orthopedic, vascular, and gynecologic surgery)[13, 15, 17]; procoagulant cytokines such as IL-1, TNF[30, 31] |
| Trauma | + + | + + | + + | Forced immobilization; direct orthopedic and vascular injuries; release of tissue thromboplastins and procoagulant cytokines such as IL-1, TNF[30, 31] |
| Advanced age | + | + | + | Impaired mobility of limbs; chronic vascular disease; enhanced baseline generation of thrombin[26] |
| Malignancy | + + | + | + + | Impaired mobility; venous compression by tumor; release of thromboplastins[32] and procoagulant cytokines such as IL-1, TNF[30, 31] |
| Advanced CHF | + + | – | – | Impaired mobility; impaired venous flow from elevated venous pressures and venous dilatation |
| Prior DVT, chronic stasis, varicose veins | + + + | + + | – | Venous pooling due to loss of valvular function and venous dilatation; prior vessel wall damage |
| Pregnancy, postpartum state | + + + | – | + | Impaired mobility; impaired venous flow from compression by gravid uterus; decreased protein S and ATIII levels[57, 96, 97] |
| Use of oral contraceptives | – | – | + + | Decreased functional protein S and ATIII levels[57, 97] |
| Lupus anticoagulant/ antiphospholipid antibody syndrome | – | + | + + | ? Vascular injury from systemic vasculitis[151]; impaired fibrinolysis[151]; impaired protein C activation[152] |

bogenesis, as originally conceived by Virchow, has been affirmed by epidemiologic and clinical data documenting an association between stasis and venous thrombosis. As discussed in the previous chapter, many of the epidemiologic risk factors for venous thromboembolism (e.g., limb immobilization, postoperative state, etc.) have in common the presence of venous stasis. The absence of muscular contraction in an immobilized or paralyzed lower extremity results in loss of the normal pumping action, which causes blood to flow centrally out of the venous sinuses of the calf and thigh. The documented antithrombotic efficacy of interventions designed to prevent venous stasis, such as the use of venous compression devices in high-risk patients, lends further credence to the concept that stasis plays a significant role in the pathogenesis of venous thrombosis.[10–12]

Despite this clinical and epidemiologic evidence, however, the precise means by which stasis contributes to thrombus formation has proved difficult to study experimentally, and still remains poorly understood. The use of various animal models to investigate the effects of stasis on vascular integrity have yielded conflicting results.[13–17] Results of many studies using venous ligation have suggested that stasis by itself, in the absence of vessel wall injury or other thrombogenic stimuli, is not sufficient to produce venous thrombosis. This has led some investigators to postulate that stasis merely creates a permissive environment for the development of venous thrombosis, with culmination in thrombus formation only if there is sufficient local thrombin generation (i.e., the presence of at least two of the three components of Virchow's triad).

In the 1990s, the use of increasingly sophisticated experimental methods has contributed to our understanding of the mechanisms by which stasis may promote thrombogenesis.[18] Studies have demonstrated that flow may augment fibrinolytic capacity by stimulating release of tissue plasminogen activator from endothelial cells; loss of flow (stasis) can therefore result in diminished fibrinolytic activity at the endothelial surface.[19] Other investigators have shown that flow stimulates release of an endogenous nitrovasodilator; loss of flow (stasis) can therefore result in vasoconstriction and loss of antiaggregatory effect on platelets.[20] Other studies indicate that flow may be a major determinant of plasma enzyme-substrate interactions, thereby playing an important role in regulating the activity of the coagulation cascade.[21, 22] Future investigations should define more precisely the mechanisms by which venous stasis contributes

to the pathogenesis of venous thromboembolism.

## THROMBORESISTANCE OF THE NORMAL ENDOTHELIUM

The normal endothelial surface is maintained in a "thromboresistant" state by several mechanisms under basal conditions. The prothrombotic and antithrombotic forces that normally interact at the endothelial surface are shown in Table 15–3. Under physiologic conditions in which no thrombogenic stimuli are operative, the various components of the hemostatic system exist in a relatively quiescent state. Platelets are prevented from interacting with components of the subendothelial matrix by the intact endothelial layer, and the normal endothelium elaborates substances such as prostacyclin and nitric oxide, which act as potent inhibitors of platelet aggregation.[23, 24] Similarly, the various clotting proteins and cofactors that comprise the coagulation cascade exist predominantly, under normal circumstances, as inactive zymogens that lack activity as serine proteases or

**Table 15–3. Overview of Endothelial Factors Contributing to the Pathogenesis of Venous Thrombosis**

| Prothrombotic | Antithrombotic |
|---|---|
| 1. Endothelial injury<br>  a. Denuding<br>  b. Nondenuding (activation by cytokines) | 1. Nonthrombogenic properties of the intact endothelium |
| 2. Platelet adhesion and aggregation | 2. Endogenous inhibitors of platelet aggregation (prostacyclin, nitric oxide) |
| 3. Activation of coagulation factors | 3. Natural anticoagulant pathways<br>  a. Heparin-ATIII mechanism<br>  b. Protein C pathway<br>  c. TFPI mechanism |
| 4. Inhibition of fibrinolysis<br>  a. Elevated plasminogen activator inhibitor-1<br>  b. Reduced plasminogen activator activity | 4. Dissolution of fibrin by the fibrinolytic pathway (plasminogen-plasminogen activator pathway) |
| 5. Stasis of blood flow | 5. Dilution of clearance of activated clotting factors by normal luminal blood flow |

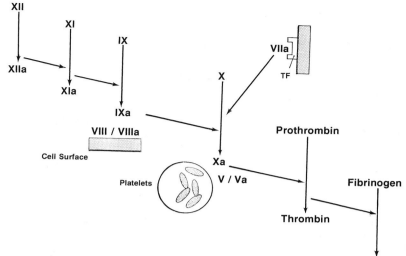

**Figure 15–1.** A schematic of the coagulation cascade.

## ACTIVATION OF BLOOD COAGULATION

In the event of endothelial cell injury or perturbation, the hemostatic system is poised to provide a burst of procoagulant activity, and the thromboresistant properties of the normal endothelium may be overcome. An overview of the process by which thrombi are formed is depicted schematically in Figure 15–1. Fibrin clot results when the coagulation mechanism becomes activated in conjunction with the activation of platelets, resulting in formation of fibrin strands and entrapped platelet aggregates, which constitute the evolving thrombus. Under physiologic (unstimulated) conditions, the individual clotting factors in the coagulation cascade exist as inactive zymogens or procofactors that can be converted to active serine proteases or active cofactors by a series of linked proteolytic reactions. These reactions take place on or near phospholipid surfaces on platelets, white blood cells, and endothelial cells.

The hemostatic mechanism has traditionally been divided into the intrinsic and extrinsic pathways of coagulation, with the two cascades overlapping in a final pathway in which the common product, factor Xa, converts prothrombin to thrombin. The generation of thrombin is a critical step in the pathogenesis of thrombus formation, causing direct conversion of the substrate fibrinogen into fibrin, and inducing platelet activation, resulting in formation of the crosslinked fibrin clot. Thrombin or factor Xa also "back activate" the procofactors, factor V and factor VIII, and thrombin also activates factor XIII, the enzyme responsible for covalent crosslinking of fibrin monomer. Platelet activation and the generation of thrombin by the coagulation cascade are therefore mutually reinforcing processes, because thrombin is a potent platelet agonist and activated platelets secrete various clotting factors, express receptors for activated clotting factors, and provide a phospholipid surface on which the reactions of the cascade take place.

Advances in our understanding of blood coagulation have resulted in modifications of the traditional two-limb clotting cascade, taking into account the fact that there is considerable "crosstalk" between the intrinsic and extrinsic pathways in vivo.[25, 27] The extrinsic pathway of coagulation is activated when factor VII binds to tissue factor, a membrane-bound glycoprotein that is present on endothelial cells, white blood cells, and components of the subendothelial matrix.[28, 29] Blood may become exposed to tissue factor as a direct result of vascular injury, with denudation of the endothelial layer and loss of the protective barrier between blood and the subendothelial matrix. Alternatively, tissue factor may be expressed by monocyte-mac-

active cofactors. Furthermore, in the absence of platelet or endothelial cell activation, the proteins in the coagulation cascade lack an appropriate phospholipid surface on which to interact with their respective substrates. Consequently, the normal endothelium is nonthrombogenic by virtue of the fact that it does not activate platelets or coagulation proteins to a sufficient degree to cause thrombus formation in the absence of prothrombotic stimuli.

rophages or endothelial cells in response to activation by endotoxin or cytokines (tumor necrosis factor and interleukin-1).[30, 31]

The association of factor VII with tissue factor allows for the generation of factor VIIa, a serine protease with substrate specificity for both factor X and factor IX. The factor VIIa-phospholipid-bound tissue factor complex may generate factor Xa either *directly*, by converting factor X to factor Xa, or *indirectly*, by first converting factor IX to factor IXa, which, in the presence of a cofactor (factor VIIIa) and calcium ions on a phospholipid surface, may then convert factor X to factor Xa. The factor Xa generated by either of these mechanisms may then associate on the phospholipid surface with another cofactor, factor Va, and, in the presence of calcium ions, forms the prothrombinase complex that efficiently converts prothrombin to thrombin.[33]

The intrinsic limb (or contact system) of the coagulation cascade, as originally defined by in vitro investigations, is initiated when factor XII in plasma comes into contact with a foreign surface. Activation of the intrinsic pathway in vivo may occur in response to vascular damage, with exposure of collagen within the subendothelium acting as a potential stimulus for conversion of factor XII to the serine protease, factor XIIa. Factor XIIa acts upon its principal substrate, factor XI, to generate the factor XIa, a serine protease that directly converts factor IX to factor IXa. The relevance of these early steps to coagulation system function is uncertain, because patients with known factor XII deficiency do not exhibit a hemorrhagic tendency, and patients with factor XI deficiency manifest excessive bleeding only in the setting of a significant hemostatic challenge. It is likely that the factor VIIa/tissue factor mechanism is the dominant pathway for activation of blood coagulation in vivo, with the early steps of the intrinsic pathway playing a less defined role.[25, 34]

The notion that the hemostatic system is completely quiescent in the absence of thrombogenic stimuli is an oversimplification. Studies employing sensitive immunologic markers of hemostatic system activation indicate that there is a continuous low level of activity of the coagulation mechanism in vivo in normal subjects.[2, 25, 26] It is possible that trace amounts of tissue factor are normally expressed on endothelial cells or monocyte-macrophages, although this has not been demonstrable using currently available techniques.[35, 36] Alternatively, there is evidence to suggest that coagulation proteins in plasma may traverse the endothelial barrier, thereby gaining access to subendothelial sites of constitutive tissue factor expression.[36, 37] In ei-

ther case, the fact that the tissue factor mechanism is continuously active under normal conditions suggests that the system is poised to respond with a burst of procoagulant activity in the event of a prothrombotic stimulus.

## NATURAL ANTICOAGULANT MECHANISMS

During the past three decades, several physiologically important anticoagulant pathways have been discovered and characterized. These pathways provide protective mechanisms to ensure that the low level of coagulation system activation is held in check under normal circumstances (i.e., in the absence of thrombotic stimuli). Furthermore, in response to a thrombogenic stimulus such as vascular injury, the natural anticoagulant mechanisms function to localize thrombus formation to the site of such injury and prevent widespread activation of coagulation. Interruption of any of these protective natural anticoagulant pathways may result in unopposed thrombin generation, with resultant pathologic thrombus formation. A thorough appreciation of the normal function of the natural anticoagulant mechanisms is therefore crucial to understanding the pathogenesis of thrombosis. The three major natural anticoagulant pathways that limit the activity of the coagulation system in vivo are (1) the heparin-antithrombin III pathway; (2) the protein C-thrombomodulin-protein S pathway; and (3) tissue factor pathway inhibitor.

### The Heparin-Antithrombin III Pathway

Antithrombin III (ATIII) is an important member of the general class of plasma proteins known as serine protease inhibitors (serpins). Although the existence of a thrombin inhibitor in plasma was hypothesized in the early part of this century, it was not until the 1970s that mechanism of action and physiologic relevance of ATIII were established.[38, 39] Human ATIII is synthesized in hepatocytes, has a molecular weight of 58 kd, and is present in plasma at a concentration of 140 μg/ml. In addition to its ability to neutralize thrombin, ATIII inhibits the other serine proteases of the coagulation cascade (factors XIIa, XIa, IXa, and Xa).[40–43] Evidence also has shown that ATIII is capable of inhibiting factor VIIa bound to tissue factor.[44, 45] ATIII thus serves a critical function as a natural anticoagulant by damping procoagulant enzyme function at several steps in the clotting cascade.

The mechanism by which ATIII functions to neutralize thrombin and the other serine proteases in the coagulation cascade involves the formation of 1:1 stoichiometric complexes with these enzymes, as shown schematically in Figure 15–2. ATIII and thrombin interact via an arginine reactive center at the carboxy terminal end of ATIII and the serine active center of thrombin, resulting in formation of a stable enzyme-inhibitor complex. Similar interactions occur with the other enzymes of the coagulation cascade, with the result that the complexed serine proteases are unable to interact with their respective zymogen substrates in the cascade.

The interaction between ATIII and thrombin occurs at a very slow rate in the absence of heparin, but is accelerated up to 1,000-fold in its presence (thus accounting for the known anticoagulant properties of heparin). The rate of interaction between ATIII and the other serine proteases is also accelerated by heparin, although the rate for factor XIIa, factor XIa, factor Xa, and factor VIIa is increased to a lesser extent than for thrombin and factor IXa.[40–45] Studies have shown that heparin reversibly binds to lysyl residues near the amino terminal end of ATIII, inducing an allosteric change in the reactive center, which enhances complex formation with the serine active center of thrombin.[39] Heparin thereby functions as a catalyst for the interactions between ATIII and the serine proteases, because it is released from ATIII after formation of enzyme-inhibitor complex occurs and is then free to bind to other ATIII molecules and initiate further rounds of complex formation.

Heparin is a sulfated glycosaminoglycan that is present within intracellular granules in mast cells. These cells are widely distributed in the interstitial tissues of various organs, including those of the pulmonary and gastrointestinal tracts (the sources of commercial preparations of heparin). There is little scientific evidence to suggest that the heparin contained within mast cells is constitutively secreted or participates in the normal physiologic functioning of ATIII in vivo. Rather, studies have shown that a related proteoglycan, heparan sulfate, is synthesized by the endothelium and contains the critical polysaccharide structures necessary to bind ATIII and catalyze its inhibitory effects in vivo.[46–48] Anticoagulantly active heparan sulfate has been identified both on the luminal surface of endothelial cells as well as in the subendothelium, where it is ideally situated to perform its function of helping to protect the endothelial surface against thrombus formation.[49] An intact heparan sulfate–ATIII pathway is therefore considered to be one of the important mechanisms by which the endothelium is maintained in a thromboresistant state.

The physiologic relevance of the heparan sulfate–ATIII pathway in the pathogenesis of thrombosis is highlighted by a number of clinical situations in which this pathway is interrupted. First is the well known association between inherited deficiencies of ATIII and the occurrence of venous thrombosis. ATIII deficiency is inherited in an autosomal dominant fashion, with affected heterozygotes having functional plasma ATIII levels in plasma of 30 to 60% of normal. The lifetime risk of thrombosis generally is over 50%, and about 1 to 3% of carefully studied patients with recurrent idiopathic thromboses has ATIII deficiency.[50–53] Deficiencies or abnormalities of vessel wall heparan sulfate have not been described, but recurrent thrombosis is known to occur in homozygous patients with ATIII deficiency with defects limited to the heparin-binding region of the molecule.[54]

In addition to inherited ATIII deficiency, there are acquired clinical disorders in which alterations in plasma ATIII levels can occur. For instance, patients with nephrotic syndrome have reduced ATIII levels as a consequence of urinary protein loss, perhaps accounting in part for the known increased risk of thrombosis in these patients.[55] Likewise, patients with severe liver disease and disseminated intravascular

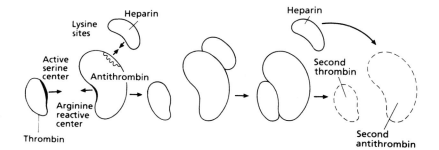

**Figure 15–2.** The mechanism of action of heparin and antithrombin III.

coagulation can have reduced plasma concentrations of ATIII, presumably on the basis of decreased synthesis and increased consumption of ATIII, respectively.[56] Finally, reductions in plasma ATIII concentration are seen in users of oral contraceptives and exogenous estrogens.[57, 58]

## The Protein C-Thrombomodulin-Protein S Pathway

### Protein C

The protein C pathway functions in parallel with the other natural anticoagulant mechanisms to regulate the thrombotic process in vivo. Human protein C is a vitamin K-dependent plasma glycoprotein that is synthesized by hepatocytes, has a molecular weight of 62 kd, and is present in plasma at a concentration of 4 µg/ ml.[59–61] It circulates in plasma primarily as a two-chain species, with the heavy and light chains joined by a single disulfide bond. Protein C is a zymogen that requires conversion to an active serine protease, activated protein C or APC, in order to function as an anticoagulant.

APC functions as an anticoagulant primarily by proteolytically cleaving and inactivating the activated cofactors, factor Va and factor VIIIa, thereby inhibiting the activation of factor X and prothrombin (Fig. 15–3).[62–65] The scission of peptide bonds within factor Va and factor VIIIa by the serine active site on the heavy chain of APC takes place on phospholipid surfaces where these cofactors normally participate in the procoagulant reactions of the coagulation mechanism. There is also evidence suggesting that APC may oppose thrombus formation by stimulating the fibrinolytic system, although the physiologic relevance of these findings remains controversial.[66–68]

Thrombin is the only physiologically relevant enzyme responsible for converting protein C from an inactive zymogen to its corresponding serine protease, APC. The rate of this reaction in plasma under in vitro conditions is extremely slow, but it is accelerated over 10,000-fold in vivo when thrombin binds to a high-affinity receptor on the endothelial surface known as thrombomodulin.[69–71] Thrombin binds to thrombomodulin to form a 1:1 complex of enzyme and cofactor, leading to a conformational change in thrombin that alters its substrate specificity. Thrombin bound to thrombomodulin has a diminished ability to convert fibrinogen to fibrin, to activate factor V, or to induce platelet activation as compared with free thrombin.[72, 73] An intact protein C-thrombo-

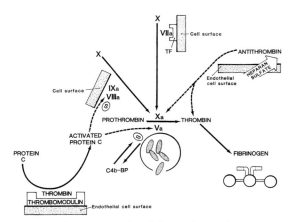

**Figure 15–3.** A schematic of the pathways that generate factor Xa and thrombin, and the natural anticoagulant mechanisms that regulate the activity of these enzymes.

Factor X can be activated by the extrinsic (factor VIIa-tissue factor [TF]) or the intrinsic (factor IXa-VIIIa-activated cell surface complex) pathways. Factor Xa binds to the factor Va on activated platelets and mediates the conversion of prothrombin to thrombin under physiologic conditions. Thrombin is then able to act upon fibrinogen to form a fibrin clot; the initial step in this conversion results in the liberation of fibrinopeptide A (FPA).

Thrombin and factor Xa are inactivated by antithrombin III bound to heparan sulfate molecules associated with the vascular endothelium resulting in the formation of factor Xa-antithrombin III and thrombin-antithrombin III complexes. Protein C is activated by thrombin bound to the endothelial cell receptor thrombomodulin. Once activated, protein C functions as a potent anticoagulant by inactivating factors VIIIa and Va. Protein S enhances the binding of activated protein C to phospholipid-containing membranes and is able to accelerate the inactivation of factors VIIIa and Va by this enzyme. The complement component, C4b-binding protein (C4b-BP), forms complexes with protein S, resulting in a reduction of protein S functional activity.

modulin pathway therefore functions as a negative regulator of unopposed thrombin generation, helping to maintain the endothelium in a thromboresistant state.

### Protein S

Another plasma protein, protein S, contributes to the normal functioning of the protein C-thrombomodulin anticoagulant mechanism by serving as a cofactor for the APC-dependent inactivation of factors Va and VIIIa.[74] Human protein S is a vitamin K–dependent protein that is synthesized by hepatocytes and endothelial cells, has a molecular weight of 69 kd, and circulates in plasma at a total concentration of 23 µg/ml.[75] Protein S is found in plasma in two forms that exist in equilibrium—the free, unbound protein, constituting about 40% of total protein S, and the bound form, which is complexed to C4b-binding protein, a component of the complement system that is an acute phase reactant.[76] C4b-binding protein serves to regulate the function of protein S because only the free form of protein S is active as a cofactor for APC.

In contrast to the other vitamin K–dependent coagulation proteins, protein S is not a zymogen of a serine protease and does not require proteolytic activation to serve as an active cofactor for APC. Protein S forms a stoichiometric complex with APC in the presence of calcium ions on a phospholipid surface, and accelerates APC-mediated cleavage of factor Va and factor VIIIa by enhancing the binding of APC to cell membranes where these reactions take place.[77, 78] Protein S may also inhibit prothrombinase activity independent of APC simply by competing with prothrombin for direct binding to factor Va.[79] The role of protein S in the overall functioning of the protein C-thrombomodulin mechanism is shown schematically in Figure 15–3.

The physiologic importance of the protein C-thrombomodulin-protein S pathway in the pathogenesis of thrombosis is substantiated by several clinical situations in which this pathway is dysfunctional. As is the case with the ATIII pathway, the most compelling evidence attesting to the importance of the protein C pathway in vivo comes from the well documented association between inherited deficiencies of protein C or protein S and the occurrence of venous thromboembolism. Both are inherited in an autosomal dominant fashion. Heterozygotes with protein C deficiency have functional protein C levels in plasma of 40 to 60% of normal, and affected members of thrombophilic kindreds have a lifetime risk of thrombotic events ranging between 60 and 75%.[80–82] Heterozygotes with protein S deficiency likewise have total plasma protein S levels of about 50% of normal, and studies of affected kindreds suggest a cumulative lifetime risk of thrombosis of about 75%.[83, 84] When patients with recurrent idiopathic venous thrombosis are carefully studied for deficiencies of the natural anticoagulant proteins, approximately 3% are found to be protein S-deficient, and another 2 to 3% are found to be protein C-deficient.[51, 52]

## APC Cofactor

Studies have identified another inherited disorder within the protein C pathway that is associated with recurrent thrombotic phenomena.[85] The existence of this hereditary defect was predicted based upon the finding of a poor anticoagulant response to addition of purified APC to plasmas from three unrelated thrombophilic patients.[85] Additional studies have found that this defect in the protein C anticoagulant pathway is present in 20 to 60% of thrombophilic patients with no other identifiable laboratory abnormality.[86–88] The basis for this disorder is an abnormal factor V molecule, which in most APC-resistant patients results from the replacement of an arginine residue at amino acid position 506 by glutamine.[89–90] The latter site is the initial APC-cleavage site of factor Va.

In addition to inherited deficiencies of protein C and protein S, a number of acquired clinical disorders exist in which reduced functional levels of these anticoagulant proteins have been observed. Acquired protein C deficiency has been identified in patients with severe liver disease, disseminated intravascular coagulation, adult respiratory distress syndrome, and the postoperative state.[91–93] Acquired protein S deficiency occurs in the setting of exogenous estrogen or oral contraceptive use, pregnancy, and disseminated intravascular coagulation.[58, 94–97] Many instances of acquired protein S deficiency may in part be related to shifts in the equilibrium between the free (active) and bound (inactive) forms of protein S, because the levels of C4b-binding protein, an acute-phase protein, may increase in these and other inflammatory disorders.[96]

Another important example of a thrombotic disorder resulting from an acquired abnormality of the protein C pathway is the phenomenon of warfarin-induced skin necrosis. In this disorder, thrombi are formed within dermal blood vessels of susceptible individuals during the first few days of oral anticoagulation with warfarin.[98–100] Studies have shown that this phenomenon is the result of the induction of a transient hypercoagulable state related to reductions in the level of proteins C by warfarin relative to levels of the vitamin K–dependent procoagulant factors (factors II, VII, IX, and X).[91, 101]

The final line of evidence substantiating a major role for the protein C pathway as a natural regulator of the thrombotic process in vivo comes from studies of immunologic markers of hemostatic system activity in patients with inherited deficiencies of proteins C and S. These studies indicate that the coagulation system is hyperactive in asymptomatic patients with deficiencies of protein C and protein S in comparison with normal subjects.[102, 103] Furthermore, when protein C concentrate is administered to patients with homozygous protein C deficiency, the level of activity of the coagulation system is brought into the normal range.[104] These data further support the view that an intact protein C-thrombomodulin-protein S pathway is of crucial importance in regulating thrombogenesis in vivo.

## Tissue Factor Pathway Inhibitor

Another natural anticoagulant that has a potential role in the regulation of thrombogenesis in vivo is tissue factor pathway inhibitor (TFPI). Although the existence in serum of an inhibitor of tissue factor was inferred from experiments done several decades ago,[105, 106] it was not until very recently that this inhibitor was identified and its mechanism of action fully characterized.[107, 108] TFPI is a 276 amino acid protein synthesized primarily in endothelial cells and megakaryocytes. It has a molecular weight of approximately 40 kd, and is present in plasma at a concentration of approximately 100 ng/ml.[109] Recent evidence suggests that TFPI in humans exists in vivo in four distinct intravascular fractions, including (1) 75% of the total intravascular pool is bound to the endothelial surface, perhaps in association with heparan sulfate and other glycosaminoglycans, and is releasable into plasma following intravenous infusion of heparin (the "heparin releasable" fraction)[110, 115]; (2) 20% is present in plasma bound to lipoproteins; (3) 2 to 3% circulates in plasma in the free, unbound form; and (4) 2 to 3% is present in platelets and may be released following exposure to platelet agonists such as thrombin.[109, 111] The relative contribution of each of these different sources of TFPI to the overall regulation of the thrombotic process in vivo has not been established.

The mechanism by which TFPI functions as a coagulation inhibitor is shown schematically in Figure 15–4. As described earlier in this chapter, blood coagulation in vivo is initiated when tissue factor becomes exposed to factor VII in plasma, with the resultant factor VIIa/tissue factor complex causing conversion of factor X to factor Xa. TFPI inhibits these enzyme-substrate interactions in a two-step process that results in the formation of a quaternary complex composed of factor Xa-TFPI-factor VIIa/tissue factor.[112] The TFPI molecule contains three domains with homology to Kunitz-type protease inhibitors. The Kunitz-2 domain of TFPI binds to, and inactivates, the serine active site of factor Xa. The factor Xa-TFPI complex then binds to the factor VIIa/tissue factor complex via the Kunitz-1 domain, thereby inhibiting its procoagulant activity.[112] Because of its ability to inhibit both factor Xa and factor VIIa/tissue factor at the endothelial surface, TFPI may serve a potentially crucial function in maintaining the endothelium in a thromboresistant state.

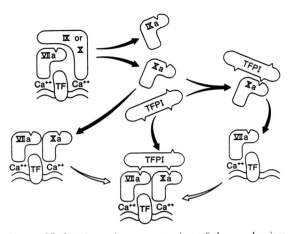

**Figure 15–4.** Schematic representation of the mechanism by which tissue factor pathway inhibitor (TFPI) inhibits factor VIIa-tissue factor activity. The indentations represent the active sites of factor VIIa and factor Xa; the protrusions represent the three Kunitz-type domains of TFPI. Two pathways for the formation of the quaternary complex are shown. In the lower left, TFPI binds to a preformed factor Xa-factor VIIa-tissue factor complex. In the lower right, TFPI binds to factor Xa and the factor Xa-TFPI complex then binds to the factor VIIa-tissue factor complex. (Used with permission from Broze GJ, Jr: The tissue factor pathway of coagulation. In Loscalzo J, Schafer AI (eds): Thrombosis and Hemorrhage. Boston, Blackwell Scientific Publications, 1994. Reprinted by permission of Blackwell Scientific Publications, Inc.)

The extent to which the TFPI mechanism contributes to the physiologic regulation of overall coagulation system activity in vivo has yet to be established. In contrast to the other natural anticoagulants, an inherited deficiency state associated with an increased risk of thrombotic disease has not been described for TFPI. This may in part be related to the fact that TFPI levels in plasma do not necessarily reflect the anticoagulantly active fraction of the total intravascular pool of TFPI in vivo, most of which is believed to be bound to the endothelium.

Evidence substantiating a physiologic role for TFPI in vivo comes primarily from animal studies. Infusion of recombinant TFPI inhibits the development of intravascular coagulation in rabbits coinfused with tissue factor,[113] whereas rabbits immunodepleted of TFPI have more profound tissue factor–induced intravascular coagulation relative to controls.[114] In patients with thrombosis, baseline immunologic levels of TFPI in plasma appear to be normal,[115] and the relative increase in functional TFPI levels in plasma following heparin injection is similar in thrombophilic compared with normal patients.[116] Similarly, studies of patients with disseminated intravascular coagulation have yielded inconsistent results, with some patients having diminished TFPI levels and others appearing normal.[117, 118]

## ABNORMALITIES IN FIBRINOLYSIS

The fibrinolytic system represents another important proteolytic enzyme pathway that may potentially play a pivotal role in the homeostatic regulation of blood coagulation. The physiologic function of the fibrinolytic system is mediated by the enzyme plasmin, a serine protease that proteolytically digests fibrin and thereby serves to limit thrombus formation. Thus, as is the case for abnormalities in each of the natural anticoagulant mechanisms discussed previously, it is plausible that impaired fibrinolysis may play a role in the pathogenesis of venous thromboembolism.

The various components of the fibrinolytic system are shown schematically in Figure 15–5.[119–121] Plasmin is generated when its precursor zymogen, plasminogen, undergoes limited proteolysis mediated by plasminogen activators. The most important physiologic activator of plasminogen is tissue plasminogen activator (t-PA), a serine protease that is synthesized and secreted by vascular endothelial cells. The affinity of t-PA for plasminogen is greatly enhanced by the presence of crosslinked fibrin, thereby ensuring that physiologic fibrinolysis occurs predominantly within the evolving clot.

Like the coagulation cascade, the overall activity of the plasminogen-plasminogen activator pathway is modulated by circulating protein inhibitors in plasma, many of which belong to the serpin family of protease inhibitors. One such inhibitor, α2-antiplasmin, forms complexes with and rapidly inactivates free plasmin that is formed in plasma. In contrast, fibrin-bound plasmin within the fibrin clot is relatively sequestered and thereby is relatively protected from inactivation by α2-antiplasmin. Another inhibitor, plasminogen activator inhibitor-1 (PAI-1), rapidly inactivates t-PA, thus blocking the activation of plasminogen and inhibiting net

fibrinolytic activity. PAI-1 is synthesized and secreted by endothelial cells, and preformed stores may be released into plasma by a variety of stimuli, including endothelial exposure to proinflammatory cytokines such as interleukin-1 and tumor necrosis factor.[122–124] This mechanism may explain the acute phase behavior of plasma PAI levels and may account in part for the conversion of the endothelial surface from a nonthrombogenic to a prothrombogenic phenotype in various disease states, such as malignancy and sepsis.[3] Thus, the vessel wall plays a central role in regulating the fibrinolytic process, because endothelial cells synthesize and secrete both t-PA and PAI-1, and are capable of binding both plasminogen and t-PA on their surface.

The extent to which abnormalities in fibrinolysis contribute to the pathogenesis of venous thromboembolism remains uncertain.[125] The weakness of the clinical association between impaired fibrinolysis and thrombosis may be related to the heterogeneity of assay methods used and the lack of uniform laboratory standardization available for assessing fibrinolytic activity in patients. The various assays used to assess fibrinolytic capacity include global assays of fibrinolysis (such as euglobulin clot lysis time, dilute whole blood clot lysis time, and euglobulin lysis of fibrin on a plate), as well as assays for specific components of the fibrinolytic system (t-PA antigen, t-PA activity, releasable t-PA following venous occlusion, plasminogen activity, PAI activity, etc.).

Several investigators have identified individuals with hereditary defects in fibrinolysis and recurrent venous thromboembolism, but the strength of this association is much weaker than is the case for inherited abnormalities of the natural anticoagulant proteins (protein C, protein S, and ATIII). For instance, several thrombophilic individuals with hereditary dysplasminogenemia or hypoplasminogenemia, inherited in an autosomal dominant fashion, have been identified whose biochemically affected family members have failed to manifest any thrombotic

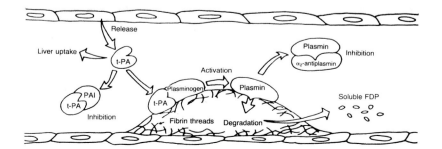

**Figure 15–5.** The fibrinolytic system leading to the generation of plasmin and the degradation of fibrin clot. (t-PA = tissue plasminogen activator.) (Reprinted with permission from Wiman B and Hamsten A: The fibrinolytic system and its role in the etiology of thromboembolic disease. Semin Thromb Hemost 16:207, 1990. Thieme Medical Publishers, Inc.)

tendency, despite careful study.[126, 127] Other family studies have described thrombophilic individuals with impaired fibrinolytic activity resulting either from increased plasma concentrations of PAI[128, 129] or defective synthesis or release of t-PA.[130, 131] The pattern of inheritance of specific defects in the fibrinolytic system has been difficult to establish from these studies. When levels of fibrinolytic capacity are compared among symptomatic and asymptomatic family members in these studies, no significant differences are demonstrable, calling into question whether these fibrinolytic defects are causal or merely coincidental.[125]

Hereditary abnormalities of fibrinolysis that appear to be more convincingly associated with thromboembolism are those involving inheritance of abnormal fibrinogens (congenital dysfibrinogenemia), although fewer than 20 cases of variant fibrinogens have been reported in association with thrombosis.[9] In vitro investigations reveal that many of these inherited fibrinogen mutations have in common either resistance to lysis of the fibrin or fibrinogen by plasmin (e.g., fibrinogen Chapel Hill III),[131] or failure of the abnormal fibrin or fibrinogen to promote plasminogen activation by t-PA (e.g., fibrinogen Dusard, fibrinogen New York I).[132-134]

Other studies involving series of patients with spontaneous, recurrent thromboembolism have suggested a possible role for acquired abnormalities of fibrinolysis in the pathogenesis of venous thromboembolism. One cohort study of patients with documented deep-vein thrombosis (DVT) found a recurrence rate of 6.3% per year in patients with impaired fibrinolytic capacity at baseline compared with 2.3% per year in patients with normal fibrinolytic capacity.[135] Numerous other studies involving either case-control or cross-sectional designs have suggested an association between impaired fibrinolysis and venous thromboembolism,[129, 136-139] although many have been criticized for including inappropriate control groups, failing to document thromboembolic events objectively, and using a heterogeneous array of assay methodologies that lack appropriate standardization.[125]

The strongest evidence suggesting a truly causal association between impaired fibrinolytic activity and venous thromboembolism comes from studies of patients with postoperative thrombosis. Global fibrinolytic activity tends to become diminished in most patients in the early postoperative period, presumably on the basis of increased synthesis or release of PAI from stimulated endothelial cells.[140, 141] Several prospective studies involving series of patients undergoing a variety of surgical procedures have documented an association between defective fibrinolytic activity at baseline (measured either pre- or postoperatively) and the development of postoperative thrombosis.[142-147] Acquired abnormalities in the fibrinolytic pathway may therefore represent the primary basis for hypercoagulability in the perioperative period. More compelling substantiation of the role of impaired fibrinolysis in the pathogenesis of venous thromboembolism, and of the clinical value of measuring fibrinolytic activity in individual patients, must await the outcome of carefully conducted prospective cohort studies.

## REFERENCES

1. Virchow R: Phlogose und thrombose in GefaBsystem. In Virchow R (ed): Gesammelte Abhandlugen zur Wissenschaftlichen Medicin. Frankfurt, von Meidinger Sohn, 1856, p 458.
2. Bauer KA, Rosenberg RD: The pathophysiology of the prethrombotic state in humans: Insights gained from studies using markers of hemostatic system activation. Blood 70:343, 1987.
3. Nachman RL, Silverstein R: Hypercoagulable states. Ann Intern Med 119:819, 1993.
4. Salzman EW, Hirsh J: The epidemiology, pathogenesis, and natural history of venous thrombosis. In Colman RW, Hirsh J, Marder VJ, and Salzman EW (eds): Hemostasis and Thrombosis: Basic Principles and Clinical Practice, ed 3. Philadelphia, JB Lippincott, 1994, pp 1275–1296.
5. Moser KM, Fedullo PF, LitteJohn JK, et al: Frequent asymptomatic pulmonary embolism in patients with deep venous thrombosis. JAMA 271:223, 1994.
6. Plate G, Ohlin P, Eklof B: Pulmonary embolism in acute iliofemoral venous thrombosis. Br J Surg 72:912, 1985.
7. Hull RD, Hirsh J, Carter CJ, et al: Pulmonary angiography, ventilation lung scanning, and venography for clinically suspected pulmonary embolism with abnormal perfusion lung scan. Ann Intern Med 98:891, 1983.
8. Schafer AI: The hypercoagulable states. Ann Intern Med 102:814, 1985.
9. Bauer KA: Pathobiology of the hypercoagulable state: Clinical features, laboratory evaluation, and management. In Hoffman J, Benz EJ, Shattil SJ, et al (eds): Hematology: Basic Principles and Practice, ed 1. New York, Churchill Livingstone, 1991, pp 1415–1430.
10. National Institutes of Health Consensus Development Conference: Prevention of venous thrombosis and pulmonary embolism. JAMA 256:744, 1986.
11. Colditz GA, Tuden RL, Oster G: Rates of venous thrombosis after general surgery: Combined results of randomized clinical trials. Lancet 2:143, 1986.
12. Scurr JH, Coleridge-Smith PD, Hasty JH: Regimen for improved effectiveness of intermittent pneumatic compression in deep venous thrombosis prophylaxis. Surgery 102:816, 1987.
13. Schaub RG, Simmons CA, Koetz MH, et al: Early events in the formation of a venous thrombus following local trauma and stasis. Lab Invest 51:218, 1984.
14. Usui Y, Wu HD, Goff SG, et al: A comparative experimental study of the organization of arterial and venous thrombi. Ann Surg 205:312, 1987.
15. Pescador R, Porta R, Conz A, et al: A quantitative

venous thrombosis model with stasis based on vascular lesion. Thromb Res 53:197, 1989.

16. Thomas DP, Merton RE, Hiller KF, et al: Resistance of normal endothelium to damage by thrombin. Br J Haematol 51:25, 1982.

17. Thomas DP, Merton RE, Wood RD, et al: The relationship between vessel wall injury and venous thrombosis: An experimental study. Br J Haematol 59:449, 1985.

18. Slack SM, Cui Y, Turitto VT: The effect of flow on blood coagulation and thrombosis. Thromb Haemost 70:129, 1993.

19. Diamond SL, Eskin SG, McIntire LV: Fluid flow stimulates tissue plasminogen activator secretion by cultured human endothelial cells. Science 243:1483, 1989.

20. Cooke JP, Rossitch E Jr, Andon NA, et al: Flow activates an endothelial potassium channel to release an endogenous nitrovasodilator. J Clin Invest 88:1663, 1991.

21. Nemerson Y: The tissue factor pathway of blood coagulation. Semin Hematol 29:170, 1992.

22. Gemmell CH, Turitto VT, Nemerson Y: Flow as a regulator of the activation of factor X by tissue factor. Blood 72:1404, 1988.

23. Moncada S, Higgs A: Mechanisms of disease: The L-arginine-nitric oxide pathway. N Engl J Med 329:2002, 1994.

24. Sinzinger H, Rauscha F, O'Grady J, et al: Prostaglandin $I_2$ and the nitric oxide donor molsidomine have synergistic effects on thromboresistance in man. Br J Clin Pharmacol 33:289, 1992.

25. Bauer KA, Kass BL, ten Cate H, et al: Factor IX is activated in vivo by the tissue factor mechanism. Blood 76:731, 1990.

26. Bauer KA, Weiss LM, Sparrow D, et al: Aging-associated changes in indices of thrombin generation and protein C activation in humans: Normative aging study. J Clin Invest 80:1527, 1987.

27. Osterud B, Rapaport SI: Activation of factor IX by the reaction product of tissue factor and factor VII: Additional pathway for initiating blood coagulation. Proc Natl Acad Sci USA 74:5260, 1977.

28. Rao LVM, Rapaport SI, Bajaj SP: Activation of human factor VII in the initiation of tissue factor-dependent coagulation. Blood 68:685, 1986.

29. Rao LVM, Rapaport SI: Activation of factor VII bound to tissue factor: A key early step in the tissue factor pathway of blood coagulation. Proc Natl Acad Sci USA 85:6687, 1989.

30. Bevilacqua MP, Pober JS, Majean GR, et al: Interleukin 1 (IL-1) induces biosynthesis and cell surface expression of procoagulant activity in human vascular cells. J Exp Med 160: 618, 1984.

31. Bevilacqua MP, Pober JS, Majean GR, et al: Recombinant tumor necrosis factor induces procoagulant activity in cultured human vascular endothelium: Characterization and comparison with action of interleukin 1. Proc Natl Acad Sci USA 83:4533, 1986.

32. Rao LVM: Tissue factor as tumor procoagulant. Cancer Metastasis Rev 11:249, 1992.

33. Mann KG, Nesheim ME, Church WR, et al: Surface-dependent reactions of the vitamin-K dependent enzyme complexes. Blood 76:1, 1990.

34. Gailani D, Broze GJ Jr: Factor XI activation in a revised model of blood coagulation. Science 253:909, 1991.

35. Wilcox JN, Smith KM, Schwartz SM, et al: Localization of tissue factor in the normal vessel wall and in the atherosclerotic plaque. Proc Natl Acad Sci USA 86:2839, 1989.

36. Weiss HJ, Turitto VT, Baumgartner HR, et al: Evidence for the presence of tissue factor on the subendothelium. Blood 73:968, 1989.

37. Dvorak HF, Senger DR, Dvorak AM, et al: Regulation of extravascular coagulation by microvascular permeability. Science 227:1059, 1985.

38. Rosenberg RD, Damus PS: The purification and mechanism of action of human antithrombin-heparin cofactor. J Biol Chem 248:6490, 1973.

39. Rosenberg RD: Actions and interactions of antithrombin and heparin. N Engl J Med 292:146, 1975.

40. Rosenberg JS, McKenna P, Rosenberg RD: Inhibition of human factor $IX_a$ by human antithrombin-heparin cofactor. J Biol Chem 250: 8883, 1975.

41. Stead N, Kaplan AP, Rosenberg RD: Inhibition of activated factor XII by antithrombin-heparin cofactor. J Biol Chem 251:6481, 1976.

42. Kurachi F, Fujikawa K, Schmeir G, et al: Inhibition of bovine factor $IX_a$ and factor $X_a$ by antithrombin III. Biochemistry 15:373, 1976.

43. Beeler DL, Marcum JA, Schiffman S, et al: Interaction of factor $XI_a$ and antithrombin in the presence and absence of heparin. Blood 67:1488, 1986.

44. Lawson JH, Butenas S, Ribarik N, et al: Complex-dependent inhibition of factor $VII_a$ by antithrombin III and heparin. J Biol Chem 268:767, 1993.

45. Rao LVM, Rapaport SI, Hoang AD: Binding of factor $VII_a$ to tissue factor permits rapid antithrombin III/heparin inhibition of factor $VII_a$. Blood 81:2600, 1993.

46. Marcum JA, Rosenberg RD: Anticoagulantly active heparin-like molecules from vascular tissue. Biochemistry 23:1730, 1984.

47. Marcum JA, McKenney JB, Rosenberg RD: The acceleration of thrombin-antithrombin complex formation in rat hindquarters via heparinlike molecules bound to the endothelium. J Clin Invest 74:341, 1984.

48. Marcum JA, Atha DH, Fritze LMS, et al: Cloned bovine aortic endothelial cells synthesize anticoagulantly active heparan sulfate proteoglycan. J Biol Chem 261: 7507, 1986.

49. deAgostino AI, Watkins SC, Slayter HS, et al: Localization of anticoagulantly active heparan sulfate proteoglycans in vascular endothelium: Antithrombin binding on cultured endothelial cells and perfused rat aorta. J Cell Biol 111:1293, 1990.

50. Demers C, Ginsberg JS, Hirsh J, et al: Thrombosis in antithrombin-III-deficient persons: Report of a large kindred and literature review. Ann Intern Med 116:754, 1992.

51. Heijboer H, Brandjes DPM, Buller HR, et al: Deficiencies of coagulation-inhibiting and fibrinolytic proteins in outpatients with deep-vein thrombosis. N Engl J Med 323:1512, 1990.

52. Malm J, Laurell M, Nilsson IM, et al: Thromboembolic disease—critical evaluation of laboratory investigation. Thromb Haemost 68:7, 1992.

53. Vikydal R, Korninger C, Kyrle PA, et al: The prevalance of hereditary antithrombin III deficiency in patients with a history of venous thromboembolism. Thromb Haemost 54:744, 1985.

54. Salem HH, Mitchell CA, Firkin BG: Current views on the pathophysiology and investigations of thrombotic disorders. Am J Hematol 25:463, 1987.

55. Kauffman RH, Veltkamp JJ, Van Tilburg NH, et al: Acquired antithrombin III deficiency and thrombosis in the nephrotic syndrome. Am J Med 65:607, 1978.

56. Damus PS, Wallace GA: Immunologic measurement of antithrombin III-heparin cofactor and $\alpha$2-macroglobulin in disseminated intravascular coagulation and hepatic failure coagulopathy. Thromb Res 6:27, 1989.

57. Weenink GH, Kahle LH, Lamping RJ, et al: Antithrombin III in oral contraceptive users and during normotensive pregnancy. Acta Obstet Gynecol Scand 63:57, 1984.

58. Caine YG, Bauer KA, Barzegar S, et al: Coagulation

activation following estrogen administration to post-menopausal women. Thromb Haemost 68:392, 1992.

59. Clouse LH, Comp PC: The regulation of hemostasis: The protein C system. N Engl J Med 314:1298, 1986.

60. Esmon CT: The roles of protein C and thrombomodulin in the regulation of blood coagulation. J Biol Chem 264:4743, 1989.

61. Esmon CT: The regulation of natural anticoagulant pathways. Science 235:1348, 1987.

62. Kisiel W, Canfield WM, Ericsson LH, et al: Anticoagulant properties of bovine plasma protein C following activation by thrombin. Biochemistry 16:5824, 1977.

63. Walker FJ, Sexton PW, Esmon CT: The inhibition of blood coagulation by activated protein C through the selective inactivation of activated factor V. Biochem Biophys Acta 571:333, 1979.

64. Fulcher CA, Gardiner JE, Griffin JH, et al: Proteolytic inactivation of human factor VIII procoagulant protein by activated protein C and its analogy with factor V. Blood 63:486, 1984.

65. Marlar RA, Kleiss AJ, Griffin JH: Mechanism of action of human activated protein C, a thrombin-dependent anticoagulant enzyme. Blood 59:1067, 1982.

66. Comp PC, Esmon CT: Generation of fibrinolytic activity by infusion of activated protein C into dogs. J Clin Invest 68:1221, 1981.

67. Sakata Y, Curriden S, Lawrence D, et al: Activated protein C stimulates the fibrinolytic activity of cultured endothelial cells and decreases antiactivator activity. Proc Natl Acad Sci USA 82:1121, 1985.

68. van Hinsbergh VWM, Bertina RM, van Wijngaarden A, et al: Activated protein C decreases plasminogen activator inhibitor activity in endothelial cell-conditioned medium. Blood 65:444, 1985.

69. Esmon CT, Owen WG: Identification of an endothelial cell cofactor for thrombin-catalyzed activation of protein C. Proc Natl Acad Sci USA 78:2249, 1981.

70. Owen WG, Esmon CT: Functional properties of an endothelial cell cofactor for thrombin catalyzed activation of protein C. J Biol Chem 256:5532, 1981.

71. Esmon NL, Owen WG, Esmon CT: Isolation of a membrane bound cofactor for thrombin-catalyzed activation of protein C. J Biol Chem 257:859, 1982.

72. Esmon CT, Esmon NL, Harris KW: Complex formation between thrombin and thrombomodulin inhibits both thrombin-catalyzed fibrin formation and factor V activation. J Biol Chem 257:7944, 1982.

73. Esmon NL, Carroll RC, Esmon CT: Thrombomodulin blocks the ability of thrombin to activate platelets. J Biol Chem 258:12238, 1983.

74. Walker FJ: The regulation of activated protein C by a new protein: The possible function of bovine protein S. J Biol Chem 255:5521, 1980.

75. DiScipio RG and Davie EW: Characterization of protein S, a carboxyglutamic acid containing protein from bovine and human plasma. Biochemistry 18:899, 1979.

76. Dahlback B, Stenflo J: High molecular weight complex in human plasma between vitamin K-dependent protein S and complement component C4b-binding protein. Proc Natl Acad Sci USA 78:2512, 1981.

77. Walker FJ: Regulation of protein C by protein S: The role of phospholipid in factor $V_a$ inactivation. J Biol Chem 256:11128, 1981.

78. Walker FJ, Chavin SI, Fay PJ: Inactivation of factor VIII by activated protein C and protein S. Arch Biochem Biophys 252:322, 1987.

79. Heeb MJ, Mesters RM, Taus G, et al: Binding of protein S to factor $V_a$ associated with inhibition of prothrombinase that is independent of activated protein C. J Biol Chem 268:2872, 1993.

80. Griffin JH, Evatt B, Zimmerman TS, et al: Deficiency

81. Broekmans AW, Veltkamp JJ, Bertina RM: Congenital protein C deficiency and venous thromboembolism: A study of three Dutch families. N Engl J Med 309:340, 1983.

82. Bovill EG, Bauer KA, Dickerman JD, et al: The clinical spectrum of heterozygous protein C deficiency in a large New England kindred. Blood 73:712, 1989.

83. Comp PC, Esmon CT: Recurrent venous thromboembolism in patients with a partial deficiency of protein S. N Engl J Med 311:1525, 1984.

84. Engesser L, Broekmans AW, Briet E, et al: Hereditary protein S deficiency: Clinical manifestations. Ann Intern Med 106:677, 1987.

85. Dahlback B, Carlsson M, Svensson PJ: Familial thrombophilia due to a previously unrecognized mechanism characterized by poor anticoagulant response to activated protein C: Prediction of a cofactor to activated protein C. Proc Natl Acad Sci USA 90:1004, 1993.

86. Koster T, Rosendaal FR, de Ronde H, et al: Venous thrombosis due to poor anticoagulant response to activated protein C: Leiden Thrombophilia Study. Lancet 342:1503, 1993.

87. Griffin JH, Evatt B, Wideman C, et al: Anticoagulant protein C pathway defective in majority of thrombophilic patients. Blood 82:1989, 1993.

88. Svensson PJ, Dahlback B: Resistance to activated protein C as a basis for venous thrombosis. N Engl J Med 330:517, 1994.

89. Dahlback B, Hildebrand B: Inherited resistance to activated protein C is corrected by anticoagulant cofactor activity found to be a property of factor V. Proc Natl Acad Sci USA 91:1396, 1994.

90. Bertina RM, Koeleman BPC, Koster T, et al: Mutation in factor V associated with resistance to activated protein C. Nature 369:64, 1994.

91. D'Angelo SV, Comp PC, Esmon CT, et al: Relationship between protein C antigen and anticoagulant activity during oral anticoagulation and in selected disease states. J Clin Invest 77:416, 1986.

92. Mannucci PM, Vigano S: Deficiencies of protein C, an inhibitor of blood coagulation. Lancet 2:463, 1982.

93. Griffin JH, Mosher DF, Zimmerman TS, et al: Protein C, an antithrombotic protein, is reduced in hospitalized patients with intravascular coagulation. Blood 60:261, 1982.

94. Comp PC, Thurnau GR, Welsh J, et al: Functional and immunologic protein S levels are decreased during pregnancy. Blood 68:881, 1986.

95. Malm J, Laurell M, Dahlback B: Change in the plasma levels of vitamin K-dependent proteins C and S and of C4b-binding protein during pregnancy and oral contraception. Br J Haematol 68:437, 1988.

96. D'Angelo A, Vigano-D'Angelo S, Esmon CT, et al: Acquired deficiencies of protein S: Protein S activity during oral anticoagulation, in liver disease, and in disseminated intravascular coagulation. J Clin Invest 81:1445, 1988.

97. Heeb MJ, Mosher DF, Griffin JH: Activation and complexation of protein C and cleavage and decrease of protein S in plasma of patients with disseminated intravascular coagulation. Blood 73:455, 1989.

98. Broekmans AW, Bertina RM, Loeliger EA, et al: Protein C and the development of skin necrosis during anticoagulant therapy (letter). Thromb Haemost 49:244, 1983.

99. McGehee WG, Klotz TA, Epstein DJ, et al: Coumarin necrosis associated with hereditary protein C deficiency. Ann Intern Med 100:59, 1984.

100. Friedman KD, Marlar RA, Houston JG, et al: Warfarin-

of protein C in congenital thrombotic disease. J Clin Invest 68:1370, 1981.

induced skin necrosis in a patient with protein S deficiency (abstract). Blood 68[suppl 1]:333, 1986.

101. Conway EM, Bauer KA, Barzegar S, et al: Suppression of hemostatic system activation by oral anticoagulants in the blood of patients with thrombotic diatheses. J Clin Invest 80:1535, 1987.

102. Bauer KA, Broekmans AW, Bertina RM, et al: Hemostatic enzyme generation in blood of patients with hereditary protein C deficiency. Blood 71:1418, 1988.

103. Mannucci PM, Tripodi A, Bottasso B, et al: Markers of procoagulant imbalance in patients with inherited thrombophilic syndromes. Thromb Haemost 67:200, 1992.

104. Conard J, Bauer KA, Gruber A, et al: Normalization of markers of coagulation activation with a purified protein C concentrate in adults with homozygous protein C deficiency. Blood 82:1159, 1993.

105. Schneider CL: The active principle of placental toxin: Thromboplastin; its inactivator in blood: Antithromboplastin. Am J Physiol 149:123, 1947.

106. Thomas L: Studies on the intravascular thromboplastin effect of tissue suspensions in mice: II. A factor in normal rabbit serum which inhibits the thromboplastin effect of the sedimentable tissue component. Bull Johns Hopkins Hosp 81:26, 1947.

107. Broze GJ Jr, Miletich JP: Characterization of the inhibition of tissue factor in serum. Blood 69:150, 1987.

108. Rao LVM, Rapaport SI: Studies of a mechanism inhibiting the initiation of the extrinsic pathway of coagulation. Blood 69:645, 1987.

109. Lindahl AK, Sandset PM, Abildgaard U: The present status of tissue factor pathway inhibitor. Blood Coagul Fibrinolysis 3:439, 1992.

110. Sandset PM, Abildgaard U, Larsen ML: Heparin induces release of extrinsic coagulation pathway inhibitor (EPI). Thromb Res 50:813, 1989.

111. Novotny WF, Girard TJ, Miletich JP, Broze GJ Jr: Platelets secrete a coagulation inhibitor functionally and antigenically similar to the lipoprotein associated coagulation inhibitor. Blood 72:2020, 1988.

112. Broze GJ Jr: The role of tissue factor pathway inhibitor in a revised coagulation cascade. Semin Hematol 29:159, 1992.

113. Day KC, Hoffman LC, Palmier MO, et al: Recombinant lipoprotein-associated coagulation inhibitor inhibits tissue thromboplastin-induced intravascular coagulation in the rabbit. Blood 76:1538, 1991.

114. Sandset PM, Warn-Cramer BJ, Rao LVM, et al: Depletion of extrinsic pathway inhibitor (EPI) sensitizes rabbits to disseminated intravascular coagulation induced with tissue factor: Evidence supporting a physiologic role for EPI as a natural anticoagulant. Proc Natl Acad Sci USA 88:708, 1991.

115. Novotny WF, Brown SG, Miletich JP, et al: Plasma antigen levels of the lipoprotein-associated coagulation inhibitor in patient samples. Blood 78:387, 1991.

116. Ariens RAS, Faioni EM, Panzeri D, et al: Heparin-releasable tissue factor pathway inhibitor in thrombophilic patients (abstract). Blood 82[Suppl 1]:273, 1993.

117. Bajaj MS, Rana SV, Wysolmerski RB, et al: Inhibitor of the factor VII$_a$-tissue factor complex is reduced in patients with disseminated intravascular coagulation but not in patients with severe hepatocellular disease. J Clin Invest 79:1874, 1987.

118. Warr TA, Rao LVM, Rapaport SI: Human plasma extrinsic pathway inhibitor activity: II. Plasma levels in disseminated intravascular coagulation and hepatocellular disease. Blood 74:994, 1989.

119. Wiman B, Hamsten A: The fibrinolytic enzyme system and its role in the etiology of thromboembolic disease. Semin Thromb Hemost 16:207, 1990.

120. Lijnen HR, Collen D: Review: Congenital and acquired deficiencies of components of the fibrinolytic system and their relationship to bleeding and thrombosis. Fibrinolysis 3:67, 1989.

121. Aoki N: Fibrinolysis. Semin Thromb Hemost 10:1, 1984.

122. Colucci M, Paramo JA, Collen D: Generation in plasma of a fast-acting inhibitor of plasminogen activator in response to endotoxin stimulation. J Clin Invest 75:818, 1985.

123. Nachman RL, Hajjar KA, Silverstein RL, et al: Interleukin 1 induces endothelial cell synthesis of plasminogen activator inhibitor. J Exp Med 163:1595, 1986.

124. van Hinsbergh VWM, Kooistra T, van den Berg EA, et al: Tumor necrosis factor increases the production of plasminogen activator inhibitor in human endothelial cells in vitro and rats in vivo. Blood 72:1967, 1988.

125. Prins MH, Hirsh J: A critical review of the evidence supporting a relationship between impaired fibrinolytic activity and venous thromboembolism. Arch Intern Med 151:1721, 1991.

126. Aoki N, Moroi M, Sakata Y, et al: Abnormal plasminogen: A hereditary molecular abnormality found in a patient with recurrent thrombosis. J Clin Invest 61:1186, 1978.

127. Miyata T, Iwanaga S, Sakata Y, et al: Plasminogen Tochigi: Inactive plasmin resulting from replacement of alanine-600 by threonine in the active site. Proc Natl Acad Sci USA 79:6132, 1982.

128. Joergensen M, Bonnevie-Nielsen V: Increased concentration of fast-acting plasminogen activator inhibitor in plasma associated with familial venous thrombosis. Br J Haematol 65:175, 1987.

129. Engesser L, Brommer EJP, Kluft C, et al: Elevated plasminogen activator inhibitor (PAI), a cause of thrombophilia? A study in 203 patients with familial or sporadic venous thrombophilia. Thromb Haemost 62:673, 1989.

130. Johansson L, Hedner U, Nilsson IM: A family with thromboembolic disease associated with deficient fibrinolytic activity in vessel wall. Acta Med Scand 203:477, 1978.

131. Carrell N, Gabriel DA, Blatt PM, et al: Hereditary dysfibrinogenemia in a patient with thrombotic disease. Blood 62:439, 1983.

132. Al-Mondhiry HAB, Bilezikian SB, Nossel HL: Fibrinogen "New York"—An abnormal fibrinogen associated with thromboembolism: Functional evaluation. Blood 45:607, 1975.

133. Soria J, Soria C, Caen JP: A new type of congenital dysfibrinogenemia with defective fibrin lysis—Dusard syndrome: Possible relation to thrombosis. Br J Haematol 53:575, 1983.

134. Collet J-P, Soria J, Mirshahi M, et al: Dusart syndrome: A new concept of the relationship between fibrin clot architecture and fibrin clot degradability: Hypofibrinolysis related to an abnormal clot structure. Blood 82:2462, 1993.

135. Korninger C, Lechner K, Niessner H, et al: Impaired fibrinolytic capacity predisposes for recurrence of thrombosis. Thromb Haemost 52:127, 1984.

136. Wiman B, Ljungberg B, Chielewska J, et al: The role of the fibrinolytic system in deep vein thrombosis. J Lab Clin Med 105:265, 1985.

137. Nilsson IM, Ljungner H, Tengborn L: Two different mechanisms in patients with venous thrombosis and defective fibrinolysis: Low concentration of plasminogen activator or increased concentration of plasminogen activator inhibitor. Br Med J 290:1453, 1985.

138. Juhan-Vague I, Alessi MC, Fossat C, et al: Clinical relevance of reduced t-PA release and elevated PA inhibitor levels in patients with spontaneous or recurrent deep venous thrombosis. Thromb Haemost 57:67, 1987.

139. Lau HKF, Teitel JM, Cheung T, et al: Hypofibrinolysis in patients with hypercoagulability: The roles of urokinase and of plasminogen activator inhibitor. Am J Hematol 44:260, 1993.

140. Comp PC, Jackocks RM, Taylor FB Jr: The dilute whole blood clot lysis assay: A screening method for identifying postoperative patients with a high incidence of deep venous thrombosis. J Lab Clin Med 93:120, 1979.

141. Crandon AJ, Peel KR, Anderson JA, et al: Postoperative deep vein thrombosis: Identifying high-risk patients. Br Med J 291:343, 1980.

142. Rocha E, Alfaro MJ, Paramo JA, et al: Preoperative identification of patients at high risk of deep venous thrombosis despite prophylaxis in total hip replacement. Thromb Haemost 59:93, 1988.

143. Kluft C, Jie AFH, Lowe GDO, et al: Association between post-operative hyperresponse in tPA-inhibition and deep vein thrombosis. Thromb Haemost 56:107, 1986.

144. Sue-Ling HM, Johnston D, McMahon MJ, et al: Pre-operative identification of patients at high risk of deep venous thrombosis after elective major abdominal surgery. Lancet 1:1173, 1986.

145. Sue-Ling HM, Johnston D, Verheijen JH, et al: Indicators of depressed fibrinolytic activity in pre-operative prediction of deep venous thrombosis. Br J Surg 74:275, 1987.

146. Sorensen JV, Borris LC, Lassen MR, et al: Association between plasma levels of tissue plasminogen activator and post-operative deep vein thrombosis: Influence of prophylaxis with low molecular weight heparin. Thromb Res 59:131, 1990.

147. Sorensen JV, Lassen MR, Borris LC, et al: Postoperative deep vein thrombosis and plasma levels of tissue plasminogen activator inhibitor. Thromb Res 60:247, 1990.

# PART ONE

# PREVENTION OF VENOUS THROMBOEMBOLISM

## Chapter 16

## Overview of Prevention

G. Patrick Clagett

Venous thrombosis and pulmonary embolism are preventable causes of death and morbidity in hospitalized patients. It has been estimated that venous thromboembolism causes death in more than 100,000 patients each year in the United States and is a contributing factor in the demise of another 100,000.[1] Although approximately 50% of these patients have terminal illnesses that are complicated by pulmonary embolism, many have treatable conditions and would have extended longevity were it not for fatal pulmonary embolism. The loss of productive lives and the economic burden imposed by dealing with the consequences of venous thromboembolism in surviving patients demand serious consideration from a public health perspective.

The estimates cited earlier are from older, crude data. However, they have been substantiated in a contemporary study conducted in 16 short-stay community hospitals in central Massachusetts, where the annual incidence of verified pulmonary embolism was 23 per 100,000 residents with an inhospital case fatality rate of 12%.[2] Extrapolation of these data to the United States population suggests that approximately 260,000 cases of *clinically diagnosed* venous thromboembolism occur each year in patients hospitalized in acute care hospitals in this country. However, this may be a "tip of the iceberg" situation; undiagnosed pulmonary embolism is

a larger problem. Fatal and nonfatal pulmonary embolisms are most often clinically silent, with the disease being unsuspected before death in 70 to 80% of patients in whom the diagnosis is made at autopsy.[3, 4] Because of the low rate of autopsy in the United States and the failure of the Massachusetts study to include nonacute care facilities such as nursing homes and rehabilitation hospitals, where the incidence of pulmonary embolism is probably even higher, the real incidence of venous thromboembolism is far greater. These estimates are justified based on data from population studies in countries where the rate of autopsy is much higher.[5]

### ARGUMENTS FOR AND AGAINST PROPHYLAXIS OF VENOUS THROMBOEMBOLISM

A fundamental rationale for using prophylaxis of venous thromboembolism is the clinically silent nature of the disease. Deep venous thrombosis and pulmonary embolism manifest few specific symptoms,[6] and the clinical diagnosis based on history and physical examination alone is insensitive and unreliable.[7] In addition, to wait until venous thromboembolism becomes clinically manifest before treating the condition exposes susceptible patients to unacceptable risks. The first sign of the disease may be fatal pulmonary embolism. Although anticoagulation is highly effective therapy, the majority of patients who die from pulmonary embolism do so within 1/2 hour of the onset of symptoms,[8] too soon for anticoagulant therapy to be effective. Unrecognized and untreated deep venous thrombosis may also lead to longterm sequelae such as chronic venous insufficiency and the postphlebitic syndrome and may predispose patients to recurrent venous thromboembolism.

In addition to saving lives and reducing morbidity, health care costs are reduced by broad application of strategies to prevent venous thromboembolism. All cost-effectiveness analyses have documented that it is far cheaper to employ routine prophylaxis rather than to pay for treatment of clinically recognized venous thromboembolism.[9–14] In a study that addressed the prevalence of risk factors for venous thromboembolism in hospitalized patients in the United States, the costs of prophylaxis to the patients at risk were assessed.[15] The authors estimated that for the 1.18 million patients over the age of 40 years undergoing major surgery each year, the total cost of prophylaxis, estimated to be $50 to 100 per patient, would be $59 million to $118 million. If effective, prophylaxis would prevent 158,000 episodes of deep venous thrombosis and 6,000 deaths from pulmonary embolism. The cost savings would be $119 million to $301 million. In addition, the authors estimated that there were 6 million patients hospitalized annually for medical and other surgical conditions who were at high risk for venous thromboembolism. In extrapolating the same data to this larger group, the general application of prophylaxis to these high risk patients may prevent 700,000 episodes of deep venous thrombosis and 25,000 to 33,000 deaths from pulmonary embolism annually. This represents a savings of $330 million to $660 million.

An alternative to prophylaxis would be to use serial surveillance tests such as duplex ultrasonography or impedance plethysmography in high-risk patients.[16, 17] Although attractive, this approach is expensive, time-consuming, and cumbersome, and, therefore, can be applied to only limited numbers of patients at risk. In addition, the sensitivity of these methods in detecting deep venous thrombosis in asymptomatic patients who may have partially occlusive or distally located clots is not as good as it is in symptomatic patients. Most experts believe that broad application of effective methods of prevention is safer and more cost-effective than selective, intensive surveillance.[9, 10]

Despite overwhelming evidence of the efficacy of a wide variety of prophylactic agents,

surveys conducted in the United States, England, and Sweden document wide practice variations among physicians; approximately one-half of surgeons in these countries use prophylaxis in less than one-fifth of their patients.[19–22] A study of more than 2,000 patients with multiple risk factors hospitalized at 16 acute care hospitals showed that only one-third of these patients received prophylaxis.[23] Use of prophylaxis was higher in teaching than nonteaching hospitals, and patients undergoing vascular, abdominal, and orthopedic operations were the most likely to receive prophylaxis. Risk factors for venous thromboembolism were highly prevalent in this population of hospitalized patients; 78% of all patients had one or more risk factors, 48% had two or more, and 19% had three or more.[15] The authors concluded that despite widespread recognition of the problem and the effectiveness of multiple preventive strategies, prophylaxis is woefully underutilized at present.

Why do physicians fail to use prophylaxis more widely? Many believe that the overall incidence of venous thromboembolism among hospitalized and postoperative patients has decreased over the past decades to the point where the incidence is too low to consider prophylaxis. These physicians frequently cite informal, retrospective surveys of their own clinical services and the rare occurrence of fatal pulmonary embolism diagnosed by autopsy at their hospital to bolster this argument. In fact, the incidence of venous thromboembolism has declined in recent years,[24] and this probably reflects the success of prophylactic strategies.[25] Even so, the incidence remains too high for a condition that is preventable, and the current estimates of the incidence of fatal pulmonary embolism based on hospital discharge data suggest the need for even wider application of prophylaxis.[26] Furthermore, the difficulties in establishing the antemortem diagnosis of pulmonary embolism have been alluded to as well as the low rate of autopsy in the United States, especially in elderly patients with chronic conditions. Data from countries where autopsy is mandated indicate that pulmonary embolism remains a significant problem.[5, 27] In addition, contemporary data from the central Massachusetts study show that clinically recognized pulmonary embolism is surprisingly common.[2]

Another reason for failure to use prophylaxis, especially in surgical patients, is the concern about bleeding complications with anticoagulants.[22] Countering this argument are the abundant data from meta-analyses and placebo-controlled, double-blind randomized trials that demonstrate no significant increase in major bleeding with the use of low-dose heparin and low-molecular-weight heparin.[28-30] The incidence of wound hematomas is increased with these agents, and this can be an important problem resulting in wound infection, dehiscence, and infection of a prosthetic device placed at the time of operation.[28] The magnitude of hematoma occurrence has, unfortunately, been downplayed or ignored by many medical advocates of prophylaxis who are not surgeons. However, alternative, mechanical methods of effective prophylaxis that carry no bleeding risk are available for such patients. Heparin-induced thrombocytopenia has also been raised as a concern with widespread use of low-dose heparin. Critical review of this problem, though, suggests that the incidence with this route of heparin administration is rare.[31] In addition, the costs of prophylaxis have also been used as an argument against its wider use; however, as argued above, every study addressing this issue has concluded that broad application of prophylaxis is highly cost-effective.

The final reason for not using prophylaxis has to do with subjective perceptions of the magnitude of the problem and the effects of prophylaxis in *individual* practices. Because venous thromboembolism is most often clinically silent, the occurrence of overt venous thromboembolism among an individual physician's patients is perceived to be rare.[22] For example, extrapolation of data from meta-analyses suggests that fatal pulmonary embolism occurs in 0.5 to 0.8% of patients over the age of 40 years,[11, 28, 29] undergoing major abdominal surgery and in many of these, the diagnosis and cause of death would not be known. Similarly, proximal or above-knee venous thrombosis is present in 6 to 7% of general surgical patients, and less than 50% of these would be clinically overt and detected. Therefore, an average busy surgeon whose practice consists of a high volume of major abdominal surgery may not perceive venous thromboembolism to be a significant problem. More importantly, this physician may have little appreciation of the effectiveness of, for example, low-dose heparin in reducing the incidence of fatal pulmonary embolism in the individual practice from 0.7 to 0.2%, as would be expected by extrapolation of data from meta-analyses dealing with large numbers of patients.[28] Thus, from an individual practice perspective, it is difficult to appreciate the effectiveness of prophylaxis, whereas failures (patients developing clinically overt venous thromboembolism who receive prophylaxis) are readily apparent. Additionally, bleeding complications are highly visible, not easily forgotten, and frequently blamed on prophylaxis.

## RISK FACTORS

Application of effective prophylaxis depends upon knowledge of specific clinical risk factors in individual patients. Clinical risk factors include age greater than 40 years; advanced age (greater than 70 years); prolonged immobility or paralysis; prior venous thromboembolism; cancer; major surgery (particularly operations involving the abdomen, pelvis, and lower extremities); obesity; varicose veins; congestive heart failure; myocardial infarction; stroke; fractures of the pelvis, hip, or leg; and high-dose estrogen use.[32-34] In addition, congenital and acquired aberrations in hemostatic mechanisms (hypercoagulable states) that ordinarily predispose to venous thromboembolism assume even greater risk when afflicted patients are hospitalized and undergo surgical procedures. Hemostatic abnormalities include antithrombin III deficiency; protein C deficiency; protein S deficiency; dysfibrinogenemia; disorders of plasminogen and plasminogen activation; antiphospholipid antibodies and lupus anticoagulant, heparin-induced thrombocytopenia; myeloproliferative disorders such as polycythemia vera; and hyperviscosity syndromes.[35]

In many patients, multiple risk factors may be present, and the risks are cumulative. For example, elderly patients with hip fractures undergoing major orthopedic operations who remain immobile in bed after operation are among the most susceptible to fatal pulmonary embolism. Awareness of the risk of venous thromboembolism in general patient categories and in clinical settings in which the risk has been defined by epidemiologic studies is also important in successful application of prophylaxis.[32] For example, the overall incidence of venous thromboembolism is higher on orthopedic services and in intensive care units than on general medical services. The levels of risk for thromboembolic events based on clinical risk factors and epidemiologic data are shown in Table 16-1.

## METHODS AND RESULTS OF PROPHYLAXIS

Just as the level of risk varies in individual patients, so too does the efficacy of various prophylactic approaches. An effective strategy in one type of patient may be relatively ineffective

Table 16–1. **Classification of Level of Risk**

| Thromboembolic Event | Low Risk | Moderate Risk | High Risk | Very High Risk |
|---|---|---|---|---|
| | Uncomplicated surgery in patients under 40 years of age with no other risk factors | Major surgery in patients over 40 years of age with no other clinical risk factors | Major surgery in patients over 40 years of age who have additional risk factors or myocardial infarction | Major surgery in patients over 40 years of age plus previous thromboembolic or malignant disease or orthopedic surgery or hip fracture or stroke or spinal cord injury |
| Calf vein thrombosis (%) | 2 | 10–20 | 20–40 | 40–80 |
| Proximal vein thrombosis (%) | 0.4 | 2–4 | 4–8 | 10–20 |
| Clinical pulmonary embolism (%) | 0.2 | 1–2 | 2–4 | 4–10 |
| Fatal pulmonary embolism (%) | 0.002 | 0.1–0.4 | 0.4–1.0 | 1–5 |

Modified from Gallus AS, Salzman EW, Hirsh J: Prevention of venous thromboembolism. In Colman RW, Hirsh J, Marder VJ, Salzman EW (eds): Hemostasis and Thrombosis: Basic Principles and Clinical Practice, ed 3, p. 1332. Philadelphia, JB Lippincott, 1994.

in another. An example is low-dose heparin that is highly effective in moderate-risk general surgery patients but is a poor choice in high-risk orthopedic patients. In addition to relative effectiveness, the risk of bleeding, other side effects, and expense vary with different agents. An underlying philosophy of broad application of prophylaxis is that many patients will be treated to spare the few who might develop venous thromboembolism. Therefore, costly strategies with significant bleeding potential should be reserved for patients at highest risk. For example, moderate-intensity warfarin (International Normalized Ratio [INR] = 2 to 3) is an excellent choice in high-risk orthopedic patients but is inappropriate in moderate-risk general surgery patients. Currently used prophylactic regimens proved to be effective are outlined in Table 16–2.

The results of prophylactic strategies in various patient groups are shown in Table 16–3. Effectiveness is defined by the relative risk reduction (% reduction) of deep venous thrombosis, the precursor to pulmonary embolism. These data were derived from pooled analyses of the results of randomized trials published in English up to 1992.[36] The following recommendations in various patient categories were made by a consensus group[36] that critically reviewed these data, applied formal statistical rules of evidence to judge efficacy,[37] extrapolated results from studies in similar patient groups when data was insufficient, and tempered their recommendations with practical concerns of cost, patient acceptance, and physician and nursing compliance.

## General Surgery

The overall incidence of thromboembolic endpoints in general surgical patients was calculated by pooling data in controlled studies of patients in published English-language trials of prophylactic methods.[28] In most trials, the bulk of these patients had elective gastrointestinal surgery. However, in some the patient populations were more heterogeneous and included those undergoing gynecologic, thoracic, urologic, and vascular operations. The overall incidence of deep venous thrombosis as assessed by the labeled fibrinogen uptake test was 25% in control subjects; in trials in which the fibrinogen uptake test was confirmed by phlebography, the incidence was 19%. Most of this represents calf or leg vein thrombosis of questionable clinical significance. The presence of more serious proximal or above-knee deep venous thrombosis was 6 to 7% in patients not treated with prophylaxis. The overall incidence of clinically recognized pulmonary embolism (fatal and nonfatal) was 1.6%, and the incidence of fatal pulmonary embolism was 0.8%.[28]

In low-risk general surgery patients who are undergoing minor operations, who are less than 40 years of age, and who have no clinical risk factors, no specific prophylaxis other than early ambulation is warranted. Elastic stockings, low-dose heparin (given every 12 hours), or intermittent pneumatic compression are appropriate for moderate-risk general surgery patients who are over 40 years of age and are undergoing major operations, but who have no additional clinical risk factors for venous thromboembolism. Low-dose heparin (given every 8 hours) or low-molecular-weight heparin should be used in higher risk general surgery patients who are over the age of 40 years, those undergoing major operations, and those who have additional risk factors.

Low-molecular-weight heparin appears to be slightly better than low-dose unfractionated heparin in preventing venous thromboembolism (see Table 16–3) and may be associated with slightly fewer bleeding complications.[30, 381, 39] Low-molecular-weight heparin is also more convenient and can be administered in a single, daily dosage regimen. However, both strategies are highly successful in preventing venous thromboembolism in general surgical patients, and the marginal advantages of low-molecular-weight heparin may be offset by its higher expense. At present prices, low-molecular-weight heparin costs about 20-fold more per dose than low-dose heparin. Low-dose heparin combined with dihydroergotamine is also effective but has been withdrawn from the market in the United States.

In higher risk general surgery patients who

are prone to wound complications such as hematoma and infection, dextran or intermittent pneumatic compression are good alternative choices for prophylaxis. These agents have been proved effective in multiple trials and carry less bleeding risk.[28] In very-high-risk general surgery patients with multiple risk factors, pharmacologic methods (low-dose heparin, low-molecular-weight heparin, or dextran) may be combined with intermittent pneumatic compression. In selected very-high-risk general surgery patients, perioperative low-to-moderate intensity warfarin may be an appropriate choice. Aspirin has been found to be ineffective[28] or marginally effective[39, 40] in preventing venous thromboembolism in general surgery patients and is not an appropriate strategy.

## Orthopedic Surgery

Orthopedic operations and orthopedic trauma are high-risk conditions in which the most frequent cause of death is pulmonary embolism. In patients not receiving prophylaxis, deep venous thrombosis complicates the postoperative course after total hip replacement in approximately 50% of patients.[29, 411, 421] Fatal pulmonary embolism occurs in up to 6% of patients who are not treated with antithrombotic prophylaxis.[43] The mortality of patients with hip fractures without prophylaxis is over 3% and may be as high as 12%, with death being most

Table 16–2. **Antithrombotic Regimens to Prevent Venous Thromboembolism**

| Method | Description |
| --- | --- |
| Low-dose heparin | 5,000 U heparin given subcutaneously every 8 to 12 hours, starting 1–2 hours before operation |
| Adjusted dose subcutaneous heparin | 3,500 U heparin given subcutaneously every 8 hours with postoperative dose adjustment by +/− 500 U to maintain APTT at high-normal values |
| Heparin/DHE (dihydroergotamine) | 2500–5000 U heparin + 0.5 mg DHE given subcutaneously every 12 hours |
| Low-molecular-weight heparin and heparinoids | Various doses, depending on preparation, given subcutaneously once or twice daily |
| Moderate-dose perioperative warfarin | Start moderate daily dose (5 mg) the day of or the day after operation; adjust dose for prothrombin time ratio 1.3–1.5 (INR 2–3) by day 5 |
| Pre- and postoperative two-step warfarin | Start 1–2.5 mg/day 5–14 days before operation aiming for 2- to 3-second increase in prothrombin time at time of operation; give 2.5–5 mg/day aiming for prothrombin time ratio of 1.3–1.5 (INR 2–3) in postoperative period |
| Minidose warfarin | Start 1 mg/day 10–14 days before operation, aiming for INR of 1.5 after operation |
| Dextran 40/70 | 500–1,000 ml dextran 40 or 70 during operation, then 500 ml daily for 3 days, then every other day |
| Aspirin | 325–3,600 mg/day |
| Intermittent pneumatic compression/elastic stocking | Start immediately before operation, and continue until fully ambulatory |

Table 16–3. **Effectiveness of Prophylaxis of Venous Thromboembolism According to Patient Category***

| Patient Category† | No Prophylaxis | | Relative Risk Reduction (%) With Prophylactic Methods | | | | | | | | |
|---|---|---|---|---|---|---|---|---|---|---|---|
| | Incidence of DVT (%) | 95% CI | Low-Dose Heparin | Low-Dose Heparin Plus Dihydroergotamine | Low-Molecular-Weight Heparin | Adjusted Dose Subcutaneous Heparin | Warfarin | Dextran | Aspirin | Intermittent Pneumatic Compression | Elastic Stockings |
| General surgery‡ | 25 | 24–26 | 68 | 64 | 86 | ? | 59 | 38 | 19 | 61 | 63 |
| Elective hip replacement | 50 | 46–55 | 32 | 26 | 68 | 77 | 63 | 41 | 11 | 60 | 25 |
| Hip fracture | 43 | 38–49 | 9 | 17 | 74 | ? | 43 | 32 | 6 | ? | ? |
| Neurosurgery | 24 | 20–28 | 75 | ? | ? | ? | ? | ? | ? | 73 | 64 |
| Spinal cord injury | 38 | 31–46 | ? | ? | ? | ? | ? | ? | ? | ? | ? |
| Multiple trauma | 48 | 43–53 | ? | ? | ? | ? | ? | ? | ? | ? | ? |
| Myocardial infarction | 24 | 18–30 | 72 | ? | ? | ? | ? | ? | ? | ? | ? |
| Stroke | 47 | 35–48 | 45 | ? | 79 | ? | ? | ? | ? | ? | ? |

*Data obtained from pooled analysis of English language trials reported through 1992 (see reference 36).
†Deep venous thrombosis (DVT) diagnosed by labeled fibrinogen uptake test in general surgical, neurosurgical, myocardial infarction, and stroke patients; by phlebography in elective hip surgery, hip fracture, and multiple trauma patients; and by impedance plethysmography in spinal cord injury patients.
‡General surgery patient includes any patient over the age of 40 years undergoing major abdominal surgery (gastrointestinal, gynecologic, and urologic complications).
?Indicates that data are too scant to make reliable estimate of risk reduction.

commonly the result of fatal pulmonary embolism.[43] After knee replacement surgery, the incidence of deep venous thrombosis is over 50% and may reach 80%.[44I, 45I, 46IV]

In patients undergoing total hip replacement, warfarin and low-molecular-weight heparin are the most effective antithrombotic agents (see Table 16–3). The results from a recent large randomized trial indicated that the small reduction in the incidence of venous thromboembolism with low-molecular-weight heparin, as compared with warfarin, was offset by an increase in bleeding complications.[47] Although other methods such as low-dose heparin, dextran, aspirin, intermittent pneumatic compression, and elastic stockings reduce the overall incidence of venous thromboembolism, they are less effective and should not be used routinely. Subcutaneous heparin given in adjusted doses to maintain the activated partial thromboplastin time in the upper normal range has also been found to be highly effective.[48I, 49I] However, this method of administration is cumbersome, requires close monitoring, and is not commonly used.

Warfarin and low-molecular-weight heparin are the most effective prophylactic agents in patients with hip fractures. Dextran, low-dose heparin, and aspirin are less effective and are not recommended for routine use (see Table 16–3). Placement of a prophylactic inferior vena cava filter may be considered and selected for high-risk orthopedic trauma patients in whom other forms of prophylaxis are contraindicated or ineffective.[50, 51]

## Neurosurgery, Acute Spinal Cord Injury, Multiple Trauma

Patients undergoing elective intracranial neurosurgery are at high risk for venous thromboembolism because they frequently have paralysis, prolonged postoperative immobility, and lengthy operations with the lower extremities in a dependent position. In control patients not treated with prophylaxis, the average incidence of deep venous thrombosis is approximately 24% (see Table 16–3). Physical methods of prophylaxis in neurosurgical patients have been preferred to anticoagulant therapy because of concern about intracranial bleeding. Intermittent pneumatic compression with or without elastic stockings is the prophylactic method of choice in these patients.

Although the high incidence of deep venous thrombosis in patients with hip and lower extremity fractures is well established, the incidence following other types of trauma is less well known. The literature is difficult to interpret because trauma patients are heterogeneous with a variety of injuries, and studies reporting a high incidence of deep venous thrombosis may have a large proportion of patients with lower extremity trauma and fractures. A recent review article suggests that patients with trauma and no additional risk factors for venous thromboembolism are at relatively low risk.[52] However, in trauma patients with clinical risk factors, the incidence is high enough to justify both prophylaxis and close surveillance.[53] In patients with multiple trauma, intermittent pneumatic compression, warfarin, or low-molecular-weight heparin may be effective, but data are limited. A recent nonrandomized study suggests that low-dose heparin is inadequate prophylaxis in patients with multiple trauma.[54] In patients with extensive trauma who have multiple risk factors but who cannot receive other forms of prophylaxis, inferior vena cava filter insertion may be considered, but there are no randomized prospective control studies to verify efficacy. Serial duplex ultrasonography to detect subclinical deep vein thrombosis may also be helpful in these patients.[53]

In patients with acute spinal cord injury, the venographic incidence of deep venous thrombosis has been reported as 18 to 90%, with an average incidence of 38% (see Table 16–3). Pulmonary embolism occurs in about 5% of patients following paralysis due to acute spinal cord injury, and the period of greatest risk appears to be during the first 2 weeks following the injury.[55] Death from pulmonary embolism is unusual 3 months or more after injury. Low-dose heparin appears to be relatively ineffective in patients with spinal cord injury, whereas low-molecular-weight heparin is clearly efficacious.[56I, 57I] Warfarin and intermittent pneumatic compression prophylaxis have not been well studied in these patients but may be effective, based on their ability to prevent venous thromboembolism in high-risk orthopedic patients[58] (see Table 16–3).

## Myocardial Infarction, Ischemic Stroke

The overall incidence of deep venous thrombosis is about 24% among myocardial infarction patients not treated with prophylaxis. From available data, low-dose heparin and full anticoagulation with heparin are effective in reducing the incidence of venous thromboembolism in these patients (see Table 16–3). Because of this and because anticoagulants reduce other thromboembolic events (mural thrombosis and systemic arterial embolism) in these patients without incurring a significant major bleeding risk, liberal use of these agents is appropriate. Although data are limited, mechanical methods of prophylaxis (elastic stockings and intermittent pneumatic compression) are also useful in patients with myocardial infarction when bleeding risk is great and conventional antithrombotic agents are contraindicated. Fibrinolytic therapy to treat myocardial infarction may also reduce the incidence of deep venous thrombosis complicating this condition.

Patients with stroke have a high risk of deep venous thrombosis in the paretic or paralyzed lower extremity. The overall incidence of leg deep venous thrombosis is 47% (see Table 16–3). Low-dose heparin and low-molecular-weight heparin have been shown to be highly effective in reducing the incidence of deep venous thrombosis in these patients.[59I, 60I, 61, 62] Because of the efficacy of intermittent pneumatic compression in neurosurgical patients, many of whom have hemiparesis, this method should also be beneficial in stroke patients. Elastic stockings may also be helpful.

In conclusion, a wide variety of effective prophylactic methods are available to prevent venous thromboembolism. These methods have been tested in numerous randomized clinical trials of immaculate scientific design. Whether these trials are considered singly or in the aggregate in the form of overview analyses, the inescapable conclusion is that the prophylactic strategies considered in this review prevent morbidity and mortality associated with venous thromboembolism.

Individual patients can be assigned a level of risk for venous thromboembolism based on clinical risk factors. The choice of prophylactic method is based on the level of risk, the potential for side effects and complications, and the overall costs. With the wide variety of proven prophylactic methods, the most appropriate method can be readily tailored to individual patients' needs, and no patient at significant risk for venous thromboembolism should be left unprotected.

## REFERENCES

1. Dalen JE, Alpert JS: Natural history of pulmonary embolism. Prog Cardiovasc Dis 17:257–270, 1975.
2. Anderson FA, Wheeler HB, Goldberg RJ, et al: A population-based perspective of the hospital incidence and case-fatality rates of deep vein thrombosis and pulmonary embolism. Arch Intern Med 151:933–938, 1991.
3. Goldhaber SZ, Hennekens CH, Evans DA, et al: Factors associated with correct antemortem diagnosis of major pulmonary embolism in a hospital population. Br J Surg 55:347–352, 1968.
4. Rubinstein I, Murray D, Hoffstein V: Fatal pulmonary emboli in hospitalized patients. Arch Intern Med 148:1425–1426, 1988.
5. Lindblad B, Eriksson A, Bergqvist D: Autopsy-verified pulmonary embolism in a surgical department: Analysis of the period from 1951 to 1988. Br J Surg 78:849–852, 1991.
6. Huisman MV, Buller H, Jan W, et al: Unexpected high prevalence of silent pulmonary embolism in patients with deep venous thrombosis. Chest 95:498–502, 1989.
7. Hirsh J, Hull RD: Diagnosis of venous thrombosis. In Venous Thromboembolism: Natural History, Diagnosis, and Management. Boca Raton, FL, CRC Press, 1987, pp 23–28.
8. Donaldson GA, Williams C, Scannell JG, et al: A reappraisal of the application of the Trendelenburg operation to massive fatal embolism: report of a successful pulmonary-artery thrombectomy using a cardiopulmonary bypass. N Engl J Med 268:171–174, 1963.
9. Hull R, Hirsh J, Sackett DL, et al: Cost-effectiveness of primary and secondary prevention of fatal pulmonary embolism in high-risk surgical patients. Can Med Assoc J 127:990–995, 1982.
10. Salzman EW, Davies GC: Prophylaxis of venous thromboembolism: Analysis of cost-effectiveness. Ann Surg 191:207–218, 1980.
11. Oster G, Tuden R, Colditz G: Prevention of venous Thromboembolism after general surgery: Cost-effectiveness analysis of alternative approaches to prophylaxis. Am J Med 82:889–899, 1987.
12. Oster G, Tuden R, Colditz G: A cost-effectiveness analysis of prophylaxis against deep-vein thrombosis in major orthopedic surgery. JAMA 257:203–208, 1987.
13. Bergqvist D, Matzsch T: Cost/benefit aspects on thromboprophylaxis. Haemostasis 23[Suppl 1]:15–19, 1993.
14. Bergqvist D, Jendteg S, Lindgren B, et al: Economics of general thromboembolic prophylaxis. World J Surg 12:349–355, 1988.
15. Anderson FA, Wheeler HB, Goldberg R, et al: The prevalence of risk factors for venous thromboembolism among hospital patients. Arch Intern Med 152:1660–1664, 1992.
16. Barnes RW, Nix ML, Barnes CL, et al: Perioperative asymptomatic venous thrombosis: Role of duplex scanning versus venography. J Vasc Surg 9:251–260, 1989.
17. Comerota AJ, Katz ML, Greenwald LL, et al: Venous duplex imaging: Should it replace hemodynamic tests for deep venous thrombosis? J Vasc Surg 9:251–260, 1989.
18. Salzman EW, Hirsh J: Prevention of venous thromboembolism. In Colman RW, Hirsh J, Marder VJ, et al (eds): Hemostasis and Thrombosis. Philadelphia, JB Lippincott, 1987, pp 1252–1265.
19. Conti S, Daschback M: Venous thromboembolism prophylaxis. Arch Surg 117:1036–1040, 1982.
20. Morris GK: Prevention of venous thromboembolism: A survey of methods used by orthopaedic and general surgeons. Lancet 2:572–574, 1980.
21. Bergqvist D: Prevention of postoperative deep vein thrombosis in Sweden: Results of a survey. World J Surg 4:489–495, 1980.
22. Laverick MD, Croal SA, Mollan RAB: Orthopaedic surgeons and thromboprophylaxis. Br Med J 303:549–550, 1991.
23. Anderson FA, Wheeler HB, Goldberg RJ, et al: Physi-

cian practices in the prevention of venous thromboembolism. Ann Intern Med 115:591–595, 1991.

24. Dismuke SE, Wagner EH: Pulmonary embolism as a cause of death: The changing mortality in hospitalized patients. JAMA 255:2039–2042, 1986.

25. Ruckley CV, Thurston C: Pulmonary embolism in surgical patients: 1959–79. Br Med J 284:1100–1110, 1982.

26. Lilienfeld DE, Chan E, Ehland J, et al: Mortality from pulmonary embolism in the United States: 1962–1984. Chest 98:1067–1072, 1990.

27. Bergqvist D, Lindblad B: A 30-year survey of pulmonary embolism verified at autopsy: An analysis of 1274 surgical patients. Br J Surg 72:105–108, 1985.

28. Clagett GP, Reisch JS: Prevention of venous thromboembolism in general surgical patients. Ann Surg 208:227–240, 1988.

29. Collins R, Scrimgeour A, Yusuf S, Peto R: Reduction in fatal pulmonary embolism and venous thrombosis by perioperative administration of subcutaneous heparin. N Engl J Med 318:1162–1173, 1988.

30. Nurmohamed MT, Rosendaal FR, Buller HR, et al: Low-molecular weight heparin versus standard heparin in general and orthopaedic surgery: A meta-analysis. Lancet 340:152–155, 1988.

31. Schmitt BP, Adelman B: Heparin-associated thrombocytopenia A critical review and pooled analysis. Am J Med Sci 305:208–215, 1993.

32. Carter C, Gent M, Leclerc JR: The epidemiology of venous thrombosis. In Colman RW, Hirsch J, Marder VJ, et al (eds): Hemostasis and Thrombosis. Philadelphia, JB Lippincott, 1987, pp 1185–1198.

33. Coon WW: Epidemiology of venous thromboembolism. Ann Surg 186:149–164, 1977.

34. Goldhaber SZ, Savage DD, Garrison RJ, et al: Risk factors for pulmonary embolism: The Framingham study. Am J Med 74:1023–1028, 1963.

35. Nachman RL, Silverstein, R: Hypercoagulable states. Ann Intern Med 119:819–827, 1993.

36. Clagett GP, Anderson FA, Levine MN, et al: Prevention of venous thromboembolism. Chest 102:391S–407S, 1992.

37. Cook D, Guyatt GH, Laupacis A, Sackett D: Rules of evidence and clinical recommendations on the use of antithrombotic agents. Chest 102:305S–311S, 1992.

I 38. Kakkar VV, Cohen AT, Edmonson RA, et al: Low molecular weight versus standard heparin for prevention of venous thrombo-embolism after major abdominal surgery. Lancet 341:259–265, 1993.

39. Jorgensen LN, Willie-Jorgensen P, Hauch O: Prophylaxis of postoperative thromboembolism with low molecular weight heparins. Br J Surg 80:689–704, 1993.

40. Lensing AWA, Hirsh J, Roberts R, Gent M: Critical review of aspirin in the prevention of postoperative venous thromboembolism. Br Med J in press.

I 41. Turpie AGG, Levine MN, Hirsh J, et al: A randomized controlled trial of a low-molecular weight heparin (Enoxaparin) to prevent deep vein thrombosis in patients undergoing elective hip surgery. N Engl J Med 315:925–929, 1986.

I 42. Gallus A, Raman K, Darby T: Venous thrombosis after elective hip replacement: the influence of preventive intermittent calf compression and of surgical technique. Br J Surg 70:17–19, 1983.

43. Haake DA, Berkman SA: Venous thromboembolic disease after hip surgery. Clin Orthop 242:212, 1989.

I 44. Hull R, Delmore TJ, Hirsh J, et al: Effectiveness of intermittent pulsatile stockings for the prevention of calf and thigh vein thrombosis in patients undergoing elective knee surgery. Thromb Res 16:37–45, 1979.

I 45. Lynch AF, Bourne RB, Rorabeck CH, et al: Deep-vein thrombosis and continuous passive motion after total knee arthroplasty. J Bone Joint Surg 70:11, 1988.

IV 46. Stulberg BN, Insall JN, Williams GW, et al: Deep-vein thrombosis following total knee replacement. J Bone Joint Surg 66:194, 1984.

47. Hull R, Raskob G, Pineo G, et al: A comparison of subcutaneous low-molecular-weight heparin with warfarin sodium for prophylaxis against deep-vein thrombosis after hip or knee implantation. N Engl J Med 329:1370–1376, 1993.

I 48. Leyvraz PF, Richard J, Bachmann F: Adjusted versus fixed-dose subcutaneous heparin in the prevention of deep vein thrombosis after total hip replacement. N Engl J Med 309:954–958, 1983.

I 49. Leyvraz PF, Bachmann F, Hoek J, et al: Prevention of deep vein thrombosis after hip replacement: Randomized comparison between unfractionated heparin and low molecular weight heparin. Br Med J 303:531–532, 1991.

50. Golueke PF, Garrett WV, Thompson JE, et al: Interruption of the vena cava by means of the Greenfield filter: Expanding the indications. Surgery 103:111–117, 1988.

51. Vaughn BK, Knezevich S, Lombardi AV, et al: Use of the Greenfield filter to prevent fatal embolism associated with total hip and knee arthroplasty (abstract). J Bone Joint Surg 71:1542, 1989.

52. O'Malley KF, Ross SE: Pulmonary embolism in major trauma patients. J Trauma 30:748–750, 1990.

53. Knudson MM, Collins JA, Goodman SB, et al: Thromboembolism following multiple trauma. J Trauma 32:2–11, 1992.

54. Ruiz AJ, Hill SL, Berry RE: Heparin, deep venous thrombosis, and trauma patients. Am J Surg 162:159–162, 1991.

55. Waring WP, Karunas RS: Acute spinal cord injuries and the incidence of clinically occurring thromboembolism in spinal cord injury. JAMA 260:1255–1258, 1988.

I 56. Green D, Lee MY, Ito VY, et al: Fixed- vs adjusted-dose heparin in the prophylaxis of thromboembolism in spinal cord injury. JAMA 260:1255–1258, 1988.

I 57. Green D, Lee MY, Lim AC, et al: Prevention of thromboembolism after spinal cord injury using low-molecular weight heparin. Ann Intern Med 113:571–574, 1990.

58. Green, D: Prophylaxis of thromboembolism in spinal cord-injured patients. Chest 102:649S–651S, 1992.

I 59. McCarthy ST, Turner JJ, Robertson D, et al: Low dose heparin as a prophylaxis against deep vein thrombosis after acute stroke. Lancet 2:800–801, 1977.

I 60. Turpie AGG, Levine MN, Hirsh J, et al: A double-blind randomized trial or ORG 10172 low molecular weight heparinoid in the prevention of deep vein thrombosis in thrombotic stroke. Lancet 1:523–526, 1987.

61. Prins MH, den Ottolander GJH, Gelsema R, et al: Deep vein thrombosis prophylaxis with a low molecular weight heparin (Kabi 2165) in stroke patients. Haemostasis 19[Suppl]:245–250, 1989.

62. Turpie AGG, Levine MN, Powers PJ, et al: A double-blind randomized trial of ORG 10172 low molecular weight heparinoid versus unfractionated heparin in the prevention of deep vein thrombosis in patients with thrombotic stroke. Thromb Haemost 65[Suppl]:753, 1991.

# Chapter 17

# Prevention of Venous Thromboembolism in General Surgery

Alexander T. Cohen and Vijay V. Kakkar

General surgery encompasses a broad spectrum of operations and specialities. This chapter covers the following areas: (1) general abdominal surgery; (2) thoracic and cardiothoracic surgery with particular emphasis on cardiac surgery, thoracoabdominal surgery being included in both these areas; (3) urologic surgery including renal transplantation; (4) gynecologic surgery; (5) female patients in general; (6) surgery for malignancy; (7) various therapeutic options; (8) anesthetic factors; and (9) the future of thromboprophylaxis.

Being a heterogeneous group, general surgical patients have a wide range of risk of developing postoperative venous thromboembolism (VTE). They therefore highlight the importance of assessing the risk and choosing the appropriate form of thromboprophylactic therapy. Those with benign conditions are generally considered to be of low to medium risk of developing VTE. Those undergoing extensive pelvic or abdominal operations for malignant disease are of high risk.

The overall frequency of postoperative deep vein thrombosis (DVT) is 25%, as diagnosed by the $^{125}$I fibrinogen uptake test and 19% as diagnosed by venography. Proximal DVT occurs in 7% of patients.[1] The frequency of DVT diagnosed by the $^{125}$I fibrinogen uptake test in various patient groups is recorded in Table 17–1.[2] The figures are for elective surgery; emergency general surgery is thought to have at least the same risk of VTE. The overall frequency of pulmonary embolism (PE) is 1.6%, and fatal pulmonary embolism (FPE) in patients not receiving thromboprophylaxis is 0.8% (0.5 to 1%).[1]

Effective prophylaxis can significantly reduce the incidence of DVT and PE in general surgical patients.[3] The main barrier to successful thromboprophylaxis is failure to use the available methods in the patients at risk. Continuing education is therefore essential.

## RISK FACTORS FOR VENOUS THROMBOEMBOLISM

Risk of thromboembolic disease increases with age, becoming significant in otherwise low-risk patients undergoing general surgery at over 40 years of age. Risk factors for venous thromboembolic disease have been covered in Chapter 16. All general surgical patients should be assessed for thromboembolic risk factors prior to surgery, because risk determines the therapy. For example, the incidence of thromboembolism in patients in the low-risk group undergoing minor surgical procedures is such that the potential complications and expense of prophylaxis may not be warranted. However, others at low risk, as determined by the type of surgery, may in fact be at much higher risk of DVT if they have one or more risk factors. Clinical findings such as varicose veins, obesity, and heart failure should be sought, because their presence is associated with an increased risk of VTE and may therefore result in modification of thromboprophylaxis.

## RISK IN GENERAL ABDOMINAL SURGERY

The majority of research has been performed in patients undergoing general abdominal surgery and has included thoracoabdominal procedures such as esophageal operations. Modalities that have been shown to be efficacious include

**Table 17–1. Frequency of DVT Diagnosed by the $^{125}$I Fibrinogen Uptake Test***

| Type of Surgery | Frequency (%) |
|---|---|
| General abdominal | 30 |
| General surgery for malignancy | 40 |
| Thoracic surgery | |
|   Malignancy | 45 |
|   Other noncardiac | 30 |
|   Cardiac | 30 |
| Gynecologic surgery | 25 |
|   Benign, abdominal hysterectomy | 12 |
|   Radical abdominal hysterectomy | 26 |
|   Surgery for ovarian, vulval cancer | 45 |
| Urologic surgery | |
|   Transvesical prostatectomy | 40 |
|   Transurethral prostatic resection | 10 |
| Herniorraphy | 5 |

(Modified from Bergqvist, D: Postoperative thromboembolism. Frequency, etiology, and prophylaxis. New York, Springer-Verlag, 1983.)

low-molecular-weight heparin (LMWH); unfractionated heparin (UFH) with and without dihydroergotamine; intermittent pneumatic compression (IPC); graduated compression stockings (GCS); oral anticoagulants such as warfarin; dextran; and antiplatelet agents. The efficacy varies; LMWH results in a large reduction in the relative risk (RR) of developing DVT (86%), whereas antiplatelet agents have the lowest efficacy, giving a 19% reduction of RR.[4]

Minimally invasive surgery is now used for many procedures previously requiring open surgery. Despite this type of surgery resulting in less tissue damage and early mobilization, VTE is known to occur. Crural thromboses have been recorded after rectosigmoid surgery,[5] and other DVT after laparoscopic Nissen fundoplication.[6] In some cases thrombosis may be the result of increased operation times and abdominal insufflation causing venous compression. However, clotting activation may be less of a problem, as shown in a study on patients undergoing videolaparoscopic surgery for cholecystectomy. Minimally invasive surgery did not induce a significant activation of the clotting system.[7]

## RISK IN THORACIC AND CARDIOTHORACIC SURGERY

Thromboembolism occurs commonly after thoracic surgery, and heparin with and without dihydroergotamine (DHE) has been investigated and found to be efficacious. In patients undergoing major thoracic surgery, such as those having thoracotomy for carcinoma of the lung or esophagus, the incidence of DVT with routine low-dose heparin prophylaxis, 10,000 U daily, remains high, around 25%. Higher doses of heparin, totalling 15,000 U daily, have resulted in a nonsignificant decrease in total DVT frequency, in conjunction with a significant reduction in the extent of thrombosis. Despite prophylaxis, DVT is common after esophagogastrectomy.[8][11] In 191 patients undergoing thoracic surgery for lung cancer, the prophylactic action of heparin-DHE and of low-dose heparin was compared in a randomized, controlled study. The thrombosis rate measured by $^{125}$I fibrinogen test was 35% in the control group, 11% in the low-dose heparin group, and 2.5% in the heparin with DHE group.[9]

Most studies in the area of cardiac surgery have investigated VTE in patients undergoing coronary artery bypass grafting (CABG).[10] These patients have many risk factors for VTE including stasis, long anesthesia, advanced age, and heart failure, resulting in a high rate of DVT, 30%,[11, 12] and a very high rate of PE, 4%.[13, 14] Mechanical methods have been employed most often and compared with no therapy. IPC appeared to be effective in one study,[11] and GCS was used in others with variable results.[12, 13]

## RISK IN UROLOGIC SURGERY

VTE is the commonest cause of death following urologic surgery.[15] The incidence of DVT is at least five times higher in those undergoing retropubic prostatectomy compared with those having transurethral operations. Intermittent pneumatic compression (IPC), oral anticoagulants, low-dose heparin (UFH) with and without dihydroergotamine, and dextran have been shown to decrease the risk of DVT.[16][11] The efficacy varies, however. IPC results in a large reduction in the RR of developing DVT (70%), whereas oral anticoagulants have shown variable efficacy.

Deep venous thrombosis occurs frequently in patients undergoing renal transplantation and is more common in those with established risk factors and those with juvenile diabetes mellitus.[17] In a retrospective study of DVT after renal transplantation, 480 consecutive renal transplant operations were reviewed to obtain the incidence of DVT or PE or both. Forty (8.3%) thrombotic events were diagnosed, comprising 25 cases of lower limb DVT alone, 11 cases of DVT with PE, and four with PE alone. Four deaths were directly attributable to PE, which was the fourth major cause of death in the review period. DVT was more common on the side of the transplant, but the difference was not significant.[18] Other studies have shown a higher incidence of fatal PE, occurring in over 4% of patients undergoing renal transplantation.[19]

## RISK IN GYNECOLOGIC SURGERY

Fully 40% of all deaths following gynecologic surgery are the result of VTE.[20] The National Confidential Enquiry into Perioperative Deaths (NCEPOD) showed that 20% of deaths following hysterectomy were the result of VTE.[21] The risk of DVT depends on the type of surgery (Table 17–1) and, overall, fatal PE occurs in 1% of patients.

Pelvic and ovarian vein thrombi are particularly common. Trials in gynecologic surgery have shown that oral anticoagulants, low-dose heparin, dextran, and IPC are effective in this situation.[22, 23II, 24I, 25I] Low-dose heparin with combined dihydroergotamine may not be more effective than low-dose heparin on its own in this setting.[26II] Bleeding is a particular problem and is seen frequently.[24] The site of heparin administration may be a factor, because a significant proportion is absorbed via the lymphatic channels. Incisions, especially transverse ones, divide some of the subcutaneous lymphatics, and thus they may result in a higher local tissue concentration of heparin, which may predispose to wound hematoma.[27I] Heparin administered subcutaneously to the upper arm instead of the abdominal wall is associated with a lower incidence of abdominal wound hematoma.[28]

## RISK IN FEMALE PATIENTS

Women on hormonal therapy or those who are pregnant require special consideration. It is important to establish whether women of reproductive age undergoing general surgery are taking the oral contraceptive pill (OCP). In a retrospective study on 5,603 women undergoing surgery, 34 of whom subsequently developed VTE, the incidence of VTE was found to be 1% (12/1,244) for pill users and 0.5% (22/4,359) for nonusers.[29] However, it does not follow that women scheduled for surgery should be advised to stop the OCP. These women may be at risk of an unplanned or unwanted pregnancy, with the subsequent risk to both mother and fetus during surgery. Patients with additional risk factors should, in most circumstances, receive thromboprophylaxis, but each case should be assessed individually. Although even low doses

of estrogen have been shown to have significant effects on coagulation parameters, the risk of thrombosis seems to be directly related to the dose of estrogen contained in oral contraceptive preparations. The progesterone-only pill does not seem to confer a greater risk of DVT.

Hormone replacement therapy (HRT) may also confer a greater risk of DVT. However, no randomized studies have been performed to confirm this. Although the HRT preparations currently in use contain much lower doses of estrogen than the combined OCP, the increased age of this group of patients makes them more likely to have additional risk factors for postoperative DVT. Consequently, although there is no evidence to suggest that withdrawal of HRT prior to surgery is necessary, this group of patients should probably receive thromboprophylaxis.

Pregnancy associated with VTE and PE is now one of the leading causes of maternal death in pregnancy and the puerperium. However, routine prophylaxis during an uncomplicated pregnancy is not justified. Obesity, age over 35, parity of three or greater, and prolonged bedrest are additional risk factors. Thromboprophylaxis should be considered for these women, especially if they are immobilized for any reason, either in the pre- or postpartum period. In most circumstances, thromboprophylaxis should be given to pregnant women undergoing surgery (including caesarean section). Pregnant women with thrombophilia are at greater risk of developing DVT and, if possible, should be referred to a specialist to advise on appropriate management throughout their pregnancy.

## RISK IN CANCER SURGERY

Patients undergoing cancer surgery have a high risk of developing both VTE and bleeding, and they require special consideration. Because of their illness, they have prolonged immobility and may have further stasis from neoplastic compression of veins. Furthermore, tumor invasion, chemotherapy, and vascular access catheters affect vessel wall integrity, and procoagulant changes occur in the coagulation cascade. The risk of developing VTE is 2 to 3 times that of benign surgery and may remain high despite thromboprophylaxis.

Various therapies have been shown to be efficacious, including LMWH, UFH in fixed and adjusted doses, dextran, oral anticoagulants, IPC, and GCS. In an overview of general surgery, the results in patients with cancer were as follows: low-dose heparin reduced the RR of developing DVT by 53% and PE by 58%; the respective figures for dextran were 46% and 57%. IPC reduced the risk of DVT by 39%; there were too few data to analyze the effect on PE.[1] Organan has been used in a trial investigating VTE in 513 patients with malignancy and was compared with low-dose UFH 5,000 U twice daily. There was no difference in bleeding complications and a nonsignificant trend toward less VTE in the Organan group, 10.4% versus 14.9%.[30II] In general, an anticoagulant and a mechanical method (for instance, LMWH and GCS) should be used for these patients.

## METHODS OF PREVENTING DEEP VEIN THROMBOSIS

Thromboprophylaxis can be directed toward the three components of Virchow's triad, namely blood flow, factors within the blood itself, and the vascular endothelium. Some methods act on all three, resulting in a reduction of venous stasis, prevention of the hypercoaguable state induced by tissue trauma and other factors, and protection of the endothelium. Regardless of the method used, thromboprophylaxis should probably be initiated prior to induction of anesthesia, because it has been demonstrated that the thrombotic process commences intraoperatively.[31]

The ideal thromboprophylactic agent would prevent all DVTs, be free from side effects, be applicable to all surgical specialities, and be simple to apply or administer. No such agent exists. The selection of a particular thromboprophylactic method therefore depends on the type of surgery, the overall risk category into which the patient falls, and the preference of the responsible clinician. For example, it may not be appropriate to treat with anticoagulants those patients at very high risk of bleeding or at risk of complications secondary to bleeding, or to use mechanical devices on patients who have peripheral ischemia. For all patients it is important to reduce tissue trauma, shorten the anesthetic time, and promote early postoperative mobilization.

## Mechanical Methods

### Graduated Compression Stockings

Graduated compression stockings are a simple, safe, and moderately effective form of thromboprophylaxis. It is by no means clear how GCS achieve a thromboprophylactic effect.

It has been shown that they increase the velocity of venous blood flow[32–34] and thus may reduce the activation of coagulation systems associated with stasis. It has also been proposed that anesthesia causes venous dilatation and that in unsupported veins this may cause microtears in the endothelium. GCS may prevent this dilatation and therefore prevent exposure of procoagulant subendothelial collagen to circulating coagulation factors.[35]

GCS are recommended in low-risk patients and as an adjunct in those with medium and high risk. The only major contraindication is peripheral vascular disease. The majority of studies in patients undergoing general abdominal and gynecologic procedures have shown a reduction in the incidence of DVT. A comprehensive meta-analysis concluded that, in studies using sound methods, there was a highly significant risk reduction of 68% in patients at moderate risk of postoperative thromboembolism.[36] However, there is no conclusive evidence that GCS are effective in reducing the incidence of fatal and nonfatal PE. It is not known whether wearing GCS following discharge from the hospital is efficacious.

### Intermittent Pneumatic Compression

Intermittent pneumatic compression (IPC) devices currently in use are more comfortable to wear, less bulky, and have been designed to allow greater knee movement than earlier ones. IPC influences all three components of Virchow's triad.[35, 37, 38] Studies comparing IPC with control, pharmacologic agents, and combined methods of prophylaxis have been performed in general abdominal, gynecologic, and urologic procedures. IPC is effective in malignant disease[39II] and after urologic surgery.[40II] However, prospective, randomized, double-blinded trials have had insufficient power to show that IPC reduces the incidence of postoperative PE.

The optimal duration of IPC application has not been firmly established. However, several studies have shown that commencing IPC in the postoperative period is not as effective as commencing it prior to surgery and maintaining it throughout the intraoperative and postoperative periods until the patient is mobile without requiring aid. Combined use of IPC with graduated compression stockings may also be more effective than either IPC or GCS alone.[41] There are few contraindications for using IPC; however, care should be taken in patients with heart failure and significant leg edema and for those patients with suspected

DVT, because compression of the leg may promote embolization of the thrombus.

## Pharmacologic Methods

### Dextran

Dextran is a high-molecular-weight glucose polymer formed by enzymatic degradation of saccharose. The molecular weight of the most commonly used "dextrans" in clinical practice are 40,000 and 70,000. Dextran is principally excreted renally at a rate proportional to its molecular weight. It exerts an antithrombotic effect by reducing red cell aggregation, providing a protective coating over the vascular endothelium and erythrocytes, reducing platelet aggregation, and by having a specific inhibitory effect on von Willebrand factor. There is also evidence that dextran may facilitate endogenous thrombolysis and reduce venous stasis by expanding plasma volume. A meta-analysis in general surgical patients showed a significant 57% reduction in the odds of developing DVT.[1]

Clinical trials in general abdominal, urologic, and gynecologic surgery comparing dextran with other anticoagulants have shown it to be less effective than low-dose UFH heparin, LMWH, and warfarin in reducing postoperative DVT. Dextran does, however, seem to be effective in reducing extension of DVT beyond the calf and may reduce the incidence of PE.

Dextran used in combination with either GCS[42I] or IPC[43I] has been shown to be more effective than dextran alone. The use of dextran is limited, possibly because of its side effects, including fluid overload, allergic reactions, and anaphylaxis. There is a risk of bleeding and wound oozing comparable to that observed with low-dose heparin. Dextran must also be administered by intravenous infusion, and the optimal dosage regimen has not been established.

### Aspirin and Other Antiplatelet Agents

Antiplatelet agents inhibit cyclooxygenase, a key enzyme involved in the formation of thromboxane $A_2$. Thromboxane $A_2$ is synthesized and released by platelets in response to various stimuli, such as adenosine diphosphate, thrombin, and collagen. By inhibiting the formation of thromboxane $A_2$, antiplatelet agents are able to reduce platelet aggregation and inhibit interaction with the vascular endothelium. Investigators in a large number of clinical trials have sought the possible thromboprophylactic effect of antiplatelet agents. Many of these have been small or poorly designed studies, and the few high-quality studies that have been performed have shown conflicting results. However, there are potential advantages of using aspirin and other antiplatelet agents. The drugs are cheap, active when given orally, and are well tolerated when given at doses that effectively inhibit platelets.

Antiplatelet agents have been recommended following a meta-analysis.[44] The results obtained with these drugs showed a risk reduction of 25% for DVT, when compared with results in control groups. However, this figure is poor when compared with the result of a similar study with heparin that showed a risk reduction of 58%.[45] The comparison of the results for PE showed similar efficacy. Furthermore, the meta-analysis included studies that were clinically and statistically heterogeneous, causing any interpretation to be open to question.[46] Antiplatelet agents used with anticoagulant thromboprophylaxis result in increased bleeding.[47I]

### Oral Anticoagulants

Oral anticoagulants antagonize the effects of vitamin K, resulting in low levels of vitamin K–dependent coagulation factors II, VII, IX, and X. Warfarin is sometimes used in very-high-risk patients and may be given in low-to-moderate doses aiming to increase mildly the international normalized ratio (INR). It is efficacious in general surgery and has resulted in a risk reduction of 59%,[4] but it is associated with a high risk of bleeding complications if not monitored carefully. Patients at very high risk may have undetected DVT prior to surgery, and prophylactic oral anticoagulant therapy has the advantage of treating them as well.[48]

### Unfractionated Heparin

Heparin, a heterogeneous mixture of sulphated acidic mucopolysaccharides, binds to antithrombin III, inducing a structural change that increases the antithrombin catalytic activity (antifactor IIa) several thousand-fold and inhibits activated factors IX, X, and XII. At higher concentrations, heparin is able to inhibit thrombin by activating heparin cofactor II and results in the release of the natural anticoagulant tissue factor pathway inhibitor (TFPI). In addition, heparin inhibits the interactions of coagulant factors on the platelet surface. Low-dose UFH has been used as a thromboprophylactic agent for over 20 years and in many centers has been the standard therapy. Used in doses of 5,000 U twice or three times daily, it is an effective prophylaxis.[49] In a meta-analysis of 62 random-ized, placebo-controlled trials in general surgi-cal and urologic procedures, the incidence of DVT was reduced by at least two-thirds.[45] UFH also reduces the incidence of PE and fatal PE.[49] However, this benefit is offset by a small but significant increase in minor bleeding complica-tions, especially wound hematomas. The above-mentioned meta-analysis showed that there was no difference in the incidence of fatal bleeding events but there was a 2% increase in the inci-dence of minor bleeding events. In addition to bleeding, standard heparin has other side ef-fects including thrombocytopenia, pain, and bruising, which may occur at the injection site. It has to be administered either two or three times daily, starting the day before surgery and continuing usually until the patient is mobile.

## Low-molecular-weight Heparin

Low-molecular-weight heparins are derived by depolymerization of heparin by either chemical or enzymatic degradation. Conventional UFH molecules have molecular weights ranging from 5,000 to 30,000 daltons, whereas LMWH mole-cules range from 2,000 to 8,000 daltons. Several laboratory studies have shown that LMWH pro-duces less bleeding than UFH while retaining an equivalent antithrombotic effect.[50, 51] This has been explained by the fact that LMWHs have a more specific effect on activated factor X (factor Xa) than on factor II (thrombin). However, the exact mechanism is far from clear.

Several meta-analyses have investigated the relative safety and efficacy of LMWH compared with UFH. One meta-analysis has compared UFH with LMWH in general surgical trials with weak and strong methodology.[52] In studies with weak methodology, risk reductions of 33% and 63% were seen for DVT and PE respectively; yet, no overall difference in efficacy and safety was seen in studies with strong methodology. This study was performed before the publica-tion of results of two large multicenter trials that reinforced the findings of the earlier labo-ratory studies.

The first was a double-blind multicenter trial in which patients undergoing major abdominal surgery were randomized to receive either LMWH once daily or UFH twice daily.[47] The study included 3,809 patients and revealed LMWH to have a thromboprophylactic effect, equivalent to that of UFH. However, less bleed-ing occurred in the LMWH group as evidenced by a reduction in the incidence of wound hema-toma (1.4% versus 2.7%, $p=.007$), severe bleed-ing (1% versus 1.9%, $p=.02$), and in the num-ber of patients requiring reoperation for bleeding (1% versus 1.7%, $p=.05$). There was no significant difference between the two groups in the overall incidence of major bleed-ing events (3.6% versus 4.8%, RR 0.77, confi-dence interval [CI] 0.56–1.04, $p=.10$). There was also less minor bleeding at the injection sites.

The other large multicenter trial produced similar findings with respect to the frequency of wound hematomas and injection site complica-tions.[53] The endpoints of these studies were as-sessed uniformly and were different from those in the meta-analysis, which did not investigate wound hematomas.[52]

## ANESTHESIA AND THROMBOEMBOLISM

Lumbar epidural anesthesia results in higher flow velocity in the femoral vein than general anesthesia (GA).[54] The same is not true for thoracic epidural anesthesia.[55] The incidence of postoperative DVT may be lower in those undergoing lumbar epidurals. In open prosta-tectomy, epidural anesthesia was compared with GA; less DVT occurred in those having epidur-als.[56] Studies comparing the incidence of DVT following GA or thoracic extradural anesthesia in general abdominal surgery have not shown significant differences.[57, 58] A randomized study of patients undergoing elective abdominal sur-gery compared morphine for analgesia and low-dose heparin with epidural analgesia with no prophylactic antithrombotic treatment.[59] The incidence of DVT ([125]I fibrinogen scan) was 32% after GA and low-dose heparin and 34% after epidural analgesia with no prophylactic antithrombotic treatment ($p<.9$).

Regional anesthesia combined with UFH or LMWH raises another issue. Spinal hematoma is a recognized complication of epidural and spinal anesthesia, and there are obvious con-cerns regarding the safety of combining these invasive techniques with anticoagulant throm-boprophylactic agents. However, intraspinal hemorrhages may occur spontaneously or in conjunction with coexisting pathology, such as bleeding disorders, spinal neoplasia, and vascu-lar abnormalities lying in close proximity to the spinal cord. They are well documented in asso-ciation with therapeutic anticoagulation.

The complications of regional anesthesia have been investigated in three studies with a total of 164,701 patients. There were no re-ported cases of spinal hematomas. A review of surgical patients in clinical trials using heparin thromboprophylaxis wherein the type of anesthesia was defined showed no intraspinal hematomas in 9,013 patients receiving LMWH in combination with epidural or spinal anesthesia.[60] There is one case report of a spinal hematoma in a patient receiving prophylactic UFH in combination with epidural anesthesia, and two case reports of spinal bleeding in patients receiving LMWH prophylaxis. However, only one of these patients had epidural catheterization. This data suggest that there is little or no increased risk associated with a combination of regional anesthesia and heparin thromboprophylaxis. In patients undergoing major surgery, particularly those at high risk of thromboembolic disease, the risks of DVT and FPE far outweigh the risks of spinal hemorrhage. Investigators concluded from their review of the literature that the combination of heparin with epidural or spinal anesthesia is safe, provided that normal safety precautions are respected.

## THE FUTURE OF THROMBOPROPHYLAXIS

Our understanding of the cellular and molecular biology of thrombosis has advanced considerably over the last few years. This, together with a greater awareness of the magnitude of the problem of thromboembolic disease and the more widespread use of thromboprophylactic agents, should lead to a reduction in the mortality from postoperative PE. There should also be a reduction in the number of patients with the chronic sequelae of DVT and PE. At present, however, all the thromboprophylactic agents currently in use have potential side effects or limitations in their application. In addition, the incidence of thromboembolic disease remains above 18% for those at highest risk despite thromboprophylactic measures. Further, large clinical trials are required to evaluate LMWHs in different types of surgery and to evaluate them against and in addition to mechanical methods of prophylaxis and antiplatelet agents. The results of studies on newer agents, such as ultra-low-molecular-weight heparins; highly specific thrombin inhibitors; specific anti-Xa inhibitors; antibodies to the fibrinogen platelet receptor; the cytoadhesin, glycoprotein IIb/IIIa, and other integrins such as the "LeuCAMs," are awaited with interest.

A range of therapies is available to prevent DVT and PE, which are major causes of morbidity and mortality in patients undergoing general surgery. Anticoagulant prophylaxis and mechanical methods both reduce the incidence of postoperative VTE, but only the former has been shown to reduce mortality from PE.[45] Thromboprophylactic agents that have been shown to reduce the incidence of DVT and PE should be used in all patients at moderate or high risk of thromboembolism. The choice of a suitable agent depends upon the type of surgery and other risk factors associated with each patient. So far, the evidence from clinical trials does not demonstrate a clear advantage of any particular agent in preventing thromboembolism. However, a combination of a pharmacologic agent with GCS has been shown to be efficacious and should probably be given to both moderate- and high-risk patients. IPC is an effective alternative, particularly in those patients for whom anticoagulants are contraindicated. Further large clinical trials and evaluation of more specific antithrombotic agents are underway.

## References

1. Clagett GP, Reisch JS: Prevention of venous thromboembolism in general surgical patients. Ann Surg 208:227–240, 1988.
2. Bergqvist D: Postoperative thromboembolism. Frequency, aetiology, prophylaxis. New York, Springer-Verlag, 1983.
3. Kakkar VV, Adams PC: Preventive and therapeutic approach to venous thromboembolism. Can death from pulmonary embolism be prevented? J Am Coll Cardiol 8:146B–158B, 1986.
4. Clagett GP, Anderson FA, Levine MN, et al: Prevention of venous thromboembolism. Chest 102(4): 391S–407S, 1992.
5. Mentges B, Buess G, Manncke K, Becker HD: Minimal invasive surgery of the colon and rectum. [Minimal Invasive Chirurgie Des Kolon und Rektum.] Zentralbl Chir 118:12, 746–753, 1993.
6. Pitcher DE, Curet MJ, Martin DT, et al: Successful management of severe gastroesophageal reflux disease with laparoscopic Nissen fundoplication. Am J Surg 168(6):547–554, 1994.
7. Vannucchi PL, Ridolfi B, Biliotti G, et al: Evaluation of prothrombin F1+2 fragment after videolaparoscopic surgery. Thromb Res 75(2):219–222, 1994.
8. Cade JF, Clegg EA, Westlake GW: Prophylaxis of venous thrombosis after major thoracic surgery. Aust N Z J Surg 53(4):301–304, 1983.
9. Kaiser D, Hau H, Strey M: Prevention of venous thromboembolism during and after surgery of lung cancer. [Peri- und Postoperative Thromboseprophylaxe Beim Bronchialkarzinom.] Prax Pneumol 35(1)918–921, 1981.
10. Malone KM: Coronary artery bypass grafting. In Goldhaber SZ (ed): Prevention of Venous Thromboembolism, 18:439–444, 1993.
11. Pogson GW, Reed W, Weinstein GS: Prevention of deep vein thrombosis. Mo Med 82(3):133–136, 1985.
12. Reis SE, Polak JF, Hirsch DR, et al: Frequency of deep venous thrombosis in asymptomatic patients with coronary bypass grafts. Am Heart J 122:478–482, 1991.

13. Rao G, Zikria EA, Miller WH, et al: Incidence and prevention of pulmonary embolism after coronary artery surgery. Vasc Surg 9:37–45, 1975.

14. Sharma GVRK, Josa M, Khuri SF: Pulmonary embolism is an important sequel of coronary bypass surgery [abstract]. Circulation 82:II-508, 1990.

15. Antila LE, Markulla H, and Iisaly E: Ten years experience of geriatric aspects of surgery of patients with benign prostatic hypertrophy. Acta Chir Scand 357[Suppl]:95, 1966.

II 16. Hansberry KL, Thompson IM (Jr), Bauman J, et al: A prospective comparison of thromboembolic stockings, external sequential pneumatic compression stockings and heparin sodium/dihydroergotamine mesylate for the prevention of thromboembolic complications in urological surgery. J Urol 145(6):1205–1208, 1991.

17. Brunkwall J, Bergqvist D, Bergentz SE, et al: Deep venous thrombosis in patients undergoing renal transplantation—effects of cyclosporine A. Postoperative deep vein thrombosis. Transplantation 43:647–649, 1987.

18. Allen RDM, Michie CA, Murie JA, Morris PJ: Deep venous thrombosis after renal transplantation. Surg Gynecol Obstet 164(2):137–142, 1987.

19. Combined Report on Regular Dialysis and Transplantation in Europe. London, European Dialysis and Transplant Association, Pitman, 1983.

20. Jeffcoate TNA, Tindall VR: Venous thrombosis and embolism in obstetrics and gynaecology. Aust N Z J Obstet Gynaecol 5:119–130, 1965.

21. The Report of the National Confidential Enquiry Into Perioperative Deaths 1990. 35-43 Lincoln's Inn Fields, London WC2A 3PN, April 1992.

22. Genton E, Turpie A: Venous thromboembolism associated with gynecologic surgery. Clin Obstet Gynecol 23:209–241, 1980.

III 23. Bonnar J, Walsh H: Prevention of thrombosis after pelvic surgery by British dextran70. Lancet 1:614–616, 1972.

I 24. Clarke-Pearson DL, Synan I, Hinshaw W, et al: Prevention of postoperative venous thromboembolism by external pneumatic calf compression in patients with gynecologic malignancy. Obstet Gynecol 63:92–97, 1984.

I 25. Taberner DA, Poller L, Burslem RW, et al: Oral anticoagulants controlled by the British Comparative Thromboplastin versus low-dose heparin in prophylaxis of deep vein thrombosis. Br Med J 1:272–274, 1978.

II 26. UrlepSalinovic V, Jelatancev B, Gorisek B: Low doses of heparin and heparin dihydergot in postoperative thromboprophylaxis in gynaecological patients. Thromb Haemost 72(1):16–20, 1994.

I 27. Kakkar VV, Murray WJG: Efficacy and safety of low molecular weight heparin (CY216) in preventing postoperative venous thromboembolism: A co-operative study. Br J Surg 72:786–791, 1985.

28. Briel RC: Low dose heparin prophylaxis and postoperative wound haematoma. Int Surg 68:241–243, 1983.

29. Vessey MP, Mant D, Smith A, et al: Oral contraceptives and venous thromboembolism: Findings in a large prospective study. Br Med J 292:526, 1986.

II 30. Gallus A, Cade J, Ockelford P, et al (ANZ-Organon Investigators' Group): Orgaran (Org 10172) or heparin for preventing venous thromboembolism after elective surgery for malignant disease? A double-blind, random- ised multicentre comparison. Thromb Haemost 70(4): 562–567, 1993.

31. Kakkar VV, Howe CT, Flanc C, et al: Natural history

of postoperative deep-vein thrombosis. Lancet 230–233, 1969.

32. Meyerowitz BR, Nelson R: Measurement of the velocity of blood in lower limb veins with and without compression surgery. Surgery 56:481–486, 1964.

33. Sigel B, Edelstein AL, Felix WR: Compression of the deep venous system of the lower leg during inactive recumbency. Arch Surg 106:38–43, 1973.

34. Lawrence D, Kakkar VV: Graduated, static, external compression of the lower limb: A physiological assessment. Br J Surg 67:119–121, 1980.

35. Comerota AJ, Stewart GJ, Alburger PD, et al: Operative venodilation: A previously unsuspected factor in the cause of postoperative deep vein thrombosis. Surgery 106:301–309, 1988.

36. Wells PS, Lensing AWA, Hirsh J: Graduated compression stockings in the prevention of postoperative venous thromboembolism. A meta-analysis. Arch Intern Med 154:67–72, 1994.

37. Blackshear VW, Precott C, LePain F, et al: Influence of sequential pneumatic compression on postoperative venous function. J Vasc Surg 5:432–436, 1987.

38. Summaria L, Caprini J, McMillan R: Relationship between postsurgical fibrinolytic parameters and deep vein thrombosis in surgical patients treated with compression devices. Am Surg 54:156–160, 1988.

II 39. Butson ARC. Intermittent pneumatic calf compression for prevention of deep vein thrombosis in general abdominal surgery. Am J Surg 142:525–527, 1981.

I 40. Salzman EW, Pleotz J, Bettmann M, et al: Intraoperative external pneumatic calf compression to afford long-term prophylaxis against deep vein thrombosis in urological patients. Surgery 87:239–242, 1980.

I 41. Nicolaides AN, Miles C, Hoare M, et al: Intermittent sequential pneumatic compression of the legs and thromboembolism-deterrent stockings in the prevention of postoperative deep venous thrombosis. Surgery 94:21–25, 1983.

I 42. Bergqvist D, Lindblad B: The thromboprophylactic effect of graded elastic compression stockings in combination with dextran 70. Arch Surg 119:1329–1331, 1984.

I 43. Smith RC, Elton RA, Orr JD: Dextran and intermittent pneumatic compression in prevention of postoperative deep vein thrombosis. Multi-unit trial. Br Med J 1:952–954, 1978.

44. Antiplatelet Trialists' Collaboration. Collaborative overview of randomised trials of antiplatelet therapy III. Reduction in venous thrombosis and pulmonary embolism by antiplatelet prophylaxis among surgical and medical patients. Br Med J 308:235–246, 1994.

45. Collins R, Scrimgeour A, Yusel S, et al: Reduction in fatal pulmonary and venous thrombosis by perioperative administration of subcutaneous heparin. Over view of randomized trials of general or orthopaedic and urological surgery. N Engl J Med 318:1162–1173, 1988.

46. Cohen AT, Skinner JA, Kakkar VV: Antiplatelet treatment for thromboprophylaxis: A step forward or backwards. Br Med J 309:1213–1217, 1994.

I 47. Kakkar VV, Cohen AT, Edmondson RA, et al: Low molecular weight versus standard heparin for the prevention of venous thrombo-embolism after major abdominal surgery. Lancet 341:259–265, 1993.

48. Hirsh J, Dalen JE, Deykin D, Poller L: Oral anticoagulants: Mechanisms of action, clinical effectiveness, and optimal therapeutic range. Chest 102[Suppl]: 312S–326S, 1992.

I 49. Kakkar VV, Corrigan TP, Fossard DP: Prevention of

fatal postoperative pulmonary embolism by low doses of heparin: An International Trial. Lancet ii:45–51, 1975.

50. Carter CJ, Kelton JG, Hirsh J, et al: The relationship between the haemorrhagic and antithrombotic properties of low molecular weight heparins and heparin. Blood 59:1239, 1982.

51. Esquivel CO, Bergqvist D, Bjork C-G, Nilsson B: Comparison between commercial heparin, low molecular weight heparin and pentosan polysulphate on haemostasis and platelets in vivo. Thromb Res 28:389, 1982.

52. Nurmohamed MT, Rosendaal FR, Buller HR, et al: Low molecular weight heparin versus standard heparin in general and orthopaedic surgery: A meta-analysis. Lancet 340:152–156, 1992.

53. Boneu B: An international multicentre study: Clivarin(R) in the prevention of venous thromboembolism in patients undergoing general surgery. Report of the International Clivarin(R) Assessment Group (Conference). Blood Coagul Fibrinolysis 4[Suppl 1]:S21–S22, 1993.

54. Polkolainen E, Hendolin H: Effects of lumbar epidural analgesia and general anaesthesia on flow velocity in the femoral vein and postoperative deep vein thrombosis. Acta Chir Scand 149:361–364, 1983.

55. Otton PE, Wilson EJ: The cardiocirculatory effects of upper thoracic epidural analgesia. Can Anaesth Soc J 13:541–549, 1966.

56. Hendolin H, Mattila MAK, Poikolainen E: The effect of lumbar epidural analgesia on the development of deep vein thrombosis of the legs after open prostatectomy. Acta Chir Scand 147:425–429, 1981.

57. Hendolin H, Tuppurainen T, Lahtinen J: Thoracic epidural analgesia and deep vein thrombosis in cholecystectomized patients. Acta Chir Scand 148:405–409, 1982.

58. Mellbring G, Dahlgren S, Reiz S, et al: Thromboembolic complications after major abdominal surgery. Effect of thoracic epidural analgesia. Acta Chir Scand 149:263–268, 1983.

59. Hjortso NC, Neumann P, Frosig F, et al: A controlled study on the effect of epidural analgesia with local anaesthetics and morphine on morbidity after abdominal surgery. Acta Anaesthesiol Scand 29(8):790–796, 1985.

60. Bergqvist D, Lindblad B, Matzsch T: Low molecular weight heparin for thromboprophylaxis and epidural/spinal anaesthesia—Is there a risk? Acta Anaesthesiol Scand 36:605–609, 1992.

# Chapter 18

# Prevention in Orthopedic Surgery and Trauma

Michael R. Lassen and Lars C. Borris

Patients suffering major trauma or undergoing orthopedic surgery are at a very high risk of developing thromboembolic complications. When compared with the risk after most other forms of surgery, the risk is highest after orthopedic surgery and surgery for fractures of the long bones and pelvis. The exact reason for these differences is not known in detail, but many indications suggest that changes in hemostasis due to activation of the coagulation and shutdown of fibrinolysis, damage to the deep veins, liberation of proteolytic activators, tissue factors, complement activation, and decreased blood velocity are among the most important etiologic factors. These factors are combined with individual risk factors.

## RISK OF THROMBOEMBOLIC COMPLICATIONS AFTER ELECTIVE ORTHOPEDIC OPERATIONS AND MAJOR TRAUMA

Based on previously published studies in unprotected patients it can be recapitulated that the risk of developing deep vein thrombosis (DVT) after total hip replacement (THR) is 39 to 54%, after total knee replacement (TKR) is 41 to 84%, and following various major traumas is 50 to 100%, with the highest incidence observed in patients with spinal fractures with tetraplegia (Table 18–1).

The risk of developing pulmonary embolism (PE) is best documented in patients undergoing THR. In these patients the risk is approximately 25%, with 1 to 3% being fatal. The rate of fatal PE in trauma patients is best known from the classic study by Sevitt and Gallagher in which 26% of patients with a fracture of the femoral

neck died of PE confirmed at autopsy.[1111] However, in a younger population suffering multiple trauma, incidences of PE up to 25% have been observed, of which 5 to 8% were fatal.

The onset of risk is well defined in elective surgery, but the length of the risk period is unknown because studies do not follow the patients beyond 1 to 2 weeks after the operation. However, the risk may last longer, depending on the type of operation and the postoperative treatment (use of plaster casts and degree of weightbearing).

The period of risk in trauma patients starts at the time of the accident before admission to the hospital. In these cases the length of risk period is unknown, but it is common practice to consider it over when the patient is mobilized (i.e., out of bed). In patients wearing plaster

Table 18–1. **Incidences of Deep Vein Thrombosis (DVT) After Elective Orthopedic Operations and Trauma***

| Patient Category | DVT (%)† |
|---|---|
| Total hip replacement | 39–54 |
| Total knee replacement | 41–84 |
| Major trauma | |
|   Face/chest/abdomen | 50 |
|   Head | 54 |
|   Spine | 62 |
| Lower limb fractures | |
|   Pelvic | 62 |
|   Femoral | 78 |
|   Tibial | 83 |
|   Ankle | 67 |

*DVT diagnoses obtained by phlebography within 14 days after operation/trauma.
†Based on previous publications.

Activation of the coagulation cascade

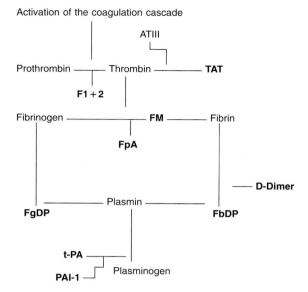

**Figure 18–1.** Essential steps in the formation and degradation of fibrin. (ATIII = antithrombin III; TAT = thrombin-antithrombin III complex; F1 + 2 = prothrombin fragment 1 + 2; FM = fibrin monomers; FpA = fibrinopeptide A; FbDP, FgDP = fibrin/ogen degradation products. All steps written in boldface are measurable.)

casts, studies have shown that approximately 25 to 30% of patients develop DVT.[21] These results give an indication that the risk period may be much longer in such cases.

## ACTIVATION OF COAGULATION AND FIBRINOLYSIS IN RELATION TO TRAUMA AND SURGERY

The hemostatic reaction to blunt trauma and surgical trauma is not essentially different. In both situations, activation of the coagulation cascade through the extrinsic pathway is induced by release of tissue thromboplastin from areas with soft tissue injury and bone fractures. The end result of the activation is formation of fibrin, which may aggregate (polymerize) into larger fibrin clots. Figure 18–1 illustrates the essential steps in the formation and degradation of fibrin in the coagulation system. In previous studies, elevated levels of fibrin degradation products (FpA, TAT, and F1 + 2) were observed during operation in patients undergoing elective hip surgery, which indicates increased fibrin formation.[3–6] In another study of hip surgery, the postoperative levels of F1 + 2 and total fibrin and fibrinogen degradation products were significantly elevated compared with the preoperative status in patients who developed postoperative

thromboembolic complications.[6] It has been suggested that impaired fibrinolysis due to reduced t-PA activity after operation as a consequence of increased plasminogen activator inhibitor (PAI) activity may be responsible for development of postoperative thromboembolism.[7, 8]

In a study of patients suffering fractures of the lower limbs, activation of the coagulation and fibrinolytic systems was indicated by high levels of F1 + 2, TAT, FM, FbDP and FgDP measured shortly after the trauma.[9] In patients with multiple trauma, high admission levels of FpA, F1 + 2, and TAT[10–12] have been reported.

These changes confirm that a substantial activation of the hemostatic system is taking place in relation to surgery and trauma. Unfortunately, none of these markers is very specific, and as a consequence it is not possible on this basis to predict which patients will suffer thromboembolic complications, although many attempts have been made to predict their occurrence. Development of hemostatic activation after surgery has been studied only in the 7 to 10 postoperative days. Thus, the duration of the activation is unknown, and whether it is even longer in patients suffering thromboembolic complications also is unknown.

## RISKS INDUCED BY SURGERY OR TRAUMA

Direct damage to the deep veins during THR has been reported previously. Twisting of the proximal veins during dislocation of the hip joint was reported in one study by the use of preoperative phlebography.[13] A cadaver study later confirmed this finding.[14IV] In theory, twisting may cause damage to the endothelium in the area and start local thrombus formation. Both studies support the common observation that the incidence of proximal thrombosis is high after THR.

Delayed stabilization of fractures results in an increased number of postoperative complications. The most important is adult respiratory distress syndrome, which can be reduced by early surgical intervention.[15] The mechanism behind this observation is largely unknown. However, it seems reasonable to suggest that early stabilization offers a distinct advantage by enabling the patient to be more mobile; the patient may be placed in an upright chest position and may avoid the forced supine position of skeletal traction. In addition, with a stable fracture the local tissue damage is lessened. Neovascularization is more likely to occur, and the local inflammatory response is reduced.

This reduces the systemic response of the wound as well.

In some studies it has been shown that in patients undergoing THR without specific thromboprophylaxis, regional anesthesia (spinal or epidural) significantly reduced the incidence of postoperative DVT compared with that in patients undergoing general anesthesia.[16, 17III] The same effect has been demonstrated in patients suffering femoral neck fractures; however, a meta-analysis did not allow a conclusion that important differences in mortality existed between patients undergoing regional versus general anesthesia.[18]

The use of a tourniquet during operation may contribute to an increased thrombosis risk, although there is no firm evidence of tourniquet effects.[19, 20] Embolization of echogenic material has been reported shortly after release of the tourniquet in patients undergoing total knee arthroplasty.[21] Beneficial effect on the fibrinolytic system has also been reported,[22] but no firm conclusion on the risks and benefits of the use of tourniquet can be made at the present time.

The risk induced by stasis caused by immobilization in plaster casts before and after operation or avoidance of weightbearing on an extremity for a time period is often neglected, and the problem has been only sporadically studied. It is widely accepted that stasis is a major factor in the cause of DVT, and it is logical to believe that reduced blood flow may prolong the contact time of activated platelets and clotting factors with the vein wall. Although direct injury may occur at the operative site in some patients undergoing orthopedic procedures, the more distant veins are not directly damaged, yet these are the most common sites for DVT. A canine study demonstrated endothelial damage after THR.[23] Although these lesions have not been directly documented in humans, the endothelial lesions may serve as sites for initiation of thrombi. Theoretically, the endothelial damage may be caused by dilation of the vein wall beyond the ability of the endothelium and basement membrane to accommodate the trauma. By the use of a system noninvasively monitoring venous diameter, dilation beyond a certain critical point was correlated with an increased incidence of venous lesions in a canine model of THR.[24]

## INDIVIDUAL RISK FACTORS

Individual risk factors for development of thromboembolic complications after elective or-

thopedic and trauma surgery are comparable with risk factors known in other surgical specialties. The most important are age (over 40 years), duration of operation (over 30 minutes), obesity, previous thromboembolism (DVT and/or PE), varicose veins, reoperations, infections, congenital or acquired disorders (deficiencies of antithrombin III, protein C, protein S; dysfibrinogenemia; abnormal fibrinolysis) predisposing patients to thrombosis, and known malignancy. In a previous anatomic study it was shown that legs having a venous valve number greater than five between the popliteal fossa and the ischial spine were at much greater risk for development of thrombosis than normal legs.[25]

The total risk of thromboembolism for a patient is the combined risk incurred by the operation or the trauma and the individual risk. When joint replacement operations are in question, the risk posed by the operation itself is so high that all patients undergoing these operations must receive adequate prophylaxis regardless of the magnitude of the individual risk.

## PRINCIPLES OF PROPHYLAXIS

Several principles can be applied to decrease the risk of thromboembolic complications after elective orthopedic and trauma surgery. These include avoidance of unnecessary immobilization, reduction of the duration of operation, use of a tourniquet only if necessary, early stabilization of fractures, use of operative methods enabling rigid fixation of fractures (i.e., interlocking intramedullary nailing systems), and immediate weightbearing.

When it is decided to use a prophylactic regimen, there are basically two types of prophylaxis, namely (1) mechanical; and (2) pharmacologic.

### Mechanical Methods

Several devices have been applied to increase velocity of venous return from the limbs to reduce venous stasis, which is a key factor in Virchow's triad. Graded compression stockings may be employed in patients undergoing low-risk procedures on a risk/benefit basis, although no data are available to support this. For optimal use it is necessary to measure the size of the legs every second day to ensure that the stockings fit properly. In high-risk patients, such as most orthopedic patients, stockings alone do not offer a sufficient protection.

Intermittent pneumatic compression (IPC) reduces the risk of venous stasis and may enhance fibrinolysis. Used alone, compression of both calf and thigh is effective even in high-risk patients such as those undergoing THR; however, to be effective IPC must be used on both legs from arrival in the recovery room until at least 14 days after operation. This regimen may result in low patient compliance.

Compression stockings or IPC may be combined with pharmacologic methods.

A venous foot pump, tested in 84 patients, reduced the incidence of DVT significantly, from 40 to 5%.[26I] By this method the venous circulation is maintained, thereby improving the emptying in the deep veins. Whether it is more effective than the other mechanical methods awaits further study.

The applicability of mechanical methods depends on the patient. Patients undergoing TKR are not suited for compression stockings or IPC, because the devices encompass the wound area. In trauma patients with fractures of the lower limbs on which external fixators have been used, or in patients with major open wounds, the mechanical methods also cannot be applied. In general, mechanical methods should be considered when contraindications to pharmacologic prophylaxis are present, such as major bleeding and head trauma with intracranial bleeding.

Compression stockings may cause ischemia of the legs in arteriosclerotic patients with borderline arterial supply.

No clinical study has shown that the mechanical methods reduce the incidence of fatal pulmonary embolism after surgical procedures or trauma.

## Pharmacologic Methods

Since the first study by Sevitt and Gallagher in 1959, reporting a significant effect of phenindione in preventing thromboembolic complications in patients with fractures of the hip,[27III] a number of different drugs with known antithrombotic capacity have been evaluated to decrease the rate of thromboembolic events after surgery or trauma. The duration of administration of the drugs in most studies is between 7 and 14 days. The accepted preparations are oral anticoagulants, low doses of unfractioned heparin, dextrans, low-molecular-weight heparins (LMWHs), or heparinoids.

Oral anticoagulants have been shown to be capable of reducing the incidence of postoperative thromboembolism compared with aspirin and dextran 40. Treatment must be started on the day before surgery, and the intensity of anticoagulation has to be monitored by re-

peated measurement of International Normalized Ratio (INR) to obtain and maintain the range between 2 and 3. However, the optimal intensity has not yet been fully established. In some countries it has become a habit to keep patients on oral anticoagulation for 3 months after a THR. However, this is based on purely empiric data and not on scientific evidence.

Fixed low-dose unfractionated heparin (LDH), 5,000 U given subcutaneously 2 to 3 times daily, reduces DVT in many patients. A meta-analysis has shown a statistically significant improvement in efficacy of LDH compared with placebo in patients undergoing THR or surgical repair of hip fractures.[28] The efficacy of LDH, however, is not optimal; more than 25% of the patients develop DVT in spite of prophylaxis. To improve the level of efficacy, the dosage has been adjusted according to the activated partial thromboplastin time (APTT), which in one study was more effective than a fixed-dose heparin regimen (3,500 U three times daily) without an increase in bleeding complications.[29I] Drawbacks of this regimen are the need for continued laboratory monitoring and difficulties in comparison between studies because of large interlaboratory variations of APTT measurements.

Dextrans have been studied in both elective and acute hip surgery. Overall the efficacy of dextran is comparable with that of oral anticoagulation but without the need for laboratory monitoring. In a study with a mixed orthopedic population, dextran 70 was as effective and safe as a regimen of heparin 5,000 U three times daily with respect to the number of deaths due to autopsy-verified pulmonary embolism.[30II] Dextran 70 causes more bleeding in both elective and acute hip surgery compared with other prophylactic regimens except oral anticoagulants.[31I, 32]

In the 1970s it was shown by several investigators that anti-IIa activity of heparin fragments decreased with decreasing molecular weight, whereas the anti-Xa activity was preserved. This observation led to development of LMWHs, which were able to prevent thrombus formation and, for an equivalent antithrombotic effect, produced less bleeding in animal models compared with unfractionated heparin.[33] Several compounds of LMWH are being manufactured with different molecular profiles and in vitro activities. They have molecular weights within the range of 4,000 to 8,000. Because of these differences it is accepted that each compound be regarded as a separate pharmacologic entity, and each must be evaluated separately in terms of efficacy and safety.

One of the first clinical studies using LMWH was prematurely stopped because of serious bleeding complications in study subjects. It appeared that the dose given (2 × 8,700 anti-Xa units) was too high. Later dose-finding studies have shown that a dosage of approximately 2,500 to 5,000 anti-Xa units has an acceptable risk/benefit ratio, although the dosage depends on the risk group of the patients. Through the 1980s many clinical studies have confirmed that LMWH is an effective and safe regimen to prevent postoperative thromboembolism in different types of surgery. In a number of published meta-analyses both in elective orthopedic and general surgery, LMWH has been found to be more effective than placebo, dextran 70, and LDH, and at least as effective as adjusted-dose unfractionated heparin and LDH combined with dihydroergotamine.[34–37]

No clinical study so far has been able to show a reduced bleeding tendency of LMWH compared with standard regimens of LDH (5,000 U two or three times daily). One reason may be that the size of the patient groups in the studies was based on efficacy outcome and not on expected blood losses and other secondary safety variables; therefore, the studies have not been large enough to demonstrate differences in safety variables. In a recent study, however, it was shown that a regimen of unfractionated heparin of 15,000 U daily (7,500 U twice daily) produced significantly more bleeding complications in patients undergoing THR than a postoperative regimen of a LMWH (enoxaparin 30 mg twice daily).[38I]

In trauma patients, few studies have been conducted with LMWH, and most of these studies were performed in patients with hip fracture. Until now, no data show a superiority of LMWH prophylaxis over LDH, and only a few studies have been published. One study showed a significantly better efficacy and safety of LMWH compared with dextran 70 in patients with hip fracture.[32] In patients with spinal cord injuries who have a very high risk of thromboembolic complications, however, LMWH prophylaxis was more effective and safe than LDH.[39I] The observation that LMWH can be safely used in these patients may suggest that LMWH can be used also in injured patients with head trauma in whom bleeding is a commonly feared complication.

In patients wearing plaster casts, LMWH seems to be effective when it is used during the period of immobilization. The concept of once-daily injection without the need for laboratory monitoring is acceptable for most patients, and LMWH has been used successfully by self-administration.[40]

It is still a controversial issue whether there is a risk by combining LMWH for thromboprophylaxis with epidural and spinal anesthesia. In a recent review on the subject it was concluded that neurologic complications after the combination of regional anesthesia with LMWH as well as LDH are extremely rare, and the combination therefore was considered to be safe.[41]

Although LMWH is a most effective prophylaxis, 10 to 25% of patients develop thromboembolism after surgery despite adequate prophylaxis. The basis for this may be suboptimal dosages, resistance to heparin, or a too-short duration of prophylactic treatment (7–14 days). A reason for this relative high number of nonresponders has not yet been found.

A heparinoid, a mixture of sulfated glycosaminoglycuronides with a mean molecular weight of approximately 6,000, has been studied in both elective and acute hip surgery and compared with LDH and dextran, respectively. Both studies showed a significantly better efficacy of the heparinoid and an acceptable level of safety.[42I, 43I] Compared with LDH combined with dihydroergotamine (DHE), the heparinoid offered a significantly better prophylaxis in elective hip surgery, with an acceptable level of safety.[44I] The combination of LDH and DHE is no longer recommended because of a definite risk of circulatory disturbances in the lower extremities, especially in patients having trauma surgery. In one study, a comparison of heparinoid and two different LMWHs was performed in patients with hip fractures; results showed a comparable efficacy against postoperative DVT of the heparinoid.[45]

In summary, the rationale behind the use of any kind of thromboprophylaxis is to save lives—in other words, to reduce mortality. It is disappointing, however, that no modern study so far has been focused on mortality, but all studies have relied on the physician-based intermediate endpoints such as DVT and PE. However, no clearcut scientific proof of a direct correlation exists between these short-term endpoints and total mortality. In future research it must be the most important issue to prove this relationship and to show that thromboprophylaxis is able to secure survival, which to the patient is the most important consideration. So far, it can be concluded that modern methods of thromboprophylaxis are effective in reducing thromboembolic complications after operation and trauma without increasing the risk of major bleeding complications.

# REFERENCES

III 1. Sevitt S, Gallagher HG: Prevention of venous thrombosis and pulmonary embolism in injured patients: A trial of anticoagulant prophylaxis with phenindione in middle-aged and elderly patients with fractured necks of femur. Lancet 2:981, 1959.

I 2. Kujath P, Spannagel U, Habscheid W, et al: Thromboseprophylaxe bei Ambulanten Patienten mit Verletzungen der unteren Extremität. Dtsch Med Wochenschr 117:6, 1992.

3. Wilson J, Grant PJ, Davies JA, et al: The relationship between plasma vasopressin and changes in coagulation and fibrinolysis during hip surgery. Thromb Res 51:439, 1988.

4. Dahl OE, Johnsen H, Kierulf P, et al: Intrapulmonary thrombin generation and its relation to monomethylmetacrylate plasma levels during hip arthroplasty. Acta Anaesthesiol Scand 36:331, 1992.

5. Dahl OE, Pedersen T, Kierulf P, et al: Sequential intrapulmonary and systemic activation of coagulation and fibrinolysis during and after total hip replacement surgery. Thromb Res 70:451, 1993.

6. Sørensen JV, Lassen MR, Borris LC, et al: Reduction of plasma levels of prothrombin fragment 1 and 2 during thromboprophylaxis with a low molecular weight heparin. Blood Coagul Fibrinolysis 3:55, 1992.

7. Sørensen JV, Borris LC, Lassen MR, et al: Association between plasma levels of tissue plasminogen activator and postoperative deep vein thrombosis—influence of prophylaxis with a low molecular weight heparin. Thromb Res 59:131, 1990.

8. Ericsson BI, Ericsson E, Risberg B: Impaired fibrinolysis and postoperative thromboembolism in orthopedic patients. Thromb Res 62:55, 1991.

9. Sørensen JV, Rahr HB, Jensen HP, et al: Markers of coagulation and fibrinolysis after fractures of the lower extremities. Thromb Res 65:479, 1992.

10. Gando S, Tedo I, Kubota M: Posttrauma coagulation and fibrinolysis. Crit Care Med 20:594, 1992.

11. Sørensen JV, Jensen HP, Rahr HB, et al: Fibrinogen and fibrin derivatives in traumatized patients; relation to injury severity and posttraumatic pulmonary dysfunction. Haemostasis 23:91, 1993.

12. Lampl L, Bock KH, Hartel W, et al: Hemostatic disorders following polytrauma—the role of physiologic coagulation inhibitors during the preclinical phase. Anaesthesiol Intensivmed Notfallmed Schmertzther 27: 31, 1992.

13. Stamatakis JD, Kakkar VV, Sagar S, et al: Femoral vein thrombosis and total hip replacement. Br Med J 2:223, 1977.

IV 14. Planes A, Vochelle N, Fagola M: Total hip replacement and deep vein thrombosis. J Bone Joint Surg 72B:9, 1990.

15. Bone L, Johnson J, Weigelt J, et al: Early versus delayed femoral fracture stabilization: A prospective randomized study. J Bone Joint Surg 71A:336, 1989.

16. Modig J, Borg T, Karlström G, et al: Thromboembolism after total hip replacement: Role of epidural and general anesthesia. Anesth Analg 62:174, 1983.

III 17. Thorburn J, Louden JR, Vallance R: Spinal and general anaesthesia in total hip replacement: Frequency of deep vein thrombosis. Br J Anaesth 52:1117, 1980.

18. Sorenson RM, Pace NL: Anesthetic techniques during surgical repair of femoral neck fractures. A meta-analysis. Anesthesiology 77:1095, 1992.

19. Cohen SH, Ehrlich GE, Kauffman MS, et al: Thrombophlebitis following knee surgery. J Bone Joint Surg 55A:106, 1973.

20. Sharrock NE, Hargett MJ, Urquhart B, et al: Factors affecting deep vein thrombosis rate following total knee arthroplasty under epidural anesthesia. J Arthroplasty 8:133, 1993.

21. Parmet JL, Berman AT, Horrow JC, et al: Thromboembolism coincident with tourniquet deflation during total knee arthroplasty. Lancet 341:1057, 1993.

22. Fahmy NR, Patel DG: Hemostatic changes and postoperative deep-vein thrombosis associated with use of a pneumatic tourniquet. J Bone Joint Surg 63A:461, 1981.

23. Stewart GJ, Alburger PD, Stone EA, Soszka TW: Total hip replacement induces injury to remote veins in a canine model. J Bone Joint Surg 65A:97, 1983.

24. Stewart GJ, Ziskin MC, Schaub RG, et al: Use of ultrasound for non invasive study of blood vessel responsiveness. Am J Physiol 253:H671, 1987.

25. Liu G-C, Ferris E, Reifsteck JR, et al: Effect of anatomic variations on deep venous thrombosis of the lower extremity. Am J Radiol 146:845, 1986.

I 26. Fordyce MJF, Ling RSM: A venous foot pump reduces thrombosis after total hip replacement. J Bone Joint Surg 74B:45, 1992.

III 27. Sevitt S, Gallagher NG: Prevention of venous thrombosis and pulmonary embolism in injured patients: A trial of anticoagulant prophylaxis with phenindione in middle-aged and elderly patients with fractured necks of femur. Lancet 2:981, 1959.

28. Collins R, Scrimgeour A, Yusuf S, Peto R: Reduction in fatal pulmonary embolism and venous thrombosis by perioperative administration of subcutaneous heparin. N Engl J Med 318:1162, 1988.

I 29. Leyvraz PF, Richard J, Bachmann F, et al: Adjusted versus fixed-dose subcutaneous heparin in the prevention of deep-vein thrombosis after total hip replacement. N Engl J Med 309:954, 1983.

II 30. Gruber UF, Salden T, Brokop T, et al: Incidence of fatal pulmonary embolism after prophylaxis with dextran 70 and low-dose heparin: An international multicentre study. Br Med J 280:69, 1980.

I 31. The Danish Enoxaparin Study Group: Low-molecular-weight heparin (Enoxaparin) vs Dextran 70. The prevention of postoperative deep vein thrombosis after total hip replacement. Arch Intern Med 151:1621, 1991.

32. Hess P, Oertly D, Dürig M, et al: Thromboembolieprophylaxe in der Hüfttraumatologie: Niedermolekulares Heparin versus Dextran. Helv Chir Acta 58:931, 1991.

33. Hirsh J, Levine M: Low molecular weight heparins. Blood 79:1, 1992.

34. Lassen MR, Borris LC, Christiansen HM, et al: Clinical trials with low molecular weight heparins in the prevention of postoperative thromboembolic complications: A meta-analysis. Semin Thromb Hemost 17[Suppl 1]:284, 1991.

35. Nurmohamed MT, Rosendaal FR, Büller H, et al: Low-molecular-weight heparin versus standard heparin in general and orthopaedic surgery: A meta analysis. Lancet 340:152, 1992.

36. Leizorovicz A, Haugh MC, Chapuis F-R, et al: Low molecular weight heparin in prevention of perioperative thrombosis. Br Med J 305:913, 1992.

37. Borris LC, Lassen MR, Jensen HP, et al: Perioperative thrombosis prophylaxis with low molecular weight heparins in elective hip surgery. Clinical and economic considerations. Int J Clin Pharmacol Ther Toxicol 32:262, 1994.

I 38. Levine MN, Hirsh J, Gent M, et al: Prevention of deep vein thrombosis after elective hip surgery. A randomized trial comparing low molecular weight heparin with standard unfractionated heparin. Ann Intern Med 114:545, 1991.

I 39. Green D, Lee MY, Lim AC, et al: Prevention of thromboembolism after spinal cord injury using low molecular weight heparin. Ann Intern Med 113:571, 1990.

40. Zagrodnock J, Kauffner HK: Prophylaxis of thromboembolism trauma surgery outpatients by self-injection of heparin. Unfallchirurgie 93:331, 1990.

41. Bergqvist D, Lindblad B, Mätzsch T: Risk of combining low molecular weight heparin for thromboprophylaxis and epidural or spinal anesthesia. Semin Thromb Hemost 19[Suppl 1]:147, 1993.

I 42. Hoek J, Nurmohamed MT, Hamelynck KJ, et al: Prevention of deep-vein thrombosis following total hip replacement by a low-molecular-weight heparinoid. Thromb Haemost 67:28, 1992.

I 43. Bergqvist D, Kettunen K, Fredin H, et al: Thromboprophylaxis in patients with hip fractures. A prospective, randomized, comparative study between ORG 10172 and dextran 70. Surgery 109:617, 1991.

I 44. Leyvraz P, Bachmann F, Bohnet J, et al: Thromboembolic prophylaxis in total hip replacement: A comparison between the low molecular weight heparinoid Lomoparan and heparin-dihydroergotamine. Br J Surg 79:911, 1992.

45. Røise O, Nurmohamed M, Reijnders P, et al: A multicentre, randomized, assessor-blind, pilot study comparing the efficacy in the prophylaxis of DVT and safety of Orgaran (ORG 10172), Fragmin, Clexane/Lovenox in patients undergoing surgery for a fractured hip (abstract 273). Thromb Haemost 69:620, 1993.

# Chapter 19

# Prevention in Neurosurgery and Spinal Cord Injury

A. G. G. Turpie and David Green

## SPINAL CORD INJURY

Deep vein thrombosis occurs in virtually every patient with acute spinal cord injury not receiving prophylaxis, and pulmonary embolism is reported in up to 10%.[1] The majority of the deep vein thrombi are clinically silent; in one series, only 9 of 53 thrombi in 41 patients were associated with clinical manifestations.[2] In an investigation of the causes of death during the first 12 years after spinal cord injury, 61 of 854 deaths were attributed to pulmonary emboli.[3] At our own institution, nine of 338 (2.7%) patients admitted with motor complete paralysis in the past 5 years died of proven pulmonary embolism.[4] This high frequency of usually unsuspected serious thromboembolic disease underlines the importance of early initiation of preventive measures. In this section, the advantages and disadvantages of the various means of prophylaxis will be discussed, and applications to particular clinical situations described.

## Methods of Prophylaxis

### Leg Compression Devices

Elastic stockings and intermittent pneumatic compression (IPC) have been the traditional method of prophylaxis for neurosurgical patients, and the efficacy of this approach has been established by several clinical trials.[5] In patients with spinal cord injury, IPC alone or combined with aspirin and dipyridamole (ASA + Dip) was compared with historic untreated controls.[6II] Thrombosis, as detected by the radiofibrinogen uptake test, was recorded in 29 of 37 (78%) control subjects. In contrast, only 6 of 15 (40%) with IPC alone, and 3 of 12 (25%) patients with IPC-ASA + Dip had thrombosis. The difference between the IPC alone

and IPC-ASA + Dip was not statistically significant. As compared with the controls, thrombi in the treated patients appeared later after injury (on days 7–15 versus days 4–12) and were more likely to be in distal (popliteal and calf) than proximal (femoral and iliofemoral) veins. One patient who received ASA + Dip had extensive bleeding during cervical fusion surgery; no other adverse effects of prophylaxis were observed.

In another small study of spinal cord injured patients, thrombosis occurred in only one of 21 subjects treated with IPC, elastic stockings, and low-dose heparin (5,000 U every 12 hours) as compared with 6 of 17 historic controls.[7IV] The results of these studies suggest that leg compression devices are moderately effective in preventing thrombosis in patients with spinal cord injury; their efficacy appears to be improved when combined with anticoagulants. A major disadvantage of IPC is the need for the leggings to be worn continuously and checked frequently for proper application and function; in the study of Green and coworkers,[6II] three patients promptly developed thrombosis when the leggings were removed 1 month after injury.

### Electric Stimulation

Functional electric stimulation of calf musculature has been shown to increase plasma fibrinolytic activity and moderately improve venous emptying in subjects with spinal cord injury.[8] In a clinical trial, 48 patients were randomly assigned to placebo, low-dose heparin (5,000 U every 8 hours), or low-dose heparin plus electric stimulation of the tibialis anterior and gastrocnemius muscles.[9I] Thrombi were detected by radiofibrinogen uptake and impedance plethysmography, and confirmed by venography. Deep vein thrombosis developed in

216

half the placebo and low-dose heparin treated patients but in only one of those receiving electric stimulation plus low-dose heparin ($p < .05$). This very promising approach is limited by the need for special equipment and expertise in the application of electric stimulation.

## Unfractionated Heparin

As noted earlier, unfractionated heparin has been combined with IPC or electric stimulation as prophylaxis for thromboembolism in patients with spinal cord injury. When used alone, it has a rate of effectiveness similar to that of IPC. For example, in a trial in which patients were randomized to receive either fixed doses of 5,000 U every 12 hours, or doses adjusted to prolong the activated partial thromboplastin time (aPTT) to about 1.5 times control, thrombosis occurred in nine of 29 (31%) receiving the fixed dose.[10I] In contrast, only two of the 29 (7%) treated with the adjusted doses had thrombosis ($p < .05$). However, bleeding occurred in seven (24%) on the adjusted dose and in none on the fixed dose ($p < .02$). Other disadvantages of the adjusted dose regimen were the need for repeated measurements of the aPTT test and frequent dose adjustments. In another trial[111] in which unfractionated heparin was given in doses of 5,000 U every 8 hours, five of 21 patients had thrombosis, including two fatal pulmonary emboli, and two additional patients had bleeding (cumulative event rate 34.7%). A large retrospective study of 97 patients receiving this dose of heparin for a 3-month period was reported.[12V] Thromboembolism was detected in 26 (27%), including 17 with deep vein thrombosis, seven with pulmonary emboli, and two with both deep vein thrombosis and pulmonary emboli. These results indicate that low-dose unfractionated heparin is relatively ineffective in thrombus prevention, and although increasing the dose improves efficacy, there is a concomitant increase in bleeding.

## Low-molecular-weight Heparin

As noted earlier, neither IPC nor unfractionated heparin has been found to be ideal for the prevention of thromboembolism in spinal cord injury; therefore, low-molecular-weight heparin (LMWH) has been studied. In a small trial of 41 patients, subjects were randomized to receive either unfractionated heparin, 5,000 U every 8 hours, or LMWH (Logiparin, Novo-Nordisk), 3,500 U once daily.[111] Treatment was begun within 72 hours of injury and continued for 8 weeks. Thrombosis was detected by venous ultrasound and confirmed by venography, and hematomas and other bleeding events were recorded. While the cumulative event rate for those receiving the unfractionated heparin was 34.7% (95% confidence interval, 13.7–55.2%), no patient treated with LMWH had thrombosis or bleeding ($p < .006$). Based on these results, all subsequent patients (n = 60) were given LMWH. Six developed deep vein thrombosis (four proximal and two distal), one had a fatal pulmonary embolus, and one patient had postoperative bleeding that did not require transfusion. The percentage of patients who were event-free after 8 weeks was 84.4%.[4] In reviewing the total experience from this spinal cord injury center, LMWH was found to be significantly safer than unfractionated heparin (only one bleeding event in 68 patients as compared with nine events in 79 patients ($p = .04$), and was at least as efficacious (seven thromboses as compared to 16, $p = .15$). These results with LMWH in spinal cord injury are consistent with those obtained in other high-risk indications such as elective hip surgery[13I]; LMWH is as effective as unfractionated heparin but provokes less bleeding.

## Inferior Vena Cava Filters

Under radiologic guidance, mechanical devices may be introduced percutaneously into the inferior vena cava to prevent emboli originating in distal veins from reaching the lung. These filters are useful in situations in which antithrombotic measures cannot be applied, such as IPC in patients with leg fractures, or anticoagulants in persons who are actively bleeding. Their use in spinal cord injury has been reviewed by Merli.[14] Although they are effective in preventing pulmonary emboli (incidence 2.7–5%) and infrequently associated with vena caval thrombosis (2–2.9%), they have a number of drawbacks, including the need for skilled placement, the possibility of migration of the device, and the formation of retroperitoneal hematoma. It must also be remembered that the device does not substitute for either prevention or treatment of leg vein thrombosis; as soon as the patient can tolerate antithrombotic agents, antithrombotic therapy must be given to avoid massive thrombosis of the proximal veins and chronic venous insufficiency.[15]

## Prophylaxis in Specific Clinical Situations

In 1992, the Consensus Conference on Deep Vein Thrombosis in Spinal Cord Injury[16] made the following recommendations for the prophylaxis of thromboembolism in spinal cord injury:

1. Mechanical compression devices should be applied to every patient for the first 10 to 14 days after injury
2. Anticoagulant drugs could be started beginning 72 hours after injury
3. Vena cava filters should be inserted in those patients who cannot wear compression devices because of lower limb fractures, and in those in whom anticoagulation is contraindicated because of sites of active bleeding, thrombocytopenia or other coagulopathy, renal or hepatic failure, or the need for multiple surgical procedures.

In consideration of the reported experience with LMWH,[4, 111] these recommendations may be modified by substituting LMWH for anticoagulant drugs, as shown in Table 19–1.

## Uncomplicated Spinal Cord Injury

For patients with uncomplicated spinal cord injury, prophylaxis with LMWH is recommended, based on the results of the clinical trials previously described. Prophylaxis should begin as soon as possible after admission, because there is some evidence that delaying prophylaxis increases the risk of thromboembolism.[12V] On the other hand, during the first week to 10 days following injury, many patients require surgical procedures such as spine fusion or tracheostomy. These interventions necessitate omitting the LMWH dose on the morning

**Table 19–1. Recommendations for Prevention of Thromboembolism in Patients With Spinal Cord Injury**

| Method of Prophylaxis | Comment |
| --- | --- |
| Leg compression devices | Apply to all patients for the first 10–14 days post-injury |
| Low-molecular-weight heparin | Safe and effective for patients with uncomplicated injuries, and can be given 10 days to 2 weeks after injury in most others |
| Vena cava filters | For patients with multiple fractures, head injury, or other contraindications to anticoagulant drugs as well as other high-risk patients (see text) |

of the procedure and resuming therapy the following day. To ensure protection from thrombus development during this period, and to enhance the effectiveness of the LMWH, it is recommended that all patients be fitted with IPC devices at the time of admission and that these be worn until the patient is no longer confined to bed.

## Spinal Cord Injury Complicated by Skull, Rib, or Long Bone Fractures

In the clinical trials of LMWH, patients with skull, rib, or long bone fractures were excluded, based on the assumption that anticoagulant therapy may aggravate intracranial bleeding in patients with head injuries, hemothorax in patients with rib fractures, and muscle hematomas in those with long bone fractures. In fact, these additional injuries are found in about 50% of patients with spinal cord injury.[4] For this large number of subjects, IPC is appropriate initial thromboprophylaxis, supplemented by electric stimulation, if available. However, because IPC devices cannot be worn continuously when patients begin rehabilitative therapies, LMWH should be initiated as soon as the risk of bleeding subsides, which is usually within 10 days to 2 weeks following injury.

## Prevention of Pulmonary Embolism

Massive pulmonary embolism is a major cause of death in spinal cord injury.[3] Therefore, recognition of patient characteristics that may predispose to this complication is of great importance. In reviewing the records of nine patients with spinal cord injury who died of pulmonary embolism, it was observed that certain features were present with greater frequency in these patients than in a control group of 42 concurrently hospitalized spinal cord injury survivors.[17] Patients with fatal emboli had fewer thoracic and lumbar injuries ($p = .04$); less spasticity ($p = .01$), and greater body mass index ($p = .01$). There was also a trend toward more advanced age ($p = .10$) and more frequent serious infections ($p = .08$). The fatal emboli occurred in from 8 to 73 days following injury (mean, 36 days). Based on this data, consideration should be given to the early placement of an inferior vena cava filter in those patients who have a high level of injury, or those who are obese, older, and have recurrent infections. LMWH may be continued in these patients to prevent leg vein thromboses.

## Duration of Prophylaxis

In patients with spinal cord injury and complete motor paralysis, thromboprophylaxis should be continued for at least 8 weeks, based on published experience showing that this is the period of greatest danger.[4, 6II] However, risk may persist beyond this interval; in one study,[4] 2 of 33 (6%) patients had thromboembolism as long as 10 weeks after injury. Prophylaxis can probably be safely discontinued if patients are beyond the period of flaccid paralysis, are free of medical complications such as infection, and are actively engaged in a rehabilitation program. As a further safeguard, all patients should be closely observed during the first few weeks after prophylaxis is stopped, using clinical examinations and, possibly, sensitive laboratory assays for thrombosis such as the D-Dimer test. When D-Dimers are measured by an enzyme-linked immunoassay method, the test has been shown to have high sensitivity for the presence of thrombosis in symptomatic patients with deep vein thrombosis.[18I, 19I] Those with abnormal values should have thrombosis confirmed by venous ultrasound or venography, because the specificity of the D-Dimer test is low.[20I]

In conclusion, patients with acute spinal cord injury frequently have unsuspected deep vein thrombosis, and massive pulmonary embolism is one of the leading causes of death in this disorder. Upon arrival at the hospital, all such patients should be fitted with calf and thigh compression devices, and those without risk of bleeding or contraindications to anticoagulant therapy should be given LMWH. Patients at especially high risk for thromboembolism, such as those with high spinal cord injury, obesity, advanced age, or other serious medical problems, should have a vena cava filter inserted. These individuals should also receive LMWH as prophylaxis against leg vein thrombosis. LMWH should be continued for at least 8 weeks, and should be given longer in patients with persistent flaccid paralysis, recurrent infections, and inability to fully participate in rehabilitation programs.

## REFERENCES

1. Weingarden SI: Deep venous thrombosis in spinal cord injury. Overview of the problem. Chest 102 [Suppl]:636S, 1992.

2. Yelnik A, Dizien O, Bussel B, et al: Systematic lower limb phlebography in acute spinal cord injury in 147 patients. Paraplegia 29:253, 1991.

3. DeVivo MJ, Black KJ, Stover SL: Causes of death during the first 12 years after spinal cord injury. Arch Phys Med Rehabil 74:248, 1993.

4. Green D, Chen D, Chmiel JS, et al. Prevention of thromboembolism in spinal cord injury: Role of low molecular weight heparin. Arch Phys Med Rehabil 75:290, 1994.

5. Clagett GP, Anderson FA Jr, Levine MN, et al: Prevention of venous thromboembolism. Chest 102 [Suppl]:391S, 1992.

II  6. Green D, Rossi EC, Yao JST, et al: Deep vein thrombosis in spinal cord injury: Effect of prophylaxis with calf compression, aspirin, and dipyridamole. Paraplegia 20:227, 1982.

IV  7. Merli GJ, Crabbe S, Doyle L, et al: Mechanical plus pharmacological prophylaxis for deep vein thrombosis in acute spinal cord injury. Paraplegia 30:558, 1992.

8. Katz RT, Green D, Sullivan T, Yarkony G: Functional electric stimulation to enhance systemic fibrinolytic activity in spinal cord injury patients. Arch Phys Med Rehabil 68:423, 1987.

I  9. Merli GJ, Herbison GJ, DiTunno JF, et al: Deep vein thrombosis: prophylaxis in acute spinal cord injured patients. Arch Phys Med Rehabil 69:661, 1988.

I  10. Green D, Lee MY, Ito VY, et al: Fixed- vs adjusted-dose heparin in the prophylaxis of thromboembolism in spinal cord injury. JAMA 260:1255, 1988.

I  11. Green D, Lee MY, Lim AC, et al: Prevention of thromboembolism after spinal cord injury using low-molecular-weight heparin. Ann Intern Med 113:571, 1990.

V  12. Kulkarni JR, Brut AA, Tromans AT, Constable PDL: Prophylactic low dose heparin anticoagulant therapy in patients with spinal cord injury: A retrospective study. Paraplegia 30:169, 1992.

I  13. Levine MN, Hirsh J, Gent M, et al: Prevention of deep vein thrombosis after elective hip surgery: A randomized trial comparing low molecular weight heparin with standard unfractionated heparin. Ann Intern Med 114:545, 1991.

14. Merli GJ: Management of deep vein thrombosis in spinal cord injury. Chest 102 [Suppl]:652S, 1992.

15. Editorialist: Post-thrombotic venous disorders. Lancet 1:1488, 1985.

16. Consensus Conference on Deep Vein Thrombosis in Spinal Cord Injury: Summary and Recommendations. Chest 102 [Suppl]:633S, 1992.

17. Green D, Twardowski P, Wei R, Rademaker AW: Fatal pulmonary embolism in spinal cord injury. Chest 105:853, 1994.

I  18. Heaton DC, Billings JD, Hickton CM: Assessment of D-Dimer assays for the diagnosis of deep vein thrombosis. J Lab Clin Med 110:588, 1987.

I  19. Carter CJ, Doyle DL, Dawson N, et al: Investigations into the clinical utility of latex D-Dimer in the diagnosis of deep venous thrombosis. Thromb Haemost 69:8, 1993.

I  20. Heijboer H, Ginsberg JS, Buller HR, et al: The use of the D-Dimer test in combination with non-invasive testing versus serial non-invasive testing alone for the diagnosis of deep-vein thrombosis. Thromb Haemost 67:510, 1992.

# Chapter 20

# Prevention in Medical Patients

A. S. Gallus

It is extremely tempting to simply take the vast body of knowledge derived from surgical venous thrombosis (VT) prevention trials and apply this directly to medical patients. There are, after all, some obvious similarities—the immediate increase in the risk of venous thromboembolism (VTE) after either an acute medical catastrophe or following major surgery, and its resolution with full functional recovery. The differences, however, are sufficient to indicate a need for a separate evaluation in medical patients of those preventive measures that are known to be effective in surgery.

First, in almost all surgical evaluations the preventive method is initiated preoperatively, before onset of the thrombogenic stimulus. This is clearly not possible in medical emergencies in which prophylaxis must wait until some time after the event, when small VT may already have been laid down.

Second, although firm conclusions can now be drawn about the impact of at least some prophylactic methods on the mortality from major pulmonary embolism (PE) after elective general surgery, this is not true for medical patients for whom most VT prevention trials have been quite small and were limited to measuring an effect on asymptomatic VT. There is also somewhat more uncertainty about the clinical importance of VTE in medical patients than is the case after surgery.

Third, chronic medical illnesses are special challenges because hospital admissions are no more than brief interludes in the longterm progression of chronic disabilities. A need for prolonged prophylaxis is thereby suggested.

## VENOUS THROMBOEMBOLISM (VTE) IN MEDICAL PATIENTS

In autopsy studies, fatal pulmonary embolism (PE) is found more often in medical than in surgical admissions (Tables 20–1 and 20–2).[1-6]

For instance, an extensive Swedish series, made especially credible by its very high autopsy rate, found fatal PE in 0.27% of general surgical and 0.42% of orthopedic surgery admissions, compared with 0.43% of admissions to an infectious diseases unit, 0.58% for internal medicine, and 1.13% in oncology.[3] From another perspective, medical conditions also predominate as the predisposing events in people presenting with venous thrombosis (VT).[7, 8]

The most important question concerns the impact of fatal PE on the underlying prognosis, because there is little gain from preventing fatal PE in medical patients if PE occurred only in people who are already terminally ill from their underlying disease. Although there was a relatively benign underlying pathology in 25 to 55% of deaths from PE recorded in two early autopsy studies, and these were therefore labeled as potentially "preventable,"[4, 9] it is uncertain whether this applies to medical patients today. Indeed, in one Danish series, a severe and probably terminal underlying disease was present in 168 of 178 medical patients with fatal, autopsy-confirmed PE[5]—clear evidence that disease prognosis must be a major determinant when selecting patients for VT prophylaxis.

## RISK FACTORS IN MEDICAL PATIENTS

Most risk factors are familiar; they include previous VTE, increasing age beyond 40 years,

Table 20–1. **Mortality from PE**

| Reference | Nonoperated Patients (%) | Surgical Patients (%) |
|---|---|---|
| Hermann et al, 1961 | 0.49 | 0.09 |
| Dismuke, Wagner, 1986 | 0.18 | 0.05 |
| Lindblad et al, 1991 | 0.47 | 0.24 |

Estimated from autopsy studies of medical and surgical admissions to university general hospitals in the United States and Sweden. The autopsy rate varied from 50–77%.

Table 20–2. **Proportion of All Fatal PE Found in Medical as Opposed to Surgical Patients at Autopsy**

| Reference | Fatal PE | Nonoperated Patients (n/%) | Surgical Patients (n/%) |
|---|---|---|---|
| Nielsen et al, 1981 | 220 | 183 (83%) | 37 (17%) |
| Hauch et al, 1990 | 74 | 58 (78%) | 16 (22%) |
| Sperry et al, 1990 | 78 | 45 (59%) | 31 (41%) |

obesity (greater than 20% overweight),[10, 11] prolonged bedrest, motor paralysis, chronic disabling cerebrovascular disease, myocardial infarction, uncontrolled heart failure,[10] severe infection, trauma, and cancer.[10, 12, 13] Two studies defined the use of multiagent cancer chemotherapy as an additional risk factor.[14, 15I]

Present formulations of estrogen-containing oral contraceptives probably remain mildly thrombogenic,[16] but there is no good evidence that postmenopausal estrogen replacement increases VT risk,[17] and neither cigarette smoking nor hypercholesterolemia predisposes to VTE.

In a few disorders like Behçet's disease and the primary antiphospholipid syndrome, VTE and artery thrombosis form part of the natural history.[18, 19] A limited number of truly "hypercoagulable" states occur because of inherited deficiency of one of the physiologic anticoagulants, including antithrombin III, protein C, or protein S.

Large-scale surveys suggest that most patients admitted to hospitals have more than one risk factor for VTE,[20] as do most patients who go on to develop VTE.[8] A number of [125]I-Fibrinogen leg scan–based studies, mostly dating from the 1970s, measured VT rates after various acute medical illnesses and reviewed the influence of clinical risk factors (Table 20–3). VT after myocardial infarction develops most often in older people and in patients with heart failure, shock, cardiac arrest, another significant arrhythmia, or continuing chest pain.[21–24] The risk is further increased by transfemoral pacemaker insertion,[25] but cigarette smoking, oddly enough, may protect from VT.[26I, 27, 28]

The risk is especially great when there is a disabling stroke or spinal injury; 25% of people with hemiplegia admitted to a rehabilitation unit have developed symptomatic VT.[29] Routine venography reveals VT in 40%[30] and leg scanning becomes abnormal in about 50% of paralyzed legs.[30] Screening after spinal cord injury reveals VT in 60 to 90% of patients.[31, 32] One unexpected risk factor after stroke is atrial fibrillation. In a 1991 report, symptomatic VTE occurred in 23% of 88 patients with stroke plus atrial fibrillation, compared with 4% of 451 patients without fibrillation ($p<.001$).[33]

Leg scanning reveals that medical admissions to intensive care units are at a moderate level of risk; 13% had VT in a small study of respiratory patients[34] and 10% had VT among controls in a larger evaluation of low-dose heparin prophylaxis.[35] In a large autopsy survey of respiratory intensive care unit patients, PE was present in 27% of postmortem examinations, with 44% of cases of PE probably contributing to death.[36] Leg scanning also revealed VT in 13% of bedridden medical inpatients, 20% when pneumonia or heart disease was present, and 4% in others.[37] Among inpatients with lung disease confined to bed for longer than 3 days, the VT rate was 26%.[38III]

Table 20–3. **Various Medical Conditions With Their Associated VT or PE Rates Determined by Leg Scanning, Routine Venography, or at Autopsy**

| Condition | Diagnosis | VT (%) | PE (%) | Reference |
|---|---|---|---|---|
| Myocardial infarction | Leg scan | 37 | | Maurer et al, 1971 |
| | Leg scan | 27 | | Simmons et al, 1973 |
| | Leg scan | 29 | | Marks, Emerson, 1974 |
| | Leg scan | 17 | | Cristal et al, 1976 |
| Stroke | Venography | 31 | | Cope et al, 1973 |
| | Leg scan | 53 | | Warlow et al, 1973 |
| | Clinical/autopsy | | 9 | Warlow et al, 1973 |
| Paraplegia | Venography | 59 | | Bors et al, 1954 |
| Respiratory | Leg scan | 13 | | Moser et al, 1981 |
| | Leg scan | 26 | | Ibarra-Perez et al, 1988 |
| Medical ICU | Leg scan | 10 | | Cade, 1982 |
| Medical | Leg scan | 13 | | Kierkegaard et al, 1987 |

Little is known about the incidence and clinical importance of VTE among chronically debilitated elderly people. Consecutive autopsies from a nursing home showed some degree of PE in 34% of deaths and major PE in 27%, none of them clinically predictable.[39]

## SOME LIMITATIONS OF VT PREVENTION TRIALS IN MEDICAL PATIENTS

One severe drawback of most VT prevention trials in medical patients is their small size; few have enrolled enough subjects to indicate an effect on the incidence of extensive VT or major PE. Most have relied, instead, on convenient tests like [125]I-fibrinogen leg scanning to screen for a high-frequency substitute endpoint, asymptomatic calf VT. This approach has at least two limitations. The available evaluations of leg scanning as a diagnostic test for VT are now quite old and largely fail to meet present-day methodologic criteria, and thus there is some doubt about its accuracy.[40] In addition it remains uncertain whether prophylactic regimens that prevent calf VT detected by leg scanning will also, of necessity, prevent PE. Leg scan–based trials cannot, therefore, yield definitive information in their own right, although they do provide justification for much larger studies with a clinically important endpoint. These must, in turn, meet the challenge of diagnostic uncertainty, which is a recurring feature of autopsy correlations.

Thus, in a recent overview of seven published clinicopathologic correlations, the clinical diagnosis of PE had a very low sensitivity of 11 to 49% but a higher specificity of 89 to 99% for the presence of PE at autopsy, whereas the accuracy of a positive clinical diagnosis was 25 to 88% compared with 87 to 99.7% for a negative diagnosis.[41] As a corollary, PE is perhaps the most frequently misdiagnosed condition relative to its actual presence at autopsy.[42] One reason is that, typically, only 30% of fatal PE cause the clinical stereotype of sudden death, whereas 70% result in a gradual deterioration that is easily mistaken for progressive heart or respiratory failure.[12] Because of the variable clinical presentation, diagnostic sensitivity is especially poor among the elderly and when the clinical presentation is complicated by pneumonia.[39, 43]

## PREVENTING VENOUS THROMBOSIS IN MEDICAL PATIENTS

Logic suggests that medical illnesses should present two clearly distinct clinical settings for VT prevention and, although not enough clinical trials have been done to validate this speculation, it seems not unreasonable to make this distinction.

1. Myocardial infarction or a mild stroke, pneumonia, or other acute problems in previously well people in whom the thrombogenic stimulus happens at a clearly defined time, there is a full or near-complete functional recovery, and effective preventive therapy during the hospital admission should make a significant impact.
2. Chronically disabling heart, lung, or other major diseases when there is a longterm risk of VTE; prophylaxis limited to hospital admissions may well have a limited impact and longterm prophylaxis may be more appropriate.

## EVIDENCE CONCERNING THE VALUE OF PREVENTIVE METHODS

Clinical trials have focused on myocardial infarction, on stroke and other neurologic disability, and on general medical unit admissions. The preventive methods that have been most extensively evaluated are low doses of unfractionated heparin or low-molecular-weight heparins given subcutaneously, and oral anticoagulant therapy, although physical measures like graded pressure elastic stockings and intermittent leg compression have also been tested in patients with intracranial pathology when anticoagulants are thought to be contraindicated.

### Myocardial Infarction and Other Heart Disease

#### Myocardial Infarction

The major finding in several early clinical trials was that a moderate level of oral anticoagulant effect, corresponding to an International Normalization Ratio (INR) of 1.5 to 2.5, prevents symptoms of VT, PE, and systemic embolism after myocardial infarction.[44, 45] Investigators failed to resolve whether this can also prevent further coronary artery occlusion.

From subsequent leg scan studies, it appears that unfractionated heparin can prevent VT after myocardial infarction (MI), regardless of whether it is given by intravenous (IV) infusion in therapeutic doses, as continuous IV heparin followed by warfarin, or in low doses given subcutaneously (sc) (5,000 U sc, injected two or three times a day),[26I, 46I, 47I, 48I, 49I, 50I] although 7,500 U of heparin given subcutaneously twice daily was ineffective in one report[51III] (Table 20–4).

One intriguing observation that, it seems, has not been followed up is that 500 U of IV heparin, infused every 12 hours, may give similar results to full-dose IV heparin.[50I]

## Is VT Prevention the Only Aim of Anticoagulant Therapy After MI?

How much heparin is given after myocardial infarction and by which route depends on the intent of therapy. To prevent mural thrombus formation and a subsequent embolic stroke, heparin 5,000 U given subcutaneously 12 hourly is not enough, and the minimum appropriate heparin dose is probably 12,500 U, given subcutaneously twice daily.[52I] To prevent coronary artery reocclusion following thrombolytic therapy, the required dose may well be higher.[53]

If, on the other hand, the sole purpose is to prevent VTE after an uncomplicated myocardial infarction, heparin 5,000 U given subcutaneously 8 or 12 hourly appears to be safe and effective.

## Heart Failure and Cardiac Pacemaker Insertion

Preventing venous and systemic thromboembolism in congestive heart failure was the focus of several early oral anticoagulant trials. At that time, a high proportion of people with severe and intractable congestive heart failure developed thrombophlebitis, pulmonary embolism, and arterial embolism, and several comparisons suggested that longterm dicoumarol therapy substantially prevents these complications.[54III, 55III, 56III]

Whether these findings remain relevant is uncertain. The extent of heart failure was extreme by today's standards (80% of people in one trial had edema, 80% had hepatomegaly, and almost 60% had pleural effusion).[54III] The diagnosis of VT and PE was based on clinical criteria alone, and case-allocation to treatment or control groups was suboptimal. Nevertheless, in a recent report, there was a dramatic decrease in pulmonary or arterial embolism after the start of oral anticoagulant therapy in people with dilated cardiomyopathy, which stood in sharp contrast to a high risk of recurrence when anticoagulants were stopped.[57V]

There are reports that low-dose heparin fails to prevent VT after pacemaker insertion.[58]

## Stroke and Other Neurologic Disorders

Disabling stroke is followed by a high risk of developing VT, especially in the paralyzed leg, but most clinicians remain reluctant to prevent VTE with anticoagulants because they fear to provoke intracranial bleeding. A number of pilot studies have been done and are the subject of a 1993 overview.[59]

Table 20–4. **The Effect of Various Unfractionated Heparin Regimens on the VT Rate After MI***

| Heparin Regimen | VT (Active) n/N (%) | VT (Control) n/N (%) | % Risk Reduction | Reference |
|---|---|---|---|---|
| Continuous IV | 0/24 (0) | 7/24 (29) | 100 | Handley et al, 1972 |
| Continuous IV, then warfarin | 3/46 (7) | 10/46 (22) | 72 [92 to −3%] | Wray et al, 1973 |
| Continuous IV | 4/35 (11) | 11/37 (30) | 66 [89 to −7%] | Pitt et al, 1980 |
| 500 U IV 12 hourly | 5/36 (14) | | 57 [85 to −23%] | |
| 7,500 U bid sc | 6/26 (23) | 7/24 (29) | 19 [73 to −140%] | Handley, 1972 |
| 5,000 U tid sc | 1/38 (3) | 9/40 (23) | 90 [17 to 99%] | Gallus et al, 1973 |
| 5,000 U bid | 2/63 (3) | 11/64 (17) | 83 [23 to 96%] | Warlow et al, 1973 |
| Low-dose heparin | 2/37 (5) | 14/41 (34) | 87 [41 to 97%] | Emerson, Marks, 1977 |

*As observed in leg scan–based randomized trials. Continuous IV = therapeutic doses of intravenous heparin; bid and tid sc = subcutaneous heparin given two or three times daily. The figures in square brackets are 95% confidence intervals for the observed risk reduction, where negative risk reduction reflects an increase in risk.

## General Medical Unit Admissions

Randomized trials suggest that both low-dose heparin (5,000 U 8 hourly or 12 hourly sc) and a low-molecular-weight heparin (LMWH) given sc once a day can prevent asymptomatic calf VT in medical inpatients with heart failure or chest infection,[60] after admission to a medical ward or coronary care unit,[35] or following admission to a general medical unit in patients over 65 years old[61I] (Table 20–5).

A direct comparison between low-dose standard heparin (5,000 U sc 8 hourly) and a LMWH (from Sandoz, given once daily subcutaneously) revealed identical VT rates in general medical inpatients expected to stay in bed for longer than 7 days, as measured by clinical examination, Doppler ultrasound examination, and impedance plethysmography.[62I] Similarly, in a double-blind randomized study of medical inpatients over 65 years of age reported in an abstract by the Geriatric Enoxaparin Study Group, leg scan evidence of VT was present in 9 of 207 patients (4.4%) given 20 mg/day of a LMWH Enoxaparin, compared with VT occurring in 10 of 216 (4.6%) patients given 5,000 U sc of unfractionated heparin twice daily. Inhospital mortality and the frequency of bleeding were similar.[63]

Other preventive measures have also been evaluated to a limited extent in a further leg scan–based randomized trial in which bedridden patients with lung disease were treated with 5,000 U sc of standard heparin sc 12 hourly (VT = 1 in 39), graded compression stockings (VT = 0 in 39), elastic bandages (VT = 4 in 33), or 0.5 g aspirin 12 hourly (VT = 2 in 35); and all were associated with a significantly lower VT rate than that previously observed in an untreated but nonrandomized control group (12 in 46 = 26%).[38III]

Two studies have also examined the possible impact of VT prophylaxis on mortality in medical inpatients. In one open comparison, low doses of subcutaneous heparin appeared to reduce inhospital mortality from 10.9% in untreated controls to 7.8% ($p = .025$). However, the study design was seriously flawed. Treatment allocation was based on "odd" or "even" medical record numbers, a significant bias led to more exclusions from the heparin group (32%, compared with 25% of controls; $p < .01$) such that only 411 of 669 people eligible for heparin actually received the drug, and it is unclear if the study size was determined in advance.[64III]

The preliminary report from a large placebo-controlled, double-blind, multicenter, randomized trial in 2,474 medical patients over the age 40 years and with limited mobility found the LMWH CY 216 (Fraxiparin) had no effect on 21-day mortality. This was similar in the CY 216 and placebo groups (10.1% and 10.3%), although prophylaxis was accompanied by nonsignificant trends toward less PE at autopsy and less VTE diagnosed clinically and/or at autopsy.[65] Further interpretation awaits full publication of this report.

It is concluded that although epidemiologic surveys and autopsy studies show that more VT and PE arise in medical patients than in patients after surgery, and although most medical inpatients have one or more clinical risk factors for VTE, few large-scale trials of VT prevention have been conducted among medical patients. Recommendations about prophylaxis therefore remain relatively insecure.

Nevertheless, it seems that low-dose sc heparin, LMWHs, oral anticoagulants, graded pressure elastic stockings, and intermittent leg compression are all effective, at least for preventing asymptomatic calf vein thrombosis detected by [125]I-fibrinogen leg scanning.

Table 20–5. **Randomized Leg Scan–Based VT Prevention Trials Comparing Active Therapy (Standard Heparin or Low-Molecular-Weight Heparin) and No Treatment in General Medical Patients**

| Preventive Regimen | VT (Active) | VT (Control) | Risk Reduction [CE %] | Reference |
|---|---|---|---|---|
| Standard Heparin | | | | |
| 5,000 U 8 hourly sc | 2/50 (4%) | 13/50 (26%) | 85% | Belch et al, 1981 |
| 5,000 U 12 hourly sc | 2% | 10% | [32 to 97%] | Cade, 1982 |
| LMW Heparin | | | | |
| Enoxaparin, 60 mg sc daily | 4/132 (3%) | 12/131 (9%) | 67% [89 to −3%] | Dahan et al, 1986 |

After myocardial infarction, the choice lies between low doses of subcutaneous heparin, if the infarct is limited and uncomplicated, high doses of subcutaneous heparin (12,500 U twice daily) when there is a need to prevent mural thrombosis, and IV heparin when the drug is given to maintain coronary artery patency.

For paralysis due to stroke or spinal injury, a LMWH or heparinoid may be the preferred option, although graded pressure stockings or intermittent leg compression are also effective.

In elderly patients with heart failure, chest infection, or general immobility, the only advantage of subcutaneous LMWHs over low doses of unfractionated heparin given subcutaneously 8 or 12 hourly appears to be the convenience of once-daily injection.

A 1986 to 1989 audit of 16 short-stay hospitals in Massachusetts found that 30% of medical inpatients with more than one risk factor for VTE received prophylaxis, usually low-dose subcutaneous heparin; that preventive therapy was used most often in teaching hospitals (44%, compared with 19% elsewhere); and that a history of PE, heart failure, trauma, myocardial infarction, increasing age, obesity, and major surgery were the most frequent triggers for prophylaxis.[13] Consensus conferences have listed disabling stroke, together with active disease in immobilized patients, as indications for routine prophylaxis,[66, 67] but the audit found no association between VT prevention and the presence of stroke or immobility,[13] so that practice differed from theory. At least in the case of disabling stroke, failure to prescribe prophylaxis was most likely the result of concerns about the safety of preventive anticoagulant therapy.

A recommendation for VT prevention in all hospitalized patients, medical or surgical, with more than one risk factor for VTE[66, 67] has major cost implications,[20] and it is hard to see physicians moving away from selective prophylaxis until they see more extensive and broadly based studies of cost-effectiveness and safety in medical patients, based on large trials that measure the effects of various preventive measures on clinically significant disease (extensive VT, PE, fatal PE, and overall mortality).

# REFERENCES

1. Dismuke SE, Wagner EH: Pulmonary embolism as a cause of death. The changing mortality in hospitalized patients. JAMA 255:2039, 1986.
2. Hermann RE, Davis JH, Holden WD: Pulmonary embolism. A clinical and pathological study with emphasis on the effect of prophylactic therapy with anticoagulants. Am J Surg 102:19, 1961.
3. Lindblad B, Sternby NH, Bergqvist D: Incidence of venous thromboembolism verified by autopsy over 30 years. Br Med J 302:709, 1991.
4. Hauch O, Jorgensen LN, Khattar SC, et al: Fatal pulmonary embolism associated with surgery. An autopsy study. Acta Chir Scand 156:747, 1990.
5. Nielsen HK, Bechgaard P, Nielsen PF, et al: 178 fatal cases of pulmonary embolism in a medical department. Acta Med Scand 209:351, 1981.
6. Sperry KL, Key CR, Anderson RE: Toward a population-based assessment of death due to pulmonary embolism in New Mexico. Hum Pathol 21:159, 1990.
7. Nordstrom M, Lindblad B, Bergqvist D, Kjellstrom T: A prospective study of the incidence of deep-vein thrombosis within a defined urban population. J Intern Med 232:155, 1992.
8. Anderson FA, Wheeler HB, Goldberg RJ, et al: A population-based perspective of the hospital incidence and case-fatality rates of deep vein thrombosis and pulmonary embolism. Arch Intern Med 151: 933, 1991.
9. Morrell MT, Dunnill MS: The post-mortem incidence of pulmonary embolism in a hospital population. Br J Surg 55:347, 1968.
10. Coon WW: Risk factors in pulmonary embolism. Surg Gynecol Obstet 143:385, 1976.
11. Goldhaber Z, Savage DD, Garrison RJ, et al: Risk factors for pulmonary embolism. The Framingham study. Am J Med 74:1023, 1983.
12. Havig, O: Deep vein thrombosis and pulmonary embolism. Acta Chir Scand 478[Suppl]:1, 1977.
13. Anderson FA, Wheeler HB, Goldberg RJ, et al: Physician practice in the prevention of venous thromboembolism. Ann Intern Med 115:591, 1991.
14. Clarke CS, Otridge BW, Carney DN: Thromboembolism. A complication of weekly chemotherapy in the treatment of non-Hodgkin's lymphoma. Cancer 66:2027, 1990.
15. Levine MN, Gent M, Hirsh J, et al: The thrombogenic effect of anticancer drug therapy in women with stage II breast cancer. N Engl J Med 318:404, 1988.
16. Quinn DA, Thompson BT, Terrin ML, et al: A prospective investigation of pulmonary embolism in women and men. JAMA 268:1689, 1992.
17. Devor M, Barrett-Connor E, Renvall M, et al: Estrogen replacement therapy and the risk of venous thrombosis. Am J Med 92:275, 1992.
18. Wechsler B, Piette JC, Conard J, et al: Les thromboses veineuses profondes dans la maladie de Behçet. Presse Med 16:661, 1987.
19. Hughes GRV: The antiphospholipid syndrome: Ten years on. Lancet 342:341, 1993.
20. Anderson FA, Wheeler HB, Goldberg RJ, Hosmer DW: The prevalence of risk factors for venous thromboembolism among hospital patients. Arch Intern Med 152:1660, 1992.
21. Cristal N, Stern J, Ronen M, et al: Identifying patients at risk for thromboembolism. Use of $^{125}$I-labeled fibrinogen in patients with acute myocardial infarction. JAMA 236:2755, 1976.
22. Hayes MJ, Morris GK, Hampton JR: Lack of effect of bed rest and cigarette smoking on development of deep venous thrombosis after myocardial infarction. Br Heart J 38:981, 1976.
23. Maurer BJ, Wray R, Shillingford JP: Frequency of venous thrombosis after myocardial infarction. Lancet 2:1385, 1971.
24. Simmons AV, Sheppard MA, Cox AF: Deep venous thrombosis after myocardial infarction. Br Heart J 35:623, 1973.
25. Pandian NG, Kosowsky BD, Gurewich V: Transfemo-

ral temporary pacing and deep vein thrombosis. Am Heart J 100:847, 1980.

I 26. Emerson PA, Marks P: Preventing thromboembolism after myocardial infarction: Effect of low dose heparin or smoking. Br Med J 1:18, 1977.

27. Handley AJ, Teather D: Influence of smoking on deep vein thrombosis after myocardial infarction. Br Med J 3:230, 1974.

28. Marks P, Emerson PA: Increased incidence of deep vein thrombosis after myocardial infarction in non-smokers. Br Med J 3:232, 1974.

29. Rentsch HP: Thromboembolische Komplikationen nach akuter Hemiplegien. Schweiz Med Wochenschr 117:1853, 1987.

30. Cope C, Reyes TM, Skversky NJ: Phlebographic analysis of the incidence of thrombosis in hemiplegia. Radiology 109:581, 1973.

31. Bors E, Conrad CC, Massell TB: Venous occlusion of the lower extremities in paraplegic patients. Surg Gynecol Obstet 99:451, 1954.

32. Brach BB, Moser KM, Cedar L, et al: Venous thrombosis in acute spinal cord paralysis. J Trauma 17:289, 1977.

33. Noel P, Gregoire F, Capon A, Lehert P: Atrial fibrillation as a risk factor for deep venous thrombosis and pulmonary emboli in stroke patients. Stroke 22:760, 1991.

34. Moser KM, LeMoine JR, Nachtwey FJ, Spragg RG: Deep venous thrombosis and pulmonary embolism. Frequency in a respiratory intensive care unit. JAMA 246:1422, 1981.

35. Cade JF: High risk of the critically ill for venous thromboembolism. Crit Care Med 10:448, 1982.

36. Neuhaus A, Bentz RB, Weg JG: Pulmonary embolism in respiratory failure. Chest 73:460, 1978.

37. Kierkegaard A, Norgren L, Olsson C-G, et al: Incidence of deep vein thrombosis in bed-ridden non-surgical patients. Acta Med Scand 222:409, 1987.

III 38. Ibarra-Perez C, Lau-Cortes E, Colmenore-Zubiate S, et al: Prevalence and prevention of deep venous thrombosis of the lower extremities in high-risk pulmonary patients. Angiology 39:505, 1988.

39. Gold G, Pervez N, Kropsky B, et al: Pulmonary embolism in the nursing home population: High frequency of autopsy in female residents. Arch Gerontol Geriatr 14:117, 1992.

40. Lensing AWA, Hirsh J: 125I-fibrinogen leg scanning: reassessment of its role for the diagnosis of venous thrombosis in post-operative patients. Thromb Haemost 69:2, 1993.

41. Anderson RE, Hill RB, Key CR: The sensitivity and specificity of clinical diagnosis during five decades. Toward an understanding of necessary fallibility. JAMA 261:1610, 1989.

42. Rao MG, Rangwala AF: Diagnostic yield from 231 autopsies in a community hospital. Am J Clin Pathol 93:486, 1990.

43. Goldhaber SZ, Hennekens CH, Evans DA, et al: Factors associated with correct antemortem diagnosis of major pulmonary embolism. Am J Med 73:822, 1982.

44. Hirsh J, Dalen JE, Deykin, D, Poller L: Oral anticoagulants. Mechanism of action, clinical effectiveness, and optimal therapeutic range. Chest 102[Suppl]:312S, 1992.

45. Clagett CP, Anderson FA, Levine MN, et al: Prevention of venous thromboembolism. Chest 102 [Suppl]:391S, 1992.

I 46. Warlow C, Beattie AG, Terry G, et al: A double-blind trial of low doses of subcutaneous heparin in the prevention of deep-vein thrombosis after myocardial infarction. Lancet 1:934, 1973.

I 47. Wray R, Maurer B, Shillingford, J: Prophylactic anticoagulant therapy in the prevention of calf-vein thrombosis after myocardial infarction. N Engl J Med 288:815, 1973.

I 48. Gallus AS, Hirsh J, Tuttle RJ, et al: Small subcutaneous doses of heparin in prevention of venous thrombosis. N Engl J Med 288:545, 1973.

I 49. Handley AJ, Emerson PA, Fleming PR: Heparin in the prevention of deep vein thrombosis after myocardial infarction. Br Med J 2:436, 1972.

I 50. Pitt A, Anderson ST, Habersberger PG, Rosengarten DS: Low dose heparin in the prevention of deep vein thrombosis in patients with acute myocardial infarction. Am Heart J 99:574, 1980.

III 51 Handley AJ: Low-dose heparin after myocardial infarction. Lancet 2:623, 1972.

I 52. Turpie AGG, Robinson JG, Doyle DJ, et al: Comparison of high-dose with low-dose subcutaneous heparin to prevent left ventricular mural thrombosis in patients with acute transmural anterior myocardial infarction. N Engl J Med 320:352, 1989.

53. Eisenberg PR: Role of heparin in coronary thrombolysis. Chest 101[Suppl]:131S, 1992.

III 54. Harvey WP, Finch CA: Dicumarol prophylaxis of thromboembolic disease in congestive heart failure. N Engl J Med 242:208, 1950.

III 55. Anderson GM, Hull E: The effect of dicumarol upon the mortality and incidence of thromboembolic complications in congestive heart failure. Am Heart J 39:697, 1950.

III 56. Griffith GC, Stagnell R, Levinson DC, et al: A study of the beneficial effects of anticoagulant therapy in congestive heart failure. Ann Intern Med 37:867, 1952.

V 57. Kyrle PA, Korninger C, Gossinger H, et al: Prevention of arterial and pulmonary embolism by oral anticoagulants in patients with dilated cardiomyopathy. Thromb Haemost 54:521, 1985.

58. Munch U, Mombelli G: Unwirksamkeit der Low-dose-Heparin-Prophylaxe bei Schrittmachereinbau. Schweiz Med Wochenschr 110:1125, 1980.

59. Sandercock PAG, van den Belt AGM, Lindley RI, Slattery J: Antithrombotic therapy in acute ischemic stroke: An overview of the completed randomised trials. J Neurol Neurosurg Psychiatry 56:17, 1993.

60. Belch JJ, Lowe GDO, Ward AG, et al: Prevention of deep vein thrombosis in medical patients by low-dose heparin. Scot Med J 26:115, 1981.

I 61. Dahan R, Houlbert D, Caulin C, et al: Prevention of deep vein thrombosis in elderly medical in-patients by a low-molecular weight heparin: A randomized double-blind trial. Haemostasis 16:159, 1986.

I 62. Harenberg J, Kallenbach B, Martin U, et al: Randomized controlled study of heparin and low molecular weight heparin for prevention of deep-vein thrombosis in medical patients. Thromb Res 59:639, 1990.

63. Mottier D: Prophylaxis of deep vein thrombosis in medical geriatric patients. Thromb Haemost 69 [Suppl]:1115, 1993.

III 64. Halkin H, Goldberg J, Modan M, Modan B: Reduction of mortality in general medical in-patients by low-dose heparin prophylaxis. Ann Intern Med 96:561, 1982.

65. Caulin C: The influence of CY 216 administration on hospital mortality of general medical in-patients. International collaborative double-blind study: Methods and preliminary results. In Breddin K,

Fareed J, Samama M (eds): Fraxiparine. First International Symposium. Analytical and Structural Data Pharmacology, Clinical trials. Stuttgart-New York; Schattauer, 1989, pp 147–152.

66. Lowe GDO, Greer IA, Dewar EP, et al: Risk of and prophylaxis for venous thromboembolism in hospital patients. Br Med J 305:567, 1992.

67. Nicolaides AN, Arcelus J, Belcaro G, et al: Prevention of venous thromboembolism. European consensus statement. Int Angiol 11:151, 1992.

# Chapter 21

# Cost-Effectiveness of Preventing Postoperative Deep Vein Thrombosis

David Bergqvist, Björn Lindgren, and Thomas Mätzsch

Economic evaluation of health care programs involves estimation of at least three types of consequences, namely, changes in resource utilization, productive capacity, and state of health, respectively. The first type, the *direct* costs and benefits, include changes in the utilization of personnel, equipment, and other health care inputs. The second type, the *indirect* costs and benefits, involve changes in the production capacity of the economy resulting from illness or absence of illness among individuals. The third type, the *intangible* costs and benefits, includes perhaps the most important consequences—changes in individual health status, quality of life, wellbeing, and the like.[1]

## ECONOMIC EVALUATION TECHNIQUES

At least four types of economic evaluation techniques are available; all belong to the cost-benefit approach. They include (1) cost (or cost minimization) analysis, (2) cost-effectiveness analysis, (3) cost-utility analysis, and (4) cost-benefit analysis.

The four different but related economic evaluation techniques are listed in order of increasing complexity and sophistication. The rule of thumb is that evaluators use the simplest technique (i.e. the least resource-consuming) that can still produce the information sufficient for making a specific decision; using a more sophisticated technique certainly adds more information, but the additional information would have no influence on the decision to be taken. In the cost-minimization analysis, the simplest economic evaluation technique available, the efficiency evaluation is essentially a search for the

least-cost alternative. The outcomes of the options under consideration are identical (or assumed to be identical) in all relevant respects; therefore, no specific valuation of outcomes is made. When health care programs do differ in costs as well as in their abilities to achieve the desired outcomes, a simple cost minimization is not sufficient as the basis for decision-making.

In cost-effectiveness analysis, costs are related to a single common effect such as lifeyears gained, and the efficiency criterion is to choose options on the basis of comparisons of costs per lifeyears gained. When health care programs do not produce some single common effect but rather produce different or multiple effects, a more sophisticated outcome measure must be used. In cost-utility analysis, different health care programs are compared according to their costs per quality-adjusted lifeyears gained. In cost-benefit analysis, finally, both costs and benefits are measured in monetary terms, the benefits ideally reflecting people's willingness to pay for the health care programs under study. This kind of analysis is the most general one of the four economic evaluation techniques available. As such, it can answer the questions of efficient resource allocations beyond those confined to the health care sector; the cost-benefit analysis also enables comparisons, at least in principle, with any other possible resource use in the community (e.g., regarding housing, food, education, culture, and military defense).

Evaluation must always rely on a number of assumptions, because complete knowledge and perfect data rarely exist. Insufficient knowledge and uncertainty of outcome, to a certain extent, can be considered through the use of sensitivity analysis. By reperforming the analysis with a range of alternative values of the variables representing resource inputs and outcomes, respectively, of each strategy, the robustness of the original results can be tested.

## ECONOMIC EVALUATION OF DEEP VEIN THROMBOSIS PROPHYLAXIS

### Identification of Prophylaxis Options for Evaluation

General cost evaluation principles will be applied to data concerning postoperative deep vein thrombosis. Although prophylaxis against postoperative venous thromboembolism has increasingly been accepted among surgeons, there is still reluctance to employ prophylaxis among a few.[2] Motivations not to use prophylaxis may vary, but usually motivations include a fear of side effects or a concern that prophylaxis is too expensive. Looking only at the costs of prophylactic medication is a serious oversimplification, however. When dealing with thromboprophylaxis, a number of treatment choices can be made, but further discussion will be restricted to just a few options. The cost-minimization technique will be used, in which no measurements of improvement in quality of life or gained years of life through prevention of fatal pulmonary embolism are considered. This latter factor, however, is important, and it is today possible to reduce mortality in pulmonary embolism.[3–5]

This chapter outlines the costs of various prophylactic options against postoperative thromboembolism. The objective is to examine whether prophylaxis reduces the costs of treating thromboses more than it adds to the total costs of treating the patient, without increasing side effects and complications from prophylaxis. These factors are compared with the cost and number of thromboses avoided. Two patient categories are studied, one in a moderate-risk

situation (elective general abdominal surgery) and one in a high-risk situation (elective hip arthroplasty). Four alternative strategies are compared for each patient category, including (1) no prophylaxis but treatment if clinical thromboembolic complications occur, (2) no prophylaxis but general surveillance with the fibrinogen uptake test and treatment of patients positive for thrombosis, (3) general prophylaxis with unfractionated standard low-dose heparin, and (4) general prophylaxis with low-molecular-weight heparin.

Basic data and assumptions on which the evaluation is based are presented in Table 21–1. The data in the table are based on a synthesis from several sources.[4, 6–8]

Basic data on the costs of surveillance test, prophylaxis, and treatment are shown in Table 21–2. The estimates of treatment costs were based on patient data from a randomized controlled trial on thromboprophylaxis.[9] A wide variation was present between patients treated for thrombosis and those with hemorrhagic complications due to prophylaxis. The most severe cases required additional bed-days, while the milder cases of thrombosis, for instance, did not require very much more than a venogram to verify the clinical diagnosis. The estimate of the costs of treating a patient with pulmonary embolism (in addition to the costs of the primary illness) was based on just two observations, both with very similar total costs, however. Based on previous studies, the total number of thromboembolisms was assumed to consist of 86% deep vein thrombosis and 14% pulmonary embolism. Regarding the costs of prophylactic medication, the mean was taken for the available substances on the market in Sweden. Four low-molecular-weight heparins are available, with a range of 40% in cost between the most expensive and the cheapest one. The doses recommended by the manufacturers were used in

Table 21–1. **Basic Data on Thromboembolism and Bleeding**

| | General Surgery | | | Hip Surgery | | |
| --- | --- | --- | --- | --- | --- | --- |
| | No Prophylaxis | UFH | LMWH | No Prophylaxis | UFH | LMWH |
| Frequency of thromboembolism | | | | | | |
|   Clinically detected | 0.115 | 0.011 | 0.010 | 0.232 | 0.066 | 0.048 |
|   FUT | 0.290 | 0.057 | 0.041 | 0.590 | 0.333 | 0.195 |
| Frequency of bleeding complications | | | | | | |
|   Prophylaxis | —— | 0.048 | 0.036 | —— | 0.048 | 0.036 |
|   Therapy | 0.11 | 0.11 | 0.11 | 0.11 | 0.11 | 0.11 |

FUT = fibrinogen uptake test; UFH = low-dose unfractionated heparin; LMWH = low-molecular-weight heparin.

Table 21–2. **Basic Data on the Costs of Surveillance Test, Prophylaxis and Treatment**

| | Mean | Range | Standard Deviation |
|---|---|---|---|
| Surveillance test | | | |
| Fibrinogen uptake test | 800 | * | * |
| Prophylaxis | | | |
| General surgery | | | |
| Low-dose unfractionated heparin | 140 | 135–145 | * |
| Low-molecular-weight heparin | 185 | 165–230 | * |
| Hip surgery | | | |
| Low-dose unfractionated heparin | 200 | 190–210 | * |
| Low-molecular-weight heparin | 265 | 235–330 | * |
| Treatment† | | | |
| Deep vein thrombosis (n = 13) | 7,765 | 3,865–34,090 | 9,580 |
| Pulmonary embolism (n = 2) | 65,080 | 64,280–65,880 | 1,125 |
| Bleeding complications due to prophylaxis (n = 9) | 8,545 | 575–26,085 | 8,700 |

*Not applicable.
†Treatment costs were estimated on the basis of the resource use of 24 patients included in a randomized control trial.[6]
Costs are expressed in SEK (Swedish crowns) and at the 1993 level of costs. When this was written (September 1993), the Swedish crown was floating; at that time SEK 100 were approximately equivalent to $12.6 or £8.2.

the calculations. The duration of prophylaxis was set to 7 days for patients after abdominal surgery and 10 days for patients after hip surgery. Low-dose heparin was given twice daily, and low-molecular-weight heparin was given once daily.

## Results of Cost Evaluation

In Tables 21–3 and 21–4, the estimated costs per patient in general surgery and hip arthroplasty are given for the various situations under study. To reach these figures, the frequencies and costs from Tables 21–1 and 21–2 were used. In both general abdominal and elective hip surgery, general prophylaxis is the least-cost alternative. In addition, using low-molecular-weight heparin is a less expensive strategy than using unfractionated low-dose heparin.

As indicated above, the costs of low-molecular-weight heparins were based on the mean price of those substances in Sweden. If the cheapest or the most expensive substance, respectively, always was used, the total expected costs per patient in the general prophylaxis strategy are either SEK 645 or SEK 710 for general surgery, and either SEK 1,360 or SEK 1,455 for hip arthroplasty.

### Sensitivity Analysis of Results

Although based on the results of prospective studies, several assumptions had to be made in this study. In addition, inherent uncertainties were present in the data. Therefore, a sensitivity analysis was performed to test the robustness of the results. Certain variables were altered one at a time, holding all others constant. Variables

Table 21–3. **Expected Cost Per Patient in Three Alternative Strategies Regarding the Risk of Thrombosis in General Surgery —Total and Distribution by Type of Cost (SEK)**

| | Total costs per patient | Surveillance test | Prophylaxis | Thromboembolism | Bleeding due to prophylaxis |
|---|---|---|---|---|---|
| No prophylaxis | 1,950 | 0 | 0 | 1,950 | 0 |
| Selective treatment after surveillance | 5,710 | 800 | 0 | 4,910 | 0 |
| General prophylaxis | | | | | |
| UFH | 735 | 0 | 140 | 185 | 410 |
| LMWH | 665 | 0 | 185 | 170 | 310 |

Table 21–4. **Expected Cost Per Patient in Three Alternative Strategies Regarding the Risk of Thrombosis in Hip Surgery. Total and Distribution by Type of Cost (SEK)**

| | Total costs per patient | Surveillance test | Prophylaxis | Thromboembolism | Bleeding due to prophylaxis |
|---|---|---|---|---|---|
| No prophylaxis | 3,930 | 0 | 0 | 3,930 | 0 |
| Selective treatment after surveillance | 10,790 | 800 | 0 | 9,990 | 0 |
| General prophylaxis | | | | | |
| UFH | 1,730 | 0 | 200 | 1,120 | 410 |
| LMWH | 1,390 | 0 | 265 | 815 | 310 |

included prophylactic effect, initial frequencies of thrombosis without prophylaxis, treatment costs for thromboembolism, treatment costs for hemorrhage complications due to prophylaxis, and prices of the low-molecular-weight heparins. For each variable, the search is for the breakeven point (i.e., for the values of the variables that make the alternatives under consideration equally expensive).

COST OF PROPHYLAXIS. In the base case analysis, the prophylactic effects were assumed to be 90% in general surgery, regardless of prophylactic substance, and 72% for low-dose unfractionated heparin (UFH) and 79% for low-molecular-weight heparin (LMWT), respectively, in hip arthroplasty. To break even, the prophylactic effect did not have to be larger than 29%, using UFH, or 24%, using LMWT, in general surgery. The corresponding numbers in hip arthroplasty would have been 32%, for either substance. Thus, general prophylaxis would be the least-cost alternative, even if the prophylactic effect were considerably lower.

INITIAL FREQUENCY OF THROMBOEMBOLISM. The initial frequency of thromboembolism in general surgery in the absence of prophylaxis was assumed to be 11.5% in the base case. With UFH as the prophylactic substance, only 3.6% would be sufficient for the general prophylaxis strategy to break even with the no-prophylaxis alternative; LMWH would require just 3.2%. In hip arthroplasty, the initial frequency was assumed to be 23.2% in the base case. UFH would, however, just require 5.0% and LMWH 4.3% to break even. Hence, general prophylaxis is the least-cost alternative, even if the initial frequencies of thromboembolism were considerably lower.

COST OF TREATMENT. In the base case analysis, the costs of treating thromboembolism were assumed to be SEK 16,935, the figure based on the costs reproduced in Table 21–2 and the assumption that 86% of these patients had deep vein thrombosis, whereas the remaining 14% had pulmonary embolism. Wide differences were apparent in costs among patients, and thus the relative importance of the cost figure used in the base case should be examined. When examined, it was found that the cost of one thromboembolic event could not be higher than SEK 4,715 for the no-prophylaxis strategy to be just as inexpensive as the general prophylaxis strategy in general surgery (using LMWH); in hip surgery, the corresponding figure was SEK 3,125. Both numbers seem to be unrealistically low at the present time.

COST OF HEMORRHAGIC COMPLICATIONS. The effect of varying the assumption of the costs of hemorrhagic complications was examined. In the base case, following the results of a randomized clinical trial, it was assumed that each hemorrhagic complication due to prophylaxis cost SEK 8,700. According to our sensitivity analysis, this figure had to be raised by more than 400% to SEK 44,305, for no prophylaxis to break even with general prophylaxis in general surgery (using LMWH): in hip arthroplasty, the corresponding figure would have to be SEK 79,165. It can be safely concluded that the results were very stable regarding changes in this variable.

PRICE OF PROPHYLAXIS SUBSTANCES. It was found that if the least expensive LMWH could reduce the frequency of thromboembolism from 23.2 to 4.8% in hip surgery, the most expensive substance would have to be able to reduce the frequency of thromboembolism by another 0.55 percentage points, to 4.25% to be as cost-effective as the least expensive substance.

EFFECT OF MULTIPLE VARIABLES. The effects of altering four of the variables mentioned earlier at the same time by as much as 25% were examined (i.e., the initial frequency of thromboembolism was assumed to be reduced from 11.5 to 8.6%, the prophylactic effect reduced from 90 to 67.5%, the costs of treating thromboembolism decreased from SEK 16,935 to SEK 12,700, and the costs for treating hemorrhagic complications due to prophylaxis increased from SEK 8,700 to SEK 10,875). For general surgery, using LMWH as the prophylactic substance, the expected costs per patient would then be SEK 1,092 for the no-prophylaxis strategy and SEK 932 for the general prophylaxis alternative. Even if the difference in the estimated expected costs between the no-prophylaxis and the general prophylaxis strategy dropped, the general prophylaxis strategy would still be roughly 15% cheaper than no prophylaxis, despite the drastic changes in assumptions made. The results for UFH and hip arthroplasty were similarly stable.

## INTERPRETATION OF THE COST EVALUATION STUDY OF THROMBOSIS

There are by now several studies in which the cost-effectiveness of thromboprophylaxis have been analyzed, all showing that general prophylaxis is a more cost-effective alternative than no prophylaxis.[6, 10–20]

General prophylaxis in most of these studies has meant prophylaxis to all patients above a certain critical age, usually 40 to 45 years. Thus, it has been shown repeatedly that with prophylaxis there are monetary savings to be made. To this effect must be added the reduction in frequency of fatal pulmonary embolism.[3, 4, 5] Although the frequency of the post-thrombotic syndrome after surgery is probably low,[21] the inclusion of costs related to this disease would make general prophylaxis a still more cost-effective alternative.

In this study, surveillance with the fibrinogen uptake test was used as one diagnostic alternative, and it always proved to be the highest cost alternative. It may be argued that the fibrinogen uptake test is not an optimal diagnostic method in patients undergoing hip surgery, but for the purpose of our study and this discussion, this drawback is of less importance. Surveillance with venography would have given a similar frequency of deep vein thrombosis, and bilateral venography certainly is more expensive than the fibrinogen uptake test. However, the fibrinogen uptake test is on its way out of the market because of the potential of transmitting viral diseases (hepatitis, HIV). Using duplex ultrasonography would probably give a lower frequency of deep vein thrombosis (missing the distal thrombosis), but again the costs of the test (SEK 620) do not make routine surveillance with this method a cost-effective alternative.

When comparing unfractionated low-dose heparin and low-molecular-weight heparin, the advantage of once-daily administration has not been taken into consideration because this simpler routine would hardly reduce the necessary number of nurses, thereby saving money. Nonetheless, less frequent injections are advantageous both for the patients and the nursing staff.

There are indications that low-molecular-weight heparins may be more effective than low-dose heparin in reducing the frequency of proximal thrombosis. This would again contribute to the improved cost-effectiveness of low-molecular-weight heparins.

In this chapter, a cost-minimization exercise was made. It is important to remember that, in addition to the cost savings to be obtained, both unfractionated low-dose heparin and low-molecular-weight heparin prophylaxis do decrease the frequency of fatal pulmonary embolism, thus saving lives.[3–5] A cost-utility approach taking quality of life into account, is more complex than the presented approach. Although infrequent after postoperative thrombosis,[21] the development of a post-thrombotic syndrome would only have made the cost-effectiveness even greater. Besides being rare, the time to develop post-thrombotic venous insufficiency is long—in the order of 5 to 10 years. However, in regard to venous ulceration, the quality of life of the patients is diminished. Nurses were required to dress the wounds 1,100 times per week per 100,000 in a Swedish study population.[22] The cost for personnel alone for this undertaking is around SEK 500 million per year in Sweden (8.5 million inhabitants). The cost of pain and suffering for the patient is certainly difficult to quantify. However, because such long-term effects were not included in this analysis, no future costs (or benefits) were discounted.

The sensitivity analysis showed that the study results were very robust. Even drastic changes in the assumptions did not alter the conclusion. However, the possible treatment option of deep vein thrombosis with a single daily injection of low-molecular-weight heparin on an ambulant basis, which could well be reality in the near future, may alter the outcome of the calculations. The cost-effectiveness of preventing postoperative deep vein thrombosis then has to be examined anew.

In the meantime, it seems fair to conclude from this study and those of others[6, 10–20] that prophylaxis against postoperative thromboembolism belongs to a fairly unique medical technology that saves lives at the same time as it saves health care money.

# REFERENCES

1. Drummond MF, Stoddart GL, Torrance GW: Methods for the economic evaluation of health care programmes. Oxford, Oxford University Press. 1987.
2. Bergqvist D: Prophylaxis against postoperative venous thromboembolism: A survey of surveys. Thromb Haemorrh Disord 2:69–67, 1990.
3. Collins R, Scrimgeour A, Yusuf S, et al: Reduction in fatal pulmonary embolism and venous thrombosis by perioperative administration of subcutaneous heparin. N Engl J Med 318:1162–1173, 1988.
4. Bergqvist D: Review of clinical trials of low molecular weight heparins. Eur J Surg 158:67–78, 1992.
5. Bergqvist D: Dextran. In Goldhaber S (ed): Prevention of Venous Thromboembolism. New York, Marcel Dekker, 1992, pp 167–215.
6. Bergqvist D, Jendteg S, Lindgren B, et al: The economics of general thromboembolic prophylaxis. World J Surg 12:349–355, 1988.
7. Kakkar VV, Cohen AT, Edmonson RA, et al: Low molecular weight versus standard heparin for prevention of venous thromboembolism after major abdominal surgery. Lancet 341:259, 1993.
8. Jørgensen LN, Wille-Jørgensen P, Hauch O: Prophylaxis of postoperative thromboembolism with low molecular weight heparins. Br J Surg 80:689, 1993.
9. Bergqvist D, Mätzsch T, Burmark US, et al: Low molecular weight heparin given the evening before surgery compared with conventional low dose heparin in the prevention of thrombosis after elective general abdominal surgery. Br J Surg 75:888, 1988.
10. Salzman EW, Davies GC: Prophylaxis of venous thromboembolism. Analysis of cost-effectiveness. Ann Surg 191:207–216, 1980.
11. Bergqvist D, Ousbäck L: Profylax eller rutinmässig screening av postoperativ thromboembolism. Läkartidn 79:3302–3306, 1982.
12. Hull RD, Hirsh J, Sacket DL, et al: Cost-effectiveness of primary and secondary prevention of fatal pulmonary embolism in high risk surgical patients. Can Med Assoc J 127:990–992, 1982.
13. Pfyl T, Gruber UF: Kosten-Nutzen-Analyse der Thromboembolieprophylaxe in der Chirurgie. Akt Chir 18:180–183, 1983.
14. Hamilton CW, Romankiewicz JA: Impact of prophylactic therapy for postoperative thromboembolism on prospective payment. Pharmacotherapy 6:23S–27S, 1986.
15. Wille-Jørgensen P, Hauch O: Tromboemboliprofylakse i Danmark. Ugeskr Læger 149:1811–1814, 1987.
16. Paiement GD, Bell D, Wessinger SJ, et al: New advances in the prevention, diagnosis, and cost effectiveness of venous thromboembolic disease in patients with total hip replacement. In Paiement D, Braod RA (eds): The Hip. St Louis, CV Mosby, 1987.
17. Oster G, Tuden RL, Colditz GA: A cost-effectiveness analysis of prophylaxis against deep-vein thrombosis in major orthopaedic surgery. JAMA 257:203–208, 1987.
18. Hillson SD, Rich EC: Two strategies for prophylaxis of fatal postoperative pulmonary embolism. Cost-effectiveness analysis. Intl J Technology Assessment in Health Care 6:470–479, 1990.
19. Hauch O, Khattar SC, Jørgensen LN: Cost-benefit analysis of prophylaxis against deep vein thrombosis in surgery. Semin Thromb Hemost 17[Suppl 3]:280–283, 1991.
20. Borris L, Lassen M: Sundheldsudgifter kan reduceres ved brug af thromboseprofylakse. Tidskrift for danske sygehuse 9:420–422, 1991.
21. Lindhagen A, Bergqvist D, Hallböök T: Deep venous insufficiency after post-operative thrombosis diagnosed with $^{125}$I-labelled fibrinogen uptake test. Br J Surg 71:511, 1984.
22. Nelzen O, Bergqvist D, Lindhagen A: Venous and non-venous leg ulcers: Clinical history and appearance in a population study. Br J Surg 81:182–187, 1994.

# PART TWO

# DIAGNOSIS OF VENOUS THROMBOEMBOLISM

## Chapter 22

## Clinical Features of Deep Venous Thrombosis and Pulmonary Embolism

Paul D. Stein

Deep venous thrombosis is common, yet often undiagnosed. Among 27 patients at autopsy, 44% had unsuspected venous thrombosis involving veins of the calves and/or thighs.[1] The clinical examination alone for deep venous thrombosis is unsatisfactory.[2] Among patients with clinically suspected deep venous thrombosis, based on the presence of pain, tenderness, or swelling, and excluding those with obvious superficial phlebitis or other causes of these signs (torn calf muscle, hematoma, ruptured Achilles tendon, cellulitis, congestive heart failure, and Baker's cyst), venography confirmed the diagnosis in 42% and excluded the diagnosis in 58%[3] This result lent further support to the conclusion that the clinical diagnosis of venous thrombosis is insensitive and nonspecific.[4]

### SIGNS OF VENOUS THROMBOSIS

Swelling of the thigh implies obstruction of the iliofemoral system.[5] Swelling of the calf, if the thigh measurements are equal, implies at least obstruction of the femoral and popliteal system. Although swelling has been reported in 100% of patients with iliofemoral vein thrombosis and 86% of patients with femoral vein thrombosis,[6] and local tenderness also correlated well with sites of venous thrombosis,[6] these findings seem not to have been confirmed with subsequent testing.[2, 3]

Homans' sign is present when active and/or passive dorsiflexion of the foot is associated with (1) pain, (2) incomplete dorsiflexion (with equal pressure applied) to prevent pain, or (3) flexion of the knee to release tension in the posterior muscles with dorsiflexion.[7] If the Homans' sign was considered positive with the slightest irritability of the posterior muscles, the test was positive in 44 to 66% of patients with venous thrombosis.[6] Inflation of a blood pressure cuff around the calf to 150 mm Hg or less,[8] or around the thigh to 40 mm Hg[9] are other tests that have been recommended for an objective assessment of tenderness, but these tests have not been shown to be more helpful than assessment of direct tenderness or leg circumference.[6]

234

## CLINICAL EVIDENCE OF VENOUS THROMBOSIS IN PATIENTS WITH PULMONARY EMBOLISM

In 80% or more of patients with pulmonary embolism (PE), the thromboemboli originate in the veins of the lower extremities.[10–13] Even so, among patients with massive or submassive PE, signs of thrombophlebitis were present in only 33% of patients.[14] Among patients with mild PE as well as those with severe PE, the frequency of clinically apparent venous thrombosis was only 15%,[15] and among those with no prior cardiopulmonary disease it was 11%.[16] Among patients with no prior cardiopulmonary disease, symptoms of leg pain (26%) were more frequent than one or more signs of venous thrombosis (edema, erythema, tenderness, palpable cord, or Homans' sign) (11%). A Homans' sign was present in only 4%.[16] Objective tests of the legs were not part of the protocol in this study.[17]

It has been suggested that if a patient has clinical features compatible with venous thrombosis, further investigation is required, with the possible exception of occasional patients with phlegmasia cerulea dolens.[4] If clinical examination shows an alternative diagnosis, such as arthritis or cellulitis, investigation for venous thrombosis may not be necessary.

## CLINICAL DIAGNOSIS OF PULMONARY EMBOLISM

Regarding the clinical manifestations of PE, particularly useful information has been derived from patients with no associated or prior cardiopulmonary disease, which eliminates confounding manifestations associated with prior illness. In the following paragraphs, clinical manifestations are described both in patients with and those without prior cardiopulmonary disease.

## SYNDROMES OF ACUTE PULMONARY EMBOLISM

Pulmonary embolism may present as (1) pulmonary hemorrhage or infarction associated with pleuritic pain or hemoptysis: (2) circulatory collapse associated with arrhythmia or shock: and (3) isolated dyspnea, not complicated by pleuritic pain, hemoptysis, or circulatory collapse. The syndrome of pulmonary hemorrhage or infarction is the most frequent (or perhaps most frequently diagnosed).[16, 18] Among all patients, regardless of associated cardiopul-

monary disease, the pulmonary hemorrhage/infarction syndrome occurred in 59%.[15] Circulatory collapse occurred in 9% of patients with PE, and the syndrome of isolated dyspnea (not accompanied by pulmonary infarction or circulatory collapse) occurred in 27%.[15, 16] Circulatory collapse, among patients with no prior cardiopulmonary disease in the Prospective Investigation of Pulmonary Embolism Diagnosis (PIOPED) (8%), was less frequent than that reported among such patients in the Urokinase Pulmonary Embolism Trial and the Urokinase-Streptokinase Embolism Trial (19%).[16, 18] This may reflect the selection of more severely ill patients in the Urokinase Pulmonary Embolism Trial and the Urokinase-Streptokinase Embolism Trial. In these trials, patients were selected for study only if the PE was massive or submassive.[19, 20]

### Predisposing Factors

More than half of patients with PE were immobilized within 3 months of the acute episode. The usual cause of immobilization was recent surgery. Among the patients immobilized, 65% were immobilized for 2 weeks or less and 7% were immobilized only 1 or 2 days.[16] Short-duration immobilization, therefore, is an important predisposing factor for PE.

Coronary heart disease was present in 20% of patients with acute PE.[15] Among patients with coronary heart disease, recent myocardial infarction seemed to predispose to PE more than heart failure.[15] Lung disease (asthma, chronic obstructive pulmonary disease, or interstitial lung disease) was associated with PE in 16%.

### Symptoms of Acute Pulmonary Embolism

Among patients with PE and no prior cardiac or pulmonary disease, dyspnea was the most common symptom, occurring in 73%.[16] Pleuritic pain (66%) occurred more often than hemoptysis (13%). Hemoptysis was characterized as blood-streaked, blood-tinged, or pure blood. Cough was common (37%); was sometimes nonproductive; and was sometimes productive of clear, bloody or occasionally purulent sputum. Purulent sputum was present in 7%.

Angina-like chest pain occurred in only 4% with PE and no prior cardiopulmonary disease.[16] Pain was usually located in the anterior chest, and it did not radiate to either arm or to the jaw in any of the patients with PE. The frequency of the various symptoms associated with PE was comparable in patients who had prior cardiopulmonary disease.[15]

## Signs of Acute Pulmonary Embolism

Among patients with no prior cardiac or pulmonary disease, tachypnea (respiratory rate ≥20/minute) was the most common sign of acute PE, occurring in 70%.[16] Tachycardia (heart rate >100/minute) occurred in 30% of patients with PE. The pulmonary component of the second sound was accentuated in 23% of patients with PE. A right ventricular lift, third heart sound, or pleural friction rub was uncommon. Each occurred in 4% or fewer with PE and no prior cardiopulmonary disease. The frequency of signs of PE was comparable among patients who had prior cardiopulmonary disease.[15]

Rales (crackles) were heard in 51% with no prior cardiopulmonary disease. Most patients with PE who had rales (88% of patients with rales) had pulmonary parenchymal abnormalities, atelectasis, or a pleural effusion on the chest radiograph.[16] Rales, therefore, appeared to be caused by the effects of pulmonary infarction or atelectasis.

Among patients with no prior cardiopulmonary disease who had either massive or submassive PE, the most severe PE, as assessed by pulmonary arteriography, occurred in patients with shock or syncope.[18] In patients with uncomplicated dyspnea, the severity of PE was almost as great. Patients with the pulmonary hemorrhage/infarction syndrome had the least severe PE.[18]

Syncope was more frequent in patients with massive PE than submassive PE (17% versus 4%).[18] Apprehension, diaphoresis, and tachypnea were also more frequent with massive PE. However, patients with massive PE, in comparison with patients with submassive PE, less frequently had pleuritic pain (67% versus 85%) or a pleural friction rub (14% versus 26%). Among all patients, regardless of the presence or absence of prior cardiopulmonary disease, syncope, accentuated pulmonary component of the second sound, third or fourth heart sound ($S_3$ or $S_4$), and cyanosis were more frequent among patients with massive PE than those with submassive PE.[14] Pleuritic pain, however, was less frequent among patients with massive PE than those with submassive PE.

## Patients With Chronic Obstructive Pulmonary Disease

In spite of the potential difficulty in reaching a clinical diagnosis in patients with chronic obstructive pulmonary disease (COPD), the clinical assessment by physicians, when they were confident that PE was present or confident that it was absent, was as likely to be correct among patients with COPD as among patients with no prior cardiopulmonary disease.[16, 21] The percentage of uncertain clinical diagnoses, surprisingly, was also similar in the assessment of patients with COPD and patients with no prior cardiopulmonary disease.[16, 21]

## Elderly Patients

Contrary to younger age groups, 11% of patients 70 years old or older were identified on the basis of unexplained radiographic findings of atelectasis, pleural effusion, or pleural-based opacities.[22] Elderly patients (≥70 years) with no associated cardiopulmonary disease showed no significant difference of signs, symptoms, chest radiographic, and most electrocardiographic (ECG) manifestations relative to young patients (<40 years) or patients in their middle years (ages 40–69).[22]

## Plain Chest Radiograph

The plain chest radiograph was normal in only 16% of patients with PE and no prior cardiac or pulmonary disease.[16] Atelectasis or pulmonary parenchymal abnormalities were the most common radiographic abnormalities in 68%. A pleural effusion occurred in 48%. Most of these patients with a pleural effusion (86%) showed only blunting of the costophrenic angle. Pleural-based opacities occurred in 35% of patients with PE. An elevated diaphragm is an easily recognized sign in patients with PE, which occurred in 24%, and in patients with massive or submassive PE, it occurred even more frequently (46%).[23] Decreased pulmonary vascularity and a prominent central pulmonary artery occurred in 21% and 15%, respectively.

Interstitial edema occurred in 3% of patients with pulmonary embolism and no prior cardiopulmonary disease.[16] Alveolar pulmonary edema occurred in only 1% of patients with PE and no prior cardiopulmonary disease. None of the radiographic abnormalities was specific for PE. Even the Westermark sign (prominent central pulmonary artery with decreased pulmonary vascularity), observed in only 7% of patients with PE, was not specific.[16] Among patients with no prior cardiopulmonary disease, the lowest pulmonary artery mean pressures were in patients with a normal chest radiograph.[24] The highest pulmonary artery mean pressures, among patients with no prior cardiopulmonary disease, were in patients with a prominent central pulmonary artery or cardiomegaly.[24]

## Combinations of Clinical Characteristics

Combinations of clinical characteristics are useful in the assessment of PE. Patients were rarely diagnosed if these clinical characteristics were absent. Dyspnea or tachypnea (respiratory rate ≥20/minute) was present in 91%.[25] Dyspnea or tachypnea or pleuritic pain was present in 97%. Dyspnea or tachypnea or pleuritic pain or radiographic evidence of atelectasis or a parenchymal abnormality was present in 99%. An additional 1% had an unexplained low $PaO_2$.

## Electrocardiogram

Among patients with no prior cardiopulmonary disease, the ECG in patients with PE showed definite abnormalities, which, however, were nonspecific.[16, 26] The most frequent abnormality was nonspecific change of the ST segment or T wave (49%).[16] Left axis deviation (left anterior hemiblock) occurred as often or more often than right axis deviation and, therefore, should not lead to an exclusion of the clinical diagnosis of pulmonary embolism.[16, 26–28] Right atrial enlargement (P pulmonale), right ventricular hypertrophy, right axis deviation and right bundle branch block each occurred in 6% or fewer patients with PE.[16]

The majority of patients (90% with no prior cardiopulmonary disease) were in sinus rhythm.[16] Atrial flutter occurred in 1%, and atrial fibrillation occurred in 4%. Atrial premature contractions were present in 4%, and ventricular premature contractions were also present in 4%.

## Partial Pressure of Oxygen in Arterial Blood

The partial pressure of oxygen in arterial blood ($PaO_2$) in patients with acute PE has been shown to be a helpful adjunct in the diagnostic assessment.[29] It was, however, normal (≥80 mm Hg) in 26% of patients with PE who had no prior cardiopulmonary disease and were able to have their blood gases measured while they were on room air.[16] Even some patients with submassive or massive PE had a normal $PaO_2$.[14]

## Alveolar Arterial Oxygen Gradient

A normal alveolar-arterial oxygen gradient does not exclude the diagnosis of PE.[16, 30]

Among patients with PE and no associated cardiopulmonary disease, the gradient was 10 mm Hg or less in 8% of patients and 11 to 20 mm Hg in 6% of patients.[16] The average alveolar arterial oxygen gradient in these patients was $37 \pm 17$ mm Hg (mean ± standard deviation).

## D-dimers

D-dimers are degradation products of fibrin that are present after stabilization of the fibrin network and subsequent lysis by plasmin.[31] They increase in any circumstance that may result in thrombus formation and lysis. Studies, not yet fully confirmed, suggest that PE is unlikely if plasma D-dimers are lower than 500 μg/l.[32] D-dimers, therefore, potentially may be useful in excluding PE. An elevated level of D-dimers (>500 μg/l), however, is not specific and, therefore, is not very useful for making a diagnosis of PE.

## Computer-based Pattern Recognition

A potential has been shown for computer-based pattern recognition to assist physicians who are inexperienced with PE in reaching a clinical impression.[33] Neural network computer-based pattern recognition predicted the clinical likelihood of PE with an accuracy comparable to that of experienced physicians.[33] The neural network was based on input variables, which readily can be obtained by physicians or physicians' assistants. These include data from the history, physical examination, chest radiograph, ECG, and arterial blood gases.

In conclusion, the signs, symptoms, chest radiograph and ancillary laboratory tests in patients with acute PE are known to be deceptively nonspecific.[34] As a constellation of findings, however, and with a sensitive level of awareness of the potential diagnosis, the clinical manifestations form a useful guide for determining the extent to which the diagnosis should be pursued, and for making a probability assessment that may lead to treatment on the basis of a noninvasive diagnosis.[35–39]

## REFERENCES

1. Stein PD, Evans H: An autopsy study of leg vein thrombosis. Circulation 35:671–681, 1967.
2. Kakkar VV: Deep vein thrombosis: Detection and prevention. Circulation 51:8–19, 1975.
3. Hull R, Hirsh J, Sackett DL, et al: Replacement of venography in suspected venous thrombosis by impe-

dance plethysmography and [135]I-fibrinogen leg scanning. Ann Intern Med 94:12–15, 1981.

4. Hirsh J, Genton E, Hull R: Venous Thromboembolism. New York, Grune & Stratton, 1981, pp 73–81.

5. Hume M, Sevitt S, Thomas DP: Venous Thrombosis and Pulmonary Embolism. Cambridge, Harvard University Press, 1970, pp 144–164.

6. DeWeese JA, Rogoff SM: Phlebographic patterns of acute deep venous thrombosis of the leg. Surgery 53:99–108, 1963.

7. Homans J: Disease of the veins. N Engl J Med 231:51–60, 1944.

8. Lowenberg RI: Early diagnosis of phlebothrombosis with aid of a new clinical test. JAMA 155:1566–1570, 1954.

9. Ortiz-Ramirez T, Serna-Ramirez R: New early diagnostic sign of phlebitis of the lower extremities. Am Heart J 50:366–389, 1955.

10. Sevitt S, Gallagher N: Venous thrombosis and pulmonary embolism: A clinico-pathological study in injured and burned patients. Br J Surg 48:475–489, 1961.

11. Cohn R, Walsh J: The incidence and anatomical site of origin of pulmonary emboli. Stanford Med Bull 4:97–99, 1946.

12. Short DS: A survey of pulmonary embolism in a general hospital. Br Med J 1:790–796, 1952.

13. Byrne JJ, O'Neil EE: Fatal pulmonary emboli: A study of 130 autopsy-proven fatal emboli. Am J Surg 84:47–54, 1952.

14. National Cooperative Study: The Urokinase Pulmonary Embolism Trial. Associated laboratory and clinical findings. Circulation 47/48[Suppl II]:81–85, 1973.

15. Stein PD: Unpublished data from the Prospective Investigation of Pulmonary Embolism Diagnosis (PIOPED) Study.

16. Stein PD, Terrin ML, Hales CA, et al: Clinical, laboratory, roentgenographic and electrocardiographic findings in patients with acute pulmonary embolism and no pre-existing cardiac or pulmonary disease. Chest 100:598–603, 1991.

17. The PIOPED Investigators: Value of the ventilation/perfusion scan in acute pulmonary embolism: Results of the Prospective Investigation of Pulmonary Embolism Diagnosis (PIOPED). JAMA 263:2753–2759, 1990.

18. Stein PD, Willis PW III, DeMets DL: History and physical examination in acute pulmonary embolism in patients without pre-existing cardiac or pulmonary disease. Am J Cardiol 47:218–223, 1981.

19. National Cooperative Study: The Urokinase Pulmonary Embolism Trial. Design of the trial. Circulation 47/48[Suppl II]:18–24, 1973.

20. National Cooperative Study: Urokinase-Streptokinase Embolism Trial. Phase 2 results. JAMA 229:1606–1613, 1974.

21. Lesser BA, Leeper KV, Stein PD, et al: The diagnosis of pulmonary embolism in patients with chronic obstructive pulmonary disease. Chest 102: 17–22, 1992.

22. Stein PD, Gottschalk A, Saltzman HA, Terrin ML: Diagnosis of acute pulmonary embolism in the elderly. J Am Coll Cardiol 18:1452–1457, 1991.

23. Stein PD, Willis PW III, DeMets DL, Greenspan RH: Plain chest roentgenogram in patients with acute pulmonary embolism and no pre-existing cardiac or pulmonary disease. Am J Noninvas Cardiol 1:171–176, 1987.

24. Stein PD, Athanasoulis C, Greenspan RH, Henry JW: Relation of plain chest radiographic findings to pulmonary arterial pressure and arterial blood oxygen levels in patients with acute pulmonary embolism. Am J Cardiol 69:394–396, 1992.

25. Stein PD, Saltzman HA, Weg JG: Clinical characteristics of patients with acute pulmonary embolism. Am J Cardiol 68:1723–1724, 1991.

26. Stein PD, Dalen JE, McIntyre KM, et al: The electrocardiogram in acute pulmonary embolism. Prog Cardiovasc Dis 17:247–257, 1975.

27. Lynch RE, Stein PD, Bruce TA: Leftward shift of frontal plane QRS axis as a frequent manifestation of acute pulmonary embolism. Chest 61:443–446, 1972.

28. Stein PD, Bruce TA: Left axis deviation as an electrocardiographic manifestation of acute pulmonary embolism. J Electrocardiol 4:67–69, 1971.

29. Szucs MM, Brooks HL, Grossman W, et al: Diagnostic sensitivity of laboratory findings in acute pulmonary embolism. Ann Intern Med 74:161–166, 1971.

30. Stein PD, Goldhaber SZ, Henry JW: Alveolar-arterial oxygen gradient in the assessment of acute pulmonary embolism. Chest 107:139–143, 1995.

31. Gaffney PJ, Creighton LJ, Callus M, Thorpe R: Monoclonal antibodies to crosslinked fibrin degradation products (XL-FDP). Br J Haematol 68:83–96, 1988.

32. Bounameaux H, Cirafici P, DeMoerloose P, et al: Measurement of D-dimer in plasma as diagnostic aid in suspected pulmonary embolism. Lancet 337:196–200, 1991.

33. Patil S, Henry JW, Rubenfire M, Stein PD: Neural network in the clinical diagnosis of acute pulmonary embolism. Chest 104:1685–1689, 1993.

34. Wenger NK, Stein PD, Willis PW III: Massive acute pulmonary embolism: The deceivingly nonspecific manifestations. JAMA 220:843–844, 1972.

35. Stein PD, Willis PW, III, Dalen JE: Importance of clinical assessment in the selection of patients for pulmonary arteriography. Am J Cardiol 43:669–671, 1979.

36. Stein PD, Hull RD, Saltzman HA, Pineo G: Strategy for diagnosis of patients with suspected acute pulmonary embolism. Chest 103:1553–1559, 1993.

37. Stein PD, Hull RD: Relative risks of anticoagulant treatment of acute pulmonary embolism based upon an angiographic diagnosis versus a ventilation/perfusion scan diagnosis. Chest 106:727–730, 1994.

38. Stein PD, Hull RD, Raskob G: Risks for major bleeding in patients with acute pulmonary embolism who are candidates for thrombolytic therapy: Consideration of noninvasive management. Ann Intern Med 12:313–317, 1994.

39. Stein PD, Henry JW, Gottschalk A: The addition of prior clinical assessment to stratification according to prior cardiopulmonary disease further optimizes the interpretation of ventilation/perfusion lung scans in pulmonary embolism. Chest 104:1472–1476, 1993.

# Chapter 23

# Objective Tests for the Diagnosis of Venous Thrombosis

Anthonie W. A. Lensing and Harry R. Büller

Deep vein thrombosis of the lower extremity is a frequent disorder that may occur either spontaneously or in the course of a high-risk situation such as following major surgical procedures or a prolonged period of immobilization. Untreated deep vein thrombosis is associated with morbidity due to pulmonary embolism and the post-thrombotic syndrome.

It was only with the introduction of contrast venography for the diagnosis of deep vein thrombosis in the 1960s that the inaccuracy of the clinical diagnosis became apparent.[1, 2] Since then, an array of noninvasive and less invasive objective diagnostic tests has been developed.[3] These diagnostic methods are distinctly different in technology and consequently in their ability to demonstrate or refute the presence of deep vein thrombi. The correct approach to the diagnosis of deep vein thrombosis differs depending on the nature of the patient group under consideration.[4] The patient categories include those with a suspected first episode of venous thrombosis, those with a suspected recurrent episode of venous thrombosis, and those who are asymptomatic but who are at high risk to develop deep vein thrombosis. Based on the characteristics of these patient groups and the diagnostic method, the clinical utility of the validated objective tests varies in these three settings. Furthermore, the features of deep vein thrombi differ depending on the patient group under consideration (Table 23–1).

Numerous studies have now demonstrated that only 20 to 30% of patients with a first episode of clinically suspected venous thrombosis have the diagnosis confirmed.[3–6I, 7] Clinical diagnosis in these patients is nonspecific because none of the symptoms or signs of venous thrombosis are unique to this condition and all

can be caused by transient abnormalities of the musculoskeletal system or skin, which mimic an acute venous thrombosis. These nonthrombotic conditions clearly do not require anticoagulant therapy. At the time of diagnosis of venous thrombosis in these patients, about 90% of the thrombi have extended into the proximal veins (i.e., popliteal vein or above). These thrombi are predominantly large and occlusive and carry a high risk for pulmonary embolism. At presentation, patients are symptomatic for a period varying between some days to several weeks.

Of patients with proven deep vein thrombosis who have been treated, approximately 25 to 50% present in the subsequent years with signs and symptoms suggestive of recurrent venous thrombosis. Various studies have revealed that these recurrent symptoms are caused by a new acute thrombosis in only approximately one-third of these patients,[8, 9] whereas the post-thrombotic syndrome or a variety of other non-thrombotic disorders is the cause of complaints in the remaining patients. Little is known about the characteristics of thrombi in these patients. It invariably involves acute lesions on old thrombi that may vary in size, but they are usually small. Because the patient is aware of the symptoms the delay before medical attention is sought is usually minimal.

Despite adequate prophylaxis for deep vein thrombosis approximately, 10 to 25% of patients at high risk for deep vein thrombosis (i.e., patients who have undergone major surgery or prolonged immobilization) develop deep vein thrombosis that is usually asymptomatic at the time of hospital discharge.[10–16] In these patients, clinical diagnosis is insensitive because many potentially dangerous venous thrombi are non-obstructive and not associated with inflamma-

Table 23–1. **Features of Deep Vein Thrombi in Symptomatic Patients With a First Episode of Deep Vein Thrombosis, Recurrent Symptomatic Deep Vein Thrombosis, or Asymptomatic Deep Vein Thrombosis**

| Patient Category | Prevalence of DVT (%) | Location | Size | Occlusiveness | Age of Thrombus |
|---|---|---|---|---|---|
| First episode of DVT | 20–30* | Mainly proximal veins | Large | Mainly occlusive | Days to weeks |
| Recurrent DVT | 20–30* | Variable | Usually limited | Mainly occlusive | Usually days |
| Asymptomatic DVT | 10–25* | Usually calf veins | Variable | Mainly nonocclusive | Days |

*Prevalence in symptomatic patients, when applying venography.

tion of the vessel wall or of the perivascular tissues and, therefore, produce few or no signs and symptoms. The thrombi in these patients are usually from recent onset; they are small and nonocclusive, and the majority are located in the deep veins of the calf. However, if the thrombus remains undetected, it may enlarge and give rise to pulmonary embolism.

As a consequence of these specific features of deep vein thrombosis in the three patient categories, different diagnostic approaches should be applied.[4] In patients with a first episode of clinically suspected deep vein thrombosis, diagnostic tests need to have a high sensitivity for proximal vein thrombosis. To safely manage the small group of patients with isolated calf vein thrombosis, diagnostic tests need to have either a high sensitivity for isolated calf vein thrombosis or the capability to detect these thrombi if they extend into the proximal veins during the ensuing days. In patients presenting with a suspected episode of recurrent deep vein thrombosis, diagnostic tests need to meet the specific requirement to distinguish old from new deep vein thrombi, whereas in the asymptomatic patient at high risk for deep vein thrombosis, the diagnostic tests should be able to simply detect small and nonocclusive isolated calf vein thrombosis, as well as proximally located, usually nonocclusive thrombi in large groups of patients.

In this chapter, a critical review is provided on the accuracy of the diagnostic approaches to venous thrombosis in different clinical settings. Results of studies were considered only when their methodology fulfilled the essential criteria for evaluation of a diagnostic test.

## EVALUATION OF A DIAGNOSTIC TEST

Evaluation of a new diagnostic technique should be performed in three separate but consecutive phases.[4] Incomplete adherence to these principles has led to the introduction of invalid or inaccurate methods into clinical practice.[17]

First, objective criteria for the presence or absence of venous thrombosis should be defined and the technical aspects of the test should be standardized. For example, the position of the patient during examination and the method of execution should be specified. The requirement of objective criteria is crucial. Subjective measurements, such as the audible signals with Doppler ultrasound, have led to considerable confusion about the proper criteria for an abnormal test. The variations in the interpretation of the objective test result between observers should be determined, because it is important to know whether other investigators performing and interpreting the diagnostic test for deep vein thrombosis in the same patients would come to an identical diagnosis. If the new method is shown to be objective and reproducible, the accuracy of the test can be assessed.

In this second phase, the outcomes of the test are compared blindly to the results of the gold standard (contrast venography), which is performed in all patients to generate the indices of accuracy (i.e., sensitivity, specificity, and predictive values). Failure to adhere to the requirement of a blind performance and analysis of the new test as well as the reference method may result in falsely high estimates of the accuracy. Care should be taken that the evaluation is performed in a broad spectrum of consecutive patients. The failure to include a broad spectrum of patients (including those with and without deep vein thrombosis, as well as patients with disorders frequently confused with venous thrombosis) hampers the applicability of the test in future patient groups. An additional aim of this phase is to determine if the new method is suitable for all categories of patients. If the test has a sufficiently high sensitivity and specificity for venous thrombosis, the clinical validity and applicability of the technique should be investigated in the third phase.

The objective of the third phase is to document the safety and effectiveness of the method in a sufficiently large sample of consecutive patients to determine whether management decisions about treatment can be based on the outcome of the test. Patients in whom the diagnosis of deep vein thrombosis is rejected on the basis of normal test results should be carefully followed to ensure that little or no morbidity from venous thromboembolism occurs. Alternatively, patients with an abnormal test should have the findings confirmed. When a new diagnostic test for venous thrombosis has complied with the requirements of each of these three phases, the test can be recommended for clinical use. The recommendation should specify the patient category for which the diagnostic test has been shown to be appropriate, because the various objective tests have different diagnostic accuracies depending on the nature of the patient category under investigation (i.e., first or recurrent episode of symptomatic venous thrombosis, or asymptomatic deep vein thrombosis).

## METHODOLOGIC CONSIDERATIONS AND ANALYSIS

We critically reviewed the articles published in the English literature that evaluated the accuracy of methods used for the diagnosis of proximal or calf vein thrombosis in patients with a clinical suspicion of a first or recurrent episode or in patients who are asymptomatic but at high risk. To minimize diagnostic suspicion bias, reports were included for this review only if the diagnostic test under consideration was independently compared with venography and the results were interpreted by observers who had no knowledge of the other outcome of the test.[17] In addition, reports needed to evaluate consecutive patients who were studied prospectively, because the failure to meet this requirement can result in the exclusion of patients in certain risk categories and thus produce false estimates of accuracy.

## ANATOMY OF THE VENOUS SYSTEM OF THE LEG

The venous system of the leg consists of deep and superficial veins. The deep venous system of the leg consists of three pairs of deep calf veins (i.e., the posterior tibial, the peroneal, and anterior tibial veins), the deep proximal veins (the popliteal, superficial femoral, deep femoral, common femoral, and iliac veins). The popliteal vein starts at the junction of the posterior tibial veins and the peroneal veins and becomes the superficial femoral vein at the junction of the proximal part of the popliteal fossa and the adductor canal in the thigh. The superficial femoral vein is joined by the deep femoral vein in the upper thigh to form the common femoral vein, which becomes the external iliac vein at the level of the inguinal ligament. The external iliac vein is joined by the internal iliac vein in the pelvis to form the common iliac vein, and the common iliac veins converge to form the inferior vena cava. The proximal venous system is defined as the deep veins in the pelvis, the thigh, and the popliteal region proximal to the trifurcation of the calf veins.

The superficial venous system consists of the long and short saphenous veins and the soleal and gastrocnemius plexus. The long and short saphenous veins drain into the common femoral and popliteal veins, respectively. The soleal plexus drains into the posterior tibial vein, and the gastrocnemius plexus drains into the popliteal vein. The superficial system is connected with the deep venous system by communicating veins that contain valves that direct flow from the superficial into the deep system.

## DIAGNOSTIC TECHNIQUES

The available techniques for the objective diagnosis of deep vein thrombosis include invasive and noninvasive methods and biochemical assays. These techniques visualize the thrombus (contrast venography, real-time B-mode ultrasonography with or without [color] Doppler facilities, and computed tomography or magnetic resonance imaging), measure venous outflow (impedance plethysmography or strain gauge plethysmography and Doppler ultrasound), measure the incorporation of radiolabeled proteins in the developing thrombus ($^{125}$I-fibrinogen leg scanning and several other isotopic methods), or detect circulating fibrin formation or breakdown products. Of these methods, ultrasound imaging, impedance plethysmography, and Doppler ultrasonography are the most widely used methods.

Contrast venography is generally considered the reference method for the presence or absence of deep vein thrombosis with which all other tests should be compared.

### Venography

With contrast venography, the entire deep venous system is visualized. Usually separate exposures are obtained of the calf and proximal veins. Although contrast venography is widely accepted as the gold standard for the diagnosis of deep vein thrombosis, several features have limited the general use of this method, including its invasive nature, the technical requirements, and the difficulty of repeating the test. In addition, the test may not be feasible or is inadequate for interpretation in approximately 10 to 20% of patients.[18, 19]

The most reliable venographic criterion is the presence of an intraluminal filling defect that is constant in all films and is seen in at least two different projections.[20] Other less reliable criteria include (1) nonfilling of a segment of the deep venous system with abrupt termination of the column of contrast medium at a constant site below the segment and reappearance of the contrast medium at a constant site above the segment, and (2) nonfilling of the deep venous system above the knee, despite repeated injections of contrast material and adequate venographic technique. The likelihood that these appearances are the result of venous thrombosis is increased if the abnormality is associated with the presence of abnormal collaterals.

Venography is a technique that requires experience to perform and interpret adequately. Unless care is taken to inject the dye into the dorsal foot vein, nonfilling of calf veins may be falsely interpreted as abnormal for thrombosis because the vein is not filled, or falsely interpreted as normal because the filling defect produced by the thrombus is not seen. The proximal part of the femoral vein and the external iliac and common iliac veins may also be inadequately filled by ascending venography.

Contrast venography is contraindicated in patients with acute or chronic renal failure, a history of a reaction to contrast material, or an obvious local infection of the foot. If venography is required in pregnant women, it should be performed with the fetus shielded from radiation by covering the patient's abdomen and upper thighs with a lead-lined apron. With the use of low osmolar contrast materials, adverse reactions have become rare.

## Ultrasonography Techniques

### Conventional Gray-scale Real-time Ultrasonography

Venous ultrasound imaging is performed with the patient in the supine position, with the head of the bed elevated approximately 30 degrees to ensure adequate venous filling of the legs. The ultrasound probe is placed in the groin to identify the common femoral vein, which is always medial to the common femoral artery. The transducer is then moved distally to visualize the superficial femoral vein throughout its course. For examination of the popliteal vein, the patient is in the prone or the lateral decubitus position with the knees flexed to prevent spontaneous collapse of the vein. The lumen of a normal vein is free of echoes and, in contrast to arteries, veins have thin walls and are held open primarily by the low venous blood pressure. Therefore, the vein lumen can be easily obliterated by a small amount of extrinsic pressure.

The most accurate and simple ultrasonic criterion for diagnosing venous thrombosis is noncompressibility of the vascular lumen under gentle probe pressure (compression ultrasound).[21, 22] Vein compressibility is considered present if no residual lumen is observed; compressibility indicates the absence of venous thrombosis. The images can be obtained in either the transverse or longitudinal plane. However, vein compressibility is best evaluated in the transverse view because it allows visualization of both the vein and the adjacent artery. With the vein imaging in the longitudinal plane, the vein may slide out of the image plane during compression with the ultrasound probe and so may falsely simulate compressibility of the venous segment. The presence of echogenic bands in the vein might be helpful to diagnose venous thrombosis, but bands are often observed in patients in whom contrast venography proves the absence of venous thrombosis. In general, the common femoral and popliteal veins can be visualized most easily because of their superficial location. The superficial femoral vein, especially its segment that passes through the adductor canal, is localized deeper and is often more difficult to evaluate. The calf veins cannot be evaluated with conventional ultrasound techniques because they cannot be visualized adequately; their small size and insufficient resolution of the current ultrasound device preclude visualization.

### Duplex Ultrasonography

Patients are examined in a manner identical to that with conventional compression ultrasound. In addition, blood flow characteristics may be evaluated using the pulsed Doppler capability. Blood flow in normal veins is spontaneous and phasic with respiration; it can be augmented by elevating the distal lower extremity or by manual compression distal to the ultrasound transducer, and it can be interrupted by performing the Valsalva maneuver. When the phasic pattern is absent, flow is defined as continuous, indicating the presence of venous outflow obstruction especially when there is little or no change after the Valsalva maneuver. Absence of spontaneous venous flow may result from complete obstruction of the vein lumen.

A major drawback of the duplex examination is the lack of objective and standardized diagnostic criteria for the Doppler assessment. Sometimes spontaneous flow cannot be detected in normal veins because of low flow velocity in small veins. Augmentation techniques do not always result in a clear venous Doppler signal. Furthermore, continuous flow with poor or no response to the Valsalva maneuver can be observed in patients without venous thrombosis. In patients with nonocclusive venous thrombosis, the normal finding—phasic spontaneous flow interrupted by the Valsalva maneuver—may be observed.

The assessment of the calf veins by duplex ultrasound is, as for the conventional gray-scale examination, hampered by the poor visualization of these veins.

## Color-coded Doppler Ultrasonography

The technique of the color-coded Doppler ultrasonography (color Doppler) examination is basically identical to that of compression ultrasound and duplex ultrasonography. With color flow sonography, pulsed Doppler signals are used to produce the images. When a Doppler shift is recognized, it is assigned a color (i.e., red or blue) according to its forward or reverse direction. Therefore, the technique of color Doppler mapping results in a display of flowing blood as a color overlay to the gray-scale ultrasound image, which has the potential to enhance the ability to identify the veins even when they are obscured by soft tissue edema or by excessive depth from the transducer. Color Doppler has the potential to visualize the calf veins.

Images in the longitudinal axis are used for the assessment with color Doppler. The interpretation of venous flow, whether with color Doppler or duplex ultrasonography, is essentially the same. The criterion for an abnormal color Doppler test is the absence of color in a vein after augmentation or a focal intraluminal filling defect.

As with the duplex examination, "venous flow" is Doppler wave information detected as a Doppler shift, rather than true flow measured in volume per unit of time. Therefore, Doppler-detected flow may be absent in normal veins because of low flow, and augmentation does not always result in a clear color image. The color Doppler examination may be falsely interpreted as normal in patients with nonocclusive thrombosis due to persistent venous flow (and, therefore, normal color coding of venous flow) around the thrombus.

## Impedance Plethysmography

Impedance plethysmography is performed with the patient supine and with the lower limb elevated 25 to 30 degrees, the knee flexed 10 to 20 degrees, and the ankle 8 to 15 cm higher than the knee. The cuff is inflated to a pressure of 50 cm $H_2O$. The test measures volume changes in the leg produced by inflation and deflation of a pneumatic thigh cuff. The volume changes in the calf are measured with the use of circumferential electrodes. The presence of proximal vein thrombosis or extensive calf vein thrombosis results in impairment of venous outflow. Objective criteria have been defined using a discriminant line that was developed by discriminant function analysis to provide optimal separation of the impedance plethysmography test result in patients with and without proximal vein thrombosis.[23] Impedance plethysmography is relatively simple to perform, and is a well standardized and easily repeatable test that detects occlusive thrombosis in the proximal veins. The method does not distinguish between thrombotic and nonthrombotic obstruction to venous outflow. A disadvantage of impedance plethysmography is that the test is relatively insensitive to isolated calf vein thrombosis and nonobstructive proximal thrombi. A reliable test result can be obtained in almost all patients except those who cannot be positioned correctly.

## Doppler Ultrasonography

The Doppler ultrasound examination is performed with the patient lying in bed in the semiupright position with the hip slightly externally rotated. The common femoral vein is located by initially placing the probe over the common femoral artery, which can be easily identified, and it is then moved medially until the low-pitched sound, typical of venous flow, is heard. The intensity of this low-pitched sound decreases with inspiration and increases with expiration, resulting in a phasic signal. Abdominal compression results in interruption of venous flow in the leg; when abdominal compression is released, there is an augmented sound as blood flow in the veins suddenly increases. Manual compression of the thigh and calf produces an augmented venous sound because of sudden acceleration of venous flow. Patency of the entire superficial femoral vein can be confirmed by moving the probe distally along this vein and repeating calf and distal thigh compression. However, care must be taken not to confuse the sounds with those produced by the long saphenous vein. Augmentation of flow is also induced by sudden release of thigh compression proximal to the probe. The probe is then placed over the posterior tibial vein, which is located adjacent to the corresponding artery behind the ankle. Augmentation of flow is produced by squeezing the foot and by suddenly releasing proximal calf compression.

Doppler ultrasound is sensitive to occlusive thrombi in the popliteal and more proximal veins, but is less sensitive to nonocclusive proximal thrombi. The ultrasonic detection of isolated calf vein thrombosis is cumbersome because of slow venous flow, which is often beyond the detection limit of the Doppler equipment and the complicated anatomy of the calf veins.

Obstruction to venous outflow may result in an absent venous signal, provided that the thrombus completely occludes the vein. Augmentation of the venous signal, in case of intravascular thrombus formation, may be diminished, high-pitched and of short duration, or absent. Deep breathing or the Valsalva maneuver may also result in increase of venous flow and may produce additional information regarding the patency of veins.

However, venous flow may be interpreted as normal in patients with nonocclusive thrombosis when it does not cause hemodynamic changes and when it occurs in patients with collateral veins. False-abnormal results may be found in patients with extrinsic venous compression or with previous deep vein thrombosis, but false abnormals may also be the result of inexperience of the examiner. The interpretation of Doppler ultrasound results is in part subjective, and the test requires considerable skill and experience to perform reliably. Recordings of the signals on a stripchart have overcome the subjective interpretation of the test.[1011]

### 125I-Fibrinogen Leg Scanning

Patients are scanned with an isotope detector probe while their legs are elevated 15 degrees above horizontal to minimize venous pooling in the calf veins. Readings are taken over both legs, and the results are expressed as a percentage of the surface radioactivity measured over the heart. The surface radioactivity is recorded over the femoral vein at 7- to 8-cm intervals, from the inguinal ligament and over the medial and posterior aspects of the popliteal fossa and calf. Venous thrombosis is suspected if there is an increase in the radioactivity of more than 20% at any point compared with the readings over the adjacent points on the limb, or with the same point on the previous day, or with the readings over the corresponding point on the opposite leg. Venous thrombosis is diagnosed if the scan remains abnormal.

## DIAGNOSIS OF SYMPTOMATIC DEEP VEIN THROMBOSIS

### Ultrasound Imaging

A total of 20 ultrasound studies were selected for this analysis. In these investigations, venography was used in all patients, including only patients with signs and symptoms of venous thrombosis of the lower extremity. Several other studies are not included in the analysis, because they did not fulfill the requirements of a systematic use of venography, clear patient selection, or independent comparison with the reference standard.[24–50, 199–201] Of the selected 20 reports, 11 evaluated compression ultrasound, five used duplex ultrasonography, and four assessed color-coded ultrasonography.

### Accuracy for Proximal Vein Thrombosis

Compression Ultrasound

Of the 11 studies evaluating compression ultrasound, nine included symptomatic outpatients and two were hospitalized patients who became symptomatic for venous thrombosis during their stay in the hospital. The combined analysis of the outpatient studies demonstrated that compression ultrasound correctly identified proximal vein thrombosis in 414 of the 430 patients, for a sensitivity of 96% (Table 23–2). Thrombosis was correctly excluded in 546 of the 559 patients with normal venograms, for a specificity of 98%. Therefore, the positive predictive value was 96%. Feasibility of the compression ultrasound test was consistently high in all studies. Inconclusive compression ultrasound test results occurred infrequently (less than 1% of patients). Two large studies limited the compression ultrasound evaluation to the common femoral and popliteal vein.[52, 551] Combining the data, the sensitivity and specificity for proximal vein thrombosis were 97% and 99%, respec-

Table 23–2. **Compression Ultrasonography in Patients With Clinically Suspected Deep Vein Thrombosis**

| Investigators | Sensitivity for Proximal DVT % (n/N) | Specificity % (n/N) |
|---|---|---|
| Dauzat et al, 1986 | 97 (89/92) | 100 (45/45) |
| Appelman et al, 1987 | 92 (48/52) | 97 (58/60) |
| Aitken and Godden, 1987 | 94 (15/16) | 100 (26/26) |
| Cronan et al, 1987 | 93 (25/27) | 100 (23/23) |
| Lensing et al, 1989 | 100 (66/66) | 99 (142/143) |
| Monreal et al, 1989 | 93 (40/43) | 86 (18/21) |
| Habscheid et al, 1990 | 95 (57/60) | 100 (91/91) |
| Gudmundsen et al, 1990 | 100 (60/60) | 97 (87/90) |
| Chance et al, 1991 | 100 (14/14) | 93 (56/60) |
| Total | 96 (414/430) | 98 (546/559) |

tively; these results are fully comparable with the results of studies that evaluated the entire proximal venous system. Both compression ultrasound studies evaluating hospitalized patients who became symptomatic for venous thrombosis during hospitalization used correct methodology.[60, 61I] In these patients, the combined sensitivity and specificity for proximal vein thrombosis were 91% (135 in 148) and 94% (102 in 109), respectively. These findings in hospitalized patients appear to be comparable with the results obtained in symptomatic outpatients.

## Duplex Ultrasonography

Of the five selected studies evaluating the accuracy of duplex ultrasonography for the diagnosis of proximal vein thrombosis (four in symptomatic outpatients, one in hospitalized patients). The combined sensitivity for the four outpatient studies was 95% (98 in 103), whereas specificity was 93% (134 in 144) (Table 23–3).[62–65] The positive predictive value was, therefore, 91%. In the single duplex ultrasonography study that evaluated hospitalized patients who became symptomatic for venous thrombosis during hospitalization, sensitivity and specificity

for proximal vein thrombosis were 97% and 98%, respectively.[66I]

## Color Doppler Ultrasonography

In the four selected studies, color Doppler correctly diagnosed proximal vein thrombosis in 123 of the 127 patients, for a sensitivity of 97% (Table 23–4).[67–70] The presence of proximal vein thrombosis was correctly excluded in 207 of the 213 patients, for a specificity of 97%. The predictive value of an abnormal test result was, therefore, 96%.

## Accuracy for Isolated Calf Vein Thrombosis

Only one study correctly evaluating accuracy investigated the use of compression ultrasound in the diagnosis of isolated calf vein thrombosis (Table 23–5).[57] In this study, isolated calf vein thrombosis was demonstrated by venography in 23 patients and compression ultrasound identified 20 of these (sensitivity, 87%). Of the duplex ultrasonography studies performed with correct methodology, the ability to detect isolated calf vein thrombosis was addressed in one small investigation.[65] In this study, duplex ultrasonogra-

Table 23–3. **Duplex Ultrasonography in Patients With Clinically Suspected Deep Vein Thrombosis**

| Investigators | Sensitivity for Proximal DVT % (n/N) | Specificity % (n/N) |
|---|---|---|
| Vogel et al, 1987 | 95 (19/20) | 100 (33/33) |
| O'Leary et al, 1988 | 92 (22/24) | 96 (25/26) |
| Mantoni et al, 1989 | 97 (34/35) | 97 (48/50) |
| Mitchell et al, 1991 | 96 (23/24) | 80 (28/35) |
| Total | 95 (98/103) | 93 (134/144) |

**Table 23–4. Color-coded Doppler Ultrasonography in Patients With Clinically Suspected Deep Vein Thrombosis**

| Investigators | Sensitivity for Proximal DVT % (n/N) | Specificity % (n/N) |
|---|---|---|
| Baxter et al, 1990 | 92 (11/12) | 100 (26/26) |
| Rose et al, 1990 | 92 (23/25) | 100 (50/50) |
| Schindler et al, 1990 | 98 (54/55) | 100 (100/100) |
| Mattos et al, 1992 | 100 (35/35) | 84 (31/37) |
| Total | 97 (123/127) | 97 (207/213) |

phy identified two of the five patients with isolated calf vein thrombosis (sensitivity, 40%). The sensitivity of color Doppler ultrasonography for isolated calf vein thrombosis was determined in two methodologically sound studies[67, 68]; color Doppler correctly identified 24 of the 32 patients with isolated calf vein thrombosis, for a sensitivity of 75%.

## Impedance Plethysmography

Thus far, the accuracy of impedance plethysmography for the diagnosis of deep vein thrombosis in symptomatic patients has been evaluated in 17 studies (including one study in hospitalized patients). The inclusion of consecutive patients and independent analysis of a standardized impedance plethysmography result with venography was used in nine studies,[72I, 74I, 77I, 78I] whereas the remaining eight studies had a potential for bias, or did not truly evaluate accuracy.[80–88] The combined analysis of the studies using proper methodology demonstrated that impedance plethysmography detected 574

of the 639 proximal thrombi, for a sensitivity of 90% (Table 23–6). False-positive results were obtained in 60 of the 1,352 patients, for a specificity of 96%. Therefore, the predictive value of an abnormal test is 89%. The sensitivity and specificity in the single study evaluating hospitalized patients were 96% and 83%, respectively.[6II]

Impedance plethysmography has a very low sensitivity (approximately 20%) for isolated calf vein thrombosis.[71, 72I, 74I, 77I, 78I]

## Doppler Ultrasonography

Nine studies correctly evaluated the accuracy of Doppler ultrasound for the diagnosis of symptomatic deep vein thrombosis,[89–97] although subjective criteria for the analysis of flow sound were used, whereas the earlier Doppler ultrasound studies had methodologic weaknesses.[98–100] The pooled results of these studies demonstrated that Doppler ultrasound detected 280 of the 315 patients with venographically proven proximal vein thrombosis, for a sensitivity of 89% (Table 23–7). The test result was falsely abnormal in 93 of the 706 patients without proximal vein thrombosis, for a specificity

**Table 23–5. Sensitivity for Isolated Calf Vein Thrombosis for Studies in Symptomatic Patients That Minimized the Potential for Bias**

| | Sensitivity % (n/N) | 95% Confidence Interval (%) |
|---|---|---|
| Gray-scale Real-time Ultrasonography | | |
| Habscheid et al, 1990 | 87 (20/23) | 65–92 |
| Duplex Ultrasonography | | |
| Mitchell et al, 1991 | 40 (2/5) | 13–93 |
| Color Doppler Ultrasonography | | |
| Baxter et al, 1990 | 100 (2/2) | 23–100 |
| Rose et al, 1990 | 73 (22/30) | 54–87 |
| Total | 75 (24/32) | 56–88 |

**Table 23–6. Impedance Plethysmography in Patients With Clinically Suspected Deep Vein Thrombosis**

| Investigators | Sensitivity % (n/N) | Specificity $ (n/N) |
|---|---|---|
| Hull et al, 1976 | 93 (124/133) | 97 (386/397) |
| Richards et al, 1976 | 81 (30/37) | 87 (78/90) |
| Hull et al, 1977 | 98 (59/60) | 95 (108/114) |
| Toy and Schrier, 1978 | 94 (15/16) | 100 (9/9) |
| Hull et al, 1978 | 92 (155/169) | 96 (305/317) |
| Hull et al, 1981 | 95 (74/78) | 98 (157/160) |
| Peters et al, 1982 | 92 (36/39) | 93 (115/124) |
| Prandoni et al, 1991 | 86 (44/51) | 95 (134/141) |
| Anderson et al, 1992 | 66 (37/56) | |
| Total | 90 (574/639) | 96 (1,292/1,352) |

Table 23–7. **Doppler Ultrasonography in Symptomatic Patients**

| Investigators | Sensitivity % (n/N) | Specificity % (n/N) |
|---|---|---|
| Yao et al, 1972 | 100 (33/33) | 88 (15/17) |
| Holmes et al, 1973 | 100 (17/17) | 94 (46/49) |
| Meadway et al, 1975 | 85 (29/34) | 72 (55/76) |
| Dosick et al, 1978 | 96 (50/52) | 93 (100/102) |
| Flanigan et al, 1978 | 65 (35/54) | 96 (94/98) |
| Sumner and Lambeth, 1979 | 94 (34/36) | 90 (35/39) |
| Hanel et al, 1981 | 92 (49/53) | 91 (118/130) |
| Zielinsky et al, 1983 | 95 (20/21) | 76 (117/153) |
| Turnbull et al, 1990 | 87 (13/15) | 78 (33/42) |
| Total | 89 (280/315) | 87 (613/706) |

of 87%. Consequently, the predictive value of an abnormal Doppler ultrasound test is 75%.

Doppler ultrasonography is not sensitive for the detection of isolated calf vein thrombosis.

Doppler ultrasound for the diagnosis of proximal vein thrombosis was evaluated using objective criteria for normal and abnormal test results.[101I, 102I] A total of 155 consecutive patients with clinically suspected deep vein thrombosis were studied. An abnormal Doppler test was obtained in 83 of the 92 patients with proximal vein thrombosis (sensitivity, 87%). A false-abnormal Doppler test result was obtained in only three of the 209 patients without deep vein thrombosis, for a specificity of 99%.

## Other Methods

Various other methods, including strain gauge plethysmography,[103, 104] liquid crystal (contact) thermography,[105, 106I, 107, 108, 109I] light reflection rheography,[110I] computed tomography scanning, and magnetic resonance scanning,[111–114I] radionuclide venography,[115–130I, 131–133I, 134I] as well as numerous blood tests (including measurements of fibrinopeptide A,[135I–137] fibrin and fibrinogen degradation products [FDP],[138, 139] degradation products of cross-linked fibrin (D-Dimer),[140I, 141, 142I, 143–149I, 150I, 151–153I] prothrombin fragments $1 + 2$ [F1 + 2] and thrombin-antithrombin III [TAT] complexes),[154–156I] and fragment E[157] have been evaluated in patients presenting with signs and symptoms of deep vein thrombosis. These methods are either still experimental or have not been properly evaluated in large series of consecutive patients. Therefore, at present none of these methods should be used for the diagnosis of deep vein thrombosis.

## Diagnostic Management of Patients with a Clinically Suspected First Episode of Venous Thrombosis

Although a normal ultrasound imaging or impedance plethysmography (IPG) result essentially excludes a diagnosis of proximal vein thrombosis, it does not exclude the presence of isolated calf vein thrombosis. Based on the premise that thrombi that are undetected by an initial normal test are not clinically important and do not need anticoagulant treatment unless they extend after initial presentation, several investigators have evaluated the clinical validity of serial testing during the following week as the only diagnostic test in patients with clinically suspected deep venous thrombosis.[86, 158–164] It should be realized that only a minority (approximately 10%) of patients presenting with their first episode of deep vein thrombosis indeed have isolated calf vein thrombosis. Hence, at a prevalence of deep vein thrombosis of 25%, only two to three patients of each group of 100 symptomatic subjects have deep vein thrombosis confined to the calf veins.

The safety of the serial testing approach with ultrasound imaging or impedance plethysmography has been confirmed by the longterm followup of over 3,000 patients, which revealed an incidence of subsequent venous thromboembolism of approximately 1 to 2%.[86, 158, 159I, 160I, 161–164I] No fatal pulmonary embolism occurred in these studies. This low incidence is identical to that observed when contrast venography is used for the exclusion of deep vein thrombosis.

The results of a randomized diagnostic study directly comparing the safety and efficacy of serial compression ultrasound (with the examination limited to the common femoral and popliteal veins) to serial IPG in a consecutive series of 985 outpatients with a first episode of clinically suspected deep vein thrombosis have been published.[164I] Patients were allocated to be tested with three sequential studies with either IPG or compression ultrasonography. The tests were performed on the day of referral, on the next day, and 1 week later. Of the 89 patients who developed an abnormal IPG over the 7 days of testing, 76 (85%) had an abnormal test on the day of referral, whereas 78 (93%) of the 84 patients who had an abnormal ultrasound test over the 7 days of testing had an abnormal test on the day of referral. Over the next 7 days of serial testing, the test become abnormal in another 13 patients of the IPG group and in six patients of the compression ultrasound group.

Thus, the ultrasound test was more efficient in detecting thrombi on the day of referral. All patients with abnormal noninvasive studies underwent contrast venography, which confirmed the presence of venous thrombosis in 83% of the IPG abnormal patients and in 94% of the compression ultrasound abnormal patients. This difference in positive predictive value was statistically significant. The results of serial testing were normal in 365 and 390 patients of the IPG and compression ultrasound groups, respectively. These patients were not treated with anticoagulants and were followed for 6 months. During followup, venous thromboembolism was confirmed in nine patients (2.5%; 95% confidence interval 0.5 to 3.3%) of the compression ultrasound group. None of these patients died as a result of pulmonary embolism. These findings indicate that both methods can be used to exclude deep vein thrombosis, but that compression ultrasound is the preferred method in view of the higher accuracy to detect thrombosis.

The results of this review indicate that for the diagnosis of symptomatic deep vein thrombosis, duplex and color ultrasonography do not offer any advantage over conventional compression ultrasound because use of the former tests does not result in an increased accuracy for proximal vein thrombosis. Duplex and color Doppler ultrasonography have the disadvantages of being less cost-effective than compression ultrasound, because these devices are more expensive and the procedures more time-consuming.

Compression ultrasound limited to the assessment of the common femoral vein and the popliteal vein is the test of choice in the evaluation of symptomatic patients. An abnormal compression ultrasound test justifies the initiation of anticoagulant treatment because the predictive value of an abnormal test outcome is high. Although a normal compression ultrasound result essentially excludes a diagnosis of proximal vein thrombosis, it does not exclude the presence of isolated calf vein thrombosis. Therefore, patients with a normal test outcome should be retested to detect the small proportion of patients (approximately 1 to 2% of patients with an initial normal ultrasound test) with proximally extending calf vein thrombosis. There appears to be no role for simple Doppler ultrasound in the diagnosis of deep vein thrombosis because the subjective interpretation limits its reliability.

A diagnostic algorithm for the noninvasive diagnosis of clinically suspected venous thrombosis could be outlined in the following manner. Compression ultrasound is performed on referral; if it is abnormal, the diagnosis of venous thrombosis is established, and the patient is treated accordingly. If the result of the initial real-time ultrasound evaluation is normal, anticoagulant therapy is withheld and the test is repeated the following day, and again at day 7. If the real-time B-mode ultrasound results become abnormal during this time, a diagnosis of venous thrombosis is made, and anticoagulant therapy is commenced. If the compression ultrasound test results remain normal during serial testing, the diagnosis of venous thrombosis is excluded and the patient is not treated with anticoagulant therapy. It needs to be demonstrated whether alternative strategies can be employed to limit the number of repeat tests.

## DIAGNOSIS OF DEEP VEIN THROMBOSIS IN ASYMPTOMATIC HIGH-RISK PATIENTS

### Ultrasound Imaging

A total of 15 studies (14 in orthopedic surgical patients; one in neurosurgical patients) reported on the accuracy of ultrasound imaging techniques for the diagnosis of asymptomatic

**Table 23–8. Compression Ultrasonography in Asymptomatic High-Risk Patients**

| Investigators | Sensitivity for Proximal DVT % (n/N) | Specificity % (n/N) | Positive Predictive Value % (n/N) |
|---|---|---|---|
| Borris et al, 1989 | 63 (15/24) | 91 (29/32) | 83 (15/18) |
| Borris et al, 1990 | 73 (8/11) | 94 (44/47) | 73 (8/11) |
| Agnelli et al, 1992 | 57 (12/21) | 99 (165/166) | 92 (12/13) |
| Ginsberg et al, 1991 | 52 (11/21) | 99 (184/186) | 89 (11/13) |
| Cronan et al, 1991 | 100 (12/12) | 100 (64/64) | 100 (12/12) |
| Tremaine et al, 1992 | 100 (2/2) | 95 (55/58) | 40 (2/5) |
| Jongbloets et al, 1992 | 38 (5/13) | 96 (83/87) | 56 (5/9) |
| Lensing et al, 1994 | 60 (15/25) | 96 (124/129) | 75 (15/20) |
| Total | 62 (80/129) | 97 (748/769) | 79 (80/101) |

Table 23–9. **Duplex Ultrasonography in Asymptomatic High-Risk Patients**

| Investigators | Sensitivity for Proximal DVT % (n/N) | Specificity % (n/N) | Positive Predictive Value % (n/N) |
|---|---|---|---|
| Froehlich et al, 1989 | 100 (5/5) | 97 (33/34) | 83 (5/6) |
| Barnes et al, 1991 | 79 (15/19) | 98 (283/289) | 71 (15/21) |
| Woolson et al, 1991 | 67 (10/15) | 99 (72/73) | 91 (10/11) |
| Elliott et al, 1993 | 100 (4/4) | 92 (85/92) | 36 (4/11) |
| Total | 79 (34/43) | 97 (473/488) | 69 (34/49) |

venous thrombosis of the leg in high-risk patients. In all these studies, venography was used systematically; consecutive patients were included, and the analysis was done independently. Various other studies have investigated the usefulness of ultrasound in the diagnosis of thrombosis in this patient category, but have failed to meet the criteria for the proper evaluation of a diagnostic test.[35, 56, 165–168I, 169I, 170–173] In the selected 15 reports, eight evaluated compression ultrasound,[174–181] four used duplex ultrasonography,[182–185] and three assessed color-coded ultrasonography.[70, 181I, 186]

### Compression Ultrasound

In the eight studies using correct methodology, compression ultrasound identified 80 of the 129 legs with proximal vein thrombosis, for a sensitivity of 62% (Table 23–8). An abnormal ultrasound test was found in 21 of the 769 legs with normal venogram results, for a specificity of 97%. The positive predictive value was 79%.

### Duplex Ultrasonography

Four studies properly evaluated the accuracy of duplex ultrasonography for the diagnosis of proximal-vein thrombosis in asymptomatic high-risk patients (Table 23–9). In these studies, the sensitivity was 79% (34 in 43), and specificity was 97% (473 in 488). The predictive value of an abnormal test was 69%.

### Color Doppler Ultrasonography

The accuracy of color Doppler ultrasonography as a screening test for proximal vein thrombosis has been investigated in three methodologically sound studies[48, 66I, 75] (Table 23–10). Color Doppler correctly diagnosed proximal vein thrombosis in only 28 of the 56 legs, for a sensitivity of 50%. The presence of proximal vein thrombosis was correctly excluded in 528 of the 548 legs, for a specificity of 96%. Proximal vein thrombosis was demonstrated by venography in only 28 of the 48 legs with an abnormal color Doppler test result, for a positive predictive value of 58%.

### Accuracy for Isolated Calf Vein Thrombosis

Of the eight compression ultrasound studies in which the potential for bias was minimized, four evaluated the accuracy for isolated calf vein thrombosis[177I, 178I, 179I, 180, 181] (Table 23–11). In these studies, compression ultrasound identified 17 of the 42 isolated calf vein thromboses, for a sensitivity of 40%. Of the four duplex ultrasonography studies, only one study evaluated the accuracy for isolated calf vein thrombosis.[185] In this study, duplex ultrasonography identified 13 of the 23 patients with isolated calf vein thrombosis (sensitivity 57%). The sensitivity of color Doppler ultrasonography for isolated calf vein thrombosis was determined in one of three methodologically sound studies.[181] In addition, a color Doppler ultrasonography

Table 23–10. **Color Doppler Ultrasonography in Asymptomatic High-Risk Patients**

| Investigators | Sensitivity for Proximal DVT % (n/N) | Specificity % (n/N) | Positive Predictive Value % (n/N) |
|---|---|---|---|
| Davidson et al, 1992 | 38 (8/21) | 94 (225/239) | 30 (8/22) |
| Mattos et al, 1992 | 50 (5/10) | 99 (179/180) | 83 (5/6) |
| Lensing et al, 1994 | 60 (15/25) | 96 (124/129) | 75 (15/20) |
| Total | 50 (28/56) | 96 (528/548) | 58 (28/48) |

**Table 23-11. Sensitivity for Isolated Calf Vein Thrombosis for Studies in Asymptomatic High-Risk Patients That Mimimized the Potential for Bias**

| | Sensitivity | 95% Confidence Interval |
|---|---|---|
| Gray-scale Real-time Ultrasonography | | |
| Cronan et al, 1991 | 0 (0/1) | |
| Tremaine et al, 1992 | 50 (2/4) | 12–100 |
| Jongbloets et al, 1994 | 38 (5/13) | 8–69 |
| Lensing et al, 1994 | 42 (10/24) | 20–63 |
| Total | 40 (17/42) | 24–57 |
| Duplex Ultrasonography | | |
| Elliott et al, 1993 | 57 (13/23) | 34–79 |
| Color Doppler Ultrasonography | | |
| Lensing et al, 1994 | 42 (10/24) | 20–63 |
| Rose et al, 1993 | 58 (14/24) | 37–80 |
| Total | 49 (24/49) | 34–64 |

study that minimized the potential for bias was identified that evaluated only patients with isolated calf vein thrombosis.[187] The combined results of these studies demonstrate that 24 of the 49 patients with isolated calf vein thrombosis (sensitivity 49%) were correctly diagnosed.

## Impedance Plethysmography

A total of three studies evaluated the accuracy of IPG for the detection of asymptomatic thrombosis in postoperative patients.[188I, 189I, 190] All three studies used correct methodology. Impedance plethysmography detected 30 of the 134 patients with proximal vein thrombosis, for a sensitivity of 22%. A false-abnormal result was obtained in 32 of the 1,713 patients without proximal vein thrombosis, for a specificity of 98%. The positive predictive value was 55% (Table 23–12). The addition of fibrinogen leg scanning to IPG in patients who have hip surgery

improves sensitivity, but only to approximately 50%.

## Doppler Ultrasound

No studies using rigorous methodology addressed the value of Doppler ultrasound for the screening of asymptomatic deep vein thrombosis.

## 125I-Fibrinogen Leg Scanning

The pooled analysis of studies correlating 125I-fibrinogen leg scanning with contrast venography in postoperative patients who had hip surgery reported a sensitivity and specificity of leg scanning for both proximal and calf vein thromboses of 45% and 92% respectively (Table 23–13).[191] Surprisingly, 125I-fibrinogen leg scanning had a sensitivity for isolated calf vein thrombosis of only 55%.

## Diagnostic Management of Patients with Asymptomatic Deep Vein Thrombosis

The need for an accurate screening test for patients at high risk for asymptomatic deep vein thrombosis is well recognized. This patient category includes those following major orthopedic neurosurgical or abdominal-thoracic intervention, as well as patients who are subjected to periods of prolonged bedrest due to stroke or other chronic medical disorders. The ideal screening test should have a high predictive value for both ruling in and ruling out venous thrombosis, particularly of the deep calf veins. Furthermore, the test should be noninvasive, easy to perform in large numbers of patients, and cost-effective. At present, none of the available noninvasive techniques is able to satisfy these requirements.

Initially, it was believed that 125I-fibrinogen leg scanning was highly accurate for the diagnosis of asymptomatic thrombosis. The more rigorously designed studies, however, have revealed

**Table 23-12. Impedance Plethysmography in Postoperative Orthopedic Patients**

| Investigators | Sensitivity for Proximal DVT % (n/N) | Specificity % (n/N) | Positive Predictive Value % |
|---|---|---|---|
| Paiement et al, 1988 | 12 (9/73) | 99 (856/864) | 53 (9/17) |
| Cruickshank et al, 1989 | 29 (14/49) | 98 (681/694) | 58 (18/31) |
| Ginsberg et al, 1990 | 58 (7/12) | 95 (144/155) | 50 (7/14) |
| Total | 22 (30/134) | 98 (1,681/1,713) | 55 (34/62) |

Table 23–13. $^{125}$I-Fibrinogen Leg Scanning in Orthopedic Surgical Patients

| Investigators | Sensitivity for Calf DVT % (n/N) | Sensitivity for All DVT % (n/N) | Specificity % (n/N) |
|---|---|---|---|
| Harris et al, 1976 | 75 (6/8) | 37 (7/19) | 90 (53/59) |
| Sautter et al, 1979 | 59 (23/39) | 58 (29/50) | 70 (67/96) |
| Sautter et al, 1983 | 59 (14/24) | 34 (20/50) | 79 (47/59) |
| Paiement et al, 1988 | 59 (78/133) | 44 (84/190) | 96 (769/804) |
| Cruickshank et al, 1989 | 51 (59/116) | 45 (78/175) | 95 (737/776) |
| Faunø et al, 1990 | 50 (30/60) | 44 (12/27)* | 87 (368/423) |
| Total | 55 (210/380) | 45 (230/511) | 92 (2,041/2,217) |

its poor sensitivity for calf as well as proximal vein thrombosis. There was an initial optimism that the ultrasound imaging techniques would resolve the diagnostic problem in patients at high risk of having asymptomatic thrombosis. Unfortunately, again, upon careful evaluation it was shown that none of the ultrasound devices had a sufficient high sensitivity, even for proximal vein thrombosis. These findings are in contrast with the high clinical utility of ultrasound in the diagnosis of symptomatic venous thrombosis. This discrepancy is most likely caused by the different features of the thrombus in the two patient categories (see Table 23–1). Therefore, at this time the only reliable technique remains contrast venography.

## DIAGNOSIS OF RECURRENT DEEP VEIN THROMBOSIS

The diagnosis of recurrent deep vein thrombosis still remains a difficult problem, because the clinical diagnosis of recurrent deep vein thrombosis is highly nonspecific and because each of the objective diagnostic tests for deep vein thrombosis has potential limitations in this setting.[8, 9] Approximately one-third of patients with an initial episode of deep vein thrombosis during the following year have signs and symptoms suggestive of recurrent deep vein thrombosis. These symptoms are indeed caused by acute recurrent deep vein thrombosis in approximately one of three patients, whereas in the remaining subjects, the suspected episode is the result of the post-thrombotic syndrome or a variety of other nonthrombotic disorders. Differentiation among these three causes for recurrent leg symptoms is important because anticoagulant therapy is not required in patients with either the post-thrombotic syndrome or a nonthrombotic cause for leg symptoms. Of the available diagnostic tests for venous thrombosis, venography, impedance plethysmography alone or in combination with $^{125}$I-fibrinogen leg scan-

ning, and ultrasound imaging have been evaluated for the diagnosis of recurrent deep vein thrombosis.

## Venography

Venography is a useful test for the diagnosis of recurrent deep vein thrombosis if films of the initial thrombotic episode are available and repeat venography demonstrates a new constant intraluminal filling defect.[8] The use of venography as a diagnostic tool for recurrent deep vein thrombosis is limited if a baseline venogram is not available or if the presence of recurrent thrombosis is masked by obliteration and recanalization of the vein as a consequence of previous disease, the latter possibly occurring in up to 30% of patients.

## Impedance Plethysmography and $^{125}$I-Fibrinogen Leg Scanning

In patients with suspected recurrent deep vein thrombosis, IPG can be used only if a normal previous test result is available. In prospective cohort studies it has been shown that 1 year after the initial thrombosis, 95% of the IPG test results have returned to normal.[9, 192] If the IPG test results become normal, the test can be used alone or in combination with fibrinogen leg scanning to confirm or refute the diagnosis of recurrent deep vein thrombosis in symptomatic patients.[17, 42] The utility of IPG in symptomatic recurrent deep vein thrombosis has been determined in two studies.[8, 9] In the first study, 270 patients were referred with clinical signs and symptoms of recurrent deep vein thrombosis. In 200 of these patients, the IPG result was normal and subsequently leg scanning was performed. The results of leg scanning were normal in 181 patients. These patients were not treated with anticoagulants. During 3 months of followup, recurrent deep vein thrombosis was demonstrated in three of the 181 patients (1.7%). In another study of patients with sus-

pected recurrent deep vein thrombosis, anticoagulants were withheld safely in all 18 patients
with repeated normal IPG tests.

## Ultrasound Imaging

The use of ultrasound imaging for the diagnosis of recurrent deep vein thrombosis is complicated by the high rate of persistent abnormal
ultrasound results. In prospective cohort studies, the compression ultrasound results became
normal in only 50 to 60% of the patients after
1 year.[193–196] An alternative quantitative compression ultrasound method based on measuring vein diameter during maximal compressibility has been introduced.[197, 198] To obtain a
baseline result, compression measurements
were performed every 3 months after a first
episode of deep vein thrombosis. If a patient
returned with recurrent symptoms, the measurements were repeated and compared with
the previous results. The hypothesis is that new
thrombosis correlates with an increase in diameter. A study is ongoing to demonstrate the safety
and effectiveness of this method in a large sample of patients with a suspected episode of recurrent deep vein thrombosis.

## Diagnostic Management of Patients with Suspected Recurrent Deep Vein Thrombosis

No general recommendations can be given
for the diagnostic management of patients with
suspected recurrent deep vein thrombosis, because the use of all available methods is limited
in this setting. Contrast venography gives indeterminate results in a substantial proportion of
patients. Impedance plethysmography alone has
been insufficiently documented as a safe approach, whereas the addition of [125]I-fibrinogen
leg scanning is hampered by the limited availability of the radiofarmacon. Finally, ultrasound
imaging has the potential to become the
method of choice.

## REFERENCES

1. Bauer G: A venographic study of thromboembolism problems. Acta Chir Scand 84 (Suppl 161):1, 1940.
2. Haeger K: Problems of acute deep venous thrombo-sis. I. The interpretation of signs and symptoms. Angiology 20:219, 1969.
3. Lensing AWA, Hirsh J, Büller HR: Diagnosis of deep vein thrombosis. In Colman RW, Hirsh J, Marder VJ, Salzman EW (eds): Hemostasis and Thrombosis. Philadelphia, JB Lippincott, 1993.
4. Büller HR, Lensing AWA, Hirsh J, ten Cate JW: Deep venous thrombosis: New noninvasive tests. Thromb Haemost 66:133, 1991.
5. Cranley JJ, Canos AJ, Sull WJ: The diagnosis of deep vein thrombosis. Fallibility of clinical signs and symp-toms. Arch Surg 111:34, 1976.
6. O'Donnel TF, Abbott WM, Athanasoulis CA, et al: Diagnosis of deep vein thrombosis in the outpatient by venography. Surg Gynecol Obstet 150:69, 1980.
7. Cogo A, Lensing AWA, Prandoni P, Hirsh J: Distribu-tion of deep vein thrombi in symptomatic patients. Arch Intern Med 153:2777, 1993.
8. Hull RD, Carter C, Jay R, et al: The diagnosis of acute recurrent deep-vein thrombosis: A diagnostic challenge. Circulation 67:901, 1983.
9. Huisman MV, Büller HR, ten Cate JW: Utility of impedance plethysmography in the diagnosis or re-current deep-vein thrombosis. Arch Intern Med 148:681, 1988.
10. Consensus Conference: Prevention of Venous Thrombosis and Pulmonary Embolism. JAMA 256:744, 1986.
11. Leyvraz PF, Richard J, Bachman F, et al: Adjusted versus fixed dose subcutaneous heparin in the pre-vention of deep vein thrombosis after total hip re-placement. N Engl J Med 309:954, 1983.
12. Francis CW, Marder VJ, Evarte CM, Yaukoolbodi S: Two step warfarin therapy. Prevention of postopera-tive venous thrombosis without excessive bleeding. JAMA 249:374, 1983.
13. Turpie AG, Levine MN, Hirsh J, et al: A randomized controlled trial of low molecular weight heparin to prevent deep vein thrombosis in patients undergo-ing elective hip surgery. N Engl J Med 315:925, 1986.
14. Hirsh J, Levine M: Prevention of venous thrombosis in patients undergoing major surgical procedures. Br J Clin Pract 43(Suppl):2, 1988.
15. Levine MN, Hirsh J, Gent M, et al: Prevention of deep vein thrombosis after elective hip surgery. A randomized trial comparing low molecular weight heparin with standard unfractionated heparin. Ann Intern Med 114:545, 1991.
16. Hull R, Raskob G, Pineo G, et al: A comparison of subcutaneous low-molecular-weight heparin with warfarin sodium for prophylaxis against deep-vein thrombosis after hip or knee implantation. N Engl J Med 329:1370, 1993.
17. Sackett DL, Haynes RB, Tugwell P: The interpreta-tion of diagnostic data. In Clinical Epidemiology. A Basic Science for Clinical Medicine. Boston/To-ronto, Little, Brown, 1985.
18. Lensing AWA, Prandoni P, Büller HR, et al: Lower extremity venography with iohexol: Results and com-plications. Radiology 177:503, 1990.
19. McLachlan MSF, Thomson JG, Taylor DW, et al: Observer variation in the interpretation of lower limb venograms. Am J Radiol 132:227, 1979.
20. Lensing AWA, Büller HR, Prandoni P, et al: Contrast venography, the gold standard for the diagnosis of deep vein thrombosis: Improvement in observer agreement. Thromb Haemost 67:8, 1992.
21. White RH, McGahan JP, Dasenbach MM, Hartling RP: Diagnosis of deep vein thrombosis using duplex ultrasound. Ann Intern Med 111:297, 1989.
22. Becker DM, Philbrick JT, Abbitt PL: Real-time ultra-sonography for the diagnosis of lower extremity deep venous thrombosis. Arch Intern Med 149:1731, 1989.
23. Hull RD, van Aken WG, Hirsh J, et al: Impedance plethysmography using the occlusive cuff technique in the diagnosis of venous thrombosis. Circulation 53:696, 1976.
24. Langsfeld M, Hershey FB, Thorpe L, et al: Duplex

B-mode imaging for the diagnosis of deep venous thrombosis. Arch Surg 122:587, 1987.

25. Rollins DL, Semrow CM, Friedell ML, et al: Progress in the diagnosis of deep venous thrombosis. J Vasc Surg 7:638, 1988.

26. Rosner NH, Doris PE: Diagnosis of femoropopliteal venous thrombosis. AJR 150:623, 1988.

27. Persson AV, Jones C, Zide R, Jewell ER: Use of triplex scanner in diagnosis of deep venous thrombosis. Arch Surg 124:593, 1989.

28. Fobbe F, Koennecke HC, Bedewi M, et al: Diagnostik der tiefen beinvenenthrombose mit der farbkodierten duplexsonosgraphie. Fortschr Roentgenstr 151:569, 1989.

29. Killewich LA, Bedford GR, Beach KW, Strandness DE Jr: Diagnosis of deep venous thrombosis. Circulation. 79:810, 1989.

30. Cavaye D, Kelly AT, Graham JC, et al: Duplex ultrasound diagnosis of lower limb venous thrombosis. Aust NZJ Surg 60:283, 1990.

31. George JE, Berry RE: Noninvasive detection of deep venous thrombosis. Am Surg 56:76, 1990.

32. Wright DJ, Shepard AD, McPharlin M, Ernst CB: Pitfalls in lower extremity venous duplex scanning. J Vasc Surg 5:675, 1990.

33. Foley WD, Middleton WD, Lawson TL, et al: Color Doppler ultrasound imaging of lower-extremity venous disease. Am J Radiol 152:371, 1991.

34. AbuRahma AF, Kennard W, Robinson PA, et al: The judicial use of venous duplex imaging and strain gauge plethysmography (single or combined) in the diagnosis of acute and chronic deep vein thrombosis. Surg Gynecol Obstet 174:52, 1992.

35. Mussurakis S, Papaioannou S, Voros D, Vrakatselis T: Compression ultrasonography as a reliable imaging monitor in deep venous thrombosis. Surg Gynecol Obstet 171:233, 1990.

36. Greer IA, Barry J, Mackon N, Allan PL: Diagnosis of deep venous thrombosis in pregnancy: A new role for diagnostic ultrasound. Br J Obstet Gynecol 97:53, 1990.

37. Ramshorst B, Legemate DA, Verzijlbergen JF, et al: Duplex scanning in the diagnosis of acute deep vein thrombosis of the lower extremity. Eur J Vasc Surg 5:255, 1991.

38. Irvine AT, Thomas ML: Colour-coded duplex sonography in the diagnosis of deep vein thrombosis: A comparison with phlebography. Phlebography 6:103, 1991.

39. Lindqvist R: Ultrasound as a complementary diagnostic method in deep vein thrombosis of the leg. Acta Med Scand 201:435, 1977.

40. Montefusco-von Kleist CM, Bakal C, Sprayregen S, et al: Comparison of duplex ultrasonography and ascending contrast venography in the diagnosis of venous thrombosis. Angiology 44:169, 1993.

41. Yucel EK, Fisher JS, Egglin TK, et al: Isolated calf vein thrombosis: Diagnosis with compression ultrasound. Radiology 179:443, 1991.

42. Effeney DJ, Friedman MD, Gooding GAW: Iliofemoral venous thrombosis: Real-time ultrasound diagnosis, normal criteria, and clinical application. Radiology 150:787, 1984.

43. Raghavendra BN, Rosen RJ, Lam S, et al: Deep venous thrombosis: detection by high resolution real-time ultrasonography. Radiology 152:789, 1984.

44. Raghavendra BN, Horii SC, Hilton S, et al: Deep venous thrombosis: detection by probe compression of veins: J Ultrasound Med 5:89, 1986.

45. Fletcher JP, Kershaw LS, Barker DS, et al: Ultra-sound diagnosis of lower limb deep venous thrombosis. Med J Aust 153:453, 1990.

46. George JE, Smith MO, Berry RE: Duplex scanning for the detection of deep venous thrombosis of lower extremities in a community hospital. Curr Surg 44:203, 1987.

47. Elias A, LeCorff G, Bouvier JL, et al: Value of real-time B-mode ultrasound imaging in the diagnosis of deep vein thrombosis of the lower limbs. Int Angiol 6:175, 1987.

48. Comerota AJ, Katz ML, Greenwald LL, et al: Venous duplex imaging: Should it replace hemodynamic tests for deep venous thrombosis. J Vasc Surg 11:53, 1990.

49. Belcaro GV, Laurora G, Cesarone MR, Errichi BM: Colour duplex scanning and phlebography in deep vein thrombosis. Panminerva Med 34:1, 1992.

50. Bradley MJ, Spencer PA, Elaxander L, Milner GR: Colour flow mapping in the diagnosis of calf deep vein thrombosis. Clin Radiol 47:399, 1993.

51. Dauzat MM, Laroche JP, Charras C, et al: Real-time B-mode ultrasonography for better specificity in the noninvasive diagnosis of deep venous thrombosis. J Ultrasound Med 5:625, 1986.

52. Appelman PT, de Jong TE, Lampman LE, et al: Deep venous thrombosis of the leg: US findings. Radiology 163:743, 1987.

53. Aitken AGF, Godden DJ: Real-time ultrasound diagnosis of deep vein thrombosis: A comparison with venography. Clin Radiol 38:309, 1987.

54. Cronan JJ, Dorfman GS, Scola FH, et al: Deep venous thrombosis: US assessment using vein compressibility. Radiology 162:191, 1987.

I 55. Lensing AWA, Prandoni P, Brandjes D, et al: Detection of deep-vein thrombosis by real-time B-mode ultrasonography. N Engl J Med 320:342, 1989.

56. Monreal M, Montserrat E, Salvador R, et al: Real-time ultrasound for diagnosis of symptomatic venous thrombosis and for screening of patients at risk. Angiology 40:527, 1989.

57. Habscheid W, Hohmann M, Wilhelm T, Epping J: Real-time ultrasound in the diagnosis of acute deep venous thrombosis of the lower extremity. Angiology 40:599, 1990.

I 58. Gudmundsen TE, Vinje B, Pedersen T: Deep vein thrombosis of lower extremities. Diagnosis by real-time ultrasonography. Acta Radiol 31:473, 1990.

59. Chance JF, Abbitt PL, Tegtmeyer CJ, Powers RD: Real-time ultrasound for the detection of deep venous thrombosis. Ann Emerg Med 20:494, 1991.

60. Pedersen OM, Aslaksen A, Vik-Mo H, Bassoe AM: Compression ultrasonography in hospitalized patients with suspected deep venous thrombosis. Arch Intern Med 151:2217, 1991.

I 61. Heijboer H, Cogo A, Büller HR, et al: Detection of deep vein thrombosis with impedance plethysmography and real-time compression ultrasonography in hospitalized patients. Arch Intern Med 152:1901, 1992.

62. Vogel P, Laing FC, Jeffrey RB, Wing VW: Deep venous thrombosis of the lower extremity: US evaluation. Radiology 163:747, 1987.

63. O'Leary DH, Kane RA, Chase BM: A prospective study of the efficacy of B-scan sonography in the detection of deep venous thrombosis in the lower extremities. J Clin Ultrasound 16:1, 1988.

64. Mantoni M: Diagnosis of deep venous thrombosis by duplex sonography. Acta Radiol 30:575, 1989.

65. Mitchell DC, Grasty MS, Stebbings WSL, et al: Comparison of duplex ultrasonography and venography

in the diagnosis of deep venous thrombosis. Br J Surg 78:611, 1991.

I 66. Quintavalla R, Larini P, Miselli A, et al: Duplex ultrasound diagnosis of symptomatic proximal deep vein thrombosis of lower limbs. Eur J Radiol 15:32, 1992.

67. Baxter GM, McKechnie S, Duffy P: Colour Doppler ultrasound in deep venous thrombosis: A comparison with venography. Clin Radiol 42:32, 1990.

68. Rose ST, Zwiebel WJ, Nelson BD, et al: Symptomatic lower extremity deep venous thrombosis: accuracy, limitations, and role of color duplex flow imaging in diagnosis. Radiology 175:639, 1990.

69. Schindler JM, Kaiser M, Gerber A, et al: Colour coded duplex sonography in suspected deep vein thrombosis of the leg. Br Med J 301:1369, 1990.

70. Mattos MA, Londey GL, Leutz DW, et al: Color-flow duplex scanning for the surveillance and diagnosis of acute deep venous thrombosis. J Vasc Surg 15:366, 1992.

71. Hull RD, van Aken WG, Hirsh J, et al: Impedance plethysmography using the occlusive cuff technique in the diagnosis of venous thrombosis. Circulation 53:696, 1976.

I 72. Richards KL, Armstrong DJ, Tikoff G, et al: Noninvasive diagnosis of deep venous thrombosis. Arch Intern Med 136:1091, 1976.

73. Hull RD, Hirsh J, Sackett DL, et al: Combined use of leg scanning and impedance plethysmography in suspected venous thrombosis: An alternative to venography. N Engl J Med 296:1497, 1977.

I 74. Toy PTC, Schrier SL: Occlusive impedance plethysmography: A non-invasive method of diagnosis of deep vein thrombosis. West J Med 129:89, 1978.

75. Hull RD, Taylor DW, Hirsh J, et al: Impedance plethysmography: The relationship between venous filling and sensitivity and specificity for proximal vein thrombosis. Circulation 58:898, 1978.

76. Hull RD, Hirsh J, Sackett DL, et al: Replacement of venography in suspected venous thrombosis by impedance plethysmography and 125I-fibrinogen leg scanning: A less invasive approach. Ann Intern Med 94:12, 1981.

I 77. Peters SHA, Jonker JJC, de Boer AC, et al: Home diagnosis of deep venous thrombosis with impedance plethysmography. Thromb Haemost 48:297, 1982.

I 78. Prandoni P, Lensing AWA, Huisman MV, et al: A new computerized impedance plethysmograph: Accuracy in the detection of proximal deep vein thrombosis in symptomatic outpatients. Thromb Haemost 65:229, 1991.

79. Anderson DR, Lensing AWA, Wells PS, et al: Limitations of impedance plethysmography in the diagnosis of clinically suspected deep-vein thrombosis. Ann Intern Med 118:25, 1993.

80. Johnston KW, Kakkar VV: Plethysmographic diagnosis of deep vein thrombosis. Gynecol Obstet 139:41, 1974.

81. Wheeler HB, Pearson D, O'Connell D, Mullick SC: Impedance phlebography: Technique, interpretation and results. Arch Surg 104:164, 1972.

82. Wheeler B, O'Donnel JA, Anderson F, et al: Bedside screening for venous thrombosis using occlusive impedance plethysmography. Angiology 26:199, 1975.

83. Flanigan DP, Goodreau JJ, Burnham SJ, et al: Vascular laboratory diagnosis of clinically suspected acute deep vein thrombosis. Lancet 2:331, 1978.

84. Cooperman M, Martin EW, Jr, Satiani B, et al: Detection of deep venous thrombosis by impedance plethysmography. Am J Surg 137:252, 1979.

85. Gross WS, Burney RE: Therapeutic and economic implications of emergency department evaluation for venous thrombosis. Ann Emerg Med 8:110, 1979.

86. Wheeler HB, Anderson FA, Cardullo PA: Suspected deep vein thrombosis. Management by impedance plethysmography. Arch Surg 117:1206, 1982.

87. Sandler DA, Martin JF, Duncan JE, et al: Diagnosis of deep vein thrombosis. Comparison of clinical evaluation, ultrasound, plethysmography and venoscan with X-ray venogram. Lancet I:716, 1984.

88. Comerota A, Katz ML, Grossy RJ, et al: Comparative value of noninvasive testing for diagnosis and surveillance of deep vein thrombosis. J Vasc Surg 7:40, 1988.

89. Yao ST, Gourmos C, Hobbs JT: Detection of proximal vein thrombosis by Doppler ultrasound flow detection. Lancet 1:1, 1972.

90. Holmes MCG: Deep venous thrombosis of the lower limbs diagnosed by ultrasound. Med J Aust 1:427, 1973.

91. Meadway J, Nicolaides AN, Walker CJ, et al: Value of Doppler ultrasound in diagnosis of clinically suspected deep vein thrombosis. Br Med J 4:552, 1975.

92. Dosick SM, Blakemore WS: The role of Doppler ultrasound in acute deep vein thrombosis. Am J Surg 136:265, 1978.

93. Flanigan DP, Goodreau JJ, Burnham SJ, et al: Vascular laboratory diagnosis of clinically suspected acute deep vein thrombosis. Lancet 2:331, 1978.

94. Sumner DS, Lambeth A: Reliability of Doppler ultrasound in the diagnosis of acute venous thrombosis both above and below the knee. Am J Surg 138:205, 1979.

95. Hanel KC, Abbott WM, Reidy NC, et al: The role of two noninvasive tests in deep venous thrombosis. Ann Surg 194:725, 1981.

96. Zielinsky A, Hull R, Carter C, et al: Doppler ultrasonography in patients with clinically suspected deep vein thrombosis. Thromb Haemost 50:153, 1983.

I 97. Turnbull T, Dymowski JJ, Zalut TE: A prospective study of hand-held Doppler ultrasonography by emergency physicians in the evaluation of suspected deep vein thrombosis. Ann Emerg Med 19:691, 1990.

98. Sigel B, Felix WR, Popky GL, Ispen J: Diagnosis of lower limb venous thrombosis by Doppler ultrasound technique. Arch Surg 104:174, 1972.

99. Evans DS: The early diagnosis of thromboembolism by ultrasound. Ann R Coll Surg Engl 49:225, 1971.

100. Strandness DE, Sumner DS: Ultrasonic velocity detector in the diagnosis of thrombophlebitis. Arch Surg 104:180, 1972.

I 101. Lensing AWA, Levi MM, Büller HR, et al: An objective Doppler method for the diagnosis of deep-vein thrombosis. Ann Intern Med 113:9, 1990.

I 102. Cogo A, Lensing AWA, Prandoni P, et al: Comparison of real-time B-mode ultrasonography and Doppler ultrasound with contrast venography in symptomatic outpatients. Thromb Haemost 70:404, 1993.

103. Barnes RW, Collicott PE, Mozersky DJ, et al: Noninvasive quantitation of maximum venous outflow in acute thrombophlebitis. Surgery 72:971, 1972.

104. Cranley JJ, Gay AY, Grass AM, Simeone FA: A plethysmographic technique for the diagnosis of deep venous thrombosis of the lower extremities. Surg Gynecol Obstet 136:385, 1973.

105. Cooke ED, Pilcher MF: Deep vein thrombosis: A preclinical diagnosis by thermography. Br J Surg 61:971, 1974.

I 106. Jensen C, Lomboldt Knudsen L, Hegedüs V: The role of contact thermography in the diagnosis of deep venous thrombosis. Europe J Radiol 3:99, 1983.

107. Sandler DA, Martin JF: Liquid crystal thermography as a screening test for deep-vein thrombosis. Lancet 1: 665, 1985.

108. Holmgren K, Jacobsson H, Johnsson H, Lofsjogard-Nilsson: Thermography and plethysmography, a noninvasive alternative to venography in the diagnosis of deep vein thrombosis. J Intern Med 228:29, 1990.

I 109. Bounameaux H, Khabiri E, Huber O, et al: Value of liquid crystal contact thermography and plasma level of D-dimer for screening of deep venous thrombosis following general abdominal surgery. Thromb Haemost 67:603, 1992.

I 110. Thomas PRS, Butler CM, Bowman J, et al: Light reflection rheography: An effective non-invasive technique for screening patients with suspected deep venous thrombosis. Br J Surg 78:207, 1991.

111. Spritzer CE, Sussman SK, Blinder RA, et al: Deep venous thrombosis evaluation with limited-flipangle, gradient-refocused MR imaging: Preliminary experience. Radiology 166:371, 1988.

112. Erdman WA, Jayson HT, Redman HC, et al: Deep venous thrombosis of extremities: Role of MR imaging in the diagnosis. Radiology 174:425, 1990.

113. Spritzer CE, Sostman HD, Wilkes DC, Coleman RE: Deep venous thrombosis: experience with gradient echo MR imaging in 66 patients. Radiology 177:235, 1990.

I 114. Evans AJ, Sostman HD, Knelson MH, et al: Detection of deep venous thrombosis: Prospective comparison of MR imaging with contrast venography. AJR 161:131, 1993.

115. Webber MM, Bennett LR, Cragin M, Webb R Jr: Thrombophlebitis demonstration by scintiscanning. Radiology 92:620, 1969.

116. Rosenthal L, Greyson ND: Observations on the use of 99mTc albumin macroaggregates for the detection of thrombophlebitis. Radiology 94:413, 1970.

117. Webber MM, Victery W, Cragin MD: Demonstration of thrombophlebitis and endothelial damage by scintiscanning. Radiology 100:93, 1971.

118. Webber MM, Pollack EW, Victery W, et al: Thrombosis detection by radionuclide particle (MAA) entrapment: Correlation with fibrinogen uptake and venography. Radiology 111:645, 1974.

119. Millar WT, Smith JFB: Localization of deep venous thrombosis using technetium-99m-labelled urokinase. Lancet 2:695, 1974.

120. Kempi V, Van Der Linden V, VonScheele C: Diagnosis of deep-vein thrombosis with 99mTc-streptokinase: A clinical comparison with phlebography. Br Med J 4:748, 1974.

121. Ryo UY, Qazi M, Srikantaswamy S, Pinsky S: Radionuclide venography: Correlation with contrast venography. J Nucl Med 18:11, 1977.

122. Knight LC, Primeau JL, Siegel BA, Welch MJ: Comparison of In-111-labelled platelets and iodinated fibrinogen for the detection of deep-vein thrombosis. J Nucl Med 19:891, 1978.

123. Bentley PG, Kakkar VV: Radionuclide venography for the demonstration of the proximal deep venous system. Br J Surg 66:687, 1979.

124. Beswick W, Chmiel R, Booth R, et al: Detection of deep venous thrombosis by scanning of 99m technetium-labelled red-cell venous pool. Br Med J 1:82, 1979.

125. Deacon JM, Ell PJ, Anderson P, Khan O: Technetium-99m-plasmin: A new test for the detection of deep-vein thrombosis. Br J Radiol 53:673, 1980.

126. Uphold RE, Knopp R, dosSantos PAL: Radionuclide

venogaphy as an outpatient screening test for deep venous thrombosis. Ann Emerg Med 9:613, 1980.

127. Fenech A, Hussey JK, Smith FW, et al: Diagnosis of deep-vein thrombosis using autologous indium-111-labelled platelets. Br Med J 282:1020, 1981.

128. Grimley RP, Rafiqi E, Hawker RJ, Drolc Z: Imaging of 111In-labelled platelets—a new method for the diagnosis of deep-vein thrombosis. Br J Surg 68: 714, 1981.

129. Lisbona R, Stern J, Derbekyan V: 99mTc red blood cell venography in deep-vein thrombosis of the legs: A correlation with contrast venography. Radiology 143:771, 1982.

I 130. Adolfsson L, Nordenfelt I, Olsson H, Torstensson I: Diagnosis of deep-vein thrombosis with 99mTcm-plasmin. Acta Med Scand 211:365, 1982.

131. Fedullo PF, Moser KM, Moser KS, et al: Indium-111-labelled platelets: Effect of heparin on uptake by venous thrombi and relationship to the activated partial thromboplastin time. Circulation 66:632, 1982.

132. Singer I, Royal HD, Uren RF, et al: Radionuclide plethysmography and Tc-99m red blood cell venography in venous thrombosis: Comparison with contrast venography. Radiology 150:213, 1984.

I 133. Zorba J, Schier D, Posmituck G: Clinical value of blood pool radionuclide venography. AJR, 146:1051, 1986.

I 134. Leclerc JR, Wolfson C, Arzoumanian A, et al: Technetium-99m red blood cell venography in patients with clinically suspected deep vein thrombosis: A prospective study. J Nucl Med 29:1498, 1988.

135. Yudelman IM, Nossel HL, Kaplan KL, Hirsh J: Plasma fibrinopeptide A levels in symptomatic venous thromboembolism. Blood 51:1189, 1978.

136. Kockum C: Radioimmunoassay of fibrinopeptide A—clinical applications. Thromb Res 8:225, 1976.

137. Yudelman IM, Nossel HL, Kaplan KL, Hirsh J: Plasma fibrinopeptide A levels in symptomatic venous thromboembolism. Blood 51:1189, 1978.

138. Tibbutt DA, Chesterman CN, Allington MJ, et al: Measurement of fibrinogen-fibrin-related antigen in serum as aid to diagnosis of deep vein thrombosis in outpatients. Br Med J 1:367, 1975.

139. Hunt FA, Rylatt DB, Hart RA, et al: Serum cross-linked fibrin (XDP) and fibrinogen/fibrin degradation products (FDP) in disorders associated with activation of the coagulation or fibrinolytic systems. Br J Haematol 60:715, 1985.

I 140. Heaton DC, Billings JD, Hickton CM: Assessment of D dimer assays for the diagnosis of deep vein thrombosis. J Lab Clin Med 110:588, 1987.

141. Declerck PJ, Mombaerts P, Holvoet P, et al: Fibrinolytic response and fibrin fragment D-dimer levels in patients with deep vein thrombosis. Thromb Haemost 58:1024, 1987.

I 142. Ott P, Astrup L, Jensen RH, et al: Assessment of D-dimer in plasma: Diagnostic value in suspected deep venous thrombosis of the leg. Acta Med Scand 224:263, 1988.

143. Bounameaux H, Schneider PA, Reber G, et al: Measurement of plasma D-dimer for diagnosis of deep venous thrombosis. Am J Clin Pathol 91:82, 1989.

144. Wilde JT, Kitchen S, Kinsey S, et al: Plasma D-dimer levels and their relationship to serum fibrinogen/fibrin degradation products in hypercoagulable states. Br J Haematol 71:65, 1989.

145. Elms MJ, Bunce IK, Bundesen PG, et al: Measurement of crosslinked fibrin degradation products—an immunoassay using monoclonal antibodies. Thromb Haemost 50:591, 1983.

146. Rowbotham BJ, Carroll P, Whitaker AN, et al: Measurement of crosslinked fibrin derivatives—use in the diagnosis of venous thrombosis. Thromb Haemost 57:59, 1987.

147. Heaton DC, Billings JD, Hickton CM: Assessment of D-dimer assays for the diagnosis of deep vein thrombosis. J Lab Clin Med 1110:588, 1987.

148. Ott P, Astrup L, Jensen RH, Nyeland B, Pederson B: Assessment of D-dimer in plasma: Diagnostic value in suspected deep venous thrombosis of the leg. Acta Med Scand 224:263, 1988.

I 149. Bounameaux H, Schneider PA, Reber G, et al: Measurement of plasma D-dimer for diagnosis of deep venous thrombosis. Am J Clin Pathol 91:82, 1989.

I 150. Speiser W, Mallek R, Koppensteiner R, et al: D-dimer and TAT measurements in patients with deep venous thrombosis: Utility in diagnosis and judgement of anticoagulant treatment effectiveness. Thromb Haemost 64:196, 1990.

151. Rowbotham BJ, Carroll P, Whitaker AN, et al: Measurement of crosslinked fibrin derivatives—use in the diagnosis of venous thrombosis. Thromb Haemost 57:59, 1987.

152. Boneu B, Bes G, Pelzer H, et al: D-dimers, thrombin-antithrombin III complexes and prothrombin fragments 1 + 2: Diagnostic value in clinically suspected deep vein thrombosis. Thromb Haemost 65:28, 1991.

I 153. Heijboer H, Ginsberg JS, Büller HR, et al: The use of the D-dimer test in combination with non-invasive testing versus serial non-invasive testing alone for the diagnosis of deep-vein thrombosis. Thromb Haemost 67:510, 1992.

154. Hoek JA, Nurmohamed MT, ten Cate JW, et al: Thrombin-antithrombin III complexes in the prediction of deep vein thrombosis following total hip replacement. Thromb Haemost 62:1050, 1989.

155. Boneu B, Bes G, Pelzer H, et al: D-dimers, thrombin antithrombin III complexes and prothrombin fragments 1 + 2: Diagnostic value in clinically suspected deep vein thrombosis. Thromb Haemost 65:28, 1991.

I 156. Cogo A, Lensing AWA, Prandoni P, et al: Failure of T-AT complexes in the diagnosis of deep vein thrombosis in symptomatic patients. Angiology 43:975, 1992.

157. Zielinsky A, Hirsh J, Hull R, et al: Evaluation of radioimmunoassay for Fragment E in the diagnosis of venous thrombosis. Thromb Haemost 42:28, 1979.

158. Hull RD, Hirsh J, Carter C, et al: Diagnostic efficacy of impedance plethysmography for clinically suspected deep-vein thrombosis: A randomized trial. Ann Intern Med 102:21, 1985.

I 159. Huisman MV, Büller HR, ten Cate JW, Vreeken J: Serial impedance plethysmography for suspected deep venous thrombosis in outpatients. The Amsterdam General Practitioner Study. N Engl J Med 314:823, 1986.

I 160. Huisman MV, Büller HR, ten Cate JW, et al: Management of clinically suspected acute venous thrombosis in outpatients with serial impedance plethysmography in a community hospital setting. Arch Intern Med 149:511, 1989.

161. Hull RD, Raskob GE, Carter CJ, et al: Serial impedance plethysmography in pregnant patients with clinically suspected deep vein thrombosis. Ann Intern Med 112:663, 1990.

162. Vaccaro JP, Cronan JJ, Dorfman GS: Outcome analysis of patients with normal compression US—examinations. Radiology 175:645, 1990.

163. Sluzewski M, Koopman MMW, Schuur KH, et al:

Influence of negative ultrasound findings on the management of in- and outpatients with suspected deep-vein thrombosis. Eur J Radiol 13:174, 1991.

I 164. Heijboer H, Büller HR, Lensing AWA, et al: A comparison of real-time compression ultrasonography with impedance plethysmography for the diagnosis of deep-vein thrombosis in symptomatic outpatients. N Engl J Med 329:1365, 1993.

165. Nix ML, Nelson CL, Harmon BH, et al: Duplex venous scanning: Image vs Doppler accuracy. J Vasc Tech 13:123, 1989.

166. Barnes RW, Nix ML, Barnes CL, et al: Perioperative asymptomatic venous thrombosis: Role of duplex scanning versus venography. J Vasc Surg 9:251, 1989.

167. Flinn WR, Sandager GP, Cerullo LJ, et al: Duplex venous scanning for the prospective surveillance of perioperative venous thrombosis. Arch Surg 124:901, 1989.

I 168. Kraay MJ, Goldberg VM, Herbener TE: Vascular ultrasonography for deep venous thrombosis after total knee arthroplasty. Clin Orthop 286:18, 1993.

I 169. Vanninen R, Manninen H, Soimakallio S, et al: Asymptomatic deep venous thrombosis in the calf: Accuracy and limitations of ultrasonography as a screening test after total knee arthroplasty. Br J Radiol 66:199, 1993.

170. Woolson ST, McCrory DW, Walter JF, et al: B-mode ultrasound scanning in the detection of proximal venous thrombosis after total hip replacement. J Bone Joint Surg 72:983, 1990.

171. Dorfman GS, Froehlich JA, Cronan JJ, et al: Lower-exterimity venous thrombosis in patients with acute hip fractures. AJR 154:851, 1990.

172. Comerota AJ, Katz ML, Greenwald LL, et al: Venous duplex imaging: Should it replace haemodynamic tests for deep venous thrombosis? J Vasc Surg 11:53, 1990.

173. White RH, Goulet JA, Bray TJ, et al: Deep-vein thrombosis after fracture of the pelvis: Assessment with serial duplex ultrasound screening. J Bone Joint Surg 4:495, 1990.

174. Borris LC, Christiansen HM, Lassen MR, et al: Comparison of real-time B-mode ultrasonography and bilateral ascending phlebography for detection of postoperative deep vein thrombosis following elective hip surgery. Thromb Haemost 61:363, 1989.

175. Borris LC, Christiansen HM, Lassen MR, et al: Real-time B-mode ultrasonography in the diagnosis of postoperative deep-vein thrombosis in non-symptomatic high-risk patients. Eur J Vasc Surg 4:473, 1990.

176. Ginsberg JS, Caco CC, Brill-Edwards P, et al: Venous thrombosis in patients who have undergone major hip or knee surgery: Detection with compression US and impedance plethysmography. Radiology 181:651, 1991.

I 177. Cronan JJ, Froehlich JA, Dorfman GS: Image-directed Doppler ultrasound: A screening technique for patients at high risk to develop deep vein thrombosis. J Clin Ultrasound 19:133, 1991.

I 178. Agnelli G, Volpato R, Radicchia S, et al: Detection of asymptomatic deep vein thrombosis by real-time B-mode compression ultrasound in hip surgery patients. Thromb Haemost 68:257, 1992.

I 179. Tremaine MD, Choroszy CJ, Gordon GH, Menking SA: Diagnosis of deep vein thrombosis by compression ultrasound in knee arthroplasty patients. J Arthroplasty 7:187, 1992.

180. Jongbloets LMM, Lensing AWA, Koopman MMW, et al: Limitations of compression ultrasound for the detection of symptomless postoperative deep vein thrombosis. Lancet 343:1142, 1994.

181. Lensing AWA, McGrath F, Doris I, et al: Color Doppler versus real-time ultrasonography in the diagnosis of postoperative asymptomatic deep-vein thrombosis. Submitted.

182. Froehlich JA, Dorfman GS, Cronan JJ, et al: Compression ultrasonography for the detection of deep venous thrombosis in patients who have a fracture of the hip. J Bone Joint Surg 71:249, 1989.

I 183. Barnes CL, Nelson CL, Nix ML, et al: Duplex scanning versus venography as a screening examination in total hip arthroplasty patients. Clin Orthop 271:180, 1991.

I 184. Woolson ST, Pottorf G: Venous ultrasonography in the detection of proximal vein thrombosis after total knee arthroplasty. Clin Orthop 273:131, 1991.

185. Elliott GC, Suchyta M, Rose SC, et al: Duplex ultrasonography for the detection of deep vein thrombi after total hip or knee arthroplasty. Angiology 44:26, 1993.

I 186. Davidson B, Elliott GC, Lensing AWA: Low accuracy of color Doppler ultrasound to detect proximal leg vein thrombosis during screening of asymptomatic high-risk patients. Ann Intern Med 117:735, 1992.

187. Rose SC, Zwiebel WJ, Murdock LE, et al: Insensitivity of color Doppler flow imaging for detection of acute calf deep venous thrombosis in asymptomatic postoperative patients. J Vasc Interv Radiol 4:111, 1993.

I 188. Paiement G, Wessinger SJ, Waltman AC, Harris WH: Surveillance of deep vein thrombosis in asymptomatic total hip replacement patients. Impedance plethysmography and fibrinogen scanning versus roentgenographic phlebography. Am J Surg 155:400, 1988.

I 189. Cruickshank MK, Levine MN, Hirsh J, et al: An evaluation of impedance plethysmography and $^{125}$I-fibrinogen leg scanning in patients following hip surgery. Thromb Haemost 62:830, 1989.

190. Ginsberg JS, Caco CC, Brill-Edwards P, et al: Venous thrombosis in patients who have undergone major hip or knee surgery: Detection with compression US and impedance plethysmography. Radiology 181:651, 1991.

191. Lensing AWA, Hirsh J: $^{125}$I-fibrinogen leg scanning: Reassessment of its role for the diagnosis of venous thrombosis in post-operative patients. Thromb Haemost 69:2, 1993.

192. Jay R, Hull RD, Carter C, et al: Outcome of abnormal impedance plethysmography results in patients with proximal-vein thrombosis: Frequency of return to normal. Thromb Res 36:259, 1984.

193. Murphy TP, Cronan JJ: Evolution of deep venous thrombosis: A prospective evaluation with US. Radiology 177:543, 1990.

194. Cronan JJ, Leen V: Recurrent deep venous thrombosis: Limitations of US. Radiology 170:739, 1989.

195. Heijboer H, Jongbloets LMM, Büller HR, et al: The clinical utility of real-time compression ultrasound in the diagnostic management of patients with recurrent venous thrombosis. Acta Radiol Scand 33:297, 1992.

I 196. Heijboer H, Ginsberg JS, Büller HR, et al: The use of the D-dimer test in combination with non-invasive testing versus serial non-invasive testing alone for the diagnosis of deep-vein thrombosis. Thromb Haemost 67:510, 1992.

197. Prandoni P, Cogo A, Bernardi E, et al: A simple approach for detection of recurrent proximal vein thrombosis. Circulation 88:1730, 1993.

198. Koopman MMW, Jongbloets LMM, Lensing AWA, et al: Clinical utility of a quantitative B-mode ultrasonography method in patients with suspected recurrent deep vein thrombosis (DVT abstract). Thromb Haemost 69:623, 1993.

199. Ezekowitz MD, Migliaccio F, Farlow D, et al: Comparison of platelet scintigraphy, impedance plethysmography, gray scale color flow duplex ultrasound and venography for the diagnosis of venous thrombosis. Radiolabelled Cellular Blood Elements 23:112, 1990.

200. de Valois JC, van Schaik CC, Verzijlbergen F, et al: Contrast venography: From gold standard to "golden backup" in clinically suspected deep vein thrombosis. Eur J Radiol 11:131, 1990.

201. Wysokinski W, Beyens G, Blockmans D, Verhaeghe R: Assessment of the patency of deep leg veins with duplex. Int Angiol 10:69, 1991.

# Chapter 24

# Ventilation-perfusion Lung Scans for the Diagnosis of Acute Pulmonary Embolism

Alexander Gottschalk, Mark A. Bisesi,
and Paul D. Stein

The first strides toward an accurate imaging test were made in the early 1960s when George Taplin developed a way of generating and radio-labeling macroaggregated particles of albumin that ranged in size from 5 to 20 microns.[1] When injected intravenously, these microemboli lodge in the first small vascular bed they encounter, in this case the pulmonary microcirculation. Thus, pulmonary artery perfusion (Q) could be determined clinically when the location of the radio-activity following intravenous injection is determined by imaging the lungs. Early clinical trials determined the feasibility of this technique.[2–4] Further specificity of the perfusion scan was obtained by defining regional ventilation abnor-malities (V). Currently, xenon-133, a radioactive gas, is the most common agent in use for this purpose. Several other agents have been devel-oped and remain in clinical usage, including technetium-99m-diethylenetriaminepentaacetic acid (Tc-99m-DTPA) and technetium-99m-methylene diphosphonate (Tc-99m-MDP) or py-rophosphate (Tc-99m-PYP) aerosols, krypton-81m, and technetium-labeled aerosolized car-bon particles (Technegas). All are discussed later.

Most pulmonary diseases such as obstructive pulmonary disease, lung masses, and pneumo-nia produce decreased pulmonary arterial per-fusion. The development of ventilation-per-fusion criteria that distinguish pulmonary em-bolism (PE) from other diseases has become of major import to investigators interested in this problem. With pulmonary emboli, results of both the regional chest radiograph and the ven-tilation scan in theory should be normal, whereas perfusion is decreased in a pulmonary segmental configuration. This is called a mis-matched segmental defect. In contrast, when both perfusion and ventilation abnormalities are congruent, a matched defect is defined. This happens in such diseases as emphysema.[5–7]

In this chapter the basic aspects of lung scan-ning are discussed. First, the technical aspects of obtaining ventilation-perfusion images are re-viewed. Next, ventilation-perfusion scan inter-pretation is discussed. New developments, both diagnostic and technical, that may further im-prove the ability to identify patients with pulmo-nary embolism are mentioned.

## TECHNICAL CONSIDERATIONS

In most circumstances, lung scanning is readily performed and is nearly innocuous for the patient. No specific patient preparation is required. The studies are of the highest techni-cal quality in patients who are alert enough to follow directions and who have some mobility, or at least the strength to sit in an erect posi-tion. Many patients, however, are too ill to do this. In these instances, chest radiographs and ventilation-perfusion images can be performed with the patient in the supine position. Al-though this position may limit the diagnostic value somewhat, any patient that can receive the necessary supportive care during the study can benefit.

## CHEST RADIOGRAPHY

Chest radiography is the first step in per-forming a ventilation-perfusion lung scan. Eval-uation of the chest radiograph is mandatory to interpret lung scans using any current criteria. The radiograph also helps rule out the possibility of coexisting disease processes. Ideally, a posterior-anterior and lateral radiograph should be obtained with the patient erect. In seriously ill patients, a supine, portable radiograph has to suffice. Regardless of how it is obtained, a recent chest radiograph is an integral part of any ventilation-perfusion scan protocol. In our opinion, the ventilation-perfusion study and the chest radiograph should be obtained at the same time.

## VENTILATION SCANS

### Xenon-133

Obtaining good quality ventilation images is the most difficult part of ventilation-perfusion imaging for most patients. When xenon-133 is used, the study is made with 15 to 20 mCi of the radiogas, and there are three phases to the ventilation images.[8]

First, a single breath image is performed after a bolus injection into the spirometer. To provide accurate information, patients must be able to inhale deeply on command and hold their breath for 20 seconds. This view is obtained with the patient's back to a wide-field (usually at least 38 cm in diameter) gamma camera. A ventilation defect is shown as a "cold spot" (a void) on this image.

After the first breath, the patient breathes normally while the xenon is circulated within a closed spirometer for 4 minutes (equilibrium phase). The face mask must be tightly sealed during this portion of the study to ensure that equilibrium is reached.[9] During this time, collateral air drift as well as normal ventilation occurs, and this portion of the study shows the total aerated lung volume. Many centers obtain posterior views during this interval. However, we suggest that obtaining a posterior and both posterior oblique views is better, because this practice allows maximal ability to assess if any lung zone has not been ventilated at all by radioxenon.

The patient must continue to breathe normally while the xenon is vented from the system (washout phase). The washout phase usually lasts approximately 5 minutes, and is accomplished by turning the spirometer valves so that the patient inhales room air while exhaling into a shielded charcoal trap that catches the xenon-133. The purpose of this phase of the study is to demonstrate areas of slow washout (air trapping), which are now shown as "hot spots."

Hot spots represent areas of abnormal ventilation wherein lung that ventilated initially by the slow process of collateral air drift cannot get rid of the radioactive xenon by expiration as fast as a normal lung does. The resulting "unevenness" is characteristic of abnormal ventilation seen commonly with disease like chronic obstructive pulmonary disease (COPD). We believe that images should be taken at about 45-second intervals during the washout phase, and posterior oblique views should be obtained during this interval as well.

Because the photon energy of xenon-133 (80 keV) is lower than that of technetium-99m (140 keV), which is used to label the macroaggregates for perfusion scans, the xenon ventilation study is usually done prior to the perfusion scan to avoid confusing down-scatter from technetium-99m. Consequently, it is not known where in the lung the perfusion defect, if any, will be. To maximize the lung volume seen, the posterior view is used primarily for the xenon-133 study. We believe that the posterior oblique views should be obtained as well to improve detection of areas of retention and to locate them in the anterior-posterior plane. The washout phase is considered to be the most likely phase of the xenon-133 study to show ventilation abnormalities.[8, 10]

### Radioaerosol Ventilation Scanning

Some centers are using alternative tracers to assess ventilation. Technetium aerosols are in common use.[11, 12, 13] This has become possible because disposable, easily shielded, efficient nebulizers are commercially available. These make possible the delivery of small radiolabeled particles that reach the central airways but form sediment more distally and diffuse into the alveoli.[14] Currently available nebulizers produce submicronic droplets that have a better penetration into the lung periphery than aerosol from nebulizers used in the past, which produced droplets in the 3- to 5-micron range that often were deposited in the central airway.[15]

The aerosol of Tc-99m-DTPA is used by many centers. This low-molecular-weight tracer comes in contact with alveoli, adheres to alveolar walls, crosses the epithelium, is absorbed into the bloodstream, and is excreted by the kidneys. The half time of this process of lung clearance is normally about 1 hour. In smokers, however, lung clearance is often faster and can cause the count rate to decrease during the ventilation study. To avoid this, aerosols of Tc-99m-MDP or Tc-99m-PYP have been used. These have a significantly longer lung clearance time.[15]

Aerosol ventilation imaging can be performed either before or after the perfusion scan. In addition, images can be made in views precisely comparable with the perfusion images, allowing direct comparisons. These advantages are offset by the problem of central deposition because the aerosol has limited peripheral penetration in some patients, especially those with chronic bronchitis. In addition, there is no washout phase with aerosol imaging because the aerosol is not exhaled but is excreted by the kidney. An additional problem is that aerosols can be swallowed and can cause confusion in interpretation if the reader mistakes gastric for pulmonary activity (Fig. 24–1).

Ventilation imaging is commonly performed using about 30 mCi of Tc-99m-DTPA in 2 to 3 ml of saline with the submicron particle nebulizer aerated at a flow rate of 8 to 10 L/minute.[131] The patient's back is positioned to the camera and the aerosol is inhaled until an appropriate count rate is achieved (e.g., 50,000 counts/minute). If the ventilation scan is obtained after the perfusion scan (post-perfusion imaging), the nebulizer dose is raised to about 45 mCi of Tc-99m-PYP (or DTPA), and the inhalation of the aerosol is continued until the count rate over the perfusion defect in question is double that of the residual counts from the perfusion scan.[15]

## Other Ventilation Techniques

Krypton-81m is an inert radiogas tracer that has been used for ventilation imaging.[16] Because of its short half life (13 seconds), images must be acquired rapidly, but they can also be re-

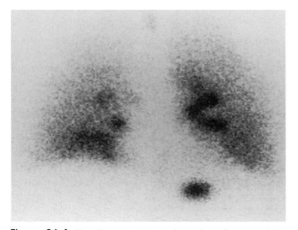

**Figure 24–1.** Ventilation scan made with technetium-99m-methylene diphosphonate aerosol. Note the central airway deposition, especially prominent on the left, and the swallowed radioactivity in the stomach.

peated if necessary. Although krypton imaging is quite accurate, clinical use is limited in North America by the short half life of the generator parent (rubidium-81, half life 4.7 hours), by lack of availability, and by high cost.

Technegas, an agent of technetium-labeled ultra small carbon particles (described as radioactive soot), has been used with increasing frequency in Australia and Europe.[17–20] Although there is good distribution of the gas because of the ultra small particle size, some reservations remain about its use. For example, transient symptomatic hypoxia has been observed.[20] It has not yet been approved by the Food and Drug Administration (FDA) for use in the United States.

Despite the many ventilation agents available, there is no clear diagnostic advantage of any one preparation. Cost, availability, and imaging logistics determine which is best suited for each institution.[9]

## PERFUSION IMAGING

Perfusion imaging is performed after the injection of technetium-99m-labeled macroaggregated albumin in a peripheral vein. The average particle size of the aggregates is about 40 to 60 microns. Approximately, 200,000 to 500,000 particles are injected. These temporarily lodge as microemboli in the small arterioles, occluding about one of every 10,000.[21] After several hours, the particles are broken down mechanically to a size of about 1 to 2 microns, which is small enough to pass through the pulmonary vascular system. Particles are then phagocytosed by the reticuloendothelial system and ultimately metabolized by the liver. Pulmonary complications are extremely rare. Because the microembolic aggregates are only temporarily present in the lung, the pulmonary microcirculation ultimately returns to normal.

To minimize gravitational gradient to blood flow, the perfusion macroaggregates are injected with the patient in the supine position,[101] during which the particles embolize the pulmonary arterioles and become "fixed." Images are obtained subsequently with the patient sitting erect when possible. Just as an erect chest radiograph is easier to interpret than a supine one (especially to evaluate lung bases) an erect ventilation-perfusion (V/Q) scan is preferable to a supine study.[101]

Perfusion images are obtained in multiple views.[22–24] In the Prospective Investigation of Pulmonary Embolism Diagnosis (PIOPED) Study, anterior, posterior, anterior oblique, and posterior oblique views were made with 750,000 counts per image using an all-purpose low-energy collimator on the gamma camera. The lateral images were timed views. The time to obtain 500,000 counts on the side with the best perfusion was used as the imaging time for the other side.[101] The usual dose of Tc-99m-macroaggregates is 4 mCi. The perfusion images require about 15 minutes to complete, yielding an overall examination time of approximately 30 minutes. The images are acquired with a gamma camera and printed on standard radiographic film. When the study is completed, the ventilation and perfusion images are interpreted together with a chest radiograph performed in close proximity to the lung scan.

## INTERPRETATION OF THE VENTILATION-PERFUSION SCAN

### General Considerations

Interpretation of V/Q lung scans begins with a review of the chest radiograph. In many cases of pulmonary embolism, the radiograph has a normal appearance, but several radiographic findings are suggestive of embolism. Findings include regional oligemia (especially with associated hilar vascular engorgement), peripheral infiltrates, and pleural effusions. None of these is specific, however. The main value of the chest radiograph is that it allows evaluation of other disease processes that may be causing the patient's symptoms.

To evaluate perfusion defects accurately, it has to be known whether there is abnormality on the chest radiograph in the region of the perfusion defect. For a V/Q abnormality to be considered characteristic of PE, the radiograph must be clear in the same area. The importance of obtaining the chest radiograph at the same time as the lung scan cannot be overemphasized. At the very least, it should have been performed within the 12 hours preceding the lung scan.[101] Chest radiography obtained prior to that time may result in an inaccurate correlation because of the rapid changes that can occur on the radiograph in the presence of evolving disease.

The appearance of the V/Q scan in a normal patient is illustrated in Figure 24–2. The perfusion scan shows homogeneous uptake throughout the aerated lung. The washout views on the xenon-133 study may show mild but symmetric retention of the tracer in the upper lung zones early during the washout phase.

Inflammation and other causes of pulmonary consolidation typically cause perfusion defects with matching radiographic and ventilation abnormalities. This includes pulmonary hemorrhage from thromboembolism (the radiographic pulmonary "infarct"), which cannot be differentiated on V/Q scans from other causes of consolidation.[9] Chronic obstructive pulmonary disease, chronic bronchitis, and most restrictive diseases cause matched ventilation and perfusion defects.

Segmental V/Q mismatched lesions with clear radiographic regions are *not* pathognomonic of PE. Diseases and conditions that mimic PE do occur. Nonembolic pulmonary vascular occlusion can occur from neoplastic compression of the pulmonary arteries (Fig. 24–3). This is often seen with bronchogenic carcinoma, which may cause a lack of perfusion in an entire lung. This would be unusual for PE, which usually causes bilateral segmental lesions.[25] Collagen disease with pulmonary vasculitis can mimic PE. Embolism of nonthrombotic material injected by intravenous drug abusers can mimic PE. The list of other causes of PE mimics is extensive, but most are rare, and many can be diagnosed from a good chest radiograph.[9, 26]

Bronchial constriction may result from PE and may cause a matched, not mismatched, defect on V/Q scan. This can be the result of substances released by the embolic material. Bronchial constriction is usually a transient response in PE, however, and is rare by the time the patient presents for V/Q scintigraphy.[27–29]

Occasionally, patients present with a diffuse generalized abnormality on the chest radiograph. The source is usually pulmonary edema, but it can be diffuse reticulonodular disease. Because the process is so symmetric, the perfusion scan may be normal. In one series, 73% of 55 patients with diffuse pulmonary disease had normal or nearly normal perfusion scans. These scans exclude PE and guide management decisions in these patients, who are frequently critically ill.[30]

### Ventilation-perfusion Scan Diagnostic Criteria

The characteristic finding of PE is a segmental rectangular, square, or triangular pleural-based perfusion defect in a *region* of the lung that has both a normal radiograph and normal ventilation scan (Fig. 24–4). The diagnostic scan categories commonly used have a rank order. High probability has precedence over intermediate probability, which has precedence over low probability, which has precedence over nor-

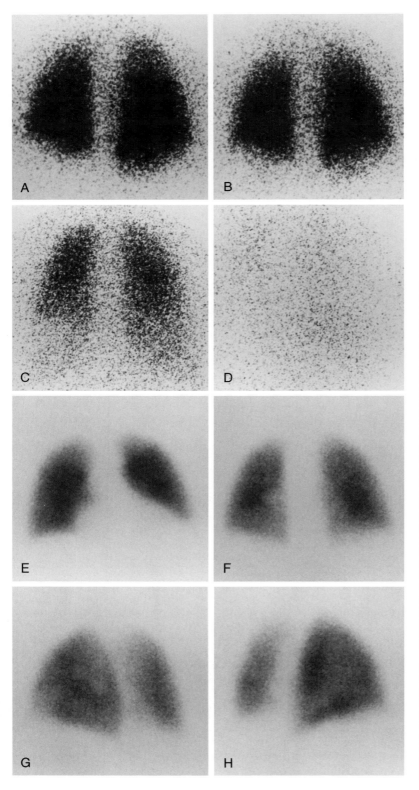

**Figure 24–2.** Normal xenon-133 ventilation and technetium-99m albumin macroaggregate perfusion scan in a patient with mild cardiomegaly, having an otherwise normal chest radiograph. The first four views (A–D) are from the xenon-133 study. (A) The posterior single breath view from the inhaled xenon bolus. Usually about 20,000 counts are obtained in about 20 seconds for this image. (B) A posterior equilibrium image taken during the 4-minute rebreathing xenon equilibration period. About 15 to 20 mCi of xenon-133 are equilibrated by breathing in a closed spirometer in this phase of the study. (C) Early washout phase (45–90 seconds). This posterior view shows more retention in the upper lung zones than in the bases. Note the uptake below the right diaphragm. Xenon-133 is fat soluble, and if the patient has a fatty liver, hepatic uptake can be seen. In this case, liver uptake is mild. In addition, the lung uptake is symmetric with no "unevenness" that would indicate air trapping. (D) Late washout phase (180–225 seconds). No air trapping is seen with virtually all the xenon-133 exhaled from the lungs. Slight hepatic uptake is still present.

E, F, G, H are anterior, posterior, left posterior oblique, and right posterior oblique perfusion images. On all the images, the heart and prominent hilar structures can be seen causing focal or diffuse diminished activity particularly prominent on the posterior scan. Comparison of the way these areas "rotate" between views indicates their mediastinal origin. The lungs perfuse normally.

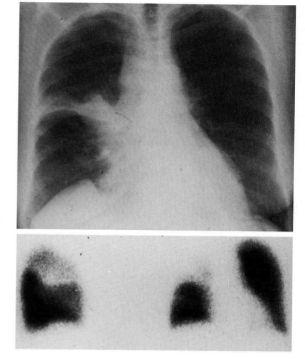

**Figure 24–3.** (Top) Posterior-anterior chest radiograph showing a right hilar bronchogenic carcinoma with slight peripheral right upper lobe atelectasis, but most of the right upper lung is normally aerated. On the xenon-133 ventilation study, the right upper lobe is ventilated normally.

(Bottom) Right lateral and anterior perfusion images show a solitary right upper lobar perfusion defect. Note some "shine through" activity from the left lung on the lateral view in the region of the upper lobe defect. This is a lobar mismatched perfusion defect. The defect is also substantially larger than the radiographic findings (i.e., Q>> than X-ray appearance, see Table 24–1). This is a pulmonary embolism mimic.

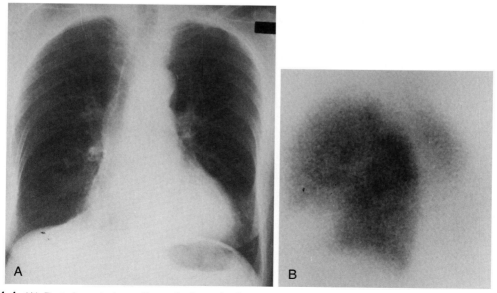

**Figure 24–4.** (A) Posterior-anterior radiograph shows the lungs are clear. The xenon-133 ventilation study was normal in this patient. (B) Left posterior oblique perfusion image. There is a solitary anterior basal segmental defect in the left lower lobe. No other abnormality was present on other views. This is a single mismatched segmental lesion. Table 24–2 shows that although this is a characteristic mismatched segmental perfusion defect, with only one such lesion, the V/Q scan will show intermediate/indeterminate probability in most of the interpretive criteria listed. In this case, the angiogram showed no pulmonary embolism.

**Table 24–1. Criteria for High Probability in the Interpretation of Ventilation-Perfusion Scans for Pulmonary Embolism**

| Biello 1987[35] | Biello et al 1979[34] | Sullivan et al[54] Based on McNeil 1980[55] | PIOPED[10] | PIOPED Revised[25] | Hull et al[32] |
|---|---|---|---|---|---|
| ≥2 Large V/Q mismatches with N1 X-ray or ≥2 Mod V/Q mismatches with N1 X-ray or ≥1 Q>>X-ray* | ≥1 Large V/Q mismatches with N1 X-ray or ≥2 Mod V/Q mismatches with N1 X-ray or ≥ Q>>X-ray* | Multiple V/Q mismatches largest being ≥ segmental | ≥2 Large V/Q mismatches or 1 Large V/Q and ≥2 mod V/Q mismatches or ≥4 Mod V/Q mismatches | ≥2 Large V/Q mismatches (2 large V/Q are borderline high prob) or 1 Large V/Q and ≥2 Mod V/Q mismatches or ≥4 Mod V/Q mismatches | ≥1 Segmental mismatch |
| Mod: 25–90% Seg Large: >90% Seg | Mod: 25–75% Seg Large: >75% Seg | | Mod: 25–75% Seg Large: >75% Seg | Mod: 25–75% Seg Large: >75% Seg | |
| V/Q mismatch = N1 V in region of Q defect | V/Q mismatch = N1 V in region of Q defect | V/Q mismatch = N1 or mildly reduced V with N1 X-ray in region of Q defect | V/Q mismatch = N1 V and N1 X-ray or Q > V or X-ray in region of Q defect | V/Q mismatch = N1 V and N1 X-ray or Q > V or X-ray in region of Q defect | |
| V/Q match = abnormal V in region of Q defect | V/Q match = abnormal V in region of Q defect | | | | |

Reprinted from Stein PD, Gottschalk A: Critical review of ventilation/perfusion lung scans in acute pulmonary embolism. Prog Cardiovasc Dis 37:13–24, 1994.
*Our interpretation of Biello's articles.
N = normal; V/Q = ventilation/perfusion; X-ray = radiographic abnormality in region of perfusion abnormality; Mod = moderate; Seg = segment.

mal. For example, if a scan shows results in some area that are those of intermediate probability, the results can never be called low probability, but they may be called high probability if mismatched segmental lesions are found in other areas.

Many investigators have either developed criteria for V/Q scan interpretation, or criteria are suggested by their publications. Tables 24–1 to 24–3 list some of these criteria. The probability for the various scan categories using these criteria is comparable and is shown in Table 24–4.[31] It must be emphasized that when the chest radiograph and the ventilation scan are called

**Table 24–2. Criteria for Intermediate Probability in the Interpretation of Ventilation-Perfusion Scans for Pulmonary Embolism**

| Biello 1987[35] | Biello et al 1979[34] | Sullivan et al[54] Based on McNeil 1980[55] | PIOPED[10] | PIOPED Revised[25] | Hull et al[32] |
|---|---|---|---|---|---|
| ≥1 Q = X-ray or 1 Large V/Q mismatch or 1 Mod V/Q mismatch or Severe COPD with Q defects | ≥1 Q = X-ray or 1 Mod V/Q mismatch with N1 X-ray or Severe COPD with Q defects | 1 Seg V/Q mismatch or ≥1 Q = X-ray or Mixed V/Q mismatched and matched defects or Multiple subsegmental V/Q mismatches | 1 Large V/Q mismatch ± 1 Mod V/Q mismatch or 2 or 3 Mod V/Q mismatches | 1 Large ± 1 Mod V/Q mismatch or 1 to 3 Mod V/Q mismatches or 1 Matched V/Q defect with N1 X-ray 2 Large V/Q mismatches are borderline intermediate to high prob | ≥1 Subsegmental* V/Q mismatch or ≥1 Segmental V/Q match or ≥1 Subsegmental V/Q match |

Reprinted from Stein PD, Gottschalk A: Critical review of ventilation/perfusion lung scans in acute pulmonary embolism. Prog Cardiovasc Dis 37:13–24, 1994.
*Our interpretation of Hull's criteria.
N = normal; V/Q = ventilation/perfusion; X-ray = radiographic abnormality in region of perfusion abnormality; Mod = moderate; Seg = segment.

**Table 24–3. Criteria for Low Probability in the Interpretation of Ventilation-Perfusion Scans for Pulmonary Embolism**

| Biello 1987[35] | Biello et al 1979[34] | Sullivan et al[54] Based on McNeil 1980[55] | PIOPED[10] | PIOPED Revised[25] | Hull et al[32] |
|---|---|---|---|---|---|
| Small V/Q mismatches or V/Q matches with N1 X-ray or Q<<X-ray | Small V/Q mismatches or V/Q matches with N1 X-ray or Q<<X-ray | 1 Subseg V/Q mismatch or ≥1 V/Q match | 1 Mod V/Q mismatch with N1 X-ray or Q<<X-ray or V/Q matches with N1 X-ray or X-ray<<Q involving ≤4 segments in 1 lung and ≤3 segments in 1 lung region or Perfusion defects due to pleural effusion, cardiomegaly, enlarged aorta, hilum, mediastinum, and elevated diaphragm or >3 Small Q with N1 X-ray or Very low probability ≤3 small Q with N1 X-ray | Q<<X-ray defect or ≥2 V/Q matches with N1 X-ray and some areas of normal perfusion in lung or Perfusion defects due to pleural effusion, cardiomegaly, enlarged aorta, hilum, mediastinum, and elevated diaphragm or Any small perfusion defects and N1 X-ray | Not reported |
| Small: <25% Seg | Small: <25% Seg |  | Small: <25% Seg |  |  |

Reprinted from Stein PD, Gottschalk A: Critical review of ventilation/perfusion lung scans in acute pulmonary embolism. Prog Cardiovasc Dis 37:13–24, 1994.

N = normal; V/Q = ventilation/perfusion; X-ray = radiographic abnormality in region of perfusion abnormality; Mod = moderate; Seg = segment.

normal in these criteria, the designation refers to the *region* of the chest radiograph or ventilation scan in which the perfusion defect is found. The chest radiograph or ventilation scan may show an abnormality elsewhere.

Many of these criteria were developed using xenon-133 as the ventilation agent. Consequently, ventilation scans were performed primarily using posterior images with only posterior oblique views providing anterior-posterior localization. Therefore, it was not always possible to define precisely in which lung segment the ventilation defect was located. Thus, many ventilation studies were interpreted using lung

zones obtained by dividing the lung craniocaudally (i.e., upper, middle, and lower zones). The slight variation in terminology between investigators is noted in Table 24–1.

Most of the studies evaluating V/Q scan efficacy were done with retrospective analysis of those patients who had both V/Q scans and pulmonary angiography. Only the McMaster University data[32] and that from the PIOPED Study[10] had patients that were prospectively recruited for V/Q scan and angiography. However, only PIOPED Study investigators evaluated their *diagnostic criteria* prospectively.

In the PIOPED Study, both the pulmonary

**Table 24–4. Probability of Pulmonary Embolism Obtained With Different Criteria for the Interpretation of Ventilation-Perfusion Scans for Pulmonary Embolism**

|  | Biello 1987[35] (%) | Biello et al 1970[34] (%) | PIOPED[10] (%) | Hull et al[32] (%) |
|---|---|---|---|---|
| High | 90 | 87–92 | 87 | 86 |
| Intermediate | 30 | 20–33 | 30 | 21–40 |
| Low | 10 | 0–8 | 14 | —— |
| Normal | 0 | 0 | 0 | 0 |

Reprinted from Stein PD, Gottschalk A: Critical review of ventilation/perfusion lung scans in acute pulmonary embolism. Prog Cardiovasc Dis 37:13–24, 1994.

angiogram and the V/Q scan were described in a computer-compatible format.[33] Consequently, it was possible to re-evaluate the criteria used in the study. Based upon this retrospective re-evaluation, the PIOPED nuclear medicine working group has recommended changes from the original criteria.[25] These can be found in Tables 24–1 to 24–3.

In the PIOPED Study a high-probability diagnosis indicated PE in 87% of patients.[10I] Other series had a range from a positive predictive value of 86 to 92% (Fig. 24–5).[32, 34, 35] (See Table 24–4.) Similarly, Table 24–4 shows that PE is present in from 20 to 40% when intermediate or indeterminate probability is diagnosed, a range that is not useful clinically.

A low-probability V/Q scan diagnosis properly excluded PE in 86% in the PIOPED Study, and 90% or more using the other criteria listed (Fig. 24–6). Twenty-one cases in the PIOPED Study were called normal. None had PE. There were 121 PIOPED Study cases called "near normal" (best thought of as very low probability), and PE was properly excluded in 95%.[10I] This rate is comparable with the precision of the pulmonary angiogram. In the PIOPED Study, 72 pulmonary angiograms had intraobserver interpretation—reader self-agreement occurred in 95% ± 5%.[36]

The distribution of the scan category readings for the V/Q scans in the PIOPED Study was 13% high probability, 39% intermediate/indeterminate probability, 34% low probability, and 14% were nearly normal (very low probability) or normal. A high probability interpretation was 97% specific but only 41% sensitive.[10I]

Although the ventilation scan is considered a cornerstone of the diagnostic technique permitting separation of perfusion defects in diseases such as chronic obstructive pulmonary disease and PE, the ventilation scan cannot always be obtained, especially in very ill or uncooperative patients. It has been shown that the perfusion scan compared only with the chest radiograph still has diagnostic value. In a series of 98 patients with perfusion scans and chest radiographs but no ventilation scans, the diagnostic reliability of both high and low probability interpretations was comparable to that in patients with a complete V/Q scan. However, the number of intermediate/indeterminate cases increased.[37I]

Associated cardiopulmonary disease increases the number of intermediate/indeterminate readings of V/Q scans. Using PIOPED Study criteria, the number of such readings was 13% in patients with normal chest radiographs,[38I] 33% in patients with no clinical assessment of prior cardiac or pulmonary disease,[39I] 43% in patients with any cardiac or pulmonary disease,[39I] and 60% in patients with COPD.[40I]

Among elderly patients (those over 70 years old) the V/Q scan performed as well as it did in younger patients. Sensitivity and specificity were comparable in the two groups for high probability readings.[41I]

## CLINICAL ASSESSMENT AND LUNG SCAN INTERPRETATION IN COMBINATION

The PIOPED Study has demonstrated that if there is congruence between the clinical probability assessment of PE and the V/Q scan interpretation, the results are reliable enough to guide therapy without further patient evaluation. However, this concordance occurred in only 28% of the patients in the PIOPED Study.[10I] In addition, in PIOPED, the clinical probability of PE was determined by experienced physicians interested in this problem. It is possible to take objective clinical information obtained by any physician or physician's assistant, process it with neural network computer intelligence, and obtain a clinical assessment as accurate as that of an experienced physician.[42]

The use of scan categories lumps together scans that may have different diagnostic power. For example, high probability is usually considered to represent an 80 to 100% likelihood of PE.[32] However, it is now possible to give a discrete probability based on the number of mismatched defects.[43–45]

An important new diagnostic refinement can be made if clinical stratification for the presence or absence of cardiopulmonary disease is used in conjunction with V/Q scan analysis. Fewer mismatched defects are needed to diagnose PE with confidence in patients with no prior cardiopulmonary disease than are needed if cardiopulmonary disease is present (Fig. 24–7).[43] No added benefit is obtained, however, if further stratification is made into either cardiac or pulmonary disease.[43]

The PIOPED investigators and others use the concept of segmental equivalents.[6] This means that a large segmental perfusion defect is equivalent to two moderate segmental perfusion defects. A large perfusion defect is defined as one that is larger than 75% of a segment, whereas a moderate perfusion defect is one involving 25 to 75% of a segment. Deciding whether a perfusion defect is large or moderate is subjective, and even with experienced observers, precision is not ideal. Often the defect size is underesti-

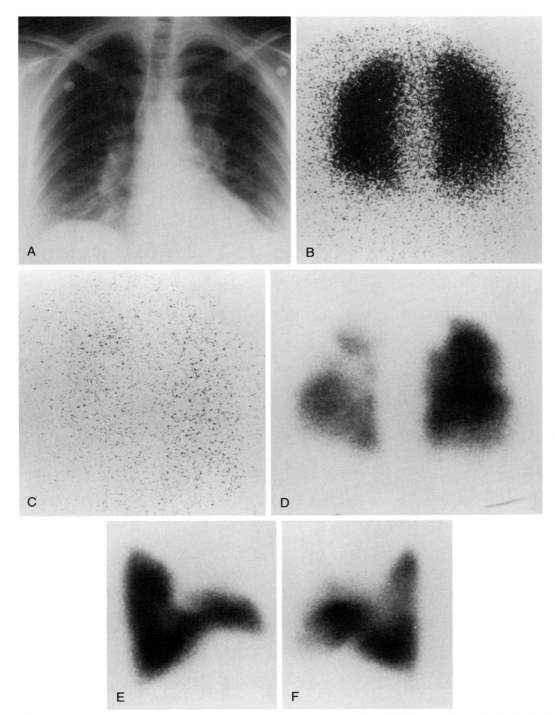

**Figure 24–5.** (A) Posterior-anterior chest radiograph with hilar fullness and possibly increased vascularity in the bases compared with that in the mid and upper lung zones. (B, C) Posterior single breath and 90- to 135-second washout view from the xenon-133 ventilation study. These are normal. (D, E, F) Posterior, right lateral, and left lateral views from the perfusion study. The right lateral view has a peculiar shape because all of the right upper lobe and some of the middle lobe are not perfused. A similar appearance is seen on the left with most of the apical lower lobe segment also unperfused. On the posterior view, additional moderate-sized segmental defects are seen on the right side. If the height of the lungs on the perfusion scan is measured and compared with the height on the single breath xenon image (B), the upper lung zones will be missing from the perfusion scan. This is a high-probability V/Q scan with multiple bilateral mismatched segmental defects. Pulmonary angiogram was terminated when a large right upper lobe embolus was identified.

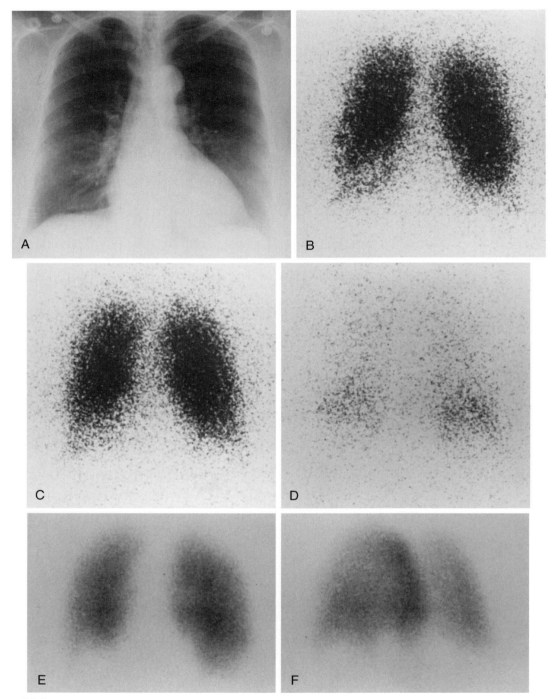

**Figure 24–6.** (A) Posterior-anterior chest radiograph showing clear lungs. (B, C, D) Posterior single breath, early equilibrium and 180- to 225-second washout views from the xenon-133 ventilation study. On the single breath image (B) there is a marked decrease in ventilation in both lower lung zones. This is beginning to fill in by collateral air drift on the early equilibrium image (C). On the washout view (D) there is air trapping in both lower lung zones. (E and F) Posterior and left posterior oblique views from the perfusion study. These illustrate perfusion defects in both lower lung zones that match the air trapping seen on the ventilation.

Tables 24–2 and 24–3 show that in the PIOPED study this presentation would meet the criteria for intermediate probability, but that in the revised PIOPED criteria this presentation would correspond to low probability because there are two areas of V/Q match, a clear chest radiograph, and normally perfused lung elsewhere (the mid and upper lungs in this case). The pulmonary angiogram showed no emboli.

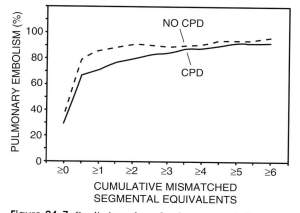

**Figure 24–7.** Predictive value of pulmonary embolism relative to the cumulative number of mismatched segmental equivalents among patients with no prior cardiopulmonary disease (NO CPD) and among patients with any prior cardiopulmonary disease (CPD). Significant differences occurred with $\geq 0.5$ and $\geq 1.0$ segmental equivalents ($p < .01$) and with $\geq 1.5$ segmental equivalents ($p < .05$). (Used with permission from Stein PD, Gottschalk A, Henry JW, Shivkumar K: Stratification of patients according to prior cardiopulmonary disease and probability assessment based upon the number of mismatched segmental perfusion defects. Chest 104:1461–1467, 1993.)

mated.[46] Data show that a moderate-size perfusion defect has the same diagnostic power as a large perfusion defect.[44] Therefore, if either a moderate or a large segmental perfusion defect is considered a vascular perfusion defect, a positive predictive value for PE comparable with that for segmental equivalents is obtained.[44] Using vascular defects should make V/Q scans easier to read, and could decrease the number of intermediate/indetermined interpretations.

## DEVELOPING NEW CONCEPTS AND MODALITIES

An interesting development in diagnostic imaging is the neural network to aid in interpretation of V/Q scans. It appears that trained neural networks can successfully arrive at the diagnosis of high, low, or intermediate probability when the scintigraphic findings are entered.[47] It remains to be seen if this technology will evolve to the point in which digitized images of the V/Q scan and chest radiographs can be accurately assessed in this way.

The noninvasive diagnosis of pulmonary embolism by new imaging modalities is currently under investigation. Conventional, spiral, and electron beam computed tomography (CT) have been suggested as possible tools for the diagnosis of pulmonary embolism.[48–50] Conventional CT can detect proximal emboli in the pulmonary artery, but this is usually an incidental finding and not the purpose for which the CT scan was ordered. Spiral CT takes advantage of the speed of spiral imaging, allowing good images of the proximal branches of the pulmonary artery to be obtained during transit of a bolus of contrast material. Theoretically, this will permit the diagnosis of embolic intraluminal filling defects using essentially the same criteria as that used for pulmonary angiography. Electron beam CT also makes possible faster scanning times, which also permits improved visualization of the pulmonary arteries.

Another area of technical advance is magnetic resonance angiography. The rate of progress has been extremely rapid over the past several years, and the final limitations of the technique are impossible to predict. Flow imaging techniques to evaluate the pulmonary arteries for PE or leg veins for deep venous thrombosis have been developed.[51, 52] As increasingly fast imaging techniques and better image postprocessing become available, it may become possible to evaluate reliably intraluminal filling defects, oligemia, or vascular cutoffs with magnetic resonance angiography. The inherent advantages of such an approach are that it is noninvasive, does not require contrast media, and does not involve ionizing radiation.

In conclusion, diagnostic approaches to the problem of pulmonary embolism continue to improve. Ventilation-perfusion imaging is an important screening test to evaluate patients with suspected pulmonary embolism. If the scan results are normal or of very low probability, or are of high probability for pulmonary embolism, no further evaluation is needed. Therapy can be started or efforts can be directed toward other possible diagnoses. In the presence of an intermediate probability scan or a low probability scan with a high clinical suspicion, a diagnosis of deep venous thrombosis or angiographically proven PE is needed to start definitive therapy. Many centers are now looking at the lower extremities in an effort to diagnose deep venous thrombosis and avoid pulmonary angiography.[53]

The PIOPED Study provided a large, prospective computerized database that will allow continued refinement of the diagnostic criteria of the V/Q scan for pulmonary embolism. As technologic advances continue in spiral computed tomography, magnetic resonance imaging, and computer processing, they may find a role in the diagnosis of pulmonary embolism. However, at this time, V/Q lung scans continue to have an important role in the diagnosis and management of patients suspected of having acute pulmonary embolism.

## REFERENCES

1. Taplin GV, Johnson DE, Dore EK, Kaplan HS: Suspensions of radioalbumin aggregates for photoscanning the liver, spleen, lung and other organs. J Nucl Med 5:259–275, 1964.
2. Wagner HN Jr, Sabiston DC Jr, Iio M, et al: Regional pulmonary blood flow in man by radioisotope scanning. JAMA 187:601–603, 1964.
3. Wagner HN Jr, Sabiston DC Jr, McAfee JG, et al: Diagnosis of massive pulmonary embolism in man by radioisotope scanning. N Engl J Med 271:377–384, 1964.
4. Quinn JL III, Whitley JE, Hudspeth AS, Watts FC: An approach to the scanning of pulmonary infarcts. J Nucl Med 5:1–8, 1964.
5. McNeil BJ, Holman L, Adelstein J: The scintigraphic definition of pulmonary embolism. JAMA 277:753–756, 1974
6. Neumann RD, Sostman HD, Gottschalk A: Current status of ventilation-perfusion imaging. Semin Nucl Med 10:198–217, 1980.
7. Alderson PO, Line BR: Scintigraphic evaluation of regional pulmonary ventilation. Semin Nucl Med 10:218–242, 1980.
8. Alderson PO, Biello DR, Khan AR, et al: Comparison of 133-Xe single-breath and washout imaging in the scintigraphic diagnosis of pulmonary embolism. Radiology 137:481–486, 1980.
9. Gottschalk A, Alderson PO, Sostman HD: Nuclear medicine techniques and applications. In Murray JF, Nadel JA (eds): Textbook of Respiratory Medicine, ed 2. Philadelphia, WB Saunders, 1994.
I 10. A Collaborative Study by the PIOPED investigators: Value of the ventilation/perfusion scan in acute pulmonary embolism—results of the prospective investigation of pulmonary embolism diagnosis (PIOPED). JAMA 263:2753–2759, 1990.
11. Smith R, Maher JM, Miller RI, Alderson PO: Clinical outcomes of patients with suspected pulmonary embolism and low-probability aerosol-perfusion scintigrams. Radiology 164:731–733, 1987.
12. Alderson PO, Line BR: Scintigraphic evaluation of regional pulmonary ventilation. Semin Nucl Med 10:218–242, 1980.
I 13. Alderson PO, Biello DR, Gottschalk A, et al: Tc-99m-DTPA aerosols and radioactive gases compared as adjuncts to perfusion scintigraphy in patients with suspected pulmonary embolism. Radiology 153:515–521, 1984.
14. Stuart BO: Deposition of inhaled aerosol. Arch Intern Med 131:60–73, 1973.
15. Krasnow AZ, Isitman AT, Collier BD, et al: Diagnostic applications of radioaerosols in nuclear medicine. In Freeman LM (ed): Nuclear Medicine Annual 1993. New York, Raven Press, 1993, pp 123–193.
16. Miller TR, Biello DR, Lee JI, et al: Ventilation imaging with Kr-81m: A comparison with Xe-133. Eur J Nucl Med 6:11–16, 1981.
17. James JM, Herman KJ, Lloyd JJ, et al: Evaluation of Tc-99m Technegas ventilation scintigraphy in the diagnosis of pulmonary embolism. Br J Radiol 64:711–719, 1991.
18. Cook G, Clarke SEM: An evaluation of Technegas as a ventilation agent compared with krypton-81m in the scintigraphic diagnosis of pulmonary embolism. Eur J Nucl Med 19:770–774, 1992.
19. James JM, Lloyd JJ, Leahy BC, et al: Tc-99m Technegas and krypton-81m ventilation scintigraphy: A comparison in known respiratory disease. Br J Radiol 65:1075–1082, 1992.
20. James JM, Lloyd JJ, Leahy BC, et al: The incidence and severity of hypoxia associated with Tc-99m Technegas ventilation scintigraphy and Tc-99m MAA perfusion scintigraphy. Br J Radiol 65:403–408, 1992.
21. Miller WS: The structure of the lungs. J Morphol 8:165, 1893. Quoted in Dalen JE, Haynes FW, Hoppin FG Jr, et al: Cardiovascular responses to experimental pulmonary embolism. Am J Cardiol 20:3–9, 1967.
22. Wellman HN, Mack JF, Saenger EL, Friedman BI: Clinical experience with oblique views in pulmonary perfusion scintiphotography in normal and pathological anatomy. J Nucl Med 9:374–379, 1968.
23. Mack JF, Wellman HN, Saenger EL: Oblique pulmonary scintiphotography in the analysis of perfusion abnormalities due to embolism. J Nucl Med 10:420, 1969.
24. Caride VJ, Puri S, Slavin JD, et al: The usefulness of posterior oblique views in perfusion lung imaging. Radiology 121:669–672, 1976.
25. Gottschalk A, Sostman HD, Coleman RE, et al: Ventilation-perfusion scintigraphy in the PIOPED study. Part II. Evaluation of the scintigraphic criteria and interpretations. J Nucl Med 34:1119–1126, 1993.
26. Velchik MG, Tobin M, McCarthy K: Non-thromboembolic causes of high-probability lung scans. Am J Physiol Imaging 4:32–36, 1989.
27. Thomas D, Stein M, Tanabe G, et al: Mechanism of bronchoconstriction produced by thromboemboli in dogs. Am J Physiol 206:1207–1212, 1964.
28. Kessler RM, McNeil BJ: Impaired ventilation in a patient with angiographically demonstrated pulmonary embolism. Radiology 114:111–112, 1975.
29. Epstein J, Taylor A, Alazraki NP, Coel M: Acute pulmonary embolus associated with transient ventilatory defect. J Nucl Med 16:1017–1020, 1976.
30. Newman GE, Sullivan DC, Gottschalk A, Putman CE: Scintigraphic perfusion patterns in patients with diffuse lung disease. Radiology 143:227–231, 1982.
31. Stein PD, Gottschalk A: Critical review of ventilation/perfusion lung scans in acute pulmonary embolism. Progr Cardiovasc Dis 37:13–24, 1994.
32. Hull RD, Hirsh J, Carter CJ, et al: Diagnostic value of ventilation-perfusion lung scanning in patients with suspected pulmonary embolism. Chest 88:819–828, 1985.
33. Gottschalk A, Juni JE, Sostman HD, et al: Ventilation-perfusion scintigraphy in the PIOPED study. Part I. Data collection and tabulation. J Nucl Med 34:1109–1118, 1993.
34. Biello DR, Mattar AG, McKnight RC, Siegel BA: Ventilation perfusion studies in suspected pulmonary embolism. Am J Radiol 133:1033–1037, 1979.
35. Biello DR: Radiological (scintigraphic) evaluation of patients with suspected pulmonary thromboembolism. JAMA 257:3257–3259, 1987.
36. Gottschalk A: Unpublished data from PIOPED. Presented to the Radiological Society of North America, Chicago, IL, December, 1992.
I 37. Stein PD, Terrin ML, Gottschalk A, et al: Value of ventilation/perfusion scans compared to perfusion scans alone in acute pulmonary embolism. Am J Cardiol 69:1239–1241, 1992.
I 38. Stein PD, Alavi A, Gottschalk A, et al: Usefulness of noninvasive diagnostic tools for diagnosis of acute

pulmonary embolism in patients with a normal chest radiograph. Am J Cardiol 67:1117–1120, 1991.

I 39. Stein PD, Coleman RE, Gottschalk A, et al: Diagnostic utility of ventilation/perfusion lung scans in acute pulmonary embolism is not diminished by preexisting cardiac or pulmonary disease. Chest 100:604–606, 1991.

I 40. Lesser BA, Leeper KV, Stein PD, et al: The diagnosis of acute pulmonary embolism in patients with chronic obstructive pulmonary disease. Chest 102:17–22, 1992.

I 41. Stein PD, Gottschalk A Saltzman HA, Terrin ML: Diagnosis of acute pulmonary embolism in the elderly. J Am Coll Cardiol 18:1452–1457, 1991.

I 42. Patil S, Henry JW, Rubenfire M, Stein PD: Neural network in the diagnosis of acute pulmonary embolism. Chest 104:1685–1689, 1993.

I 43. Stein PD, Gottschalk A, Henry JW, Shivkumar K: Stratification of patients according to prior cardiopulmonary disease and probability assessment based upon the number of mismatched segmental equivalent perfusion defects: Approaches to strengthen the diagnostic value of ventilation/perfusion lung scans in acute pulmonary embolism. Chest 104:1461–1467, 1993.

I 44. Stein PD, Henry JW, Gottschalk A: Mismatched vascular defects: A new approach to the interpretation of ventilation/perfusion lung scans in pulmonary embolism. Chest 104:1468–1471, 1993.

I 45. Stein PD, Henry JW, Gottschalk A: The addition of prior clinical assessment to stratification according to prior cardiopulmonary disease further optimizes the interpretation of ventilation/perfusion lung scans in pulmonary embolism. Chest 104:1472–1476, 1993.

46. Morrell NW, Nijran KS, Jones BE, et al: The underesti-mation of segmental defect size in radionuclide lung scanning. J Nucl Med 34:370–374, 1993.

47. Scott JA, Palmer EL: Neural network analysis of ventilation-perfusion lung scans. Radiology 186:661–664, 1993.

48. Verschakelen JA, Vanwijck E, Bogaert J, Baert AL: Detection of unsuspected central pulmonary embolism with conventional contrast-enhanced CT. Radiology 188:847–850, 1993.

49. Tiegen CL, Maus TP, Sheedy PF, et al: Pulmonary embolism: Diagnosis with electron-beam CT. Radiology 188:839–845, 1993.

50. Remy-jardin M, Remy J, Wattinne L, Giraud F: Central pulmonary thromboembolism: Diagnosis with spiral volumetric CT with single breath-hold technique: Comparison with pulmonary angiography. Radiology 185:381–387, 1992.

51. Sostman HD: Deep venous thrombosis: Experience with new techniques. In Pulmonary Radiology. Potchen EJ, Grainger RG, Greene R (eds): Philadelphia, WB Saunders, 1993, pp 107–112.

52. Sostman HD, MacFall JR, Foo TKF: Pulmonary arteries and veins. In Magnetic Resonance Angiography: Concepts and Applications. Potchen EJ, Haacke EM, Siebert, JE, Gottschalk A (eds): St. Louis, CV Mosby, 1993, pp 546–572.

53. Stein PD, Hull RD, Saltzman HA, Pineo G: Strategy for diagnosis of patients with suspected acute pulmonary embolism. Chest 103:1553–1559, 1993.

54. Sullivan DC, Coleman RE, Mills SR, et al: Lung scan interpretation: Effect of different observers and different criteria. Radiology 149:803–807, 1983.

55. McNeil BJ: Ventilation-perfusion studies and the diagnoses of pulmonary embolism: Concise communication. J Nucl Med 21:319–323, 1980.

# Chapter 25

# Laboratory Tests for the Diagnosis of Venous Thromboembolism

## M. H. Horellou, J. Conard, and M. M. Samama

For years, both the clinician and the biologist have been searching for blood tests that can be used to predict thrombosis in high-risk patients (predictive test) or to confirm or exclude the diagnosis of thrombosis when it is suspected clinically (diagnostic test). Sensitive and specific biochemical and immunochemical tests have been developed for detecting activation of coagulation and fibrinolysis. Detection of circulating activated clotting factors, activation peptides, complexes of activated clotting factors and their inhibitors, and products of degradation of fibrin (resulting from the action of thrombin and plasmin on fibrinogen) have been investigated in the diagnosis of venous thrombosis.

## MARKERS OF THE ACTIVATION OF COAGULATION AND FIBRINOLYSIS

Several groups of tests are available for assessing in vivo coagulation (Fig. 25–1). The first measures plasma concentration of prothrombin fragments $1+2$ (F1+2), released during the conversion of prothrombin to thrombin. The second group includes tests measuring the interaction of thrombin with its substrates (fibrinopeptide A, FpA) and/or in vivo inhibitors (complexes thrombin–antithrombin III = TAT). Following conversion of fibrinogen into fibrin by thrombin in vivo, the fibrinolytic system is stimulated to lyse the fibrin, with a subsequent increase in the levels of fibrin degradation products in plasma (D-Dimer). Markers of fibrinolysis such as plasmin $\alpha_2$-antiplasmin complexes also provide information on in vivo coagulation. Blood cells including platelets participate in coagulation by serving as surfaces for assembling clotting factors. Moreover, platelets

activated by thrombin release a variety of granular contents, some of which have been evaluated as markers of increased in vivo coagulation and thrombosis. These molecular markers elaborated by activated platelets have been studied in patients with arterial thrombosis and are not discussed in this review on laboratory tests for the diagnosis of venous thrombosis.

## Prothrombin Fragment 1 + 2

Prothrombinase, including factor Xa (enzyme) and factor Va (cofactor for factor Xa), bound to procoagulant surfaces (phospholipids), converts prothrombin into equimolar concentrations of thrombin and prothrombin fragment $1+2$. These prothrombin fragments can be detected by immunoassays including Enzyme-linked ImmunoSorbent Assay (ELISA). The concentration of F1+2 in normal adult citrated plasma varies between 0.3 and 1.5 nmol/L and increases significantly with age.[1-3] F1+2 can be measured on blood collected into citrate because no specialized anticoagulant appears to be necessary.[4] The half life of F1+2 is 90 minutes. High levels of F1+2 in the plasmas of patients with deep vein thrombosis (DVT) are observed, and heparin therapy causes a rapid reduction of their concentration. Oral anticoagulant treatment suppresses the production of F1+2, correlating with the prolongation of the prothrombin time.[3]

## Fibrinopeptide A

The fibrinopeptide FpA, one of the two amino terminal peptides cleaved from fibrinogen by thrombin, can be identified by an immunoassay.[5] The half life of FpA is very short (3

272

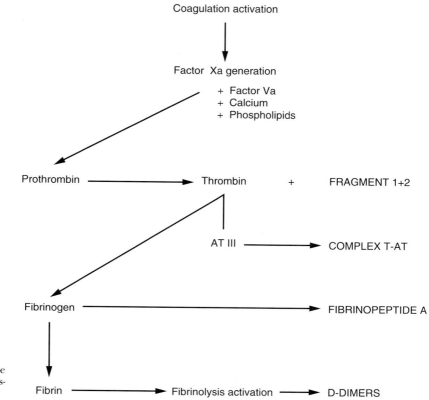

**Figure 25–1.** Coagulation cascade and markers of hemostatic systemic activation.

minutes). Normal individuals have a concentration up to 1.5 nmol/L. There is considerable overlap between the values in patients with and without detectable thrombosis that limits the clinical relevance of this assay.

## Thrombin-antithrombin III Complexes

Thrombin is rapidly inactivated by antithrombin III, and the endogenous concentrations of TAT reflect the amount of thrombin generated. The concentrations of TAT in normal volunteers using commercial ELISA kits vary between 15 and 32 pmol/l.[1, 3] The half life of TAT is 3 minutes—as short as that of FpA.

## D-Dimer

The blood of patients with active thrombotic and fibrinolytic disorders contains a large spectrum of fibrin or fibrinogen derivatives as a consequence of the separate or combined actions of thrombin, factor XIIIa, and plasmin on fibrinogen.[6] Plasmin digestion of crosslinked fibrin produces the D-Dimer fragment, which is not found in digests of fibrinogen or noncrosslinked fibrin. Thus, the presence in blood

of crosslinked fragments such as D-Dimer indicates active fibrinolysis. Monoclonal antibodies specific for antigenic determinants on D-Dimer are used in the latex agglutination and enzyme immunoassays for the specific measurement of D-Dimer. The lack of crossreactivity for the monoclonal antibody with fibrinogen allows these assays to be performed in plasma.

The minimum detectable amount of D-Dimer in plasma using latex agglutination is approximately 400 ng/ml, and by ELISA approximately 10 ng/ml. Half life of D-Dimer is 8 hours.[6]

## LABORATORY TESTS FOR THE PREDICTION OF VENOUS THROMBOSIS (PREDICTIVE TESTS)

### Preoperative Prediction of Thrombosis

Several risk factors including preoperative parameters, physical examination, and laboratory tests have been proposed to predict preoperatively a patient who will experience venous thrombosis after surgical procedures.[8] Among the different laboratory tests, fibrinolytic variables, especially prolonged clot lysis time, raised serum or plasma levels of fibrin and fibrinogen degradation products, and increased plasminogen activator inhibitor-1 (PAI-1) levels can predict postoperative DVT.[8–12] Predictive indices have been proposed.[8] For example, in a prospective study, Clayton and coworkers investigated 124 patients undergoing gynecologic surgery.[10] The thrombosis incidence was 16%, as assessed by leg scanning followed by venography in all patients with a positive scan. They concluded that, of all the preoperatively collected clinical and laboratory data, the euglobulin clot lysis time (a) was the best predictor for postoperative thrombosis. Other variables that added to the prediction power were age (b), presence of varicose veins (c), FDP levels (d), and high weight/height ratio (e). The Clayton risk factor formula is as follows:

$$I = 11.3 + 0.0090a + 0.22d + 0.085b + 0.043e + 2.19c$$

It was calculated that, with an index of $-5$, all patients with postoperative thrombosis were correctly identified. Using the Clayton index with a cutoff point of $-5$, prophylaxis could be safely withheld in 21% (27 out of 127) of the total patient group. However, the illness for which surgery is performed also influences preoperative results of hematologic tests.[13] Preoperative predictive indices are not widely used by surgeons.

## Postoperative Prediction of Thrombosis

Increased plasma TAT levels are observed after surgery, in particular in the first postoperative day (to days 14–16) with lower levels in patients receiving heparin prophylaxis.[14] Significantly higher levels were observed in patients developing DVT (proven by venography) when compared with patients without DVT, but the predictive power in individual patients to rule in or rule out DVT is unsatisfactorily low.[14]

In contrast, Ofosu and coworkers found higher concentrations of TAT in the plasma of patients who developed postoperative DVT than in plasma of patients who remained DVT-negative.[17] Comparable concentrations of TAT were observed in plasma after administration of unfractionated and low-molecular-weight heparin.

Marked increase of D-Dimer levels is also observed after orthopedic surgery[16] or general abdominal surgery.[18] This increase of D-Dimer level had no predictive value for DVT in 11 total knee replacement patients.[16] In general surgery,

the most accurate cutoff of D-Dimer (ELISA) for discriminating patients with or without DVT was 3,000 ng/ml, as determined by receiver operating characteristic (ROC) curve analysis. Sensitivity of a D-Dimer level of more than 3,000 ng for the presence of venographically documented DVT on the eighth postoperative day was 89% for a specificity of 48% with a positive predictive value of 35%.[18]

## Prediction of Thrombosis in Thrombophilic Patients

In asymptomatic patients with heterozygous antithrombin III deficiency, it was initially reported that F1+2 levels on anticoagulant solution containing heparin are frequently increased as compared with age-matched unaffected siblings,[19] $3.91 \pm 1.13$ versus $1.51 \pm 0.63$ nmol/L. Subsequently, it was shown that the high concentration of the fragment resulted from an in vitro anticoagulant effect resulting from the action of low amounts of heparin in the presence of reduced levels of antithrombin III.[20] A study of 26 antithrombin III deficient subjects did not show significant elevation in citrated plasma F1+2[21]; four patients had high F1+2 values (15%) and nine had high FpA values (35%). In contrast, in 63 members of a large family with normal level of antithrombin III antigen and reduced protease inhibitory activity, mean level of F1+2 in citrated plasma was significantly higher in the deficient adults ($0.87 \pm 0.26$ nmol/L) as compared with both the nondeficient adults ($0.70 \pm 0.21$, $p = 0.03$) and the deficient adults receiving warfarin ($0.16 \pm 0.01$). The differences in the mean values of TAT complexes and FpA between deficient and nondeficient individuals were not statistically significant.[22] Therefore, overall, the present evidence indicates that patients with antithrombin deficiency do not have excessive thrombin generation in the basal state, as measured by the F1+2 assay.

In 23 nonanticoagulated patients with an isolated deficiency of protein C, mean levels of F1+2 were significantly elevated, 2.54 versus $1.51 \pm 0.68$ nmol/L, with minimal FpA increase.[23] Approximately one-third of patients had F1+2 levels greater than the upper limit of normal control, and FpA levels were elevated in 20% of patients. A similar frequency of elevated F1+2 and FpA levels was noted by Mannucci and coworkers[21] in 57 patients with asymptomatic protein C deficiency, 25% and 18%, respectively. The predictive values of the increase of F1+2 levels, for the prediction of a thrombotic event, is not determined.

During oral anticoagulant therapy, when equivalent levels of intensity of oral anticoagulant were achieved, the mean plasma F1+2 level in patients with antithrombin III deficiency was significantly elevated as compared with the one subject with protein C deficiency or with the group of anticoagulated persons without inherited thrombotic disorder, 0.714, 0.205, and 0.231 nmol/L, respectively.[3] These immunochemical techniques should be useful in designing optimal therapeutic regimens for suppressing the in vivo generation of thrombin in such individuals. Normalization of markers of coagulation activation have been obtained after infusion of a purified protein C concentrate in two adults with homozygous protein C deficiency.[24]

## LABORATORY TESTS FOR THE DIAGNOSIS OF DEEP VENOUS THROMBOSIS (DIAGNOSTIC TESTS)

Clinical diagnosis of DVT is unreliable, and objective testing of the venous system is needed to confirm the diagnosis of DVT before starting anticoagulant treatment. Contrast venography remains the gold standard. However, this test had several major limitations including patient discomfort, allergic reactions, limited outpatient availability, and cost. A variety of noninvasive tests has been developed such as venous occlusion plethysmography and ultraDoppler scanning examinations. Published comparisons with contrast venography show that in most centers, a sensitivity for the detection of proximal venous thrombosis of approximately 90% can be obtained with these techniques. In addition to these physical techniques, the usefulness of plasma markers reflecting an activation of hemostasis has been evaluated. A rapid blood test that could be done in the emergency room or office and that could exclude clinically significant DVT would greatly simplify patient management. At the present time, the most promising results have been obtained with the measurement of D-Dimer.

### Fibrinopeptide A Determination

Nossel and coworkers were the first to report elevated levels of FpA in the plasmas of patients with thrombosis, with an increase by up to 30 times the normal level. However, FpA assays have been found to be of poor sensitivity and specificity for the diagnosis of DVT.[25]

### D-Dimer Determination

Several studies have evaluated D-Dimer in patients with clinically suspected DVT (Table 25–1), confirmed by contrast venography or noninvasive methods. D-Dimer can be measured by ELISA or by a latex agglutination assay.[26–36] On cumulative results,[37] the performances (sensitivity, specificity, positive and negative values) of the test were calculated with respect to the presence of DVT. D-Dimer ELISA tests have a high sensitivity of 96.8% (95% CI: 95.2–98.4) and a high negative predictive value of 95%, with a low specificity of 35.2% (95% CI: 32.0–38.4). Therefore, the measurement of D-Dimer by ELISA method in symptomatic patients with clinically suspected DVT allows exclusion of diagnosis of DVT when the results are negative (less than 500 ng/ml), with a predictive value of 95%. An increased value (>500 ng/ml) of D-Dimer by ELISA test could be explained by other conditions (septicemia, malignant and inflammatory diseases) and needs to be confirmed by other objective tests.

Although the ELISA test is very reliable, excluding the diagnosis of DVT when negative, it does not provide a rapid result and cannot be used as a routine screening test. The measurement of plasma D-Dimer using the latex immunoassay method is more practical and suitable for emergencies. On cumulative results,[37] the sensitivity of the latex D-Dimer assay is only 82.9% (CI 95%: 78.4–87.4) with a specificity of 67.9% (CI 95%: 63.7–72.1). This sensitivity of only 82% is not sufficient to allow this type of assay to be used as an exclusion test for DVT. A rapid test with a sensitivity of approximately 185 ng/ml as shown by a mathematic model (ROC analysis), could exclude the diagnosis of DVT in 62% of patients with a 98% sensitivity.[38]

### D-Dimer Test Combined With a Noninvasive Test

D-Dimer test measurement combined with a noninvasive test has also been studied for the diagnosis of DVT and pulmonary embolism. The diagnostic value of a combination of two noninvasive tests (i.e., computerized impedance plethysmography and a latex test) for D-Dimer measurement in plasma was assessed in 112 consecutive patients.[39] One or both tests was positive in 59 of 60 patients with positive venograms (sensitivity of 98%) and both were negative in 36 of 52 patients with negative venograms (specificity of 69%). The positive predictive value of both test results being positive was 100% (39/39) and of the negative test results was 97% (36/37). Test combinations are useful in patients with clinically suspected DVT because of the very high accuracy of concordant test results. Venography should be performed only in

**Table 25–1. Sensitivity, Specificity, Positive and Negative Predictive Values of the D-Dimer (ELISA and Latex Assay) for the Diagnosis of Deep Vein Thrombosis**

| Study | n | n (DVT) | Se (%) | Sp (%) | PPV (%) | NPV (%) |
|---|---|---|---|---|---|---|
| | | D-Dimer Latex Test | | | | |
| | | DVT Confirmed by Venography | | | | |
| Heaton | 57 | 26 | 73 | 69 | 63 | 78 |
| Ott | 108 | 39 | — | — | 59 | 98 |
| Bounameaux | 53 | 21 | 76 | 87 | 80 | 85 |
| de Boer | 33 | 21 | 43 | 100 | 100 | 52 |
| Achkar | 119 | 58 | 80 | 70 | 68 | 80 |
| | DVT Confirmed by Noninvasive Methods (Doppler Ultrasound, Impedance Phlethysmography) | | | | | |
| Elias | 100 | 45 | 98 | 22 | 50 | 92 |
| Boneu | 116 | 34 | 76 | 58 | 43 | 85 |
| Lesprit | 44 | 22 | 96 | 77 | 81 | 94 |
| Carter | 190 | 36 | 80 | 84 | 54 | 95 |
| | | D-Dimer ELISA Test | | | | |
| | | DVT Confirmed by Venography | | | | |
| Heaton | 57 | 26 | 100 | 47 | 53 | 100 |
| Rowbotham | 104 | 45 | 100 | 34 | 54 | 100 |
| Ott | 108 | 39 | 97 | 37 | 61 | 98 |
| Bounameaux | 53 | 21 | 95 | 47 | 54 | 94 |
| Mossaz | 112 | 64 | 98 | 6 | 57 | 75 |
| Heijboer | 309 | 70 | 100 | 29 | 29 | 100 |
| Achkar | 119 | 58 | 90 | 68 | 68 | 80 |
| | DVT Confirmed by Noninvasive Methods | | | | | |
| Van Bergen | 239 | 60 | 92 | 20 | 28 | 87 |
| Elias | 100 | 45 | 98 | 29 | 53 | 94 |
| Boneu | 116 | 34 | 94 | 51 | 44 | 95 |

Se = sensitivity; Sp = specificity; PPV = positive predictive value; NPV = negative predictive value.

patients with discordant test results (36 of 112 patients).

When applying the combined approach, the diagnosis of DVT could be either established (positive impedance plethysmography) or refuted (normal level of D-Dimer) in 42% of 309 referred patients on entry, in contrast to only 19% of patients using serial noninvasive testing alone.[40]

Studies have evaluated D-Dimer testing in patients with clinically suspected PE. Investigators reported that the ELISA using a cutoff of 145 ng/ml to 500 ng/ml has a sensitivity of 89 to 100% with a specificity ranging between 39% and 81%.[41–44] In the diagnostic approach of pulmonary embolism, plasma measurement of D-Dimer by ELISA is particularly useful in patients with inconclusive lung scans. Inconclusive scans represent about two-thirds of all scintigraphic examinations. When the level is less than 500 ng/ml (a cutoff that should be validated for each assay) the diagnosis of pulmonary embolism can be ruled out.[45]

## Thrombin-antithrombin III or Prothrombin Fragments 1 + 2

Determination of TAT complexes[31, 33] and F1 + 2[33] were less sensitive than D-Dimer assays in the diagnosis of DVT. The relatively longer D-Dimer half life and the rapid decrease of TAT and F1 + 2 levels during heparin therapy can explain the greater accuracy of D-Dimer for the diagnosis of DVT. Comparative evaluation of the usefulness of D-Dimer, TAT complexes, and F1 + 2 has been performed for the diagnosis of clinically suspected DVT.[33] The most accurate assay was the D-Dimer ELISA, which had both a higher sensitivity (94%) and a higher negative predictive value (95%), with values of 64% and 84% for the TAT complexes, and 47% and 78% for F1 + 2 respectively. Despite positive and significant correlations between the levels of the three different markers, their association did not improve their overall accuracy for DVT detection.[33]

Heparin significantly decreases plasma levels of F1 + 2 and TAT complexes in less than 3 days; thus, heparin rapidly improves the hypercoagulable state associated with acute venous thrombosis.[46] High levels of D-Dimer persist during the 9 days of heparin therapy[46] and until 35 days of oral anticoagulant treatment,[47] suggesting a very longterm fibrinolytic process that occurs independent of thrombin generation. Eight days after the initiation of oral anticoagulant treatment, despite a correctly adjusted treatment (International Normalized Ratio [INR] 2 to 3), increased levels of TAT complexes were associated with subnormal levels of F1+2, suggesting the persistence of a hypercoagulable state. After the first month, TAT complexes were normalized and F1+2 levels were at least three times lower than those of the young control population.[47] Monitoring of the intensity and the duration of oral anticoagulant treatment based on F1+2 and TAT complexes levels could be determined by prospective clinical trials.

In summary, highly sensitive immunologic assays for quantifying in vivo coagulation and/or fibrinolysis, namely F1+2, and TAT complexes, FpA, and D-Dimer are available. These tests have been used to confirm or refute the existence of a hypercoagulable state in patients with high risk or with symptoms of thrombosis. With the exception of D-Dimer ELISA, these markers are of limited value for the diagnosis of DVT. When the level of D-Dimer ELISA is normal, less than 500 ng/ml, the diagnosis of DVT can be ruled out with a risk of error of less than 5%. The lower sensibility (80%) of the latex D-Dimer test is not sufficient to allow this type of assay to be used as an exclusion test for DVT. ELISA is not a rapid test and is not suitable for immediate clinical decision-making. Attempts should be made to simplify and shorten the time that is necessary to perform the ELISA before the assay can be effectively used in emergencies. A rapid test with a high sensitivity could be a highly economical way to screen outpatients as to whether they need direct vascular testing for the management of suspected acute venous thrombosis.

Suppression of the in vivo coagulation markers by anticoagulants in patients with thrombosis or in those at high risk for developing DVT has been well documented. Whether it is possible to reduce the intensity of the anticoagulant treatment by the measurement of these markers must be determined by prospective clinical trials.

## REFERENCES

1. Lau HK, Rosenberg JS, Beeler DL, Rosenberg RD: The isolation and characterization of a specific antibody population directed against the prothrombin activation fragments F2 and F1+2. J Biol Chem 254:8751–8756, 1979.
2. Teitel JM, Bauer KA, Lau H, Rosenberg RD: Studies of the prothrombin activation pathway utilizing radioimmuno assays for the F1+2 and thrombin-antithrombin III. Blood 59: 1086 1097, 1982.
3. Bauer KA, Rosenberg RD: The pathophysiology of the prethrombotic state in humans: Insights gained from studies using markers of hemostatic system activation. Blood 70(2):343–349, 1987.
4. Pelzer H, Schwarz A, Stuber W: Determination of human prothrombin activation fragment 1+2 in plasma with an antibody against a synthetic peptide. Thromb Haemost 65:153–159, 1991.
5. Nossel HL, Yudelman I, Canfiel RE, et al: Measurement of fibrinopeptide A in human blood. J Clin Invest 54: 43–55, 1974.
6. Gaffney PJ: The occurrence and clinical relevance of fibrin fragments in blood. Ann NY Acad Sci 408:407–422, 1983.
7. Francks JJ, Kirsch RE, Kao B, Koppel TM: Fibrinogen and fibrinogen related peptides in cancer. In Mariani G (ed): Pathophysiology of Plasma Protein Metabolism. London: Macmillan, pp 265–269, 1984.
8. Ninet J, Horellou MH, Darjinoff JJ, et al: Assessment of preoperative risk factors. Ann Fr Anesth Reanim 11:252–281, 1992.
9. Crandon AJ, Peel KR, Anderson JA: Post operative deep vein thrombosis identifying high risk patients. Br Med J 2:343–344, 1976.
10. Clayton JK, Anderson JA, McNicol GP: Preoperative prediction of postoperative deep vein thrombosis. Br Med J 2:910–912, 1976.
11. Sue-Ling HM, Johnston D, McMahon MJ: Preoperative identification of patients at high risk of deep venous thrombosis after elective major abdominal surgery. Lancet 1:1173–1176, 1986.
12. Paramo JA, Alfaro MJ, Rocha E: Post operative changes in the plasmatic levels of tissue type plasminogen activator and its fast acting inhibitor. Relationship to deep vein thrombosis and influence of prophylaxis. Thromb Haemost 57:713, 1985.
13. Lowe GDO, McArdle BM, Carter DC, et al: Prediction and selective prophylaxis of venous thrombosis in elective gastrointestinal surgery. Lancet 1:409–412, 1982.
14. Hoek JA, Nurmohamed MT, ten Cate JW, et al: Thrombin-Antithrombin III complexes in the prediction of deep vein thrombosis following total hip replacement. Thromb Haemost 62:4, 1050–1052, 1989.
15. Bogaty-Yver J, Samama M: Thrombin-Antithrombin III complexes for the detection of postoperative hypercoagulable state in surgical patients receiving heparin prophylaxis. Thromb Haemost 61(3):538, 1989.
16. De Prost D, Ollivier V, Vie P, et al: D-Dimer and thrombin-antithrombin III complex levels uncorrelated with phlebographic findings in 11 total knee replacement patients. Ann Biol Clin 48:235–238, 1990.
17. Ofosu FA, Levine M, Craven S, et al: Prophylactically equivalent doses of Enoxaparin and unfractionated heparin inhibit in vivo coagulation to the same extent. Br J Haematol 82:400–405, 1992.
18. Bounameaux H, Khabiri E, Huber O, et al: Value of liquid crystal contact thermography and plasma level of D-Dimer for screening of deep venous thrombosis following general abdominal surgery. Thromb Haemost 67(6):603–606, 1992.
19. Bauer KA, Goodman TL, Kass BL, Rosenberg RD: Elevated factor Xa activity in the blood of asymptomatic patients with congenital antithrombin deficiency. J Clin Invest 76:826–836, 1985.

20. Bauer KA, Barzegar S, Rosenberg RD: Influence of anti-coagulants used for blood collection on plasma pro-thrombin fragment F1+2 measurements. Thromb Res 63:617–628, 1991.

21. Mannucci PM, Tripodi A, Bottasso B, et al: Markers of procoagulant imbalance in patients with inherited thrombophilic syndromes. Thromb Haemost 67(2):200–202, 1992.

22. Demers C, Ginsberg J, Henderson P, et al: Measurement of markers of activated coagulation in antithrombin III deficient subjects. Thromb Haemost 67(5):542–544, 1992.

23. Bauer KA, Broekmans AW, Bertina RM, et al: Hemostatic enzyme generation in the blood of patients with hereditary protein C deficiency. Blood 71(5):1418–1426, 1988.

24. Conard JC, Bauer KA, Griffin JH, et al: Normalization of markers of coagulation activation with a purified protein C concentrate in adults with homozygous protein C deficiency. Blood 82(4):1159–1164, 1993.

25. Wojchechoswski IJ, Olausson M, Korsan-Bengtsen K: Fibrinopeptide A, beta thromboglobulin and fibrin degradation products as screening test for the diagnosis of deep venous thrombosis. Haemostasis 13:254–261, 1983.

26. Rowbotham BJ, Carroll P, Whitaker AN: Measurement of cross linked fibrin derivatives—Use in the diagnosis of venous thrombosis. Thromb Haemost 57:59–61, 1987.

27. Heaton DC, Billings JD, Hickton CM: Assessment of D-dimer assays for the diagnosis of deep vein thrombosis. J Lab Clin Med 110:588–591, 1987.

28. Ott P, Astrup L, Hartvin G, et al: Assessment of D-Dimer in plasma: Diagnostic value in suspected deep venous thrombosis of the leg. Acta Med Scand 224:263–267, 1988.

29. Bounameaux H, Schneider PA, Reber G, et al: Measurement of plasma D-Dimer for diagnosis of deep venous thrombosis. Am J Clin Path 91:82–85, 1989.

30. Mossaz A, Gandrille S, Vitoux JF, et al: Valeur des D-Dimères dans le diagnostic en urgence des thromboses veineuses. Presse Med 19:1055, 1990.

31. Van Bergen PFMM, Ear K, Jonker JJC, et al: Is quantitative determination of fibrin(ogen) degradation products and thrombin-antithrombin III complexes useful to diagnose deep venous thrombosis in out patients. Thromb Haemost 62:1043–1045, 1989.

32. Elias A, Aillaud MF, Roul C, et al: Assessment of D-Dimer measurement by ELISA or latex methods in deep vein thrombosis diagnosed by ultrasonic duplex scanning. Fibrinolysis 4:237–240, 1990.

33. Boneu B, Bes G, Pelzer I, Sie P, Boccalon H: D-Dimers thrombin-antithrombin III complexes and prothrombin fragments 1+2 diagnostic value in clinically suspected deep vein thrombosis. Thromb Haemost 65:28–32, 1991.

34. De Boer WA, De Haan MA, Huisman JW, Klaassen CHL: D-Dimer latex assay as screening method in suspected deep venous thrombosis of the leg. A clinical study and the review of the literature. Neth J Med 38:65–69, 1991.

35. Achkar A, Laaban JP, Horellou MH, et al: Evaluation of repeated measurements of D-Dimers in the diagnosis of venous thromboembolic diseases (abstract). Thromb Haemost 69(6):620, 1993.

36. Lesprit P, Gepner P, Piette AM, et al: Phlebites profondes des membres inférieurs. Intérêt diagnostic du dosage des D-Dimerérs. Presse Med 20:1927–1929, 1991.

37. Bounameaux H, De Moerloose P, Perrier D, Reber G: Plasma measurement of D-Dimer as diagnostic aid in suspected venous thrombosis: An overview. Thromb Haemost 71:6, 1994.

38. Carter CJ, Doyle DL, Dawson N, et al: Investigations into the clinical utility of Latex D-Dimer in the diagnosis of deep venous thrombosis. Thromb Haemost 69(1):8–11, 1993.

39. Pini M, Biazzi A, Pattacini C, et al: Combined use of impedance plethysmography and plasma D-Dimer determination in clinically suspected deep venous thrombosis (abstract). Thromb Haemost 65(6):1176, 1991.

40. Heijboer H, Ginsberg J, Buller H, et al: The use of the D-Dimer test in combination with non invasive testing versus serial noninvasive testing alone for the diagnosis of deep vein thrombosis. Thromb Haemost 67(5):510–513, 1992.

41. Bounameaux H, Slosman D, De Moerloose P, Reber G: Laboratory diagnosis of pulmonary embolism. Value of increased levels of plasma D-Dimer and thrombin-antithrombin III complexes. Biomed Pharmacother 43:385–338, 1989.

42. Bridey F, Philipotteau C, Dreyfus M, Simonneau G: Plasma D-Dimer and pulmonary embolism. Lancet 1:791–792, 1989.

43. Speiser W, Leitha T, Dudczak R, Lechner K: Plasma D-Dimer levels in patients with pulmonary embolism (letter). Lancet 1:792, 1989.

44. Goldhaber SZ, Vaughan DE, Tumeh SS, Loscalzo J: Utility of cross linked fibrin degradation products in the diagnosis of pulmonary embolism. Am Heart J 116:505–508, 1988.

45. Bounameaux H, Cirafici P, De Moerloose P, et al: Measurement of D-Dimer in plasma as diagnostic aid in suspected pulmonary embolism. Lancet 337:196–200, 1991.

46. Estivals M, Pelzer H, Sie P, et al: Prothrombin fragment 1+2, thrombin-antithrombin III complexes and D-Dimers in acute deep vein thrombosis. Effects of heparin treatment. Br J Haematol 78:421–424, 1991.

47. Elias A, Bonfils S, Daoud-Elias M, et al: Influence of long term oral anticoagulants upon prothrombin fragment 1+2, thrombin-antithrombin III complex and D-Dimer levels in patients affected by proximal deep vein thrombosis. Thromb Haemost 69(4):302–305, 1993.

# Chapter 26

# Cost-effectiveness of Diagnosis

## Deep Vein Thrombosis in Symptomatic Patients

Russell D. Hull, William Feldstein, Graham F. Pineo, and Gary E. Raskob

Doppler ultrasonographic imaging of the lower extremities has become the dominant test for deep vein thrombosis since the late 1980s. It has largely replaced impedance plethysmography for noninvasive testing. Data from trials indicate that serial negative findings by impedance plethysmography or Doppler ultrasonography are equivalent.[1-6] The positive predictive value of impedance plethysmography is slightly less than that of Doppler ultrasonography.[3] However, most causes of a falsely positive impedance result (for example, congestive cardiac failure, hematoma, severe vascular disease) can be readily identified if a clinical examination at the bedside is performed.[4, 6]

Objective diagnosis of deep vein thrombosis allows treatment of these patients and avoids unnecessary treatment and prolonged hospital stays for patients in whom the diagnosis is not confirmed by objective tests.[7] Proximal vein thrombosis is much more likely to lead to fatal pulmonary embolism[8, 9] than is calf vein thrombosis; the incidence of fatal pulmonary embolism can be markedly reduced if deep vein thrombosis is treated with anticoagulant therapy.[10-12] Another important complication of deep vein thrombosis is the postphlebitic syndrome. Because no reliable information is available on its prevalence in treated versus untreated patients with deep vein thrombosis, however, this important complication is not considered in the cost-effectiveness analysis.

Economic evaluation helps decision makers maximize the health of the population served within the confines of the available resources. Cost-effectiveness analysis is an economic tool that ranks alternative approaches to the same health problem to determine which is "best."[13] The best approach in economic terms is defined as the approach that (1) accomplishes the desired health effect at minimal cost (cost minimization), (2) produces maximal health benefit for a given cost, or (3) carries the maximal effectiveness-to-cost ratio.

Cost-effectiveness analysis can be applied to the diagnosis of deep vein thrombosis using cost minimization.[7] The diagnostic approaches can be ranked from "worst" to "best," with the best approach defined as that which accomplishes the desired health effect at minimal cost.

Effectiveness (health benefit) is defined as the number or proportion of patients with deep vein thrombosis correctly identified by objective testing, or the number or proportion in whom treatment was correctly withheld. The latter group is important because large outcome studies have confirmed the safety of withholding or withdrawing anticoagulant therapy in symptomatic patients who have negative sonographic results or whose results are negative by serial noninvasive leg testing.[1-3, 14, 15] We also examine the impact of the analysis on the use of objective testing in outpatient care.

## METHODS

### Objective Tests for Deep Vein Thrombosis

Deep vein thrombosis in symptomatic patients is diagnosed from clinical findings, venography, and one or more noninvasive approaches. The best evaluated of the diagnostic approaches are ascending contrast venography, impedance plethysmography, and Doppler ultrasonography with B-mode imaging.[1-6, 14, 15] Data for this cost-effectiveness analysis were derived from a prospective study of approximately 500 patients who had had a first episode of clinically suspected deep vein thrombosis and who had been referred to a regional thromboembolism program.[7] All were assessed clinically and then investigated by venography and impedance plethysmography. Adequate venograms were obtained in 478 of these patients.[7]

Doppler ultrasonography with B-mode imaging, a highly sensitive and specific technique for detecting proximal vein thrombosis in symptomatic patients,[3, 5] was not available at the time this prosective study was performed. However, like impedance plethysmography, it is relatively insensitive for identifying calf vein thrombosis; serial testing is, therefore, required. Clinical trials comparing serial impedance plethysmography with Doppler ultrasonography with B-mode imaging have been subsequently completed.[3, 5] Serial Doppler ultrasonography is at least as effective as serial impedance plethysmography, and may be more so because of a higher positive predictive value.[3, 5] Doppler ultrasonography using B-mode imaging is formally evaluated in our study from these direc comparisons against impedance plethysmography.[3, 5]

## Cost-effectiveness

COST. The cost of each diagnostic alternative has been defined as the direct cost of administering the diagnostic test plus the treatment cost associated with a positive test result. The treatment cost consisted of the cost of anticoagulant therapy (including drugs and laboratory tests for monitoring anticoagulant therapy), and "hotel" costs of hospitalization (rooming, laundry, food, and the like). The costs of treating the complications and side effects of the diagnostic tests and of the anticoagulant therapy are not included because the costs involved were relatively minor.

The cost-effectiveness findings shown in the Results section are expressed both in 1992 Canadian (CDN) and United States (US) dollars (to the nearest dollar), according to the costs at the urban-based hospital site in Canada and the charges at the urban-based hospital site in the United States respectively. Detailed cost items for both countries were determined at the point

at which the study was completed. At the time, one Canadian dollar was equivalent to $0.80 US.

UNIT COSTS AT AN UBRAN TEACHING HOSPITAL IN CANADA. The cost data used in the study are based on actual quantities. The costs were derived from the operating costs incurred in an urban hospital affiliated with a university medical school. The costs were $542.50 per day for hotel costs, $137 for venography, and $150 and $400 for serial impedance plethysmography or serial Doppler ultrasonography with B-mode imaging, respectively. The cost of administering intravenous heparin therapy for 6 days was $142.78 for each patient and consisted of $48.91 for heparin (5,000 U initial bolus; constant infusion of 30,000 U for 6 days) and $93.87 for partial thromboplastin time tests (three during the initial 24 hours and daily thereafter).

The cost of longterm therapy with warfarin sodium for 3 months was $471.72 for each patient and consisted of $44.21 for warfarin sodium, $153.51 for prothrombin-time monitoring (five daily prothrombin time tests for days 2–6 followed by one test weekly for 12 weeks), and $274.00 for physicians' fees.

UNIT CHARGES AT AN URBAN TEACHING HOSPITAL IN THE UNITED STATES. We repeated this economic analysis using actual 1992 charges in United States dollars at an urban hospital in the midwestern United States. Teaching hospital hotel and diagnostic charges were derived from standard stepdown cost accounting and work sampling procedures. The ranking of these estimates of costs (although they differ from true economic costs) is similar in order of magnitude to the costs observed for Canada (for instance, this facility's hotel charge was US $575.00 per day compared with CDN $542.50 per day for the facility in Canada). The economic evaluation of each therapeutic approach was the same as that used for Canada (see Appendix).

EFFECTIVENESS. Three criteria of effectiveness were used and involved the correct identification of (1) deep vein thrombosis (thrombosis involving the calf, popliteal, femora, or iliac veins), (2) thrombosis involving the proximal veins (popliteal, femoral, or iliac veins) with or without calf-vein thrombosis, and (3) the number of patients in whom treatment was correctly withheld.

## Sensitivity Analysis

Multiple sensitivity analyses were performed. The variables examined were the (1) prevalence of deep vein thrombosis, (2) cost of the hospital bed, (3) cost of treatment, and (4) cost of the diagnostic tests used. For prevalence, a range of five to 80 cases of deep vein thrombosis per 100 symptomatic patients with clinically suspected deep vein thrombosis was used; this range exceeds the prevalence of deep vein thrombosis reported in the literature. For the costs of the hospital bed and treatment, a range of 40 to 300% was used, and for objective testing a range of 50 to 195% was used, reflecting regional variations in costs in Canada. For the 7% of patients in whom venograms were inadequate, the costs of other objective tests were examined by sensitivity analysis. For the inpatients who had deep vein thrombosis while they were convalescing from some other disorder, the number of extra days in the hospital attributed to the diagnosis of deep vein thrombosis ranged from 1 to 6.

The impact of false-positive results by noninvasive testing was also examined by sensitivity analysis.

## RESULTS

The 516 patients with clinically suspected venous thrombosis who were referred to the venous thromboembolism program ranged from 15 to 86 years of age (mean 53 years). The male-to-female ratio was 41:55. Two hundred and sixty-eight (52%) were outpatients at the time of referral to the program, and 248 (48%) were inpatients. Of the 248 symptomatic patients who were inpatients at the time of referral, 165 were admitted to the hospital for suspected deep vein thrombosis. The remaining 83 patients (16% of the population studied) had symptoms of deep vein thrombosis while convalescing from an acute surgical or medical illness, and management based on the clinical diagnosis would have prolonged their hospital stays; for this reason, these patients were included in the analysis.

Ascending venograms were technically adequate in 478 of the 516 patients (93%), and it

is in these patients that the cost-effectiveness comparison was performed. In 277 of the 478 patients (58%) venography was negative. Of the remining 201 patients, 139 had proximal vein thrombosis with or without calf vein thrombosis on venography and 62 had thrombosis that was limited to the calf.

A detailed analysis of the cost-effectiveness of clinical diagnosis, venography, and noninvasive testing is shown in the Appendix. Total costs and results of the alternative strategies to diagnose deep vein thrombosis are shown in Table 26–1. Total costs of the alternative strategies for each patient correctly managed are shown in Table 26–2.

## Cost-effectiveness of Diagnostic Approaches for Deep Vein Thrombosis

### Clinical Diagnosis

According to the clinical diagnosis alone, 478 symptomatic patients would have received care and treatment in the hospital. Because the venograms were normal in 277 (58%) of these 478 patients with clinically diagnosed deep vein thrombosis, more than one-half of these patients would have been incorrectly labeled and treated in the hospital on the basis of the clinical diagnosis alone. The total Canadian dollar cost of diagnosis and treatment in 478 patients for a correct diagnosis in 201 patients with deep vein thrombosis in 1992 would be CDN $1,590,784 (US $2,624,220). The cost per patient with deep vein thrombosis that was correctly identified and treated would be CDN $7,914 (US $13,055), the cost per patient with proximal vein thrombosis would be CDN $11,444 (US $18,879), and the cost incurred per patient correctly withheld from therapy would be CDN $5,743 (US $9,474).

Table 26–1. **Total Costs and Results of the Alternative Strategies to Diagnose Deep-vein Thrombosis**

| | Number of Correct Diagnoses | Cost | |
|---|---|---|---|
| | | Canadian $ | US $ |
| Clinical diagnosis | 201 | 1,590,784 | 2,624,220 |
| Inpatient venography | 201 | 1,207,707 | 2,087,417 |
| Outpatient venography | 201 | 734,314 | 1,450,040 |
| Doppler ultrasonography | 142 | 618,265 | 1,326,180 |
| Combined Doppler and impedance plethysmography | 142 | 551,065 | 1,124,580 |
| Impedance plethysmography | 142 | 527,165 | 1,052,880 |

Table 26–2. **Total Costs of the Alternative Strategies for Each Patient Correctly Managed**

| | | Cost/Patient Correctly Withheld From Treatment | Cost/Patient With Correct Diagnosis of Proximal Deep-Vein Thrombosis | Cost/Patient With Correct Diagnosis of Deep-Vein Thrombosis |
|---|---|---|---|---|
| Clinical diagnosis | CDN $ | 5,743 | 11,444 | 7,914 |
| | US $ | 9,474 | 18,879 | 13,055 |
| Inpatient venography | CDN $ | 4,360 | 8,689 | 6,008 |
| | US $ | 7,536 | 15,017 | 10,385 |
| Outpatient venography | CDN $ | 2,651 | 5,283 | 3,653 |
| | US $ | 5,235 | 10,432 | 7,214 |
| Doppler ultrasonography | CDN $ | 1,840 | 4,684 | 4,354 |
| | US $ | 3,947 | 10,047 | 9,339 |
| Combined Doppler and impedance plethysmography | CDN $ | 1,640 | 4,175 | 3,881 |
| | US $ | 3,347 | 8,520 | 7,920 |
| Impedance plethysmography | CDN $ | 1,569 | 3,994 | 3,712 |
| | US $ | 3,134 | 7,976 | 7,415 |

## Venography

Venography is accepted as the diagnostic reference standard for identifying venous thrombosis against which noninvasive tests are measured. However, venography has disadvantages. It is invasive and is associated with patient morbidity; if it is not readily available on an outpatient basis, it requires admission to the hospital. Costs are considered on the basis of outpatient and inpatient diagnosis.

**VENOGRAPHY AS AN OUTPATIENT DIAGNOSTIC APPROACH.** In 277 of the 478 patients, venography was negative; these 277 patients would have been spared inpatient care and therapy. The cost incurred in this group would be the cost of venography. The diagnosis of deep vein thrombosis was confirmed in 201 patients, and in these patients the costs incurred included those of venography, inpatient care, and treatment. The total Canadian dollar cost of outpatient venography in 478 patients yielding a diagnosis of deep-vein thrombosis in 201 in 1992 would be CDN $734,314 (US $1,450,040). The cost per patient with deep vein thrombosis correctly identified and treated would be CDN $3,653 (US $7,214), the cost per patient with proximal deep vein thrombosis would be CDN $5,283 (US $10,432), and the cost incurred per patient correctly withheld from therapy would be CDN $2,651 (US $5,235).

**VENOGRAPHY AS AN ELECTIVE INPATIENT DIAGNOSTIC APPROACH.** If immediate outpatient venography is not available, symptomatic patients may have to be admitted to the hospital for elective venography. Patients with clinically suspected deep vein thrombosis subsequently ruled out by elective venography had an average hospital stay of 3 days.

If all 478 symptomatic patients were admitted to the hospital for elective venography, 277 patients would have been hospitalized unnecessarily, incurring the costs of anticoagulant therapy and hospitalization for 3 days.

The total Canadian dollar cost of using inpatient venography in 478 patients to yield a diagnosis in 201 patients in 1992 would be CDN $1,207,707 (US $2,087,417). The cost per patient with deep vein thrombosis correctly identified and treated would be CDN $6,008 (US $10,385), the cost per patient with proximal deep vein thrombosis would be CDN $8,689 (US $15,017), and the cost incurred per patient correctly withheld from therapy would be CDN $4,360 (US $7,536).

## Serial Occlusive Cuff Impedence Plethysmography

Impedance plethysmography using the occlusive cuff technique is sensitive and specific for detecting proximal vein thrombosis but is insensitive for identifying calf thrombi. Impedance plethysmography is an objective diagnostic method that can be carried out in the oupatient clinic, ward, or emergency room.

Impedance plethysmography detected the disease in 132 (95%) of 139 patients with proximal vein thrombosis and in 10 (16%) of 62 patients with calf vein thrombosis. Thus, a correct diagnosis was made in 142 of 201 patients with deep vein thrombosis (71%). Impedance plethysmography was falsely positive in five patients (2%) in whom there was no obvious clinical cause.

The total Canadian dollar cost of using impedance plethysmography in 478 patients for a diagnosis in 142 patients in 1992 would be CDN $527,165 (US $1,052,880). The cost per patient with deep vein thrombosis correctly identified and treated was CDN $3,712 (US $7,415), the cost per patient with proximal deep vein thrombosis was CDN $3,994 (US $7,976), and the cost incurred per patient correctly withheld from therapy would be $1,569 (US $3,134).

## Ultrasonography

B-mode imaging is sensitive and specific for detecting proximal vein trombosis but is insensitive for identifying calf thrombi. B-mode imaging is an objective diagnostic method that can be carried out in the outpatient clinic, ward, or emergency room in some centers. In many centers, however, this test is done in a centralized facility.

Ultrasonography would have detected the disease in 132 (95%) of 139 patients with proximal vein thrombosis and in 10 (16%) of 62 patients with calf vein thrombosis. Thus, a correct diagnosis would have been made in 142 of 201 patients with deep vein thrombosis (71%). Ultrasonography would have been falsely positive in two patients.

The total Canadian dollar cost of using ultrasonography in 478 patients for a diagnosis in 142 patients in 1992 would be CDN $618,265 (US $1,326,180). The cost per patient with deep vein thrombosis correctly identified and treated would be CDN $4,354 (US $9,339), the cost per patient with proximal deep vein thrombosis would be CDN $4,684 (US $10,047), and the cost incurred per patient correctly withheld from therapy would be CDN $1,840 (US $3,947).

## Initial Negative Doppler Ultrasonography Examination Leading to Serial Impedance Plethysmography

Because of the higher positive predictive value observed with ultrasonography, an efficient approach may be an initial B-mode image evaluation followed by less costly serial impedance plethysmography if the initial evaluation was negative.

The total Canadian dollar cost of using this combined ultrasonography/impedance plethysmography approach in 478 patients for a diagnosis in 142 patients in 1992 would be CDN $551,065 (US $1,124,580). The cost per patient with deep vein thrombosis correctly identified and treated would be CDN $3,881 (US $7,920), the cost per patient with proximal deep vein thrombosis would be CDN $4,175 (US $8,520),

and the cost incurred per patient correctly withheld from therapy would be CDN $1,640 (US $3,347).

## Sensitivity Analysis

We performed multiple sensitivity analyses using the variables outlined in the Methods section, and this procedure did not alter the findings of this study.

## DISCUSSION

The diagnostic approaches to deep vein thrombosis include clinical diagnosis, venography, and serial noninvasive approaches. The clinical diagnosis of deep vein thrombosis is nonspecific and insensitive.[4, 14] In approximately 50% or more of the patients with clinically diagnosed deep vein thrombosis, the results of objective testing are negative.[7] Therefore, this approach is not cost-effective because one of two patients with clinically diagnosed deep vein thrombosis is inappropriately admitted to the hospital and given anticoagulant therapy. Patients with deep vein thrombosis can be accurately identified using venography[14] or noninvasive leg testing using either impedance plethysmography or Doppler ultrasonography with B-mode imaging.[1–7, 15]

At present, venography is the standard diagnostic reference test against which the noninvasive tests are evaluated.[1–7, 14] The disadvantages of venography are that it is invasive, is associated with patient discomfort, and induces postvenography phlebitis in approximately 1 to 3% of patients. In many centers, venography is readily available on an outpatient basis, thus avoiding the unnecessary costs associated with inpatient testing.

In ranking the approaches discussed, it is evident that clinical diagnosis is the least cost-effective. Noninvasive testing is the most cost-effective. Serial impedance plethysmography is less expensive than venography or Doppler ultrasonography with B-mode imaging. It is also more versatile than venography, and can be carried out in the outpatient clinic, ward, or emergency room. In many centers, B-mode imaging is carried out in a centralized facility. Noninvasive testing with serial impedance plethysmography or B-mode imaging avoids the risk of unnecessary anticoagulant therapy in those patients without proximal vein thrombosis.[1–3, 5, 15]

Serial B-mode imaging has the disadvantage of being more costly than serial impedance plethysmography, even though it is equally effective in ruling out proximal vein thrombosis. It has the advantage, however, that a bedside examination of the patient is not required to rule out clinical disorders known to produce false-positive results, which is the case when impedance plethysmography is used.[3] Accordingly, it would make economic sense in patients without clinical disorders known to produce a false-positive impedance plethysmography result to use serial impedance plethysmography in this large patient population. On the other hand, in patient subgroups (for example, those in the intensive care unit) who frequently suffer from cardiac failure, the use of serial B-mode imaging would avoid the otherwise high false-positive rates associated with impedance plethysmography testing in such a patient population.

Recent observations[16] suggest that B-mode imaging may be more sensitive to popliteal extension of calf vein thrombosis than impedance plethysmography. Large outcome studies, however, showed equivalent safety in patients with negative outcomes when either serial impedance plethysmography or ultrasonography was used.[3, 15] Thus, our cost-effectiveness analyses suggest that impedance plethysmography and B-mode imaging, if used selectively in the appropriate patient populations, would maximize effectiveness but would avoid the excessive cost associated with routine use of B-mode imaging in all patients. A strategy that would optimize both effectiveness and cost would be an initial Doppler ultrasonography B-mode examination, and if this initial evaluation were negative, mandatory serial testing could be employed using impedance plethysmography. The result would be significant cost savings. Thus, the inferences drawn from our cost-effectiveness analysis suggest that Doppler ultrasonography with B-mode imaging and impedance plethysmography are complementary rather than competitive.

It should be noted that serial testing is mandatory in patients whose results are initially negative by impedance plethysmography or B-mode imaging to detect nonocclusive proximal thrombi that subsequently extend or isolated calf vein thrombi that propagate proximally.[1–3, 5, 15, 16] Finally, in patients with a negative noninvasive test result (either by impedance plethysmography or B-mode imaging) in whom the clinical suspicion of deep vein thrombosis remains high, it is likely that a diagnosis of a nonocclusive thrombus could be made earlier by adjunctive ascending venography as an alternative to serial testing.[16]

Serial testing is feasible only on an outpatient basis in patients who are geographically accessible and are willing to return for followup. In outpatients who are unwilling or unable to return for serial followup, outpatient ascending venography remains the diagnostic method of choice.

Although the actual cost of each component will be dictated by regional differences and will change in the future, the proportion each parameter contributes (to the total cost) will remain linked. Thus, ranking of the diagnostic approaches from worst to best as determined by cost-effectiveness analysis should continue to be relevant. Because inpatient diagnosis is likely to remain a major cost, emphasis should be placed on outpatient diagnosis.

## APPENDIX

The cost-effectiveness findings for Canada, shown in the Results section, are expressed in 1992 Canadian dollars to the nearest dollar, using the Canadian dollar cost described in the Methods section. The findings for the United States are expressed in United States dollars and are calculated using the dollar cost described in the Methods section.

### Canadian Costs

#### Treatment Costing Details

HOTEL COST. The hotel cost was $542.50 per day.

INTRAVENOUS HEPARIN BY CONTINUOUS INFUSION FOR 5 TO 6 DAYS. The 1992 Canadian dollar cost per patient for initial treatment with intravenous heparin for 5 to 6 days was $142.78 and consisted of $0.61 for a drug bolus ($0.61 × 1), $0.01 for a bolus swab ($0.007 × 1), $0.12 for a bolus syringe with needle ($0.12 × 1), $48.10 for infusion bags with heparin drug ($4.81 × 10); $0.07 for infusion swabs ($0.007 × 10), $92.70 for partial thromboplastin time (PTT) tests ($10.30 × 9), and $1.17 for PTT blood vials with needles ($0.13 × 9).

INTRAVENOUS HEPARIN BY CONTINUOUS INFUSION FOR 3 DAYS. The 1992 Canadian dollar cost per patient for initial treatment with intravenous heparin for 3 days was $81.05 and consisted of $0.61 for a drug bolus ($0.61 × 1), $0.01 for a bolus swab ($0.007 × 1), $0.12 for a bolus syringe with needle ($0.12 × 1), $28.86 for infusion bags with heparin drug ($4.81 × 6), $0.04 for infusion swabs ($0.007 × 6), $51.50 for PTT tests ($10.30 × 5), and $0.65 for PTT blood vials with needles ($0.13 × 5).

LONGTERM TREATMENT WITH WARFARIN SODIUM. Longterm treatment with warfarin sodium for patients in this study ranged between 2 and 15 mg per day. The 1992 Canadian dollar cost per patient for this 12-week warfarin sodium treatment was $471.72 and consisted of $1.92 for the drug while the patient was in the hospital ($0.32 × 6), a one-time cost of $42.29 for warfarin drug prescription (this includes the cost of 90 5-mg tablets, plus dispensing fee), $151.30 for prothrombin time/International Normalization Ratio (PT/INR) tests ($8.90 × 17), $2.21 for PT/INR blood vials with needles (0.13 × 17), $100.00 for inhospital physician fees ($20.00 × 5), and $174.00 for outpatient physician fees ($14.50 × 12).

## Clinical Diagnosis

The cost for each patient with the clinical diagnosis of deep vein thrombosis would consist of the intrinsic technical cost of $0, a hospital room for 5 to 6 days (at $542.50 per day) for a cost of $2,713, plus the $615 combined cost of anticoagulant therapy, laboratory testing, and monitoring for 3 months (initial treatment with intravenous heparin costing $143 plus longterm treatment with warfarin sodium costing $472), for an overall cost of $3,328. The cost for 478 patients was 478 × $3,328 = $1,590,784.

EFFECTIVENESS. The desired result is the correct diagnosis and treatment of each patient with deep vein thrombosis. Only 201 of the 478 patients had deep vein thrombosis; 139 had proximal deep vein thrombosis and 62 had deep vein thrombosis involving only calf veins.

COST-EFFECTIVENESS. The cost for each patient with a correct diagnosis of deep vein thrombosis would be $1,590,784 ÷ 201 = $7914. The cost for each patient with a correct diagnosis of proximal deep-vein thrombosis would be $1,590,784 ÷ 139 = $11,444. The cost per patient correctly withheld from treatment would be $1,590,784 ÷ 277 = $5,743.

## Ascending Venography for Outpatient Diagnosing

The intrinsic cost of venography at $137 per patient in 478 patients would be $65,486. For 201 patients with deep vein thrombosis the cost of the hospital rooms for 5 to 6 days per patient (at $542.50 per day would be $545,213 and the cost of anticogualant therapy, laboratory tests, and monitoring (at a total of $615 per patient) would be $123,615. The total cost for 478 patients would be $734,314.

EFFECTIVENESS. In 201 patients with deep vein thrombosis, venography correctly identified the

disease; 139 patients had proximal deep vein thrombosis and 62 had calf vein thrombosis.

COST-EFFECTIVENESS. The cost for each patient with a correct diagnosis of deep vein thrombosis would be $734,314 ÷ 201 = $3,653. The cost for each patient with a correct diagnosis of proximal deep vein thrombosis would be $734,314 ÷ 139 = $5,283. The cost per patient correctly withheld from treatment would be $734,314 ÷ 277 = $2,651.

## Ascending Venography for Inpatient Diagnosing

The intrinsic cost of venography at $137 per patient in 478 patients would be $65,486. For 201 patients with deep vein thrombosis the cost of the hospital rooms for 5 to 6 days per patient (at $542.50 per day) would be $545,213 and the cost of anticoagulant therapy, laboratory tests, and monitoring (at a total of $615 per patient) would be $123,615. In addition, each of the 277 patients in whom venography was subsequently negative would receive 3 days of hospital care (3 × $542.50 = $1,628) plus anticoagulant therapy and monitoring ($81) at a cost of $1,709. The cost for 277 patients would be 277 × $1,709 = $473,393. The total cost for the 478 patients would be $1,207,707.

EFFECTIVENESS. In 201 patients with deep vein thrombosis, venography correctly identified the disease: 139 patients had proximal deep vein thrombosis and 62 had calf vein thrombosis.

COST-EFFECTIVENESS. The cost for each patient with a correct diagnosis of deep vein thrombosis would be $1,207,707 ÷ 201 = $6,008. The cost for each patient with a correct diagnosis of proximal deep vein thrombosis would be $1,207,707 ÷ 139 = $8,689. The cost per patient correctly withheld from treatment would be $1,207,707 ÷ 277 = $4,360.

## Impedance Plethysmography

The intrinsic cost of impedance plethysmography at $30 per test per patient in 478 patients would be $14,340. For the 336 negative patients the cost of serial impedance plethysmography (four tests) would be $120 × 336 = $40,320. For the 142 patients in whom impedance plethysmography was positive, the cost of the hospital rooms for 5 to 6 days per patient (at $542.50 per day) would be $385,175 and the cost of anticoagulant therapy, laboratory testing, and monitoring at a cost of $615 per patient would be $87,330. The total cost for the 478 patients would be $527,165.

EFFECTIVENESS. In 142 patients, deep vein

thrombosis was correctly identified; 132 had proximal deep vein thrombosis and 10 had calf vein thrombosis.

**COST-EFFECTIVENESS.** The cost for each patient with a correct diagnosis of deep vein thrombosis would be $527,165 ÷ 42 = $3,712. The cost for each patient with a correct diagnosis of proximal deep vein thrombosis would be $527,165 ÷ 132 = $3,994. The cost per patient correctly withheld from treatment would be $527,165 ÷ 336 = $1,569.

## Ultrasonography

The intrinsic cost of Doppler ultrasonography at $80 per test per patient in 478 patients would be $38,240. For the 336 negative patients the cost of serial ultrasonography (four tests) would be $320 × 336 = $107,520. For the 142 patients in whom ultrasonography was positive, the cost of the hospital rooms for 5 to 6 days per patient (at $542.50 per day) would be $385,175 and the cost of anticoagulant therapy, laboratory testing, and monitoring at a cost of $615 per patient would be $87,330. The total cost for the 478 patients would be $618,265.

**EFFECTIVENESS.** In 142 patients, deep vein thrombosis was correctly identified; 132 had proximal deep vein thrombosis and 10 had calf vein thrombosis.

**COST-EFFECTIVENESS.** The cost for each patient with a correct diagnosis of deep vein thrombosis would be $618,265 ÷ 142 = $4,354. The cost for each patient with a correct diagnosis of proximal deep vein thrombosis would be $618,265 ÷ 132 = $4,684. The cost per patient correctly withheld from treatment would be $618,265 ÷ 336 = $1,840.

## Initial Negative Doppler Ultrasonography Examination Leading to Serial Impedance Plethysmography

The intrinsic cost of Doppler ultrasonography at $80 per test per patient in 478 patients would be $38,240. For the 336 patients with negative results the cost of serial impedance plethysmography (four tests) would be $120 × 336 = $40,320. For the 142 patients in whom ultrasonography was positive, the cost of the hospital rooms for 5 to 6 days per patient (at $542.50 per day) would be $385,175 and the cost of anticoagulant therapy, laboratory testing, and monitoring at a cost of $615 per patient would be $87,330. The total cost for the 478 patients would be $551,065.

**EFFECTIVENESS.** In 142 patients, deep vein

thrombosis was correctly identified; 132 had proximal deep vein thrombosis and 10 had calf vein thrombosis.

**COST-EFFECTIVENESS.** The cost for each patient with a correct diagnosis of deep vein thrombosis would be $551,065 ÷ 142 = $3,881. The cost for each patient with a correct diagnosis of proximal deep vein thrombosis would be $551,065 ÷ 132 = $4,175. The cost per patient correctly withheld from treatment would be $551,065 ÷ 336 = $1,640.

## United States

### Treatment Costing Details

**HOTEL CHARGE.** The hotel charge was $575.00 per day.

**INTRAVENOUS HEPARIN BY CONTINUOUS INFUSION FOR 5 TO 6 DAYS.** The 1992 US dollar charge per patient for initial treatment with intravenous heparin for 5 to 6 days was $966.36 and consisted of $0.36 for a drug bolus ($0.36 × 1), $3.00 for a bolus swab ($3.00 × 1), $1.50 for a bolus syringe with needle ($1.50 × 1), $20.00 pharmacy charge for dispensing of the bolus ($20.00 × 1), $396.50 for infusion bags with heparin drug ($39.65 × 10), $30.00 for infusion swabs ($3.00 × 10), $200.00 in pharmacy charges for dispensing the infusion bags ($20.00 × 10), and $315.00 for PTT tests ($35.00 × 9), which includes the cost of blood vials and needles.

**INTRAVENOUS HEPARIN BY CONTINUOUS INFUSION FOR 3 DAYS.** The 1992 US dollar cost per patient for initial treatment with intravenous heparin for 3 days was $575.76 and consisted of $0.36 for a drug bolus ($0.36 × 1), $3.00 for a bolus swab ($3.00 × 1), $1.50 for a bolus syringe with needle ($1.50 × 1), $20.00 pharmacy charge for dispensing of the bolus ($20.00 × 1), $237.90 for infusion bags with heparin drug ($39.65 × 6), $18.00 for infusion swabs ($3.00 × 6), $120.00 in pharmacy charges for dispensing the infusion bags ($20.00 × 6), and $175.00 for PTT tests ($35.00 × 5), which includes the cost of blood vials and needles.

**LONGTERM TREATMENT WITH WARFARIN SODIUM.** Longterm treatment with warfarin sodium for patients in this study ranged between 2 and 15 mg per day. The 1992 US dollar charge per patient for this 12-week warfarin sodium treatment was $1,649.40 and consisted of $10.80 for the inhospital drug ($1.80 × 6), a one-time $79.60 drug prescription charge ($79.60 × 1), $323.00 for PT/INR tests ($19.00 × 17), which includes the cost of blood vials and needles, $600.00 for inhospital physician fees ($120.00 × 5), and $636.00 for out-patient physician fees ($53.00 × 12).

## Clinical Diagnosis

The charge for each patient with the clinical diagnosis of deep vein thrombosis would consist of the intrinsic technical cost of $0, a hospital room for 5 to 6 days (at $575.00 per day) for a cost of $2,875, plus the $2,615 combined cost of anticoagulant therapy, laboratory testing, and monitoring for 3 months (initial treatment with intravenous heparin costing $966 plus longterm treatment with warfarin sodium costing $1,649) for an overall charge of $5,490. The cost for 478 patients would be 478 × $5,490 = $2,624,220.

**EFFECTIVENESS.** The desired result is the correct diagnosis and treatment of each patient with deep vein thrombosis. Only 201 of the 478 patients had deep vein thrombosis; 139 had proximal deep vein thrombosis and 62 had calf vein thrombosis only.

**COST-EFFECTIVENESS.** The charge for each patient with a correct diagnosis of deep vein thrombosis would be $2,624,220 ÷ 201 = $13,055. The charge for each patient with a correct diagnosis of proximal deep vein thrombosis would be $2,624,220 ÷ 139 = $18,879. The cost per patient correctly withheld from treatment would be $2,624,220 ÷ 277 = $9,474.

## Ascending Venography for Outpatient Diagnosing

The intrinsic cost of venography at $725 per patient in 478 patients would be $346,550. For 201 patients with deep vein thrombosis, the cost of the hospital rooms for 5 to 6 days per patient (at $575 per day) would be $577,875 and the cost of anticoagulant therapy, laboratory tests, and monitoring (at a total of $2,615 per patient) in 201 patients with deep vein thrombosis would be $525,615. The total charge for 478 patients would be $1,450,040.

**EFFECTIVENESS.** In 201 patients with deep vein thrombosis, venography correctly identified the disease; 139 patients had proximal deep vein thrombosis, and 62 had calf vein thrombosis.

**COST-EFFECTIVENESS.** The charge for each patient with a correct diagnosis of deep vein thrombosis would be $1,450,040 ÷ 201 = $7,214. The charge for each patient with a correct diagnosis of proximal deep vein thrombosis would be $1,450,040 ÷ 139 = $10,432. The cost per patient correctly withheld from treatment would be $1,450,040 ÷ 277 = $5,235.

## Ascending Venography for Inpatient Diagnosing

The intrinsic cost of venography at $725 per patient in 478 patients would be $346,550. For 201 patients with deep vein thrombosis the cost of the hospital rooms for 5 to 6 days per patient (at $575 per day) would be $577,875 and the cost of anticoagulant therapy, laboratory tests, and monitoring (at a total of $2,615 per patient) in 201 patients with deep vein thrombosis would be $525,615. In addition, each of the 277 patients in whom venography was subsequently negative would receive 3 days of hospital care (3 × $575 = $1,725) plus anticoagulant therapy and monitoring ($576) at a cost of $2,301. The cost for 277 patients would be 277 × $2,301 = $637,377. The total charge for the 478 patients would be $2,087,417.

**EFFECTIVENESS.** In 201 patients with deep vein thrombosis, venography correctly identified the disease; 139 patients had proximal deep vein thrombosis and 62 had calf vein thrombosis.

**COST-EFFECTIVENESS.** The charge for each patient with a correct diagnosis of deep vein thrombosis would be $2,087,417 ÷ 201 = $10,385. The charge for each patient with a correct diagnosis of proximal deep vein thrombosis would be $2,087,417 ÷ 139 = $15,017. The cost per patient correctly withheld from treatment would be $2,087,417 ÷ 277 = $7,536.

## Impedance Plethysmography

The intrinsic cost of impedance plethysmography at $150 per test per patient in 478 patients would be $71,700. For the 336 negative patients the cost of serial impedance plethysmography (four tests) would be $600 × 336 = $201,600. For the 142 patients in whom impedance plethysmography was positive, the cost of the hospital rooms for 5 to 6 days per patient (at $575 per day) would be $408,250 and the cost of anticoagulant therapy, laboratory testing, and monitoring at a cost of $2,615 per patient would be $371,330. The total charge for the 478 patients would be $1,052,880.

**EFFECTIVENESS.** In 142 patients, deep vein thrombosis was corectly identified; 132 had proximal deep vein thrombosis and 10 had calf vein thrombosis.

**COST-EFFECTIVENESS.** The charge for each patient with a correct diagnosis of deep vein thrombosis would be $1,052,880 ÷ 142 = $7,415. The charge for each patient with a correct diagnosis of proximal deep vein thrombosis would be $1,052,880 ÷ 132 = $7,976. The cost per patient correctly withheld from treatment would be $1,052,880 ÷ 336 = $3,134.

## Ultrasonography

The intrinsic cost of Doppler ultrasonography at $300 per test per patient in 478 patients would be $143,400. For the 336 negative patients the cost of serial ultrasonography (four tests) would be $1,200 × 336 = $403,200. For the 142 patients in whom ultrasonography was positive the cost of the hospital rooms for 5 to 6 days per patient (at $575 per day) would be $408,250 and the cost of anticoagulant therapy, laboratory testing, and monitoring at a cost of $2,615 per patient in 142 patients would be $371,330. The total charge for the 478 patients would be $1,326,180.

**EFFECTIVENESS.** In 142 patients, deep vein thrombosis was correctly identified; 132 had proximal deep vein thrombosis and 10 had calf vein thrombosis.

**COST-EFFECTIVENESS.** The charge for each patient with a correct diagnosis of deep vein thrombosis would be $1,326,180 ÷ 142 = $9,339. The charge for each patient with a correct diagnosis of proximal deep vein thrombosis would be $1,326,180 ÷ 132 = $10,047. The cost per patient correctly withheld from treatment would be $1,326,180 ÷ 336 = $3,947.

## Initial Negative Doppler Ultrasonography Examination Leading to Serial Impedance Plethysmography

The intrinsic cost of Doppler ulrasonography at $300 per test per patient in 478 patients would be $143,400. The cost of serial impedance plethysmography (four tests) in the 336 negative patients would be $600 × 336 = $201,600. The cost of the hospital rooms for 5 to 6 days per patient (at $575 per day) for 142 patients in whom ultrasonography was positive would be $408,250. The cost of anticoagulant therapy, laboratory testing and monitoring at a cost of $2,615 per patient in 142 patients would be $371,330. The total charge for the 478 patients would be $1,124,580.

**EFFECTIVENESS.** In 142 patients, deep vein thrombosis was correctly identified; 132 had proximal deep vein thrombosis and 10 had calf vein thrombosis.

**COST-EFFECTIVENESS.** The charge for each patient with a correct diagnosis of deep vein thrombosis would be $1,124,580 ÷ 142 = $7,920. The charge for each patient with a correct diagnosis of proximal deep vein thrombosis would be $1,124,580 ÷ 132 = $8,520. The cost per patient correctly withheld from treatment would be $1,124,580 ÷ 336 = $3,347.

## REFERENCES

1. Huisman MV, Buller HR, ten Cate JW, Vreeken J: Serial impedance plethysmography for suspected deep venous thrombosis in outpatients. The Amsterdam General Practitioner study. N Engl J Med 314:823–822, 1986.
2. Huisman MV, Buller HR, ten Cate JW, et al: Management of clinically suspected acute venous thrombosis in outpatients with serial impedance plethysmography in a community hospital setting. Arch Intern Med 149:511–513, 1989.
3. Heijboer H. Buller HR, Lensing AWA, et al: A comparison of real-time compression ultrasonography with impedance plethysmography for the diagnosis of deep vein thrombosis in symptomatic outpatients. N Engl J Med 329:1365–1369, 1993.
4. Wheeler HB, O'Donnell JA, Anderson FA, Benedict K, Jr: Occlusive impedance phlebography: A diagnostic procedure for venous thrombosis and pulmonary embolism. Prog Cardiovasc Dis 17:199–205, 1974.
5. Heijboer H, Cogo A. Buller HR, et al: Detection of deep vein thrombosis with impedance plethysmography and real-time compression ultrasonography in hospitalized patients. Arch Intern Med 152:1901–1903, 1992.
6. Hull RD, Van Aken WG, Hirsh J, et al: Impedance plethysmography using the occlusive cuff technique in the diagnosis of venous thrombosis. Circulation 53:697–700, 1976.
7. Hull RD, Hirsh J, Sackett DL, Stoddart G: Cost effectiveness of clinical diagnosis, venography, and noninvasive testing in patients with symptomatic deep vein thrombosis. N Engl J Med 304:1561–1567, 1981.
8. Kakkar W, Howe CT, Flanc C, Clarke MB: Natural history of postoperative deep vein thrombosis. Lancet 2:230–232, 1969.
9. Moser KM, LeMoine JR: Is embolic risk conditioned by location of deep venous thrombosis? Ann Intern Med 94:439–444, 1981.
10. Hull RD, Raskob GE, Hirsh H, et al: Continuous intravenous heparin compared with intermittent subcutaneous heparin in the initial treatment of proximal vein thrombosis. N Engl J Med 315:1109–1114, 1986.
11. Hull RD, Delmore T, Genton E, et al: Warfarin sodium versus low-dose heparin in the long-term treatment of venous thrombosis. N Engl J Med 301:855, 1979.
12. Brandjes DPM, Heijboer H, Buller HR, et al: Acenocoumarol and heparin compared with acenocoumarol alone in the initial treatment of proximal vein thrombosis. N Engl J Med 327:1485–1489, 1992.
13. Weinstein MC, Stason WB: Foundations of cost effectiveness analysis for health and medical practices. N Engl J Med 296:716, 1977.
14. Hull RD, Hirsh J, Sackett DL, et al: Clinical validity of a negative venogram in patients with clinically suspected venous thrombosis. Circulation 64:622, 1981.
15. Hull RD, Hirsh J. Carter CJ, et al: Diagnostic efficacy of impedance plethysmography for clinically suspected deep vein thrombosis. Ann Intern Med 102:21–28, 1985.
16. Kearon C, Hirsh H: Factors influencing the reported sensitivity and specificity of impedance plethysmography for proximal deep vein thrombosis. Thromb Haemost 72:652–658, 1994.

# Pulmonary Embolism

Russell D. Hull, William Feldstein, Paul D. Stein, and Graham F. Pineo

Pulmonary embolism is a frequently oc-curring disorder. In a 1991 population study, the incidence of pulmonary embolism was 21 patients per 100,000 (0.021%).[1] The nonspe-cificity of clinical findings[2-7] combined with the diagnostic uncertainties and challenges pre-sented by both ventilation-perfusion lung scan-ning[2, 3, 5-14] and pulmonary angiography[2, 3, 8, 15, 16] have made the diagnosis of pulmonary embo-lism one of the most challenging diagnostic problems facing clinicians.

In symptomatic patients, ventilation-perfusion lung scanning plays a key role in the diagnosis of pulmonary embolism.[2, 3, 5-14] Pioneering retro-spective studies have introduced the concept of high-, intermediary-, indeterminate-, and low-probability lung scan patterns.[12, 13] Recent pro-spective studies have demonstrated that the low-probability lung scan pattern is associated with an unacceptably high frequency of pulmonary embolism (14 to 30%).[5-8] Indeed, these rigorous studies suggest that it would be more appro-priate to categorize results in patients with ab-normal perfusion lung scans as high-probability or nondiagnostic, as suggested by Moser.[2]

In recent years, the clinician's ability to diag-nose pulmonary embolism has been enhanced by the use of objective tests to detect venous thrombosis and by improvements in clinical trial methodology. Many patients with pulmonary embolism have residual deep vein thrombosis in the lower extremities.[7, 8] Indeed, Bone[17] has stated that the noninvasive diagnosis of deep venous thrombi (which are the usual anteced-ents to pulmonary emboli), using either imped-ance studies or duplex ultrasound studies of the legs, has been a major advance in the diagnosis of pulmonary embolism. As noted by Dalen,[18] incorporating lower limb diagnostics for venous thrombosis enhances the clinician's ability to achieve a cost-effective diagnosis of pulmonary embolism.

We have reported a practical noninvasive strategy[19] in patients with adequate cardiorespi-ratory reserve and nondiagnostic lung scans. This strategy (1) avoids pulmonary angiogra-phy, (2) identifies patients with proximal vein thrombosis who require treatment, and (3)

avoids the need for treatment and further inves-tigation in the majority of patients. Our find-ings supported two biologic concepts: (1) local thrombotic extension in the lung of submassive pulmonary embolism is not an important cause of morbidity or mortality in patients with ade-quate cardiorespiratory reserve, and (2) recur-rent pulmonary embolism comes from proximal vein thrombosis of the lower extremities in most patients. Our findings are not applicable to pa-tients with nondiagnostic lung scans and inade-quate cardiorespiratory reserve who require ei-ther treatment or further investigation with selective pulmonary angiography.

Economic evaluation is designed to help deci-sion-makers maximize the health of the pop-ulation served, subject to the available re-sources.[20-25] Cost-effectiveness analysis is an eco-nomic tool that ranks alternative approaches to the same health problem to determine "which is best." The best approach in economic terms can be defined as the approach that (1) accom-plishes the desired health effect at minimal cost (cost minimization), (2) produces maximal health benefit for a given cost, or (3) carries the maximal effectiveness-to-cost ratio.

We have performed a cost-effectiveness analy-sis of the recommended strategies for pulmo-nary embolism diagnosis and management. Two criteria of effectiveness are used: (1) the correct identification of pulmonary embolism, and (2) the correct identification of the number of pa-tients in whom treatment was correctly with-held.

Our findings in an era of health care cost constraints guided by managed care provide a rational comparison of the commonly used strategies for pulmonary embolism diagnosis and management in symptomatic patients.

## METHODS

### Objective Tests for Pulmonary Embolism

Methods for diagnosing pulmonary embolism in symptomatic patients include clinical findings, ventilation-perfusion lung scanning, pulmonary angiography, and noninvasive leg tests.[4-20] If serial noninvasive leg testing is negative in patients with a nondiagnostic lung scan pattern and adequate cardiorespiratory reserve, therapy can be withheld or withdrawn.[19] This is because recurrent venous thrombosis in such patients is detected by serial testing, which prevents the morbidity and mortality associated with recurrent venous thromboembolism.[19]

This cost-effectiveness analysis is based on data from a decision analysis that has been published separately (i.e., a collaborative study, Prospective Investigation of Pulmonary Embolism Diagnosis [PIOPED],[5, 26] in which 662 patients participated). Patients were prospectively evaluated by ventilation-perfusion lung scanning and pulmonary angiography. The following diagnostic strategies were used.

### Strategy 1—Ventilation-perfusion Lung Scans and Pulmonary Angiography

Patients with a high-probability lung scan result would be treated. In patients with a near-normal lung scan, treatment would be withheld or withdrawn. Patients with nondiagnostic lung scan results (regardless of cardiorespiratory reserve) would receive pulmonary angiography, and treatment would be based on the result of the angiogram.

### Strategy 2—Ventilation-perfusion Lung Scans, Single Noninvasive Leg Test, and Pulmonary Angiography

Patients with a high-probability lung scan result would be treated. In patients with a near-normal lung scan, treatment would be withheld or withdrawn. Patients with nondiagnostic lung scan results would receive a single noninvasive leg test. Those patients with a positive noninvasive leg test result would receive treatment, and those with a negative test result would receive pulmonary angiography.

### Strategy 3—Ventilation-perfusion Lung Scans, Serial Noninvasive Leg Tests, and Pulmonary Angiography

Patients with a high-probability lung scan result would be treated. In patients with a near-normal lung scan, treatment would be withheld or withdrawn. Patients with nondiagnostic lung scan results who had poor cardiorespiratory reserve would receive pulmonary angiography. Patients with nondiagnostic lung scans who had adequate cardiorespiratory reserve would receive serial noninvasive leg tests.

## Cost-effectiveness

### Cost

The cost of each diagnostic alternative was defined as the direct cost of administering the diagnostic test plus the treatment cost associated with a positive test result. All diagnostic testing charges included physician/specialist charges for interpretation. The treatment cost consisted of (1) the cost of anticoagulant therapy (including drugs, laboratory tests for monitoring anticoagulant therapy, and physician fees); and (2) the "hotel" costs of hospitalization (rooming, laundry, food, and the like). The costs of complications and side effects associated with anticoagulant therapy, as measured empirically in a recent double-blinded, multicenter clinical trial, are included and are detailed within the Appendix. The costs of treating the complications and side effects of pulmonary angiography are not included because they were relatively minor.[27]

The economic viewpoint of this analysis[22] was that of a third-party payer (in the United States, an insurance company or self-pay patient; in Canada, the Ministry of Health). The cost-effectiveness findings shown in the Results section are expressed both in 1992 United States and Canadian dollars (to the nearest dollar), according to the charges at an urban-based hospital site in the United States and one in Canada, respectively.

UNIT CHARGES AT AN URBAN TEACHING HOSPITAL IN THE UNITED STATES. The cost data used in the study are based on actual quantities. The costs were derived from the operating charges incurred in a midwestern urban hospital affiliated with a university medical school. Detailed charges are shown in the Appendix. Because clinical examination was the starting point for all patients in each strategy, the charge for the initial physician's fee was not included in this analysis. This facility's charges were US $575 per day for hotel charges, US $510 for ventilation-perfusion lung scans, US $2,553 for pulmonary angiography (which includes two additional days in the hospital), US $150 for a single impedance plethysmography, US $300 for a single Doppler ultrasonograph with B-mode imaging, and US $750 and US $1,500 for serial impedance plethysmography or serial Doppler ultrasonography with B-mode imaging, respectively. The total charges for treating each patient with intravenous heparin therapy followed by longterm warfarin sodium were US $6,522, as detailed in the Appendix.

UNIT COSTS AT AN URBAN TEACHING HOSPITAL IN CANADA. This economic analysis was also performed using actual 1992 costs in Canadian dollars at an urban hospital in western Canada. Although the Canadian costs are lower, their ranking in order of magnitude is similar to the charges in the United States (for instance, this facility's hotel charge was CDN $543 per day compared with US $575 per day for the facility in the United States).

This facility's costs were CDN $258 for ventilation-perfusion lung scans, CDN $828 for pulmonary angiography (which includes two additional days in the hospital), CDN $30 for a single impedance plethysmograph, CDN $80 for a single Doppler ultrasonograph with B-mode imaging, and CDN $150 and CDN $400 for serial impedance plethysmography or serial Doppler ultrasonography with B-mode imaging, respectively. The total costs for treating each patient with intravenous heparin therapy followed by longterm warfarin sodium were CDN $4,160, as detailed in the Appendix.

EFFECTIVENESS. Two criteria of effectiveness were used: (1) the correct identification of pulmonary embolism, and (2) the correct identification of the number of patients in whom treatment was correctly withheld.

## Sensitivity Analysis

Multiple sensitivity analyses[20, 22] were performed. Variables examined included charges for the hospital bed, charges for treatment, and charges for diagnostic tests. For prevalence, a range of 10 to 80 cases of pulmonary embolism per 100 symptomatic patients with clinically suspected pulmonary embolism was used; this range exceeds the prevalence of pulmonary embolism reported in the literature. For the charges for the hospital bed and treatment, a range of 40 to 300% was used, and for objective testing, a range of 55 to 195% was used, reflecting regional variations in charges in the United States.

The impact of false-positive results by noninvasive testing was also examined by sensitivity analysis.

The costs incurred by ancillary investigations such as chest x-rays, electrocardiograms, and baseline biochemistry during the initial work-up were the same for all strategies; these minor costs were evaluted by sensitivity analysis.

## RESULTS

The results of applying the three strategies to this 662-patient group are summarized in Table 26–3. A detailed analysis of the charges in the

Table 26–3. **United States Dollar Charges, Canadian Dollar Costs, and Effectiveness of the Alternative Strategies for Diagnosing Pulmonary Embolism in 662 Patients**

| Strategy | Number of Patients Requiring Treatment | | Total US $ Charges or CDN $ Costs | US $ Charge or CDN $ Cost Per Patient Requiring Treatment | US $ Charge or CDN $ Cost Per Patient Correctly Withheld from Treatment |
|---|---|---|---|---|---|
| 1 | 194 | US | 2,797,692 | 14,421 | 5,978 |
|   |     | CDN | 1,873,120 | 9,655 | 4,002 |
| 2a | 195 | US | 2,739,105 | 14,047 | 5,865 |
|   |     | CDN | 1,789,931 | 9,179 | 3,833 |
| 2b | 195 | US | 2,809,305 | 14,407 | 6,016 |
|   |     | CDN | 1,813,331 | 9,299 | 3,883 |
| 3a | 169 | US | 2,135,967 | 12,639 | 4,333 |
|   |     | CDN | 1,283,725 | 7,596 | 2,604 |
| 3b | 169 | US | 2,339,367 | 13,842 | 4,745 |
|   |     | CDN | 1,351,525 | 7,997 | 2,741 |

Strategy Descriptions:
  1 = Ventilation-perfusion lung scans and pulmonary angiography.
  2a = Ventilation-perfusion lung scans, single noninvasive leg test with impedance plethysmography, and pulmonary angiography.
  2b = Ventilation-perfusion lung scans, single noninvasive leg test with Doppler ultrasonography with B-mode imaging, and pulmonary angiography.
  3a = Ventilation-perfusion lung scans, serial noninvasive leg tests with impedance plethysmography, and pulmonary angiography.
  3b = Ventilation-perfusion lung scans, serial noninvasive leg tests with Doppler ultrasonography with B-mode imaging, and pulmonary angiography.

United States (or costs, in the case of Canada) is shown in the Appendix.

In all three strategies, all 662 patients would have undergone ventilation-perfusion lung scanning; the result would have been 89 with high-probability, 105 with near-normal, and 468 with nondiagnostic (intermediate- and low-probability) lung scan results.

## Strategy 1—Ventilation-perfusion Lung Scans and Pulmonary Angiography

All 89 patients with a high-probability lung scan result would receive treatment. The 105 patients with a near-normal lung scan result would receive no treatment. All 468 patients with a nondiagnostic lung scan result would have undergone pulmonary angiography, resulting in positive angiograms in 105 patients who would then receive treatment. Patients with a negative pulmonary angiogram would not receive treatment. In total, this strategy results in 194 patients requiring treatment, and treatment would be correctly withheld or withdrawn from 468 patients.

The total United States dollar charges (or Canadian dollar costs) for administering this strategy to yield a diagnosis of pulmonary embolism in 194 patients in 1992 would be US $2,797,692 (or CDN $1,873,120). Therefore, the charges in the United States (or costs in Canada) for each patient requiring treatment would be US $14,421 (or CDN $9,655). The charges (or costs) incurred per patient correctly withheld from treatment would be US $5,978 (or CDN $4,002).

## Strategy 2—Ventilation-perfusion Lung Scans, Single Noninvasive Leg Test, and Pulmonary Angiography

All 89 patients with a high-probability lung scan result would receive treatment. The 105 patients with a near-normal lung scan result would receive no treatment. All 468 patients with a nondiagnostic lung scan result would have undergone a single noninvasive leg test (impedance plethysmography or Doppler ultrasound with B-mode imaging), resulting in positive outcomes in 53 patients who would then receive treatment. In the 415 patients with a negative single noninvasive leg test result, pulmonary angiography would be performed, yielding 53 patients with positive angiogram results who would then receive treatment. Patients with a negative pulmonary angiogram result would

not receive treatment. In total, this strategy would reveal 195 patients requiring treatment, and treatment would be correctly withheld or withdrawn from 467 patients.

The total United States dollar charges (or Canadian dollar costs) for administering this strategy to yield a diagnosis of pulmonary embolism in 195 patients in 1992 would be US $2,739,105 (or CDN $1,789,931) if impedance plethysmography were used, and would be US $2,809,305 (or CDN $1,813,331) if Doppler ultrasonography were used. Therefore, the charges in the United States (or costs in Canada) for each patient requiring treatment would be US $14,047 (or CDN $9,179) if impedance plethysmography were used, and would be US $14,407 (or CDN $9,299) if Doppler ultrasonography were used. The charges (costs) incurred per patient correctly withheld from treatment would be US $5,865 (CDN $3,833) if impedance plethysmography were used, and would be US $6,016 (CDN $3,883) if Doppler ultrasonography were used.

## Stategy 3—Ventilation-perfusion Lung Scans, Serial Noninvasive Leg Tests, and Pulmonary Angiography

All 89 patients with a high-probability lung scan result would receive treatment. The 105 patients with a near-normal lung scan result would receive no treatment. All 468 patients with a nondiagnostic lung scan result would have undergone a single noninvasive leg test (impedance plethysmography or Doppler ultrasound with B-mode imaging), yielding positive test outcomes for 53 patients who would then require treatment. Of the 415 patients with a negative single noninvasive leg test result, 222 patients would have adequate cardiorespiratory reserve and would then undergo serial noninvasive leg testing; this would result in seven patients with positive test outcomes who would then require treatment. The 193 patients who would have inadequate cardiorespiratory reserve would receive pulmonary angiography; this would result in 20 patients with positive angiogram results who would then require treatment. Patients (with adequate cardiorespiratory reserve) with negative results subsequent to serial noninvasive leg testing as well as patients (with inadequate cardiorespiratory reserve) with a negative pulmonary angiogram result would not receive treatment. In total, this strategy reveals 169 patients requiring treatment, and treatment would be correctly withheld or withdrawn from 493 patients.

The total United States dollar charges (or Canadian dollar costs) for administering this strategy to the 662 patient group would be US $2,135,967 (or CND $1,283,725) if impedance plethysmography were used, and would be US $2,339,367 (or CND $1,351,525) if Doppler ultrasonography were used. Therefore, the charges in the United States (or costs in Canada) for each patient requiring treatment would be US $12,639 (or CDN $7,596) if impedance plethysmography were used, and US $13,842 (or CDN $7,997) if Doppler ultrasonography were used. The charges (or costs) incurred per patient correctly withheld from treatment would be US $4,333 (or CDN $2,604) if impedance plethysmography were used, and US $4,745 (CDN $2,741) if Doppler ultrasonography were used.

## Sensitivity Analysis

Sensitivity analysis showed that the sequence of ventilation-perfusion lung scans, serial noninvasive leg tests using impedance plethysmography, and pulmonary angiography are the most cost-effective approaches. The ranking of the other strategies is less able and may vary according to the differences in charges (or costs) for impedance plethysmography, ultrasonography, pulmonary angiography, or treatment. It is likely, however, that any potential change in charges or costs will be proportionately similar at participating centers, leaving the actual ranking observed by cost-effectiveness analysis unchanged.

## DISCUSSION

The strategy requiring pulmonary angiography in the least number of patients is a combination of ventilation-perfusion lung scans and serial noninvasive leg testing.[2-5, 10] It proved to be effective in identifying those patients requiring anticoagulant therapy and those not requiring treatment and was the least costly.

A diagnostic strategy that minimizes the need for pulmonary angiography (which is invasive and requires expertise for safe and effective imaging[5] has considerable clinical appeal. Therefore, the combination of ventilation-perfusion lung scanning with noninvasive leg testing has gained widespread acceptance.[3, 17, 19, 28]

If all patients with nondiagnostic lung scans receive pulmonary angiography, such invasive technology will be used in up to 70% of symptomatic patients; this is a costly approach. The use of ventilation-perfusion lung scans and serial noninvasive leg tests avoids the need for pulmonary angiography in 70% or more of patients with suspected pulmonary embolism and is the most cost-effective approach. The use of a single noninvasive leg test to detect deep vein thrombosis avoids the need for pulmonary angiography in approximately 20% of patients with nondiagnostic scans; this approach is intermediary in its cost-effectiveness.

In ranking the approaches discussed, it is evident that noninvasive leg testing with serial impedance plethysmography is less expensive than Doppler ultrasonography with B-mode imaging. Serial impedance plethysmography is versatile; it can be carried out in the outpatient clinic, ward, or emergency room.[19] In many centers, B-mode imaging is carried out in a centralized facility. Serial B-mode imaging is more costly than serial impedance plethysmography. B-mode imaging and impedance plethysmography have been shown to be equally effective in ruling out deep vein thrombosis.[29] B-mode imaging has the advantage, however, that a bedside examination is not required to rule out clinical disorders known to produce false-positive results, as is the case with impedance plethysmography.[30] In patients who do not have disorders that might produce false-positive impedance plethysmography results, it would make sense clinically and economically to use serial impedance plethysmography. In some patient subgroups, for example in the intensive care unit where patients frequently suffer from cardiac failure, the use of serial B-mode imaging would avoid the otherwise high false-positive rates associated with impedance plethysmography testing.

Recent observations suggest that B-mode imaging may be more sensitive to popliteal extension of calf vein thrombosis than impedance plethysmography.[31] Large outcome studies, however, show equivalent safety in symptomatic patients with negative test outcomes using either serial impedance plethysmography or ultrasonography.

Our cost-effectiveness analyses suggest that impedance plethysmography and B-mode imaging, if selected appropriately for various populations, would maximize effectiveness without the excessive costs associated with the routine use of B-mode imaging in all patients. A strategy that would optimize cost and effectiveness would be to employ B-mode ultrasonography as the initial noninvasive leg test, to be followed by impedance plethysmography if serial leg tests are necessary. Thus, the inferences drawn from our cost-effectivness analysis suggest that Dopper ultrasonography with B-mode imaging and impedance plethysmography are complementary rather than competitive.

Serial testing is feasible only in patients who are geographically accessible and are willing to return for followup. Otherwise, pulmonary angiography remains the diagnostic method of choice. Furthermore, if it is necessary to be certain whether pulmonary embolism has occurred, pulmonary angiography will be required if lung scanning is nondiagnostic.

Although the actual cost of each component in the diagnostic strategies will be dictated by regional differences and will change in the future, the proportion that each parameter contributes to the total cost will remain linked. Thus, ranking the strategies from most to least expensive, as determined by cost-effectiveness analysis, should continue to be relevant.

## APPENDIX

### United States Charges

#### Diagnostic Testing

The charges were US $510 for ventilation-perfusion lung scans, $150 for impedance plethysmography, $300 for Doppler ultrasonography with B-mode imaging, and $2,553 for pulmonary angiography. All diagnostic charges included physician/specialist charges.

#### Hotel Charge

The hotel charge was $575 per day.

#### Charges for Treatment With Intravenous Heparin and Warfarin Sodium

The total charge per patient for inhospital treatment for 6 days of intravenous heparin therapy and 3 months of outpatient longterm treatment with warfarin sodium was $6,522. The charges per patient were US $966 for intravenous heparin therapy (including physician fee, drug bolus, infusion bags, and partial thromboplastin time [PTT] tests), US $3,450 for 6 days hospital stay and $1,649 for longterm therapy with warfarin sodium (including PT/INR and physician fees). This total charge also includes the charges incurred (empirically derived from our treatment data) for the approximately 6% of patients who had a recurrent venous thromboembolic event as well as for the 5% of patients who had a major bleeding event. Minor bleeding occurred infrequently, as did other side effects of anticoagulant therapy (e.g., thrombocytopenia) and were unimportant compared with the other charges.

### Strategy 1—Ventilation-perfusion Lung Scans and Pulmonary Angiography

The total charge for administering strategy-1 diagnosis to 662 patients was US $2,797,692 and consisted of the following charges: $337,620 for ventilation-perfusion lung scans (662 × $510), $1,194,804 for pulmonary angiography (468 × $2,553), and $1,265,268 for treatment charges (194 × $6,522). The charge per patient requiring treatment was $14,421 ($2,797,692 ÷ 194), and the charge per patient in whom treatment was correctly withheld or withdrawn because of negative angiography or near-normal lung scan results was $5,978 ($2,797,692 ÷ 468).

### Strategy 2—Ventilation-perfusion Lung Scans, Single Noninvasive Leg Test, and Pulmonary Angiography

The total charge for administering strategy-2 diagnosis using impedance plethysmography to 662 patients was US $2,739,105 and consisted of the following charges: $337,620 for ventilation-perfusion lung scans (662 × $510), US $70,200 for impedance plethysmography (468 × $150), $1,059,495 for pulmonary angiography (415 × $2,553), and $1,271,790 for treatment charges (195 × $6,522). The charge per patient requiring treatment was $14,047 ($2,739,105 ÷ 195), and the charge per patient in whom treatment was correctly withheld or withdrawn was $5,865 ($2,739,105 ÷ 467).

The total charge for administering strategy-2 diagnosis using Doppler ultrasonography with B-mode imaging to 662 patients was $2,809,305 and consisted of the following charges: $337,620 for ventilation-perfusion lung scans (662 × $510), $140,400 for impedance plethysmography (468 × $300), $1,059,495 for pulmonary angiography (415 × $2,553), and $1,271,790 for treatment charges (195 × $6,522). The charge per patient requiring treatment was $14,407 ($2,809,305 ÷ 195), and the charge per patient in whom treatment was correctly withheld or withdrawn was $6,016 ($2,809,305 ÷ 467).

### Strategy 3—Ventilation-perfusion Lung Scans, Serial Noninvasive Leg Testing, and Pulmonary Angiography

The total charge for administering strategy-3 diagnosis using impedance plethysmography to 662 patients was US $2,135,967 and consisted of the following charges: $337,620 for ventilation-perfusion lung scans (662 × $510), $70,200 for the initial impedance plethysmography performed on all patients with a nondiagnostic lung scan result (468 × $150), $133,200 for the subsequent impedance plethysmography performed serially on the 222 patients with adequate cardiorespiratory reserve (222 × 4 × $150), $492,729 for pulmonary angiography performed on the 193 patients with inadequate cardiorespiratory reserve (193 × $2,533), and $1,102,218 for treatment charges (169 × $6,522). The charge per patient requiring treatment was $12,639 ($2,135,967 ÷ 169), and the charge per patient in whom treatment was correctly withheld or withdrawn was $4,333 ($2,135,967 ÷ 493).

The total charge for administering strategy-2 diagnosis using Doppler ultrasonography with B-mode imaging to 662 patients was US $2,339,367 and consisted of the following charges: $337,620 for ventilation-perfusion lung scans (662 × $510), US $140,400 for the initial Doppler ultrasound with B-mode imaging performed on all patients with a nondiagnostic lung scan result (468 × $300), $266,400 for the subsequent Doppler ultrasonography performed serially on the 222 patients with adequate cardiorespiratory reserve (222 × 4 × $300), $492,729 for pulmonary angiography performed on the 193 patients with inadequate cardiorespiratory reserve (193 × $1,403), and $1,102,218 for treatment charges (169 × $6,522). The charge per patient requiring treatment was $13,842 ($2,339,367 ÷ 169), and the charge per patient in whom treatment was correctly withheld or withdrawn was $4,745 ($2,339,367 ÷ 493).

## Canadian Costs

### Diagnostic Testing

The costs were CDN $258 for ventilation-perfusion lung scans, $30 for impedance plethysmography, $80 for Doppler ultrasonography with B-mode imaging, and $1,913 for pulmonary angiography. All diagnostic costs included physician/specialist costs.

### Hotel Cost

The hotel cost was CDN $543 per day.

### Costs for Treatment With Intravenous Heparin and Warfarin Sodium

The total cost per patient for inhospital treatment for 6 days of intravenous heparin therapy and 3 months of outpatient longterm treatment with warfarin sodium was $4,160. The costs per patient were $143 for intravenous heparin therapy (including physician fee, drug bolus, infusion bags, and PTT tests), $3,255 for 6 days hospital stay, and $472 for longterm therapy with warfarin sodium (including PT/INR and physcian fees). The total cost also includes the costs incurred (empirically derived from our treatment data) for the approximately 6% of patients who had a recurrent venous thromboembolic event as well as for the 5% of patients who had a major bleeding event. Minor bleeding occurred infrequently, as did other side effects of anticoagulant therapy (e.g., thrombocytopenia) and were unimportant as compared with the other costs.

### Strategy 1—Ventilation-perfusion Lung Scans and Pulmonary Angiography

The total cost for administering strategy-1 diagnosis to 662 patients was CDN $1,873,120 and consisted of the following costs: $170,796 for ventilation-perfusion lung scans (662 × $258), $895,284 for pulmonary angiography (468 × $1,913), and $807,040 for treatment costs (194 × $4,160). The cost per patient requiring treatment was $9,655 ($1,873,120 ÷ 194), and the cost per patient in whom treatment was correctly withheld or withdrawn because of negative angiography or near-normal lung scan results was $4,002 ($1,873,120 ÷ 468).

### Strategy 2—Ventilation-perfusion Lung Scans, Single Noninvasive Leg Tests, and Pulmonary Angiography

The total cost for administering strategy-2 diagnosis using impedance plethysmography to 662 patients was CDN $1,789,931 and consisted of the following costs: $170,796 for ventilation-perfusion lung scans (662 × $258), $14,040 for impedance plethysmography (468 × $30), $793,895 for pulmonary angiography (415 × $1,913), and $811,200 for treatment costs (195 × $4,160). The cost per patient requiring treatment was $9,179 ($1,789,931 ÷ 195), and the cost per patient in whom treatment was correctly withheld or withdrawn was $3,833 ($1,789,931 ÷ 467).

The total cost for administering strategy-2 diagnosis using Doppler ultrasonography with B-mode imaging to 662 patients was CDN $1,813,331 and consisted of the following costs: $170,796 for ventilation-perfusion lung scans (662 × $258), $37,440 for impedance plethysmography (468 × $80), $793,895 for pulmonary angiography (415 × $1,913), and $811,200 for treatment costs (195 × $4,160). The cost per patient requiring treatment was $9,299 ($1,813,331 ÷ 195), and the cost per patient in whom treatment was correctly withheld or withdrawn was $3,883 ($1,813,331 ÷ 467).

## Strategy 3—Ventilation-perfusion Lung Scans, Serial Noninvasive Leg Tests, and Pulmonary Angiography

The total cost for administering strategy-3 diagnosis using impedance plethysmography to 662 patients was CDN $1,283,725 and consisted of the following costs: $170,796 for ventilation-perfusion lung scans (662 × $258); $14,040 for the initial impedance plethysmography performed on all patients with a nondiagnostic lung scan (468 × $30); $26,640 for the subsequent impedance plethysmography performed serially on the 222 patients with adequate cardiorespiratory reserve (222 × 4 × $30); $369,209 for pulmonary angiography performed on the 193 patients with inadequate cardiorespiratory reserve (193 × $1,913); and $703,040 for treatment costs (169 × $4,160). The cost per patient requiring treatment was $7,596 ($1,283,725 ÷ 169); and the cost per patient in whom treatment was correctly withheld or withdrawn was $2,604 ($1,283,725 ÷ 493).

The total cost for administering strategy-3 diagnosis using Doppler ultrasonography with B-mode imaging to 662 patients was CDN $1,351,525 and consisted of the following costs: $170,796 for ventilation-perfusion lung scans (662 × $258); $37,440 for the initial Doppler ultrasound with B-mode imaging performed on all patients with a nondiagnostic lung scan (468 × $80); $71,040 for the subsequent Doppler ultrasonography performed serially on the 222 patients with adequate cardiorespiratory reserve (222 × 4 × $80); $369,209 for pulmonary angiography performed on the 193 patients with inadequate cardiorespiratory reserve (193 × $1,913); and $703,040 for treatment costs (169 × $4,160). The cost per patient requiring treatment was $7,997 ($1,351,525 ÷ 169); and the cost per patient in whom treatment was correctly withheld or withdrawn was $2,741 ($1,351,525 ÷ 493).

## REFERENCES

1. Anderson FF, Wheeler, HB, Goldberg RJ, et al: A population-based perspective of the hospital incidence and case-fatality rates of deep vein thrombosis and pulmonary embolism: The Worcester DVT study. Arch Intern Med 151:933–938, 1991.

2. Moser KM: Venous thromboembolism. Am Rev Respir Dis 141:235–249, 1990.

3. Kelley MA, Carson JL, Palevsky HI, Schwartz JS: Diagnosing pulmonary embolism: New facts and strategies. Ann Intern Med 114:300–306, 1991.

4. Stein PD, Saltzman HA, Weg JG: Clinical characteristics of patients with acute pulmonary embolism. Am J Cardiol 68:1723–1724, 1991.

5. Prospective Investigation of Pulmonary Embolism Diagnosis Investigators: Value of the ventilation-perfusion scan in acute pulmonary embolism: Results of the prospective investigation of pulmonary embolism diagnosis (PIOPED). JAMA 263:2753–2759, 1990.

6. Hull R, Raskob G: Low probability lung scan findings: A need for change. Ann Intern Med 114:142–143, 1991.

7. Hull RD, Hirsh J, Carter CJ, et al: Diagnostic value of ventilation-perfusion lung scanning in patients with suspected pulmonary embolism. Chest 88:819–828, 1995.

8. Hull RD, Hirsh J, Carter CJ, et al: Pulmonary angiography ventilation lung scanning and venography for clinically suspected pulmonary embolism with abnormal perfusion lung scan. Ann Intern Med 98:891–899, 1983.

9. Gottschalk A: Lung scan interpretation: A physiologic, user-friendly approach. J Nucl Med 33:1422–1424, 1992.

10. Sacker-Walker RH: On purple emperors, pulmonary embolism and venous thrombosis. Ann Intern Med 98:1006–1008, 1983.

11. Cheely R, McCartney WH, Perry JR, et al: The role of noninvasive tests versus pulmonary in the diagnosis of pulmonary embolism. Am J Med 70:17–22, 1981.

12. McNeil BJ: Ventilation-perfusion studies and the diagnosis of pulmonary embolism. Concise communication. J Nucl Med 21:319–323, 1980.

13. Biello DR, Mattar AG, McKnight RC, Siegel BA: Ventilation-perfusion studies in suspected pulmonary embolism. AJR Am J Roentgenol 133:1033–1037, 1979.

14. Alerson PO, Rujanavech N, Secker-Walker RH, McKnight RC: The role of ¹³³Xe ventilation studies in the scintigraphic detection of pulmonary embolism. Radiology 120:633–640, 1976.

15. Dalen JE, Brooks HL, Johnson LW, et al: Pulmonary angiography in acute pulmonary embolism: Indications, techniques, and results in 367 patients. Am Heart J 81:175–185, 1971.

16. Stein PD, Athanasoulis C, Alavi A, et al: Complications and validity of pulmonary angiography in acute pulmonary embolism. Circulation 85:462–468, 1992.

17. Bone RC: Ventilation-perfusion scan in pulmonary embolism: The emperor is incompletely attired. JAMA 263:2794–2795, 1990.

18. Dalen J: When can treatment be withheld in patients with suspected pulmonary embolism. Arch Intern Med 153:1415–1418, 1993.

19. Hull R, Raskob G, Ginsberg J, et al: A noninvasive strategy for the treatment of patients with suspected pulmonary embolism. Arch Intern Med 154:289–297, 1994.

20. Weinstein MC: Economic assessment of medical practices and technologies. Med Decis Making 1:309–330, 1981.

21. Weinstein MC, Stason WB: Foundations of cost-effectiveness analysis for health and medical practices. N Engl J Med 298:716–721, 1977.

22. Drummond MF, Stoddart GL, Torrance GW: Methods for the Economic Evaluation of Health Care Programs. Oxford, UK, Oxford University Press, 1987.

23. Eddy DM: Principles for making difficult decisions in difficult times. JAMA 271:1792–1798, 1994.

24. Eisenberg JM: Clinical economics: A guide to economic analysis of clinical practices. JAMA 262:2879–2886, 1989.

25. Detsky AS, Naglie IG: A clinical guide to cost-effectiveness analysis. Ann Intern Med 113:147–154, 1990.

26. Stein PD, Hull RD, Pineo GF: Strategy that includes serial noninvasive leg tests for diagnosis of thromboembolic disease in patients with suspected acute pulmonary embolism based on data from PIOPED. Accepted for publication, Arch Intern Med, 1995.

27. Hull RD, Raskob GE, Pineo GF, et al: Subcutaneous low-molecular-weight heparin compared with continuous intravenous heparin in the treatment of proximal-vein thrombosis. N Engl J Med 326:975–982, 1992.

28. Oupkerk M, Van Breek EJR, Van Putten WLJ, Buller HR: Cost-effectiveness of various strategies in the diagnostic management of pulmonary embolism. Ann Intern Med 153:947–954, 1993.

29. Heyboer H, Buller HR, Lensing AWA, et al: A randomized comparison of the clinical utility of real-time compression ultrasonography versus impedance plethysmography in the diagnosis of deep-vein thrombosis in symptomatic outpatients. N Engl J Med 329:511–513, 1993.

30. Huisman MV, Buller HR, ten Cate JW, Vreeken J: Serial impedance plethysmography for suspected deep venous thrombosis in outpatients: The Amsterdam General Practitioner study. N Engl J Med 814:823–828, 1986.

31. Kearon C, Hirsh H: Factors influencing the reported sensitivity and specificity of impedance plethysmography for proximal deep vein thrombosis. Thromb Haemost 72:652–658, 1994.

# PART THREE

# TREATMENT OF VENOUS THROMBOEMBOLISM

## Chapter 27

## Heparin Treatment of Venous Thromboembolism

### Russell D. Hull, Graham F. Pineo, and Gary E. Raskob

The standard anticoagulant therapy for venous thromboembolism (deep vein thrombosis and/or pulmonary embolism) is a combination of continuous intravenous heparin and oral warfarin sodium.[1-31] For all patients with venous thromboembolism who are medically stable, the standard clinical practice is to use heparin and warfarin simultaneously.[4, 51] There are exceptions: patients who require immediate medical or surgical intervention such as thrombolysis or insertion of a vena cava filter, patients in the intensive care unit who have multiple invasive lines, and patients with conditions that predispose them to major bleeding. A shortening of the hospital stay to 5 days for initial intravenous heparin therapy has led to significant cost savings.[41, 51] Although heparin and warfarin are given together, they are discussed separately for the purpose of this review.

## HEPARIN THERAPY FOR VENOUS THROMBOEMBOLISM

Standard unfractionated heparin remains the anticoagulant of choice for the treatment of acute thrombotic disorders because its onset of action is immediate when it is administered intravenously.[1-31] The basic biochemistry, pharmacology, and pharmacokinetics of heparin have been reviewed,[6, 7] and the uses of heparin in the prevention of venous thrombosis have been well established by consensus conferences.[8, 9] Important advances in heparin therapy have been made as a result of well designed randomized clinical trials conducted over the past 10 years.[41, 51, 101, 111] Most of the uncertainties that are commonly encountered in selecting an appropriate course of heparin therapy have now been resolved.

## HEPARIN—MECHANISM OF ACTION AND PHARMACOLOGY

The anticoagulant activity of unfractionated heparin depends upon a unique pentasaccharide that binds to antithrombin III (ATIII) and potentiates the inhibition of thrombin and activated factor X ($X_a$) by ATIII.[12-15] In addition, heparin catalyses the inactivation of thrombin by another plasma cofactor, heparin cofactor II, which acts independently of ATIII.[16] Heparin has several other effects such as binding to numerous plasma and platelet proteins, binding to endothelial cells and leukocytes, and increasing vascular permeability.[7] These latter effects may explain some of the nonanticoagulant effects as well as the hemorrhagic effects of heparin. It may also help to explain why relative heparin resistance develops in some individuals.[7] It is clear that there is a wide variability in the response of individuals to heparin and that frequent monitoring with laboratory tests (e.g., activated partial thromboplastin time [APTT]) is necessary.

## HEPARIN THERAPY FOR VENOUS THROMBOEMBOLISM

The development of accurate objective tests to detect venous thromboembolism and advances in clinical trial methodology have led to clinical trials to evaluate heparin therapy for venous thromboembolism.[4I, 5I, 10I, 11I] These clinical trials have established the need for initial heparin treatment[10I, 17V] and the optimal duration for this treatment.[4I, 5I] In addition, adequate intensity of heparin treatment is required to prevent recurrent venous thromboembolism[5I]; therefore, the anticoagulant response to heparin must be monitored and the dose must be titrated in the individual patient, because the anticoagulant response to a standard dose of heparin varies widely between patients.[19, 20] Clinical trials have provided important information on the appropriate therapeutic range for laboratory monitoring of heparin therapy.[11I]

## LABORATORY MONITORING AND THERAPEUTIC RANGE

The laboratory test most commonly used to monitor heparin therapy is the APTT. In a traditional and widely used approach, the heparin infusion dose is adjusted to maintain the APTT within a defined "therapeutic range." Over the years, the clinical custom has been to use an upper and lower limit (an APTT ratio of 1.5 to 2.5 times control). Maintaining the APTT response within this range is based on the two concepts (1) that maintaining the APTT ratio above the lower limit of 1.5 minimizes recurrent venous thromboembolic events, and (2) that maintaining the APTT ratio below the upper limit of 2.5 minimizes the risk of bleeding complications. Rigorously designed clinical trials have led to firm recommendations about the appropriate therapeutic range for the APTT. Failure to exceed the lower limit (an APTT ratio of 1.5) is associated with an unacceptably high risk of recurrent venous thromboembolism[5I]; in

contrast, no association exists between supratherapeutic APTT responses (an APTT ratio of 2.5 or more) and the risk of bleeding.[11I]

## VARIABILITY OF APTT RESULTS AND HEPARIN BLOOD LEVELS WITH DIFFERENT APTT REAGENTS

Experimental studies and clinical trials have shown that the efficacy of heparin therapy depends upon achieving a critical therapeutic level of heparin within the first 24 hours of treatment. The critical therapeutic level of heparin as measured by the APTT is 1.5 times the mean of the control value, or a heparin blood level of 0.2 to 0.4 U/ml measured by the protamine sulphate titration assay.[19] However, the APTT and heparin blood levels vary widely with different reagents and even with different batches of the same reagent. It is therefore vital that each laboratory establish the minimal therapeutic level of heparin (measured by the APTT) that provides a heparin blood level of at least 0.2 U/ml (measured by the protamine titration assay) for each batch of thromboplastin reagent being used, and particularly if the reagent is provided by a different manufacturer.

Variability in the APTT response to different heparin blood levels supports the need for an aggressive approach to heparin therapy to ensure that all patients achieve adequate therapy early in the course of their treatment. The use of low-molecular-weight heparin, which does not require laboratory monitoring, eliminates this problem. However, until these agents are approved for use, the problem of APTT standardization will remain.

## EVIDENCE FOR THE LOWER LIMIT OF THE THERAPEUTIC RANGE

Data from three randomized clinical trials[5I, 21I, 22I] provide firm support for using an APTT ratio of 1.5 as the lower limit of the therapeutic range.

The first randomized trial evaluated clinical outcomes in patients with proximal vein thrombosis who were treated with either continuous intravenous heparin or intermittent subcutaneous heparin adjusted to prolong the APTT to greater than 1.5 times the control value.[5I] The subcutaneous regimen resulted in an initial anticoagulant response below the lower limit in the majority (63%) of patients. There was also a high frequency of recurrent venous thromboembolism (11 of 57 patients, 19.3%); this was virtually confined to patients with a subtherapeutic anticoagulant response.[51] In contrast, continuous intravenous heparin resulted in an adequate anticoagulant response in the majority (71%) of patients, and a low frequency of recurrent thromboembolic events (three of 58 patients, 5.2%); the recurrences in this group were also limited to patients with an initial subtherapeutic anticoagulant response.[51] Thirteen of 53 patients (24.5%) who had an APTT response below the lower limit for 24 hours or more had recurrent venous thromboembolism compared with only one of 62 patients (1.6%) in whom the APTT ratio was 1.5 or more ($p < .001$); the relative risk for recurrent venous thromboembolism was 15:1. Similar results were found when a weight-based heparin dosing nomogram (starting dose 80 U/kg bolus and 18 U/kg/hour infusion) was compared with a standard care nomogram (starting dose 5,000 U bolus and 1,000 U/hour infusion).[221] When the weight-based nomogram was used, the therapeutic threshold was exceeded in 60 of 62 patients (97%) within 24 hours compared with 37 of 48 (77%) of patients in the standard care group ($p < .002$). Recurrent thromboembolism in the 3-month treatment period was more frequent in the standard care group; relative risk was 5.0 (95% confidence interval [CI] 1.1–21.9).[221]

These findings are strongly supported by a recent randomized trial in which intravenous heparin was compared with oral anticoagulants alone for the initial treatment of patients with proximal vein thrombosis.[211] Because of the nature of treatment in the latter group, the APTT response was inadequate for at least the first 48 hours because the onset of the anticoagulant effect of oral anticoagulants was delayed. Recurrent venous thromboembolism occurred in 12 of 60 patients (20%) treated with oral anticoagulants alone over the subsequent 3 months, compared with four of 60 patients (6.7%) who received initial intravenous heparin plus oral anticoagulants ($p = .058$).[211]

Because recurrent thromboembolism typically occurred between 3 and 12 weeks in all of these trials, it may not be recognized that these recurrent clinical events relate to the failure of initial therapy.

## LACK OF ASSOCIATION BETWEEN THE UPPER LIMIT OF THE THERAPEUTIC RANGE AND THE RISK OF BLEEDING

In contrast to the strong association between a subtherapeutic APTT response and recurrent venous thromboembolism, evidence supporting the use of an upper limit of the therapeutic range is weak. Until recently, randomized clinical trials were not able to provide clear guidelines on an upper limit to the therapeutic range. The use of an upper limit, and the clinical practice of reducing the heparin dose when the APTT results exceed this limit, have been based on clinical custom and the intuitive belief that this practice will minimize the risk of bleeding.

A randomized trial provides important information on the upper limit of the therapeutic range for the APTT.[111] Clinical outcomes in patients with proximal vein thrombosis who were randomized to receive initial treatment with either intravenous heparin alone, or intravenous heparin with simultaneous warfarin sodium, were evaluated. The combined heparin and warfarin group received more intensive anticoagulation, and the majority of patients exceeded the predefined upper limit (an APTT ratio of 2.5) for sustained periods of time.[111] This was shown by the finding that 69 of 99 patients (69%) in the combined group had a supratherapeutic APTT value (a ratio of 2.5 or more) persisting for 24 hours or more, compared with 24 of 100 patients (24%) receiving heparin alone ($p < .001$). Despite the more intense therapy in the combined group, bleeding complications occurred with similar frequency in the two groups: nine of 99 patients in the combined group (9.1%) had bleeding complications, compared with 12 of 100 patients (12.0%) in the group given heparin alone.[111] Major bleeding occurred in three of 93 patients (3.2%) with supratherapeutic APTT findings, compared with 10 of 106 patients (9.4%) without supratherapeutic APTT findings (relative risk 0.3 $p = .09$).[111]

These results indicate a lack of association between a supratherapeutic APTT result (ratio 2.5 or more) and the risk of clinically important bleeding complications. On the other hand, when the incidence of major bleeding was related to the clinical risk of bleeding, patients considered at low risk for bleeding, and who received the higher heparin dose, had a low frequency of major bleeding (1%); those considered at high risk for bleeding who received a lower dose of heparin had a higher frequency of major bleeding (11%) ($p = .007$).[111]

## THE NEED FOR QUALITY ASSURANCE OF HEPARIN THERAPY

Audits of heparin therapy suggest that administration of intravenous heparin is fraught with difficulties,[17l, 23lV, 24] and that using an ad hoc or intuitive approach to heparin dose-titration frequently results in inadequate therapy. For example, in a survey of physician practices at three university-affiliated hospitals,[24] an adequate APTT response (a ratio of 1.5) was not obtained during the initial 24 hours of therapy, and further, 30% to 40% of patients remained in a subtherapeutic range over the next 3 to 4 days. A common theme leading to inadequate therapy is an exaggerated fear of bleeding complications on the part of clinicians. Consequently, it has been common practice for many clinicians to start treatment with a low heparin dose and to cautiously increase this dose over several days to achieve the therapeutic range. Clinical trial data indicate that this practice is inappropriate, and indeed dangerous, because it places the patient at an unacceptably high risk for recurrent venous thromboembolism.[1ll]

## APPROACHES TO QUALITY ASSURANCE OF INTRAVENOUS HEPARIN THERAPY

A prescriptive approach or protocol for administering intravenous heparin therapy has been evaluated in three studies in patients with venous thromboembolism.[1ll, 22l, 23lV]

Cruickshank and coworkers[23lV] evaluated a dosing nomogram for intravenous heparin. It was designed to achieve an early therapeutic APTT response, to prevent prolonged periods of inadequate anticoagulation, and to avoid periods of over-anticoagulation. Compared with a historic control group, the use of the nomogram resulted in an increase in the proportion of patients in whom the APTT result was within the therapeutic range at 24 hours (from 37–66%) and at 48 hours (from 58–81%). These differences are clinically important and statistically significant. Even when the dosing nomogram was used, a relatively high proportion (19%) of patients had subtherapeutic APTT responses early in therapy that persisted for 24 hours or more. Recurrent venous thromboembolism and bleeding were not reported on in this study.

A randomized clinical trial in which patients were randomized to two groups—initial heparin therapy alone (100 patients) or heparin therapy with simultaneous warfarin sodium therapy (99 patients)—was recently reported.[1ll] The study had two objectives (1) to validate a prescriptive approach designed to minimize the proportion of patients receiving subtherapeutic doses of heparin within the first 24 hours in the presence or absence of oral anticoagulant therapy; and (2) to determine the effectiveness and safety of decreasing the amount of heparin infused (based on the prolongation of the APTT) to reflect both the heparin effect and alteration of the vitamin K clotting factors owing to warfarin sodium. This prescriptive approach is summarized in Tables 27–1 and 27–2.

Only 2% and 1% of the patients received subtherapeutic doses for more than 24 hours in the heparin and warfarin group, and the heparin group, respectively.[1ll] Recurrent venous thromboembolism (objectively documented) occurred infrequently in both groups (7%),[1ll] and these rates are similar to those previously reported.[4l, 51, 1ll] Subtherapy was avoided in most patients, and the prescriptive heparin protocol resulted in effective delivery of heparin therapy in both groups. Further, because of the influence of warfarin on the APTT response, patients

Table 27–1. **Intravenous Heparin Protocol for Patients With Venous Thromboembolism***

1. Initial intravenous heparin bolus: 5000 units.
2. Continuous intravenous heparin infusion: commence at 42 mL/hour of 20,000 units (1680 units/hour) in 500 mL of diluent (a 24-hour heparin dose of 40,320 units), except in the following patients, in whom the heparin infusion is commenced at a rate of 31 mL/hour (1240 units/hour) (i.e., a 24 hour dose of 29,760 units).
   a. Patients who have undergone surgery within the previous two weeks.
   b. Patients with a previous history of peptic ulcer disease, gastrointestinal bleeding or genitourinary bleeding.
   c. Patients with recent stroke (i.e., thrombotic stroke within two weeks previously).
   d. Patients with a platelet count $< 150 \times 10^9$ per liter.
   e. Patients with miscellaneous reasons for a high risk of bleeding (e.g., invasive line, hepatic failure, etc.)
3. The APTT is performed in all patients as outlined below:
   a. 4 hours after commencing heparin; the heparin dose is then adjusted according to the nomogram shown.
   b. 4–6 hours after implementing the first dosage adjustment.
   c. The APTT is then performed as indicated by a nomogram for the first 24 hours of therapy.
   d. Thereafter, the APTT is performed once daily, unless the patient is subtherapeutic, in which case, the APTT should be repeated 4 hours after increasing the heparin dose.

*Used with permission from Hull R, Raskob G, Rosenbloom D, et al: Optimal therapeutic level of heparin therapy in patients with venous thrombosis. Arch Intern Med 152:1589–1595, 1992. Copyright 1992, American Medical Association.

Table 27-2. **Intravenous Heparin Dose-titration Nomogram Using the APTT for Patients with Venous Thromboembolism***

| APTT (secs) | IV Infusion | | Additional Action |
| | Rate Change (ml/hr)† | Dose Change (units/24 hrs) | |
| --- | --- | --- | --- |
| ≤ 45 | +6 | +5,760 | Repeat APTT in 4-6 hrs |
| 46-54 | +3 | +2,880 | Repeat APTT in 4-6 hrs |
| 55-85 | 0 | 0 | None¶ |
| 86-110 | -3 | -2,880 | Stop heparin for 1 hour<br>Repeat APTT 4-6 hours after restarting heparin<br>Stop heparin for 1 hour |
| > 110 | -6 | -5,760 | Repeat APTT 4-6 hours after restarting heparin |

*Using Actin-FS thromboplastin APTT reagent (Dade).
†Heparin concentration 20,000 units in 500 ml = 40 U/ml.
¶During the first 24 hours, repeat APTT in 4-6 hours. Thereafter, the APTT is done once daily, unless subtherapeutic.
Used with permission from Hull R, Raskob G, Rosenbloom D, et al: Optimal therapeutic level of heparin therapy in patients with venous thrombosis. Arch Intern Med 152:1589-1595, 1992. Copyright 1992, American Medical Association.

in the combined treatment group received less heparin per 24 hours than those in the group given heparin alone, with no adverse outcome.[111]

The frequencies of bleeding were 9% in the group treated with heparin and warfarin simultaneously, and 12% in the group that received heparin alone.[111] These frequencies are similar to rates of bleeding reported previously.[31, 41, 51] The heparin nomogram was also used in a randomized clinical trial in which fixed-dose subcutaneous low-molecular-weight heparin was compared with continuous intravenous heparin in the initial treatment of proximal venous thrombosis.[251] Warfarin was started on day 2 in all patients. Use of the heparin nomogram in the 15 different treatment centers ensured that the vast majority of patients were within the therapeutic range within 24 hours. Findings from one of the treatment centers indicated that 91% of patients were within the therapeutic range (PTT > 1.5 × control) within 24 hours compared with 60% of the patients who were treated without the use of a heparin protocol.[261]

In another randomized clinical trial, a weight-based heparin dosing nomogram was compared with a standard-care nomogram.[221] Patients on the weight-adjusted heparin nomogram received a starting bolus of 80 U/kg and infusion

of 18 U/kg/hour. Patients on the standard-care nomogram received a bolus of 5,000 U followed by infusion of 1,000 U/hour. The heparin dose was intended to maintain an APTT of 1.5 to 2.3 times control. The results to be measured were (1) the time to exceed the therapeutic threshold of an APTT greater than 1.5 times control, and (2) the time to achieve the therapeutic range (an APTT of 1.5 to 2.3 times control). In the weight-based heparin group, 97% of patients exceeded the therapeutic threshold within 24 hours compared with 77% in the standard-care group ($p = .082$).[221] In the weight-adjusted group, 89% of patients achieved the therapeutic range within 24 hours compared with 75% in the standard-care group.[221] The risk of recurrent thromboembolism was more frequent in the standard-care group. In addition to patients with venous thromboembolism, this study included patients with unstable angina and arterial thromboembolism, indicating that the principles used in the heparin nomogram for treating venous thromboembolism may be generalized to other clinical conditions.

In summary, the appropriate use of heparin and warfarin in the treatment of venous thromboembolism has been revolutionized by the findings of clinical trials performed over the past decade. The use of a heparin nomogram as opposed to the intuitive ordering of heparin guarantees that virtually all patients achieve a therapeutic heparin level as measured by the APTT within the first 24 hours. This minimizes the threat of recurrent venous thromboembolism and possibly the development of heparin resistance. In the past, fear of bleeding with an APTT level above the therapeutic range led to inadequate treatment in a large number of patients. However, bleeding on heparin is more dependent on underlying clinical risk factors than the level of the APTT. Thus, it is more important to avoid subtherapeutic doses of heparin rather than being overly concerned with achieving supratherapeutic APTT levels. Furthermore, because the APTT varies widely with different reagents and even with different batches of the same reagent, it is vital that each laboratory establish the minimal therapeutic level of heparin as measured by the APTT that will provide a heparin blood level of at least 0.2 U/ml as measured by the protamine titration assay. This exercise must be repeated with each batch of thromboplastin reagent being used, particularly if the reagent is provided by a different manufacturer.

Unfractionated heparin remains the drug of choice for the initial management of venous thromboembolism. However, because the dose must be titrated for each patient, the use of intravenous heparin is labor-intensive and expensive. The advent of the low-molecular-weight heparins, some of which have been shown to be effective and safe and to have the convenience of a once-daily subcutaneous injection without laboratory monitoring, indicates that unfractionated heparin will soon be relegated to a secondary role in the treatment of venous thromboembolism.[251]

## REFERENCES

1. Hyers TM, Hull RD, Weg J: Antithrombotic therapy for venous thromboembolic disease. Chest 102:408S–425S, 1992.
2. Moser KM: Venous thromboembolism. Am Rev Respir Dis 141:235–249, 1990.
I 3. Salzman EW, Deykin D, Shapiro RM, et al: Management of heparin therapy: Controlled prospective trial. N Engl J Med 292:1046–1050, 1976.
I 4. Gallus A, Jackaman J, Tillett J, et al: Safety and efficacy of warfarin started early after submassive venous thrombosis or pulmonary embolism. Lancet 2:1293–1296, 1986.
I 5. Hull RD, Raskob GE, Rosenbloom D, et al: Heparin for 5 days as compared with 10 days in the initial treatment of proximal venous thrombosis. N Engl J Med 322:1260–1264, 1990.
6. Colvin BT, Barrowcliffe TW on behalf of BCSH Haemostasis and Thrombosis Task Force: The British Society for Haematology Guidelines on the use and monitoring of heparin 1992: Second revision. J Clin Pathol 46:97–103, 1993.
7. Hirsh J, Dalen JE, Deykin D, et al: Heparin: Mechanism of action, pharmacokinetics, dosing consideration, monitoring, efficacy, and safety. Chest 102(4): 337S–351S, 1992.
8. Clagett GP, Anderson, FA Jr, Levine MN, et al: Prevention of venous thromboembolism. Chest 102(4):391S–407S, 1992.
9. Nicolaides AN (Chairman), European Consensus Statement 1–5 Nov 1991: Prevention of venous thromboembolism. Int Angio 11(3):151–159, 1992.
I 10. Hull RD, Raskob GE, Hirsh J, et al: Continuous intravenous heparin compared with intermittent subcutaneous heparin in the initial treatment of proximal-vein thrombosis. N Engl J Med 315:1109–1114, 1986.
I 11. Hull RD, Raskob GE, Pineo GF, et al: Subcutaneous low-molecular weight heparin compared with continuous intravenous heparin in the treatment of proximal-vein thrombosis. N Engl J Med 326:975–982, 1992.
12. Bjork I, Lindahl U: Mechanism of the anticoagulant action of heparin. Mol Cell Biochem 48:161–182, 1982.
13. Lindahl U, Backstrom G, Cook M, et al: Structure of the antithrombin-binding site of heparin. Proc Natl Acad Sci USA 76:3198–3202, 1979.
14. Rosenberg RD, Damus PS: The purification and mechanism of action of human antithrombin-heparin cofactor. J Biol Chem 248:6490–6506, 1973.
15. Rosenberg RD, Lam L: Correlation between structure and function of heparin. Proc Natl Acad Sci USA 76:1218–1222, 1979.
16. Tollefsen DM, Majerus DW, Blank MK: Heparin cofactor II: Purification and properties of thrombin in human plasma. J Biol Chem 257:2162–2169, 1982.
V 17. Fennerty A, Thomas P, Backhouse G, et al: Audit of control of heparin treatment. Br Med J 290:27–28, 1985.
18. Cipolle RJ, Seifert RD, Neilan BA, et al: Heparin kinetics: Variables related to disposition and dosage. Clin Pharmacol Ther 29:387–393, 1981.
19. Brill-Edwards P, Ginsberg S, Johnston M, Hirsh J: Establishing a therapeutic range for heparin therapy. An Intern Med 119:104–109, 1993.
20. Hirsh J, van Aken WG, Gallus AS, et al: Heparin kinetics in venous thrombosis and pulmonary embolism. Circulation 53:691–695, 1976.
I 21. Brandjes DPM, Heijboer H, Buller HR, et al: Acenocoumarol and heparin compared with acenocoumarol alone in the initial treatment of proximal-vein thrombosis. N Engl J Med 327:1485–1489, 1992.
I 22. Raschke RA, Reilly BM, Guidry JR, et al: The weight-based heparin dosing nomogram compared with a "standard care" nomogram. Ann Intern Med 119:874–881, 1993.
IV 23. Cruickshank MK, Levine MN, Hirsh J, et al: A standard nomogram for the management of heparin therapy. Arch Intern Med 151:333–337, 1991.
24. Wheeler AP, Jaquiss RD, Newman JH: Physician practices in the treatment of pulmonary embolism and deep-venous thrombosis. Arch Intern Med 148:1321–1325, 1988.
I 25. Hull RD, Raskob GE, Rosenbloom DR, et al: Optimal therapeutic level of heparin therapy in patients with venous thrombosis. Arch Intern Med 152:1589–1595, 1992.
I 26. Elliott CG, Hiltunen SJ, Suchyta M, et al: Physician guided treatment compared with a heparin protocol for deep vein thrombosis. Arch Intern Med 154:999–1004, 1994.

# Chapter 28

# Treatment of Venous Thromboembolism With Low-molecular-weight Heparin

Graham F. Pineo and Russell D. Hull

The accepted initial treatment of acute venous thromboembolism is now understood to be intravenous heparin given continuously for 5 to 6 days[1I, 2II, 3] and warfarin started on day 1 or 2[4I, 5I] and continued for 3 months. The therapeutic range for heparin is indicated by an activated partial thromboplastin time (APTT) value of 1.5 to 2.5 times the mean of the control value to provide a heparin blood level of 0.2 to 0.4 U/ml (using the protamine sulphate titration assay). The targeted International Normalization Ratio (INR) for warfarin is 2.0 to 3.0.

A series of randomized clinical trials to evaluate various methods of treatment of venous thromboembolism have resulted from improvements in clinical trials methodology as well as the availability of accurate objective tests for detecting venous thromboembolism. From these studies, therapeutic ranges for intravenous heparin and oral warfarin have been established. This development has been effective in decreasing the recurrence rate of venous thromboembolism as well as providing an acceptably low incidence of major bleeding. Patients in whom the APTT did not reach a therapeutic level (greater than 1.5 times the control value) within the initial 24 hours or more had a much greater tendency to develop recurrent venous thromboembolism during the following 3-month period.[3I, 8I, 9I] Most of the symptomatic recurrences fell after the first month of treatment. A less intense form of warfarin (INR 2.0–3.0) was as effective as higher intensity warfarin (INR 3.0–4.5), and there was a markedly reduced incidence of major bleeding.[7I] Bleeding in patients on warfarin can be directly related to elevation of the INR above its therapeutic

range,[7I] but there is little evidence that bleeding in patients on heparin is associated with an APTT above its therapeutic range (>2.5 times control).[6I] However, there is a direct correlation between bleeding in patients on heparin and the existence of a clinical risk for bleeding (such as recent surgery, peptic ulcer disease, or recent stroke) in these patients.[6I]

Unless a heparin protocol is used, the levels of many patients remain in a subtherapeutic range for extended periods of time, and thus these patients are at significant risk of recurrent venous thromboembolism and death.[10, 11] A heparin protocol ensures that the therapeutic range of APTT is achieved in virtually all patients (98–99%) within the initial 24 hours of treatment, and thereby decreases the likelihood of recurrent thromboembolism with no added risk of bleeding.[6I, 9I]

In the past, a number of randomized clinical trials compared the effectiveness and safety of heparin given twice daily by subcutaneous injection with that of continuous intravenous heparin. From meta-analysis, it was concluded that subcutaneous heparin was at least as effective and safe as intravenous heparin.[12] In view of the well-established need to achieve a lower limit for the therapeutic range of APTT or heparin level[6I, 9I, 13] and the demonstration that subcutaneous heparin frequently results in subtherapeutic ranges (as indicated by the APTT or heparin level), subcutaneous heparin cannot be recommended in the initial treatment of proximal venous thrombosis. Furthermore, there is growing evidence that if heparin is used inadequately in the initial stages, markedly increased heparin doses may be required over the subsequent 5 or 6 days. Such heparin resistance was most evident in patients who subsequently developed recurrent venous thromboembolism.[14]

## LOW-MOLECULAR-WEIGHT HEPARIN

The possible role of low-molecular-weight heparin in the initial treatment of venous thromboembolism has been anticipated with great interest. In recent years, several low-molecular-weight heparin derivatives of commercial heparin have been prepared. The mean molecular weight of the low-molecular-weight heparins ranges from 4,000 to 5,000 daltons (the molecular weight for unfractionated heparin is 12,000 to 16,000 daltons[15]). Pharmacokinetic studies[16–21] and small clinical trials in selected patients with venous thrombosis[22–24, 25I, 26] have indicated that the availability of low-molecular-weight heparin fractions after subcutaneous injection was very high. In studies on healthy volunteers,[18] the bioavailability of low-molecular-weight heparin after a single subcutaneous injection of 120 factor Xa U/kg was approximately 90% of an equivalent intravenous dose. This excellent bioavailability of low-molecular-weight heparin, along with the longer half life of its anticoagulant activity (as measured by anti-factor Xa activity) compared with unfractionated heparin,[16–19, 21, 27] suggested that an effective regimen for the initial treatment of venous thromboembolism using a once-daily subcutaneous injection of low-molecular-weight heparin may be possible. Furthermore, there was also a high correlation between the anticoagulant response (measured by factor Xa inhibitor U/ml) observed with a given dose of low-molecular-weight heparin and body weight.[21] This suggested that low-molecular-weight heparin could be given by a fixed dose (in terms of factor Xa U/kg) with no laboratory monitoring. Studies in experimental animal models of venous thrombosis have shown that some low-molecular-weight heparin fractions have equal (or greater) antithrombotic efficacy and fewer hemorrhagic effects than unfractionated heparin.[15, 28–31] Low-molecular-weight heparins have been shown to be effective prophylactic agents following a number of moderate- or high-risk surgical procedures.[32, 33, 34I, 35I, 36]

## RANDOMIZED CLINICAL TRIALS EVALUATING THE USE OF LOW-MOLECULAR-WEIGHT HEPARIN FOR THE TREATMENT OF PROXIMAL VENOUS THROMBOSIS

A number of randomized clinical trials have compared low-molecular-weight heparin with unfractionated heparin for the initial treatment of patients with proximal venous thrombosis. In many of these studies, continuous intravenous low-molecular-weight heparin was compared with continuous intravenous unfractionated heparin.[37I, 38I, 39II, 43II] Two trials compared subcutaneous low-molecular-weight heparin with subcutaneous unfractionated heparin,[26, 49I] and three studies compared subcutaneous low-molecular-weight heparin with continuous intravenous unfractionated heparin.[46I, 47I, 48I] The findings are summarized in the following paragraphs.

In an exploratory study evaluating the effectiveness of low-molecular-weight heparin in the treatment of venous thrombosis, patients with venographically proven deep vein thrombosis (DVT) were randomized to receive continuous intravenous infusion of either low-molecular-weight heparin or unfractionated heparin.[39II] The initial dose was 240 U (anti-Xa) per kg per 12 hours. This initial study was stopped after 27 patients had been entered because two postoperative patients in the low-molecular-weight heparin group had major bleeding. The factor Xa levels assayed retrospectively were found to be much higher in the low-molecular-weight heparin group than in the unfractionated heparin group (1.6–2.0 anti-Xa U/ml versus 0.5–0.8 anti-Xa/ml, respectively).

In a subsequent study in patients with venous thrombosis, low-molecular-weight heparin 120 U (anti-Xa) per kg per 12 hours was compared with unfractionated heparin 340 U/kg/12 hours, both given intravenously.[39II] In this study of 27 patients, the mean activity was higher in the low-molecular-weight heparin group (0.9–1.2 anti-Xa U/ml) than in the unfractionated group (0.5–0.7 anti-Xa U/ml). Repeat venography showed progression of thrombus size in three (11%) patients on unfractionated heparin in both these studies (n = 29) and improvement in 14 (48%). There was no progression of thrombus size in any of the patients on low-molecular-weight heparin, six (50%) had improved in the first study, and 10 (77%) had improved in the second study. However, the mean decrease of thrombus size score (according to the Marder classification)[50] during treatment did not differ between the three groups. Antithrombin III levels decreased significantly in the unfractionated heparin group but not in the low-molecular-weight heparin groups. Amino transferase levels were transiently increased in all three groups. There was no difference in mean capillary bleeding between the three treatment groups.

Forty-four patients with venographically

proven DVT were randomized to receive either intravenous unfractionated heparin (240 anti-Xa U/kg/12 hours) or low-molecular-weight heparin (Fragmin) 120 or 240 anti-Xa U/kg/12 hours.[43II] Repeat venography showed improvement in 48% of patients treated with unfractionated heparin and in 50% and 77%, respectively, of the Fragmin-treated patients. Progression of thrombus size was seen in 11% of the unfractionated heparin-treated patients but not in patients on low-molecular-weight heparin. Bleeding complications occurred in two patients receiving the high dose of Fragmin (240 anti-Xa U/kg/12 hours). In the low-molecular-weight heparin group there was no correlation between the anti-Xa activity in plasma and the APTT.

To compare both the efficacy and safety of low-molecular-weight heparin, intravenous Fragmin was compared with unfractionated heparin in a prospective randomized double-blind trial in 194 unselected patients with acute venous thromboembolism.[38II] Ninety-six patients received intravenous Fragmin and 98 patients received continuous intravenous heparin, both for 5 to 10 days. Doses were adjusted to maintain anti-Xa levels between 0.3 and 0.6 U/ml for patients with a high risk of bleeding, and between 0.4 and 0.9 U/ml for patients at low risk of bleeding. Treatment was stopped when the therapeutic range was reached using warfarin (INR>3.5). Major bleeding was seen in 13 patients on heparin and 10 patients on Fragmin. The difference in the combined incidence of major and minor bleeding complications was 10.4% (95% CI for the difference $= -3.5$ to $+24.2\%$), which corresponds to a relative risk reduction of 21.2% for the patients on low-molecular-weight heparin. New high-probability lung scan defects were observed in six of the 46 patients in the heparin group and three of 34 patients in the Fragmin group (95% CI for the difference $= -9.4$ to $+17.8\%$). It was concluded that low-molecular-weight heparin (Fragmin) given by adjusted continuous intravenous doses was safe and effective in the initial treatment of acute venous thromboembolism compared with unfractionated heparin. There was a trend in risk reduction for bleeding in favor of low-molecular-weight heparin.

The Collaborative European Multicentre Study,[37I] compared subcutaneous low-molecular-weight heparin (CY216 Fraxiparine) with intravenous heparin over a 10-day period. Unfractionated heparin was started at 20 IU/kg/hour and adjusted to maintain an APTT between 1.5 and 2.0 times control. The dosage of low-molecular-weight heparin was 225 anti-Xa International Choay Units (ICU) per kg every 12 hours

with adjustment for high or low body weight. The trial was not double-blinded. Day 1 and day 10 venograms were assessed to show quantitative and qualitative changes by measuring the Marder[50] and Arnesen[51] and Marder[52I] scores. Perfusion lung scans were also done on days 0 and 10. In the 166 patients, by both an efficacy analysis and an intention-to-treat analysis, the study showed that low-molecular-weight heparin was more effective than continuous intravenous unfractionated heparin according to the Arnesen[50] and Marder[51] venographic scores. There was no increase in the risk of pulmonary embolism, hemorrhage, or extension of thrombosis.

Three large randomized clinical trials demonstrated that unmonitored low-molecular-weight heparin given subcutaneously was as effective and as safe as monitored continuous intravenous heparin. In the largest clinical trial carried out so far, patients with venographically proven DVT were randomized to receive a fixed dose of low-molecular-weight heparin (Logiparin 175 Xa U/kg) once daily or intravenous unfractionated heparin by continuous infusion adjusted to maintain an APTT of 1.5 to 2.5 times the mean control value using a heparin nomogram.[46I] Warfarin sodium was started on day 2 and continued for 3 months. At presentation all patients had a chest radiograph, ventilation-perfusion lung scans, and impedance plethysmography (IPG). The IPG was repeated every 3 weeks until it normalized. The outcome events included objectively documented venous thromboembolism (recurrence or extension of DVT or pulmonary embolism), major or minor bleeding, thrombocytopenia, and death.

New episodes of venous thromboembolism were seen in 6 of 213 patients receiving low-molecular-weight heparin (2.8%) and in 15 of 219 patients receiving intravenous unfractionated heparin (6.9%; $p=.07$; 95% CI for the difference $=0.02$ to $+8.1\%$).[46I] Major bleeding associated with initial therapy occurred in one patient receiving low-molecular-weight heparin (0.5%) and in 11 patients receiving intravenous unfractionated heparin (5.0%), a reduction in risk of 95% ($p=.006$). During longterm warfarin therapy, major hemorrhage was seen in five patients who had received low-molecular-weight heparin (2.3%) and in none of those receiving intravenous heparin ($p=.028$). Ten patients who received low-molecular-weight heparin (4.7%) died, compared with 21 patients who received intravenous unfractionated heparin (9.6%), a risk reduction of 51% ($p=.049$).[46I] Analysis by the log rank test, taking into account the length of time to an event, demonstrated a significant difference ($p=.024$) in the frequency of thromboembolic events and deaths (Fig. 28–1). The most striking difference was in abrupt deaths in patients with metastatic carcinoma, the majority of these deaths occurring within the first 3 weeks. It is possible that the longterm use of low-molecular-weight heparin in place of warfarin sodium may have a greater impact on recurrent thromboembolic events, bleeding, and death, particularly in patients with metastatic carcinoma.

A cost-effectiveness analysis using real costs as well as a sensitivity analysis showed that low-molecular-weight heparin was more cost-effective than unfractionated heparin in the treatment of proximal venous thrombosis.[521] Further substantial cost saving was possible in that about 37% of these patients could have had all of their treatment outside of the hospital, thus increasing the cost-effectiveness of low-molecular-weight heparin.

Prandoni and coworkers[471] reported a randomized trial in consecutive symptomatic patients with proximal vein thrombosis. The relative effectiveness and risk of bleeding were compared using fixed-dose low-molecular-weight heparin (CY216 Fraxiparine) and adjusted-dose intravenous unfractionated heparin for 10 days, followed by oral warfarin sodium for 3 months. Patients in the low-molecular-weight heparin groups received subcutaneous injections every 12 hours according to body weight (12,500 anti-Xa ICU for patients less than 55 kg; 15,000 anti-Xa ICU for patients

between 55 and 80 kg; and 17,500 anti-Xa ICU for patients more than 80 kg). In patients on adjusted-dose intravenous heparin, the APTT was maintained at 1.5 to 2.0 times the mean normal control value by continuous infusion. All patients had baseline perfusion lung scans and chest radiographs. Contrast venography was repeated on day 10 or earlier if new symptoms developed. The principal endpoint to assess efficacy was symptomatic recurrent venous thrombosis or symptomatic pulmonary embolism. Secondary endpoints to assess efficacy were changes between day 0 and day 10 in the venograms and perfusion lung scans.

The frequency of objectively diagnosed recurrent venous thromboembolism did not differ significantly between the unfractionated heparin and the low-molecular-weight heparin groups (12 [14%] versus 6 [7%]; 95% CI = − 3 to + 15%; $p$ = .13).[471] There was no significant difference in clinically evident bleeding between the two groups (3.5% for unfractionated heparin versus 1.1% for low-molecular-weight heparin; $p$ > .2).[471] In the 6-month followup period, there were 12 deaths in the unfractionated heparin group and six in the CY216 group; this difference was largely the result of cancer deaths (eight of 18 in the unfractionated heparin group and one of 15 in the low-molecular-weight heparin group).[471]

The third multicenter randomized clinical trial compared subcutaneous Enoxaparin 1 mg/ kg subcutaneously every 12 hours with continuous intravenous heparin starting at 500 U/kg/ 24 hours. Both agents were continued for 10 days; at this time oral anticoagulation was started and continued for 3 months.[481] The primary efficacy assessment was the change in the size of the thrombus shown by repeat venograms on day 10. Major bleeding during the 10 days of treatment was the primary safety outcome measurement. Patients were assessed clinically at 3 months for recurrent thromboembolism, bleeding, or death. Patients on Enoxaparin showed greater venographic improvement after 10 days compared with those on heparin, and the incidence of recurrent thromboembolic disease during the 10-day treatment was higher in the heparin group ($p$<.002). There was no major bleeding and there were no deaths during the 10-day trial.

In the Polish multicenter trial, 149 consecutive patients with venographically proven venous thrombosis (proximal and/or distal) were randomized to receive fixed-dose low-molecular-weight heparin (Fraxiparine) 225 anti-Xa IU/kg every 12 hours or subcutaneous unfractionated heparin adjusted to maintain the APTT between

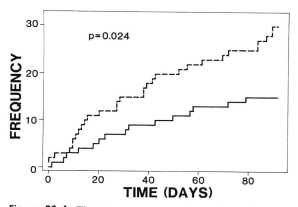

**Figure 28–1.** Time-to-event analysis for patients who had recurrent venous thromboembolism or died. Fifteen of 213 patients receiving low-molecular-weight heparin (7.0%) had objectively documented recurrent venous thromboembolism or died, as compared with 30 of 219 patients receiving intravenous heparin (13.7%; $p$ = .024). In each group the majority of these events occurred within the first 6 weeks. (Used with permission from Hull RD, et al. Subcutaneous low-molecular-weight heparin compared with continuous intravenous heparin in the treatment of proximal-vein thrombosis. N Engl J Med 326:975–982, 1992.)

1.5 and 2.5 times the control value. Oral antico-agulants were started on day 7 and continued for 3 months. The primary outcome assessment was a repeat venogram on day 10, and the main safety assessment was major or minor bleeding. Patients were followed for 3 months to monitor their anticoagulant treatment and to assess thrombotic recurrence. In this study, the mean venographic score after 10 days was significantly decreased in both groups ($p<.001$), but there was no difference between the two groups. During followup, there were two recurrences in the unfractionated heparin group but none in the low-molecular-weight heparin group. Investigators for this study concluded that subcutaneous low-molecular-weight heparin and unfractionated heparin were equally effective and safe.[49]

## FUTURE USES OF LOW-MOLECULAR-WEIGHT HEPARIN IN THE TREATMENT OF VENOUS THROMBOEMBOLISM

In patients who are unable to tolerate oral anticoagulants, longterm use of low-molecular-weight heparin has been shown to be safe.[53V]

The use of low-molecular-weight heparin has been reported in small case series of pregnant patients. Because anticoagulant activity does not cross the placenta, low-molecular-weight heparins are considered to be safe in pregnancy.[54–58] Clinical trials in pregnant patients with active DVT or a history of previous DVT are awaited with interest. Low-molecular-weight heparins are also being studied in patients who have unstable angina or who have had coronary angioplasty.

## SAFETY ISSUES

Thrombocytopenia was seen in 1.7% and 2.8% of patients receiving low-molecular-weight heparin for either prophylaxis[34] or treatment[46I] of venous thrombosis, respectively. No thrombotic disease related to thrombocytopenia was seen in these two trials. However, this complication has been reported with the administration of low-molecular-weight heparin.[59] Further prospective clinical trials are necessary to establish the exact incidence of heparin-induced thrombocytopenia related to low-molecular-weight heparins. Elevation of liver enzymes has been observed in patients receiving both low-molecular-weight heparin and unfractionated heparin, but the exact incidence and nature of this complication compared with the use of unfraction-ated heparin has not been established.[60V] The low-molecular-weight heparins have been shown to affect bone mineral metabolism in experimental models, but the relevance of these findings to patients on longterm low-molecular-weight heparin is unclear.[61]

In summary, there is now ample evidence to justify giving certain low-molecular-weight heparins subcutaneously rather than administering continuous intravenous unfractionated heparin for the initial treatment of venous thromboembolism. Given subcutaneously, the low-molecular-weight heparins have a predictably high absorption rate and a prolonged duration of action. Thus, they can be administered once or twice daily by injection to prevent or treat venous thrombosis. Furthermore, treatment does not require laboratory monitoring. Eliminating the need for continuous intravenous infusion and for laboratory monitoring should allow patients to be discharged earlier, and eventually should lead to the outpatient treatment of venous thromboembolism. Studies to date indicate that low-molecular-weight heparin is more cost-effective than unfractionated heparin, and the cost-effectiveness will be increased by out-of-hospital treatment. At present, because the findings associated with any individual low-molecular-weight heparin preparation cannot be extrapolated to different low-molecular-weight heparins, each preparation must be evaluated in separate clinical trials. The information to date is that low-molecular-weight heparin is safer and more effective than continuous intravenous unfractionated heparin in the treatment of proximal venous thrombosis. The decreased mortality rate seen in two clinical trials, particularly in patients with metastatic cancer, was quite unexpected. This requires further confirmation in larger prospective randomized trials.

## REFERENCES

I  1. Salzman EW, Deykin D, Shapiro RM, et al: Management of heparin therapy: Controlled prospective trial. N Engl J Med 315:1109–1114, 1986.

II  2. Wilson JR, Lampman J: Heparin therapy: A randomized prospective study. Am Heart J 97:155–158, 1979.

I  3. Hull RD, Raskob GE, Hirsh J, et al: Continuous intravenous heparin compared with intermittent subcutaneous heparin in the initial treatment of proximal vein thrombosis. N Engl J Med 315:1109–1114, 1986.

I  4. Gallus AS, Jackaman J, Tillett J, et al: Safety and efficacy of warfarin started early after submassive venous thrombosis or pulmonary embolism. Lancet 2:1293–1296, 1986.

I  5. Hull RD, Raskob GE, Rosenbloom D, et al: Heparin for 5 days as compared with 10 days in the initial treatment of proximal venous thrombosis. N Engl J Med 322:1260–1264, 1990.

I  6. Hull RD, Raskob GE, Rosenbloom D, et al: Optimal therapeutic levels of heparin therapy in patients with venous thrombosis. Arch Intern Med 152:1589–1595, 1992.

I  7. Hull R, Hirsh J, Jay R, et al: Different intensities of oral anticoagulant therapy in the treatment of proximal-vein thrombosis. N Engl J Med 307:1676–1681, 1982.

I  8. Basu D, Gallus A, Hirsh J, et al: A prospective study of value of monitoring heparin treatment with the activated partial thromboplastin time. N Engl J Med 287:324–327, 1972.

I  9. Raschke P, Reilly BM, Guidry JR, et al: The weight-based heparin dosing nomogram compared with a "standard care" nomogram. Ann Intern Med 327:1128–1133, 1992.

10. Fennerty A, Thomas P, Backhouse G, et al: Audit of control of heparin treatment. Br Med J 290:27, 1985.

11. Wheeler AP, Jaquiss RD, Newman JH: Physician practices in the treatment of pulmonary embolism and deep-venous thrombosis. Arch Intern Med 148:1321, 1988.

12. Hommes DW, Bura A, Mazzolai L, et al: Subcutaneous heparin compared with continuous intravenous heparin administration in the initial treatment of deep vein thrombosis. Ann Intern Med 116:279–284, 1992.

13. Brill-Edwards P, Ginsberg S, Johnston M, et al: Establishing a therapeutic range for heparin therapy. Ann Intern Med 119:104–110, 1993.

14. Hull R, Brant R, Pineo G, et al: Heparin (H) resistance as a predictor of recurrent venous thromboembolism (RVTE) (abstract 1611). Blood 82(10):406, 1993.

15. Verstraete M: Pharmacotherapeutic aspects of unfractionated and low-molecular-weight heparin. Drugs 40:498–530, 1990.

16. Bara L, Billaud E, Gramond G, et al: Comparative pharmacokinetics of a low-molecular-weight heparin and unfractionated heparin after intravenous and subcutaneous administration. Thrombosis Res 39:631–636, 1985.

17. Bergqvist D, Hedner U, Sjorin E, et al: Anticoagulant effects of two types of low-molecular-weight heparin administered subcutaneously. Thrombosis Res 32:381–391, 1983.

18. Bratt G, Tornebohm E, Widlund L, et al: Low-molecular-weight heparin (Kabi 2165; Fragmin): pharmacokinetics after intravenous and subcutaneous administration in human volunteers. Thrombosis Res 42:613–620, 1986.

19. Frydman AM, Bara L, LeRoux Y, et al: The antithrombotic activity and pharmacokinetics of enoxaparine, a low-molecular-weight, in humans given single subcutaneous doses of 20 to 80 mg. J Clin Pharmacol 28:609–618, 1988.

20. Harenberg J, Wurzner B, Zimmermann R, et al: Bioavailability and antagonization of the low-molecular-weight heparin CY216 in man. Thromb Res 44:549–554, 1986.

21. Matzsch T, Bergqvist D, Hedner U: Effects of an enzymatically depolymerized heparin as compared with conventional heparin in healthy volunteers. Thromb Haemost 57:97–101, 1987.

22. Albada J, Neuwenhuis HK, Sixma JJ: Fragmin pharmacokinetics in human volunteers (abstract 13). Thromb Res [Suppl VII] p. 17, 1987.

23. Arneson KE, Handeland GF, Abildgaard U, et al: What is the optimal dosage of LMW heparin in the subcutaneous treatment of deep vein thrombosis? (abstract 794), Thromb Haemost 58:214, 1987.

24. Bratt G, Aberg W, Tornebohm E, et al: Subcutaneous KABI 2165 in the treatment of deep venous thrombosis of the leg (abstract). Thromb Res [Suppl] 7:24, 1987.

II 25. Bratt G, Tornebohm E, Granqvist S, et al: A comparison between low-molecular-weight heparin (KABI 2165) and standard heparin in the intravenous treatment of deep venous thrombosis. Thromb Haemost 54:813–817, 1985.

26. Holm HA, Ly B, Handeland GF, et al: Subcutaneous heparin treatment of deep venous thrombosis: A comparison of unfractionated and low-molecular-weight heparin. Haemostasis 16:30–37, 1986.

27. Aiach M, Michaud A, Balian JL, et al: A new low-molecular-weight heparin derivative, in vitro and in vivo studies. Thromb Res 31:611–621, 1983.

28. Cade JF, Buchanan MR, Boneau B, et al: A comparison of the antithrombotic and haemorrhagic effects of low molecular heparin fractions: The influence of the method of preparation. Thromb Res 35:613–625, 1984.

29. Carter CJ, Kelton JR, Hirsh J, et al: Relationship between the antithrombotic and anticoagulant effects of low-molecular-weight heparin. Thromb Res 21:169–174, 1981.

30. Carter CJ, Kelton JG, Hirsh J, et al: The relationship between the hemorrhagic and antithrombotic properties of low-molecular-weight heparin in rabbits. Blood 59:1239–1245, 1982.

31. Holmer E, Mattsson C, Nilsson S: Anticoagulant and antithrombotic effects of heparin and low-molecular-weight heparin fragments in rabbits. Thromb Res 25:475–485, 1982.

32. Nurmohamed MT, Rosendal FR, Buller HR, et al: Low-molecular-weight heparin in the prophylaxis of venous thrombosis: A meta-analysis. Lancet 340:152–156, 1992.

33. Leizorovicz A, Haugh MC, Chapuis F-R, et al: Low-molecular-weight heparin in prevention of perioperative thrombosis. Br Med J 305:913–920, 1992.

I 34. Hull RD, Raskob GE, Pineo GF, et al: A comparison of subcutaneous low-molecular-weight heparin with warfarin sodium for prophylaxis against deep-vein thrombosis after hip or knee implantation. N Engl J Med 329:1370–1376, 1993.

II 35. Kakkar VV, Cohen AT, Edmonson RA, et al: Low molecular weight versus standard heparin for prevention of venous thromboembolism after major abdominal surgery. Lancet 341:259–265, 1993.

36. Thomas DP: Prevention of post-operative thrombosis by low-molecular-weight heparin in patients undergoing hip replacement. Thromb Haemost 67:491–493, 1992.

I 37. A Collaborative European Multicentre Study: A randomized trial of subcutaneous low-molecular-weight heparin (CY216) compared with intravenous unfractionated heparin in the treatment of deep-vein thrombosis. Thromb Haemost 65:251–256, 1991.

II 38. Albada J, Nieuwenhuis HK, Sixma JJ: Treatment of acute venous thromboembolism with low-molecular-weight heparin (Fragmin). Results of a double-blind randomized study. Circulation 80:935–940, 1989.

II 39. Bratt G, Aberg W, Johansson M, et al: Two daily subcutaneous injections of Fragmin as compared with intravenous standard heparin in the treatment of deep venous thrombosis (DVT). Thromb Haemost 64:506–510, 1990.

V 40. Handeland GF, Abildgaard U, Holm HA, et al: Dose-adjusted heparin treatment of deep venous thrombosis: A comparison of unfractionated and low-molecular-weight heparin. Eur J Clin Pharmacol 39:107–112, 1990.

II 41. Harenberg J, Huck K, Bratsch H, et al: Therapeutic application of subcutaneous low-molecular-weight heparin in acute venous thrombosis. Haemostasis 20 [Suppl 1]:205–219, 1990.

V 42. Huet Y, Janvier G, Bendriss PH, et al: Treatment of established venous thromboembolism with Enoxaparin: Preliminary report. Acta Chir Scand 556 [Suppl]:116–120, 1990.

II 43. Lockner D, Bratt G, Tornebohm E, et al: Intravenous and subcutaneous administration of Fragmin in deep venous thrombosis. Haemostasis 16:25–29, 1986.

I 44. Prandoni P, Vigo M, Cattelan AM, et al: Treatment of deep venous thrombosis by fixed doses of a low-molecular-weight heparin (CY216). Haemostasis 20 [Suppl 1]:220–223, 1990.

I 45. Siegbahn A, Y-Hassan S, Boberg J, et al: Subcutaneous treatment of deep venous thrombosis with low-molecular-weight heparin. A dose finding study with LMWH-Novo. Thromb Res 55:767–778, 1989.

I 46. Hull RD, Raskob GE, Pineo GF, et al: Subcutaneous low-molecular-weight heparin compared with continuous intravenous heparin in the treatment of proximal-vein thrombosis. N Engl J Med 326:975–983, 1992.

I 47. Prandoni P, Lensing AW, Buller HR, et al: Comparison of subcutaneous low-molecular-weight heparin with intravenous standard heparin in proximal deep-vein thrombosis. Lancet 339:411–415, 1992.

I 48. Simonneau G, Charbonnier B, Decousus H, et al: Subcutaneous low-molecular-weight heparin compared with continuous intravenous unfractionated heparin in the treatment of proximal deep vein thrombosis. Arch Intern Med 153:1541–1546, 1993.

I 49. Lopaciuk S, Meissner AJ, Filipecki S, et al: Subcutaneous low-molecular-weight heparin versus subcutaneous unfractionated heparin in the treatment of deep vein thrombosis: A Polish multicentre trial. Thromb Haemost 68(1):14–18, 1992.

50. Arnesen H, Heilo A, Jakobsen E, et al: A prospective study of streptokinase and heparin in the treatment of deep vein thrombosis. Acta Med Scand 203:457–463, 1978.

51. Marder VJ, Soulen RL, Atchartakarn V, et al: Quantitative venographic assessment of deep vein thrombosis in the evaluation of streptokinase and heparin therapy. J Lab Clin Med 89(5):1018–1029, 1977.

I 52. Hull RD, Rosenbloom D, Pineo GF, et al: A cost-effectiveness analysis of low-molecular-weight heparin compared with continuous intravenous heparin in the treatment of proximal-vein thrombosis (abstract 2777). Circulation 88(4 Part 2):I–516, 1993.

V 53. Harenberg J, Leber G, Dempfle CE, et al: Long-term anticoagulation with low-molecular-weight heparin in outpatients with side effects on oral anticoagulants. Nouv Rev Fr Hematol 31:363–369, 1989.

54. Omri A, Delaloye JF, Andersen H, et al: Low-molecular-weight heparin Novo (LHN-1) does not cross the placenta during the second trimester of pregnancy. Thromb Haemost 61:55–56, 1989.

55. Bergqvist D, Hedner U, Sjorin E, et al: Anticoagulant effects of two types of low-molecular-weight heparin administered subcutaneously. Thromb Res 32:381–391, 1983.

56. Forestier F, Daffos F, Capella-Pavlovsky M: Low-molecular-weight heparin (PK 10169) does not cross the placenta during the second trimester of pregnancy. Study by direct fetal blood sampling under ultrasound. Thromb Res 34:557–560, 1984.

57. Forestier F, Daffos F, Rainaut M, et al. Low-molecular-weight heparin (CY 216) does not cross the placenta during the third trimester of pregnancy. Thromb Haemost 57:234, 1987.

58. Andrew M, Cade J, Buchanan MR, et al: Low-molecular-weight heparin does not cross the placenta (abstract). Thromb Haemost 50:225, 1983.

59. Mohr VD, Lenz J: Heparin-assoziierte thrombocytopenie, thrombose und embolie. Unerwünschte wirkung der thromboembolieprophylaxe mit dem niedermolekularen heparin Enoxaparin? Chirug 62: 686–690, 1991.

V 60. Monreal M, Lafoz E, Salvador R, et al: Adverse effects of three different forms of heparin therapy: Thrombocytopenia, increased transaminases, and hyperkalaemia. Eur J Clin Pharmacol 37:415–418, 1989.

61. Matzsch T, Bergqvist D, Hedner U, et al: Effects of an enzymatically depolymerized heparin as compared with conventional heparin in healthy volunteers. Thromb Haemost 57:97–101, 1987.

# Chapter 29

# Oral Anticoagulants for the Treatment of Venous Thromboembolism

Jack E. Ansell

As demonstrated throughout this section of the text, venous thromboembolism is a significant health hazard with a prevalence in the general population estimated to be approximately 2 to 5%[1, 2] and a 1% incidence in hospitalized patients.[2] Pulmonary embolism occurs in more than 600,000 cases per year, resulting in approximately 200,000 deaths.[3] The rationale for treatment of venous thrombosis of the lower extremities is to avert the three most common sequelae—recurrence of venous thrombosis, development of the postphlebitic syndrome, and occurrence of pulmonary embolism. The rationale for treating pulmonary embolism (PE) is the same, because the majority of PEs originate from the lower extremities, but there is also the need to prevent sudden death or longterm pulmonary dysfunction.

A number of modalities are available for the treatment of venous thromboembolism. All antithrombotic therapy is considered prophylactic in nature (primary prophylaxis when no disease is present and secondary prophylaxis in the presence of established disease), because anticoagulants have little effect on established thrombi. Thrombolytic therapy has a direct effect on established thrombi, whereas vena caval interruption is directed to the primary or secondary prevention of embolism to the lungs.

This chapter focuses on the use of oral anticoagulants for the therapy of *established* venous thromboembolism (secondary prophylaxis). The reader is referred to the previous chapter for a detailed discussion of the use of heparin or low-molecular-weight heparin for the initial treatment of such disease, and to other chapters for a discussion of the use of oral anticoagulants for the primary prophylaxis of venous thromboembolism.

## RATIONALE FOR ANTICOAGULANT THERAPY

It is not surprising that the early demonstration of therapeutic efficacy for anticoagulants lacks the support of large randomized prospective studies with placebo control groups. Anticoagulants (heparin in the 1930s and dicoumarol in the 1940s) came into use with meager clinical data for their therapeutic effectiveness but with theoretical support.[4] Deykin and coworkers[5] presented the first high quality in vitro data for an antithrombotic effect of dicoumarol in a serum-induced rabbit thrombosis model. This effect was achieved at specific anticoagulant levels as indicated by the prothrombin time without hemorrhagic side effects, suggesting the existence of a safe and effective therapeutic range. Hoak and coworkers[6] monitored coagulation factor levels in patients receiving coumarin drugs and suggested that reduced levels of factors IX and X correlated better with an antithrombotic effect than a reduction in other affected factors. Additional in vitro data for effectiveness and the existence of a therapeutic range was generated more recently by Gitel and Wessler[7, 8] in a similar rabbit model but with a much lower intensity of anticoagulation, as determined by measuring the vitamin K–dependent factors.

Barritt and Jordan[91] conducted the first randomized clinical trial of anticoagulants in patients with PE, showing a significant reduction in mortality and recurrence of embolism in patients treated with heparin and an oral anticoagulant compared with those who received no anticoagulant therapy. Kernohan and Todd[10V] presented evidence for a beneficial effect of initial treatment with heparin compared with oral anticoagulants alone, and Kanis[11] retrospectively identified a greater benefit of early heparinization versus the use of oral anticoagulants with or without heparin. More recently, Hull and coworkers[12I] confirmed the benefit of initial heparin therapy by continuous infusion, at least compared with a fixed subcutaneous dose of heparin, which resulted in a less than therapeutic target level of anticoagulation in many cases, and a high frequency of recurrent venous thromboembolism. Brandjes and coworkers[13I] again demonstrated the benefit of early heparinization by prospectively comparing two groups, one treated with an oral anticoagulant alone as initial therapy for proximal vein thrombosis versus a group treated with heparin plus an oral anticoagulant. The former group experienced a significant increase in asymptomatic extension of venous thrombosis and a borderline significant increase in symptomatic events. Studies of this nature established the benefit of the initial treatment of venous thromboembolism with intravenous heparin and identified that a similar benefit was not achievable by substituting an oral anticoagulant for heparin therapy at this stage of the disease.

The rationale for the longterm treatment of venous thromboembolism with oral anticoagulants (secondary prophylaxis) was initially an outgrowth of the beneficial effect demonstrated for the initial treatment with heparin. In a retrospective analysis of data, however, Coon and coworkers[14] presented the first evidence that longterm oral anticoagulation may reduce recurrence compared with no longterm treatment. In a well-designed prospective study with objectively documented endpoints, Hull and coworkers[15I] demonstrated a significant reduction in recurrent venous thromboembolism in patients receiving oral anticoagulation versus a group receiving a fixed dose of low-dose heparin after initial treatment.

Perhaps a more appropriate question is just how long anticoagulation must be given to reduce the recurrence rate of venous thromboembolism to that of the normal population, or to balance the rate of hemorrhagic complications with that of recurrent thromboembolism. In 1972, O'Sullivan[16II] demonstrated that 6 weeks was as satisfactory as 6 months of therapy to prevent recurrent venous thromboembolism in 186 nonstratified patients with deep vein thrombosis (DVT) or PE divided into two groups. In another retrospective analysis, Coon and Willis[17] suggested that 4 months was the optimal duration of therapy. Lagerstedt and coworkers[18I] prospectively studied patients with symptomatic calf vein thrombosis and showed that oral anticoag-

ulant therapy for 3 months significantly decreased the incidence of recurrence compared with results in those who were not treated after hospital discharge (8 of 28 versus 0 of 23, $p < .01$). Holmgren and coworkers,[19II] however, failed to show any difference in recurrent thromboembolism with 1 or 6 months of treatment in two groups of patients following the first episode of DVT. Schulman and coworkers[20II] stratified their patients according to risk factors and number of episodes and found no difference in outcome between those treated for 1.5 versus 3 months (first episode with transient risk factor), 3 or 6 months (first episode with permanent risk factor), or 6 versus 12 months (second episode). Petitti and coworkers[21] studied patients with a first episode of DVT in a retrospective analysis over a period of 10 years (n = 370) and found no benefit for treatment of greater than 6 weeks compared with treatment limited to 1 to 6 weeks. They did show that the risk of hemorrhagic complications increased linearly with the duration of treatment in these patients. The British Thoracic Society[22I] conducted a prospective study in 712 patients with DVT or PE treated for either 4 weeks or 3 months. They found that 4 weeks was adequate treatment for patients with postoperative DVT in whom the risk presumably resolved, but that 3 months was more beneficial in *medical* patients with DVT and PE.

Based on these studies, there is broad agreement for the necessity of post-acute treatment with oral anticoagulants to prevent recurrent thromboembolism. Although 3 months seems to be the most commonly cited interval, a number of patient-specific variables may influence the optimal duration of treatment in specific groups, including those with proximal or distal venous thrombosis,[15I] prior history of thromboembolism,[20, 21] persistent risk factors for recurrence,[20, 21] and the presence or absence of PE.[23] The ideal handling of each of these groups remains to be defined. In general, patients with calf vein thrombosis without persistent risk factors should be considered for shorter courses of therapy (about 1 month), whereas those with proximal vein thrombosis, especially those with persistent risk factors, should be treated for 3 months or longer in some cases.

## ORAL ANTICOAGULANTS IN CLINICAL PRACTICE FOR THE TREATMENT OF VENOUS THROMBOEMBOLISM

In a previous chapter, Becker and Ansell summarized the information pertaining to the mechanism of action and pharmacokinetics of warfarin, and this will not be repeated here. The following discussion will focus on the practical aspects of managing warfarin therapy in patients with venous thromboembolic disease.

Warfarin therapy is commenced using an average maintenance dose or slightly higher (e.g., 5 or 10 mg) for the first 2 or 3 days when beginning therapy. A loading dose (>20 mg) produces a rapid and excessive reduction of factor VII, putting patients at risk for hemorrhage early in therapy, without a more rapid achievement of a full reduction of the vitamin K–dependent factors, as demonstrated by O'Reilly and Aggeler.[24] As discussed earlier, heparin is the recommended initial treatment for venous thromboembolism, but warfarin therapy must overlap with heparin therapy for a period of 3 to 5 days, because it takes that long to lower the vitamin K–dependent coagulation factors with a longer half life (factors II, IX, and X).[24] With a therapeutic prothrombin time (PT) after 3 to 5 days, heparin can be discontinued. A number of studies have shown that for PE[25I, 26V, 27II] or for lower extremity DVT,[27II, 28I] the traditional approach of a 10-day course of heparin therapy with warfarin started on day 5 or 6 is unnecessary. Starting warfarin simultaneously or soon after heparin is initiated produces no short- or longterm differences in outcome and leads to shorter hospital stays, thus being a more cost-effective approach to treatment. Such treatment may even be safer in that the tendency for heparin-induced thrombocytopenia, thrombosis, or bleeding may be less.[27]

Estimation of the maintenance dose is often based on observations of the PT response following a fixed dose of warfarin over a few days' interval.[29] An individual who rapidly achieves a high therapeutic PT (International Normalization Ratio [INR]>2.5) after two doses of 10 mg of warfarin is likely to require a low maintenance dose. The opposite holds for those who show little elevation of the PT (INR<1.5) after two doses.

Outpatient management of warfarin therapy should aim for simplicity and clarity to avoid patient confusion, poor compliance, and dosing errors that may result in complications.[30] It is recommended that a limited number of warfarin tablet strengths be used in clinical practice and that patients clearly understand the various dosing patterns that are used, such as alternate day doses or dosing levels based on days of the week.[30]

The prothrombin time is the method of choice for monitoring oral anticoagulant therapy, but differences in the sensitivity of thromboplastin reagents have led to inconsistencies in PT results, noncomparability of results from different laboratories or even within the same laboratory as reagents change, and unknowingly higher levels of anticoagulation when the PT ratio is used to guide therapy.[31] The uniform acceptance of the International Normalized Ratio as a means of equilibrating PT ratios should lead to safer and more effective therapy. The INR simply converts prothrombin time ratios to an internationally accepted norm based on the sensitivity of the thromboplastin used in the assay.[32] The thromboplastin sensitivity is derived by the manufacturer from an international reference preparation and is called the International Sensitivity Index (ISI). Any PT ratio can be converted to an INR by the formula indicated in Table 29–1.

The concept of that which constitutes a therapeutic range above which the risk of hemorrhage or below which the risk of recurrent thromboembolism is unacceptable developed as a consequence of trial and error and clinical empiricism in studies of primary and secondary prophylaxis. Loeliger[33] provides an excellent review of the early history pertaining to development of a therapeutic range. Well-designed, randomized prospective studies have confirmed and further refined earlier recommendations. Wright,[34III] Moschos and coworkers,[35III] and Sevitt and Gallagher[36III] used a PT ratio of approximately 1.5 to 3 times a control or normal range in their studies of primary prophylaxis in patients at risk and obtained good results. This range quickly became the standard for treating patients with thromboembolic disease.[37] However, as early as 1947, Allen[38V] warned clinicians about the inconsistencies of thromboplastins and that identical PTs may indicate entirely dif-

Table 29–1. **Calculation of INR**

ISI = International Sensitivity Index; a comparative rating of different thromboplastins

INR = International Normalized Ratio; a comparative rating of prothrombin time ratios for individuals with stable therapeutic anticoagulation

To convert a prothrombin time (PT) ratio to an INR equivalent:

$$INR = PT \, Ratio^{isi}$$

Example:

PT = 17.9s
Mean of normal range = 12.2s
ISI of thromboplastin = 2.3

Then:

$$17.9 \div 12.3 = 1.47 \, PT \, ratio$$
$$1.47^{2.3} = 2.4 \, INR$$

ferent levels of anticoagulation. Tang and Poller,[39] in their 1975 international survey of dosing and PT monitoring, aptly demonstrated the consequence of thromboplastin inconsistencies as well as reporting methodologies, in that "the upper limit in one country may be the lower limit in another," and that "in many centers doses of anticoagulant drugs are advocated which elsewhere are considered either inadequate anticoagulation or dangerous overdosage."[39] These differences in therapeutic range and their potential impact on clinical studies did not go unrecognized by others. Bailey and coworkers[40] showed that a therapeutic range with a sensitive thromboplastin represented a PT ratio of 1.8 to 3.0, whereas that with an insensitive reagent was 1.25 to 1.75.

As recently as the early 1990s, the consequences of relying on a therapeutic range defined by the PT ratio were demonstrated in the publication of a respected multi-institutional clinical trial of warfarin prophylaxis in atrial fibrillation, showing a greater variability of therapeutic control than originally suspected because of the variability of thromboplastin reagent.[41] Perhaps the most important study to bring this discrepancy to the attention of physicians in North America was the prospective study of patients with venous thrombosis by Hull and coworkers,[42] showing that patients managed in a similar therapeutic range by PT ratio (but different range according to INR), using a sensitive and insensitive reagent, actually represented a degree of over-anticoagulation in the "insensitive" group, leading to a higher rate of hemorrhagic complications. As a result of this study, recommendations were proposed in the early 1980s to aim for a lower PT ratio of approximately 1.2 to 1.5 when using an insensitive rabbit brain thromboplastin compared with a sensitive human brain thromboplastin in which the therapeutic ratio was 2.0 to 3.0 for most indications.[43] However, it quickly became apparent that rabbit-derived thromboplastins differed substantially in their responsiveness and that nothing short of reporting all PT ratios as INRs would resolve this problem of PT ratio comparability.[44] Based on reviews of published data and recommendations made by the British Society of Hematology[45] and subsequently refined by the American College of Chest Physicians,[44] there is abundant evidence that a less intense therapeutic range as defined by an INR of 2.0 to 3.0 is effective in the primary prophylaxis of venous thromboembolism in patients at risk. In addition, this range is effective in the prevention of systemic embolism after acute myocardial infarction and in patients with tissue heart valves, and that this same range is effective in the secondary prevention of recurrent disease in those with a recent venous thromboembolic event. Similarly, there is evidence that in patients with a more thrombogenic stimulus, a somewhat higher therapeutic range is recommended, as defined by an INR of 2.5 to 3.5.

The physician managing oral anticoagulation is often presented with the need to correct excessive degrees of anticoagulation or simply to reverse anticoagulation before an invasive procedure. There is abundant evidence that the incidence of bleeding increases with more intense anticoagulation,[46] but the question as to how best and how rapidly to reverse anticoagulation remains unanswered. The American College of Chest Physicians has made specific recommendations for reversing the INR in patients excessively anticoagulated, as summarized in Table 29–2.[44] However, the applicability of these guidelines in outpatients receiving warfarin is doubtful unless serious clinical bleeding is pres-

**Table 29–2. Recommendations for Correcting Excessive Anticoagulation Proposed by the American College of Chest Physicians[44]**

| INR/Clinical Situation | ACCP Recommendation |
| --- | --- |
| INR >3.5 <6.0 No bleeding Rapid reversal not required | Omit next few doses; restart warfarin at lower dose when PT therapeutic |
| INR >6.0 <10.0 No bleeding More rapid reversal desired | 0.5–1.0 mg vitamin $K_1$; can be repeated at 24 hr if INR still too high |
| INR >10.0 <20.0 No bleeding | 3.0–5.0 mg vitamin $K_1$; check INR every 6–12 hr; vitamin K can be repeated as needed |
| For rapid reversal of anticoagulation because of serious bleeding or major overdose (INR >20.0) | 10.0 mg vitamin $K_1$; check INR every 6 hr; vitamin K can be repeated every 12 hr and supplemented with fresh frozen plasma or factor concentrates depending on urgency |
| For life-threatening bleeding or overdose | Replace with factor concentrates supplemented with IV vitamin $K_1$, 10.0 mg as needed |
| For continued warfarin therapy after high doses of vitamin K if indicated | Heparin can be given until the effects of vitamin K have been reversed and patient becomes responsive to warfarin |

ent or the risk for such bleeding is overwhelming. A more practical approach is indicated in Table 29–3. This approach is based on personal experience in managing a large number of anticoagulated outpatients over many years. Important in managing excessive anticoagulation is knowledge of the patient's usual maintenance dose of warfarin. Patients maintained on a low average daily dose (≤2.5 mg daily) take longer to return to a therapeutic range when warfarin is held than those who are maintained on a higher average daily dose (≥7.5 mg daily). This information may influence the tendency to use vitamin K if more rapid reversal is required. When vitamin K is used, small parenteral doses have been shown to adequately correct the PT and are preferable (≤1 mg),[47IV] unless there is no need to reanticoagulate the patient once the PT is corrected. Larger doses often lead to relative states of warfarin resistance and often make re-establishment of a therapeutic range difficult.

Because of the fluctuation in anticoagulant response, warfarin therapy requires frequent

monitoring. One of the challenges of management is the problem of determining the cause of nontherapeutic PTs, especially in patients who are stable for long periods of time.[48, 49] Table 29–4 identifies two principal considerations when a nontherapeutic PT is encountered. Although warfarin and vitamin K are not biochemical antagonists, they clinically behave as such. Thus, the PT varies inversely with the amount of vitamin K absorbed from the diet[50] and directly with the amount of warfarin absorbed. A simple history assessing these two variables often clarifies the cause of over or underresponsiveness. Table 29–5 summarizes the approximate content of vitamin K in various foods.[51]

Of course, other factors can influence the PT response to warfarin therapy, as identified in Table 29–4. Drug interactions are of particular concern and can lead to difficulty in achieving therapeutic anticoagulation[52] or may predispose to instability of control.[53, 54] Most drugs mediate their deleterious effects by altering warfarin pharmacokinetics and, thus, the pharmacodynamic response,[55] or by affecting other aspects of hemostasis resulting in an altered anticoagulant response. Table 29–6 lists most drug interactions and identifies those for which a mechanism seems well established. Drug interactions not only interfere with warfarin pharmacokinetics, but may also disturb vitamin K homeostasis by affecting its cyclic conversion to a reduced form or by interfering with absorption or bacterial vitamin K synthesis in the gastrointestinal tract. Drugs may also alter the metabolism of coagulation factors, inhibit coagulation factor interactions by other mechanisms (heparin), or inhibit other aspects of hemostasis (aspirin's effect on platelet function) and lead to a greater risk of bleeding. In general, most interactions are not problematic unless medications are added or deleted from a patient's regimen.

With increasing frequency, physicians are confronted with the problem of handling anticoagulation in individuals requiring noncardiac surgery or other invasive procedures, especially in individuals with prosthetic heart valves. There are few critical studies examining the alternative choices for managing anticoagulation in this setting, but some have shown that excessive blood loss is not necessarily a risk in certain invasive procedures in patients who are fully anticoagulated, such as in dental procedures.[56III, 57I] Similarly, invasive procedures in patients with mechanical prosthetic heart valves can be done with a temporary cessation of warfarin, allowing the PT to return to normal or a subtherapeutic range,[58V] although the brief use

**Table 29–3. Alternative Means of Managing Excessive Anticoagulation in the Outpatient Setting**

| INR | Recommendation |
|---|---|
| >3.5 <6.0 | Omit one or more doses of warfarin; consider restarting at reduced dose |
| >6.0 <10.0 | Omit warfarin until INR is therapeutic, then reinstitute at reduced dose |
| >10.0 <20.0 | Consider vitamin K₁ 0.5–2.0 mg IV*; check INR in 12–24 hr and repeat vitamin K if necessary; reinstitute warfarin at reduced dose |
| >20.0 | Consider vitamin K₁ 1.0–5.0 mg IV; maintain close observation and consider fresh frozen plasma depending on degree of INR elevation and specific patient risks for bleeding; reinstitute warfarin at lower dose when INR becomes therapeutic† |

- Serious bleeding requires the use of fresh frozen plasma to replace missing factors as well as the administration of parenteral vitamin K₁; factor concentrates may be considered in life-threatening or intracranial hemorrhage

*Because of the potential for hypersensitivity reactions or anaphylaxis to IV vitamin K, it should be given slowly (not > 1.0 mg/min); alternatively, it can be given by the subcutaneous route, although response may be delayed if absorption is impaired.

†Vitamin K can lead to a brief period of relative warfarin resistance and difficulty re-establishing a therapeutic range; brief periods of heparin administration may be needed or higher doses of warfarin may be required, but frequent monitoring of the INR is imperative.

**Table 29–4. Causes of Nontherapeutic Prothrombin Times (INR)**

| Major Considerations | |
|---|---|
| **Too Much or Too Little Vitamin K** | |
| Decrease in dietary vitamin K | Increase |
| Malabsorption of vitamin K | Increase |
| Suppression of gut bacteria | Increase |
| Increase in dietary vitamin K | Decrease |
| **Too Much or Too Little Warfarin** | |
| Decrease in absorption | Decrease |
| Changes in metabolism due to illness | Increase/Decrease |
| Changes in metabolism due to drugs | Increase/Decrease |
| **Minor Considerations** | |
| **Changes in Factor Production/Metabolism** | |
| Liver disease | Increase |
| Hypermetabolic states (fever) | Increase |
| Other illnesses | Increase |
| **Technical/Laboratory Factors** | |
| Phlebotomy technique | Increase/Decrease |
| Evacuated collection tube problems | Increase/Decrease |
| Handling of specimen problems | Increase/Decrease |
| Instrumentation variability | Increase/Decrease |
| Different thromboplastin reagents | Increase/Decrease |

of heparin may be indicated in patients with mechanical prosthetic mitral valves, which tend to be more thrombogenic.[59V] In each case, the physician must determine what the risk of thromboembolism is with a temporary cessation of anticoagulation versus the risk of bleeding with full or partial correction of the PT during the surgical procedure. In most cases, warfarin can simply be held a few days before the procedure, allowing the PT to return to normal or a subtherapeutic range with prompt reinstitution of the maintenance dose following the procedure. In some cases, particularly when the risk of thromboembolism is high if the patient is off anticoagulants, warfarin must be stopped; the patient is started on a continuous infusion of heparin (usually in the hospital), and the heparin is stopped approximately 4 hours preoperatively and reinstituted postoperatively when it is considered safe to do so. Then, warfarin anticoagulation needs to be re-established. This will provide the shortest interval free of anticoagulation if surgery cannot be done on an anticoagulated patient and the risk of thromboembolism is high. The cost-effectiveness of this latter approach in all cases is questionable.[60]

Of great importance to the success of oral anticoagulation is effective patient education. Patients should understand the reason for their treatment; the anticoagulant's effect on blood; the importance of PT monitoring; the concern about drug interactions; and guidelines pertaining to diet, alcohol use, and commonsense safety rules. Many patients are managed by health professionals working in specialized anticoagulation clinics, usually in large medical centers. These programs are ideal for medical practices with a large number of patients on oral anticoagulation. They are usually equipped for patient education with helpful patient aids and these centers may provide better care and may be more cost-effective than traditional models of care.[61V, 62, 63V]

As might be expected, the potential for hemorrhagic complications of oral anticoagulant therapy can be great. Such adverse affects of oral anticoagulants are reviewed in depth in Chapter 7. By optimizing therapy through the use of specialized clinics, clinicians can hope that complications will be reduced.

The management of oral anticoagulant therapy tends to be labor-intensive and costly both for the physician and the patient. The cost-benefit ratio of treating patients with anticoagulants is reviewed elsewhere in this text, but once again, specialized anticoagulation clinics may be more cost-effective than traditional models of care.[63] The use of oral anticoagulants in specific medical conditions may also present special problems such as anticoagulation during pregnancy or in patients with cancer, and these issues are dealt with elsewhere in this text.

Table 29–5. **Content of Vitamin K in Different Food Products**

| Vit. K* | Product | Vit. K* | Product |
|---|---|---|---|
| | Beverages | | Milk, Other |
| 0.7 | coffee, dry—1 rd t (1.8 g) 99 tea, | 0.6 | human—1 fl oz (30 g) |
| 199 | green, dry—1 oz (28 g) | | |
| | Eggs, Chicken | | Sweeteners |
| 25 | whole, fresh/frzn—1 large (50 g) | 5 | honey—1 T (21 g) |
| 25 | yolk, fresh—yolk or 1 large egg (17 g) | | |
| | Fats & Oils | | Vegetables |
| | Vegetable Oils | | asparagus spears |
| 1 | coconut oil—1 T (14 g) | 16 | frzn, boiled—4 spears (60 g) |
| 8 | corn oil—1 T (14 g) | 23 | raw—4 spears (58 g) |
| 0 | cottonseed oil—1 T (14 g) | 3 | beet, raw—½ cup (68 g) |
| 0 | olive oil—1 T (14 g) | | broccoli |
| 1 | palm oil—1 T (14 g) | 58 | raw—½ cup chopped (44 g) |
| 0 | peanut oil—1 T (14 g) | 63 | frzn—½ cup (92 g) |
| 0 | safflower oil, linoleic—1 T (14 g) | 52 | cabbage, green, raw—½ cup shredded (35 g) |
| 0.4 | safflower oil, oleic—1 T (14 g) | 9 | carrot, raw—1 med (72 g) |
| 76 | soybean oil—1 T (14 g) | 96 | cauliflower, raw—½ cup pieces (50 g) |
| | Fruits | | chickpeas (garbanzo beans) |
| 4 | apple, raw w/skin—1 med (138 g) | 74 | mature seeds, dry—1 oz (28 g) |
| 7 | orange, raw—1 med (131 g) | 13 | sprouted seeds, raw—1 oz (28 g) |
| 21 | strawberries, raw—1 cup (149 g) | 2 | corn, yellow, raw 1 oz (28 g) |
| | | 3 | cucumber, raw—½ cup slices |
| | Grain Fractions | | (⅙ cucumber) (52 g) |
| 18 | oats, dry—1 oz (28 g) | | green beans (snap beans) |
| 23 | wheat bran—1 oz (28 g) | 22 | frzn, boiled—½ cup (68 g) |
| 36 | wheat flour, whole wheat—1 cup (120 g) | 8 | raw—1 oz (28 g) |
| 10 | wheat germ—1 oz (28 g) | | lentils |
| | | 62 | mature seeds, dry—1 oz (28 g) |
| | Infant Formulas | 11 | sprouted seeds, raw—1 oz (28 g) |
| 4 | cocentrate, reconstituted—1 fl oz (30 g) | 22 | lettuce, iceberg, raw—1 leaf (2 g) |
| 5 | powder, reconstituted—1 fl oz (30 g) | | mung beans |
| 4 | ready-to-feed—1 fl oz (30 g) | 48 | mature seeds, dry—1 oz (28 g) |
| | | 17 | sprouted seeds, raw—½ cup (52 g) |
| | | 3 | mushrooms, raw—½ cup pieces (35 g) |
| | Meats | 104 | nettle leaves, raw 1 oz (28 g) |
| | Beef | | peas |
| 4 | ground, regular, raw—3.5 oz (100 g) | 23 | mature seeds, dry 1 oz (28 g) |
| | | 7 | sprouted seeds, raw—1 oz (28 g) |
| | Variety Cuts | | potato |
| | liver, raw | 18 | raw—1 potato (112 g) |
| 104 | beef—3.5 oz (100 g) | 6 | baked—1 potato (156 g) |
| 80 | chicken—3.5 oz (100 g) | | seaweed |
| 0 | lamb—3.5 oz (100 g) | 1700 | dulse, dried—3.5 oz (100 g) |
| 0 | pigeon—3.5 oz (100 g) | 1700 | rockweed, dried—3.5 oz (100 g) |
| 88 | pork—3.5 oz (100 g) | 246 | seagrass—3.5 oz (100 g) |
| 35 | rabbit—3.5 oz (100 g) | 68 | sealettuce—3.5 oz (100 g) |
| 0 | turkey—3.5 oz (100 g) | 53 | soybeans, mature, raw—1 oz (28 g) |
| 27 | veal—3.5 oz (100 g) | | spinach |
| | | 74 | raw—½ cup chopped (28 g) |
| | Milk, Cow | 131 | frzn—½ cup (95 g) |
| 10 | skim—8 fl oz (245 g) | | tomato |
| 3 | skim, dry— ¼ cup (30 g) | 58 | green, raw—1 tomato (123 g) |
| 10 | whole, 3.7% fat—8 fl oz (244 g) | 28 | red, raw—1 tomato (123 g) |
| | | 182 | turnip greens, raw—½ cup shopped (28 g) |
| | | 10 | watercress, raw—½ chopped (17 g) |

Used with permission from Pennington JAT: Food Values of Portions Commonly Used, ed 16. Philadelphia, JB Lippincott, 1994, p 421.
*In mcg.

**Table 29–6. Drug Interactions With Warfarin and Their Mechanism of Action**

| Drug | Mechanism of Action |
|---|---|
| *Prolongs Prothrombin Time* | |
| Amiodarone | Decreases clearance (nonstereoselective) |
| Anabolic steroids | Unknown |
| Cephalosporins (2nd/ 3rd generation) | Interferes with vitamin K recycling |
| Cimetidine | Decreases clearance (inhibits R isomer) |
| Clofibrate | Unknown |
| Disulfiram | Decreases clearance (inhibits S isomer) |
| Erythromycin | Unknown |
| Fluoroquinolones | Displace binding to albumin |
| Fluconazole | Unknown |
| Glucagon | Unknown |
| Metronidazole | Decreases clearance (inhibits S isomer) |
| Miconazole | Decreases clearance (nonstereoselective) |
| Omeprazole | Decreases clearance (inhibits R isomer) |
| Phenytoin | Unknown |
| Piroxicam | Unknown |
| Quinidine | Unknown |
| Phenylbutazone | Decreases clearance (inhibits S isomer) |
| Salicylates | Enhances hypoprothrombinemia (large doses) |
| Sulfinpyrazone | Decreases clearance (inhibits S isomer) |
| Tamoxifen | Unknown; ? inhibits metabolism |
| Thyroxine | Increases metabolism of coagulation factors |
| Trimethoprim- Sulfamethoxazole | Decreases clearance (inhibits S isomer) |
| Vitamin E | Unknown |
| *Reduces Prothrombin Time* | |
| Alcohol | Increases clearance (stimulates metabolism) |
| Barbiturates | Increases clearance (stimulates metabolism) |
| Carbamazepine | Increases clearance (stimulates metabolism) |
| Cholestyramine | Decreases absorption |
| Griseofulvin | Increases clearance (stimulates metabolism) |
| Nafcillin | Increases clearance (stimulates metabolism) |
| Rifampin | Increases clearance (stimulates metabolism) |
| Sucralfate | Decreases absorption |
| *Enhances Risk of Bleeding* | |
| Aspirin | Inhibits platelet function |
| Heparin | Inhibits other coagulation factors |
| Penicillins | Inhibits platelet function |

References to above-cited drug interactions can be found in Ansell J: Oral anticoagulant therapy, *In* R Hull, G Pineo, G Raskob (eds): Venous Thromboembolism. Futura Publishing, Mt. Kisco, NY, 1995, in press.

In summary, the achievement of the goals of safe and effective therapy not only requires knowledge of when to use oral anticoagulants and for what indications, but also how to use them and how to properly manage therapy. With their proper use, the goals of efficacy and safety can easily be achieved.

## REFERENCES

1. Coon WW, Willis PW, Keller JB: Venous thromboembolism and other venous disease in the Tecumseh Community Health study. Circulation 48:839–846, 1973.
2. Anderson FA, Wheeler HB: Physician practices in the management of venous thromboembolism: A community-wide survey. J Vasc Surg 16:707–714, 1992.
3. Dalen JE, Paraskos JA, Ockene IS, et al: Venous thromboembolism: Scope of the problem. Chest 89[Suppl]:370S–373S, 1989.
4. Wright IS, Prandoni A: The dicoumarin 3,3′-methylene-bis-(4-hydroxycoumarin): Its pharmacologic and therapeutic action in man. JAMA 120:1015–1021, 1942.
5. Deykin D, Wessler S, Reimer SM: Evidence for an antithrombotic effect of dicumarol. Am J Physiol 199:1161–1164, 1960.
6. Hoak JC, Connor WE, Warner ED, Carter JR: The antithrombotic properties of coumarin drugs. Ann Intern Med 54:73–81, 1961.
7. Gitel SN, Wessler S: The antithrombotic effects of warfarin and heparin following infusions of tissue thromboplastin in rabbits: Clinical implications. J Lab Clin Med 94:481–488, 1979.
8. Gitel SN, Wessler S: Dose-dependent antithrombotic effect of warfarin in rabbits. Blood 61:435–438, 1983.
I 9. Barritt DW, Jordan SC: Anticoagulant drugs in the treatment of pulmonary embolism: A controlled trial. Lancet 1:1309–1312, 1960.
V 10. Kernohan RJ, Todd C: Heparin therapy in thromboembolic disease. Lancet 1:621–623, 1966.
11. Kanis JA: Heparin in the treatment of pulmonary thromboembolism. Thromb Diathes Haemorr 32:519–527, 1974.
I 12. Hull RD, Raskob GE, Hirsh J, et al: Continuous intravenous heparin compared with intermittent subcutaneous heparin in the initial treatment of proximal vein thrombosis. N Engl J Med 315:1109–1114, 1986.
I 13. Brandjes DPM, Heijboer H, Buller HR, et al: Acenocoumarol and heparin compared with acenocoumarol alone in the initial treatment of proximal-vein thrombosis. N Engl J Med 327:1485–1489, 1992.
14. Coon WW, Willis PW, Symons MJ: Assessment of anticoagulant treatment of venous thromboembolism. Ann Surg 170:559–568, 1969.
I 15. Hull R, Delmore T, Genton E, et al: Warfarin sodium versus low-dose heparin in the longterm treatment of venous thrombosis. N Engl J Med 301:855–858, 1979.
II 16. O'Sullivan EF: Duration of anticoagulant therapy in venous thrombo-embolism. Med J Aust 2:1104–1107, 1972.
17. Coon WW, Willis PW: Recurrence of venous thromboembolism. Surgery 73:823–827, 1973.
I 18. Lagerstedt CI, Olsson CG, Fagher BO, et al: Need for long-term anticoagulant treatment in symptomatic calf-vein thrombosis. Lancet 2:515–518, 1985.
II 19. Holmgren K, Andersson G, Fagrell B, et al: One-month versus six-month therapy with oral anticoag-

ulants after symptomatic deep vein thrombosis. Acta Med Scand 218:279–284, 1985.

II 20. Schulman S, Lockner D, Juhlin-Dannfelt A: The duration of oral anticoagulation after deep vein thrombosis. Acta Med Scand 217:547–552, 1985.

21. Petitti DB, Strom BL, Melmon KL: Duration of warfarin anticoagulant therapy and the probabilities of recurrent thromboembolism and hemorrhage. Am J Med 81:255–259, 1986.

I 22. Research Committee of the British Thoracic Society: Optimum duration of anticoagulation for deep-vein thrombosis and pulmonary embolism. Lancet 340:873–876, 1992.

23. Wessler S, Gitel SN: Rethrombosis: Warfarin or low-dose heparin. N Engl J Med 301:889–891, 1979.

24. O'Reilly RA, Aggeler PM: Studies on coumarin anticoagulant drugs: Initiation of warfarin therapy without a loading dose. Circulation 38:169–177, 1968.

I 25. Gallus A, Jackaman J, Tillett J, et al: Safety and efficacy of warfarin started early after submassive venous thrombosis or pulmonary embolism. Lancet 2:1293–1296, 1986.

V 26. Rosiello RA, Chan CK, Tencza F, Matthay RA: Timing of oral anticoagulation therapy in the treatment of angiographically proven acute pulmonary embolism. Arch Intern Med 147:1469–1473, 1987.

II 27. Mohiuddin SM, Hilleman DE, Destache CJ, et al: Efficacy and safety of early versus late initiation of warfarin during heparin therapy in acute thromboembolism. Am Heart J 123:729–732, 1992.

I 28. Hull RD, Raskob GE, Rosenbloom D, et al: Heparin for 5 days as compared with 10 days in the initial treatment of proximal venous thrombosis. N Engl J Med 322:1260–1264, 1990.

29. Miller DR, Brown MA. Predicting warfarin maintenance dosage based on initial response. Am J Hosp Pharm 36:1351–1355, 1979.

30. Ansell J: Oral anticoagulant therapy—50 years later. Arch Intern Med 153:586–596, 1993.

31. Hirsh J: Is the dose of warfarin prescribed by American physicians unnecessarily high? Arch Intern Med 147:769–771, 1987.

32. Kirkwood TBL: Calibration of reference thromboplastins and standardization of the prothrombin time ratio. Thromb Haemost 49:238–244, 1983.

33. Loeliger EA: The optimal therapeutic range in oral anticoagulation: History and proposal. Thromb Haemost 42:1141–1152, 1979.

III 34. Wright IS, Beck DF, Marple CD: Myocardial infarction and its treatment with anticoagulants. Lancet 1:92–95, 1954.

III 35. Moschos CB, Wong PCY, Sise HS: Controlled study of the effective level of long-term anticoagulation. JAMA 190:799–805, 1964.

III 36. Sevitt S, Gallagher NG: Prevention of venous thrombosis and pulmonary embolism in injured patients. Lancet 1:981–989, 1959.

37. Miale JB: Laboratory control of anticoagulant therapy. JAMA 180:736–738, 1962.

V 38. Allen EV: The clinical use of anticoagulants. JAMA 134:323–329, 1947.

39. Lam-Po-Tang PRLC, Poller L: Oral anticoagulant therapy and its control: An international survey. Thromb Diathes Haemorr 34:419–425, 1975.

40. Bailey EL, Harper TA, Pinkerton PH: The "therapeutic range" of the one-stage prothrombin time in the control of anticoagulant therapy: The effect of different thromboplastin preparations. Can Med Assoc 105:1041–1043, 1971.

41. Bussey HI, Force RW, Bianco TM, Leonard AD: Reliance on prothrombin time ratios causes significant errors in anticoagulation therapy. Arch Intern Med 152:278–282, 1992.

I 42. Hull R, Hirsh J, Jay R, et al: Different intensities of oral anticoagulant therapy in the treatment of proximal-vein thrombosis. N Engl J Med 307:1676–1681, 1982.

43. Hirsh J, Deykin D: Therapeutic range for oral anticoagulant therapy. Chest 89[Suppl]:11S–15S, 1986.

44. Hirsh J, Dalen JE, Deykin D, Poller L: Oral anticoagulants: Mechanism of action, clinical effectiveness, and optimal therapeutic range. Chest 102:312S–326S, 1992.

45. British Society for Haematology: Guidelines on oral anticoagulation: Second edition. J Clin Pathol 43:177–183, 1990.

46. Levine MN, Hirsh J, Landefeld S, Raskob G: Hemorrhagic complications of anticoagulant treatment. Chest 120:352S–363S, 1992.

IV 47. Shetty HG, Backhouse G, Bentley OP, et al: Effective reversal of warfarin-induced excessive anticoagulation with low dose vitamin K₁. Thromb Hemost 67:13–15, 1992.

48. Loeliger EA, van Dijk-Wierda CA, van den Besselaar AMHP, et al: Anticoagulant control and the risk of bleeding. In Meade TW, (ed): Anticoagulants and Myocardial Infarction: A Reappraisal, New York, John Wiley & Sons, pp 135–177, 1984.

49. Breckenridge AM: Interindividual differences in the response to oral anticoagulants. Drugs 14:367–375, 1977.

50. Qureshi GD, Reinders TP, Swint JJ, Slate MB: Acquired warfarin resistance and weight-reducing diet. Arch Intern Med 141:507–509, 1981.

51. Pennington JAT: Food Values of Portions Commonly Used, ed 16. Philadelphia, JB Lippincott, p 421, 1994.

52. O'Malley K, Stevenson IHN, Ward CA, et al: Determinants of anticoagulant control in patients receiving warfarin. Br J Clin Pharmacol 4:309–314, 1977.

53. Williams JRB, Griffin JP, Parkins A: Effect of concomitantly administered drugs on the control of long-term anticoagulant therapy. Q J Med 45:66–73, 1976.

54. O'Reilly RA, Aggeler PA: Determinants of the response to oral anticoagulant drugs in man. Pharmacol Rev 22:35, 1970.

55. O'Reilly RA: Warfarin metabolism and drug-drug interactions. In Wessler S, Becker CG, Nemerson Y (eds): The New Dimensions of Warfarin Prophylaxis. Advances in Experimental Medicine and Biology, Vol 214. New York, Plenum Press, pp 205–212, 1986.

III 56. McIntyre H: Management during dental surgery of patients on anticoagulants. Lancet 2:99–100, 1966.

I 57. Rustad H, Myhre E: Surgery during anticoagulant treatment. Acta Med Scand 173:115–119, 1963.

V 58. Tinker JH, Tarhan S: Discontinuing anticoagulant therapy in surgical patients with cardiac valve prosthesis. JAMA 239:738–739, 1978.

V 59. Katholi RE, Nolan SP, McGuire LB: The management of anticoagulation during noncardiac operations in patients with prosthetic heart valves. Am Heart J 96:163–165, 1978.

60. Eckman MH, Beshansky JR, Durand-Zaleski I, et al: Anticoagulation for noncardiac procedures in patients with prosthetic heart valves. JAMA 263:1513–1521, 1990.

V 61. Garabedian-Ruffalo SM, Gray DR, Sax MJ, Ruffalo RL: Retrospective evaluation of a pharmacist-managed warfarin anticoagulation clinic. Am J Hosp Pharm 42:304–308, 1985.

62. Gray DR, Garabedian-Ruffalo SM, Chretien SD: Cost justification of a clinical pharmacist-managed anticoagulation clinic. Drug Intel Clin Pharm 19:575–580, 1985.

V 63. Bussey HI, Rospond RM, Quandt CM, Clark GM: The safety and effectiveness of long-term warfarin therapy in an anticoagulation clinic. Pharmacotherapy 9:214–219, 1989.

# Chapter 30

# Thrombolytic Therapy for Venous Thromboembolism

Samuel Z. Goldhaber

The hemodynamic response to pulmonary embolism (PE) depends upon the size of the embolus, the presence of coexistent cardiopulmonary disease, and the degree of vasoconstriction and bronchospasm caused by neurohumoral mediators. Pulmonary artery obstruction and the subsequent release of neurohumoral substances (primarily serotonin and thromboxane $A_2$) constrict the pulmonary vascular bed and cause an increase in right ventricular afterload. As right ventricular and pulmonary artery pressures rise, the right ventricle dilates, becomes hypokinetic, and ultimately fails. Sudden increases in right ventricular pressure adversely affect left ventricular function because of the anatomic juxtaposition of the two ventricles and "ventricular interdependency." Moderate right ventricular hypertension can displace the interventricular septum toward the left ventricle, resulting in decreased left ventricular diastolic filling and end-diastolic volume (Fig. 30–1). As a result, the cardiac output is reduced, leading to a possible downhill spiral of cardiogenic shock and death.

By relieving obstruction to pulmonary artery blood flow, thrombolysis can rapidly lower the abnormally elevated pulmonary artery pressure, thereby reversing cardiogenic shock and possibly reducing the mortality rate from PE. Because of interventricular dependency, improved right ventricular function usually leads to better left ventricular function, which helps improve cardiac output. PE thrombolysis may also reduce the rate of recurrent PE by lysing the source of the PE in situ, usually thrombus in the pelvic or deep leg veins.

Among patients with major PE who are treated with anticoagulation alone, pulmonary artery clots may fail to resolve completely in 75% after 1 to 4 weeks[1] and in 50% after 4 months of followup.[2] Dissolution of the thrombus should improve pulmonary tissue perfusion, which, in turn, should prevent chronic pulmonary hypertension as a late effect of PE and should improve the quality of life.

## PROGNOSIS WITH HEPARIN ALONE

Among patients treated with heparin alone, the rate of death or recurrent PE within 2 weeks of diagnosis is at least 10%, based on a report of 399 carefully selected patients from the Prospective Investigation of Pulmonary Embolism Diagnosis (PIOPED) group that excluded patients who were "too ill" to undergo pulmonary angiography.[3] Only 2.5% died, and most deaths were caused by recurrent PE. Overall, the rate of PE recurrence was 8.3%. Very few of these PIOPED Study patients were gravely ill; therefore, in unselected groups of PE patients, the reported rates of death and recurrent PE are usually higher.

## INITIAL CLINICAL TRIALS

In phase I of the Urokinase Pulmonary Embolism Trial (UPET), a 24-hour urokinase (UK) infusion dissolved PE more rapidly than heparin alone and, in certain instances, reversed clinical shock.[41] There was a trend with UK toward reduction of mortality and recurrent PE, but this did not achieve statistical significance. In the Urokinase-Streptokinase PE Trial, acute thrombolysis of PE followed by heparin improved pulmonary capillary blood volume at 2 weeks and at 1 year more than heparin alone.[51] Among a subgroup followed for an average of 7 years, those assigned initially to thrombolysis appeared to have a more complete resolution of PE as assessed by preservation of the normal pulmonary vascular response to exercise.[6]

321

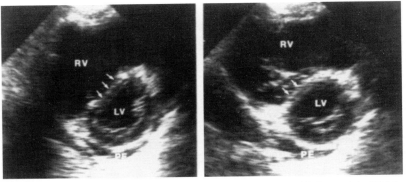

**Figure 30–1.** Parasternal short axis views of the right ventricle (RV) and left ventricle (LV) in diastole (left) and systole (right). There is diastolic and systolic bowing of the interventricular septum (arrows) into the left ventricle compatible with right ventricular volume and pressure overloads, respectively. The right ventricle is appreciably dilated and markedly hypokinetic, with little change in apparent right ventricular area from diastole to systole. PE = small pericardial effusion. (Used with permission from Come PC: Echocardiographic evaluation of pulmonary embolism and its response to therapeutic interventions. Chest 101:151S–162S, 1992.)

## LATER CLINICAL TRIALS

In the 1980s, recombinant tissue plasminogen activator (rt-PA) was developed for PE treatment after initial laboratory studies suggested that it was more potent than urokinase (UK) or streptokinase (SK) and possibly safer.[7, 8] When peripheral intravenous and local pulmonary arterial infusion of rt-PA were compared, both routes of administration caused similar rates of lysis, bleeding, and changes in coagulation parameters.[9I] Therefore, rt-PA can be administered through a peripheral vein, and infusion through a pulmonary arterial catheter appears to be unnecessary.

In 1992, the Plasminogen Activator Italian Multicenter Study (PAIMS-2) investigators in Italy[10I] reported the results of their clinical trial in which 36 patients with angiographically proven PE were randomized to receive 100 mg of rt-PA over 2 hours or heparin alone. Clot lysis at post-treatment angiography, assessed by the Miller index, occurred in the rt-PA group (with the Miller index improving from $28.3 \pm 2.9$ to $24.8 \pm 5.2$), but not in the patients who received heparin alone. Mean pulmonary artery pressure decreased from $30.2 \pm 7.8$ mm Hg to $21.4 \pm 6.7$ mm Hg in the rt-PA group, but increased in patients who received heparin alone. Two patients given rt-PA died (one from renal failure following cardiac tamponade and one from intracranial bleeding), and one patient who received heparin alone died from recurrent PE.

European Cooperative Study Group Investigators compared 100 mg of rt-PA over 2 hours with a 12-hour weight-adjusted infusion of UK (4,400 U/kg bolus, followed by 4,400 U/kg/ hour for 12 hours).[11I] The principal endpoint was reduction in total pulmonary resistance, defined as pulmonary artery mean pressure divided by cardiac index. At 2 hours, total pulmonary resistance decreased by 36% in the rt-PA group, compared with a decrease of 18% in the UK-treated patients ($p = .0009$). However, by 6 hours, UK appeared to "catch up" to rt-PA, and hemodynamic differences between the two groups did not persist.

In Boston, we have coordinated five trials of PE thrombolysis.[12V, 13I, 14II, 15I, 15aII] This fifth trial included investigators from Canada, Italy, and the United States and tested the hypothesis that a smaller bolus of rt-PA (0.6 mg/kg/15 min) is equally effective and safer than a larger dose (100 mg/2 hours).[16I]

During our first trial, we noted that hemodynamic and angiographic improvement (Fig. 30–2) was accompanied by recovery in pulmonary perfusion.[17V] One day after rt-PA, there was a 57% increase in perfusion among the 19 patients who had followup lung scans. We also observed dramatic improvement in right ventricular function.[18V] Come and colleagues performed Doppler echocardiography on seven patients with PE before and after they received rt-PA (Figs. 30–3 and 30–4). Within a day of treatment, the right ventricular end-diastolic diameter was halved from an average of 3.9 to 2.0 cm. Right ventricular wall motion, initially graded as mildly, moderately, or severely hypokinetic in one, two, and four patients, respectively, normalized in five and improved to mild hypokinesis in two. Tricuspid regurgitation was present before lytic therapy in six patients, but was detected after the completion of lytic therapy in only two patients and had disappeared

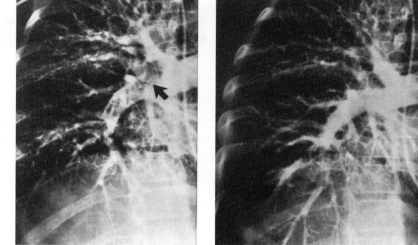

**Figure 30–2.** (Left) A large embolus is present in the right pulmonary artery (arrow). (Right) After a 2-hour infusion of rt-PA through a peripheral vein, there is pronounced resolution, with only a small amount of residual thrombus in segmental branches. (Used with permission from Goldhaber SZ, et al: Acute pulmonary embolism treated with tissue plasminogen activator. Lancet 2:886–889, 1986. © by Lancet Ltd., 1986.)

by restudy 5 days later in one of these two patients. The rapid reversal of right heart failure suggested a mechanism by which thrombolytic agents may reduce the mortality from acute PE.

The study of Come and coworkers[18V] was a case series of consecutive patients who received rt-PA to treat pulmonary embolism. It was conceivable that the observed improvement of right heart failure, although dramatic, could have been the result of heparin plus "tincture of time" rather than a result of rt-PA therapy. Therefore, we believed that Come's observations needed to be tested in a randomized controlled trial of rt-PA followed by heparin versus heparin alone. We undertook this fourth PE Trial (Fig. 30–5) as a multicentered United States study with the a priori hypothesis that

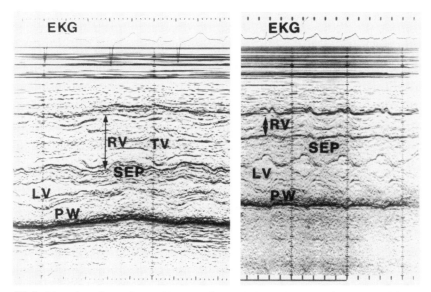

**Figure 30–3.** M-mode echocardiographic recordings of the right ventricle (RV) and left ventricle (LV), from a subcostal transducer position, in a patient before (left) and after (right) thrombolytic therapy for pulmonary embolism. Prior to rt-PA treatment, the patient had a markedly enlarged right ventricle, reduced left ventricular chamber size, and paradoxical movement of the interventricular septum. The right ventricle also appears markedly hypokinetic. After dissolution of intrapulmonary thrombi, documented by pulmonary angiography, the right ventricle has become much smaller in size, and the left ventricle has become larger. Paradoxical systolic septal movement is no longer present, and right ventricular wall movement has normalized. PW = posterior wall; SEP = septum; TV = tricuspid valve. (Used with permission from Come PC, et al: Early reversal of right ventricular dysfunction in patients with acute pulmonary embolism after treatment with intravenous tissue plasminogen activator. J Am Coll Cardiol 10:971–978, 1987.)

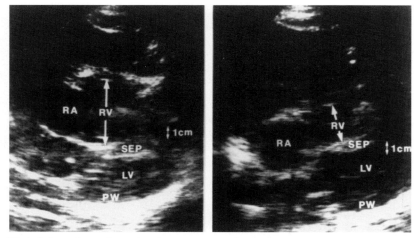

**Figure 30–4.** Subcostal two-dimensional images at end-diastole in a patient with PE from our first PE trial who presented with syncope and "heart failure." Before rt-PA (left), the right ventricle (RV) is markedly enlarged and the diameter of the left ventricle (LV) is reduced. After rt-PA (right), a remarkable decrease in RV size and a corresponding increase in LV size are apparent. RA = right atrium; SEP = septum; PW = posterior wall. (Used with permission from Come PC, et al: Early reversal of right ventricular dysfunction in patients with acute pulmonary embolism after treatment with intravenous tissue plasminogen activator. J Am Coll Cardiol 10:971–978, 1987.)

rt-PA followed by anticoagulation does, in fact, accelerate the improvement of right ventricular function and pulmonary perfusion after PE more rapidly than anticoagulation alone.

Right ventricular wall motion was assessed qualitatively, and right ventricular end-diastolic area from the apical four-chamber view was planimetered on serial echocardiograms at baseline, at 3 hours, and at 24 hours. (An abnormally large right ventricular end diastolic area indicates right ventricular dilatation.) Pulmo-

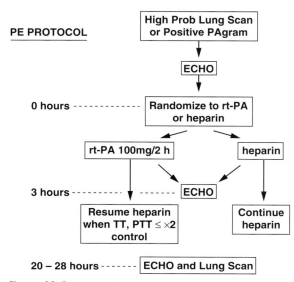

**Figure 30–5.** Protocol for our fourth pulmonary embolism trial (see text).

nary perfusion scans were obtained at baseline and at 24 hours. The results indicated that rt-PA (100 mg/2 hours) followed by heparin provided striking improvement in right ventricular function and pulmonary perfusion compared with heparin anticoagulation alone.

Overall, 101 patients were enrolled in this randomized trial; 46 received rt-PA 100 mg/2 hours followed by heparin, and 55 received heparin alone.[151] Thus, this constitutes the largest thrombolysis versus heparin trial that has been undertaken since phase I of the Urokinase Pulmonary Embolism Trial.[41] At entry, all patients were hemodynamically stable; no patient presented with an initial systolic arterial pressure less than 90 mm Hg. Only 20% of the patients underwent diagnostic pulmonary angiograms. The others were enrolled on the basis of high probability lung scans.

At baseline, about half of the patients with PE had entirely normal right ventricular function. Qualitative assessment of right ventricular wall motion at baseline versus 24 hours demonstrated that 39% of the rt-PA patients improved and 2.4% worsened, compared with 17% improvement and 17% worsening among those who received heparin alone ($p = .005$). Quantitative assessment showed that rt-PA patients had a significant decrease in right ventricular end diastolic area during the 24 hours after randomization compared with none among those allocated to heparin alone ($p = .01$) (Fig. 30–6). Patients who received rt-PA also had an absolute improvement in pulmonary perfusion of 14.6%

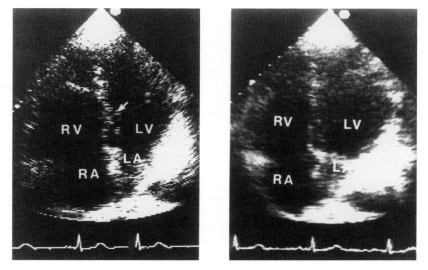

**Figure 30–6.** Echocardiograms (four-chamber view) in a 53-year-old previously healthy man with a high probability lung scan for pulmonary embolism. (Left) Right ventricular enlargement before treatment. The right ventricular end diastolic area was 42.9 cm², and the interventricular septum (arrow) was displaced toward the left ventricle. (Right) Three hours after initiating rt-PA therapy, the right ventricle was normal in size (with a planimetered area of 25.7 cm²), and the interventricular septum regained its normal configuration.

at 24 hours, compared with 1.5% improvement among patients receiving heparin alone ($p<.0001$).

Most importantly, no clinical episodes of recurrent PE occurred among patients receiving rt-PA, but there were five (two fatal and three nonfatal) clinically suspected recurrent PEs within 14 days in patients randomized to receive heparin alone ($p=.06$). All five presented initially with right ventricular hypokinesis on echocardiogram, suggesting that patients with this initial echocardiographic finding constitute a high-risk group.

We studied the relationship between right ventricular (RV) hypokinesis on echocardiography and defects on the initial perfusion lung scan.[19] The degree of the perfusion defect was greater in those patients with baseline RV hypokinesis ($54\pm16\%$ of the lung nonperfused) than in those patients with normal RV wall motion at baseline ($30\pm18\%$ nonperfused lung; $p<.001$). Receiver-operating characteristic curve analysis revealed a perfusion lung scan defect score of 0.3 (i.e., 30% of the lung nonperfused) to have a 92% sensitivity for predicting RV hypokinesis; this finding carried a relative risk for observing RV hypokinesis of 6.8 times greater than that among those patients with a perfusion scan score of less than 0.3 (Fig. 30–7). Considering that all patients with recurrent symptomatic PE were in the subgroup with RV hypokinesis (13% versus 0% for those with normal RV wall motion; $p=.01$), a strategy of performing echocardiography in those patients with a perfusion scan defect score of 0.3 or more appears to identify patients at increased risk for recurrent PE.

In summary, results of this trial suggest that rapid improvement in right ventricular function and pulmonary perfusion, accomplished with thrombolytic therapy followed by heparin, may lead to a lower rate of death and recurrent PE, especially among patients who present with right ventricular hypokinesis. Furthermore, echocardiography (or extensive perfusion defects on lung scanning) appears to identify a subgroup of PE patients at high risk of adverse clinical outcomes if treated with heparin alone. These patients, in particular, appear to be excellent candidates for thrombolytic therapy in the absence of contraindications.

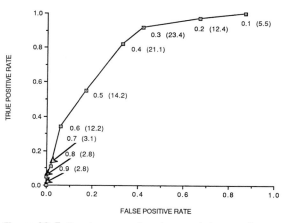

**Figure 30–7.** Receiver-operating characteristic curve for segmental pulmonary perfusion scan scores for the discrimination of the presence or absence of right ventricular hypokinesis on baseline echocardiography. Numbers in parentheses represent the chi-square values for the corresponding perfusions can score. (Used with permission from Wolfe MW, et al: Prognostic significance of right ventricular hypokinesis and perfusion lung scan defects in pulmonary embolism. Am Heart J 127:1371–1375, 1994.)

## PRACTICAL POINTS

The United States Food and Drug Administration approved streptokinase (SK) in 1977 and UK in 1978 for treatment of pulmonary embolism. The agent rt-PA was approved for this use in 1990. All three regimens (Table 30–1) utilize fixed or weight-adjusted doses of thrombolytic agents. Therefore, there is no need to obtain laboratory tests during the thrombolytic infusion because no dosage adjustments are made.

For patients with a high clinical suspicion of PE and high probability results on ventilation-perfusion lung scans, thrombolytic therapy can be administered without angiographic confirmation of the diagnosis.[20] However, angiography should be performed among patients with nonhigh probability scan results prior to administering thrombolytic therapy. For hemodynamically stable patients admitted in the evening or at night, we defer angiography until the next morning and initiate heparin empirically. Heparin is held for several hours prior to angiography, which is usually performed with a single wall puncture of the right femoral vein; for blood sampling, we use a Cordis sheath with a side arm.[21]

When considering PE thrombolysis, we do not have an arbitrary upper age limit. We have found that patients with PE have a wide "window" for effective use of thrombolysis. Specifically, patients who receive thrombolysis 6 to 14 days after new symptoms or signs have as effective a response as those patients who receive thrombolytic therapy within 5 days after the onset of PE. Therefore, we consider patients suspected of PE as potentially eligible for thrombolysis if they have had any new symptoms or signs within the 2 weeks prior to presentation.

Table 30–1. **FDA-Approved Thrombolytic Regimens for PE**

| Streptokinase |
|---|
| 250,000 U as a loading dose over 30 minutes, followed by 100,000 U/hour for 24 hours—approved in 1977. |
| Urokinase |
| 4,400 U/kg as a loading dose over 10 minutes, followed by 4,400 U/kg/hour for 12–24 hours—approved in 1978. |
| rt-PA |
| 100 mg as a continuous peripheral intravenous infusion administered over 2 hours—approved in 1990. |

None of the Food and Drug Administration- (FDA-) approved regimens for PE thrombolysis employs concomitant heparin therapy—an important difference when compared with the usual approach to thrombolysis in myocardial infarction. At the conclusion of the thrombolytic infusion, a partial thromboplastin time (PTT) should be obtained. Usually, the PTT is less than twice the upper limit of normal, and heparin therapy can be initiated (or resumed) as a continuous intravenous infusion without a loading dose. Occasionally, after termination of the thrombolytic infusion, the PTT exceeds twice the upper limit of normal. In these circumstances, the test should be repeated every 4 hours until it declines into the range in which heparin therapy is safe. We leave the Cordis sheath in place until the next morning and discontinue the heparin infusion for several hours before removing the sheath. Heparin administration is resumed without a bolus after adequate hemostasis is achieved at the catheterization site.

### Bleeding Complications

Of greatest concern is the risk of intracranial bleeding, which occurs in 0.5 to 1.0% of patients treated with thrombolytic therapy. If intracranial bleeding is suspected, thrombolytic therapy or heparin should be discontinued immediately, and both neurologic and neurosurgical consultation should be obtained. Retroperitoneal hemorrhage can also be life-threatening because the bleeding is often sustained, brisk, and difficult to diagnose. This complication can occur during the femoral vein catheterization for pulmonary angiography if an artery is inadvertently punctured above the inguinal ligament.

During the past decade, appropriate patient selection and minimizing the "handling" of patients during the thrombolytic infusion have lessened the bleeding rate. By 1987, the rate of severe bleeding in a multicentered European study of UK for PE had decreased to 4%.[22ll]

### Contemporary PE Thrombolysis

PE thrombolysis used to require automatic admission to an intensive care unit (ICU) for careful clinical and laboratory monitoring of prolonged thrombolytic infusions. However, with short 2-hour infusions of thrombolytic agents, many patients can be treated safely in an intermediate care ("step-down") unit.

Many clinicians who practiced in the early and mid 1970s remember PE thrombolysis as a heroic and often thankless measure of desperation that consumed hospital resources and physicians' peace of mind. Often, thrombolysis would not be started until the patient became hemodynamically unstable owing to progressive right heart failure. At that point, efficacy was less certain and bleeding complications seemed to increase. For example, more than one in every four patients suffered a major hemorrhagic complication when a 24-hour thrombolysis dosing regimen was utilized in the UPET population of massive and submassive PE.[41]

Fortunately, recently completed clinical trials have taught us many ways to make thrombolytic therapy safer, more streamlined, and more economical. Our rt-PA vs. heparin alone PE trial[15I] provides a rationale for administering thrombolytic therapy to patients who are hemodynamically stable but who, nevertheless, have echocardiographic evidence of right ventricular hypokinesis. Contemporary PE thrombolysis is characterized by a 2-week "time window," a brief infusion administered through a peripheral vein, and no special laboratory tests.

Future studies will require international collaboration and must utilize relevant clinical endpoints such as reduction of mortality, recurrent PE, and chronic pulmonary hypertension.[23] Such trials should focus not only on patients with massive embolism but also on those with smaller emboli that so often herald catastrophic events.[24]

## Treatment of Venous Thrombosis of the Extremities

The therapy for venous thrombosis should depend upon the patient's risk for pulmonary embolism, recurrent venous thrombosis, and chronic venous insufficiency. For large above-calf thrombosis and for upper extremity superior vena caval, subclavian, or axillary vein thrombosis (especially to preserve the patency of an indwelling central venous catheter that is thrombosed), thrombolytic therapy should be considered. This latter approach may provide more rapid and complete resolution of the clot than anticoagulation alone. New dosing regimens are currently being investigated that utilize "bursts" of high concentrations of drug over short periods of time. For example, our research group has successfully tested urokinase (Abbokinase) for upper extremity and leg venous thrombosis with a regimen of 1 million U over 10 minutes, administered through a peripheral vein three times over 24 hours.[25V] We have now embarked upon a trial of recombinant urokinase followed by heparin versus heparin alone. The recombinant form of urokinase does not appear to be associated with rigors that sometimes occurred with urokinase prepared from human cell cultures.

## REFERENCES

1. Dalen JE, Banas JS, Jr, Brooks HL, et al: Resolution rate of acute pulmonary embolism in man. N Engl J Med 280:1194–1199, 1969.
2. Tow DE, Wagner NH Jr: Recovery of pulmonary arterial blood flow in patients with pulmonary embolism. N Engl J Med 276:1053–1059, 1967.
3. Carson JL, Kelley MA, Duff A, et al: The clinical course of pulmonary embolism. N Engl J Med 326:1240–1245, 1992.
I 4. The Urokinase Pulmonary Embolism Trial: A national cooperative study. Circulation 47:II1–108, 1973.
I 5. Sharma GVRK, Burleson VA, Sasahara AA: Effect of thrombolytic therapy on pulmonary-capillary blood volume in patients with pulmonary embolism. N Engl J Med 303:842–845, 1980.
6. Sharma GVRK, Folland ED, McIntyre KM, Sasahara AA: Longterm hemodynamic benefit of thrombolytic therapy in pulmonary embolic disease (abstract). J Am Coll Cardiol 15:65A, 1990.
7. Agnelli G, Buchanan MR, Fernandez F, et al: A comparison of the thrombolytic and hemorrhagic effects of tissue-type plasminogen activator and streptokinase in rabbits. Circulation 72:178–182, 1985.
8. Prewitt RM, Hoy C, Kong A, et al: Thrombolytic therapy in canine pulmonary embolism. Am Rev Respir Dis 141:290–295, 1990.
I 9. Verstraete M, Miller GAH, Bounameaux H, et al: Intravenous and intrapulmonary recombinant tissue-type plasminogen activator in the treatment of acute massive pulmonary embolism. Circulation 77:353–360, 1988.
I 10. Dalla-Volta S, Palla A, Santolicandro A, et al: PAIMS 2: Alteplase combined with heparin versus heparin in the treatment of acute pulmonary embolism. Plasminogen Activator Italian Multicenter Study 2. J Am Coll Cardiol 20:520–526, 1992.
I 11. Meyer G, Sors H, Charbonnier B, et al, on behalf of the European Cooperative Study Group for Pulmonary Embolism: Effects of intravenous urokinase versus alteplase on total pulmonary resistance in acute massive pulmonary embolism: A European multicenter double-blind trial. J Am Coll Cardiol 19:239–245, 1992.
V 12. Goldhaber SZ, Vaughan DE, Markis JE, et al: Acute pulmonary embolism treated with tissue plasminogen activator. Lancet 2:886–889, 1986.
I 13. Goldhaber SZ, Kessler CM, Heit J, et al: A randomized controlled trial of recombinant tissue plasminogen activator versus urokinase in the treatment of acute pulmonary embolism. Lancet 2:293–298, 1988.
II 14. Goldhaber SZ, Kessler CM, Heit JA, et al: Recombinant tissue-type plasminogen activator versus a novel dosing regimen of urokinase in acute pulmonary embolism: A randomized controlled multicenter trial. J Am Coll Cardiol 20:24–30, 1992.
I 15. Goldhaber SZ, Haire WD, Feldstein ML, et al: Alteplase versus heparin in acute pulmonary embolism: Randomised trial assessing right ventricular function and pulmonary perfusion. Lancet 341:507–511, 1993.

II 15a. Goldhaber SZ, Agnelli G, Levine MN: The Bolus Atleplase Pulmonary Embolism Group. Reduced dose bolus alteplase vs. conventional alteplase infusion for pulmonary embolism thrombolysis. An International Multicenter Randomized Trial. Chest 106:718–724, 1994.

I 16. Levine MN, Hirsh J, Weitz J, et al: A randomized trial of a single bolus dosage regimen of recombinant tissue plasminogen activator in patients with acute pulmonary embolism. Chest 98:1473–1479, 1990.

V 17. Parker JA, Markis JE, Palla A, et al, on behalf of the Participating Investigators: Early improvement in pulmonary perfusion after rt-PA therapy for acute embolism: Segmental perfusion scan analysis. Radiology 166:441–445, 1988.

V 18. Come PC, Kim D, Parker JA, et al, and Participating Investigators: Early reversal of right ventricular dysfunction in patients with acute pulmonary embolism after treatment with intravenous tissue plasminogen activator. J Am Coll Cardiol 10:971–978, 1987.

19. Wolfe MW, Lee RT, Feldstein ML, et al: Prognostic significance of right ventricular hypokinesis and perfusion lung scan defects in pulmonary embolism. Am Heart J 127:1371–1375, 1994.

20. PIOPED Investigators: Value of the ventilation/perfusion scan in acute pulmonary embolism. Results of the Prospective Investigation of Pulmonary Embolism Diagnosis (PIOPED). JAMA 263:2753–2759, 1990.

21. Meyerovitz M: How to maximize the safety of coronary and pulmonary angiography in patients receiving thrombolytic therapy. Chest 97:132S–135S, 1990.

II 22. The UKEP Study Research Group: The UKEP study: Multicentre clinical trial on two local regimens of urokinase in massive pulmonary embolism. Eur Heart J 8:2–10, 1987.

23. Goldhaber SZ: Pulmonary embolism thrombolysis: A clarion call for international collaboration. J Am Coll Cardiol 19:246–247, 1992.

24. Thrombolysis for pulmonary embolism. Lancet 2:21–22, 1992.

V 25. Goldhaber SZ, Polak JF, Feldstein ML, et al: Efficacy and safety of repeated boluses of urokinase in the treatment of deep venous thrombosis. Am J Cardiol 73:75–79, 1994.

# Chapter 31

# Vena Caval Filters

Greg Elliott and Bo Eklof

## HISTORIC OVERVIEW

Trousseau proposed ligation of the inferior vena cava to treat recurrent pulmonary thromboembolism in 1868. Recognition that vena cava ligation led to chronic venous insufficiency with attendant ulceration stimulated the development of surgical techniques that simultaneously filtered the vena cava and preserved blood flow. Transvenous devices soon replaced external suture plication and serrated clips (Adams-DeWeese clips) applied externally to the vena cava. These early transvenous devices, such as the Hunter balloon and the Mobin-Uddin umbrella, were subsequently discontinued because of unacceptable morbidity caused by occlusion of the inferior vena cava. In 1973 a stainless steel cone-shaped device, the Greenfield filter, replaced the more primitive early transvenous filters. This device had, as its principal advance, a shape that optimized the capture of thrombi while permitting the preservation of blood flow.

## CURRENT DEVICES

Technologic advances have provided a variety of intravascular vena cava filters for modern use (Fig. 31–1). These filters vary in design, materials, length, diameter, delivery system, and clot-filtering efficiency. Filter designs include a conical shape (Greenfield or LGM); a tangle with hooks to engage the vena cava wall (Gianturco-Roehm "bird's nest"), a "clover leaf," and a pyramidal structure (Amplatz-Spider or Simon-nitinol). Materials include stainless steel, titanium, eligiloy, and nickel titanium alloy. Titanium possesses thrombogenicity similar to that of stainless steel, but its increased tolerance to flexion stress allows it to be compressed into a smaller carrier.[1] Current introducer systems are smaller (9–14 French) than older devices, a feature that decreases the risk of thrombosis at the insertion site.[2, 3] Differences in filter diameter are important clinically. The bird's nest filter can be placed in larger vena cava (up to 40 mm diameter) than the other filters.[4]

Differences in clot-filtering efficiency also may be important clinically. However, adequately controlled direct clinical comparisons are nonexistent. Results of in vitro studies suggest that the Greenfield filter is less likely to trap smaller thrombi (2–4 mm × 20–30 mm) than the bird's nest filter[5] or the clover leaf filter.[6] Furthermore, eccentric positioning of the Greenfield filter markedly diminishes its clot-trapping efficiency. More efficient filters, such as the bird's nest filter, may increase the risk for obstruction of the inferior vena cava.[7V]

### Insertion Technique

Percutaneous venotomy is currently the most widely used approach to inferior vena cava filtration. The right femoral vein is the preferred site for venous access because the left iliac vein may be partially compressed by the right iliac artery, and the internal jugular veins pose the risk of air embolism. The latter occurred in 1% of internal jugular insertions.[8V] Because of the potential danger of air embolism, the left common femoral vein should be used when the right common femoral vein is not available or when severe levoscoliosis is present.[9] In addition, use of femoral veins allows the same puncture site to be used for pulmonary angiography and cavography.

A vena cavagram is important to identify caval size, anatomy, and thrombi between the venotomy site and the proposed point of filter placement. Vena cavagrams frequently identify cavae that are too large for standard Greenfield filters, inferior vena cava thrombi, or anatomic variations that influence filter placement.[10, 11V, 12]

## INDICATIONS

Prevention of pulmonary embolism constitutes the rationale for vena cava filtration. Avail-

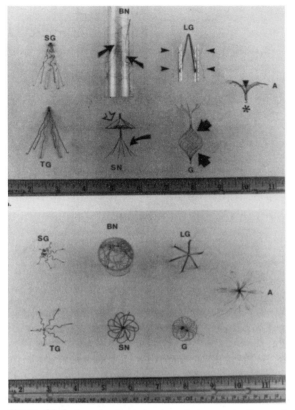

**Figure 31–1.** Longitudinal (top) and short axis (bottom) views of seven current vena cava filters. The Bird's nest (BN) is designed for use in vena cava up to 40 mm in diameter. SG = stainless steel Greenfield; LG = LGM filter; A = Amplatz filter; TG = titanium Greenfield; SN = Simon nitinol; and G = Gunther filter. (Used with permission from Dorfman GS: Percutaneous inferior vena caval filters. Radiology 174:987–992, 1990.)

tion of anticoagulant therapy (Table 31–1). Active bleeding that cannot be easily controlled is one absolute contraindication to anticoagulation. Situations in which life-threatening bleeding is likely (e.g., recent central nervous system trauma) also contraindicate anticoagulant therapy. Serious complications of anticoagulant therapy such as major bleeding or heparin-induced thrombocytopenia with thromboses also warrant vena cava filter placement.

In some situations, the contraindication to anticoagulant therapy is relative. Examples include recently treated gastrointestinal ulceration or active inflammatory bowel disease. In these circumstances, clinicians must decide whether to anticoagulate based upon available clinical information. Vena caval filtration is appropriate when the risk of anticoagulation is excessive.

The need to operate upon a patient with incompletely treated proximal deep vein thrombosis is another clinical problem that requires insertion of a vena cava filter. Interruption of anticoagulant therapy increases the risk for recurrent thromboembolism, and prophylactic doses of anticoagulant (e.g., subcutaneous heparin 5,000 U bid) are insufficient in the setting of active thrombosis. In this situation, placement of a vena cava filter is necessary, just as it is when anticoagulation is contraindicated because of recent major surgery.

Surgery for patients with chronic large vessel thromboembolic pulmonary hypertension is another proposed indication for vena caval filtra-

able data suggest that recurrent pulmonary embolism is unlikely after proper placement of a vena cava filter. Becker and coworkers reported recurrent pulmonary emboli in 26 of 1,094 patients after vena cava filtration, with eight deaths (0.7%) attributed to pulmonary embolism.[13] In subsequent studies, investigators report similar low rates of recurrent thromboembolism and death due to pulmonary embolism with a variety of vena cava filters.[14] Such data compare favorably with recurrence rates and deaths following anticoagulant treatment of acute proximal deep vein thrombi[15, 16] and acute pulmonary embolism.[17] These comparisons, although imperfect, provide the basis for placement of vena cava filters.

Two widely accepted indications for vena cava filtration are (1) an absolute contraindication to anticoagulation, and (2) a serious complica-

### Table 31–1. Indications for Vena Caval Filter

Absolute contraindication to anticoagulation
  Active bleeding of clinical consequence
  Life-threatening or serious bleeding likely e.g., CNS surgery or trauma within 2 weeks
Complications of anticoagulant therapy
  Major bleeding
  Heparin-induced thrombocytopenia with thromboses
Emergency surgery for a patient with incompletely treated proximal deep vein thrombosis
Thromboendarterectomy with chronic large vessel thromboembolic pulmonary hypertension
Objectively documented recurrent pulmonary embolism in the presence of adequate anticoagulant therapy
Acute massive thromboembolism treated by thrombectomy *or* treated by thrombolysis with residual proximal deep vein thrombi
? Free-floating iliofemoral or vena cava thrombi
? Prophylactic placement for high-risk patients prior to orthopedic surgery or following trauma

Table 31–2. **The Clinical Significance of Unattached Venous Thrombi**

| Author, Date | Method | Imaging Technique | N-Total | N-Free-floating Thrombi | Observations |
|---|---|---|---|---|---|
| Voet, 1991 | Retrospective | Serial duplex ultrasound 2 weeks and 3 months (D) | — | 30 | 4 suffered massive PE ≤4 days after duplex diagnosis (2 were fatal) |
| Norris, 1985 | Retrospective | Venography (L) | 78 | 5 | 3 of 5 had symptomatic PE in spite of anticoagulation |
| Berry, 1990 | Retrospective | Duplex ultrasound (D) | 65 | — | 17 (26%) developed PE |
| Baldridge, 1990 | Retrospective | Duplex ultrasound (D) | 732 | 73 | 2 (3%) developed PE |

*Inferior vena cava; D = Dynamic movement; L = Length of tail > 5 cm

tion. Although active thrombosis does not exist, Moser and coworkers advocate placement of vena cava filters prior to surgical thromboendarterectomy.[18] Filter placement, instead of more conventional prophylactic measures, may be justified by the risks of anticoagulants after cardiopulmonary bypass; by the possibility that recurrent thromboemboli may not dissolve; and by the fact that these patients have a demonstrated predisposition to serious venous thromboembolism.

Recurrent thromboembolism despite anticoagulant treatment also may warrant the insertion of a vena cava filter. However, several caveats apply. First, objective proof of recurrent pulmonary thromboembolism is important. Objectively documented recurrent pulmonary embolism is rare when adequate initial doses of anticoagulants are given.[15l, 16l, 17] Symptoms and signs that suggest a recurrence are nonspecific and may reflect complications of a prior pulmonary embolism or anxiety. Furthermore, up to 50% of patients who present with acute deep vein thrombosis have lung scan patterns suggestive of occult pulmonary embolism prior to the initiation of anticoagulant therapy.[19–21] When recurrent pulmonary embolism complicates inadequate initial anticoagulant therapy, the clinician may choose not to place a vena cava filter, particularly if the patient is young and has ample cardiopulmonary reserve and little remaining clot burden, and if an adequate anticoagulant effect can be achieved.

Acute massive pulmonary embolism is another clinical problem for which placement of vena cava filter deserves consideration. Thrombectomy for acute massive pulmonary embolism justifies vena cava filter placement,[22, 23] because anticoagulation is contraindicated and the risk of recurrent thromboembolism is high. Vena cava filtration also should be considered if extensive thrombus remains in the lower extremities and thrombolysis is planned. In this situation, partial lysis of loosely attached venous thrombi can produce fatal thromboemboli.[24]

The presence of unattached tails of adherent thrombi, often referred to as "floating thrombi," presents a controversial indication for vena cava filtration.[25, 26] The risks posed by such thrombi remain uncertain (Table 31–2). Some investigators have reported that most free-floating thrombi do not embolize,[27] while others have reported a high rate of pulmonary embolism when thrombi with nonadherent segments are treated with anticoagulants alone.[28, 29] Difficulties of diagnosis[30] and coexisting conditions that influence prognosis (e.g., advanced cancer) add complexity to the decision to place a vena cava filter when free-floating thrombi are identified. Thus, in the absence of compelling data, the decision to place a vena cava filter for a free-floating thrombus must be individualized. The decision should take into account the size of the unattached segment; the presence and nature of preexisting cardiopulmonary compromise; the presence of coexisting disease (e.g., advanced malignancy) that limits the prognosis; and the patient's wishes. When unattached thrombus extends into the vena cava and thrombectomy is planned, a filter should be placed proximal to the thrombus.[31]

Prophylactic placement of vena cava filters has been suggested for selected "high risk" patients. Examples include multiorgan trauma victims or patients undergoing hip or knee arthroplasty who have a number of risk factors for venous thromboembolism.[32] However, at present no clinical trials have examined these indications, and the low rates of fatal pulmonary emboli that follow widely accepted prophylactic measures make the use of vena cava filters difficult to justify in these circumstances.

## CONTRAINDICATIONS

There are few contraindications to placing a vena cava filter. Uncooperative or unwilling patients cannot have filters placed, and patients without suitable venous access cannot have filters inserted percutaneously. The latter circumstance requires operative filter placement. Under such circumstances, coagulopathy or thrombocytopenia contraindicates filter placement.

Sepsis does not contraindicate insertion of a vena cava filter.[33, 34V] However, thrombus trapped by a filter can become infected, necessitating treatment with parenteral antibiotics and surgical removal of the filter.[33, 35] Therefore, in the presence of sepsis, clear and compelling indications for vena cava filtration are necessary.

## COMPLICATIONS

Fatal complications rarely follow vena cava filtration.[13] Reported deaths have accompanied massive embolism of thrombus attached to a filter,[7] sudden cardiopulmonary collapse,[10] and misplacement of a Greenfield filter.[36V] Fatalities also result from recurrent venous thromboembolism in spite of vena cava filtration.[14, 37, 38V] Recurrent thromboemboli may arise from the vena cava filter (Fig. 31–2); or they may pass through a malpositioned filter.[39]

Nonfatal complications include those related to the insertion procedure, such as infection, thrombosis, and hematoma; and those that occur later, such as filter migration, erosion of a hook through the vena cava, or vena cava obstruction. Thrombosis at the insertion site was a common complication when large-bore introducer systems were used. The advent of 12 to 14 French delivery systems has reduced the incidence of this complication to approximately 10 to 30%.[40] Infections occur uncommonly, and hematomas are rarely of clinical consequence. Migration of vena cava filters occurs commonly,[41V] but is seldom clinically important. Rarely, caudal migration beyond the bifurcation of the inferior vena cava may permit fatal pulmonary embolism from the opposite iliac vein.[11V] Erosion of anchoring filter struts can cause chronic neuralgia[8V, 11V] or intestinal perforation[42]; but often perforation of the vena cava is asymptomatic and clinically unimportant.[11V, 43]

Vena cava obstruction in lower extremities is a potentially serious complication. The reported incidence has varied between 0 and 21%. The wide variation in reported incidence reflects different methods used to detect caval obstruction as well as differences in filter design, anticoagu-

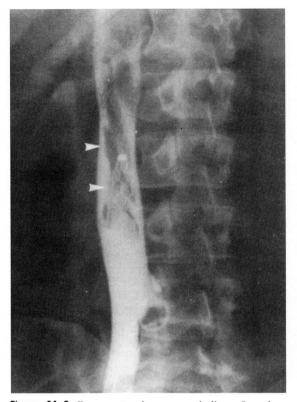

**Figure 31–2.** Recurrent pulmonary embolism after placement of a Greenfield filter prompted this venacavogram, which demonstrates extensive thrombus that has propagated above the vena cava filter. (Used with permission from Braun TI, et al: An unusual thromboembolic complication of a Greenfield vena caval filter. Chest 87:127–129, 1985.)

lation practice, and duration of followup. Caval obstruction may contribute to chronic venous stasis with swelling, ulceration, and even venous gangrene that necessitates amputation.[11V] Acute caval obstruction causes sudden cyanosis of the lower extremities, swelling, and pain; acute obstruction appears more likely to occur within a few weeks after filter placement.[44] Treatment of acute vena caval obstruction includes volume replacement to avoid hypotension and thrombolysis to relieve the obstruction whenever possible.

## LONGTERM ANTICOAGULATION

The use of anticoagulants following vena cava filter placement must be guided by assessment of risk and benefit for the individual patient. No well-designed clinical trials have provided insight for this management issue. Risks such as vena caval thrombosis and recurrent thromboemboli favor continued anticoagulation, particularly when the risks for bleeding complications are minimal. Because the filter does not prevent thrombosis, and because the risk of recurrent thromboembolism is substantial without anticoagulation, we recommend anticoagulants in the absence of strong contraindications or bleeding complications. The presence of a vena cava filter does not contraindicate anticoagulant therapy, because clinically important hemorrhage at the site where the filter anchors to the vena cava is rare. Furthermore, contraindications to anticoagulants (e.g., recent surgery) often resolve within several weeks after vena cava filters are placed, allowing anticoagulant therapy to resume.

## Infections

Pyophlebitis involving a vena cava filter may occur.[35] Such infections may present the clinical picture of persistent generalized septicemia following bacteremia. Successful treatment may require both parenteral antibiotics and surgical removal of the filter. Although infections appear to be exceedingly infrequent, the presence of an intravascular foreign body has led some authors to recommend antimicrobial prophylaxis during procedures that may give rise to bacteremia.[33] Furthermore, although sepsis is not an absolute contraindication to placement of a vena caval filter, the risk of pyophlebitis involving the filter must be considered.

## Upper Extremity Thrombosis

The deep veins of the upper extremities must be considered potential sources of venous thromboembolism. Indwelling catheters have increased the incidence of upper extremity thrombosis. Thrombi involving the subclavian and axillary veins may complicate the course of more than one-fourth of patients with subclavian catheters, with a substantial fraction resulting in pulmonary emboli,[45] some of which have proven fatal.[46] Thus, treatment of upper extremity thrombosis is often necessary, and anticoagulants may be contraindicated. Under such circumstances, a Greenfield filter can be placed in the superior vena cava,[47] although the exact indications for this procedure remain poorly defined.

## Magnetic Resonance Imaging

Vena caval filters may complicate magnetic resonance images (MRI). The ferromagnetic components of these filters degrade MRI studies.[48] In addition, magnetic forces can move ferromagnetic structures. To date, the application of forces up to 1.5 T have not affected patients with Greenfield,[49] Simon-nitinol,[50, 51] and bird's nest filters.[48] However, caution is appropriate within the first several weeks after filter placement, before fibrin and endothelial proliferation stabilize the filter.

## Thrombolytic Therapy

Severe bleeding is the major risk associated with thrombolytic therapy. Because the hooks or barbs that secure the vena cava filter penetrate the vessel wall, significant retroperitoneal hemorrhage is a potential risk for patients who receive thrombolytic therapy shortly after vena caval filtration. However, major hemorrhage has not been reported for the few patients who have received thrombolytic agents after insertion of vena caval filters with hooks or barbs.[36V, 44] Removable vena cava filters also have been used successfully when thrombolytic therapy has been used for deep vein thrombosis.[52V]

## Suprarenal Placement

Suprarenal placement of vena caval filters is necessary when thrombus arises at or above the renal veins (Table 31–3). Thrombus arising from the left ovarian vein can be managed either by suprarenal filter placement or by ligation of the ovarian vein. Thromboemboli following renal transplant may arise from the iliac vein on the grafted side, necessitating placement of vena cava filters above the anastomosis of the renal and iliac veins.

Most patients tolerate suprarenal filter placement.[53V, 54] Greenfield and coworkers reported no deaths from recurrent thromboembolism or renal failure among 60 patients who had filters placed above the renal veins.[53V] However, thrombotic obstruction of a suprarenal vena cava filter can precipitate acute renal failure or even rupture of a renal transplant.[55]

Table 31–3. **Indications for Suprarenal Placement of Vena Cava Filter**

Renal vein thrombosis
Infrarenal vena cava thrombosis
Large patent left ovarian vein (pregnancy *or* childbearing)
Thrombus propagating proximal to a filter below the renal veins

# REFERENCES

1. Greenfield LJ, Cho KJ, Procter M, et al: Results of a multicenter study of the modified hook-titanium Greenfield filter. J Vasc Surg 14:253–257, 1991.
2. Mewissen MW, Erickson SJ, Foley WD, et al: Thrombosis at venous insertion sites after inferior vena caval filter placement. Radiology 173:155–157, 1989.
3. Dorfman GS, Cronan JJ, Paolella LP, et al: Iatrogenic changes at the venotomy site after percutaneous placement of the Greenfield filter. Radiology 173:159–162, 1989.
4. Gianturco-Roehm Bird's Nest Vena Cava Filter; Suggested Instructions for Placement. Product brochure, Cook Incorporated; Bloomington, IN.
5. Katsamouris AA, Waltman AAC, Delichatsios MA, Athanasoulis CA: Inferior vena cava filters: In vitro comparison of clot trapping and flow dynamics. Radiology 166:361–366, 1988.
6. Palestrant AM, Faykus MH: Clover leaf inferior vena cava filter: In vitro evaluation of filter deployment and comparison of emboli—capturing ability. J Vasc Intervent Radiol 2:117–121, 1991.
V 7. Roehm JOF, Johnsrude IS, Barth MH, Gianturco C: The bird's nest inferior vena cava filter: Progress report. Radiology 168:745–749, 1988.
V 8. Greenfield LJ, Michna BA: Twelve-year clinical experience with the Greenfield vena caval filter. Surgery 104:706–712, 1988.
9. Dorfman GS: Percutaneous inferior vena caval filters. Radiology 174:987–992, 1990.
10. Pais SO, Tobin KD, Austin CB, Queral L: Percutaneous insertion of the Greenfield inferior vena cava filter: Experience with 96 patients. J Vasc Surg 8:460–464, 1988.
V 11. Carabasi RA, Moritz MJ, Jarrell BE: Complications encountered with the use of the Greenfield filter. Am J Surg 154:163–168, 1987.
12. Smith DC, Kohne RE, Taylor FC: Steel coil embolization supplementing filter placement in a patient with a duplicated inferior vena cava. J Vasc Intervent Radiol 3:577–580, 1992.
13. Becker DM, Philbrick JT, Selby JB: Inferior vena cava filters: Indications, safety, effectiveness. Arch Intern Med 152:1985–1994, 1992.
14. Ferris EJ, McCowan TC, Carber DR, Mcfarland DR: Percutaneous inferior vena caval filters: Follow up of seven designs in 320 patients. Radiology 188:851–856, 1993.
I 15. Hull RD, Raskob GE, Rosenbloom D, et al: Heparin for 5 days as compared with 10 days in the initial treatment of proximal venous thrombosis. N Engl J Med 322:1260–1264, 1990.
I 16. Hull RD, Raskob GE, Pineo FT, et al: Subcutaneous low-molecular-weight heparin compared with continuous intravenous heparin in the treatment of proximal vein thrombosis. N Engl J Med 326:975–982, 1992.
17. Carson JL, Kelley MA, Duff A, et al: The clinical course of pulmonary embolism. N Engl J Med 326:1240–1245, 1992.
18. Moser KM, Auger WR, Fedullo PF, et al: Chronic thromboembolic pulmonary hypertension: Clinical picture and surgical treatment. Eur Respir J 5:334–342, 1992.
19. Monreal M, Ruiz J, Olazabal A, et al: Deep venous thrombosis and the risk of pulmonary embolism. Chest 102:677–681, 1992.
20. Dorfman GS, Cronan JJ, Tupper TB, et al: Occult pulmonary embolism: A common occurrence in deep venous thrombosis. AJR 148:263–266, 1987.
21. Huisman MV, Buller HR, ten Cate JW, et al: Unexpected high prevalence of silent pulmonary embolism in patients with deep venous thrombosis. Chest 95:498–502, 1989.
22. Meyns B, Sergeant P, Flameng W, Daenen W: Surgery for massive pulmonary embolism. Acta Cardiologies 47:487–493, 1992.
23. Kieny R, Charpentier A, Kieny MT: What is the place of pulmonary embolectomy today? J Cardiovasc Surg 32:549–554, 1991.
24. Goldsmith JC, Lollar P, Hoak JC: Massive fatal pulmonary emboli with fibrinolytic therapy. Circulation 64:1068–1069, 1982.
25. Page Y, Decourus H, Tardy B, et al: Criteria for prophylactyic caval interruption in venous thromboembolism. Am Rev Respir Dis 147(4):A1001, 1993.
26. Girard P, Hauuy MP, Musset D, et al: Acute inferior vena cava thrombosis. Chest 95:284–291, 1989.
27. Baldridge ED, Martin MA, Welling RE: Clinical significance of free-floating venous thrombi. J Vasc Surg 11:62–67, 1990.
28. Norris CS, Greenfield LJ, Barnes RW: Free-floating iliofemoral thrombus: A risk of pulmonary embolism. Arch Surg 120:806–808, 1985.
29. Voet DA, Afschrift M: Floating thrombi: Diagnosis and follow-up by duplex ultrasound. Br J Radiol 64:1010–1014, 1991.
30. Schmidt JA, Gartenschlager M, Joseph U, et al: The diagnosis of floating venous thrombi: A comparison between venography, sonography and so-called phlebo-computer-tomography. Am Rev Respir Dis 147(4):A998, 1993.
31. Eklof B, Juhan C: Revival of thrombectomy in the management of acute iliofemoral venous thrombosis. Contemp Surg 40:21–30, 1992.
32. Vaughn BK, Knezevich S, Lombardi AV, Mallory TH: Use of the Greenfield filter to prevent fatal pulmonary embolism associated with total hip and knee arthroplasty. J Bone Joint Surg 71:1542–1548, 1989.
33. Peyton JWR, Hylemon MB, Greenfield LJ, et al: Comparison of Greenfield filter and vena caval ligation for experimental septic thromboembolism. Surgery 93:533–537, 1983.
V 34. Kantor A, Glanz S, Gordon DH, Sclafani SJA: Percutaneous insertion of the Kimray-Greenfield filter: Incidence of femoral vein thrombosis. AJR 149:1065–1066, 1987.
35. Scott JH, Anderson CL, Shankar PS: Septicemia from infected filter. JAMA 243:1133–1134, 1980.
V 36. Scurr JH, Jarrett PE, Wastell C: The treatment of recurrent pulmonary embolism: Experience with the Kimray-Greenfield vena cava filter. Ann R Coll Surg Engl 65:233–234, 1983.
37. Geisinger MA, Zelch MG, Risius B: Recurrent pulmonary embolism after Greenfield filter placement. Radiology 165:383–384, 1987.
V 38. Cohen JR, Grella L, Citron M: Greenfield filter instead of heparin as primary treatment for deep venous thrombosis or pulmonary embolism in patients with cancer. Cancer 70:1993–1996, 1992.
39. Greenfield LJ, Peyton R, Crute S, Barnes R: Greenfield vena caval filter experience. Arch Surg 116:1451–1456, 1981.
40. Molgaard CP, Yucel EK, Geller SC, et al: Access site thrombosis after placement of inferior vena cava filters with 12-14-F delivery sheaths. Radiology 185:257–261, 1992.

V 41. Rose BS, Simon DC, Hess ML, Van Aman ME: Percutaneous transfemoral placement of the Kimray-Greenfield vena cava filter. Radiology 165:373–376, 1987.

42. Sidoway AN, Menzoian JO: Distal migration and deformation of the Greenfield vena cava filter. Surgery 99:369–372, 1986.

43. Long W, Schweiger H, Fietkau R, Hofmann-Preiss K: Spontaneous disruption of two Greenfield vena caval filters. Radiology 174:445–446, 1990.

44. Greenfield LJ: Current indications for and results of Greenfield filter placement. J Vasc Surg 1:502–504, 1984.

45. Horattas MC, Wright DJ, Fenton AH, Evans DM: Changing concepts of deep venous thrombosis of the upper extremity—report of a series and review of the literature. Surgery 104:561–567, 1988.

46. Lindblad B, Tengborn L, Bergqvist D: Deep vein thrombosis of the axillary-subclavian veins: Epidemiologic data, effects of different types of treatment and late sequelae. Eur J Vasc Surg 2:161–165, 1988.

47. Hoffman MJ, Greenfield LJ: Central venous septic thrombosis managed by superior vena cava Greenfield filter and venous thrombectomy: A case report. J Vasc Surg 4:606–611, 1986.

48. Watanobe AT, Teitelbaum GP, Gomes AS, Roehm JOF: MR imaging of the bird's nest filter. Radiology 177:578–579, 1990.

49. Liebman CE, Messersmith RN, Levin DN, Chien-Tai L: MR imaging of inferior vena cava filters: Safety and artifacts. AJR 150:1174–1176, 1988.

50. Teitelbaum GP, Bradley WG Jr, Klein BD: MR imaging artifacts, ferromagnetism, and magnetic torque of intravascular filters, stents, and coils. Radiology 166:657–664, 1988.

51. Teitelbaum GP, Ortega HV, Vinitski S, et al: Optimization of gradient echo imaging parameters for intracaval filters and trapped thromboemboli. Radiology 174:1013–1019, 1990.

V 52. Thery C, Asseman P, Amrouni N, et al: Use of a new removable vena cava filter in order to prevent pulmonary embolism in patients submitted to thrombolysis. Eur Heart J 11:334–341, 1990.

V 53. Greenfield JL, Cho KJ, Proctor MC, et al: Late results of suprarenal Greenfield vena cava filter placement. Arch Surg 127:969–973, 1992.

54. Pasquale MD, Abrams JH, Najarian JS, Cerra FB: Use of Greenfield filters in renal transplant patients—are they safe? Transplantation 55:439–442, 1993.

55. Swanson RJ, Carlson RE, Olcott C, et al: Rupture of the left kidney following renosplenic shunt. Surgery 79:710, 1976.

# SECTION III

# Special Problems

# Chapter 32

# Congenital and Acquired Hypercoagulable States

Philip C. Comp

A variety of patients suffer from recurrent venous thromboembolic disease. Some of these patients not only have a personal history of thrombophlebitis and pulmonary embolism but also a family history of these conditions. In these patients it is now possible to identify biochemical abnormalities in the blood coagulation system associated with the development of thrombosis.

Other patients develop thromboembolism in particular high-risk clinical settings, such as the postoperative surgical period. Although no coagulation marker can specifically identify patients before developing the blood clots, a variety of changes in the coagulation system do occur in these settings. Subtle alterations in the balance between hemorrhage and thrombosis may be involved in triggering clot formation. Unlike the hereditary hypercoagulable states, acquired conditions combine not just a single coagulation abnormality but they encompass a variety of physical changes as well. Changes include immobility and local vein trauma, which can create additional predisposition to blood clot formation.

The biochemistry of the clotting factors involved in hereditary and acquired hypercoagulable states has been the subject of frequent excellent reviews and will not be reiterated here, other than to outline basic principles of the relevant coagulation mechanisms.[1–5]

Advances in our understanding of blood clotting now allow the identification of an underlying hereditary cause of thrombosis in a minimum of 30% of patients with recurring thromboembolic disease. As will be discussed, the identification of an inherited defect characterized by an insensitivity to the anticoagulant effect of activated protein C may explain the propensity to thrombosis in an even higher percentage of affected patients. Besides these abnormalities, other abnormalities of the blood clot lysis system also contribute to inherited venous thrombosis.

As a complicating factor, a variety of acquired clinical conditions can result in acquired deficiencies of the plasma proteins involved in hereditary thrombosis. Therefore, although providing assurance in certain cases to the physician and patient that an explanation exists for recurrent thrombosis, the use of newly developed laboratory tests to screen for these inherited abnormalities presents a new set of clinical problems. Specifically, a variety of medical conditions result in acquired abnormalities of these clinical parameters. This can lead to the overdiagnosis of inherited disease in acutely ill individuals. Secondly, the proper clinical use of the test results has yet to be demonstrated, especially in the proper treatment of asymptomatic deficient individuals and the optimal duration of treatment of affected individuals with a single episode of venous thrombosis.

Other acquired coagulation–associated abnormalities are found in patients with venous thrombosis. They are the lupus anticoagulant and anticardiolipin antibodies. Both of these conditions are characterized by antibodies in the blood that interfere with blood clotting tests or bind to negatively charged phospholipids. The need for prospective demonstration of the thrombotic risk imposed by these antibodies remains a major area of interest in clinical coagulation.

## HEREDITARY DEFECTS ASSOCIATED WITH RECURRENT VENOUS THROMBOSIS

The blood clotting system in the body may be divided into three sets of plasma proteins. First

339

are the blood clotting factors that, by way of both the intrinsic and extrinsic clotting pathway, produce blood clots. The second system consists of natural anticoagulant proteins that prevent blood clot formation and hold the clotting system in check. The third system consists of the fibrinolytic proteins that dissolve clots once they are formed. The hereditary absence of a blood clotting protein, such as factor VIII, results in a bleeding diathesis, whereas a deficiency for the natural anticoagulant proteins predisposes to uncontrolled blood clot formation. Unfortunately, deficiencies of anticoagulant proteins do not affect routinely used coagulation tests. This significantly delayed the discovery of these abnormalities.

The best characterized deficiencies of the natural anticoagulant proteins are of antithrombin III (ATIII), protein C, and protein S. The most recent abnormality predisposing to thrombosis involves abnormal factor V molecules. Factor V plays not only a critical role in blood clot formation, but, as does protein S, also serves as a cofactor for the anticoagulant effects of activated protein C. In the thrombophiliacs who inherit this abnormality, the clotting promoting function of factor V functions correctly but the ability to potentiate the anticoagulant activity of activated protein C is missing.

## Antithrombin III Deficiency

Antithrombin III deficiency was the first abnormality identified with recurrent venous and arterial thrombosis.[6-9] ATIII functions in concert with heparin to inhibit the vitamin K–dependent clotting factors when they are in the enzymatically active forms (e.g., factor Xa). The frequency with which thromboembolic events occur in deficient patients varies with the baseline level of ATIII. The lower the level of ATIII, the higher the frequency of thromboembolic events. ATIII deficiency is inherited as autosomal dominant trait. Patients with ATIII deficiency frequently present with their first thromboembolic event between puberty and middle age, with a median age of onset of 27 years. Approximately half of the thromboembolic events appear spontaneously, whereas the remainder are associated with conditions of increased risks such as pregnancy and surgery. ATIII deficiency is more common than previously supposed (Table 32–1). Studies have demonstrated that ATIII levels lower than 50% are present in approximately one in 200 to one in 500 individuals in the normal population.[10, 11] The vast majority of these deficient individuals do not have venous thrombosis (Table 32–1).

Table 32–1. **Frequency of Natural Anticoagulant Deficiencies**

|  | Thrombophiliacs (%) | Normals (%) |
|---|---|---|
| Antithrombin III | 2 | 0.2 |
| Protein C | 4 | 0.5 |
| Protein S | 5 | ? |
| APC resistance | 20–30 | 5–7 |
| **Total** | **31–41** | **6–8** |

The relative percentage of given abnormality will increase as the number of patients with a strong family history of recurrent thrombosis increases.

Modified from Kolodziej M, Comp PC: Hypercoagulable states due to natural anticoagulant deficiencies. In Anderson JW (ed). Current Opinion in Hematology. Philadelphia, Current Science, 1993, pp 301–307.

## Protein C Deficiency

Protein C is a vitamin K–dependent plasma protein. On the endothelial cell surface, the clotting enzyme thrombin binds to a receptor protein thrombomodulin, and the bound thrombin then converts protein C to activated protein C.[3, 12] Activated protein C functions as an anticoagulant by inhibiting the clotting cascade at the levels of factor V and factor VIII.

Hereditary protein C deficiency is associated with recurrent venous thrombosis. The majority of deficient individuals have a heterozygous deficiency state with protein C levels of between 50 and 65% that of normal individuals. Homozygous deficient infants with essentially no detectable protein C develop a severe thrombotic condition termed purpura fulminans neonatalis.[13, 14] This condition occurs shortly after birth and is characterized by extensive thrombosis in the small veins of the skin. This results in large necrotic areas of the skin and underlying fatty tissue. The heterozygous deficient individuals have much milder thrombotic complications, primarily venous thrombosis.

Two distinct types of protein C heterozygous deficient kindreds exist. The majority of protein C–deficient kindreds do not exhibit venous thrombosis.[15] Affected families may be relatively common, because the frequency of protein C deficiency is relatively high and may be present in as many as one out of every 250 people in the normal population (see Table 32–1). The latter figure is conservative, because it is based on antigenic measurements of protein C alone and does not account for other individuals in the population who may have functionally abnormal protein C molecules or who may already be on chronic oral anticoagulation and therefore cannot be tested.

The second, or symptomatic, type of protein

C–deficient families have a high incidence of thromboembolic complications, typically venous thrombosis of the leg veins. There is to date no biochemical or genetic difference between these two types of families. The reason one type of family develops venous thrombosis while the other does not is not clear. The coinheritance of another trait predisposing to thrombosis may play a role. However, the autosomal dominant nature of the inheritance pattern indicated that the two coinherited traits would need to be very tightly linked.

Coumarin-induced skin (or tissue) necrosis has been associated with protein C deficiency,[16] as well as deficiencies of protein S[17] and ATIII.[18] Coumarin necrosis is a rare condition characterized by necrosis of the skin and underlying fatty tissue shortly after the initiation of oral anticoagulant therapy.[19] The association with deficiencies of the natural anticoagulant proteins is thought to occur from the rapid decrease in protein C following the initiation of such therapy. During this initial 12- to 18-hour period, the antithrombotic effects of the protein C system are lost before the patient is fully anticoagulated, and blood clot formation occurs in the small venules of the skin. This drop in protein C occurs in all individuals undergoing oral anticoagulation, but the hypercoagulable state may be exaggerated in protein C–deficient individuals. As is the case with purpura fulminans neonatalis associated with homozygous protein C deficiency, the reason why the skin is the target organ for this intravascular clot formation is unknown. Coumarin necrosis occurs most frequently in the setting of acute deep vein thrombosis.[20] The majority of patients who develop coumarin necrosis do not have a demonstrable underlying abnormality of the natural anticoagulant proteins. An association with hereditary activated protein C resistance has not yet been demonstrated.

## Measurement of Protein C Levels

Laboratory measurement of protein C is relatively straightforward. However, care must be taken in interpretation of results obtained from patients on oral anticoagulation. Protein C is a vitamin K–dependent plasma protein; therefore, the levels of protein C normally drop during oral anticoagulation. This makes the measurement of protein C in affected patients difficult and, although various measures have been proposed to estimate the baseline protein C data of such individuals, the results must be regarded as an estimate of baseline protein C status. Obtaining protein C levels at a time when

the patient is no longer on oral anticoagulation is the useful approach, as is measuring protein C levels of other family members who are not receiving chronic anticoagulation.

Care must be taken not to overinterpret the protein C levels that are obtained in critically ill individuals.[21] Low protein C levels have been found in conditions such as sepsis or extensive trauma, and they do not indicate an underlying hereditary deficiency. Acquired protein C deficiency has been well documented in bacterial sepsis,[22] and this has resulted in the therapeutic use of protein C concentrate in these settings. The acquired protein C deficiency is associated with purpuric skin lesions that respond rapidly to administration of the protein C concentrate.

## Protein S Deficiency

Protein S is a vitamin K–dependent plasma protein that serves as a cofactor for anticoagulant effects of activated protein C.[23] Patients deficient in protein S appear very similar to those with a deficiency in protein C and are at risk of recurrent venous thrombosis and pulmonary embolism.[24, 25] Unlike protein C deficiency, no protein S–deficient kindreds have been identified who are completely free of thromboembolic complications.

Protein S differs from the other vitamin K–dependent plasma proteins in that two forms of protein S are found in normal plasma.[26] Free protein S serves as the cofactor for activated protein C. The remaining approximately 50% of protein S is bound to C4b binding protein, an inhibitor of the classic complement pathway. The protein S that is bound to C4b binding protein is functionally inactive. Heterozygous protein S deficiency can result in approximately 50% of the normal level of total protein S and a corresponding reduction of free protein S. Some deficient patients have been identified who have essentially normal total protein S levels, but a disproportionate amount of protein S is bound to C4b binding protein with a resulting low level of free protein S.[27]

The C4b binding protein is an acute phase protein, and abrupt shifts in the level of protein S from the free (active) to the bound (inactive) form can occur during inflammatory events as the level of C4b binding protein rises. Whether this transient shift in protein S results in thrombotic complications is unknown. However, this shift does cause difficulty in the diagnosis of protein S in acutely ill individuals, because free protein S levels may be transiently reduced. Caution must be employed in making a diagnosis of hereditary protein S deficiency based on single plasma determinations. Again, as with protein C deficiency, measuring the protein S levels of family members not receiving oral anticoagulation may be useful.

## Other Plasma Protein Disorders

Two other plasma protein disorders have been associated with recurrent venous thrombosis—plasminogen deficiency and abnormal fibrinogen molecules. Plasminogen is converted to the active enzyme plasmin by tissue plasminogen activator, and the resulting plasmin enzymatically degrades fibrin clots. If the plasminogen molecules are abnormal or missing, inadequate clot lysis occurs and thrombophlebitis results, because the body cannot eliminate growing clots. Structurally abnormal fibrinogen molecules can also result in blood clot accumulation. The abnormal fibrinogen is converted to structurally abnormal fibrin clot, which is not subject to normal fibrinolysis. This resistance to fibrinolysis is thought to result in clot propagation.

Plasminogen abnormalities can be detected by laboratory testing. Fibrinogen abnormalities are more difficult to detect and involve testing for fibrinogen, which does not clot at the normal rate (i.e., the thrombin clotting time is prolonged). This test obviously may miss potential fibrinogen abnormalities that affect the rate of fibrinolysis but not the rate of clot formation.

## Hereditary Resistance to Activated Protein C

An inherited coagulation defect that is associated with the development of venous thrombosis has been identified.[28] The plasma of affected individuals is not anticoagulated by activated protein C, although protein S is functioning properly. This resistance to the anticoagulant effects of activated protein C is inherited as an autosomal dominant trait. The inherited defect involves coagulation factor V.[29] A single amino acid mutation in factor V prevents activated protein C from inactivating Factor Va, in the coagulation cascade.[30] Unopposed blood clotting occurs and thrombosis results (Fig. 32–1).

Protein S also serves as a cofactor for activated protein C, but is normal in activated protein C–resistant individuals. This defect in the protein C system was initially identified in 33% of patients with recurrent and/or familial venous thrombosis.[31] In a cohort of 301 unselected consecutive patients under 70 years of age presenting with their first episode of documented deep vein thrombosis, resistance to activated

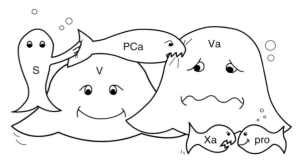

**Figure 32–1.** A fanciful marine depiction of the final step in blood coagulation. Activated Factor V (Va) is positioning Factor Xa so that Factor Xa can convert prothrombin (pro) to thrombin, which will then convert fibrinogen to fibrin to form a clot. Factor Va is disturbed because activated protein C (PCa) is about to take a bite out of Factor Va and make it drop prothrombin and Factor Xa. Thus, anticoagulation will occur and a clot will not form. Activated protein C cannot do this difficult job alone and must stand on the back of another Factor V molecule and must receive a helping shove from protein S in order to bite Factor Va. If protein S is absent (protein S deficiency) or the Factor V has an abnormal back (activated protein C resistance), activated protein C cannot "bite" Factor Va. Anticoagulation does not take place, and unwanted blood clots form.

protein C was found in 21%.[32] A small series of highly selected thrombophilic patients demonstrated the abnormality in half the patients studied[33] as well as in two of 22 patients with concomitant protein C or protein S deficiency. Approximately 5 to 7% of the normal population also carries this trait,[31, 32] suggesting that factors other than this trait alone are necessary for the development of thrombosis. The finding of resistance to activated protein C in patients with systemic lupus erythematosus who have thrombosis[34] has prompted speculation that autoantibodies may arise in patients with lupus to induce an acquired resistance to activated protein C.[33]

The newly postulated role for factor V as not only a procoagulant but also as a potent participant in the protein C anticoagulant pathway may explain why a significant number of patients with severe plasma factor V deficiency do not bleed.[35] In affected patients, the bleeding tendencies induced by low levels of factor V could be balanced by the clot-forming tendencies resulting from the factor V–dependent activated protein C resistance. Disseminated intravascular coagulation has been reported in association with acquired antibodies directed against factor V[36]; this intravascular coagulation may reflect the loss of regulation of the coagulation cascade by the protein C system, as has been reported in protein C deficiency states.[37–39] Future considerations of the treatment of disseminated intravascular coagulation should involve increased emphasis on replenishing factor V, which may have a major effect on restoring hemostatic balance.

Laboratory tests to measure resistance to activated protein C are not licensed for clinical use in the United States. However, the assay is technically easy to perform and is available in an increasing number of research reference laboratories.

## ACQUIRED DEFICIENCIES OF THE NATURAL ANTICOAGULANT PROTEINS

Acquired deficiencies of the natural anticoagulant proteins can occur. Because protein C, protein S, and ATIII are all produced in the liver, severe liver disease can decrease the levels of these proteins. Both protein C and protein S are vitamin K–dependent plasma proteins and are decreased in vitamin K deficiency and during the administration of oral anticoagulants. During disseminated intravascular coagulation, the levels of protein C, protein S, and ATIII drop, presumably because they are consumed in the intravascular clotting process.

### Acquired Protein S Deficiencies

The best characterized acquired deficiency of protein S is that seen during normal pregnancy.[40–42] Both the total and free levels of protein S decrease significantly during pregnancy and can drop to as low as 40% of the normal level. This decrease in protein S may represent a protective mechanism to help ensure that hemorrhage does not occur during pregnancy. The decrease in this natural anticoagulant protein is accompanied by an elevation of plasminogen activator inhibitor II, which results in inhibition of the fibrinolytic system, with a resulting decrease in the body's ability to dissolve blood clots. To determine whether the relative protein S deficiency is a risk factor for thrombophlebitis, which occurs as frequently as one in 1,200 pregnancies, would require an extensive prospective study. The predictable decrease in protein S during pregnancy makes measurement of this natural anticoagulant difficult during pregnancy, and at present there are no standard criteria for making the diagnosis of hereditary protein S deficiency during pregnancy.

Decreased levels of protein S have been reported in diabetes mellitus[43–47] in the majority of studies. Decreased levels of free protein S have been observed in patients with sickle cell disease,[48] as well as in a variety of severely ill hospitalized patients.[21] Decreased protein S levels are found in patients with the acquired immune deficiency syndrome.[49, 50] The mechanism responsible for decreased protein S levels in these conditions is not known, but it may include decreased hepatic synthesis of protein S, as well as a shift of protein S from the free to the bound form because of an elevation of C4b binding protein. The contribution that low protein S levels make to the thrombotic complications associated with these conditions is also unknown and will require prospective examination.

Free protein S deficiency is found in patients with acute stroke.[51–62] Evidence for the transient nature of free protein S deficiency has been provided in a study that examined stroke patients at times well after the acute event. The results showed that free protein S levels were not significantly decreased, compared with those of other hospitalized patients.[63] This suggests that the acute changes seen in protein S status revert to normal as the acute inflammatory effects of the stroke resolve. In addition, a high incidence of stroke is not reported in families with hereditary protein S deficiency, again suggesting that the changes seen following stroke are acquired. The possibility that acutely decreased free protein S levels may contribute to further extension of the stroke needs further examination.

## ANTIBODIES AGAINST PHOSPHOLIPID

Antibodies directed against phospholipid are present in the plasma of certain patients with a history of thrombosis. There are two distinct types of these antibodies—the lupus anticoagulant and antiphospholipid antibodies. The antibodies are defined by the laboratory tests used to detect them. The lupus anticoagulant is an immunoglobulin that binds to the phospholipid used in clotting assays. As a result of this binding, the phospholipid is no longer able to catalyze the clotting reaction, and the clotting time is prolonged. For example, the activated partial thromboplastin time is prolonged from a normal of 29 seconds to 58 seconds. Antiphospholipid antibodies are identified by their ability to bind to immobilized negatively charged phospholipids (for example, cardiolipin and phosphatidylserine) in an enzyme-linked immunoassay.

In patients there is a significant overlap in these antibodies. Approximately one-third of patients have lupus anticoagulant only, one-third have both lupus anticoagulant and anti-phospholipid antibodies, and the remaining one-third have antiphospholipid antibody alone.[64] These antibodies are seen in patients with systemic lupus erythematosus, acute infections including that from human immunodeficiency virus (HIV),[65] and malignancy[66]; in association with various medications including cardiac medications and major tranquilizers; in normal individuals; and in individuals with a history of arterial and venous thrombosis.[67, 68] An association between anticardiolipin antibodies and spontaneous abortions is recognized.[69]

The association between the presence of the lupus anticoagulant and venous and arterial thrombosis has been observed.[67, 68, 70] Unfortunately, these observations have been based on a limited number of cases reviewed retrospectively; the lupus anticoagulant has been detected after the thrombotic complication occurred. Antiphospholipid antibodies have also been detected in patients with venous thrombosis and in patients with stroke. However, again, these antibodies are detected after the clinical event. Given the high frequency with which the lupus anticoagulant and antiphospholipid antibodies are observed in patients with systemic lupus erythematosus (an average prevalence of 34% and 44%, respectively[62]), if the antibodies carry a high risk for the development of thrombotic complications, the complications should be more common in this population than is currently observed clinically. This does not appear to be the case. Similarly, both antibodies are detected in other disease groups, as well as in normal individuals. A marked increased risk of thrombotic complications is not clinically apparent in these individuals. The absence of thrombotic complications in patients who develop antiphospholipid antibodies in response to medication or acute infection further brings into question a causal relationship between these antibodies and the development of thrombosis. Clinical definition of the risk imposed by the lupus anticoagulant and antiphospholipid antibodies will require prospective study, preferably in a study of a large nonselected population. Such a study would help determine if the lupus anticoagulant and antiphospholipid antibodies have a causal relationship to thrombosis or are epiphenomena associated with thrombotic complications.

## CANCER AND VENOUS THROMBOSIS

Patients with cancer are prone to the development of thromboembolism. A variety of proco-

agulant mechanisms may be at work in cancer patients that predispose to blood clot formation.[71–73] The occurrence of deep vein thrombosis in middle-aged or older individuals should raise the clinical suspicion of a possible underlying malignancy.[74–78] At present there is no consensus of how extensive the search for a hidden cancer should be in such patients. At a minimum, a chest radiograph, a stool guaiac test, and a thorough pelvic examination for female patients should be carried out in addition to a comprehensive physical examination.

## TESTING FOR UNDERLYING CAUSES OF THROMBOSIS

An initial workup for an underlying abnormality should include determination of protein S, protein C, ATIII, and, soon, activated protein C resistance.[79, 80] Ideally, a plasma sample should be obtained from a patient presenting with venous thrombosis prior to the initiation of heparin and oral anticoagulation. On this sample, a baseline activated partial thromboplastin time (APTT) should be obtained. This will detect the presence of a lupus anticoagulant and will prevent basing heparin therapy on a prolonged, preheparin APTT. If a patient has an undetected baseline APTT of 80 seconds, the administration of intravenous heparin with a resulting clotting time of 80 seconds represents an inadequate level of anticoagulation.

Protein C and protein S levels drop when oral anticoagulation is started and activated protein C resistance is no longer measurable. ATIII levels are also affected by anticoagulant administration.

If a patient is already receiving oral anticoagulation, the measurement of these factors may wait until several weeks after oral anticoagulation therapy is discontinued. Measuring the ratio of protein C antigen to prothrombin antigen while patients are on oral anticoagulation has been proposed,[81] but such laboratory tests are dependent on very stable oral anticoagulation therapy.

Although many physicians only see a limited number of patients with venous thrombosis, a number of issues should be considered regarding testing for hereditary and acquired abnormalities associated with thrombosis. Clearly, a patient with a third episode of deep vein thrombosis requires longterm oral anticoagulation, regardless of any test results. For a patient with the first episode of deep vein thrombosis, there is no conclusive evidence that patients with an identifiable coagulation abnormality should be treated differently than those without such an abnormality. The possible benefits of preventing some future recurrence of thrombosis may or may not outweigh the risks of bleeding associated with lifetime oral anticoagulation.

Measurement of these coagulation parameters is useful in detecting other affected family members. No firm evidence exists that asymptomatic carriers of these abnormalities should be treated prophylactically for prolonged periods of time. The possible benefits of remaining thrombosis-free versus the risks associated with longterm oral anticoagulation are unknown in this group. Consideration should be given to the possibility that asymptomatic carriers will be labeled as such and that this may affect their future insurability and eligibility for military service. Asymptomatic individuals who are identified can be treated with maximal clot prevention measures at times of particularly high risk, for example, following orthopedic surgery. However, considering all that we do not know about the development of thrombosis, this treatment is wise in the case of the other, ostensibly normal, family members as well. Longterm oral anticoagulation carries significant risks in women of childbearing potential. No information is available on the advisability of prophylactic heparin administration during pregnancy in asymptomatic women with an underlying coagulation abnormality.

## MANAGEMENT OF THROMBOPHILIA

The presence of an identifiable coagulation abnormality predisposing to thrombosis does not alter the clinical management of affected patients. All suspected thromboembolic events must be documented by objective means, both in patients with previous thrombotic episodes and in previously asymptomatic individuals. As with any chronic illness, patient education remains of paramount importance, both in therapy and in recognition of the signs and symptoms of disease.

## REFERENCES

1. Davies MG, Hagen PO: The vascular endothelium. A new horizon. Ann Surg 218:593–609, 1993.
2. Esmon CT: Cell mediated events that control blood coagulation and vascular injury. Annu Rev Cell Biol 9:1–26, 1993.
3. Esmon CT: Molecular events that control the protein C anticoagulant pathway. Thromb Haemost 70:29–35, 1993.
4. Miletich JP, Prescott SM, White R, et al: Inherited predisposition to thrombosis. Cell 72:477–480, 1993.
5. Sala N, Fontcuberta J, Rutllant ML: New biological concepts on coagulation inhibitors. Intensive Care Med 19[Suppl 1]:S3–S7, 1993.
6. Sas G: The Biology of Antithrombins. Boca Raton, FL, CRC Press, 1989.
7. Hirsh J, Piovella F, Pini M: Congenital antithrombin III deficiency. Incidence and clinical features. Am J Med 87:34S–38S, 1989.
8. Meade TW, Cooper J, Miller GJ, et al: Antithrombin III and arterial disease. Lancet 338:850–851, 1991.
9. Hathaway WE: Clinical aspects of antithrombin III deficiency. Semin Hematol 28:19–23, 1991.
10. Tait RC, Walker ID, Davidson JF, et al: Antithrombin III activity in healthy blood donors: Age and sex related changes and prevalence of asymptomatic deficiency. Br J Haematol 75:141–142, 1990.
11. Meade TW, Dyer S, Howarth DJ, et al: Antithrombin III and procoagulant activity: Sex differences and effects of the menopause. Br J Haematol 74:77–81, 1990.
12. Esmon CT: The protein C anticoagulant pathway. Arterioscler Thromb 12:135–145, 1992.
13. Marlar RA, Neumann A: Neonatal purpura fulminans due to homozygous protein C or protein S deficiencies. Semin Thromb Hemost 16:299–309, 1990.
14. Marlar RA, Montgomery RR, Broekmans AW: Diagnosis and treatment of homozygous protein C deficiency. Report of the Working Party on Homozygous Protein C Deficiency of the Subcommittee on Protein C and Protein S, International Committee on Thrombosis and Haemostasis. J Pediatr 114:528–534, 1989.
15. Miletich J, Sherman L, Broze G Jr: Absence of thrombosis in subjects with heterozygous protein deficiency. N Engl J Med 317:991–996, 1987.
16. McGehee WG, Klotz TA, Epstein DJ, et al: Coumarin necrosis associated with hereditary protein C deficiency. Ann Intern Med 101:59–60, 1984.
17. Grimaudo V, Gueissaz F, Hauert J, et al: Necrosis of skin induced by coumarin in a patient deficient in protein S. Br Med J 298:233–234, 1989.
18. Scheffler P, Kiehl R, Braun B, et al: [Thromboembolism complications and coumarin necrosis in a patient with congenital antithrombin III deficiency]. Internist (Berlin) 29:54–57, 1988.
19. Comp PC, Elrod JP, Karzenski S: Warfarin-induced skin necrosis. Semin Thromb Hemost 16:293–298, 1990.
20. Comp PC: Coumarin-induced skin necrosis. Incidence, mechanisms, management and avoidance. Drug Saf 8:128–135, 1993.
21. Sheth SB, Carvalho AC: Protein S and C alterations in acutely ill patients. Am J Hematol 36:14–19, 1991.
22. Powars D, Larsen R, Johnson J, et al: Epidemic meningococcemia and purpura fulminans with induced protein C deficiency. Clin Infect Dis 17:254–261, 1993.
23. Clouse LH, Comp PC: The regulation of hemostasis: The protein C system. N Engl J Med 314:1298–1304, 1986.
24. Comp PC, Nixon RR, Cooper MR, et al: Familial protein S deficiency is associated with recurrent thrombosis. J Clin Invest 74:2082–2088, 1984.
25. Comp PC, Esmon CT: Recurrent venous thromboembolism in patients with a partial deficiency of protein S. N Engl J Med 311:1525–1528, 1984.
26. Dahlback B: Protein S and C4b-binding protein: Components involved in the regulation of the protein C anticoagulant system. Thromb Haemost 66 (1):49–61, 1991.
27. Comp PC, Doray D, Patton D, et al: An abnormal plasma distribution of protein S occurs in functional protein S deficiency. Blood 67:504–508, 1986.
28. Dahlback B, Carlsson M, Svensson PJ: Familial thrombophilia due to a previously unrecognized mechanism characterized by poor anticoagulant response to acti-

vated protein C: Prediction of a cofactor to activated protein C. Proc Natl Acad Sci USA 90:1004–1008, 1993.

29. Dahlback B, Hildebrand B: Inherited resistance to activated protein C is corrected by anticoagulant cofactor activity found to be a property of factor V. Proc Natl Acad Sci USA 91:1396–1400, 1994.

30. Bertina RM, Koeleman BP, Koster T, Rosendaal FR: Mutation in blood coagulation factor V associated with resistance to activated protein C. Nature 369:64–67, 1994.

31. Svensson PJ, Dahlback B: Resistance to activated protein C as a basis for venous thrombosis. N Engl J Med 330:517–522, 1994.

32. Koster T, Rosendaal FR, de Ronde H, et al: Venous thrombosis due to poor anticoagulant response to activated protein C: Leiden Thrombophilia Study. Lancet 342:1503–1506, 1993.

33. Griffin JH, Evatt B, Wideman C, et al: Anticoagulant protein C pathway defective in majority of thrombophilic patients. Blood 82:1989–1993, 1993.

34. Potzsch B, Kawamura H, Preissner KT, et al: Thrombophilia in patients with lupus anticoagulant correlates with the impaired anticoagulant activity of activated protein C but not with decreased activation of protein C (abstract). Blood 80:267, 1992.

35. Nesheim ME, Nichols WL, Cole TL, et al: Isolation and study of an acquired inhibitor of human coagulation factor V. J Clin Invest 77:405–415, 1986.

36. Lane TA, Shapiro SS, Burka ER: Factor V antibody and disseminated intravascular coagulation. Ann Intern Med 89:182–185, 1978.

37. Deguchi K, Tsukada T, Iwasaki E, et al: Late-onset homozygous protein C deficiency manifesting cerebral infarction as the first symptom at age 27. Intern Med 31:922–925, 1992.

38. Pescatore P, Horellou HM, Conard J, et al: Problems of oral anticoagulation in an adult with homozygous protein C deficiency and late onset of thrombosis. Thromb Haemost 69:311–315, 1993.

39. Gerson WT, Dickerman JD, Bovill EG, et al: Severe acquired protein C deficiency in purpura fulminans associated with disseminated intravascular coagulation: Treatment with protein C concentrate. Pediatrics 91:418–422, 1993.

40. Comp PC, Thurnau GR, Welsh J, et al: Functional and immunologic protein S levels are decreased during pregnancy. Blood 68:881–885, 1986.

41. Malm J, Laurell M, Dahlback B: Changes in the plasma levels of vitamin K–dependent proteins C and S and of C4b-binding protein during pregnancy and oral contraception. General Hospital, Sweden. Br J Haematol 68:437–443, 1988.

42. Warwick R, Hutton RA, Goff L, et al: Changes in protein C and free protein S during pregnancy and following hysterectomy. J R Soc Med 82:591–594, 1989.

43. Schwarz HP, Schernthaner G, Griffin JH: Decreased plasma levels of protein S in well-controlled type I diabetes mellitus. Thromb Haemost 57:240, 1987.

44. Saito M, Kumabashiri I, Jokaji H, et al: The levels of protein C and protein S in plasma in patients with type II diabetes mellitus. Thromb Res 52:479–486, 1988.

45. Ceriello A, Giugliano D, Quatraro A, et al: Possible role for increased C4b-binding-protein level in acquired protein S deficiency in type I diabetes. Diabetes 39:447–449, 1990.

46. Takahashi H, Tatewaki W, Wada K, et al: Plasma protein S in disseminated intravascular coagulation, liver disease, collagen disease, diabetes mellitus, and under oral anticoagulant therapy. Clin Chim Acta 182:195–208, 1989.

47. Lee P, Jenkins A, Bourke C, et al: Prothrombotic and antithrombotic factors are elevated in patients with type 1 diabetes complicated by microalbuminuria. Diabet Med 10:122–128, 1993.

48. Francis RB Jr: Protein S deficiency in sickle cell anemia. J Lab Clin Med 111:571–576, 1988.

49. Bissuel F, Berruyer M, Causse X, et al: Acquired protein S deficiency: Correlation with advanced disease in HIV-1-infected patients. J Acquir Immune Defic Syndr 5:484–489, 1992.

50. Stahl CP, Wideman CS, Spira TJ, et al: Protein S deficiency in men with long-term human immunodeficiency virus infection. Blood 81:1801–1807, 1993.

51. Israels SJ, Seshia SS: Childhood stroke associated with protein C or S deficiency. J Pediatr 111:562–564, 1987.

52. Wallis DE, Godwin J: Mitral valve prolapse, cerebral ischemia, and protein S deficiency. Am J Med 84:974, 1988.

53. Sacco RL, Owen J, Tatemichi TK, et al: Protein S deficiency and intracranial vascular occlusion (abstract). Ann Neurol 22:115, 1987.

54. Allaart CF, Aronson DC, Ruys T, et al: Hereditary protein S deficiency in young adults with arterial occlusive disease. Thromb Haemost 64:206–210, 1990.

55. Sacco RL, Owen J, Mohr JP, et al: Free protein S deficiency: A possible association with cerebrovascular occlusion. Stroke 20:1657–1661, 1989.

56. Girolami A, Simioni P, Lazzaro AR, et al: Severe arterial cerebral thrombosis in a patient with protein S deficiency (moderately reduced total and markedly reduced free protein S): A family study. Thromb Haemost 61:144–147, 1989.

57. Green D, Otoya J, Oriba H, et al: Protein S deficiency in middle-aged women with stroke. Neurology 1029–1033, 1992.

58. Comp PC: The natural anticoagulant proteins and cardiovascular disease. In Francis RB (ed): Atherosclerotic Cardiovascular Disease, Hemostasis, and Endothelial Function. New York, Marcel Dekker, 1992, pp 87–106.

59. Barinagarrementeria F, Cantu-Brito C, De La Pena A, et al: Prothrombotic states in young people with idiopathic stroke. A prospective study. Stroke 25:287–290, 1994.

60. Carr ME Jr, Zekert SL: Protein S and C4b-binding protein levels in patients with stroke: Implications for protein S regulation. Haemostasis 23:159–167, 1993.

61. Brown DC, Livingston JH, Minns RA, et al: Protein C and S deficiency causing childhood stroke. Scott Med J 38:114–115, 1993.

62. Coull BM, Clark WM: Abnormalities of hemostasis in ischemic stroke. Med Clin North Am 77:77–94, 1993.

63. Mayer SA, Sacco RL, Hurlet-Jensen A, et al: Free protein S deficiency in acute ischemic stroke. A case-control study. Stroke 24:224–227, 1993.

64. Triplett DA, Brandt J: Laboratory identification of the lupus anticoagulant. Br J Haematol 73:139–142, 1989.

65. Doweiko JP: Management of the hematologic manifestations of HIV disease. Blood Rev 7:121–126, 1993.

66. Kunkel LA: Acquired circulating anticoagulants in malignancy. Semin Thromb Hemost 18:416–423, 1992.

67. Kunkel LA: Acquired circulating anticoagulants. Hematol Oncol Clin North Am 6:1341–1357, 1992.

68. Creagh MD, Greaves M: Lupus anticoagulant. Blood Rev 5:162–167, 1991.

69. Sammaritano LA, Gharavi AE, Lockshin MD: Pregnancy and aPL. Bull Rheum Dis 3–6, 1991.

70. Tobelem G, Cariou R, Camez A: The lupus anticoagulant and its role in thrombosis. Blood Rev 1:21–24, 1987.

71. Dhami MS, Bona RD: Thrombosis in patients with cancer. Postgrad Med 93:131–133, 137–140, 1993.

72. Edwards RL, Silver J, Rickles FR: Human tumor procoagulants: Registry of the Subcommittee on Haemostasis

and Malignancy of the Scientific and Standardization Committee, International Society on Thrombosis and Haemostasis. Thromb Haemost 69:205–213, 1993.

73. Bick RL: Coagulation abnormalities in malignancy: A review. Semin Thromb Hemost 18:353–372, 1992.

74. Gore JM, Appelbaum JS, Greene HL, et al: Occult cancer in patients with acute pulmonary embolism. Ann Intern Med 96:556–560, 1982.

75. Griffin MR, Stanson AW, Brown ML, et al: Deep venous thrombosis and pulmonary embolism. Risk of subsequent malignant neoplasms. Arch Intern Med 147:1907–1911, 1987.

76. Goldberg RJ, Seneff M, Gore JM, et al: Occult malignant neoplasm in patients with deep venous thrombosis. Arch Intern Med 147:251–253, 1987.

77. Prandoni P, Lensing AWA, Buller HR, et al: Deep-vein thrombosis and the incidence of subsequent symptomatic cancer. N Engl J Med 327:1128–1133, 1992.

78. Prandoni P: Deep vein thrombosis and occult cancer. Ann Med 25:447–450, 1993.

79. Comp PC: Laboratory evaluation of protein S status. Semin Thromb Hemost 16:177–181, 1990.

80. Comp PC: Measurement of the natural anticoagulant protein S. How and when. Am J Clin Pathol 94:242–243, 1990.

81. Griffin JH, Evatt B, Zimmerman TS, et al: Deficiency of protein C in congenital thrombotic disease. J Clin Invest 68:1370–1373, 1981.

82. Kolodziej M, Comp PC: Hypercoagulable states due to natural anticoagulant deficiencies. In Anderson JW (ed): Current Opinion in Hematology. Philadelphia, Current Science, 1993, pp 301–307.

# Chapter 33

# Management of Common Thrombotic Disorders During Pregnancy

Karen Valentine, Linda Barbour, Jeffrey Pickard, Russell D. Hull, and Graham F. Pineo

## VENOUS THROMBOEMBOLISM

Thromboembolic disease remains an important cause of obstetric morbidity and mortality. Pulmonary embolism is the leading cause of maternal mortality in Wales and England,[1] and of death after a live birth in the United States.[2] Pregnancy increases the risk of venous thrombosis five-fold.[3] Because the absolute risk is low, very few prospective studies have been published.[4][11] The literature consists of mostly retrospective studies and case reports. Many of the inferences drawn from these data are contradictory.

The purpose of this review is to present the quality of the evidence upon which current recommendations are based and to highlight the reasons for these clinical contradictions. It is hoped that a better understanding of this important complication of pregnancy will lead to multicenter trials addressing the burning issues identified by this report. Our review also provides the clinician with an understanding of the underlying rationale for current clinical practice in this area.

## Methodologic Considerations

In the nonpregnant patient, most of the uncertainties that a clinician commonly encounters in selecting appropriate management for common thrombotic disorders have now been resolved. For example, in the context of venous thromboembolism it has become clear that clinically effective treatment using heparin therapy is dependent on the intensity of the heparin anticoagulant effect as measured by the acti-vated partial thromboplastin time (APTT) or the heparin blood level.[51]

The strength of evidence from clinical trials provides a keystone for making specific recommendations that affect clinical practice.[6] To qualify the strength of the evidence, we have used the "levels of evidence" approach[6] devised by the American College of Chest Physicians for the consensus conference on antithrombotic therapy.

The development of evidence-based[6] guidelines for antithrombotic therapy and prophylactic treatment of women who are pregnant is problematic. This is because there is a complete absence of level I data in the literature to support firm recommendations in this area. Indeed, in the context of pregnancy, much uncertainty remains unless the wealth of literature reporting level I trials evaluating antithrombotic management of the nonpregnant patient is incorporated into the decision-making process. An overriding caveat of using these level I data (from the nonpregnant situation) is the safety of the developing baby (for example, risk of warfarin toxicity), as well as the mother's well-being.

## Epidemiology

The absolute risk in pregnancy of venous thrombosis is small; in women without a prior history of venous thromboembolism, the estimated risk is 0.5 to 3.0 per thousand.[7, 8]

Women with a prior history of venous thromboembolism are considered to be a high-risk group for further events during pregnancy.[9V, 10V]

Venous thromboembolism may occur at any time during pregnancy in addition to the puerperium.[10V, 11, 12, 13V, 14V, 15] The complication of pulmonary embolism may occur more frequently in the postpartum period, particularly in patients undergoing a caesarean section.[7] Peculiar to pregnancy is the striking predilection for pregnancy-associated deep vein thrombosis to occur in the left leg.[10, 16] Factors that may significantly increase the risk of pregnancy-associated thromboembolism are mode of delivery, age and parity, obesity, prolonged hospitalization, operative procedures, underlying hypercoagulable states (e.g., antiphospholipid antibody syndrome), and prior venous thromboembolism.[3, 14V, 17, 18I]

## Diagnosis

Pregnancy compounds the difficulties of clinically differentiating between nonthrombotic disorders and deep vein thrombosis in patients with clinically suspected venous thrombosis.[19] Venography remains the gold standard for making the diagnosis of venous thrombosis, even in pregnancy. The quantity of radiation associated with limited venography (using pelvic shielding) is low (<.05 rads).[20] Two noninvasive methods of diagnosing deep vein thrombosis—impedance plethysmography[16I, 21, 22, 23I, 24, 25I] and duplex ultrasonography—show promise in the pregnant patient. Impedance plethysmography was recently studied prospectively in 152 consecutive pregnant women with clinically suspected deep vein thrombosis.[16I] Patients were studied during the third trimester as they were positioned in the left lateral decubitus position because of possible external compression of the pelvic vessels by the gravid uterus.[16I] Patients with abnormal impedance plethysmographies had their diagnoses confirmed by venography and were treated with anticoagulation. Those women with negative impedance plethysmographies initially were retested on days 1, 3, and 5, or 7, 10, and 14 following the initial examination, and all were followed until 3 months postpartum. Results of impedance plethysmography were negative in 139 of 152 patients who were followed as described above, without any therapy. None of these women developed clinical evidence of pulmonary embolism or deep vein thrombosis, leading the authors to conclude that it is safe to withhold therapy in pregnant women who have negative results after serial impedance plethysmography.

Duplex ultrasonography is a proven noninvasive technique for diagnosing deep vein thrombosis in nonpregnant patients,[22, 23I, 24, 25I] but remains to be evaluated during pregnancy.

The ventilation-perfusion lung scan remains the pivotal test for diagnosing pulmonary embolism during pregnancy; the dose of ionizing radiation is low, particularly if the ventilation scan can be avoided in patients with a normal perfusion scan. The role of pulmonary angiography for diagnosing pulmonary embolism during pregnancy is controversial; its use must be decided on an individual basis while weighing the risks and benefits.

## Anticoagulant Therapy

### Heparin

Classical heparin therapy remains the initial treatment of choice in patients with documented venous thromboembolism.[26, 27I, 28I, 29I] Heparin has the advantage that it is unable to cross the placenta and therefore on pharmacologic evidence, it is very unlikely to affect the fetus. Retrospective studies, however, have reported conflicting observations about the safety of heparin during pregnancy. Investigators in one series concluded that heparin adversely affected fetal outcome. This study did not control for the serious confounding maternal conditions that were present and known to seriously adversely affect the fetus.[30V] A more recent retrospective series controlled for confounding variables and reported that the rate of adverse fetal or neonatal outcomes was similar in pregnant patients treated with heparin to outcomes in those who were not.[31IV]

Because warfarin sodium therapy is contraindicated throughout pregnancy, therapeutic adjusted-dose heparin therapy has become the standard longterm therapy. Patients suffering venous thromboembolism during pregnancy are treated with initial heparin therapy for 6 days followed by adjusted-dose subcutaneous heparin every 12 hours.[32] The duration of long-term therapy is mandated by the need to protect the patient during the remainder of pregnancy and for 4 to 6 weeks postpartum. Subcutaneous heparin therapy every 12 hours is monitored by the APTT, adjusting the midinterval APTT to the therapeutic range.[33I] A special concern arising from the prolonged use of therapeutic doses of heparin is osteoporosis.

Heparin-induced osteoporosis in pregnancy is poorly documented. The literature contains scattered case reports of women with vertebral fractures clinically associated with heparin therapy.[14V, 34, 35] Retrospective studies suggest that approximately 15 to 20% of pregnant women exposed to significant heparin doses may suffer osteoporosis.[36] A recent prospective series using dual photon bone densitometry was done in a small series of 14 pregnant women requiring heparin therapy and 14 pregnant controls matched for age, race, and smoking status.[37IV] Proximal femur measurements were taken at entry during pregnancy, immediately postpartum, and at 6 months postpartum. Five of 14 patients on heparin (36%) developed at least a 10% decrease from their baseline proximal femur measurements to immediate postpartum values as compared with none of the 14 matched controls. Mean proximal femur bone density also decreased in the patients and this difference continued to be statistically significant at 6 months postpartum. No dose-response relationship could be demonstrated, which was similar to findings in Dahlman's study. Pregnancy alone does not appear to affect bone density.[38]

Subcutaneous heparin prophylaxis is recommended during pregnancy and the postpartum period for 4 to 6 weeks in women with a past history of venous thromboembolism.[32] The use of subcutaneous heparin prophylaxis is based on extrapolation from the knowledge that low-dose heparin prophylaxis is effective in other moderate-risk patient groups,[39] and adjusted-dose subcutaneous heparin is effective in high-risk groups.[40I, 41I] It is uncertain whether low-dose or adjusted-dose subcutaneous heparin is required for prophylaxis in pregnant patients.[32] It is well documented by extrapolation from other patient groups at high risk for venous thrombosis that low-dose heparin is relatively ineffective by comparison with adjusted doses of heparin in these high-risk patients.[42I] Current recommendations assume that pregnant patients with prior venous thromboembolism are at moderate risk and should receive low-dose heparin prophylaxis throughout pregnancy and the postpartum period.[32]

## Warfarin

The use of warfarin therapy is contraindicated throughout pregnancy. Warfarin exposure during the first trimester is associated with embryopathies (e.g., stippled epiphyses, nasal and limb hypoplasia).[43] Central nervous system abnormalities including dorsal midline dysplasia (agenesis of the corpus callosum and Dandy-Walker malformations), midline cerebellar atrophy, and ventral midline dysplasia manifested by optic atrophy and hemorrhage have been noted in patients exposed to warfarin in the second trimester.[44] Rates of spontaneous abortions and stillbirths are elevated in the third trimester, probably as a result of hemorrhage.[45V, 46, 47III] A review of 1,325 pregnancies from 186 different studies reported a 16.9% incidence of adverse outcomes with the use of warfarin dur-ing pregnancy after excluding pregnancies with maternal comorbid conditions and prematurity with normal outcomes.[30V] Selection bias may affect the accuracy of this figure.

Warfarin is thought to be safe in women who breast-feed their babies. Studies, although small, have found little or no warfarin activity in breast milk or in the infants' circulation.[48, 49]

## Other Therapies

Streptokinase and urokinase are relatively contraindicated in pregnancy and within the first 10 days after delivery.[50–55] Although little streptokinase crosses the placenta,[56] placental abruption and excessive blood loss in the puerperium have been noted with its use.[57]

Low-molecular-weight heparin promises advantages for antithrombotic therapy or prophylaxis during pregnancy. The long half-life of some of the low-molecular-weight heparin preparations, and the observation that monitoring is not required, offer the possibility of a once-daily subcutaneous approach without monitoring.[58] Low-molecular-weight heparin does not cross the placenta.[59–62III] Additionally, one study suggested a lower risk of osteoporosis when used in the longterm management of nonpregnant individuals.[63V] Low-molecular-weight heparin has been used in a small number of pregnant women who had adverse reactions to heparin.[59–61] Because the molecular weight and activity of low-molecular-weight heparin vary widely depending on the preparation, individual preparations need to be tested independently during pregnancy.

## THROMBOEMBOLIC COMPLICATIONS OF PROSTHETIC HEART VALVES

In pregnant women, prosthetic mechanical valves pose major concerns because of the need for continued therapeutic anticoagulation. Oral anticoagulant therapy is contraindicated during pregnancy yet is the accepted standard of care for preventing valve thrombosis and systemic embolism. At present, the practical alternative is full therapeutic doses of heparin administered subcutaneously and monitored by the APTT to ensure achievement of the therapeutic range. The use of subcutaneous heparin therapy in this context is based on extrapolation of heparin use in other patient groups.[40I, 41I]

Some information is available from observation studies. A study of 156 women with prosthetic valves who had 223 pregnancies suggested that antiplatelet agents alone are inadequate prophylaxis against systemic embolism.[64]

Limited data suggest that adjusted-dose heparin to keep the APTT in the therapeutic range at midinterval may be adequate in preventing thromboembolism,[65, 66I, 67] but considerable uncertainty persists.

## References

1. Department of Health, Welsh Office, Scottish Home and Health Department and Department of Health and Social Services, Northern Ireland: Report on Confidential Enquiries into Maternal Deaths in the United Kingdom 1985–87, London, HMSO, 1991.
2. Atrash HK, Koonin LM, Lawson HW, et al: Maternal mortality in the United States 1979–1986. Obstet Gynecol 76(6):1055–1060, 1990.
3. Bonnar J: Venous thromboembolism in pregnancy. Clin Obstet Gynecol 8(2):455–473, 1981.
II 4. Howell R, Fidler J, Letsky E, et al: The risks of antenatal subcutaneous heparin prophylaxis: A controlled trial. Br J Obstet Gynaecol 90:1124–1128, 1983.
I 5. Hull RD, Raskob GE, Rosenbloom D, et al: Optimal therapeutic level of heparin therapy in patients with venous thrombosis. Arch Intern Med 152:1589–1595, 1992.
6. Cook DJ, Guyatt GH, Laupacis A, et al: Rules of evidence and clinical recommendations on the use of antithrombotic agents. Chest 1024[Suppl]:305S–311S, 1992.
7. Rutherford S, Montoro M, McGehee W, et al: Thromboembolic disease associated with pregnancy: An 11 year review (abstract). Am J Obstet Gynecol 164(1):286, 1991.
8. Dixon JE: Pregnancies complicated by previous thromboembolic disease. Br J Hosp Med 37:449–452, 1987.
V 9. Badaracco MA, Vessey MP: Recurrence of venous thromboembolic disease and use of oral contraceptives. Br Med J 1:215–217, 1974.
V 10. Tengborn L, Bergqvist D, Mätzsch T, et al: Recurrent thromboembolism in pregnancy and puerperium. Am J Obstet Gynecol 28(1):107–118, 1985.
11. Department of Health and Social Services: Report on Confidential Enquiries into Maternal Deaths in England and Wales 1976–1978. London, HMSO, 1980.
12. Aaro LA, Juergens JL: Thrombophlebitis associated with pregnancy. Am J Obstet Gynecol 109(8):1128–1133, 1971.
V 13. Bergqvist A, Bergqvist D, Holböök T: Deep vein thrombosis during pregnancy: A prospective study. Acta Obstet Gynecol Scand 62:443–448, 1983.
V 14. Hellgren M, Nygards EB: Long-term therapy with subcutaneous heparin during pregnancy. Gynecol Obstet Invest 13:76–89, 1982.
15. Ginsberg JS, Brill-Edwards P, Burrows RF, et al: Venous thrombosis during pregnancy: Leg and trimester of presentation. Thromb Haemost 67(5):519–520, 1992.
I 16. Hull RD, Raskob GE, Carter CJ: Serial impedance plethysmography in pregnant patients with clinically suspected deep-vein thrombosis. Ann Intern Med 112:663–667, 1990.
17. de Swiet M: Thromboembolism. Clin Hematol 14(3):643–661, 1985.
I 18. Moseley P, Kerstein M: Pregnancy and thrombophlebitis. Surg Gynecol Obstet 150:593–599, 1980.
19. Lee RV, McComb LE, Mezzadri FC: Pregnant patients, painful legs: The obstetrician's dilemma. Obstet Gynecol Surg 45:290–298, 1990.
20. Ginsberg JS, Hirsh J, Rainbow AJ, Coates G: Risk to the fetus of radiologic procedures used in the diagnosis of maternal thromboembolic disease. Thromb Hemost 61:189–196, 1989.
21. Clarke-Pearson DL, Jelovsek FR: Alterations of occlusive cuff impedance plethysmography results in the obstetric patient. Surgery 89:594–598, 1981.
22. Cronan JJ, Dorfman GS, Scola FH, et al: Deep venous thrombosis: US assessment using vein compressibility. Radiology 162:191–194, 1987.
I 23. Lensing AWA, Prandoni P, Brandjes D, et al: Detection of deep-vein thrombosis by real-time B-mode ultrasonography. N Engl J Med 320:342–345, 1989.
24. Rose ST, Zwiebel WJ, Nelson BD, et al: Symptomatic lower extremity deep venous thrombosis: Accuracy, limitations, and role of colour duplex flow imaging in diagnosis. Radiology 175:639–644, 1990.
I 25. Heijboer H, Buller HR, Lensing AWA, et al: A comparison of real-time compression ultrasonography with impedance plethysmography for the diagnosis of deep-vein thrombosis in symptomatic outpatients. N Engl J Med 329(19):1365–1369, 1993.
26. Hyers TM, Hull RD, Weg J: Antithrombotic therapy for venous thromboembolic disease. Chest 102:408S–425S, 1992.
I 27. Salzman EW, Deykin D, Shapiro RM, et al: Management of heparin therapy: Controlled prospective trial. N Engl J Med 292:1046–1050, 1976.
I 28. Gallus A, Jackaman J, Tillett J, et al: Safety and efficacy of warfarin started early after submassive venous thrombosis or pulmonary embolism. Lancet 2:1293–1296, 1986.
I 29. Hull RD, Raskob GE, Rosenbloom D, et al: Heparin for 5 days as compared with 10 days in the initial treatment of proximal venous thrombosis. N Engl J Med 322:1260–1264, 1990.
V 30. Ginsberg JS, Hirsh J, Turner DC, et al: Risks to the fetus of anticoagulant therapy during pregnancy. Thromb Hemost 61(2):197–203, 1989.
IV 31. Ginsberg JS, Kowalchuk G, Hirsh J, et al: Heparin therapy during pregnancy: Risks to the fetus and mother. Arch Intern Med 149:2233–2236, 1989.
32. Ginsberg JS, Hirsh J. Use of antithrombotic agents during pregnancy. Chest 102(4)[Suppl]:385S–390S, 1992.
I 33. Hull R, Delmore T, Carter C, et al: Adjusted subcutaneous heparin versus warfarin sodium in the long-term treatment of venous thrombosis. N Engl J Med 306:189–193, 1982.
34. Aarskog D, Aksnes L: Low 1,25-dihydroxy vitamin D in heparin-induced osteopenia. Lancet 650–651, 1980.
35. Zimran A, Shilo S, Fisher D, et al: Histomorphometric evaluation of reversible heparin-induced osteoporosis in pregnancy. Arch Intern Med 46:386–388, 1986.
36. Dahlman TC, Lindvall N, Hellgren M: Osteopenia in pregnancy during long-term heparin treatment: A radiological study post partum. Br J Obstet Gynaecol 97:221–228, 1990.
IV 37. Barbour LA, Kick SD, Steiner JF, et al: A prospective study of heparin induced osteoporosis in pregnancy using bone densitometry. Am J Obstet Gynecol 170:862–869, 1994.
38. Sowers M, Crutchfield M, Jannausch M, et al: A

prospective evaluation of bone mineral change in pregnancy. Obstet Gynecol 77(6):841–845, 1991.

39. Collins R, Scrimgeour A, Yusuf S, et al: Reduction in fatal pulmonary embolism and venous thrombosis by perioperative administration of subcutaneous heparin. N Engl J Med 318:1162–1173, 1988.

I 40. Leyvraz PF, Richard J, Bachmann F: Adjusted versus fixed-dose subcutaneous heparin in the prevention of deep vein thrombosis after total hip replacement. N Engl J Med 309:954–958, 1983.

I 41. Hull RD, Delmore TJ, Carter C, et al: Adjusted subcutaneous heparin versus warfarin sodium in the long-term treatment of venous thrombosis. N Engl J Med 306:189–194, 1982.

I 42. Hull RD, Delmore TJ, Genton E, et al: Warfarin sodium versus low-dose heparin in the long-term treatment of venous thrombosis. N Engl J Med 301:855–858, 1979.

43. Hall JG, Pauli RM, Wilson KM: Maternal and fetal sequelae of anticoagulation during pregnancy. Am J Med 68:122–140, 1980.

44. Stevenson RE, Burton OM, Ferlauto GJ, et al: Hazards of oral anticoagulants during pregnancy. JAMA 243:1549–1551, 1980.

V 45. Chen WWC, Chan CS, Lee PK, et al: Pregnancy in patients with prosthetic heart valves: An experience with 45 pregnancies. Q J Med 203:358–365, 1982.

46. Chong MKB, Harvey D, deSwiet M: Follow-up study of children whose mothers were treated with warfarin during pregnancy. Br J Obstet Gynaecol 91:1070–1073, 1984.

III 47. Iturbe-Alesio I, del Carmen Fonseca M, Mutchinik O, et al: Risks of anticoagulant therapy in pregnant women with artificial heart valves. N Engl J Med 22(315):1390–1393, 1986.

48. Orme M, Lewis PJ, deSwiet M, et al: May mothers given warfarin breast-feed their infants? Br Med J 1:1564–1565, 1977.

49. McKenna R, Cole E, Vasan U: Is warfarin sodium contraindicated in the lactating mother? J Pediatr 103(2):325–327, 1983.

50. Pfeifer GW: The use of thrombolytic therapy in obstetrics and gynaecology. Australas Ann Med 19 [Suppl]:28–31, 1970.

51. McTaggart DR, Engram TG: Massive pulmonary embolism during pregnancy treated with streptokinase. Med J Aust 1:18–20, 1977.

52. Amias AG: Streptokinase, cerebral vascular disease—and triplets. Br Med J 1:1414–1415, 1977.

53. Delclos GL, Davila F: Thrombolytic therapy for pulmonary embolism in pregnancy: A case report. Am J Obstet Gynecol 155:375–376, 1986.

54. Hall RJC, Young C, Sutton GC, et al: Treatment of acute massive pulmonary embolism by streptokinase during labor and delivery. Br Med J 4:647–649, 1972.

55. Birger F, Mats A, Birger A: Acute massive pulmonary embolism treated with streptokinase during labor and the early puerperium. Acta Obstet Gynecol Scand 69:659–662, 1990.

56. Pfeifer GW: Distribution and placental transfer of [131]I streptokinase. Australas Ann Med 19[Suppl]:17–18, 1970.

57. Fagher B, Ahlgren M, Astedt B: Acute massive pulmonary embolism treated with streptokinase during labor and the early puerperium. Acta Obstet Gynecol Scand 69:659–662, 1990.

58. Hirsh J, Levine MN: Low molecular weight heparin. Blood 79:1–17, 1992.

59. de Boer K, Heyboer H, ten Cate JW, et al: Low molecular weight heparin treatment in a pregnant woman with allergy to standard heparins and heparanoid. Thromb Haemost 61(1):148, 1989.

60. Priollet P, Roncato M, Aiach M, et al: Low molecular-weight heparin in venous thrombosis during pregnancy. Br J Haematol 63:605–606, 1986.

61. Henny CP, ten Cate H, ten Cate JW, et al: Thrombosis prophylaxis in an AT-III deficient pregnant woman: Application of a low molecular weight heparinoid. Thromb Haemost 55:301, 1986.

III 62. Omri A, Delaloye JF, Anderson H, et al: Low molecular weight heparin Novo (LHN-1) does not cross the placenta during the second trimester of pregnancy. Thromb Haemost 61(1):55–56, 1989.

V 63. Monreal M, Lafoz E, Olive A, et al: Comparison of subcutaneous unfractionated heparin with a low molecular weight heparin (Fragmin) in patients with venous thromboembolism and contraindications to coumarin. Thromb Haemost 71:7–11, 1994.

64. Salazar E, Zajarias A, Gutierrez N, et al: The problem of cardiac valve prostheses, anticoagulants and pregnancy. Circulation 70[Suppl I]:169–177, 1984.

65. Levine HJ, Pauker SE, Salzman EW: Antithrombotic therapy in valvular heart disease. Chest 89[Suppl 2]:36S–45S, 1986.

I 66. Wang RYC, Lee PK, Chow JSF, et al: Efficacy of low dose, subcutaneously administered heparin in treatment of pregnant women with artifical heart valves. Med J Aust 2:126–128, 1983.

67. Chesebro JH, Adams PC, Fuster V: Antithrombotic therapy in patients with valvular heart disease. J Am Coll Cardiol 8(6[Suppl B]):41B–56B, 1986.

# Chapter 34

# Anticoagulants and Bone Demineralization

David A. Hanley and Melvin A. Andersen

The two major classes of drugs used for long-term anticoagulant therapy in clinical medicine, heparin and the coumarin derivatives, may both have significant effects on bone. As the clinical indications for their use expand, it becomes increasingly important to understand their potential interactions with bone, and if longterm use of these drugs is planned, the potential for development of metabolic bone disease (specifically, osteopenia) must be examined. This chapter briefly reviews normal bone physiology and some of the experimental data on anticoagulants and bone, and concludes with a discussion of clinical bone disorders that may be related to the use of anticoagulants.

## NORMAL BONE PHYSIOLOGY

Bone tissue is predominantly composed of extracellular matrix, with only a very small cellular component. The bone matrix primarily consists of type I collagen, which is uniquely layered so that the collagen fibrils overlap each other with spaces left where the inorganic matrix mineral crystal is incorporated into the structure. The mineral of bone is predominantly a complex calcium phosphate crystal, similar to hydroxyapatite, but also containing small amounts of sodium, magnesium, potassium, zinc, citrate, and carbonate. About 10% of the matrix is made up of a variety of noncollagen proteins, some of which are thought to play significant roles in the regulation of mineralization of bone. At least two of these proteins, osteocalcin and matrix GLA protein, require vitamin K for normal synthesis and may therefore be affected by use of coumarin anticoagulants (see later).

Collagen and most of the other matrix proteins of bone are synthesized by the *osteoblast*, a cell of mesenchymal origin. As these cells lay down the normal bone matrix, they eventually become surrounded by matrix and are then termed osteocytes. The osteocyte appears to maintain communication with the bone-forming surface through the extracellular fluid in canaliculi, and the osteocyte may serve the function of rapidly mobilizing calcium from bone adjacent to the osteocyte into the extracellular fluid and the circulation. It has been speculated that the osteocyte may be the cell that senses physical strains within bone tissue and modulates bone modeling and remodeling in response to biomechanical factors.[1]

The other major cell of bone is the *osteoclast,* which is a multinucleated cell of probable monocyte/macrophage origin. These migratory cells are stimulated to enter a small localized area of bone and begin the process of resorption of bone. This is done by the release of acid, acid hydrolases, and acid phosphatase into the underlying bone matrix. It is presumed that the osteoclast is recruited to the area for bone resorption in response to a signal from osteoblasts in the same area. This process of recruitment involves differentiation of the osteoclast from precursor cells and activation of the bone resorption function of the cells. The osteoclasts resorb bone down to a preset depth, then osteoblastic activity takes over. New bone matrix is synthesized, mineralized, and approximately the same amount of bone that was removed is restored. The packet of bone that undergoes this cycle is often referred to as a basic structural unit or basic multicellular unit of bone. In the adult skeleton, this process is termed remodeling, and the sequence of resorption followed by formation is followed in normal and even many abnormal states of bone physiology, such as Paget's disease of bone. Bone resorption and formation are said to be "coupled." Abnormal loss of bone occurs whenever bone resorption exceeds formation, or if the processes become uncoupled so that bone resorption proceeds without subsequent bone formation. The latter set of circumstances may occur in heparin-induced osteoporosis.

On a macroscopic level, two major forms of bone are present, including trabecular (also called cancellous or spongy bone) and cortical bone. Trabecular bone also contains marrow, is more actively remodeled, and is found primarily in the axial skeleton (vertebral bodies) and ends of long bones. Cortical bone is the extremely dense thick outer layer of long bones, providing major structural support and protection against fracture from bending forces. Cortical bone remodels much more gradually than trabecular bone, which can be turned over at a rate of more than 5% per year in some parts of the skeleton. A good review of normal bone physiology is available to readers.[2]

## HEPARIN EFFECTS ON BONE

A number of studies, in vitro and in vivo, indicate that heparin increases osteoclast activity and bone resorption.[3–5] Earlier work suggested that heparin may do this through potentiating the effects of parathyroid hormone (PTH) on bone,[6] but this line of investigation has not been pursued. Heparin may certainly amplify the effect of factors that may be found in serum, such as PTH or osteoclast resorption stimulating activity (ORSA),[8] but the studies by Chowdhury and coworkers[4] suggest an independent effect of heparin on chick and rat osteoclasts, increasing the number of differentiated (multinucleated) osteoclasts, and increasing the resorption activity of osteoclasts as measured by resorption pits per osteoclast number in bone slices. How heparin actually stimulates differentiation of the osteoclasts or increases activity is not known, but its acidic nature and its structural similarity to heparan sulphate[9] suggest that it may create a favorable environment for osteoclast adhesion to bone surfaces and subsequent bone resorption.

As noted earlier, bone resorption is normally coupled with subsequent bone formation. However, there is in vitro evidence that heparin reduces collagen synthesis and bone formation in cultures of fetal rat calvaria.[10, 11] This combination of increased bone resorption with reduced bone formation would be particularly hazardous to skeletal health.

Because of the association between heparin therapy and bone disease, there has been an interest in whether the newer low-molecular-weight heparins (LMWH) have effects on bone. Simmons and Raisz[12] recently examined the effect of LMWH on bone resorption induced by acid and basic fibroblast growth factor, two growth factors that are known to bind heparin. In the presence of LMWH, these growth factors stimulated $^{45}Ca$ release from cultured fetal rat long bone, suggesting that LMWH, like standard preparations of heparin, also is associated with increased bone resorption. Similarly, Hurley and coworkers[11] demonstrated that several LMWHs and standard heparin preparations had similar inhibitory effects on collagen synthesis, suggesting that LMWHs are unlikely to offer a bone-sparing advantage over standard heparin. Mätzsch and coworkers found that when the dose of unfragmented heparin is matched with LMWH with respect to factor Xa inhibitory activity, the two forms of heparin were equipotent in causing osteoporosis on a rat model of heparin-induced osteoporosis.[13] This study also found reduced zinc content in bone ash of heparin-treated rats.

## VITAMIN K AND BONE

Vitamin K metabolism and the effects of the coumarin derivatives on gamma carboxylation of glutamic acid–containing proteins are reviewed elsewhere in this volume. The role of vitamin K in skeletal metabolism has been reviewed.[14] A deficiency of vitamin K (or the use of coumarin derivatives) results in the reduction in gamma carboxylation of glutamic acid residues in a variety of vitamin K–dependent proteins, and gamma carboxylation is probably a key to the function of these molecules. Effects of this deficiency would predictably be seen in two of the major noncollagen proteins of bone—osteocalcin (OC) and matrix GLA protein (MGP)—both of which are gamma carboxylated. Much more is known about OC than MGP in this regard. A third vitamin K–dependent protein, protein S, has been shown to be synthesized and secreted by osteoblast cell lines and has been extracted from human bone matrix,[15] but the significance of its presence in bone is not known.

Delmas and coworkers have called attention to the finding of incompletely carboxylated OC in patients with osteoporosis,[16, 17] and this could be presumed to be a consequence of either vitamin K deficiency or a resistance to vitamin K–mediated gamma carboxylation of OC. Furthermore, several studies have demonstrated reduced blood levels of vitamin K in patients with osteoporosis.[18, 19] Vitamin K treatment of postmenopausal women with low levels of circulating osteocalcin and elevated urinary calcium excretion (suggesting reduced bone formation and increased bone resorption) corrected these abnormalities,[20] and preliminary studies suggest that vitamin K may have use as an osteoporosis therapy.[21] In vitro studies of osteoblasts in culture indicate that vitamin $K_2$ has a stimulatory effect on osteoblast proliferation and functions.[22] Hara and coworkers have recently demonstrated that the vitamin K metabolite menatetrenone inhibits interleukin-1–induced bone resorption in mouse calvaria.[23] These findings suggest that vitamin K may have a role in stimulating bone formation and reducing bone resorption, which obviously implies a beneficial effect of vitamin K on the maintenance of bone mass.

## CLINICAL BONE DISORDERS RELATED TO ANTICOAGULANTS

### Heparin

In the late 1950s and early 1960s, chronic subcutaneous heparin therapy was fairly widely used in the treatment and secondary prevention of ischemic cardiac and cerebrovascular disease. The more recent resurgence of interest in a role for anticoagulants in the prevention of these disorders makes a better understanding of anticoagulant-associated osteopenia of great clinical importance. The first systematic documentation of a link between heparin and osteoporosis was published in 1965.[24] Griffith and coworkers reviewed their experience with patients receiving self-administered chronic subcutaneous heparin for recurrent thrombophlebitis as well as coronary artery disease and cerebrovascular disease. This paper is the origin of the generally held view that daily doses of heparin under 15,000 U are not associated with heparin-induced osteoporosis. Of 117 patients, the authors identified 10 who were treated with 15,000 U of heparin per day or more. In this group (which, interestingly, included six physicians and one nurse), six patients suffered spontaneous vertebral and/or rib fractures. The other four were treated prophylactically with calcium supplements and "anabolic steroids." None of the 107 patients who received less than 15,000 U per day experienced fractures. No measures of bone density were available to the authors, so it cannot be known with certainty that bone was not compromised at the lower heparin doses.

Most individuals receiving longterm subcutaneous heparin have been pregnant women who have had deep vein thrombosis and pulmonary embolism. Most of the literature has consisted of case reports of a significant fracturing osteoporosis in these patients,[25–27] including one report of osteoporotic fractures in a patient receiving 10,000 U of heparin daily during pregnancy.[28] More recently, larger series of patients have been reported,[29, 30] including two prospective case-controlled studies in pregnancy.[31, 32] The latter two reports include the use of bone density measurements as an endpoint, rather than osteoporotic fracture. The first of these two studies, by Barbour and coworkers,[31] assessed 14 women who were started on heparin therapy (mean dose 12,000–21,000 U daily) at 20 weeks gestation because of a prior history of venous thromboembolism. A comparable group of controls was also studied. The authors measured proximal femur bone density by dual energy x-ray absorptiometry at the time of recruitment into the study, at 30 to 34 weeks gestation, immediately postpartum, and at 6 months postpartum. Mean proximal femur bone density decreased in the treated patients compared with controls ($p<.01$), and this difference remained significant 6 months postpartum ($p<.03$). Five of the 14 heparin-treated patients showed a 10% or greater decline in bone density during heparin therapy, compared with none of the control subjects ($p<.04$). This study raises the possibility that recovery of bone after treatment with heparin may not be complete.

The second study, by Dahlman and coworkers,[32] measured single photon bone densitometry of the distal (cortical bone) and ultradistal (trabecular bone) radius in 39 consecutive women treated with heparin (average dose 17,300 U daily) for a mean of 28 weeks during pregnancy and 6 weeks postpartum. A control group of 34 women matched for age, height, weight, parity, and smoking habits was also studied. In the heparin group, there was a 5% decline in trabecular bone during heparin therapy ($p<.01$), and a tendency to recover the bone loss following cessation of therapy was also seen.

Mechanism of bone loss in heparin-induced osteoporosis has not been well established, but based on the animal and bone cell culture studies outlined earlier, an imbalance of bone remodeling can be predicted, with increased bone resorption and a concomitant decrease in bone formation, resulting in accelerated bone loss. Interestingly, heparin may also affect vitamin D metabolism. Aarskog and coworkers found reduced levels of 1,25-dihydroxy-vitamin D in heparin-treated patients.[25, 33] If there is reduced formation of 1,25-dihydroxy-vitamin D, reduced calcium absorption and increased parathyroid hormone synthesis and subsequent secretion may be expected,[34] further increasing the likelihood of bone resorption.

The issue of whether a specific dose-relationship exists for heparin-induced osteoporosis has not been settled, although it appears dose and duration of heparin therapy are important variables in the development of the bone disease. Results of most clinical studies seem to suggest that the daily "threshold dose" for the risk of development of fractures is around 10,000 to 15,000 U of heparin, with greater than 3 months duration of therapy. Although several studies have been unable to establish a clear dose-relationship for heparin's effect on bone,[31, 35] the weight of available evidence suggests increased osteoporosis risk with higher doses, especially more than 15,000 U per day for more than 1 month. It is hoped that the use of LMWH may allow lower doses of actual heparin activity and perhaps prevent the bone risks of chronic heparin therapy. One study of chronic LMWH use in pregnancy (from very early pregnancy to at least 12 weeks postpartum) suggested that the drug could be used safely from the standpoint of fetal development, and bone density measured after therapy was not significantly different from that of matched control subjects.[36] However, this trial was not designed to examine changes in bone density during therapy, and there are animal and in vitro data to suggest that LMWH may have deleterious effects on bone.[11, 13]

The more recent development of sensitive measurements of bone-related variables such as bone density and biochemical markers of bone turnover has allowed better assessment of the clinical effects of heparin dose on bone. The above studies of bone density demonstrated a significant effect of heparin even though no fractures occurred.[31, 32, 35] A short-term study of the effects of 5,000 U of heparin twice daily for 10 days in six normal male adult volunteers found no effect on urinary hydroxyproline or serum type I collagen crosslink C-terminal telopeptide, two biochemical markers of bone resorption. However, there was a small but significant fall in alkaline phosphatase, a marker of bone formation.[37]

To summarize, almost all of the osteoporotic fractures associated with heparin use have been reported in uncontrolled retrospective studies or isolated case reports. Prospective studies of heparin effects on bone are starting to appear,[31, 32] but these studies must rely on matching their treatment group with similar untreated control subjects. There has been one randomized controlled trial of heparin prophylaxis in 40 pregnant women.[38] This study found one case of symptomatic osteoporosis in the 20 patients who received 20,000 U of heparin daily. The numbers of patients in this study is too small to make predictions of the incidence of heparin-induced osteoporosis, and present clinical guidelines for anticoagulant use in pregnancy make a randomized placebo-controlled trial of heparin in pregnancy unethical. The only way to perform a randomized prospective controlled trial examining heparin osteopenia is to compare heparin therapy with an anticoagulant that does not have a significant effect on bone. The coumarin derivatives do not meet this criterion, and because of the close ties between proteins involved in coagulation and the noncollagen matrix proteins of bone, it is unlikely that a new anticoagulant without bone effects will be available in the near future.

The prospect of heparin-induced osteopenia is important because of the increasing indications for chronic heparin therapy, and the effects of age on bone mass. It is believed that peak bone mass is attained at around age 25 to 35 years. After that, a gradual age-related decline in measured bone density occurs. After a certain age we do not seem to be able to fully replace bone that has been resorbed as part of the normal remodeling process.[2] Age-related loss of bone (and risk of osteoporotic fracture) is greater in those individuals who have a higher overall rate of bone turnover, or those who have had times of increased bone turnover such as menopause or courses of bone-depleting drugs such as corticosteroids. Patients over the age of attainment of peak bone mass who lose bone because of heparin therapy may not restore this loss, and prolonged heparin therapy may therefore increase the risk of later symptomatic osteoporosis even if it does not cause serious problems while it is being administered. Although in some studies it appears that recovery of bone does occur after completion of heparin treatment,[27, 31, 32] the extent of recovery is not certain, with one study of heparin use in pregnancy showing persistent cortical bone loss 24 weeks after the heparin was stopped.[30]

No specific therapy of heparin-induced osteoporosis can be recommended. General measures, such as assurance of adequate calcium and vitamin D intake are appropriate. One small randomized study of heparin use in pregnancy (6 months of treatment) found preservation of bone mass in nine women receiving a unique calcium supplement, Ossein-hydroxyapatite (available in Europe), whereas 11 patients who did not receive the supplement had a significant loss of bone mass.[39] Because heparin-induced bone disease is primarily associated with increased bone resorption, a case may be made for treatment or prevention with an anti-resorptive therapy such as a bisphosphonate or calcitonin.[40] However, the bisphosphonates are contraindicated in pregnancy, and even if calcitonin were approved for use in pregnancy, its usual route of administration (injection) would not make it favored by patients receiving anticoagulants.

It seems clear that prolonged heparin therapy of more than 3 months duration, using dose levels often required for effective anticoagulant effect, is likely to cause some degree of osteopenia, and rarely some patients may develop fractures. Clinicians must be aware of this potential serious problem. More research is needed in several key areas, including pathogenesis, dose-relationship, prediction of risk for individual patients, and development of prevention and treatment strategies.

## Coumarin Derivatives

A large literature is developing that indicates a role for vitamin K in normal skeletal physiology, and there is a serious fetal bone developmental abnormality caused by warfarin.[41] Therefore a significant potential exists for deleterious effects of coumarin derivatives on the skeleton. Despite this, few studies exist indicating that use of coumarin derivatives for anticoagulant therapy may be associated with bone disease. Fiore and coworkers studied 56 women receiving acenocoumarol as an anticoagulant following aortic valve surgery and found that they had significantly reduced bone density when compared with 61 similar patients not taking oral anticoagulants.[42] They found no difference between the groups in serum levels of the vitamin K–dependent protein, osteocalcin (OC), but they did not have access to techniques to examine whether there was decreased gamma-carboxylation of OC in the coumarin-treated group. Other investigators have found low OC levels in phenprocoumon-treated patients, and a reduction in proportional carboxylation of OC in the treated group.[43] However, no evidence of clinical bone disease was present in these patients. Warfarin has also been shown to impair carboxylation of osteocalcin in humans.[44] Plantalech and coworkers found that young patients on chronic warfarin therapy had levels of undercarboxylated OC similar to those found in elderly osteoporotic women.[17] At present, there is a need for large well-designed studies to address the issue of whether coumarins

can be implicated in the development of bone disease, because of the renewed interest in long-term anticoagulant therapy.

## REFERENCES

1. Lanyon LE: Biomechanical properties of bone and response of bone to mechanical stimuli: Functional strain as a controlling influence on bone modelling and remodelling behavior. In Hall BK, (ed): Bone, vol. 3: Bone Matrix and Bone Specific Products. Boca Raton, FL, CRC Press, 1991, pp 79–108.
2. Aurbach GD, Marx SJ, Spiegel AM: Metabolic bone disease. In Wilson JD, Foster DW, (eds): Williams Textbook of Endocrinology, ed 8. Philadelphia, WB Saunders, 1992, pp 1477–1516.
3. Glowacki J: The effects of heparin and protamine on resorption of bone particles. Life Sci 33:1019–1024, 1983.
4. Chowdhury MH, Hamada C, Dempster DW: Effects of heparin on osteoclast activity. J Bone Min Res 7:771–777, 1992.
5. Mätzsch T, Bergqvist D, Hedner U, Nilsson B, Østergaard P: Heparin-induced osteoporosis in rats. Thromb Haemostas 56:293–294, 1986.
6. Goldhaber P: Heparin enhancement of factors stimulating bone resorption in tissue culture. Science 147:407–408, 1965.
7. Wolinsky I, Cohn DV: The stimulation by heparin and parathyroid hormone of bone resorption in tissue culture. Israel J Med Sci 6:691–696, 1970.
8. Fuller K, Chambers TJ, Gallagher AC: Heparin augments osteoclast resorption-stimulating activity in serum. J Cell Physiol 147:208–214, 1991.
9. Gallagher JT, Lyon M, Steward WP: Structure and function of heparin sulfate proteoglycans. Biochem J 236:313–325, 1986.
10. Hurley MM, Gronowicz G, Kream BE, Raisz LG: Effect of heparin on bone formation in cultured fetal rat calvaria. Calcif Tiss Int 46:183–188, 1990.
11. Hurley MM, Kream BE, Raisz LG: Structural determinants of the capacity of heparin to inhibit collagen synthesis in 21 day fetal rat calvariae. J Bone Min Res 5:1127–1133, 1990.
12. Simmons HA, Raisz LG: Effects of acid and basic fibroblast growth factor and heparin on resorption of cultural fetal rat long bones. J Bone Miner Res 6:1301–1305, 1991.
13. Mätzsch T, Bergqvist D, Hedner U, et al: Effects of low molecular weight heparin and unfragmented heparin on induction of osteoporosis in rats. Thromb Haemostas 63:505–509, 1990.
14. Rosen HN, Maitland LA, Suttie JW, et al: Vitamin K and maintenance of skeletal integrity in adults. Am J Med 94:62–68, 1993.
15. Maillard C, Berruyer M, Serre CM, et al: Protein-S, a vitamin K-dependent protein, is a bone matrix component synthesized and secreted by osteoclasts. Endocrinology 130:1599–1604, 1992.
16. Szulc P, Chapuy MC, Meunier PJ, Delmas PD: Serum undercarboxylated osteocalcin as a marker of the risk of hip fracture in elderly women. J Clin Invest 91:1769–1774, 1993.
17. Plantalech L, Guillaumont M, Leclerq M, Delmas PD: Impaired carboxylation of serum osteocalcin in elderly women. J Bone Min Res 6:1211–1216, 1991.
18. Hart JP, Catterall A, Dodds RA, et al: Circulating vitamin K₁ levels in fractured neck of the femur. Lancet 2(8397):283, 1984.

19. Hodges SJ, Pilkington MJ, Stamp TCB, et al: Depressed levels of circulating menaquinones in patients with osteoporotic fractures of the spine and femoral neck. Bone 12:387–389, 1991.

20. Knapen MHJ, Hamulyak K, Vermeer L: The effect of vitamin K supplementation on circulating osteocalcin (bone Gla protein) and urinary calcium excretion. Ann Intern Med 111:1001–1005, 1989.

21. Orimo H, Fujita T, Onomura T, et al: Clinical evaluation of vitamin K in the treatment of involutional osteoporosis. In Christiansen C, Riis B (eds): Proceedings of the Fourth International Symposium on Osteoporosis, Hong Kong, 1993. Handelstrykkeriet Aalborg Aps, Aalborg, Denmark, 1993, pp 148–149.

22. Akedo Y, Hosoi T, Inoue S, et al: Vitamin $K_2$ modulates proliferation and function of osteoblastic cells in vitro. Biochem Biophys Res Comm 187(2):814–820, 1992.

23. Hara K, Akiyama Y, Tajima T, Shiraki M: Menatetrenone inhibits bone resorption partly through inhibition of $PGE_2$ synthesis in vitro. J Bone Miner Res 8:535–542, 1993.

24. Griffith GC, Nichols G Jr, Asher JD, Flanagan B: Heparin osteoporosis. JAMA 193:91–94, 1965. (See also editorial p 152, same issue.)

25. Aarskog D, Aksnes L, Lehmann V: Low 1,25-dihydroxyvitamin D in heparin-induced osteoporosis. Lancet 2:650–651, 1980.

26. Wise PH, Hall AJ: Heparin-induced osteoporosis in pregnancy. Br Med J 281:110–111, 1980.

27. Zimran A, Shilo S, Fisher D, Bab I: Histomorphometric evaluation of reversible heparin-induced osteoporosis in pregnancy. Arch Intern Med 146:386–388, 1976.

28. Griffith HT, Liu DTY: Severe heparin osteoporosis in pregnancy. Postgrad Med J 60:424–425, 1984.

29. Rupp WM, McCarthy HB, Rohde TD, et al: Risk of osteoporosis in patients treated with long-term intravenous heparin therapy. Curr Surg 39:419–422, 1982.

30. deSwiet M, Dorrington Ward P, Fidler J, et al: Prolonged heparin therapy in pregnancy causes bone demineralization. Br J Obstet Gynaecol 90:1129–1134, 1983.

31. Barbour LA, Kick SD, Steiner JF, et al: A prospective study of heparin-induced osteoporosis in pregnancy using bone densitometry. Am J Obstet Gynecol 170:862–869, 1994.

32. Dahlman TC, Sjöberg HE, Ringertz H: Bone mineral density during long-term prophylaxis with heparin in pregnancy. Am J Obstet Gynecol 170:1315–1320, 1994.

33. Aarskog D, Aksnes L, Markestad T, et al: Heparin-induced inhibition of 1,25-dihydroxyvitamin D formation. Am J Obstet Gynecol 148:1141–1142, 1984.

34. Watson PH, Hanley DA: Parathyroid hormone: Regulation of synthesis and secretion. Clin Invest Med 16:58–77, 1993.

35. Ginsberg JS, Kowalchuk G, Hirsh J, et al: Heparin effect on bone density. Thromb Haemostas 64:286–289, 1990.

36. Melissari E, Parker CJ, Wilson NV, et al: Use of low molecular weight heparin in pregnancy. Thromb Haemostas 68:652–656, 1992.

37. van der Wiel HE, Lips P, Huijgens PC, Netelenbos JC: Effects of short-term low-dose heparin administration on biochemical parameters of bone turnover. Bone Miner 22:27–32, 1993.

38. Howell R, Fidler J, Letsky E, de Swiet M: The risk of antenatal subcutaneous heparin prophylaxis: A controlled trial. Br J Obstet Gynaecol 90:1124–1128, 1983.

39. Ringe JD, Keller A: Risk of osteoporosis in long-term heparin therapy of thromboembolic diseases in pregnancy: attempted prevention with ossein-hydroxyapatite. Geburtshilfe Frauenheilkd 52:426–429, 1992.

40. Riggs BL, Melton LJ: Drug therapy: The prevention and treatment of osteoporosis. N Engl J Med 327:620–627, 1992.

41. Hall JG, Pauli RM, Wilson KM: Maternal and fetal sequelae of anticoagulation during pregnancy. Am J Med 68:122–140, 1980.

42. Fiore CE, Tamburino C, Foti R, Grimaldi D: Reduced axial bone mineral content in patients taking an oral anticoagulant. South Med J 83:538–542, 1990.

43. Pietschmann P, Woloszczuk W, Panzer S, et al: Decreased serum osteocalcin levels in phenprocoumon-treated patients. J Clin Endocrinol Metab 66:1071–1074, 1988.

44. Menon RK, Gill DS, Thomas M, et al: Impaired carboxylation of osteocalcin in warfarin-treated patients. J Clin Endocrinol Metab 64:59–61, 1987.

# Chapter 35

# Heparin-associated Thrombocytopenia

James N. George

Heparin-associated thrombocytopenia is common, yet its pathogenesis remains undefined. Prospective studies have demonstrated the occurrence of decreased platelet counts with heparin administration, occasionally to very low levels, but the estimated frequency of thrombocytopenia varies widely. The clinical manifestations of heparin-associated thrombocytopenia are also extremely variable, from common, minimal, and transient decreases of the platelet count to reports of severe thrombocytopenia that may be accompanied by arterial thromboembolism and disseminated intravascular coagulation (DIC). Consistent with the variable clinical manifestations is uncertainty about the etiology. Minimal, transient thrombocytopenia may be caused by heparin-induced platelet aggregation; severe thrombocytopenia may involve heparin-dependent antibodies. Laboratory assays for heparin-dependent antibodies have been developed, but their interpretation and clinical role remain undefined. Contributing to the uncertainty about heparin-associated thrombocytopenia is the inconsistency of clinical observations over the past 30 years, with dramatic abnormalities in early reports yet negligible impact on current clinical practice.

## HISTORY

### Thrombocytopenia Associated With Heparin

The effect of heparin on blood platelets was initially investigated by Copley and Robb in 1942[1] to determine if heparin's therapeutic activity was related to inhibition of platelet procoagulant activity, specifically by diminishing the platelet count. The first experiments demonstrated that collection of dog blood in heparin, 10 U/ml, resulted in consistently lower platelet counts compared with blood anticoagulated with sodium citrate.[1] In subsequent experiments, some dogs given intravenous heparin, 100 or 200 U/kg, became thrombocytopenic, decreasing their platelet counts by up to 40%.[2] Thrombocytopenia occurred within a few minutes and spontaneously recovered within 2 hours, a pattern parallel to the prolongation of the whole blood clotting time (Fig. 35–1).[2] These observations were confirmed in 1948 by Fidlar and Jaques,[3] who also demonstrated thrombocytopenia in dogs given heparin. All dogs became thrombocytopenic, but there was marked individual variability and little or no correlation between the dose of heparin (50 to 1,500 U/kg) and the resulting thrombocytopenia. Continuous heparin injection resulted in continued thrombocytopenia, an observation that suggested to the authors "that as long as heparin remained in the blood stream the (platelet) counts would remain depressed." The effect of heparin on the platelet count was reproduced by injection of heparin into Dr. Jacques, 40 U/kg intravenously on one occasion and 40 U/kg subcutaneously on another.[3] His platelet count fell from 255,000/μl to 155,000/μl at 7 minutes after the intravenous injection and recovered to 255,000/μl at 30 minutes; after the subcutaneous injection his platelet count fell from 190,000/μl to 90,000/μl at 150 minutes and recovered in 43 hours. In the same year, Quick, Shanberge, and Stefanini[4] performed similar experiments in dogs and two of the authors. No thrombocytopenia occurred in the human subjects, at doses of approximately 80 U/kg, but in dogs heparin injections at doses above 55 U/kg, from five different manufacturers, caused reproducible, transient thrombocytopenia. Platelet clumping was observed within 1 minute of the heparin injection, maximal thrombocytopenia occurred at 5 minutes, and

359

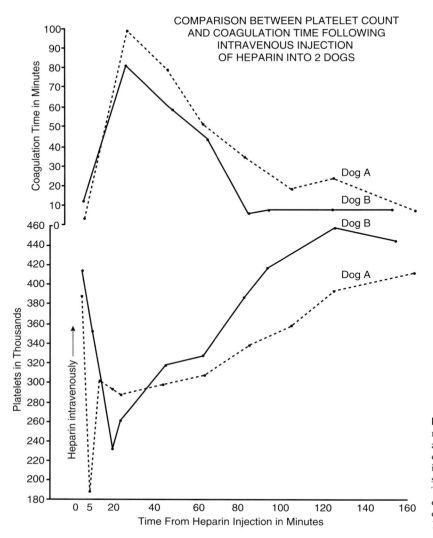

COMPARISON BETWEEN PLATELET COUNT
AND COAGULATION TIME FOLLOWING
INTRAVENOUS INJECTION
OF HEPARIN INTO 2 DOGS

**Figure 35–1.** Effect of an intravenous bolus administration of heparin, 100 U/kg, on whole blood clotting times and platelet counts in two dogs. (Used with permission from Copley AL and Robb TP: Studies on platelets. II. The effect of heparin on the platelet count in vitro. Am J Clin Pathol 12:563–570, 1942.)

platelet counts returned to normal by 30 minutes.[4]

Further investigation of heparin-associated thrombocytopenia did not occur until 1962 when, to investigate a possible role of heparin in the etiology of thrombocytopenia accompanying cardiopulmonary bypass surgery, seven normal subjects were given intravenous injections of 4,000 U of heparin.[5] In each subject there was an immediate decrease of the platelet count, averaging 33%, which was maximal at 30 minutes and returned to normal by 120 minutes. Whether the observed thrombocytopenia was real, or whether heparin caused platelet clumping that resulted in a systematic counting error, was the basis of an experiment by Davey and Lander in 1968.[6] Six normal subjects with circulating autologous [51]Cr-labeled platelets were given 5,000 or 10,000 U of hepa-

rin intravenously; an immediate decrease of the platelet count was noted, but there was no change in blood radioactivity. These data were interpreted to indicate that heparin caused an artefactually decreased platelet count without true thrombocytopenia, although no in vitro platelet clumping was actually observed.

Until 1969, there had been no documentation of heparin-associated thrombocytopenia as a clinically important problem. Then, between 1969 and 1974, five patients were reported with severe thrombocytopenia that seemed clearly related to heparin therapy[7–9]; four of the patients also had evidence of thrombosis or DIC.[8, 9] This led to the initial prospective study, conducted in 1974 and 1975, which documented thrombocytopenia in 16 of 52 patients treated with intravenous heparin for venous thromboembolism or coronary artery disease[10, 11] (see Table 35–2).

This remarkable observation and the continued case reports of thrombocytopenia[12–15] stimulated many prospective clinical trials and much investigation into the mechanism of heparin interactions with platelets.

Conclusions from the initial observations on heparin-associated thrombocytopenia from 1942 to 1976 may be summarized as follows: (1) Heparin can cause platelet clumping. (2) In some experiments in dogs and man, heparin caused prompt, transient thrombocytopenia. (3) Whether the observed thrombocytopenia was real, or the result of an artefactually low platelet count caused by platelet clumping, was unclear. (4) Despite these experimental observations beginning in 1942, thrombocytopenia in patients treated with heparin was not recognized until 1969. (5) After heparin-associated thrombocytopenia was recognized, a prospective trial documented the occurrence of significant thrombocytopenia (platelet counts <100,000/μl on two consecutive days) in 31% of patients. (6) Subsequent prospective studies involving more than 2,000 patients have never duplicated this high frequency. In fact, the reported frequency of heparin-associated thrombocytopenia has steadily diminished over the subsequent 17 years.

## Thrombosis Associated With Heparin

The initial observations that therapeutic heparin may be associated with thrombosis, specifically arterial thromboembolism, were in two reports in 1958[16] and 1964.[17] Weismann and Tobin[16] reported 10 patients seen during 3 years who developed arterial emboli while on anticoagulating doses of heparin, typically 150 to 500 mg (approximately 20,000–60,000 U) given subcutaneously in divided doses to achieve a whole blood clotting time of 30 to 40 minutes. Six of the patients were being anticoagulated for arterial thromboembolism, four for venous thromboembolism. Multiple arterial emboli occurred in nine of 10 patients, six patients died, and two of the survivors required amputations. In 1964, Roberts and coworkers reported on 11 patients seen during 9 years who developed arterial emboli while on heparin,[17] with clinical features similar to those in the earlier report of Weismann and Tobin. Over the next 15 years, several additional publications presented patients who developed arterial thromboses and DIC while on heparin.[8, 9, 11, 13, 15] Despite the dramatic nature of these observations, subsequent prospective clinical trials have not clearly demonstrated the occurrence of heparin-associated arterial thromboembolism.

## PATHOGENESIS

### Heparin-associated Thrombocytopenia in Normal Subjects

The occurrence of heparin-associated thrombocytopenia in patients must be assessed from the perspective that heparin causes decreased platelet counts in normal subjects. In one study, intravenous heparin caused a transient decrease of platelet counts in all of seven subjects.[5] In a subsequent study,[18] investigators treated 30 normal subjects with intermittent intravenous bolus heparin to achieve plasma heparin concentrations of 0.2 to 0.4 U/ml for 10 days; 10 control subjects received saline by the same regimen. The treated subjects had a lower mean platelet count compared with control subjects at days 6 to 10, and eight of the 30 treated subjects had a significant decrease of their platelet counts compared with pretreatment values (Fig. 35–2). In a third study, investigators treated 39 normal subjects with 5,000 U of heparin subcutaneously every 12 hours for 10 days.[19] Although no subject became thrombocytopenic, as a group there was a significant linear decrease of the platelet count throughout the period of heparin administration, with a sharp increase after discontinuation of heparin (Fig. 35–3). These effects in normal subjects may be less apparent in patients in whom illness or surgery would cause an acute phase response with increased plasma interleukin-6 (IL-6) concentrations and a compensatory thrombocytosis.[20]

### Interaction of Heparin With Platelets

Heparin binds to a single class of saturable sites on platelets with a dissociation constant equivalent to the therapeutic level in plasma (0.1–0.2 U/ml).[21] Higher molecular weight fractions of heparin bind with higher affinity, probably because of their increased total negative charge,[22] and are more active in causing platelet aggregation in plasma.[23–25] Heparin at therapeutic concentrations in either citrate or hirudin-anticoagulated plasma can also potentiate platelet activation by physiologic agonists.[23, 25–27] However, in vitro platelet responses to heparin vary widely among normal subjects,[23] even among subjects who have never received heparin.[26] In

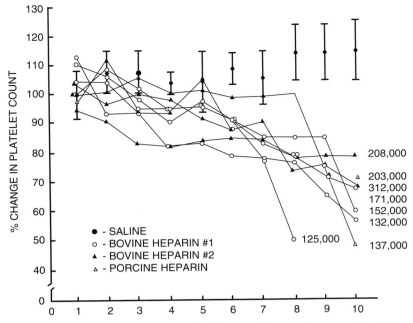

**Figure 35–2.** Effect of intravenous heparin on platelet counts in normal human subjects. Heparin was administered by intravenous bolus every 6 hours for 10 days to achieve plasma heparin concentrations of 0.2 to 0.4 U/ml. Twenty subjects received either one of two preparations of beef lung heparin, and ten subjects received porcine mucosal heparin. Individual platelet counts are presented on eight subjects whose platelet counts significantly decreased during heparin therapy. Platelet counts in the other 22 subjects did not change during heparin therapy. Ten subjects received a saline placebo injection; their mean platelet values (± standard deviation) are presented at the top of the figure. (From Schwartz KA, Royer G, Kauffman DB, et al: Complications of heparin administration in normal individuals. Am J Hematol 19:355–363, 1985. Copyright © 1985. Reprinted by permission of Wiley-Liss, Inc., a subsidiary of John Wiley & Sons, Inc.)

studies using heparin concentrations greater than therapeutic levels, 5 to 12 U/ml, platelet aggregates formed in whole blood samples in some normal subjects and in all patients who had recently received heparin.[28, 29] This caused a significantly lower apparent platelet count in the patients' samples, a phenomenon that also could be induced in most normal heparinized blood samples after 4 hours at 4 degrees C.[29]

These observations suggest that the common observation of diminished platelet counts in both normal subjects and patients may be simply a result of predictable heparin-induced platelet aggregation, and furthermore that the variability among normal subjects may reflect inherent differences in the reactivity of platelets to heparin.

Heparin reacts not only with platelets; abnormalities of liver function regularly occur in normal subjects given heparin as well as in patients in clinical studies.[18, 19, 30] This is consistent with the many biologic activities of heparin, mediated by its high negative charge density that results in interactions with clusters of basic amino acids on many proteins and cells.[31–33] Heparin has been implicated in numerous ad-

hesion reactions of extracellular matrix proteins, interactions with lipoproteins and proteins of the complement system, and regulation of growth factors and angiogenesis.[33]

## Evidence for the Existence of Antiheparin Antibodies

Although the common, mild thrombocytopenia that accompanies heparin administration may be the result of nonimmune platelet aggregation by heparin, heparin-dependent antiplatelet antibodies may be responsible for the uncommon occurrences of severe thrombocytopenia.[12, 34, 35] Many reports have demonstrated that immunoglobulin G (IgG) from patients with heparin-associated thrombocytopenia causes platelet aggregation and secretion in the presence of heparin, and these observations have formed the basis for laboratory assays. However, the molecular mechanisms involved in the interactions of these three components—patient serum, normal donor platelets, and heparin—remain obscure. The complexity of these interactions is increased by variability with each component; that is, plate-

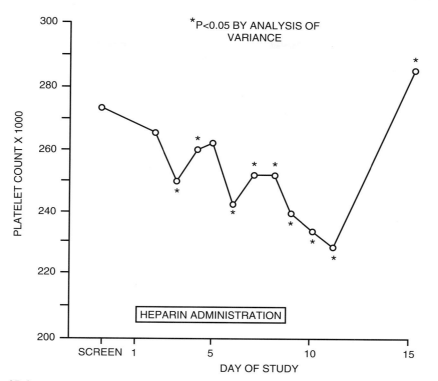

**Figure 35–3.** Effect of subcutaneous heparin on platelet counts in normal human subjects. The mean platelet counts in 39 normal volunteers are presented. Heparin was administered in a dose of 5,000 U subcutaneously every 12 hours for 10 days. Heparin from beef lung was used for 25 subjects; heparin from porcine intestinal mucosa was used for 14. There was no difference in the platelet counts between these two groups. Asterisks indicate values that were significantly different from the pretreatment value ($p < .05$). Note that the range of platelet counts on the abscissa is only from 200,000/$\mu$l to 300,000/$\mu$l. No subjects became thrombocytopenic. (Used with permission from Saffle JR, Russo J, Dukes GE, Warden GD: The effect of low-dose heparin therapy on serum platelet and transaminase levels. J Surg Res 28:297–308, 1980.)

lets from different normal donors may or may not aggregate in the presence of patient serum and heparin.[36, 37] Platelets from some normal donors are aggregated by heparin without patient sera and some patient sera can aggregate normal platelets without heparin.[36] Heparin can be replaced by other anionic molecules[38, 39] or subaggregating concentrations of agonists such as epinephrine[36]; and the interactions are dependent on the heparin concentration, with higher concentrations inhibiting some platelet responses[38, 40] but also causing nonspecific platelet responses in other studies.[41, 42] Further complicating the understanding of these interactions has been the inability to isolate specific antiheparin antibodies or heparin-immune complexes from patients[38] combined with the difficulty of distinguishing immune interactions from nonspecific heparin-IgG electrostatic interactions.[43] Although specific antiheparin antibodies have not been isolated and characterized,[38] the possibility that development of antibodies to heparin may be ubiquitous is suggested by the observation that patients who have

been treated with heparin demonstrate consistent in vitro platelet aggregation by heparin compared with patients who have not previously been treated.[29] However, the occurrence of thrombocytopenia does not appear to be greater in patients who have been previously treated with heparin.[11, 44]

From many experimental studies, a consensus mechanism appears to involve the development in some patients of clinically important antiplatelet antibodies that require heparin or related polyanionic molecules[38, 39, 45] for optimal interaction with platelet antigens. The role of heparin appears to involve alteration of the platelet surface, facilitating the binding of antibody to platelet antigens and antigen-antibody complexes to platelet Fc receptors.[38, 42, 46–48] Multiple platelet surface antigens may be involved in these interactions,[38, 49] and heparin complexed to platelet factor 4, the platelet's strongest cationic heparin-binding protein, which is secreted and rebound to the platelet surface,[50] may be an additional target for antibodies.[51] IgG from patients with heparin-associated thrombocytopenia may also bind to endothelial cells in the presence of heparin,[52] an observation that could have relevance to the occurrence of DIC[9, 11] and thrombotic complications.[8, 15–17]

## Platelet Immunoglobulin Fc Receptors are Potential Modulators of Heparin-platelet Interactions

A potential mechanism to explain why some patients may be at greater risk for heparin-associated thrombocytopenia was suggested by observations on differences in platelet surface concentrations of the immunoglobulin Fc receptor, FcRII, which would affect the magnitude of platelet interactions with heparin-antiheparin antibody immune complexes.[53] In a study, platelet concentrations of FcRII were found to be greater in patients with heparin-associated thrombocytopenia compared with those in a group of nonthrombocytopenic patients who had comparable disorders similarly treated with heparin.[53] Both the thrombocytopenic and nonthrombocytopenic patients had greater platelet concentrations of FcRII than normal subjects,[53] further suggesting that patients with acute inflammatory illnesses may be at greater risk for heparin-associated thrombocytopenia. In vitro activation of platelets increases surface expression of FcRII,[54] but not to the extent seen in patients with acute illnesses.[53] IL-6, a cytokine that mediates the acute phase response, stimulates the production of larger platelets[55] that are more responsive to agonists.[56] These observations suggest that in the presence of acute illness, platelets may be more reactive with heparin-antibody complexes. The basis for different susceptibilities to heparin-associated thrombocytopenia among normal individuals may be related to inherent differences in the platelet surface concentration and responsiveness of FcRII.[57, 58] Among normal subjects, both the number of FcRII expressed on the platelet surface and the responsiveness of receptor molecules coded by different alleles define the observed variability of in vitro platelet activation by immune complexes.[57, 58]

The role of FcRII in platelet responses to heparin-antibody complexes is consistent with observations suggesting that the platelet membrane glycoprotein (GP) Ib-IX is involved in these reactions.[46, 48] This appears to be related to the proximity of GP Ib-IX and FcRII on the platelet surface, because platelet aggregation and secretion induced by crosslinking of FcRII[59] can be blocked by monoclonal antibodies to the membrane GP Ib-IX complex.[60]

## CLINICAL FEATURES

Heparin-associated thrombocytopenia is commonly described as two syndromes,[14, 35] although the clinical distinction between them is unclear. Minimal thrombocytopenia, with platelet counts not less than 50,000/μl, probably represents the common occurrence of diminished platelet counts seen in studies of normal subjects (see Figs. 35–2 and 35–3).[18, 19] The platelet count may begin to fall soon after heparin administration is begun and may continue to decrease throughout treatment, although commonly the platelet count recovers despite continued heparin treatment. This subsequent compensation may occur by the increased platelet production stimulated by IL-6 and other cytokines involved in the acute phase response to the illness for which heparin was prescribed.[20, 55] Mild thrombocytopenia, or a decreased platelet count that remains within the normal range, is the most common abnormality associated with heparin therapy. The actual frequency of thrombocytopenia with heparin therapy is unclear, in part because of variability of the definition of thrombocytopenia in prospective trials.[61] Some define thrombocytopenia as the occurrence of any platelet count less than normal (150,000/μl), whereas others require the occurrence of platelet counts less than 100,000/μl for at least 2 consecutive days. Severe thrombocytopenia, with platelet counts less than 50,000/μl, is less common. More severe thrombocytopenia seems to appear later during the course of heparin therapy than mild thrombocytopenia, which may only reflect the continued accumulation of the effect of heparin-induced platelet aggregation (see Figs. 35–2 and 35–3). In these patients a plasma activity, presumably antibody, is often demonstrated by platelet aggregation or secretion in the presence of heparin. In addition, it is in these patients that the thrombocytopenia seems to have a greater risk for recurrence upon readministration of heparin.[11] Severe thrombocytopenia may also accompany other signs of an immunologic reaction, such as skin necrosis[62] and acute febrile reactions to heparin[63] or related glycosaminoglycans.[39] Although these two categories of heparin-associated thrombocytopenia are commonly described, the prospective studies reviewed later do not support a clear distinction.

Thrombocytopenia can occur with any heparin preparation, dose, and route of administration. Thrombocytopenia has been reported during treatment with unfractionated heparin, low-molecular-weight heparins,[64] chondroitin sulfate–like glycosaminoglycan agents,[39] heparin-like compounds, such as pentosan (poly-sulfated plant polypentose),[65, 66] and the "heparinoid" glycosaminoglycan agent, Organon 10172.[67] The in vitro studies described earlier predict that higher molecular fractions of heparin would interact more readily with platelets and thereby cause more thrombocytopenia,[22, 23] but also that any polyanionic molecule can mimic the heparin effect.[38, 39, 45] Heparin isolated from beef lung appears to cause thrombocytopenia more often than heparin from pork intestinal mucosa (see later). Thrombocytopenia has occurred even when heparin was used only to flush indwelling intravenous catheters in doses as low as 100 U/day[68–70] and with the use of heparin-coated pulmonary catheters.[71] However, no relationship appears between the dose of administered heparin and the occurrence of thrombocytopenia. More patients receive low doses of heparin for thrombosis prevention, but thrombocytopenia more commonly occurs in patients receiving higher doses of heparin for treatment of thromboembolism. Certainly, even more patients are exposed to heparin to keep indwelling intravenous catheters free of clot than are actually treated with heparin, but the occurrence of thrombocytopenia in these situations appears to be much less common. In one study of 54 patients with heparin-associated thrombocytopenia, 50% of the patients had received heparin for treatment of thromboembolic disease, 20% for prophylaxis, 11% each for catheter flushing or for extracorporeal circulation, and others for plasma exchange and coronary arteriography.[70]

The clinical spectrum of heparin-associated thrombocytopenia is described by the prospective trials summarized in Tables 35–1 and 35–2. Table 35–1 describes the results from nine reports[19, 30, 72–78] of 490 patients given subcutaneous heparin as prophylaxis for venous thromboembolism in surgical patients or patients in coronary care units, or, in one study, 39 normal volunteer subjects.[19] The overall occurrence of thrombocytopenia was 4%, but this figure overestimates the clinical importance because in only one of the 20 thrombocytopenic patients was the platelet count less than 90,000/$\mu$l (this patient had a platelet count of 83,000/$\mu$l). Although the information is not complete, it appears that the platelet count recovered to normal in all patients while herapin therapy was continued. No significant bleeding and no thrombotic complications was reported.

Table 35–2 presents the data from 21 reports[11, 14, 18, 30, 44, 64, 72–74, 78–89] on 2,453 patients treated with intravenous heparin for venous or arterial thromboembolic disease. In one report,

213 patients were treated with subcutaneous low-molecular-weight heparin for proximal vein thrombosis,[64] and these patients are included in Table 35–2. The patients received approximately twice as much heparin per day as the patients represented in Table 35–1. Although the overall frequency of thrombocytopenia, 5%, is similar to that in patients treated prophylactically with heparin, the range of reported abnormalities is greater. Among these reports, the initial prospective study of the occurrence of thrombocytopenia in patients treated with heparin by Bell and coworkers[11] is distinct from the others. Sixteen of 52 patients (31%) became thrombocytopenic, defined as platelet counts less than 100,000/$\mu$l on 2 consecutive days, and 10 of these 16 thrombocytopenic patients had laboratory evidence of DIC. Platelet counts returned to normal 3 to 5 days after discontinuation of heparin. No patients had clinically important bleeding. This high frequency has never been reproduced, even though the definition of thrombocytopenia used in this initial study was more stringent than in most subsequent studies. The evidence for DIC noted in this study has also not been reproduced. Other early studies reported frequencies of thrombocytopenia of 11 to 24%,[14, 73, 81, 82] but in the five reports since 1986[30, 64, 78, 88, 89] only 17 of 857 patients (2%) became thrombocytopenic, and in most of these patients the criteria for determining thrombocytopenia was only an isolated platelet count of less than 150,000/$\mu$l.

The reason for the decreased occurrence of heparin-associated thrombocytopenia over the 16-year period from 1976 to 1992 is unknown. A change in the composition of commercial heparin preparations may have occurred. In many of the earlier studies, heparin prepared from bovine lung was used and in several studies this was directly compared with heparin prepared from porcine intestinal mucosa. As shown in Table 35–2, bovine lung heparin appears to be associated with a greater risk for thrombocytopenia, suggesting the importance of the heparin preparation. One report suggested that heparin-associated thrombocytopenia accompanied by venous thromboembolic complications was related to the use of a specific lot of beef lung heparin from a single manufacturer.[90] Current commercial heparin preparations are essentially all isolated from porcine intestinal mucosa. Another possible explanation is that recent studies have used shorter durations of heparin treatment. In earlier studies, the average duration of heparin therapy was 8 to 10 days[72–74] and the typical time for the onset of thrombocytopenia was after 5 to 7 days.[11, 74, 81] In one study, throm-

Table 35–1. **Subcutaneous, Prophylactic Heparin: Frequency of Thrombocytopenia and Thrombosis in Prospective Studies**

| Reference | Heparin Treatment | | Patients | | Thrombo-cytopenia | Thrombosis | Comments |
|---|---|---|---|---|---|---|---|
| | Type* | Dose, Duration† | Number | Diagnosis** | | | |
| Malcolm, 1978[72] | PM | 15,000 U; 6 days | 10 | CCU | 0 | 0 | No platelet counts <100,000/μl |
| Malcolm, 1979[73] | PM | 15,000 U; 10 days | 38 | CCU | 4 | 0 | Four patients with platelet counts of 90,000–150,000/μl. Asymptomatic and possibly unrelated to heparin |
| Saffle, 1980[19] | NS | 10,000 U; 10 days | 39 | Normal volunteers | 0 | 0 | No platelet counts <150,000/μl, however mean platelet count less than pretreatment mean value on days 3–11 (see Fig. 35–2) |
| Gallus, 1980[74] | NS | 10,000–15,000 U; 5–10 days | 51 | Elective surgery | 1 | 0 | One patient with platelet count <100,000/μl (83,000/μl), resolved on continued treatment |
| Romeril, 1982[75] | PM | 15,000 U; NS | 45 | CCU | 0 | 0 | Mean plasma fibrinogen level and platelet count increased from day 1 to day 10: 400 mg/dl to 600 mg/dl; 210,000/μl to 300,000/μl |
| Weitberg, 1982[76] | PM | 10,000 U; 3–15 days | 50 | CCU | 0 | 0 | No platelet counts <150,000/μl. Mean platelet count unchanged |
| Johnson, 1984[77] | PM | 10,000 U; 7 days | 66 | CCU | 10 | 0 | Nine patients with platelet count <150,000/μl at day 2–5; one patient with thrombocytopenia twice. All returned to >150,000/μl on continued heparin. No platelet count <100,000/μl |
| Monreal, 1989[30] | BL | 15,000 U; >10 days | 49 | Hip fracture | 0 | 0 | No platelet counts <150,000/μl |
| Monreal, 1989[30] | BL/LMW | 5000 U; 10 days | 43 | Hip fracture | 0 | 0 | No platelet counts <150,000/μl |
| Rao, 1989[78] | PM | 10,000 U; >5 days | 99 | NS | 5 | 0 | Five patients with platelet counts of 100,000–140,000/μl for 1 day, recovered on next day with continued treatment |
| **Summary** | | | 490 | | 20 (4%) | 0 | Only one of 20 thrombocytopenic patients had a platelet count <90,000/μl (83,000/μl) and apparently all recovered while on continued heparin treatment |

*Heparin type: PM, pork mucosa; BL, bovine lung; NS, not stated or not distinguished.
†Dose is the total daily dose given for the number of days indicated. NS, not stated.
**CCU, admission to coronary care unit; NS, not stated.

bocytopenia was observed only in patients treated with heparin for longer than 10 days.[44] In current clinical practice, intravenous heparin is usually given only for 5 days.[64, 89]

Although some of the patients represented in Table 35–2 developed severe thrombocytopenia, only one patient was specifically reported to have bleeding associated with the thrombocytopenia, but the nature or severity of the bleeding was not described.[81] This lack of symptomatic bleeding is especially striking, because heparin therapy alone, even without thrombocytopenia, may be associated with major bleeding episodes in 5 to 10% of patients.[64, 89] Many of the patients in Table 35–2 had mild thrombocytopenia that resolved while heparin therapy was continued. When heparin was discontinued upon discovery of thrombocytopenia, thrombocytopenia characteristically resolved in 2 to 5 days.

Arterial emboli are the most serious reported complications of heparin therapy. These usually occur with severe thrombocytopenia and may have severe and fatal complications. Although case reports of arterial thromboembolism were frequent among the early descriptions of heparin-associated thrombocytopenia,[8, 9, 16, 17] the incidence of heparin-associated thrombosis is unknown. Among the 2,943 patients represented in Tables 35–1 and 35–2, eight were reported to have thrombotic complications that were possibly related to heparin therapy. However, the etiology of the thrombosis is difficult to define in these critically ill patients, and often the clinical descriptions of the patients were incomplete. It is possible that the thrombotic episodes were unrelated to heparin therapy in all eight patients, because all occurred in clinical settings in which other potential etiologies were present. No studies developed a priori criteria for defining thrombotic complications.[61]

A problem in the diagnosis of heparin-associated thrombosis is that patients have a high incidence of pre-existing symptomatic vascular disease. In one series of 54 patients, 33 had already experienced a myocardial infarction, stroke, or peripheral arterial thrombosis.[70] Others have also noted that venous thrombosis attributed to heparin occurred in patients who were at high risk for thrombosis because of recent surgery.[91] Furthermore, recurrent venous thromboembolism occurs in about 7% of patients treated with conventional heparin for venous thromboembolic disease.[64, 89] The occurrence of arterial thromboembolism in patients on heparin treatment continues to be reported and attributed to heparin,[92] but whether heparin actually causes thrombosis remains unproved.

## LABORATORY FEATURES

The complexity of the laboratory evaluation of heparin-associated thrombocytopenia can be anticipated from the description of pathogenesis. The principle of the typical laboratory assays is straightforward—patient serum with added heparin is incubated with platelet-rich plasma from a normal subject and an aggregation or secretion response of the platelets is measured. However, the execution of the assays may be difficult.[93] The amount of platelet aggregation may vary among different normal donors[37, 94]; platelets from some normal donors appear completely unresponsive to patient serum plus heparin, whereas other donor platelets aggregate in the presence of heparin even without patient serum.[42, 94] Furthermore, a result may be defined as positive when the platelet aggregation is actually quite minimal, such as a 10% change from baseline light transmission.[70] Techniques have been changed in an attempt to simplify the interpretation of aggregation responses.[95] Another assay measures the secretion of [14]C-serotonin from normal platelets at two concentrations of heparin; therapeutic heparin concentrations support secretion but higher concentrations do not.[96] Similar dependence on heparin concentration has been reported for assays using an endpoint of platelet aggregation, with heparin-dependent aggregation occurring at a heparin concentration of 0.1 U/ml but not at 100 U/ml.[94] The explanation provided for these observations is that immune complexes of heparin plus antiheparin antibodies form at low heparin concentrations, but these complexes are disrupted by higher heparin concentrations.[96] However, these higher concentrations of heparin may also inhibit platelet aggregation by collagen and adenosine diphosphate (ADP) by an unknown mechanism that does not involve immune complexes.[42] Apparent spontaneous platelet aggregation or secretion in these assays may be caused by trace amounts of heparin in the patient's blood; this heparin may then interact with a heparin-dependent antibody[97] or prevent complete coagulation and leave residual thrombin in the patient's serum, which could itself cause platelet aggregation.[70] Thrombin may also be present in serum derived from severely thrombocytopenic blood.[98] Although clinical studies have demonstrated a correlation of these laboratory assays with the occurrence of heparin-associated thrombocytopenia,[96, 99] oth-

Table 35-2. Intravenous, Therapeutic Heparin: Frequency of Thrombocytopenia and Thrombosis in Prospective Studies

| Reference | Heparin Treatment | | Patients | | Thrombo-cytopenia | Thrombosis | Comments |
|---|---|---|---|---|---|---|---|
| | Type* | Dose, Duration† | Number | Diagnosis** | | | |
| Bell, 1976[11] | BL | 25,000–43,000 U; >5 days | 52 | VTE, 45 CAD, 7 | 16 | 0 | Platelet counts in 16 patients decreased from >150,000/μl to <100,000/μl for 2 consecutive days; nadir <50,000/μl in 9 patients. 10/16 had increased FDP; 5 of these 10 patients had decreased fibrinogen. 2/16 had recurrent thrombocytopenia with subsequent heparin. No important bleeding episodes. All recovered in 3–5 days after heparin stopped. |
| Nelson, 1978[14] | PM | 300–450 U/kg; NS | 37 | CCU | 9 | 0 | Platelet counts <150,000/μl in 9 patients, lowest = 88,000/μl. Three resolved on continued heparin. No DIC, no bleeding. |
| Malcolm, 1978[72] | PM | 30,000 U; 10 days | 10 | CCU | 0 | 0 | No platelet counts <100,000/μl for 2 consecutive days. |
| Malcolm, 1979[73] | PM | NS; 8 days | 49 | CCU, VTE | 9 | 0 | Only two patients with platelet counts <90,000/μl (64,000/μl and 26,000/μl). In only this latter patient was thrombocytopenia clearly related to heparin, and she also had evidence for DIC. |
| Powers, 1979[79] | PM | 20,000–25,000 U; >5 days | 117 | VTE | 1 | 0 | Four patients with platelet counts <150,000/μl, but in only one was heparin a probable etiology. |
| Gallus, 1980[74] | PM | 10,000–50,000 U; 3–30 days | 166 | VTE, 139 Arterial, 27 | 5 | 0 | Platelet counts of 7,000–73,000/μl in five patients, recovered 3–10 days after heparin stopped. Four other patients developed platelet counts of 15,000–88,000/μl probably not caused by heparin. |
| Eika, 1980[80] | PM | 10,000–50,000 U; >5 days | 77 | VTE | 1 | 0 | Two patients with mild thrombocytopenia; no recurrence in one with subsequent heparin. Three other patients with minimal, transient thrombocytopenia. |
| | BL | 10,000–50,000 U; >5 days | 52 | | 1 | 0 | |
| Bell, 1980[81] | PM | 24,000 U; >3 days | 99 | VTE, 130 CAD, 15 Arterial, 4 | 8 | 0 | Platelet counts <100,000/μl, on at least 2 consecutive days in 19/21 patients. Three patients recovered on continued heparin; three patients had laboratory evidence of DIC; one patient had symptomatic bleeding. |
| | BL | 25,000 U; >3 days | 50 | | 13 | 0 | |
| Ansell, 1980[82] | PM | NS; 10 days | 22 | VTE | 1 | 0 | One patient on PM heparin had platelet count of 140,000/μl that recovered on continued heparin. The four patients on BL heparin had platelet counts of 90,000–150,000/μl that recovered 1–6 days after heparin stopped. No evidence of DIC. |
| | BL | NS; 10 days | 21 | | 4 | 0 | |
| Cipolle, 1983[83] | PM | NS; >3 days | 111 | VTE, CAD, Stroke | 1 | 0 | Thrombocytopenia with platelet counts of 39,000–98,000/μl developed after 2–10 days of heparin and recovered 1–4 days after heparin stopped. |
| | BL | NS; >3 days | 100 | | 10 | 0 | |
| Powers, 1984[84] | PM | 24,000 U; >8 days | 66 | VTE | 0 | 0 | Nadir platelet counts, 40,000–138,000/μl. No evidence of DIC. |
| | BL | 24,000 U; >8 days | 65 | | 5 | 0 | |

368

| Study | Heparin type[*] | Dose[†] | No. patients | Diagnoses[**] | Thrombocytopenia | (?) | Comments |
|---|---|---|---|---|---|---|---|
| Green, 1984[85] | PM | 15,000–40,000 U; >5 days | 44 | VTE, 39; Stroke, 5 | 0 | 0 | The two thrombocytopenic patients had nadir platelet counts of 14,000/μl and 15,000/μl. One 67-year-old hypertensive patient developed a stroke on day 7 of heparin treatment for VTE when platelet count was 236,000/μl. The platelet count was 83,000/μl on day 8 and 14,000/μl on day 11. |
| | BL | 15,000–40,000 U; >5 days | 45 | VTE, 42; Stroke 3 | 2 | 1 (?) | |
| Ramirez-Lassepos, 1984[86] | PM, BL | NS; >3 days | 137 | Stroke, TIA | 7 | 1 (?) | Nadir platelet counts, 45,000–98,000/μl. No evidence for DIC, no bleeding. One thrombocytopenic patient (76,000/μl) extended her cerebral infarct while on heparin. |
| Schwartz, 1985[18] | PM | Footnote 2: 10 days | 10 | Normal | 0 | 0 | Three normal subjects on BL heparin developed platelet counts of 126,000–137,000/μl on days 8–10. |
| | BL | Footnote 2: 10 days | 20 | Normal | 3 | 0 | |
| Kakkasseril, 1985[44] | BL | 12,000–53,000 U; >3 days | 142 | VTE, 70; Arterial, 72 | 9 | 4 (?) | Nadir platelet counts, 32,000–70,000/μl. In two patients, thrombocytopenia was associated with pulmonary emboli. In two other patients, leg arterial emboli occurred; the pretreatment diagnosis and occurrence of thrombocytopenia was not stated. |
| Ansell, 1985[87] | PM | NS; >4 days | 50 | VTE, 31; Arterial, 14; Other, 5 | 2 | 0 | Nadir platelet counts, 44,000–98,000/μl. Seven other patients developed platelet counts of 100,000–150,000/μl that resolved on continued heparin. |
| | BL | NS; >4 days | 54 | VTE, 26; Arterial, 20; Other, 8 | 1 | 0 | |
| Bailey, 1986[88] | PM | NS; >5 days | 21 | VTE, 14; Arterial, 7 | 0 | 0 | The one thrombocytopenic patient received heparin for 13 days throughout a postoperative course complicated by sepsis, and multiple cerebral infarcts, and death. |
| | BL | NS; >5 days | 22 | VTE, 11; Arterial, 11 | 1 | 1 (?) | |
| Monreal, 1989[30] | BL | 600 U/kg; >8 days | 89 | VTE | 2 | 1 (?) | Nadir platelet counts, 21,000/μl and 33,000/μl. One patient had accompanying "symptoms suggestive of pulmonary embolism." |
| Rao, 1989[78] | PM | 21,000 U; >4 days | 94 | NS | 0 | 0 | No patients with platelet counts <100,000/μl. |
| Hull, 1990[89] | PM | NS; 5 days | 99 | VTE | 3 | 0 | Thrombocytopenia defined as any platelet count <150,000/μl. |
| | PM | NS; 10 days | 100 | VTE | 2 | 0 | |
| Hull, 1992[64] | PM | NS; 5 days | 219 | VTE | 3 | 0 | Thrombocytopenia defined as any platelet count <150,000/μl. |
| | PM/LMW | 175 U/kg; 5 days | 213 | VTE | 6 | 0 | |

| Summary | | No. patients | Thrombocytopenia | (?) |
|---|---|---|---|---|
| PM | | 973 | 37 (4%) | — |
| BL | | 712 | 67 (9%) | — |
| PM OR BL | | 137 | 7 (5%) | — |
| **Total** | | 2453 | 125 (5%) | ? |

*Heparin type: PM, pork mucosa; BL, bovine lung; NS, not stated or not distinguished.

†Dose is the total daily dose given for the number of days indicated. NS, not stated. Studies used both continuous intravenous administration and intravenous bolus administration every 4–6 hours. In studies where doses were not stated, the dose was adjusted according to PTT assays. In the study on normal subjects, heparin doses were adjusted to achieve plasma levels of 0.2–0.4 U/ml.

**Diagnoses: VTE, venous thromboembolism; CAD, coronary artery disease; CCU, admission to coronary care unit; Arterial, arterial embolism.

ers have not confirmed these observations.[98] Detection of heparin-dependent antibodies has been used to retrospectively assess patient groups,[100] but the conclusions of such studies are questionable because there are no prospective data to support the importance of laboratory assays in clinical outcomes. At the present time, assays for heparin-dependent antibodies remain investigative tools and are not required for the management of thrombocytopenic patients.

## PREVENTION, DIAGNOSIS, AND THERAPY

Awareness of the potential for thrombocytopenia with heparin use, with frequent performance of platelet counts, is the most important preventive measure. The diagnosis of heparin-associated thrombocytopenia should be made on the basis of platelet counts less than $100,000/\mu l$ on 2 consecutive days[11, 98] in the absence of other etiologies. If this occurs, heparin may be discontinued, depending on the clinical assessment of the relative risks of extension or recurrence of the underlying thrombotic disease compared with the potential risk from the thrombocytopenia. There are many reports of patients with platelet counts of $50,000/\mu l$ to $100,000/\mu l$ whose platelet counts returned to normal while heparin was continued. Heparin must be discontinued if the platelet count is less than $50,000/\mu l$. Evidence for DIC should be assessed, which may itself be caused by the heparin.[9, 11, 81] All heparin-associated platelet and coagulation changes should reverse within several days of stopping heparin. If laboratory assays for heparin-dependent antibodies are available, they may provide supportive information, but they are unlikely to alter clinical decisions.

In almost all patients, the thrombocytopenia is mild and self-limited, and it is discovered at a time in the course of therapy when heparin can be safely discontinued. In the uncommon patients in whom alternative antithrombotic therapy is required, options include fibrinolytic agents,[101, 102] ancrod (a defibrinogenating venom available only by compassionate release in the United States),[103-105] low-molecular-weight heparins (which may have some crossreactivity with heparin-dependent antibodies),[104, 106] and heparinoids (which appear to have less cross-reactivity with heparin-dependent antibodies).[107, 108] The latter class of compounds, such as Organon 10172, may be important in the management of pregnant patients who have severe heparin-associated thrombocytopenia be-cause the compounds do not cross the placenta.[108] It can be anticipated that new synthetic thrombin inhibitors will soon be available for clinical use, and they may effectively maintain anticoagulation in patients with heparin-associated thrombocytopenia.[109, 110] Treatment for severe thrombocytopenia may also include the use of intravenous IgG[111] or plasmapheresis.[112, 113] No reports of adverse reactions to platelet transfusions have emerged, but their use in the presence of an antibody that may aggregate platelets could theoretically result in thrombosis, as has been described in thrombotic thrombocytopenic purpura.[114] The requirement for any of these therapeutic modalities is rare, and their efficacy is supported by anecdotal evidence.

## REFERENCES

1. Copley AL, Robb TP: Studies on platelets. II. The effect of heparin on the platelet count in vitro. Am J Clin Pathol 12:416–423, 1942.
2. Copley AL, Robb TP: The effect of heparin in vivo on the platelet count in mice and dogs. Am J Clin Pathol 12:563–570, 1942.
3. Fidlar E, Jaques LB: The effect of commercial heparin on the platelet count. J Lab Clin Med 33:1410–1423, 1948.
4. Quick AJ, Shanberge JN, Stefanini M: The effect of heparin on platelets in vivo. J Lab Clin Med 33:1424–1430, 1948.
5. Gollub S, Ulin AW: Heparin-induced thrombocytopenia in man. J Lab Clin Med 59:430–434, 1962.
6. Davey MG, Lander H: Effect of injected heparin on platelet levels in man. J Clin Pathol 21:55–59, 1968.
7. Natelson EA, Lynch EC, Alfrey CP, Gross JB: Heparin-induced thrombocytopenia. An unexpected response to treatment of consumption coagulopathy. Ann Intern Med 71:1121–1125, 1969.
8. Rhodes GR, Dixon RH, Silver D: Heparin induced thrombocytopenia with thrombotic and hemorrhagic manifestations. Surg Gynecol Obstet 136:409–416, 1973.
9. Klein HG, Bell WR: Disseminated intravascular coagulation during heparin therapy. Ann Intern Med 80:477–481, 1974.
10. Bell WR: Thrombocytopenia occurring during heparin therapy. N Engl J Med 295:276–277, 1976.
11. Bell WR, Tomasulo PA, Alving BA, Duffy TP: Thrombocytopenia occurring during the administration of heparin. A prospective study of 52 patients. Ann Intern Med 85:155–160, 1976.
12. Fratantoni JC, Pollet R, Gralnick HR: Heparin-induced thrombocytopenia: Confirmation of diagnosis with in vitro methods. Blood 45:395–401, 1975.
13. Babcock RB, Dumper CW, Scharfman WB: Heparin-induced immune thrombocytopenia. N Engl J Med 295:237–241, 1976.
14. Nelson JC, Lerner RG, Goldstein R, Cagin NA: Heparin-induced thrombocytopenia. Arch Intern Med 138:548–552, 1978.
15. Cimo PL, Moake JL, Weinger RS, et al: Heparin-induced thrombocytopenia: Association with a platelet aggregating factor and arterial thromboses. Am J Hematol 6:125–133, 1979.
16. Weismann RE, Tobin RW: Arterial embolism oc-

curring during systemic heparin therapy. Arch Surg 76:219–227, 1958.

17. Roberts B, Rosato FE, Rosato EF: Heparin—a cause of arterial emboli? Surgery 55:803–808, 1964.

18. Schwartz KA, Royer G, Kaufman DB, Penner JA: Complications of heparin administration in normal individuals. Am J Hematol 19:355–363, 1985.

19. Saffle JR, Russo J, Dukes GE, Warden GD: The effect of low-dose heparin therapy on serum platelet and transaminase levels. J Surg Res 28:297–305, 1980.

20. Hollen CW, Henthorn J, Koziol JA, Burstein SA: Elevated serum interleukin-6 levels in patients with reactive thrombocytosis. Br J Haematol 79:286–290, 1991.

21. Horne MK III, Chao ES: Heparin binding to resting and activated platelets. Blood 74:238–243, 1989.

22. Horne MK III, Chao ES: The effect of molecular weight on heparin binding to platelets. Br J Haematol 74:306–312, 1990.

23. Salzman EW, Rosenberg RD, Smith MH, et al: Effect of heparin and heparin fractions on platelet aggregation. J Clin Invest 65:64–73, 1980.

24. Saba HI, Saba SR, Morelli GA: Effect of heparin on platelet aggregation. Am J Hematol 17:295–306, 1984.

25. Westwick J, Scully MF, Poll C, Kakkar VV: Comparison of the effects of low molecular weight heparin and unfractionated heparin on activation of human platelets in vitro. Thromb Res 42:435–447, 1986.

26. Brace LD, Fareed J: An objective assessment of the interaction of heparin and its fractions with human platelets. Semin Thromb Hemost 11:190–198, 1985.

27. Chen J, Karlberg K-E, Sylvén C: Heparin enhances platelet aggregation irrespective of anticoagulation with citrate or with hirudin. Thromb Res 67:253–262, 1992.

28. Eika C: Platelet refractory state induced by heparin. Scand J Haematol 9:665–672, 1972.

29. Shojania AM, Turnbull G: Effect of heparin on platelet count and platelet aggregation. Am J Hematol 26:255–262, 1987.

30. Monreal M, Lafoz E, Salvador R, et al: Adverse effects of three different forms of heparin therapy: Thrombocytopenia, increased transaminases, and hyperkalemia. Eur J Clin Pharmacol 37:415–418, 1989.

31. Jaques LB: Heparin: An old drug with a new paradigm. Science 206:528–533, 1979.

32. Linhardt RJ: Heparin: An important drug enters its seventh decade. Chemistry and Industry 2:45–50, 1991.

33. Lane DA, Adams L: Non-anticoagulant uses of heparin. N Engl J Med 329:129–130, 1993.

34. Green D, Harris K, Reynolds N, et al: Heparin immune thrombocytopenia: Evidence for a heparin-platelet complex as the antigenic determinant. J Lab Clin Med 91:167–175, 1978.

35. Chong BH, Pitney WR, Castaldi PA: Heparin-induced thrombocytopenia: Association of thrombotic complications with heparin-dependent IgG antibody that induces thromboxane synthesis and platelet aggregation. Lancet 2:1246–1248, 1982.

36. Pfueller SL, David R: Different platelet specificities of heparin-dependent platelet aggregating factors in heparin-associated immune thrombocytopenia. Br J Haematol 64:149–159, 1986.

37. Warkentin TE, Hayward CPM, Smith CA, et al: Determinants of donor platelet variability when testing for heparin-induced thrombocytopenia. J Lab Clin Med 120:371–379, 1992.

38. Anderson GP: Insights into heparin-induced thrombocytopenia. Br J Haematol 80:504–508, 1992.

39. Greinacher A, Michels I, Schafer M, et al: Heparin-associated thrombocytopenia in a patient treated with polysulphated chondroitin sulphate: Evidence for im-

munological crossreactivity between heparin and polysulphated glycosaminoglycan. Br J Haematol 81:252–254, 1992.

40. Kelton JG, Sheridan D, Santos A: Heparin-induced thrombocytopenia: Laboratory studies. Blood 72:925–930, 1988.

41. Cines DB, Kaywin P, Bina M, et al: Heparin-associated thrombocytopenia. N Engl J Med 303:788–795, 1980.

42. Isenhart CE, Brandt JT: Platelet aggregation studies for the diagnosis of heparin-induced thrombocytopenia. Am J Clin Pathol 99:324–330, 1993.

43. Levy DE, Horner AA, Solomon A: Immunoglobulin-sulfated polysaccharide interactions. J Exp Med 153:883–896, 1981.

44. Kakkasseril JS, Cranley JJ, Panke T, Grannan K: Heparin-induced thrombocytopenia: A prospective study of 142 patients. J Vasc Surg 2:382–384, 1985.

45. Greinacher A, Michels I, Mueller-Eckhardt C: Heparin associated thrombocytopenia: Immune complexes are bound to platelets by the negative charge of highly sulfated oligosaccharides. Blood 80:62a, 1992.

46. Adelman B, Sobel M, Fujimura Y, et al: Heparin-associated thrombocytopenia: Observations on the mechanism of platelet aggregation. J Lab Clin Med 113:204–210, 1989.

47. Chong BH, Castaldi PA, Berndt MC: Heparin-induced thrombocytopenia: Effects of rabbit IgG, and its Fab and Fc fragments on antibody-heparin-platelet interaction. Thromb Res 55:291–295, 1989.

48. Chong BH, Fawaz I, Chesterman CN, Berndt MC: Heparin-induced thrombocytopenia: Mechanism of interaction of the heparin-dependent antibody with platelets. Br J Haematol 73:235–240, 1989.

49. Lynch DM, Howe SE: Heparin-associated thrombocytopenia: Antibody binding specificity to platelet antigens. Blood 66:1176–1181, 1985.

50. George JN, Onofre AR: Human platelet surface binding of endogenous secreted factor VIII-von Willebrand factor and platelet factor 4. Blood 59:194–197, 1982.

51. Amiral J, Bridey F, Dreyfus M: Platelet factor 4 complexed to heparin is the target for antibodies generated in heparin-induced thrombocytopenia. Thromb Haemost 68:95–96, 1992.

52. Cines DB, Tomaski A, Tannenbaum S: Immune endothelial-cell injury in heparin-associated thrombocytopenia. N Engl J Med 316:581–590, 1987.

53. Chong BH, Pilgrim RL, Cooley MA, Chesterman CN: Increased expression of platelet IgG Fc receptors in immune heparin-induced thrombocytopenia. Blood 81:988–993, 1993.

54. McCrae KR, Shattil SJ, Cines DB: Platelet activation induces increased Fc gamma receptor expression. J Immunol 144:3920–3927, 1990.

55. Burstein SA, Downs T, Friese P, et al: Thrombocytopoiesis in normal and sublethally irradiated dogs: Response to human interleukin-6. Blood 80:420–428, 1992.

56. Peng JP, Friese P, George JN, et al: Alteration of platelet function in dogs mediated by interleukin-6. Blood 83:398–403, 1994.

57. Rosenfeld SL, Ryan DH, Looney RJ, et al: Human Fc gamma receptors: Stable inter-donor variation in quantitative expression on platelets correlates with functional responses. J Immunol 138:2869, 1987.

58. Tomiyama Y, Kunicki TJ, Zipf TF, et al: Response of human platelets to activating monoclonal antibodies: Importance of FcγRII (CD32) phenotype and level of expression. Blood 80:2261–2268, 1992.

59. Anderson GP, Anderson CL: Signal transduction by the platelet Fc receptor. Blood 76:1165–1172, 1990.

60. Sullam PM, Lopez JA: Thrombosis: Glycoprotein Ib-IX

and von Willebrand Factor. Circulation 86:1–414, 1992.

61. Schmitt BP, Adelman B: Heparin-associated thrombocytopenia: A critical review and pooled analysis. Am J Med Sci 305:208–215, 1993.

62. Fowlie J, Stanton PD, Anderson JR: Heparin-associated skin necrosis. Postgrad Med J 66:573–575, 1990.

63. Warkentin TE, Soutar RL, Panju A, Ginsberg JS: Acute systemic reactions to intravenous bolus heparin therapy: Characterization and relationship to heparin-induced thrombocytopenia. Blood 80:160a, 1992.

64. Hull RD, Raskob GE, Pineo GF, et al: Subcutaneous low-molecular-weight heparin compared with continuous intravenous heparin in the treatment of proximal-vein thrombosis. N Engl J Med 326:975–982, 1992.

65. Follea G, Hamandjian I, Trzeciak MC, et al: Pentosane polysulphate associated thrombocytopenia. Thromb Res 42:413–418, 1986.

66. Goad KE, Horne MK, Gralnick HR: Platelet heparin binding in pentosan induced thrombocytopenia. Blood 80:62a, 1992.

67. Magnani HN: Compassionate use of Lomoparan in patients with HIT. Br J Haematol 77:65, 1991.

68. Doty JR, Alving BM, McDonnell DE, Ondra SL: Heparin-associated thrombocytopenia in the neurosurgical patient. Neurosurg 19:69–72, 1986.

69. Potter C, Gill JC, Scott JP, McFarland JG: Clinical and laboratory observations. Heparin-induced thrombocytopenia in a child. J Pediatr 121:135–138, 1992.

70. Lepine-Martin M, Nichols WL, Heit JA, Bowie EJW: Heparin-associated thrombocytopenia: Clinical and laboratory features of 54 patients tested for heparin-dependent platelet aggregation. Blood 80:61a (abstract), 1992.

71. Laster JL, Nichols WK, Silver D: Thrombocytopenia associated with heparin-coated catheters in patients with heparin-associated antiplatelet antibodies. Arch Intern Med 149:2285–2287, 1989.

72. Malcolm ID, Wigmore TA: Thrombocytopenia induced by low-dose subcutaneous heparin. Lancet 1:444, 1978.

73. Malcolm ID, Wigmore TA, Steinbrecher UP: Heparin-associated thrombocytopenia: Low frequency in 104 patients treated with heparin of intestinal mucosal origin. Can Med Assoc J 120:1086–1088, 1979.

74. Gallus AS, Goodall KT, Beswick W, Chesterman CN: Heparin-associated thrombocytopenia: Case report and prospective study. Aust N Z J Med 10:25–31, 1980.

75. Romeril KR, Hickton CM, Hamer JW, Heaton DC: Heparin induced thrombocytopenia: Case reports and a prospective study. N Z Med J 95:267–269, 1982.

76. Weitberg AB, Spremulli E, Cummings FJ: Effect of low-dose heparin on the platelet count. South Med J 75:190–192, 1982.

77. Johnson RA, Lazarus KH, Henry DH: Heparin-induced thrombocytopenia: A prospective study. Am J Hematol 17:349–353, 1984.

78. Rao AK, White GC, Sherman L, et al: Low incidence of thrombocytopenia with porcine mucosal heparin. A prospective multicenter trial. Arch Intern Med 149:1285–1288, 1989.

79. Powers PJ, Cuthbert D, Hirsh J: Thrombocytopenia found uncommonly during heparin therapy. JAMA 241:2396–2397, 1979.

80. Eika C, Godal HC, Laake K, Hamborg T: Low incidence of thrombocytopenia during treatment with hog mucosa and beef lung heparin. Scand J Haematol 25:19–24, 1980.

81. Bell WR, Royall RM: Heparin-associated thrombocytopenia: A comparison of three heparin preparations. N Engl J Med 303:902–907, 1980.

82. Ansell J, Slepchuk N Jr, Kumar R, et al: Heparin induced thrombocytopenia: A prospective study. Thromb Haemost 43:61–65, 1980.

83. Cipolle RJ, Rodvold KA, Seifert R, et al: Heparin-associated thrombocytopenia: A prospective evaluation of 211 patients. Therap Drug Monitoring 5:205–211, 1983.

84. Powers PJ, Kelton JG, Carter CJ: Studies on the frequency of heparin-associated thrombocytopenia. Thromb Res 33:439–443, 1984.

85. Green D, Martin GJ, Shoichet SH, et al: Thrombocytopenia in a prospective, randomized, double-blind trial of bovine and porcine heparin. Am J Med Sci 288:60–64, 1984.

86. Ramirez-Lassepas M, Cipolle RJ, Rodvold KA, et al: Heparin-induced thrombocytopenia in patients with cerebrovascular ischemic disease. Neurology 34:736–740, 1984.

87. Ansell JE: Heparin-induced thrombocytopenia. What is its real frequency? Chest 88:878–882, 1985.

88. Bailey RT, Ursick JA, Heim KL, et al: Heparin-associated thrombocytopenia: A prospective comparison of bovine lung heparin, manufactured by a new process, and porcine intestinal heparin. Drug Intell Clin Pharm 20:374–378, 1986.

89. Hull RD, Raskob GE, Rosenbloom D, et al: Heparin for 5 days as compared with 10 days in the initial treatment of proximal venous thrombosis. N Engl J Med 322:1260–1264, 1990.

90. Stead RB, Schafer AI, Rosenberg RD, et al: Heterogeneity of heparin lots associated with thrombocytopenia and thromboembolism. Am J Med 77:185–188, 1984.

91. Boshkov LK, Warkentin TE, Hayward CPM, et al: Heparin-induced thrombocytopenia and thrombosis: Clinical and laboratory studies. Br J Haematol 84:322–328, 1993.

92. Hunter JB, Lonsdale RJ, Wenham PW, Frostick SP: Lesson of the week: Heparin induced thrombosis: An important complication of heparin prophylaxis for thromboembolic disease in surgery. Br Med J 307:53–55, 1993.

93. Edson JR: Heparin-induced thrombocytopenia. J Lab Clin Med 120:355–356, 1992.

94. Chong BH, Burgess J, Ismail F: The clinical usefulness of the platelet aggregation test for the diagnosis of heparin-induced thrombocytopenia. Thromb Haemost 69:344–350, 1993.

95. Greinacher A, Michels I, Kiefel V, Mueller-Eckhardt C: A rapid and sensitive test for diagnosing heparin-associated thrombocytopenia. Thromb Haemost 66:734–736, 1991.

96. Sheridan D, Carter C, Kelton JG: A diagnostic test for heparin-induced thrombocytopenia. Blood 67:27–30, 1986.

97. McCabe White M, Siders L, Jennings LK, White FL: The effect of residual heparin on the interpretation of heparin-induced platelet aggregation in the diagnosis of heparin-associated thrombocytopenia. Thromb Haemost 68:88, 1992.

98. Bell WR: Heparin-associated thrombocytopenia and thrombosis. J Lab Clin Med 111:600–604, 1988.

99. Kelton JG, Sheridan D, Brain H, et al: Clinical usefulness of testing for a heparin-dependent platelet-aggregating factor in patients with suspected heparin-associated thrombocytopenia. J Lab Clin Med 103:606–612, 1984.

100. Walls JT, Curtis JJ, Silver D, et al: Heparin-induced thrombocytopenia in open heart surgical patients: Sequelae of late recognition. Ann Thorac Surg 53:787–791, 1992.

101. Dieck JA, Rizo-Patron C, Unisa A, et al: A new manifes-

tation and treatment alternative for heparin-induced thrombosis. Chest 98:1524–1526, 1990.

102. Mehta DP, Yoder EL, Appel J, Bergsman KL: Heparin-induced thrombocytopenia and thrombosis: Reversal with streptokinase A case report and review of literature. Am J Hematol 36:275–279, 1991.

103. Demers C, Ginsberg JS, Brill-Edwards P, et al: Rapid anticoagulation using ancrod for heparin-induced thrombocytopenia. Blood 78:2194–2197, 1991.

104. Warkentin TE, Kelton JG: Heparin-induced thrombocytopenia. Prog Hemost Thromb 10:1–34, 1991.

105. Soutar RL, Ginsberg JS: Uses of heparin. Ancrod for heparin induced thrombocytopenia. Br Med J 306:1410, 1993.

106. Murdoch IA, Beattie RM, Silver DM: Heparin-induced thrombocytopenia in children. Acta Paediatr 82:495–497, 1993.

107. Chong BH, Ismail F, Cade J, et al: Heparin-induced thrombocytopenia: Studies with a new low molecular weight heparinoid, Org 10172. Blood 73:1592–1596, 1989.

108. Greinacher A, Eckhardt T, Mussmann J, Mueller-Eckhardt C: Pregnancy complicated by heparin associated thrombocytopenia: Management by a prospectively in vitro selected heparinoid (Org 10172). Thromb Res 71:123–126, 1993.

109. Matsuo T, Kario K, Chikahira Y, et al: Treatment of heparin-induced thrombocytopenia by use of argatroban, a synthetic thrombin inhibitor. Br J Haematol 82:627–629, 1992.

110. Nand S: Hirudin therapy for heparin-associated thrombocytopenia and deep venous thrombosis. Am J Hematol 43:310–311, 1993.

111. Grau E, Linares M, Olaso MA, et al: Heparin-induced thrombocytopenia—Response to intravenous immunoglobulin in vivo and in vitro. Am J Hematol 39:312–313, 1992.

112. Nand S, Robinson JA: Plasmapheresis in the management of heparin-associated thrombocytopenia with thrombosis. Am J Hematol 28:204–206, 1988.

113. Brady J, Riccio JA, Yumen OH, et al: Plasmapheresis: A therapeutic option in the management of heparin-associated thrombocytopenia with thrombosis. Am J Clin Pathol 96:394–397, 1991.

114. Harkness DR, Byrnes JJ, Lian ECY: Hazard of platelet transfusion in thrombotic thrombocytopenia purpura. JAMA 246:1931–1933, 1981.

# Chapter 36

# Thrombosis and Cancer

Richard L. Edwards and Frederick R. Rickles

The increased frequency of subclinical and clinical thromboembolic disorders in patients with cancer has been recognized for over 100 years. Professor Armand Trousseau, for whom the clinical syndrome of migratory thrombophlebitis associated with cancer was named, first noted in 1865 that in patients with cancer, "There appears in the cachexia . . . a particular condition of the blood which predisposes it to spontaneous coagulation . . ."[1] Since then, much has been learned about the prethrombotic state present in many patients with cancer,[2] although many questions remain unanswered. This chapter examines several of these questions, including (1) the true incidence of thromboembolic disorders (TED) in patients with cancer and whether the occurrence of TED is sufficient justification to initiate a search for underlying malignancy; (2) the important factors in the pathogenesis of thromboembolism in cancer; (3) those tests (if any) that are helpful in defining the presence of the prethrombotic state in cancer; and (4) how thromboembolic disorders should be treated in the patient with cancer.

## THROMBOEMBOLIC DISEASE IN PATIENTS WITH CANCER

Hemostatic abnormalities are present in a high proportion of cancer patients, and the risk of TED rises in patients with advanced or metastatic disease. In several studies, TED has been shown to complicate the clinical course of from 1 to 11% of patients with cancer.[3, 4] Autopsy studies have demonstrated an even higher incidence of subclinical TED.[5] Although mucin-producing tumors of the gastrointestinal tract have long been associated with TED, hematologic malignancies and other types of solid tumors may also be implicated in TED and/or bleeding. Immobility, surgery, and chemotherapy are likely contributing risk factors for TED in many cancer patients.

The risk of thromboembolic complications in the post-surgical period is markedly increased in patients with cancer. In one large meta-analysis, Clagett and Reisch observed a 29.1% incidence of deep venous thrombosis (DVT) in 546 cancer patients undergoing a variety of surgical procedures. This compared with a 6.9% incidence of DVT in all patients in that study and suggested a greater than two-fold increase in the rate of postoperative DVT in cancer patients.[6] This high rate of TED following cancer surgery has been confirmed in many studies and has been reviewed recently.[7] Substantial evidence also exists that implicates chemotherapy as an independent risk factor for the development of TED. Indeed, hormonal as well as cytotoxic chemotherapy has been noted to increase the TED rate in patients with a variety of tumor types including prostate and breast cancer and lymphoma.[8-10]

Thrombosis of the deep venous system of the lower extremity and pulmonary embolism are the most common and dangerous forms of TED in cancer patients. However, other thrombotic complications have been reported, some of which have a particular association with cancer. The syndrome of migratory superficial thrombophlebitis was first described by Trousseau in a patient with gastric carcinoma. This syndrome has been found to occur primarily in patients with mucin-secreting carcinomas of the gastrointestinal tract, particularly of pancreatic origin. Trousseau's syndrome may involve superficial veins (including unusual sites such as the upper extremities and chest wall) and has a high incidence of recurrence despite conventional anticoagulant therapy.

Thrombotic nonbacterial endocarditis (marantic endocarditis) is also found more commonly in patients with cancer.[11] The major clinical sequelae, which are the result of embolization to the brain, heart, and peripheral vessels, include

374

stroke, myocardial infarction, and distal ischemia. Hepatic vein thrombosis and portal vein thrombosis have been reported most frequently among cancer patients in those with myeloproliferative disorders and solid tumors of the liver, kidney, and adrenal glands.[12, 13] Thrombosis of the superior vena cava, secondary to caval obstruction, usually occurs in patients with mediastinal tumors. Other thrombotic complications of malignant disease are related to iatrogenic factors such as presence of indwelling venous catheters and administration of chemotherapy.

The high incidence of TED in cancer patients adds significantly to morbidity and may be a contributing factor in up to 50% of cancer deaths.[5] Conversely, it has also been suggested that the presence of unexplained TED may be a useful marker for undiagnosed cancer. Several recent studies have examined the incidence of cancer in patients who initially present with TED. Gore and coworkers have observed a 14.7% incidence of cancer in a 2-year followup of 128 patients presenting with angiographically proven pulmonary embolism.[14] The incidence of cancer was zero in an age- and sex-matched control group who presented with similar symptoms but did not have angiographic evidence of pulmonary embolism. Similarly, a 5-year followup study of 370 patients with DVT demonstrated a 6.3% incidence of cancer, whereas cancer was diagnosed in only 2.4% of 1,073 patients with symptoms of venous thrombosis but negative impedance plethysmography.[15] In a more recent study, Prandoni and coworkers followed 250 patients with venographically documented DVT for 2 years. The incidence of cancer in patients with secondary venous thrombosis (thrombosis associated with well recognized risk factors) was compared with the incidence of cancer in patients with idiopathic thrombosis (no known risk factors) and no previous history of DVT. At the time of diagnosis, 3.3% of patients with idiopathic thrombosis had evidence of cancer on routine examination, whereas none of those with secondary thrombosis had cancer. During the 2-year followup period, 7.6% of patients with idiopathic thrombosis developed evidence of cancer as compared with only 1.9% of patients with secondary thrombosis. The incidence of cancer was also greater in the patients with pulmonary embolism and/or recurrent venous thrombosis.[16]

In contrast to these studies, Griffen and coworkers found no evidence of increased cancer risk in 76 patients with venous thrombosis or 37 patients with pulmonary embolism as compared with control groups with negative venograms and lung scans followed for up to 5 years.[17]

At this time, the question of whether to pursue the diagnosis of occult cancer in all patients presenting with unexplained TED remains unresolved. Until the results of large, prospective, well controlled clinical trials are available, it would seem prudent to follow such patients closely and to aggressively evaluate those patients with symptoms suggestive of malignant disease (e.g., weight loss, bleeding, pain). Patients with unusual types of TED (migratory superficial thrombophlebitis, hepatic vein thrombosis, etc.) as well as recurrent or refractory TED should be evaluated at the time of presentation for an occult neoplasm.

## THE PATHOGENESIS OF THROMBOSIS IN CANCER

Rudolf Virchow first recognized that thrombosis could be precipitated by primary abnormalities of the vessel wall, reduction of blood flow (stasis), or changes in the composition of the blood itself.[18] His observations have been validated repeatedly over the past 135 years and remain particularly relevant to classifying the defects that lead to thromboembolic disorders in cancer patients. Cancer patients often have defects in one or more of these basic components of the hemostatic system, and many (if not all) of these individuals have evidence for a "prethrombotic state."[19] When physiologic antithrombotic mechanisms are overwhelmed by this prethrombotic process, thrombosis occurs.

The endothelial surface of the vessel wall, in addition to its physical properties as a "nonwettable" surface, is normally well suited to prevent thrombus formation through the expression of naturally occurring antithrombotic mediators including heparin and heparans, thrombomodulin, prostacyclin, and plasminogen activators. Direct vascular invasion by tumor cells may damage this metabolically active thromboresistant endothelium, leading to development of the prethrombotic state.

Normal laminar blood flow is important for minimizing contact between the endothelial surface and red cells or platelets. Moreover, the flow of blood helps prevent the local accumulation of activated clotting factors by carrying them away to the liver where they can be cleared. Several clinical conditions lead to an increased incidence of venous stasis in cancer patients, including prolonged periods of bedrest, vascular compromise by bulky tumors, and immobility due to pain. Moreover, certain tumor types are associated with hyperviscosity due to either increased concentration of plasma proteins (e.g., myeloma and Waldenstrom's macroglobulinemia) or cellular elements (e.g., polycythemia vera, essential thrombocytosis). This increase in viscosity may further impair blood flow and enhance the development of the prethrombotic state.

Much effort has been devoted to studies of the factors leading to "hypercoagulability" of the blood in patients with cancer. It is now clear that the pathogenesis of tumor-related thrombosis is extremely complex and may vary depending upon the characteristics of the individual patient and the tumor type. Several mechanisms have been described in experimental and human tumors, including (1) expression of direct and indirect procoagulant activities by tumor cells; (2) expression of specific and/or nonspecific procoagulant activities by tumor-associated leukocytes; and (3) expression of mediators of platelet adhesion or aggregation by tumor cells.

## Procoagulant Activities of Tumor Cells

Many publications have identified and characterized procoagulant activity (PCA) in extracts or sonicates of human and animal tumors or tumor cell lines. Several different PCAs have been described, all of which may activate blood coagulation at different sites in the coagulation cascade. The properties of these tumor PCAs have been compiled in registries maintained by the Scientific and Standardization Committee of the International Society on Thrombosis and Haemostasis.[20, 21] The two best characterized of the tumor cell-associated PCAs are tissue factor (TF) and activators of factor X.

Tissue factor is a nonproteolytic cofactor for factor VIIa in the activation of either factor IX or factor X. Although human leukemia cells were suspected to possess substantial thromboplastic activity as early as 1954,[22] it was not until 1973 that Gralnick and Abrell identified tissue factor–like activity in the buffy coat of patients with progranulocytic leukemia.[23] Tissue factor has since been identified in intact cells, extracts, and shed vesicles obtained from many human tumors and cell lines.[24] Tissue factor also appears to be a more potent activator of blood coagulation than the factor X activators and may be the single most important tumor cell procoagulant.[25]

Factor X activators have the characteristics of cysteine proteases and were originally identified in extracts of the rabbit $V_2$ carcinoma.[26, 27] Factor X activators have subsequently been described in tumors of the breast, lung, kidney, and colon.

Although not unique to tumor tissue, this procoagulant may be partly responsible for the fibrin deposition observed in some tumors.[28] A nonproteolytic factor X-activator has also been described in extracts of mucin-producing tumors as well as in mucus from normal tissue.[29] Francis and colleagues demonstrated that much of the "direct" factor X–cleaving activity in tumor extracts is contributed by a complex of TF and factor VII rather than by a specific tumor-derived, factor X–activating enzyme.[30] Nevertheless, both TF and factor X activators have been implicated in the pathogenesis of clotting abnormalities associated with human malignancy. The relative contribution of TF and factor X activators to tumor-related coagulopathy remains the subject of intense interest.

## Procoagulant Activity of Tumor-associated Leukocytes

The contribution of leukocyte-derived procoagulants to thrombogenesis in inflammation and neoplasia has been assessed in several recent reviews.[2, 31] The inflammatory host response to neoplasia may provide a source of procoagulant activity equally important to that expressed by tumor cells. Leukocytes are capable of expressing procoagulant activity when stimulated in vitro and in vivo. Most authors now agree that the monocyte is the cell responsible for the in vitro generation of procoagulant activity in studies of mixed leukocyte populations.[31, 32]

Several different types of monocyte procoagulant activity have been identified. Activated monocytes express TF activity[33, 34] and have also been shown to synthesize factor VII, express functional factor V/Va, and demonstrate high affinity binding sites for factor X/Xa and fibrinogen.[35] The presumed receptor-ligand interactions that may occur on the monocyte/macrophage surface may provide a unifying explanation for the cell-associated fibrin localization characteristic of inflammatory and neoplastic disorders. Several studies have clearly demonstrated TF antigen expression by monocyte/macrophages within the tumor milieu,[36] whereas others have demonstrated increased TF procoagulant expression by peripheral blood monocytes obtained from cancer patients.[36, 37] Immunohistologic studies have shown cross-linked fibrin to be primarily associated with tumor-associated monocyte/macrophages rather than the tumor cells themselves.[24, 35, 38] Thus, the relative importance of tumor cell procoagulants and leukocyte procoagulants in the pathogenesis of tumor-associated activation of blood coagulation remains to be defined.

## Platelet Activation and Cancer

Platelets appear to play a role in the development of metastatic disease. Pathologic studies have frequently demonstrated platelet aggregates surrounding tumor deposits. Many studies have shown that thrombocytopenia or inhibition of platelet function may provide protection against metastasis formation in experimental models.[39-41] Subsequently, it has been shown that tumor cells may cause platelet activation in vitro via several mechanisms.

Platelet aggregating activity (PAA) has been identified in a variety of tumor cell lines as well as in whole tumor cells and cell extracts.[42-44] Several mechanisms have been described for tumor cell–mediated platelet aggregation, including tumor-related generation of thrombin,[45] production of adenosine diphosphate,[46] and activation of prostaglandin metabolism.[47] However, thrombin is known to be a potent platelet activator, and recent studies suggest that tumor-induced thrombin generation may be the most important PAA in cancer patients.[48]

## ABNORMALITIES OF BLOOD COAGULATION TESTS IN PATIENTS WITH CANCER

Because thromboembolic disorders lead to greatly increased morbidity and mortality in patients with cancer, methods for early detection of the prethrombotic state would be helpful in the design of clinical trials of the prophylaxis of thrombosis in this high-risk group. Abnormalities of the so-called *routine* tests of blood coagulation have been described in upwards of 90% of patients with cancer.[4, 49] Commonly, these include elevation of plasma clotting factor levels (fibrinogen, factors V, VIII, IX, and XI), elevated fibrin and fibrinogen degradation products (FDP),[4, 49-51] and thrombocytosis.[3, 49] Because many of these findings were based on retrospective analyses of small numbers of patients referred to the coagulation laboratory, they may not accurately represent the frequency of abnormal coagulation tests in the patient population at large. Moreover, in some of the smaller studies, the potential confusing effect of cancer treatment on the abnormalities of coagulation tests could not be determined. Nevertheless, two studies have demonstrated a correlation between the extent of disease and serial fibrinogen levels and platelet counts in patients

with advanced malignancy independent of the effects of chemotherapy.[49, 52]

Edwards and colleagues analyzed the results of routine clotting tests in 431 patients enrolled consecutively in a multi-institutional prospective Veterans Administration Cooperative Trial (VA CSP #75) of warfarin anticoagulation as adjunctive therapy in patients with cancer.[49] In that study, only 8% of untreated patients had elevated levels of FDP and 14% had abnormal prothrombin times (PT) at the time of entry into the study (shortly following diagnosis of cancer). Of the patients with advanced carcinoma of the lung, colon, prostate, or head and neck, 48% had elevated fibrinogen levels and 36% had thrombocytosis at the time of presentation.

In a subsequent study (VA CSP #188), the same group performed routine and specialized clotting studies in 719 consecutive patients with advanced cancer.[53] At the time of diagnosis, 53% of patients had elevated fibrinogen levels, 54% had elevated platelet counts, and 28% had elevated FDP levels, whereas only 3.5% had prolongation of the activated partial thromboplastin time (APTT). Coagulation tests were repeated on each patient at monthly intervals. The mean platelet count in this group of patients with lung or colon cancer increased as disease progressed and reached a maximum 1 month prior to death. Despite the progressive upward trend, the difference between the mean platelet count 1 month prior to death and that obtained at entry into the study did not reach statistical significance. A similar rise in plasma fibrinogen levels was observed in these patients. Overall, the results the coagulation tests performed in these two large clinical trials suggested the presence of low-grade activation of blood coagulation in most patients with advanced cancer. However, neither overt disseminated intravascular coagulation (DIC) nor clinical thromboembolic episodes were observed in these patients.

More sensitive and specific tests of blood coagulation have been utilized in studies of cancer patients and tumor-bearing experimental animals in an attempt to assess subclinical activation of the coagulation system. Such studies have measured radiolabeled fibrinogen turnover,[54-57] plasma fibrinopeptide A (FpA),[56-65] and/or prothrombin fragment 1 + 2 (F1 + 2)[61] levels in cancer patients. FpA is a small peptide released following cleavage of fibrinogen by thrombin, whereas F1 + 2 is a product released following cleavage of prothrombin by factor Xa. Other studies have examined plasma levels of fibrin D-dimer (the crosslinked fibrin degradation product), and thrombin-antithrombin (TAT) complex levels in patients with leukemia or solid tumors.[61, 64–67] Virtually all of these studies have suggested that patients with leukemia and solid tumors have laboratory evidence of activation of blood coagulation, or low-grade (compensated) DIC.[68] The evidence for low-grade activation of blood coagulation was observed regardless of the presence or absence of clinical evidence for TED and was generally noted at the time of tumor diagnosis, prior to the initiation of chemotherapy.

Consistent with these observations, 67% of the patients in the VA CSP Trial #75 and 75% of patients in VA CSP #188 had elevated FpA levels at the time they entered the studies.[49] FpA levels were also compared with the results of routine coagulation studies. Elevated fibrinogen levels and platelet counts were observed more frequently in those patients who presented with elevated FpA levels. This data may suggest a relationship between low levels of circulating thrombin and the regulation of platelet production and fibrinogen synthesis.

The results of other specialized tests of blood coagulation have suggested a shift in the normal balance of hemostasis toward thrombosis in patients with cancer. Several studies have addressed the potential significance of reduced plasma levels of a number of antithrombotic proteins including antithrombin III,[52, 62, 69–71] protein C,[52, 62, 71, 72] and free protein S.[72] Others have examined the significance of increased levels of some of the prothrombotic proteins, such as plasminogen activator inhibitor-1 (PAI-1)[65, 66] or von Willebrand factor (vWF).[66, 73] At this time, lacking studies in which coagulation tests and tests for asymptomatic venous thrombosis were performed simultaneously, it is difficult to draw conclusions regarding the predictive value of serial levels of any of these putative ''thrombotic markers'' and their relationship to development of TED in an individual patient.

As suggested by the relationship between fibrinogen levels, platelet counts, and tumor burden, it is possible that sensitive markers for the hypercoagulable state may provide information on the status of tumor growth. Several studies have demonstrated a correlation between plasma FpA levels and the extent of disease or disease activity in some patients with solid tumors.[60, 63, 65] In the VA CSP #75 trial, serial FpA levels appeared to correlate with disease progression, supporting the results of the single-institution studies reported previously.[56–59] In the larger study (CSP #188), FpA levels, which were elevated de novo, remained initially stable or decreased toward the normal range in those patients who responded to therapy. As in the initial study, the FpA levels increased progressively over time as tumor burden increased. One month prior to death, FpA levels were increased in 118 of 135 patients available for study (87%), and the mean FpA level had risen significantly when it was compared with the values determined at the time of randomization. In addition, it has been suggested that serial FpA levels may allow the prediction of relapse in acute leukemia.[59]

Similarly, it has been claimed that tumor growth may be predicted by elevations of other marker proteins for activation of clotting such as D-dimer,[65] which may reflect ongoing fibrin deposition at the site of a growing tumor, or vWF,[73] which may reflect endothelial cell perturbation by tumor products.

Thus, although the measurement of sensitive indicators of blood coagulation may not be useful for predicting thrombotic complications in individual patients,[62] some combination of these tests may be useful for monitoring disease progression in selected patients, particularly those in large clinical trials.

## TREATMENT OF THROMBOEMBOLIC DISORDERS IN CANCER PATIENTS

The primary treatment goals in patients with thromboembolic disease are to prevent death from pulmonary embolism, reduce morbidity associated with thrombus, minimize occurrence of postphlebitic syndrome, and prevent recurrence of thrombosis. The same principles apply to cancer patients with TED, possibly with the added goal of slowing primary tumor growth and delaying development of metastatic disease.

Heparin anticoagulation remains the mainstay of therapy for acute venous thrombosis in cancer patients as well as in the general population.[74, 75] Heparin may be administered by continuous intravenous infusion, intermittent intravenous bolus injection, or subcutaneous injection. Although all methods are effective if a sufficient dose is administered, continuous infusion appears to have a lower rate of bleeding complications than intermittent intravenous bolus therapy.[76] Results of several studies have suggested that intermittent subcutaneous heparin therapy is of equivalent safety and efficacy to continuous intravenous therapy.[77, 78] Generally, heparin is administered at a dose sufficient to prolong the APTT to 1.5 to 2 times the control. The risk of significant bleeding is approximately 5% and occurs most frequently in patients with an excessively prolonged APTT.[79]

In most patients with uncomplicated DVT, initial therapy with heparin is followed by an extended course of treatment with oral anticoagulants (vitamin K antagonists). Bleeding is the most common complication of oral anticoagulant therapy, although newer regimens using less intense therapy (maintaining the International Normalized Ratio in the range of 2.0) have shown good efficacy with a significantly reduced risk of bleeding.[80] An alternative is adjusted dose subcutaneous heparin, which is equally effective in preventing recurrent thrombosis and may have a lower bleeding risk as compared with full-dose oral anticoagulant therapy.[81]

For several reasons, the therapy of TED may be more complex in patients with cancer. Several authors have described a state of relative heparin resistance in cancer patients and a dissociation between plasma heparin level and APTT. It has been suggested that patients may be better managed by adjusting heparin dose to maintain the plasma heparin level between 0.3 and 0.5 U/ml.[76] Cancer patients also are likely to remain at high risk for recurrent thrombosis because, in the absence of effective cancer therapy, the cancer-related prethrombotic stimuli persist. Moreover, it has been suggested that oral anticoagulants, in normal doses, are often inadequate for prevention of recurrent thrombosis in the cancer patient.[82–85] Although the reasons for resistance to oral anticoagulant therapy are not clear, these drugs do not have the antiprotease activity of heparin and may be incapable of adequately suppressing the thrombin generated by the tumor-associated procoagulants described in the previous sections of this review. Low-molecular-weight heparin is promising as chronic therapy for these patients because it may require no laboratory monitoring and it appears to cause less frequent bleeding complications than unfractionated heparin.[85] Of interest also is the recent observation that overall cancer mortality was decreased in one group of patients treated with low-molecular-heparin as compared with unfractionated heparin.[86] The role of low-molecular-weight heparin as an antitumor agent and in the chronic therapy of cancer-related thrombosis remains unclear and awaits further study in large, well-controlled prospective clinical trials.

Some patients with cancer are at high risk of bleeding when treated with either heparin or oral anticoagulants. In one study, 50% of cancer patients treated for deep venous thrombosis or pulmonary embolism developed hemorrhagic complications of anticoagulant therapy.[87] Other patients are in the terminal stages of their disease and prefer not to be burdened with the need for heparin injections or frequent laboratory monitoring for regulation of oral anticoagulant therapy. In such patients, interruption of the vena cava is effective in preventing pulmonary embolization from thrombi in the deep veins of the leg.

The Greenfield filter has become the method of choice for caval interruption because of its ease of insertion, efficacy, and low complication rate.[88] Several studies have demonstrated caval interruption to be an effective method for chronic therapy of venous thrombosis in cancer patients. Cohen and coworkers have reported the results of Greenfield filter placement in 41 cancer patients who presented with DVT or pulmonary embolism.[89] There was no operative mortality; however, 46% of the patients died of cancer during the followup period. Leg swelling improved in 76% and remained unchanged in 22% of evaluable patients. In another study, Calligaro and coworkers examined the course of 30 cancer patients who developed DVT.[90] Twenty patients were treated with anticoagulation and 10 were treated primarily with Greenfield filter placement. Of the 20 anticoagulant-treated patients, 15 developed complications and 10 ultimately required Greenfield filter placement. Of the 10 patients initially treated with a Greenfield filter, three progressed and required anticoagulant therapy. These authors suggest that Greenfield filter placement is appropriate primary therapy for DVT in patients with advanced cancer.

The treatment of TED in patients with advanced cancer remains controversial. The decision whether to initiate therapy with heparin or vena cava interruption will be best resolved through prospective, randomized clinical trials. Until such trials have been performed, decisions must be made on the basis of the physician's assessment of each patient's clinical condition, risk factors, and individual preferences. In general, caval interruption should be considered in those patients who have bled at normal levels of anticoagulation and in those patients who have suffered recurrent venous thrombosis or pulmonary embolism while they were effectively anticoagulated.

## REFERENCES

1. Trousseau A: Phlegmasia alba dolens. In Clinique Medicale de l'Hotel-Dieu de Paris. Paris, JB Balliere et Fils, 3:654–712, 1865.
2. Rickles FR, Edwards RL: Leukocytes and tumor cells in thrombosis. In Colman RW, Hirsh J, Marder VJ, Salz-

man EW (eds): Hemostasis and Thrombosis, ed 3. Philadelphia, J B Lippincott, 1994, pp 1164–1179.

3. Rickles FR, Edwards RL: Activation of blood coagulation in cancer: Trousseau's syndrome revisited. Blood 62:14–31, 1983.

4. Sun NC, McAfee WM, Hum GJ, Weiner JM: Hemostatic abnormalities in malignancy, a prospective study in one hundred eight patients. Part I. Coagulation studies. Am J Clin Pathol 71:10–16, 1979.

5. Ambrus JL, Ambrus CM, Mink IB, et al: Causes of death in cancer patients. J Med 6:61–64, 1975.

6. Clagett GP, Reisch JS: Prevention of venous thromboembolism in general surgical patients. Ann Surg 208:227–240, 1988.

7. Rickles FR, Levine M, Edwards, RL: Hemostatic alterations in cancer patients. Cancer Metastasis Rev 11:237–248, 1992.

8. Kasimis BS, Spiers AD: Thrombotic complications in patients with advanced prostate cancer treated with chemotherapy. Lancet 1:159, 1979.

9. Levine M, Gent M, Hirsh J, et al: The thrombogenic effect of anticancer drug therapy in women with Stage II breast cancer. N Engl J Med 318:404–407, 1988.

10. Seifter E, Young RC, Longo DL: Deep venous thrombosis during therapy for Hodgkin's disease. Cancer Treat Rep 69:1011–1013, 1985.

11. Min KW, Gyorkey F, Sato C: Mucin producing adenocarcinomas and nonbacterial thrombotic endocarditis. Cancer 1980; 45:2374–2382, 1980.

12. Mitchell MC, Boitnott JK, Kaufman S, et al: Budd-Chiari syndrome: Etiology, diagnosis and management. Medicine (Baltimore) 61:199–218, 1982.

13. Valla D, Casadevall N, Huisse MG, et al: Etiology of portal vein thrombosis in adults. Gastroenterology 94:1063–1069, 1988.

14. Gore JM, Appelbaum JS, Greene HL, et al: Occult cancer in patients with acute pulmonary embolism. Ann Intern Med 96:556–560, 1982.

15. Goldberg RJ, Seneff M, Gore JM, et al: Occult malignant neoplasm in patients with deep venous thrombosis. Arch Intern Med 147:251–253, 1987.

16. Prandoni P, Lensing AWA, Buller HR, et al: Deep vein thrombosis and the incidence of subsequent symptomatic cancer. N Engl J Med 327:1128–1133, 1992.

17. Griffen MR, Stanson AW, Brown ML, et al: Deep venous thrombosis and pulmonary embolism. Risk of subsequent malignant neoplasm. Arch Intern Med 147:1907–1911, 1987.

18. Virchow R: Gesammelte Abhaldungen zur Wissenschaftlichen Medecin. Frankfurt, FRG, Meidinger Sohn, 1856, p 477.

19. Luzzatto G, Schafer A: The prethrombotic state in cancer. Semin Oncol 17:147–159, 1990.

20. Edwards RL, Morgan DL, Rickles FR: Animal tumor procoagulants: Registry of the Subcommittee on Haemostasis and Malignancy of the Scientific and Standardization Committee, International Society on Thrombosis and Haemostasis. Thromb Haemost 63:133–138, 1990.

21. Edwards RL, Silver J, Rickles FR: Human tumor procoagulants. Registry of the Subcommittee on Haemostasis and Malignancy of the Scientific and Standardization Subcommittee, International Society on Thrombosis and Haemostasis. Thromb Haemost 69:205–213, 1993.

22. Eiseman G, Stefanini M: Thromboplastic activity of leukemic white cells. Proc Soc Exp Biol Med 86:763, 1954.

23. Gralnick HR, Abrell E: Studies of the procoagulant and fibrinolytic activity of promyelocytes in acute promyelocytic leukemia. Br J Haematol 24:89–99, 1973.

24. Rickles FR, Hancock WW, Edwards RL, Zacharski LR: Antimetastatic agents. I. Role of cellular procoagulants in the pathogenesis of fibrin deposition in cancer and the use of anticoagulants and/or antiplatelet drugs in cancer treatment. Semin Thromb Hemost 14:88–94, 1988.

25. Falanga A, Gordon SG: Comparison of the properties of cancer procoagulant and human amnion-chorion procoagulant. Biochem Biophys Acta 831:161–166, 1985.

26. Falanga A, Gordon SG: Isolation and characterization of cancer procoagulant A: A cysteine protease from malignant tissue. Biochemistry 24:5558, 1975.

27. Gordon SG, Cross BA: A factor X-activating cysteine protease from malignant tissue. J Clin Invest 67:1665–1671, 1981.

28. Gordon SG, Hasiba U, Cross BA, et al: Cysteine protease procoagulant from amnion-chorion. Blood 66:1261, 1985.

29. Pineo GF, Brain MC, Gallus AS: Tumor's mucus production and hypercoagulability. Ann NY Acad Sci 230:262–272, 1974.

30. Francis JL, El-Baruni K, Roath OS, Taylor I: Factor X-activating activity in normal and malignant colorectal tissue. Thromb Res 52:207, 1988.

31. Edwards RL, Rickles FR: The role of leukocytes in the activation of blood coagulation. Semin Hematol 29:202–212, 1992.

32. Rothberger H, McGee MP: Generation of coagulation factor V activity by cultured rabbit alveolar macrophages. J Exp Med 160:1880, 1984.

33. Edwards RL, Rickles FR, Bobrove AMG: Mononuclear cell tissue factor: Cell of origin and requirements for activation. Blood 54:359–370, 1979.

34. Gregory SA, Morrissey JH, Edgington TS: Regulation of tissue factor gene expression in the monocyte procoagulant response to endotoxin. Mol Cell Biol 9:2752–2755, 1989.

35. Hancock WW, Colby A, Kobzik L, et al: Localization of coagulation proteins and activated mononuclear leukocytes in lung carcinoma (abstract). Lab Invest 56:29, 1987.

36. Edwards RL, Rickles FR, Cronlund M: Abnormalities of blood coagulation in patients with cancer: Mononuclear cell tissue factor generation. J Lab Clin Med 98:917–928, 1981.

37. Morgan D, Edwards RL, Rickles FR: Monocyte procoagulant activity as a peripheral marker of clotting activation in cancer patients. Hemostasis 18:55, 1988.

38. Costantini V, Zacharski LR, Memoli VA, et al: Fibrinogen deposition and macrophage-associated fibrin formation in malignant and non-malignant lymphoid tissue. Blood 74[Suppl]:37a, 1989.

39. Gasic GJ, Gasic TB, Stewart TD: Antimetastatic effects associated with platelet reduction. Proc Natl Acad Sci USA 61:46–52, 1968.

40. Gasic GJ, Gasic TB, Galanti N, et al: Platelet tumor interactions in mice. The role of platelets in spread of malignant disease. Int J Cancer 11:704–708, 1973.

41. Gordon SG, Witul M, Cohen H, et al: Studies on platelet aggregation inhibitors in vivo. VIII. Effect of pentoxifylline on spontaneous tumor metastases. J Med 10:35–41, 1979.

42. Karpatkin S, Pearlstein E: Role of platelets in tumor cell metastasis. Ann Intern Med 95:636–641, 1981.

43. Marcum JM, McGill M, Bastida E, et al: The interaction of platelet, tumor cells, and vascular endothelium. J Lab Clin Med 96:1046–1053, 1980.

44. Bastida E: The metastatic cascade: Potential approaches for the inhibition of metastasis. Semin Thromb Hemost 14:66–72, 1988.

45. Bastida E, Ordinas A, Escolar G, et al: Tissue factor in microvesicles shed from U87MG human glioblastoma cells induces coagulation, platelet aggregation, and thrombogenesis. Blood 64:177–184, 1984.

46. Grignani G, Jamieson GA: Platelets in tumor metastasis: Generation of adenosine diphosphate by tumor cells is specific but unrelated to metastatic potential. Blood 71:844–849, 1988.

47. Honn KV, Busse WD, Sloane BF: Prostacyclin and thromboxanes. Implications for their role in tumor cell metastasis. Biochem Pharmacol 32:1–11, 1983.

48. Cavanaugh PG, Sloane BF, Bajkowski AS, et al: Purification and characterization of platelet aggregating activity from tumor cells: Copurification with procoagulant activity. Thromb Res 37:309, 1985.

49. Edwards, RL, Rickles FR, Moritz TE, et al: Abnormalities of blood coagulation tests in patients with cancer. Am J Clin Pathol 88:596–602, 1987.

50. Carlsson S: Fibrinogen degradation products in serum from patients with cancer. Acta Chir Scand 139:499–502, 1973.

51. Okajima K, Okabe H, Inoue M, Takasuki K: Characterization of the fibrinolytic state by measuring stable cross-linked fibrin degradation products in disseminated intravascular coagulation associated with acute promyelocytic leukemia. Acta Haematologica 81:15–18, 1989.

52. Wajima T, Mukhopadhyay P: Serial coagulation profiles in patients with small cell carcinoma of the lung (abstract). Thromb Haemost 62[Suppl]:136, 1989.

53. Zacharski LR, Moritz TE, Baczek LA, et al: Effect of Mopidamol on survival in carcinoma of the lung and colon: Final report of Veterans Administration Cooperative Study No. 188. J Natl Cancer Inst 80:90–97, 1988.

54. Al-Mondhiry H, Lawlor BA, Sadula D: Fibrinogen survival and fibrinolysis in acute leukemia. Cancer 35:432–435, 1975.

55. Lyman GH, Bettigole RE, Robson E, et al: Fibrinogen kinetics in patients with neoplastic disease. Cancer 41:1113–1122, 1978.

56. Yoda Y, Abe T: Fibrinopeptide A (FPA) level and fibrinogen kinetics in patients with malignant disease. Thromb Haemost 46:706–709, 1981.

57. Mombelli G, Roux A, Haeberli A, Straub PW: Comparison of $^{125}$I-fibrinogen kinetics and fibrinopeptide A in patients with disseminated neoplasias. Blood 60:381–388, 1982.

58. Peuscher FW, Cleton FJ, Armstrong L, et al: Significance of plasma fibrinopeptide A (FPA) in patients with malignancy. J Lab Clin Med 96:5–14, 1980.

59. Myers TJ, Rickles FR, Barb C, Cronlund M: Activation of blood coagulation in acute leukemia—fibrinopeptide A (FPA) generation as an indicator of disease activity. Blood 57:518–525, 1981.

60. Rickles FR, Edwards RL, Barb C, Cronlund M: Abnormalities of blood coagulation in patients with cancer: Fibrinopeptide A generation and tumor growth. Cancer 51:301–307, 1983.

61. Bauer KA, Rosenberg RD: Thrombin generation in acute promyelocytic leukemia. Blood 64:791–796, 1984.

62. Nand S, Fisher SG, Salgia R, Fisher RI: Hemostatic abnormalities in untreated cancer: Incidence and correlation with thrombotic and hemorrhagic complications. J Clin Oncol 12:1998–2003, 1987.

63. Auger MJ, Galloway MJ, Leinster SJ, et al: Elevated fibrinopeptide A levels in patients with clinically localized breast carcinoma. Haemostasis 17:336–339, 1987.

64. Lindahl AK, Sandset PM, Abildgaard U: Indices of hypercoagulation in cancer as compared with those in acute inflammation and acute infarction. Haemostasis 20:253–262, 1990.

65. Gadducci A, Baicchi U, del Bravo B, et al: The assessment of the hemostasis system in patients with ovarian and cervical carcinoma. Cancer J 4:183–187, 1991.

66. Uchiyama T, Matsumoto M, Kobayashi N: Studies of the pathogenesis of coagulopathy in patients with arterial thromboembolism and malignancy. Thromb Res 59:955–965, 1990.

67. Abshire TC, Gold SH, Odom LF, et al: The coagulopathy of childhood leukemia. Thrombin activation or primary fibrinolysis? Cancer 66:716–721, 1990.

68. Bick RL: Disseminated intravascular coagulation and related syndromes: A clinical review. Semin Thromb Hem 14:65–81, 1988.

69. Rubin RN, Kies MS, Posch JJ: Measurements of antithrombin III in solid tumor patients with and without hepatic metastases. Thromb Res 18:353–360, 1980.

70. Honegger H, Anderson N, Hewitt LA, Tullis JL: Antithrombin III profiles in malignancy, relationship to primary tumors and metastatic sites. Thromb Haemost 46:500–503, 1981.

71. Rodeghiero F, Mannucci PM, Vigano S, et al: Liver dysfunction rather than intravascular coagulation as the main cause of low protein C and antithrombin III in acute leukemia. Blood 63:965–969, 1984.

72. Troy K, Essex D, Rand J, et al: Protein C and S levels in acute leukemia. Am J Hematol 37:159–162, 1991.

73. Sweeney JD, Killion KM, Pruet CF, Spaulding MB: von Willebrand factor in head and neck cancer. Cancer 66:2387–2389, 1990.

74. Scates SM: Diagnosis and treatment of cancer-related thrombosis. Hematol Oncol Clin North Am 6:1329–1339, 1992.

75. Hull RD, Raskob GE, Hirsh J, et al: A double-blind randomized trial of intravenous versus subcutaneous heparin in the initial treatment of proximal-vein thrombosis. N Engl J Med 315:1109–1114, 1986.

76. Levine M, Hirsh J: The diagnosis and treatment of thrombosis in the cancer patient. Semin Oncol 17:160–171, 1990.

77. Doyle DJ, Turpie AGG, Hirsh J, et al: Adjusted subcutaneous heparin or continuous intravenous heparin in patients with acute deep vein thrombosis: A randomized trial. Ann Intern Med 107:441–445, 1987.

78. Bently PG, Kakkar VV, Scully MF, et al: An objective study of alternative methods of heparin administration. Thromb Res 18:177–187, 1980.

79. Levine M, Hirsh J: Hemorrhagic complications of anticoagulant therapy. Semin Thromb Hemost 12:39–57, 1986.

80. Hull R, Hirsh J, Jay R, et al: Different intensities of oral anticoagulant therapy in the treatment of proximal vein thrombosis. N Engl J Med 307:1676–1681, 1982.

81. Hull R, Delmore T, Carter C, et al: Adjusted subcutaneous heparin versus warfarin sodium in the long term treatment of venous thrombosis. N Engl J Med 306:189–194, 1982.

82. Bell WR, Starksen NF, Tong S, et al: Trousseau's syndrome. Devastating coagulopathy in the absence of heparin. Am J Med 79:423–430, 1985.

83. Mosesson MW, Coleman RW, Sherry S: Chronic intravascular coagulation syndrome. N Engl J Med 278:815–821, 1968.

84. Kazmier FJ, Bowie EJW, Hagedorn AB, et al: Treatment of intravascular coagulation and fibrinolysis syndrome. Mayo Clin Proc 49:665–672, 1974.

85. Hirsh J, Levine M: Low molecular weight heparin. Blood 79:1–17, 1992.

86. Green D, Hull RD, Brant R, Pineo G: Lower mortality in cancer patients treated with low-molecular-weight versus standard heparin. Lancet 339:1476, 1992.

87. Moore DF, Osteen TR, Karp DD, et al: Anticoagulants, venous thromboembolism, and the cancer patient. Arch Surg 116:405–407, 1981.

88. Greenfield JL, Michna AB, Arbor A: Twelve-year clinical experience with the Greenfield filter. Surgery 104:706–712, 1983.

89. Cohen JR, Grella L, Citron M: Greenfield filter instead of heparin as primary treatment for deep venous thrombosis or pulmonary embolism in patients with cancer. Cancer 70:1993–1996, 1992.

90. Calligaro KD, Bergen WS, Haut MJ, et al: Thromboembolic complications in patients with advanced cancer: Anticoagulation versus Greenfield filter placement. Ann Vasc Surg 5:186–189, 1991.

# Chapter 37

# Chronic Pulmonary Thromboembolism

Gordon T. Ford, Sid M. Viner, Brent R. Bagg, and William R. Auger

Acute pulmonary embolism is a common, well known disorder and is an important cause of morbidity and mortality in patients who develop venous thrombosis. It afflicts an estimated 600,000 people every year in the United States alone and, of these patients, approximately 50,000 will not survive the acute event.[1, 2, 3, 4IV, 5] In the vast majority who do survive, the pulmonary emboli and, to a large extent, the thrombus at the venous site from which the embolus arose, resolve rapidly and substantially owing to the endogenous fibrinolytic system. This usually results in no symptoms and no significant sequelae.

In a small minority of patients, the emboli fail to resolve and undergo fibrovascular organization, leaving endothelialized residua that cause chronic obstruction to pulmonary arterial blood flow. This can result in a condition known as chronic pulmonary thromboembolic hypertension (CPTH). Patients with this complication develop unrelenting symptoms of progressive right ventricular failure and hypoxemia. In the past, these patients received only medical management for the secondary pulmonary hypertension and had a particularly poor prognosis. It is now recognized that CPTH is amenable to surgical therapy, with a successful thromboendarterectomy offering the best chance of long-term survival. This chapter offers a brief historic perspective of this condition, its pathophysiology, clinical presentation, and diagnosis, and a discussion of the current supportive medical and surgical treatment and outcomes.

## HISTORIC PERSPECTIVE

The existence of pulmonary thrombi was first identified by pathologists in the early 1800s.

They believed that all pulmonary thrombi originated in situ rather than in the peripheral venous system. In 1819, Laennec used the term "pulmonary apoplexy" to describe the clinical characteristics and resulting pathologic changes of acute pulmonary embolism. He did not associate peripheral vein thrombi with this condition.[6] It was not until 1858 that the concept of pulmonary embolism was established by Virchow, who coined the term "Embolia," and demonstrated that foreign material placed in the peripheral venous system of dogs was found in pulmonary arteries at postmortem examination. He also demonstrated that occlusion of the pulmonary arteries did not always result in infarction and concluded that the lungs were also perfused by systemic bronchial artery collaterals.[7, 8]

The concept of chronic pulmonary thromboembolism (CPT) was suspected at the turn of the century by Hart (1916) and Moller (1920).[8] An association of CPT with progressive respiratory insufficiency was made in 1928 by Ljungdahl, who reported two patients with progressive cor pulmonale and, at autopsy, organized chronic emboli obstructing the pulmonary arteries. He was the first to associate the radiologic findings of a dilated pulmonary artery and increased right ventricular size with the clinical observations of pulmonary hypertension.[8] The condition was largely regarded as an autopsy curiosity, and antemortem diagnosis was unusual. In the mid 1900s, several case reports appeared on chronic cor pulmonale, which was thought to be the result of chronic pulmonary emboli.[5] In 1950, Carroll reported a series of five patients with this condition. He provided the first detailed description of the clinical signs and symptoms and results of diagnostic tests, including right heart catheterization and pulmonary angiography.[9] The small number of patients who were diagnosed with this condition received only medical management for secondary pulmonary hypertension, including oxygen, vasodilator, fibrinolytic and anticoagulant therapy. Long-term prognosis was very poor.

This changed as advances in cardiac surgical techniques led to the ability to perform thromboendarterectomy, which offered a surgical "cure." The history of a surgical approach to thromboembolism dates back to 1908, when Trendelenburg described a surgical treatment for acute pulmonary embolism.[10] Subsequent case reports described different surgical techniques for chronic pulmonary thromboembolic disease, but it was not until 1956 that Hollister proposed pulmonary thromboendarterectomy as the favored approach because of the adherent and endothelialized nature of the organized thrombus. He noted that the use of anticoagulant and enzyme therapy would make possible some degree of prevention and control of thromboembolic disease.[11] The procedure was first performed successfully in 1958 by Allison, at Oxford, and subsequent pioneering work by Snyder in 1961 and Houk in 1963 established pulmonary thromboendarterectomy as the treatment of choice for chronic pulmonary embolism.[12–14] The first reported procedure utilizing cardiopulmonary bypass to assist in the surgical approach was in 1964 by Castleman.[15] Over the next two decades the surgical procedure was advanced significantly. There have been more than 400 cases of pulmonary endarterectomy reported, with the vast majority coming from the University of California Medical Center at San Diego (UCSD). The rate of surgical correction at that institution has been steadily increasing each year and surgeons are currently operating on two or three patients a week (Fig. 37–1).[4IV]

The establishment of an early diagnosis of CPTH has become more important because of the availability of a potential surgical treatment. Early diagnosis has been facilitated by an increased awareness among physicians of the characteristic clinical presentation and natural history of the disorder and by advances in diagnostic techniques such as lung scanning, pulmonary angiography, and right heart catheterization. The diagnosis of CPT involving the major pulmonary vessels is now made more often during life, and it is apparent that CPTH is more common than was once previously thought. Although the exact incidence of pulmonary hypertension secondary to unresolved emboli is not known, Jamieson and coworkers have esti-

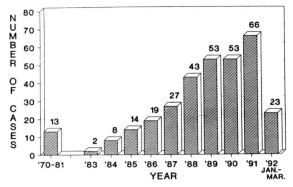

**Figure 37–1.** Number of patients with CPTH who have received pulmonary thromboendarterectomy at UCSD since 1970. Annualized projection for 1992 is 90 patients. (Used with permission from Jamieson SW, Auger WR, Fedullo PF, et al: Experience and results with 150 pulmonary thromboendarterectomy operations over a 29-month period. J Thorac Cardiovasc Surg 106:116–127, 1993.)

mated that this sequela may develop in 0.1 to 0.2% of survivors of an acute embolic event, or 540 to 1,080 patients a year in the United States.[4IV]

## PATHOPHYSIOLOGY

The natural history of chronic thromboembolic pulmonary vascular disease has been difficult to accurately define, given the subtleties of presentation and the frequently asymptomatic, initial acute thromboembolic events. For unclear reasons, the intrinsic ability to resolve acute pulmonary thromboemboli is inadequate in these patients, with a consequent clinical course that is divergent from that of most acute embolic survivors.

Throughout the 1960s and 1970s, the natural history of acute pulmonary thromboembolic disease was extensively described. Numerous studies examined the resolution of acute pulmonary emboli prior to therapy, following treatment with intravenous heparin and oral anticoagulation, or following thrombolytic therapy and longterm anticoagulation.[16–21] The information that is available is based primarily on sequential lung scan studies. Review of these studies supports the concept that in the majority of embolic survivors, on appropriate therapy, thrombus dissolution can be seen to begin within the first several days of the acute event, with significant resolution of the thrombus burden over the subsequent 2 to 4 weeks.[22] Despite reported exceptions, complete resolution of acute pulmonary thromboemboli within the first 2 weeks is distinctly unusual.[23–25] Conversely, the persistence of perfusion deficits by scintigraphic studies months following the occurrence of acute thromboemboli is generally underrecognized, although well described.

Tow and Wagner described 69 patients with various degrees of thromboembolic burden, who were followed for 4 months after their acute event.[21] In those individuals with minimal involvement (defined as 1–15% of lung involved with thromboemboli), 67% had complete return of blood flow at 120 days; 75% showed significant improvement. In 31 patients with intermediate involvement of their pulmonary vascular bed, only 38% had complete return of perfusion, and 51% demonstrated significant improvement. In a group of nine patients who had marked thromboembolic burden, only 20% experienced normalization of perfusion over the 4-month period, with 70% showing a substantial reduction in the severity of perfusion deficits. The implication of these observations is that even in a patient population receiving adequate anticoagulation, a high percentage of patients fail to completely normalize pulmonary blood flow over several months. This is more often the case in patients experiencing a significant thromboembolic burden.

In 1968, Murphy and Bulloch found that lung perfusion scans up to 5 months after an acute pulmonary embolic event demonstrated significant perfusion deficits in patients who experienced a massive pulmonary embolic event.[18] In 15 of these 25 patients, complete resolution was seen during the 20-week period of observation, although the rate of resolution was quite variable. Persistent perfusion abnormalities by scintigraphic studies have also been noted by other investigators. In a study of 69 acute pulmonary embolic patients, Palla and coworkers documented persistent perfusion defects in all patients at 6 months following the acute thromboembolic event, although substantial perfusion recovery was seen within the first 4 weeks.[19] Similar observations were made by Prediletto and coworkers, who followed 33 acute embolic event survivors over a 180-day period.[20]

These data suggest that the resolution of acute pulmonary thromboembolic disease has a variable time course, most likely dependent on multiple factors including the level of organization of the thrombus prior to embolization, the overall embolic burden in the pulmonary vascular bed, and the presence of associated cardiopulmonary disorders. Although thrombus dissolution may be prompt, it is important to recognize that persistent abnormalities on perfusion scanning may be observed months after adequate anticoagulation, and in some cases,

minor perfusion abnormalities may persist indefinitely. In the majority of patients, these residual perfusion deficits are typically minor and are associated with normal pulmonary vascular pressure and right ventricular function, but in a minority of patients, the residua may be extensive enough to lead to hemodynamic sequelae and thereafter cardiopulmonary symptoms.[16]

Recent research has focused on the mechanisms of poor thrombus dissolution. It has been established that fibrin thrombi are degraded in large part by the proteolytic action of plasmin. This serine protease circulates in plasma as a proenzyme, plasminogen, and current information indicates that its major endogenous activator is tissue-type plasminogen activator (TPA).[26–28] The activity of plasmin within the vasculature is regulated either via endogenous synthesis and release from endothelial cells or by complex formation and inactivation by its primary physiologic inhibitor, type 1 plasminogen activator inhibitor (PAI-1). PAI-1 is secreted by a variety of cells, including endothelial cells, smooth muscle cells, and fibroblasts. Its synthesis is regulated by a wide spectrum of physiologic compounds.[29, 30]

Although abnormalities of the fibrinolytic system have been implicated as causing arterial and venous thrombosis, studies investigating the endogenous fibrinolytic system in patients with CPT revealed neither excessive PAI-1 activity in peripheral blood nor inadequate production of TPA.[31–34] However, other data indicate that rather than occurring at a systemic level, the regulation of plasminogen activation may occur as a localized event within the vascular wall.[35, 36]

Lang and coworkers have demonstrated that high levels of PAI-1 are present within pulmonary thromboendarterectomy specimens from CPTH patients. This suggests that PAI-1 expression by cells within thromboemboli may play a role in the stabilization of thrombi.[37] Little is known about the source and localization of PAI-1 expression in the local environment within a thrombus. Because deep venous thrombi are the source for pulmonary thromboemboli, it is possible that cells expressing PAI-1 play a role in the resistance of the thrombi to lysis after embolization and to the persistence of thrombi residing in the deep venous system. Future experiments directed at defining the factors and conditions associated with a high level of PAI-1 expression by cells contained within chronic thromboemboli may contribute to our understanding of the pathophysiology of this disease.[37]

In an effort to better understand the pathophysiology of CPTH, investigators have searched for other hypercoagulable disorders in these patients. The presence of a lupus anticoagulant has been identified in about 10% of CPTH patients, but less than 1% manifest deficiencies of protein C, protein S, or antithrombin III.[38, 39]

Greengard and coworkers have reported that the most common laboratory-based cause of deep vein thrombosis (DVT) is resistance to activated protein C. The cause of this resistance is a mutation in the factor V gene by a single amino acid substitution. They described an example of familial thrombosis and resistance to active protein C by this mutation. This important observation may indicate a genetic role in the development of venous thrombosis.[39a]

The pathophysiology of CPTH may also be related to abnormalities of the vascular endothelium. The endothelium and endothelial-platelet interactions may play an important role not only in clot formation, but also in clot lysis and the development of secondary pulmonary arteriolar hypertensive changes in some patients. The endothelium is known to produce a variety of substances having antiplatelet, anticoagulant, vasodilating, and vasoconstricting properties.[40] The endothelial product prostacyclin causes vasodilation and inhibition of platelet aggregation. As previously noted, endothelial cells also produce TPA, which in turn can have both aggregatory and inhibitory effects on platelets.[40, 41] If aggregatory effects predominate, lysis of clot may be followed by rethrombosis. Activated platelets can also release PAI-1, which, as previously noted, has been found locally in increased quantities in chronic thrombus.

Endothelial-derived relaxing factor, now known to be nitric oxide (NO), is a potent biologic messenger with several unique properties.[42, 43] NO has antithrombotic effects related to inhibition of platelet aggregation and adhesion. It inhibits the proliferation of smooth muscle cells (antimitogenic effect) that may otherwise contribute to the development of secondary pulmonary hypertension. Furthermore, endogenous NO may be largely responsible for vasodilator tone in the systemic and pulmonary circulations. Exogenous NO administration by inhalation has been shown to decrease pulmonary artery pressure in patients with secondary pulmonary hypertension associated with hypoxia, chronic obstructive pulmonary disease (COPD), and adult respiratory distress syndrome.[44]

In addition to the relaxing factors prostacyclin and NO, the endothelium produces several potent vasoconstrictors. Endothelin-1 is produced by endothelial cells and is the most potent vasoconstrictor known in man.[45] Giaid

and coworkers have shown an increased expression of endothelin-1 in vascular endothelial cells in patients with pulmonary hypertension (particularly primary pulmonary hypertension), suggesting that local production of this mediator contributes to the vascular abnormalities associated with pulmonary hypertension.[46]

Although supposition as to the cause for pulmonary hypertension in patients with CPTH is related to proximal thrombi causing a net loss of cross-sectional area of the pulmonary vascular bed, endothelial dysfunction and endothelial-platelet interaction may play an important role in the persistence of clot in some patients and the development of secondary pulmonary hypertensive changes in small pulmonary arterioles. This is an area that will be subject to intense investigation in the future.

In patients with CPT, the degree of residual embolic obstruction varies widely, leaving some with minor residua, whereas others retain extensive vascular occlusion of the major (main, lobar, and segmental) pulmonary vessels. In the presence of partial or complete obstruction of only a few vessels, pulmonary hypertension does not occur. However, when there is more extensive loss of a cross-sectional area of the pulmonary vascular bed, pulmonary hypertension appears initially with exertion, then eventually at rest. The pulmonary hypertension that develops is the result of a critical reduction in the effective cross-sectional area for blood flow. No predictable correlation exists between the extent to which the pulmonary arteries are occluded and the observed elevation in pulmonary vascular resistance. It has been suggested that over an unknown duration of time, the relatively high flow of blood through the nonoccluded pulmonary vascular bed may incite secondary hypertensive changes in the precapillary pulmonary arterioles.[39] More distal, muscular pulmonary arteries may undergo medial hypertrophy and plexiform changes as seen in patients with primary pulmonary hypertension.[47] These changes may play a substantial role in further increases in pulmonary vascular resistance that lead to pulmonary hypertension and increased right ventricular demand.[39, 47]

On gross examination, pathology demonstrates that the proximal pulmonary arteries involved with chronic thrombi are dilated and filled with gray-to-yellow, friable, laminated thrombotic material that is firmly adherent to the vessel wall. A thin rim of superimposed fresh red thrombus may also layer the surface. Partial recanalization often occurs, resulting in the formation of intra-arterial cords, bands and webs (Fig. 37–2).[48] Partially organized and chronic

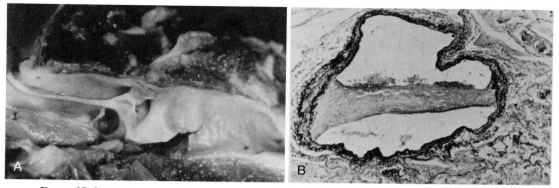

**Figure 37–2.** (A) A gross specimen demonstrating a vestige of a resolving embolus with a web-like structure partially obstructing the pulmonary artery. (B) Photomicrograph of a pulmonary embolus that has undergone partial resolution, leaving a fibrous band in an elastic pulmonary artery. (Used with permission from Wagenvoort CA, Wagenvoort N: Pathology of Pulmonary Hypertension. New York, John Wiley & Sons, 1977.)

emboli are simultaneously present in many patients. Histology shows changes characteristic of chronic thrombosis with proliferation of fibrous connective tissue and small blood vessels penetrating a variable distance into the thrombus, attaching it to the intimal surface of the vessel wall. The endothelium proliferates at the margins of the thrombus, but complete endothelialization does not occur. Complete fibrovascular organization may occur, resulting in a classic recanalized fibrous mass obstructing the arterial lumen as the thrombus extends into smaller lobar arteries. In these arteries, the muscular media demonstrates basophilic degenerative changes as seen in aortic cystic medial necrosis. The smooth muscle and elastic fibers of the arterial wall are displaced by cleft-like cystic spaces containing basophilic myxoid ground substance (Fig. 37–3).[8, 49]

The prognosis in patients with pulmonary hypertension is generally poor and proportional to the degree of hypertension. Riedel and co-workers studied 147 patients with serial right heart studies and reported that patients with mean pulmonary artery pressures over 30 mm Hg had a 30% 5-year survival and patients with mean pressures over 50 mm Hg had a 10% 5-year survival (Fig. 37–4).[50]

## CLINICAL PRESENTATION

The clinical presentation of patients with CPTH is variable. This is the result of the wide variation in the degree of embolic obstruction that may occur. Pulmonary hypertension does not result from complete or partial obstruction of only a few vessels in the pulmonary arterial system, although an increased dead space may result. When the loss of the cross-sectional area

of the pulmonary vascular bed is more extensive, pulmonary hypertension appears at rest, or with minimal levels of exertion. Therefore, patients that are left with minor residual obstruction may have virtually no symptoms, whereas those with extensive vascular occlusion may present with severe pulmonary hypertension and right-heart failure.

Many patients do not relate an obvious past history of venous thrombosis or acute pulmonary embolus. On direct questioning, patients may recall a nonspecific event such as a "muscle strain or cellulitis" that in retrospect may have been a venous thrombotic event. The acute embolic event may have been misdiagnosed as pneumonia, pleurisy, or some other disease.[39, 51] Therefore, the diagnosis of CPTH cannot be excluded on the basis of a negative history of a

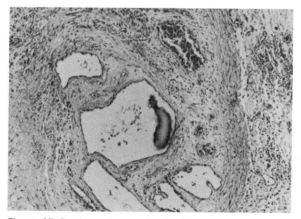

**Figure 37–3.** Photomicrograph of a chronic pulmonary embolus that has become organized and attached to the intimal surface of the pulmonary arterial wall. (×40). (Used with permission from Chitwood WR, Sabiston DC, Wechsler AS: Surgical treatment of chronic unresolved pulmonary embolism. Clin Chest Med 5:507–536, 1984.)

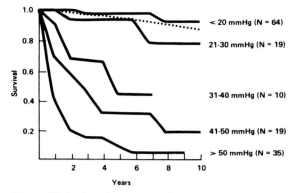

**Figure 37-4.** Cumulative survival curves in patients with chronic pulmonary thromboembolic hypertension according to the initial mean pulmonary artery pressure. The dotted line represents predicted survival among men 40–50 years old. (Used with permission as modified from Reidel M, Stanek V, Widinsky J, et al: Long-term follow-up of patients with pulmonary thromboembolism: Late prognosis and evaluation of hemodynamic and respiratory data. Chest 81:151–158, 1982.)

prior venous thrombotic event. A family history of thrombosis may occasionally be found in these patients.[39a]

Dyspnea is the one common presenting symptom in all patients. Initially, dyspnea may occur only on exertion and is often attributed to poor physical conditioning. Because pulmonary vascular resistance is relatively fixed, the increase in cardiac output that occurs during exertion leads to a further increase in pulmonary artery pressure causing symptoms that may not be present at rest.[52] As pulmonary hypertension worsens, dyspnea occurs with lesser amounts of exertion and at rest.

Following an acute symptomatic embolic event, patients may enjoy a "honeymoon period" (a term coined by Moser) during which pulmonary hypertension is present, but symptoms are few.[51] It is believed that during this period, compensatory right ventricular hypertrophy develops, allowing for maintenance of an adequate cardiac output despite the presence of pulmonary hypertension and increased pulmonary vascular resistance.[39] After a period of months to years, right ventricle function deteriorates, and the patient enters a period of symptomatic decline. Contributing to this decline is the development of secondary pulmonary hypertensive changes leading to a further increase in pulmonary vascular resistance and right ventricular afterload. Embolic recurrence or in situ extension of chronic emboli may also increase pulmonary vascular resistance. These changes limit cardiac output, producing symptoms of fatigue, presyncope and, less commonly, syn-

cope. Chest pain may be present and pleuritic in nature, or it may be associated with myocardial ischemia. Atypical substernal pain may be caused by acute dilatation of the pulmonary outflow tract.[53] Hemoptysis is uncommon. Ultimately, patients may exhibit all of the features of severe right heart failure.

The physical signs may be few until overt pulmonary hypertension and cor pulmonale develop. With progressive disease, jugular venous pressure is commonly elevated with a positive hepatojugular reflex. Precordial examination may reveal a right ventricular heave and a palpable pulmonary artery and $P_2$. Patients may have an increased $P_2$; murmurs associated with a tricuspid insufficiency; and/or an ejection systolic murmur, which is related to turbulent flow across the pulmonary valve. There may be signs of right ventricular dysfunction including a right ventricular $S_3$, $S_4$, or summation gallop. With progressive right heart failure, a pulsatile liver and increasing peripheral edema may be present. Patients may demonstrate peripheral and central cyanosis. Clubbing is uncommon. Flow murmurs or bruits characteristic of this disease may be present over the major pulmonary arteries rather than the normal cardiac auscultory areas.[54, 55] These high-pitched, continuous or systolic bruits may be inaudible during respiration and are best heard by having patients hold their breath for short periods. They are believed to be caused by flow through pulmonary arteries partially obstructed by organized thrombi.

## DIAGNOSIS

The diagnosis of CPTH can be difficult because of the infrequent number of cases and a general lack of awareness of the clinical entity. The development of CPTH is often insidious and slowly progressive in nature, which also contributes to this difficulty. The key to making the correct diagnosis is to consider CPTH in any patient with exertional dyspnea for which no compelling cause can be found. A history of a prior embolic event or venous thrombotic event should then be sought. Impedance plethysmography may show findings compatible with chronic venous thrombosis. In many patients, the venous thrombotic event may be sufficiently old that such tests, even venography, may not confirm the diagnosis. Other findings may suggest an alternative diagnosis. Patients are often thought to suffer from coronary artery disease because they may have effort-induced chest pain due to right ventricular ischemia, and the electrocardiogram of severe right ventricular hypertrophy and strain may suggest an old anterior myocardial infarction. Some patients may carry a "diagnosis" of primary pulmonary hypertension.

Routine blood work is usually normal until the development of severe right heart failure occurs. With progressive disease, results of liver and renal function tests may be abnormal. Polycythemia may develop because of chronic hypoxemia. Arterial blood gas test results at rest may be normal, with desaturation occurring during exercise. When hypoxemia is present, it is usually related to ventilation/perfusion $(\dot{V}/\dot{Q})$ abnormalities and exacerbated by a reduction in cardiac output and mixed venous $P_{O_2}$.[56]

The electrocardiogram is also often normal in the early stages of the disease. As the disease progresses, abnormalities including sinus tachycardia, right axis deviation, P pulmonale, or results indicative of right ventricular hypertrophy or strain may develop. There may be marked T wave inversion across the precordium associated with right ventricular hypertrophy. This is sometimes misinterpreted as anterior myocardial ischemia.

The chest radiograph may appear surprisingly unremarkable, especially in the early stages of the disease. Abnormal findings include decreased vascular markings causing increased radiolucency of either an entire lung or of localized areas. In addition, radiographs may reveal areas of hyperperfusion often interpreted as interstitial fibrosis and bilateral enlargement of the pulmonary artery trunks at the hilum, as seen in patients with pulmonary hypertension. However, in CPTH, the presence of organized thrombus in one or both main pulmonary arteries may prevent such enlargement. When the central pulmonary arteries are asymmetric in the presence of pulmonary hypertension, the diagnosis of CPT should be considered. If pulmonary infarction has occurred, pleural thickening may be seen. With disease progression, there will be evidence of right ventricular and right atrial enlargement that is best demonstrated on the lateral radiograph (Fig. 37–5).

Pulmonary function tests are commonly within normal limits, but approximately 20% of patients exhibit a restrictive pulmonary defect with a reduction in lung volumes to below 80% of predicted levels.[57, 58] This restrictive defect may be the result of a combination of pleural

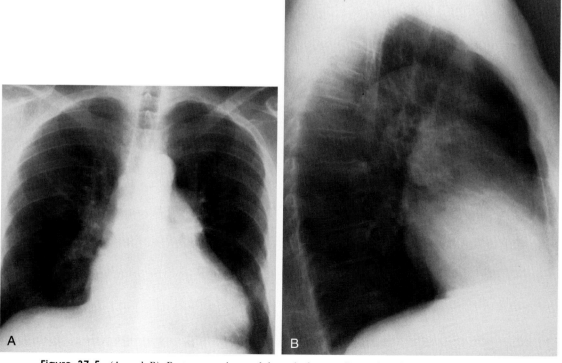

**Figure 37–5.** (A and B) Posteroanterior and lateral chest radiographs of a patient with chronic thromboembolic pulmonary hypertension. Features include central pulmonary artery enlargement, increased vascular markings to both upper lobes with oligemia of the lower lung fields, cardiomegaly, and a prominent pulmonary outflow tract. The latter finding is best appreciated by "filling" of the retrosternal space on the lateral view.

disease and small infarcts scattered throughout the lung lobes, which can lead to the erroneous diagnosis of interstitial lung disease. Surprisingly, the diffusing capacity for carbon monoxide in a significant number of patients may be within the normal range, even when there is severe disease and ablation of the pulmonary vascular bed. This may be the result of extensive bronchial artery collateral flow, which may be up to 10% of the cardiac output, and may backperfuse into the capillary bed and achieve substantial carbon monoxide transfer.[39] A normal diffusing capacity for carbon monoxide does not exclude the diagnosis of CPTH.

Echocardiography usually demonstrates signs of right atrial and right ventricular enlargement and right ventricular pressure overload in symptomatic patients. Tricuspid regurgitation is often present and allows estimation of pulmonary artery systolic pressure. Thrombus in the right atrium or ventricle and right or left atrial myxoma may be visualized. Transesophageal echocardiography with "bubble" studies may be useful in ruling out an occult atrial septal defect or other right to left shunt that may cause secondary pulmonary hypertension.

The most definitive noninvasive test for the diagnosis of CPT is the $\dot{V}/\dot{Q}$ lung scan, which can be safely performed even in the presence of severe pulmonary hypertension.[59] $\dot{V}/\dot{Q}$ scans of these patients show at least one segmental sized or larger perfusion defect, with most patients showing several segmental or lobar defects bilaterally (Fig. 37–6). Perfusion defects

are usually mismatched and larger than ventilation abnormalities. In primary pulmonary hypertension, $\dot{V}/\dot{Q}$ scans may be normal or show patchy, subsegmental abnormalities with a "mottled" appearance. Therefore, the $\dot{V}/\dot{Q}$ scan often provides a noninvasive means of differentiating between these two disorders.[59, 60I, 61] The extent of perfusion defects cannot be used reliably to predict the severity of central vessel obstruction. In fact, perfusion scans have been shown to consistently underestimate the severity of large vessel obstruction and pulmonary hypertension.[62] Fibrosing mediastinitis or pulmonary arteritis may mimic the lung scan of CPT, underlining the importance of following up an abnormal lung scan with pulmonary angiography.[63, 64]

Right heart catheterization should be performed to determine the severity of pulmonary hypertension and to rule out other causes of pulmonary hypertension such as left to right shunting, pulmonary venous congestion, or hypertension. Cardiac output needs to be measured and pulmonary vascular resistance calculated, because some patients may have a misleadingly low pulmonary artery pressure owing to a marked diminution of cardiac output. During right heart catheterization, exercise can be useful to see how well the right heart can augment cardiac output and to determine the degree to which pulmonary vascular resistance is fixed.[52] Pulmonary capillary wedge pressure can be measured to provide information regarding left ventricular function. The absence of a substantial rise in pulmonary capillary wedge pressure during exercise excludes the presence of significant left heart dysfunction. It may be difficult to measure the pulmonary capillary wedge pressure accurately because of wedging of the catheter in a proximal pulmonary artery partially or totally occluded by thrombus.

The "gold standard" test for the diagnosis of CPT is pulmonary angiography. It confirms the diagnosis and defines extent of thrombus and its location, thus determining the feasibility of thromboendarterectomy. The procedure can be performed safely with a low risk of mortality and morbidity even in patients with severe pulmonary hypertension and right sided cardiac failure.[65–67] A mortality of 0.2% and complication rate of 4.5% in 1,350 studies done at Duke University Medical Center (Durham, NC) has been reported.[65] The only complication in 50 patients undergoing pulmonary angiography was one episode of hypotension recorded in the Primary Pulmonary Hypertension Registry.[66] Few complications have been reported as a result of pulmonary angiography in patients with

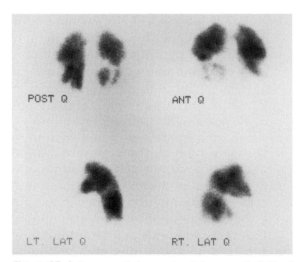

**Figure 37–6.** Lung perfusion study of the same individual shown in Figure 37–5. Multiple segmental and subsegmental defects are apparent, principally involving both lower lobes, the right middle lobe and lingula. The ventilation scan (not shown) was normal.

primary or thromboembolic pulmonary hypertension, even though the right ventricular end diastolic pressure was equal to or exceeded 20 mm Hg in 14 of these patients.[67]

The interpretation of pulmonary angiograms of patients with CPTH can be difficult, because these images are significantly different from those seen in acute embolism in which sharply bordered, rounded, well defined filling defects and cutoffs are the diagnostic standard.[68] Chronic thrombi appear in highly variable locations and may organize in an unpredictable way, producing unusual radiographic images. Chronic thrombi are often incorporated into the arterial wall and retract the vessel wall.[67, 69] Obstructions in CPT present as bands or webs causing narrowed segmental pulmonary arteries, sometimes accompanied by poststenotic dilatation. Irregularities of intima, rounded termination of segmental branches, luminal narrowing of the central vessels, and oddly shaped pulmonary arteries are reliable indicators of chronic emboli (Fig. 37–7).[67, 69, 70]

Left heart catheterization and coronary angiography may be performed to establish that left ventricular and atrial pressures are normal and to rule out coexisting coronary artery disease. When significant coronary artery disease is present, it is often necessary to perform coronary artery bypass surgery in conjunction with pulmonary thromboendarterectomy in view of the prolonged bypass time and cardioplegia necessary to perform surgical thromboendarterectomy.

Pulmonary fiberoptic angioscopy allows direct visualization of the pulmonary vascular bed and is important prior to surgery in which pulmonary angiographic findings do not clearly define the surgical accessibility of the chronic thromboemboli.[71] Investigational procedures includ-

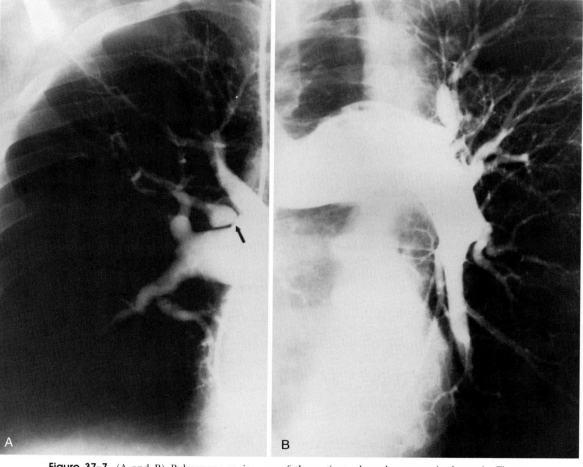

**Figure 37–7.** (A and B) Pulmonary angiogram of the patient whose lung scan is shown in Figure 37–6. Several typical angiographic features of chronic thromboembolic disease include an abrupt narrowing of this patient's left descending pulmonary artery, several occluded right lower lobe vessels, a vascular "web" involving a right upper lobe artery (black arrow), and an irregularly contoured left upper lobar vessel. The main pulmonary arteries are also markedly enlarged.

ing intravascular ultrasound imaging, ultrafast computed tomographic scanning, and magnetic resonance imaging are currently being tested as imaging techniques to precisely define the presence and location of chronic thromboembolic lesions.

## SUPPORTIVE MEDICAL THERAPY

Significant limitations influence the medical treatment of patients with severe CPTH, because medical therapy fails to address the basic underlying problem of fixed pulmonary vascular obstruction. Nonetheless, not all patients are candidates for surgical therapy. In patients awaiting surgery, it is important to institute measures to prevent further embolization of clot to the lung and to treat cor pulmonale. In all patients with CPTH, anticoagulation is initiated immediately and maintained for life. Thrombolytic therapy is of no value because the clot within the lung is fibrotic and organized and often covered by a layer of endothelium. Except in rare patients in whom emboli are known to have originated in the upper extremities or right side of the heart, or in whom inferior vena caval (IVC) obstruction is shown to be present with venous return occurring via collaterals, insertion of an IVC filter is performed.[72] Oxygen should always be administered if hypoxemia is present. Standard therapy for right heart failure includes a low salt diet and judicious use of loop diuretics.

There is limited data on the role of pulmonary vasodilator therapy in patients with CPTH. Vasodilators are not expected to affect the proximal, fixed pulmonary vascular obstruction. It is known, however, that if the pulmonary vasculature of "normal lung" is subjected to increased pressure or flow, secondary pulmonary hypertensive changes may develop. Studies suggest that vasodilators such as prostacyclin, calcium channel blockers, and NO may be of benefit in preventing and treating these secondary changes.[44, 73–76] Any potential benefit of pulmonary vasodilators in CPTH is speculative. If patients with secondary pulmonary hypertension due to CPT are given a trial of vasodilators, the trial should only be performed with the guidance of invasive monitoring of pulmonary artery pressure and cardiac output. Pulmonary vasodilators can be considered to be of possible benefit if it was demonstrated that there was a fall in the pulmonary artery pressure with no significant fall in systemic blood pressure and no change or an increase in cardiac output. Experience in patients with primary pulmonary hypertension has shown that prostacyclin and NO are ideal agents for assessing acute vasodilator responses, whereas orally administrated calcium channel blockers are more suitable for longterm therapy.[76, 77] It should be emphasized that medical therapy may play an adjunctive role but must not delay surgical assessment and therapy. Surgical thromboendarterectomy is the first-line treatment for CPT.

## TREATMENT AND OUTCOMES

An increasing body of literature supports pulmonary thromboendarterectomy as the treatment of choice for patients with CPTH.[4IV] The criteria for selecting patients who are candidates to undergo pulmonary thromboendarterectomy have been established, but they are not considered absolute and continue to evolve with experience (Table 37–1). At present, most patients referred for surgery have New York Heart Association (NYHA) class III or IV dyspnea and a pulmonary vascular resistance of greater than 300 dynes/sec/cm$^{-5}$. Younger patients with a pulmonary vascular resistance less than 300 dynes/sec/cm$^{-5}$ and significant symptoms are also candidates for surgery. Current surgical techniques allow only for removal of chronic thrombi residing in main, lobar, or segmental arteries, and thus surgical accessibility must be confirmed by angiography or angioscopy. The patient and his family must also be willing to accept the significant risks of surgery. Severe right ventricular dysfunction is not a contraindication to surgery because right ventricular function improves dramatically if the pulmonary vascular obstructions are successfully removed.[78]

The exact nature of the surgical procedure has been well described elsewhere.[4IV] Surgery is performed by median sternotomy. The procedure involves the use of cardiopulmonary bypass and periods of cardioplegia, deep hypothermia, and circulatory arrest. A true thromboendarterectomy is performed with removal of the orga-

Table 37–1. **Selection Criteria for Thromboendarterectomy**

1. Chronic thrombi judged to be surgically accessible
2. The absence of significant comorbid disease
3. Pulmonary vascular resistance > 300 dynes/sec/cm$^{-5}$
4. Symptomatic, high dead space ventilation in the presence of surgically accessible chronic thrombi
5. A willingness of the patient and the family to accept the significant risks of surgery

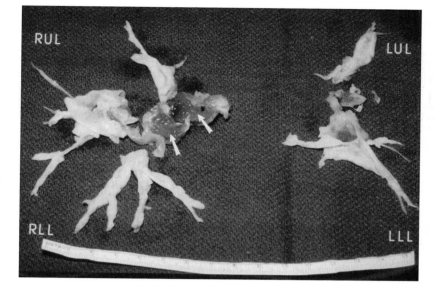

**Figure 37–8.** Gross specimen of chronic thrombi removed by thromboendarterectomy in the patient featured in Figures 37–5 to 37–7. The fibrotic organized material that involved the right main pulmonary artery is lined by a small amount of partially organized thrombus (arrows).

nized thrombus along with its lining of neointima while leaving the media and most of the original intima intact (Fig. 37–8). The procedure in no way resembles an acute embolectomy. Careful dissection down to the native intima is imperative for an optimal surgical outcome. At present, the surgery is performed at a limited number of centers because of the complexities involved. In inexperienced hands, incomplete thromboendarterectomies have been performed, leading to an inadequate postoperative pulmonary hemodynamic outcome.

The postoperative management of these patients can be difficult and complex. The usual problems associated with open heart surgery are encountered, including hemodynamic instability, cardiac arrhythmias, bleeding, electrolyte disturbance, infection, pericarditis, and pericardial effusion. Problems unique to thromboendarterectomy include persistent pulmonary hypertension from an inability to remove a sufficient amount of organized thrombus at the time of surgery and reperfusion pulmonary edema. The causes of reperfusion edema have yet to be determined, but ongoing investigations indicate that similar mechanisms implicated in other types of high-permeability lung injury seem to be involved.[79, 80] Radiographically, the edema has been shown to involve lung areas distal to where organized thrombi have been removed. The edema may appear at any time up to 72 hours postoperatively. The severity ranges from acute hemorrhage with fatal consequences to mild edema associated with modest hypoxemia. Perfusion of the edematous areas continues, resulting in significant shunting and hy-

poxemia, as demonstrated on $\dot{V}/\dot{Q}$ scans. Mechanical ventilation and increased oxygen concentrations for periods from a few days to a few weeks may be required to manage this lung injury. Corticosteroids have been used with observed clinical benefit.[39] Anticoagulant therapy should be started in the immediate postoperative period unless there are major bleeding problems. Most patients are weaned and extubated within 3 days, discharged from intensive care at 5 days, and from the hospital at 14 days following surgery.[39] Common postoperative complications are summarized in Table 37–2.

With increased experience and refinements in surgical techniques and perioperative management, the last reported operative mortality at UCSD Medical Center had dropped to 8.7%.[41V] This relatively high mortality rate reflects the critical status of many of these patients at the time they are referred for surgery. Many of the patients undergoing the operation are severely limited with New York Heart Association (NYHA) functional class IV dyspnea. Few

Table 37–2. **Postoperative Complications**

Delerium
Reperfusion pulmonary edema
Persistent pulmonary hypertension from the inability to remove sufficient thrombotic material at the time of surgery
Bleeding
Cardiac supraventricular arrythmias
Pleuropericarditis
Pericardial effusions

**Table 37-3. Hemodynamic Values Obtained in 47 of the First 150 Patients Who Returned for Followup Cardiac Catheterization at 6-24 Months After Surgery**

|  | Preoperative | Postoperative | Followup |
|---|---|---|---|
| PA mean (mm Hg) | 48 ± 12 | 27 ± 8* | 24 ± 10 |
| PA systolic (mm Hg) | 80 ± 21 | 44 ± 15* | 39 ± 17** |
| CO (L/mm) | 3.7 ± 1.17 | 6.0 ± 1.1* | 4.8 ± 1.0† |
| PVR (dynes/sec/cm⁻⁵) | 971 ± 551 | 232 ± 111* | 282 ± 251 |

Data from University of California, San Diego Medical Center.
Used with permission from Moser KM, Auger WR, Fedullo PF, Jamieson SW: Chronic thromboembolic pulmonary hypertension: Clinical picture and surgical treatment. Eur Respir J 5:334–342, 1992.
*$p<0.001$ vs preoperative value.
**$p<0.0015$ vs postoperative value.
†$p<0.0001$ vs postoperative value.
PA = pulmonary artery; CO = cardiac output; PVR = pulmonary vascular resistance. Values are mean ± SD.

patients have been turned down on the basis of age or significant collateral disease because patients with CPT and severe pulmonary hypertension have an extremely poor prognosis without surgery. The presence of concomitant coronary artery disease, obstructive lung disease, renal or liver disease, or hematologic abnormalities influences peri-operative mortality and longterm outcome. Nonetheless, patients with extreme hemodynamic compromise have undergone surgery with good outcomes.

Substantial improvement is seen postoperatively. Hemodynamic studies demonstrate a decline in pulmonary artery pressure, an increase in cardiac output, and a significant reduction in pulmonary vascular resistance, which is sustained or improved over the long term (Table 37-3).[39] Postoperative echocardiograms also reflect these hemodynamic changes with a reduction in right atrial and right ventricular size, a return of the interventricular septum to a normal position with loss of paradoxical motion, and minimal or no tricuspid regurgitation.[78, 81] On physical examination, signs of pulmonary hypertension and right heart failure quickly regress. Functionally, patients show significant improvement typically within a few weeks after surgery, with continued improvement occurring over the ensuing 9 to 12 months. The gradual improvement is thought to be related to resolution of postoperative edema, anemia, and the deconditioned state. At 12 months, 95% of patients are in NYHA class I or II (Table 37-4).[39] Postoperative lung perfusion scans and angiography show marked improvements in perfusion. In a study of 34 postendarterectomy patients, cardiac catheterization and angiography results were either normal or showed minimal residual distal obstruction in one or more segmental arteries.[51] In that group, only one patient failed to show significant restoration of vascular patency.

As previously noted, patients are maintained on lifelong anticoagulation therapy. Longterm followup of these patients (up to 18 years) has revealed only three patients who have suffered recurrent venous thrombosis, and in each case the patient had discontinued warfarin therapy.[39] There have been no instances of thrombosis of the IVC filter during postdischarge followup.[51]

In summary, chronic pulmonary thromboembolism is one of the rare treatable causes of pulmonary hypertension. Because the surgical treatment has been so successful, clinicians should be aware of this condition so that it may be diagnosed early. Suspected cases should be referred to specialized centers for definitive diagnosis and treatment.

Further research into the underlying pathophysiology and possible endogenous fibrinolytic defects needs to be undertaken. Advances in adjunctive medical therapy including specific vasodilator therapy (e.g., NO) may help ameliorate ongoing pulmonary hypertension until definitive surgical therapy can be performed. In

**Table 37-4. New York Heart Association Functional Classification of 117 Patients of the First 150 Who Were Evaluated at One Year Following Surgery**

| Class | Preoperative | Followup |
|---|---|---|
| IV | 63 | 0 |
| III | 49 | 6 |
| II | 5 | 26 |
| I | 0 | 85 |
| Total | 117 | 117 |

Data from University of California, San Diego Medical Center.

Used with permission from Moser KM, Auger WR, Fedullo PF, Jamieson SW: Chronic thromboembolic pulmonary hypertension: Clinical picture and surgical treatment. Eur Respir J 5:334–342, 1992.

patients with conditions that are inoperable, adjunctive medical therapy may prolong life and improve functional status, although this has yet to be tested.

## REFERENCES

1. Moser KM: Venous thromboembolism. Am Rev Resp Dis 141:235–249, 1990.
2. Benotti JR, Dalen JE: The natural history of pulmonary embolism. Clin Chest Med 5:403–410, 1984.
3. Anderson FA, Wheeler HB, Goldberg RJ, et al: A population-based perspective of the hospital incidence and case-fatality rates of deep vein thrombosis and pulmonary embolism. Arch Intern Med 151:933–938, 1991.
IV  4. Jamieson SW, Auger WR, Fedullo PF, et al: Experience and results with 150 pulmonary thromboendarterectomy operations over a 29-month period. J Thorac Cardiovasc Surg 106:116–127, 1993.
5. Viner SM, Bagg BR, Auger WR, Ford GT: The management of pulmonary hypertension secondary to chronic thromboembolic disease. Prog Cardiovasc Dis 37:79–92, 1994.
6. Laennec RTH: De l'ausculation Mediate. Paris, Brossen et Chaude, 1819.
7. Virchow R: Cellular Pathology. Translated by Frank Chance. New York, Robert M. Debit, 1860.
8. Chitwood WR, Sabiston DC, Wechsler AS: Surgical treatment of chronic unresolved pulmonary embolism. Clin Chest Med 5:507–536, 1984.
9. Carroll D: Chronic obstruction of major pulmonary arteries. Am J Med 9:175–185,1950.
10. Trendelenburg F: Ueber die operative behandlung der embolie der lungenarterie. Arch Klin Chir 24:687–700, 1908.
11. Hollister LE, Cull VL: The syndrome of chronic thrombosis of the major pulmonary arteries. Am J Med 21:312–320, 1956.
12. Allison PR, Dunhill MS, Marshall R: Pulmonary embolism. Thorax 15:273–283, 1960.
13. Snyder WH, Kent DC, Baisch BF: Successful endarterectomy of chronically occluded pulmonary artery: Clinical report and physiologic studies. J Thorac Cardiovasc Surg 45:482–489, 1964.
14. Houk VN, Hufnagel CA, McClenathan JE, Moser KM: Chronic thrombosis obstruction of major pulmonary arteries. Report of a case successfully treated by thromboendarterectomy and review of the literature. Am J Med 35:269–282, 1963.
15. Castleman B, McNeely BU, Scannell G: Case records of the Massachusetts General Hospital. Case 32–1964. N Engl J Med 271:40–50, 1964.
16. Sutton GC, Hall RJC, Kerr IH: Clinical course and late prognosis of treated subacute massive, acute minor, and chronic pulmonary thromboembolism. Br Heart J 39:1135–1142, 1977.
17. Dalen JE, Banas JS, Brooks HL, et al: Resolution rate of acute pulmonary embolism in man. N Engl J Med 280:1194–1199, 1969.
18. Murphy ML, Bulloch RT: Factors influencing the resolution of blood flow following pulmonary embolization as determined by angiography and scanning. Circulation 1116–1126, 1966.
19. Palla A, Donnamaria V, Petruzzelli S, Giuntini C: Follow-up of pulmonary perfusion recovery after embolism. J Nucl Med Allied Sci 30:23–28, 1986.
20. Prediletto R, Paoletti P, Fornal E, et al: Natural course of treated pulmonary embolism. Chest 97:554–561, 1990.
21. Tow DE, Wagner HN Jr: Recovery of pulmonary arterial blood flow in patients with pulmonary embolism. N Engl J Med 276:1053–1059, 1967.
22. Benotti JR, Dalen JE: The natural history of pulmonary embolism. Clin Chest Med 5:403–410, 1984.
23. Fred HL, Axelrad MA, Leis JM, Alexander JK: Rapid resolution of pulmonary thromboemboli in man. JAMA 196:1137–1139, 1966.
24. James S, Menn SJ, Moser KM: Rapid resolution of a pulmonary embolism in man. West J Med 128:60–64, 1976.
25. Langer JE, Velchik MG: Rapid resolution of massive pulmonary embolism due to streptokinase therapy: Documented by ventilation/perfusion imaging. Clin Nucl Med 13:874–877, 1988.
26. Astrup T: Fibrinolysis in the organism. Blood 11:781, 1956.
27. Collen D: On the regulation and control of fibrinolysis. Thromb Haemost 43:77–89, 1980.
28. Kluft C: T-PA in fibrin dissolution and hemostasis. In Kluft C (ed): Tissue-type Plasminogen Activator (t-PA): Physiological and Clinical Aspects. Boca Raton, FL, CRC Press, 1988, pp 47–82.
29. Loskutoff DJ, Sawdey M, Mimuro J: Type 1 plasminogen activator inhibitor. In Coller B (ed): Progress in Hemostasis and Thrombus. Philadelphia, WB Saunders, 1989, pp 87–115.
30. Sprengers ED, Kluft C: Plasminogen activator inhibitors. Blood 69:381–387, 1987.
31. Nilsson IM, Ljungner H, Tegborn L: Two different mechanisms in patients with venous thrombosis and defective fibrinolysis: Low concentration of plasminogen activator or increased concentration of plasminogen activator inhibitor. Br Med J 290:1453–1456, 1985.
32. Wiman B, Ljungberg B, Chmielewska J, et al: The role of the fibrinolytic system in deep vein thrombosis. J Lab Clin Med 105:265–270, 1985.
33. Grimuado V, Bachmann F, Hauert J, et al: Hypofibrinolysis in patients with a history of idiopathic deep vein thrombosis and/or pulmonary embolism. Thromb Haemost 67:397–401, 1992.
34. Olman MA, Marsh JJ, Lang IM, et al: The endogenous fibrinolytic system in chronic large-vessel thromboembolic pulmonary hypertension. Circulation 86:1241–1248, 1992.
35. Loskutoff DJ, Sadey M, Keeton M, Schneiderman J: Regulation of PAI-1 gene expression in vivo. Thromb Haemost 70:135–137, 1993.
36. Loskutoff DJ: Regulation of the thrombolytic potential of the vascular wall by plasminogen activator inhibitor-1 (PAI-1). Can J Cardiol 9:1–3, 1993.
37. Lang IM, James JM, Mitchell A, et al: Expression of type 1 plasminogen activator inhibitor in chronic pulmonary thromboemboli. Circulation 89:2715–2721, 1994.
38. Rich S, Levitsky S, Brundage BH: Pulmonary hypertension from chronic pulmonary thromboembolism. Ann Intern Med 108:425–434, 1988.
39. Moser KM, Auger WR, Fedullo PF, et al: Chronic thromboembolic pulmonary hypertension: Clinical picture and surgical treatment. Eur Respir J 5:334–342, 1992.
39a. Greengard JS, Eichinger S, Griffin JH, Bauer KA: Brief report: Variability of thrombosis among homozygous siblings with resistance to activated protein C due to an Arg→Gln mutation in the gene for factor V. N Engl J Med 331:1559–1569, 1994.

40. Ware JA, Heistad DD: Platelet-endothelium interactions. N Engl J Med 328:628–635, 1993.

41. Coller BS: Platelets and thrombolytic therapy. N Engl J Med 322:33–42, 1990.

42. Lowenstein CJ, Dinerman JL, Snyder SH: Nitric oxide: A physiologic messenger. Ann Intern Med 120:227–237, 1994.

43. Moncada S, Higgs A: The l-arginine-nitric oxide pathway. N Engl J Med 329:2002–2012, 1993.

44. Zapol WM, Falke KJ, Hurford WE, Roberts JD: Inhaling nitric oxide: A selective pulmonary vasodilator and bronchodilator. Chest 105:87S–91S, 1994.

45. Vane JR, Anggard EE, Botting RM: Regulatory functions of the vascular endothelium. N Engl J Med 323:27–36, 1990.

46. Giaid A, Yanagisawa M, Langleben D, et al: Expression of endothelin-1 in the lungs of patients with pulmonary hypertension. N Engl J Med 328:1732–1739, 1993.

47. Moser KM, Bloor CM: Pulmonary vascular lesions occurring in patients with chronic major vessel thromboembolic pulmonary hypertension. Chest 103:685–692, 1993.

48. Wagenvoort CA, Wagenvoort N (eds): Pathology of Pulmonary Hypertension. New York, John Wiley & Sons, 1977.

49. Presti B, Berthrong M, Sherwin M: Chronic thrombosis of major pulmonary arteries. Hum Pathol 21:601–606, 1990.

50. Riedel M, Stanek V, Widinsky J, Prevosky I: Long-term follow-up of patients with pulmonary thromboembolism: Late prognosis and evaluation of hemodynamic and respiratory data. Chest 81:151–158, 1982.

51. Moser KM, Auger WR, Fedullo PF: Chronic major vessel thromboembolic pulmonary hypertension. Circulation 81:1735–1743, 1990.

52. Fedullo PF, Auger WR, Moser KM, et al: Hemodynamic response to exercise in patients with chronic, major vessel thromboembolic pulmonary hypertension (abstract). Am Rev Resp Dis 141:A890, 1990.

53. DeGowin EL, DeGowin RL: Bedside Diagnostic Examination. New York, Macmillan, 1981, p 235.

54. Auger WR, Moser KM: Pulmonary flow murmurs: A distinctive physical sign found in chronic pulmonary thromboembolic disease (abstract). Clin Res 37:145A, 1989.

55. Perloff JK: Auscultatory and phonocardiographic manifestations of pulmonary hypertension. Prog Cardiovasc Dis 9(4):303–340, 1967.

56. Kapitan KS, Buchbinder M, Wagner PD, Moser KM: Mechanism of hypoxemia in chronic thromboembolic pulmonary hypertension. Am Rev Resp Dis 139:1149–1154, 1989.

57. Horn M, Ries AL, Neveu C, Moser KM: Restrictive ventilatory pattern in precapillary pulmonary hypertension. Am Rev Resp Dis 128:163–165, 1983.

58. Ryan KL, Fedullo PF, Clausen J, Moser KM: Pulmonary function in chronic thromboembolic pulmonary hypertension. Am Rev Resp Dis 84:679–683, 1986.

59. Hull RD, Hirsch J, Carter CJ, et al: Pulmonary angiography, ventilation lung scanning, and venography for clinically suspected pulmonary embolism with abnormal perfusion lung scan. Ann Intern Med 98:891–899, 1983.

I 60. D'Alonzo GE, Bower JS, Dantzker DR: Differentiation of patients with primary and thromboembolic pulmonary hypertension. Chest 85:457–461, 1984.

61. Fishman AJ, Moser KM, Fedullo PF: Perfusion lung scans versus pulmonary angiography in evaluation of suspected primary pulmonary hypertension. Chest 84:679–683, 1983.

62. Ryan KL, Fedullo PF, David GB, et al: Perfusion scans underestimate the severity of angiographic and hemodynamic compromise in chronic thromboembolic pulmonary hypertension. Chest 93:1180–1185, 1988.

63. Berry DF, Buccigrossi D, Peabody J, et al: Pulmonary vascular occlusion and fibrosing mediastinitis. Chest 89:296–301, 1986.

64. Lupi E, Sanchez G, Horwitz S, Gutierrez E: Pulmonary arteritis involvement in Takayasu's arteritis. Chest 67:69–74, 1975.

65. Mills SR, Jackson DC, Older RA, et al: The incidence, etiologies and avoidance of complications of pulmonary angiography in a large series. Radiology 136:295–299, 1980.

66. Rich S, Dantzker DR, Ayers SM, et al: Primary pulmonary hypertension: A natural prospective study. Ann Intern Med 107:216–223, 1987.

67. Nicod P, Moser KM, Peterson KL, et al: Pulmonary angiography in severe pulmonary hypertension. Ann Intern Med 107:565–568, 1987.

68. Greenspan RH: Angiography in pulmonary embolism. In Abrams HL (ed): Angiography: Vascular and Interventional Radiology, ed 3. Boston, Little, Brown, 1983, pp 803–816.

69. Owen WR, Thomas WA, Castleman B, et al: Unrecognized emboli to the lungs associated with subsequent cor pulmonale. N Engl J Med 249:919–926, 1953.

70. Auger WR, Fedullo PF, Moser KM, et al: Chronic major-vessel thromboembolic pulmonary artery obstruction: Appearance at angiography. Radiology 182:393–398, 1992.

71. Shure D, Gregoratos G, Moser KM: Fiberoptic angioscopy: Role in the diagnosis of chronic pulmonary arterial obstruction. Ann Intern Med 103:844–850, 1985.

72. Greenfield LJ, Scher LA, Elkins RC: KMA-Greenfield filter placement for chronic pulmonary hypertension. Ann Surg 93:170–175, 1979.

73. Adnot S, Kouyoumdjian C, Eddahibi S, et al: Continuous inhalation of nitric oxide protects against development of pulmonary hypertension in chronically hypoxic rats (abstract). Am Rev Resp Dis 147:A494, 1993.

74. Serraf A, Labat C, Herve P, et al: Surgical model of pulmonary hypertension in the neonatal piglet: Hemodynamic, morphological and endothelial features (abstract). Am Rev Resp Dis 147:A496, 1993.

75. Schiller L, Ward H, Archer S, et al: Endothelial dysfunction in a canine model of high flow pulmonary hypertension (abstract). Am Rev Resp Dis 147:A497, 1993.

76. Rich S, Brundage BH: High-dose calcium channel blocking therapy for primary pulmonary hypertension: Evidence for long-term reduction in pulmonary arterial pressure and regression of right ventricular hypertrophy. Circulation 76:135–141, 1987.

77. Pepke-Zaba J, Higenbottam TW, Dinh-Xuan AT, et al: Inhaled nitric oxide as a cause of selective pulmonary vasodilation in pulmonary hypertension. Lancet 338:1173–1174, 1991.

78. Chow LC, Dittrich HC, Hoit BO, et al: Doppler assessment of changes in right-sided cardiac hemo-

dynamics after pulmonary thromboendarterectomy. Am J Cardiol 61:1092–1097, 1988.

79. Levinson RM, Shure D, Moser KM: Reperfusion pulmonary edema following pulmonary artery thromboendarterectomy. Am Rev Res Dis 134:1241–1245, 1986.

80. Auger WR, Smith RM, Spragg, RG: Protease release

and antiprotease inactivation in a clinical model of acute high permeability lung injury (abstract). Am Rev Resp Dis 137:A146, 1988.

81. Dittrich HC, Nicod PH, Chow LC, et al: Early changes of right heart geometery after pulmonary thromboendarterectomy. J Am Coll Cardiol 11:937–943, 1988.

# Chapter 38

# Calf-vein Thrombosis

Gary E. Raskob

Major advances have been made in the diagnosis, treatment, and prevention of venous thromboembolism during the past 15 years.[1, 2] An important advance has been the concept that proximal-vein thrombosis—popliteal, femoral, or iliac vein thrombosis—is a distinct prognostic category from deep-vein thrombosis confined to the calf veins.[1–7]

Proximal-vein thrombosis is a serious and potentially lethal disorder. Inadequately treated proximal-vein thrombosis is associated with a 20 to 50% risk of clinically important recurrent venous thromboembolic events.[8I, 9I, 10I, 11I] There is a strong association between proximal-vein thrombosis and fatal pulmonary embolism. This association has been documented in studies of patients having major orthopedic surgery such as hip or knee replacement without preventive measures. These studies document a rate of proximal-vein thrombosis of 20 to 30%,[12, 13] and a rate of fatal pulmonary embolism of 2 to 3%.[14I, 15] Thus, the data support a 10% rate of fatal pulmonary embolism associated with untreated proximal-vein thrombosis.

In contrast, the available data from clinical trials support the inference that thrombosis remaining confined to the calf veins is associated with a low risk of clinically important pulmonary embolism.[3, 4, 16I, 17I, 18I, 19I, 20I] In the context of this chapter, "clinically important" pulmonary embolism refers to either fatal pulmonary embolism or nonfatal symptomatic pulmonary embolism.

The management of patients with calf-vein thrombosis is an issue that continues to attract attention in the literature.[5, 6, 21, 22] This literature is potentially confusing and contains divergent, contradictory recommendations. The reasons are (1) the low risk of important pulmonary embolism in patients with thrombosis that remains confined to the calf veins may be incorrectly inferred to mean "no further management" is required; (2) case reports[22] and autopsy studies[23, 24] attributing pulmonary

embolism to a source in the calf veins create doubt about the validity of the concept that isolated calf-vein thrombosis has a low risk of important pulmonary embolism; and (3) the observation that patients with calf-vein thrombosis may develop extension into the proximal veins has led to the suggestion that all patients with calf-vein thrombosis should be treated with anticoagulant therapy.[21]

This chapter reviews the available data on the clinical course of untreated calf-vein thrombosis and the evidence supporting three alternative management strategies: (1) no further intervention, (2) antithrombotic therapy with heparin and oral anticoagulants, and (3) serial noninvasive leg testing to monitor for proximal extension.

## SCOPE OF THE PROBLEM

The incidence of calf-vein thrombosis in symptomatic patients is well documented from prospective studies in which venography was performed in consecutive patients presenting with symptoms or signs suggesting deep-vein thrombosis.[25I, 26, 27I, 28I, 29] These studies have shown that 4 to 13% of such patients have deep-vein thrombosis confined to the calf, about 30% have proximal-vein thrombosis (popliteal, femoral, or iliac thrombosis), and 57 to 66% of patients have normal venograms. Thus, most patients with confirmed thrombosis have proximal-vein thrombosis (with or without associated calf thrombosis), and a minority of patients have thrombosis confined to the calf veins.

Since the mid-1980s, noninvasive testing has replaced venography in most centers as first-line tests for evaluating patients who present with symptoms or signs of venous thrombosis.[16I, 17I, 18I, 19I, 20I] The most commonly used noninvasive tests are B-mode or duplex ultrasound and impedance plethysmography. These tests fail to detect most patients with deep-vein thrombosis confined to the calf.[30, 31] Consequently, the patient with symptomatic calf-vein thrombosis is less commonly encountered by physicians than in the past when venography was used as the first-line objective test. In centers where noninvasive tests are not available, or where there is a preference for venography, thrombosis confined to the calf is identified more commonly.

In recent years, the incidence of asymptomatic calf-vein thrombosis in high-risk patients has been well documented by clinical trials performed to evaluate preventive approaches in which venography was used routinely as the diagnostic endpoint. For example, thrombosis confined to the calf veins is present in 10 to 40% of patients undergoing hip or knee replacement who receive prophylaxis with either warfarin or low-molecular-weight heparin.[32I, 33I, 34I] Calf-vein thrombosis is present in 10 to 30% of patients over the age of 40 years undergoing abdominal or thoracic surgery, neurosurgery, or urologic surgery without prophylaxis,[13, 14III, 15] and in up to 50% of patients with stroke causing paralysis.[15] Most of these patients are asymptomatic, and therefore thrombosis remains undetected in most centers, unless casefinding with venography is performed as part of routine care or as part of clinical trials. The asymptomatic calf-vein thrombi are usually clinically unimportant as long as they remain confined to the calf veins. However, in some patients, these thrombi may extend proximally (see later) and may lead to important and even fatal pulmonary embolism.

Data indicate that most patients with symptomatic proximal-vein thrombosis or pulmonary embolism are outpatients at the time of presentation,[16I, 35I] and most of them have a history of surgery or hospital admission for medical illness during the previous 6 months.[36, 37I] It is likely that many of these patients had asymptomatic calf-vein thrombosis at the time of discharge from the hospital, but these thrombi evolved during the subsequent weeks to months, leading to symptomatic proximal-vein thrombosis or pulmonary embolism. This inference is further supported by the findings of a study using venography performed preoperatively and then serially postoperatively in patients undergoing knee replacement.[38] The results indicate that in 90% of patients with thrombosis, the thrombus is present within 24 hours postoperatively, and is present when the patient is discharged several days later. The length of hospital stay has decreased markedly for most surgical procedures, including hip or knee replacement, procedures which are high

risk for venous thromboembolism. Many patients who in the past would have presented with symptomatic venous thromboembolism during the hospital stay are now presenting as outpatients or, during their convalescence at rehabilitation hospitals. The result is a shift in the burden of illness of venous thromboembolism from the acute-care hospital setting to the community and nonacute-care setting.

## CLINICAL COURSE OF UNTREATED CALF-VEIN THROMBOSIS

This section summarizes the available data on the clinical course of untreated calf-vein thrombosis for two outcomes: (1) the extension of thrombosis into the proximal-veins, and (2) the incidence of clinically important pulmonary embolism.

The post-phlebitic syndrome is a potentially important longterm outcome. The incidence of the post-phlebitic syndrome in patients with calf-vein thrombosis is currently uncertain.[7] It is also uncertain whether thrombi that remain confined to the calf lead to post-phlebitic symptoms, or whether calf thrombi must first extend into the proximal veins to be associated with subsequent post-phlebitic problems. Post-phlebitic symptoms are common sequelae in patients with symptomatic proximal-vein thrombosis.[7] Because untreated calf-vein thrombosis may extend proximally and lead to symptomatic proximal-vein thrombosis, at least some patients with calf-vein thrombosis subsequently develop the post-phlebitic syndrome owing to proximal progression of thrombosis. However, it is possible that thrombosis confined to the calf also contributes to post-phlebitic symptoms. Further studies are required to resolve these issues.

### Proximal Extension of Calf-vein Thrombosis

Extension of thrombosis into the popliteal vein or more proximally occurs in 15 to 25% of patients with calf-vein thrombosis.[3, 21, 39I] This rate applies to patients with either symptomatic or asymptomatic calf-vein thrombosis. The data for the rate of proximal extension comes from two types of studies: (1) studies including a series of consecutive patients with untreated calf-vein thrombosis who were monitored for proximal extension using objective tests including [125]I-fibrinogen leg scanning, impedance plethysmography, duplex ultrasound, or venography[3, 4, 21]; and (2) a randomized trial (level 1) evaluating alternative regimens for the treatment of calf-vein thrombosis.[39] The studies evaluating the clinical course of untreated calf-vein thrombosis are summarized in Table 38–1.

In the randomized trial by Lagerstedt and coworkers,[39I] patients were treated with an initial course of intravenous heparin for 5 days, and then randomly allocated to receive continued longterm treatment with warfarin or no longterm anticoagulant treatment. Of the 28 patients who did not receive warfarin, five (18%) had proximal extension confirmed by venography. Two additional patients had "recurrence of" thrombosis, but the venographic findings were not described in detail. In contrast, none of the 23 patients treated with warfarin had proximal extension of thrombosis or recurrent thromboembolism. These results indicate that calf-vein thrombosis may extend proximally, even when it is treated with initial heparin but not followed by oral anticoagulant therapy. The results have important implications for patients in whom a decision is made to treat with anticoagulants (see later under Antithrombotic Therapy).

## Incidence of Clinically Important Pulmonary Embolism

The incidence of clinically important pulmonary embolism is low (1% or less) in patients in whom thrombosis remains confined to the calf veins. This inference is supported by two lines of evidence: (1) studies in relatively small numbers of consecutive patients with untreated calf-vein thrombosis who are followed to document the incidence of pulmonary embolism[3, 4]; and (2) five large prospective studies[16I, 17I, 18I, 19I, 20I] in patients with symptoms or signs suggesting deep-vein thrombosis who are managed based on noninvasive tests that are insensitive for calf-vein thrombosis, and in whom anticoagulant therapy was withheld if these tests remained negative.

In the studies by Kakker and coworkers,[3] and by Moser and LeMoine,[4] no patient in whom thrombosis remained confined to the calf developed clinically evident pulmonary embolism (rates of 0/31 and 0/21, respectively). In the trial by Lagerstedt and coworkers,[39I] one of the 28 patients presented with symptomatic pulmonary embolism confirmed by ventilation-perfusion lung scanning, but the lung scan criteria for this diagnosis were not described. In this study, the patients were not monitored for proximal extension using objective testing, and so it is unknown whether the patient developed proximal extension of thrombosis before pulmonary embolism occurred. The study by Lohr and coworkers[21] did not report whether patients developed pulmonary embolism or which objective tests were used to confirm or exclude this diagnosis.

The large prospective studies evaluating noninvasive testing in patients with clinically suspected venous thrombosis provide data on the incidence of important pulmonary embolism.[16I, 17I, 18I, 19I, 20I] These data are summarized in Table 38–2. The results are relevant to the issue of calf-vein thrombosis because each of these studies evaluated the safety of withholding anticoagulant therapy in patients in whom noninvasive tests that are sensitive for proximal-vein thrombosis but insensitive for calf-vein thrombosis remained negative. None of more than 1600 patients evaluated in these studies died from pulmonary embolism (95% confidence interval 0 to 0.2%), and only three patients (0.3%) had symptomatic nonfatal pulmonary embolism.

Table 38–1. **Studies Evaluating Extension of Calf-vein Thrombosis**

| Study and Year | Number of Patients | Patient Status | Test Used to Detect Extension | Number (%) With Extension into Proximal Veins |
|---|---|---|---|---|
| Kakkar et al, 1969[3] | 40 | Asymptomatic Postoperative elective surgery | [125]I-fibrinogen scan and venography | 9 (22.5) |
| Moser and LeMoine, 1981[4] | 21 | Mixed symptomatic and asymptomatic high-risk | [125]I-fibrinogen scan impedance plethysmography, venography | 0 |
| Lagerstedt et al, 1985[39] | 28 | Symptomatic | Venography | 5 (18)* |
| Lohr et al, 1991[21] | 75 | Symptomatic (62) and asymptomatic (13), 36 outpatients, 39 inpatients | Duplex ultrasound | 11 (15) |

*Two additional patients had "recurrence" but the venographic findings were not described; if these two patients are included, the rate is 7/28 (25%).

Table 38–2. **Incidence of Clinically Important Pulmonary Embolism in Patients With Suspected Venous Thrombosis and Negative Results by Serial Noninvasive Testing; Prospective Studies**

| Study and Year | Diagnostic Test | Number of Patients With Negative Results | Fatal PE Number of Patients | Symptomatic Nonfatal PE Number of Patients (%) |
|---|---|---|---|---|
| Hull et al, 1985[16] | IPG | 311 | 0 | 0 |
| Huisman et al, 1986[17] | IPG | 289 | 0 | 0 |
| Huisman et al, 1989[18] | IPG | 131 | 0 | 0 |
| Hull et al, 1990[19] | IPG | 139 | 0 | 0 |
| Heijboer et al, 1993[20] | IPG | 361 | 0 | 2 (0.6) |
| | C-US | 390 | 0 | 1 (0.3) |
| Total | | 1621 | 0* | 3 (0.2)* |

IPG = impedance plethysmography, C-US = compression ultrasound, PE = pulmonary embolism.
*95% confidence intervals: 0/1621, 0% to 0.2%; 3/1621, 0.07% to 0.4%.

The data provide support for the strategy of serial testing for proximal extension as one approach for managing patients with deep-vein thrombosis confined to the calf.

How can the above data be reconciled with case reports or autopsy studies that reveal important pulmonary embolism associated with calf-vein thrombosis?[22–24] This issue has been clarified by the findings of recent prospective studies in patients with clinically suspected pulmonary embolism who underwent routine objective testing for deep-vein thrombosis.[37I, 40I, 41I] These studies used objective testing with venography or impedance plethysmography. Impedance plethysmography is sensitive for proximal-vein thrombosis in patients with suspected pulmonary embolism.[40] The results indicate that proximal-vein thrombosis is absent in about 50% of patients with confirmed pulmonary embolism.[40I, 41I] The explanation for this finding is that all or most of the thrombus is embolized, leaving no or little residual thrombosis in the legs detectable by objective testing at the time of presentation with clinical symptoms or signs of pulmonary embolism.

This explanation is strongly supported by the findings of a large prospective study evaluating serial noninvasive testing for proximal-vein thrombosis in patients with suspected pulmonary embolism and nondiagnostic lung scans.[35, 37I] The findings indicate that anticoagulant therapy can be safely withheld in such patients who have adequate cardiorespiratory reserve at presentation, provided the results of objective testing for proximal-vein thrombosis are negative, and remain negative on serial testing for 10 to 14 days. Of 627 patients with nondiagnostic lung scans, adequate cardiorespiratory reserve, and serially negative results by noninvasive leg testing, only four patients (0.6%) returned with clinically important pulmonary embolism during followup for 3 months.

Because the noninvasive test used in this study is insensitive for calf-vein thrombosis, the findings support the inference that isolated calf-vein thrombosis is associated with a low risk of clinically important pulmonary embolism, and that serial testing with impedance plethysmography can be used to identify patients with proximal extension of calf-vein thrombosis who require treatment with anticoagulants.

Thus, the aggregate data in patients with suspected venous thrombosis[16I, 17I, 18I, 19I, 20I] and in those with clinically suspected pulmonary embolism[35, 37I, 40I, 41I] support the inference that proximal-vein thrombosis is the key prognostic marker for clinically important pulmonary embolism. If thrombosis remains confined to the calf, the risk of clinically important pulmonary embolism is low.[16I, 17I, 18I, 19I, 20I, 35, 37I] The finding of isolated calf-vein thrombosis in a patient with confirmed pulmonary embolism does not establish that the embolus originated directly from deep veins in the calf. All of the available data[3, 4, 16I, 17I, 18I, 19I, 20I, 35, 37I] support the explanation that such calf thrombi represent the residua of larger proximal-vein thrombosis that embolized.

## MANAGEMENT OF CALF-VEIN THROMBOSIS

### No Further Intervention

The outcomes for a "no intervention" strategy can be estimated from the available data on the rates of proximal extension[3, 4, 21] and the randomized trial data (level 1) for inadequately managed proximal-vein thrombosis.[8I, 9I, 10I, 11I] Of

100 patients with calf-vein thrombosis who are managed using "no further intervention," extension into the proximal veins would be expected in 20 of these patients.[3, 4, 21] Because inadequately treated or untreated proximal-vein thrombosis is associated with a 20 to 50% rate of recurrent venous thromboembolic events[8I, 9I, 10I, 11I] and a 10% risk of fatal pulmonary embolism, the outcomes in the 20 patients with proximal-vein thrombosis can be predicted. It is expected that two patients would die from pulmonary embolism, and five to 10 patients would return with either symptomatic pulmonary embolism or symptomatic recurrent deep-vein thrombosis. Thus, of 100 patients with untreated calf-vein thrombosis, the expected mortality from pulmonary embolism is 2%, and the expected frequency of nonfatal symptomatic pulmonary embolism is approximately 5%.

## Antithrombotic Therapy

Anticoagulant therapy with intravenous heparin followed by oral warfarin is effective for preventing extension and/or recurrence of thromboembolism in patients with calf-vein thrombosis.[39I] The trial by Lagerstedt and coworkers[39I] establishes the need for longterm treatment following the initial course of heparin. In this trial, extension and/or recurrence of venous thromboembolism occurred in eight of 28 patients (29%) who did not receive longterm warfarin, compared with none of the 23 patients given longterm therapy ($p < .01$). All cases of thrombosis extension and recurrence occurred within the first 3 months, and five of eight occurred in the first 6 weeks.

Certain low-molecular-weight heparin preparations given subcutaneously once or twice daily have been shown to be as effective as intravenous unfractionated heparin for initial treatment of patients with proximal-vein thrombosis.[42I, 43I] These low-molecular-weight heparin preparations should also be effective for treatment in patients with calf-vein thrombosis (a lower risk group than proximal-vein thrombosis). If low-molecular-weight heparin is available, it can be used for initial treatment of calf-vein thrombosis based on the data from clinical trials in patients with proximal-vein thrombosis.

Treatment with oral anticoagulants alone is not recommended for patients with documented calf-vein thrombosis. Although convenient, the effectiveness of oral anticoagulant therapy alone for preventing extension of calf-vein thrombosis remains uncertain. Furthermore, treatment with oral anticoagulants alone is less effective than treatment with initial heparin and oral anticoagulants in patients with proximal-vein thrombosis.[10] This observation suggests that oral anticoagulant treatment alone may not be effective for preventing extension in patients with documented calf-vein thrombosis.

The available data from clinical trials indicates that oral anticoagulant therapy should be continued for at least 6 weeks in patients with calf-vein thrombosis.[8I, 39I] Hull and coworkers reported that none of 32 patients with calf-vein thrombosis who received anticoagulant therapy for 6 weeks developed symptomatic venous thromboembolism during the subsequent year (0/32, 95% confidence interval 0 to 11%).[8I] In the trial by Lagerstedt, only one of 23 patients (4%) with calf-vein thrombosis treated for 3 months developed recurrent venous thromboembolism during the subsequent year (1/23, 95% confidence interval 0 to 15%).[39I] The data indicate that patients with calf-vein thrombosis should be treated for 6 weeks to 3 months, and, in many patients, 6 weeks is probably sufficient. It may be prudent to continue treatment for longer than 6 weeks in selected patients with continuing risk factors. Moderate doses of subcutaneous heparin provide an effective and safe alternative to warfarin for longterm treatment in patients in whom warfarin is contraindicated or for whom prothrombin time monitoring is not feasible.[44I]

The risk of major bleeding during treatment with initial intravenous heparin is about 5%.[9I, 10I, 42I, 43I] However, there is a marked difference in the risk of major bleeding among patients without risk factors (1%) compared with patients who have had recent surgery or other risk factors in whom the risk for major bleeding is 11%.[45I] The risk of major bleeding during longterm treatment with warfarin (International Normalized Ratio [INR] 2.0 to 3.0) is about 2% during the initial 3 months.[46I] The risk of fatal bleeding during either initial heparin or longterm warfarin therapy is low (<1%) based on multiple randomized trials in large numbers of patients with venous thrombosis.[47] These risks of bleeding with current anticoagulant therapy are outweighed by the estimated risk of fatal pulmonary embolism of 2% and the risk of nonfatal symptomatic pulmonary embolism of 5% if patients with calf-vein thrombosis receive no further intervention.

The availability of low-molecular-weight heparin for the initial treatment of deep-vein thrombosis will likely shift the risk/benefit calculation markedly in favor of treating patients with calf-vein thrombosis, because certain low-molecular-weight heparin preparations are associated with a markedly reduced risk of major bleeding compared with use of intravenous unfractionated heparin.[421, 431] In the trial by Hull and coworkers,[431] 11 of 219 patients (5%) who received continuous intravenous heparin had major bleeding, compared with only one of 213 patients (0.5%) given the low-molecular-weight heparin tinzaparin (a risk reduction of 90%, $p < .01$). This trial included a substantial number of patients at high risk of bleeding because of the presence of risk factors such as recent surgery, a history of gastrointestinal or genitourinary bleeding, thrombocytopenia, or other disorders predisposing to bleeding. Low-molecular-weight heparin can be given subcutaneously once or twice daily without the need for laboratory monitoring and dose adjustment.[421, 431] This simplified therapy will enable patients to be managed in the outpatient setting and is likely to be more cost-effective than treatment in hospital with intravenous heparin for 4 to 5 days. These factors are likely to shift future practice towards treating most patients with documented calf-vein thrombosis.

## Monitoring for Proximal Extension

Repeated testing with impedance plethysmography or B-mode ultrasound is effective for detecting extension of calf-vein thrombosis into the popliteal or more proximal veins. The approach of monitoring for proximal extension is supported by the findings of several prospective studies[16I, 17I, 18I, 19I, 20I, 35, 37I] that document the safety of withholding anticoagulant therapy in patients in whom repeated noninvasive testing remains negative. These studies used repeated testing over a 10- to 14-day period.

The potential advantage of monitoring for proximal extension, rather than treating all patients with anticoagulant therapy, is that treatment can be confined to patients who develop proximal-vein thrombosis. In patients in whom thrombosis remains confined to the calf, the risk of bleeding with anticoagulant therapy can be avoided, because these thrombi are associated with a low risk of subsequent clinically important venous thromboembolic events.

At present, serial testing for proximal extension may be preferred in selected patients with calf-vein thrombosis at high risk of bleeding (e.g., surgery within the previous week). If serial testing is used, the test should be repeated every 2 to 3 days for at least a 10- to 14-day period. This may not be practical in some patients who live a far distance from the hospital or clinic.

## RECOMMENDATIONS

1. Patients with thrombosis confined to the calf either should be treated with anticoagulant therapy to prevent extension, or should undergo monitoring for proximal extension using serial noninvasive testing with either impedance plethysmography or compression ultrasound imaging.

2. The choice between anticoagulant treatment or monitoring for extension depends on the risk of bleeding, and on the availability and feasibility of performing serial noninvasive testing.

3. The strategy of "no further intervention" (i.e., neither treatment or serial noninvasive testing) is not recommended. This approach exposes patients to an unacceptable risk of clinically important pulmonary embolism.

4. If the decision to treat with anticoagulant therapy is made, at 1995 standards, this should consist of intravenous heparin for 4 to 5 days followed by oral warfarin sodium for 6 weeks to 3 months. If available, certain low-molecular-weight heparin preparations given subcutaneously could be used in place of intravenous unfractionated heparin, based on their established effectiveness in patients with proximal-vein thrombosis.

## REFERENCES

1. Weinmann E, Salzman EW: Deep-vein thrombosis. N Engl J Med 331:1630–1641, 1994.
2. Moser KM: Venous thromboembolism. Am Rev Respir Dis 141:235–249, 1990.
3. Kakkar VV, Howe CT, Flanc C, Clarke MB: Natural history of postoperative deep-vein thrombosis. Lancet 2:230–233, 1969.
4. Moser KM, LeMoine JR: Is embolic risk conditioned by location of postoperative deep-vein thrombosis? Ann Intern Med 94:439–444, 1981.
5. Philbrick JT, Becker DM: Calf deep venous thrombosis. A wolf in sheep's clothing? Arch Intern Med 148:2131–2138, 1988.
6. Powers LR: Distal deep vein thrombosis. What's the best treatment? J Gen Intern Med 3:288–292, 1988.
7. Hirsh J, Lensing AWA: Natural history of minimal calf deep-vein thrombosis. In Berstein EF: Vascular Diagnosis, ed 4. St. Louis, CV Mosby, 1993, pp 779–781.
I 8. Hull R, Delmore T, Genton E, et al: Warfarin sodium versus low-dose heparin in the long-term treatment of venous thrombosis. N Engl J Med 301:855–858, 1979.
I 9. Hull R, Raskob G, Hirsh J, et al: Continuous intravenous heparin compared with intermittent subcutaneous heparin in the initial treatment of proximal-vein thrombosis. N Engl J Med 315:1109–1114, 1986.
I 10. Brandjes DPM, Heijboer H, Buller HR, et al: Acenocoumarol and heparin compared with acenocoumarol alone in the initial treatment of proximal-vein thrombosis. N Engl J Med 327:1485–1489, 1992.

I  11. Raschke RA, Reilly BM, Guidry JR, et al: The weight-based heparin dosing nomogram compared with a "standard care" nomogram. A randomized controlled trial. Ann Intern Med 119:874–881, 1993.

12. Imperiale TF, Speroff T: A meta-analysis of methods to prevent venous thromboembolism following total hip replacement. JAMA 271:1780–1785, 1994.

13. Gallus AS, Salzman EW, Hirsh J: Prevention of venous thromboembolism. In Coleman RW, Hirsh J, Marder V, Salzman EW: Hemostasis and Thrombosis: Basic Principles and Clinical Practice, ed 3. Philadelphia, JB Lippincott, 1994, pp 1331–1345.

III 14. Coventry MB, Nolan DR, Beckenbaugh RD: "Delayed" prophylactic anticoagulation: A study of results and complications in 2,012 total hip arthroplasties. J Bone Joint Surg 55A:1487–1492, 1973.

15. Clagett GP, Anderson FA, Levine MN, et al: Prevention of venous thromboembolism. Chest 102[Oct Suppl]:391–407, 1992.

I  16. Hull R, Hirsh J, Carter C, et al: Diagnostic efficacy of impedance plethysmography for clinically suspected deep-vein thrombosis: A randomized trial. Ann Intern Med 102:21–28, 1985.

I  17. Huisman MV, Buller HR, ten Cate JW, Vreeken J: Serial impedance plethysmography for suspected deep venous thrombosis in outpatients. The Amsterdam General Practitioner Study. N Engl J Med 314:823–828, 1986.

I  18. Huisman MV, Buller HR, ten Cate JW, et al: Management of clinically suspected acute venous thrombosis in outpatients with serial impedance plethysmography in a community hospital setting. Arch Intern Med 149:511–513, 1989.

I  19. Hull R, Raskob G, Carter CJ: Serial impedance plethysmography in pregnant patients with clinically suspected deep-vein thrombosis. Clinical validity of negative findings. Ann Intern Med 112:663–667, 1990.

I  20. Heijboer H, Buller HR, Lensing AWA, et al: A comparison of real-time compression ultrasonography with impedance plethysmography for the diagnosis of deep-vein thrombosis in symptomatic outpatients. N Engl J Med 329:1365–1369, 1993.

21. Lohr JM, Kerr TM, Lutter KS, et al: Lower extremity calf thrombosis: To treat or not to treat? J Vasc Surg 14:618–623, 1991.

22. Chapman WHH, Lee MYT, Foley KT: Pulmonary embolism from a venous thrombosis distal to the popliteal vein. Mil Med 156:252–254, 1991.

23. Havig GO: Source of pulmonary emboli. Acta Chir Scand 478[Suppl]:42–47, 1977.

24. Giachino A: Relationship between deep-vein thrombosis in the calf and fatal pulmonary embolism. Can J Surg 31:129–130, 1988.

I  25. Hull R, Hirsh J, Sackett DL, et al: Combined use of leg scanning and impedance plethysmography in suspected venous thrombosis. An alternative to venography. N Engl J Med 296:1497–1500, 1977.

26. O'Donnell TF, Abbott WM, Athanasoulis CA, et al: Diagnosis of deep venous thrombosis in the outpatient by venography. Surg Gynecol Obstet 150:69–74, 1980.

I  27. Hull R, Hirsh J, Sackett DL, et al: Replacement of venography in suspected venous thrombosis by impedance plethysmography and $^{125}$I-fibrinogen leg scanning. A less invasive approach. Ann Intern Med 94:12–15, 1981.

I  28. Lensing AWA, Prandoni P, Brandjes D, et al: Detection of deep-vein thrombosis by real-time B-mode ultrasonography. N Engl J Med 320:342–345, 1989.

29. Cogo A, Lensing AWA, Prandoni P, Hirsh J: Distribution of thrombosis in patients with symptomatic deep vein thrombosis. Arch Intern Med 153:2777–2780, 1993.

30. Wheeler HB, Hirsh J, Wells P, Anderson FA: Diagnostic tests for deep vein thrombosis. Clinical usefulness depends on probability of disease. Arch Intern Med 154:1921–1928, 1994.

31. White RW, McGahan J, Daschbach M, Hartling RP: Diagnosis of deep-vein thrombosis using Duplex ultrasound. Ann Intern Med 111:297–304, 1989.

I  32. Hull R, Raskob G, Pineo G, et al: A comparison of subcutaneous low-molecular weight heparin with warfarin sodium for prophylaxis against deep-vein thrombosis after hip or knee implantation. N Engl J Med 329:1370–1376, 1993.

I  33. RD Heparin Arthroplasty Group: RD heparin compared with warfarin for prevention of venous thromboembolic disease following total hip or knee arthroplasty. J Bone Joint Surg 76A:1174–1185, 1994.

I  34. Leclerc JR, Geerts WH, Desjardins L, et al: Prevention of venous thromboembolism (VTE) after knee arthroplasty—a randomized double-blind trial comparing a low molecular weight heparin fragment (enoxaparin) to warfarin. Blood 84[Suppl 1]:246a, 1994.

I  35. Hull R, Raskob G, Ginsberg J, et al: A noninvasive strategy for the treatment of patients with suspected pulmonary embolism. Arch Intern Med 154:289–297, 1994.

36. Anderson FA, Wheeler HB, Goldberg RJ, et al: A population-based perspective of the hospital incidence and case-fatality rates of deep-vein thrombosis and pulmonary embolism. The Worcester DVT Study. Arch Intern Med 151:933–938, 1991.

I  37. Hull R, Raskob G, Coates G, et al: A new noninvasive management strategy for patients with suspected pulmonary embolism. Arch Intern Med 149:2549–2555, 1989.

38. Maynard M, Sculco TP, Ghelman B: Progression and regression of deep-vein thrombosis after total knee arthroplasty. Clin Orthop 273:125–130, 1991.

I  39. Lagerstedt CI, Olsson CG, Fagher BO, et al: The need for long-term anticoagulant treatment in symptomatic calf-vein thrombosis. Lancet 2:515–518, 1985.

I  40. Hull R, Hirsh J, Carter C, et al: Pulmonary angiography, ventilation lung scanning and venography for clinically suspected pulmonary embolism with abnormal perfusion lung scan. Ann Intern Med 98:891–899, 1983.

I  41. Hull R, Hirsh J, Carter C, et al: Diagnostic value of ventilation-perfusion lung scanning in patients with suspected pulmonary embolism. Chest 88:819–828, 1985.

I  42. Prandoni P, Lensing AWA, Buller HR, et al: Comparison of subcutaneous low molecular weight heparin with intravenous standard heparin in proximal deep-vein thrombosis. Lancet 339:441–445, 1992.

I  43. Hull R, Raskob G, Pineo G, et al: Subcutaneous low molecular weight heparin compared with continuous intravenous heparin in the treatment of proximal vein thrombosis. N Engl J Med 326:975–982, 1992.

I  44. Hull R, Delmore T, Carter C, et al: Adjusted subcutaneous heparin versus warfarin sodium in the long-term treatment of venous thrombosis. N Engl J Med 306:189–194, 1982.

I  45. Hull RD, Raskob GE, Rosenbloom D, et al: Heparin

for 5 days as compared with 10 days in the initial treatment of proximal venous thrombosis. N Engl J Med 322:1260–1264, 1990.

I 46. Hull R, Hirsh J, Jay R, et al: Different intensities of oral anticoagulant therapy in the treatment of proximal-vein thrombosis. N Engl J Med 307:1676–1681, 1982.

47. Levine M, Raskob G, Landefeld S, Hirsh J: Hemorrhagic complications of anticoagulant treatment. Chest, 1995, in press.

# Chapter 39

# New Antithrombotic Drugs

Jawed Fareed, Debra Hoppensteadt, Walter Jeske,
Demetra Callas, and Jeanine M. Walenga

The pathophysiology of thrombotic events has multiple components and involves blood, vascular system, and target sites. Initially, vascular injury results in the localized alterations of the vessels and subsequent activation of platelets. Activated cells mediate several direct or signal transduction-induced processes resulting in the activation of platelets. Cellular activation also results in the release of various mediators, which amplify vascular spasm and the coagulation process. Thus, anaphylatoxins ($C_3a$ and $C_5a$), superoxide, leukotrienes (LTC4), thromboxane $B_2$ ($TxB_2$), serotonin, platelet factor 3 (PF3), platelet factor 4 (PF4), platelet activating factor (PAF), endothelin-1, and numerous cytokines play a role in the overall pathophysiology of the thrombotic process. Drugs that target various sites of the activation process can be developed to control thrombotic events. Because of the coupled pathophysiology, a single drug may not be able to target these sites to produce therapeutic actions. Furthermore, many of these mediators produce localized actions at cellular and subcellular levels. The feedback amplification process also plays an important role in the pathology of these disorders. This understanding has led to the concept of polytherapy in the management of thrombotic disorders.

Venous insufficiency, blood plasma–related disorders, fibrinolytic deficit, and an imbalance of regulatory proteins result in the activation of the hemostatic process. Postsurgical trauma, inflammation, and sepsis also result in the activation of the hemostatic process leading to venous thrombosis. The primary process in venous thrombosis is the generation of thrombin. Thus, drugs targeting coagulation protease activation are useful in the treatment of venous disorders.[21] However, platelet and cellular activation contribute significantly to arterial thrombotic events, and therefore, drugs targeting those sites are important in the management of arterial thrombosis and microangiopathic disorders.

The newer developments in antithrombotic drugs are significant. Many advanced techniques to develop antithrombotic drugs are used at the present time. Advances in biotechnology and separation techniques have also contributed to the development of newer antithrombotic drugs.[18–25] These drugs may prove to have a better efficacy in the control of thrombogenesis and its treatment. Drugs and devices that have been or are being developed based on newer concepts can be classified into the groups as listed below. The drugs marked with an asterisk (*) may be useful in trauma patients because their safety/efficacy index is claimed to be higher than that of conventional anticoagulants.

I. Heparin-related Drugs
   1. *Low-molecular-weight heparins
   2. Medium-molecular-weight heparins
   3. High-molecular-weight heparins
   4. Chemically modified heparins
   5. Dermatans
   6. *Heparans
   7. Semisynthetic heparin derivatives (suleparoide)
   8. Chemically synthesized antithrombotic oligosaccharides
   9. Sulfated dextrans
   10. Synthetic hypersulfated compounds
   11. Polyanionic agents
   12. Marine polysaccharides
   13. Heparinoids (Lomoparan)

II. Antiplatelet Drugs
   1. *(Ticlopidine)-related antiplatelet drugs
   2. *(Pletaal)-related phosphodiesterase inhibitors
   3. (Iloprost) prostanoid modulators
   4. Eicosanoids and related drugs

5. ω-3 fatty acids and fish oil–related products
6. Antibodies targeting membrane glycoproteins
7. Peptides and proteins modulating platelet function
III. Endothelial Lining Modulators
   1. *Nucleic acid derivatives (defibrotide)
   2. Sulfomucopolysaccharide mixtures
   3. DDAVP and related peptides
   4. Growth factor–related peptides
   5. Protein digests
   6. Vitamins
IV. Viscosity Modulators
   1. Synthetic and natural polymers
   2. *Pentoxifylline
   3. Venoms defibrinating agents (ancrod)
   4. Polyelectrolytes
V. Biotechnology-based Proteins
   1. t-PA and mutants
   2. *Hirudin, mutants, and fragments
   3. Protein C and protein S
   4. Thrombomodulin
   5. Thrombomodulin-thrombin complex
   6. Antithrombin III (ATIII)
   7. Antithrombin III–heparin complex
   8. Recombinant heparin cofactor II
   9. Glycoprotein-targeting proteins and peptides
   10. Protease specific inhibitors
   11. Recombinant tissue factor pathway inhibitor
VI. Peptides and Related Antithrombotic Agents
   1. *Hirulogs
   2. D-Me-Phe-Pro-Arg–derived antithrombotic drugs
   3. Argatroban
   4. Borohydride derivatives
VII. Optimized Polytherapy of Trauma-induced Thrombotic Disorders
   1. Heparin/antiplatelet drugs
   2. Coumadin/antiplatelet drugs
   3. Thrombolytic agents/heparin
   4. Thrombolytic agents/antiplatelet drugs
   5. Thrombolytic agents/Hirudin and other thrombin inhibitors
   6. Recombinant drug conjugates
   7. Hirudin/antithrombotic agents
   8. Hirudin/glycoprotein targeting antibodies
VIII. Newer Drug Delivery Systems and Formulations
   1. Oral
   2. Ointments
   3. Transdermal
   4. Sustained release
   5. Transdermal
   6. Target-specific antithrombotic drugs (antibody-directed)
   7. Catheters and devices capable of targeted drug delivery

It can be appreciated from the above survey that antithrombotic drugs represent a wide spectrum of natural, synthetic, semisynthetic, and biotechnology-produced agents with marked differences in chemical composition, physicochemical properties, biochemical actions, and pharmacologic effects. The use of physical means to treat thrombotic disorders, and an advanced means of drug delivery, add to the expanding nature of this area.

The endogenous actions of the antithrombotic drugs are remarkably complex. It is no longer valid to assume that an antithrombotic drug must produce an anticoagulant action in blood like that of conventional heparin and oral anticoagulants. Many of the drugs listed in various categories do not produce any alteration of blood clotting parameters, yet they are effective therapeutic agents because of their interactions with the various elements of the vascular and other blood components. Another perspective is that several of these agents require endogenous transformation to become active products. Therefore, it becomes important to rely on the pharmacodynamic actions of these agents rather than on their in vitro characteristics to assess potency or efficacy of the product. Hematologic modulation plays a key role in the mediation of the antithrombotic actions of these drugs involving red cells, white cells, platelets, and blood proteins. This is particularly true for the case of trauma-induced thrombotic disorders in which multiple processes are involved in thrombogenesis.

## THE NEW HEPARINS

### The Development of Low-molecular-weight Heparins

The development of low-molecular-weight heparin (LMWH) has added a new dimension to the clinical management of thrombotic disorders. These agents have revolutionized the prophylaxis of postsurgical thrombosis.[38, 53, 59] More recently, these drugs have been used for the treatment of trauma-related thrombosis. In particular, their relative effects on platelets are minimal in comparison to the effects of heparin. Thus, these agents are of value in platelet-compromised patients. In addition to the low-molecular-weight heparins, several other agents such as the chemically synthesized analogues of heparin and nonheparin glycosaminoglycans such as dermatan sulfate, heparan sulfate, and various other antithrombotic agents have also become available for the management of thrombotic disorders. In the United States, however, most of these agents are in clinical trials and are not yet available for general use in patients.

For the past few decades, heparin has been widely used for the prevention of postoperative thromboembolism.[32, 36, 37] However, there are several adverse side effects associated with the use of heparin such as bleeding, heparin-induced thrombocytopenia, heparin-induced thrombosis,[42, 64] and osteoporosis.[28] In addition, the regimen of prophylactic heparin used in the prevention of deep venous thrombosis (DVT) is tedious, requiring 2 to 3 daily injections because of the limited bioavailability and short half life of heparin administered subcutaneously.

The many clinical problems associated with heparin led several investigators to study the structure of heparin and to identify the active components of this agent. The observation that only low-molecular-weight heparins are absorbed after subcutaneous administration has led to the development of LMWHs. Experimental studies revealed that the first LMWHs had a subcutaneous bioavailability of about 90% compared with 15 to 25% for unfractionated heparin (UFH).[4] Furthermore, these agents exhibit a much longer biologic half life in contrast to heparin.[22] Thus, LMWH preparations could be administered with a single daily injection, making them easy to administer as a prophylactic agent. Eight LMWHs have already been approved for the prophylaxis of thrombosis in the European community. Several of these LMWHs are under clinical trials in the United States. One was approved in 1993 for use in post orthopedic surgery prophylaxis of DVT. It is expected that two other agents will be approved for clinical use in 1994.

Low-molecular-weight components in UFH were identified long before the development of clinically effective agents. However, because of technologic problems, they were not made available for clinical use. The very first LMWH was obtained by a fractionation method.[13] However, this method yielded only a limited amount of the active product and was cost-prohibitive. During the past decade, different chemical processes have been developed to obtain LMWH from the parent UFH.

Table 39–1 lists some of the commercially available LMWHs. Fraxiparin was originally obtained by a fractionation method. However, it is now obtained by an optimized nitrous acid depolymerization.[14] Lovenox is obtained by benzylation followed by alkaline depolymerization (β-elimination). Large amounts of sodium bisulfite are added to prevent oxidation of the terminal groups, because Enoxaparine contains a double bond at the reducing end.[21] A recent formulation does not contain any sodium bisulfate, and the new formulation is claimed to exhibit pharmacologic effects similar to those of the original product.[24, 25] Fragmin is obtained by nitrous acid depolymerization followed by ion exchange chromatography. It markedly differs from the other LMWHs in physicochemical characteristics and pharmacologic profile.[21] Fluxum is obtained from beef mucosa by a peroxidative depolymerization process. This agent has been found to mediate some of its actions through non-antithrombin III (ATIII)–mediated pathways.[22] Ardeparin, a product prepared

Table 39–1. **Currently Available Low-molecular-weight Heparins**

| Trade Name | Manufacturer/Supplier | Method of Preparation |
|---|---|---|
| Fraxiparin, Seleparin | Sanofi; Paris, France | Fractionation, optimized nitrous acid depolymerization |
| Enoxaparin, Clexane, Lovenox | Rhone Poulenc; Paris, France | Benzylation followed by alkaline hydrolysis |
| Fragmin | Kabi; Stockholm, Sweden | Controlled nitrous acid depolymerization |
| Fluxum | Opocrin; Corlo, Italy | Peroxidative cleavage |
| Ardeparin, Normiflo | Wyeth; Philadelphia, PA, USA | Peroxidative cleavage |
| Logiparin | Novo; Copenhagen, Denmark | Heparinase digestion |
| Innohep | Leo; Copenhagen, Denmark | Heparinase digestion |
| Sandoparin | Sandoz AG; Nurenberg, Germany | Isoamyl nitrate digestion |
| Reviparin, Clivarin | Bioiberica; Palafolls, Spain | β-elimination |
| Boxol | Rovi; Madrid, Spain | β-elimination or nitrous acid digestion |
| Miniparin | Syntex; Buenos Aires, Argentina | Nitrous acid digestion |
| Clivarin | Knoll; Ludwigshafen, Germany | Controlled nitrous acid depolymerization followed by chromatographic purification |

Table 39–2. **A Comparison of UFH and LMWH Efficacy in General Surgery in Randomized Studies**

| Reference | LMWH | UFH | Incidence of Thrombosis LMWH (%) | UFH (%) | p Value |
|---|---|---|---|---|---|
| European Fraxiparin Group[17] | Fraxiparin 7,500 AXa U/daily | 5,000 IU tid | 2.8 | 4.5 | <.05 |
| Caen[11] | Fragmin 2,500 AXa U/daily | 5,000 IU bid | 3.1 | 3.7 | NS |
| Bergqvist[7] | Fragmin 5,000 AXa U/daily | 5,000 IU bid | 5.0 | 9.2 | <.05 |
| Verardi[70] | Fluxum 4,000 IU or 8,000 AXa U/daily | 5,000 IU bid or tid | 3.2 | 6.3 | NS |
| Kakkar[41] | Sandoz LMWH/DHE 1,500 APTT U/daily | UFH/DHE 5,000 IU bid | 11.4 | 11.0 | NS |
| Hartl[31] | Fragmin 2,500 AXa U/daily | 5,000 IU bid | 7.9 | 8.1 | NS |
| Samama[62] | Enoxaparin 60 mg daily 40 mg daily t.i.d. 20 mg daily | 5,000 IU | 2.9 2.9 3.8 | 3.8 2.7 7.6 | NS NS NS |
| Baumgartner[5] | Sandoz LMWH/DHE 1,500 APTT U/daily | UFH/DHE 2,500 IU bid | 3.1 | 3.7 | NS |

NS = nonsignificant

by peroxidative digestion procedures by Hepar (KabiVitrum), has been developed by Wyeth laboratories for clinical use. The Novo LMWH (Logiparin) is prepared by enzymatic digestion using *Flavobacterium heparinicum* heparinase. This drug also contains large amounts of sodium bisulfite as an antioxidant.[22] Innohep is also prepared by a heparinase digestion method and is an identical product to Logiparin.

Embolex NM is a LMWH that is prepared by isoamyl nitrite digestion and is supplemented with dihydroergotamine. A monosubstance that does not contain dihydroergotamine has also been introduced. Reviparin (Clivarin) is a product of Knoll Laboratories (Ludwigshafen, Germany) and is also prepared by nitrous acid digestion. Bioparin is a LMWH from Bioiberica (Barcelona, Spain) and is prepared by a β-elimination method. Boxol is a product of Rovi Pharmaceutical (Madrid, Spain) and is prepared by either β-elimination or nitrous acid digestion method. Marked differences in the two different batches of this product have been observed. Miniparin is a product of Syntex Argentina that is prepared by a nitrous acid digestion method.

Recent studies have shown that the individual LMWHs obtained from each process exhibit chemical and pharmacologic differences.[2, 9, 27, 34, 39]

## Low-molecular-weight Heparins in the Management of Thrombosis

In the past, LMWHs have been used for the postsurgical prophylaxis of DVT. However,

these agents are now also used in the treatment of pre-existing events utilizing both the subcutaneous[37] and intravenous* routes of administration.

Table 39–2 summarizes some of the randomized studies in which LMWHs have been compared with UFH in patients undergoing abdominal surgery. In two studies a significant decrease in DVT was observed in patients receiving LMWHs compared with UFH.[7, 10, 17, 29] There was no statistical difference in efficacy observed between the two treatments in the other studies.[5, 11, 31, 32, 41, 58, 62, 70] In most studies there was no significant difference between the observed bleeding effects of the LMWHs and UFH. In all of these studies, LMWH was given as a single daily dose, whereas UFH was administered two or three times daily. The results of these studies suggest that LMWHs are effective and well tolerated in patients undergoing general surgery. The advantage of LMWHs over heparin was primarily in the reduced number of injections per day.

The most extensively studied method of prophylaxis of DVT in orthopedic patients in recent years has been with LMWH. Evidence that this treatment is both effective and safe is quickly accumulating.

Ten randomized trials using venography or [125]I fibrinogen uptake as the endpoint are summarized in Table 39–3. Four studies compared LMWH with dextran. In two of these studies

*(Breddin, personal communication)

**Table 39–3. Comparison Between LMWHs and Control Group Efficacy in Patients Undergoing Hip Surgery**

| Reference | LMWH | Control Drug | % DVT | | |
|---|---|---|---|---|---|
| | | | LMWH | Control | p Value |
| Matzsch[51] | Logiparan 35 AXa U/kg/daily | Dextran 70 500 ml alt. day | 23 | 37 | NS |
| Pini[57] | Fluxum 7500 AXa U/bid | UFH 5,000 tid | 20 | 29 | NS |
| Monreaul[55] | Fragmin 5,000 AXa U/daily | UFH 5,000 tid | 30 | 13.6 | <.05 |
| Planes[58] | Enoxaparin 40 mg/daily | UFH 5,000 tid | 12.5 | 25 | <.05 |
| Eriksson[16] | Fragmin 2500 AXa U/bid | Dextran 70 500 ml alt. day | 20 | 45 | <.05 |
| Matzsch[52] | Logiparin 35 AXa U/kg/daily | Dextran 500 ml alt. day | 28 | 39 | NS |
| Sorensen[66] | Logiparin 50 IU/kg/daily | Placebo/daily | 27 | 39 | NS |
| Borris[10] | Enoxaparin 40 mg/daily | Dextran 60 mg/ml alt. day | 6 | 21 | <.05 |
| Haas[29] | Sandoz LMWH/ DHE 1,500 APTT U/daily | UFH/DHE 5000 IU bid | 20.5 | 20.5 | NS |
| Turpie[69] | Enoxaparin 30 mg/bid | Placebo bid | 12 | 43 | <.05 |

NS = nonsignificant

results showed no significant difference between the LMWH and the dextran groups. However, in the other two studies, LMWH was more effective than dextran. The different results obtained in these studies are probably the consequence of the different dosages selected for dextran as well as the difference in the dosages and composition of the different LMWHs. Two other studies compared LMWH with placebo. In one study, a difference in the incidence of DVT was found, but in the other study there was no significant difference.

Many surgeons and physicians around the world now appreciate that a large number of cases of venous thromboembolism, particularly those following surgery, can be avoided by correct use of prophylaxis. With additional education and with the introduction of newer and more efficacious agents, it should become routine for all patients undergoing surgery to be assessed for their risk of venous thrombosis and protected accordingly.

Of the many drugs used as prophylactic antithrombotic agents, heparin has a long history as therapy for both DVT and pulmonary embolism (PE). Many studies have shown that in moderate- and high-risk patients, heparin can prevent postoperative DVT and PE.[16, 38, 46, 47, 51, 52, 55, 71] Now, with the introduction of LMWHs, these benefits can be had together with easier dosing and potentially less risk of bleeding.

Many surgeons still, however, harbor fears and doubts about using thromboprophylaxis. One of the most common fears is that of bleeding. There are still some surgeons who are not convinced that the benefits of prophylaxis outweigh the risks.

During the 1980s great advances have aided our understanding of how heparin-like compounds work. It is known that LMWHs are less anticoagulant (in vitro clot-inhibiting) in their actions than heparin but retain their antithrombotic (in vivo thrombosis-inhibiting) potential.[33, 56, 67, 72] This makes the potential risk of bleeding less with LMWHs than with heparin when LMWHs are properly used, particularly with patient-adjusted dosages. However, minor wound bleeding after a successful operation is preferable to death caused by PE.

In the United States, postsurgical and medical thromboembolic disorders affect over 1 million Americans yearly, requiring hospitalization. Approximately 10% of these individuals develop serious PE. Because of this problem, the United States National Institutes of Health (NIH) called a consensus meeting in March, 1986 to discuss the magnitude of thromboembolic disorders and the need for prophylactic therapy.

The consensus conference was effective in identifying the magnitude of medical and postsurgical thromboembolic disorders. Participants made a strong recommendation to use prophylactic measures. Although participants of the consensus meeting reviewed various pharmacologic and physical methods for the prophylaxis of thromboembolic disease, they specifically discussed the use of low-dose heparin therapy for prophylaxis and made the following recommendations:

1. Low-dose heparin can be used for the prophylaxis of DVT in general surgical patients (patients with medium risk).
2. Individualized dosages of low-dose heparin should be given to high-risk patients (trauma and orthopedic surgery).
3. None of the available (1986) prophylactic regimens were considered optimal.

At the time these recommendations were made, only one LMWH was commercially available in France, and very limited information was available in the United States on LMWHs. Today, LMWHs are commonly used in many European countries for the prophylaxis of thromboembolic disorders in both surgical and medical patients. Several LMWHs are currently being evaluated in phase II and phase III clinical trials in the United States.

Available clinical data suggest that LMWHs can be safely substituted for low-dose heparin. To validate this, several trials throughout the world comparing low-dose heparin and LMWHs are in progress. In several European clinical trials, the efficacy of LMWHs in the prevention of postsurgical DVT has now been proven, and these agents are considered to be the drug of choice for this indication.[7, 40, 41, 45]

When used for prophylactic treatment (subcutaneously), most LMWHs mediate their actions in a similar manner; however, their efficacy and tolerability profiles differ markedly, as discussed earlier, and the recommended dosages for the various products differ. Because of the differences between products, such practices as standardization by a single in vitro assay and assignment of a single International Normalization Ratio (INR) designation are deemed invalid for LMWHs as a group. The individualized agent approach to all LMWHs has recently been adopted by the World Health Organization (WHO), the United States Food and Drug Administration (FDA), and the Scientific and Standardization Subcommittee of the International Society of Thrombosis and Hemostasis (ISTH). The recognition of the individuality of each of the LMWHs is extremely important to avoid excessively high or low doses of a product. Dose-finding studies are essential and will have a major impact on the prophylactic and therapeutic acceptance of LMWHs.

Having satisfactorily passed their first step in clinical use, LMWHs are now being applied to other clinical situations. LMWH treatment is moving into the area of established DVT and therapeutic approach to thrombosis. LMWHs may be therapeutic alternatives to heparin in some, but not all, patients who develop a sensitivity to heparin or who develop heparin-induced thrombocytopenia. At optimal dosages, these agents produce their antithrombotic effects, but whether they have fewer adverse effects than standard heparin may vary with the product and is unproved for many of them. LMWHs have proved to be equally effective as heparin in general surgery and orthopedic surgery.[17, 31, 41, 43, 71]

Based on data from several studies, it is proposed that in addition to their antithrombotic effects, the LMWH-mediated profibrinolytic effects may be responsible for the therapeutic actions of these agents.[3, 25, 35] However, this claim requires verification in well-designed experimental and clinical studies.

LMWHs are being used for specific indications such as percutaneous transluminal coronary angioplasty (PTCA), as adjuncts to thrombolytic agents in disseminated intravascular coagulation (DIC), and for the hypercoagulable state. A recent study has reported on the inhibition of cellular proliferation after experimental balloon angioplasty by LMWH in rabbits.[30] There are several other indications such as the treatment of cardiovascular disorders in which these agents may also prove to be useful.

## CURRENTLY USED ANTITHROMBOTIC AGENTS

For the prophylaxis of medical and surgical thromboembolic disorders, several pharmacologic means other than heparin and certain physical methods are currently being used clinically. A comparison of some of the newer antithrombotic drugs that are currently used for the prophylaxis of postsurgical thrombosis is given in Table 39–4.

Oral anticoagulants are often used for the prophylaxis of thrombosis. Patient compliance is generally good, because one oral dosage is sufficient for the daily prophylaxis of thrombotic complications; however, the need for laboratory monitoring and dosage adjustment are drawbacks to this mode of therapy. Dextrans are generally administered intravenously. However, prolonged usage of dextran often results in hypervolemia, bleeding, and platelet dysfunction. Although aspirin is useful for prophylaxis of

**Table 39–4. A Comparison of Current Agents for Prophylaxis of Postsurgical and Medical Thromboembolism**

| Agent | Advantages | Disadvantages |
|---|---|---|
| Heparin | Subcutaneous administration (2–3 dosages) | Dosage adjustment, bleeding, thrombocytopenia |
| LMWH | Single, subcutaneous administration, sustained actions, outpatient usage | Dosage adjustment in high-risk patients, bleeding, products not readily interchangeable |
| Warfarin | Oral administration | Bleeding, delayed action, need for laboratory monitoring |
| Dextran | High efficacy | Hypervolemia, bleeding, cost, IV administration |
| Aspirin | Low cost, ease of administration | Questionable efficacy, bleeding |
| Compression devices | Few complications/side effects | Low compliance, rehabilitation, ineffective in high-risk patients |

arterial thrombosis, it is of questionable value in the prophylaxis of venous thrombosis. Furthermore, it may cause bleeding or gastric ulcers. Sequential compression devices have been used for the prophylaxis of postsurgical thrombosis. Several advantages of these mechanical devices include minor or no adverse effects, no pharmacologic manipulation, and activation of the patient's own physiologic systems. However, these devices are bulky, patient compliance is not as high as desired, and there is questionable efficacy in high-risk patients.

## NEWER ANTITHROMBOTIC AGENTS

### Heparin-related and Other Antithrombotic Agents

Several newer drugs to prevent thromboembolic disorders have been or are being developed. A list of some of these newer drugs is given in Table 39–5. Most of these drugs are in their early phases of development, and it will take some time before their clinical efficacy is proved.

A very LMWH fraction (CY 222) has been developed for clinical trials. This agent produces its effects by multiple mechanisms. Pentasaccharide is a synthetic material whose structure is based on the critical binding region of heparin to antithrombin (AT). It functions by inhibiting activated factor X. These agents do not impair primary hemostasis, and they exhibit a high bioavailability. They do not exhibit any anticoagulant effect at antithrombotic dosages.

Currently, several dermatan sulfates are under development for the prophylaxis of venous thromboembolism. Although similar in structure to heparin, these agents do not produce any effect on platelets. Furthermore, these agents are poorly absorbed after subcutaneous administration. More recently some low-molecular-weight dermatans have been produced that are absorbed subcutaneously, unlike dermatan sulfate.

Heparan sulfates have been developed as prophylactic antithrombotic agents. These agents are not homogeneous and contain other chondroitin sulfates. They bind to AT (AT III is officially being designated as antithrombin; AT) and heparin cofactor II but to a lesser degree than heparin, and they are weakly anticoagulant. Thus, large dosages of heparan are needed for effective antithrombotic treatment. Depolymerized heparans have better bioavailability than native heparans.

A synthetic hypersulfated lactobionic acid amide (Aprosulate) has been developed for prophylactic antithrombotic use. This agent produces its action via heparin cofactor II and by inhibiting protease generation. The bioavailability of this agent is better than that of dermatan and heparan sulfates.

Many other glycosaminoglycans are being developed for the prophylaxis of thromboembolism. Some of these represent mixtures of glycosaminoglycans with varying molecular weight profiles. Noteworthy are Lomoparan and Suleparoide, which are depolymerized heparan preparations. These agents exert their antithrombotic actions via unknown mechanisms; however, these are clinically very effective drugs. Other agents, such as Hemoclar and Arteparon, are sulfated polymers of natural origin with antithrombotic activities. Although these agents have been in existence for many years, the data on the prophylactic antithrombotic actions is not clearly known at this time.

Defibrotide is a polydeoxyribonucleotide derivative that has been used for the prophylaxis of both venous and arterial thrombosis. This agent primarily acts by modulating endothelial/

Table 39–5. **Newer Pharmacologic Strategies for the Management of Thrombotic Disorders**

| Drug | Advantages | Disadvantages |
|---|---|---|
| Very-low-molecular-weight heparins | Better bioavailability, promotes endogenous fibrinolysis | Polycomponent GAGs with poor bioavailability, mechanism of action is unknown |
| Pentasaccharide | Synthetic well-defined antithrombotic agent | Cost, efficacy not yet proved |
| Dermatan sulfate and derivatives | No effect on platelets, do not require ATIII | Polycomponent GAGs with poor bioavailability, mechanism of action is unknown |
| Heparan sulfate and derivatives | Modulate endogenous cellular and plasmatic functions independent of HCII and ATIII | Poorly defined agents whose mechanism of action is unknown, poor bioavailability |
| Synthetic lactobionic acid derivatives | Synthetic, homogeneous antithrombotic agents | Hypersulfated may bind to endogenous sites |
| Depolymerized heparinoids | Contain mixtures of GAGs with multiple sites of action | Polycomponent drugs with several activities |
| Polydeoxyribonucleotide derivatives | DNA-derived agents with endogenous modulatory actions on blood/vascular cells | Mechanism of action is unknown, poor bioavailability via SC route |
| Synthetic peptides and related drugs | Specific inhibitors of thrombin and other proteases, good bioavailability | Short half life, pharmacologic antagonist is unknown |
| Recombinant hirudin and related anticoagulants | Specific antithrombotic agents, extremely potent inhibitors | Highly specific inhibitors of thrombin, limited bioavailability |

GAG = glycosaminoglycan

cellular function. Much work is needed to understand its mechanism of action.

More recently, synthetic peptides have been used for the prophylaxis of thromboembolic phenomenon. Several peptides have been developed in Japan and in the United States for this indication. A peptide based on the structure of hirudin is now undergoing phase I clinical trials for its anticoagulant and antithrombotic actions.

One of the major advances in the development of antithrombotic drugs is the application of molecular biology techniques. Through this technology, several naturally occurring anticoagulants have been developed. One of these is recombinant hirudin, which is almost three times as potent as heparin in producing antifactor IIa activity. Although this inhibitor may be useful as an anticoagulant, because of its limited bioavailability and excessive specificity, this agent may not prove to be an effective prophylactic antithrombotic agent. Additional studies may be needed to modify its structure to obtain a desirable biologic behavior for prophylactic antithrombotic activity.

## Nonheparin Glycosaminoglycans

In addition to the development of LMWH, many significant developments in the area of nonheparin glycosaminoglycan–derived products as antithrombotic drugs have also taken place. Many drugs are developed as byproducts of heparin, and several newer agents are being developed. It is no longer believed that a sulfomucopolysaccharide of natural origin must exhibit some interaction with antithrombin to have effective antithrombotic properties. Several agents without this interaction have been found to produce therapeutic effects on the blood and vascular system.[8, 35, 49] Several mammalian glycosaminoglycan-derived drugs are currently being used in European countries as antithrombotic, antilipemic, and anti-atherosclerotic agents.[65] These agents represent mixtures of native sulfomucopolysaccharides or their derivatives obtained by depolymerization and/or fractionation. At present, the chemistry and pharmacology of these drugs is not fully understood.

Table 39–6 lists several important issues in the development of glycosaminoglycans as drugs. Most of the currently available agents are mixtures of mammalian glycosaminoglycans that are obtained as side products or specific products during the manufacturing of heparin. Specific glycosaminoglycans can be obtained from various organs such as the spleen, pancreas, kidney, and skin. Fractionation and chemical depolymerization along with extraction methods have been used to obtain these agents in large quantities for clinical usage. Despite

**Table 39–6. Important Issues in the Development of Glycosaminoglycans as Drugs**

1. Mixtures of glycosaminoglycans of natural origin (degree of heterogeneity; batch control)
2. Mechanisms of therapeutic clinical effects
3. Pharmacologic profiling in established models
4. Standardization and cross-referencing
5. Indications in various thrombotic conditions
6. Clinical acceptance

claims that some of these agents may be homogeneous, the molecular profile of these agents suggests that each is a polycomponent drug with both structural and molecular heterogeneity that widely varies from product to product. Thus, concerns exist over reproducible batch-to-batch composition as well as product-to-product differences in mechanism of action and potency.

Because of the composition variations, the mechanisms of pharmacologic and clinical actions of each of these agents differ markedly. As with LMWHs, each product must be individually characterized. The pharmacologic action of these agents is mediated by several endogenous interactions in which both humoral and cellular receptors are involved. In addition to plasmatic effects, these agents are capable of producing several cellular actions. The measure of a single plasma parameter, therefore, cannot be a true reflection of the overall pharmacologic action.

The initial development of these drugs was mostly empiric, and much needed pharmacologic information on their application was not available. These agents may be useful in several clinical indications; however, only very limited data exist on their pharmacologic characterization. These agents represent complex mixtures of linear polymers with varying endogenous interactions. Thus, their efficacy in the common pharmacokinetic models for antithrombotic effects, bleeding, pharmacodynamics, and biotransformation may differ from the clinical reality. With the use of newer biochemical and pharmacologic screening methods, valid pharmacologic screening can be used to develop these agents for specific clinical indications. A cautious approach should be taken when interpreting data from experimental models and when extrapolating to the clinical setting. With these complex drugs, direct correlations may not be possible in all situations as was possible with the development of earlier drugs in which simpler action-reactions were studied.

Because of these complexities, the glycosami-

noglycan-derived drugs cannot be standardized as a single or multiple group. Rather, each drug should be considered as a separate entity. Such issues as the bioavailability and mechanism of action have been targeted by regulatory agencies to standardize these agents. Several other issues such as the clinical indications for use and route of administration should be considered in the standardization of the new drugs.

When first developed, each of these agents was accepted as a derivative of heparin. However, with an increase in our knowledge of their structure and functional activity, preliminary pharmacologic studies were carried out to determine the proper indications for individual drugs. The glycosaminoglycan-derived drugs are generally used as antithrombotic agents; however, several other indications such as atherosclerosis, stroke, hyperlipemia, and senile dementia are now being considered.

## Currently Available Nonheparin Glycosaminoglycans

A partial list of some of the available glycosaminoglycan-derived drugs is given in Table 39–7. Most of the agents listed in this table are in clinical development or actual usage at this time. Several agents that are in preclinical development are not listed in this table. The described agents are mainly of mammalian origin with the exception of SP 54 (Hemoclar), which is obtained from a plant. However, SP 54 is a hypersulfated pentosan polysulfate with structural and functional characteristics similar to those of other sulfated glycosaminoglycans.

ORG 10172 is a depolymerized mixture of heparans, dermatans, heparin, and other chondroitin sulfates. It has been currently developed under the commercial name of Lomoparan by Organon, of Oss, The Netherlands. This agent is undergoing clinical trials for the prophylaxis of DVT after general and orthopedic surgery. This agent is also being used in the prevention of ischemic complications associated with stroke. It is claimed to have a better safety to efficacy ratio than heparin such that it produces minimal antihemostatic effects at antithrombotic doses.[54]

The code name MF 701 identifies a dermatan preparation that is being developed by Mediolanum Laboratories in Milan, Italy. This heterogeneous mixture of dermatan sulfate is claimed to be of mammalian mucosal origin. It is being developed for prophylaxis against thrombosis after general and orthopedic surgery. Because the bioavailability of this agent via subcutaneous administration is rather limited, it is being ad-

Table 39–7. **Development of Glycosaminoglycans-Derived Drugs**

| Drug | Composition | Status |
|------|-------------|--------|
| ORG 10172 | Depolymerized mixture of GAGs mainly containing heparan sulfate | Prophylactic antithrombotic drug; ongoing clinical trials |
| MF 701 | Mixture of native and depolymerized dermatans | Prophylactic antithrombotic drug; ongoing clinical trials |
| Suleparoide | Semisynthetic GAG | Available for various indications |
| OP 435 | Mixture of dermatans | Prophylactic antithrombotic; preclinical |
| OP 370 | Low-molecular-weight dermatans | Prophylactic antithrombotic; preclinical |
| SP 54 | Hypersulfated pentosan polysulfate | Prophylactic antithrombotic; clinically used |
| MPS | Depolymerized hypersulfated mixture of GAGs | Antithrombotic agent; developed for animal use |
| Sulfomucopolysaccharide mixtures | Mixture of GAGs | Clinically used |

GAGs = glycosaminoglycans

ministered intramuscularly. Several clinical trials are ongoing.

Suleparoide is a widely used semi-synthetic glycosaminoglycan that has been employed for prophylaxis of both arterial and venous thromboses.

Another dermatan preparation is under development at Opocrin Laboratories in Corlo, Italy. This dermatan preparation (OP 435) is extracted from bovine mucosa. It is being developed for prophylactic antithrombotic usage in patients undergoing general surgery.

Several questions have been posed on the safety and efficacy of the higher-molecular-weight dermatans such as the MF 701 and OP 435. Both of these agents exhibit rather limited bioavailability and have thus been administered in rather large dosages. Considering these issues, low-molecular-weight dermatan preparations have been recently introduced. One such preparation is OP 370, or Desmin, currently developed by Alfa-Wasserman Company in Modena, Italy. This agent exhibits a much better bioavailability than high-molecular-weight dermatan sulfate and may also exhibit a longer duration of action. This agent is being developed for prophylactic antithrombotic usage.

Hemoclar (SP 54) or pentosan polysulfate is a linear cationic polymer of beechwood tree origin that has been used for the prophylaxis of DVT. The agent is developed by Bene Chemical Company of Munich, Germany. Because of its origin, this agent can be obtained in relatively large quantities and may prove to be useful in various indications.

The agent MPS represents a mixture of mucopolysaccharides obtained from mammalian trachea. It is manufactured by Luitpold-Werk of Munich, Germany, for both human and equine usage for the treatment of joint diseases. Only limited data is available on the structure-activity relationship of this agent. MPS may have various applications as an antithrombotic agent. Additional pharmacologic studies may be needed for other indications.

The sulfated mucopolysaccharides or SMPS represent a large class of drugs that are currently sold under various commercial names. SMPS are noncharacterized glycosaminoglycans that contain dermatan, heparan, chondroitin sulfate, and other noncharacterized glycosaminoglycans. Although the composition of these agents does not differ markedly, each product is marketed for a specific indication. The mechanism of action and pharmacodynamics are not understood, and the pharmacology of these mucopolysaccharides is also poorly understood.

It is interesting to note that in Italy, six or seven mucopolysaccharide preparations of similar chemical composition are being used clinically. A list of these agents is given in Table 39–8. Despite similar composition, different companies are making these agents available for different clinical indications.

Table 39–8. **Commercially Available Sulfomucopolysaccharide Preparations**

| Brand Name | Indication |
|------------|------------|
| Ateroid (Crinos) | Senile dementia |
| Prisma (Alfa-Wasserman) | Antilipemic |
| Wessel (Mediolanum) | Vascular disease |
| Mesoglycan | Antithrombotic |
| Others | Several indications |

## Biologic Sources of Nonheparin Glycosaminoglycans

Table 39–9 lists various biologic sources from which glycosaminoglycans are extracted. These agents can be obtained from various animal tissues, such as porcine, bovine, and sheep sources, but bovine tissues provide the most abundant source. Besides mucosal tissue, organs such as spleen, kidney, and pancreas also provide raw material for the isolation of various glycosaminoglycans. It is difficult to distinguish the products isolated from different species and origins. However, the products of plant origin can be easily differentiated from the mammalian products on the basis of chemical structure. The pharmacopoeial specifications for the current products are rather flexible and do not require molecular profiles or other chemical characterization studies. It may be necessary in the future to provide data on the molecular profile and chemical structure of glycosaminoglycan products.

## Pharmacologic Aspects of Nonheparin Glycosaminoglycans

The pharmacologic aspects of various glycosaminoglycan-derived drugs is shown in Table 39–10. Besides the molecular weight profile, several behavioral characteristics have to be taken into account in the development of these agents. The bioavailability of these agents varies widely and is largely dependent on the molecular weight. For example, lower-molecular-weight glycosaminoglycans such as ORG 10172 and OP 370 exhibit a much better bioavailability than MF 701 and OP 435. The duration of action of each of the glycosaminoglycans varies according to molecular weight as well, and the lower-molecular-weight agents produce a longer duration

of action. The exact mechanism by which these agents produce a longer duration of action is not known at this time.

Most of the available nonheparin glycosaminoglycans do not exhibit any significant interaction with AT. If there is any activity observed, this may primarily be the result of contamination by heparin. Varying degrees of interaction with heparin cofactor II have been obtained with these glycosaminoglycans. Native dermatans such as MF 701 and OP 435 produce a significant activation of heparin cofactor II. However, the lower-molecular-weight derivatives exhibit much weaker effects. This suggests that the activation of heparin cofactor II is probably related to the molecular weight.

Almost all of the glycosaminoglycans exhibit some degree of neutralization by platelet factor 4 and protamine sulfate. However, in contrast to heparin, relatively higher amounts of both protamine sulfate and platelet factor 4 are needed.

## Synthetic Analogues Of Nonheparin Glycosaminoglycans

With the knowledge of various viral contaminants in the natural products of livestock origin such as bovine spongiform encephalopathy and foot and mouth virus, there is increasing fear that products from bovine or livestock origin may be contaminated. Thus, some countries in Europe have barred bovine products completely. This has introduced a new developmental strategy within the pharmaceutical industry. Many synthetic analogues of glycosaminoglycans are, therefore, being developed at this time. Some of these analogues are (1) heparin pentasaccharide; (2) sulfated lactobionic acid amides; and (3) sulfonated polyphenolic compounds.

These agents have been shown to produce dose-dependent antithrombotic effects in animal models. Although similar to heparin, these agents exhibit markedly different antithrombotic effects in comparison with heparin. Thus, each agent is developed in a defined manner for certain indications. The development of these agents may, therefore, have a major impact on approaches for the management of thrombosis.

## Clinical Applications of Nonheparin Glycosaminoglycans

Despite the unresolved basic pharmacologic issues, developments in the area of glycosaminoglycans are progressing. Although the thrust

Table 39–9. **Sources of Natural Glycosaminoglycans**

| Source | Glycosaminoglycan |
|---|---|
| Porcine tissues | |
| Mucosa | Dermatans |
| Skin | Dermatans |
| Trachea | Others |
| Bovine tissues | |
| Mucosa | Dermatan, SMPS |
| Skin | Dermatans |
| Spleen | Heparans |
| Pancreas | Heparins |
| Lungs | Heparin |
| Trachea | MPS |
| Sheep tissues | |
| Plants | SP 54 |

Table 39–10. **Pharmacologic Aspects of Various GAG-derived Drugs**

| Drug | Bioavailability | Sustained Action | AT Dependence | HCII Dependence | Protamine Neutralization | TFPI Release |
|---|---|---|---|---|---|---|
| ORG 10172 | + + + + | + + | ± | ± | + + | ± |
| MF 701 | + | + + | ± | + + + | + + | + |
| OP 435 | + + + | + | ± | + + + | + | + |
| OP 370 | + + + | + + | ± | + + | + | + |
| SP 54 | + + | + | ± | + + | + | + + |
| MPS | + + | + | − | + | + | + + |

is to develop an antithrombotic agent, these agents may also be used as an alternate drug in conditions in which heparin may not be safe, especially in the heparin-induced thrombocytopenia and heparin-induced thrombosis related syndromes. A list of various clinical indications is shown in Table 39–11. Some of the newer indications for these agents include anti-inflammatory and anti-atherosclerotic applications, treatment of vascular disorders, as topical agents for wound healing, and as a treatment for acquired immunodeficiency syndrome (AIDS). Other indications may include senile dementia and as a cytoprotective agent in surgery or transplant.

Several small-scale clinical trials have been done to study nonheparin glycosaminoglycans for these different indications.[1, 6, 12, 15, 44, 60, 61, 63] Heparan sulfate has been studied in DVT, chronic venous insufficiency, and intermittent claudication.[1, 61, 63] Although small numbers of patients were included in these trials, positive results appear to be obtained with this agent.

Dermatan sulfate has also been studied in several small-scale clinical trials.[15, 44] Most recently a pilot study was completed using dermatan sulfate in acute leukemia to control DIC.[15] Other clinical trials on some of the previously mentioned agents are also underway to prove the effectiveness of nonheparin glycosaminoglycans.

Table 39–11. **Clinical Applications of Glycosaminoglycan-derived Drugs**

1. Antithrombotic
2. Anti-inflammatory
3. Anti-atherosclerotic
4. Vascular deficit
5. Topical agents
   Wound healing
6. AIDS
7. Senile dementia
8. Cytoprotective actions

## Recombinant and Synthetic Antithrombin Drugs

Thrombin is known to play a crucial role in the overall thrombotic events leading to both arterial and venous thrombosis.[26] Besides mediating the transformation of fibrinogen to fibrin, this enzyme is claimed to mediate the activation of platelets and macrophages and produces on-site vascular effects leading to ischemia and vascular contraction. Furthermore, this enzyme is also linked with cellular proliferation and related events leading to restenosis. Thus, the development of agents that can solely target this enzyme is considered to be an important approach in providing newer drugs for the treatment of venous and arterial thrombosis.

With the availability of molecular biology techniques, it has become possible to produce pharmaceutical quantities of recombinant equivalent of hirudin, a potent antithrombin agent which was originally isolated from the medicinal leech, *Hirudo medicinalis.*[50] This anticoagulant is a 65 amino acid protein, which is much stronger in producing its anticoagulant effects than heparin. Furthermore, it does not require any endogenous factors for producing its effects. A comparison of this new anticoagulant with heparin is given on Table 39–12.

Recombinant hirudin (r-hirudin) represents a new anticoagulant agent in a field where heparin has been the only available drug. From a practical perspective, r-hirudin will probably be compared with heparin. However, because the mechanism of action of r-hirudin differs from that of heparin, caution must be used in the applications of this new agent. Being a monocomponent, single-acting drug, r-hirudin should offer certain advantages over heparin, which has many and varied activities. Although r-hirudin is a stronger antithrombin agent than heparin, the thrombin generation pathways in the coagulation cascade appear to be inhibited only under certain conditions. Thus, a very high dose of r-hirudin as compared with a dose of heparin may be needed for effective antithrombotic ac-

**Table 39-12. Comparison of r-Hirudin and Heparin**

| r-Hirudin | Heparin |
|---|---|
| Monocomponent protein with single target (thrombin) | Polycomponent drug with multiple sites of action |
| Thrombin-mediated amplification of coagulation is effected only under certain conditions | Thrombin and factor Xa feedback amplification of clotting is affected. Fibrinolysis and platelet function are affected |
| No known interactions with endothelium other than blocking thrombin-thrombomodulation mediated activation of protein C | Significant interactions with endothelium. Both physical and biochemical modulation of endothelial function |
| Shorter half life via IV route | Short half life via IV route |
| Functional bioavailability is variable and dependent on the structure of r-hirudin | Functional bioavailability is 20–30%. LMWHs are better absorbed |
| Endogenous factors (PF4, FVIII) do not alter its antithrombotic action | Marked modulation by the endogenous factors. Several factors may alter the anticoagulant action |
| Relatively inert proteins not altered by metabolic processes | Transformed by several enzyme systems and reduces its anticoagulant actions |
| Information on cellular uptake and depo formation is not presently known | Significant cellular uptake and depo formation |

tivity because only one target site can be inhibited. By inhibiting thrombin, the bioregulatory actions of thrombin such as protein C activation, the release of t-PA, and cellular function may also be inhibited. This may have certain additional physiologic effects beyond the anticoagulation response; the additional effects must be addressed before this agent is used clinically.

Recombinant hirudin has a relatively short half life when given intravenously, shorter than that of heparin as measured by antithrombin assays. Because of the multiple activities associated with heparin, other pharmacologic effects remain, although the antithrombin activity is no longer detectable. This should not be the case with r-hirudin, because the thrombin inhibition activity is the only effect of this agent.

The subcutaneous bioavailability of r-hirudin is low, being somewhat similar to that of standard heparin. Based on this and the short half life, it is unlikely that r-hirudin will have an important role in prophylaxis. However, the short-term therapeutic role of r-hirudin seems very promising. Coupled with the fact that the bleeding effects are apparently minor, particularly compared with those of heparin, the efficacy/tolerance index of this agent is very favorable.

A synthetic analogue of hirudin, hirulog (Biogen), has also been developed and tested in various clinical trials in which anticoagulation is indicated.[48] A report has described its use as an anticoagulant during angioplasty.[68] This agent represents a completely synthetic anticoagulant whose anticoagulant actions are comparable to those of heparin. However, it does not require any plasmatic factors for its anticoagulant actions. Hirulog is being evaluated for various indications such as in the management of unstable angina and interventional cardiology-related occlusive phenomenon. Besides hirulog, many other synthetic peptides are also being developed for use as anticoagulant and antithrombotic drugs.

Both recombinant and synthetic antithrombin drugs may be extremely useful as alternate anticoagulants for heparin-compromised patients because many of the adverse effects (thrombocytopenia and white clot syndrome) are not found to be produced by these agents. However, their therapeutic efficacy in several other indications must be tested in parallel with heparin prior to formulating recommendations.

In summary, remarkable progress has been made by both pharmaceutical companies and academic institutions to develop many newer anticoagulant and antithrombotic drugs. These developments are only possible owing to the introduction of newer technology such as molecular biology, improved isolation methods, and utilization of newer synthetic organic chemistry methods. Newer drugs such as LMWHs, hirudin, hirulog, and many other synthetic antiplatelet drugs have been introduced.

The use of LMWH for management of venous thrombosis has added a new dimension in this area. LMWHs are being tested in various cardiovascular indications such as treatment of unstable angina and prevention of post-PTCA restenosis. Although derived from heparin, these drugs exhibit different pharmacologic actions and exhibit individual behavior. Thus, unlike heparin, these agents are not interchangeable.

Nonheparin glycosaminoglycans such as dermatan sulfate and heparan sulfate have also been developed for various indications. However, investigations of these drugs have not provided convincing clinical evidence on their safety and efficacy. Mixtures of glycosaminoglycans such as Lomoparan have been tested extensively in the management of thrombosis; however, additional data is needed for their clinical applications.

The introduction of recombinant and synthetic antithrombin agents such as hirudin and hirulog offers a potentially useful alternate anticoagulant approach that once was considered to be solely manageable by heparin. These agents are stronger than heparin and do not exhibit some of the adverse effects that are associated with the use of heparin. Newer anticoagulant may, therefore, be very useful in acute anticoagulation protocols. Because they are markedly different than heparin, some of the therapeutic effects seen with heparin are not observed with these agents. Thus, it is important to know that the clinical effects of these agents are not comparable with those of heparin. Additional clinical trials are needed for the true validation of these antithrombin agents in medical indications.

The remainder of the 1990s will witness progressive growth in the area of anticoagulant and antithrombotic therapy. Many newer drugs will become available for the management of venous and arterial thrombosis. However, it should be kept in mind that conventional anticoagulants such as heparin and oral anticoagulants, and antiplatelet drugs such as aspirin, have provided us with remarkably useful drugs that have only been used in limited indications. Newer information on their use, optimization of dosage in newer indications, and an understanding of their therapeutic effects also represent equally important areas in which additional clinical data and research are needed.

## REFERENCES

1. Agrati AM, DeBartolo G, Palmieri G: Heparan sulfate: Efficacy and safety in patients with chronic venous insufficiency. Minerva Cardioangiologica 39(10):395–400, 1991.
2. Atha DH, Stephens AW, Rimon A, Rosenberg RD: Sequence variation in heparin octasaccharides with high affinity for antithrombin III. Biochemistry 23:5801–5812, 1984.
3. Bacher P, Welzel D, Iqbal O, et al: The thrombotic potency of LMW-heparin compared to urokinase in a rabbit jugular vein clot lysis model. Thromb Res 66:151–158, 1992.
4. Bara L, Billaud E, Gramond G, et al: Comparative pharmacokinetics of low molecular weight heparin (PK 10169) and unfractionated heparin after intravenous and subcutaneous administration. Thromb Res 39:631–636, 1985.
5. Baumgartner A, Jacot N, Moser G, et al: Prevention of postoperative deep vein thrombosis by one daily injection of low molecular weight heparin and dihydroergotamine. Vasa 18(2):152–156, 1989.
6. Bergqvist D, Kettunen K, Fredin H, et al: Thromboprophylaxis in patients with hip fractures: A prospective, randomized, comparative study between Org 10172 and dextran 70. Surgery 109(5):617–622, 1991.
7. Bergqvist D, Matzsch T, Burmark US, et al: Low molecular weight heparin given the evening before surgery compared with conventional low-dose heparin in prevention of thrombosis. Br J Surg 75(9):888–891, 1988.
8. Bianchini P: Therapeutic potential of non-heparin glycosaminoglycans of natural origin. Semin Thromb Hemost 15:365–369, 1989.
9. Bianchini P, Osima B, Parma B, et al: Pharmacological activities of heparins obtained from different tissues: Enrichment of heparin fractions with high lipoprotein lipase, anti-hemolytic and anticoagulant activities by molecular sieving and antithrombin III affinity chromatography. J Pharmacol Exper Therap 220:406–410, 1982.
10. Borris LC, Hauch O, Jorgensen LN, Lassen MR, et al: Enoxaparin versus dextran 70 in the prevention of postoperative deep vein thrombosis after total hip replacement. A Danish multicentre study. Proceeding of the Danish Enoxaparin Symposium, Feb 3, 1990.
11. Caen JP: A randomized double-blind study between a low molecular weight heparin Kabi 2165 and standard heparin in the prevention of deep vein thrombosis in general surgery. A French multicenter trial. Thromb Haemost 59(2):216–220, 1988.
12. Caramelli L, Mirchioni R, Carini: Effectiveness of short-term sulodexide treatment on peripheral vascular disease clinical manifestations. Rivista Europea per le Scienze Mediche e Farmacologiche 10(1):55–58, 1988.
13. Choay J, Lormeau JC, Sinay P, et al: Structure activity relationship in heparin: A synthetic pentasaccharide with high affinity for antithrombin III and eliciting high anti-Xa activity. Biochem Biophys Res Comm 116:491–499, 1983.
14. Choay J, Lormeau JC, Sinay P, et al: Anti-Xa active heparin oligosaccharides. Thromb Res 18:573–578, 1980.
15. Cofrancesco E, Boschetti C, Leonardi P, et al: Dermatan sulphate in acute leukaemia. Lancet 339(8802):1177–1178, 1992.
16. Eriksson BI, Zachrisson BE, Teger-Nilsson AC, et al: Thrombosis prophylaxis with low molecular weight heparin in total hip replacement. Br J Surg 75(11):1053–1057, 1988.
17. European Fraxiparin Study Group: Comparison of low molecular weight heparin and unfractionated heparin for the prevention of deep vein thrombosis in patients undergoing abdominal surgery. Br J Surg 75:1058–1063, 1988.
18. Fareed J, Walenga JM, Pifarre R: Newer approaches to the pharmacologic management of acute myocardial infarction. Cardiac Surgery: State of the Art Reviews 6(1):101–111, 1992.
19. Fareed J, Walenga JM, Pifarre R, et al: Some objective considerations for the neutralization of the anticoagulant actions of recombinant hirudin. Haemostasis 21(1):64–72, 1991.

20. Fareed J, Bacher P, Messmore HL, et al: Pharmacological modulation of fibrinolysis by antithrombotic and cardiovascular drugs. Prog Cardiovasc Dis 6:379–398, 1992.

21. Fareed J: Antithrombotic drugs in vascular disorders; newer developments and future perspectives. Minerva Angiol 17(2):41–47, 1992.

22. Fareed J, Walenga JM, Hoppensteadt D, et al: Chemical and biochemical heterogeneity in low molecular weight heparins: Implications for clinical use and standardization. Semin Thromb Hemost 15:440–463, 1989.

23. Fareed J, Walenga JM, Racanelli A, et al: Validity of the newly established low molecular weight heparin standard in cross-referencing low molecular weight heparins. Haemostasis 18:33–47, 1988.

24. Fareed J, Walenga JM, Hoppensteadt D, et al: Comparative preclinical studies on various low molecular weight heparins. Haemostasis 18:3–25, 1988.

25. Fareed J, Walenga JM, Lassen M, et al: Pharmacologic profile of a low molecular weight heparin (Enoxaparin): Experimental and clinical validation of the prophylactic antithrombotic effects. Acta Chir Scand 156[Suppl 556]:75–90, 1990.

26. Fareed J, Walenga JM, Iyer L, et al: An objective perspective on recombinant hirudin: A new anticoagulant and antithrombotic agent. Blood Coag Fibrinolysis 2:135–147, 1991.

27. Fussi F, Federli G: Oligoheteropolysaccharides with heparin-like effects. Ger Offen 2:833–898, 1977.

28. Griffith GC, Nichols G Jr, Asher JD, et al: Heparin osteoporosis. JAMA 193:85–94, 1965.

29. Haas S, Stemberger A, Fritsche HM, et al: Prophylaxis of deep vein thrombosis in high risk patients undergoing total hip replacement with low molecular weight heparin plus dihydroergotamine. Arzneimittel-Forschung 37(7):839–843, 1987.

30. Hanke H, Oberhoff M, Hanke S, et al: Inhibition of cellular proliferation after experimental balloon angioplasty by low molecular weight heparin. Circulation 85:1548–1556, 1992.

31. Hartl P, Brucke P, Dienstl E, et al: Prophylaxis of thromboembolism in general surgery: Comparison between standard heparin and Fragmin. Thromb Res 57(40):577–584, 1990.

32. Hirsh J, Levine M: The development of low molecular weight heparins for clinical use. In Verstraete M, et al (eds): Thrombosis and Haemostasis. Leuven, Leuven University Press, 1987, pp 425–448.

33. Holmer E, Mattson C, Nilsson S: Anticoagulant and antithrombotic effects of heparin and low molecular weight heparin fragments in rabbits. Thromb Res 25:475–485, 1982.

34. Hook M, Bjork I, Hopwood J, et al: Anticoagulant activity of heparin: Separation of high activity and low activity heparin species by affinity chromatography on immobilized antithrombin. FEBS Letters 66:90–93, 1976.

35. Hoppensteadt D, Racanelli A, Walenga JM, et al: Comparative antithrombotic and hemorrhagic effects of dermatan sulfate, heparan sulfate and heparin. Semin Thromb Hemost 15:378–385, 1989.

36. Hull R, Delmore T, Carter C, et al: Adjusted subcutaneous heparin versus warfarin sodium in the long-term treatment of venous thrombosis. N Engl J Med 306:954–958, 1983.

37. Hull R, Nieuwenhuis HK, Albada J, et al: Identification of risk factor for bleeding during treatment of acute venous thrombolysis with heparin or low molecular weight heparin. Blood 78(9):2337–2343, 1991.

38. Hull R, Raskob G, Pineo G: Subcutaneous low molecular weight heparin compared with continuous intravenous heparin in the treatment of proximal vein thrombosis. N Engl J Med 326(15):975–982, 1992.

39. Hurst RE, Poon M, Griffith MJ: Structure-activity relationships of heparin. J Clin Invest 72:1042–1045, 1983.

40. Kakkar VV, Murray WJG: Efficacy and safety of low molecular weight heparin (CY 216) in preventing postoperative venous thrombo-embolism: A cooperative study. Br J Surg 72:786–791, 1985.

41. Kakkar W, Stringer MD, Hedges AR, et al: Fixed combinations of low molecular weight or unfractionated heparin plus dihydroergotamine in the prevention of postoperative deep vein thrombosis. Am J Surg 157(4):413–418, 1989.

42. Kelton JG: Heparin induced thrombocytopenia. Haemostasis 16:173–186, 1986.

43. Koppenhagen K, Adolf J, Matthes M, et al: Low molecular weight heparin and prevention of postoperative thrombosis in abdominal surgery. Thromb Haemost 67(6):627–630, 1992.

44. Lane DA, Ryan K, Ireland H, Curtis JR, et al: Dermatan sulphate in haemodialysis. Lancet 339(8789):334–335, 1992.

45. Levine MN, Hirsh J: An overview of clinical trials with low molecular weight heparin fractions. Acta Chir Scand 154(543):73–79, 1988.

46. Leyvraz PF, Richard J, Bachmann F, et al: Adjusted versus fixed subcutaneous heparin in the prevention of deep vein thrombosis after total hip replacement. N Engl J Med 309:954–958, 1983.

47. Lindblad B: Prophylaxis of postoperative thromboembolism with low dose heparin alone or in combination with dyhydroergotamine: A review. Acta Chir Scand 154(543):31–42, 1988.

48. Maraganore JM, Bourdon P, Jablonski J, et al: Design and characterization of hirulogs: A novel class of bivalent peptide inhibitors of thrombin. Biochemistry 29:7095–7101, 1990.

49. Marcum JA, Rosenberg RD: Role of endothelial cell surface heparin-like polysaccharides. In Ofosu FA, Danishefsky I, Hirsh J (eds): Heparin and Related Polysaccharides. Structure and activities. NY, The New York Academy of Sciences, 1989, pp. 81–94.

50. Markwardt F, Fink G, Kaiser B, et al: Pharmacological survey of recombinant hirudin. Pharmazie 43:202–207, 1988.

51. Matzsch T, Bergqvist D, Fredin H, et al: Safety and efficacy of a low molecular weight heparin (Logiparin) versus dextran as prophylaxis against thrombosis after total hip replacement. Acta Chir Scand 543:80–84, 1988.

52. Matzsch T, Bergqvist D, Fredin H, et al: Low molecular weight heparin compared with dextran as prophylaxis against thrombosis after total hip replacement. Acta Chir Scand 156(6–7):445–450, 1990.

53. Messmore HL: Clinical efficacy of heparin fractions: Issues and answers. CRC Clin Rev Clin Lab Sci 23:77–94, 1986.

54. Meuleman DG, Dinther TV, Hobbelen PM, et al: Effects of the low molecular weight heparinoid, ORG 10172, in experimental thrombosis and bleeding models: Comparison with heparin. Thromb Haemorrhagic Dis 2(1):25–29, 1990.

55. Monreaul M, Lafoz E, Navarro A, et al: A prospective double-blind trial of a low molecular weight heparin once daily compared with conventional low-dose heparin three times daily to prevent pulmonary embolism and venous thrombosis in patients with hip fracture. J Trauma 29(6):873–875, 1989.

56. Ockelford PA, Carter CJ, Mitchell L, et al: Discordance between the anti-Xa activity and antithrombotic activi-

ties of an ultra-low molecular weight heparin fraction. Thromb Res 28:401–409, 1982.

57. Pini M, Tagliaferri A, Manotti C, et al: Low molecular weight heparin (Alfa LMWH) compared with unfractionated heparin in prevention of deep-vein thrombosis after hip fractures. Int Angiol 8(3):134–139, 1989.

58. Planes A, Vochelle N, Mazas F, et al: Prevention of postoperative venous thrombosis: A randomized trial comparing unfractionated heparin with low molecular weight heparin in patients undergoing total hip replacement. Thromb Haemost 60(3):407–410, 1988.

59. Prandoni P, Lensing A, Buller H, et al: Comparison of subcutaneous standard low-molecular weight heparin with intravenous standard heparin in proximal deep-vein thrombosis. Lancet 339:441–445, 1992.

60. Rowlings PA, Mansberg R, Rozenberg MC, et al: The use of a low molecular weight heparinoid (Org 10172) for extracorporeal procedures in patients with heparin dependent thrombocytopenia and thrombosis. Aust N Z J Med 21(1):52–54, 1991.

61. Romeo S, Grasso A, Costanzo C: A controlled clinical experiment "within subjects" with heparan sulfate in intermittent claudication. Minerva Cardioangiol 39(9):345–352, 1991.

62. Samama M, Combe-Tamazali S: Prevention of thromboembolic disease in general surgery with Enoxaparin. Br J Clin Pract 65:9–15, 1989.

63. Seccia M, Bellomini MG, Goletti O, et al: The prevention of postoperative deep venous thrombosis with heparan sulfate per os. A controlled clinical study vs. heparin calcium. Minerva Chir 47(1–2):45–48, 1992.

64. Silver D, Kapsch D, Tosi E: Heparin induced thrombocytopenia, thrombosis and haemorrhage. Ann Surg 198:301–305, 1983.

65. Sirtori CR: Pharmacology of sulfomucopolysaccharides in atherosclerosis prevention and treatment. In Ricci G, et al (eds): Selectivity and Risk-Benefit Assessment of Hyperlipidemia Drugs. New York, Raven Press, 1982, pp 189–194.

66. Sorensen JV, Lassen MR, Borris LC, et al: Reduction of plasma levels of prothrombin fragments 1 and 2 during thrombophylaxis with a low-molecular-weight heparin. Blood Coag Fibrinol 3(1):55–59, 1992.

67. Thomas DP, Merton RE, Gray E, et al: The relative antithrombotic effectiveness of heparin, in a low molecular weight heparin and a pentasaccharide fragment in an animal model. Thromb Haemost 61:204–207, 1989.

68. Topol EJ, Bonan R, Jewitt D, et al: Use of a direct antithrombin, hirulog, in place of heparin during coronary angioplasty. Circulation 87:1622–1629, 1993.

69. Turpie AGG, Levine MN, Hirsh J, et al: A randomized controlled trial of low molecular weight heparin (Enoxaparin) to prevent deep vein thrombosis in patients undergoing elective hip surgery. N Engl J Med 315:925–929, 1987.

70. Verardi S, Casciani CU, Nicora E, et al: A multicentre study on LMW-heparin effectiveness in preventing postsurgical thrombosis. Int Angiol 7(3):19–24, 1988.

71. Verstraete M: Pharmacotherapeutic aspects of unfractionated and low molecular weight heparins. Drugs 40(4):498–530, 1990.

72. Walenga JM, Petitou M, Lormeau JC, et al: Antithrombotic activity of a synthetic heparin pentasaccharide in a rabbit stasis thrombosis model using different thromogenic challenges. Thromb Res 46:187–198, 1987.

# Chapter 40

# Novel Thrombolytic Agents

Marc Verstraete and H. Roger Lijnen

Four thrombolytic agents are approved by the United States Food and Drug Administration (FDA) for the treatment of acute myocardial infarction and some other thrombotic conditions. These agents are streptokinase, the complex of streptokinase with anisoylated human plasminogen (APSAC, anistreplase), urokinase, and tissue-type plasminogen activator (t-PA, alteplase). Those novel thrombolytic agents that are currently investigated in clinical trials but not yet approved by the FDA or other drug licensing agencies are discussed in this chapter.

## SINGLE-CHAIN UROKINASE-TYPE PLASMINOGEN ACTIVATOR

Single-chain urokinase-type plasminogen activator (scu-PA, pro-urokinase) is a naturally occurring human protein first isolated from natural sources[1] and then produced through recombinant deoxyribonucleic acid (DNA) technology.[2] The human gene responsible for its synthesis is located on chromosome 10, is about 6.4 Kb long, is organized in 11 exons, and gives rise to a 2.5-Kb long messenger RNA, which transcribes a single-chain glycosylated polypeptide.[3–5] Evidence for the signal transduction pathways involved in regulation of the urokinase gene has to date demonstrated three mechanisms that are dependent respectively on activation of c-AMP protein kinase, protein kinase C, and an as yet uncharacterized protein kinase.[6]

The single-chain protein is synthesized principally by renal and vascular endothelial cells but also by a variety of cultured normal, transformed, and malignant cell types.[7, 8] The level of production of scu-PA is circa 10 times higher in tumor cell lines compared with normal tissues and is further stimulated by prolactin and pituitary gland extracts,[9] interleukin-1,[10] a number of cytokines including phorbol esters, tumor growth factor beta (TGFβ), lipopolysaccharides (LPS), and tumor necrosis factor-alpha

(TNFα).[11] The protein scu-PA has also been expressed by gene cloning techniques in *Escherichia coli* bacteria.[12]

### Physicochemical Properties

The glycosylated natural scu-PA is a single-chain glycoprotein with a molecular weight of 54,000 daltons containing 411 amino acid residues. The N-terminal domain has a homology with the growth factor domain of other proteins, followed by a kringle domain, homologous to plasminogen, tissue plasminogen activator, and other proteins involved in coagulation.[13, 13a] However, the single disulfide bonded kringle domain of scu-PA does not contain a lysine-binding site, and it does not confer fibrin-binding properties to the enzyme.[14]

The single glycosylation site of the glycoprotein is located at asparagine 302. The molecule expressed by *E. coli* lacks the glycosyl group that reduces the molecular weight to 47,000 daltons.

The plasminogen activator scu-PA is the native zymogenic precursor of urokinase. Limited hydrolysis by plasmin or kallikrein of the $Lys^{158}$-$Ile^{159}$ peptide bond converts the molecule to two-chain urokinase-type plasminogen activator (tcu-PA, urokinase), which is held together by one disulfide bond that is essential for the thrombolytic activity (Fig. 40–1). A fully active tcu-PA derivative is obtained after additional proteolysis at position $Lys^{135}$-$Lys^{136}$.

The activation of scu-PA by full-length plasmin has been reported not to follow Michaelis kinetics, whereas addition of epsilon-amino caproic acid changes the kinetic pattern to the Michaelis model.[15] Plasmin, which is lacking the kringle domains 1 to 4 (mini-plasmin), activates scu-PA according to Michaelis kinetics, leading to the hypothesis of an interaction between scu-PA and the kringles of plasmin.[15]

Specific hydrolysis of the $Glu^{143}$-$Leu^{144}$ peptide bond in scu-PA yields a low-molecular-weight scu-PA of 32,000 daltons (scu-PA-32k).[16] Throm-

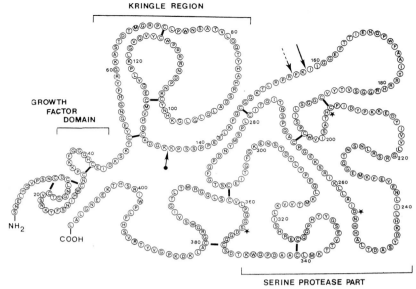

**Figure 40–1.** Schematic representation of the primary structure of scu-PA. The amino acids are represented by their single-letter symbols, and black bars indicate disulfide bonds. The active site residues His 204, Asp 255, and Ser 356 are indicated with an asterisk. The arrows indicate the plasmin cleavage sites for conversion of Mr 54,000 scu-PA to Mr 54,000 tcu-PA and of Mr 54,000 tcu-PA to Mr 33,000 tcu-PA (arrow), for conversion to inactive Mr 54,000 tcu-PA by thrombin (dotted arrow) and for conversion to Mr 32,000 scu-PA by an unidentified protease (circled arrow). (Modified from Holmes WE, Pennica D, Blaber M, et al: Cloning and expression of the gene for pro-urokinase in Escherichia coli. Biotechnology 3:923–929, 1985.)

bin, on the other hand, cleaves the $Arg^{156}$-$Phe^{157}$ peptide bond in scu-PA, resulting in an inactive double-chain molecule.[17]

## Mechanism of Plasminogen Activation

Studies on the intrinsic functional activity of scu-PA have been hampered because the single-chain form is too readily activated by plasmin to the two-chain form of urokinase. Therefore, aprotinin has been used to block plasmin and dansyl-glutamyl-glycyl-arginine-chloromethylketone to inhibit tcu-PA, or site-directed mutant forms of scu-PA were used, rendering these molecules incapable of conversion by plasmin to tcu-PA. scu-PA does not have a specific affinity for fibrin.[15] In purified systems, scu-PA has some intrinsic plasminogen-activating potential, which is, however, 1% or less of that of tcu-PA.[18] Conversion of scu-PA to tcu-PA in the vicinity of a fibrin clot apparently constitutes a significant positive feedback mechanism for clot lysis in human plasma in vitro.[13, 18] This conversion may, however, play a less important role in in vivo thrombolysis because of preferential fibrin-associated activation of plasminogen by scu-PA.

Several cell types express specific high-affinity binding sites on their surface for scu-PA and tcu-PA as human peripheral monocytes, fibroblasts, and Bowes melanoma cells. The interaction between these plasminogen activators and the receptor were recently summarized.[19] (1) Receptor binding does not require the active site of the enzymes; (2) scu-PA binds with the same affinity as tcu-PA; (3) receptor-bound scu-PA can be activated at the site of the receptor; (4) the region of scu-PA that binds to the receptor is located in the cysteine-rich amino-terminal peptide (residues 12–32); (5) this region shows sequence homology to that part of the epidermal growth factor (EGF) that is responsible for the binding of EGF to the EGF receptor (but EGF does not bind to the scu-PA receptor); (6) bound scu-PA dissociates very slowly from the cell surface and is not appreciably degraded; and (7) receptor binding does not shield urokinase (tcu-PA) from the action of plasminogen activation inhibitor (PAI)-1 and PAI-2. Enzyme-inhibitor complexes are bound with about 10 times lower affinity compared with the enzyme itself. Cell-bound scu-PA and tcu-PA are thought to be involved in the generation of pericellular proteolysis during cell migration and tissue remodeling.[20, 21]

## Studies With scu-PA in Thrombotic Animal Models

Low-molecular-weight scu-PA (scu-PA-32k), purified from the conditioned medium of a human lung adenocarcinoma cell line[17] or prepared by recombinant DNA technology[22] has a fibrinolytic capacity in a rabbit jugular vein thrombosis model comparable to that of wild-type recombinant scu-PA.[23] The relative fibrin specificity of scu-PA, in contrast to that of tcu-PA, was maintained at thrombolytic doses. Provided this relative fibrin specificity also holds for patients with thromboembolic disease, scu-PA-32k may be a practical alternative molecule for the large-scale production of a fibrin-specific thrombolytic agent by recombinant DNA technology.

## Pharmacokinetics

In man, scu-PA is rapidly cleared from the blood following disappearance kinetics, which can be described by two exponential terms with half lives of 7.9 ($\pm$ 1.2) and 48 ($\pm$ 8) minutes, respectively. NH$_2$-terminal recognition sites and carbohydrate moieties appear not to be critical for clearance, because the pharmacokinetics of natural glycosylated scu-PA,[23] of recombinant nonglycosylated scu-PA, and of the truncated low-molecular-weight variant, scu-PA-32k, are indeed identical. These findings suggest the need for continuous intravenous infusion to achieve and maintain steady-state plasma levels required for thrombolytic efficacy. Postinfusion clearance of scu-PA occurs with similar rapidity, suggesting nonsaturability of the clearance mechanism.

## Dose of Saruplase

Clinical experience with recombinant scu-PA is still limited. The generic name for full-length unglycosylated human recombinant scu-PA obtained from *E. coli* is saruplase (Grünenthal). With a preparation containing 160,000 U/mg, the dose used successfully in patients with acute myocardial infarction was 20 mg given as a bolus and 60 mg in the next hour, immediately followed by an intravenous heparin infusion (20 IU/kg/hour) for 72 hours.[24–26] This dosage regimen was found to cause a clear systemic activation of the fibrinolytic system and fibrinogen degradation. Activation may be the result, at least in part, of conversion of scu-PA to tcu-PA in the circulation.

Another glycosylated recombinant pro-urokinase (Abbott-74187) was studied in 122 patients with acute myocardial infarction to evaluate the effect of infusion duration (60 versus 90 minutes) and of a "primary" (using 250,000 U) dose on initial patency and extent of clot lysis.[27] With a 60-minute infusion the patency was 79% and 75% at 60 minutes and 90 minutes; a 90-minute infusion resulted in 56% and 76% patency at 60 minutes and 90 minutes, respectively. Fibrinogen decreased by 24% with a 60-minute infusion (60 mg) and by 38% with a 90-minute infusion (90 mg). Priming had no effect on patency rate and fibrinogenolysis.

The same glycosylated pro-urokinase (Abbott-74187) was infused directly into an occluded peripheral artery at 3 mg/hour.[28] Success, defined as 95% clot lysis followed by balloon angioplasty and/or atherectomy, was achieved in 12 of 13 patients (92%) with an infusion time of 2.0 to 16.4 hours (mean 6.3 $\pm$ 3.4) and at a mean total dose of 18.8 ($\pm$ 10.2) mg. The fibrinogen levels remained unchanged in the first 24 hours.[28]

An unglycosylated pro-urokinase from a different source (Farmitalia Carlo Erba) was tested first in an open trial in 23 patients receiving a single dose of 12.8 million (M) IU administered intravenously (3.2 M IU as a bolus and 9.6 M IU over 1 hour) within 4 hours after onset of a first myocardial infarction.[27] The 75 to 90-minute patency rate was 90%. In a second, double-blind phase, 96 patients were randomly allocated within the same time window to either 6.4 M, 9.6 M, or 12.8 M IU pro-urokinase intravenously, 25% of the total dose being administered as a bolus and the remaining dose over 1 hour. Heparin was administered at a dose of 1,000 IU/hour after a bolus injection of 7,500 IU. In addition, patients were given oral aspirin 100 to 160 mg, intravenous atenolol 6 to 10 mg, and a nitroglycerin infusion. The 75- to 90-minute coronary patency rate (TIMI grade 2 and 3) of the infarct-related artery was centrally and blindly determined. The three regimens resulted in patency rates of, respectively, 60% (19/32), 79% (26/33), and 83% (25/30). Fibrinogen levels, expressed as percent of baseline values, were respectively 78%, 46%, and 47%. Five patients suffered from bleeding complications requiring transfusion and 34 patients (28.6%) had minor bleeding.

## Adverse Effects of Saruplase

In a direct double-blind comparison between intravenous saruplase (80 mg over 60 minutes) and streptokinase (1.5 M IU over 60 minutes) in 401 patients with acute myocardial infarction, a somewhat smaller reduction in circulating fibrinogen levels was observed in patients treated with saruplase. There were significantly less bleeding episodes in the saruplase group versus the streptokinase group (14 vs. 25%), and less transfusion requirement (4 vs. 11%).[24]

## KRINGLE 2 AND PROTEASE DOMAINS OF t-PA

The agent BM 06.022 (Reteplase) is produced in *E. coli* cells using an expression vector containing a cDNA derived from the Bowes human melanoma cell line. The cDNA is coded for a protein of 356 amino acids. The N-terminal methionine was removed by the *E. coli* methionine aminopeptidase, leaving serine as the N-

## OTHER MUTANTS AND VARIANTS OF TISSUE-TYPE PLASMINOGEN ACTIVATOR

terminal amino acid. Therefore, the primary structure of the resulting protein comprised the N-terminal amino acids[1-3] attached to the complete kringle 2 domain (176–275) and the protease amino acid sequence (276–527).[29, 30] The final product, unglycosylated because of the *E. coli* expression, is completely in the single-chain form (MW 39 kd). The thrombolytic effects of BM 06.022 after intravenous bolus injection were investigated in the rabbit model of jugular vein thrombosis.[31] Equipotent doses (50% thrombolysis, $ED_{50}$) obtained by half-logarithmic regression analysis was 163 kU/kg (0.28 mg/kg) for BM 06.022 and 871 kU/kg (1.09 mg/kg) for alteplase. At equipotent doses the residual concentration of fibrinogen were 74% and 76%, those of plasminogen 67% and 69%, and those of $\alpha_2$-antiplasmin of 47% and 46% for BM 06.022 and alteplase, respectively. Pharmacokinetic analysis for plasma activity revealed a half life of 18.9 ($\pm$ 1.5) minutes for BM 06.022, whereas alteplase was distributed with a half life of 2.1 ($\pm$ 0.1) minutes, accounting for 86.7% ($\pm$ 1.9%) of the total area under the curve, followed by a β-phase with a half life of 13.8 ($\pm$ 0.9) minutes. Plasma clearance of BM 06.022 was 4.7 ($\pm$ 0.7) ml/min$^{-1}$kg$^{-1}$ compared with 20 ($\pm$ 1.2) ml/min$^{-1}$kg$^{-1}$ for alteplase.

Also in a canine stenotic model of electrically induced coronary artery occlusion, a model known to develop a platelet-rich thrombus, intravenous bolus injections of BM 06.022 and alteplase revealed that the equipotent dose ($LD_{50}$) of BM 06.022 (83 kU/kg) was 11.6-fold lower than that of alteplase (951 kU/kg).[32] Comparison with infusion experiments showed that intravenous injection of 140 kU/kg of BM 06.022 was equi-effective to a 90-minute infusion of 800 kU/kg (1 mg/kg) of alteplase regarding reperfusion rate (66%) and time to reperfusion (16 $\pm$ 6 vs. 18 $\pm$ 8 minutes).[33] At equi-effective doses, residual fibrinogen and bleeding time were not different between the two drugs. In the absence of a systemic fibrinolytic state, reocclusion within the first 90 minutes is frequent but can be avoided with an intravenous bolus of heparin.[34-35]

A dose-ranging study with 10 and 15 megaunits BM 06.022 was conducted in 143 patients with acute myocardial infarction.[37, 38] With 10 megaunits, the patency rates (TIMI grades 2 or 3) were at 30 minutes 73%, at 60 minutes 74%, and at 90 minutes 62% (n=43). With 15 megaunits BM 06.022, the corresponding rates were 66%, 75%, and 76% (n=100). In the absence of heparin, the reocclusion rate between the 30- and 90-minute angiogram was 20% or 12.5%.

Several rt-PA mutants have been constructed with altered pharmacokinetic properties or with altered functional properties, including binding to fibrin and stimulation by fibrin, and resistance to plasma protease inhibitors.[39] rt-PA mutants with deletion of the finger (F), epidermal growth factor (E), and/or kringle 1 ($K_1$) domains were shown to have a significantly reduced plasma clearance in several animal models. This is, however, frequently associated with a reduced specific thrombolytic activity, resulting in an unchanged or only marginally improved thrombolytic potency.[39]

Mutants consisting of the kringle 2 ($K_2$) and protease (P) domains of t-PA ($K_2$P, BM 06.022, LY 210825) (compare with supra) were shown to have a longer half life in animals.[40-42] Prolonged half lives have also been obtained by substitution or deletion of one or a few selected amino acids in the finger or EGF domains.[39] Such mutants have a better preserved specific thrombolytic activity than domain deletion mutants. One of such t-PA molecules (E6010) in which $Cys^{84}$ in the E-domain is replaced by Ser has a half life in man of more than 20 minutes, as compared with 6 minutes for native t-PA. This compound has been used successfully for bolus administration at less than half of the dose of native t-PA in a multicenter trial in 96 patients with acute myocardial infarction.[43]

An rt-PA mutant in which $Thr^{103}$ is substituted by Asn and the sequence $Lys^{296}$-His-Arg-Arg is mutagenized to Ala-Ala-Ala-Ala was found to have both a prolonged half life and resistance to PAI-1. This mutant was shown to have an increased potency on platelet-rich plasma clots (rich in PAI) in animal models.[44] Thus, it appears to be possible to engineer several properties into human t-PA to produce a molecule with an enhanced therapeutic potential.

The t-PA of saliva from the vampire bat *Desmodus rotundus* (bat-PA) was found to constitute a potent and fibrin-specific thrombolytic agent in rabbits and dogs with femoral arterial thrombosis.[45] From a family of four Desmodus plasminogen activators encoded by four distinct genes, one of the two larger forms, rDSPA$_{\alpha1}$, was shown to be an efficient and fibrin-specific thrombolytic agent in rats with experimental pulmonary embolism[46] and in a canine model of arterial thrombolysis.[47]

It remains to be shown in direct comparative studies whether, in addition to BM 06.022 and E6010, these rt-PA mutants or variants offer advantages over wild-type rt-PA for the treatment of patients with thromboembolic disease.

## RECOMBINANT CHIMERIC PLASMINOGEN ACTIVATORS

Recombinant chimeric plasminogen activators have been constructed primarily using different domains of t-PA on the one hand and of the serine protease part of scu-PA on the other.[48–54] It was found that $K_1K_2P_u$, a chimera consisting of amino acids 1 to 3 and 87 to 274 of t-PA ($K_1$ and $K_2$ domains) and of amino acids 144 to 411 of scu-PA (serine protease domain) (Fig. 40–2) had a markedly increased thrombolytic potency in vivo as compared with that of recombinant t-PA (rt-PA, alteplase) and of recombinant scu-PA (rscu-PA, saruplase).[55] The increased thrombolytic potency of $K_1K_2P_u$ appeared to be mainly the result of reduced plasma clearance in the presence of a relative maintenance of the specific thrombolytic activity. $K_1K_2P_u$ also appeared to be suitable for administration by bolus injection, as demonstrated in a hamster pulmonary embolism model[56] and in a combined femoral arterial eversion graft thrombosis and femoral vein thrombosis model in the dog.[54] Thus, this chimera seemed to have the characteristics of an improved thrombolytic agent. Therefore, a procedure for the production of centigram quantities of $K_1K_2P_u$ was established.[55] Analysis of the purity, sterility, endotoxin content, viral contamination, heat stability, and acute toxicity in mice indicated that this material was suitable for the investigation, on a pilot scale, of its pharmacokinetic and thrombolytic properties in patients.

The feasibility of the use of $K_1K_2P_u$ by bolus injection for coronary thrombolysis in six patients with acute myocardial infarction was investigated.[57] In two patients given an intravenous bolus of 10 mg $K_1K_2P_u$ over 5 minutes, persistent coronary artery recanalization was not observed within 30 minutes. In two of four patients given a second bolus of 10 mg $K_1K_2P_u$ 15 minutes after the first one, persistent coronary recanalization occurred within 30 minutes. The four patients without recanalization within 30 minutes were immediately given 100 mg t-PA over 90 minutes. In all patients, the infarct-related artery was patent at 24 hours and the hospital course was uneventful. The bolus injections did not produce significant fibrinogen breakdown or $\alpha_2$-antiplasmin consumption within 30 minutes. The plasma $K_1K_2P_u$ level increased to 2 to 3 µg/ml after injection of the first bolus and to 4 to 5 µg/ml after injection of the second bolus. $K_1K_2P_u$ disappeared from the plasma with an initial half life of 9 minutes and a clearance of approximately 50 ml per minute. Thus, bolus injection of 20 mg $K_1K_2P_u$

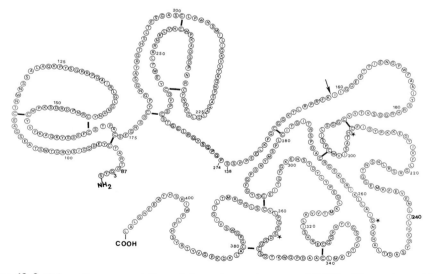

**Figure 40–2.** Schematic representation of the primary structure of $K_1K_2P_u$. The amino acids are represented by their single-letter symbols, and black bars indicate disulfide bonds. The active site residues in the protease domain of scu-PA are indicated with an asterisk. The chimera consists of amino acids Ser[1]-Glu[3] and Asp[87]-Phe[274] of t-PA and amino acids Ser[138]-Leu[411] of scu-PA. The arrow indicates the plasmin cleavage site for conversion to a two-chain molecule. (Modified from Holmes WE, Pennica D, Blaber M, et al: Cloning and expression of the gene for pro-urokinase in Escherichia coli. Biotechnology 3:923–929, 1985; Pennica D, Holmes WE, Kohr WJ, et al: Cloning and expression of human tissue-type plasminogen activator cDNA in E. coli. Nature 301:214–221, 1983.)

is well tolerated and can induce clot-selective coronary thrombolysis in patients with acute myocardial infarction.

## RECOMBINANT STAPHYLOKINASE

The fibrinolytic potential of some staphylococci strains was already recognized in 1948 and attributed to the production of an enzyme, named staphylokinase, that was able to dissolve human thrombin-fibrinogen clots.[58] Staphylokinase was shown not to lyse fibrin directly, but rather to act as a plasminogen activator.[58]

In 1951 the differential in vitro sensitivity of the fibrinolytic system of various species to staphylokinase was described.[59] Staphylokinase was found to activate dog, human, cat, rabbit, and guinea pig plasminogen. No activation of rat or bovine plasminogen was observed.[59] The first in vivo studies conducted in dogs in 1964 were hampered by a high incidence of bleeding and subsequent mortality.[60] Moreover, a wide range of inhibitor activity was found in the population,[61] which, in analogy with what was known for streptokinase, was attributed to staphylokinase-neutralizing antibodies and presumed to interfere with a fixed dosing schedule, rendering staphylokinase treatment impractical and unpredictable. Hence, because of the high fatality rate of early animal experiments and to the extensive dose-response variability in humans, interest in staphylokinase as a thrombolytic agent faded.

### Structure, Mechanism of Action and Fibrin-Specificity

The nucleotide sequence of the staphylokinase gene and the deduced amino acid sequence are elucidated.[62–65] They do not relate to those of streptokinase. Published staphylokinase molecules differ only in three amino acids, depending on the strain used.[62–65] The molecular weight of this 136 amino acid protein is only one-third that of streptokinase. This evoked the speculation that thrombus penetration might be better.

Like streptokinase, staphylokinase as such is not an enzyme; it does not directly convert plasminogen to plasmin but rather forms a 1:1 stoichiometric complex with plasminogen that then activates other plasminogen molecules.[66–69] Hence, staphylokinase may be classified as a profibrinolytic agent.

Several mechanisms may contribute to the fibrin specificity and the potency of staphylokinase in a plasma milieu. First, in contrast to the plasminogen-streptokinase complex, the plasminogen-staphylokinase complex is rapidly neutralized by $\alpha_2$-antiplasmin in plasma in the absence of fibrin, thus avoiding systemic plasminogen activation and the ensuing systemic lytic state. In the presence of fibrin, the plasminogen-staphylokinase complex binds to the clot via the lysine-binding sites of the plasminogen moiety. Consequently, the inhibition rate by $\alpha_2$-antiplasmin is markedly reduced, thus allowing preferential plasminogen activation at the fibrin surface.[66] Second, staphylokinase dissociates in active form from the plasmin-staphylokinase complex after its inhibition by $\alpha_2$-antiplasmin, and the released staphylokinase molecules are recycled to other plasminogen molecules.[69] Third, the plasminogen-staphylokinase complex is inactive and unable to convert to active plasmin-staphylokinase complex at appreciable rates in the presence of excess inhibitor. This observation may provide some explanation for the remarkable stability of plasminogen in the presence of relatively high concentrations of staphylokinase.[70] Fourth, fibrin disturbs the stability of staphylokinase in a plasma milieu, producing fibrin-specific clot lysis. Indeed, staphylokinase was shown to induce clot lysis without associated $\alpha_2$-antiplasmin consumption or systemic fibrinogen breakdown, in in vitro models,[71] in several animal studies,[72] and in a pilot study in patients with evolving myocardial infarction.[73]

### In Vitro Studies

Lack[58] reported that certain staphylococci strains are able to lyse human plasma clots. He extracted the moiety responsible for this fibrinolytic action and showed that the lytic activity depended upon the presence of plasminogen, concluding that staphylococci can produce a plasminogen activator. Sweet and coworkers[61] demonstrated that staphylokinase is a potent and rapid activator of human plasminogen if used in sufficiently high concentrations. However, he questioned its relevance as a thrombolytic drug because of the wide variation of inhibitor level in the population. The fibrinolytic potential of recombinant staphylokinase, t-PA, and streptokinase was compared in an in vitro system consisting of a radioactive human plasma clot suspended in circulating citrated plasma.[74, 75] The fibrinolytic potency of staphylokinase, on a molar basis, was found to be about two times higher than that of streptokinase, but only half that of t-PA. Systemic fibrinolytic activation and fibrinogen breakdown occurred with streptokinase, but not with staphylokinase, nor with t-PA.

These findings were confirmed by comparing the lysis rate of staphylokinase and streptokinase using a 0.12-ml radioactive human plasma clot submersed in 0.5 ml of citrated plasma.[71] Staphylokinase induced a dose-dependent lysis. A 50% lysis in 2 hours was obtained with 17 nM staphylokinase and was associated with only 5% plasma fibrinogen degradation. Corresponding values for streptokinase were 68 nM and more than 90% fibrinogen degradation. In the absence of a fibrin clot, 50% fibrinogen degradation in human plasma in 2 hours requires 700 nM staphylokinase, but only 4.4 nM streptokinase.

Staphylokinase derives its fibrin specificity largely from the discriminative inhibition of $\alpha_2$-antiplasmin that neutralizes the circulating but not the fibrin-associated plasminogen-staphylokinase complex.[66, 74] Consequently, plasminogen activation by staphylokinase is limited to the fibrin surface. In contrast, $\alpha_2$-antiplasmin does not hinder the circulatory streptokinase-plasminogen complex, thus allowing systemic plasminogen activation and the resulting hemostatic breakdown.

In a human plasma milieu in vitro, staphylokinase has a comparable fibrinolytic activity versus platelet-rich and platelet-poor plasma, whereas streptokinase is very inefficient toward platelet-rich plasma clots.[70] When retraction of platelet-rich plasma clots was prevented by a glycoprotein IIb-IIIa antagonist, platelet-poor and platelet-rich plasma clots become equally sensitive to lysis with streptokinase. Likewise, mechanically compressed human plasma clots were found to be resistant to in vitro lysis by streptokinase but not by staphylokinase. The potency of staphylokinase towards platelet-rich plasma clots, as suggested by these in vitro experiments, might be clinically important because aggregated platelets contribute largely to arterial thrombi such as those found in the coronary or cerebral arterial circulation during ischemic events. Furthermore, platelets are held responsible for resistance to lysis with current thrombolytic regimens and for the early reocclusion hazard.[76]

The in vitro fibrinolytic and fibrinogenolytic properties of streptokinase and staphylokinase were compared, revealing marked interspecies variability.[71] Streptokinase appears to be a very poor plasminogen activator toward autologous plasma clots submersed in baboon, rabbit, hamster, rat, or dog plasma. Staphylokinase, in contrast, induces very efficient clot lysis in all these species except the rat. The plasma fibrinolytic system of baboon, rabbit, and hamster react comparably to the human system to staphylokinase, whereas the dog system seems to be much more sensitive. These findings are in agreement with what Lewis and Ferguson reported in 1951.[59] Furthermore, except in the dog, clot lysis by staphylokinase is achieved without systemic fibrinogen degradation. The marked sensitivity of dog plasma to staphylokinase and the lack of fibrin specificity may account for the high incidence of lethal hemorrhagic events encountered during the very first in vivo experiments with staphylokinase, in which a dog model was used.[60, 77]

## Pharmacokinetics

In hamsters and rabbits, staphylokinase is cleared from the circulation in a biphasic manner, with an initial half life of 1.8 minutes and a plasma clearance of 7.4 ml/minute in hamsters and corresponding values of 1.7 minutes and 14 ml/minute in rabbits.[72]

The organ distribution of both staphylokinase and streptokinase documents a rapid uptake in muscle and kidney, but not in liver. The less important role of the liver in the clearance mechanism is substantiated by the finding that functional hepatectomy in rabbits only results in a three- to four-fold reduced clearance.[72]

In five patients with acute myocardial infarction treated with an intravenous infusion of 10 mg recombinant staphylokinase over 30 minutes, the postinfusion disappearance of staphylokinase-related antigen from plasma occurred in a biphasic manner with an alpha half life of 6.3 minutes and a beta half life of 37 minutes, corresponding to a plasma clearance of 270 ml/minute.[73]

## Thrombolysis Experiments in Animals

The thrombolytic properties of streptokinase and (recombinant) staphylokinase were compared in several animal thrombosis models. In hamsters with pulmonary emboli consisting of preformed human plasma clots containing standardized platelet concentrations, the relative thrombolytic potencies, on a weight basis of staphylokinase versus streptokinase, were comparable when using platelet-poor and platelet-rich plasma clots, but five- and two-fold higher in the platelet-enriched and in the mechanically compressed plasma clots, respectively.[78]

The thrombolytic potency on a molar basis of staphylokinase versus streptokinase was similar in a rabbit[72] and in a baboon jugular vein thrombosis model[79] and five-fold higher in a dog femoral vein model. As compared with streptokinase, staphylokinase induced recanalization significantly more frequently and more persistently in a platelet-rich femoral arterial eversion graft thrombosis model, performed both in dogs and in baboons.[78, 79]

The immunogenicity of staphylokinase as compared with streptokinase was studied in a dog[78] and in a baboon[79] extracorporeal loop thrombosis model. Plasma of both species at baseline contained measurable streptokinase, but apparently no staphylokinase-neutralizing activity. Weekly administration of either agent to dogs induced neutralizing antibodies and an increasing resistance to clot lysis, although less rapidly with staphylokinase as compared with streptokinase.[78] Weekly administration of streptokinase to baboons induced a marked increased in neutralizing antibody production that was associated with severe hypotensive reactions and with a progressive waining of thrombolytic efficacy. A five times repeated weekly staphylokinase administration provoked neutralizing antibodies in only one of four baboons, while mean thrombolytic potency was maintained and no hypotensive or allergic reactions occurred.[79]

## A Pilot Study in Five Patients With Evolving Myocardial Infarction

In four of five patients with acute myocardial infarction, 10 mg recombinant staphylokinase, given intravenously over 30 minutes, was found to induce angiographically documented coronary artery recanalization within 40 minutes.[73] Plasma fibrinogen and $\alpha_2$-antiplasmin levels were unaffected, and allergic reactions were not observed.

Although the small number of patients included in this pilot study precludes valid estimation of the frequency of coronary artery recanalization with recombinant staphylokinase and of the adequacy of the dose used, this pilot study suggests that intravenous infusion of 10 mg recombinant staphylokinase may produce fibrin-specific coronary thrombolysis.

Definition of the relative therapeutic benefit will require more detailed dose-finding studies followed by randomized clinical trials comparing recombinant staphylokinase with other thrombolytic agents.

## Immunogenicity

As previously described, animal experiments (performed in dogs and baboons) suggested a rather low-grade immunogenicity of repeated staphylokinase administration.[78, 79] Unfortunately, this cannot be extrapolated to man. In a study dating back to 1962, a rise in antistaphylokinase titer was observed in nine of 35 patients with staphylococcal osteomyelitis.[58] Sweet and coworkers,[61] although convinced of the potent and rapid plasminogen activating properties of staphylokinase, doubted its role as a routinely used thrombolytic agent because they found a wide variation in inhibitor level to staphylokinase in the population, which they assumed to be the result of antistaphylokinase antibodies. Consequently, as they believed, the loading dose of staphylokinase may have to be individualized to overcome the inhibitor activity and, following the anticipation of a marked rise in inhibitor level after an initial administration, repeated use would be precluded for several months. In the five patients with acute myocardial infarction who received an intravenous infusion of 10 mg recombinant staphylokinase over 30 minutes, no neutralizing antibodies against staphylokinase could be demonstrated at baseline and up to 6 days after infusion, but antibodies were consistently demonstrated in plasma from 14 to 35 days onward.[73]

The prevalence of antistaphylokinase in the general population appears to be much lower than that of antistreptokinase antibodies.[80] Thus, the initial anticipation that recombinant staphylokinase may produce fewer allergic reactions than streptokinase is not definitively validated by the present demonstration of its immunogenicity. Although the restriction to single use as a result of antibody production would probably apply to both streptokinase and recombinant staphylokinase, the absence of cross-reactivity of induced antibodies[80] suggests that the use of both substances would not be mutually exclusive.

## REFERENCES

1. Bernik MB, Oller EP: Plasminogen activator and proactivator (urokinase precursor) in lung cultures. J Am Med Wom Assoc 31:465–472, 1976.
2. Nolli ML, Sarubbi E, Corti A, et al: Production and characterization of human recombinant single chain urokinase-type plasminogen activator from mouse cells. Fibrinolysis 3:101–106, 1989.
3. Günzler WA, Steffens GJ, Ötting F, et al: Structural relationship between human high and low molecular mass urokinase. Hoppe-Seylers Z Physiol Chem 363:1155–1165, 1982.
4. Tripputi P, Blasi F, Verde P, et al: Human urokinase gene is located on the long arm of chromosome 10. Proc Natl Acad Sci USA 82:4448–4452, 1985.
5. Verde P, Stoppelli MP, Galeffi P, et al: Identification of primary sequence of an unspliced human urokinase poly(A) + RNA. Proc Natl Acad Sci USA 81:4727–4731, 1988.

6. Scully MF: Plasminogen activator-dependent pericellular proteolysis. Br J Haemotol 79:537–543, 1991.

7. Eaton DL, Scott RW, Baker JB: Purification of human fibroblast urokinase proenzyme and analysis of its regulation by proteases and protease nexin. J Biol Chem 259:6241–6247, 1984.

8. Nielsen LS, Hansen JG, Skriver L, et al: Purification of zymogen to plasminogen activator from human glioblastoma cells by affinity chromatography with monoclonal antibody. Biochemistry 24:6410–6415, 1982.

9. Mira-y-Lopez R, Reich E, Ossowski L: Modulation of plasminogen activators in rodent mammary tumors by hormones and other effectors. Cancer Res 43:5467–5477, 1983.

10. Michel JB, Quertermous T: Modulation of mRNA levels for urinary- and tissue-type plasminogen activator and plasminogen activator inhibitors 1 and 2 in human fibroblasts by interleukin 1. J Immunol 143:890–895, 1989.

11. Sawdy M, Podor TJ, Loskutoff DJ: Regulation of type I plasminogen activator inhibitor gene expression in cultured bovine aortic endothelial cells. J Biol Chem 264:10396–10401, 1989.

12. Holmes WE, Pennica D, Blaber M, et al: Cloning and expression of the gene for pro-urokinase in Escherichia coli. Biotechnology 3:923–929, 1985.

13. Declerck PJ, Lijnen HR, Verstreken M, et al: A monoclonal antibody specific for two-chain urokinase-type plasminogen activator. Application to the study of the mechanism of clot lysis with single-chain urokinase-type plasminogen activator in plasma. Blood 75:1794–1800, 1990.

13a. Patthy L, Traxler M, Vali Z, et al: Kringles: Modules specialized for protein binding. Homology of the gelatin-binding region of fibronectin with the kringle structures of proteins. FEBS Lett 171:131–136, 1984.

14. Lijnen HR, Zamarron C, Blaber M, et al: Activation of plasminogen by pro-urokinase. I. Mechanism. J Biol Chem 261:1253–1258, 1986.

15. Scully MF, Ellis V, Watahiki Y, Kakkar VV: Activation of pro-urokinase by plasmin: Non-Michaelian kinetics indicates a mechanism of negative cooperation. Arch Biochem Biophys 268:438–446, 1989.

16. Stump DC, Lijnen HR, Collen D: Purification and characterization of single-chain urokinase-type plasminogen activator from human cell cultures. J Biol Chem 261:1274–1278, 1986.

17. Ichinose A, Fujikawa K, Suyama T: The activation of pro-urokinase by plasma kallikrein and its inactivation by thrombin. J Biol Chem 261:3486–3489, 1986.

18. Lijnen HR, Van Hoef B, De Cock F, Collen D: The mechanism of plasminogen activation and fibrin dissolution by single chain urokinase-type plasminogen activator in a plasma milieu in vitro. Blood 73:1864–1872, 1989.

19. Kirchheimer JC, Binder BR: Function of receptor-bound urokinase. Semin Thromb Hemost 17:246–250, 1991.

20. Saksela O, Rifkin DB: Cell-associated plasminogen activation: Regulation and physiological functions. Annu Rev Cell Biol 4:93–126, 1988.

21. Danø K, Andreasen PA, Grondahl-Hansen J, et al: Plasminogen activators, tissue degradation and cancer. Adv Cancer Res 44:139–266, 1985.

22. Lijnen HR, Nelles L, Holmes WE, Collen D: Biochemical and thrombolytic properties of a low molecular weight form (comprising Leu144 through Leu411) of recombinant single-chain urokinase-type plasminogen activator. J Biol Chem 263:5594–5598, 1988.

23. Collen D, De Cock F, Lijnen HR: Biological and thrombolytic properties of proenzyme and active forms of human urokinase. II. Turnover of natural and recombinant urokinase in rabbits and squirrel monkeys. Thromb Haemost 52:24–26, 1984.

24. PRIMI Trial Study Group: Randomised double-blind trial of recombinant pro-urokinase against streptokinase in acute myocardial infarction. Lancet 1:863–868, 1989.

25. Kasper W, Meinertz T, Hohnloser S, et al: Coronary thrombolysis in man with pro-urokinase: Improved efficacy with low dose urokinase. Klin Wochenschr 66[Suppl XII]:109–114, 1988.

26. Diefenbach C, Erbel R, Pop T, et al: Recombinant single-chain urokinase-type plasminogen activator during acute myocardial infarction. Am J Cardiol 61:966–970, 1988.

27. Weaver WD, Hartman JK, Reddy PS, Anderson J, for the Pro-UK Study Group: Prourokinase achieves rapid and sustained patency for treatment of acute myocardial infarction (abstract). J Am Coll Cardiol 21[Suppl A]:397, 1993.

28. Hartmann JR, Enger EL, Thomas O, et al: Pro-urokinase (A-74187): Highly effective, rapid thrombolysis of peripheral arterial occlusions without fibrinogenolysis (abstract). Circulation 86:3078, 1992.

29. Kohnert U, Rudolph H, Prinz H, et al: Production of a recombinant human tissue plasinogen activator variant (BM 06.022) from Escherichia coli using a novel renaturation technology (abstract). Fibrinolysis 4[Suppl 3]:116, 1990.

30. Kohnert U, Rudolph R, Verheijen JH, et al: Biochemical properties of the kringle-2 and protease domains are maintained in the refolded t-PA deletion variant BM 06.022. Protein Eng 5:93–100, 1992.

31. Martin U, Fischer S, Kohnert U, et al: Thrombolysis with an Escherichia coli-produced recombinant plasminogen activator (BM 06.022) in the rabbit model of jugular vein thrombosis. Thromb Haemost 65:560–564, 1991.

32. Martin U, Fischer S, Kohnert U, et al: Coronary thrombolytic properties of a novel recombinant plasminogen activator (BM 06.022) in a canine model. J Cardiovasc Pharmacol 18:111–119, 1991.

33. Martin U, Fischer S, Sponer G: Influence of heparin and systemic lysis on coronary blood flow after reperfusion induced by the novel recombinant plasminogen activator BM 06.022 in a canine model of coronary thrombosis. J Am Coll Cardiol 22:914–920, 1993.

34. Martin U, Sponer G, König R, et al: Double bolus administration of the novel recombinant plasminogen activator BM 06.022 improves coronary blood flow after reperfusion in a canine model of coronary thrombosis. Blood Coagul Fibrinolysis 3:139–147, 1992.

35. Martin U, Sponer G, Strein K: Evaluation of thrombolytic and systemic effects of the novel recombinant plasminogen activator BM 06.022 compared with alteplase, anistreplase, streptokinase and urokinase in a canine model of coronary artery thrombosis. J Am Coll Cardiol 19:433–440, 1992.

36. Martin U, von Möllendorff E, Akpan W, et al: Dose-ranging study of the novel recombinant plasminogen activator BM 06.022 in healthy volunteers. Clin Pharmacol Ther 50:429–436, 1991.

37. Seifried E, Müller M, Ziesche S, et al: Influence of a novel recombinant plasminogen activator on the hemostatic system: Dose-ranging multicenter study (GRECO) (abstract). Fibrinolysis 6[Suppl 2]:146, 1992.

38. Neuhaus KL, von Essen R, Vogt A, et al: Dose-ranging study of a novel recombinant plasminogen activator in patients with acute myocardial infarction: Results of the GRECO-study (abstract). Circulation 84[Suppl II]:II-573, 1991.

39. Lijnen HR, Collen D: Strategies for the improvement

of thrombolytic agents. Thromb Haemost 66:88–110, 1991.

40. Jackson CV, Frank JD, Craft TJ, et al: Comparison of the thrombolytic activity of the novel plasminogen activator, LY210825, to anisoylated plasminogen-streptokinase activator complex in a canine model of coronary artery thrombolysis. J Pharmacol Exper Therap 260:64–70, 1992.

41. Martin U, Koehler J, Sponer G, Strein K: Pharmacokinetics of the novel recombinant plasminogen activator BM 06.022 in rats, dogs, and non-human primates. Fibrinolysis 6:39–43, 1992.

42. Nicolini FA, Nichols WW, Mehta JL, et al: Sustained reflow in dogs with coronary thrombosis with K2P, a novel mutant of tissue-plasminogen activator. J Am Coll Cardiol 20:228–235, 1992.

43. Kawai C, Hosoda S, Motomiya T, et al for the E6010 Investigators: Multicenter trial of a novel modified t-PA, E6010, by i.v. bolus injection in patients with acute myocardial infarction (AMI). Circulation 86[Suppl]: I–409, 1992.

44. Refino CJ, Paoni NF, Keyt BA, et al: A variant of t-PA (T103N, KHRR-296-299 AAAA) that, by bolus, has increased potency and decreased systemic activation of plasminogen. Thromb Haemost 70:313–319, 1993.

45. Gardell SJ, Ramjit DR, Stabilito II, et al: Effective thrombolysis without marked plasminemia after bolus intravenous administration of vampire bat salivary plasminogen activator in rabbits. Circulation 84:244–253, 1991.

46. Witt W, Baldus B, Bringmann P, et al: Thrombolytic properties of Desmodus rotundus (vampire bat) salivary plasminogen activator in experimental pulmonary embolism in rats. Blood 79:1213–1217, 1992.

47. Mellott MJ, Stabilito II, Holahan MA, et al: Vampire bat salivary plasminogen activator promotes rapid and sustained reperfusion without concomitant systemic plasminogen activation in a canine model of arterial thrombosis. Arterioscler Thromb 12:212–221, 1992.

48. Gheysen D, Lijnen HR, Pierard L, et al: Characterization of a recombinant fusion protein of the finger domain of tissue-type plasminogen-activator with a truncated single chain urokinase-type plasminogen activator. J Biol Chem 262:11779–11784, 1987.

49. Piérard L, Jacobs P, Gheysen D, et al: Mutant and chimeric recombinant plasminogen activators: Production in eukaryotic cells and preliminary characterization. J Biol Chem 262:11771–11778, 1987.

50. Nelles L, Lijnen HR, Collen D, Holmes WE: Characterization of a fusion protein consisting of amino acids 1 to 263 of tissue-type plasminogen activator and amino acids 144 to 411 of urokinase-type plasminogen activator. J Biol Chem 262:10855–10862, 1987.

51. Lijnen HR, Nelles L, Van Hoef B, et al: Characterization of a chimeric plasminogen activator consisting of amino acids 1 to 274 of tissue-type plasminogen activator and amino acids 138 to 411 of single-chain urokinase-type plasminogen activator. J Biol Chem 263:19083–19091, 1988.

52. Collen D, Stassen JM, Demarsin E, et al: Pharmacokinetics and thrombolytic properties of chimaeric plasminogen activators consisting of the NH2-terminal region of human tissue-type plasminogen activator and the COOH-terminal region of human single-chain urokinase-type plasminogen activator. J Vasc Med Biol 1:234–240, 1989.

53. Nelles L, Lijnen HR, Van Nuffelen A, et al: Characterization of domain deletion and/or duplication mutants of a recombinant chimera of tissue-type plasminogen activator and urokinase-type plasminogen activator (rt-PA/u-PA). Thromb Haemost 64:53–60, 1990.

54. Collen D, Lu HR, Lijnen HR, et al: Thrombolytic and pharmacokinetic properties of chimeric tissue-type and urokinase-type plasminogen activators, Circulation 84:1216–1234, 1991.

55. Collen D, Nelles L, De Cock F, et al: $K_1K_2P_u$, a recombinant t-PA/u-PA chimera with increased thrombolytic potency, consisting of amino acids 1 to 3 and 87 to 274 of human tissue-type plasminogen activator (t-PA) and amino acids 138 to 411 of human single-chain urokinase-type plasminogen activator (scu-PA). Purification in centigram quantities and conditioning for use in man. Thromb Res 65:421–438, 1992.

56. Lu HR, Lijnen HR, Stassen JM, Collen D: Comparative thrombolytic properties of bolus injections and continuous infusions of a chimeric (t-PA/u-PA) plasminogen activator in a hamster pulmonary embolism model. Blood 78:125–131, 1991.

57. Van de Werf F, Lijnen HR, Collen D: Coronary thrombolysis with $K_1K_2P_u$, a chimeric tissue-type and urokinase-type plasminogen activator. A feasibility study in six patients with acute myocardial infarction. Coron Art Dis 4:929–933, 1993.

58. Lack CH: Staphylokinase: An activator of plasma protease. Nature 161:559–560, 1948.

59. Lewis JH, Ferguson JH: A proteolytic enzyme system of the blood. III. Activation of dog serum profibrinolysin by staphylokinase. Am J Physiol 166:594–602, 1951.

60. Lewis JH, Kerber CW, Wilson JH: Effects of fibrinolytic agents and heparin on intravascular clot lysis. Am J Physiol 207:1044–1052, 1964.

61. Sweet B, McNicol P, Douglas AS: In vitro studies of staphylokinase. Clin Sci 29:375–382, 1965.

62. Collen D, Zhao ZA, Holvoet P, et al: Primary structure and gene structure of staphylokinase. Fibrinolysis 6:226–231, 1992.

63. Sako T, Sawaki S, Sakurai T: Cloning and expression of the staphylokinase gene of Staphyloccus aureus in Escherichia coli. Mol Gen Genet 190:271–277, 1983.

64. Sako T: Overproduction of staphylokinase in Escherichia coli and its characterization. Eur J Biochem 149:557–563, 1985.

65. Behnke D, Gerlach D: Cloning and expression in Escherichia coli, Bacillus subtilis and Streptococcus sanguis of a gene for staphylokinase—a bacterial plasminogen activator. Mol Gen Genet 210:528–534, 1987.

66. Lijnen HR, Van Hoef B, De Cock F, et al: On the mechanism of fibrin-specific plasminogen activation by staphylokinase. J Biol Chem 266:11826–11832, 1991.

67. Lijnen HR, Van Hoef B, Matsuo O, et al: On the molecular interactions between plasminogen-staphylokinase, $\alpha_2$-antiplasmin and fibrin. Biochim Biophys Acta 1118:144–148, 1992.

68. Collen D, Schlott B, Engelborghs Y, et al: On the mechanism of the activation of human plasminogen by recombinant staphylokinase. J Biol Chem 268:11, 1993.

69. Silence K, Collen D, Lijnen HR: Interaction between staphylokinase, plasmin(ogen) and $\alpha_2$-antiplasmin. Recycling of staphylokinase after neutralization of the plasmin-staphylokinase complex by $\alpha_2$-antiplasmin. J Biol Chem 268:13, 1993.

70. Lijnen HR, Van Hoef B, Vandebossche L, et al: Biochemical properties of natural and recombinant staphylokinase. Fibrinolysis 6:214–225, 1992.

71. Lijnen HR, De Cock F, Matsuo O, et al: Comparative fibrinolytic and fibrinogenolytic properties of staphylokinase and streptokinase in plasma of different species in vitro. Fibrinolysis 6:33–37, 1992.

72. Lijnen HR, Stassen JM, Vanlinthout I, et al: Comparative fibrinolytic properties of staphylokinase and streptokinase in animal models of venous thrombosis. Thromb Haemost 66:468–473, 1991.

73. Collen D, Van de Werf F: Coronary thrombolysis with

recombinant staphylokinase in patients with evolving myocardial infarction. Circulation 87:1850–1853, 1993.

74. Sakai M, Watanaki M, Matsuo O: Mechanism of fibrin-specific fibrinolysis by staphylokinase: Participation of $\alpha_2$-plasmin inhibitor. Biochem Biophys Res Commun 162:830–837, 1989.

75. Matsuo O, Okada K, Fukao H, et al: Thrombolytic properties of staphylokinase. Blood 76:925–929, 1990.

76. Parise P, Agnelli V: Thrombus resistance to lysis and reocclusion after thrombolysis: The role of platelets. Blood Coagul Fibrinolysis 2:745–758, 1991.

77. Kanae K: Fibrinolysis by staphylokinase in vivo (abstract 65436). Biol Abstr AB748, 1986.

78. Collen D, De Cock F, Van Linthout I, et al: Comparative thrombolytic and immunogenic properties of staphylokinase and streptokinase. Fibrinolysis 6:232–242, 1992.

79. Collen D, De Cock F, Stassen JM: Comparative immunogenicity and thrombolytic properties towards arterial and venous thrombi of streptokinase and recombinant staphylokinase in baboons. Circulation 87:996–1006, 1993.

80. Declerck PJ, Vanderschueren S, Billiet J, et al: Prevalance and induction of circulating antibodies against recombinant staphylokinase. Thromb Haemost 71:129–133, 1994.

81. Pennica D, Holmes WE, Kohr WJ, et al: Cloning and expression of human tissue-type plasminogen activator cDNA in E. coli. Nature 301:214–221, 1983.

# Index

Note: Page numbers in *italics* refer to illustrations; page numbers followed by t refer to tables.

433

ISBN 0-7216-5278-6